SIXTH EDITION
VOLUME I

ART HISTORY

MARILYN
STOKSTAD

MICHAEL W.
COTHREN

SIXTH EDITION
VOLUME I

ART HISTORY

MARILYN
STOKSTAD

MICHAEL W.
COTHREN

This sixth edition of **ART HISTORY** *is dedicated
to the memory of Marilyn Stokstad (1929–2016) who
conceived and created the first edition, published in 1995.*

Editor-in-Chief: Sarah Touborg
Sponsoring Editor: Helen Ronan
Product Marketing Manager: Jeremy Intal
Product Marketing Assistant: Frank Alarcon
Executive Field Marketer: Wendy Albert
Project Management Team Lead: Melissa Feimer
Content Producer: Barbara Cappuccio
Senior Producer, REVEL: Rich Barnes
Digital Imaging Technician: Corin Skidds

This book was designed and produced by Laurence King Publishing Ltd., London
www.laurenceking.com

Editorial Manager: Kara Hattersley-Smith
Senior Editor: Sophie Wise
Production Manager: Simon Walsh
Designer: Ian Hunt
Picture Researchers: Katharina Gruber and Julia Ruxton

Cover image: Hildegard of Bingen, *The Choir of Angels*
1927–1933 facsimile of Vision 6 of the Liber Scivias of Hildegard of Bingen. Original (lost in World War II) 1150–1175.

Acknowledgments of third party content appear on page 600, which constitutes an extension of this copyright page.

Copyright © 2018, 2014, 2011 by Pearson Education, Inc. or its affiliates. All Rights Reserved. Printed in the United States of America. This publication is protected by copyright, and permission should be obtained from the publisher prior to any prohibited reproduction, storage in a retrieval system, or transmission in any form or by any means, electronic, mechanical, photocopying, recording, or otherwise. For information regarding permissions, request forms, and the appropriate contacts within the Pearson Education Global Rights & Permissions department, please visit www.pearsoned.com/permissions.

PEARSON™, ALWAYS LEARNING™, and REVEL™ are exclusive trademarks in the U.S. and/or other countries owned by Pearson Education, Inc. or its affiliates, please visit pearsoned.com/permissions.

Unless otherwise indicated herein, any third-party trademarks that may appear in this work are the property of their respective owners and any references to third-party trademarks, logos, or other trade dress are for demonstrative or descriptive purposes only. Such references are not intended to imply any sponsorship, endorsement, authorization, or promotion of Pearson's products by the owners of such marks, or any relationship between the owner and Pearson Education, Inc. or its affiliates, authors, licensees, or distributors.

Library of Congress Cataloging-in-Publication Data
Names: Stokstad, Marilyn, 1929-2016, author. | Cothren, Michael Watt, author.
Title: Art History / Marilyn Stokstad, Michael W. Cothren.
Description: Sixth edition. | Upper Saddle River : Pearson, [2018] |
Includes
    bibliographical references and index.
Identifiers: LCCN 2016034108| ISBN 9780134475882 (combined volume) | ISBN 0134475887 (combined volume) |
    ISBN 9780134479279 (student edition volume 1) | ISBN 0134479270 (student edition volume 1) |
    ISBN 9780134479262 (student edition volume 2) | ISBN 0134479262 (student edition volume 2)
Subjects: LCSH: Art--History--Textbooks.
Classification: LCC N5300 .S923 2018 | DDC 709--dc23
LC record available at https://lccn.loc.gov/2016034108

3   17

Student Edition Volume 1
ISBN-10:   0-13-447927-0
ISBN-13: 978-0-13-447927-9

Books a la Carte Volume 1
ISBN-10:   0-13-448464-9
ISBN-13: 978-0-13-448464-8

MN 11.21.2018 1140

Brief Contents

Contents

7 Jewish and Early Christian Art 216

8 Byzantine Art 236

9 Islamic Art 268

10 Art of South and Southeast Asia before 1200 298

Letter from the Author

Dear Colleagues,

When Marilyn Stokstad wrote the first edition of *Art History* in the early 1990s, it represented an historical advance in the conception and teaching of the history of art. The discipline had recently gone through a period of crisis and creativity that challenged the assumptions behind the survey course and questioned the canon of works that had long been its foundation. We all rethought what we were doing, and this soul searching made us better teachers—more honest and relevant, more passionate and inclusive. With characteristic energy and intelligence, Marilyn stepped up to the task of conceiving and creating a new survey book for a new generation of students ready to reap the benefits of this refined notion of art history. From the beginning, she made it global in scope, inclusive in coverage, warm and welcoming in tone. Marilyn highlighted the role of women in the history of art both by increasing the number of women artists and by expanding the range of art to focus on media and genres that had traditionally engaged female artists and patrons.

my students to slow down and spend extended time studying the illustrations of the works of art, what I call "slow looking." I thought memorizing the IDs would accomplish this. But I have grown to realize that there are more effective ways to make this happen, especially in the new online REVEL format that is transforming this textbook into an interactive learning experience. REVEL is more like a classroom than a book. It is based on the premise that students will focus more effectively on a series of changing formats tailored to the content being presented. When I piloted REVEL in my survey classroom last Fall, I discovered that my students were "slow looking" while taking advantage of interactive REVEL features such as the pan/zoom figures (which allow them to zoom in on details) and the architectural panoramas (which allow them to explore the interacting spaces of architectural interiors from multiple viewpoints). I doubted my students would take advantage of these opportunities while doing "assigned reading," but I was wrong. The first week of class a student's hand shot up to ask if I could explain a detail she had seen when using the pan/zoom. Within the same week, another student shared his surprise at the small size of a work of art discovered when clicking on the pan/zoom's scale feature. In three decades of teaching art history survey, never had a student brought to class an observation or question about scale, even though measurements were included in captions. I love books, I really do, but in my experience REVEL is a more effective teaching resource.

It was an honor to become part of her project almost a decade ago, and it is my sad responsibility to acknowledge her passing, just as this sixth edition went to press. To me, she was more than a brilliant art historian; she was a loyal and compassionate colleague, a great friend. The warmth and trust with which she welcomed me into the writing of *Art History* was one of the great experiences of my professional life. I will truly miss her, and I will work faithfully to continue her legacy as this book moves into the future. I promised her I would.

After all, reconsidering and refining what we do never ceases. Like art, learning and teaching change as we and our culture change, responsive to new objectives and new understandings. Opportunities for growth sometimes emerge in unexpected situations. One day, while I was inching through sluggish suburban traffic with my daughter Emma—a gifted teacher—I confessed my disappointment about my survey students' struggle with mastering basic information. "Why," I asked rhetorically, "is it so difficult for them to learn these facts?" Emma's unexpected answer shifted the question and reframed the discussion. "Dad," she said, "you are focusing on the wrong aspect of your teaching. What are you trying to accomplish by asking your students to learn those facts? Clarify your objectives first, then question whether your assessment is actually the best way to encourage its accomplishment."

Emma's question inspired me to pause and reflect on what it is we seek to accomplish in art history survey courses. One of my primary goals has been encouraging

I urge you to continue thinking with me about how the study of art history can be meaningful and nourishing for students. Our discipline originated in dialogue and is founded on the desire to talk with each other about why works of art matter and why they affect us so deeply. I would love to hear from you—mcothre1@swarthmore.edu.

Warm regards,

Michael

What's New

WHY USE THIS NEW EDITION?

Art history—what a fascinating and fluid discipline,which evolves as the latest research becomes available for debate and consideration. The sixth edition of *Art History* has been revised to reflect such new discoveries, recent research, and fresh interpretive perspectives, and also to address the changing needs of the audience—both students and educators. With these goals in mind and by incorporating feedback from our many users and reviewers, we have sought to make this edition an improvement in sensitivity, readability, and accessibility without losing anything in comprehensiveness, in scholarly precision, or in its ability to engage readers.

To facilitate student learning and understanding of art history, the sixth edition is centered on six key Learning Objectives. These overarching goals helped steer and shape this revision with their emphasis on the fundamental reasons we teach art history to undergraduates, and they have been repeated at the beginning of each chapter, tailored to the subject matter in that section of the book so that the student will be continually reminded of the goals and objectives of the study of art history.

LEARNING OBJECTIVES FOR *ART HISTORY*

1. Identify the visual hallmarks of regional and period styles for formal, technical, and expressive qualities.

2. Interpret the meaning of works of art from diverse cultures, periods, and locations based on their themes, subjects, and symbols.

3. Relate artists and works of art to their cultural, economic, and political contexts.

4. Apply the vocabulary and concepts used to discuss works of art, artists, and art history.

5. Interpret art using appropriate art historical methods, such as observation and inductive reasoning.

6. Select visual and textual evidence to support an argument or interpretation.

DESIGNING *ART HISTORY* IN REVEL

One of the principal objectives of the current edition has been to advance the transformation of the traditional narrative into an interactive learning experience in REVEL. REVEL is conceived to promote learning in a digital platform that is engaging and meaningful to today's student. Along with traditional narrative text passages, features such as pan/zoom images, videos, architectural panoramas, and audio text are integrated to better explain and present concepts key to understanding the history of art.

- **Pan/zooms** appear with a simple click for most of the figures, allowing students to zoom in and examine details with stunning clarity and resolution, and then return to the overall view of the work of art, so they can relate these details to the whole.

- The pan/zooms' **scale feature** opens a window where works of art appear next to a scaled human figure (or for small works a scaled human hand), giving students an instant sense of the size of what they are studying. Since all works of art are scaled in a fundamental sense to the size of human creators and viewers (rather than to an arbitrary measuring system),

this intuitive communication of size is more instructive for students than the specific measurements found in the captions.

- There are three kinds of **writing prompts** in each chapter. All are keyed to specific works of art and appear in conjunction with figures that illustrate the works. **Journaling** prompts focus on building skills of visual analysis; **Shared Writing** responses relate the material in the chapter to today's world; and **Writing Space** prompts encourage students to engage in cross-cultural thinking, often across chapters.

NEW TO THIS EDITION OF REVEL

- **3D animations of architectural and art historical techniques** depict and explain processes and methods that are difficult for students to grasp simply through narrative text.

- **New panoramas from global sites** sourced from 360Cities have been integrated, bringing students into the setting of major buildings and monuments such as the Taj Mahal and Great Zimbabwe.

- **Each and every Closer Look** has been transformed into a REVEL video presentation, where students are guided through a detailed examination of the work, coordinated with the interpretive material about style, subject matter, and cultural context as it unfolds.

SOME ADDITIONAL CONTENT HIGHLIGHTS OF THE NEW EDITION

- **Global coverage has been deepened** with the addition of new works of art and revised discussions that incorporate new scholarship. This is especially true in the cases of South and Southeast Asia, as well as Africa—the chapters addressing these areas have been significantly reworked and expanded.

- **Chapter 33 on contemporary art** has been rethought, reorganized, and reworked for greater clarity and timeliness. Numerous new works have been incorporated.

- Throughout, **images have been updated** whenever new and improved images were available or works of art have been cleaned or restored.

- The **language used to characterize works of art**—especially those that attempt to capture the lifelike appearance of the natural world—has been **refined and clarified** to bring greater precision and nuance.

- In response to readers' requests, **discussion of many major monuments** has been revised and expanded.

- **New works have been added** to the discussion in many chapters to enhance and enrich what is said in the text. These include the Standard of Ur, the Great Mosque of Damascus, a painting from the tomb of Nebamun, the Ardabil Carpet, the burial mask of Pakal the Great, Mesa Verde, Kim Hongdo's scene of roof tiling, Imogen Cunningham's *Two Callas*, and the works of many additional contemporary artists. In addition, the following artists are now discussed through new, and more representative, works: Zhao Mengfu, Rosalba Carriera, Antonio Canova, Georgia O'Keeffe, Vladimir Tatlin, Paula Modersohn-Becker, Suzuki Harunobu, and Mary Cassatt.

Acknowledgments and Gratitude

Art History, originally written by Marilyn Stokstad and first published by Harry N. Abrams, Inc. and Prentice Hall, Inc. in 1995, has relied, each time it has been revised, on the contributions of colleagues . Their work is reflected here, and they deserve enduring gratitude since this sixth edition represents the cumulative efforts of the distinguished group of scholars and educators who contributed to the previous five editions. The work of Stephen Addiss, Chutsing Li, Marylin M. Rhie, and Christopher D. Roy for the original book has been updated by David Binkley and Patricia Darish (Africa); Claudia Brown and Robert Mowry (China and Korea); Patricia Graham (Japan); Rick Asher (South and Southeast Asia); D. Fairchild Ruggles (Islamic); Claudia Brittenham (Americas); Sara Orel and Carol Ivory (Pacific cultures); and Bradford R. Collins, David Cateforis, Patrick Frank, and Joy Sperling (Modern). For this sixth edition, Robert DeCaroli reworked the chapters on South and Southeast Asia; Susan Kart extensively rethought and revised the chapters on African art; and Virginia Spivey did the same for the final chapter, "The International Scene since the 1950s".

Words can hardly express the depth of my own gratitude to Marilyn Stokstad, who welcomed me in 2008 with enthusiasm and trust into the collaborative adventure of revising this historic textbook, conceived for students in the 21st century. We worked together on *Art History* since the fourth edition, and with her passing in 2016 as this sixth edition was going to press, I have lost a treasured colleague.

Marilyn would want me to thank her University of Kansas colleagues Sally Cornelison, Susan Craig, Susan Earle, Charles Eldredge, Kris Ercums, Sherry Fowler, Stephen Goddard, Saralyn Reece Hardy, Marsha Haufler, Marni Kessler, Amy McNair, John Pulz, Linda Stone Ferrier, and John Younger for their help and advice; and also her friends Katherine Giele and Katherine Stannard, William Crowe, David Bergeron, and Geraldo de Sousa for their sympathy and encouragement. Very special thanks go to Marilyn's sister, Karen Leider, and her niece, Anna Leider, without whose enduring support, this book would not have seen the light of day.

At Pearson, I have collaborated closely with two gifted and dedicated editors, Sarah Touborg and Helen Ronan, whose almost daily support in so many ways was at the center of Marilyn's and my work for years. I cannot imagine working on this project without them. Also working with me at Pearson were Barbara Cappuccio, Joe Scordato, Melissa Feimer, Cory Skidds, Victoria Engros, and Claire Ptaschinski. At Laurence King Publishing, Sophie Wise, Kara Hattersley-Smith, Julia Ruxton, Katharina Gruber, and Simon Walsh oversaw the production of this new edition. Much appreciation also goes to Wendy Albert, Marketing Manager extraordinaire, as well as the entire Social Sciences and Arts team at Pearson. My work has been greatly facilitated by the research assistance and creative ideas of Fletcher Coleman, Andrew Finegold, Moses Hanson-Harding, and Zoe Wray, who helped with previous editions. I also have been supported by a host of colleagues at Swarthmore College. Generations of students challenged me to hone my pedagogical skills and steady my focus on what is at stake in telling the history of art. My colleagues in the Art Department—especially Stacy Bomento, Syd Carpenter, June Cianfrana, Randall Exon, Logan Grider, Laura Holzman, Constance Hungerford, Brian Meunier, Thomas Morton, Derek Burdette, Patricia Reilly, and Tomoko Sakomura—have answered questions, shared insights on works in their areas of expertise, and offered unending encouragement and support. I am so lucky to work with them.

Many art historians have provided assistance, often at a moment's notice, and I am especially grateful to Betina Bergman, Claudia Brown, Elizabeth Brown, Brigitte Buettner, David Cateforis, Madeline Caviness, Sarah Costello, Cynthia Kristan-Graham, Joyce de Vries, Cheri Falkenstien-Doyle, Sharon Gerstel, Kevin Glowaki, Ed Gyllenhaal, Julie Hochstrasser, Vida J. Hull, Penny Jolly, Padma Kaimal, Barbara Kellum, Alison Kettering, Benton Kidd, Ann Kuttner, Anne Leader, Steven LeBlanc, Cary Liu, Elizabeth Marlowe, Samuel Morse, Thomas Morton, Kathleen Nolan, David Shapiro, Mary Shepard, Larry Silver, David Simon, Donna Sadler, Jeffrey Smith, Mark Tucker, and Tarynn Witten.

I am fortunate to have the support of many friends especially John Brendler, David Eldridge, Fiona Harrison, Stephen Lehmann, Mary Marissen, Denis Ott, Bruce and Carolyn Stephens, and Rick and Karen Taylor.

My preparation for this work runs deep. My parents, Mildred and Wat Cothren, showered me with unconditional love and made significant sacrifices to support my education, from pre-school through graduate school. Sara Shymanski, elementary school librarian at St. Martin's Episcopal School in Metairie, Louisiana, gave me courage through her example and loving encouragement to pursue unexpected passions for history, art, and the search to make them meaningful in both past and present. Françoise Celly, my painting professor during a semester abroad in Aix-en-Provence, sent me to study the Romanesque sculpture of Autun, initiating my journey toward a career in art history. At Vanderbilt University, Ljubica Popovich fostered this new interest by unlocking the mysteries of Byzantine art. My extraordinary daughters Emma and Nora remain a constant inspiration. I am so grateful for their delight in my passion for art's history, and for their dedication to keeping me from taking myself too seriously. But deepest gratitude is reserved for Susan Lowry, my wife and soul-mate, who brings joy to my life on a daily basis. She is not only patient and supportive during the long distractions of my work on this book; she provides help in countless ways. The greatest accomplishment of my life in art history occurred on the day I met her in graduate school at Columbia University in 1973.

It seems fitting in this sixth edition of *Art History*, dedicated to the memory of the scholar who created it, to conclude with the statement that ended Marilyn's "Preface" for the first edition in 1995, since it captures in her inimitable style my own thoughts as well. "As each of us develops a genuine appreciation of the arts, we come to see them as the ultimate expression of human faith and integrity as well as creativity. I have tried here to capture that creativity, courage, and vision in such a way as to engage and enrich even those encountering art history for the very first time. If I have done that, I will feel richly rewarded."

Michael W. Cothren
Sedona, AZ, and Philadelphia, PA

IN GRATITUDE: As its predecessors did, this sixth edition of *Art History* benefited from the reflections and assessments of a distinguished team of scholars and educators. The authors and Pearson are grateful to the following academic reviewers for their numerous insights and suggestions for improvement: Victor Coonin, Rhodes College; Sarah Blick, Kenyon College; Elizabeth Adan, California Polytechnic State University, San Luis Obispo; Sara Orel, Truman State University; Carolyn E. Tate, Texas Tech University; April Morris, University of Alabama; Catherine Pagani, University of Alabama; Jennie Klein, Ohio University; Rebecca Stone, Emory University; Tanja Jones, University of Alabama; Keri Watson, University of Central Florida; Stephany Rimland, Harper College; Elizabeth Sutton, University of Northern Iowa; Elizabeth Carlson, Lawrence University; Laura Crary, Presbyterian College; Camille Serchuk, Southern Connecticut State University; Lydia Host, Bishop State Community College; K.C. Williams, Northwest Florida State College; Elissa Graff, Lincoln Memorial University; Ute Wachsmann-Linnan, Columbia College; Amy Johnson, Otterbein University; Lisa Alembik, Georgia Perimeter College; Virginia Dacosta, West Chester University; Megan Levacy, Georgia Perimeter College; Victor Martinez, Monmouth College; Julia Sienkewicz, Duquesne University; Jamie Ratliff, University of Minnesota Duluth; Maureen McGuire, Full Sail University; Heather Vinson, University of West Georgia.

This edition has continued to benefit from the assistance and advice of scores of other teachers and scholars who generously answered questions, gave recommendations on organization and priorities, and provided specialized critiques during the course of work on previous editions.

We are grateful for the detailed critiques from the following readers across the country who were of invaluable assistance during work on the third, fourth, and fifth editions:

Craig Adcock, University of Iowa; Charles M. Adelman, University of Northern Iowa; Fred C. Albertson, University of Memphis; Kimberly Allen-Kattus, Northern Kentucky University; Frances Altvater, College of William and Mary; Kirk Ambrose, University of Colorado, Boulder; Michael Amy, Rochester Institute of Technology; Lisa Aronson, Skidmore College; Susan Jane Baker, University of Houston; Jennifer L. Ball, Brooklyn College, CUNY; Samantha Baskind, Cleveland State University; Tracey Boswell, Johnson County Community College; Mary Brantl, St. Edward's University; Jane H. Brown, University of Arkansas at Little Rock; Denise Budd, Bergen Community College; Stephen Caffey, Texas A&M University; Anne Chapin, Brevard College; Michelle Moseley Christian, Virginia Tech; Charlotte Lowry Collins, Southeastern Louisiana University; Sarah Kielt Costello, University of Houston; Roger J. Crum, University of Dayton; Brian A. Curran, Penn State University; Cindy B. Damschroder, University of Cincinnati; Michael T. Davis, Mount Holyoke College; Juilee Decker, Georgetown College; Laurinda Dixon, Syracuse University; Rachael Z. DeLue, Princeton University; Anne Derbes, Hood College; Sheila Dillon, Duke University; Caroline Downing, State University of New York at Potsdam; Laura Dufresne, Winthrop University; Suzanne Eberle, Kendall College of Art & Design of Ferris State University; April Eisman, Iowa State University; Dan Ewing, Barry University; Allen Farber, State University of New York at Oneonta; Arne Flaten, Coastal Carolina University; William Ganis, Wells College; John Garton, Cleveland Institute of Art; Richard Gay, University of North Carolina, Pembroke; Regina Gee, Montana State University; Sharon Gerstel, University of California, Los Angeles; Rosi Gilday, University of Wisconsin, Oshkosh; Kevin Glowacki, Texas A&M University; Amy Golahny, Lycoming College; Steve Goldberg, Hamilton College; Bertha Gutman, Delaware County Community College; Deborah Haynes, University of Colorado, Boulder; Mimi Hellman, Skidmore College; Julie Hochstrasser, University of Iowa; Eva Hoffman, Tufts University; Eunice D. Howe, University of Southern California; Phillip Jacks, George Washington University; Kimberly Jones, University of Texas, Austin; Evelyn Kain, Ripon College; Nancy Kelker, Middle Tennessee State University; Barbara Kellum, Smith College; Patricia Kennedy, Ocean County College; Jennie Klein, Ohio University; Katie Kresser, Seattle Pacific University; Cynthia Kristan-Graham, Auburn University; Barbara Platten Lash, Northern Virginia Community College; Paul Lavy, University of Hawaii at Manoa; William R. Levin, Centre College; Susan Libby, Rollins College; Henry Luttikhuizen, Calvin College; Lynn Mackenzie, College of DuPage; Elisa C. Mandell, California State University, Fullerton; Elizabeth Mansfield, New York University; Pamela Margerm, Kean University; Elizabeth Marlowe, Colgate University; Marguerite Mayhall, Kean University; Katherine A. McIver, University of Alabama at Birmingham; Dennis McNamara, Triton College; Gustav Medicus, Kent State University; Lynn Metcalf, St. Cloud State University; Janine Mileaf, Swarthmore College; Jo-Ann Morgan, Coastal Carolina University; Eleanor Moseman, Colorado State University; Johanna D. Movassat, San Jose State University; Sheila Muller, University of Utah; Beth A. Mulvaney, Meredith College; Dorothy Munger, Delaware Community College; Jacqueline Marie Musacchio, Wellesley College; Bonnie Noble, University of North Carolina at Charlotte; Elizabeth Olton, University of Texas at San Antonio; Leisha O'Quinn, Oklahoma State University; Lynn Ostling, Santa Rosa Junior College; David Parrish, Purdue University; Willow Partington,

Hudson Valley Community College; Martin Patrick, Illinois State University; Ariel Plotek, Clemson University; Patricia V. Podzorski, University of Memphis; Albert Reischuck, Kent State University; Margaret Richardson, George Mason University; James Rubin, Stony Brook University; Jeffrey Ruda, University of California, Davis; Tomoko Sakomura, Swarthmore College; Donna Sandrock, Santa Ana College; Erika Schneider, Framingham State University; Michael Schwartz, Augusta State University; Diane Scillia, Kent State University; Joshua A. Shannon, University of Maryland; David Shapiro; Karen Shelby, Baruch College; Susan Sidlauskas, Rutgers University; Jeffrey Chipps Smith, University of Texas, Austin; Royce W. Smith, Wichita State University; Stephanie Smith, Youngstown State University; Stephen Smithers, Indiana State University; Janet Snyder, West Virginia University; Richard Sundt, University of Oregon; Laurie Sylwester, Columbia College (Sonora); Carolyn Tate, Texas Tech University; Rita Tekippe, University of West Georgia; James Terry, Stephens College; Tilottama Tharoor, New York University; Sarah Thompson, Rochester Institute of Technology; Michael Tinkler, Hobart and William Smith Colleges; Amelia Trevelyan, University of North Carolina at Pembroke; Rebecca Turner, Savannah College of Art and Design; Julie Tysver, Greenville Technical College; Mary Jo Watson, University of Oklahoma; Reid Wood, Lorain County Community College; Jeryln Woodard, University of Houston; Linda Woodward, LSC Montgomery.

Our thanks also to additional expert readers including: Susan Cahan, Yale University; David Craven, University of New Mexico; Marian Feldman, University of California, Berkeley; Dorothy Johnson, University of Iowa; Genevra Kornbluth, University of Maryland; Patricia Mainardi, City University of New York; Clemente Marconi, Columbia University; Tod Marder, Rutgers University; Mary Miller, Yale University; Elizabeth Penton, Durham Technical Community College; Catherine B. Scallen, Case Western University; Kim Shelton, University of California, Berkeley.

Many people reviewed the original edition of *Art History* and have continued to assist with its revision. Every chapter was read by one or more specialists. For work on the original book and assistance with subsequent editions thanks go to: Barbara Abou-el-Haj, SUNY Binghamton; Roger Aiken, Creighton University; Molly Aitken; Anthony Alofsin, University of Texas, Austin; Christiane Andersson, Bucknell University; Kathryn Arnold; Julie Aronson, Cincinnati Art Museum; Michael Auerbach, Vanderbilt University; Larry Beck; Evelyn Bell, San Jose State University; Janetta Rebold Benton, Pace University; Janet Berlo, University of Rochester; Sarah Blick, Kenyon College; Jonathan Bloom, Boston College; Suzaan Boettger; Judith Bookbinder, Boston College; Marta Braun, Ryerson University; Elizabeth Broun, Smithsonian American Art Museum; Glen R. Brown, Kansas State University; Maria Elena Buszek, Kansas City Art Institute; Robert G. Calkins; Annmarie Weyl Carr; April Clagget, Keene State College; William W. Clark, Queens College, CUNY; John Clarke, University of Texas, Austin; Jaqueline Clipsham; Ralph T. Coe; Robert Cohon, The Nelson-Atkins Museum of Art; Alessandra Comini; James D'Emilio, University of South Florida; Walter Denny, University of Massachusetts, Amherst; Jerrilyn Dodds, City College, CUNY; Lois Drewer, Index of Christian Art; Joseph Dye, Virginia Museum of Art; James Farmer, Virginia Commonwealth University; Grace Flam, Salt Lake City Community College; Mary D. Garrard; Paula Gerson, Florida State University; Walter S. Gibson; Dorothy Glass; Oleg Grabar; Randall Griffey, Amherst College; Cynthia Hahn, Florida State University; Sharon Hill, Virginia Commonwealth University; John Hoopes, University of Kansas; Reinhild Janzen, Washburn University; Wendy Kindred, University of Maine at Fort Kent; Alan T. Kohl, Minneapolis College of Art; Ruth Kolarik, Colorado College; Carol H. Krinsky, New York University; Aileen Laing, Sweet Briar College; Janet LeBlanc, Clemson University; Charles Little, The Metropolitan Museum of Art; Laureen Reu Liu, McHenry County College; Loretta Lorance; Brian Madigan, Wayne State University; Janice Mann, Bucknell University; Judith Mann, St. Louis Art Museum; Richard Mann, San Francisco State University; James Martin; Elizabeth Parker McLachlan; Tamara Mikailova, St. Petersburg, Russia, and Macalester College; Anta Montet-White; Anne E. Morganstern, Ohio State University; Winslow Myers, Bancroft School; Lawrence Nees, University of Delaware; Amy Ogata, Cleveland Institute of Art; Judith Oliver, Colgate University; Edward Olszewski, Case Western Reserve University; Sara Jane Pearman; John G. Pedley, University of Michigan; Michael Plante, Tulane University; Eloise Quiñones-Keber, Baruch College and the Graduate Center, CUNY; Virginia Raguin, College of the Holy Cross; Nancy H. Ramage, Ithaca College; Ann M. Roberts, Lake Forest College; Lisa Robertson, The Cleveland Museum of Art; Barry Rubin; Charles Sack, Parsons, Kansas; Jan Schall, The Nelson-Atkins Museum of Art; Tom Shaw, Kean College; Pamela Sheingorn, Baruch College, CUNY; Raechell Smith, Kansas City Art Institute; Lauren Soth; Anne R. Stanton, University of Missouri, Columbia; Michael Stoughton; Thomas Sullivan, OSB, Benedictine College (Conception Abbey); Pamela Trimpe, University of Iowa; Richard Turnbull, Fashion Institute of Technology; Elizabeth Valdez del Alamo, Montclair State College; Lisa Vergara; Monica Visoná, University of Kentucky; Roger Ward, Norton Museum of Art; Mark Weil, St. Louis; David Wilkins; Marcilene Wittmer, University of Miami.

Use Notes

The various features of this book reinforce each other, helping you to become comfortable with terminology and concepts that are specific to art history.

Starter Kit and Introduction The Starter Kit is a very concise primer of basic concepts and tools. The Introduction explores the way they are used to come to an understanding of the history of art.

Captions There are two kinds of captions in this book: short and long. Short captions include information specific to the work of art or architecture illustrated:

> artist (when known)
>
> title or descriptive name of work
>
> date
>
> original location (if moved to a museum or other site)
>
> material or materials a work is made of
>
> size (height before width) in feet and inches, with meters and centimeters in parentheses
>
> present location

The order of these elements varies, depending on the type of work illustrated. Dimensions are not given for architecture, for most wall paintings, or for most architectural sculpture. Some captions have one or more lines of small print below the identification section of the caption that gives museum or collection information. This is rarely required reading; its inclusion is often a requirement for gaining permission to reproduce the work.

Some longer captions also include information that complements the discussion of a work in the main text.

Definitions of Terms You will encounter the basic terms of art history in three places:

> **In the text,** where words appearing in boldface type are defined, or glossed, at their first use.
>
> **In features on technique and other subjects,** where labeled drawings and diagrams visually reinforce the use of terms.
>
> **The glossary** contains all the words in boldface type in the text and features.

Maps At the beginning of most chapters you will find a map with all the places mentioned in the chapter.

Other In-Chapter Features Throughout the chapters is special material set off from the main text that complements, explains, or extends the chapter narrative.

"Art and its Contexts" features tell you more about selected works or issues from the chapter. "Closer Look" features help you learn more about specific aspects of important works. "Elements of Architecture" features clarify specific architectural features, often explaining engineering principles or building technology. "Technique" features outline how certain types of art are created.

Bibliography The bibliography lists books in English, organized by general works and by chapter, that are basic to the study of art history today, as well as books cited in the text.

Learning Objectives At the beginning of each chapter is a list of its key learning objectives: what the authors hope you will learn by studying the chapter.

Think About It These critical thinking questions appear at the end of each chapter and help you assess your mastery of the learning objectives by thinking through and applying what you have learned.

Dates, Abbreviations, and Other Conventions This book uses the designations BCE and CE, abbreviations for "Before the Common Era" and "Common Era," instead of BC ("Before Christ") and AD ("Anno Domini," "the year of our Lord"). The first century BCE is the period from 99 BCE to 1 BCE; the first century CE is from the year 1 CE to 99 CE. Similarly, the second century BCE is the period from 199 BCE to 100 BCE; the second century CE extends from 100 CE to 199 CE.

100's	**99–1**	**1–99**	**100's**
second century BCE	first century BCE	first century CE	second century CE

Circa ("about") is used with approximate dates, abbreviated to "c." This indicates that an exact date (or date range) is not yet verified.

An illustration is called a "figure," abbreviated as "fig." Thus, figure 6–7 is the seventh numbered illustration in Chapter 6, and figure Intro–3 is the third figure in the Introduction. There are two types of figures: photographs of artworks or models, and line drawings. Drawings are used when a work cannot be photographed or when a diagram or simple drawing is the clearest way to illustrate aspects of an object or a place.

When introducing artists, we use the words *active* and *documented* with dates, in addition to "b." (for "born") and "d." (for "died"). "Active" means that an artist worked during the years given. "Documented" means that documents link the person to that date.

Accents are used for words in French, German, Italian, and Spanish only. With few exceptions, names of cultural institutions in Western European countries are given in the form used in that country.

Titles of Works of Art It was only over the last 500 years that paintings and works of sculpture created in Europe and North America were given formal titles, either by the artist or by critics and art historians. Such formal titles are printed in italics. At other times, and in other traditions and cultures in which single titles are not important or even recognized, the descriptive titles used here are not italicized. Most often formal titles are given in English, but if a non-English title is commonly used for the work (as in FIG. 31–17, Manet's *Luncheon on the Grass*), that title (*Le déjeuner sur l'herbe*) will appear in parentheses after the English title. In all cases, titles of works that are particularly important in a chapter are shown in all capital letters and bold type.

Starter Kit

Art history focuses on the visual arts—painting, drawing, sculpture, prints, photography, ceramics, metalwork, architecture, and more. This Starter Kit addresses the basic, underlying information and concepts of art history; you can use it as a quick reference guide to the vocabulary used to classify and describe art objects. Understanding these terms is indispensable because you will encounter them again and again in reading, talking, and writing about art.

Let us begin with the basic properties of art. A work of art is a material object having both *form* and *content*. It is often described and categorized according to its *style* and *medium*.

FORM

Referring to purely visual aspects of art and architecture, the term *form* encompasses qualities of *line*, *shape*, *color*, *light*, *texture*, *space*, *mass*, *volume*, and *composition*. These qualities are known as *formal elements*. When art historians use the term *formal*, they mean "relating to form."

Line and **shape** are attributes of form. Line is an element—usually drawn or painted—the length of which is so much greater than the width that we perceive it as having only length. Line can be actual (when the line is visible), or it can be implied (when the movement of the viewer's eyes over the surface of a work follows a path encouraged by the artist). Shape, on the other hand, is the two-dimensional, or flat, area defined by the borders of an enclosing *outline* or *contour*. Shape can be *geometric*, *biomorphic* (suggesting living things; sometimes called *organic*), *closed*, or *open*. The *outline* or *contour* of a three-dimensional object can also be perceived as line.

Color has several attributes. These include *hue*, *value*, and *saturation*.

Hue is what we think of when we hear the word *color*; the terms are interchangeable. We perceive hues as a result of differing wavelengths of electromagnetic energy. The visible spectrum, which can be seen in a rainbow, runs from red through violet. When the ends of the spectrum are connected through the hue red-violet, the result may be diagrammed as a color wheel. The primary hues (numbered 1 in the diagram) are red, yellow, and blue. They are known as primaries because all other colors are made by combining these hues. Orange, green, and violet result from the mixture of two primaries and are known as secondary hues (numbered 2). Intermediate hues, or tertiaries (numbered 3), result from the mixture of a primary and a secondary. Complementary colors are the two colors directly opposite one another on the color wheel, such as red and green. Red, orange, and yellow are regarded as warm colors and appear to advance toward us. Blue, green, and violet, which seem to recede, are called cool colors. Black and white are considered neutrals, not colors but, in terms of light, black is understood as the absence of color and white as the mixture of all colors.

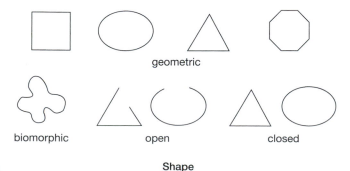

geometric

biomorphic   open   closed

Shape

Value is the relative degree of lightness or darkness of a given color and is created by the amount of light reflected from an object's surface. A dark green has a deeper value than a light green, for example. In black-and-white reproductions of colored objects, you see only value, and some artworks—for example, a drawing made with black ink—possess only value, not hue or saturation.

Value scale from white to black.

+ WHITE   PURE HUE   + BLACK

Value variation in red.

Saturation, also sometimes referred to as *intensity*, is a color's quality of brightness or dullness. A color described as highly saturated looks vivid and pure; a hue of low saturation looks muddy or grayed.

PURE HUE   DULLED   PURE HUE

Intensity scale from bright to dull.

Texture, another attribute of form, is the tactile (or touch-perceived) quality of a surface. It is described by words such as *smooth, polished, rough, prickly, grainy,* or *oily*. Texture takes two forms: the texture of the actual surface of the work of art and the implied (illusionistically described) surface of objects represented in the work of art.

Technique

PICTORIAL DEVICES FOR DEPICTING RECESSION IN SPACE

overlapping

In overlapping, partially covered elements are meant to be seen as located behind those covering them.

diminution

In diminution of scale, successively smaller elements are perceived as being progressively farther away than the largest ones.

vertical perspective

Vertical perspective stacks elements, with the higher ones intended to be perceived as deeper in space.

atmospheric perspective

Through atmospheric perspective, objects in the far distance (often in bluish-gray hues) have less clarity than nearer objects. The sky becomes paler as it approaches the horizon.

orthogonals

divergent perspective

In divergent or reverse perspective, forms widen slightly and imaginary lines called orthogonals diverge as they recede in space.

intuitive perspective

Intuitive perspective takes the opposite approach from divergent perspective. Forms become narrower and orthogonals converge the farther they are from the viewer, approximating the optical experience of spatial recession.

one-point

vanishing point   horizon line   vanishing point

two-point

linear perspective

Linear perspective (also called scientific, mathematical, one-point and Renaissance perspective) is a rationalization or standardization of intuitive perspective that was developed in fifteenth-century Italy. It uses mathematical formulas to construct images in which all elements are shaped by, or arranged along, orthogonals that converge in one or more vanishing points on a horizon line.

Space is what contains forms. It may be actual and three-dimensional, as it is with sculpture and architecture, or it may be fictional, represented illusionistically in two dimensions, as when artists represent recession into the distance on a flat surface—such as a wall or a canvas—by using various systems of *perspective*.

Mass and **volume** are properties of three-dimensional things. Mass is solid matter—whether sculpture or architecture—that takes up space. Volume is enclosed or defined space and may be either solid or hollow. Like space, mass and volume may be illusionistically represented on a two-dimensional surface, such as in a painting or a photograph.

Composition is the organization, or arrangement, of forms in a work of art. Shapes and colors may be repeated or varied, balanced symmetrically or asymmetrically; they may be stable or dynamic. The possibilities are nearly endless, and the artist's choices depend both on the time and place where the work was created and the objectives of individual artists. Pictorial depth (spatial recession) is a specialized aspect of composition in which the three-dimensional world is represented on a flat surface, or *picture plane*. The area "behind" the picture plane is called the *picture space* and conventionally contains three "zones": *foreground*, *middle ground*, and *background*.

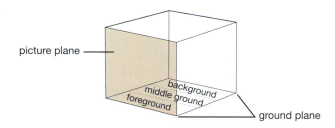

picture plane

background
middle ground
foreground

ground plane

Various techniques for conveying a sense of pictorial depth have been devised by artists in different cultures and at different times (see "Pictorial Devices for Depicting Recession in Space" opposite). In some European art, the use of various systems of perspective has sought to create highly convincing illusions of recession into space. At other times and in other cultures, indications of recession have been suppressed or avoided in order to emphasize surface rather than space.

CONTENT

Content includes *subject matter*, but not all works of art have subject matter. Many buildings, paintings, sculptures, and other art objects include no recognizable references to things in nature nor to any story or historical situation, focusing instead on lines, colors, masses, volumes, and other formal elements. However, all works of art—even those without recognizable subject matter—have content, or meaning, insofar as they seek to communicate ideas, convey feelings, or affirm the beliefs and values of their makers, their patrons, and usually the people who originally viewed or used them.

Content may derive from the social, political, religious, and economic *contexts* in which a work was created, the *intention* of the artist, and the *reception* of the work by beholders (the audience). Art historians, applying different methods of *interpretation*, often arrive at different conclusions regarding the content of a work of art, and single works of art can contain more than one meaning because they are occasionally directed at more than one audience.

The study of subject matter is called *iconography* (literally, "the writing of images") and includes the identification of *symbols*—images that take on meaning through association, resemblance, or convention.

STYLE

Expressed very broadly, *style* is the combination of form and composition that makes a work distinctive. *Stylistic analysis* is one of art history's most developed practices, because it is how art historians recognize the work of an individual artist or the characteristic manner of groups of artists working in a particular time or place. Some of the most commonly used terms to discuss *artistic styles* include *period style, regional style, personal style, representational style, abstract style, linear style,* and *painterly style*.

Period style refers to the common traits of works of art and architecture from a particular historical era. It is good practice not to use the words "style" and "period" interchangeably. Style is the sum of many influences and characteristics, including the period of its creation. An example of proper usage is "an American house from the Colonial period built in the Georgian style."

Regional style refers to stylistic traits that persist in a geographic region. An art historian whose specialty is medieval art can recognize Spanish style through many successive medieval periods and can distinguish individual objects created in medieval Spain from other medieval objects that were created in, for example, Italy.

Personal style refers to stylistic traits associated with an individual artist.

Representational styles are those that describe the appearance of recognizable subject matter in ways that make it seem lifelike.

> **Realism** and **naturalism** are terms that some people use interchangeably to characterize artists' attempts to represent the observable world in a manner that appears to describe its visual appearance accurately. When capitalized, Realism refers to a specific period style (see Chapter 31).

Idealization strives to create images of physical perfection according to the prevailing values or tastes of a culture. An artist may work in a representational style and idealize it to capture an underlying value or expressive effect.

Illusionism refers to a highly detailed style that seeks to create a convincing illusion of physical reality by describing its visual appearance meticulously.

Abstract styles depart from mimicking lifelike appearance to capture the essence of a form. An abstract artist may work from nature or from a memory image of nature's forms and colors, which are simplified, stylized, perfected, distorted, elaborated, or otherwise transformed to achieve a desired expressive effect.

Nonrepresentational (or nonobjective) is a term used for works of art that do not aim to mimic lifelike appearances.

Expressionism refers to styles in which the artist exaggerates aspects of form to draw out the beholder's subjective response or to project the artist's own subjective feelings.

Linear describes both styles and techniques. In linear styles artists use line as the primary means of definition. But linear paintings can also incorporate *modeling*—creating an illusion of three-dimensional substance through shading, usually executed so that brushstrokes nearly disappear.

Painterly describes a style of representation in which vigorous, evident brushstrokes dominate, and outlines, shadows, and highlights are brushed in freely.

MEDIUM AND TECHNIQUE

Medium (plural, *media*) refers to the material or materials from which a work of art is made. Literally anything can be used to make a work of art, including not only traditional materials like paint, ink, and stone, but also rubbish, food, and the earth itself.

Technique is the process that transforms media into a work of art. Various techniques are explained throughout this book in "Technique" features. Two-dimensional media and techniques include painting, drawing, printmaking, and photography. Three-dimensional media and techniques are sculpture (using, for example, stone, wood, clay, or metal), architecture, and small-scale arts (such as jewelry, containers, or vessels) in media such as ceramics, metal, or wood.

Painting includes wall painting and fresco, illumination (the decoration of books with paintings), panel painting (painting on wood panels), painting on canvas, and handscroll and hanging scroll painting. The paint in these examples is pigment mixed with a liquid vehicle, or binder. Some art historians also consider pictorial media such as mosaic and stained glass—where the pigment is arranged in solid form—as a type of painting.

Graphic arts are those that involve the application of lines and strokes to a two-dimensional surface or support, most often paper. Drawing is a graphic art, as are the various forms of printmaking. Drawings may be sketches (quick visual notes, often made in preparation for larger drawings or paintings); studies (more carefully drawn analyses of details or entire compositions); cartoons (full-scale drawings made in preparation for work in another medium, such as fresco, stained glass, or tapestry); or complete artworks in themselves. Drawings can be made with ink, charcoal, crayon, or pencil. Prints, unlike drawings, are made in multiple copies. The various forms of printmaking include woodcut, the intaglio processes (engraving, etching, drypoint), and lithography.

Photography (literally, "light writing") is a medium that involves the rendering of optical images through a recording of light effects. Photographic images are typically recorded by a camera.

Sculpture is three-dimensional art that is carved, modeled, cast, or assembled. Carved sculpture is subtractive in the sense that the image is created by taking away material. Wood, stone, and ivory are common materials used to create carved sculptures. Modeled sculpture is considered additive, meaning that the object is built up from a material, such as clay, that is soft enough to be molded and shaped. Metal sculpture is usually cast or is assembled by welding or a similar means of permanent joining.

Sculpture is either free-standing (that is, surrounded by space) or pictorial relief. Relief sculpture projects from the background surface of the same piece of material. High-relief sculpture projects far from its background; low-relief sculpture is only slightly raised; and sunken relief, found mainly in ancient Egyptian art, is carved into the surface, with the highest part of the relief being the flat surface.

Ephemeral arts include processions, ceremonies, and ritual dances (often with décor, costumes, or masks); performance art; earthworks; cinema and video art; and some forms of digital or computer art. All impose a temporal limitation—the artwork is viewable for a finite period of time and then disappears forever, is in a constant state of change, or must be replayed to be experienced again.

Architecture creates enclosures for human activity or habitation. It is three-dimensional, highly spatial, functional, and closely bound with developments in technology and materials. Since it is difficult to capture in a photograph, several types of schematic drawings are commonly used to enable the visualization of a building:

Plans depict a structure's masses and voids, presenting a view from above of the building's footprint as if it had been sliced horizontally at about waist height.

Plan: Philadelphia, Vanna Venturi House

Sections reveal the interior of a building as if it had been cut vertically from top to bottom.

Section: Rome, Sta. Costanza

Isometric drawings show buildings from oblique angles either seen from above ("bird's-eye view") to reveal their basic three-dimensional forms (often cut away so we can peek inside) or from below ("worm's-eye view") to represent the arrangement of interior spaces and the upward projection of structural elements.

Isometric cutaway from above: Ravenna, San Vitale

Isometric projection from below: Istanbul, Hagia Sophia

Introduction

I.a Explain the cultural foundations of the diverse ways art has been defined and characterized.

I.b Distinguish four ways art historians investigate works of art.

I.c Identify the components of the four-part method of art historical investigation that leads to the historical interpretation of a work of art.

The title of this book seems clear. It defines a field of academic study and scholarly research that has achieved a secure place in college and university curricula across North America. But *Art History* couples two words—even two worlds—that are less well focused when separated. What is art? In what sense does it have a history? Students of art and its history should pause and engage, even if briefly, with these large questions before beginning the journey surveyed in the following chapters.

What is Art?

What are the cultural foundations of the diverse ways art has been defined and characterized?

Artists, critics, art historians, and the general public all grapple with this thorny question. The *Random House Dictionary* defines "art" as "the quality, production, expression, or realm of what is beautiful, or of more than ordinary significance." Others have characterized "art" as something human-made that combines creative imagination and technical skill and satisfies an innate desire for order and harmony—perhaps a human hunger for the beautiful. This seems relatively straightforward until we start to look at modern and contemporary art, where there has been a heated and extended debate concerning "What is art?" The focus is often far from questions of transcendent beauty, ordered design, or technical skill; it centers instead on the conceptual meaning of a work for an elite target audience or the attempt to pose challenging questions or unsettle deep-seated cultural ideas.

The works of art discussed in this book represent a privileged subset of artifacts produced by past and present cultures. They were usually meant to be preserved, and they are currently considered worthy of conservation and display. The determination of which artifacts are exceptional—which are works of art—evolves through the actions, opinions, and selections of artists, patrons, governments, collectors, archaeologists, museums, art historians, and others. Labeling objects as art is usually meant to signal that they transcended or now transcend in some profound way their practical function, often embodying cherished cultural ideas or asserting foundational values. Sometimes it can also mean they are considered beautiful, well designed, and made with loving care, but this is not always the case. We will discover that at various times and places, the complex notion of what art is has little to do with standards of skill or beauty. Some critics and historians argue broadly that works of art are tendentious embodiments of power and privilege, hardly sublime expressions of beauty or truth. After all, art can be unsettling as well as soothing, challenging as well as reassuring, whether made in the present or surviving from the past.

Increasingly, we are realizing that our judgments about what constitutes art—as well as what constitutes beauty—are conditioned by our own education and experience. Whether acquired at home, in classrooms, in museums, at the movies, or on the Internet, our responses to art are learned behaviors influenced by class, gender, race, geography, and economic status as well as education. Even art historians find that their definitions of what constitutes art—and what constitutes artistic quality—evolve with additional research and understanding. Exploring works by twentieth-century painter Mark Rothko and nineteenth-century quilt-makers Martha Knowles and Henrietta Thomas demonstrates how definitions of art and artistic value are subject to change over time.

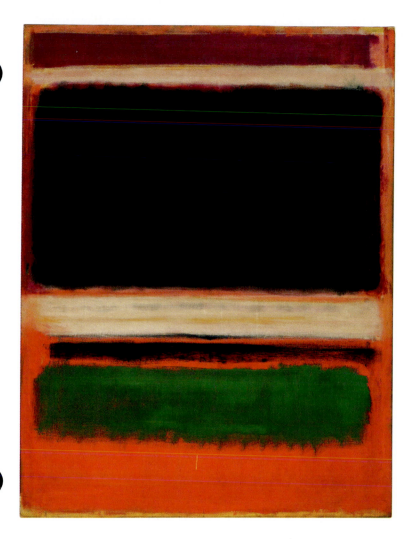

INTRO–1 Mark Rothko **MAGENTA, BLACK, GREEN ON ORANGE (NO. 3/NO. 13)**
1949. Oil on canvas, 7′1⅜″ × 5′5″ (2.165 × 1.648 m). Museum of Modern Art, New York.

Credit: © 2016. Digital Image, The Museum of Modern Art, New York/Scala, Florence. © 1998 Kate Rothko Prizel & Christopher Rothko/Artists Rights Society (ARS), New York

vision." In part because they are carefully crafted by an established artist who provided these kinds of intellectual justifications for their character and appearance, Rothko's abstract paintings are broadly considered works of art and are treasured possessions of major museums across the globe.

Works of art, however, do not always have to be created by individuals who perceive themselves as artists. Nor are all works produced for an art market surrounded by critics and collectors ready to explain, exhibit, and disperse them, ideally to prestigious museums. Such is the case with this quilt (**FIG. Intro–2**) made by Martha Knowles and Henrietta Thomas a century before Rothko's painting. Their work is similarly composed of blocks of color, and, like Rothko, they produced their visual effect by arranging these flat chromatic shapes carefully and regularly on a rectangular field. But this quilt was not meant to hang on the wall of an art museum. It is the social product of a friendship, intended as an intimate

Rothko's painting **NO. 3/NO. 13 (MAGENTA, BLACK, GREEN ON ORANGE)** (**FIG. Intro–1**), is a well-known example of the sort of abstract painting that was considered the epitome of artistic sophistication by the mid-twentieth-century New York art establishment. It was created by an artist who meant it to be a work of art. It was acquired by the Museum of Modern Art in New York, and its position on the walls of that museum is a sure sign of its acceptance as art by a powerful cultural institution. However, outside the context of the American artists, dealers, critics, and collectors who made up Rothko's art world, such paintings were often received with skepticism. They were seen by many as incomprehensible—lacking both technical skill and recognizable subject matter, two criteria that were part of the general public's definition of art at the time. Abstract paintings inspired a popular retort: "That's not art; my child could do it!" Interestingly enough, Rothko saw in the childlike character of his own paintings one of the qualities that made them works of art. Children, he said, "put forms, figures, and views into pictorial arrangements, employing out of necessity most of the rules of optical **perspective** and geometry but without the knowledge that they are employing them." He characterized his own art as childlike, as "an attempt to recapture the freshness and naiveté of childish

INTRO–2 Martha Knowles and Henrietta Thomas **MY SWEET SISTER EMMA**
1843. Cotton quilt, 8′11″ × 9′1″ (2.72 × 2.77 m). International Quilt Studies Center and Museum, University of Nebraska, Lincoln.

gift presented to a loved one for use in her home. An inscription on the quilt itself makes this clear: "From M.A. Knowles to her Sweet Sister Emma, 1843." Thousands of such friendship quilts were made by women during the middle years of the nineteenth century for use on beds, either to provide warmth or as a covering spread. Whereas quilts were sometimes displayed to a broad and enthusiastic audience of producers and admirers at competitions held at state and county fairs, they were not collected by art museums or revered by artists until relatively recently.

In 1971 at the Whitney Museum in New York—an establishment bastion of the art world of which Rothko had been a part—art historians Jonathan Holstein and Gail van der Hoof mounted an exhibition entitled "Abstract Design in American Quilts," demonstrating the artistic affinity we have already noted in comparing the way Knowles and Thomas, like Rothko, create abstract patterns with fields of color. Quilts were later accepted—or perhaps **appropriated**—as works of art and hung on the walls of a New York art museum because of their visual similarities with the avant-garde, abstract works of art created by elite New York artists.

Art historian Patricia Mainardi took the case for quilts one significant step further in a pioneering article of 1973 published in *The Feminist Art Journal*. Entitled "Quilts: The Great American Art," her argument was rooted not only in the aesthetic affinity of quilts with the esteemed work of contemporary abstract painters, but also in a political conviction that the definition of art had to be broadened. What was at stake here was historical veracity. Mainardi began, "Women have always made art. But for most women, the arts highest valued by male society have been closed to them for just that reason. They have put their creativity instead into the needlework arts, which exist in fantastic variety wherever there are women, and which in fact are a universal female art, transcending race, class, and national borders." She argued for the inclusion of quilts within the history of art to give deserved attention to the work of women artists who had been excluded from discussion because they created textiles and because they worked outside the male-dominated professional structures of the art world—because they

were women. Quilts now hang as works of art on the walls of museums and appear with regularity in books that survey the history of art.

As these two examples demonstrate, definitions of art are rooted in cultural systems of value that are subject to change. And as they change, the list of works considered by art historians is periodically revised. Determining what to study is a persistent part of the art historian's task.

Architecture

This book contains much more than paintings and textiles. Within these pages you will also encounter sculpture, vessels, books, churches, jewelry, tombs, chairs, temples, photographs, houses, and more. But as with Rothko's *No. 3/No. 13 (Magenta, Black, Green on Orange)* (SEE FIG. Intro-1) and Knowles and Thomas's *My Sweet Sister Emma* (SEE FIG. Intro-2), criteria have been used to determine which works are selected for inclusion in a book titled *Art History*. Architecture—which includes churches, tombs, temples, and houses, as well as many other kinds of buildings—presents an interesting case.

Buildings meet functional human needs by enclosing human habitation or activity. Many works of architecture, however, are considered "exceptional" because they transcend functional demands by manifesting distinguished architectural design or because they embody in important ways the values and goals of the culture that built them. Such buildings are usually produced by architects influenced, like painters, by great works and traditions from the past. In some cases they harmonize with, or react to, their natural or urban surroundings. For such reasons, they are discussed in books on the history of art.

INTRO-3 Le Corbusier
NÔTRE-DAME-DU-HAUT

Ronchamp, France. 1950–1955.

Credit: © F.L.C./ADAGP, Paris/Artists Rights Society (ARS), New York 2016. Photo © Michal Sikorski/123 RF

Typical of such buildings is the church of Nôtre-Dame-du-Haut in Ronchamp, France, designed and constructed between 1950 and 1955 by Swiss architect Charles-Edouard Jeanneret, better known by his pseudonym, Le Corbusier (**FIG. Intro-3**). This building is the product of a significant historical moment, rich in international cultural meaning. A pilgrimage church on this site had been destroyed during World War II, and the creation here of a new church symbolized the end of a devastating war, embodying hopes for a brighter global future. Le Corbusier's design—drawing on sources that ranged from Algerian mosques to imperial Roman villas, from crab shells to airplane wings—is sculptural as well as architectural. Built at the crest of a hill, it soars toward the sky but at the same time seems solidly anchored in the earth. And its coordination with the curves of the natural landscape creates an outdoor setting for religious ceremonies (to the right in the figure) to supplement the spaces of the church interior. In fact, this building is so renowned today as a monument of modern architecture that the bus-loads of pilgrims who arrive at the site are mainly architects and devotees of architectural history.

What is Art History?

What are four ways art historians investigate works of art?

There are many ways to study or appreciate works of art. Art history represents one specific approach, with its own goals and its own methods of assessment and interpretation. Simply put, art historians seek to understand the meaning of art from the past within its original cultural contexts, both from the point of view of its producers—artists, architects, and patrons—as well as from the point of view of its consumers—those who formed its original audience. Coming to an understanding of the cultural meaning of a work of art requires detailed and patient investigation on many levels, especially with art that was produced long ago and in societies distinct from our own. This is a scholarly rather than an intuitive exercise. In art history, the work of art is seen as an embodiment of the values, goals, and aspirations of its time and place of origin. It is a part of culture.

Art historians use a variety of theoretical perspectives and interpretive strategies to do their work. But as a place to begin, the work of art historians can be divided into four types of investigation:

1. assessment of physical properties,
2. analysis of visual or formal structure,
3. identification of subject matter or conventional symbolism, and
4. integration within cultural context.

Assessing Physical Properties

Of the methods used by art historians to study works of art, this is the most objective, but it requires close access to the work itself. Physical properties include shape, size, materials, and technique. For instance, many pictures are rectangular (SEE FIG. Intro-1), but some are round (see **FIG. C** in "Closer Look" on page xxvii). Paintings as large as Rothko's require us to stand back if we want to take in the whole image, whereas some paintings (see **FIG. A** in "Closer Look" on page xxvi) are so small that we are drawn up close to examine their detail. Rothko's painting and Knowles and Thomas's quilt are both rectangles of similar size, but they are distinguished by the materials from which they are made—oil paint on canvas versus cotton fabric joined by stitching. In art history books, most physical properties can only be understood from descriptions in captions, but when we are in the presence of the work of art itself, size and shape may be the first thing we notice. To fully understand **medium** and technique, however, it may be necessary to employ methods of scientific analysis or documentary research to figure out the details of the practices of artists at the time when and place where the work was created.

Analyzing Formal Structure

Art historians explore the visual character that artists give their works—using the materials and the techniques chosen to create them—in a process called **formal analysis**. On the most basic level, it is divided into two parts:

- assessing the individual visual elements or formal vocabulary that make up pictorial or sculptural communication, and

- discovering the overall arrangement, organization, or structure of an image, a design system that art historians often refer to as **composition**.

THE ELEMENTS OF VISUAL EXPRESSION   Artists control and vary the visual character of works of art to give their subjects and ideas meaning and expression, vibrancy and persuasion, challenge or delight (see "Closer Look" on pages xxvi–xxvii). For example, the motifs, objects, figures, and environments in paintings can be sharply defined by line (SEE FIGS. Intro-2, Intro-4), or they can be suggested by a sketchier definition (SEE FIGS. Intro-1, Intro-5). Painters can simulate the appearance of three-dimensional form through **modeling** or shading (SEE FIG. Intro-4 and **FIG. C** in "Closer Look" on page xxvii), that is, by imitating the way light from a single source will highlight one side of a solid while leaving the other side in shadow. Alternatively, artists can avoid any strong sense of three-dimensionality by emphasizing patterns on a surface rather than forms in space (SEE FIG. Intro-1 and **FIG. A** in "Closer Look" on page xxvi).

A Closer Look

VISUAL ELEMENTS OF PICTORIAL EXPRESSION: LINE, LIGHT, FORM, AND COLOR

LINE

A. CARPET PAGE FROM THE LINDISFARNE GOSPELS

From Lindisfarne, England. c. 715–720. Ink and tempera on vellum, 13⅜ × 9⁷⁄₁₆″ (34 × 24 cm). The British Library, London.

Credit: © The British Library Board (Cotton Nero D. IV, f.26v)

Every element in this complicated painting is sharply outlined by abrupt changes between light and dark or between one color and another; there are no gradual or shaded transitions. Since the picture was created in part with pen and ink, the linearity is a logical extension of medium and technique. And although line itself is a "flattening" or two-dimensionalizing element in pictures, a complex and consistent system of overlapping gives the linear animal forms a sense of shallow but carefully worked-out three-dimensional relationships to one another.

LIGHT

B. Georges de la Tour **THE EDUCATION OF THE VIRGIN**

c. 1650. Oil on canvas, 33″ × 39½″ (83.8 × 100.4 cm). The Frick Collection, New York. Purchased by the Frick Collection 1948. (1948.1.155).

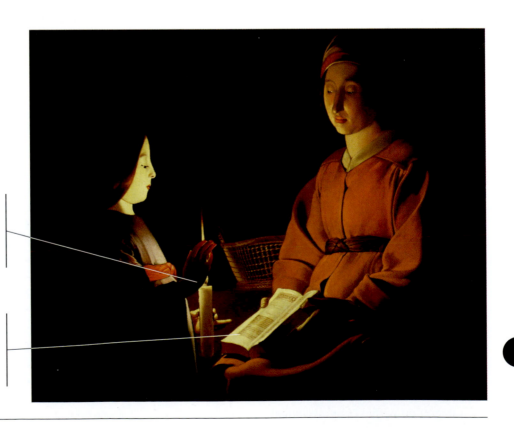

The source of illumination is a candle depicted within the painting. The young girl's raised right hand shields its flame, allowing the artist to demonstrate his virtuosity in painting the translucency of human flesh.

Since the candle's flame is partially concealed, its luminous intensity is not allowed to distract from those aspects of the painting most brilliantly illuminated by it—the face of the girl and the book she is reading.

FORM

C. Michelangelo
THE HOLY FAMILY (DONI TONDO)

c. 1503. Oil and tempera on panel, diameter 3′11¼″ (1.2 m). Galleria degli Uffizi, Florence.

Credit: © Studio Fotografico Quattrone, Florence

The complex overlapping of their highly three-dimensionalized bodies conveys the somewhat contorted positions and spatial relationship of these three figures.

Through the use of modeling or shading—a gradual transition from lights to darks—Michelangelo imitates the way solid forms are illuminated from a single light source—the side closest to the light source is bright while the other side is cast in shadow—and gives a sense of three-dimensional form to his figures.

In a technique called **foreshortening**, the carefully calculated angle of the Virgin's elbow makes it seem to project out toward the viewer.

The actual three-dimensional projection of the sculpted heads in medallions around the frame—designed for this painting by Michelangelo himself—heightens the illusion of three-dimensionality in the figures painted on its flat surface.

Junayd chose to flood every aspect of his painting with light, as if everything in it were illuminated from all sides at once. As a result, the emphasis here is on jewel-like color. The vibrant tonalities and dazzling detail of the dreamy landscape are not only more important than the simulation of three-dimensional forms within a space, they actually upstage the human drama taking place against a patterned, tipped-up ground in the lower third of the picture.

COLOR

D. Junayd **HUMAY AND HUMAYUN**

From a manuscript of the Divan of Kwaju Kirmani. Made in Baghdad, Iraq. 1396. Color, ink, and gold on paper, 12⅝ × 9⁷⁄₁₆″ (32 × 24 cm). The British Library, London.

Credit: © The British Library Board (Add. 18113, f.23)

INTRO–4 Raphael **MADONNA OF THE GOLDFINCH (MADONNA DEL CARDELLINO)**
1506. Oil on panel, 42 × 29½″ (106.7 × 74.9 cm).
Galleria degli Uffizi, Florence.

The vibrant colors of this important work were revealed in the course of a careful, ten-year restoration, completed in 2008.

Credit: © Studio Fotografico Quattrone, Florence. Courtesy of the Ministero Beni e Att. Culturali

In addition to revealing the solid substance of forms through modeling, dramatic lighting can also guide viewers' attention to specific areas of a picture see **FIG. B** in "Closer Look" on page xxvi), or it can be lavished on every aspect of a picture to reveal all its detail and highlight the vibrancy of its color (see **FIG. D** in "Closer Look" on page xxvii). Color itself can be muted or intensified, depending on the mood artists want to create or the tastes and expectations of their audiences.

Thus, artists communicate with their viewers by making choices in the way they use and emphasize the elements of visual expression, and art historical analysis seeks to reveal how these choices bring meaning to a work of art. For example, in two paintings of women with children (SEE FIGS. Intro–4, Intro–5), Raphael and Renoir work with the same visual elements of line, form, light, and color in the creation of their images, but they employ these shared elements to different expressive ends. Raphael concentrates on line to clearly differentiate each element of his picture as a separate form. Careful modeling describes these outlined forms as substantial solids surrounded by space. This gives his subjects a sense of clarity, stability, and grandeur. Renoir, on the other hand, focuses on the flickering of light and the play of color as he minimizes the sense of three-dimensionality in individual forms. This gives his image a more ephemeral, casual sense. Art historians pay close attention to such variations in the use of visual elements—the building blocks of artistic expression—and use visual analysis to characterize the expressive effect of a particular work, a particular artist, or a general period defined by place and date.

COMPOSITION   When art historians analyze composition, they focus not on the individual elements of visual expression but on the overall arrangement and organizing design or structure of a work of art. In Raphael's **MADONNA OF THE GOLDFINCH** (**FIG. Intro–4**), for example, the group of figures has been arranged in a triangular shape and placed at the center of the picture. Raphael emphasized

this central focus by opening the clouds to reveal a patch of blue in the middle of the sky and by flanking the figural group with lacelike trees. Since the Madonna is at the center and the two boys are divided between the two sides of the triangle, roughly—though not precisely—equidistant from the center of the painting, this is a bilaterally symmetrical composition: on either side of an implied vertical line at the center of the picture, there are equivalent forms on left and right, matched and balanced in a mirrored correspondence. Art historians refer to such an implied line—around which the elements of a picture are organized—as an **axis**. Raphael's painting has not only a vertical, but also a horizontal axis, indicated by a line of demarcation between light and dark—as well as between degrees of color saturation—in the landscape. The belt of the Madonna's dress is aligned with this horizontal axis, and this correspondence, taken with the coordination of her head with the blue patch in the sky, relates her harmoniously to the natural world in which she sits, lending a sense of stability, order, and balance to the picture as a whole.

The main axis in Renoir's painting of **MME. CHARPEN-TIER AND HER CHILDREN** (FIG. Intro-5) is neither vertical nor horizontal, but diagonal, running from the upper right to the lower left corner of the painting. All major elements of the composition are aligned along this axis—dog, children, mother, and the table and chair that represent the most complex and detailed aspect of the setting. The upper left and lower right corners of the painting balance each other on either side of the diagonal axis as relatively simple fields of neutral tone, setting off and framing the main subjects between them. The resulting arrangement is not bilaterally symmetrical, but blatantly asymmetrical, with the large figural mass pushed into the left side of the picture. And unlike Raphael's composition, where the spatial relationship of the figures and their environment is mapped by the measured placement of elements that become increasingly smaller in scale and fuzzier in definition as they recede into the background, the relationship of Renoir's figures to their spatial environment is less clearly defined as they recede into the background along the dramatic diagonal axis. Nothing distracts us from the bold informality of this family gathering.

Both Raphael and Renoir arrange their figures carefully and purposefully, but they use distinctive compositional systems that communicate different notions of the way these figures interact with each other and the world around them. Art historians pay special attention to how pictures are arranged, because composition is one of the principal ways artists give their paintings expressive meaning.

Identifying Subject Matter

Art historians have traditionally sought subject matter and meaning in works of art with a system of analysis that was outlined by Erwin Panofsky (1892–1968), an influential German scholar who was expelled from his academic position by the Nazis in 1933 and spent the rest of his career of research and teaching in the United States. Panofsky proposed that when we seek to understand the subject of a work of art, we derive meaning initially in two ways:

- First we perceive what he called "natural subject matter" by recognizing forms and situations that we know from our own experience.

- Then we use what he called "**iconography**" to identify the conventional meanings associated with forms and figures as bearers of narrative or symbolic content, often specific to a particular time and place.

Some artworks, like Rothko's abstractions and Knowles and Thomas's quilt, do not contain subjects drawn from the world around us, from stories, or from conventional symbolism, but Panofsky's scheme remains a standard method of investigating meaning in works of art that present narrative subjects, portray specific people or places, or embody cultural values with iconic imagery or allegory.

NATURAL SUBJECT MATTER We recognize some things in works of visual art simply by virtue of living in a world similar to that represented by the artist. For example, in the two paintings by Raphael and Renoir just examined (SEE FIGS. Intro-4, Intro-5), we immediately recognize the principal human figures in both as a woman and two children—boys in the case of Raphael's painting, girls in Renoir's. We can also make a general identification of the animals: a bird in the hand of Raphael's boys, and a pet dog under one of Renoir's girls. And natural

INTRO-5 Auguste Renoir
MME. CHARPENTIER AND HER CHILDREN
1878. Oil on canvas, 60½ × 74⅞" (153.7 × 190.2 cm). Metropolitan Museum of Art, New York.

Credit: © 2016. Image copyright The Metropolitan Museum of Art/Art Resource/Scala, Florence

subject matter can extend from an identification of figures to an understanding of the expressive significance of their postures and facial features. We might see in the boy who snuggles between the knees of the woman in Raphael's painting, placing his own foot on top of hers, an anxious child seeking the security of physical contact with a trusted caretaker—perhaps his mother—in response to fear of the bird he reaches out to touch. Many of us have seen insecure children take this very pose in response to potentially unsettling encounters.

The closer the work of art is in both time and place to our own situation temporally and geographically, the easier it sometimes is to identify what is represented. However, it's not always that simple. Although Renoir painted his picture almost 140 years ago in France, the furniture in the background still looks familiar, as does the book in the hand of Raphael's Madonna, painted five centuries before our time. But the object hanging from the belt of the scantily clad boy at the left in Raphael's painting will require identification for most of us. Iconographic investigation is necessary to understand the function of this form.

ICONOGRAPHY Some subjects are associated with conventional meanings established at a specific time or place, some of the human figures portrayed in works of art have specific identities, and some of the objects or forms have symbolic or allegorical meanings in addition to their natural subject matter. Discovering these conventional meanings of art's subject matter is called iconography (see "Closer Look" opposite).

For example, the woman accompanied in the outdoors by two boys in Raphael's *Madonna of the Goldfinch* (SEE FIG. INTRO-4) would have been immediately recognized by members of its intended early sixteenth-century Florentine audience as the Virgin Mary. Viewers would have identified the naked boy standing between her knees as her son Jesus and the boy holding the bird as Jesus's cousin John the Baptist, sheathed in the animal skin garment that he would wear in the wilderness and equipped with a shallow cup attached to his belt, ready to be used in baptisms. Such attributes of clothing and equipment are often critical in making iconographic identifications. The goldfinch in the Baptist's hand was at this time and place a symbol of Christ's death on the cross, an allegorical implication that makes the Christ Child's retreat into secure contact with his mother—already noted on the level of natural subject matter—understandable in relation to a specific story. The comprehension of conventional meanings in this painting would have been almost automatic among those for whom it was painted, but for us, separated by time and place, some research is necessary to recover associations that are no longer part of our everyday world.

Although it may not initially seem as unfamiliar, the subject matter of Renoir's 1878 portrait of *Mme.* *Charpentier and her Children* (SEE FIG. INTRO-5) is in fact even more obscure. There are those in twenty-first-century American culture for whom the figures and symbols in Raphael's painting are still recognizable and meaningful, but Marguérite-Louise Charpentier died in 1904, and no one living today would be able to identify her based on the likeness Renoir presumably gave to her face in this family portrait commissioned by her husband, the wealthy and influential publisher Georges Charpentier. We need the painting's title to make that identification. And Mme. Charpentier is outfitted here in a gown created by English designer Charles Frederick Worth, the dominant figure in late nineteenth-century Parisian high fashion. Her clothing was a clear attribute of her wealth for those who recognized its source; most of us need to investigate to uncover its meaning. But a greater surprise awaits the student who pursues further research on her children. Although they clearly seem to our eyes to represent two daughters, the child closest to Mme. Charpentier is actually her son Paul, who at age 3, following standard Parisian bourgeois practice, has not yet had his first haircut and still wears clothing comparable to that of his older sister Georgette, perched on the family dog. It is not unusual in art history to encounter situations where our initial conclusions on the level of natural subject matter will need to be revised after some iconographic research.

Integration within Cultural Context

Natural subject matter and iconography were only two of three steps proposed by Panofsky for coming to an understanding of the meaning of works of art. The third step he labeled "**iconology.**" Its aim is to interpret the work of art as an embodiment of its cultural situation, to place it within broad social, political, religious, and intellectual contexts. Such integration into history requires more than identifying subject matter or conventional symbols; it requires a deep understanding of the beliefs and principles or goals and values that underlie a work of art's cultural situation as well as the position of an artist and patron within it.

In the "Closer Look" on iconography, the subject matter of two **still life** paintings (pictures of inanimate objects and fruits or flowers taken out of their natural contexts) is identified and elucidated, but to truly understand these two works as bearers of cultural meaning, more knowledge of the broader context and specific goals of artists and audiences is required. For example, the fact that Zhu Da (1626–1705) became a painter was rooted more in the political than the artistic history of China at the middle of the seventeenth century. As a member of the imperial family of the Ming dynasty, his life of privilege was disrupted when the Ming were overthrown during the Manchu conquest of China in 1644. Fleeing for his life, he sought refuge in a Buddhist monastery, where he wrote poetry and painted.

A Closer Look

ICONOGRAPHY

These grapes sit on an imported, Italian silver *tazza*, a luxury object that may commemorate northern European prosperity and trade. This particular object recurs in several of Peeters's other still lifes.

An image of the artist herself appears on the reflective surface of this pewter tankard, one of the ways that she signed her paintings and promoted her career.

Luscious fruits and flowers celebrate the abundance of nature, but because these fruits of the earth will eventually fade, even rot, they could be moralizing references to the transience of earthly existence.

Detailed renderings of insects showcased Peeters's virtuosity as a painter, but they also may have symbolized the vulnerability of the worldly beauty of flowers and fruit to destruction and decay.

These coins, including one minted in 1608–1609, help focus the dating of this painting. The highlighting of money within a still life could reference the wealth of the owner—or it could subtly allude to the value the artist has crafted here in paint.

This knife—which appears in several of Peeters's still lifes—is of a type that is associated with wedding gifts.

A. Clara Peeters **STILL LIFE WITH FRUIT AND FLOWERS**
c. 1612. Oil on copper, 25⅕ × 35″ (64 × 89 cm). Ashmolean Museum, Oxford.

Credit: Bridgeman Images

Quince is an unusual subject in Chinese painting, but the fruit seems to have carried personal significance for Zhu Da. One of his friends was known as the Daoist of Quince Mountain, a site in Hunan Province that was also the subject of a work by one of his favorite authors, Tang poet Li Bai.

The artist's signature reads "Bada Shanren painted this," using a familiar pseudonym in a formula and calligraphic style that the artist ceased using in 1695.

This red block is a seal with an inscription drawn from a Confucian text: "Teaching is half of learning." This was imprinted on the work by the artist as an aspect of his signature, a symbol of his identity within the picture, just as the reflection and inscribed knife identify Clara Peeters as the painter of her still life.

B. Zhu Da (Bada Shanren) **QUINCE (MUGUA)**
1690. Album leaf mounted as a hanging scroll; ink and colors on paper, 7⅞ × 5¾″ (20 × 14.6 cm). Princeton University Art Museum.

Credit: © 2016. University Art Museum/Art Resource/Scala, Florence. Photo: Bruce M. White.

Almost 40 years later, in the aftermath of a nervous break-down (that could have been staged to avoid retribution for his family background), Zhu Da abandoned his monastic life and developed a career as a professional painter, adopting a series of descriptive pseudonyms—most notably Bada Shanren ("mountain man of eight greatnesses") by which he is most often known today. His paintings are at times saturated with veiled political commentary; at times they seek to accommodate the expectations of collectors to assure their marketability; and in paintings like FIGURE B, the artist seems to hark back to the contemplative, abstract, and spontaneous paintings associated with great Zen masters such as Muqi (c. 1201–after 1269), whose calligraphic pictures of isolated fruits seem almost like acts of devotion or detached contemplations on natural forms, rather than the works of a professional painter.

Clara Peeters's still life (see FIG. A in "Closer Look" on page xxxi), on the other hand, fits into a developing Northern European painting tradition within which she was an established and successful professional, specializing in portrayals of food, flowers, fruit, and reflective objects. Still-life paintings in this tradition could be jubilant celebrations of the abundance of the natural world and the wealth of luxury objects available in the prosperous mercantile society of the Netherlands. Or they could be moralizing **vanitas** paintings, warning of the ephemeral meaning of those worldly possessions or even of life itself. But this painting has also been interpreted in a more personal way. Because the type of knife that sits in the foreground near the edge of the table was a popular wedding gift and is inscribed with the artist's own name, some have suggested that this still life could have celebrated Peeters's marriage. Or this could simply be a witty way to sign her picture. It certainly could be personal and at the same time participate in the broader cultural meaning of still-life paintings.

INTRO-6 Rogier van der Weyden **CRUCIFIXION WITH THE VIRGIN AND ST. JOHN THE EVANGELIST** c. 1460. Oil on oak panels, 71 × 73" (1.8 × 1.85 m). John G. Johnson Collection, Philadelphia Museum of Art.

Credit: © 2016. Photo The Philadelphia Museum of Art/Art Resouce/Scala, Florence

Mixtures of private and public meanings have been proposed for Zhu Da's paintings as well. Some have seen his picture of quince as part of a series of allegorical self-portraits that extend across his career as a painter. Art historians frequently discover multiple meanings when interpreting single works. Art often represents complex cultural and personal situations.

A Case Study: Rogier van der Weyden's Philadelphia *Crucifixion*

How does the four-part art historical method lead to an art historical interpretation of a specific work of art?

The basic, four-part method of art historical investigation and interpretation just outlined and explored may become clearer when its extended use is traced in relation to one specific work of art. A particularly revealing subject for such a case study is a seminal and somewhat perplexing painting now in the Philadelphia Museum of Art—the **CRUCIFIXION WITH THE VIRGIN AND ST. JOHN THE EVANGELIST** (**FIG. Intro-6**) by the Flemish artist Rogier van der Weyden (c. 1400–1464) (see Chapter 19). Each of the four levels of art historical inquiry reveals important information about this painting—information that has been used by art historians to reconstruct its relationship to its artist, its audience, and its broader cultural setting. The resulting interpretation is rich, but also complex. An investigation this extensive will not be possible for all the works of art in the following chapters, where the text will focus only on one or two facets of more expansive research. Because of the amount and complexity of information involved in a thorough art historical interpretation, it is sometimes only in a second reading that we can follow the subtleties of its argument, after a first reading has provided a basic familiarity with the work of art, its conventional subjects, and its general context.

Physical Properties

Perhaps the most striking aspect of this painting's physical appearance is its division into two separate tall rectangular panels, joined by a frame to form a coherent, almost square composition. These are oak panels, prepared with chalk to form a smooth surface on which to paint with mineral pigments suspended in oil. A technical investigation of the painting in 1981 used infrared reflectography to reveal a very sketchy underdrawing beneath the surface of the paint, indicating that this painting is almost entirely the work of Rogier van der Weyden himself. Famous and prosperous artists of this time and place employed many assistants to work in large production workshops, and

they would make detailed underdrawings to ensure that assistants replicated the **style** of the master. But in cases where the masters themselves intended to execute the work, only sketchy compositional outlines were needed. In addition, modern technical investigation of Rogier's painting used **dendrochronology** (the dating of wood based on the patterns of the growth rings) to date the oak panels and consequently the painting itself, now securely situated near the end of the artist's career, c. 1460.

The most recent restoration of the painting—during the early 1990s by Mark Tucker, senior conservator at the Philadelphia Museum of Art—returned it, as close as possible, to what experts currently believe was its original fifteenth-century appearance (see "De-restoring and Restoring Rogier van der Weyden's *Crucifixion*" on page xxxiv). This project included extensive technical analysis of almost every aspect of the picture, during which a critical clue emerged, one that may lead to a sharper understanding of its original use. X-rays revealed dowel holes and plugs running in a horizontal line about one-fourth of the way up from the bottom across the entire expanse of the two-panel painting. Tucker's convincing research suggested that the dowels would have attached these two panels to the backs of wooden boxes or to carved tracery to form a complex work of art that combined sculpture and painting and was hung over the altar in a fifteenth-century church. Recently, Tucker worked collaboratively with art historian Griet Steyaert to identify two paintings that were originally on the reverse of these two panels, demonstrating that the Philadelphia **diptych** (two-panel painting) formed part of the exterior of the wings of the original **polyptych** (multiple-panel painting), visible only when it was closed (SEE FIGS. 19–13, 19–14 for views of another polyptych altarpiece with wings open and closed).

Formal Structure

The visual organization of this two-part painting emphasizes both connection and separation. It is at the same time one painting and two. Continuing across both panels are the strip of midnight blue sky and the stone wall that constricts space within the picture to a shallow corridor, pushing the figures into the foreground and close to the viewer. The shallow strip of mossy ground under the two-figure group in the left panel continues its sloping descent into the right panel, as does the hem of the Virgin's ice-blue garment. We look into this scene as if through a window with a mullion down the middle and assume that the world on the left continues behind this central strip of frame into the right side.

On the other hand, strong visual forces isolate the figures within their respective panels, setting up a system of "compare and contrast" that seems to be at the heart of

RECOVERING THE PAST

DE-RESTORING AND RESTORING ROGIER VAN DER WEYDEN'S *CRUCIFIXION*

Ever since Rogier van der Weyden's strikingly asymmetrical, two-panel rendering of the *Crucifixion* (SEE FIG. Intro-6) was purchased by Philadelphia lawyer John G. Johnson in 1906 for his spectacular collection of European paintings, it has been recognized not only as one of the greatest works by this master of fifteenth-century Flemish painting, but also as one of the most important European paintings in North America. Soon after the Johnson Collection became part of the Philadelphia Museum of Art in 1933, however, this painting's visual character was significantly transformed. In 1941, the museum employed freelance restorer David Rosen to work on the painting. Deciding that Rogier's work had been seriously marred by later overpainting and disfigured by the discoloration of old varnish, Rosen subjected the painting to a thorough cleaning. He also removed the strip of dark blue paint forming the sky above the wall at the top—identifying it as an eighteenth-century restoration—and replaced it with gold leaf to conform with remnants of gold in this area that he thought were surviving fragments of the original background. Rosen's restoration of Rogier's painting was uncritically accepted for almost half a century, and the gold background became a major factor in the interpretations of art historians as distinguished as Erwin Panofsky and Meyer Schapiro.

In 1990, in preparation for a new installation of the work, Rogier's painting received a thorough technical analysis by Mark Tucker, the museum's senior conservator. There were two startling discoveries:

- The dark blue strip that had run across the top of the picture before Rosen's intervention was actually original to the painting. Remnants of paint left behind in 1941 proved to be the same azurite blue that also appears in the clothing of the Virgin, and in no instance did the traces of gold discovered in 1941 run under aspects of the original paint surface. Rosen had removed Rogier's original midnight blue sky.

- What Rosen had interpreted as disfiguring varnish streaking the wall and darkening the brilliant cloths of honor hanging over it were actually Rogier's careful painting of lichens and water stains on the stone and his overpainting on the fabric that had originally transformed a vermillion undercoat into deep crimson cloth.

In meticulous work during 1992–1993, Tucker cautiously restored the painting based on the evidence he had uncovered. Neither the lost lichens and water stains nor the toning crimson overpainting of the hangings were replaced, but a coat of blue-black paint was laid over Rosen's gold leaf at the top of the panels, taking care to apply the new layer in such a way that should a later generation decide to return to the gold leaf sky, the midnight tonalities could be easily removed. That seems an unlikely prospect. The painting as exhibited today comes as close as possible to the original appearance of Rogier's *Crucifixion*. At least we think so for now.

the painting's design. The striking red cloths that hang over the wall are centered directly behind the figures on each side, forming internal frames that highlight them as separate groups and focus our attention back and forth between them rather than on the pictorial elements that unite their environments. As we begin to compare the two sides, it becomes increasingly clear that the relationship between figures and environment is quite distinct on each side of the divide.

The dead figure of Christ on the cross, elevated to the very top of the picture, is strictly centered within his panel, as well as against the cloth that hangs directly behind him. The grid of masonry blocks and creases in the cloth emphasizes his rectilinear integration into a system of balanced, rigid regularity. His head is aligned with the cap of the wall, his flesh largely contained within the area defined by the cloth. His elbows mark the juncture of the wall with the edge of the hanging, and his feet extend just to the end of the cloth, where his toes substitute for the border of fringe they overlap. The environment is almost as balanced. The strip of dark sky at the top is equivalent in size to the strip of mossy earth at the bottom

of the picture, and both are visually bisected by centered horizontals—the cross bar at the top and the alignment of bone and skull at the bottom. A few disruptions to this stable, rectilinear, symmetrical order draw the viewer's attention to the panel at the left: the downward fall of the head of Christ, the visual weight of the skull, the downturn of the fluttering loin cloth, and the tip of the Virgin's gown that transgresses over the barrier to move in from the other side.

John and Mary merge on the left into a single figural mass that could be inscribed into a half-circle. Although set against a rectilinear grid background comparable to that behind Jesus, they contrast with, rather than conform to, the regular sense of order. Their curving outlines offer unsettling unsteadiness, as if they are toppling to the ground, jutting into the other side of the frame. This instability is reinforced by their postures. The projection of Mary's knee in relation to the angle of her torso reveals that she is collapsing into a curve, and the crumpled mass of drapery circling underneath her only underlines her lack of support. John reaches out to catch her, but he has not yet made contact with her body. He strikes a stance of strident instability without even touching the ground, and he looks blankly out into space with an unfocused expression, distracted from, rather than concentrating on, the task at hand. Perhaps he will come to his senses and grab her. But will he be able to catch her in time, and even then support her, given his unstable posture? The moment is tense; the outcome is unclear. But we are moving into the realm of natural subject matter. The poignancy of this concentrated portrayal seems to demand it.

Iconography

The subject of this painting is among the most familiar themes in the history of European art. The dead Jesus has been crucified on the cross, and two of his closest associates—his mother and John, one of his disciples—mourn his loss. Although easily recognizable, the austere and asymmetrical presentation is unexpected.

More usual is an earlier painting of this subject by the same artist, **CRUCIFIXION TRIPTYCH WITH DONORS AND SAINTS** (FIG. Intro–7), where Rogier situates the crucified Christ at the center of a symmetrical arrangement, the undisputed axial focus of the composition. The scene unfolds here in an expansive landscape with a wider cast of participants, each of whom takes a place with symmetrical decorum on either side of the cross. Most crucifixions follow some variation on this pattern, so Rogier's two-panel portrayal (SEE FIG. Intro–6)—in which the cross is asymmetrically placed and the two figures near it are relegated to a separately framed and severely restricted space—requires some explanation, as does the mysterious,

dark world beyond the wall and the artificial backdrop of the textile hangings.

This scene is not only austere and subdued, it is also sharply focused, and the focus relates it to a specific moment in the story that Rogier decided to represent. The Christian Bible contains four accounts of Jesus's crucifixion, one in each of the four Gospels. Rogier took two verses in John's account as his painting's text (John 19:26–27), cited here in the Douai-Reims literal English translation (1582, 1609) of the Latin Vulgate Bible that was used by Western European Christians during the fifteenth century:

> When Jesus therefore had seen his mother and the disciple standing whom he loved, he saith to his mother: Woman, behold thy son. After that, he saith to the disciple: Behold thy mother. And from that hour, the disciple took her to his own.

Even the textual source uses conventions that need explanation, specifically the way the disciple John is consistently referred to in this Gospel as "the disciple whom Jesus loved." Rogier's painting, therefore, seems to focus on Jesus's call for a newly expanded relationship between his mother and a beloved follower. More specifically, he has projected us slightly forward in time to the moment when John needs to respond to that call—Jesus has died; John is now in charge.

There are, however, other conventional iconographic associations with the crucifixion that Rogier has folded into this spare portrayal. Fifteenth-century viewers would have understood the skull and femur that lie at the base of the cross as the bones of Adam—the first man in the

INTRO–7 Rogier van der Weyden **CRUCIFIXION TRIPTYCH WITH DONORS AND SAINTS**

c. 1440. Oil on wooden panels, 39¾ × 55" (101 × 140 cm). Kunsthistorisches Museum, Vienna.

Credit: © KHM-Museumsverband

Hebrew Bible account of creation—on whose grave Jesus's crucifixion was believed to have taken place. This juxtaposition embodied the Christian belief that Christ's sacrifice on the cross redeemed believers from the death that Adam's original sin had brought to human existence.

Mary's swoon would have evoked another theological idea, the *co-passio*, in which Mary's anguish while witnessing Jesus's suffering and death was seen as a parallel passion of mother with son, both critical for human salvation. Their connection in this painting is underlined visually by the similar bending of their knees, inclination of their heads, and closing of their eyes. They even seem to resemble each other in facial likeness, especially when compared to John.

Cultural Context

In 1981 art historian Penny Howell Jolly published an interpretation of Rogier's Philadelphia *Crucifixion* as the product of a broad personal and cultural context. In addition to building on the work of earlier art historians, she pursued two productive lines of investigation to explain the rationale for this unusually austere presentation:

- the prospect that Rogier was influenced by the work of another artist, and

- the possibility that the painting was produced in a context that called for a special mode of visual presentation and a particular iconographic focus.

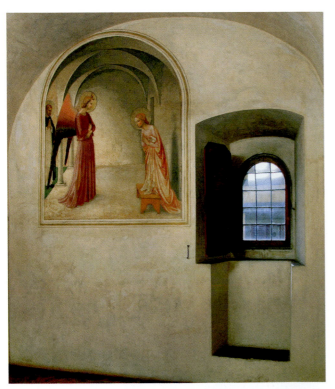

INTRO–8 VIEW OF A MONK'S CELL IN THE MONASTERY OF SAN MARCO, FLORENCE

Including Fra Angelico's fresco of the *Annunciation*. c. 1438–1445.

Credit: © Studio Fotografico Quattrone, Florence

INTRO–9 Fra Angelico **MOCKING OF CHRIST WITH THE VIRGIN MARY AND ST. DOMINIC**

Monastery of San Marco, Florence. c. 1441–1445.

Credit: © 2016 Photo Scala, Florence - courtesy of the Ministero Beni e Att. Culturali

FRA ANGELICO AT SAN MARCO We know very little about the life of Rogier van der Weyden, but we do know that in 1450, when he was already established as one of the principal painters in northern Europe, he made a pilgrimage to Rome. Either on his way to Rome or during his return journey home, he stopped in Florence and saw the **altarpiece**, and presumably also the frescos, that Fra Angelico (c. 1400–1455) and his workshop had painted during the 1440s at the monastery of San Marco. The evidence of Rogier's contact with Fra Angelico's work is found in a work Rogier painted after he returned home based on a panel of the San Marco altarpiece. For the Philadelphia *Crucifixion*, however, it was Fra Angelico's devotional frescos on the walls of the monks' individual rooms (or cells) that seem to have had the greatest impact (**FIG. Intro–8**). Jolly compared the Philadelphia *Crucifixion* with a scene of the Mocking of Christ at San Marco to demonstrate the connection (**FIG. Intro–9**). Fra Angelico presented the sacred figures with a quiet austerity that recalls Rogier's unusual composition. More specific parallels are the use of an expansive stone wall to restrict narrative space to a shallow foreground corridor, the description of the world beyond that wall as a dark sky that contrasts with the brilliantly illuminated foreground, and the use of a draped cloth of honor to draw attention to a narrative vignette from the life of Jesus, to separate it out as an object of devotion.

THE CARTHUSIANS   Having established a possible connection between Rogier's painting and frescos by Fra Angelico that he likely saw during his pilgrimage to Rome in 1450, Jolly reconstructed a specific context of patronage and meaning within Rogier's own world in Flanders that could explain why the paintings of Fra Angelico would have had such an impact on him at this particular moment in his career.

During the years around 1450, Rogier developed a personal and professional relationship with the monastic order of the Carthusians, and especially with the Belgian Charterhouse (or Carthusian monastery) of Hérrines, where his oldest son was invested as a monk in 1450. Rogier gave money to Hérrines, and texts document his donation of a painting to its chapel of St. Catherine. Jolly suggested that the Philadelphia *Crucifixion* could be that painting. Its subdued colors and narrative austerity are consistent with Carthusian aesthetic attitudes, and the walled setting of the scene recalls the enclosed gardens that were attached to the individual dormitory rooms of Carthusian monks. The reference in this painting to the *co-passio* of the Virgin provides supporting evidence, since this theological idea was central to Carthusian thought and devotion. The *co-passio* was even reflected in the monks' own initiation rites, during which they re-enacted and sought identification with both Christ's sacrifice on the cross and the Virgin's parallel suffering.

In Jolly's interpretation, the religious framework of a Carthusian setting for the painting emerges as a personal framework for the artist himself, since this *Crucifixion* seems to be associated with important moments in his own life—his religious pilgrimage to Rome in 1450 and the initiation of his oldest son as a Carthusian monk at about the same time. The sense of loss and separation that Rogier evoked in his portrayal of a poignant moment in the life of St. John (**FIG. Intro–10**) could have been especially meaningful to the artist himself at the time this work was painted.

ART HISTORY: A CONTINUING PROJECT   The final word has not been spoken in the interpretation of Rogier's Philadelphia *Crucifixion*. Mark Tucker's recent work on the physical evidence points toward it having been part of a large sculptured altarpiece. Even if this rules out the prospect that it is the **panel painting** Rogier donated to

INTRO–10 DETAIL OF FIG. **INTRO–6 SHOWING PART OF THE LEFT WING**

Credit: © 2004. Photo The Phildelphia Museum of Art/Scala, Florence

Hérrines, it does not negate the relationship Jolly drew with Fra Angelico, nor the Carthusian context she outlined. It simply reminds us that our understanding of works such as this will evolve when new evidence about them emerges.

As the history of art unfolds in this book, it will be important to keep two things in mind as you read about individual works of art and their broader cultural contexts. Art historical interpretations are built on extended research comparable to what we have just surveyed for Rogier van der Weyden's Philadelphia *Crucifixion*. But the work of interpretation is never complete. Art history is a continuing project, a work perpetually in progress.

Think About It

1   Analyze the composition of one painting illustrated in this Introduction.
2   Characterize the difference between natural subject matter and iconography, focusing your discussion on a specific work of art.
3   What are the four separate steps proposed here for art historians to interpret works of art? Characterize

the cultural analysis in step four by showing how it expands our understanding of one of the still lifes in the second "Closer Look."

4   What aspect of the case study of Rogier van der Weyden's Philadelphia *Crucifixion* was most interesting to you? Why? How did it affect your understanding of what you will learn in this course?

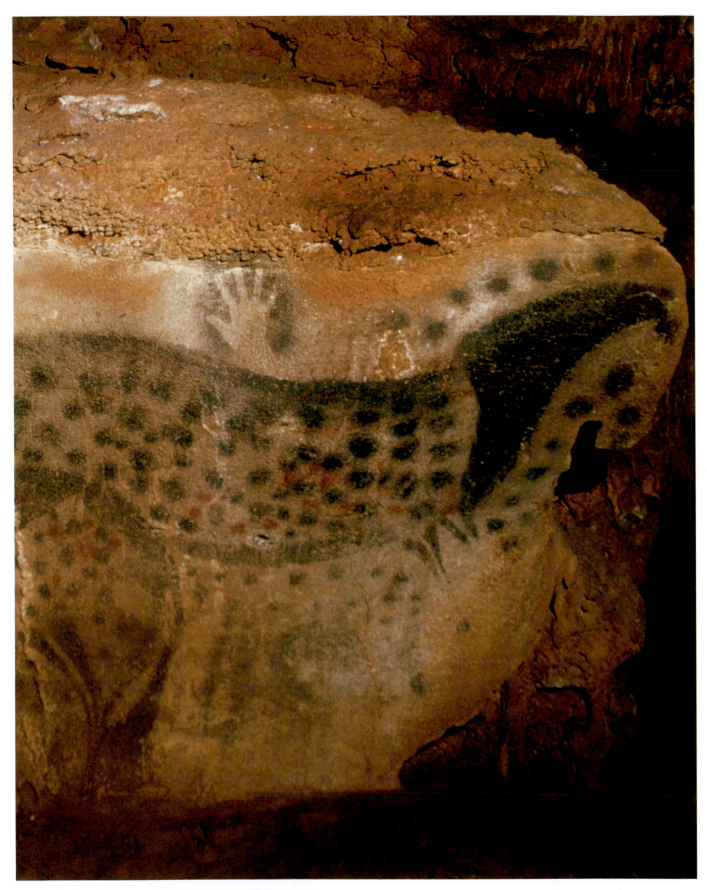

1-1 SPOTTED HORSES AND HUMAN HANDS

Pech-Merle Cave. Dordogne, France. Horses 25,000–24,000 BCE; hands c. 15,000 BCE. Paint on limestone, individual horses over 5′ (1.5 m) in length.

Credit: © 2016 Photo Scala, Florence/bpk, Bildagentur für Kunst, Kultur und Geschichte, Berlin

Chapter 1
Prehistoric Art

1.a Identify the visual hallmarks of Paleolithic, Neolithic, and Bronze Age art for formal, technical, and expressive qualities.

1.b Interpret the meaning of works of Paleolithic, Neolithic, and Bronze Age art based on their themes, subjects, and symbols.

1.c Relate Paleolithic, Neolithic, and Bronze Age artists and art to their cultural, economic, and political contexts.

1.d Apply the vocabulary and concepts used to discuss Paleolithic, Neolithic, and Bronze Age art, artists, and art history.

1.e Interpret Prehistoric art using appropriate art historical methods, such as observation, comparison, and inductive reasoning.

1.f Select visual and textual evidence in various media to support an argument or an interpretation of Prehistoric art.

This detail shows one of two horses positioned back-to-back on the wall of a chamber within the Pech-Merle Cave, located in the Dordogne region of France (**FIG. 1-1**). The tapering head of this horse follows the natural shape of the rock. Black dots surround portions of its contours and fill most of its body, a striking feature that was believed to be decorative until DNA analysis of the remains of prehistoric horses, published in 2011, proved that one species flourishing at this time actually was spotted. In this instance, at least, prehistoric painters were painting what they saw.

At a later date, a large fish (58 inches long and very difficult to see here) was painted in red on top of the spots. Yet the painters left more than images of horses and fish; they left their own handprints in various places around the animals. These images, and many others hidden in chambers at the ends of long, narrow passages within the cave, connect us to an almost unimaginably ancient world of 25,000 BCE.

Prehistory includes all of human existence before the emergence of writing. When our ancestors were carving objects, painting images, and creating shelters and other structures 30,000 years ago, they were not making "works of art," and there were no "artists" as we use the term today. They were flaking, chipping, and polishing flint into tools—spear points, knives, and scrapers—not sculptures, even if we find these artifacts pleasing to the eye and to the touch

today. Wall paintings must have seemed equally important to their prehistoric makers in terms of everyday survival, not visual delight.

For art historians, archaeologists, and anthropologists, prehistoric "art" provides significant clues—along with fossils, pollen, and other artifacts—to understanding early human life and culture. Specialists continue to discover more about when and how these works were created. In 2012, for instance, an international team of scientists used a refined dating technology known as the uranium-thorium method (see "How Early Art is Dated" on page 12) to prove that some paintings in a Spanish cave known as El Castillo are at least 40,000 years old and probably much older—raising the possibility that they could have been painted by Neanderthals rather than *Homo sapiens*.

We may never know exactly why prehistoric paintings were made. In fact, there may be no single meaning or use for any one image on a cave wall; perhaps it meant different things to different people, depending on their age, their experience, or their specific needs and desires. And the sculpture, paintings, and structures that survive are but a tiny fraction of what must have been created over a very long time span. The conclusions and interpretations we draw from them are only educated guesses, making prehistoric art one of the most speculative, but dynamic and exciting, areas of art history.

The Stone Age

What are the cultural and historical contexts that led to the first artistic impulses of the Stone Age?

How and when modern humans evolved is the subject of ongoing debate, but anthropologists now agree that the species called *Homo sapiens* appeared about 400,000 years ago and that the subspecies to which we belong, *Homo sapiens sapiens* (usually referred to as modern humans), evolved as early as 120,000 years ago. Based on archaeological evidence, it is now clear that modern humans spread from Africa across Asia, into Europe, and finally to Australia and the Americas. This vast movement of people took place between 100,000 and 35,000 years ago.

Scholars began the systematic study of prehistory only about 200 years ago. Nineteenth-century archaeologists, struck by the wealth of stone tools, weapons, and figures found at ancient sites, named the whole period of early human development the Stone Age. Today, researchers divide the Stone Age into two parts: Paleolithic (from the Greek *paleo-*, "old," and *lithos*, "stone") and Neolithic (from the Greek *neo-*, "new"). They divide the Paleolithic period into three phases reflecting the relative position of objects found in layers of excavation: Lower (the oldest), Middle, and Upper (the most recent). In some places archaeologists can identify a transitional, or Mesolithic (from the Greek *meso-*, "middle"), period.

The dates for the transition from Paleolithic to Neolithic vary with geography and with local environmental and social circumstances. For some of the places discussed in this chapter, such as Western Europe, the Neolithic way of living did not emerge until 3000 BCE; in others, such as the Near East, it appeared as early as 8000 BCE. Archaeologists denote time in numbers of years BP ("before present"). However, to ensure consistent style throughout the book, which reflects the usage of art historians, this chapter uses the notations BCE (before the Common Era) and CE (the Common Era) to mark time.

Much is yet to be discovered about prehistoric art. In Australia, some of the world's very oldest images have been dated to between 50,000 and 40,000 years ago, and

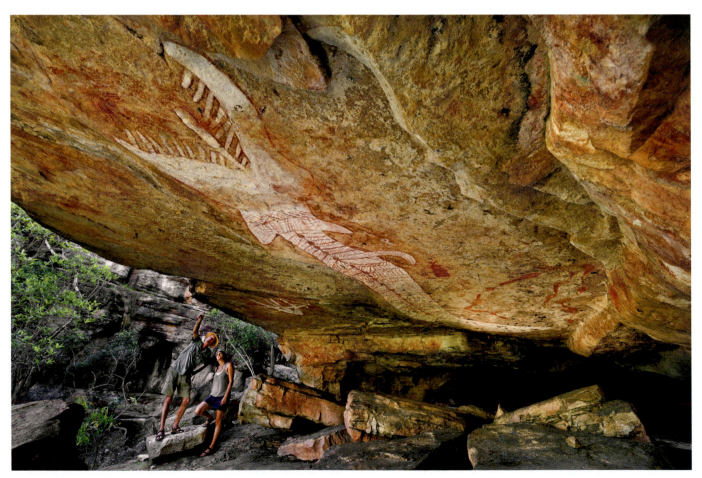

1-2 RAINBOW SERPENT ROCK
Western Arnhem Land, Australia.

Appearing in Australia as early as 6000 BCE, images of the Rainbow Serpent play a role in rituals and legends of the creation of human beings, the generation of rains, storms, and floods, and the reproductive power of nature and people.

Credit: © Marc Dozier/Corbis

MAP 1–1 PREHISTORIC EUROPE

As the Ice Age glaciers receded, Paleolithic, Neolithic, Bronze Age, and Iron Age settlements increased from south to north.

the tradition of transient communities who marked the land in complex, yet stunningly beautiful ways continues into historical time. In western Arnhem Land (**FIG. 1–2**), rock art images of the Rainbow Serpent have their origins in prehistory. They were perhaps first created during times of substantial changes in the environment.

Africa, as well, is home to ancient rock art in both its northern and southern regions. And most recently, archaeologists have dated cave paintings on the Indonesian island of Sulawesi to between 35,000 and 40,000 years ago, including stenciled hands very similar to those appearing in Europe at Pech-Merle (SEE FIG. 1–1).

It is the cognitive capability to create and recognize symbols and imagery that sets modern humans apart from all our predecessors and all our contemporary animal relatives. We are defined as a species by our abilities to make and understand art. This chapter focuses primarily on prehistoric European art from the Paleolithic and Neolithic periods and into the Bronze Age (**MAP 1–1**). Later chapters

consider some prehistoric art on other continents and from other cultures, such as China (Chapter 11) and sub-Saharan Africa (Chapter 14).

Tools or Art?

Human beings made tools long before they made what today we call "art." Art, in the sense of image making, is the hallmark of the Upper Paleolithic period and the emergence of our subspecies, *Homo sapiens sapiens*; representational images appear in the archaeological record beginning about 38,000 BCE in Australia, Africa, and Europe. Before that time, during the Lower Paleolithic period in Africa, early humans made tools by flaking and chipping (knapping) flint pebbles into blades and scrapers that had sharp edges. Dating to 2.5 million years ago, the earliest objects made by our human ancestors were simple stone tools used to cut animal skin and meat, smash open bones to reveal the marrow, and cut wood and other plant

1-3 PALEOLITHIC HAND-AXE

From Isimila Korongo, Tanzania. 60,000 years ago. Stone, height 10" (25.4 cm).

Credit: Werner Forman Archive

By 1.65 million years ago, significant changes in our ancestors' cognitive abilities and manual dexterity can be seen in sophisticated stone tools, such as the teardrop-shaped hand-axes (**FIG. 1-3**) that have been found at sites across Eurasia. These extraordinary objects, symmetrical in form and produced by a complex multistep process, were long thought of as nothing more than tools (or perhaps even as weapons)—but the most recent analysis suggests that they had a social function as well. Some sites (such as Olorgesailie in Kenya) contain hundreds of hand-axes, far more than would have been needed in functional terms, suggesting that they served to announce an individual's skills, status, and standing in his or her community. Although these ancient hand-axes are clearly not art in the representational sense, it is important to see them in terms of performance and process. These concepts, so central to modern Western art, have deep prehistoric roots.

The Paleolithic Period

What do we know about the shelters and representational images from the Paleolithic period?

By 400,000 years ago, during the late Middle Paleolithic period, a *Homo sapiens* subspecies called Neanderthal inhabited Europe. Its members used a wider range of stone tools and may have carefully buried their dead with funerary offerings. Neanderthals survived for thousands of years and overlapped with modern humans, *Homo sapiens sapiens*, which had evolved and spread out of Africa some 300,000 years after the Neanderthals and eventually replaced them, probably between 38,000 and 33,000 BCE.

Critical cognitive abilities set modern humans apart from their predecessors; *Homo sapiens sapiens* outlasted Neanderthals as a species because they had the mental capacity to solve problems of human survival. The new cognitive abilities included improvements in recognizing and benefiting from variations in the natural environment and in managing social networking and alliance making—skills that enabled organized hunting. The most important new ability, however, was the capacity to think symbolically: to create representational analogies between one person, animal, or object, and another and to recognize and remember those analogies. This cognitive development marks the evolutionary origin of what we call art.

materials. These first tools have been found at sites such as Olduvai Gorge in Tanzania. Although not art, they document a critical development in our evolution: humans' ability to create specific tools and objects that could be used to complete a task.

1-4 DECORATED OCHER

From Blombos Cave, southern Cape coast, South Africa. 77,000 years ago.

Credit: Image courtesy of Prof Christopher Henshilwood, University of Bergen, Norway

1–5 RECONSTRUCTION DRAWING OF MAMMOTH-BONE HOUSES
Ukraine. c. 16,000–10,000 BCE

Credit: Jack Unruh/National Geographic Creative

The world's earliest examples of art come from South Africa: two 77,000-year-old, engraved blocks of red ocher (probably used as crayons) found in the Blombos Cave (**FIG. 1–4**). Both blocks are engraved in an identical way with cross-hatched lines on their sides. Archaeologists argue that the similarity of the engraved patterns means these two pieces were intentionally made and decorated following a common pattern. Thousands of fragments of ocher have been discovered at Blombos; there is little doubt that people were using it to draw patterns and images, the remains of which have long since disappeared. It is highly likely that the ocher was used to decorate peoples' bodies, as well as to color objects such as tools or shell ornaments. In an earlier layer on the same site, archaeologists uncovered more than 36 shells, each of which had been perforated so that it could be hung from a string or thong, or attached to clothing or a person's hair; these shells would have been used for personal decoration. An ostrich eggshell bead from the same site would have served the same purpose. The Blombos finds are enormously important. Here our early ancestors, probably modern humans but possibly their predecessors, used the earth's raw materials to decorate themselves with jewelry and body art.

Shelter or Architecture?

"Architecture" usually refers to the enclosure of spaces with some aesthetic intent, and building even a simple shelter requires a degree of imagination and planning deserving of this term. In the Upper Paleolithic period, humans in some regions used great ingenuity to build shelters that were far from simple. In woodlands, evidence of floors indicates that our ancestors built circular or oval huts of light branches and hides that measured as much as 15 to 20 feet in diameter. (Modern tents to accommodate 6 people vary from 10- by 11-foot ovals to 14- by 7-foot rooms.)

In the treeless grasslands of Upper Paleolithic Russia and Ukraine, builders created settlements of up to ten houses using the bones of the now extinct woolly mammoth, whose long, curving tusks made excellent roof supports and arched door openings (**FIG. 1–5**). This bone framework was probably covered with animal hides and turf. Most activities centered around the inside fire pit, or hearth, where food was prepared and tools were made. Larger houses might have had more than one hearth, and spaces were set aside for specific uses—working stone, making clothing, sleeping, and dumping refuse. Inside the largest dwelling on a site in Mezhirich, Ukraine, archaeologists found 15 small hearths that still contained ashes and charred bones left by the last occupants. Some people colored their floors with powdered ocher in shades that ranged from yellow to red to brown. These Upper Paleolithic structures are important because of their early date: The widespread appearance of durable architecture concentrated in village communities did not occur until the beginning of the Neolithic period in the Near East and southeastern Europe.

Artifacts or Works of Art?

As early as 30,000 BCE small figures, or figurines, of people and animals made of bone, ivory, stone, and clay appeared in Europe and Asia. Today we interpret such self-contained, three-dimensional pieces as examples of **sculpture in the round**. Prehistoric carvers also produced **relief sculpture** in stone, bone, and ivory. In relief sculpture, part of the surrounding material is retained to form a background for the projecting figure.

THE LION-HUMAN An early and puzzling example of a sculpture in the round is a human figure—probably male—with a feline head (**FIG. 1–6**), made about 30,000–26,000 BCE. Archaeologists excavating at Hohlenstein-Stadel, Germany, found broken pieces of ivory (from a mammoth tusk) that they realized were parts of an entire figure. Nearly a foot tall, this remarkable statue surpasses most early figurines in size and complexity.

Instead of copying what he or she saw in nature, the carver created a unique creature, part human and part beast. The figure may have been intended to represent a person wearing a ritual lion mask—or someone who had actually taken on the appearance of an animal. Archaeologists now think that the people who lived at this time held very different ideas than ours about what it meant to be a human and how humans were distinct from animals; it is quite possible that they thought of animals and humans as parts of one common group of beings who shared the world. What is absolutely clear is that the Lion-Human is evidence of the uniquely human ability to conceive and represent a creature never seen in nature.

FEMALE FIGURES While a number of figurines representing men have been found recently, most human figures from the Upper Paleolithic period are female. The most famous of these, the **WOMAN FROM WILLENDORF** (**FIG. 1–7**), Austria, dates from about 24,000 BCE (see "The Power of Naming" opposite). Carved from limestone and originally colored with red ocher, the statuette's swelling,

1–6 LION-HUMAN
From Hohlenstein-Stadel, Germany. c. 40,000–35,000 BCE. Mammoth ivory, 12¼″ × 2⅞″ (31.1 × 7.3 cm). Ulmer Museum, Ulm, Germany.
Credit: Photo: Yvonne Mühleis © Landesamt für Denkmalpflege im RP Stuttgart

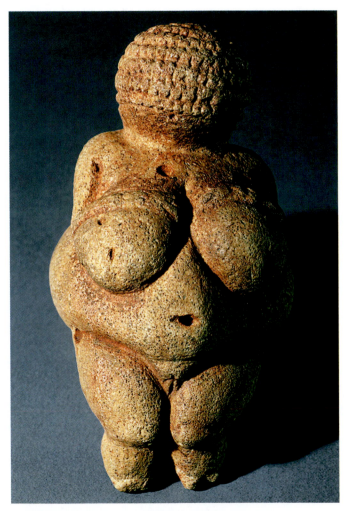

1–7 WOMAN FROM WILLENDORF
Austria. c. 24,000 BCE. Limestone, height 4⅜″ (11 cm). Naturhistorisches Museum, Vienna.
Credit: © akg-images/Erich Lessing

Art and its Contexts
THE POWER OF NAMING

Words are only symbols for ideas, and it is no coincidence that the origins of language and of art are often linked in human evolutionary development. But the very words we invent—or our ancestors invented—reveal a certain view of the world and can shape our thinking. Today, we exert the power of naming when we select a name for a baby or call a friend by a nickname. Our ideas about art can also be affected by names. Before the twentieth century, artists usually did not name, or title, their works. Names were eventually supplied by the works' owners or by art historians writing about them, and thus often express the cultural prejudices of the labelers or of the times in which they lived.

An excellent example of such distortion is the naming of the hundreds of small prehistoric statues of women that have been found. Earlier scholars called them by the Roman name Venus. For example, the sculpture in **FIGURE 1–7** was once called the

Venus of Willendorf after the place where it was found. Using the name of the Roman goddess of love and beauty sent a message that this figure was associated with religious belief, that it represented an ideal of womanhood, and that it was one of a long line of images of "classical" feminine beauty. In a short time, most similar works of sculpture from the Upper Paleolithic period came to be known as Venus figures. The name was repeated so often that even experts began to assume that the statues had to be fertility figures and Mother Goddesses, although there is no proof that this was so.

Our ability to understand and interpret works of art responsibly and creatively is easily compromised by distracting labels. Calling a prehistoric figure a woman instead of Venus encourages us to think about the sculpture in new and different ways.

rounded forms make it seem much larger than its actual 4⅜-inch height. The sculptor exaggerated the figure's female attributes by giving it pendulous breasts, a big belly with a deep navel (actually a natural indentation in the stone), wide hips, and dimpled knees and buttocks. By carving a woman with a well-nourished body, the artist may have been expressing health and fertility, which could ensure the ability to produce strong children, thus guaranteeing the survival of the clan.

The most recent analysis of the Paleolithic female sculptures, however, has replaced the traditional emphasis on fertility with more nuanced understandings of how and why the human figure is represented in this way, and who may have had these kinds of objects made. According to archaeologist Clive Gamble, these little sculptures were subtle forms of nonverbal communication among small, isolated groups of Paleolithic people spread out across vast regions. Gamble noted the tremendous (and unusual) similarity in the shapes of figures, even among those found in widely distant parts of Europe. He suggested that when groups of Paleolithic hunter-gatherers did occasionally meet up and interact, the female statues may have been among several signature objects that signaled whether a group was friendly and acceptable for interaction and, probably, for mating. As symbols, these figures would have provided reassurance of shared values about the body, and their size would have demanded engagement at a close personal level. It is not a coincidence, then, that the largest production of these figurines occurred during a period when climatic conditions were at their worst and the need for interaction and alliance building would have been at its greatest.

Another figure, the **WOMAN FROM DOLNÍ VĚSTONICE** (**FIG. 1–8**), takes our understanding of these objects further

1-8 WOMAN FROM DOLNÍ VĚSTONICE
Moravia, Czech Republic. 23,000 BCE. Fired clay, 4¼ × 1⁷⁄₁₀″ (11 × 4.3 cm). Moravske Museum, Brno, Czech Republic.

Credit: © akg-images/De Agostini Picture Lib./A. Dagli Orti still. The site of Dolní Věstonice is important because it holds evidence of a very early date (23,000 BCE) for the use of fire to make objects out of mixtures of water and soil. What makes the figures from this site in the Czech Republic and others in the region (Pavlov and Prědmosti) unusual is how they were made. But by mixing soil with water according to a very particular recipe and then placing the wet figures in a hot kiln to bake, the makers were not intending to create durable, well-fired statues. On the contrary, the recipe and firing procedure indicate that the intention was to make the figures explode in the kilns before the firing process was complete—before a "successful" figure could be produced. There are very few complete figures, but there are numerous fragments that bear the traces of explosions at high temperatures at these sites. The Dolní Věstonice fragments are records of performance and process art in their rawest and earliest forms.

Another remarkable female image, discovered in the Grotte du Pape in Brassempouy, France, is the tiny ivory head known as the **WOMAN FROM BRASSEMPOUY** (**FIG. 1–9**). Though the finders did not record its archaeological

context, recent studies prove it to be authentic and date it as early as 30,000 BCE. The carver captured the essence of a head, or what psychologists call the memory image—those generalized elements that reside in our memory of a human head. An egg shape rests on a long neck. A wide nose and strongly defined browline suggest deep-set eyes, and an engraved square patterning may be hair or a headdress. The image is an abstraction (what has come to be known as **abstract** art): the reduction of shapes and appearances to basic yet recognizable forms that are not intended to be exact replications of nature. The result in this case looks uncannily modern to contemporary viewers. Today, when such a piece is isolated in a museum case or as a book illustration we enjoy it as an aesthetic object, but we lose its original cultural context.

Cave Painting

Art in Europe entered a rich and sophisticated phase well before 40,000 years ago, when images began to be painted on the walls of caves in central and southern France and northern Spain. No one knew of the existence of prehistoric cave paintings until one day in 1879, when a young girl, exploring with her father in Altamira in northern Spain, crawled through a small opening in the ground and found herself in a chamber whose ceiling was covered with painted animals (SEE FIG. 1–13). Her father, a lawyer and amateur archaeologist, searched the rest of the cave, told authorities about the remarkable find, and published his discovery the following year. Few people believed that these amazing works could have been made by "primitive" people, and the scientific community declared the paintings a hoax. They were accepted as authentic only in 1902, after many other cave paintings, drawings, and engravings had been discovered at other places in northern Spain and in France.

TECHNIQUE OF PREHISTORIC WALL PAINTING In a dark cave, presumably working by the light of an animal-fat lamp, prehistoric artists chewed a piece of charcoal to dilute it with saliva and water. Then they blew out the mixture on the surface of a wall, using their hands as stencils. This drawing demonstrates how cave archaeologist Michel Lorblanchet and his assistant used this step-by-step process of the original makers of a cave painting at Pech-Merle (SEE FIG. 1–1) in France to create a complex design of spotted horses.

By turning himself into a human spray can, Lorblanchet produced clear lines on the rough stone surface much more easily than he could with a brush. To create the line of a horse's back, for example, with its clean upper edge and blurry lower one, he blew pigment below his hand. To capture its angular rump, he placed his hand vertically against the wall, holding it slightly curved. To produce the sharpest lines, such as those of the upper hind leg and tail,

1–9 WOMAN FROM BRASSEMPOUY
Grotte du Pape, Brassempouy, Landes, France. Probably c. 30,000 BCE. Ivory, height 1¼" (3.6 cm). Musée des Antiquités Nationales, Saint-Germain-en-Laye, France.

Credit: © akg-images/De Agostini Picture Lib./G. Dagli Orti

MICHEL LORBLANCHET SIMULATING THE TECHNIQUE OF PREHISTORIC CAVE PAINTERS

he placed his hands side by side and blew between them. To create the forelegs and the hair on the horses' bellies, he fingerpainted. A hole punched in a piece of leather served as a stencil for the horses' spots. It took Lorblanchet only 32 hours to reproduce the Pech-Merle painting of spotted horses, his speed suggesting that a single artist could have created the original.

Homo sapiens sapiens artists used three painting techniques: the spraying demonstrated by Lorblanchet, drawing with fingers or blocks of ocher, and daubing with a paintbrush made of hair or moss. In some prehistoric caves, three other stages of image creation can be seen: engraved lines using flakes of flint, followed by a color wash of ocher and manganese, and a final engraving to emphasize shapes and details.

THE MEANING OF CAVE PAINTINGS What caused people to paint such dramatic imagery on the walls of caves? The idea that human beings have an inherent desire to decorate themselves and their surroundings—that an aesthetic sense is somehow innate to the human species—found ready acceptance in the nineteenth century. Many believed that people create art for the sheer love of beauty. Scientists now agree that human beings have an aesthetic impulse, but the effort required to accomplish the great cave paintings suggests their creators were motivated by more than simple visual pleasure. Since the discovery at Altamira, anthropologists and art historians have devised several hypotheses to explain the existence of cave art. Like the search for the meaning of prehistoric female figurines, these explanations depend on the cultural views of those who advance them.

In the early twentieth century, scholars believed that art has a social function and that aesthetics are culturally relative. They proposed that cave paintings might be products both of rites to strengthen clan bonds and of ceremonies to enhance the fertility of animals used for food. In 1903, French archaeologist Salomon Reinach suggested that cave paintings were expressions of sympathetic magic: the idea, for instance, that a picture of a reclining bison would ensure that hunters found their prey asleep. Abbé Henri Breuil took these ideas further and concluded that caves were places of worship and settings for initiation rites. During the second half of the twentieth century, scholars rejected these ideas and rooted their interpretations in rigorous scientific methods and then-current social theory. André Leroi-Gourhan and Annette Laming-Emperaire, for example, dismissed the sympathetic magic theory because statistical analysis of debris from human settlements revealed that the animals used most frequently for food were not the ones traditionally portrayed in caves.

Researchers continue to discover new cave images and to correct earlier errors of fact or interpretation. A study of the Altamira Cave in the 1980s led anthropologist Leslie G. Freeman to conclude that the artists had faithfully represented a herd of bison during the mating season. Instead of being dead, asleep, or disabled—as earlier observers had thought—the animals were dust-wallowing, common behavior during the mating season. Similar thinking has led to a more recent interpretation of cave art by archaeologist Steve Mithen. In his detailed study of the motifs of the art and its placement within caves, Mithen argued that hoofprints, patterns of animal feces, and hide colorings were recorded and used as a "text" to teach novice hunters within a group about the seasonal appearance and behavior of the animals they hunted. The fact that so much cave art is hidden deep in almost inaccessible parts of caves—indeed, the fact that it is placed within caves at all—suggested to Mithen that this knowledge was intended for a privileged group and that certain individuals or groups were excluded from acquiring that knowledge.

South African rock-art expert David Lewis-Williams has suggested a different interpretation. Using a deep comparative knowledge of art made by hunter-gatherer communities that are still in existence, Lewis-Williams argued that Upper Paleolithic cave art is best understood in terms of shamanism: the belief that certain people (shamans) can travel outside of their bodies in order to mediate between the worlds of the living and the spirits. Traveling under the ground as a spirit, particularly within caves, or conceptually within the stone walls of the cave, Upper Paleolithic shamans would have participated in ceremonies that involved hallucinations. Images conceived during this trancelike state would likely combine recognizable (the animals) and abstract (the nonrepresentational) symbols. In addition, Lewis-Williams interprets the stenciled human handprints on the cave walls (SEE FIG. 1–1) as traces of the nonshaman participants in the ritual reaching toward and connecting with the shaman spirits traveling within the rock.

Although the hypotheses that seek to explain cave art have changed and evolved over time, there has always been agreement that decorated caves must have had a special meaning because people returned to them time after time over many generations, in some cases over thousands of years. Perhaps Upper Paleolithic cave art was the product of rituals intended to gain the favor of the supernatural. Perhaps because much of the art was made deep inside the caves and nearly inaccessible, its significance may have had less to do with the finished painting than with the very act of creation. Artifacts and footprints suggest that the subterranean galleries, which were far from living quarters, had a religious or magical function. Perhaps the experience of exploring the cave may have been significant to the image-makers. Musical instruments, such as bone flutes, have been found in the caves, implying that even acoustical properties may have had a role to play.

CHAUVET One of the earliest known sites of prehistoric cave paintings is the Chauvet Cave (named after one of the persons who found it) near Vallon-Pont-d'Arc in southeastern France. Discovered in December 1994, it is a trove of hundreds of paintings (**FIG. 1–10**). The most dramatic of the images depict grazing, running, or resting animals, including wild horses, bison, mammoths, bears, panthers, owls, deer, aurochs, woolly rhinoceroses,

and wild goats (or ibex). Also included are occasional humans, both male and female, many handprints, and hundreds of geometric markings such as grids, circles, and dots. Footprints in the Chauvet Cave, left in soft clay by a child, go to a "room" containing bear skulls. The charcoal used to draw the rhinos has been radiocarbon-dated to 32,410 years old, plus or minus 720 years.

LASCAUX The abundant cave paintings found in 1940 at Lascaux, in the Dordogne region of southwest France, have been dated to about 15,000 BCE.

Opened to the public after World War II, the prehistoric "museum" at Lascaux soon became one of the most popular tourist sites in France—too popular, because the visitors brought heat, humidity, exhaled carbon dioxide, and other contaminants. The cave was closed to the public in 1963 so that conservators could battle an aggressive fungus. Eventually they won, but instead of reopening the site, authorities created a facsimile of it. Visitors to what is called Lascaux II may now view copies of the paintings without harming the precious originals.

The scenes they view are remarkable. Lascaux has about 600 paintings and 1,500 engravings. In the **HALL OF BULLS** (**FIG. 1–11**), the Lascaux painters depicted cows, bulls, horses, and deer along the natural ledges of the rock, where the smooth white limestone of the ceiling and upper wall meets a rougher surface below. They also used the curving wall to suggest space. The animals appear singly, in rows, face to face, tail to tail, and even painted on top of

1–10 WALL PAINTING WITH HORSES, RHINOCEROSES, AND AUROCHS

Chauvet Cave. Vallon-Pont-d'Arc, Ardèche Gorge, France. c. 32,000–30,000 BCE. Paint on limestone.

Credit: © J. Clottes - MCC.

1–11 HALL OF BULLS

Lascaux Cave. Dordogne, France. c. 15,000 BCE. Paint on limestone, length of largest auroch (bull) 18′ (5.50 m).

Credit: © akg-images

one another. Their most characteristic features have been emphasized. Horns, eyes, and hooves are shown as seen from the front, yet heads and bodies are rendered in profile, in a system known as a **composite pose**. The animals are full of life and energy, and the accuracy in the drawing of their silhouettes, or outlines, is impressive.

Painters worked not only in large caverns, but also far back in the smallest chambers and recesses, many of which are almost inaccessible today. Over 100 small stone lamps have been found at Lascaux, indicating that the artists worked in flickering light obtained from burning animal fat. Although 1 pound of fat would burn for 24 hours and produce no soot, the light would not have been as strong as that created by a candle.

One scene at Lascaux was discovered in a remote setting on a wall at the bottom of a 16-foot shaft that contained a stone lamp and spears. The scene is unusual because it is the only painting in the cave complex that seems to tell a story (**FIG. 1–12**), and it is stylistically different from the other paintings at Lascaux. A figure who could be a hunter, greatly simplified in form but recognizably male and with

1–12 BIRD-HEADED MAN WITH BISON

Shaft scene in Lascaux Cave. c. 15,000 BCE. Paint on limestone, length approx. 9′ (2.75 m).

Credit: Photo © Hans Hinz/ARTOTHEK

the head of a bird or wearing a bird's-head mask, appears to be lying on the ground. A great bison looms above him. Below him lie a staff and a spear-thrower, the outer end of which has been carved in the shape of a bird. The long, diagonal line slanting across the bison's hindquarters may be a spear. The bison has been disemboweled and will soon die. To the left of the cleft in the wall a woolly rhinoceros seems to run off. It is unknown why the man was portrayed as a sticklike figure while the bison was rendered with such accurate detail—or whether the painting illustrates a myth, an actual event, or the vision of a shaman.

ALTAMIRA The cave paintings at Altamira, near Santander in the Cantabrian Mountains in Spain—the first to be discovered and attributed to the Upper Paleolithic period—are now dated to about 12,500 BCE, as discussed below. The Altamira artists created sculptural effects by painting over and around natural irregularities in the cave walls and ceilings. To produce the herd of bison on the ceiling of the main cavern (**FIG. 1-13**), they used red and brown ocher to paint the large areas of the animals' shoulders, backs, and flanks, then sharpened the contours of the rocks and added the details of the legs, tails, heads, and horns in black and brown. They mixed yellow and brown from iron-based ocher to make the red tones, and they derived black from manganese or charcoal.

HOW EARLY ART IS DATED Since the first discoveries at Altamira, archaeologists have developed increasingly sophisticated ways of dating cave paintings and other excavated objects. Today, they primarily use two approaches to determine an artifact's age. **Relative dating** relies on the relationships among objects in a single excavation or among several sites. If archaeologists have determined, for example, that pottery types A, B, and C follow each other chronologically at one site, they can apply that knowledge to another site. Even if type B is the only pottery present, it can still be assigned a relative date. **Absolute dating**, on the other hand, aims to determine a precise span of calendar years in which an artifact was created.

The most accurate method of absolute dating is **radiometric dating**, which measures the degree to which radioactive materials have disintegrated over time. Used for dating organic (plant or animal) materials—including some pigments used in cave paintings—one radiometric method measures a carbon isotope called radiocarbon, or carbon-14, which is constantly replenished in a living organism. When an organism dies, it starts to lose its store of carbon-14 at a predictable rate. Under the right circumstances, the amount of carbon-14 remaining in organic material can tell us how long ago an organism died.

This method has serious drawbacks for dating works of art. Using carbon-14 dating on a carved antler or wood sculpture shows only when the animal died or when the tree was cut down, not when the artist created the work using those materials. Also, some part of the object must be destroyed in order to conduct this kind of test—something that is never desirable in relation to works of art. For this reason, researchers frequently test organic materials found in the same context as the work of art rather than sacrificing part of the work itself. Radiocarbon dating is most accurate for materials no more than 30,000 to 40,000 years old.

Potassium-argon dating, which measures the decay of a radioactive potassium isotope into a stable isotope of argon, an inert gas, is most reliable with materials over a million years old. **Uranium-thorium dating** measures the decay of uranium into thorium in the deposits of calcium carbonate that cover

1-13 BISON
Ceiling of a cave at Altamira, Spain.
c. 12,500 BCE. Paint on limestone, length approx. 8'3" (2.5 m).

Credit: Sisse Brimberg/National Geographic Creative

1–14 BISON
Le Tuc d'Audoubert, France.
c. 13,000 BCE. Unbaked clay,
length 25″ (63.5 cm) and 24″
(60.9 cm).

Credit: Yvonne Vertut

the surfaces of cave walls, to determine the minimum age of paintings under the crust. **Thermo-luminescence dating** measures the irradiation of the crystal structure of a material subjected to fire, such as pottery, and the soil in which it is found, determined by the luminescence produced when a sample is heated. **Electron spin resonance** techniques use a magnetic field and microwave irradiation to date a material such as tooth enamel and the soil around it.

Recent experiments have helped to date cave paintings with increasing precision. Radiocarbon analysis has determined, for example, that the animal images at Lascaux are 17,000 years old—to be more precise, 17,070 years, plus or minus 130 years.

Cave Sculptures

Caves were sometimes adorned with relief sculpture as well as paintings. At Altamira, an artist simply heightened the resemblance of a natural projecting rock to a similar and familiar animal form. Other reliefs were created by modeling, or shaping, the damp clay of the cave's floor. An excellent example of such work in clay dating to 13,000 BCE is preserved at Le Tuc d'Audoubert, south of the Dordogne region of France. Here the sculptor created two bison leaning against a ridge of rock (**FIG. 1–14**). Although the beasts are modeled in very high relief (they extend well forward from the background), they display the same conventions as earlier painted ones, with emphasis on the broad masses of the meat-bearing flanks and shoulders. To make the animals even more lifelike, their creator engraved short parallel lines below their necks to represent their shaggy coats. Numerous small footprints found in the clay floor of this cave suggest that group rites took place here.

The Neolithic Period

How does the development of prehistoric art and architecture relate to the social and cultural changes of the Neolithic period?

Today, advances in technology, medicine, transportation, and communication change human experience in a generation. Many thousands of years ago, change took place much more slowly. In the tenth millennium BCE the world had already entered the present interglacial period; our modern climate was taking shape. The world was warming up, and this affected the distribution and stability of plant and animal life as well as marine and aquatic resources. However, the Ice Age ended so gradually and unevenly among regions that people could not have known what was happening.

One of the fundamental changes that took place in our prehistoric past was in the relationship people had with their environment. After millennia of established interactions between people and wild plants and animals—ranging from opportunistic foraging to well-scheduled gathering and collecting—people gradually started to exert increasing control over the land and its resources. Seen from the modern perspective, this change in economy (archaeologists use "economy" to refer to the ways people gathered or produced food) seems abrupt and complete. Different communities adopted and adapted new sets of technologies, skills, and plant and animal species that allowed them to produce food. This was the origin of plant and animal domestication. Wheat and barley were cultivated; sheep, goats, cattle, and pigs were bred. This new economy appeared at different rates and to varying degrees of completeness in different parts of the Near East and Europe, and no community relied exclusively on the cultivation of plants or on breeding animals. Instead they balanced hunting, gathering, farming, and animal breeding in order to maintain a steady food supply.

Architecture

At the same time as these new food technologies and species appeared, people began to establish stronger, more lasting connections to particular places in the landscape. The beginnings of architecture in Europe are marked by human social environments made up of simple but durable structures constructed of clay, mud, dung, and straw interwoven among wooden posts. While some of these buildings were simple huts used for no more than a season at a time, others were much more substantial, with foundations made of stone, set into trenches, and supporting walls of large timbers. Some were constructed from simple bricks made of clay, mud, and straw, shaped in rectangular molds and then dried in the sun. Regardless of the technique, the result was the same: People developed a new attachment to the land, and with settlement came a new kind of social life.

At the site of Lepenski Vir, on the Serbian bank of the Danube River, rows of trapezoidal buildings made of wooden posts, branches, mud, and clay—set on stone foundations and with stone-faced hearths—face the river from which the inhabitants took large fish (**FIG. 1–15**). Although this site dates to between 6300 and 5500 BCE, there is little evidence for the domestication of plants and animals that might be expected at this time in association with an architectural settlement. Archaeologists found human burials under the floors of these structures, as well as in the spaces between individual buildings.

1–15 RECONSTRUCTION DRAWING OF LEPENSKI VIR HOUSE/SHRINE

Serbia. 6300–5500 BCE.

Credit: Illustration: John Gordon Swogger

1–16 HUMAN–FISH SCULPTURE

From Lepenski Vir, Serbia. c. 6300–5500 BCE.

Credit: © akg-images/Erich Lessing

In some houses extraordinary art was found, made of carefully shaped river boulders (**FIG. 1–16**). Some of the boulders appear to represent human forms. Others look more like fish. A few seem to consist of mixtures of human and fish features. Here we have a site with a confusing combination of architecture with a nondomesticated economy, very distinctive art, and many burials. Archaeologists interpret such sites as temporary habitations where people carried out special rites and activities linked to death and to the natural and wild worlds.

In some places early architecture was dramatic and long-lasting, with the repeated building—sometimes over 1,000 years or more—of house upon house in successive architectural generations, resulting in the gradual rise of great mounds of villages referred to as tells or mound settlements. A particularly spectacular example is Çatalhöyük (Chatal Huyuk) in the Konya Plain in central Turkey, where the first traces of a village date to 7400 BCE in the early Neolithic period. The oldest part of the site consists of many densely clustered houses separated by areas of rubbish. They were made of rectangular mud bricks held together with mortar; walls, floors, and ceilings were covered with plaster and lime-based paint and were frequently replastered and repainted (see "Closer Look" opposite). The large site was home to as many as 3,000 people at any one time. Beyond the early date of the site and its size and population, the settlement at Çatalhöyük is important to the history of art for two reasons: the picture it provides of the use of early architecture and the sensational art that has been found within its buildings.

A Closer Look

A HOUSE IN ÇATALHÖYÜK

Large wooden beams of juniper or oak supported the roof and the activities that took place above.

The only entrance to the house was through the roof and down a ladder. Natural light was limited to what came through this opening because the house had no windows.

Walls up to 1 foot 4 inches thick and 16 feet high were made of rows of mortared brick. The interior sides of the walls were replastered annually up to 100 times.

Village residents were often buried under house floors.

The walls were used to display special objects. Cattle skulls and horns (bucrania) were attached to the wall as relief art. Conical repositories held special objects.

Domed ovens were placed both on the roof and in the house. The roof was used for cooking and other activities in the summer months.

Side rooms were used for storage, food preparation, and other domestic tasks.

Short walls and ridges created separate areas for different activities or social groups. Within some areas, raised platforms were coated with white plaster and covered with textile mats.

1–17 A HOUSE IN ÇATALHÖYÜK

Reconstruction drawing. Çatalhöyük, Turkey. c. 7400–6200 BCE.

Credit: Illustration: John Gordon Swogger, originally published in Ian Hodder, *The Leopard's Tale: Revealing the Mysteries of Çatalhöyük*. London: Thames & Hudson, 2006, fig. 5.8.

HOUSES AND COMMUNITIES Archaeologists and anthropologists often assume that the decision to create buildings such as the houses at Neolithic sites came from a universal need for shelter from the elements. However, as suggested by the special nature of the activities at Lepenski Vir, recent work at Çatalhöyük also shows clearly that while structures did provide shelter, early houses had much more significant functions. For the Neolithic people of Çatalhöyük, their houses were the key component of their worldview. Most importantly, they became an emblem of the spirit and history of a community. The building of house upon house created a historical continuity that outlasted any human lifetime; some house-rebuilding sequences lasted many hundreds of years. And the seasonal replastering and repainting of walls and floors only enhanced the sense of long-term continuity that made these buildings history-makers. In fact, Ian Hodder, the director of excavations at Çatalhöyük, and his colleagues call some of them "history houses" and have found no evidence to suggest that they were shrines or temples as earlier interpreters had mistakenly concluded.

As at Lepenski Vir, the dead were buried under the floors of many of the buildings at Çatalhöyük, another way that the site connected the community's past and present. While there were no burials in some houses, a few contained between 30 and 60 bodies (the average is about 6 per house), and one had 62 burials, including people who had lived their lives in other parts of the village. Periodically, perhaps to mark special community events and ceremonies, people dug down into the floors of their houses and removed the heads of the long-deceased, then buried the skulls in new graves under the floors. Skulls were also placed in the foundations of new houses as they were built and rebuilt, and in other special deposits around the settlement. In one extraordinary burial, a deceased woman holds in her arms a man's skull that had been plastered and painted. Perhaps it, too, had been removed from an earlier underfloor grave.

The houses of Çatalhöyük were powerful places not only because of the (literal) depths of their histories, but also because of the art that decorated their interiors. Painted on the walls of some of the houses are violent and wild scenes. In some, humans are represented without heads as if they had been decapitated. Vultures or other birds of prey appear huge next to them, and narratives seem to highlight dangerous interactions between people and animals. In one painting (**FIG. 1–18**) a huge, horned wild animal (probably a deer) is surrounded by small humans who are jumping or running; one of them is pulling on something sticking out of the deer's mouth, perhaps its tongue. There is an emphasis on maleness: some of the human figures are bearded and the deer has an erect penis. Archaeologists have interpreted this scene as a dangerous game or ritual of baiting and taunting a wild animal. In other paintings, people hunt or tease boars or bulls. Conservation of the wall paintings is highly complex, and since many of the most dramatic examples were excavated before modern preservation techniques existed, we must rely on the archaeologist's narrative descriptions or quick field sketches.

Other representations of wild animals, most frequently the heads and horns of bulls, are modeled in relief on the interior walls. In some houses, people placed boar tusks, vulture skulls, and fox and weasel teeth under the floors; in at least one case, they dug into previous house generations to retrieve the plastered and painted heads of bulls.

Sites such as Lepenski Vir and Çatalhöyük have forced archaeologists to think in new ways about the role of architecture and art in prehistoric communities. Critically, the mixture of shelter, architecture, art, spirit, ritual, and ceremony at these and many other Neolithic settlements makes us realize that we cannot easily distinguish between "domestic" and "sacred" architecture. This point re-emerges from the recent work at Stonehenge in England. In addition, the clear and repeated emphasis on death, violence, wild animals, and male body parts at Çatalhöyük has challenged traditional interpretations of the Neolithic worldview that concentrated on representations of the female body, human fertility, and cults of the Mother Goddess.

Most Neolithic architectural sites were not as visually sensational as Çatalhöyük. At the site of Sesklo in northern Greece, dated to 6500 BCE, people built stone-based, long-lasting structures (**FIG. 1–19**) in one part of a village and less substantial mud, clay, and wood buildings in another part. The stone-based buildings may have had a special function within the community—whether ritual, crafts-based, or political is difficult to determine. Since they were rebuilt again and again over a long period of time, the part of the village where they were located "grew" vertically into a mound or tell. Some buildings had parts with easily recognizable functions, such as a place for making ceramic vessels. The distinction between the area of the longer-lasting, often rebuilt buildings and the more temporary structures is clear in the style of architecture as well as in the quality of artifacts found. Finer, decorated pottery is more abundant in the former.

1–18 MEN TAUNTING A DEER (?)
Detail of a wall painting from Çatalhöyük, Turkey. c. 6000 BCE. Museum of Anatolian Civilization, Ankara, Turkey.

Credit: © akg-images/De Agostini Picture Lib./M. Seemuller

1–19 SESKLO STONE-FOUNDATION HOUSE

Sesklo, northern Greece. 6500 BCE.

Credit: From: Stella G. Souvatzi, *A Social
Archaeology of Households in Neolithic Greece.
An Anthropological Approach*. 2009, fig. 4.8b.
Cambridge University Press. After D.R. Theocharis,
Neolithiki Hellas, National Bank of Greece, Athens, 1973

In different regions of Europe, people created architecture in different ways. The crowded buildings of Çatalhöyük differed from the structures at Sesklo, and these differed from the trapezoidal huts at Lepenski Vir. To the northwest, in Germany and central Europe, Neolithic villages typically consisted of three or four long timber buildings, each up to 150 feet long, housing 45 to 50 people. The structures were rectangular, with a row of posts down the center supporting a **ridgepole**, a long horizontal beam against which the slanting roof poles were braced. The walls were probably made of **wattle and daub** and roofed with **thatch**, plant material such as reeds or straw tied over a framework of poles. These houses also included large granaries, or storage spaces for the harvest; some buildings contained sections for animals and for people. Around 4000 BCE, Neolithic settlers began to locate their communities at defensible sites—near rivers, on plateaus, or in swamps. For additional protection, they also frequently surrounded their settlements with wooden walls, earth embankments, and ditches.

While much research has focused on the origins and construction technology of the earliest architecture—as at Çatalhöyük, Lepenski Vir, and other sites—some of the most exciting new work has come from studies of how Neolithic houses were destroyed. Excavations of settlements dating to the end of the Neolithic period in eastern and central Europe commonly reveal a level of ash and other evidence for great fires that burned down houses at these sites. The common interpretation had been that

invaders, coming on horseback from Ukraine and Russia, had attacked these villages and burned the settlements.

In one of the most innovative recent studies, Mira Stevanović and Ruth Tringham employed the methods of modern forensic science and meticulously reconstructed the patterns of Neolithic house conflagrations. The results proved that the fires were not part of village-wide destructions, but were individual events, confined to particular houses. Most significantly, they showed that each fire had been deliberately set. In fact, in order to get the fires to consume the houses completely, buildings had been stuffed with combustibles before they were set alight. Repeated tests by experimental archaeologists have supported these conclusions. Each intentional, house-destroying fire was part of a ritual killing of the house and a rupture of the historical and social entity that the house had represented for the community. Critically, even in their destruction, prehistoric buildings played important and complex roles in relation to the ways that individuals and communities created (and destroyed) social identities and continuities.

CEREMONIAL AND TOMB ARCHITECTURE In western and northern Europe, people erected huge stones to build ceremonial structures and tombs. In some cases, they had to transport these great stones over long distances. The monuments thus created are examples of what is known as **megalithic** architecture, the descriptive term derived from the Greek words for "large" (*mega-*) and "stone" (*lithos*).

Archaeologists disagree about the nature of the societies that created these monuments. Some believe they reflect complex, stratified societies in which powerful religious or political leaders dictated the design of these monuments and inspired (and coerced) large numbers of people to contribute their labor to such engineering projects. Skilled "engineers" would have devised the methods for shaping, transporting, and aligning the stones. Other interpreters argue that these massive monuments are clear evidence for collaboration within and between groups on a common project, the successful completion of which fueled social cohesion in the absence of a powerful individual.

Many of these megalithic structures are associated with death. Most recent interpretations stress the role of death and burial as fundamental, public performances in which individual and group identity, cohesion, and disputes were played out. In this reasoning, death and its rituals are viewed as theater, with the deceased as well as grave goods perceived as props, the monument as a stage, the celebrants and mourners as actors, and the entire event proceeding in terms of an (unwritten) script with narrative and plot.

Elaborate megalithic tombs first appeared in the Neolithic period. Some were built for single burials; others had multiple burial chambers. The simplest type was the **dolmen**, formed in **post-and-lintel** construction (construction in which two uprights—the posts—support a horizontal element—the lintel). The tomb chamber was formed of huge upright stones supporting one or more tablelike rocks, or **capstones**. The structure was then mounded over with smaller rocks and dirt to form a **cairn** or artificial hill. A more imposing type of structure was the **passage grave**, in which narrow, stone-lined passageways led into a large room at the center.

At Newgrange, in Ireland, the mound of an elaborate passage grave (**FIG. 1–20**) originally stood 44 feet high and measured about 280 feet in diameter. The mound was built of sod and river pebbles and was set off by a circle of engraved standing stones around its perimeter. Its passageway, 62 feet long and lined with standing stones, leads into a three-part chamber with a **corbeled vault** (an arched structure that spans an interior space) rising to a height of 19 feet.

Some of the stones are engraved with linear designs, mainly rings, spirals, and diamond shapes. These patterns may have been marked out using strings or compasses, then carved by picking at the rock surface with tools made of antlers. Recent detailed analysis of the art engraved on passage graves like Newgrange, but also at Knowth in Ireland, suggest that the images are entoptic (meaning that their significance and function relate to the particularities of perception by the eye), and that we should understand them in terms of the neuropsychological effect they would have had on people visiting the tomb. These effects may

have included hallucinations. Archaeologists argue that key entoptic motifs were positioned at entrances and other important thresholds inside the tomb, and that they played important roles in ritual or political ceremonies that centered around death, burial, and the commemoration and visitation of the deceased by the living.

STONEHENGE Of all the megalithic monuments in Europe, the one that has stirred the imagination of the public most strongly is **STONEHENGE**, on Salisbury Plain in southern England (**FIGS. 1–21, 1–22**). A **henge** is a circle of stones or posts, often surrounded by a ditch with built-up embankments. Laying out such circles with accuracy would have posed no particular problem. Architects likely relied on the human compass, a simple but effective surveying method that persisted well into modern times. All that is required is a length of cord either cut or knotted to mark the desired radius of the circle. A person holding one end of the cord is stationed in the center; a coworker, holding the other end and keeping the cord taut, steps off the circle's circumference. By the time of Stonehenge's construction, cords and ropes were readily available.

Stonehenge is not the largest such circle from the Neolithic period, but it is one of the most complex, with eight different phases of construction and activity, starting in 3000 BCE during the Neolithic period and stretching over a millennium and a half through the Bronze Age. The site started as a cemetery of cremation burials marked by a circle of bluestones. Through numerous sequences of alterations and rebuildings, it continued to function as a domain of the dead. Between 2900 and 2600 BCE, the bluestones were rearranged into an arc. Around 2500 BCE, a circle of sarsen stones—sarsen is a gray sandstone—gave the site its well-known appearance using post-and-lintel construction. At the same time, the bluestones were rearranged within the sarsens. The center of the site was now dominated by a horseshoe-shaped arrangement of five sandstone, post-and-lintel trilithons— pairs of upright stones topped by **lintels**. The one in the middle stood considerably taller than the rest, rising to a height of 24 feet, and its lintel was more than 15 feet long and 3 feet thick. This group was surrounded by the so-called sarsen circle,

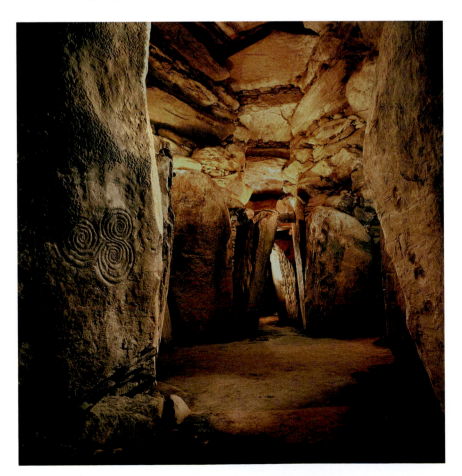

1–20 TOMB INTERIOR WITH CORBELING AND ENGRAVED STONES
Newgrange, Ireland. c. 3000–2500 BCE.

Credit: ©National Monuments Service. Dept of Arts, Heritage and the Gaeltacht

heel stone   arc of bluestones

sarsen circle

sarsen trilithon

1-21 RECONSTRUCTION DRAWING OF STONEHENGE FROM THE AIR

Salisbury Plain, Wiltshire, England. c. 3000–1500 BCE.

a ring of sandstone uprights weighing up to 26 tons each and averaging 13 feet 6 inches tall. This circle, 106 feet in diameter, was capped by a continuous lintel. The uprights taper slightly toward the top, and the gently curved lintel sections were secured by **mortise-and-tenon** joints, that is, joints made by a conical projection at the top of each upright that fits like a peg into a hole in the lintel. Over the next thousand years people continued to alter the arrangement of the bluestones, and cremation burials continued in pits at the site.

The differences in the types of stone used in the different phases of construction are significant. The use of bluestone in the early phases (and maintained and rearranged through the sequence) is particularly important. Unlike the sarsen stone, bluestone was not locally available and would have been transported over 150 miles from the west, where it had been quarried in the mountains of west Wales. The means of transporting the bluestones such distances remains a source of great debate. Some argue that they were floated around the coast on great barges; others hold that they traveled over land on wooden rollers. Regardless, the use of this material tells us that the people who first transformed the Stonehenge landscape into a ceremonial site probably had their ancestral origins in the west. By bringing the bluestones and using them in the early Stonehenge cemetery, these migrants made a powerful connection with their homelands.

Through the ages, many theories have been advanced to explain Stonehenge. In the Middle Ages, people thought that Merlin, the legendary magician of King Arthur, had built it. Later, the site was erroneously associated with the rituals of the Celtic druids (priests). Because it is oriented in relation to the movement of the sun, some people have argued that it may have been an observatory or that it had special importance as a calendar for regulating early agricultural schedules. None of these ideas is supported by the current evidence.

We now believe that Stonehenge was the site of ceremonies linked to death and burial. This theory comes from evidence that looks not only at the stone circles but also at the nearby sites dating from the periods when Stonehenge was in use (**FIG. 1-23**). A new generation of archaeologists, led by Mike Parker Pearson, has pioneered this contextual approach.

The settlements built near Stonehenge follow circular layouts, connecting them in plan to the ceremonial site

1-22 STONEHENGE FROM THE GROUND

Credit: © Peter Adams/The Image Bank/Getty Images

1-23 PLAN OF STONEHENGE AND ITS SURROUNDING SETTLEMENTS

Credit: © 1998 Antiquity Publications Ltd. Reprinted with the permission of Cambridge University Press

(FIG. 1-24). Unlike the more famous monument, however, these habitations were built primarily of wood, in particular large posts and tree trunks. A mile from Stonehenge is Durrington Walls, which was a large inhabited settlement (almost 1,500 feet across) surrounded by a ditch. Inside are a number of circles—made not from stone but from wood—and many circular houses constructed with wooden posts. The rubbish left behind at this and similar sites provides archaeologists with insights into the lives of the inhabitants. Chemical analysis of animal bone debris, for example, indicates that the animals consumed came from great distances before they were slaughtered, and therefore that the people who stayed here had come from regions far removed from the site.

Significantly, both Stonehenge and Durrington Walls are connected to the Avon River by banked avenues (SEE FIG. 1-23). These connected the worlds of the living (the wood settlement) with the domain of the dead (the stone circle). Neolithic people would have moved between these worlds as they walked the avenues, sometimes bringing the deceased to be buried or cremated, other times approaching the stone circle for ceremonies and rituals dedicated to the memories of the deceased and the very ancient ancestors. The meaning of Stonehenge therefore rests within an understanding of the larger landscape that contained not only other ritual sites but also sites of habitation.

Ceramics

In addition to domestic and ceremonial architecture and a food-producing economy, the other critical component of the Neolithic way of life was the ability to make ceramic vessels. This "pot revolution" marked a shift from a complete reliance on skin, textile, and wooden containers to the use of pots made by firing clay. Pottery provided a new medium of extraordinary potential for shaping and decorating durable objects.

The terms pottery and ceramics may be used interchangeably—and often are. Because it covers all baked-clay wares, **ceramics** is technically a more inclusive term than pottery. Pottery includes all baked-clay wares except **porcelain**, which is the most refined product of ceramic technology.

Pottery vessels can be formed in several ways. It is possible, though difficult, to raise up the sides from a ball of raw clay. Another method is to coil long rolls of soft, raw clay, stack them on top of each other to form a container, and then smooth them by hand. A third possibility is simply to press the clay over an existing form, a dried

1-24 RECONSTRUCTION DRAWING OF DURRINGTON WALLS

The settlement at Durrington Walls, near Stonehenge, southern England. 2600 BCE. Private collection.

Credit: © Historic England/Bridgeman Images

gourd for example. By about 4000 BCE, Egyptian potters had developed the potter's wheel, a round, spinning platform on which a lump of clay is placed and then formed with the fingers while rotating, making it relatively simple to produce a uniformly shaped vessel in a very short time. The potter's wheel appeared in the ancient Near East about 3250 BCE and in China about 3000 BCE.

After forming, a pot is allowed to dry completely before it is fired. Special ovens for firing pottery, called **kilns**, have been discovered at prehistoric sites in Europe dating from as early as 26,000 BCE (as at Dolní Věstonice). For effective firing, the temperature must be maintained at a relatively uniform level. Raw clay becomes porous pottery when heated to at least 500° Centigrade. It then holds its shape permanently and will not disintegrate in water. Fired at 800° Centigrade, pottery is technically known as **earthenware**. When subjected to temperatures between 1,200° and 1,400° Centigrade, certain stone elements in the clay vitrify, or become glassy, and the result is a stronger type of ceramic called **stoneware**.

Pottery is relatively fragile, and new vessels were constantly in demand to replace broken ones, so fragments of low-fired ceramics—fired at a hearth, rather than a higher-temperature kiln—are the most common artifacts found in excavations of prehistoric settlements. Pottery fragments, or **potsherds**, serve as a major key in dating sites and reconstructing human living and trading patterns.

Ceramic technology emerged independently, at different times, across the globe. The earliest examples have

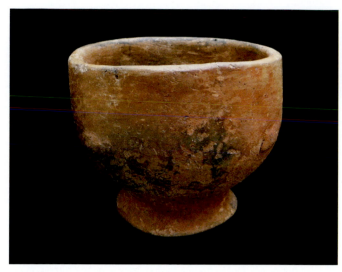

1-26 EARLY POTTERY FROM THE FRANCHTHI CAVE, GREECE
6500 BCE.

Credit: Catherine Perlès

been excavated in southern China's Jiangxi Province and date from 20,000 years ago; surviving examples from Japan's Jomon culture date from 12,000 BCE (**FIG. 1-25**). It is extremely difficult to determine with certainty why pottery was first invented or why subsequent cultures adopted it. The idea that pottery would only emerge out of farming settlements has been disproven by recent archaeology. It seems that there was no one set of social, economic, or environmental circumstances that led to the invention of ceramics.

It is likely that the technology for producing ceramics evolved in stages. Archaeologist Karen Vitelli's detailed studies of the early Neolithic site of Franchthi Cave in Greece have shown that pottery making at this site started with an experimental stage during which nonspecialist potters produced a small number of pots. These early pots were used in ceremonies, especially those where medicinal or narcotic plants were consumed (**FIG. 1-26**). Only later did specialist potters share manufacturing recipes to produce enough pots for standard activities such as cooking and eating. A similar pattern may have occurred in other early potting communities.

SCULPTED HUMAN FIGURES In addition to firing clay to make pots, cups, pitchers, and large storage containers, Neolithic people made thousands of miniature figures of humans. While it was once thought that these figurines refer to fertility cults and matriarchal societies, archaeologists now agree that they had many different functions—for example, as toys, portraits, or votives. More importantly, specialists have shown that there are great degrees of similarity in figurine shape and decoration within distinct cultural regions. Such regional similarities, and the huge numbers of Neolithic figurines that would have been in circulation at any one place and time, have

1-25 EARLY POTTERY FROM JAPAN'S JOMON CULTURE
Approx 7,000 BCE. Excavated at Choshichiyama Shell Midden, Hachinohe, Aomori prefecture.

Art and its Contexts

FIGURES OF A WOMAN AND A MAN

For all we know, the person who created these figurines in around 4500 BCE (**FIG. 1–27**) had nothing particular in mind— people had been modeling clay figures in southeastern Europe for a long time. Perhaps a woman who was making cooking and storage pots out of clay amused herself by fashioning images of the people she saw around her. But because these figures were found in the same grave in Cernavodă, Romania, they suggest to us an otherworldly message.

The woman, wide-hipped and big-bellied, sits directly on the ground, expressive of the mundane world. She exudes stability, and her ample hips and thighs seem to ensure the continuity of her family. But in a lively gesture, she joins her hands on one raised knee, curls up her toes, and tilts her head upward. Her upwardly tilted head could suggest that she is watching the smoke rising from the hearth, worrying about holes in the roof,

gazing adoringly at her partner, or communing with heaven. The man is rather slim, with massive legs and shoulders. He rests his head on his hands, evoking thoughtfulness, weariness, boredom, or sorrow.

We can interpret the Cernavodă woman and man in many ways, but we cannot know what they meant to their makers or owners. Depending on how they are displayed, we make up different stories about them, broadening the potential fields of meaning. When they are set facing each other, or side by side as they are here, we tend to think of them as a couple—a woman and man in a relationship. In fact, we do not know whether the artist conceived of them in this way, or even made them at the same time. For all their visual eloquence, their secrets remain hidden from us, but it is difficult not to speculate.

1–27 FIGURES OF A WOMAN AND A MAN
From Cernavodă, Romania. c. 4500 BCE. Ceramic, height 4½" (11.5 cm). National History Museum, Bucharest.

Credits: © akg-images/Erich Lessing

convinced experts that the critical significance of these objects is that they mark the emergence of the human body as the core location of human identity. Thus, the central role the body has played in the politics, philosophy, and art, of historical and modern times began over 8,000 years ago with Neolithic figurines.

Neolithic figures of humans were most numerous and diverse in central and eastern Europe, and among the most extraordinary are two figures of a man and woman from around 4500 BCE, excavated in Romania (see "Figures of a Woman and a Man" opposite).

In the Near Eastern site of 'Ain Ghazal in present-day Jordan, archaeologist Gary Rollefson found 32 large **HUMAN FIGURES** (**FIG. 1–28**). Dated to 6500 BCE and constructed by covering bundled-twig cores with layers of plaster, the statues were found in two pits. One contained 12 busts and 13 full figures, and in the other were two full figures, two fragmental busts, and three figures with two heads.

1–28 HUMAN FIGURE

From 'Ain Ghazal, Jordan. 6500 BCE. Fired lime plaster with cowrie shell, bitumen, and paint, height approx. 35″ (90 cm). National Museum, Amman, Jordan.

Credit: © akg-images/Erich Lessing

The stylized faces of these statues are startling for many modern viewers. The eyes—made with cowrie shells outlined with bitumen (a natural asphalt), also used to represent pupils—are wide open, giving them a lifelike appearance. Nostrils are also clearly defined, even exaggerated, but the mouths are discreet and tight-lipped. Clothes and other features were painted on the bodies. The powerful legs and feet are clearly modeled independently with plaster, but the strangely spindly arms and tiny, tapering hands cling closely to the body. The impression is of living, breathing individuals who are unable (or unwilling) to gesture or speak.

Scholars have searched for clues about the function of these figures. The people who lived in 'Ain Ghazal built and rebuilt their houses, replastered walls, buried their dead under house floors, and dug down through the floors to retrieve skulls—just like the inhabitants of Çatalhöyük. They used the same plaster both to coat the walls of their houses and to make the human figures. The site also contains buildings that may have served special, potentially ceremonial functions, and some scholars suggest that the figures are linked to these rites. In addition to the figures' lifelike appearance, the similarity between the burial of bodies under house floors and the burial of the plaster figures in pits is striking. At the same time, however, there are significant differences: The statues are buried in groups while the human bodies are not; the statues are buried in pits, not in houses; and the eyes of the statues are open, as if they are alive and awake. It is difficult to know with certainty how the figures of 'Ain Ghazal were used and what they meant to the people who made them.

Metallurgy

The technology of metallurgy is closely allied to that of ceramics. Although Neolithic culture persisted in northern Europe until about 2000 BCE (and indeed all of its key contributions to human evolution—farming, architecture, and pottery—continue through present times), the age of metals made its appearance in much of Europe about 3000 BCE. In central and southern Europe and in the Aegean region, copper, gold, and tin had been mined, worked, and traded even earlier. Smelted and cast copper beads and ornaments dated to 4000 BCE have been discovered in Poland.

Metals were first used for ornamentation, and gold was one of the first among them; it was used to make jewelry (ear, lip, and nose rings) and to decorate clothing (appliqués sewn onto fabric). Toward the end of the Neolithic period, people shaped simple beads by cold-hammering malachite, a green-colored, copper carbonate mineral that can be found on the surface of the ground in many regions.

Over time, the objects made from gold and copper became more complicated, and technologies of extraction

1–29 GOLD-ADORNED FACE MASK

From Tomb 3, Varna I, Bulgaria. Neolithic, 3800 BCE. Terra cotta and gold. Archaeological Museum, Plovdiv, Bulgaria.

Credit: © akg-images/Erich Lessing

(the mining of copper in Bulgaria) and metalworking (casting copper) improved. Ivan Ivanov discovered some of the most sensational and earliest prehistoric gold and copper objects in the late Neolithic cemetery at Varna on Bulgaria's Black Sea coast. While the cemetery consisted of several hundred graves of men, women, and children, a few special burials contained gold and copper artifacts (**FIGS. 1–29, 1–30**). Objects such as gold-covered scepters, bracelets, beads, arm rings, lip-plugs, and copper axes and chisels distinguish the graves of a small number of adult males. In a very few of those graves, no skeleton was present. Instead, the body was represented by a clay mask richly decorated with gold adornments (SEE FIG. 1-29), and the grave contained extraordinary concentrations of metal and special marine-shell ornaments. As in other prehistoric contexts, death and its attendant ceremonies were the focus for large and visually expressive displays of status and authority.

1–30 GOLD SCEPTERS

From Varna, Bulgaria. 3800 BCE. National Museum of History, Sofia, Bulgaria.

Credit: © akg-images/Erich Lessing

The Bronze Age

How does the Bronze Age transform prehistoric culture and art?

The period that followed the introduction of metalworking is commonly called the Bronze Age. Although copper is relatively abundant in central Europe and in Spain, objects fashioned from it are too soft to be functional and therefore usually have a ceremonial or representational use and value. However, bronze—an **alloy**, or mixture, of tin and copper—is a stronger, harder substance with a wide variety of uses.

The development of bronze, especially for weapons such as daggers and short swords, changed the peoples of Europe in fundamental ways. While copper ore was widely available across Europe, either as surface outcrops or easily mined, the tin that was required to make bronze had a much more limited natural distribution and often required extraction by mining. Power bases shifted within communities as the resources needed to make bronze were not widely available to all. Trade and intergroup contacts across the continent and into the Near East increased, and bronze objects circulated as prized goods.

Rock Carvings

Bronze Age artistry is not limited to metalworking; indeed, some of the most exciting imagery of the period is found in the rock art of northern Europe. For a thousand years starting around 1500 BCE, people created designs by scratching outlines and pecking and grinding the surface of exposed rock faces using stone hammers and sometimes grains of sand as an abrasive. The Swedish region of northern Bohuslän is especially rich in rock carvings dating to this period; archaeologists have recorded over 40,000 individual images from more than 1,500 sites. The range of motifs is wide, including boats, animals (bulls, elk, horses, a few snakes, birds, and fish), people (mostly sexless, some with horned helmets, but also men with erect penises), wheeled

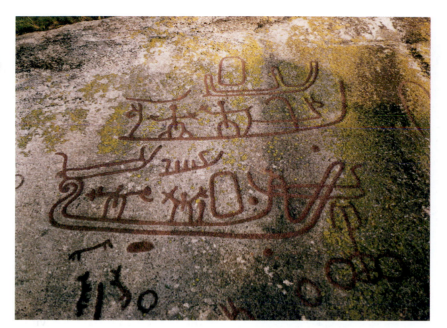

1–31 ROCK ART: BOAT AND SEA BATTLE
Fossum, northern Bohuslän, Sweden. Bronze Age, c. 1500–500 BCE.

Credit: Bridgeman Images

or past shorelines is the critical clue to their meaning. Archaeologist Richard Bradley suggests that rock art connects sky, earth, and sea, perhaps visualizing the community's view of the three-part nature of the universe. Others suggest that the art is intentionally located between water and earth to mark a boundary between the world of the living and the world of spirits. In this view, the permanent character of the rock, grounded deep in the earth, provided a means of communication and connection between distant and distinct worlds.

vehicles and plows (and unassociated disks, circles, and wheels), and weapons (swords, shields, and helmets). Within this range, however, the majority of images are boats (**FIG. 1–31**), not just in Sweden but across northern Europe. Interestingly, the boat images are unlike the boats that archaeologists have excavated. The rock-engraved images do not have masts, nor are they the dugouts or log boats that are known from this period. Instead they represent boats made from wooden planks or with animal skins.

What is the meaning of these boat images? Most agree that the location of the majority of the rock art near current

For people of the prehistoric era, representational and abstract art had critical symbolic importance, justifying the labor required to paint in the deep recesses of caves, move enormous stones great distances, or create elaborately ornamented masks. Prehistoric art and architecture connected the earthly with the spiritual, established social power hierarchies, and perhaps helped people learn and remember information about the natural world that was critical for their survival. This art represents one of the fundamental elements of our development as a human species.

Think About It

1   Prehistoric artists created representations of human figures using a variety of media, styles, and techniques. Compare two examples drawn from different times and places by discussing the relationship between style or technique and expressive character.

2   What are the common motifs found in cave paintings such as those at Lascaux and Altamira? Summarize the current theories about their original meaning and purpose.

3   Many examples of prehistoric art and architecture express relationships between the living and the dead. Discuss how this theme is evoked in one work of architecture and one example of sculpture discussed in this chapter. Why do you think this theme was so important?

4   How did the emergence of ceramics and metallurgy transform art making in the Neolithic era? Select and analyze a work discussed in this chapter that was made in one of these new media and discuss the unique properties of the medium.

Crosscurrents

Although we have limited information about the meanings prehistoric people associated with sacred spaces, art historians and archaeologists have linked these two famous sites with specific social practices and rituals. Discuss and compare current interpretations of Lascaux and Stonehenge, including evidence as well as conclusions.

FIG. 1–11

FIG. 1–22

2–1 STELE OF NARAM-SIN

From Sippar; found at Susa
(present-day Shush, Iran).
Naram-Sin (r. 2254–2218 BCE).
Limestone, height 6′6″ (1.98 m).
Musée du Louvre, Paris.

Credit: Photo © RMN-Grand Palais
(Musée du Louvre)/Les frères Chuzeville

Chapter 2
Art of the Ancient Near East

Learning Objectives

2.a Identify the visual hallmarks of early Mesopotamian, Assyrian, Neo-Babylonian, and Persian art for formal, technical, and expressive qualities.

2.b Interpret the meaning of works of early Mesopotamian, Assyrian, Neo-Babylonian, and Persian art based on their themes, subjects, and symbols.

2.c Relate early Mesopotamian, Assyrian, Neo-Babylonian, and Persian artists and art to their cultural, economic, and political contexts.

2.d Apply the vocabulary and concepts used to discuss ancient Near Eastern art, artists, and art history.

2.e Interpret ancient Near Eastern art using appropriate art historical methods, such as observation, comparison, and inductive reasoning.

2.f Select visual and textual evidence in various media to support an argument or an interpretation of ancient Near Eastern art.

In public works such as this stone **stele** (upright stone slab), the artists of Mesopotamia developed a sophisticated symbolic visual language—a kind of conceptual art—that both communicated and celebrated the political stratification that gave order to their world. Akkadian ruler Naram-Sin (ruled 2254–2218 BCE) is pictured proudly here (**FIG. 2-1**). His preeminence is signaled by his size: he is by far the largest person in the scene, conforming to an artistic practice we call **hierarchic scale**, where relative size indicates relative importance. Naram-Sin is also elevated well above the other figures and boldly silhouetted against blank ground. Even the shape of the stone slab is an active part of the composition. Its tapering top perfectly accommodates the carved mountain within it, and Naram-Sin is posed to reflect the profile of both, increasing his grandeur. He clasps a full arsenal of weaponry—spear, battleaxe, bow, and arrow—and his helmet sprouts horns, an attribute previously reserved for gods. By wearing such a helmet, he is claiming divinity for himself. Art historian Irene Winter has gone even further, pointing to his eroticized pose and well-formed body. In ancient Mesopotamian culture, male potency and vigor were

directly related to mythical heroism and kingship. Thus every aspect of the representation of this ruler supports his authority as leader of the state.

This stele is more than an emblem of Naram-Sin's divine right to rule, however. It also tells the story of one of his important military victories. The ruler stands above a crowded scene of smaller figures. Those to the left, dressed and posed like Naram-Sin, represent his army, marching in diagonal bands up the hillside into battle. The artist has included identifiable native trees to heighten the sense that this portrays an actual event rather than a generic battle scene. In front of and under Naram-Sin are the enemy, in this case the Lullubi people from eastern Mesopotamia (present-day Iran). One has taken a fatal spear to the neck, while others beg for mercy.

Taller than most viewers who might stand in front of it and carved of eye-catching pink stone, this sumptuous work of art communicates with us forcefully and directly even after more than four millennia. Powerful symbolism and dynamic storytelling are not unique to this stele; they are key characteristics of royal art in the ancient Near East.

Early Mesopotamia

How do early Mesopotamian art and architecture develop through the Sumerian and Akkadian empires?

In the sixth or fifth millennium BCE, well before farming communities appeared in Europe, people in Asia Minor and the ancient Near East were already domesticating grains in an area known today as the Fertile Crescent (**MAP 2-1**). These alluvial plains between the Tigris and Euphrates rivers, which the Greeks called *Mesopotamia*, meaning the "land between the rivers," are now in present-day Iraq. Because of problems with periodic flooding as well as drought, there was a need for large-scale systems to control and supply water. Meeting this need may have contributed to the development of the first cities.

Between 4000 and 3000 BCE, a major cultural shift seems to have taken place. Agricultural villages in both northern and southern Mesopotamia evolved into cities simultaneously and independently. These prosperous cities joined with their surrounding territories to create what are known as city-states, each with its own gods and government. As people developed specialized skills beyond those needed for agricultural work, social hierarchies emerged that divided rulers and workers. To grain mills and ovens were added kilns for brick and pottery, and workshops for textiles and metals. With extra goods and increasing wealth came more trade and contact with other cultures.

Organized religion played an important role, and the people who controlled rituals and sacred sites eventually became full-time priests. Numerous gods and goddesses were worshiped. (The names of comparable deities varied over time and place—for example, Inanna, the Sumerian goddess of fertility, love, and war, was equivalent to the Babylonians' Ishtar.) Every city had its special protective deity, and the fate of the city was seen as dependent on the power of that deity. Large complexes of religious, administrative, and service buildings developed in each city as centers of worship and government.

Although the stone-free alluvial plain of southern Mesopotamia was prone to floods and droughts, it was a fertile bed for agriculture, which supported successive,

MAP 2-1 THE ANCIENT NEAR EAST

The green areas represent fertile land that could support early agriculture, notably the area between the Tigris and Euphrates rivers and the strips of land on either side of the Nile in Egypt.

interlinked societies. But Mesopotamia's wealth and agricultural resources, as well as its few natural defenses, made it vulnerable to political upheaval. Over the centuries, the balance of power shifted between north and south and between local powers and outside invaders. First the Sumerians controlled the south, filling their independent city-states with new technology, developed literacy, and impressive art and architecture. But their neighbors to the north, the Akkadians, eventually eclipsed them. When invaders from farther north in turn conquered the Akkadians, the Sumerians regained power locally. During this period the city-states of Ur and Lagash thrived. The Amorites were next to dominate the south. Under them and their king, Hammurabi, a new, unified society arose with its capital in the city of Babylon.

Sumer

The cities and city-states that developed along the rivers of southern Mesopotamia between about 3500 and 2340 BCE are known collectively as Sumer. The Sumerians are credited with important technological and cultural advances. They may have invented the wagon wheel and the plow. But perhaps their greatest contribution was the invention in 3400–3200 BCE of the first form of written script.

WRITING The Sumerians appear to have invented writing as a business accounting system for traded goods. The symbols were pictographs, simple pictures cut into moist clay slabs with a pointed tool called a **stylus**. Eventually the symbols evolved from pictures into a writing system known as **cuneiform** ("wedge-shaped"),

stylus

	pictograph c. 3100 BCE	early cuneiform sign c. 2400 BCE	later cuneiform sign c. 700 BCE	
bull's head				bull
bowl				bread, food
head bowl				to eat

composed of phonograms—representations of syllable sounds—and thus became a writing system comparable to ours.

Thousands of surviving Sumerian tablets have allowed scholars to trace the gradual evolution of writing and arithmetic, another tool of commerce, as well as the Sumerians' organized system of justice. The world's first literary epic is Sumerian in origin, although the fullest surviving version of this tale is written in Akkadian, the language of Sumer's neighbors to the north. The *Epic of Gilgamesh* records the adventures of Gilgamesh, a legendary Sumerian king of Uruk, and his companion Enkidu. When Enkidu dies, the despondent Gilgamesh sets out to find the secret of eternal life from the only man and woman allowed by the gods to survive a great flood. Gilgamesh ultimately accepts his own mortality, abandons his quest, and returns to Uruk, recognizing the majestic city as his lasting accomplishment.

THE ZIGGURAT The Sumerians' most impressive surviving archaeological remains are **ziggurats**, huge, usually stepped structures with a temple or shrine on top. The first ziggurats may have developed from the practice of repeated rebuilding at a sacred site, with rubble from one structure serving as the foundation for the next. Elevating the buildings also protected the shrines from flooding.

Whatever the origin of their design, ziggurats towering above the flat plain proclaimed the wealth, prestige, and stability of a city's rulers and glorified its gods. Ziggurats also functioned symbolically as bridges between the earth and the heavens—a meeting place for humans and their gods. They were given names such as "House of the Mountain" and "Bond between Heaven and Earth."

TEMPLES Two large temple complexes in the 1,000-acre city at Uruk (present-day Warka, Iraq) mark the first independent Sumerian city-state. One was dedicated to Inanna, the goddess of love and war, while the other belonged to the sky god Anu. The temple platform of Anu, built up in stages over the centuries, ultimately became a ziggurat about 40 feet high. Around 3400 BCE, the priests of Uruk erected on top of the platform a whitewashed mud-brick temple that modern archaeologists refer to as the White Temple (FIG. 2-2). This now-ruined structure was a simple rectangle with an off-center doorway that led into a large chamber containing an altar; smaller spaces opened to each side.

Statues of gods and donors were placed in Sumerian temples. A striking life-size marble face from Uruk (FIG. 2-3) may represent a temple goddess. It could have been attached to a wooden head on a full-size wooden body. Now stripped of its original paint, wig, and the **inlay** set in for brows and eyes, it appears as a

2–2A RUINS OF THE ANU ZIGGURAT AND WHITE TEMPLE

Uruk (present-day Warka, Iraq). c. 3400–3200 BCE.

Many ancient Near Eastern cities still lie undiscovered. In most cases an archaeological site in the region is signaled by a large mound—known locally as a *tell*, *tepe*, or *huyuk*—that represents the accumulated debris of generations of human habitation. When properly excavated, such mounds yield evidence about the people who inhabited the site.

Credit: World Tourism Organization: Iraq

Anu District of Uruk

1. White Temple
2. altar
3. processional stairs
4. NW terrace

2–2B PLAN OF THE ANU ZIGGURAT AND WHITE TEMPLE

Uruk (present-day Warka, Iraq). c. 3400–3200 BCE.

2–3 HEAD OF A WOMAN

From Uruk (present-day Warka, Iraq). c. 3300–3000 BCE. Marble, height approx. 8″ (20.3 cm). Iraq Museum, Baghdad.

Credit: © 2016. Photo Scala, Florence/bpk, Bildagentur für Kunst, Kultur und Geschichte, Berlin

stark white mask. Shells may have formed the whites of the eyes, and lapis lazuli the pupils. The hair may have been gold.

A tall vessel of carved alabaster (a fine-grained, white stone) found in the temple complex of Inanna at Uruk (**FIG. 2-4**) shows how early Mesopotamian sculptors told stories in stone with great clarity and energy. They organized this visual narrative in three **registers**, or horizontal bands, and condensed the story to its essential elements.

The lowest register shows the sources of life in the natural world, beginning with water and plants (variously identified as date palm and barley, wheat and flax) and continuing in a superimposed upper strip, where alternating rams and ewes march single file along a solid groundline. In the middle register naked men carry baskets of foodstuffs, and in the top register, the goddess Inanna accepts an offering from two standing figures. Inanna stands in front of the gate to her richly filled shrine and storehouse, identified by two reed door poles hung with banners. The two men who face her are probably a naked priest or acolyte presenting an offering-filled basket, followed by a partially preserved, ceremonially dressed figure of the priest-king (not visible in FIG. 2-4). The scene may be a re-enactment of the ritual marriage between the goddess and Dumuzi, her consort—a role taken by the priest-king—that took place during the New Year's festival to ensure the fertility of crops, animals, and people, and thus the continued survival of Uruk.

2-4 CARVED VESSEL

From Uruk (present-day Warka, Iraq). c. 3300–3000 BCE.
Alabaster, height 36" (91 cm). Iraq Museum, Baghdad.

Credits: (left) © 2016. Photo Scala, Florence/bpk, Bildagentur für Kunst, Kultur
und Geschichte, Berlin; (right) © 2016. Photo Scala, Florence

VOTIVE FIGURES   Limestone statues dated to about
2900–2600 BCE from the Square Temple in Eshnunna (**FIG.
2-5**), excavated in 1932–1933, reveal another aspect of
Sumerian religious art. These **votive figures**—images dedicated to the gods—of men and women are directly related
to an ancient Near Eastern devotional practice in which
individual worshipers could set up images of themselves
in a shrine before a larger, more elaborate image of a god.
A simple inscription might identify a votive figure as "one
who offers prayers." Longer inscriptions might recount in
detail all the things a donor had accomplished in a god's
honor. Each sculpture served as a stand-in for the donor,
locked in eye contact with the god, perpetually in the act
of worship.

The sculptors of these votive statues followed **conventions** (traditional ways of representing forms) that were
important in Sumerian art. Figures have stylized faces and
bodies and are dressed in clothing that emphasizes pure
cylindrical shapes. They stand solemnly, hands clasped,
perhaps a posture expected in devotional contexts. The
huge, wide-open eyes may relate to contemporary Sumerian texts that advise worshipers to approach their gods
with an attentive gaze. As in the face of the woman from
Uruk, arched brows were inlaid with dark shell, stone, or
bitumen that emphasized the eyes. The male figures, barechested and dressed in what appear to be sheepskin skirts,
are stocky and muscular, with heavy legs, large feet, big
shoulders, and cylindrical bodies. The female figures are
as massive as the men. Their long sheepskin skirts reveal
sturdy legs and feet.

**2-5 TWELVE VOTIVE
FIGURES**

From the Square Temple,
Eshnunna (present-day Tell
Asmar, Iraq). c. 2900–2600 BCE.
Limestone, alabaster, and
gypsum, height of largest
figure approx. 30" (76.3 cm).
The Oriental Institute Museum,
University of Chicago.

Credit: Courtesy of the Oriental
Institute of the University of Chicago

ROYAL TOMBS The British archaeologist Sir Leonard Woolley's excavations at Ur (present-day Muqaiyir, Iraq), south of Uruk during the 1920s initially garnered international attention because of the association of this ancient Mesopotamian city with the biblical patriarch Abraham. It was not long, however, before Woolley's exciting discoveries themselves moved to center stage. Sixteen royal burials yielded spectacular gold objects and lurid evidence of the human sacrifices associated with Sumerian royal burial practices, when retainers were seemingly buried with the rulers they served.

Woolley's work at Ur was a joint venture of the University of Pennsylvania Museum in Philadelphia and the British Museum in London. To conform with Iraq's Antiquities Law of 1922, the uncovered artifacts were divided between

2-6A RECONSTRUCTION OF THE GREAT LYRE WITH BULL'S HEAD

From Royal Tomb (PG 789), Ur (present-day Muqaiyir, Iraq). c. 2600–2500 BCE. Wood with gold, silver, lapis lazuli, bitumen, and shell, reassembled in modern wood support; height of head 14″ (35.6 cm); height of front panel 13″ (33 cm); maximum length of lyre 55½″ (140 cm); height of upright back arm 46½″ (117 cm). University of Pennsylvania Museum of Archaeology and Anthropology, Philadelphia.

Credit: Courtesy of the Penn Museum, image #160104

2-6B FRONT PANEL ON SOUND BOX OF THE GREAT LYRE WITH BULL'S HEAD

Credit: Courtesy of the Penn Museum, image #150888

the sponsoring institutions and Iraq itself. Although Woolley worked with a large team of laborers and assistants during 12 seasons of digging at Ur, he and his wife Katherine reserved for themselves the painstakingly delicate process of uncovering the most important finds. Woolley's own account of work within one tomb outlines the practice: "Most of the workmen were sent away … so that the final work with knives and brushes could be done by my wife and myself in comparative peace. For ten days the two of us spent most of the time from sunrise to sunset lying on our tummies brushing and blowing and threading beads in their order as they lay…. You might suppose that to find three-score women all richly bedecked with jewelry could be a very thrilling experience, and so it is, in retrospect, but I'm afraid that at the moment one is much more conscious of the toil than of the thrill" (quoted in Zettler and Horne, p. 31).

One of the most spectacular discoveries in the royal burials at Ur was an elaborate lyre—a kind of harp—which rested over the body of the woman who had presumably played it during the funeral ceremony for the royal figure buried nearby (FIG. 2-6A). Like nine other lyres Woolley found at Ur, the wooden sound box of this one had long since deteriorated and disappeared, but an exquisitely crafted bull's-head finial of gold and lapis lazuli survived, along with a plaque of carved shell inlaid with bitumen, depicting at the top a heroic image of a man interlocked with and in control of two bulls, and below them three scenes of animals mimicking the activities of humans (FIG. 2-6B). On one register, a seated donkey plucks the strings of a bull lyre—similar to the instrument on which this set of images originally appeared—stabilized by a standing bear, while a fox accompanies him with a rattle. On the register above, upright animals bring food and drink for a feast. A hyena to the left—assuming the role of a butcher with a knife in his belt—carries a table piled high with meat. A lion follows, toting a large jar and pouring vessel.

The top and bottom registers are particularly intriguing in relation to the *Epic of Gilgamesh*, a 3,000-line poem that is Sumer's great contribution to world literature. Rich in descriptions of heroic feats and fabulous creatures, Gilgamesh's story probes the question of immortality and expresses the heroic aim to understand hostile surroundings and to find meaning in human existence. Gilgamesh encounters scorpion-men like the one pictured in the lowest register, and it is easy to see the hero himself in the commanding but unprotected bearded figure centered in the top register controlling the two human-headed bulls that flank him. Because the poem was first written down 700 years after this lyre was created, this plaque may document a very long oral tradition.

On another level, because we know lyres were used in funeral rites, this imagery might depict a heroic image

of the deceased in the top register and a funeral banquet in the realm of the dead at the bottom. Cuneiform tablets preserve songs of mourning, perhaps chanted by priests accompanied by lyres at funerals. One begins, "Oh, lady, the harp of mourning is placed on the ground," a particularly poignant statement considering that the lyres of Ur may have been buried on top of the sacrificed bodies of the women who originally played them.

Sumerian artists worked in various precious metals and in bronze, often combining them with other materials. Many of these creations were decorated with or shaped like animals or composite animal-human-bird creatures. Archaeologists discovered superb examples of their skill during the excavations of the 16 royal burials from the city of Ur. As we have seen, among the most impressive is the lyre combining wood, gold, lapis lazuli, and shell. Projecting from the base is a wood-sculpted head of a bearded bull overlaid with gold, intensely lifelike despite the blue beard created from the semiprecious gemstone lapis lazuli. Since lapis lazuli had to be imported from Afghanistan, the work documents widespread trade in the region at this time.

The Standard of Ur (FIG. 2-7)—a wooden box from the royal tombs at Ur—employs the same techniques and sumptuous materials. Here the theme is Sumerian success in battle on one side and the subsequent banquet celebrating victory on the other. The function of this box is uncertain, but its three registers of scenes are among the best surviving examples of the kind of pictorial narrative that captured the Sumerian imagination and conveyed the culture's most important messages.

The story begins on one of the plaques with a battle scene spread across the bottom register (SEE FIG. 2-7A). The action increases in intensity from left to right as the chariot animals (onagers, or wild asses) progress from a calm walk to a run, trampling over the fallen enemy soldiers. In the middle register, rows of Sumerian soldiers move in locked formation toward the removal of armor from the enemy at center, while the defeated shuffle toward the right with conspicuously less order and disjointed postures. The defeated army arrives from the right of the top register, moving toward the Sumerian ruler, easily recognized because hierarchic scale makes him the largest figure in the scene as well as the central figure within the frieze.

On the bottom two registers of the other side of the box (SEE FIG. 2-7B), servants carry the provisions necessary for a large celebration banquet. Across the top register, the ruler—this time placed off center, but clearly singled out by hierarchic scale—presides over the banquet, facing his guests, each of whom hoists a drinking cup. At far right, a woman sings to entertain the royal guests, accompanied by the playing of a bull's head lyre similar to the one in FIGURE 2-6A.

2–7A SCENES OF WAR

The front of a box known as the Standard of Ur. c. 2600–2500 BCE. Shell, lapis lazuli, and red limestone inlaid in bitumen, originally attached to the large sides of a rectangular wooden box, each 8 × 19″ (20.3 × 48.3 cm). British Museum, London.

Credit: © The Trustees of the British Museum. All rights reserved.

2–7B SCENES OF THE CELEBRATION OF VICTORY

The back of a box known as the Standard of Ur. c. 2600–2500 BCE. Shell, lapis lazuli, and red limestone inlaid in bitumen, originally attached to the large sides of a rectangular wooden box, each 8 × 19″ (20.3 × 48.3 cm). British Museum, London.

Credit: © The Trustees of the British Museum. All rights reserved.

CYLINDER SEALS About the time written records appeared, Sumerians developed stamp seals for identifying documents and establishing property ownership. By 3300–3100 BCE, record keepers redesigned the stamp seal as a cylinder. Sumerian **cylinder seals**, usually less than 2 inches high, were generally made of a hard stone so that their tiny but intricate scenes would not wear away during repeated use. Rolled across documents on clay tablets or over the soft clay applied to a closure that needed sealing—a jar lid, a knot securing a bundle, or a door to a room—the cylinders left a raised mirror image of the design incised (cut) into their surface. Such sealing

proved the authenticity or accuracy of a text or made sure that no unauthorized person could gain access to a room or container. Individuals often acquired seals as signs of status or on appointment to a high administrative position, and the seals were buried with them along with other important possessions. The lapis lazuli **CYLINDER SEAL** (**FIG. 2–8**) is one of over 400 found in excavations of the royal burials at Ur.

This seal comes from the tomb of a powerful royal woman known as Puabi and was found leaning against the right arm of her body. The modern clay impression of its incised design shows two registers of a convivial banquet

2–8 CYLINDER SEAL AND ITS MODERN IMPRESSION

From the tomb of Queen Puabi (PG 800), Ur (present-day Muqaiyir, Iraq). c. 2600–2500 BCE. Lapis lazuli, height 1⁹⁄₁₆" (4 cm), diameter ²⁵⁄₃₂" (2 cm). University of Pennsylvania Museum of Archaeology and Anthropology, Philadelphia.

Credit: Courtesy of the Penn Museum, image #10872

at which all the guests appear to be women, with fringed skirts and long hair gathered up in buns. Two seated figures in the upper register raise their glasses, accompanied by standing servants, one of whom, at far left, holds a fan. The single seated figure in the lower register sits in front of a table piled with food, while a figure behind her offers a cup of drink presumably drawn from the jar she carries in her other hand, reminiscent of the container held by the lion on the lyre plaque (SEE FIG. 2–6B). Four women standing to the far right provide background music.

Akkad

A people known as the Akkadians inhabited an area north of Uruk. During the Sumerian period, they adopted Sumerian culture, but unlike the Sumerians, the Akkadians spoke a Semitic language (the family of languages that includes Arabic and Hebrew). Under the powerful military and political figure Sargon I (ruled c. 2332–2279 BCE), they conquered most of Mesopotamia. For more than half a century, Sargon, "King of the Four Quarters of the World," ruled this empire from his capital at Akkad, the actual site of which is yet to be discovered.

DISK OF ENHEDUANNA   A partially preserved circular relief sculpture in alabaster, another of the many objects excavated at Ur by Woolley, is one of the most extraordinary surviving works of ancient Near Eastern art (**FIG. 2–9**). An inscription on the back identifies the central figure on the front—slightly larger than the others and wearing a flounced wool garment and the headgear of a high priestess—as Enheduanna, daughter of Sargon I and high priestess of the moon god Nanna at his temple in Ur. Enheduanna's name also appears in other surviving Akkadian inscriptions, most notably as the author of a series of poems and hymns dedicated to the gods Nanna and Inanna. Hers is the earliest recorded name of an author in human history.

The procession on the front of the disk commemorates the dedication of a dais (raised platform) donated by Enheduanna to the temple of Inanna in Ur. The naked man in front of her pours a ritual libation in front of a ziggurat, while Enheduanna and her two followers—probably female attendants—raise their right hands before their faces in a common gesture of pious greeting (SEE FIG. 2–12). Sargon's appointment of his daughter to this important religious office followed an established tradition, but it may also have been the ruler's attempt to bolster his support and assert dynastic control in the southern part of his domain, largely populated by Sumerians.

2–9 DISK OF ENHEDUANNA

From Ur (present-day Muqaiyir, Iraq). c. 2300–2275 BCE. Alabaster, diameter 10" (25.6 cm). University of Pennsylvania Museum of Archaeology and Anthropology, Philadelphia.

Credit: Courtesy of the Penn Museum, image #150424

HEAD OF A RULER   A life-size bronze head (**FIG. 2-10**) found in the northern city of Nineveh (present-day Ninua, Iraq) and thought to date from the time of Sargon is the earliest known work of hollow-cast sculpture using the **lost-wax casting** process (see "Lost-Wax Casting" in Chapter 14 on page 428). Its artistic and technical sophistication is spectacular.

The facial features and hairstyle may reflect a generalized ideal rather than the unique likeness of a specific individual, although the sculpture was once identified as Sargon himself. The enormous curling beard and elaborately braided hair (circling the head and ending in a knot at the back) indicate both royalty and ideal male appearance. The deliberate damage to the left side of the face and eye suggests that the head was symbolically mutilated at a later date to destroy its power. The ears and the inlaid eyes appear to have been removed to deprive the head of its ability to hear and see.

THE STELE OF NARAM-SIN   The concept of imperial authority was literally carved in stone by Sargon's grandson Naram-Sin (SEE FIG. 2-1). This stele memorializing one of his military victories is one of the first works of art created to celebrate a specific achievement of an individual ruler. The original inscription—framed in a rectangular box just above Naram-Sin's head—states that the stele commemorates his victory over the Lullubi people of the Zagros Mountains. Watched over by sun gods (symbolized by the rayed suns at the top of the stele) and wearing the horned helmet-crown previously associated only with gods, the hierarchically scaled king stands proudly above his soldiers and his fallen foes, silhouetted against the sky next to the smooth surface of a mountain.

This expression of physical prowess and political power was erected by Naram-Sin in the courtyard of the temple of the sun god Shamash in Sippar, but it did not stay there permanently. During the twelfth century BCE—over a thousand years after the end of Akkadian rule—the Elamite king Shutruk-Nahhunte conquered Sippar and transported the stele of Naram-Sin back to his own capital in Susa, where he rededicated it to an Elamite god. Shutruk-Nahhunte also added a new explanatory inscription in a diagonal band on the mountain in front of Naram-Sin, recounting his own victory and claiming the monument as a statement of his own military and political prowess. The stele remained in Susa until the end of the nineteenth century, when it was excavated by a French archaeologist and taken once more, this time for exhibition in Paris at the Louvre.

Ur and Lagash

The Akkadian Empire fell around 2180 BCE to the Guti, a mountain people from the northeast. For a brief time, the Guti controlled most of the Mesopotamian plain, but ultimately Sumerians under the leadership of King Urnammu of Ur regained control of the region and expelled the Guti in 2112 BCE. Urnammu sponsored magnificent building campaigns, notably a ziggurat dedicated to the moon god Nanna, also called Sin (**FIG. 2-11**). Although located on the site of an earlier temple, this imposing structure—mud-brick faced with kiln-dried brick set with bitumen—was not the accidental result of successive rebuilding. Its base is a rectangle of 205 by 141 feet, with three sets of stairs converging at an imposing entrance gate atop the first of what were three platforms. Each platform's walls slope outward from top to base, probably to prevent rainwater from forming puddles and eroding the mud-brick pavement below. The first two levels of the ziggurat and their retaining walls are recent reconstructions.

2-10 HEAD OF A MAN (KNOWN AS AN AKKADIAN RULER)

From Nineveh (present-day Ninua, Iraq). c. 2300–2200 BCE. Copper alloy, height 14⅜" (36.5 cm). Iraq Museum, Baghdad.

Credit: © 2016 Photo Scala, Florence

2–11 NANNA ZIGGURAT

Ur (present-day Muqaiyir, Iraq). c. 2100–2050 BCE.

Credit: © Michael S. Yamashita/CORBIS

One large Sumerian city-state remained independent throughout this period: Lagash, whose capital was Girsu (present-day Telloh, Iraq), on the Tigris River. Lagash's ruler, Gudea, built and restored many temples, and within them, following the venerable Mesopotamian tradition, he placed votive statues representing himself as governor and embodiment of just rule (**FIG. 2–12**). The statues are made of diorite, a very hard stone; the difficulty of carving it may have prompted sculptors to use compact, simplified forms for the portraits. Or perhaps it was the desire for powerful, stylized images that inspired the choice of this imported stone. Twenty of the statues survive, making Gudea a familiar figure in the study of ancient Near Eastern art.

Images of Gudea present him as a strong, peaceful, pious ruler worthy of divine favor. Whether sitting or standing, he wears a long garment, which provides plenty of smooth space for long cuneiform inscriptions. In this imposing statue, only 2½ feet tall, his right shoulder is bare, and he wears a cap with a wide brim carved with a pattern to represent fleece. He holds a vessel in front of him from which life-giving water flows in two streams, each filled with leaping fish. The text on his garment states that he dedicated himself, the statue, and its temple to the goddess Geshtinanna, the divine poet and interpreter of dreams. The sculptor has emphasized the power centers of the human body: the eyes, head, and arms. Gudea's face is youthful and serene, and his eyes—oversized and wide open—perpetually meet the gaze of the deity with intense concentration.

2–12 VOTIVE STATUE OF GUDEA

From Girsu (present-day Telloh, Iraq). c. 2090 BCE. Diorite, height 29″ (73.7 cm). Musée du Louvre, Paris.

Credit: Photo © RMN/D. Arnaudet/Louvre, Paris

Babylon

For more than 300 years, political turmoil and stable government alternated in Mesopotamia, until the Amorites (a Semitic-speaking people from the Syrian desert to the west) reunited the region under Hammurabi (ruled 1792–1750 BCE). Hammurabi's capital city was Babylon, and his subjects were called Babylonians. Among Hammurabi's achievements was a written legal code that detailed the laws of his realm and the penalties for breaking them.

THE CODE OF HAMMURABI   The Babylonian ruler Hammurabi's systematic codification of his people's rights, duties, and punishments for wrongdoing was engraved on a black basalt slab known as the **STELE OF HAMMURABI** (FIG. 2-13). This imposing artifact, therefore, is both a work of art that depicts a legendary event and a precious historical document.

At the top of the stele, we see Hammurabi standing in an attitude of prayer before Shamash, the sun god and god of justice. Rays rise from Shamash's shoulders as he sits on a backless throne, crowned by a conical horned cap and holding additional symbols of his power—the measuring rod and the rope circle. Shamash gives the law to the king, his intermediary, and the codes of justice flow forth underneath them in horizontal bands of exquisitely engraved cuneiform signs. The idea of god-given laws engraved on

2-13 STELE OF HAMMURABI
Probably from Sippar; found at Susa (present-day Shush, Iran).
c. 1792–1750 BCE. Basalt, height of stele approx. 7'4" (2.25 m),
height of figural relief 28" (71.1 cm). Musée du Louvre, Paris.

Credit: Photo © RMN/Hervé Lewandowski

stone tablets will have a long tradition in the ancient Near East. About 500 years later, Moses, the lawgiver of Israel, received two stone tablets containing the Ten Commandments from God on Mount Sinai (Exodus 32:19).

A prologue on the front of the stele lists the temples Hammurabi has restored, and an epilogue on the back glorifies him as a peacemaker, but most of the stele "publishes" the laws themselves, guaranteeing uniform treatment of people throughout his kingdom. Within the inscription, Hammurabi declares that he intends "to cause justice to prevail in the land and to destroy the wicked and the evil, that the strong might not oppress the weak nor the weak the strong." Most of the 300 or so entries that follow deal with commercial and property matters. Only 68 relate to domestic problems, and a mere 20 deal with physical assault.

The wealth, class, and gender of the parties determine the nature of their punishment—the rights of the wealthy are favored over the poor, citizens over slaves, men over women. Most famous are instances when punishments are specifically tailored to fit crimes—an eye for an eye, a tooth for a tooth, a broken bone for a broken bone. Crimes such as stealing from a temple or palace, helping a slave to escape, or being insubordinate in the army merit the death penalty. Trial by water and fire could also be imposed, such as when an adulterous woman and her lover were thrown into the water; if they did not drown, they were considered innocent. Although some of the punishments may seem excessive today, Hammurabi was breaking new ground by regulating laws and punishments rather than leaving them to the whims of rulers or officials.

Assyrians and Neo-Babylonians

How do the design, ornament, and meaning of great palace complexes and urban development projects express the power of Assyrian and Neo-Babylonian rulers?

Around 1400 BCE, a people called the Assyrians rose to dominance in northern Mesopotamia. After about 1000 BCE, they began to conquer neighboring regions. By the end of the ninth century BCE, the Assyrians controlled most of Mesopotamia, and by the early seventh century BCE they had extended their influence as far west as Egypt. Soon afterward they succumbed to internal weakness and external enemies, and by 600 BCE their empire had collapsed.

Assyrian rulers built huge palaces atop high platforms inside a series of fortified cities that served at one time or another as Assyrian capitals. They decorated these palaces with shallow stone reliefs of battle and hunting scenes, Assyrian victories, presentations of tribute to the king, and religious imagery.

Assurnasirpal II

During his reign (883–859 BCE), the Assyrian ruler Assurnasirpal II established his capital at Kalhu (present-day Nimrud, Iraq), on the east bank of the Tigris River, and undertook an ambitious building program. His architects

2-14 ASSURNASIRPAL II KILLING LIONS
From the palace complex of Assurnasirpal II, Kalhu (present-day Nimrud, Iraq). c. 875–860 BCE. Alabaster, height approx. 39" (99.1 cm). British Museum, London.

Credit: © The Trustees of the British Museum. All rights reserved.

fortified the city with mud-brick walls 5 miles long and 42 feet high, and his engineers constructed a canal that irrigated fields and provided water for the expanded population of the city. According to an inscription commemorating the event, Assurnasirpal gave a banquet for 69,574 people to celebrate the dedication of the new capital in 863 BCE.

Most of the buildings in Kalhu were made from mud bricks, but limestone and alabaster slabs—more impressive and durable—covered the walls with architectural decoration. Colossal guardian figures flanked the grand and often decorated major **portals**, and the panels covering the brick walls were carved with scenes in **low relief** (sculpted relief that projects only slightly from a recessed background) of the king participating in religious rituals, war campaigns, and hunting expeditions.

In a vivid lion-hunting scene (**FIG. 2-14**), Assurnasirpal II stands in a chariot pulled by galloping horses and draws his bow against an attacking lion, advancing from the rear with arrows already protruding from its body. Another expiring beast collapses on the ground under the horses. This was probably a ceremonial hunt, in which the king, protected by men with swords and shields, rode back and forth killing animals as they were released one by one into an enclosed area. The immediacy of this image marks a shift in Mesopotamian art away from a sense of timeless solemnity and toward a more dramatic, even emotional, involvement with the event portrayed.

A Closer Look

ENEMIES CROSSING THE EUPHRATES TO ESCAPE ASSYRIAN ARCHERS

These Assyrian archers are outfitted in typical fashion with protective boots, short "kilts," pointed helmets, and swords, as well as bows and quivers of arrows. Their smaller scale conveys a sense of depth and spatial positioning in this relief, reinforced by the size and placement of the trees.

The detailed landscape setting documents the swirling water of the river, its rocky banks, and the airy environment of the trees, one of which is clearly a palm.

The oblique line of the river bank and the overlapping of the swimmers convey a sense of depth.

If this is the ruler of the enemy citadel, he seems shocked into powerlessness by the Assyrian invasion. Note the contrast between his lowered weapon and those of the archers of the Assyrian vanguard.

The long robes of the three enemy swimmers show their high status. They are not ordinary foot soldiers.

The two lower swimmers were clearly taken by surprise. Already in retreat, they are still blowing through tubes to inflate their flotation devices, made from sewn animal skin.

This beardless swimmer is probably a eunuch, many of whom served as high officials in ancient Near Eastern courts.

Two figures raise their hands in despair, reacting to the fate of their arrow-riddled comrades.

2-15 ENEMIES CROSSING THE EUPHRATES TO ESCAPE ASSYRIAN ARCHERS
Palace complex of Assurnasirpal II, Kalhu (present-day Nimrud, Iraq). c. 875–860 BCE. Alabaster, height approx. 39″ (99.1 cm). British Museum, London.

Credit: © The Trustees of the British Museum. All rights reserved.

citadel gate A   Nabu temple   ziggurat   palace   throne room

city wall

palace entrance

citadel gate B

citadel wall

2-16 RECONSTRUCTION DRAWING OF THE CITADEL AND PALACE COMPLEX OF SARGON II

Dur Sharrukin (present-day Khorsabad, Iraq). c. 721–706 BCE. The Oriental Institute Museum, University of Chicago.

Credit: Courtesy of the Oriental Institute of the University of Chicago

In another palace relief, the scene shifts from royal ceremony to the heat of battle, set within a detailed landscape (see "Closer Look" opposite). Three of the Assyrians' enemies—two using flotation devices made of inflated animal skins—swim across a raging river, retreating from a vanguard of Assyrian archers who kneel at its banks to launch their assault. The scene evokes a specific event from 878 BCE described in the annals of Assurnasirpal. As the Assyrian king overtook the army of an enemy leader named Kudurru near the present-day town of Anu, both leader and soldiers escaped into the Euphrates River in an attempt to save their lives.

Sargon II

Sargon II (ruled 721–706 BCE) built a new Assyrian capital at Dur Sharrukin (present-day Khorsabad, Iraq). On the northwest side of the capital a walled citadel, or fortress, straddled the city wall (**FIG. 2-16**). Within the citadel Sargon's **palace complex** (the group of buildings where the ruler governed and resided) stood on a raised, fortified platform about 40 feet high—demonstrating the use of art as political propaganda.

Guarded by two towers, the palace complex could be entered only by a wide ramp leading up from an open

square, around which the homes of important government and religious officials were clustered. Beyond the ramp was the main courtyard with service buildings on the right and temples on the left. The heart of the palace lay past the main courtyard, protected by a reinforced wall with only two small, off-center doors. Within the inner compound was a second courtyard lined with narrative relief panels showing tribute bearers. Visitors would have waited to see the king in this courtyard that functioned as an open-air audience hall; once granted access to the royal throne room, they would have passed through a stone gate flanked, like the other gates of the citadel and palace (**FIG. 2-17**), by awesome guardian figures. These colossal beings, known as **lamassus**, combined the bearded head of a man, the powerful body of a lion or bull, the wings of an eagle, and the horned headdress of a god.

In an open space between the palace complex and temple complex at Dur Sharrukin rose a ziggurat declaring the might of Assyria's kings and symbolizing their claim to empire. It probably had seven levels, each about 18 feet high and painted a different color (SEE FIG. 2-16). The four levels still remaining were once white, black, blue, and red. Instead of separate flights of stairs between the levels, a single, squared-off spiral ramp rose continuously around the exterior from the base.

2-17 GUARDIAN FIGURES AT GATE A OF THE CITADEL OF SARGON II DURING ITS EXCAVATION IN THE 1840S

Dur Sharrukin (present-day Khorsabad, Iraq). c. 721–706 BCE.

Credit: World Tourism Organization: Iraq

Assurbanipal

Assurbanipal (ruled 669–c. 627 BCE), king of the Assyrians three generations after Sargon II, maintained his capital at Nineveh. Like that of Assurnasirpal II two centuries earlier, his palace walls were faced with alabaster panels carved with pictorial narratives in low relief. Most show Assurbanipal and his subjects in battle or hunting.

Occasionally, there are also scenes of palace life. An unusually peaceful example shows the king and queen relaxing in a pleasure garden (**FIG. 2-18**). The king reclines on a couch, the queen sits in a chair at his feet, and a musician plays at far left. Three servants arrive from the left with trays of food, while others wave whisks to protect the royal couple from insects. The king has taken off his rich necklace and hung it on his couch, and he has laid his weapons—a sword, a bow, and a quiver of arrows—on the table behind him. However, this apparently tranquil domestic scene is actually a victory celebration. The severed head of his vanquished enemy hangs from a tree at the far left.

2-18 ASSURBANIPAL AND HIS QUEEN IN THE GARDEN

From the palace at Nineveh (present-day Ninua, Iraq). c. 647 BCE. Alabaster, height approx. 21″ (53.3 cm). British Museum, London.

Credit: © The Trustees of the British Museum. All rights reserved.

Neo-Babylonia

At the end of the seventh century BCE, Assyria was invaded by the Medes, a people from western Iran who were allied with the Babylonians and the Scythians, a nomadic people from northern Asia (present-day Russia and Ukraine). In 612 BCE, the Medes' army captured Nineveh. When the dust had settled, Assyria was no more and the Neo-Babylonians—so named because they recaptured the splendor that had marked Babylon 12 centuries earlier under Hammurabi—controlled a region that stretched from present-day Turkey to northern Arabia and from Mesopotamia to the Mediterranean Sea.

The most famous Neo-Babylonian ruler was Nebuchadnezzar II (ruled 605–562 BCE), notorious today for his suppression of the Jews as recorded in the book of Daniel in the Hebrew Bible, in which he may have been confused with the final Neo-Babylonian ruler, Nabonidus. A great patron of architecture, Nebuchadnezzar II built temples dedicated to the Babylonian gods throughout his realm and transformed Babylon—the cultural, political, and economic hub of his empire—into one of the most splendid cities of its day.

Babylon straddled the Euphrates River, its two sections joined by a bridge. The older, eastern sector was traversed by the Processional Way, the route taken by religious processions honoring the city's patron god, Marduk (**FIG. 2-19**). This street, paved with large stone slabs set in a bed of bitumen, was up to 66 feet

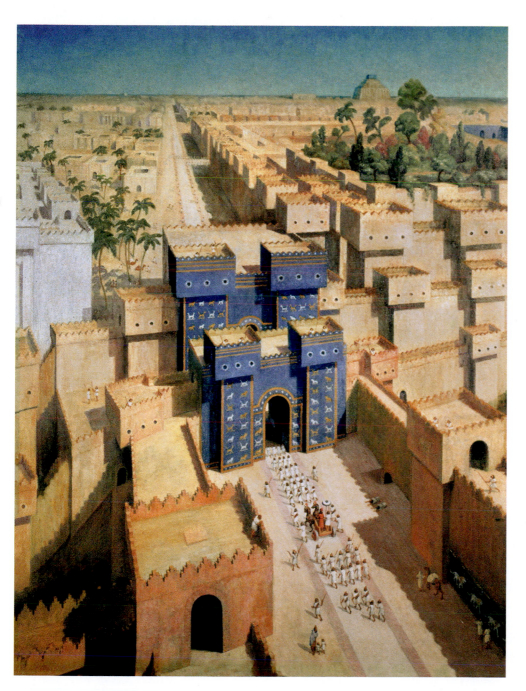

2-19 RECONSTRUCTION DRAWING OF BABYLON IN THE 6TH CENTURY BCE

The Oriental Institute Museum, University of Chicago.

The palace of Nebuchadnezzar II, with its famous Hanging Gardens, can be seen just behind and to the right of the Ishtar Gate, west of the Processional Way. The Marduk Ziggurat looms in the far distance on the east bank of the Euphrates.

Credit: Courtesy of the Oriental Institute of the University of Chicago

2–20 ISHTAR GATE AND THRONE ROOM WALL

Reconstruction; originally from Babylon (present-day Babil, Iraq). c. 575 BCE. Glazed brick, height of gate originally 40′ (12.2 m) with towers rising 100′ (30.5 m). Vorderasiatisches Museum, Staatliche Museen zu Berlin, Preussischer Kulturbesitz.

The Ishtar Gate is decorated with tiers of dragons (with the head and body of a snake, the forelegs of a lion, and the hind legs of a bird of prey) that were sacred to Marduk; bulls associated with Adad, the storm god; and lions associated with Ishtar. Now reconstructed in a Berlin museum, it is installed next to a panel from the throne room in Nebuchadnezzar's nearby palace, in which lions walk beneath stylized palm trees.

Credit: © 2016 Photo Scala, Florence/ bpk, Bildagentur für Kunst, Kultur und Geschichte, Berlin

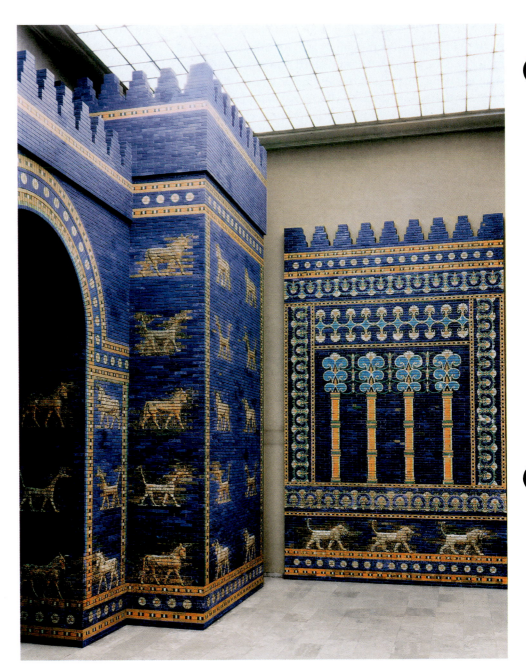

wide at some points. It ran from the Euphrates bridge through the temple district and palaces and finally through the Ishtar Gate, the ceremonial entrance to the city.

The Ishtar Gate's four **crenellated** towers (crenellations are notched walls for military defense) symbolized Babylonian power (**FIG. 2-20**). Beyond the Ishtar Gate, dark blue glazed bricks covered the walls on either side of the route. The glaze on the bricks was a film of colored glass adhered to their surface after firing, a process used since about 1600 BCE. Against that blue background, specially molded turquoise-, blue-, and gold-colored bricks formed images of striding lions, mascots of the goddess Ishtar, as well as the dragons that were associated with Marduk.

Persia

What is the impact of the Persian conquest on the history of ancient Near Eastern architecture?

In the sixth century BCE the Persians, a formerly nomadic Indo-European-speaking people, began to seize power in Mesopotamia. From the region of Parsa, or Persis (present-day Fars, Iran), they established a vast empire. The rulers of this new empire traced their ancestry to a semilegendary Persian king named Achaemenes, and consequently they are known as the Achaemenids.

The dramatic expansion of the Achaemenids began in 559 BCE with the ascension of a remarkable leader, Cyrus II (Cyrus the Great, ruled 559–530 BCE). By the

2-21 AERIAL VIEW OF THE CEREMONIAL COMPLEX, PERSEPOLIS
Iran. 518–c. 460 BCE.

Credit: Arazu/Fotolia

time of his death, the Persian Empire included Babylonia, Media (which stretched across present-day northern Iran through Anatolia), and some of the Aegean islands far to the west. Only the Greeks stood fast against them (see Chapter 5). When Darius I (ruled 521–486 BCE) took the throne, he could proclaim, "I am Darius, great King, King of Kings, King of countries, King of this earth."

An able administrator, Darius organized the Persian lands into 20 tribute-paying areas under Persian governors. He often left local rulers in place beneath the governors. This practice, along with a tolerance for diverse native customs and religions, won the Persians the loyalty of large numbers of their subjects. Like many powerful rulers, Darius created palaces and citadels as visible symbols of his authority. He made Susa his first capital and built a 32–acre administrative compound there.

In about 515 BCE, Darius began construction of Parsa, a new capital in the Persian homeland, today known by its Greek name: **PERSEPOLIS**. It is one of the best-preserved and most impressive ancient sites in the Near East (**FIG. 2-21**). Darius imported materials, workers, and artists from all over his empire. He even ordered work to be executed in Egypt and transported to his capital. The result was a new multicultural style of art that combined many different traditions—Persian, Median, Mesopotamian, Egyptian, and Greek.

In Assyrian fashion, the imperial complex at Persepolis was set on a raised platform 40 feet high and measuring 1,500 by 900 feet, accessible only via a single approach made of wide, shallow steps that could be ascended on horseback. Its rectangular grid plan is comparable to Egyptian and Greek cities. Darius lived to see the completion only of the Apadana (audience hall), a treasury, and a very small palace for himself. The **APADANA**, set above the rest of the complex on a second terrace (**FIG. 2-22**), had open porches on three sides and a square hall large enough to hold several thousand people. Darius's son Xerxes I (ruled 485–465 BCE) added a sprawling palace complex for himself, enlarged the treasury building, and began a vast new public reception space, the Hall of 100 Columns.

The central stair of Darius's Apadana displays reliefs of animal combat, tiered ranks of royal guards (the "10,000 Immortals"), and delegations of tribute-bearers. Here, lions attack bulls on either side of the Persian generals. Such animal combats (a theme found throughout the Near East) emphasize the ferocity of the leaders and their men. Ranks of warriors cover the walls with repeated patterns and seem ready to defend the palace. The elegant drawing, balanced composition, and sleek modeling of figures reflect the Persians' knowledge of Greek art and perhaps the use of Greek artists. Other reliefs throughout

2-22 APADANA (AUDIENCE HALL) OF DARIUS AND XERXES

Ceremonial complex, Persepolis, Iran. 518–c. 460 BCE.

Credit: © Melba Photo Agency/Alamy Stock Photo

2-23 DARIUS AND XERXES RECEIVING TRIBUTE

Detail of a relief from the stairway leading to the Apadana, Persepolis, Iran. 491–486 BCE. Limestone, height 8′4″ (2.54 m). The Oriental Institute Museum, University of Chicago.

Credit: Courtesy of the Oriental Institute of the University of Chicago

Persepolis depict displays of allegiance or economic prosperity. In one example, once the centerpiece, Darius holds an audience while his son and heir, Xerxes, listens from behind the throne (**FIG. 2-23**). Such panels would have looked quite different when they were freshly painted in bright colors, with metal objects such as Darius's crown and necklace covered in **gold leaf** (sheets of hammered gold).

At its height, the Persian Empire extended from Africa to India. From Persepolis, Darius in 490 BCE and Xerxes in 480 BCE sent their armies west to conquer Greece, but mainland Greeks successfully resisted the armies of the Achaemenids, preventing them from advancing into Europe. Indeed, it was a Greek who ultimately put an end to their empire. In 334 BCE, Alexander the Great of Macedonia (d. 323 BCE) crossed into Anatolia and swept through Mesopotamia, defeating Darius III and nearly destroying Persepolis in 330 BCE. Although the Achaemenid Empire was at an end, Persia eventually revived. The Persian style in art continued to influence Greek artists (see Chapter 5) and ultimately became one of the foundations of Islamic art (see Chapter 9).

Think About It

1   Describe and characterize the way human figures are represented in the Sumerian votive figures of Eshnunna. What are the potential relationships between style and function?
2   Discuss the development of relief sculpture in the ancient Near East. Choose two specific examples, one from the Sumerian period and one from the Assyrian period, and explain how symbols and stories are combined to express ideas that were important to these two cultures.
3   Select two rulers discussed in this chapter and explain how each preserved his legacy through commissioned works of art and/or architecture.
4   How did the excavations of Sir Leonard Woolley contribute to our understanding of the art of the ancient Near East?

Crosscurrents

Both of these works depict a social gathering involving food and drink, but they are vastly different in scale, materials, and physical context. How do the factors of scale and materials contribute to the visual appearance of the scenes? How does physical context and audience affect the meaning of what is portrayed?

FIG. 2–8

FIG. 2–18

3–1 FUNERARY MASK OF TUTANKHAMUN

From the tomb of Tutankhamun, Valley of the Kings. Eighteenth Dynasty (Tutankhamun ruled c. 1332–1322 BCE), c. 1327 BCE. Gold inlaid with glass and semiprecious stones, height 21¼″ (54.5 cm), weight 24 pounds (11 kg). Egyptian Museum, Cairo. (JE 60672).

Credit: © Leokos/Shutterstock

Chapter 3
Art of Ancient Egypt

⌄ Learning Objectives

3.a Identify the visual hallmarks of Early Dynastic, Old Kingdom, Middle Kingdom, New Kingdom, and Late Egyptian art for formal, technical, and expressive qualities.

3.b Interpret the meaning of works of Early Dynastic, Old Kingdom, Middle Kingdom, New Kingdom, and Late Egyptian art based on their themes, subjects, and symbols.

3.c Relate Early Dynastic, Old Kingdom, Middle Kingdom, New Kingdom, and Late Egyptian artists and art to their cultural, economic, and political contexts.

3.d Apply the vocabulary and concepts used to discuss ancient Egyptian art, artists, and art history.

3.e Interpret ancient Egyptian art using appropriate art historical methods, such as observation, comparison, and inductive reasoning.

3.f Select visual and textual evidence in various media to support an argument or an interpretation of ancient Egyptian art.

On February 16, 1923, *The Times* of London cabled the *New York Times* with dramatic news of a discovery: "This has been, perhaps, the most extraordinary day in the whole history of Egyptian excavation. The entrance today was made into the sealed chamber of [Tutankhamun's] tomb … and yet another door opened beyond that. No eyes have seen the King, but to practical certainty we know that he lies there close at hand in all his original state, undisturbed." And indeed he did. A collar of dried flowers and beads covered the chest, and a linen shroud was draped around the head. A gold **FUNERARY MASK (FIG. 3-1)** had been placed over the head and shoulders of his mummified body, which was enclosed in three nested coffins, the innermost made of gold (SEE FIG. 3-32). The coffins were placed in a yellow quartzite **sarcophagus** (stone coffin) that was itself encased within gilt wooden shrines nested inside one another.

The discoverer of this treasure, the English archaeologist Howard Carter, had worked in Egypt for more than 20 years before he undertook a last expedition, sponsored by the wealthy British amateur Egyptologist Lord Carnarvon. Carter was convinced that the tomb of Tutankhamun, one of the last Eighteenth-Dynasty royal burial places still unidentified, lay hidden in the Valley of the Kings. After 15 years of digging, on November 4, 1922, he unearthed the entrance to Tutankhamun's tomb and found unbelievable treasures in the antechamber: jewelry, textiles, gold-covered furniture, a carved and inlaid throne, and four gold chariots. In February 1923, Carter pierced the wall separating the anteroom from the actual burial chamber and found the greatest treasure of all, Tutankhamun himself.

Since ancient times, tombs have tempted looters; more recently, they also have attracted archaeologists and historians. The first large-scale "archaeological" expedition in history landed in Egypt with the armies of Napoleon in 1798. The French commander must have realized that he would find great wonders there, for he took French scholars with him to study ancient sites. The military adventure ended in failure, but the scholars eventually published richly illustrated volumes of their findings, unleashing a craze for all things Egyptian that has not dimmed since. In 1976, the first blockbuster museum exhibition was born when treasures from the tomb of Tutankhamun began a tour of the United States and attracted over 8 million visitors. Most recently, in 2006, Otto Schaden excavated a tomb containing seven coffins in the Valley of the Kings, the first tomb to be found there since Tutankhamun's in 1922.

The Gift of the Nile

What are the cultural and historical backgrounds for ancient Egyptian art and architecture?

The Greek traveler and historian Herodotus, writing in the fifth century BCE, remarked, "Egypt is the gift of the Nile." This great river, the longest in the world, winds northward from equatorial Africa and flows through Egypt in a relatively straight line to the Mediterranean (**MAP 3–1**). There it forms a broad delta before emptying into the sea. Before it was dammed in 1970 by the Aswan High Dam, the lower (northern) Nile, swollen with the runoff of heavy seasonal rains in the south, overflowed its banks for several months each year. Every time the floodwaters receded, they left behind a new layer of rich silt, making the valley and delta a continually fertile and attractive habitat.

By about 8000 BCE, the valley's inhabitants had become relatively sedentary, living off the abundant fish, game, and wild plants. Not until about 5000 BCE did they adopt the agricultural village life associated with Neolithic culture (see Chapter 1). At that time, the climate of north Africa grew increasingly dry. To ensure adequate resources for agriculture, the farmers along the Nile began to manage flood waters in a system called basin irrigation.

The Predynastic period, from roughly 5000 to 2950 BCE, was a time of significant social and political transition that preceded the unification of Egypt under a single ruler. (After unification, Egypt was ruled by a series of family dynasties and is therefore characterized as "dynastic.") Rudimentary federations emerged and began conquering and absorbing weaker communities. By about 3500 BCE, there were several larger states, or chiefdoms, in the lower Nile Valley and a centralized form of leadership had emerged. Rulers were expected to protect their subjects, not only from outside aggression, but also from natural catastrophes such as droughts and insect plagues.

The surviving art of the Predynastic period consists chiefly of ceramic figurines, decorated pottery, and reliefs carved on stone plaques and pieces of ivory. A few examples of wall painting—lively scenes filled with small figures of people and animals—were found in a tomb at Hierakonpolis, a Predynastic town of mud-brick houses in Upper Egypt that was once home to as many as 10,000 people.

MAP 3–1 ANCIENT EGYPT

Upper Egypt is below Lower Egypt on this map because the designations "upper" and "lower" refer to the directional flow of the Nile, not to our conventions for south and north in drawing maps. The two kingdoms were united c. 3000 BCE, just before the Early Dynastic period.

Early Dynastic Egypt

How are the foundations of ancient Egyptian art established during the Early Dynastic period in the conventions of figural representation and funerary architecture?

Around 3000 BCE, Egypt became a consolidated state. According to legend, the country had previously evolved into two major kingdoms—the Two Lands—Upper Egypt in the south (upstream on the Nile) and Lower Egypt in the north (downstream). But a powerful ruler from Upper Egypt conquered Lower Egypt and unified the two kingdoms. In the art of the subsequent Early Dynastic period we see the development of fundamental and enduring ideas about kingship and the cosmic order. Since the works of art and architecture that survive from ancient Egypt come mainly from tombs and temples—the majority of which were located in secure places and built with the most durable materials—most of what we now know about the ancient art of Egypt is rooted in religious beliefs and practices.

The God-Kings

The Greek historian Herodotus thought the Egyptians were the most religious people he had ever encountered. In their worldview, the movements of heavenly bodies, the workings of gods, and the humblest of human activities were all believed to be part of a balanced and harmonious grand design. Death was to be feared only by those who lived in such a way as to disrupt that harmony. Upright souls could be confident that their spirits would live on eternally.

By the Early Dynastic period, Egypt's kings were revered as gods in human form. A royal jubilee, the *heb sed* or *sed* festival, held in the thirtieth year of the living king's reign, renewed and reaffirmed his divine power, and when kings died, they rejoined their father, the sun god Ra, and rode with him in the solar boat as it made its daily journey across the sky.

In order to please the gods and ensure their continuing goodwill toward the state, kings built splendid temples and provided priests to maintain them. The priests saw to it that statues of the gods, placed deep in the innermost rooms of the temples, were never without fresh food and clothing. Egyptian gods and goddesses were depicted in various forms, some as human beings, others as animals, and still others as humans with animal heads. For example, Osiris, the overseer of the realm of the dead, regularly appears in human form wrapped in linen as a mummy. His son, the sky god Horus, is usually depicted as a falcon or falcon-headed man (see "Egyptian Symbols" below).

Over the course of ancient Egyptian history, Amun (chief god of Thebes, represented as blue and wearing a plumed crown), Ra (of Heliopolis), and Ptah (of Memphis) became the primary national gods. Other gods and their manifestations included Thoth (ibis), god of writing, science, and law; Ma'at (feather), goddess of truth, order, and justice; Anubis (jackal), god of embalming and cemeteries; and Bastet (cat), daughter of Ra.

Artistic Conventions

Egyptian artists followed a set of fairly strict conventions, often based on conceptual principles rather than on the observation of the natural world with an eye to rendering it in lifelike fashion. Eventually a system of mathematical formulas was developed to determine design and proportions (see "Conventions and Technique of Egyptian

Art and its Contexts

EGYPTIAN SYMBOLS

Three crowns symbolize kingship in early Egyptian art: the tall, clublike white crown of Upper Egypt (sometimes adorned with two plumes); the flat or scooped red cap with projecting spiral of Lower Egypt; and the double crown representing unified Egypt.

A striped gold and blue linen head cloth, known as the **nemes headdress**, having a cobra and a vulture at the center front, was also commonly used as royal headgear. The upright form of the cobra, known as the *uraeus*, represents the goddess Wadjet of Lower Egypt and is often included in king's crowns as well (SEE FIG. 3-1). The queen's crown included the feathered skin of the vulture goddess Nekhbet of Upper Egypt.

The god Horus, king of the earth and a force for good, is represented as a falcon or falcon-headed man. His eyes symbolize the sun and moon; the solar eye is called the *wedjat*. The looped cross, called the **ankh**, is symbolic of everlasting life. The **scarab** beetle (*khepri*, meaning "he who created himself") was associated with creation, resurrection, and the rising sun.

white crown
of Upper Egypt
(the South)

red crown
of Lower Egypt
(the North)

double crown
of unified Egypt

scepter

ankh

Horus

wedjat
(eye of Horus)

falcon
(the god Horus)

ankh

scarab

Technique

CONVENTIONS AND TECHNIQUE OF EGYPTIAN PICTORIAL RELIEF

Painting usually relies on color and line for its effect, while relief sculpture often depends on the play of light and shadow alone, but in Egypt, relief sculpture was also painted (SEE FIG. 3–17). The walls and closely spaced columns of Egyptian tombs and temples were almost completely covered with colorful scenes and hieroglyphic texts. Until the Eighteenth Dynasty (c. 1539–1292 LMO), the only colors used were black, white, red, yellow, blue, and green. Modeling might be indicated by overpainting lines in a contrasting color, although the sense of three-dimensionality was conveyed primarily by the carved forms and incised inscriptions underneath the paint. The crisp outlines created by such carving assured the primacy of line in Egyptian pictorial relief.

With very few exceptions, figures, scenes, and texts were composed in bands, or registers. The scenes were first laid out with inked lines, using a squared grid to guide the designer in proportioning the human figures. The sculptor who executed

the carving followed these drawings, and it may have been another person who smoothed the carved surfaces of the relief and eventually covered them with paint.

The lower left corner of the unfinished Twelfth-Dynasty **STELE OF THE SCULPTOR USERWER** shown here still maintains its preliminary underdrawings. In some figures there are also the tentative beginnings of the relief carving. The figures are delineated with black ink, and the grid lines are rendered in red. Every body part had its designated place on the grid. For example, figures are designed 18 squares tall, measuring from the soles of their feet to their hairline; the tops of their knees conform with the sixth square up from the ground-line. Their shoulders align with the top of square 16 and are six squares wide. Slight deviations exist within this structured design format, but this **canon of proportions** represents an ideal system that was standard in pictorial relief throughout the Middle Kingdom.

DETAIL OF THE STELE OF THE SCULPTOR USERWER IN FIG. 3-17

Credit: © The Trustees of the British Museum. All rights reserved.

Pictorial Relief" above). The underlying conventions that govern ancient Egyptian art appear early, however, and are maintained, with subtle but significant variations, over almost three millennia of its history.

THE PALETTE OF NARMER   This historically and artistically significant work of art (see "Closer Look" opposite) dates from the Early Dynastic period and was found in the temple of Horus at Hierakonpolis. It is commonly

interpreted as representing the unification of Egypt and the beginning of the country's growth as a powerful nation-state. It uses many of the representational conventions that would dominate royal Egyptian art from this point on.

On the reverse side of the palette, as in the stele of Naram-Sin (SEE FIG. 2–1), hierarchic scale signals the importance of Narmer by showing him overwhelmingly larger than the other human figures around him. He is also boldly silhouetted against a blank ground, just like Naram-Sin, distancing details of setting and story so they will not distract from his pre-eminence. He wears the white crown of Upper Egypt while striking the enemy who kneels before him with a mace. Above this foe, the god Horus—depicted as a falcon with a human hand—holds a rope tied around

the neck of a man whose head is attached to a block sprouting stylized papyrus, a plant that grew thickly along the Nile and symbolized Lower Egypt. This combination of symbols made the central message clear: Narmer, as ruler of Upper Egypt, is in firm control of Lower Egypt.

A Closer Look

THE PALETTE OF NARMER

This figure, named by hieroglyphic inscription and standing on his own ground-line, holds the king's sandals. Narmer is barefoot because he is standing on sacred ground, performing sacred acts. The same sandal-bearer, likewise labeled, follows Narmer on the other side of the palette.

Phonetic **hieroglyphs** centered at the top of each side of the palette name the king: a horizontal fish (*nar*) above a vertical chisel (*mer*). A depiction of the royal palace—seen simultaneously from above, as a groundplan, and frontally, as a **façade** (front wall of a building)—surrounds Narmer's name to signify that he is king.

Narmer wears the red crown of Lower Egypt and is identified by the hieroglyph label next to his head, as well by as his larger size in relation to the other figures (hierarchic scale).

The royal procession inspects two rows of beheaded enemies with their heads tucked between their feet.

Narmer attacks a figure of comparable size, also identified by a hieroglyphic label, indicating that he is an enemy of real importance, likely the ruler of Lower Egypt.

Next to the heads of these two defeated enemies are, on the left, an aerial depiction of a fortified city, and on the right, a gazelle trap, perhaps to show Narmer's dominion over both city and countryside.

A bull symbolizing the might of the king—he wears a bull's tail on both sides of the palette—tramples another enemy in front of a fortified city.

Palettes were tablets with circular depressions where eye makeup was ground and prepared. Although this example was surely ceremonial rather than functional, a mixing saucer is framed by the elongated, intertwined necks of lions, perhaps signifying the union of Upper and Lower Egypt.

3-2 THE PALETTE OF NARMER

From Hierakonpolis. Early Dynastic Period, c. 2950 BCE. Green schist, height 25″ (64 cm). Egyptian Museum, Cairo. (JE 32169 = CG 14716).

Credit: © akg-images/Erich Lessing

Many of the figures on the palette are shown in composite poses, so that each part of the body is portrayed from its most characteristic viewpoint. Heads are shown in profile, to capture most clearly the nose, forehead, and chin, while eyes are rendered frontally, from their most recognizable and expressive viewpoint. Hips, legs, and feet are drawn in profile, and the figure is usually striding, to reveal both legs. The torso, however, is fully frontal. This conceptualized artistic convention for representing the human figure was to be followed for millennia in Egypt, when depicting royalty and other dignitaries. People of lower social rank engaged in active tasks (compare the figure of Narmer with those of his standard-bearers) tend to be represented in ways that seem to us more lifelike.

Funerary Architecture

Ancient Egyptians believed that an essential part of every human personality is its life force, or soul, called the *ka*, which lived on after the death of the body, forever engaged in the activities it had enjoyed in its former existence. But the *ka* needed a body to live in, either the mummified body of the deceased or, as a substitute, a sculpted likeness in the form of a statue. The Egyptians developed elaborate funerary practices to ensure that their deceased moved safely and effectively into the afterlife.

It was especially important to provide a comfortable home for the *ka* of a departed king, so that even in the afterlife he would continue to ensure the well-being of Egypt. Egyptians preserved the bodies of the royal dead with care and placed them in burial chambers filled with sculpted body substitutes and all the supplies and furnishings the *ka* might require throughout eternity (see "Preserving the Dead" below).

MASTABA AND NECROPOLIS In Early Dynastic Egypt, the most common tomb structure—used by the upper level of society, the king's family and relatives—was the **mastaba**, a flat-topped, one-story building with slanted walls erected above an underground burial chamber (see "Mastaba to Pyramid" opposite). Mastabas were at first constructed of mud brick, but toward the end of the Third Dynasty (c. 2650–2575 BCE), many incorporated cut stone, at least as an exterior facing.

In its simplest form, the mastaba contained a **serdab**, a small, sealed room housing the *ka* statue of the deceased, and a chapel designed to receive mourning relatives and offerings. A vertical shaft led from the top of the mastaba down to the actual burial chamber, where the remains of the deceased reposed in a coffin—at times placed within a larger stone sarcophagus—surrounded by appropriate grave goods. This chamber was sealed off after interment. Mastabas sometimes had numerous underground burial chambers to accommodate whole families, and mastaba burial remained the standard for Egyptian elites for centuries.

Mastabas tended to be grouped together in a **necropolis**—literally, a "city of the dead"—at the edge of the desert on the west bank of the Nile, for the land of the dead was believed to be in the direction of the setting sun. Two of the most extensive of these early necropolises are at Saqqara and Giza, just outside present-day Cairo.

DJOSER'S COMPLEX AT SAQQARA For his tomb complex at Saqqara, the Third-Dynasty King Djoser (c. 2650–2631 BCE) commissioned the earliest-known monumental architecture in Egypt (**FIG. 3-3**). The designer of the complex was Imhotep, who served as Djoser's prime minister. Imhotep is the first architect in

Technique
PRESERVING THE DEAD

Egyptians developed mummification techniques to ensure that the *ka*, the soul or life force, could live on in the body in the afterlife. No recipes for preserving the dead have been found, but the basic process seems clear enough from images found in tombs, descriptions of later Greek writers such as Herodotus and Plutarch, scientific analysis of mummies, and modern experiments.

By the time of the New Kingdom, the routine was roughly as follows: The body was taken to a mortuary, a special structure used exclusively for embalming. Under the supervision of a priest, workers removed the brains, generally through the nose, and emptied the body cavity—except for the heart—through an incision in the left side. They then covered the body with dry natron, a naturally occurring salt, and placed it on a

sloping surface to allow liquids to drain. This preservative caused the skin to blacken, so workers often used paint or powdered makeup to restore some color, using red ocher for a man, yellow ocher for a woman. They then packed the body cavity with clean linen soaked in various herbs and ointments, provided by the family of the deceased. The major organs were wrapped in separate packets and stored in special containers called **canopic jars** to be placed in the tomb chamber.

Workers next wound the trunk and each of the limbs separately with cloth strips before wrapping the whole body in additional layers of cloth to produce the familiar mummy shape. Charms and other smaller objects were often inserted among the wrappings.

Elements of Architecture

MASTABA TO PYRAMID

As the gateway to the afterlife for Egyptian kings and members of the royal court, the Egyptian burial structure began as a low, solid, rectangular mastaba with an external niche that served as the focus of offerings. Later mastabas had either an internal *serdab* (the room where the *ka* statue was placed) and chapel (as in the drawing) or an attached chapel and *serdab* (not shown). Eventually, mastaba forms of decreasing size were stacked over an underground burial chamber to form the step pyramid. The culmination of this development is the pyramid, in which the actual burial site may be within the pyramid—not below ground—with false chambers, false doors, and confusing passageways to foil potential tomb robbers.

MASTABA

chapel

offering table

serdab with statue of *ka*

shaft

underground burial chambers

blockage

STEPPED PYRAMID

original mastaba

shaft

burial chamber

blockage

weight-relieving chamber

air shaft?

air shaft?

burial chamber

gallery to chambers

ascending corridor

abandoned burial chamber

air shaft?

escape route?

descending corridor

PYRAMID

history to be identified; his name is inscribed together with Djoser's on the base of a statue of the king found near the Step Pyramid.

It appears that Imhotep first planned Djoser's tomb as a single-story mastaba, only later deciding to enlarge upon the concept. The final structure is a step pyramid formed by six mastaba-like elements of decreasing size stacked on top of each other (**FIG. 3-4**). Although the Step Pyramid resembles the ziggurats of Mesopotamia, it differs in both meaning (a stairway to the sun god Ra) and purpose (protecting a tomb). A 92-foot shaft descended from the original mastaba enclosed within the pyramid. A descending corridor at the base of the Step Pyramid provided an entrance from outside to a granite-lined burial vault.

step pyramid

mortuary temple

sed-festival complex

enclosure wall

south tomb

entrance complex

3-3 RECONSTRUCTION DRAWING OF DJOSER'S FUNERARY COMPLEX, SAQQARA

Third Dynasty, c. 2630–2575 BCE.

Situated on a level terrace, this huge commemorative complex—some 1,800' (544 m) long by 900' (277 m) wide—was designed as a replica in stone of the wood, brick, and reed buildings used in rituals associated with kingship. Inside the wall, the Step Pyramid dominated the complex.

Credit: © Dorling Kindersley

3-4 THE STEP PYRAMID AND SHAM BUILDINGS, FUNERARY COMPLEX OF DJOSER

Limestone, height of pyramid 204' (62 m).

Credit: © Jim Henderson/Alamy Stock Photo

The adjacent funerary temple, where priests performed rituals before placing the king's mummified body in its tomb, was used for continuing worship of the dead king. In the form of his *ka* statue, Djoser intended to observe these devotions through two peepholes in the wall between the *serdab* and the funerary chapel. To the east of the pyramid, buildings filled with debris represent actual structures in which the spirit of the dead king could continue to observe the *sed* rituals that had ensured his long reign.

The Old Kingdom

How does the development of ancient Egyptian figural and architectural conventions express political power in the Old Kingdom?

Historians have divided the long royal history of ancient Egypt after the Early Dynastic Period (c. 2950–2575) into three long kingdoms of stability separated by two briefer interludes of instability: the Old Kingdom (c. 2575–2150 BCE), the First Intermediate Period (c. 2125–1975 BCE), the Middle Kingdom (c. 1975–1640 BCE), the Second Intermediate Period (c. 1630–1520 BCE), and the New Kingdom (c. 1539–1075 BCE). This span of close to two millennia —Early Dynastic plus three kingdoms—is further subdivided into 20 family dynasties.

The Old Kingdom was a time of social and political stability, despite increasingly common military excursions to defend the borders. The growing wealth of ruling families of the period is reflected in the enormous and elaborate tomb complexes they commissioned for themselves. Kings were not the only patrons of the arts, however. Upper-level government officials also could afford tombs decorated with elaborate carvings.

The Great Pyramids at Giza

The architectural form most closely identified with Egypt is the true pyramid with a square base and four sloping triangular faces, first erected in the Fourth Dynasty (2575–2450 BCE). The angled sides may have been meant to represent the slanting rays of the sun, for inscriptions on the walls of pyramid tombs built in the Fifth and Sixth Dynasties tell of deceased kings climbing up the rays to join the sun god Ra.

Although not the first pyramids, the most famous are the three great pyramid tombs at Giza (**FIG. 3-5**). These were built by three successive Fourth-Dynasty kings: Khufu (ruled c. 2551– 2528 BCE), Khafre (ruled 2520–2494 BCE), and Menkaure (ruled c. 2490– 2472 BCE). The oldest and largest pyramid at Giza is that of Khufu, which covers 13 acres at its base. It was originally finished with a thick veneer of polished limestone that lifted its apex to almost 481 feet, some 30 feet above the present summit. The pyramid of Khafre is slightly smaller than Khufu's, and Menkaure's is considerably smaller.

3-5 GREAT PYRAMIDS, GIZA
Fourth Dynasty, c. 2575–2450 BCE. Erected by (from the left) Menkaure, Khafre, and Khufu. Limestone and granite, height of pyramid of Khufu, 450′ (137 m).
Credit: © Olga Kostenko/Shutterstock

The site was carefully planned to follow the sun's east–west path. Next to each of the pyramids was a funerary temple connected by a causeway—an elevated and enclosed pathway or corridor—to a valley temple on the bank of the Nile (**FIG. 3–6**). When a king died, his body was embalmed and ferried west across the Nile from the royal palace to his valley temple, where it was received with elaborate ceremonies. It was then carried up the causeway to his funerary temple and placed in its chapel, where family members presented offerings of food and drink, and priests performed rites in which the deceased's spirit consumed a meal. These rites were to be performed at the chapel in perpetuity. Finally, the body was entombed in a vault deep within the pyramid at the end of a long, narrow, and steeply rising passageway. This tomb chamber was sealed off after the burial with a 50-ton stone block. To further protect the king from intruders, three false passageways obscured the location of the tomb.

CONSTRUCTING THE PYRAMIDS   Building a pyramid was a formidable undertaking. A large workers' burial ground discovered at Giza attests to the huge labor force that had to be assembled, housed, and fed. Most of the cut stone blocks—each weighing an average of 2.5 tons—used in building the Giza complex were quarried either on the site or nearby. Teams of workers transported them by sheer muscle power, employing small logs as rollers or pouring water on mud to create a slippery surface over which they could drag the blocks on sleds.

Scholars and engineers have various theories about how the pyramids were raised. Some ideas have been tested in computerized projections and a few models on a small but representative scale have been constructed. The most efficient means of getting the stones into position might have been to build a temporary, gently sloping ramp around the body of the pyramid as it grew higher. The ramp could then be dismantled as the stones were smoothed out or slabs of veneer were laid.

The designers who oversaw the building of such massive structures were capable of the most sophisticated mathematical calculations. They oriented the pyramids to the points of the compass and may have incorporated other symbolic astronomical calculations as well. There was no room for trial and error. The huge foundation layer had to be absolutely level and the angle of each of the slanting sides had to remain constant so that the stones would meet precisely in the center at the top.

KHAFRE'S COMPLEX   Khafre's funerary complex is the best preserved. Its pyramid is the only one of the three to have maintained some of its veneer facing at the top. But the complex is most famous for the **GREAT SPHINX** that sits just behind Khafre's valley temple. This colossal portrait of the king—65 feet tall—combines his head with the long body of a crouching lion, seemingly merging notions of human intelligence with animal strength (**FIG. 3–7**).

In the adjacent **VALLEY TEMPLE**, massive blocks of red granite form walls and piers supporting a flat roof

pyramid of Menkaure   pyramid of Khafre   pyramid of Khufu   Great Sphinx

valley temple of Khafre

mortuary temple of Khafre

causeway

3-6 RECONSTRUCTION DRAWING OF THE GIZA PLATEAU SEEN FROM ABOVE
From left to right: the temples and pyramids of Menkaure, Khafre, and Khufu.

Credit: *Russell Barnett © Dorling Kindersley*

3-7 GREAT SPHINX, FUNERARY COMPLEX OF KHAFRE
Giza. Old Kingdom, c. 2520–2494 BCE. Limestone, height approx. 65′ (19.8 m).

Credit: © Orlandin/ Shutterstock

(**FIG. 3-8**). A **clerestory** (a row of tall, narrow windows in the upper walls, not visible in the figure), lets in light that reflects off the polished Egyptian alabaster floor.

Within the temple were a series of over-life-size statues portraying **KHAFRE** as an enthroned king (**FIG. 3-9**). The falcon god Horus perches on the back of the throne, protecting the king's head with his wings. Lions—symbols of regal authority—form the throne's legs, and the intertwined lotus and papyrus plants beneath the seat symbolize the king's power over Upper (lotus) and Lower (papyrus) Egypt.

Khafre wears the traditional royal costume—a short, pleated kilt, a linen headdress, and a false beard symbolic of royalty. He exudes a strong sense of dignity, calm, and above all permanence. In his right hand, he holds a cylinder, probably a rolled piece of cloth. His arms are pressed tightly within the contours of his body, which is firmly anchored in the stone block from which it was carved. The statue was created from an unusual stone, a type of gneiss (related to diorite) imported from Nubia that produces a rare optical effect: When illuminated by sunlight entering through the temple's clerestory, it glows a deep blue, the celestial color of Horus, filling the space with a blue radiance.

3-8 VALLEY TEMPLE OF KHAFRE
Giza. Old Kingdom, c. 2520–2494 BCE. Limestone and red granite.

Credit: Werner Forman Archive

3–9 KHAFRE

From Giza, valley temple of Khafre. Fourth Dynasty, c. 2520–2494 BCE. Diorite-gabbro gneiss, height 5'6⅛" (1.68 m). Egyptian Museum, Cairo. (JE 10062 = CG 14).

Credit: Index Ricerca Iconografica/Araldo de Luca

wearing the royal kilt and headcloth—stands in a conventional, balanced pose, striding with the left foot forward, his arms straight at his sides, and his fists clenched over cylindrical objects. His equally youthful queen, taking a smaller step forward, echoes his striding pose. Her sheer, close-fitting garment reveals the curves of her gently swelling body, a foil for the tight muscularity of the king. The time-consuming task of polishing this double statue was never completed, suggesting that the work may have

Sculpture

As the surviving statues of Khafre's valley temple demonstrate, Egyptian sculptors were adept at creating lifelike figures that also express a feeling of strength and permanence consistent with the unusually hard stones from which they were carved.

MENKAURE AND A QUEEN Dignity, calm, and permanence also characterize a sleek double portrait of Khafre's heir King Menkaure and a queen, probably Khamerernebty II, discovered in Menkaure's valley temple (**FIG. 3–10**). The couple's separate figures, close in size, are joined by the stone from which they emerge, forming a single unit. They are further united by the queen's symbolic embrace. Her right hand comes from behind to clasp the king's torso, and her left hand rests over his upper arm.

The king—depicted in accordance with Egyptian ideals as an athletic, youthful figure, nude to the waist and

3–10 MENKAURE AND A QUEEN, PROBABLY KHAMERERNEBTY II

From Giza. Fourth Dynasty, 2490–2472 BCE. Graywacke with traces of red and black paint, height 54½" (142.3 cm). Museum of Fine Arts, Boston. Harvard University—Museum of Fine Arts Expedition. (11.1738).

Credit: Photograph © 2017 Museum of Fine Arts, Boston

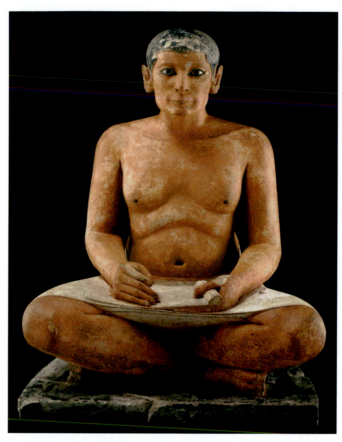

3-11 SEATED SCRIBE
Found near the tomb of Kai, Saqqara. Fifth Dynasty,
c. 2450–2325 BCE. Painted limestone with inlaid eyes of rock crystal,
calcite, and magnesite mounted in copper, height 21″ (53 cm).
Musée du Louvre, Paris. (N 2290 = E 3023).

High-ranking scribes could hope to be appointed to one of several
"houses of life," where they would copy, compile, study, and repair
valuable sacred and scientific texts.

Credit: Photo © RMN-Grand Palais (Musée du Louvre)/Franck Raux

been undertaken only a few years before Menkaure's
death in about 2472 BCE. Traces of red paint remain on the
king's face, ears, and neck (male figures were traditionally
painted red), as do traces of black on the queen's hair.

SEATED SCRIBE Old Kingdom sculptors also produced
statues of less prominent people, rendered in a more
relaxed, lifelike fashion. This less formal mode is seen in the
statue of a **SEATED SCRIBE** from early in the Fifth Dynasty
(**FIG. 3-11**)—with round head, alert expression, and close-
cropped hair—that was discovered near the tomb of a government official named Kai. It could be a portrait of Kai
himself. The irregular contours of his engaging face project
a sense of individual likeness and human presence.

The scribe's sedentary vocation has made his sagging
body slightly flabby, proof of a life free from hard physical
labor. As an ancient Egyptian inscription advises, "Become
a scribe so that your limbs remain smooth and your hands
soft and you can wear white and walk like a man of standing whom [even] courtiers will greet" (cited in Strouhal,

p. 216). This scribe sits holding a papyrus scroll partially
unrolled on his lap, his right hand clasping a now-lost
reed brush used in writing. The alert expression on his face
reveals more than a lively intelligence. Because the pupils
are slightly off-center in the irises, the eyes give the illusion of being in motion, and the reflective quality of the
polished crystal inlay reproduces with eerie fidelity the
contrast between the moist surface of eyes and the surrounding soft flesh in a living human face.

STATUETTES OF SERVANTS Even more lifelike than
the scribe were smaller figures of servants at work that
were made for inclusion in Old Kingdom tombs so that the
deceased could be provided for in the next world. Poses
are rooted directly in the labor these figures were expected
to perform throughout eternity. A painted limestone statuette from the Fifth Dynasty (**FIG. 3-12**) captures a butcher
raised up on the balls of his feet to bend down and lean
forward, poised, knife in hand, over the throat of an ox
that he has just slaughtered. He looks up to acknowledge
us, an action that enhances his sense of lifelike presence.
The emphasis on active poses and engagement with the
viewer may have been an attempt to underscore the ability
of such figures to perform their assigned tasks, or perhaps

3-12 BUTCHER
Perhaps from the tomb of the official Ni-kau-inpu and his wife
Hemet-re, Giza? Fifth Dynasty, c. 2450–2325 BCE. Painted limestone
(knife restored), height 14⅝″ (37 cm). The Oriental Institute Museum,
University of Chicago. (10626).

Although statues such as this have been assumed to represent
the deceased's servants, it has recently been proposed that instead
they depict relatives and friends of the deceased in the role of
servants, allowing these loved ones to accompany the deceased
into the next life.

Credit: © akg-images/Erich Lessing

it was meant to indicate their lower social status by showing them involved in physical labor—or both. The contrast between the detached stylization of upper-class figures and the engaging lifelikeness of laborers can be seen in Old Kingdom pictorial relief works as well.

Pictorial Relief in Tombs

To provide the *ka* with the most pleasant possible living quarters for eternity, wealthy families often had the interior walls and ceilings of their tombs decorated with paintings and reliefs. This decoration carried religious meaning, but it could also show the deceased's everyday life or ceremonial events that proclaimed the deceased's importance. Tombs therefore provide a wealth of information about ancient Egyptian culture.

THE TOMB OF TI On the walls of the large mastaba of a wealthy Fifth-Dynasty government official named Ti, a painted relief shows him watching a hippopotamus hunt—an official duty of royal courtiers (**FIG. 3-13**). It was believed that Seth, the god of chaos, disguised himself as a hippo. Hippos were also destructive, wandering into fields and damaging crops. Tomb depictions of such hunts therefore proclaimed the valor of the deceased and the triumph of good over evil, or at least of order over destruction.

The artists who created this painted limestone relief used a number of established Egyptian representational conventions. The river is shown as if seen from above, a band of parallel wavy lines below the boats. The creatures in this river, however—fish, a crocodile, and hippopotamuses—are shown in profile for easy identification. The shallow boats carrying Ti and his men are shown straight on in relation to the viewer's vantage point, and the papyrus stalks that choke the marshy edges of the river are disciplined into a regular pattern of projecting, linear, parallel, vertical forms that highlight the contrastingly crisp and smooth contour of Ti's body. At the top of the papyrus grove, however, this patterning

3-13 TI WATCHING A HIPPOPOTAMUS HUNT
Tomb of Ti, Saqqara. Fifth Dynasty, c. 2450–2325 BCE. Painted limestone relief, height approx. 45″ (114.3 cm).

Credit: Araldo de Luca

relaxes while animals of prey—perhaps foxes—stalk birds among the leaves and flowers. The hierarchically scaled and sleekly stylized figure of Ti, rendered in the conventional composite pose, looms over all. In a separate boat ahead of him, the actual hunters, being of lesser rank and engaged in more strenuous activities, are rendered in a more lifelike and lively fashion than their master. They are captured at the moment of closing in on their prey, spears at the ready and legs extended for the critical lunge forward.

The Middle Kingdom

How does Middle Kingdom Egyptian art reveal more about individuals and their lives?

The collapse of the Old Kingdom, with its long succession of powerful kings, was followed by roughly 150 years of political turmoil, fragmentation, and warfare traditionally referred to as the First Intermediate period (c. 2125–1975 BCE). About 2010 BCE, a series of kings named Mentuhotep (Eleventh Dynasty, c. 2010–c. 1938 BCE) gained power in Thebes, and the country was reunited under Nebhepetre Mentuhotep, who reasserted royal power and founded the Middle Kingdom.

The Middle Kingdom was another high point in Egyptian history. Arts and writing flourished in the Twelfth Dynasty (1938–1756 BCE), while reflecting a growing awareness of the political upheaval from which the country had just emerged. Using a strengthened military, Middle Kingdom rulers expanded and patrolled the borders, especially in lower Nubia, south of present-day Aswan (SEE MAP 3-1).

By the Thirteenth Dynasty (c. 1755–1630 BCE), however, central control by the government was weakened by a series of short-lived kings and an influx of foreigners, especially in the delta.

Portraits of Senusret III

Some royal portraits from the Middle Kingdom appear to acknowledge the hardship and fragility of human existence. Statues of Senusret III, a king of the Twelfth Dynasty, who ruled from c. 1836 to 1818 BCE, reflect this new sensibility. Old Kingdom rulers such as Khafre (SEE FIG. 3-9) gaze into eternity confident and serene, whereas the portrait **HEAD OF SENUSRET III** seems to capture a monarch preoccupied and emotionally drained (**FIG. 3-14**). Creases line his cheeks, his eyes are sunken, his eyelids droop, his forehead is flexed, and his jaw is sternly set—a bold image of a resolute ruler, tested but unbowed.

Senusret was a dynamic king and successful general who led four military expeditions into Nubia, overhauled the Egyptian central administration, and regained control

3-14 HEAD OF SENUSRET III
Twelfth Dynasty, c. 1836–1818 LᴍO. Yellow quartzite, 17¾ × 13½ × 17" (45.1 × 34.3 × 43.2 cm). The Nelson-Atkins Museum of Art, Kansas City, Missouri. Purchase: William Rockhill Nelson Trust (62-11).

over the country's increasingly independent nobles. To modern viewers, his portrait raises questions of interpretation. Are we looking at the face of a man wise in the ways of the world but saddened, and burdened by the weight of his responsibilities? Or are we looking at a reassuring statement: In spite of troubled times that have clearly left their mark on the face of the ruler himself, royal rule endures in Egypt? Given what we know about Egyptian history at this time, it is difficult to be sure.

Rock-Cut Tombs

During the Eleventh and Twelfth Dynasties, high-level officials and members of the nobility commissioned tombs hollowed out of the face of cliffs. A typical rock-cut tomb included an entrance **portico** (projecting porch), a main hall, and a shrine with a burial chamber under the offering chapel. The chambers of these tombs, as well as their ornamental columns, lintels, false doors, and niches, were all carved into the solid rock. An impressive necropolis was created in the cliffs at **BENI HASAN** on the east bank of the Nile (**FIG. 3-15**).

Painted scenes cover the interior walls of many tombs. Among the best preserved are those in the Twelfth-Dynasty

3-15 ROCK-CUT TOMBS, BENI HASAN
Twelfth Dynasty, 1938–1756 BCE.

At the left is the entrance to the tomb of a provincial governor and the commander-in-chief Amenemhat.

Credit: © www.BibleLandPictures. com/Alamy Stock Photo

tomb of local noble Khnumhotep, some of which portray vivid vignettes of farm work on his estates. In one painting two men harvest figs, rushing to compete with three baboons who relish the fruit from their perches in the trees (**FIG. 3–16**). One man reaches for a fig to add to the ordered stack in his basket, while his companion arranges the harvest in a larger box for transport. Like the hunters in the much earlier painted relief in the tomb of Ti (SEE FIG. 3–13), the upper torsos of these farm workers take a more lifelike profile posture, deviating from the strict frontality of the royal composite pose.

3-16 PICKING FIGS
Wall painting from the tomb of Khnumhotep, Beni Hasan. Twelfth Dynasty, c. 1890 BCE. Tempera facsimile by Nina de Garis.

Credit: © 2016. Photo Josse/Scala, Florence

Funerary Stelai

Only the wealthiest and noblest of ancient Egyptians could afford elaborately decorated mastabas or rock-cut tombs. Prosperous people, however, could still commission funerary stelai depicting themselves, their family, and offerings of food—meant to preserve the memory of the deceased and inspire the living to make offerings to them. An unfinished stele made for the tomb of the **SCULPTOR USERWER** (**FIG. 3–17**) presents three levels of decoration: one large upper block with five bands of hieroglyphs, beneath which are two registers with figures, each identified by inscription.

The text is addressed to the living, imploring them to make offerings to Userwer: "O living ones who are on the earth who pass by this tomb, as your deities love and favor you, may you say: 'A thousand of bread and beer, a thousand of cattle and birds, a thousand of alabaster [vessels] and clothes, a thousand of offerings and provisions that go forth before Osiris'" (Robins, p. 103).

At left, on the register immediately below this inscription, Userwer sits before a table piled with offerings of food. Behind him is his wife Satdepetnetjer and facing him on the other side of the offering table is Satameni, a standing woman also identified as his wife. (Userwer could have had more than one wife, but one of these women might also be the sculptor's deceased first wife.) At the other side of the stele on this same register but facing the opposite direction sits another couple before another table heaped with food. They are identified as Userwer's parents, and

3-17 STELE OF THE SCULPTOR USERWER

Twelfth Dynasty, c. 1850 BCE. Limestone, red and black ink, 20½ × 19″ (52 × 48 cm). British Museum London. (EA 579).

Credit: © The Trustees of the British Museum. All rights reserved.

the figure on the other side of their offering table is his son, Sneferuweser. In the lowest register are representations of other family members (probably Userwer's children) and his grandparents.

One of the most striking features of the lowest register of this stele is its unfinished state. The two leftmost figures were left uncarved, but the stone surface still maintains the preparatory ink drawing meant to guide the sculptor, preserving evidence of the system of canonical figure proportions that was established in the Middle Kingdom (see "Conventions and Technique of Egyptian Pictorial Relief" on page 52). The unfinished state of this stele has led to the suggestion that Userwer might have been in the process of carving it for himself when his death left it incomplete.

A more modest stele for a man named **AMENEMHAT** was brought to completion as a vibrantly painted relief (**FIG. 3-18**). Underneath an inscription inviting food offerings for the deceased Amenemhat is a portrait of his family. Amenemhat sits on a lion-legged bench between his wife Iyi and their son Antef, embraced by both. Next to the trio is an offering table heaped with meat, topped with onions, and sheltering two loaves of bread on the floor. On the far right is Amenemhat and Iyi's daughter Hapy, completing this tableau of family unity. The painter of this relief follows the established Egyptian convention of differentiating gender by skin tonality: dark red-brown for men and lighter yellow-ocher for women.

Town Planning

Although Egyptians used durable materials in the construction of tombs, they built their own dwellings with simple mud bricks, which have either disintegrated over time or been carried away for fertilizer by farmers. Only the foundations of these dwellings now remain.

Archaeologists have unearthed the remains of Kahun, a town built by Senusret II (ruled c. 1842–1837 BCE) for the many officials, priests, and workers who built and maintained his pyramid complex. Parallel streets were laid out on a **grid**,

3-18 STELE OF AMENEMHAT

From Assasif. Late Eleventh Dynasty, c. 2000 BCE. Painted limestone, 11 × 15″ (30 × 50 cm). Egyptian Museum, Cairo. (JE 45626).

Credit: Photo: Jürgen Liepe

forming rectangular blocks divided into lots for homes and other buildings. The houses of priests, court officials, and their families were large and comfortable, with private living quarters and public rooms grouped around central courtyards. The largest had as many as 70 rooms spread out over half an acre. Workers and their families made do with small, five-room row houses built back-to-back along narrow streets.

A New Kingdom workers' village, discovered at Deir el-Medina on the west bank of the Nile near the Valley of the Kings, has provided us with detailed information about the lives of the people who created the royal tombs. Workers lived together here under the rule of the king's chief minister. During a ten-day week, they worked for eight days and had two days off and also participated in many religious festivals. They lived a good life with their families, were given clothing, sandals, grain, and firewood by the king, and had permission to raise livestock and birds as well as tend a garden. The residents had a council, and the many written records that survive suggest a literate and litigious society that required many scribes. Because the men were away for most of the week working on the tombs, women had a prominent role in the town.

The New Kingdom

How are the conventions of ancient Egyptian art and architecture both refined and transformed during the New Kingdom?

During the Second Intermediate period (1630–1520 BCE)—another turbulent interruption in the succession of dynasties ruling a unified Egypt—an eastern Mediterranean people called the Hyksos invaded Egypt's northernmost regions. The kings of the Eighteenth Dynasty (c. 1539–1292 BCE) eventually regained control of the entire Nile region, extending from Nubia in the south to the Mediterranean Sea in the north, and restored Egypt's political and economic strength. Roughly a century later, one of the same dynasty's most dynamic kings, Thutmose III (ruled 1479–1425 BCE), extended Egypt's influence along the eastern Mediterranean coast as far as present-day Syria. His accomplishment was the result of 15 or more military campaigns and his own skill at diplomacy. The heartland of ancient Egypt was now surrounded by a buffer of empire.

Thutmose III was the first ruler to refer to himself as "pharaoh," a term that literally meant "great house." Egyptians used it in the same way that Americans say "the White House" to mean the current U.S. president and his staff. The successors of Thutmose III continued to call themselves pharaohs, and the term ultimately found its way into the Hebrew Bible—and modern usage—as the title for the kings of Egypt.

The Great Temple Complexes

At the height of the New Kingdom, rulers undertook extensive building programs along the entire length of the Nile. Their palaces, forts, and administrative centers disappeared long ago, but remnants of temples and tombs of this great age have endured. Thebes was Egypt's religious center throughout most of the New Kingdom, and worship of the Theban triad of deities—Amun, his wife Mut, and their son Khons—had spread throughout the country. Temples to these and other gods were a major focus of royal patronage, as were tombs and temples erected to glorify the kings themselves.

THE NEW KINGDOM TEMPLE PLAN As the home of the god, an Egyptian temple originally took the form of a house—a simple, rectangular, flat-roofed building approached through a courtyard and gateway. The builders of the New Kingdom enlarged and multiplied these elements. The gateway became a massive **pylon** with tapering walls; the semipublic courtyard was surrounded by columns (a **peristyle** court); and the temple itself included an outer **hypostyle hall** (a vast hall filled with columns) and an inner offering hall and sanctuary. The design was symmetrical and axial—that is, all its separate elements were symmetrically arranged along a dominant center line, creating a processional path from the outside straight into the sanctuary. The rooms became smaller, darker, and more exclusive as they neared the sanctuary, where the cult image of the god was housed. Only the pharaoh and the priests entered these inner rooms.

Two temple districts consecrated primarily to the worship of Amun, Mut, and Khons arose within the area of Thebes: a huge complex at Karnak to the north and, joined to it by an avenue of sphinxes, a more compact temple at Luxor to the south.

KARNAK Karnak was a long-standing sacred site where temples were built and rebuilt for over 1,500 years. During the nearly 500 years of the New Kingdom, successive kings renovated and expanded the complex of the **GREAT TEMPLE OF AMUN** until it covered about 60 acres, an area as large as a dozen football fields (**FIG. 3-19**).

Access to the heart of the temple, a sanctuary containing the statue of Amun, was from the west (on the left side of the reconstruction drawing) through a principal courtyard, a hypostyle hall, and a number of smaller halls and courts. Pylons set off each of these separate elements. Between the reigns of Thutmose I (Eighteenth Dynasty, ruled c. 1493–1482 BCE) and Ramses II (Nineteenth Dynasty, ruled c. 1279–1213 BCE), this area of the complex underwent a great deal of construction and renewal. Most of the pylons leading to the sanctuary and the halls and courts behind them were renovated or newly built and embellished with colorful pictorial wall reliefs. A sacred

hypostyle hall

sanctuary

pylon

3-19 RECONSTRUCTION DRAWING OF THE GREAT TEMPLE OF AMUN AT KARNAK SEEN FROM ABOVE
New Kingdom, c. 1579–1075 BCE.

lake was also added south of the complex, where the king and priests might undergo ritual purification before entering the temple. Thutmose III erected a court and festival temple to his own glory behind the sanctuary of Amun. His great-grandson Amenhotep III (ruled 1390–1353 BCE) placed a large stone statue of the god Khepri—the scarab (beetle) symbolic of the rising sun, rebirth, and everlasting life—next to the sacred lake.

In the sanctuary of Amun, priests washed the god's statue every morning and clothed it in a new garment. Because the god was thought to derive nourishment from the spirit of food, his statue was provided with tempting meals twice a day, which the priests then removed and ate themselves. Ordinary people entered the temple precinct only as far as the forecourts of the hypostyle halls, where they found themselves surrounded by inscriptions and images of kings and the god on columns and walls. During religious festivals, they lined the waterways and submitted petitions to the priests for requests they wished the gods to grant, as statues of the gods circulated along the water in ceremonial boats.

THE GREAT HALL AT KARNAK One of the most prominent features of the complex at Karnak is the enormous hypostyle hall set between two pylons at the end of the main forecourt. Nineteenth-Dynasty rulers Sety I (ruled c. 1290–1279 BCE) and his son Ramses II (ruled c. 1279–1213 BCE) erected this "Temple of the Spirit of Sety, Beloved of Ptah in the House of Amun," and it may have been used for royal coronation ceremonies. Ramses II referred to it as "the place where the common people extol the name of his majesty." The hall was 340 feet wide and 170 feet long. Its 134 closely spaced columns supported a roof of flat stones, the center section of which rose some 30 feet higher than the broad sides (**FIG. 3-20**).

papyrus capitals

clerestory

bud capitals

3-20 RECONSTRUCTION DRAWING OF THE HYPOSTYLE HALL, GREAT TEMPLE OF AMUN AT KARNAK
Nineteenth Dynasty, c. 1292–1190 BCE.

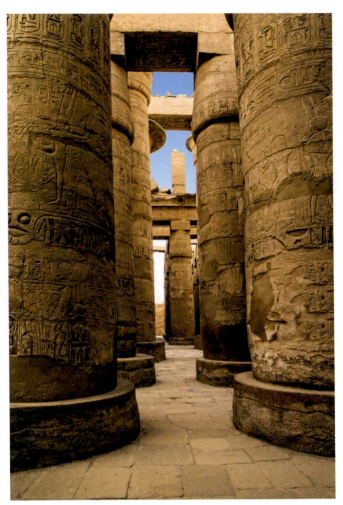

3-21 COLUMNS WITH PAPYRUS AND BUD CAPITALS, HYPOSTYLE HALL, GREAT TEMPLE OF AMUN AT KARNAK

Credit: © pakhnyushchyy/123RF

The columns supporting this higher roof section are 69 feet tall and 12 feet in diameter, ending in huge papyrus **capitals** (**FIG. 3-21**). On each side, smaller columns with bud capitals seem to march off into the darkness. In each of the side walls of the higher center section, a long row of window openings created a clerestory. These openings were filled with stone grillwork, so cannot have provided much light, but they did permit a cooling flow of air through the hall. Despite the dimness of the interior, artists covered nearly every inch of the columns, walls, and cross-beams with painted pictorial reliefs and inscriptions.

Hatshepsut

Across the Nile from Karnak and Luxor lay Deir el-Bahri and the Valleys of the Kings and Queens. These valleys on the west bank of the Nile held the royal necropolis, including the tomb of the pharaoh Hatshepsut. The dynamic Hatshepsut (Eighteenth Dynasty, ruled c. 1473–1458 BCE) is a notable figure in a period otherwise dominated by male warrior-kings. Besides Hatshepsut,

very few women ruled Egypt—they included the little-known Sobekneferu and Tausret, and much later, the well-known Cleopatra VII.

The daughter of Thutmose I, Hatshepsut married her half brother, who then reigned for 14 years as Thutmose II. When he died in c. 1473, she became regent for his underage son—Thutmose III—born to one of his concubines. Within a few years, Hatshepsut had herself declared "king" by the priests of Amun, a maneuver that made her co-ruler with Thutmose III for 20 years.

There was no artistic formula for a female pharaoh in Egyptian art, yet Hatshepsut had to be portrayed in her new role. What happened reveals something fundamentally important about the art of ancient Egypt. She was represented as a male king (**FIG. 3-22**) wearing a kilt and linen headdress, and occasionally even a king's false beard. The formula for portraying kings was not adapted to suit one individual; her appearance was adapted to conform to convention. There could hardly be a more powerful demonstration of the priority given to tradition in Egyptian royal art.

At the height of the New Kingdom, rulers undertook extensive personal building programs, and Hatshepsut was responsible for one of the most spectacular: her **FUNERARY TEMPLE** located at Deir el-Bahri, about a mile away from her actual tomb in the Valley of the Kings (**FIG. 3-23**). This imposing complex was designed for funeral rites and commemorative ceremonies and is much larger and more prominent than the tomb itself,

3-22 HATSHEPSUT KNEELING

From Deir el-Bahri. Eighteenth Dynasty, c. 1473–1458 BCE. Red granite, height 8′6″ (2.59 m). Metropolitan Museum of Art, New York.

Credit: © 2016. Image copyright The Metropolitan Museum of Art/Art Resource/ Scala, Florence reversing the scale relationship we saw in the Old Kingdom pyramid complexes.

Magnificently sited and sensitively reflecting the natural three-part layering in the rise of the landscape—from flat desert, through a sloping hillside, to the crescendo of sheer stone cliffs—Hatshepsut's temple was constructed on an axial plan (**FIG. 3-24**). A causeway lined with sphinxes once ran from a valley temple on the Nile to the huge, open space of the first court, where rare myrrh trees were planted in the temple's garden terraces. From there, visitors went up a long, straight ramp to a second court where shrines to Anubis and Hathor occupy the ends of the columned porticos. On the temple's uppermost court, colossal royal statues fronted another **colonnade** (a row of columns supporting a lintel or a series of arches), and behind this lay a large hypostyle hall with chapels

3-23 FUNERARY TEMPLE OF HATSHEPSUT, DEIR EL-BAHRI

Eighteenth Dynasty, c. 1473–1458 BCE.

At the far left, ramp and base of the funerary temple of Mentuhotep III. Eleventh Dynasty, ruled c. 2009–1997 BCE.

Credit: © Brian Lawrence/Getty Images

Temple of Thutmose III

Chapel of Hathor

Temple of Hatshepsut

Temple of Mentuhotep II

Avenue of Sphinxes leading to Karnak

3-24 RECONSTRUCTION DRAWING OF THE FUNERARY TEMPLE OF HATSHEPSUT FROM ABOVE

Deir el-Bahri.

Credit: © Dorling Kindersley

dedicated to Hatshepsut, her father, and the gods Amun and Ra-Horakhty—a powerful form of the sun god Ra combined with Horus. Centered in the hall's back wall was the entrance to the innermost sanctuary, a small chamber cut deep into the cliff.

Tombs of the Elite

The traditional art of pictorial relief, using a representational system that had dominated Egyptian figural art since the time of Narmer, reached a high degree of aesthetic refinement and technical sophistication during the reign of Amenhotep III (Eighteenth Dynasty, ruled c. 1390–1353 BCE), especially in the reliefs carved for the unfinished tomb of Ramose near Thebes (**FIG. 3-25**).

As mayor of Thebes and principal royal advisor to both Amenhotep III and Amenhotep IV (ruled 1353–c. 1336 BCE), Ramose was second only to the pharaoh in power and prestige. Soon after he gained political prominence, he began construction of an elaborate Theban tomb comprised of four rooms, including an imposing hypostyle hall 82 feet wide. Walls were covered with paintings or with shallow pictorial relief carvings celebrating the accomplishments, affiliations, and lineage of Ramose and his wife Merytptah or visualizing the funeral rites that would take place after their death. But the tomb was not used by Ramose. Work on it ceased in the fourth year of Amenhotep IV's reign, when, renamed Akhenaten, he relocated the court from Thebes to the new city of Akhetaten. Presumably Ramose moved with the court to the new capital, but neither his name nor a new tomb has been discovered there.

When the tomb was abandoned, the reliefs had not been painted, and some walls preserve only the preliminary sketches that would have guided sculptors. But the works that were executed are among the most

3-25 RAMOSE'S BROTHER MAY AND HIS WIFE WERENER
From the tomb of Ramose, Thebes. Eighteenth Dynasty, c. 1375–1365 BCE. Limestone relief.

Credit: © 2016. Photo Scala, Florence

3–26 NEBAMUN HUNTING BIRDS IN THE MARSHES

From the tomb of Nebamun, Thebes. Eighteenth Dynasty, c. 1350 BCE. Wall painting on dry plaster, 31⅝ × 38⅝" (83 × 98 cm). British Museum, London.

Credit: © The Trustees of the British Museum. All rights reserved.

sophisticated relief carvings in the history of art. On one wall, Ramose and his wife Merytptah appear, hosting a banquet for their family. All are portrayed at the same moment of youthful perfection, even though they represent two successive generations. Carvers lavished their considerable technical virtuosity on the portrayal of these majestic couples, creating clear textural differentiation of skin, hair, clothes, and jewelry. The easy elegance of linear fluidity is not easy to obtain in this medium, and the convincing sense of three-dimensionality in forms and their placement is managed within an extraordinarily shallow depth of relief. In the detail of Ramose's brother May and sister-in-law Werener in FIGURE 3–25, the traditional ancient Egyptian marital embrace (SEE FIGS. 3–10, 3–18) takes on a new tenderness, especially within the eternal stillness of a tomb.

The conceptual conventions of Egyptian royal art are rendered in these carvings with such warmth and refinement that they become almost believable. Our awareness of their artificiality is momentarily eclipsed by their sheer beauty.

But even lesser Eighteenth-Dynasty officials who were less powerful than Ramose created impressive tombs, lined with painted decoration. The walls of the tomb of Nebamun (a common New Kingdom name meaning "my lord is Amun"), who was scribe and grain accountant at the Temple of Amun in Karnak, included scenes of the elite leisure activities of his family during his eternal life after earthly life. In one (FIG. 3–26) he strides confidently on a pontoon boat, gliding through the marshes as he hunts for birds. Behind him stands his wife Hatshepsut; his daughter sits under him, grasping his left leg as a gesture of affection or a sign of stability. Just in front of Nebamun, his hunting cat snares three birds, and Nebamun himself holds three egrets. The painters have described the natural environment of Nebamun's hunt with astonishing detail, both on the land and under the water. The composition recalls the hippopotamus hunt of Ti, an Old Kingdom relief (SEE FIG. 3-13) created almost a thousand years before this painting, but employing the same conventions for representing humans and their world—alternately naturalistic and stylized. This New Kingdom version of the scene, however, is more gentle and graceful, freer and energized by spontaneity. To this refined world of convention, however, would come momentous change during the reign of Amenhotep III's successor, Amenhotep IV.

Akhenaten and the Art of the Amarna Period

Amenhotep IV was surely the most unusual ruler in the history of ancient Egypt. During his 17-year reign (c. 1353–1336 BCE), he radically transformed the political, spiritual, and cultural life of the country. He founded a new religion honoring a supreme god, the life-giving sun deity Aten (represented by the sun's disk), and changed his own name in about 1348 BCE to Akhenaten ("One Who Is Effective on Behalf of the Aten"). Abandoning Thebes, the capital of Egypt since the beginning of his dynasty and a city firmly in the grip of the priests of Amun, Akhenaten built a new capital much farther north, calling it Akhetaten ("Horizon of the Aten"). Using the modern name for this site, Tell el-Amarna, historians refer to Akhenaten's reign as the Amarna period.

THE NEW AMARNA STYLE   Akhenaten's reign not only saw the creation of a new capital and the rise of a new religious focus, it also led to radical changes in royal artistic conventions. In portraits of the king, artists used startling stylizations, even physical distortions. The new royal figure style can be seen in a colossal statue of Akhenaten, about 16 feet tall, created for a new temple to the Aten that he built near the temple complex of Karnak, openly challenging the state gods (FIG. 3-27). This portrait was placed in one of the porticos of a huge courtyard (c. 426 by 394 feet), oriented to the movement of the sun.

The sculpture's strange, softly swelling forms suggest androgyny to modern viewers. The sagging stomach and inflated thighs contrast with spindly arms, protruding collarbones, and an attenuated neck, on which sits a stylized head. Facial features are exaggerated: Slitlike eyes turn slightly downward, and the bulbous, sensuous lips are flanked by dimples that seem to express emotion. Such stark deviations from convention are disquieting, especially since Akhenaten holds the flail and

shepherd's crook, traditional symbols of the pharoah's super-human sovereignty.

The new Amarna style was used not only in official royal portraits, but also in pictorial relief sculpture portraying the family life of Akhenaten and Queen Nefertiti. In one panel the king and queen sit on cushioned stools playing with their nude daughters (FIG. 3-28), whose elongated, shaved heads conform to the new figural

3-27 COLOSSAL FIGURE OF AKHENATEN
From the temple known as the Gempaaten, built early in the reign of Akhenaten (ruled c. 1353–1336 BCE) just southeast of the Temple of Karnak. Sandstone with traces of polychromy, height of remaining portion about 13′ (4 m). Egyptian Museum, Cairo. (JE 49528).

Credit: © akg-images/De Agostini Picture Lib./A. Dagli Orti

3-28 AKHENATEN AND HIS FAMILY

From Akhetaten (present-day Tell el-Amarna). Eighteenth Dynasty, c. 1353–1336 BCE.
Painted limestone relief, 12¼ × 15¼″ (31.1 × 38.7 cm). Staatliche Museen zu Berlin, Preussischer Kulturbesitz, Ägyptisches Museum. (14145).

Egyptian relief sculptors often employed the **sunken relief** technique seen here. In ordinary reliefs, the background is carved back so that the figures project out from the finished surface. In sunken relief, the original flat surface of the stone is reserved as background, and the outlines of the figures are deeply incised, permitting the development of three-dimensional forms within them.

Credit: © 2016. Photo Scala, Florence/bpk, Bildagentur für Kunst, Kultur und Geschichte, Berlin

convention. The royal couple receives the blessings of the Aten, whose rays end in hands that come into the open pavilion to offer ankhs before their nostrils, giving them the "breath of life." The king holds one child and cradles her head while she pulls herself forward to kiss him. The youngest of the three perches on Nefertiti's shoulder, trying to attract her mother's attention by stroking her cheek, while the oldest sits on the queen's lap, tugging at her mother's hand and pointing to her father. In a striking contrast with the serene relief from Ramose's tomb, this artist has conveyed the fidgety behavior of children and the loving involvement of their parents in a manner not even hinted at in earlier royal portraiture.

PORTRAITS OF QUEENS   Akhenaten's goals were actively supported not only by Nefertiti but also by his mother, **QUEEN TIY** (**FIG. 3–29**). She had been the chief wife of the king's father, Amenhotep III, and had played a significant role in affairs of state during his reign. Queen Tiy's personality seems to emerge from a miniature portrait head that highlights the exquisite bone structure of her dark-skinned face with its arched brows, tilted eyes, and full lips. Originally, this portrait included a funerary silver headdress covered with gold cobras and gold jewelry. But after her son came to power and established his new religion, the portrait was altered: A brown cap covered with blue glass beads was placed over the original headdress.

3–29 QUEEN TIY
From Kom Medinet el-Ghurab (near el-Lahun). Eighteenth Dynasty, c. 1352 BCE. Wood (perhaps yew and acacia), ebony, glass, silver, gold, lapis lazuli, cloth, clay, and wax, height 3¾″ (9.4 cm). Staatliche Museen zu Berlin, Preussischer Kulturbesitz, Ägyptisches Museum. (21834).

Credit: © 2016. Photo Scala, Florence/bpk, Bildagentur für Kunst, Kultur und Geschichte, Berlin

3–30 NEFERTITI
From Akhetaten (present-day Tell el-Amarna). Eighteenth Dynasty, reign of Akhenaten c. 1353–1336 BCE. Painted limestone, height 20″ (51 cm). Staatliche Museen zu Berlin, Preussischer Kulturbesitz, Ägyptisches Museum. (21300).

Credit: © 2016. Photo Scala, Florence/bpk, Bildagentur für Kunst, Kultur und Geschichte, Berlin

The famous head of **NEFERTITI** (**FIG. 3–30**) was discovered in 1912 in the Akhetaten studio of the sculptor Thutmose, along with drawings and other items related to commissions for the royal family. It may have served as a model for full-length sculptures or paintings of the queen. In 2007, analysis using a CT scan revealed the existence of a delicately carved limestone sculpture underneath the modeled **stucco** that forms its outer surface. The two likenesses differ slightly. The sculptor seems to have smoothed out in stucco some of the facial irregularities in the underlying limestone carving—including a bump in Nefertiti's nose and creases around her mouth—and increased the prominence of her cheekbones, probably to bring the queen's face into conformity with contemporary notions of beauty, much in the way we would retouch a photographic image.

The proportions of Nefertiti's refined, regular features, long neck, and heavy-lidded eyes appear almost too ideal to be human, but are eerily consistent with standards of beauty in our own culture. Part of the appeal of this portrait bust, in addition to its stunning beauty, may be the artist's dramatic use of color. The hues of the blue headdress and its striped band are repeated in the rich red, blue, green, and gold of the jeweled necklace. The queen's brows, eyelids, cheeks, and lips are heightened with color, as they no doubt were heightened with cosmetics in real life.

GLASS No one knows precisely when or where the technique of glassmaking first developed, but the basics of the process are quite clear. Heating a mixture of sand, lime, and sodium carbonate or sodium sulfate to a very high temperature produces glass. The addition of other minerals can make the glass transparent, translucent, or opaque, as well as create a vast range of colors.

The first objects to be made entirely of glass in Egypt were produced with the technique known as core-formed glass. A lump of sandy clay molded into the desired shape was wrapped in strips of cloth, then skewered on a fireproof rod. It was then briefly dipped into a pot of molten glass. When the resulting coating of glass had cooled, the clay core was removed through the opening left by the skewer. To decorate the vessel, glassmakers frequently heated thin rods of colored glass and fused them on and flattened them against the surface in strips.

3–31 FISH-SHAPED PERFUME BOTTLE

From Akhetaten (present-day Tell el-Amarna). Eighteenth Dynasty, reign of Akhenaten, c. 1353–1336 BCE. Core-formed glass, length 5¾" (14.5 cm). British Museum, London. (EA 55193).

Credit: © The Trustees of the British Museum. All rights reserved.

This fish-shaped bottle (**FIG. 3–31**) is an example of core-formed glass from the New Kingdom's Amarna period. The body was created from glass tinted with cobalt, and the surface was then decorated with small rods of white and orange glass. A pointed tool was dragged along the surface to achieve the wavy pattern that resembles fish scales, then two slices of a rod of spiraled black and white glass were fused to the surface to create its eyes.

Glassmaking could only be practiced by artists working for the king, and Akhenaten's new capital had its own glass-making workshops, where this bottle was made. Meant to hold scented oil, it was fashioned in the shape of a bolti, a species of fish that carries its eggs in its mouth and spits out its offspring when they hatch. The bolti was a common symbol for birth and regeneration, complementing the self-generation that Akhenaten attributed to the sun disk Aten.

The Return to Tradition: Tutankhamun's Tomb

Akhenaten's new religion and revolutionary reconception of pharaonic art outlived him by only a few years. The priesthood of Amun quickly regained its former power, and Akhenaten's young son Tutankhaten (Eighteenth Dynasty, ruled c. 1332–1322 BCE) returned to traditional religious beliefs, changing his name to Tutankhamun—"Living Image of Amun"—and moving the court back to Thebes. He died at age 19 and was buried in the Valley of the Kings, across the Nile from Thebes.

Although some had doubted the royal lineage of the young Tutankhaten, DNA testing of a series of royal mummies from this period has confirmed that he was the son of Akhenaten and one of his sisters. His death at such a young age seems to have been the result of poor health and serious injury. The DNA analysis documented his struggles with malaria, and CT scans revealed a badly broken and seriously infected leg, as well as a series of birth defects that have been ascribed to royal inbreeding.

The sealed inner chamber of Tutankhamun's tomb was never plundered, and when it was found in 1922 its incredible riches were just as they had been left at his interment. His mummified body, crowned with a spectacular mask preserving his likeness (SEE FIG. 3–1), lay inside three nested coffins that identified him with Osiris, the god of the dead. The innermost coffin, in the shape of a mummy, is the richest of the three (**FIG. 3–32**).

Made of over 240 pounds of gold, its surface is decorated with colored glass and semiprecious gemstones,

3–32 INNER COFFIN FROM TUTANKHAMUN'S SARCOPHAGUS

From the tomb of Tutankhamun, Valley of the Kings. Eighteenth Dynasty, c. 1332–1322 BCE. Gold inlaid with glass and semiprecious stones, height 6'7⁄8" (1.85 m), weight nearly 243 pounds (110.4 kg). Egyptian Museum, Cairo. (JE 60671).

Credit: Araldo de Luca

Art and its Contexts

THE TEMPLES OF RAMSES II AT ABU SIMBEL

Many art objects are subtle, captivating us through their enduring beauty or complexity. Monuments such as Ramses II's temples at Abu Simbel, however, engage us across the ages with raw power born of sheer scale. This god-king of Egypt, ruler of a vast empire, a virile wonder who fathered nearly a hundred children, is described in an inscription he had carved into an obelisk (now standing in the heart of Paris): "Son of Ra: Ramses-Meryamun ['Beloved of Amun']. As long as the skies exist, your monuments shall exist, your name shall exist, firm as the skies." So far, this is true.

Abu Simbel was an auspicious site for Ramses II's great temples. It is north of the second cataract of the Nile, in Nubia, the ancient land of Kush, which Ramses ruled and which was the source of his gold, ivory, and exotic animal skins. The monuments were carved directly into the rock of the sacred hills. The larger temple is dedicated to Ramses and the Egyptian gods Amun, Ra-Horakhty, and Ptah (**FIG. 3–33**). A row of four colossal seated statues of the king, 65 feet high, dominate the monument, flanked by relatively small statues of family members, including his principal wife Nefertari. Inside the temple, eight 23-foot statues of the god Osiris with the face of Ramses further proclaim Ramses's divinity. The corridor they form leads to seated figures of Ptah, Amun, Ramses II, and Ra.

The corridor was oriented so that twice a year the first rays of the rising sun shot through it to illuminate statues of the king and the three gods placed against the back wall (**FIG. 3–34**).

About 500 feet away, Ramses ordered a smaller temple to be carved into a mountain sacred to Hathor, goddess of fertility, love, joy, and music, and dedicated to Hathor and Nefertari. The two temples were oriented so that their axes crossed in the middle of the Nile, suggesting that they may have been associated with the annual life-giving flood.

Ironically, rising water nearly destroyed them both. Half-buried in the sand over the ages, the temples were only rediscovered early in the nineteenth century. But in the 1960s, construction of the Aswan High Dam flooded the Abu Simbel site. An international team of experts mobilized to find a way to safeguard Ramses II's temples, deciding in 1963 to cut them out of the rock in blocks (**FIG. 3–35**) and re-erect them on higher ground, secure from the rising waters of Lake Nasser. The projected cost of $32 million was financed by UNESCO, with Egypt and the United States each pledging $12 million. Work began in 1964 and was completed in 1968. Thanks to this international cooperation, modern technology, and hard labor, Ramses II's temples were saved to engage future generations.

3-33 TEMPLE OF RAMSES II
Abu Simbel. Nineteenth Dynasty, c. 1279–1213 BCE.
Credit: Bradhenge/Fotolia

**3-34 SCHEMATIC DRAWING
OF THE TEMPLE OF RAMSES II**
Abu Simbel.

Credit: © Dorling Kindersley

inner
sanctuary

vestibule with
scenes of Ramses
and Nefertari
making offerings

statues of Osiris
with the face of
Ramses

storerooms

INTERIOR

a row of baboons
greeting the rising sun

statue of
Ra-Horakhty

colossal statues
of Ramses II

entrance to temple

EXTERIOR

**3-35 REMOVAL OF THE FACE OF ONE OF THE
COLOSSAL SCULPTURES OF RAMSES II AT ABU
SIMBEL IN THE MID-1960S**

Credit: © Terrence Spencer/Time & Life Pictures/Getty Images as well as finely incised linear designs and hieroglyphic inscriptions. The king holds a crook and a flail, symbols that were associated with Osiris and had become a traditional part of the royal regalia. A nemes headdress with projecting cobra and vulture covers his head, and a blue, braided beard is attached to his chin. Nekhbet and Wadjet, vulture and cobra goddesses of Upper and Lower Egypt, spread their wings across his body. The king's features as reproduced on the coffin and masks are those of a very young man, and the unusually full lips, thin-bridged nose, and pierced earlobes suggest the continuing vitality of some Amarna stylizations.

RAMSES II AND NEFERTARI   By Egyptian standards Tutankhamun was a rather minor king. Ramses II (Nineteenth Dynasty, ruled c. 1279–1213 BCE), on the other hand, was both powerful and long-lived. He was a bold leader and an effective political strategist and under him, Egypt was a mighty empire. Although he did not win every battle, he was a master of propaganda, able to turn military defeats into glorious victories. He also triumphed diplomatically by making peace with the Hittites, a rival power centered in Anatolia that had tried to expand to the west and south at Egypt's expense. Ramses twice reaffirmed that peace by marrying Hittite princesses.

In the course of a long and prosperous reign, Ramses II initiated building projects on a scale rivaling the Old Kingdom pyramids at Giza. Today, the most awe-inspiring of his many architectural monuments are found at Karnak and Luxor and at Abu Simbel in Egypt's southernmost region (see "The Temples of Ramses II at Abu Simbel" on pages 76–77). At Abu Simbel, Ramses ordered two large temples to be carved into natural rock, one for himself and the other for his principal wife, Nefertari.

The temples at Abu Simbel were not funerary monuments. Ramses's and Nefertari's tombs are in the Valleys

3-36 QUEEN NEFERTARI MAKING AN OFFERING TO HATHOR
Wall painting in the tomb of Nefertari, Valley of the Queens. Nineteenth Dynasty, 1290–1224 BCE.

Credit: © akg-images

3-37 JUDGMENT OF HUNEFER BEFORE OSIRIS

Illustration from a Book of the Dead. Nineteenth Dynasty, c. 1285 BCE. Painted papyrus, height 15⅝″ (39.8 cm).
British Museum, London. (EA 9901).

Credit: © The Trustees of the British Museum. All rights reserved.

of the Kings and Queens. The walls of Nefertari's tomb are covered with exquisite paintings. In one mural, Nefertari offers jars of perfumed ointment to the goddess Hathor, known as the "Mistress of the West," who welcomes the dead into their new life (**FIG. 3-36**). The queen wears the vulture-skin headdress and jeweled collar that indicate her royal position and a long, semitransparent white linen gown. Hathor, seated on her throne behind a table heaped with offerings, holds a long scepter in her left hand and the ankh in her right. She wears her signature headdress with horns framing a sun disk. This cow goddess was especially associated with femininity and fertility.

The artists responsible for decorating the tomb diverged very subtly but distinctively from earlier stylistic conventions. The outline drawing and use of pure colors within the lines reflect traditional practices, but quite new is the slight modeling of the body forms by small changes of **hue** to enhance the appearance of three-dimensionality. The skin color of these women is much darker than that conventionally used for females in earlier periods, and lightly brushed-in shading emphasizes their eyes and lips.

The Books of the Dead

Papyrus scrolls visualized New Kingdom beliefs about the final judgment that awaited souls after death. Early collectors of Egyptian artifacts called these scrolls "Books of the Dead." By the time of the New Kingdom, Egyptians had come to believe that only a person free from wrongdoing could enjoy an afterlife. The dead were thought to undergo

a last judgment consisting of two tests presided over by Osiris, the god of the underworld, and supervised by Anubis, the jackal-headed god of embalming and cemeteries. After the deceased were questioned about their behavior in life, their hearts—which the Egyptians believed to be the seat of the soul—were weighed on a scale against an ostrich feather, the symbol of Ma'at, goddess of truth, order, and justice.

Family members commissioned scrolls containing magical texts or spells, which embalmers sometimes placed among the wrappings of mummified bodies. A scene in one that was created for a man named Hunefer (Nineteenth Dynasty) shows three successive stages in his induction into the afterlife (**FIG. 3-37**). At the left, Anubis leads Hunefer by the hand to the spot where he will weigh Hunefer's heart against the "feather of Truth." Ma'at appears atop the balancing arm of the scales wearing the feather as a headdress. To the right of the scales, Ammit, the dreaded "Eater of the Dead"—part crocodile, part lion, and part hippopotamus—watches eagerly for a sign from the ibis-headed god Thoth, who prepares to record the result of the weighing.

But Hunefer passes the test, and Horus, on the right, presents him to the enthroned Osiris, who floats on a lake of natron (see "Preserving the Dead" on page 54). Behind the throne, the goddesses Nephthys and Isis support the god's left arm, while in front of him Horus's four sons, each entrusted with the care of one of the deceased's vital organs, stand on a huge lotus blossom rising out of the lake. In the top register, Hunefer, finally accepted into the afterlife, kneels before 14 gods of the underworld.

3-38 KAROMAMA

Third Intermediate period, Twenty-Second Dynasty, c. 945–715 BCE. Bronze inlaid with gold, silver, electrum, glass, and copper; height 23½" (59.5 cm). Musée du Louvre, Paris.

Credit: Photo © RMN-Grand Palais (musée du Louvre)/Hervé Lewandowski

Late Egyptian Art

What traditional and innovative visual and thematic qualities are seen in the later art of ancient Egypt?

After the end of the New Kingdom—during the Third Intermediate Period, c. 1075–715 BCE—Egypt was ruled by a series of new dynasties whose leaders continued the traditional patterns of royal patronage and pushed figural conventions in new and interesting directions. One of the most extraordinary, and certainly one of the largest, surviving examples of ancient Egyptian bronze sculpture (FIG. 3-38) dates from this period. An inscription on the base identifies the subject as Karomama, divine consort of Amun and member of a community of virgin priestesses selected from the pharaoh's family or retinue who were dedicated to him. Karomama herself was the granddaughter of King Osorkan I (Twenty-First Dynasty, ruled c. 985–978 BCE). These priestesses amassed great power, held property, and maintained their own court, often passing on their positions to their nieces. The *sistra* (ritual rattles) that Karomama once carried in her hands would have immediately identified her as a priestess rather than a princess.

The main body of this statue was cast in bronze and subsequently covered with a thin sheathing of bronze, which was then exquisitely engraved with patterns inlaid with gold, silver, and electrum (a natural alloy of gold and silver). Much of the inlay has disappeared, but we can still make out the elaborately incised drawing of the bird wings that surround Karomama and accentuate the fullness of her figure, conceived to embody a new female ideal. Her slender limbs, ample hips, and prominent breasts contrast with the uniformly slender female figures of the late New Kingdom (SEE FIG. 3-36).

Foreign Domination

The latest period in the history of ancient Egypt saw the country and its art in the hands and service of foreigners. Nubians, Persians, Macedonians, Greeks, and Romans were all attracted to Egypt's riches and seduced by its art. In the eighth century, Nubians from the powerful kingdom of Kush—ancient Egypt's neighbor to the south—conquered Egypt, establishing capitals at Memphis and Thebes (712–657 BCE) and adopting Egyptian religious, artistic, and architectural practices. The sphinx of the Nubian king Taharqo (ruled c. 690–664 BCE) (FIG. 3-39) expresses royal power in a tradition dating back to the Old Kingdom (SEE FIG. 3-7), the two cobras on his forehead perhaps representing Taharqo's two kingdoms—Kush and Egypt. The facial features, however, clearly show him to be African, and an inscription on his chest provides his specific identity.

In 332 BCE, Macedonian Greeks led by Alexander the Great conquered Egypt, and after Alexander's death in 323 BCE, his generals divided up his empire. Ptolemy, a Greek, took Egypt, declaring himself king in 305 BCE. The Ptolemaic dynasty ended with the death of Cleopatra VII (ruled 51–30 BCE), when the Romans succeeded as Egypt's rulers and made it the breadbasket of Rome.

3-39 SPHINX OF TAHARQO

From Temple T, Kawa, Nubia (present-day Sudan). Twenty-Fifth Dynasty, c. 680 BCE. Granite, height 16″ (40.6 cm), length 28¾″ (73 cm). British Museum, London.

Credit: © The Trustees of the British Museum. All rights reserved.

Think About It

1 Explain the pictorial conventions for representing the human figure in ancient Egypt, using the Palette of Narmer (see "Closer Look" on page 53) as an example.

2 Summarize the religious beliefs of ancient Egypt with regard to the afterlife, and explain how their beliefs inspired traditions in art and architecture, citing specific examples both early and late.

3 How do depictions of royalty differ from those of more ordinary people in ancient Egyptian art? Focus your answer on one specific representation of each.

4 Characterize the stylistic transformation that took place during the rule of Akhenaten by comparing **FIGURES 3-25** and **3-28**. Why would there be such a drastic change?

Crosscurrents

What do these two scenes of hunting express about the wealthy and powerful people who commissioned them? How do the artists make their messages clear? How is location related to meaning?

FIG. 2-14

FIG. 3-13

4–1 GIRL GATHERING SAFFRON CROCUS FLOWERS
Detail of wall painting, Room 3 of House Xeste 3, Akrotiri, Thera, Cyclades. Before 1650 BCE. Thera Foundation, Petros M. Nomikos, Greece.

Credit: © 2016. White Images/Scala, Florence

Chapter 4

Art of the Ancient Aegean

4.a Identify the visual hallmarks of Bronze Age Aegean Cycladic, Minoan, and Mycenaean art for formal, technical, and expressive qualities.

4.b Interpret the meaning of works of Bronze Age Aegean Cycladic, Minoan, and Mycenaean art based on their themes, subjects, and symbols.

4.c Relate Bronze Age Aegean Cycladic, Minoan, and Mycenaean artists and art to their cultural, economic, and political contexts.

4.d Apply the vocabulary and concepts used to discuss Bronze Age Aegean art, artists, and art history.

4.e Interpret ancient Aegean art using appropriate art historical methods, such as observation, comparison, and inductive reasoning.

4.f Select visual and textual evidence in various media to support an argument or an interpretation of ancient Aegean art.

This elegantly posed and sharply silhouetted girl, reaching to pluck the crocus flowers blooming on the hillside in front of her (**FIG. 4–1**), offers us a window into life in the ancient Aegean world. The image is from a **fresco** of c. 1650 BCE found in a house in Akrotiri, a town on the Aegean island of Thera that was said to be famous for the saffron harvested from its crocuses. Saffron was valued in the Bronze Age Aegean mainly as a yellow dye in textile production, but it also had medicinal properties and was used to alleviate menstrual cramps. The latter use may be referenced in this image, since the fresco was part of the elaborate painted decoration of a room that some scholars believe housed the coming-of-age ceremonies of young women at the onset of menses. The crocus gatherer's shaved head and looped long ponytail are attributes of childhood, but the light blue color of her scalp indicates that her hair is beginning to grow out, suggesting that she is entering adolescence.

The house that contained this painting disappeared suddenly more than 3,600 years ago when the volcano that formed the island of Thera erupted, spewing pumice that filled and sealed every crevice of Akrotiri—fortunately, after the residents had fled. The rediscovery of the lost town in 1967 was among the most significant archaeological events of the second half of the twentieth century, and excavation of the city is still under way. The opportunity

that Thera affords archaeologists to study works of art and architecture in context has allowed for a deeper understanding of the Bronze Age cultures of the Aegean. As the image of the girl gathering crocuses illustrates, wall paintings may reflect the ritual uses of a room or building, and the meanings of artifacts are better understood by considering where they are found and how they are grouped with one another.

From before 3000 BCE until about 1100 BCE, several Bronze Age cultures flourished simultaneously across the Aegean: on a cluster of small islands (including Thera) called the Cyclades, on Crete and other islands in the eastern Mediterranean, and on mainland Greece (**MAP 4–1**).

To learn about these cultures, archaeologists have studied shipwrecks, homes, and grave sites, as well as the ruins of architectural complexes. Archaeology—uncovering and interpreting material culture to reconstruct its original context—is our principal means of understanding the Bronze Age culture of the Aegean, since only one of its three written languages has been decoded. In recent years, archaeologists and art historians have collaborated with researchers in such areas of study as the history of trade and the history of climate change to provide an ever-clearer picture of ancient Aegean society. But many sites await excavation, or even discovery. The history of the Aegean Bronze Age is still being written.

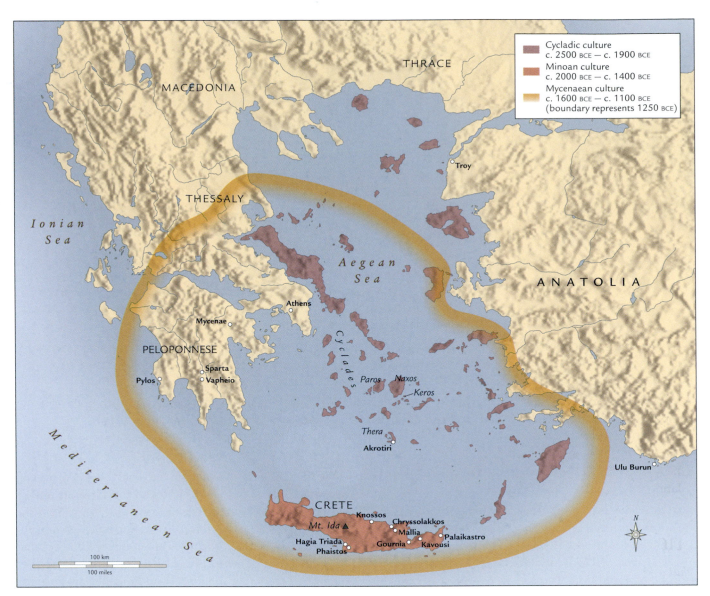

MAP 4–1 THE ANCIENT AEGEAN WORLD

The three main cultures in the ancient Aegean were the Cycladic, in the Cyclades; the Minoan, on Thera and Crete; and the Helladic, including the Mycenaean, on mainland Greece but also encompassing the regions that had been the center of the two earlier cultures.

The Bronze Age in the Aegean

How have scholars learned about the art and culture of the Aegean Bronze Age?

Using metal ores imported from Europe, Arabia, and Anatolia, Aegean peoples created exquisite objects of bronze that were prized for export. This early period when the manufacture of bronze tools and weapons became widespread is known as the Aegean Bronze Age. (See Chapter 1 for the Bronze Age in northern Europe.)

For the ancient Aegean peoples, the sea provided an important link not only between the mainland and the islands, but also to the world beyond. In contrast to the landlocked civilizations of the Near East and to the Egyptians, who used river transportation, the peoples of the Aegean were seafarers, and their ports welcomed ships from other cultures around the Mediterranean. For this reason shipwrecks are a rich source of information about the material culture of these societies. For example, the wreck of a trading vessel (probably from the Levant, the Mediterranean coast of the Near East) thought to have sunk in or soon after 1306 BCE and discovered in the vicinity of Ulu Burun, off the southern coast of present-day Turkey, carried an extremely varied cargo: metal ingots, bronze weapons and tools, aromatic resins, fruits and spices, jewelry and beads, African ebony, ivory tusks, ostrich eggs, disks of blue glass ready to be melted down for reuse, and ceramics from the Near East, mainland Greece, and Cyprus. Among the gold objects was a scarab associated with Nefertiti, wife of the Egyptian pharaoh Akhenaten.

The cargo suggests that this vessel cruised from port to port along the Aegean and eastern Mediterranean seas, loading and unloading goods as it went. It also suggests that the peoples of Egypt and the ancient Near East were trading partners.

Probably the thorniest problem in Aegean archaeology is that of dating the finds. In the case of the Ulu Burun wreck, the dating of a piece of freshly cut firewood on the ship to 1306 BCE—using a technique called dendrochronology that analyzes the spaces between growth rings—allowed unusual precision in pinpointing the moment this ship sunk. But archaeologists are not always able to find such easily datable materials. They usually rely on a relative dating system for the Aegean Bronze Age that is based largely on pottery, but assigning specific dates to sites and objects with this system is complicated and controversial. One cataclysmic event has helped: A huge volcanic explosion on the Cycladic island of Thera, as we have seen, devastated Minoan civilization there and on Crete, only 70 miles to the south. Evidence from tree rings from Ireland and California and traces of volcanic ash in ice cores from Greenland put the date of the eruption about 1650–1625 BCE. Sometimes in this book you will find periods cited without attached dates and in other books you may encounter different dates from those given for objects shown here. You should expect dating to change in the future as our knowledge grows and new techniques of dating emerge.

The Cycladic Islands

What stylistic features characterize Bronze Age Cycladic sculpted figures and how do the objects reflect Cycladic culture?

On the Cycladic islands, late Neolithic and early Bronze Age people developed a thriving culture. They engaged in agriculture, herding, crafts, and trade, using local stone to build fortified towns and hillside burial chambers. Because they left no written records, their artifacts are our principal source of information about them. From about 6000 BCE, Cycladic artists used a coarse, poor-quality local clay to make a variety of ceramic objects, including engaging ceramic figurines of humans and animals as well as domestic and ceremonial wares. Some 3,000 years later, they began to produce marble sculptures.

The Cyclades, especially the islands of Naxos and Paros, had ample supplies of a fine and durable white marble. Sculptors used it to create sleek, abstracted representations of human figures ranging from a few inches to almost 5 feet tall. They were shaped—perhaps by women—with scrapers made of obsidian and smoothed using emery polishing stones, both materials easily available on the Cyclades.

These sculptures have been found almost exclusively in graves, and, although there are a few surviving male figures, the overwhelming majority represent nude women and conform to a consistent representational convention (**FIG. 4–2**). They are presented in poses of strict symmetry, with arms folded just under gently protruding breasts, as if they were clutching their abdomens. Necks are long, heads tilted back, and faces featureless except for a prominent, elongated nose. All body parts are pared down to essentials, and some joints are indicated with incised lines. The sculptors carefully designed these figures, laying them out with a compass in conformity to three evenly spaced and equally sized circles—the first delineated by the upper arch of the head and the waist, the second by the sloping shoulders and the line of the knees, and the third beginning with the curving limit of the feet and meeting the bottom of the upper circle at the waist.

For us, these stylizations recall works of modern sculpture, but originally their smooth marble surfaces were enlivened by painted motifs in blue, red, and, more rarely, green paint, emphasizing their surfaces

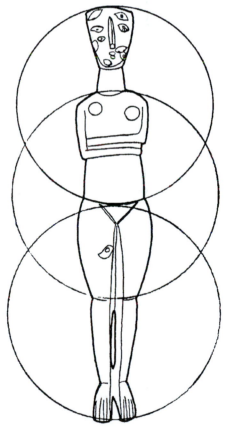

4–2 FIGURE OF A WOMAN WITH A DRAWING SHOWING EVIDENCE OF ORIGINAL PAINTING AND OUTLINING DESIGN SCHEME

From the Cyclades. c. 2600–2400 BCE. Marble, height 24¾" (62.8 cm).
Figure: Metropolitan Museum of Art, New York.
Gift of Christos G. Bastis (68.148). Drawing: Elizabeth Hendrix.

Credit: © 2016. Image copyright The Metropolitan Museum of Art/Art Resource/Scala, Florence

rather than their three-dimensional shapes. Today, evidence of such painting is extremely faint, but many patterns have been recovered using controlled lighting and microscopic investigation. Unlike the forms themselves, the painted features are often asymmetrical in organization. In the example illustrated here, wide-open eyes appear on forehead, cheeks, and thigh, as well as on either side of the nose.

Art historians have proposed a variety of explanations for these painted motifs. The angled lines on some figures' bodies could reflect the way Cycladic peoples decorated their own bodies—whether permanently with tattoos or scarification or temporarily with body paint, applied either during their lifetimes or to prepare their bodies for burial. The staring eyes, which seem to demand the viewer's return gaze, may have been a way of connecting these figures to those who owned or used them. And eyes on locations other than faces may aim to draw viewers' attention—perhaps even healing powers—to a particular area of the body. Some have associated eyes on bellies with pregnancy.

Art historian Gail Hoffman has argued that patterns of vertical red lines painted on the faces of some figures (**FIG. 4-3**) were related to Cycladic rituals of mourning their dead. Perhaps these sculptures were used in relation to a succession of key moments throughout their owners' lifetimes—such as puberty, marriage, and death—and were continually repainted with motifs associated with each ritual, before finally following their owners into their graves at death. Since there is no written evidence from Cycladic culture and no information on the archaeological contexts of many works, it is difficult to be certain, but these sculptures were clearly important to Bronze Age Cycladic peoples and seem to have taken on meaning in relationship to their use.

Although some Cycladic islands retained their distinctive artistic traditions, by the Middle and Later Bronze Age, the art and culture of the Cyclades as a whole was overtaken first by Minoan and later by Mycenaean culture.

The Minoan Civilization on Crete

What characterizes the art and architecture of the Minoan Old and New Palace periods, even beyond the island of Crete?

As early as the Neolithic period, there was large-scale migration to and permanent settlement on Crete, the largest of the Aegean islands (155 miles long and 36 miles wide). By the Bronze Age, Crete was economically self-sufficient, producing its own grains, olives and other fruits, cattle, and sheep. With many safe harbors and a convenient location, Crete became a wealthy sea power, trading with mainland Greece, Egypt, the Near East, and Anatolia, thus acquiring the ores necessary for producing bronze.

Between about 1900 BCE and 1375 BCE, a distinctive culture flourished on Crete. The British archaeologist Sir Arthur Evans (see "Pioneers of Aegean Archaeology" opposite) named it Minoan after the legend of Minos, a king who had ruled from the capital, Knossos. According to this legend, a half-man, half-bull monster called the Minotaur—son of the wife of King Minos and a bull belonging to the sea god Poseidon—lived at Knossos in a maze called the Labyrinth. To satisfy the Minotaur's appetite for human flesh, King Minos ordered the mainland kingdom of Athens to send a yearly tribute of 14 young men and women, a practice that ended when the Athenian hero Theseus killed the beast.

Minoan chronology is divided into two main periods, the Old Palace period from about 1900 to 1700 BCE and the New Palace period from around 1700 to 1450 BCE.

4-3 HEAD WITH REMAINS OF PAINTED DECORATION
From the Cyclades. c. 2500–2200 BCE. Marble and red pigment, height 9¹¹⁄₁₆″ (24.6 cm). National Museum, Copenhagen. (4697).

Credit: National Museum, Copenhagen (4697)

RECOVERING THE PAST

PIONEERS OF AEGEAN ARCHAEOLOGY

Heinrich Schliemann (1822–1890) is seen by some as the founder of the modern study of Aegean civilization. Schliemann was the son of an impoverished German minister and a largely self-educated man who spoke several languages. He worked hard, grew rich, and retired in 1863 to pursue his lifelong dream of becoming an archaeologist, inspired by the Greek poet Homer's epic tales, the *Iliad* and the *Odyssey*. In 1869, he began conducting fieldwork in Greece and Turkey. Scholars of that time considered Homer's stories pure fiction, but by studying the descriptions of geography in the *Iliad*, Schliemann located a multilayered site at Hissarlik, in present-day Turkey, whose sixth level up from the bedrock is now generally accepted as the closest chronological approximation of Homer's Troy. After his success in Anatolia, Schliemann pursued his hunch that the grave sites of Homer's Greek royal family would be found inside the citadel at Mycenae. But the graves he found were too early to contain the bodies of Atreus, Agamemnon, and their relatives—a fact only established through recent scholarship, after Schliemann's death.

The uncovering at Knossos of what Schliemann had thought was the palace of the legendary King Minos fell to a British archaeologist, Sir Arthur Evans (1851–1941), who led the excavation between 1900 and 1905. Evans gave the name Minoan—after legendary King Minos—to Bronze Age culture on Crete. He also made a first attempt to establish an absolute chronology for Minoan art, basing his conjectures on datable Egyptian artifacts found in the ruins on Crete and on Minoan artifacts found in Egypt. Later scholars, though, have revised and refined both his dating and his interpretations of what he found at Knossos.

Evans was not the only pioneering archaeologist drawn to excavate on Crete. Boston-born Harriet Boyd Hawes (1871–1945), after graduating from Smith College in 1892 with a major in Classics and a subsequent year of post-graduate study in Athens, traveled to Crete to find a site where she could begin a career in archaeology. She was in Knossos in 1900 to observe Evans's early work and was soon supervising her own excavations, first at Kavousi and then at Gournia, where she directed work from 1901 until 1904. She is famous for the timely and thorough publication of her findings, accomplished while she was not only supervising these Bronze Age digs, but also pursuing her career as a beloved professor of the liberal arts, first at Smith and later at Wellesley College.

The Old Palace Period, c. 1900–1700 BCE

Minoan civilization remained very much a mystery until 1900 CE, when Sir Arthur Evans began uncovering the buried ruins of the architectural complex at Knossos, on Crete's north coast, that had been occupied in the Neolithic period, then built over with a succession of Bronze Age structures.

ARCHITECTURAL COMPLEXES Like the nineteenth-century excavators before him, Evans called these great architectural complexes "palaces." He believed they had been occupied by a succession of kings. While some scholars continue to believe this, the evidence has suggested to others that Minoan society was not ruled by kings drawn from a royal family, but by a confederation of aristocrats or aristocratic families who established a fluid and evolving power hierarchy. In this light, some scholars interpret these elaborate complexes as sites of periodic religious ritual, perhaps enacted by a community that gathered within the courtyards that are their core architectural feature.

The walls of early Minoan buildings were made of rubble and mud bricks faced with cut and finished local stone, the first evidence of **dressed stone** used as a building material in the Aegean. Columns and other interior elements were made of wood. Both in large complexes and in the surrounding towns, timber appears to have been used for framing and bracing walls. Its strength and flexibility would have minimized damage from the earthquakes common to the area. Nevertheless, an earthquake in c. 1700 BCE severely damaged buildings at several sites, including Knossos and Phaistos.

CERAMICS During the Old Palace period, Minoans developed elegant new types of ceramics, spurred in part by the introduction of the potter's wheel early in the second millennium BCE. One type is called Kamares ware after the cave on Mount Ida overlooking the architectural complex at Phaistos, in southern Crete, where it was first discovered. The hallmarks of this select ceramic ware—so sought-after that it was exported as far away as Egypt and Syria—were its extreme thinness, its use of color, and its graceful, stylized painted decoration. An example from about 2000–1900 BCE has a globular body and a "beaked" pouring spout (**FIG. 4-4**). Created from brown, red, and creamy white pigments on a black body, the bold, curving forms—derived from plant life—that decorate this jug seem to swell with its bulging contours.

4-4 KAMARES WARE JUG

From Phaistos, Crete. Old Palace period, c. 2000–1900 BCE. Ceramic, height 10⅝″ (27 cm). Archaeological Museum, Iraklion, Crete.

Credit: © Craig & Marie Mauzy, Athens

The New Palace Period, c. 1700–1450 BCE

The early architectural complex at Knossos, erected about 1900 BCE, formed the core of an elaborate new one built after a terrible earthquake shook Crete in c. 1700 BCE. This rebuilding, at Knossos and elsewhere, belonged to the New Palace period and is considered by many scholars to be the highest point of Minoan civilization. In its heyday, the Knossos complex covered six acres (**FIG. 4-5**).

Damaged structures were repaired and enlarged, and the resulting new complexes shared a number of features. Multistoried, flat-roofed, and with many columns, they were designed to maximize light and air, as well as define access and circulation patterns. Daylight and fresh air entered through staggered levels, open stairwells, and strategically placed air shafts and light-wells (**FIG. 4-6**).

Large, central courtyards—not audience halls or temples—were the most prominent components of these rectangular complexes. Suites of rooms were arranged around them. Corridors and staircases led from the central and subsidiary courtyards through apartments, ritual areas, and storerooms. Walls were coated with plaster, and some were painted with murals. Floors were plaster, or plaster mixed with pebbles, stone, wood, or beaten earth. The residential quarters had many luxuries: sunlit courtyards

4-5 RECONSTRUCTION DRAWING OF THE "PALACE" COMPLEX, KNOSSOS, CRETE

As it would have appeared during the New Palace period. Site occupied since the Neolithic period; the Minoan complex of the Old Palace period (c. 1900–1700 BCE) was rebuilt during the New Palace period (c. 1700–1450 BCE) after earthquakes and fires; final destruction c. 1375 BCE.

Credit: Illustration: Peter Bull

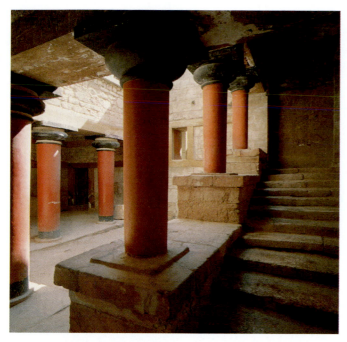

4–6 EAST WING STAIRWELL

"Palace" complex, Knossos, Crete. New Palace period, c. 1700–1450 BCE.

Credit: © Roger Wood/Corbis

or light-wells, richly colored murals, and sophisticated plumbing systems.

Workshops clustered around the complexes formed commercial centers. Storeroom walls were lined with enormous clay jars for oil and wine, and in their floors stone-lined pits from earlier structures were used for the storage of grain. The huge scale of the centralized food management became apparent when excavators at Knossos found in a single (although more recent) storeroom enough ceramic jars to hold 20,000 gallons of olive oil.

Because double-axe motifs were used in its architectural decoration, the Knossos "palace" was referred to in later Greek legends as the Labyrinth, meaning the "House of the Double Axes" (Greek *labrys*, "double axe"). The organization of the complex seemed so complicated that the word labyrinth eventually came to mean "maze" and became part of the Minotaur legend.

This complicated layout provided the complex with its own internal security system: a baffling array of doors leading to unfamiliar rooms, stairs, yet more corridors, or even dead ends. Admittance could be denied by blocking corridors, and some rooms were accessible only from upper terraces. Close analysis, however, shows that the builders had laid out a square grid following predetermined principles and that the now-confusing layout may partially be the result of later earthquake destruction and rebuilding over the centuries.

In typical Minoan fashion, the rebuilt Knossos complex was organized around a large central courtyard (SEE FIG. 4–5). A few steps led from the courtyard down into

the so-called Throne Room to the west, and a great staircase on the east side descended to the Hall of the Double Axes, an unusually grand example of a Minoan hall. (Evans gave the rooms their misleading but romantic names.) This hall and others were supported by the unique Minoan-type wooden columns that became standard in Aegean palace architecture (SEE FIG. 4–6). The tree trunks from which the columns were made were inverted so that they tapered toward the bottom; they were topped with a broad, flattened capital.

Rooms, following tradition, were arranged around a central space rather than along an axis, as we have seen in Egypt and will see in mainland Greece. During the New Palace period, suites functioned as archives, business centers, and residences. Some must also have had a religious function, though the temples, shrines, and elaborate tombs seen in Egypt are not found in Minoan architecture.

BULL LEAPING AT KNOSSOS Minoan painters worked on a large scale, covering entire walls of rooms with geometric borders, views of nature, and scenes of human activity.

Murals can be painted on a still-wet plaster surface (**buon fresco**) or a dry one (**fresco secco**). The wet technique binds pigments to the wall, but forces the painter to work very quickly. On a dry wall, the painter need not hurry, but the pigments tend to flake off over time. Minoans used both techniques.

Minoan wall painting displays elegant drawing, and Minoan painters, like the Egyptians, filled these linear contours with bright and unshaded fields of pure color. They preferred profile or full-faced views, and they turned natural forms into decorative patterns. One of the most famous paintings of Knossos depicts one of the most prominent subjects in Minoan art: **BULL LEAPING** (**FIG. 4–7**). The panel—restored from excavated fragments—is one of a group of paintings of bulls from a room in the east wing of the complex. The action—perhaps representing an initiation or fertility ritual—shows three scantily clad youths around a gigantic, dappled bull, which is charging in the **"flying-gallop"** pose. The pale-skinned person at the right—her paleness probably identifying her as a woman—is prepared to catch the dark-skinned man in the midst of his leap, and the pale-skinned woman at the left grasps the bull by its horns, perhaps to help steady it or to begin her own vault. Framing the action are strips of overlapping shapes filled with ornament set within striped bands.

STATUETTE OF A MALE FIGURE FROM PALAIKASTRO Surviving Minoan sculpture consists mainly of small, finely executed work in wood, ivory, precious metals, stone, and ceramic. **Faience** (colorfully glazed fine ceramic) female figurines holding serpents are among the most characteristic images and may have been associated with water, regenerative power, and protection of the

4–7 BULL LEAPING

Wall painting with areas of modern reconstruction, from the "palace" complex, Knossos, Crete. Late Minoan period, c. 1450–1375 BCE. Height approx. 24½" (62.3 cm). Archaeological Museum, Iraklion, Crete.

Careful sifting during excavation preserved many fragments of the paintings that once covered the walls at Knossos. The pieces were painstakingly sorted and cleaned by restorers and reassembled into puzzle pictures; more pieces were missing than found. Areas of color have been used in this reconstruction to fill the gaps, making it obvious which bits are the restored portions, but allowing us to have a sense of the original image.

Credit: © Craig & Marie Mauzy, Athens

home. But among the most impressive works is an unusually large male figure that has been reconstructed from hundreds of fragments excavated in eastern Crete at Palaikastro between 1987 and 1990 (**FIG. 4-8**). The blackened state of the remains is evidence of a fire that must have destroyed the building where it was kept, since fire damage pervades the archaeological layer in which these fragments were found. The cause or meaning of this fire is a mystery.

The statuette is a multimedia work assembled from a variety of mostly precious materials. The majority of the body was carved in exquisite anatomical detail—including renderings of subcutaneous veins, tendons, and bones—from the ivory of two hippopotamus teeth, with a gap in the lower torso for a wooden insert to which was attached a kilt made of gold foil. Miniature gold sandals slipped onto the small, tapering feet. The head was carved of gray serpentine with inset eyes of rock crystal, just as inlaid wooden nipples

detail the figure's torso. The ivory and gold may have been imported—perhaps from Egypt—but the style is characteristically Minoan (COMPARE FIG. 4-7). We know very little about the context and virtually nothing about the meaning or use of this figure, but the nature of the materials and the large size suggest that it was important. Some have interpreted this as the cult statue of a young god, while others have proposed it was a votive effigy for a religious ceremony, but these remain speculations.

STONE RHYTONS   Almost certainly of ritual significance are a series of stone **rhytons**—vessels used for pouring

4–8 STATUETTE OF A MALE FIGURE

From Palaikastro, Crete. c. 1500–1475 BCE. Ivory, gold, serpentine, rock crystal, and wood; height 19½" (50 cm). Archaeological Museum, Siteia, Crete.

Credit: British School at Athens by permission of the Management Committee (courtesy of the Department of Classics, University of Columbia USA. Photo © L.H.Sackett)

4–9 TWO VIEWS OF THE HARVESTER RHYTON

From Hagia Triada, Crete. New Palace period, c. 1650–1450 BCE. Steatite, greatest diameter 4½″ (11.3 cm). Archaeological Museum, Heraklion, Crete.

Credit: (left) © Craig & Marie Mauzy, Athens; (right) © 2016. Marie Mauzy/Scala, Florence

liquids—that Minoans carved from steatite (a greenish or brown soapstone) and serpentine (usually dull green in color). These have been found in fragments and reconstructed by archaeologists. **THE HARVESTER RHYTON** was a cone-shaped vessel, barely 4½ inches in diameter (**FIG. 4–9**). Only the upper part is preserved.

THE HARVESTER Rhyton may have been covered with gold leaf, a technically demanding process in which artists affix paper-thin sheets of hammered gold to the surface being **gilded** (see "Aegean Metalworking" on page 93).

A rowdy procession of 27 men has been crowded onto its curving surface. The piece is exceptional for relationships among the figures, who overlap and jostle one another instead of marching in patterned single file in the manner of some Near Eastern or Egyptian art. The exuberance of this scene is especially notable in the emotions expressed on the men's faces. They march and chant to a *sistrum*—a rattlelike percussion instrument—lifted by a man whose wide-open mouth seems to signal singing at the top of his lungs. The men have large, bold features and sinewy bodies so trim we can see their ribs. One stands out from the crowd because of his long hair, scale-covered ceremonial cloak, and commanding staff. Archaeologists have proposed a variety of interpretations for the scene—a spring planting or fall harvest festival, a religious procession, a dance, a crowd of warriors, or a gang of forced laborers.

Bulls are a recurrent theme in Minoan art, and rhytons were also made in the form of a bull's head (**FIG. 4–10**). The sculptor carved this one from a block of greenish-black serpentine to create an image that approaches animal portraiture.

4–10 BULL'S-HEAD RHYTON

From Knossos, Crete. New Palace period, c. 1550–1450 BCE. Serpentine with shell, rock crystal, and red jasper; the gilt-wood horns are restorations, height 12″ (30.5 cm). Archaeological Museum, Iraklion, Crete.

Credit: © akg-images/Nimatallah

Lightly engraved lines, filled with white powder to make them visible, enliven the animal's coat: short, curly hair on top of the head; longer, shaggy strands on the sides; and circular patterns along the neck suggest its dappled coloring. White bands of shell outline the nostrils, and painted rock crystal and red jasper form the eyes. The horns (here restored) were made of wood covered with gold leaf. This rhyton was filled with liquid through a hole in the bull's neck, and during rituals, fluid was poured out through its mouth.

CERAMICS   The ceramic arts, so splendidly realized early on in Kamares ware, continued throughout the New Palace period. Some of the most striking ceramics are characterized as Marine style because of the depictions of sea life on their surfaces. In a stoppered bottle of this type known as the **OCTOPUS FLASK**, made about 1500–1450 BCE (FIG. 4–11), the painter created a dynamic arrangement of marine life, in seeming celebration of Minoan maritime skill. Like microscopic life teeming in a drop of pond water, sea creatures float around an octopus's tangled tentacles. The decoration on the earlier Kamares ware jug (SEE FIG. 4–4) had reinforced the solidity of its surface, but here the pottery surface seems to dissolve. The painter captured the grace and energy of natural forms while presenting them as a stylized design in harmony with the vessel's bulging shape.

4–11 OCTOPUS FLASK

From Palaikastro, Crete. New Palace period, c. 1500–1450 BCE. Marine-style ceramic, height 11″ (28 cm). Archaeological Museum, Heraklion, Crete.

Credit: © Craig & Marie Mauzy, Athens

4–12 PENDANT OF GOLD BEES

From Chryssolakkos, near Malia, Crete. New Palace period, c. 1700–1550 BCE. Gold, height approx. 1¹³⁄₁₆″ (4.6 cm). Archaeological Museum, Heraklion, Crete.

Credit: Studio Kontos Photostock

METALWORK   By about 1700 BCE, Aegean metalworkers were producing objects that rivaled those of Near Eastern and Egyptian jewelers, whose techniques they may have learned and adopted. For a pendant in gold found at Chryssolakkos, the artist arched a pair of easily recognizable but geometrically stylized bees (or perhaps wasps) around a honeycomb of gold granules, providing their sleek bodies with a single pair of outspread wings (FIG. 4–12). The pendant hangs from a spiderlike filigree form with what appear to be long legs encircling a tiny gold ball. Small disks dangle from the ends of the wings and the point where the insects' bodies meet.

The Spread of Minoan Culture

About 1450 BCE, a conquering people from mainland Greece known as Mycenaeans arrived in Crete. They occupied the buildings at Knossos and elsewhere until a final catastrophe and the destruction of Knossos about 1375 BCE caused them to abandon the site. But by 1400 BCE, the center of political and cultural power in the Aegean had shifted to mainland Greece.

The skills of Minoan artists, particularly metalsmiths, had made them highly sought after on the mainland. A pair of magnificent gold cups found in a large tomb at Vapheio, on the Greek mainland south of Sparta, were made sometime between 1650 and 1450 BCE either by Minoan artists or by locals trained in Minoan style and techniques. One

Technique

AEGEAN METALWORKING

Aegean artists created exquisite luxury goods from imported gold. Their techniques included lost-wax casting (see "Lost-Wax Casting" in Chapter 14 on page 428), inlay, filigree, granulation, repoussé, niello, and gilding.

The early Minoan pendant with a pair of gold bees (SEE FIG. 4–12) exemplifies early sophistication in **filigree** (delicate decoration with fine wires) and **granulation** (minute granules or balls fused to underlying forms), the latter used to enliven the surfaces and to outline or even create three-dimensional shapes.

The Vapheio Cup (SEE FIG. 4–13) and the funerary mask (SEE FIG. 4–21) are examples of **repoussé**, in which artists gently pushed up relief forms (perhaps by hammering) from the back of a thin sheet of gold. Experienced goldsmiths may have formed simple designs freehand or used standard wood forms or punches. For more elaborate decorations they would first have sculpted the entire design in wood or clay and then used this form to mold the gold sheet.

The artists who created the Mycenaean dagger blade (SEE FIG. 4–22) not only inlaid one metal into another, but also employed a special technique called **niello**, still a common method of metal decoration. Powdered nigellum—a black alloy of lead, silver, and copper with sulfur—was rubbed into very fine engraved lines in a silver or gold surface, then fused to the surrounding metal with heat. The resulting lines appear as black drawings.

---

side of one cup is shown here (FIG. 4–13). The relief designs were executed in repoussé—the technique of pushing up a sheet of metal from the back. The handles were attached with rivets, and the cup was then lined with sheet gold. In the scenes circling the cups, men are depicted trying to capture bulls in various ways. Here, a scantily clad man has roped a bull's hind leg. The figures dominate the landscape and bulge from the surface with a muscular vitality that belies the cup's small size—it is only 4½ inches tall. The depiction of olive trees could indicate that the scene is set in a sacred grove. The cups may illustrate exploits in some long-lost heroic tale—or just commonplace herding scenes.

WALL PAINTING AT AKROTIRI ON THERA Minoan cultural influences seem to have spread to the Cyclades as well as mainland Greece. Thera, for example, was so heavily under Crete's influence in the New Palace period that it was a veritable outpost of Minoan culture. A girl picking crocuses in a fresco in a house at Akrotiri (SEE FIG. 4–1) wears a typically colorful Minoan flounced skirt with a short-sleeved, open-breasted bodice, large earrings, and bracelets. This wall painting demonstrates the sophisticated decorative sense found in Minoan art, both in color selection and in surface detail. The room in which this painting appears seems to have been dedicated to young women's coming-of-age ceremonies, and its frescos provided the visual context for ritual activity, just as the courtyards of architectural complexes in Crete had.

In another Akrotiri house, an artist created an imaginative landscape of hills, rocks, and flowers (FIG. 4–14), the first pure landscape painting we have encountered in ancient art. A viewer standing in the center of the room is surrounded by orange, rose, and blue rocky hillocks sprouting oversized, deep-red lilies. Swallows, sketched by a few deft lines, swoop above and around the flowers. The artist unified the rhythmic flow of the undulating landscape, the stylized patterning of the natural forms, and the decorative use of bright colors alternating with darker, neutral tones, perhaps meant to represent areas of shadow. The colors may seem fanciful to us, but present-day sailors attest to their accuracy, suggesting that these artists recorded the actual colors of Thera's wet rocks in the sunshine—a celebration of the natural world very different from the cool, stable elegance of Egyptian wall painting.

Direct references to the geology of Thera also appear in a long strip of wall painting known as the "Flotilla Fresco" (see "Closer Look" on pages 94–95) running along the tops of the walls in the room of a house in Akrotiri, a domestic context comparable to that of the fresco of the girl gathering crocuses.

This expansive tableau was for years interpreted as a long-distance voyage with a military flavor, but in 2010 art

4–13 VAPHEIO CUP
One of two cups found near Sparta, Greece. c. 1650–1450 BCE. Gold, height 4½" (11.3 cm). National Archaeological Museum, Athens.

Credit: © Craig & Marie Mauzy, Athens

4–14 LANDSCAPE ("SPRING FRESCO")

Wall painting with areas of modern reconstruction, from Akrotiri, Thera, Cyclades. Before 1630 BCE. National Archaeological Museum, Athens.

Credit: © akg-images/Nimatallah

historian Thomas Strasser argued convincingly that this is a specific seascape viewed from the eastern interior of the island of Thera itself, looking toward the western opening between two peninsular mountainous landmasses, populated by local ships and the dolphins that leap around them. The land and sea of Thera may be the principal subject of this painting.

A Closer Look

THE "FLOTILLA FRESCO" FROM AKROTIRI

The **depiction of lions chasing deer**, perhaps signifying heroism or political power, has a long history in Aegean art.

This block of land seems to represent one of two spits of land in Thera that separate the sea from an enclosed area of water in a volcanic basin at the center of the island. Both the volcanic quality of the painted rocks and their division into horizontal registers as bands of color reproduce the actual geological appearance of this terrain.

The arrangement of ships and leaping dolphins in the center uses vertical perspective (see Starter Kit on page xviii) to indicate spatial recession. In this system, higher placement is given to things that are in the distance, while those placed lower are closer to the viewer.

4–15 "THE FLOTILLA FRESCO"

Detail of the left part of a mural from Room 5 of West House, Akrotiri, Thera. New Palace period, c. 1650 BCE. Height 14⁵⁄₁₆″ (44 cm). National Archaeological Museum, Athens.

Credit: © akg-images/Nimatallah

The Mycenaean (Helladic) Culture

What features distinguish the art and architecture of the Mycenaeans on the Greek mainland from other Aegean Bronze Age cultures?

Archaeologists use the term *Helladic* (from *Hellas*, the Greek name for Greece) to designate the Aegean Bronze Age on mainland Greece. The Helladic period extends from about 3000 to 1000 BCE, contemporary with Cycladic and Minoan cultures. In the early part of the Aegean Bronze Age, Greek-speaking peoples, probably from the northwest, moved into the area. They brought with them advanced techniques for metalworking, ceramics, and architectural design, and they displaced the local Neolithic culture. Later in the Aegean Bronze Age, the people of the mainland city of Mycenae rose to power and extended their influence into the Aegean islands as well.

Helladic Architecture

Mycenaean architecture developed in ways distinct from those of the Minoans. Mycenaeans built fortified strongholds called citadels to protect the palaces of their rulers. These palaces contained a characteristic architectural unit called a **megaron** that was axial in plan, consisting of a large room entered through a porch with columns and sometimes a vestibule. The Mycenaeans also buried their dead in magnificent vaulted tombs, round in floor plan and crafted of cut stone.

MYCENAE Later Greek writers called the walled complex of Mycenae (**FIG. 4-16**) the home of Agamemnon, legendary Greek king and leader of the Greek army that conquered the great city of Troy, as described in Homer's epic poem the *Iliad*. The site was occupied from the Neolithic period to around 1050 BCE. The walls were rebuilt three times—c. 1340 BCE, c. 1250 BCE, and c. 1200 BCE—each

Each of the seven vessels of the fleet (only four can be seen in this partial view) is unique in size, decoration (this one has lions painted on its side), and rigging. This tableau may show a single moment from a nautical festival, perhaps a spring ceremony to kick off a new season of sailing.

Note the difference between the surviving fragments of the original fresco and the modern infill in this restored presentation of a dolphin swimming alongside the ships.

4–16 CITADEL AT MYCENAE

Peloponnese, Greece. Aerial view. Site occupied c. 1600–1200 BCE; walls built c. 1340, 1250, 1200 BCE, creating a progressively larger enclosure.

Credit: © akg-images/Albatross/Duby Tal

time stronger and enclosing more space than the last. The second walls were pierced by the monumental Lion Gate (at bottom left in this view of the archaeological site from above). The final walls were extended to protect the water supply, an underground cistern. These walls were about 25 feet thick and nearly 30 feet high. Their drywall masonry, using largely unworked boulders, is known as **cyclopean**, because at one time it was believed that only the enormous Cyclopes (legendary one-eyed giants) could have moved such massive stones.

Even today, the monumental gateway to the citadel at Mycenae (**FIG. 4-17**) is an impressive reminder of the importance of the city. As in Near Eastern citadels, the Lion Gate was provided with guardian figures, which stand above the door rather than to the sides in the door jambs. The gate is today a simple opening, but its importance is indicated by the material of the flanking walls, a conglomerate stone that can be polished to glistening multicolors. A corbeled relieving **arch** above the lintel forms a triangle filled with a limestone panel bearing a grand heraldic composition—guardian beasts flanking a single Minoan column that swells upward to a large, bulbous capital.

The archival photograph (SEE FIG. 4-17) shows a group posing jauntily outside the gate, including Heinrich Schliemann standing at the left, and his wife and partner in archaeology, Sophia, sitting at the right. Schliemann had already "discovered" Troy, and when he turned his attention to Mycenae in 1876, he unearthed graves containing rich treasures, including gold masks. The grave circle he excavated lay just inside the Lion Gate.

The Lion Gate has been the subject of much speculation in recent years. What are the animals? What does the architectural feature mean? How is the imagery to be interpreted? The beasts supporting and defending the column are magnificent, supple creatures rearing up on hind legs. Their faces must once have been turned toward the visitor, but today only the attachment holes from their heads remain.

A metaphor for power, the lions rest their feet on Minoan-style altars. Between them stands the mysterious Minoan column, also on the altar base. Clearly the Mycenaeans are borrowing symbolic vocabulary from Crete. But scholars do not agree on what this composition means: It may represent a temple, a palace, the entire city, or the god of the place. The column and capital support a lintel or architrave, which in turn supports the butt ends of logs forming rafters of the horizontal roof, so the most likely theory is that the structure is the symbol of a palace or a temple. But some scholars suggest that by extension it becomes the symbol of a king or a deity. If so, the imagery of the Lion Gate, with its combination of guardian beasts and divine or royal palace, signifies the legitimate power of the ruler of Mycenae.

From the Lion Gate, the Great Ramp led up the hillside past a grave circle to the courtyard for the building occupying the highest point in the center of the city, which may have been the residence of a ruler. From the courtyard one entered a porch, a vestibule, and finally the megaron, which seems to be the intended destination, in contrast to Minoan complexes where the courtyard itself seems to be the destination. The great room of a typical megaron had a central hearth surrounded by four large columns that supported the ceiling. The roof above the hearth was probably raised to admit light and air and permit smoke to escape (SEE FIG. 4–18). Some architectural historians think that the megaron eventually came to be associated with royalty. The later Greeks adapted its form when building temples, which they saw as earthly palaces for their gods.

PYLOS   The rulers of Mycenae fortified their city, but the people of Pylos, in the extreme southwest of the Peloponnese, perhaps felt that their more remote and defensible location made them less vulnerable to attack. This seems not to have been the case, for within a century of its construction in c. 1340 BCE, the palace at Pylos was destroyed by fires, apparently set during the violent upheavals that brought about the collapse of Mycenae itself.

4–17 LION GATE, MYCENAE

c. 1250 BCE. Limestone relief, height of sculpture approx. 9′ 6″ (2.9 m).

In this historic photograph Heinrich Schliemann, director of the excavation beginning in 1876, stands to the left of the gate, and his wife and partner in archaeology, Sophia, sits to the right.

Credit: Deutsches Archaeologisches Institut, Athens (D-DAI-ATH-Mykene63). All rights reserved.

4–18 RECONSTRUCTION DRAWING OF THE CITADEL AT MYCENAE AT ITS MOST DEVELOPED STATE

Unlike at Knossos and Akrotiri, where we can understand multistory structures because multiple levels survived and have been excavated, at Mycenae we have, for the most part, only foundations. To a certain extent, we can only speculate about the upper portions of these buildings.

Credit: © Dorling Kindersley

4-19 PLAN OF THE MEGARON OF THE PYLOS PALACE
c. 1300–1200 BCE.

The architectural complex at Pylos was built on a raised site without fortifications, organized around a special area that included an archive, storerooms, workshops, and a megaron (**FIG. 4-19**) with a formal throne room that may also have been used to host feasting rituals involving elite members of the community. Including a porch and vestibule facing the courtyard, the Pylos megaron was a magnificent display of architectural and decorative skill.

The reconstruction shown here (**FIG. 4-20**) shows how it might have looked. Every inch was painted—floors, ceilings, beams, and door frames with brightly colored abstract designs, and walls with paintings of large mythical animals and highly stylized plant and landscape forms. Flanking the throne (on the back wall of the reconstruction) are monumental paintings of lions and griffins. A circular hearth sits in the middle, set into a floor finished with plaster painted with imitations of stone and tile patterns. There was a spot in the megaron where priests and priestesses poured libations to a deity from a ceremonial

rhyton, fostering communication between the people of Pylos and their god or gods.

Clay tablets found in the ruins of the palace include an inventory of its elegant furnishings. The listing on one tablet reads: "One ebony chair with golden back decorated with birds; and a footstool decorated with ivory pomegranates. One ebony chair with ivory back carved with a pair of finials and with a man's figure and heifers; one footstool, ebony inlaid with ivory and pomegranates."

Mycenaean Tombs

SHAFT GRAVES Tombs were given much greater prominence in the Helladic culture of the mainland than they were by the Minoans, and ultimately they became the most architecturally sophisticated monuments of the entire Aegean Bronze Age. The earliest burials were in **shaft graves**, vertical pits 20 to 25 feet deep. In Mycenae, the graves of important people were enclosed in a circle of standing stone slabs. In these graves, the ruling families laid out their dead in opulent dress and jewelry and surrounded them with ceremonial weapons, gold and silver wares, and other articles indicative of their status, wealth, and power.

Among the 30 pounds of gold objects Schliemann found in the shaft graves of Mycenae were five funerary masks, one of which he identified as the face of Agamemnon, commander-in-chief of the Greek forces in Homer's account of the Trojan War (**FIG. 4-21**). We now know the masks have nothing to do with the heroes of the Trojan War, since the Mycenae graves are about 300 years older than Schliemann believed and the burial practices they display were different from those described by Homer.

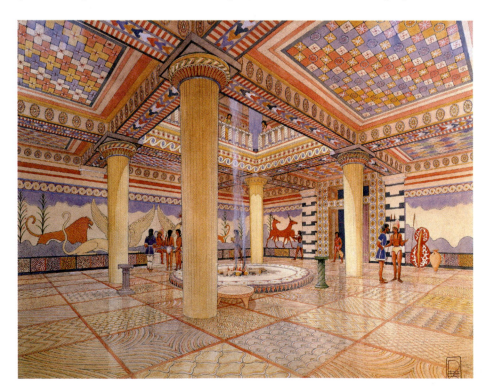

4-20 RECONSTRUCTION DRAWING OF THE MEGARON (GREAT ROOM) OF THE PYLOS PALACE

c. 1300–1200 BCE. Watercolor by Piet de Jong.

English artist Piet de Jong (1887–1967) began his career as an architect, but his service in the post-World War I reconstruction of Greece inspired him to focus his talents on recording and reconstructing Greek archaeological excavations. In 1922, Arthur Evans called him to work on the reconstructions at Knossos. Piet de Jong spent the rest of his life creating fanciful but archaeologically informed visions of the original appearance of some of the greatest twentieth-century discoveries of ancient Greece and the Aegean during a long association with the British School of Archaeology in Athens.

Credit: © akg-images/De Agostini Picture Lib./G. Dagli Orti

RECOVERING THE PAST

THE "MASK OF AGAMEMNON"

One of Heinrich Schliemann's most famous discoveries in the shaft graves in Mycenae was a solid gold mask that had been placed over the face of a body he claimed was the legendary Agamemnon (SEE FIG. 4–21), uncovered on November 30, 1876. But Schliemann's identification of the mask with this king of Homeric legend has been disproven, and even the authenticity of the mask itself has been called into question over the last 30 years.

Doubts are rooted in a series of stylistic features that separate this mask from the other four excavated by Schliemann in Grave Circle A: the treatment of the eyes and eyebrows, the cut-out separation of the ears from the flap of gold around the face, and, most strikingly, the beard and handlebar mustache that have suspicious parallels with nineteenth-century fashion in facial hair. Suspicions founded on such anomalies are reinforced by Schliemann's own history of deceit and embellishment when characterizing his life and discoveries,

not to mention his freewheeling excavation practices when judged against current archaeological standards.

Some specialists have claimed a middle ground between genuine or fake for the mask, suggesting that the artifact itself may be authentic, but that Schliemann quickly subjected it to an overzealous restoration to make the face of "Agamemnon" seem more heroic and noble—at least to viewers in his own day—than the faces of the four other Mycenaean funerary masks. But another scholar has argued that, in fact, this particular mask is not the one Schliemann associated with Agamemnon, undercutting some of the principal arguments for questioning its authenticity in the first place.

The resolution of these questions awaits a full scientific study to determine the nature of the alloy (gold was regularly mixed with small amounts of other metals to make it stronger) from which this mask was made, as well as a microscopic analysis of its technique and the appearance of its surface.

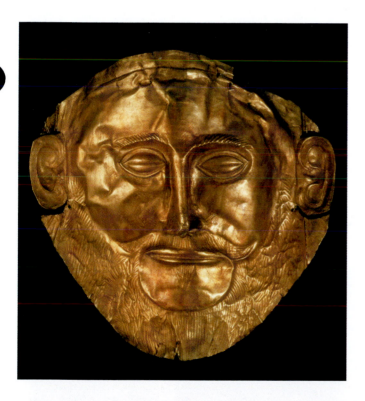

4-21 "MASK OF AGAMEMNON"

Funerary mask, from Shaft Grave V, Grave Circle A, Mycenae, Greece. c. 1600–1550 BCE. Gold, height approx. 12″ (35 cm). National Archaeological Museum, Athens.

Credit: © Craig & Marie Mauzy, Athens

Also found in these shaft graves were bronze **DAGGER BLADES** (FIG. 4-22) decorated with inlaid scenes, further evidence of the wealth of the Mycenaean ruling elite. To form the decoration of daggers like this, Mycenaean artists cut shapes out of different-colored metals (copper, silver, and gold), inlaid them in the bronze blade, and then added fine details in niello (see "Aegean Metalworking" on page 93). In Homer's *Iliad*, the poet describes similar decoration on Agamemnon's armor and Achilles' shield. The blade shown here depicts four lunging hunters—Minoan in style—attacking a charging lion that has already downed one of their companions, who lies under the lion's front legs. Two other lions retreat in full flight. Like the bull in the Minoan fresco (SEE FIG. 4-7), these fleeing animals stretch out in the "flying-gallop" pose to indicate speed and energy.

4-22 DAGGER BLADE WITH LION HUNT

From Shaft Grave IV, Grave Circle A, Mycenae, Greece. c. 1550–1500 BCE. Bronze inlaid with gold, silver, and niello; length 9⅜″ (23.8 cm). National Archaeological Museum, Athens.

Credit: © akg-images/Nimatallah

4-23 CUTAWAY DRAWING OF THOLOS, THE SO-CALLED TREASURY OF ATREUS

Credit: © Dorling Kindersley

THOLOS TOMBS By about 1600 BCE, members of the elite class on the mainland had begun building large above-ground burial places commonly referred to as **tholos** tombs (popularly known as **beehive tombs** because of their rounded, conical shape). More than 100 such tombs have been found, nine of them in the vicinity of Mycenae. Possibly the most impressive is the so-called **TREASURY OF ATREUS** (**FIGS. 4-23, 4-24**), which dates from about 1300 to 1200 BCE.

A walled passageway through the earthen mound covering the tomb, about 114 feet long and 20 feet wide and open to the sky, led to the entrance, which was 34 feet high and had a door 16½ feet high faced with bronze plaques. On either side of the entrance were columns created from a green stone found near Sparta and carved with decoration. The section above the lintel had smaller engaged columns on each side, and the relieving triangle was disguised behind a red-and-green engraved marble panel. The main tomb chamber (**FIG. 4-25**) is a circular room, 47½ feet in diameter and 43 feet high.

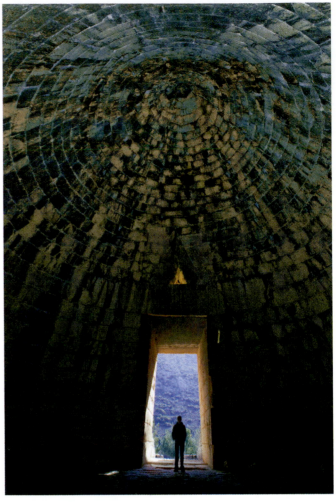

4-25 CORBEL VAULT, INTERIOR OF THOLOS, THE SO-CALLED TREASURY OF ATREUS

Limestone vault, height approx. 43′ (13 m), diameter 47′6″ (14.48 m).

For over a thousand years after it was constructed, this vast vaulted chamber remained the largest unobstructed interior space built in Europe. It was exceeded in size only by the Roman Pantheon (SEE FIG.6–48), built 110–128 CE.

Credit: © Craig & Marie Mauzy, Athens

4-24 EXTERIOR VIEW OF THOLOS, THE SO-CALLED TREASURY OF ATREUS

Mycenae, Greece. c. 1300–1200 BCE.

Credit: © Craig & Marie Mauzy, Athens

It is roofed with a **corbeled vault.** The vault is built up in regular **courses,** or layers, of **ashlar**—precisely cut blocks of stone—smoothly leaning inward and carefully calculated to meet in a single capstone (the topmost stone that joins the sides and completes the structure) at the peak. Covered with earth, the tomb became a conical hill. It was a remarkable engineering feat.

Ceramics

In the final phase of the Helladic Bronze Age, Mycenaean potters created highly refined ceramics. A large **krater**—a bowl for mixing water and wine, used both in feasts and as grave markers—is an example of the technically sophisticated wares being produced on the Greek mainland between 1300 and 1100 BCE. Decorations could be highly stylized, like the scene of marching men on the **WARRIOR KRATER** (FIG. 4-26). On the side shown here, a woman at the far left bids farewell to a group of helmeted men with lances and large shields marching off to the right. The vibrant energy of the Harvester Rhyton or the Vapheio Cup has changed to the regular rhythm inspired by the tramping feet of disciplined warriors. The only indication of the woman's emotions is the gesture of an arm raised to her head, a symbol of mourning. The men seem to be interchangeable parts in a rigidly disciplined war machine.

The succeeding centuries, between about 1100 and 900 BCE, were a time of transformation in the Aegean

4-26 WARRIOR KRATER

From Mycenae, Greece. c. 1300–1100 BCE. Ceramic, height 16" (41 cm). National Archaeological Museum, Athens.

Credit: © Craig & Marie Mauzy, Athens

marked by less political, economic, and artistic complexity and control. A new culture was forming, one that looked back upon the exploits of the Helladic warrior-kings as the glories of a heroic age, while setting the stage for a new Greek civilization.

Think About It

1   Choose a picture or sculpture of a human figure from two of the ancient Aegean cultures examined in this chapter. Characterize how the artist represents the human form and how that representation could be related to the cultural significance of the works in their original contexts.

2   Assess the methods of two archaeologists whose work is discussed in this chapter. How have they recovered, reconstructed, and interpreted the material culture of the Aegean Bronze Age?

3   What explanations have art historians proposed for the use and cultural significance of the figures of women that have been excavated in the Cyclades?

4   Compare the plans of the architectural complexes at Knossos and Mycenae. How have the arrangements of the buildings helped archaeologists to think about how these complexes were related to their cultural contexts and ritual or political uses?

Crosscurrents

Discuss the differences in style between these two works of ancient painting. Consider the different modes of representing human figures as well as the ways those figures are related to their surroundings. Could there be a relationship between the architectural context and the style of presentation?

FIG. 3–36

FIG. 4–1

5–1 Exekias (potter and painter) **AJAX AND ACHILLES PLAYING A GAME**
c. 540–530 BCE. Black-figure painting on a ceramic amphora, height of amphora 24″ (61 cm). Musei Vaticani, Rome.

Credit: Photo © Musei Vaticani/IKONA

Chapter 5
Art of Ancient Greece

Learning Objectives

5.a Identify the visual hallmarks of Greek Geometric, Orientalizing, Archaic, Classical, and Hellenistic period art for formal, technical, and expressive qualities.

5.b Interpret the meaning of works of Greek Geometric, Orientalizing, Archaic, Classical, and Hellenistic period art based on their themes, subjects, and symbols.

5.c Relate artists and works of the distinct periods of Greek Geometric, Orientalizing, Archaic, Classical, and Hellenistic period art to their cultural, economic, and political contexts.

5.d Apply the vocabulary and concepts used to discuss ancient Greek art, artists, and art history.

5.e Interpret ancient Greek art using appropriate art historical methods, such as observation, comparison, and inductive reasoning.

5.f Select visual and textual evidence in various media to support an argument or an interpretation of ancient Greek art.

This elegantly contoured **amphora** was conceived and created to be more than the all-purpose storage jar signaled by its shape, substance, and size (**FIG. 5–1**). A strip around the belly of its bulging form was reserved by Exekias—the mid-sixth-century BCE Athenian artist who signed it proudly as both potter and painter—for a narrative episode from the Trojan War, one of the central stories of the ancient Greeks' mythical conception of their past. Two heroic warriors, Achilles and Ajax, sit across from each other, supporting themselves on their spears as they lean in toward the block between them that serves as a makeshift board for their game of dice. Ajax, to the right, calls out "three"—the spoken word written out on the pot's surface as if coming from his mouth. Achilles counters with "four," the winning number, his victory already suggested by the visual prominence of the boldly silhouetted helmet on his head. (Ajax's headgear has been set aside on his shield, leaning behind him.) Ancient Greek viewers, however, would have understood the tragic irony of Achilles's victory. When these two warriors returned from this playful diversion into the serious contest of battle, Achilles would be killed—and soon afterward, the grieving Ajax would take his own life in despair.

The poignant narrative on this amphora is also a masterful composition. Crisscrossing diagonals and compressed overlapping of spears, bodies, and table describe spatial complexity as well as surface pattern. The varying textures of hair, armor, and clothing are dazzlingly evoked by the alternation between expanses of unarticulated surface and dense patterns of finely incised lines. Careful contours convey a sense of three-dimensional human form. And the arrangement coordinates with the shape of the vessel itself, its curving outline matched by the warriors' bending backs, the line of its handles continued in the tilt of the leaning shields.

There is no hint here of gods or kings. Focus rests on the private diversions of heroic warriors as well as on the identity and personal style of the artist who portrayed them. Supremely self-aware and self-confident, the ancient Greeks developed a concept of human capacity and responsibility that required a new visual expression. Greek art was centered in the material world, but it also conformed to strict ideals of beauty and mathematical concepts of design. This paralleled Greek philosophers' search for the human values of truth, virtue, and harmony, qualities that imbue both subject and style in this celebrated work.

The Emergence of Greek Civilization

What aspects of Greek geography, history, and religion create the background for the emergence of its ancient art and architecture?

Ancient Greece was a mountainous land of spectacular natural beauty. Olive trees and grapevines grew on the steep hillsides, producing oil and wine, but there was little good farmland. In towns, skilled artisans produced metal and ceramic wares to trade abroad for grain and raw materials. Greek merchant ships carried pots, olive oil, and bronzes from Athens, Corinth, and Aegina around the Mediterranean Sea, extending the Greek cultural orbit from mainland Greece south to the Peloponnese, north to Macedonia, and east to the Aegean islands and the coast of Asia Minor (**MAP 5–1**). Greek colonies in Italy, Sicily, and Asia Minor rapidly became powerful, independent commercial and cultural centers, but they remained tied to the homeland by language, heritage, religion, and art.

Within a remarkably brief time, Greek artists developed focused and distinctive ideals of human representation and architectural design that continue to exert a profound influence today. From about 900 BCE until about 100 BCE, they concentrated on a new, rather narrow range of subjects and produced an impressive body of work in a variety of media. Greek artists were restless. They continually sought to change and improve existing artistic trends, resulting in a striking stylistic evolution over the course of a few centuries. This is in stark contrast to the art of ancient Egypt, where a desire for continuity maintained stable artistic conventions for nearly 3,000 years.

Historical Background

In the ninth and eighth centuries BCE, long after Mycenaean dominance in the Aegean had come to an end, the Greeks began to form independently governed city-states. Each city-state was an autonomous region with a city—Athens, Corinth, Sparta—as its political, economic, religious, and cultural center. Each had its own form of government and

MAP 5–1 ANCIENT GREECE

The cultural heartland of ancient Greece consisted of the Greek mainland, the islands of the Aegean, and the west coast of Asia Minor, but colonies on the Italic peninsula and the island of Sicily extended Greek cultural influence farther west into the Mediterranean.

Art and its Contexts

GREEK AND ROMAN DEITIES

(The Roman form of the name is given after the Greek name.)

The Five Children of Earth and Sky

Zeus (Jupiter), supreme Olympian deity. Mature, bearded man, often holding scepter or lightning bolt; sometimes represented as an eagle.

Hera (Juno), goddess of marriage. Sister/wife of Zeus. Mature woman; cow and peacock are sacred to her.

Hestia (Vesta), goddess of the hearth. Sister of Zeus. Her sacred flame burned in communal hearths.

Poseidon (Neptune), god of the sea. Holds a three-pronged spear (trident).

Hades (Pluto), god of the underworld, the dead, and wealth.

The Seven Sky Gods, Offspring of the First Five

Ares (Mars), god of war. Son of Zeus and Hera.

Hephaistos (Vulcan), god of the forge, fire, and metal handcrafts. Son of Hera (in some myths, also of Zeus); husband of Aphrodite.

Apollo (Phoebus), god of the sun, light, truth, music, archery, and healing. Sometimes identified with Helios (the Sun), who rides a chariot across the daytime sky. Son of Zeus and Leto (a descendant of Earth); brother of Artemis.

Artemis (Diana), goddess of the hunt, wild animals, and the moon. Sometimes identified with Selene (the Moon), who rides a chariot or oxcart across the night sky. Daughter of Zeus and Leto; sister of Apollo. Carries bow and arrows and is accompanied by hunting dogs.

Athena (Minerva), goddess of wisdom, war, victory, and the city. Also goddess of handcrafts and other artistic skills. Daughter of Zeus; sprang fully grown from his head. Wears helmet and carries shield and spear.

Aphrodite (Venus), goddess of love. Daughter of Zeus and the water nymph Dione; alternatively, born of sea foam; wife of Hephaistos.

Hermes (Mercury), messenger of the gods, god of fertility and luck, guide of the dead to the underworld, and god of thieves and commerce. Son of Zeus and Maia, the daughter of Atlas, a Titan who supports the sky on his shoulders. Wears winged sandals and hat; carries caduceus, a wand with two snakes entwined around it.

Other Important Deities

Demeter (Ceres), goddess of grain and agriculture. Daughter of Kronos and Rhea, sister of Zeus and Hera.

Persephone (Proserpina), goddess of fertility and queen of the underworld. Wife of Hades; daughter of Demeter.

Dionysos (Bacchus), god of wine, the grape harvest, and inspiration. His female followers are called **maenads** (Bacchantes).

Eros (Cupid), god of love. In some myths, the son of Aphrodite. Shown as an infant or young boy, sometimes winged, carrying bow and arrows.

Pan (Faunus), protector of shepherds, god of the wilderness and of music. Half-man, half-goat, he carries panpipes.

Nike (Victory), goddess of victory. Often shown winged and flying.

---

economy, and each managed its own domestic and foreign affairs. The power of these city-states initially depended at least as much on their manufacturing and commercial skills as on their military might.

Among the emerging city-states, Corinth, located on major land and sea trade routes, was one of the oldest and most powerful. By the sixth century BCE, Athens rose to commercial and cultural preeminence. Soon it had also established a representative government in which every community had its own assembly and magistrates. Citizenship was open only to Athenian men, but all citizens participated in the assembly, and all had an equal right to own private property, exercise freedom of speech, vote, hold public office, and serve in the army or navy. The census of 309 BCE in Athens listed 21,000 citizens, 10,000 foreign residents, and 400,000 others—that is, women, children, and slaves.

Religious Beliefs and Sacred Places

According to ancient Greek legend, the creation of the world involved a battle between the earth gods, called Titans, and the sky gods. The victors were the sky gods, whose home was believed to be atop Mount Olympus in the northeast corner of the Greek mainland. The Greeks saw their gods as immortal and endowed with supernatural powers, but they also visualized them in human form and attributed to them human weaknesses and emotions to a greater extent than the Egyptians and peoples of the ancient Near East had done. Among the most important deities were the supreme god and goddess, Zeus and Hera, and their offspring (see "Greek and Roman Deities" above).

Many sites throughout Greece, called **sanctuaries**, were thought to be sacred to one or more gods. The earliest sanctuaries included outdoor altars or shrines and a sacred natural element such as a tree, a rock, or a spring. As more buildings were added, a sanctuary might become a palatial home for the gods, with one or more temples, several treasuries for storing valuable offerings, various monuments and statues, housing for priests and visitors, an outdoor dancefloor or permanent theater for ritual performances and literary competitions, and a stadium for athletic events. The Sanctuary of Zeus near Olympia, in the western Peloponnese, housed an extensive athletic facility with training rooms and arenas for track-and-field events. It was here that athletic competitions, prototypes of today's Olympic Games, were held.

Greek sanctuaries (SEE FIGS. 5-5, 5-6) are quite different from the religious complexes of the ancient Egyptians (see, for example, the Temple of Amun at Karnak, FIG. 3-19). Egyptian builders dramatized the power of gods or god-rulers by organizing their temples along straight, processional ways. The Greeks, in contrast, treated each building and monument as an independent element to be integrated with the natural features of the site in an irregular arrangement that emphasized the exterior of each building as a discrete sculptural form on display.

Greek Art c. 900–c. 600 BCE

What are the distinguishing features of ancient Greek art during its Geometric and Orientalizing periods?

Around the mid eleventh century BCE, a new culture began to form on the Greek mainland. Athens began to develop as a major center of ceramic production, creating both sculpture and vessels decorated with organized abstract designs. In this Geometric period, the Greeks, as we now call them, were beginning to create their own architectural forms and were trading actively with their neighbors to the east. By c. 700 BCE, in a phase called the Orientalizing period, they began to incorporate exotic foreign motifs into their native art.

The Geometric Period

What we call the Geometric period flourished in Greece between 900 and 700 BCE, especially in the decoration of ceramic vessels with linear motifs, such as spirals, diamonds, and cross-hatching. This abstract vocabulary is strikingly different from the stylized plants, birds, and sea creatures that had characterized Minoan pots (SEE FIGS. 4-4, 4-11).

Large funerary vessels like the krater illustrated here (**FIG. 5-2**) were developed at this time for use as grave markers, many of which have been uncovered at the ancient cemetery of Athens just outside the Dipylon Gate, once the main western entrance into the city. This krater seems to provide a detailed pictorial record of funerary rituals associated with the important person whose death is commemorated by it. On the top register, the body of the deceased is shown lying on its side on a funeral bier, perhaps awaiting the relatively new Greek practice of cremation. Male and female figures stand on each side of the body, their arms raised and both hands placed on top of their heads in a gesture of anguish, as if they were literally

tearing their hair out with grief. In the register underneath, horse-drawn chariots and foot soldiers, who look like walking shields with tiny antlike heads and muscular legs, move in solemn procession.

The geometric shapes used to represent human figures on this pot—triangles for torsos; more triangles for the heads in profile; round dots for eyes; long, thin rectangles for arms; tiny waists; and long legs with bulging thigh and calf muscles—are what has given the Geometric style its name. Figures are shown in either full-frontal or full-profile views that emphasize flat patterns and crisp outlines. Any sense of the illusion of three-dimensional forms occupying real space has been avoided. But the artist has captured a deep sense of human loss through the stylized solemnity and strong rhythmic accents of the carefully arranged elements.

Egyptian funerary art reflected the strong belief that the dead in the afterworld could continue to engage in activities they enjoyed while alive. For the Greeks, the deceased entered a place of mystery and obscurity that living humans could not define precisely, and their funerary art, in contrast, focused on the emotional reactions of the survivors. The scene of mourning on this pot contains no

5-2 Attributed to the Hirschfeld Workshop FUNERARY KRATER

From the Dipylon Cemetery, Athens. c. 750–735 BCE. Ceramic, height 42⅝" (108 cm). Metropolitan Museum of Art, New York. Rogers Fund, 1914. (14.130.14).

Credit: © 2016. Image copyright The Metropolitan Museum of Art/Art Resource/ Scala, Florence

5–3 MAN AND CENTAUR
Perhaps from Olympia. c. 750 BCE. Bronze, height 4⁵/₁₆″ (11.1 cm).
Metropolitan Museum of Art, New York. Gift of J. Pierpont Morgan, 1917.
(17.190.2072).

Credit: © 2016. Image copyright The Metropolitan Museum of Art/Art Resource/
Scala, Florence

supernatural beings, nor any identifiable reference to an afterlife, only poignant evocations of the sentiments and rituals of those left behind on earth.

Greek artists of the Geometric period also produced figurines of wood, ivory, clay, and cast bronze. These small statues of humans and animals are similar in appearance to those painted on pots. A tiny bronze of this type, depicting a **MAN AND CENTAUR**—a mythical creature, part man and part horse (**FIG. 5–3**)—dates to about the same time as the funerary krater. Although there were wise and good centaurs in Greek lore, this work takes up the theme of battling man and centaur, prominent throughout the history of Greek art (**SEE FIG. 5–39**). The two figures confront each other after the man—perhaps Herakles—has stabbed the centaur; the spearhead is visible on the centaur's left side. Like the painter of the funerary krater from the same period, the sculptor has abstracted the body parts of these figures to basic geometric shapes, arranging them in a composition of solid forms and open, or negative, spaces that makes the piece interesting from multiple viewpoints. Most such sculptures have been found in sanctuaries, suggesting that they may have served as votive offerings to the gods.

The Orientalizing Period

By the seventh century BCE, painters in major pottery centers in Greece had moved away from the dense linear decoration of the Geometric style, preferring more open compositions built around large motifs—real and imaginary animals, abstract plant forms, and human figures. The source of these motifs can be traced to the arts of the Near East, Asia Minor, and Egypt. Greek painters did not simply copy the work of Eastern artists, however. Instead, they drew on work in a variety of media—including sculpture, metalwork, and textiles—to invent an entirely new approach to painting vessels.

The Orientalizing style (c. 700–600 BCE) began in Corinth, a port city where luxury wares from the Near East and Egypt inspired artists. The new style is evident in a Corinthian **olpe**, or wide-mouthed pitcher, dating to about 650–625 BCE (**FIG. 5–4**). Silhouetted creatures—lions, panthers, goats, deer, bulls, boars, and swans—stride in

5–4 OLPE (PITCHER)
From Corinth. c. 650–625 BCE. Ceramic with black-figure decoration, height 12⁷/₈″ (32.8 cm). J. Paul Getty Museum, Villa Collection, Pacific Palisades, CA (85.AE.89)

horizontal bands against a light background with stylized flower forms called **rosettes** filling the spaces around them. An early example of the **black-figure** technique (see "Black-Figure and Red-Figure" on page 120), dark shapes define the silhouettes of the animals against a background of very pale buff, the natural color of the Corinthian clay. The artist incised fine details inside the silhouetted shapes with a sharp tool and added touches of white and red slip to enliven the design.

The Archaic Period, c. 600–480 BCE

What are the characteristic stylistic features of ancient Greek art and architecture during the Archaic period?

The Archaic period does not deserve its name. "Archaic" means "antiquated" or "old-fashioned," even "primitive," and the term was chosen by art historians who wanted to stress the contrast between what they perceived as the undeveloped art of this time and the subsequent Classical period, once thought to be the most admirable and highly developed phase of Greek art. But the Archaic period was a time of great new achievement in Greece. In literature, Sappho wrote her inspired poetry on the island of Lesbos, while on another island the legendary storyteller, Aesop, crafted his animal fables. Artists and architects shared in the growing prosperity as city councils and wealthy individuals sponsored the creation of extraordinary sculpture and fine ceramics and commissioned elaborate civic and religious buildings in cities and sanctuaries.

The Sanctuary at Delphi

According to Greek myth, Zeus was said to have released two eagles from opposite ends of the earth, and they met exactly at the rugged mountain site of Apollo's sanctuary (**FIG. 5-5**). From very early times, the sanctuary at Delphi was renowned as an oracle, a place where the god Apollo was believed to communicate with humans by means of cryptic messages delivered through a human intermediary, or medium (the Pythia). The Greeks and their leaders routinely sought advice at oracles and attributed many twists of fate to misinterpretations of the Pythia's statements. Even foreign rulers journeyed to request help at Delphi.

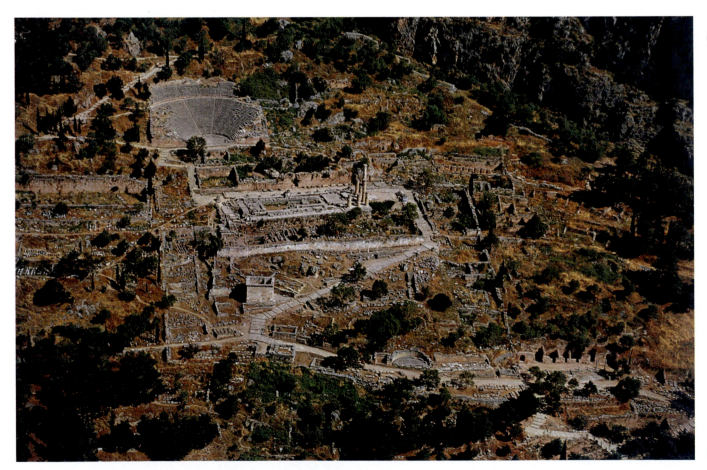

5-5 AERIAL VIEW OF THE SANCTUARY OF APOLLO, DELPHI
Greece, 6th–3rd century BCE.

Credit: © DeAgostini/Superstock

5–6 RECONSTRUCTION DRAWING OF THE SANCTUARY OF APOLLO, DELPHI

Credit: © Dorling Kindersley

theater

Temple of Apollo

Treasury of the Athenians

Meeting Hall of the Knidians

Siphnian Treasury

Sikyonian Treasury

Stoa of Attalos

Arkadian monument

Altar of the Chians

Stoa of the Athenians

Sacred Way

Delphi was the site of the Pythian Games, which, like the Olympian Games, attracted participants from all over Greece. The principal events were athletic, music, dance, and poetry competitions in honor of Apollo. As at Olympia, hundreds of statues dedicated to the victors of the competitions, as well as mythological figures, filled the sanctuary grounds. The sanctuary of Apollo was significantly developed during the Archaic period and included the main temple, performance and athletic areas, treasuries, and other buildings and monuments, which made full use of limited space on the hillside (**FIG. 5-6**).

After visitors had climbed the steep path up the lower slopes of Mount Parnassos, they entered the sanctuary by a ceremonial gate in the southeast corner. From there they zigzagged up the Sacred Way, so named because it was the route of religious processions during festivals. Moving past the numerous treasuries and memorials built by the city-states, they arrived at the long colonnade of the Temple of Apollo, rebuilt in c. 530 BCE on the site of an earlier temple. Below the temple was a **stoa**, a columned pavilion open on three sides, built by the people of Athens. There visitors rested, talked, or watched ceremonial dancing. At the top of the sanctuary hill was a stadium area for athletic contests.

TREASURY OF THE SIPHNIANS Sanctuaries also included treasuries built by the citizens of Greek city-states to house their offerings. The small but luxurious **TREASURY OF THE SIPHNIANS** (**FIG. 5–7**) was built in the sanctuary of Apollo at Delphi by the residents of the island of Siphnos in the Cyclades, between about 530 and 525 BCE.

5–7 RECONSTRUCTION DRAWING OF THE TREASURY OF THE SIPHNIANS

Sanctuary of Apollo, Delphi. c. 530–525 BCE.

This small treasury building at Delphi was originally elegant and richly ornamented. The figure sculpture and decorative moldings were once painted in strong colors, mainly dark blue, bright red, and white, with touches of yellow to resemble gold.

5-8 BATTLE BETWEEN THE GODS AND THE GIANTS
Fragments of the north frieze of the Treasury of the Siphnians, Sanctuary of Apollo, Delphi. c. 530–525 BCE. Marble, height 26″ (66 cm).
Archaeological Museum, Delphi.

Credit: © Craig & Marie Mauzy, Athens

It survives today only in fragments housed in the museum at Delphi. Instead of columns, the builders used two stately **caryatids**—columns carved in the form of women clothed in finely pleated, flowing garments, raised on **pedestals**, and balancing elaborately carved capitals on their heads. The capitals support a tall **entablature** conforming to the **Ionic order**, which features a plain, or three-panel, **architrave** and a continuous carved **frieze** set off by richly carved moldings (see "The Greek Orders" opposite).

Both the continuous frieze and the **pediments** of the Siphnian Treasury were originally filled with relief sculpture. A surviving section of the frieze from the building's north side, which shows a scene from the legendary **BATTLE BETWEEN THE GODS AND THE GIANTS**, is notable for its complex representation of space (**FIG. 5-8**). To give a sense of three-dimensional recession, the sculptors overlapped the figures—sometimes three deep—and varied the depth of the relief to convey different placements in space. Originally such sculptures were painted with bright colors to enhance the lifelike effect.

Temples

For centuries ancient Greeks had worshiped at sanctuaries where an outdoor altar stood within an enclosed sacred area called a **temenos** reserved for worship. Sometimes temples sheltering a statue of a god were incorporated into these sanctuaries, often as later additions to an established sanctuary. A number of standardized temple plans evolved, ranging from simple, one-room structures with columned **porches** (a covered, open space in front of an entrance) to buildings with double porches (located at front and back) surrounded entirely by columns. Builders also experimented with the design of temple

elevations—the arrangement, proportions, and appearance of the columns and the lintels—which now grew into elaborate entablatures. Two specific elevation designs emerged during the Archaic period: the **Doric order** and the Ionic order. The **Corinthian order**, a variant of the Ionic order, would develop later (see "The Greek Orders" opposite).

A particularly well-preserved Archaic Doric temple, built around 550 BCE, still stands at the former Greek colony of Poseidonia (Roman Paestum) about 50 miles south of the present-day city of Naples, Italy (**FIG. 5-9**). Dedicated to Hera, the wife of Zeus, it is known today as Hera I to distinguish it from a second, adjacent temple to Hera built about a century later. A row of columns called the peristyle surrounded the main room, the **cella**. The columns of Hera I are especially robust—only about four times as high as their maximum diameter—and topped with a widely flaring capital and a broad, blocky **abacus**, creating an impression of great stability and permanence. As the column shafts rise, they swell in the middle and contract again toward the top, a refinement known as **entasis**, giving them a sense of energy and lift. Hera I has an uneven number of columns—nine—across the short ends of the peristyle, with a column instead of a space at the center of the two ends. The entrance to the **pronaos** (enclosed vestibule) has three columns in antis (between flanking wall piers), and a row of columns runs down the center of the wide cella to help support the ceiling and roof. The unusual two-aisle, two-door arrangement leading to the small room at the end of the cella suggests that the temple had two presiding deities: Hera and Poseidon (patron of the city), Hera and Zeus, or perhaps Hera in her two manifestations (as warrior and protector of the city and as mother and protector of children).

Elements of Architecture

THE GREEK ORDERS

Each of the three Classical Greek architectural **orders**—Doric, Ionic, and Corinthian—constitutes a system of interdependent parts whose proportions are based on mathematical ratios. No element of an order could be changed without producing a corresponding change in other elements.

The basic components are the **column** and the entablature, which function as post and lintel in the structural system. All three types of columns have a **shaft** and a capital; Ionic and Corinthian also have a base. The shafts are formed of stacked round sections, or **drums**, which are joined inside by metal pegs. In Greek temple architecture, columns stand on the **stylobate**, the "floor" of the temple, which rests on top of a set of steps that form the temple's base, known as the **stereobate**.

In the Doric order, shafts sit directly on the stylobate without a base. They are **fluted**, or channeled, with sharp edges. The height of the substantial columns ranges from five-and-a-half to seven times the diameter of the base. A necking at the top of the shaft provides a transition to the capital itself, composed

of the rounded **echinus** and the tabletlike abacus. The entablature includes the architrave, the distinctive frieze of alternating **triglyphs** and **metopes**, and the **cornice**, the topmost, projecting horizontal element. The roofline may have decorative waterspouts and terminal decorative elements called **acroteria**.

The Ionic order has more elongated proportions than the Doric, the height of a column being about nine times the diameter of its base. The flutes on the columns are deeper and are separated by flat surfaces called **fillets**. The capital has a distinctive, spiral-scrolled **volute**; the entablature has a three-panel architrave, continuous sculptured or decorated frieze, and richer decorative moldings.

The Corinthian order, a variant of the Ionic order originally developed by the Greeks for use in interiors, was eventually used on temple exteriors as well. Its elaborate capitals are sheathed with stylized **acanthus** leaves that rise from a convex band called the **astragal**.

Doric order   **Ionic order**   **Corinthian order**

5-9A PLAN OF THE TEMPLE OF HERA I, POSEIDONIA (ROMAN PAESTUM)

Southern Italy. c. 550–540 BCE.

5-9B EXTERIOR VIEW OF THE TEMPLE OF HERA I, POSEIDONIA (ROMAN PAESTUM)

Southern Italy. c. 550–540 BCE.

Credit: © Fotografica Foglia, Naples

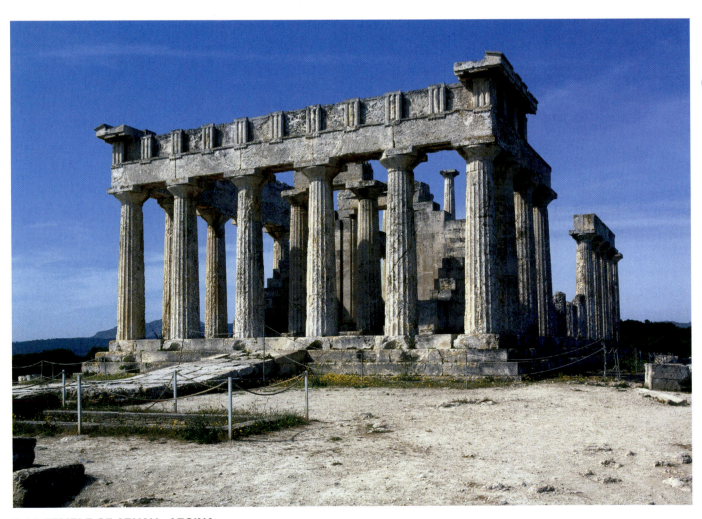

5-10 TEMPLE OF APHAIA, AEGINA

View from the east. c. 500 or c. 475 BCE. Column height about 17′ (5.18 m).

Credit: © Craig & Marie Mauzy, Athens

5-11 RECONSTRUCTION DRAWING OF THE TEMPLE OF APHAIA, AEGINA

c. 500 or c. 475 BCE.

Credit: Courtesy of Laurence King Publishing, John Griffiths Pedley, *Greek Art and Archaeology*, 4th edition ©2007

THE TEMPLE OF APHAIA ON AEGINA A fully developed and somewhat sleeker Doric temple than the one from Poseidonia was built on the island of Aegina during the first quarter of the fifth century BCE in a sanctuary dedicated to a local goddess named Aphaia (**FIG. 5-10**). Spectacularly sited on a hill overlooking the sea, the temple is reasonably well preserved, in spite of the loss of pediments, roof, and sections of its colonnade. Enough evidence remains to form a reliable reconstruction of its original appearance (**FIG. 5-11**).

The plan combines 6 columns on the façades with 12 on the sides, and the cella—whose roof was supported by superimposed colonnades—could be entered from porches on both short sides. The slight swelling of the columns (entasis) seen at Poseidonia is evident here as well, and the outside triglyphs are pushed to the ends of frieze, out of alignment with the column underneath them, to avoid the awkwardness of half a metope (rectangular panel with a relief or painting) at the corner.

Like most Greek temples, this building was neither isolated nor situated in open space, but set in relation to an outside altar where religious ceremonies were focused (**FIG. 5-12**). By enclosing the temple within a walled area, or temenos, the designer could control the viewer's initial experience of the temple. As the viewer entered the sacred space through a gatehouse—the propylon—the temple would be seen at an oblique angle. Unlike ancient Egyptian temples, where long processional approaches led visitors directly to the flat entrance façade of a building (SEE FIGS. 3-19, 3-23), the Greek architect revealed from the outset the full shape of a closed, compact, sculptural mass, inviting viewers not to enter seeking something within, but rather to walk around the exterior, exploring the rich sculptural embellishment on the pediments and frieze. Cult ceremonies, after all, took place at an altar outside Greek temples.

5-12 PLAN OF COMPLEX OF THE TEMPLE OF APHAIA, AEGINA

c. 500 or c. 475 BCE.

ARCHITECTURAL SCULPTURE AT AEGINA Modern viewers will not find exterior sculpture at Aegina. Nothing remains from the metopes, and substantial surviving portions of the two pediments were purchased in the early nineteenth century by the future Ludwig I of Bavaria and are now exhibited in Munich. The triangular pediments in Greek temples created challenging compositional problems for sculptors intent on fitting figures into the tapering spaces at the outside corners, since the scale of figures could not change, only their poses. The west pediment from Aegina (**FIG. 5-13**)—traditionally dated about 500–490 BCE, before its eastern counterpart—represents a creative solution that became a design standard, appearing with variations throughout the fifth century BCE. The subject of the

5–13 WEST PEDIMENT OF THE TEMPLE OF APHAIA, AEGINA

c. 500–490 or 470s BCE. Width about 49′ (15 m). Surviving fragments as assembled in the Staatliche Antikensammlungen und Glyptothek, Munich (early restorations removed).

Credit: Staatliche Antikensammlungen, Munich

pediment, rendered in fully three-dimensional figures, is the participation of local warriors in the military expedition against Troy. Fallen warriors fill the angles at both ends of the pediment base, while others crouch and lunge, rising in height toward an image of Athena as warrior goddess—who can fill the elevated, pointed space at the center peak since she is allowed to be represented larger (hierarchic scale) than the humans who flank her.

Among the best-preserved fragments from the west pediment is the **DYING WARRIOR** from the far right corner (**FIG. 5–14**). This tragic figure struggles to rise up, supported on bent leg and elbow, in order to extract an arrow from his chest even though his death seems certain. The figure originally would have been painted and fitted with authentic bronze accessories, heightening the sense of reality.

A similar figure appeared on the east pediment (**FIG. 5–15**), traditionally seen as postdating the west pediment by a decade or so. The sculptor of this dying warrior also exploited the difficult framework of the pediment corner, only here, instead of an uplifted frontal form in profile, we see a body turning in space. The figure is more precariously balanced on his shield, clearly about to collapse. There is an increased sense of softness in the portrayal of human flesh and a greater sophistication in fitting the bodily posture not only to the tapering shape of the pediment, but also to the expression of the warrior's own agony and vulnerability, which in turn inspires a sense of pathos or empathy in the viewer.

For decades, art historians taught that over the course of a decade, two successive sets of sculptures on Aegina allow us to trace the transition from Archaic toward Early Classical art. Recently, however, Andrew Stewart has reviewed the archaeological evidence on the Athenian Akropolis and Aegina and reached a very different conclusion. He questions the traditional dating of key works from the transition between Archaic and Early Classical

art—notably the Aegina pediment sculpture and the Kritios Boy (SEE FIG. 5–27)—placing them after the Persian invasion of 580–579 BCE and raising the question of whether Greek victory over this outside enemy might have been a factor in the stylistic change. In the case of the Aegina temple, this re-dating becomes especially interesting. Instead of assuming that the difference in style between the western and eastern pediments represents a time gap separating their production, Stewart proposes that the ensembles were both produced during the 470s by two workshops, one conservative and one progressive.

COLOR IN GREEK SCULPTURE For many modern viewers, it comes as a real surprise, even a shock, that the stone sculptures of ancient Greece did not always have stark white marble surfaces, comparable in appearance to—and consistent in taste with—the more recent, but still classicizing sculptures of Michelangelo or Canova (SEE FIGS. 21–14, 2–15; 30–14). But they were originally painted with brilliant colors. A close examination of Greek sculpture and architecture has long revealed evidence of polychromy, even to the unaided eye, but our understanding of the original appearance of these works has been greatly enhanced by the work of German scholar Vinzenz Brinkmann. Since the 1980s, Brinkmann has used visual and scientific analysis to evaluate the traces of painting that remain on ancient Greek sculpture, employing tools such as ultraviolet and x-ray fluorescence, microscopy, and pigment analysis. Based on this research, he and his colleague Ulrike Koch-Brinkmann have made reconstructions to show the exuberant effect these works would have had when they were new. Illustrated here is their painted reconstruction of a kneeling archer (**FIGS. 5–16, 5–17**) from about 500 (or during the 470s) BCE that once formed part of the west pediment of the Temple of Aphaia at Aegina.

5-14 DYING WARRIOR

From the right corner of the west pediment of the Temple of Aphaia, Aegina. c. 500–490 or 470s BCE. Marble, length 5′6″ (1.68 m). Staatliche Antikensammlungen und Glyptothek, Munich.

Credit: Staatliche Antikensammlungen, Munich/Studio Koppermann

5-15 DYING WARRIOR

From the left corner of the east pediment of the Temple of Aphaia, Aegina. c. 490–480 or 470s BCE. Marble, length 6′ (1.83 m). Staatliche Antikensammlungen und Glyptothek, Munich.

Credit: Staatliche Antikensammlungen, Munich/Studio Koppermann

5-16 Vinzenz Brinkmann and Ulrike Koch-Brinkmann **RECONSTRUCTION OF ARCHER**

From the west pediment of the Temple of Aphaia, Aegina. 2004 CE. Staatliche Antikensammlungen und Glyptothek, Munich.

Credit: Staatliche Antikensammlungen, Munich/Studio Koppermann

5-17 ARCHER ("PARIS")

From the west pediment of the Temple of Aphaia, Aegina. c. 500–490 or 470s BCE. Marble. Staatliche Antikensammlungen und Glyptothek, Munich.

Credit: Staatliche Antikensammlungen, Munich/Studio Koppermann

To begin with, they have replaced features of the sculpture that had been lost—ringlet hair extensions, a bow, a quiver, and arrows—probably originally made of bronze or lead and attached to the stone after it was carved, using the holes still evident in the figure's hip and head. The biggest surprise, however, is the restoration of the diamond-shaped patterns originally painted on the archer's leggings and sleeves using pigments derived from malachite, azurite, arsenic, cinnabar, and charcoal. These were not simply colored in. The Greek artists created a sophisticated integration of three-dimensional form, color, and design: The patterning of the figure's leggings actually changes in size and shape in relation to the body beneath it, stretching out on the thighs and constricting on the ankles. Ancient authors indicate that sculpture was painted to make figures more lifelike, and these reconstructions certainly back up their description of the effect.

Free-Standing Sculpture

In addition to statues designed for temple exteriors, sculptors of the Archaic period created a new type of large, free-standing statue made of wood, **terra cotta** (clay fired over low heat), limestone, or white marble from the islands of Paros and Naxos. These figures were brightly painted and sometimes bore inscriptions indicating that individual men or women had commissioned them for a commemorative purpose. They have been found marking graves and in sanctuaries, where they lined the sacred way from the entrance to the main temple.

A female statue of this type is called a **kore** (plural, *korai*), Greek for "young woman," and a male statue is called a **kouros** (plural, *kouroi*), Greek for "young man." Archaic *korai*, always clothed, probably represented deities, priestesses, and nymphs (young female immortals who served as attendants to gods). *Kouroi*, nearly always nude, have been variously identified as gods, warriors, and victorious athletes. Because the Greeks associated young, athletic males with fertility and family continuity, the *kouroi* figures may have symbolized ancestors.

5–18 METROPOLITAN KOUROS

From Attica, Greece. c. 600–590 BCE. Marble, height 6′4⅝″ (1.95 m). Metropolitan Museum of Art, New York. Fletcher Fund, 1932. (32.11.1).

Credit: © 2016. Image copyright The Metropolitan Museum of Art/Art Resource/ Scala, Florence

METROPOLITAN KOUROS A *kouros* dated about 600 BCE (**FIG. 5–18**) recalls the pose and proportions of Egyptian sculpture. As with Egyptian figures such as the statue of Menkaure (SEE FIG. 3–10), this young Greek stands rigidly upright, arms at his sides, fists clenched, and one leg slightly in front of the other. However, the Greek artist has cut away all stone from around the body to make the human form free-standing. Archaic *kouroi* are also much less lifelike than their Egyptian forebears. Anatomy is delineated with linear ridges and grooves that form regular, symmetrical patterns. The head is ovoid and schematized, and the wiglike hair evenly knotted into tufts and tied back with a narrow ribbon. The eyes are relatively large and wide open, and the mouth forms a conventional closed-lip expression known as the **Archaic smile**. In Egyptian sculpture, male figures usually wore clothing associated with their status, such as the headdresses, necklaces, and kilts that identified them as kings. The total nudity of the Greek *kouroi* is unusual in ancient Mediterranean cultures, but it is acceptable—even valued—in the case of young men. Not so with women.

BERLIN KORE Early Archaic *korai* are as severe and stylized as the male figures. The **BERLIN KORE**, a funerary statue found in a cemetery at Keratea and dated about 570–560 BCE, stands more than 6 feet tall (**FIG. 5–19**). The erect, full-bodied figure takes an immobile pose—accentuated by a bulky crown and thick-soled clogs. The thick robe and tasseled cloak over her shoulders fall in regularly spaced, symmetrically arranged, parallel folds like the fluting on a Greek column. This drapery masks her body but mimics its contours. Traces of red—perhaps the red clay used to attach thin sheets of gold—indicate that the robe was once painted or gilded. The figure holds a pomegranate in her right hand, a symbol of Persephone, who was abducted by Hades, the god of the underworld, and whose annual return brought the springtime.

5–19 BERLIN KORE
From the cemetery at Keratea, near Athens. c. 570–560 BCE. Marble with remnants of red paint, height 6′3″ (1.9 m). Staatliche Museen zu Berlin, Preussischer Kulturbesitz, Antikensammlung.

Credit: © 2016.Photo Scala, Florence/bpk, Bildagentur für Kunst, Kultur und Geschichte, Berlin

5-20 ANAVYSOS KOUROS

From the cemetery at Anavysos, near Athens. c. 530 BCE. Marble with remnants of paint, height 6′4″ (1.93 m). National Archaeological Museum, Athens.

Credit: © Craig & Marie Mauzy, Athens

5-21 "PEPLOS" KORE

From the Akropolis, Athens. c. 530 BCE. Marble, height 4′ (1.21 m). Akropolis Museum, Athens.

Credit: © Craig & Marie Mauzy, Athens/Acropolis Museum, Athens, Greece

ANAVYSOS KOUROS   The powerful, rounded, athletic body of a *kouros* from Anavysos, dated about 530 BCE, documents the increasing interest of artists and their patrons in a more lifelike rendering of the human figure (**FIG. 5-20**). The pose, wiglike hair, and Archaic smile echo the earlier style, but the massive torso and limbs have carefully rendered, bulging muscularity, suggesting heroic strength. The statue, a grave monument for a fallen war hero, has been associated with a base inscribed "Stop and grieve at the tomb of the dead Kroisos, slain by wild Ares [god of war] in the front rank of battle." However, there is no evidence that the figure was meant to preserve the likeness of Kroisos or anyone else. It is a symbolic type, not a specific individual.

"PEPLOS" KORE   The kore in **FIG. 5-21** is dated about the same time as the Anavysos Kouros, though she is a votive rather than a funerary statue. Like the *kouros*, she has rounded body forms, but unlike him, she is clothed. She has the same motionless, vertical pose of the Berlin Kore (SEE FIG. 5-19), but her bare arms and head convey a sense of soft flesh covering a real bone structure, and her smile and hair are much less stylized. The original painted colors on both body and clothing must have made her seem even more lifelike, and she also once wore a metal crown and jewelry.

The name we use for this figure is based on an assessment of her clothing as a young girl's peplos—a draped rectangle of cloth pinned at the shoulders and belted to give a bloused effect—but it has recently been argued that this *kore* is actually not wearing a peplos but a sheathlike garment, originally painted with a frieze of animals, identifying her not as a young girl but a goddess, perhaps Athena or Artemis. Her missing left forearm—which was made of a separate piece of marble fitted into the still-visible socket—would have extended forward horizontally, and may have held an attribute that identified her.

Painted Pots

Greek potters created beautiful vessels whose standardized shapes were tailored to specific utilitarian functions (**FIG. 5-22**). Occasionally, these potters actually signed their work, as did the artists who painted scenes on the pots. Greek ceramic painters became highly accomplished at composing their pictures to fit the often awkward fields on utilitarian shapes, and they usually showcased scenes of human interaction evoking a story, rather than isolated figures.

5-22 SOME STANDARD SHAPES OF GREEK VESSELS

Technique

BLACK-FIGURE AND RED-FIGURE

The two predominant techniques for painting on Greek ceramic vessels were black-figure (**FIG. 5–23**) and red-figure (**FIG. 5–24**). Both involved applying **slip** (a mixture of clay and water) to the surface of a pot and carefully manipulating the firing process in a kiln (a closed oven) to control the amount of oxygen reaching the ceramics. This firing process involved three stages. In the first stage, oxygen was allowed into the kiln, which "fixed" the whole vessel in one overall shade of red depending on the composition of the clay. Then, in the second (reduction) stage, the oxygen in the kiln was cut back (reduced) to a minimum, turning the vessel black, and the temperature was raised to the point at which the slip partially vitrified (became glasslike). Finally, in the third stage, oxygen was allowed back into the kiln, turning the unslipped areas back to a shade of red. The areas where slip had been applied, however, were sealed against the oxygen and remained black.

In the black-figure technique, artists silhouetted the forms with slip against the unpainted clay of the background. Then, using a sharp tool (a stylus), they cut through the slip to the body of the vessel, **incising** linear details within the silhouetted shape by revealing the unpainted clay underneath. The characteristic color contrast only appeared after firing. Sometimes touches of white and reddish-purple gloss—made of metallic pigments mixed with slip—enhanced the decorative effect.

In the **red-figure** technique, the approach was reversed. Artists painted not the shapes of the forms themselves but the background around forms (negative space), reserving unpainted areas for silhouetted forms. Instead of engraving details, painters drew on the reserved areas with a fine brush dipped in slip. The result was a lustrous black vessel with light-colored figures delineated in fluid black lines.

The contrasting effects obtained by these two techniques are illustrated here in details of two sides of a single amphora of about 525 BCE, both portraying the same figural composition, one painted by an artist using black-figure, and the other painted by an innovative proponent of red-figure technique. The sharp precision and flattened decorative richness of black-figure contrasts strikingly here with the increased fluidity and greater sense of three-dimensionality possible with the red-figure technique.

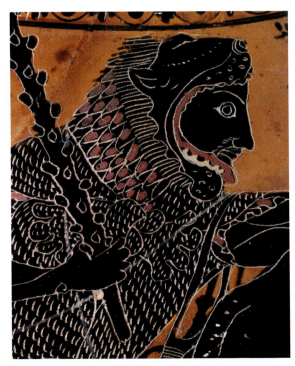

5–23 Lysippides Painter **HERAKLES DRIVING A BULL TO SACRIFICE**

c. 525–520 BCE. Black-figure decoration on an amphora. Ceramic, height of amphora 20¹⁵⁄₁₆″ (53.2 cm). Museum of Fine Arts, Boston. Henry Lillie Pierce Fund (99.538).

Credit: Photograph © 2017 Museum of Fine Arts, Boston

5–24 Andokides Painter **HERAKLES DRIVING A BULL TO SACRIFICE**

c. 525–520 BCE. Red-figure decoration on an amphora. Ceramic, height of amphora 20¹⁵⁄₁₆″ (53.2 cm). Museum of Fine Arts, Boston. Henry Lillie Pierce Fund (99.538).

Credit: Photograph © 2017 Museum of Fine Arts, Boston

BLACK-FIGURE VESSELS During the Archaic period, Athens became the dominant center for pottery manufacture and trade in Greece, and Athenian painters adopted Corinthian black-figure techniques (SEE FIG. 5-4), which became the principal mode of decoration throughout Greece in the sixth century BCE. At first, Athenian vase painters retained the horizontal banded composition that was characteristic of the Geometric period. Over time, however, they decreased the number of bands and increased the size of figures until a single narrative scene dominated each side of the vessel.

THE AMASIS PAINTER A mid-sixth-century BCE amphora—a large, all-purpose storage jar—with bands of decoration above and below a central figural composition illustrates this development (**FIG. 5-25**). The painting on this amphora has been attributed to an artist we call the Amasis Painter, since this distinctive style was first recognized on vessels such as this one that are signed by a prolific potter named Amasis.

Two maenads (female worshipers of the wine god Dionysos), intertwined with arms around each other's shoulders, skip forward to present their offerings—a long-eared rabbit and a small deer—to the god. (Amasis's signature is just above the rabbit.) The maenad holding the deer wears the skin of a spotted panther or leopard, its head still attached, draped over her shoulders and secured with a belt at her waist. The imposing, richly dressed god clasps a large **kantharos** (wine cup). This encounter between humans and a god appears to be a joyful, celebratory occasion rather than one of reverence or fear. The Amasis Painter favored strong shapes and patterns over conventions for making figures appear to occupy real space. He emphasized fine details, such as the large, delicate petal and spiral designs below each handle, the figures' meticulously arranged hair, and the bold patterns on their clothing.

EXEKIAS Perhaps the most famous of all Athenian black-figure painters, Exekias, signed many of his vessels as both potter and painter. He took his subjects from Greek mythology, which he and his patrons probably considered to be history. On the body of the amphora we saw at the beginning of this chapter, he portrayed Trojan War heroes Ajax and Achilles in a rare moment of relaxation playing dice (SEE FIG. 5-1). This is an episode not included in any literary source, but for Greeks familiar with the story, this anecdotal portrayal of friendly play would have been a poignant reminder that before the end of the war, the heroes would be parted by death. Knowing the story was critical to engaging with such paintings; artists often included identifying labels beside the characters to guide viewers so they could delight in the painters' rich renderings of familiar stories.

5-25 Amasis Painter **DIONYSOS WITH MAENADS**
c. 540 BCE. Black-figure decoration on an amphora. Ceramic, height of amphora 13″ (33.3 cm). Bibliothèque Nationale, Paris.

Credit: Bibliothèque nationale de France

RED-FIGURE VESSELS In the last third of the sixth century BCE, while many painters were still creating handsome black-figure wares, some turned to the new, more fluid technique called red-figure (see "Black-Figure and Red-Figure" opposite). The greater freedom and flexibility that resulted from painting rather than engraving details led ceramic painters to adopt the red-figure technique widely in a relatively short time. It allowed them to create livelier human figures with a more developed sense of bodily form—qualities that were increasingly popular in several media.

EUPHRONIOS One of the best-known red-figure artists was Euphronios. His rendering of the death of Sarpedon, about 515 BCE (see " Closer Look" on page 122), is painted on a krater—called a **calyx krater** because its handles curve up like a flower's calyx. Such a vessel was used as a punchbowl during a **symposium**, a social gathering of rich and powerful men. According to Homer's *Iliad*, Sarpedon, a son of Zeus and a mortal woman, was killed by the Greek warrior Patroclus while fighting for the Trojans. Euphronios captures the scene in which the warrior is being carried off to the underworld, the land of the dead.

Euphronios has created a balanced composition of verticals and horizontals that take the shape of the vessel into account. The bands of decoration above and below the

A Closer Look

THE DEATH OF SARPEDON

Hypnos (Sleep) and Thanatos (Death), identified by inscriptions that seem to emerge from their mouths, face each other on either side of the fallen body of Sarpedon, gently raising the slain warrior.

The god Hermes is identified not only by inscription, but also by his caduceus (staff with coiled snakes) and winged headgear. The attention to contours, distribution of drapery folds, and overlapping of forms give the twisting figure three-dimensionality.

Euphronios makes it appear as if Sarpedon's left leg is projecting into the viewer's space through the technique of foreshortening.

The painting's field is framed by bands of detailed ornament, placed to highlight the contours of the krater.

Sarpedon's body twists up toward the viewer, allowing Euphronios to outline every muscle and ligament of the torso, showing off both his knowledge of anatomy and his virtuosity in the newly developed red-figure technique.

Blood continues illogically to pour from the wounds in Sarpedon's corpse, not out of ignorance on the part of the artist but to heighten the dramatic effect of the scene.

5-26 Euphronios (painter) and Euxitheos (potter) **THE DEATH OF SARPEDON** c. 515 BCE. Red-figure decoration on a calyx krater. Ceramic, height of krater 18″ (45.7 cm). Museo Nazionale di Villa Giulia, Rome.

Credit: © 2016. Photo Scala, Florence - courtesy of the Ministero Beni e Att. Culturali

scene echo the long horizontal of the dead fighter's body, which seems to levitate in the gentle grasp of its bearers, and the inward-curving lines of the handles mirror the arching backs and extended wings of Hypnos (Sleep) and Thanatos (Death). The upright figures of the lance-bearers on each side and Hermes in the center balance the horizontal and diagonal elements of the composition. While conveying a sense of the mass and energy of human subjects, Euphronios also portrayed the elaborate details of their clothing, musculature, and facial features with the fine tip of a brush. And he created the impression of real space around the figures by gently foreshortening Sarpedon's left leg, which appears to be coming toward the viewer's own space. Such formal features, as well as the scene's sense of pathos, seem to connect Euphronios's work with the dying warriors of the pediments from Aegina (SEE FIGS. 5–14, 5–15).

The Early Classical Period, c. 480–450 BCE

How do increasing naturalism and idealization of the human figure transform sculpture and painting during the Early Classical Period?

Over the brief span of 160 years between c. 480 and 323 BCE, the Greeks established an ideal of beauty that has endured in the Western world to this day. Scholars have associated Greek Classical art with three general concepts: humanism, rationalism, and idealism (see "Classic and Classical" on page 124). The ancient Greeks believed the words of their philosophers and expected to see them embodied in their art: "Man is the measure of all things," that is, seek an ideal based on the human form; "Know thyself," seek the inner significance of forms; and "Nothing in excess," reproduce only essential forms. In their embrace of humanism, the Greeks even imagined their gods as perfect human beings. But the Greeks valued human reason over human emotion. They saw all aspects of life, including the arts, as having meaning and pattern; in their view, nothing happened by accident. It is not surprising that great Greek artists and architects were not only practitioners but also theoreticians. In the fifth century BCE, the sculptor Polykleitos and the architect Iktinos both wrote books on the theory underlying their practices.

Art historians usually divide the Classical into three phases based on the formal qualities of the art: the Early Classical period (c. 480–450 BCE), the High Classical period (c. 450–400 BCE), and the Late Classical period (c. 400–323 BCE). The Early Classical period begins with the defeat of the Persians in 480–479 BCE by an alliance of city-states led by Athens and Sparta. The expanding Persian Empire had posed a formidable threat to the independence of the city-states, and the two sides had been locked in battle for decades until the Greek alliance was able to repulse a Persian invasion and score a decisive victory. Some scholars have argued that success against the Persians gave the Greeks a self-confidence that accelerated artistic development, inspiring artists to seek new and more effective ways to express their cities' accomplishments. In any case, the period that followed the Persian Wars, extending to about 450 BCE, saw the emergence of a new stylistic direction, away from elegant stylizations and toward a sense of greater faithfulness to the natural appearance of human beings and their world.

Marble Sculpture

In the remarkably short time of only a few generations, Greek sculptors had moved far from the stiff postures and rigid frontality of the Archaic *kouroi* to more relaxed poses in lifelike figures such as the so-called **KRITIOS BOY** of about 480 BCE (**FIG. 5-27**). The softly rounded body forms, broad facial features, and calm expression give the figure an air of self-confident seriousness. His weight rests on his left, or engaged, leg, while his right, or relaxed, leg bends slightly at the knee, and a noticeable curve in his spine counters

5-27 KRITIOS BOY

From the Akropolis, Athens. c. 480 BCE. Marble, height 3'10" (1.17 m). Akropolis Museum, Athens.

The damaged figure, excavated from the debris on the Athenian Akropolis, was thought by its finders to be by the Greek sculptor Kritios, whose work they knew only from Roman copies.

Credit: (left) © Craig & Marie Mauzy, Athens
Credit: (right) Studio Kontos Photostock

Art and its Contexts

CLASSIC AND CLASSICAL

The English words "classic" and "classical" both come from the Latin word *classis*, referring to the division of people into classes based on wealth. But they do not mean the same thing today. "Classic" has come to mean "first class" or "the standard of excellence," and in the most general usage, a "classic" is something—a book, a car, a film, even a soft drink—thought to be of lasting quality and universal esteem. However, the meaning of "Classical" is different. In art history, it refers to the work of Greek artists in the fifth century BCE, who sought to create ideal images based on strict mathematical proportions. Since Roman artists were inspired by the Greeks, "Classical" also often refers to the culture of ancient Rome. By extension, the word may also mean "in the style of ancient Greece and Rome," whenever or wherever that style is used. (You will notice that when "Classical" is used in these contexts, it is capitalized.)

the slight shifting of his hips and a subtle drop of one of his shoulders. We see here the beginnings of **contrapposto**, the convention (later developed in full by High Classical sculptors such as Polykleitos) of presenting standing figures with opposing alternations of tension and relaxation around a central axis that will dominate Classical art. The slight turn of the head invites the spectator to move around the figure and admire the small marble statue from every angle.

Bronze Sculpture

Development of the lost-wax process in hollow-cast bronze gave Greek sculptors the potential to create more complex action poses with outstretched arms and legs. These were very difficult to create in marble, since unbalanced figures might topple over and extended limbs might break off due to their weight. Bronze figures were easier to balance, and the metal's greater tensile strength made complicated poses and gestures technically possible.

The painted underside of an Athenian **kylix** (broad, flat drinking cup) portrays work in a late Archaic foundry for casting life-size figures (**FIG. 5-28**), providing clear evidence that the Greeks were creating large bronze statues in active poses as early as the first decades of the fifth century BCE. The walls of the workshop are filled with hanging tools and other foundry paraphernalia including several sketches: a horse, human heads, and human figures in different poses. One worker, wearing what looks like a present-day construction helmet, squats to tend the furnace on the left, perhaps aided by an assistant who peeks from behind. The man in the center, possibly the supervisor, leans on a staff, while a third worker assembles a leaping figure that is braced against a molded support. The unattached head lies between his feet.

THE CHARIOTEER A spectacular and rare life-size bronze, the **CHARIOTEER** (**FIG. 5-29**), cast about 470 BCE, documents the skills of Early Classical bronze-casters. It was found in the sanctuary of Apollo at Delphi together with fragments of a bronze chariot and horses, all buried during an earthquake in 373 BCE that may have saved them from the fate of most ancient bronzes, which were

5–28 Foundry Painter
A BRONZE FOUNDRY
490–480 BCE. Red-figure decoration on a kylix from Vulci, Italy. Ceramic, diameter of kylix 12″ (31 cm). Staatliche Museen zu Berlin, Preussischer Kulturbesitz, Antikensammlung.

The Foundry Painter has masterfully organized this workshop scene within the flaring space that extends upward from the foot of the vessel and along its curving underside to the lip, thereby using a circle as the ground-line for his composition.

Credit: © 2016. Photo Scala, Florence/bpk, Bildagentur für Kunst, Kultur und Geschichte, Berlin. Photo: Ingrid Geske melted down so the material could be recycled into new works. According to its inscription, the sculptural group commemorated a victory in the Pythian Games of 478 or 474 BCE, though it was the team of horses and the owner—not the charioteer—who were being celebrated.

The face of this youth is highly idealized, but there is a lifelike quality to the way his head turns slightly to one side, and the glittering onyx eyes and fine copper eyelashes enhance his intense expression. He stands at attention, sheathed in a long robe with rippling folds that appear to fall naturally under their own weight, varying in width and depth, yet seemingly capable of swaying with the charioteer's movement. The feet, with their closely observed toes, toenails, and swelling veins over the instep, are so realistic that they seem to have been cast from molds made from the feet of a living person.

THE RIACE WARRIORS   Shipwreck as well as earthquake has protected ancient bronzes from recycling. As recently as 1972, divers recovered a pair of heavily corroded, larger-than-life-size bronze figures from the seabed off the coast of Italy, dating from about 460–450 BCE.

Initially, a scuba diver in the Ionian Sea near the beach resort of Riace thought he had found a human elbow and upper arm protruding from sand about 25 feet beneath the sea. Taking a closer look, he discovered that the arm was made of metal, not flesh, and was part of a large statue. He uncovered a second statue nearby, and underwater salvagers soon raised the statues: bronze warriors more than 6 feet tall, complete in every respect, except for swords, shields, and one helmet.

5-29 CHARIOTEER

From the Sanctuary of Apollo, Delphi. c. 470 BCE. Bronze, copper (lips and lashes), silver (hand), onyx (eyes); height 5′11″ (1.8 m). Archaeological Museum, Delphi.

The setting of a work of art affects the impression it makes. Today, the *Charioteer* is exhibited on a low base in the peaceful surroundings of a museum, isolated from other works and spotlighted for close examination. Its effect would have been very different in its original outdoor location, standing in a horse-drawn chariot atop a tall monument. Viewers in ancient times, tired from the steep climb to the sanctuary and jostled by crowds of fellow pilgrims, could have absorbed only its overall effect, not the fine details of the face, robe, and body visible to today's viewers.

Credit: © Craig & Marie Mauzy, Athens/Archeological Museum, Delphi

5-30 WARRIOR
Found in the sea off Riace, Italy. c. 460–450 BCE. Bronze with bone and glass eyes, silver teeth, and copper lips and nipples; height 6′9″ (2.05 m). National Archeological Museum, Reggio Calabria, Italy.

Credit: © akg-images/Nimatallah

After centuries underwater, however, the bronze *Warriors* were corroded and covered with accretions. The clay cores from the casting process were still inside, adding to the deterioration by absorbing lime and sea salts. Conservators first removed all the exterior corrosion and lime encrustations using surgeon's scalpels, pneumatic drills, and high-technology equipment such as sonar (soundwave) probes and micro-sanders. Then they painstakingly removed the clay core through existing holes in the heads and feet using hooks, scoops, jets of distilled water, and concentrated solutions of peroxide. Finally, they cleaned the figures thoroughly by soaking them in solvents and sealed them with a fixative specially designed for use on metals before exhibiting them in 1980.

The **WARRIOR** in **FIG. 5-30** reveals a striking balance between the idealized smoothness of "perfected" anatomy conforming to Early Classical standards and the reproduction of details observed from nature, such as the swelling veins in the backs of the hands. Contrapposto is further developed here than in the Kritios Boy, with a more pronounced counterbalance between tension (right leg and left arm) and relaxation (left leg and right arm), seeming to raise the possibility of movement and life. The lifelike quality of this bronze is further heightened by inserted eyeballs of bone and colored glass, copper inlays on lips and nipples, silver plating on the teeth that peek between parted lips, and attached eyelashes and eyebrows of separately cast strands of bronze. This accommodation of the intense study of the human figure to an idealism that belies the irregularity of nature will be continued by artists in the High Classical period.

Ceramic Painting

Greek potters and painters continued to work with the red-figure technique throughout the fifth century BCE, refining their ability to create supple, rounded figures posed in ever more complicated and dynamic compositions. One of the most prolific Early Classical artists was Douris, whose signature appears on over 40 surviving pots decorated with scenes from everyday life as well as mythological subjects. His conspicuous skill in composing complex figural scenes that respond to the available pictorial fields of a variety of vessel types is evident in a frieze of frisky satyrs that he painted c. 480 BCE around the perimeter of a **psykter** (**FIG. 5-31**). This strangely shaped pot was a wine cooler, made to float in a krater (see "Closer Look" on page 122) filled with chilled water, its extended bottom serving as a keel to keep it from tipping over.

Like the krater, the psykter was a vessel meant for use in drinking parties know as symposia—lively, elite male gatherings that focused on wine, music, games, and love

5-31 Douris **FROLICKING SATYRS**

c.480 BCE. Red-figure decoration on a psykter. Ceramic, height 11¹⁵⁄₁₆″ (28.7 cm). British Museum, London.

Credit: © The Trustees of the British Museum. All rights reserved.

making—and the decoration was chosen with this context in mind. The seeming acrobatic virtuosity of the satyrs' movements is matched by the artist's own virtuosity in composing them as an interlocking set of diagonal gestures that alternately challenge and follow the bulging form around which they are painted. The playful interaction of satyrs with their kylixes must have amused the tipsy revelers, especially when the pot was gently bobbing within a krater, making the satyrs seem to be walking around in circles on top of the wine. One satyr cups his kylix to his buttocks, juxtaposing convex and concave shapes. Another, balanced in a precarious handstand, seems to be observing his own reflection within the wine of his kylix.

But Douris was also capable of more lyrical compositions, as seen in the painting he placed inside a kylix (**FIG. 5-32**) similar in shape to those used as props by the satyrs on the psykter. This **tondo** (circular painting) was an intimate picture. It became visible only to the user of the cup when he tilted up the kylix to drink from it; otherwise, sitting on a table, the painting would have been obscured by the dark wine pool within it. A languidly posed and elegantly draped youth stands behind an altar pouring wine from an **oinochoe** (wine jug) into the kylix of a more dignified, bearded older man. Euphronios's tentative foreshortening of Sarpedon's bent leg on his krater (see "Closer Look" on page 122) blossoms in the work of Douris to become full-scale, formal projection as the graceful youth

on this kylix bends his arm from the background to project his tipping oinochoe over the laterally held kylix of his seated companion.

For the well-educated reveler using this cup at a symposium, there were several possible readings for the scene. This could be the legendary Athenian king Kekrops, who appears, identified by inscription, in the scene Douris painted on the underside of the kylix. Also portrayed there are Zeus and the young Trojan prince Ganymede, whom the supreme god abducted to Olympus to serve as his cupbearer. Or, since the symposia themselves were sites of amorous interactions between older and younger men, the user of this cup might have found his own situation mirrored in what he was observing at the bottom of the cup while he drank.

Wall Painting

Although ancient Greek commentators describe elaborate, monumental wall paintings and discuss the output and careers of illustrious painters from the fifth and fourth centuries BCE, almost nothing of this art has survived. We rely heavily on ceramics to fill gaps in our knowledge of Greek painting, assuming that the decoration of these more modest, utilitarian vessels reflects the glorious painting tradition documented in texts. There are also tantalizing survivals in provincial Greek sites. Principal among

5–32 Douris **A YOUTH POURING WINE INTO THE KYLIX OF A COMPANION**
c. 480 BCE. Red-figure decoration on a kylix. Ceramic, height 12¾" (32.4 cm). The Soprintendenza Speciale per i Beni Archeologici di Napoli e Pompei.

Credit: Courtsy Ministero dei Beni e delle Attività Culturali e del Turismo - Museo Archeologico Nazionale di Napoli

5–33 RECONSTRUCTION DRAWING OF THE TOMB OF THE DIVER, POSEIDONIA (ROMAN PAESTUM)
c. 480 BCE.

Credit: Illustration: Peter Bull

On one short side (visible in the reconstruction drawing), a striding nude youth has filled the oinochoe in his right hand with the mixture of wine and water that was served from large kraters (portrayed on the table behind him) as the featured beverage of the symposium. He extends his arm toward a group of revelers reclining along one of the long walls (**FIG. 5–34**), each of whom has a kylix waiting to be filled. The man at the left reclines alone, raising his kylix to salute a couple just arriving—or perhaps toasting their departure—on the other short side. Behind him, the two couples on the long frieze—in each case a bearded, mature man paired with a youthful companion—are already engaged in the party. The young man in the middle pairing is slinging his upraised kylix, presumably to throw the dregs of his wine toward a target, a popular symposium game. His partner turns in the opposite direction to ogle at the amorous pair at the right, who have abandoned their cups on the table in front of them and turned to embrace, gazing into each other's eyes.

The significance of these paintings in relationship to a young man's tomb is not absolutely clear. They may demonstrate the deceased's elevated social status, since only wealthy aristocrats participated in such gatherings. The symposium could also represent funerary feasting or a vision of the pleasures that await the deceased in a world beyond death.

them are the well-preserved Early Classical wall paintings of c. 480–470 BCE in the Tomb of the Diver, discovered in 1968 just south of the Greek colony of Poseidonia (Roman Paestum) in southern Italy.

The paintings cover travertine slabs that formed the four walls and roof of a tomb submerged into the natural rock (**FIG. 5–33**), approximately 7 feet long, 3½ feet wide, and 2½ feet deep. Painted in *buon fresco* (water-based pigments applied to wet plaster) on a white ground in earthy browns, yellows, and blacks with accents of blue, the scenes on the walls surrounded the occupant of this tomb with a group of reclining men assembled for a symposium. Many of the most distinguished of surviving Greek ceramic vessels were made for use in these playfully competitive parties, and they are highlighted in the tomb paintings.

5–34 A SYMPOSIUM SCENE
From the Tomb of the Diver, Poseidonia (Roman Paestum). c. 480 BCE. Fresco on travertine slab, height 31″ (78 cm). Paestum Museum.

Credit: © akg-images/Andrea Baguzzi

5-35 A DIVER

From the Tomb of the Diver, Poseidonia (Roman Paestum). c. 480 BCE. Fresco on travertine slab, height 3'4" (1.02 m). Paestum Museum.

Credit: © akg-images/Erich Lessing

The transition between this world and the next certainly seems to be the theme of the spare but energetic painting on the roof of the tomb, where a naked boy is caught in mid-dive, poised to plunge into the water portrayed as a blue mound underneath him (**FIG. 5-35**). Whereas the symposium scene follows an ancient Greek pictorial tradition, especially prominent on ceramic vessels made for use by its male participants, this diver finds his closest parallels in Etruscan tomb painting (SEE FIG. 6–5), flourishing at this time farther north in Italy. Since the scene was located directly over the body of the man entombed here, it is likely that it mirrors his own plunge from life into death. And since it combines Greek and Etruscan traditions, perhaps this tomb was made for an Etruscan citizen of Poseidonia, whose tomb was commissioned from a Greek artist working in this flourishing provincial center.

The High Classical Period, c. 450–400 BCE

What qualities constitute the High Classical moment of Greek art and architecture in Athens?

The High Classical period of Greek art lasted only a half-century, 450–400 BCE. The use of the word "high" to qualify the art of this time reflects the value judgments of art historians who have considered this period a pinnacle of artistic refinement, producing works that set a standard of unsurpassed excellence. Some have even referred to this half-century as Greece's "Golden Age," although these decades were also marked by turmoil and destruction. Without a common enemy, Sparta and Athens turned on each other in a series of conflicts known as the Peloponnesian War. Sparta dominated the Peloponnese peninsula and much of the rest of mainland Greece, while Athens controlled the Aegean and became the wealthy and influential center of a maritime empire. Today we remember Athens more for its cultural and intellectual brilliance and its experiments with democratic government, which reached its zenith in the fifth century BCE under the charismatic leader Perikles (c. 495–429 BCE), than for the imperialistic tendencies of its considerable commercial power.

Except for a few brief interludes, Perikles dominated Athenian politics and culture from 462 BCE until his death in 429 BCE. Although comedy writers of the time sometimes mocked him, calling him "Zeus" and "The Olympian" because of his haughty personality, he was a dynamic, charismatic political and military leader. He was also a great patron of the arts, supporting the use of Athenian wealth for the adornment of the city and encouraging artists to promote a public image of peace, prosperity, and power. Perikles said of his city and its accomplishments, "Future generations will marvel at us, as the present age marvels at us now." It was a prophecy he himself helped fulfill.

The Akropolis

Athens originated as a Neolithic **akropolis**, or "city on top of a hill" (*akro* means "high" and *polis* means "city"), that later served as a fortress and sanctuary. As the city grew, the Akropolis became the religious and ceremonial center devoted primarily to the goddess Athena, the city's patron and protector.

After Persian troops destroyed the Akropolis in 480 BCE, the Athenians vowed to keep it in ruins as a memorial, but Perikles convinced them to rebuild it, arguing that this project honored the gods, especially Athena, who had helped the Greeks defeat the Persians. Perikles intended to create a visual expression of Athenian values and civic pride that would bolster the city's status as the capital of the empire. He chose his close friend Pheidias, a renowned sculptor, to supervise the rebuilding and assembled under him the most talented artists in Athens.

The cost and labor involved in this undertaking were staggering. Large quantities of gold, ivory, and exotic woods had to be imported. Some 22,000 tons of marble were transported 10 miles from mountain quarries to city workshops. Perikles was severely criticized by his political opponents for this extravagance, but it never cost

him popular support. In fact, many working-class Athenians-—laborers, carpenters, masons, sculptors, and the farmers and merchants who kept them supplied and fed—benefited from his expenditures.

Work on the **AKROPOLIS** continued throughout the fifth century BCE (**FIG. 5–36**). Visitors in 400 BCE would have climbed a steep ramp on the west side of the hill (in the foreground of FIG. 5–36) to the sanctuary entrance, perhaps pausing to admire the small temple dedicated to Athena Nike (Athena as goddess of victory in war) displayed on a projection of rock above the ramp. After passing through an impressive porticoed gatehouse called the Propylaia, they would have seen a huge bronze figure of Athena Promachos (the Defender) designed and executed by Pheidias between about 465 and 455 BCE. Sailors entering the Athenian port of Piraeus, about 10 miles away, could see the sun reflected off her helmet and spear tip. Behind this statue was a walled area that enclosed the Erechtheion, a temple dedicated to several deities, and to its right was the largest building on the Akropolis: the Parthenon, a temple dedicated to Athena Parthenos (the Virgin). Visitors approached the temple from its northwest corner, instantly grasping the imposing width and depth of this building, isolated like a work of sculpture elevated on a pedestal.

5-36 THE AKROPOLIS, ATHENS
Reconstruction drawing as it appeared
c. 447–432 BCE.

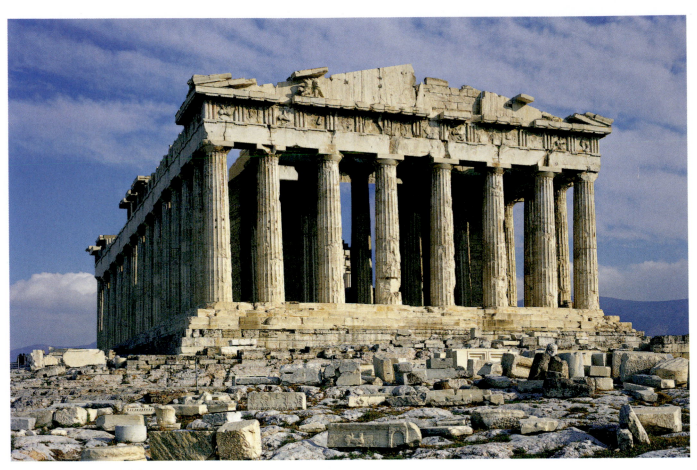

5-37A Kallikrates and Iktinos **THE PARTHENON**

Akropolis, Athens. 447–432 BCE. Pentelic marble. Photograph: view from the northwest.

Credit: © Craig & Marie Mauzy, Athens

The Parthenon

Sometime around 490 BCE, Athenians began work on a temple to Athena Parthenos that was still unfinished when the Persians sacked the Akropolis a decade later. In 447 BCE Perikles commissioned the architects Kallikrates and Iktinos to design a larger temple using the existing foundation and stone elements. The finest white marble was used throughout—even on the roof, in place of the more usual terra-cotta tiles (**FIG. 5-37**). The planning and execution of the Parthenon (dedicated in 438 BCE) required extraordinary mathematical, mechanical, and artistic skills from a large number of architects, builders, sculptors, and painters. The result is as much a testament to Pheidias's administrative talent as his artistic vision, since he supervised the entire project.

One key to the Parthenon's sense of harmony and balance is an attention to proportions—especially the ratio of 4:9, expressing the relationship of breadth to length and the relationship of column diameter to space between columns. Also important are subtle refinements of design, deviations from absolute regularity made to create a harmonious effect when the building was actually viewed. For example, since long, straight horizontal lines seem to

5-37B PLAN OF THE PARTHENON

Akropolis, Athens. 447–432 BCE.

opisthodomos

stereobate

stylobate

cella

peristyle colonnade

pronaos

sag when seen from a distance, the Parthenon's base and entablature curve slightly upward to correct this optical distortion. The columns have a gentle swelling (entasis) and tilt inward slightly from bottom to top; the corners are strengthened visually by reducing the space between columns at those points. These refinements give the Parthenon a buoyant, organic appearance and prevent it from looking like a heavy, lifeless stone box. The significance of their achievement was clear to its builders—Iktinos wrote a book on the proportions of this masterpiece.

The sculptural decoration of the Parthenon reflects Pheidias's unifying aesthetic vision, but it also conveys a number of political and ideological themes: the triumph of the democratic Greek city-states over imperial Persia, the preeminence of Athens thanks to the favor of Athena, and the victory of an enlightened Greek civilization over despotism and barbarism.

PEDIMENTS   As with most temples, sculpture in the round filled both pediments of the Parthenon, set on the deep shelf of the cornice and secured to the wall with metal pins. Unfortunately, much of the sculpture has been damaged, lost, or removed to museums over the centuries. Using the locations of the pinholes and weathering marks on the cornice, as well as drawings made by French artist Jacques Carrey (1649–1726) on a visit to Athens in 1674, however, scholars have been able to determine the placement of surviving statues and infer the poses of missing ones. We know the subjects from the descriptions of the second-century CE Greek writer Pausanias. The west pediment sculpture, facing the entrance to the Akropolis, presented the contest Athena won over the sea god Poseidon for rule over the Athenians. The east pediment figures, above the entrance to the cella, portrayed the birth of Athena, fully grown and clad in armor, from the brow of her father, Zeus.

The statues from the east pediment are the best preserved of the two groups (**FIG. 5-38**). Flanking the missing central figures—probably Zeus seated on a throne with the newborn adult Athena standing at his side—were groups of goddesses and a single male figure. In the left corner was the sun god Helios in his horse-drawn chariot rising from the sea, while at the right the moon goddess Selene descended in her chariot to the sea, the head of her tired horse hanging over the cornice. The reclining male nude, whose relaxed pose fits so easily into the left pediment, has been identified as either Herakles with his lion's skin or Dionysos (god of wine) lying on a panther skin. The two seated women may be the earth and grain goddesses Demeter and Persephone. The running female figure just to the left of center is Iris, messenger of the gods, spreading the news of Athena's birth.

The three interlocked female figures on the right who seem to be awakening from a deep sleep, two sitting upright and one reclining, are probably Hestia (a sister of Zeus and the goddess of the hearth), Dione (one of Zeus's many consorts), and her daughter, Aphrodite. The sculptor expertly rendered the female forms beneath the draperies, which both cover and reveal the three figures' bodies while uniting them into a single mass.

METOPES   The all-marble Parthenon had two sculptured friezes, one above the outer peristyle and another atop the cella wall inside. The Doric frieze on the exterior had 92 metope reliefs depicting legendary battles symbolized by combat between two representative figures: a centaur against a Lapith (a mythical people of pre-Hellenic times); a god against a Titan; a Greek against a Trojan; and a Greek against an Amazon (one of the mythical tribe of female warriors sometimes said to be the daughters of the war god Ares). Each of these struggles represented for the Greeks the triumph of reason over passion.

Among the best-preserved metope reliefs are several depicting the battle between Lapiths and centaurs from

Art and its Contexts

WHO OWNS THE ART? THE ELGIN MARBLES AND THE EUPHRONIOS KRATER

At the beginning of the nineteenth century, Thomas Bruce, the British Earl of Elgin and ambassador to Constantinople, acquired much of the surviving sculpture from the Parthenon, which was at that time being used for military purposes. He shipped it back to London in 1801 to decorate a lavish mansion for himself and his wife, but by the time he returned to England, his wife had left him and the ancient treasures were at the center of a financial dispute and had to be sold. Referred to as the Elgin Marbles, most of the sculpture is now in the British Museum, including all the elements seen in FIGURE 5-38. The Greek government has tried unsuccessfully to have the Elgin Marbles returned.

Another Greek treasure has been in the news more recently. In 1972, a krater painted by Euphronios (see "Closer Look" on page 122) and depicting the death of the warrior Sarpedon during the Trojan War was purchased by the Metropolitan Museum of Art in New York. Museum officials were told that it had come from a private collection, and it became the centerpiece of the museum's galleries of Greek vessels. But in 1995, Italian and Swiss investigators raided a warehouse in Geneva, Switzerland, where they found documents showing that the krater had been stolen from an Etruscan tomb near Rome. The Italian government demanded its return. The controversy was not resolved until 2006. The krater, along with other objects known to have been stolen from Italian sites, was returned, and the Metropolitan Museum is displaying pieces "of equal beauty" under long-term loan agreements with Italy.

5–38 PHOTOGRAPHIC MOCK-UP OF THE EAST PEDIMENT OF THE PARTHENON (USING PHOTOGRAPHS OF THE EXTANT MARBLE SCULPTURE)

c. 447–432 BCE. The gap in the center represents the space that would have been occupied by the missing sculpture. The pediment is over 90 feet (27.45 m) long; the central space of about 40 feet (12.2 m) is missing. British Museum, London.

Credit: © The Trustees of the British Museum. All rights reserved.

the south side of the Parthenon. The panel shown here (**FIG. 5–39**) presents a pause within the struggle, a timeless image standing for an extended historical episode. Forms are reduced to their most characteristic essentials, and so dramatic is the X-shaped composition that we easily accept its visual contradictions. The Lapith is caught at an instant of total equilibrium. What could be a grueling tug-of-war between a man and a man-beast has been transformed into an athletic ballet, choreographed to show off the Lapith warrior's flexed muscles and graceful movements against the implausible backdrop of his carefully draped cloak.

PROCESSIONAL FRIEZE Enclosed within the Parthenon's Doric peristyle, a continuous, 525–foot-long Ionic frieze ran along the exterior wall of the cella. Since the eighteenth century, its subject has been seen as a procession celebrating the festival that took place in Athens every four years, when the women of the city wove a new wool peplos and carried it to the Akropolis to clothe an ancient wooden cult statue of Athena. Both the skilled riders in the procession (**FIG. 5–40**) and the graceful but sturdy young walkers (**FIG. 5–41**) are representative types, ideal inhabitants of a successful city-state. The underlying message of the frieze is that Athenians are a healthy, vigorous people united in a democratic civic body favored by the gods. The people are inseparable from and symbolic of the city itself.

5–39 LAPITH FIGHTING A CENTAUR

Metope relief from the Doric frieze on the south side of the Parthenon. c. 447–432 BCE. Marble, height 56″ (1.42 m). British Museum, London.

Credit: © The Trustees of the British Museum. All rights reserved.

Credit: © The Trustees of the British Museum. All rights reserved.

5–40 HORSEMEN

Detail of the Procession, from the Ionic frieze on the north side of the Parthenon. c. 447–432 BCE. Marble, height 41¾″ (106 cm).
British Museum, London.

Credit: © The Trustees of the British Museum. All rights reserved.

5–41 YOUNG WOMEN AND MEN

Detail of the Procession, from the Ionic frieze on the east side of the Parthenon. c. 447–432 BCE. Marble, height 3′6″ (1.08 m).
Musée du Louvre, Paris.

Credit: Bridgeman Images

A more recent interpretation by art historian Joan Connelly, however, has challenged the traditional reading of the frieze as an ideal rendering of a contemporary event. She argues that—consistent with what we know of temple decoration elsewhere—what is portrayed is not contemporary but mythological: the legendary Athenian king Erechtheus, who, following the advice of the oracle at Delphi, sacrificed one of his own daughters to save the city of Athens from an external enemy. This theme, also incorporating a procession, would have had obvious resonance with the recent Athenian victory over the Persians.

As with the metope relief of a Lapith fighting a centaur (SEE FIG. 5–39), viewers of the processional frieze easily accept its disproportions, spatial compression, and incongruities, including men and women standing as tall as rearing horses. Carefully planned rhythmic variations contribute to the effectiveness of the frieze. Horses plunge ahead at full gallop; women proceed with a slow, stately step; and men pause to look back at the progress of those behind them.

In executing the frieze, the sculptors took into account the spectators' low viewpoint and the dim lighting inside the peristyle. They carved the top of the frieze band in higher relief than the lower part, thus tilting the figures out to catch the reflected light from the pavement, permitting a clearer reading of the action. The subtleties in the sculpture may not have been as evident to Athenians in the fifth century BCE as they are now: the frieze, seen at the top of a high wall and between columns, was originally completely painted. Figures in red and ocher, accented with glittering gold and real metal details, were set against a contrasting background of dark blue.

STATUE OF ATHENA PARTHENOS After having explored the considerable richness of sculpture on the exterior of the Parthenon, viewers with permission could have climbed the east steps to look into the cella, where they would have seen Pheidias's colossal gold and ivory statue of Athena—outfitted in armor and holding a shield in one hand and a winged Nike (Victory) in the other—which was installed in the temple and dedicated in 438 BCE (**FIG. 5–42**). The original has vanished, but descriptions and later copies allow us a clear sense of its appearance and its imposing size, nearly 40 feet tall.

5-42 RE-CREATION OF PHEIDIAS'S HUGE GOLD AND IVORY FIGURE OF ATHENA

Royal Ontario Museum, Toronto.

Credit: With permission of the Royal Ontario Museum © ROM

"The Canon" of Polykleitos

Just as Greek architects defined and followed a set of standards for ideal temple design, Greek sculptors sought an ideal for representing the human body. Studying actual human beings closely and selecting the attributes they considered most desirable—such as regular facial features, smooth skin, and particular body proportions—sculptors combined them into a single ideal of physical perfection.

The best-known theorist of the High Classical period was the sculptor Polykleitos of Argos. About 450 BCE, balancing careful observation with generalizing **idealization**, he developed a set of rules for constructing what he considered the ideal human figure, which he set down in a treatise called the Canon (kanon is Greek for "measure," "rule," or "law"). To illustrate his theory, Polykleitos created a bronze statue of a standing man carrying a spear—perhaps the hero Achilles. Neither the treatise nor the original statue has survived, but both were widely discussed in the writings of his contemporaries, and later Roman artists made marble copies of the *Spear Bearer* (*Doryphoros*). By studying these copies, scholars have tried to determine the set of measurements that defined ideal human proportions in Polykleitos's Canon.

The Canon included a system of ratios between a basic unit and the length of various body parts. Some studies suggest that this basic unit may have been the length of the figure's index finger or the width of its hand across the knuckles; others suggest that it was the height of the head from chin to hairline. The Canon also included guidelines for *symmetria* ("commensurability"), by which Polykleitos meant the relationship of body parts to one another. In the *Spear Bearer*, he explored not only proportions, but also the diagonally counterbalanced relationships between weight-bearing and relaxed legs and arms around a central axis, referred to as contrapposto.

The Roman marble copy of the **SPEAR BEARER** (**FIG. 5-43**) shows a male athlete perfectly balanced with the whole weight of the upper body supported over the tense and straight ("engaged") right leg. The relaxed left leg is bent at the knee, with the left foot poised on the ball of the foot, suggesting the weight shift that comes before and after movement. The pattern of tension and relaxation is reversed in the arrangement of the arms, with the right relaxed on the engaged side, and the left bent to support the weight of the (missing) spear. The pronounced tilt of the *Spear Bearer*'s hipline accommodates the raising of the left foot onto its ball, and the head is turned toward the same side as the engaged leg. Hints of this dynamically balanced body pose—characteristic of High Classical standing figure sculpture—had already appeared in the Kritios Boy (SEE FIG. 5-27), and it was developed further in the Riace *Warrior* (SEE FIG. 5-30).

5-43 Polykleitos **SPEAR BEARER (DORYPHOROS)**
Roman copy after the original bronze of c. 450–440 BCE. Marble, height 6′11″ (2.12 m); tree trunk and brace strut are Roman additions. National Archaeological Museum, Naples.

Credit: © akg-images/De Agostini Picture Lib./G. Nimatallah

The Propylaia and the Erechtheion

Upon completion of the Parthenon, work began in 437 BCE on the monumental gatehouse, the Propylaia (**FIG. 5-44**), that had been part of the original design of the Akropolis complex. The Propylaia had no sculptural decoration, but its north wing was originally a dining hall that later became the earliest known museum (meaning "home of the Muses"), a gallery built specifically to house a collection of paintings for public view.

Construction of the **ERECHTHEION** (**FIG. 5-45**), the second important temple erected on the Akropolis under Perikles's building program, began in the 430s BCE and ended in 406 BCE, just before the fall of Athens to Sparta. The asymmetrical plan reflects the building's multiple functions in housing several shrines, and also conformed to the sharply sloping terrain on which it is located. The Erechtheion stands on the site of the mythical contest between the sea god Poseidon and Athena for patronage over Athens. During this contest, Poseidon struck a rock with his trident (three-pronged harpoon), bringing forth a spout of water, but Athena gave an olive tree to Athens and won the contest. The Athenians enclosed what they believed to be this sacred rock, bearing the marks of the trident, in the Erechtheion's north porch. The Erechtheion also housed the venerable wooden cult statue of Athena that was the center of the Panathenaic festival.

The north and east porches of the Erechtheion came to epitomize the Ionic order and have served as an important model for European architects since the eighteenth

5-44 THE MONUMENTAL ENTRANCE TO THE AKROPOLIS, ATHENS
The Propylaia (Mnesikles) with the Temple of Athena Nike (Kallikrates) on the bastion at the right. c. 437–423 BCE.

Credit: Studio Kontos Photostock

5-45 ERECHTHEION

Akropolis, Athens. 430s–406 BCE. View from the east. Porch of the Maidens at left; the north porch can be seen through the columns of the east wall.

Credit: © S.Borisov/Shutterstock

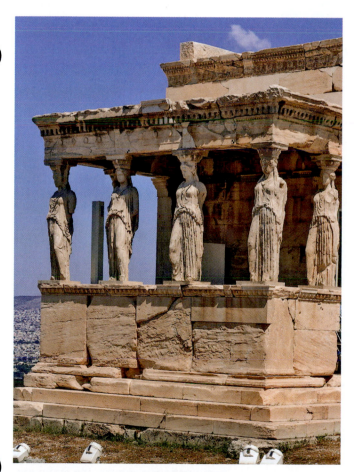

5-46 PORCH OF THE MAIDENS (SOUTH PORCH), ERECHTHEION

Akropolis, Athens. c. 420–410 BCE.

Credit: © Boris17/Shutterstock

century. Taller and more slender in proportion than the Doric, the Ionic order also has richer and more elaborately carved decoration (see "The Greek Orders" on page 111). The columns rise from molded bases and end in volute (spiral) capitals; the frieze is continuous.

The **PORCH OF THE MAIDENS** (FIG. 5–46), on the south side facing the Parthenon, is even more famous. Raised on a high base, its six stately caryatids support an Ionic entablature made up of bands of carved molding. In a pose characteristic of Classical figures, each caryatid's weight is supported on one engaged leg, while the free leg, bent at the knee, rests on the ball of the foot. The three caryatids on the left have their right legs engaged, and the three on the right have their left legs engaged, creating a sense of closure, symmetry, and rhythm.

THE TEMPLE OF ATHENA NIKE The Ionic Temple of Athena Nike (victory in war), located south of the Propylaia, was designed and built about 425 BCE, probably by Kallikrates (SEE FIG. 5–44). Reduced to rubble during the Turkish occupation of Greece in the seventeenth century CE, the temple has since been rebuilt. Its diminutive size—about 27 by 19 feet—and refined Ionic decoration are in marked contrast to the weightier Doric Propylaia adjacent to it.

Between 410 and 405 BCE, this temple was surrounded by a parapet or low wall faced with sculptured panels depicting Athena presiding over the preparation of a celebration by winged Nikes (victory figures). The parapet no longer exists, but some panels have survived, including

5-47 NIKE (VICTORY) ADJUSTING HER SANDAL

Fragment of relief decoration from the parapet (now destroyed), Temple of Athena Nike, Akropolis, Athens. Last quarter of the 5th century (perhaps 410–405) BCE. Marble, height 3'6" (1.06 m). Akropolis Museum, Athens.

Credit: © Craig & Marie Mauzy, Athens/Akropolis Museum, Athens

the celebrated **NIKE (VICTORY) ADJUSTING HER SANDAL** (FIG. 5-47). The figure bends forward gracefully, allowing her chiton (tunic) to slip off one shoulder. Her large, overlapping wings effectively balance her unstable pose. Unlike the decorative swirls of heavy fabric covering the Parthenon goddesses and the weighty, pleated robes of the Erechtheion caryatids, the textile covering this Nike appears delicate and light, clinging to her body like wet silk, one of the most discreetly erotic images in ancient art.

The Athenian Agora

In Athens, as in most cities of ancient Greece, commercial, civic, and social life revolved around the marketplace, or **agora**. The Athenian Agora, at the foot of the Akropolis, began as an open space where farmers and artisans displayed their wares. Over time, public and private structures were erected on both sides of the Panathenaic Way, a ceremonial road used during an important festival in honor of Athena (FIG. 5-48). A stone drainage system was installed to prevent flooding, and a large fountain house was built to provide water for surrounding homes, administrative buildings, and shops (see "Women at a Fountain House" on page 142). By 400 BCE, the Agora contained several religious and administrative structures and even a small racetrack. The Agora also had the city mint, its military headquarters, and two buildings devoted to court business.

In design, the stoa, a distinctively Greek structure found nearly everywhere people gathered, ranged from a simple roof held up by columns to a substantial and sometimes architecturally impressive building with two stories and shops along one side. Stoas offered protection from the sun and rain and provided a place for strolling and talking business, politics, or philosophy. While city business could be, and often was, conducted in the stoas, agora districts also came to include buildings with specific administrative functions.

In the Athenian Agora, the 500-member *boule*, or council, met in a building called the *bouleuterion*. This structure, built before 450 BCE but probably after the

new *bouleuterion*

Temple of Hephaistos

Stoa of Zeus

Royal Stoa

Altar of the Twelve Gods

Painted Stoa

old *bouleuterion*

courtroom

tholos

racetrack

South Stoa

fountain house

mint

to the Acropolis

Panathenaic Way

5–48 RECONSTRUCTION DRAWING OF THE AGORA (MARKETPLACE), ATHENS
c. 400 BCE.

Persian destruction of Athens in 480 BCE, has a simple, rectangular plan with a vestibule and large meeting room. Near the end of the fifth century BCE, a new *bouleuterion* was constructed west of the old one. This too had a rectangular plan. The interior, however, may have had permanent tiered seating arranged in an ascending semicircle around a ground-level **podium**, or raised platform.

Nearby was a small, round building with six columns supporting a conical roof, a type of structure known as a tholos. Built about 465 BCE, this tholos was the meeting place of the 50-member executive committee of the boule. The committee members dined there at the city's expense, and a few of them always spent the night there in order to be available for any pressing business that might arise.

Private houses surrounded the Agora. Compared with the often grand public buildings, houses of the fifth century BCE in Athens were rarely more than simple rectangular structures of stucco-faced mud brick with wooden posts and lintels supporting roofs of terra-cotta tiles. Rooms were small and included a dayroom in which women could sew, weave, and do other chores, a dining room with couches for reclining around a table, a kitchen, bedrooms, and occasionally an indoor bathroom. Where space was not limited, houses sometimes opened onto small courtyards or porches.

City Plans

In older Greek cities such as Athens, buildings and streets developed in conformance to the needs of their inhabitants and the requirements of the terrain. As early as the eighth century BCE, however, builders in some western Greek settlements began to use a mathematical concept of urban development based on the **orthogonal** (or grid) plan. New cities or rebuilt sections of old cities were laid out on straight, evenly spaced parallel streets that intersected at right angles to create rectangular blocks. These blocks were then subdivided into identical building plots.

During the Classical period, Hippodamos of Miletos, a major urban planner of the fifth century BCE, held views on the reasoned perfectibility of urban design akin to those of the Athenian philosophers (such as Socrates) and artists (such as Polykleitos). He believed the ideal city should be limited to 10,000 citizens divided into three

Art and its Contexts

WOMEN AT A FOUNTAIN HOUSE

Since most women in ancient Greece were confined to their homes, their daily trip to the communal well or fountain house in the agora was an important event. The Archaic ceramic artist known as the Priam Painter recorded a vignette from this aspect of Greek city life on a black-figure **hydria** (water jug) (**FIG. 5–49**). In the shade of a Doric-columned porch, three women fill hydriae just like the one on which they are painted. A fourth balances her empty jug on her head as she waits, while a fifth woman without a jug seems to be waving a greeting to someone. The building is designed like a stoa, open on one side, but having animal-head spigots on three walls. The Doric columns support a Doric entablature with an architrave above the colonnade and a colorful frieze—here black-and-white blocks replace carved metopes.

5–49 Priam Painter **WOMEN AT A FOUNTAIN HOUSE**

520–510 BCE. Black-figure decoration on a hydria. Ceramic, height 20⅞" (53 cm). Museum of Fine Arts, Boston. William Francis Warden Fund. (61.195).

Credit: Photograph © 2017 Museum of Fine Arts, Boston

classes—artists, farmers, and soldiers—and three zones—sacred, public, and private. The basic Hippodamian plot was a square 600 feet on each side, divided into quarters. Each quarter was subdivided into six rectangular building plots measuring 100 by 150 feet, a scheme still widely used in American and European cities and suburbs.

Stele Sculpture

Upright stone slabs called stelai (singular, stele) were used in Greek cemeteries as gravestones, carved in low relief with an image (actual or allegorical) of the person or people to be remembered. Instead of the proud warriors or athletes used in the Archaic period, however, Classical stelae place figures in personal or domestic contexts that often feature women and children. A touching mid-fifth-century BCE example found on the island of Paros portrays

a young girl seemingly bidding farewell to her pet birds, one of which she kisses on the beak (**FIG. 5–50**). She wears a loose peplos, which is open at the side to reveal parts of her body and clings elsewhere over her form to reveal its three-dimensionality. The extraordinary carving recalls the contemporary reliefs of the Parthenon frieze; like them, this stele would have been painted with color to provide details such as the straps of the girl's sandals or the feathers on her birds.

Another, somewhat later, stele commemorates the relationship between a couple identified by name across an upper frieze resting on two Doric pilasters (**FIG. 5–51**). The husband, Ktesilaos, stands casually with crossed legs and joined hands, gazing at his wife, Theano, who sits before him on a bench, pulling at her gauzy wrap with her right hand in a gesture that is often associated with Greek brides. Presumably this was a tombstone for a joint grave, since both names are inscribed on it, but we do not know which of the two might have died first, leaving behind a mate to mourn and memorialize by commissioning this stele. The air of introspective melancholy here, as well as the softness and delicacy of both flesh and fabric, seem to point forward out of the High Classical period and into the increased sense of narrative and delicacy that was to characterize the fourth century BCE.

5-51 GRAVE STELE OF KTESILAOS AND THEANO

c. 400 BCE. Marble, height 36⅝" (93 cm). National Archaeological Museum, Athens.

Credit: © 2016. Photo Scala, Florence

Painting

The Painted Stoa built on the north side of the Athenian Agora (SEE FIG. 5-48) about 460 BCE is known to have been decorated with paintings (hence its name) by the most famous artists of the time, including Polygnotos of Thasos (active c. 475–450 BCE). His contemporaries praised his talent for creating the illusion of spatial recession in landscapes, rendering female figures clothed in transparent draperies, and conveying through facial expressions the full range of human emotions. Ancient writers enthusiastically described his painting, as well as other famous works, but nothing survives for us to see.

White-ground ceramic painting, however, may echo the style of lost contemporary wall and panel painting.

5-50 GRAVE STELE OF A LITTLE GIRL

c. 450–440 BCE. Marble, height 31½" (80 cm). Metropolitan Museum of Art, New York.

Credit: © 2016. Image copyright The Metropolitan Museum of Art/Art Resource/Scala, Florence

5-52 Style of the Achilles Painter **WOMAN AND MAID**
c. 450–440 BCE. White-ground lekythos. Ceramic, with additional painting in tempera, height 15⅛″ (38.4 cm). Museum of Fine Arts, Boston. Francis Bartlett Donation of 1912. (13.201).

Credit: Photograph © 2017 Museum of Fine Arts, Boston

In this technique, painters applied refined white slip as a ground on which they painted designs with liquid slip. High Classical white-ground painting became a specialty of Athenian potters. Artists enhanced the fired vessel with a full range of colors using paints made by mixing tints with white clay, and also using **tempera**, an opaque, water-based medium mixed with glue or egg white. This fragile decoration deteriorated easily, and for that reason seems to have been favored for funerary, votive, and other non-utilitarian vessels.

Tall, slender, one-handled white-ground **lekythoi** were used to pour libations during religious rituals. Some convey grief and loss, with scenes of departing figures bidding farewell. Others depict grave stelai draped with garlands. Still others envision the deceased returned to the prime of life and engaged in a seemingly everyday activity. A white-ground lekythos dated about 450–440 BCE shows a young servant girl carrying a stool for a small chest of valuables to a well-dressed woman of regal bearing, the dead person whom the vessel memorializes (**FIG. 5–52**). As on the stele of Ktesilaos and Theano (SEE FIG. 5–51), the scene portrayed here contains no overt signs of grief, but a quiet sadness pervades it. The two figures seem to inhabit different worlds, their glances somehow failing to meet.

The Late Classical Period, c. 400–323 BCE

What features separate the style and subjects of Late Classical art from the art of the High Classical period?

After the Spartans defeated Athens in 404 BCE, they set up a pro-Spartan government so oppressive that within a year the Athenians rebelled against it, killed its leader, Kritias, and restored democracy. Athens recovered its independence and its economy revived, but it never regained its dominant political and military status. It did, however, retain its reputation as a center of artistic and intellectual life. In 387 BCE, the great philosopher-teacher Plato founded a school just outside Athens, as his student Aristotle did later. Among Aristotle's students was young Alexander of Macedon, known to history as Alexander the Great.

In 359 BCE, a crafty and energetic warrior, Philip II, had come to the throne of Macedon. In 338, he defeated Athens and rapidly conquered the other Greek cities. When he was assassinated two years later, his kingdom passed to his 20-year-old son, Alexander, who consolidated his power and led a united Greece in a war of revenge and conquest against the Persians. In 334 BCE, he crushed the Persian army and conquered Syria and Phoenicia. By 331, he had occupied Egypt and founded the seaport he named

MAP 5-2 HELLENISTIC GREECE

Alexander the Great created a Greek empire that extended from the Greek mainland and Egypt across Asia Minor and as far east as India.

Alexandria. The Egyptian priests of Amun recognized him as the son of a god, an idea he readily adopted. That same year, he reached the Persian capital of Persepolis and continued east until reaching present-day Pakistan in 326 BCE; his troops then refused to go any farther (**MAP 5-2**). On the way home in 323 BCE, Alexander died of a fever. He was only 33 years old.

Changing political conditions never seriously dampened the Greeks' artistic creativity. Indeed, artists experimented widely with new subjects and styles. Although they maintained a Classical approach to composition and form, they relaxed its conventions, supported by a sophisticated new group of patrons drawn from the courts of Philip and Alexander, wealthy aristocrats in Asia Minor, and foreign aristocrats eager to import Greek works and, sometimes, Greek artists.

Sculpture

Throughout the fifth century BCE, sculptors had accepted and worked within standards for the ideal proportions and forms of the human figure as established by Pheidias

and Polykleitos at mid century. But fourth-century BCE artists began to challenge and modify those standards. On mainland Greece, in particular, a new canon of proportions associated with the sculptor Lysippos emerged for male figures—now eight or more "heads" tall rather than the six-and-a-half or seven-head height of earlier works. The calm, noble detachment characteristic of High Classical figures gave way to more sensitively rendered expressions of wistful introspection, dreaminess, even fleeting anxiety or lightheartedness.

PRAXITELES   According to the Greek traveler Pausanias, writing in the second century CE, the Late Classical sculptor Praxiteles (active in Athens from about 370 to 335 BCE or later) carved a "Hermes of stone who carries the infant Dionysos" for the Temple of Hera at Olympia. In 1875, just such a statue depicting the messenger god Hermes teasing the baby Dionysos with a bunch of grapes was discovered in the ruins of this temple (**FIG. 5-53**). Initially accepted as an original work of Praxiteles because of its high quality, recent studies hold that it is probably an excellent Roman or Hellenistic copy.

5-53 Praxiteles or his followers **HERMES AND THE INFANT DIONYSOS**

Probably a Hellenistic or Roman copy after a Late Classical 4th-century BCE original. Marble, with remnants of red paint on the lips and hair, height 7'1" (2.15 m). Archaeological Museum, Olympia.

Discovered in the rubble of the ruined Temple of Hera at Olympia in 1875, this statue is now widely accepted as an outstanding Roman or Hellenistic copy. Support for this conclusion comes from certain elements typical of Roman sculpture: Hermes's sandals, which recent studies suggest are not accurate for a fourth-century BCE date; the supporting element of crumpled fabric covering a tree stump; and the use of a reinforcing strut, or brace, between Hermes's hip and the tree stump.

Credit: © Craig & Marie Mauzy, Athens/Archaeological Museum, Olympia

The sculpture highlights the differences between the fourth- and fifth-century BCE Classical styles. Hermes has a smaller head and a more sensual and sinuous body than Polykleitos's *Spear Bearer* (FIG. 5-43). His off-balance, S-curving pose, requires him to lean on a post—a clear contrast with the balanced posture of Polykleitos's work. Praxiteles also created a sensuous play of contrasting textures over the figure's surface, juxtaposing the smooth flesh with crumpled draperies and rough locks of hair. Praxiteles humanizes his subject with a hint of narrative—two gods, one a loving adult and the other a playful child, caught in a moment of absorbed companionship.

Around 350 BCE, Praxiteles created a daring statue of Aphrodite for the city of Knidos in Asia Minor. Although artists of the fifth century BCE had begun to hint boldly at the naked female body beneath tissue-thin drapery—as in the panel showing a Nike adjusting her sandal (SEE FIG. 5-47)—this Aphrodite was apparently the first statue by a well-known Greek sculptor to depict a fully nude woman, and it set a new standard (FIG. 5-54). Although nudity among athletic young men was admired in Greek society, nudity among women was seen as a sign of low character. The acceptance of nudity in statues of Aphrodite may be related to the gradual merging of the Greeks' concept of this goddess with some of the characteristics of the Phoenician goddess Astarte (the Babylonian Ishtar), who was nearly always shown nude in Near Eastern art.

In the version of Praxiteles's statue seen here (actually a composite of two Roman copies), the goddess is preparing to take a bath, with a water jug and her discarded clothing at her side. Her hand is caught in a gesture of modesty that only calls attention to her nudity. Her strong and well-toned body leans forward slightly, with one projecting knee in a seductive pose that emphasizes the swelling forms of her thighs and abdomen. According to an old legend, the sculpture was so realistic that Aphrodite herself journeyed to Knidos to see it and cried out in shock, "Where did Praxiteles see me naked?" The Knidians were so proud of their Aphrodite that they placed it in an open shrine where people could view it from every side. Hellenistic and Roman copies probably numbered in the hundreds, and nearly 50 survive in various collections today.

LYSIPPOS Compared to Praxiteles, more details of Lysippos's life are known, and, although none of his original works has survived, there are many copies of the sculpture he produced between c. 350 and 310 BCE. Although he claimed to be entirely self-taught and asserted that "nature" was his only model, he must have received some technical training in the vicinity of his home, near Corinth. He expressed great admiration for Polykleitos, but his own figures reflect a different ideal and different proportions. For his famous portrayal of a **MAN SCRAPING HIMSELF (APOXYOMENOS)**, known today only from Roman copies

(**FIG. 5–55**), he chose a typical Classical subject—a nude, male athlete. But instead of a figure actively engaged in his sport, striding, or standing at ease, Lysippos depicted a young man after his workout, methodically removing oil and dirt from his body with a scraping tool called a strigil.

This tall and slender figure with a relatively small head makes a telling comparison with Polykleitos's *Spear Bearer* (SEE FIG. 5–43). Not only does it reflect a different canon of proportions, but the legs are in a wider stance

5–54 Praxiteles **APHRODITE OF KNIDOS**

Composite of two similar Roman copies after the original marble of c. 350 BCE. Marble, height 6′8″ (2.04 m). Musei Vaticani, Museo Pio Clementino, Gabinetto delle Maschere, Rome.

The head of this figure is from one Roman copy, the body from another. Seventeenth- and eighteenth-century CE restorers added the nose, the neck, the right forearm and hand, most of the left arm, and the feet and parts of the legs. This kind of restoration would rarely be undertaken today, but it was frequently done and considered quite acceptable in the past, when archaeologists were trying to put together a body of work documenting the appearance of lost Greek statues.

Credit: © 2016. Photo Scala, Florence

5–55 Lysippos **MAN SCRAPING HIMSELF (APOXYOMENOS)**

Roman copy after the original bronze of c. 350–310 BCE. Marble, height 6′9″ (2.06 m). Musei Vaticani, Museo Pio Clementino, Gabinetto dell'Apoxyomenos, Rome.

Credit: © akg-images/Nimatallah

to counterbalance the outstretched arms, and there is a pronounced curve to the posture. The *Spear Bearer* is contained within fairly simple, compact contours and oriented toward a center-front viewer. In contrast, the arms of the *Man Scraping Himself* break free into the surrounding space, inviting the viewer to move around the statue. Roman authors, who may have been describing the bronze original rather than a marble copy, remarked on the subtle modeling of the statue's elongated body and the spatial extension of its pose.

When Lysippos was summoned to create a portrait of Alexander the Great, he portrayed Alexander as a standing figure with an upraised arm holding a scepter, the same way he posed Zeus. Based on description and later copies, we know Lysippos idealized the ruler as a ruggedly handsome, heavy-featured young man with a large Adam's apple and short, tousled hair. According to the Roman historian Plutarch, Lysippos presented Alexander in a meditative pose, perhaps contemplating grave decisions, waiting to receive divine advice.

Metalwork

The detailed, small-scale work of Greek goldsmiths followed the same stylistic trends and achieved the same high standards of technique and execution characterizing other arts. A specialty of Greek goldsmiths was the design of earrings in the form of tiny works of sculpture. They were often placed on the ears of marble statues of goddesses, but they adorned the ears of living women as well. **EARRINGS** dated about 330–300 BCE depict the abducted youth Ganymede caught in the grasp of an eagle (Zeus) (**FIG. 5–56**),

5-56 EARRINGS
c. 330–300 BCE. Hollow-cast gold, height 2⅜" (6 cm). Metropolitan Museum of Art, New York. Harris Brisbane Dick Fund, 1937. (37.11.9–10).

Credit: © 2016, Image copyright The Metropolitan Museum of Art/Art Resource/ Scala, Florence

a technical *tour-de-force*. Slightly more than 2 inches high, they were hollow-cast using the lost-wax process, no doubt to make them light on the ear. Despite their small size, they capture the drama of their subject, evoking swift movement through space.

Painting

Roman observers such as Pliny the Elder praised Greek painters for their skill in capturing the appearance of the real world. Roman patrons also admired Greek murals, and they commissioned copies in fresco or **mosaic** to decorate their homes. (Mosaics—created from **tesserae**, small cubes of colored stone or marble—provide a permanent, waterproof surface that the Romans used for floors in important rooms.) A first-century CE Roman mosaic, **ALEXANDER THE GREAT CONFRONTS DARIUS III AT THE BATTLE OF ISSOS** (**FIG. 5-57**), for example, replicates a Greek painting of about 310 BCE. Pliny the Elder mentions a painting of this subject by Philoxenos of Eretria, but a new theory claims the original as a work of Helen of Egypt.

Such copies document a growing taste for dramatic narrative subjects in late fourth-century BCE Greek painting. The scene here is one of violent action, where diagonal disruption and radical foreshortening draw the viewer in and elicit an emotional response. Astride a rearing horse at the left, his hair blowing free and his neck bare, Alexander challenges the helmeted and armored Persian leader, who stretches out his arm in a gesture of defeat and apprehension as his charioteer whisks him back toward safety within the Persian ranks. The mosaicist has created an illusion of solid figures through modeling, mimicking the play of light on three-dimensional surfaces with highlights and shading.

The interest of fourth-century BCE artists in creating believable illusions of the real world was the subject of anecdotes repeated by later writers. One popular legend involved a floral designer named Glykera—widely praised for her artistry in weaving blossoms and greenery into wreaths, swags, and garlands for religious processions and festivals—and Pausias—the foremost painter of his day. Pausias challenged Glykera to a contest, claiming that he could paint a picture of one of her complex works that would appear as lifelike to the spectator as her real one. According to the legend, he succeeded. It is not surprising, although perhaps unfair, that the opulent floral borders so popular in later Greek painting and mosaics are described as "Pausian" rather than "Glykeran."

A Pausian design frames a mosaic floor from a palace at Pella (Macedonia) dated about 300 BCE (**FIG. 5-58**). The floor features a series of hunting scenes, such as the **STAG HUNT** seen here, prominently signed by an artist named Gnosis. The blossoms, leaves, spiraling tendrils, and twisting, undulating stems that frame this scene echo the linear patterns formed by the hunters, the dog, and

5–57 ALEXANDER THE GREAT CONFRONTS DARIUS III AT THE BATTLE OF ISSOS

Floor mosaic, Pompeii, Italy. 1st-century BCE Roman copy of a Greek wall painting of c. 310 BCE, perhaps by Philoxenos of Eretria or Helen of Egypt. Entire panel 8'10" × 17' (2.7 × 5.2 m). Museo Archeologico Nazionale, Naples.

Credit: © Fotografica Foglia, Naples

the struggling stag. The human and animal figures are modeled in light and shade, and the dog's front legs are expertly foreshortened to create the illusion that the animal is turning at a sharp angle into the picture. The work is all the more impressive because it was not made with uniformly cut marble in different colors, but with a carefully selected assortment of natural pebbles.

The Hellenistic Period, 323–31/30 BCE

What distinguishes the styles and subjects of Hellenistic art from the Classical art that preceded it?

When Alexander died unexpectedly at age 33 in 323 BCE, he left a vast empire with no administrative structure and no accepted successor. Almost immediately his generals turned against one another, local leaders fought to

5–58 Gnosis STAG HUNT

Detail of mosaic floor decoration from Pella, Macedonia (in present-day Greece). c. 300 BCE. Pebbles, central panel 10'7½" × 10'5" (3.24 × 3.17 m). Signed at top: "Gnosis made it." Archaeological Museum, Pella.

Credit: Studio Kontos Photostock

regain their lost autonomy, and the empire began to break apart. By the early third century BCE, three of Alexander's generals—Antigonus, Ptolemy, and Seleucus—had carved out kingdoms. The Antigonids controlled Macedonia and mainland Greece; the Ptolemies ruled Egypt; and the Seleucids controlled Asia Minor, Mesopotamia, and Persia.

Over the course of the second and first centuries BCE, these kingdoms succumbed to the growing empire centered in Rome. Ptolemaic Egypt endured the longest, and its capital, Alexandria, flourished as a prosperous seaport and great center of learning and the arts. Its library is estimated to have contained 700,000 papyrus and parchment scrolls. The Battle of Actium in 31 BCE and the death in 30 BCE of Egypt's last Ptolemaic ruler, the remarkable Cleopatra, marks the end of the Hellenistic period.

Alexander's lasting legacy was the spread of Greek culture far beyond its original borders, but artists of the Hellenistic period developed visions discernibly distinct from those of their Classical Greek predecessors. Where earlier artists sought to codify a generalized artistic ideal, Hellenistic artists shifted focus to the individual and the specific. They turned increasingly away from the heroic to the everyday, from gods to mortals, from aloof serenity to individual emotion, and from decorous drama to emotional melodrama. Their works appeal to the senses through luscious or lustrous surface treatments and to our hearts as well as our intellects through expressive subjects and poses. Although such tendencies are already evident during the fourth century BCE, they become more pronounced in Hellenistic art.

Architecture

In the architecture of the Hellenistic period, a variant of the Ionic order that had previously been reserved for interiors—called Corinthian by the Romans and featuring elaborate foliate capitals—challenged the dominant Doric and Ionic orders (see "The Greek Orders" on page 111). In Corinthian capitals, curly acanthus leaves and coiled flower spikes surround a basket-shaped core. Above the capitals, the Corinthian entablature, like the Ionic, has a stepped-out architrave and a continuous frieze, but it includes additional bands of carved moldings.

The Corinthian **TEMPLE OF OLYMPIAN ZEUS** (**FIG. 5-59**), located in the lower city of Athens at the foot of the Akropolis, was designed by the Roman architect Cossutius in the second century BCE on the foundations of an earlier Doric temple, but it was not completed until three centuries later, under the patronage of the Roman emperor Hadrian. Viewed through these huge columns—55 feet 5 inches tall—the Parthenon seems modest in comparison. But the new temple followed long-established conventions. It was an enclosed rectangular building surrounded by a screen of columns standing on a three-stepped base. It is simply a Greek temple grown very large.

GREEK THEATERS In ancient Greece, the theater was more than mere entertainment: It was a vehicle for the communal expression of religious beliefs through music, poetry, and dance. In very early times, theater performances took place on the hard-packed dirt or stone-surfaced pavement

5-59 TEMPLE OF OLYMPIAN ZEUS, ATHENS

View from the southeast with the Akropolis in the distance. Building and rebuilding phases: foundation c. 520–510 BCE, using the Doric order; temple designed by Cossutius begun 175 BCE, left unfinished 164 BCE, completed 132 BCE using Cossutius's design. Height of columns 55'5" (16.89 m).

Credit: © Amanaimages Inc./123RF

of an outdoor threshing floor—the same type of floor later incorporated into religious sanctuaries. Whenever feasible, dramas were also presented facing a steep hill that served as elevated seating for the audience. Eventually such sites were made into permanent open-air auditoriums. At first, tiers of seats were simply cut into the side of the hill. Later, builders improved them with stone.

During the fifth century BCE, the plays were usually tragedies in verse based on popular myths and were performed at festivals dedicated to Dionysos; the three great Greek tragedians—Aeschylus, Sophocles, and Euripides—created works that would define tragedy for centuries. Because they were used continuously and frequently modified over many centuries, early theaters have not survived in their original form.

The theater at Epidauros (**FIG. 5–60**), built in the second half of the fourth century BCE, is characteristic. A semicircle of tiered seats built into the hillside overlooked the circular performance area, called the orchestra, at the center of which was an altar to Dionysos. Rising behind the orchestra was a two-tiered stage structure made up of the vertical *skene* (scene)—an architectural backdrop for performances that also screened the backstage area from view—and the *proskenion* (**proscenium**), a raised platform in front of the *skene* that was increasingly used over time as an extension of the orchestra. Ramps connecting the *proskenion* with lateral passageways provided access for performers. Steps gave the audience access to the 55 rows of seats and divided the seating area into uniform, wedge-shaped sections. The tiers of seats above the wide corridor, or gangway, were added at a much later date. This design provided uninterrupted sight lines and good acoustics and allowed for the efficient entrance and exit of the 12,000 spectators. No better design has ever been created.

**5–60 OVERALL VIEW (A)
AND RECONSTRUCTION DRAWING (B)
OF THE THEATER, EPIDAUROS**

Peloponnese, Greece. 4th century BCE and later.

Credit: (above) © Craig & Marie Mauzy, Athens
(right) © Dorling Kindersley

Sculpture in Pergamon

Hellenistic sculptors produced an enormous variety of work in a wide range of materials, techniques, and styles. The period was marked by two broad and conflicting trends. One trend emulated earlier Classical models; sculptors selected aspects of favored works of the fourth century BCE and incorporated them into their own work. The other (sometimes called anti-Classical or Baroque) abandoned Classical strictures and experimented freely with new forms and subjects. This style was especially strong in Pergamon and other eastern centers of Greek culture.

The Anatolian city of Pergamon was the capital of a breakaway state within the Seleucid realm established in the early third century BCE, and it quickly became a leading center of the arts and the hub of an experimental sculptural style that had far-reaching influence throughout the Hellenistic period. This radical style characterizes a monument commemorating the victory in 230 BCE of Attalos I (ruled 241–197 BCE) over the Gauls, a Celtic people (see "The Celts" below). The monument extols the dignity and heroism of the defeated enemies and, by extension, the power and virtue of the Pergamenes.

The bronze figures of Gauls mounted on the pedestal of this monument are known today only from Roman copies in marble. One captures the slow demise of a wounded Celtic soldier-trumpeter (**FIG. 5-62**), whose lime-spiked hair, mustache, and twisted neck ring or **torc** (reputedly the only thing the Gauls wore into battle) identify him as a **barbarian** (a label the ancient Greeks used for all foreigners, whom they considered uncivilized). But the sculpture also depicts his dignity and heroism in defeat, inspiring in viewers both admiration and pity for this fallen warrior. Fatally injured, he struggles to rise, but the slight bowing

Art and its Contexts

THE CELTS

During the first millennium BCE, Celtic peoples inhabited most of central and western Europe. The Celtic Gauls portrayed in the Hellenistic Pergamene victory monument moved into Asia Minor from Thrace during the third century BCE. Pushed out by migrating people, attacked and defeated by challenged kingdoms like that at Pergamon, and then again by the Roman armies of Julius Caesar, the Celts were pushed into the northwesternmost parts of the continent—Ireland, Cornwall, and Brittany. Their wooden sculpture and dwellings and colorful woven textiles have disintegrated, but spectacular funerary goods such as jewelry, weapons, and tableware survive.

This golden **TORC**, dating sometime between the third and first centuries BCE (**FIG. 5-61**), was excavated in 1866 from a Celtic tomb in northern France, but it is strikingly similar to the neck ring worn by the dying trumpeter illustrated in FIGURE 5-62. Torcs were worn by noblemen and were sometimes awarded to warriors for heroic performance in combat. Like all Celtic jewelry, the decorative design of this work consists not of natural forms but of completely abstract ornament, in this case created by the careful twisting and wrapping of strands of pure gold, resolved securely in the definitive bulges of two knobs. In Celtic hands, pattern becomes an integral part of the object itself, not an applied decoration. In stark contrast to the culture of the ancient Greeks, where the human figure was at the heart of all artistic development, here it is abstract, nonrepresentational form and its continual refinement that is the central artistic preoccupation.

5-61 TORC

Found at Soucy, France. Celtic Gaul, 3rd–1st century BCE. Gold, height 5″ (12.7 cm), length 5⅝″ (14.5 cm). Musée Nationale du Moyen-Âge, Paris.

Credit: Photo © RMN/ Jean-Gilles Berizzi

5-62 Epigonos (?) **DYING GALLIC TRUMPETER**

Roman copy (found in Julius Caesar's garden in Rome) after the original bronze of c. 220 BCE. Marble, height 36½" (93 cm). Museo Capitolino, Rome.

Pliny the Elder described a work like the *Dying Gallic Trumpeter*, attributing it to an artist named Epigonos. Recent research indicates that Epigonos probably knew the early fifth-century BCE sculpture of the Temple of Aphaia on Aegina, which included the *Dying Warriors* (SEE FIGS. 5–14, 5–15), and could have had it in mind when he created his own works.

Credit: © Vincenzo Pirozzi, Rome
fotopirozzi@inwind.it

of his supporting right arm and his unseeing, downcast gaze indicate that he is on the point of death. This kind of deliberate attempt to elicit a specific emotional response in the viewer is known as **expressionism**, and it was to become a characteristic of Hellenistic art.

The sculptural style and approach seen in the monument to the defeated Gauls became more pronounced and dramatic in later works, culminating in the sculptured frieze wrapped around the base of a Great Altar on a mountainside at Pergamon (**FIG. 5-63**). Now reconstructed inside a Berlin museum, the original altar was enclosed within a single-story Ionic colonnade raised on a high podium reached by a monumental staircase 68 feet wide and nearly 30 feet deep. The sculptural frieze, over 7 feet in height and probably executed during the reign of Eumenes II (197–159 BCE), depicts the battle between the gods and

the giants, a mythical struggle that the Greeks saw as a metaphor for their conflicts with barbarians. In this case it evokes the Pergamenes' victory over the Gauls.

The Greek gods fight here not only with giants, but also with monsters with snakes for legs that are emerging from the bowels of the earth. In a detail from it (**FIG. 5-64**), the goddess Athena at the left has grabbed the hair of a winged male monster and forced him to his knees. Inscriptions along the base of the sculpture identify him as Alkyoneos, a son of the earth goddess Ge. Ge rises from the ground on the right in fear as she reaches toward Athena, pleading for her son's life. At the far right, a winged Nike rushes to crown Athena with a victor's wreath.

The figures in the Pergamon frieze not only fill the space along the base of the altar, they also break out of their architectural boundaries and invade the spectators'

5-63 RECONSTRUCTED WEST FRONT OF THE ALTAR FROM PERGAMON (IN PRESENT-DAY TURKEY)
c. 175–150 BCE. Marble, height of frieze 7'7" (2.3 m). Staatliche Museen zu Berlin.

Credit: © 2016. Photo Scala, Florence/bpk, Bildagentur für Kunst, Kultur und Geschichte, Berlin

5-64 ATHENA ATTACKING THE GIANTS

Detail of the frieze from the east front of the altar from Pergamon. c. 175–150 BCE. Marble, frieze height 7'7" (2.3 m). Staatliche Museen zu Berlin.

Credit: © 2016. Photo Scala, Florence/bpk, Bildagentur für Kunst, Kultur und Geschichte, Berlin

5-65 Hagesandros, Polydoros, and Athenodoros of Rhodes **LAOCOÖN AND HIS SONS**

Original of 1st century BCE or a Roman copy, adaptation, or original of the 1st century BCE. Marble, height 8' (2.44 m). Musei Vaticani, Museo Pio Clementino, Cortile Ottagono, Rome.

Credit: © 2016. Photo Scala, Florence

space, crawling out onto the steps that visitors climbed on their way to the altar. Many consider this theatrical and complex interaction of space and form to be a benchmark of the Hellenistic style, just as they consider the balanced restraint of the Parthenon sculpture to be the epitome of the High Classical style. Where fifth-century BCE artists sought horizontal and vertical equilibrium and control, Pergamene artists sought to balance opposing forces in three-dimensional space along dynamic diagonals. Classical preference for smooth, evenly illuminated surfaces has been replaced by dramatic contrasts of light and shade playing over complex forms carved with deeply undercut high relief. The composure and stability admired in the Classical style have given way to extreme expressions of pain, stress, wild anger, fear, and despair. Whereas the Classical artist asked only for an intellectual commitment, the Hellenistic artist demanded that the viewer also empathize.

THE LAOCOÖN Pergamene artists may have inspired the work of Hagesandros, Polydoros, and Athenodoros, three sculptors on the island of Rhodes named by Pliny the Elder as the creators of the famed **LAOCOÖN**

AND HIS SONS (**FIG. 5-65**). This work has been assumed by many art historians to be a Hellenistic original from the first century BCE, although others argue that it is a brilliant copy, a creative adaptation, or a Hellenistic-style invention commissioned by an admiring Roman patron in the first century CE.

The complex sculptural composition illustrates an episode from the Trojan War when the priest Laocoön warned the Trojans not to bring within their walls the giant wooden horse left behind by the Greeks. The gods who supported the Greeks retaliated by sending serpents from the sea to destroy Laocoön and his sons as they walked along the shore. The struggling figures, anguished faces, intricate diagonal movements, and skillful unification of diverse forces in a complex composition all suggest a strong relationship between Rhodian and Pergamene sculptors. Although sculpted in the round, the Laocoön was composed to be seen frontally and from close range, and the three figures resemble the relief sculpture on the altar from Pergamon.

Three Statues of Women

THE NIKE OF SAMOTHRACE This winged figure of Victory (**FIG. 5-66**) is even more theatrical than the Laocoön. In its original setting—in a hillside niche high above the theater in the Sanctuary of the Great Gods at Samothrace, perhaps drenched with spray from a fountain—this huge goddess must have reminded visitors of the god in Greek plays who descends from heaven to determine the outcome of the drama. The forward momentum of the Nike's heavy body is balanced by the powerful backward

5-66 NIKE (VICTORY) OF SAMOTHRACE
Sanctuary of the Great Gods, Samothrace. c. 180 BCE (?). Marble, height 8′1″ (2.45 m). Musée du Louvre, Paris.

The wind-whipped costume and raised wings of this Nike indicate that she has just alighted on the prow of the stone ship that formed the original base of the statue. The work probably commemorated an important naval victory, perhaps the Rhodian triumph over the Seleucid king Antiochus III in 190 BCE. The Nike (lacking its head and arms) and a fragment of its stone ship base were discovered in the ruins of the Sanctuary of the Great Gods by a French explorer in 1863 (additional fragments were discovered later). Soon after, the sculpture entered the collection of the Louvre Museum in Paris.

Credit: Photo © RMN-Grand Palais (musée du Louvre)/Gérard Blot/Christian Jean

5-67 OLD WOMAN

Roman 1st century BCE copy of a Greek work of the 2nd century BCE. Marble, height 49½″ (1.25 m). Metropolitan Museum of Art, New York. Rogers Fund, 1909. (09.39).

Credit: © 2016. Image copyright The Metropolitan Museum of Art/Art Resource/ Scala, Florence

5-68 Alexandros from Antioch-on-the-Orontes APHRODITE OF MELOS (VENUS DE MILO)

c. 150–100 BCE. Marble, height 6′8″ (2.04 m). Musée du Louvre, Paris.

The original appearance of this famous statue's missing arms has been much debated. When it was dug up in a field on the Cycladean island of Milos in 1820, some broken pieces (now lost) found with it indicated that the figure was holding out an apple in its right hand. Many judged these fragments to be part of a later restoration, not part of the original statue. Another theory is that Aphrodite was admiring herself in the highly polished shield of the war god Ares, an image that was popular in the second century BCE. This theoretical "restoration" would explain the pronounced S-curve of the pose and the otherwise unnatural forward projection of the knee.

Credit: Photo © RMN/Hervé Lewandowski

thrust of her enormous wings. The large, open movements of the figure, the strong contrasts of light and dark on the deeply sculpted forms, and the contrasting textures of feathers, fabric, and skin typify the finest Hellenistic art.

OLD WOMAN   The Hellenistic world was varied and multicultural, and some artists turned from generalizing idealism to an attempt to portray the world as they saw it, including representations of people from every level of society, unusual types as well as ordinary individuals. Traditionally, this figure of an aged woman (**FIG. 5-67**) has been seen as a seller on her way to the agora, carrying three chickens and a basket of produce. Despite the bunched and untidy disposition of her dress, however, it is elegant in design and made of fine fabric, and her hair is not in total disarray. These characteristics, along with the woman's sagging lower jaw, unfocused stare, and lack of concern for her exposed breasts, have led to a more recent interpretation that sees her as an aging, dissolute follower of Dionysos on her way to a religious festival, carrying offerings and wearing on her head the ivy wreath associated with the cult of this god of wine. Either way, she is the antithesis of the *Nike of Samothrace*. Yet in formal terms, both sculptures stretch out assertively into the space around them, both demand an emotional response from the viewer, and both display technical virtuosity in the rendering of forms and textures.

APHRODITE OF MELOS   Not all Hellenistic artists followed the descriptive and expressionist tendencies of the artists of Pergamon and Rhodes. Some turned to the past, creating an eclectic style by reexamining and borrowing elements from earlier Classical styles and combining them in new ways. Many looked back to Praxiteles and Lysippos for their models. This was the case with Alexandros, son of Menides, the sculptor of an *Aphrodite* (better known as the **VENUS DE MILO**) (**FIG. 5-68**) found on the island of Melos by French excavators in the early nineteenth century. The dreamy gaze recalls Praxiteles's work (SEE FIG. 5-54), and the figure has the heavier proportions of High Classical sculpture, but the twisting stance and the strong projection of the knee are typical of Hellenistic art, as is the rich three-dimensionality of the drapery. The juxtaposition of soft flesh and crisp drapery, seemingly in the process of slipping off the figure, adds a note of erotic tension.

By the end of the first century BCE, the influence of Greek painting, sculpture, and architecture had spread to the artistic communities of the emerging Roman Empire. Roman patrons and artists maintained their enthusiasm for Greek art into Early Christian and Byzantine times. The urge to emulate the work of great Greek artists was so strong that, as we have seen throughout this chapter, much of our knowledge of Greek achievements comes from Roman replicas of Greek artworks and descriptions of Greek art by Roman writers.

Think About It

1   Discuss the development of a characteristically Greek approach to the representation of the male nude by comparing the Anavysos Kouros (**FIG. 5-20**), the Kritios Boy (**FIG. 5-27**), the *Spear Bearer* (**FIG. 5-43**), and *Hermes and the Infant Dionysos* (**FIG. 5-53**). What changes and what remains constant?

2   Choose a work from this chapter that illustrates a scene from a Greek myth or a scene from daily life in ancient Greece. Discuss the nature of the story or event, the particular aspect chosen for illustration by the artist, and the potential meaning of the episode in relation to its cultural context.

3   What ideals are embodied in the term "High Classicism," and what are the value judgments that underlie this art historical category? Select one sculpture and one building discussed in the chapter and explain why these works are regarded as High Classical.

4   Distinguish the attributes of the Doric and Ionic orders, focusing your discussion on a specific building representing each.

Crosscurrents

What is the common theme found in the heroic subjects depicted on these two very different works? What does the specific function and location of each indicate about the importance of that theme in each culture?

FIG. 2–6b

FIG. 5–39

6–1 Novios Plautios **THE FICORONI CISTA**

350–300 BCE. Bronze, height 2′6¼″ (78.6 cm). Museo Nazionale di Villa Giulia, Rome.

Credit: © Vincenzo Pirozzi, Rome fotopirozzi@inwind.it

Chapter 6
Etruscan and Roman Art

Learning Objectives

6.a Identify the visual hallmarks of Etruscan and Roman styles for formal, technical, and expressive qualities.

6.b Interpret the meaning of works of Etruscan and Roman art based on their themes, subjects, and symbols.

6.c Relate Etruscan and Roman artists and art to their cultural, economic, and political contexts.

6.d Apply the vocabulary and concepts relevant to Etruscan and Roman art, artists, and art history.

6.e Interpret a work of Etruscan or Roman art using the art historical methods of observation, comparison, and inductive reasoning.

6.f Select visual and textual evidence in various media to support an argument or an interpretation of a work of Etruscan or Roman art.

Long before the Romans ruled the entire Italic peninsula as the center of an expanding empire, the Etruscans created a thriving culture in northern and central Italy. Etruscan artists were known throughout the Mediterranean world for their special sophistication in casting and engraving on bronze. Some of their most extraordinary works were created for domestic use, including a group of surviving **cistae**—cylindrical containers used by wealthy women as cases for toiletry articles such as mirrors, cosmetics, and perfume.

This exquisitely wrought and richly decorated example—**THE FICORONI CISTA**, named after an eighteenth-century owner—was made in the second half of the fourth century BCE and excavated in Palestrina (**FIG. 6-1**). It was commissioned by an Etruscan woman named Dindia Macolnia as a gift for her daughter, perhaps on the occasion of her marriage. The artist Novios Plautios signed the precisely engraved drawings around the cylinder, accomplished while the hammered bronze sheet from which it was constructed was still flat. First he incised lines within the metal, then filled them with a white substance to make them stand out. The cista's legs and handle—created by the figural group of Dionysus between two satyrs—were cast as separate pieces, attached during the assembly process.

The natural poses and individualization of these figures—both incised and cast—recalls the relaxed but lively naturalism of Etruscan wall paintings, but the Classicizing idealization of bodies and poses seems to come directly from contemporary Greek art. Furthermore, the use of broad foliate and ornamental bands to frame the frieze of figural narrative running around the cylinder matches the practice of famous Greek ceramic painters like Euphronios (see "Closer Look" on page 122). As with Greek pots, the most popular subjects for cistae were Greek myths. Here Novios has engraved sequential scenes drawn from an episode in the story of the Argonauts' quest for the Golden Fleece. The sailors sought water in the land of King Amykos, but the hostile king would give them water from his spring only if they beat him in a boxing match. After the immortal Pollux defeated Amykos, the Argonauts tied the king to a tree, the episode highlighted on the side of the cista seen here.

Novios Plautios probably based this scene on a monumental, mid-fourth-century BCE Greek painting of the Argonauts by Kydias that seems to have been in Rome at this time—perhaps explaining why the artist tells us in his incised signature that he executed this work in Rome. The combination of cultural components coming together in the creation of this cista—Greek stylistic sources in the work of an Etruscan artist living in Rome—will continue as Roman art develops out of the native heritage of Etruria and the emulation of the imported Classical heritage of the Greeks.

The Etruscans

How do the Etruscans develop distinctive types of architecture, tombs, and works in bronze?

At the end of the Bronze Age (about 1000 BCE), a central European people known as the Villanovans occupied the northern and western regions of the boot-shaped Italian peninsula, while the central area was home to people who spoke a closely related group of Italic languages, Latin among them. Beginning in the eighth century BCE, Greeks established colonies on the Italian mainland and in Sicily. From the seventh century BCE, people known as Etruscans, probably related to the Villanovans, gained control of the north and much of today's central Italy, an area known as Etruria. They reached the height of their power in the sixth century BCE, when they expanded into the Po River Valley to the north and the Campania region to the south (**MAP 6–1**).

Etruscan wealth came from fertile soil and an abundance of metal ore. Besides being farmers and metalworkers, the Etruscans were also sailors and merchants, and they exploited their resources in trade with the Greeks and with other people of the eastern Mediterranean. Etruscan artists knew and drew inspiration from Greek and Near Eastern art, assimilating such influences to create a distinctive Etruscan style.

Architecture

In architecture, the Etruscans established patterns of building that would be adopted later by the Romans. Cities were laid out on grid plans, like cities in Egypt and Greece, but more regularly. Two main streets—one usually running north–south and the other east–west—divided the city into quarters, with the town's business district centered at their intersection. We know something about Etruscan domestic architecture within these quarters, because they created house-shaped funerary urns and also decorated the interiors of tombs to resemble houses. Dwellings were designed around a central courtyard (or **atrium**) that was open to the sky, with a pool or cistern fed by rainwater.

MAP 6–1 THE ANCIENT ROMAN WORLD

This map shows the Roman Empire at its greatest extent, which was reached in 106 CE under the emperor Trajan.

6-2 PORTA AUGUSTA
Perugia, Italy. 3rd–2nd century BCE.

Credit: © 2016. Photo Scala, Florence

TEMPLES The Etruscans incorporated Greek deities and heroes into their pantheon and, like the ancient Mesopotamians, used divination to predict future events. Beyond this and their burial practices (as revealed by the findings in their tombs), we know little about their religious beliefs. Our knowledge of the appearance of Etruscan temples comes from a few excavated foundations, from ceramic votive models, and from the later writings of the Roman architect Vitruvius, who sometime between 33 and 23 BCE compiled descriptions of the nature of Etruscan architecture (see "Roman Writers on Art" on page 168).

Walls with protective gates and towers surrounded Etruscan cities. The third- to second-century BCE city gate of Perugia, called the **PORTA AUGUSTA**, is one of the few surviving examples of Etruscan monumental architecture (**FIG. 6-2**). A tunnel-like passageway between two huge towers, this gate is significant for anticipating the Roman use of the round arch, which is here extended to create a semicircular barrel vault over the passageway. A square frame surmounted by a horizontal decorative element resembling an entablature sets off the entrance arch, which is accentuated by a molding. The decorative section is filled with a row of circular panels, or **roundels**, alternating with rectangular, columnlike upright strips called **pilasters** in an effect reminiscent of the Greek Doric frieze.

Etruscans built their temples with mud-brick walls; columns and entablatures were made of wood or a quarried volcanic rock (tufo) that hardens upon exposure to air. Vitruvius indicates that like the Greeks, Etruscan builders used the post-and-lintel structure and gable roofs, with bases, column shafts, and capitals recalling the Doric or Ionic order and entablatures resembling a Doric frieze (**FIG. 6-3**). Vitruvius used the term "**Tuscan order**" to describe the characteristic Etruscan variation of Doric—an unfluted shaft and simplified base, capital, and entablature (see "Roman Architectural Orders" on page 162).

6-3A MODEL OF AN ETRUSCAN TEMPLE
Based on descriptions by Vitruvius. Università della Sapienza, Rome.

Credit: © akg-images/Pirozzi

6-3B PLAN OF AN ETRUSCAN TEMPLE
Based on descriptions by Vitruvius.

Elements of Architecture

ROMAN ARCHITECTURAL ORDERS

The Etruscans and Romans adapted Greek architectural orders (see "The Greek Orders" on page 111) to their own tastes, often using them as applied decoration on walls. The Etruscans developed the Tuscan order by modifying the Doric order, adding a base under the shaft, which was often left unfluted. This system was subsequently adopted by the Romans. Later, the Romans created the **Composite order** by combining the volutes of Greek Ionic capitals with the acanthus leaves from the Corinthian order. In this diagram, the two Roman orders are shown on pedestals, which consist of a **plinth**, a **dado**, and a cornice.

Tuscan order   Composite order

Like the Greeks, the Etruscans built rectangular temples on a high platform, but they often imbedded them within urban settings. Rather than surrounding temples uniformly on all sides with a stepped stereobate and peristyle colonnade, as was the practice in Greece (SEE FIGS. 5-10, 5-37), Etruscans built a single flight of stairs leading to a columned porch on one short side. Etruscan siting and orientation also constitutes an important difference from Greek temples, which were built toward the center of an enclosed sacred precinct (SEE FIGS. 5-12, 5-36), rather than the Etruscan practice of siting them on the edge of a courtyard or public square. Also, there was an almost even division in Etruscan temples between porch and interior space, which was often divided into three rooms, presumably for cult statues (SEE FIG. 6-3B).

Although Etruscan temples were simple in form, they were embellished with dazzling displays of painting and terra-cotta sculpture. The temple roof, rather than the pediment, served as a base for large statue groups. Etruscan artists excelled at the imposing technical challenge of making huge terra-cotta figures for placement on temples. A splendid example is a life-size figure of **APULU (APOLLO)** (**FIG. 6-4**). To make such large clay sculptures, artists had to know how to construct figures so that they did not collapse under their own weight while the raw clay was still wet. They also had to regulate the kiln temperature during the long firing process. The names of some Etruscan terra-cotta artists have come down to us, including that of a sculptor from Veii (near Rome) called Vulca, in whose workshop this figure of Apulu may have been created.

Dating from about 510–500 BCE and originally part of a four-figure scene depicting one of the labors of Hercle (Hercules), this boldly striding Apulu comes from the temple dedicated to Menrva (Minerva) and other gods in the sanctuary of Portonaccio at Veii. Four figures on the temple's ridgepole (horizontal beam at the peak of the roof) depicted Apulu and Hercle fighting for possession of a deer sacred to Aritimi (Diana), while she and Turms (Mercury) looked on.

Apulu's well-developed body and his "Archaic smile" clearly demonstrate that Etruscan sculptors were familiar with the *kouroi* of their Archaic Greek counterparts. But a comparison of the Apulu and a figure such as the Greek Anavysos Kouros (SEE FIG. 5-20) reveals telling differences. Unlike the Greek *kouros*, the body of the Etruscan Apulu is partially concealed by a rippling robe that cascades in knife-edged pleats to his knees. The forward-moving pose of the Etruscan statue also has a dynamic vigor that is avoided in the balanced, rigid stance of the Greek figure. This sense of energy expressed in purposeful movement is a defining characteristic of Etruscan sculpture and painting.

6–4 Master Sculptor Vulca (?) **APULU (APOLLO)**
From the temple of Minerva, Portonaccio, Veii. c. 510–500 BCE.
Painted terra cotta, height 5′10″ (1.8 m). Museo Nazionale di Villa Giulia, Rome.

Credit: © Vincenzo Pirozzi, Rome

Tombs

Like the Egyptians, the Etruscans seem to have conceived tombs as homes for the dead. The Etruscan cemetery of La Banditaccia at Cerveteri, in fact, was laid out as a small town, with "streets" running between the grave mounds. The tomb chambers were partially or entirely excavated below the ground, and some were hewn out of bedrock. They were roofed over, sometimes with corbel vaulting, and covered with dirt and stones.

Etruscan painters had a remarkable ability to envision their subjects inhabiting a bright, tangible world just beyond the tomb. Vividly colored scenes of playing, feasting, dancing, hunting, fishing, and other leisure activities decorated the walls. In a late sixth-century BCE tomb from Tarquinia, wall paintings show two boys spending a day in the country, surrounded by the graceful flights of brightly colored birds (**FIG. 6-5**). The boy to the left is climbing a hillside to the promontory of a cliff, soon to put aside his clothes and follow his naked companion, caught by the artist in mid-dive, plunging toward the water below. Such charming scenes of carefree diversions, removed from the routine demands of daily life, seem to promise a pleasurable post-mortem existence to the occupant of this tomb. But this diver could also symbolize the deceased's own plunge from life into death (AS IN FIG. 5–35).

In a painted frieze in the **TOMB OF THE TRICLINIUM**, somewhat later but also from Tarquinia, the diversions are more mature in focus as young men and women frolic to the music of the lyre and double flute within a room whose ceiling is enlivened with colorful geometric decoration (**FIG. 6-6**). These dancers line the side walls, composed within a carefully arranged setting of stylized trees and birds, while at the end of the room couples recline on couches enjoying a banquet as cats prowl underneath the table looking for scraps. The immediacy of this wall painting is striking. Dancers and diners—women as well as men—are engaging in the joyful customs and diversions of human life as we know it.

Some tombs were carved out of the rock to resemble rooms in a house. The **TOMB OF THE RELIEFS**, for example, seems to have a flat ceiling supported by square stone posts (**FIG. 6-7**). Its walls were plastered and painted, and it was fully furnished. Couches were carved from stone, and other fittings were formed of stucco, a slow-drying type of plaster that can be easily molded and carved. Simulated pots, jugs, robes, axes, and other items were molded and carved to look like real objects hanging on hooks—even including what may be a family pet rendered in low relief at the bottom of the post just left of center.

The remains of the deceased were placed in urns or sarcophagi (coffins) made of clay or stone. On the terracotta **SARCOPHAGUS FROM CERVETERI**, dating from

6-5 BOYS CLIMBING ROCKS AND DIVING, TOMB OF HUNTING AND FISHING

Tarquinia, Italy. Late 6th century BCE.

Credit: © 2016. Photo Scala, Florence – courtesy of the Ministero Beni e Att. Culturali

about 520 BCE (**FIG. 6–8**), a husband and wife are shown reclining comfortably on a dining couch. The smooth, life-like forms of their upper bodies are vertical and square-shouldered, but their hips and extended legs seem to sink into the softness of the couch. Rather than a somber memorial to the dead, we encounter two lively individuals with alert eyes and warm smiles. The man once raised a drinking vessel, addressing the viewer with the lively and engaging gesture of a genial host, perhaps offering an invitation to dine with them for eternity or to join them in the sort of convivial festivities recorded in the paintings on the walls of Etruscan tombs.

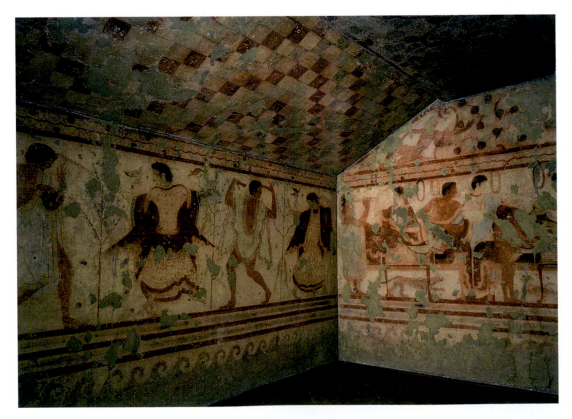

6-6 DANCERS AND DINERS, TOMB OF THE TRICLINIUM

Tarquinia, Italy. c. 480–470 BCE.

Credit: © akg-images/ De Agostini Picture Lib./G. Nimatallah

6–7 BURIAL CHAMBER, TOMB OF THE RELIEFS

Cerveteri, Italy. 3rd century BCE.

Credit: © 2016. Photo Scala, Florence - courtesy of the Ministero Beni e Att. Culturali

6–8 RECLINING COUPLE ON A SARCOPHAGUS FROM CERVETERI

c. 520 BCE. Terra cotta, length 6′7″ (2.06 m). Museo Nazionale di Villa Giulia, Rome.

Portrait sarcophagi like this one evolved from earlier terra-cotta cinerary urns with sculpted heads of the deceased whose ashes they held.

Credit: © Araldo de Luca/ Corbis

The lid of another Etruscan sarcophagus—slightly later in date and carved of marble rather than molded in clay—also portrays a reclining Etruscan couple, but during a more private moment (**FIG. 6–9**). Dressed only in their jewelry and just partially sheathed by the light covering that clings to the forms of their bodies, this loving pair has been caught for eternity in a tender embrace, absorbed with each other rather than looking out to engage the viewer. The sculptor of this relief was clearly influenced by Greek Classicism in the rendering of human forms, but the human intimacy that is captured here is far removed from the cool, idealized detachment characterizing Greek funerary stelai (SEE FIG. 5–51).

6-9 MARRIED COUPLE (LARTH TETNIES AND THANCHVIL TARNAI) EMBRACING

Lid of a sarcophagus. c. 350–300 BCE. Marble, length 7′ (2.13 m). Museum of Fine Arts, Boston. Museum purchase with funds donated by Mrs Gardner Brewer and by contribution and the Benjamin Pierce Cheney Fund (86.145a-b).

Credit: Photograph © 2017 Museum of Fine Arts, Boston

Works in Bronze

The Etruscans were particularly skilled in casting and engraving on bronze. The richly decorated Ficoroni Cista, dated to the second half of the fourth century BCE and found in Palestrina, is inscribed with the words *Dindia Macolnia filea dedit/Novios Plautios med Romai Fecid* ("Novios Plautios made me in Rome/Dindia Macolnia gave [me] to her daughter") (SEE FIG. 6–1).

Since Etruscan bronze artists went to work for Roman patrons after Etruscan lands became part of the Roman Republic, distinguishing between Etruscan and early Roman art is often difficult. A head that was once part of a bronze statue of a man may be an example of an important Roman commission from an Etruscan artist (**FIG. 6–10**). Since it is over life size, this head may have been part of a commemorative work honoring a great man, and the downturned tilt of the head, as well as the flexing of the neck, have led many to propose that it was part of an equestrian figure. Traditionally dated to about 300 BCE, this rendering of a strong, broad face with heavy brows, hawk nose, firmly set lips, and clear-eyed expression is scrupulously detailed. The commanding, deep-set eyes are created with ivory inlay, within which float irises created of glass paste within a ring of bronze. The lifelike effect

6-10 HEAD OF A MAN (TRADITIONALLY KNOWN AS "BRUTUS")

c. 300 BCE. Bronze, eyes of painted ivory, height 12½″ (31.8 cm). Palazzo dei Conservatori, Rome.

Credit: © Araldo de Luca/Corbis

6–11 CAPITOLINE SHE-WOLF

c. 500 BCE or c. 800 CE? (Boys underneath, 15th century CE). Bronze, height 33½" (85 cm). Museo Capitolino, Rome.

Credit: © 2016 Photo Scala, Florence

is further enhanced by added eyelashes of separately cut pieces of bronze. This work is often associated with a set of male virtues that would continue to be revered by the Romans: stern seriousness, strength of character, the age-worn appearance of a life well lived, and the wisdom and sense of purpose it confers.

A famously ferocious she-wolf has long been considered an—if not the—outstanding example of Etruscan bronze sculpture (**FIG. 6–11**), lauded for its technical sophistication and expressive intensity and traditionally dated to c. 500–470 BCE. The animal confronts us with a vicious snarl, her tense body, thin flanks, and protruding ribs contrasting with her pendulous, milk-filled teats. Since she currently suckles two chubby human boys—Renaissance additions of the fifteenth century—the ensemble now evokes the story of the twins Romulus and Remus, legendary founders of Rome, who were nursed back to health by a she-wolf after having been left to die on the banks of the Tiber.

However, when the bronze she-wolf was restored and cleaned during 1997–2000 under the supervision of archaeologist Anna Maria Carruba, Carruba mounted a serious challenge to its Etruscan pedigree. She argues that it dates not from antiquity, but from the Middle Ages. Technical as well as stylistic evidence supports her conclusions, specifically the fact that this unusual work, created by the lost-wax process, was formed in the medieval technique of single-pour casting, whereas all surviving Etruscan and Roman bronzes were assembled from separate pieces soldered together. Carruba's proposal of a date of c. 800 CE for the she-wolf has certainly caught the attention of specialists in ancient art, many of whom have revised their assessment of the work. Others are waiting for the full publication of the scientific evidence before removing the she-wolf from the Etruscan canon.

Etruscan art and architectural forms left an indelible stamp on the art and architecture of early Rome that was rivaled only by the influence of Greece. By 88 BCE, when the Etruscans were granted Roman citizenship, their art had already been absorbed into that of Rome.

The Roman Republic, 509–27 BCE

What are the distinctive modes of human representation and architectural design that emerge during the Roman Republic?

At the same time that the Etruscan civilization was flourishing, the Latin-speaking inhabitants of Rome began to develop into a formidable power. For a time, kings of Etruscan lineage ruled them, but in 509 BCE the Romans overthrew them and formed a republic centered in Rome. The Etruscans themselves were absorbed by the Roman Republic at the end of the third century BCE, by which time Rome had steadily expanded its territory in many directions. The Romans unified what is now Italy and, after defeating their rival, the North African city-state of Carthage, they established an empire that encompassed the entire Mediterranean region (SEE MAP 6–1).

At its greatest extent, in the early second century CE, the Roman Empire reached from the Euphrates River in southwest Asia to Scotland. It ringed the Mediterranean Sea— *mare nostrum,* or "our sea," the Romans called it. Those who were conquered by the Romans gradually assimilated Roman legal, administrative, and cultural structures that endured for some five centuries—in the eastern Mediterranean until the fifteenth century CE—and left a lasting mark on the civilizations that emerged in Europe.

The Romans themselves assimilated Greek gods, myths, and religious beliefs and practices into their state religion. During the imperial period, they also deified some of their emperors posthumously. Worship of ancient gods mingled with homage to past rulers, while oaths of allegiance to the living ruler made the official religion a political duty. Religious worship became increasingly ritualized, perfunctory, and distant from the everyday life of most people.

Many Romans adopted the so-called mystery religions of the people they had conquered. Worship of Isis and Osiris from Egypt, Cybele (the Great Mother) from Anatolia, the hero-god Mithras from Persia, and the single, all-powerful God of Judaism and Christianity from Palestine challenged the Roman establishment. These unauthorized religions flourished alongside the state religion with its Olympian deities and deified emperors, despite occasional government efforts to suppress them.

Early Rome was governed by kings and an advisory body of leading citizens called the Senate. The population was divided into two classes: a wealthy and powerful upper class, the patricians, and a lower class, the plebeians. In 509 BCE, Romans overthrew the last Etruscan king and established the Roman Republic as an oligarchy, a government by aristocrats, that would last about 450 years.

As a result of its stable form of government and especially of its encouragement of military conquest, by 275 BCE Rome controlled the entire Italian peninsula. By 146 BCE Rome had defeated its great rival, Carthage, on the north coast of Africa and taken control of the western Mediterranean. By the mid second century BCE Rome had taken Macedonia and Greece, and by 44 BCE it had conquered most of Gaul (present-day France) as well as the eastern Mediterranean (SEE MAP 6–1). Egypt remained independent until Octavian defeated Mark Antony and Cleopatra at the Battle of Actium in 31 BCE.

Art and its Contexts

ROMAN WRITERS ON ART

Only one book devoted specifically to the arts survives from antiquity. (All our other written sources consist of digressions and insertions in works on other subjects.) That one book, the *Ten Books on Architecture* by Vitruvius (c. 80–c. 15 BCE) is invaluable. Written for Augustus in the first century BCE, it is a practical handbook for builders that discusses such things as laying out cities, siting buildings, and using the Greek architectural orders. Vitruvius argued for appropriateness and rationality in architecture, and he also made significant contributions to art theory, including studies on proportion.

Pliny the Elder (c. 23–79 CE) wrote a vast encyclopedia of "facts, histories, and observations" known as *Naturalis Historia* (*Natural History*) that often included discussions of art and architecture. Pliny occasionally used works of art to make his points—for example, citing sculpture within his essays on stone and metals. His scientific turn of mind led to his death, for he was overcome while observing the eruption of Mount Vesuvius that buried Pompeii. His nephew, Pliny the Younger (c. 61–113 CE), a voluminous letter writer, added to our knowledge of Roman domestic architecture with his meticulous descriptions of villas and gardens.

Valuable bits of information can also be found in books by travelers and historians. Pausanias, a second-century CE Greek traveler, wrote descriptions that are basic sources on Greek art and artists. Flavius Josephus (c. 37–100 CE), a historian of the Flavians, wrote in his *Jewish Wars* a description of the triumph of Titus that includes the treasures looted from the Temple in Jerusalem (SEE FIG. 6–36).

During the Republic, Roman art was rooted in its Etruscan heritage, but territorial expansion brought wider exposure to the arts of other cultures. Like the Etruscans, the Romans admired Greek art. As Horace wrote (*Epistulae* ii, 1): "Captive Greece conquered her savage conquerors and brought the arts to rustic Latium." The Romans used Greek designs and Greek orders in their architecture, imported Greek art, and employed Greek artists. In 146 BCE, for example, they stripped the Greek city of Corinth of its art treasures and shipped them back to Rome.

Roman Portraiture

Portrait sculptors of the Republican period created lifelike images seemingly based on the careful observation of their subjects. The strong emphasis on portraiture in Roman art may stem from the early practice of creating likenesses—in some cases actual wax death masks—of revered figures and distinguished ancestors for display on public occasions, most notably funerals. Contemporary historians left colorful evocations of this distinctively Roman custom. Polybius, a Greek exiled to Rome in the middle of the second century BCE, wrote home with the following description:

> … after the interment [of the illustrious man] and the performance of the usual ceremonies, they place the image of the departed in the most conspicuous position in the house, enclosed in a wooden shrine. This image is a mask reproducing with remarkable fidelity both the features and the complexion of the deceased. On the occasion of public sacrifices, they display these images, and decorate them with much care, and when any distinguished member of the family dies they take them to the funeral, putting them on men who seem to bear the closest resemblance to the original in stature and carriage…. There could not easily be a more ennobling spectacle for a young man who aspires to fame and virtue. For who would not be inspired by the sight of the images of men renowned for their excellence, all together and as if alive and breathing?… By this means, by the constant renewal of the good report of brave men, the celebrity of those who performed noble deeds is rendered immortal, while at the same time the fame of those who did good services to their country becomes known to the people and a heritage for future generations. (The Histories, 7.53, 54, trans. W.R. Paton, Loeb Library ed.)

Growing out of this heritage, Roman Republican portraiture is frequently associated with the notion of **verism**—an interest in the faithful reproduction of the immediate visual and tactile appearance of subjects. Since

6-12 PORTRAIT HEAD OF AN ELDER FROM SCOPPITO

1st century BCE. Marble, height 11″ (28 cm). Museo Nazionale, Chieti.

Credit: Canali Photobank, Milan, Italy

we find in these portrait busts the same sorts of individualizing physiognomic features that allow us to differentiate among the people we know in our own world, it is easy to assume that they are exact likenesses of their subjects as they appeared during their lifetime. Of course, this is impossible to verify, but our strong desire to believe it must realize the intentions of the artists who made these portraits and the patrons for whom they were made. From this emphasis on verism in the republican period develops a new Roman artistic ideal in human representation, an ideal quite different from the one we encountered in Greek Classicism. Instead of generalizing a human face, smoothed of its imperfections and caught in a moment of detached abstraction, this new Roman idealization emphasized—rather than suppressed—the hallmarks of advanced age and the distinguishing aspects of individual likenesses. This mode is most prominent in portraits of Roman patricians (**FIG. 6-12**), whose time-worn faces embody the wisdom and experience that come with old age. Frequently we take these portraits of wrinkled elders at face value, as highly realistic and faithful descriptions of actual human beings—contrasting Roman realism with Greek idealism—but there is good reason to think that these portraits actually conform to a particularly Roman type of idealization that underscores the effects of aging on the human face.

PORTRAIT SCULPTURE   The life-size bronze portrait of **AULUS METELLUS**—the Roman official's name is inscribed on the hem of his garment in Etruscan letters (**FIG. 6–13**)—dates to about 80 BCE. The statue, known from early times as *The Orator*, depicts a man addressing a gathering, his arm outstretched and slightly raised, a pose expressive of rhetorical persuasiveness. The orator wears sturdy laced leather boots and a folded and draped toga, the characteristic garment of a Roman senator. Perhaps the statue was mounted on an inscribed base in a public space by officials grateful for Aulus's benefactions on behalf of their city.

6–13 AULUS METELLUS (THE ORATOR)
Found near Perugia. c. 80 BCE. Bronze, height 5′11″ (1.8 m). Museo
Credit: © Quattrone, Florence

6–14 DENARIUS WITH PORTRAIT OF JULIUS CAESAR
44 BCE. Silver, diameter approximately ¾″ (2 cm). Ashmolean
Museum, Oxford.

Credit: Bridgeman Images

THE DENARIUS OF JULIUS CAESAR The propaganda value of portraits was not lost on Roman leaders. In 44 BCE, Julius Caesar issued a **DENARIUS** (a widely circulated coin) bearing his portrait (**FIG. 6–14**) conforming to the Roman ideal of advanced age, with notable wrinkles of flesh on the neck and sunken areas on the face. He was the first Roman leader to place his own image on a coin, initiating a practice that would be adopted by his successors, but at the time when this coin was minted it smacked of the sort of megalomaniacal behavior that would ultimately lead to his assassination. Perhaps it is for this reason that Caesar underscores his age, and thus his old-fashioned respectability, in this portrait, which reads as a mark of his traditionalism as a senator. The inscription placed in front of his face—CAESAR IMP—refers to his title of "imperator" or military commander, and the two objects behind him—the spiraling lituus employed by augurs to interpret divine will, and the simpulum or sacrificial jug used for libations—signify his priestly role in religious ceremony.

PATRICIAN CARRYING PORTRAIT BUSTS OF TWO ANCESTORS   A life-size marble statue of a Roman **PATRICIAN** (**FIG. 6–15**) dating from the period of the Emperor Augustus reflects the practices documented much earlier by Polybius and links the man portrayed with a revered tradition and its laudatory associations. The large marble format emulates a Greek notion of sculpture, and its use here signals not only this man's wealth but also his sophisticated artistic tastes, characteristics he shared with the emperor himself. His toga, however, is not Greek but indigenous and signifies his respectability as a Roman

6–15 PATRICIAN CARRYING PORTRAIT BUSTS OF TWO ANCESTORS (KNOWN AS THE BARBERINI TOGATUS)
End of 1st century BCE or beginning of 1st century CE. Marble, height 5′5″ (1.65 m). Palazzo de Conservatori, Rome.

The head of this standing figure, though ancient Roman in origin, is a later replacement and not original to this statue. The separation of head and body in this work is understandable since in many instances the bodies of full-length portraits were produced in advance, waiting in the sculptor's workshop for a patron to commission a head with his or her own likeness that could be attached to it. Presumably the busts carried by this patrician were likewise only blocked out until they could be carved with the faces of the commissioner's ancestors. These faces share a striking family resemblance, and the stylistic difference reproduced in the two distinct bust formats reveals that these men lived in successive generations. They could be the father and grandfather of the man who carries them.

Credit: © Araldo de Luca/Corbis

citizen of some standing. The busts of ancestors that he holds in his hands document his distinguished lineage in the privileged upper class (laws regulated which members of society could own such collections), and the statue as a whole proclaims his adherence to the family tradition by having his own portrait created.

The Roman Arch

The round arch was not an Etruscan or Roman invention, but the Etruscans and Romans were the first to make widespread use of it (SEE FIG. 6–2)—both as an effective structural idea and an elegant design motif.

Round arches displace most of their weight, or downward **thrust** (see arrows on diagram), along their curving sides, transmitting that weight to adjacent supporting uprights (door or window jambs, columns, or piers). From there, the thrust goes to, and is supported by, the ground. To create an arch, brick or cut stones are formed into a curve by fitting together wedge-shaped pieces, called **voussoirs**, until they meet and are locked together at the top center by the final piece called the **keystone**. These voussoirs exert an outward as well as a downward thrust, so arches may require added support, called **buttressing**, from adjacent masonry elements.

Until the keystone is in place and the mortar between the bricks or stones dries, an arch is held in place by wooden scaffolding called **centering**. The points from which the curves of the arch rise are called **springings**, and their support is often reinforced by **impost blocks**. The wall areas adjacent to the curves of the arch are **spandrels**. In a succession of arches, called an **arcade**, the space encompassed by each arch and its supports is called a **bay**.

keystone

spandrel · spandrel · extrados

voussoirs · intrados

impost · springing

centering

jamb · pier · pier

bay

round arch

6–16 PONT DU GARD

Nîmes, France. Late 1st century BCE. Height above river 160′ (49 m), width of road bed on lower arcade 20′ (6 m).

Credit: © Filipa Fuxa/Shutterstock

A stunning example of the early Roman use of the round arch is a bridge known as the **PONT DU GARD** (**FIG. 6–16**), part of an aqueduct built in the late first century BCE near Nîmes, in southern France. An ample water supply was essential for a city, and the Roman invention to supply this water was the aqueduct, built with arcades—a linear series of arches. This aqueduct brought water from springs 30 miles to the north using a simple gravity flow, and it provided 100 gallons a day for every person in Nîmes. Each arch buttresses its neighbors and the huge arcade ends solidly in the hillsides. The structure conveys the balance, proportions, and rhythmic harmony of a great work of art, and although it harmonizes with its natural setting, it also makes a powerful statement about Rome's ability to control nature in order to provide for its cities. Both structure and function are marks of Roman civilization.

Temples

Architecture during the Roman Republic reflected both Etruscan and Greek practices. Like the Etruscans, the Romans built urban temples in commercial centers as well as in special sanctuaries. An early example is a small rectangular temple standing on a raised platform, or podium, beside the Tiber River in Rome (**FIG. 6–17**), probably from the second century BCE and perhaps dedicated to Portunus, the god of harbors and ports. This temple uses the Etruscan system of a rectangular cella and a front porch at one end reached by a broad, inviting flight of steps, but the Roman architects have adopted the Greek Ionic order, with full columns on the porch and half-columns **engaged** (set into the wall) around the exterior walls of the cella (SEE FIG. 6–17B) and a continuous frieze in the entablature. The overall effect resembles a Greek temple, but there are two major differences. First, Roman architects liberated the form of the column from its post-and-lintel structural roots and engaged it onto the surface of the wall as a decorative feature. Second, while a Greek temple encourages viewers to walk around the building and explore its uniformly articulated sculptural mass, Roman temples are defined in relation to interior spaces, which visitors are invited to enter through one opening along the longitudinal axis of a symmetrical plan.

By the first century BCE nearly a million people lived in Rome, which had evolved into the capital of a formidable commercial and political power with a growing overseas empire. As long as Republican Rome was essentially a large city-state, its form of government—an oligarchy under the control of a Senate—remained feasible. But as the empire around it grew larger and larger, a government of competing senators and military commanders could not enforce taxation and maintain order in what was becoming a vast and complicated territorial expanse. As governance of the Republic began to fail, power became concentrated in fewer and fewer leaders, until it was ruled by one man, an emperor, rather than by the Senate.

The Early Empire, 27 BCE–96 CE

What changes and innovations in art and architecture take place when Rome becomes an empire?

The first Roman emperor was born Octavian in 63 BCE. When he was only 18 years old, his brilliant great-uncle, Julius Caesar, adopted him as son and heir, recognizing in him qualities that would make him a worthy successor. Shortly after Julius Caesar refused the Senate's offer of the imperial crown early in 44 BCE, a group of conspirators murdered him, and the 19-year-old Octavian stepped up to take his place. Over the next 17 years, acting as a

general, politician, and public-relations genius, Octavian vanquished warring internal factions and brought peace to fractious provinces. By 27 BCE the Senate had conferred on him the title of Augustus (meaning "exalted," or "sacred"). Assisted by his astute and pragmatic second wife, Livia, Augustus led the state and the empire for 45 years. He established efficient rule and laid the foundation for an extended period of stability, domestic peace, and economic prosperity known as the *Pax Romana* ("Roman Peace"), which lasted more than 200 years (27 BCE to 180 CE). In 12 BCE he became Pontifex Maximus ("High Priest"), the empire's highest religious official, as well as its political leader.

Conquering and maintaining a vast empire required not only the inspired leadership and tactics of Augustus, but also careful planning and great administrative skill, backed by massive logistical support. These qualities are reflected in some of Rome's most enduring contributions to Western civilization: its system of law, its governmental and administrative structures, and its sophisticated civil engineering and architecture.

To facilitate the development and administration of the empire, as well as to make city life comfortable and attractive to its citizens, the Roman state undertook building programs of unprecedented scale and complexity, mandating the construction of central administrative and legal centers (forums and basilicas), recreational facilities

6–17A EXTERIOR VIEW OF A TEMPLE, PERHAPS DEDICATED TO PORTUNUS
Forum Boarium (Cattle Market), Rome. Late 2nd century BCE.

Credit: © Vincenzo Pirozzi, Rome

6–17B PLAN OF A TEMPLE, PERHAPS DEDICATED TO PORTUNUS
Forum Boarium (Cattle Market), Rome. Late 2nd century BCE.

6–18 AUGUSTUS OF PRIMAPORTA

Early 1st century CE. Perhaps a copy of a bronze statue of c. 20 BCE. Marble, originally painted with color, height 6′8″ (2.03 m). Musei Vaticani, Braccio Nuovo, Rome.

Credit: © Araldo de Luca/Corbis

(racetracks, stadiums), temples, markets, theaters, public baths, aqueducts, middle-class housing, and even entire new towns. To accomplish these tasks without sacrificing beauty, efficiency, and human well-being, Roman builders and architects developed rational plans using easily worked but durable materials and highly sophisticated engineering methods.

To move their armies about efficiently, to speed communications between Rome and the farthest reaches of the empire, and to promote commerce, the Romans built a vast and complex network of roads and bridges. Many modern European streets and highways still follow the lines laid down by Roman engineers; some Roman bridges are even still in use.

Art in the Age of Augustus

Roman artists of the Augustan age created a new style—a new Roman form of idealism that, though still grounded in the appearance of the everyday world, revived Greek Classical ideals. They enriched the art of portraiture in both official images and representations of private individuals, they recorded contemporary historical events on public monuments, and they contributed unabashedly to Roman imperial propaganda.

AUGUSTUS OF PRIMAPORTA   In the sculpture known as **AUGUSTUS OF PRIMAPORTA (FIG. 6-18)**—because it was discovered in Livia's villa at Primaporta, near Rome (SEE FIG. 6-31)—we see the emperor as he wanted to be seen and remembered. This work demonstrates the creative combination of earlier sculptural traditions that is a hallmark of Augustan art. In its idealization of a specific ruler and his prowess, the sculpture also illustrates the way Roman emperors would continue to use portraiture for propaganda that not only expressed their authority directly, but rooted it in powerfully traditional stories and styles.

The sculptor of this larger-than-life marble statue adapted the standard pose of a Roman orator (SEE FIG. 6-13) by melding it with the contrapposto and canonical proportions developed by the Greek High Classical sculptor Polykleitos, as exemplified by his *Spear Bearer* (SEE FIG. 5-43). Like the heroic Greek figure, Augustus's portrait captures him in the physical prime of youth, far removed from the image of advanced age idealized in the coin portrait of Julius Caesar (SEE FIG. 6-14). Although Augustus lived almost to age 76, in his portraits he is always a vigorous ruler, eternally young. But like Caesar, and unlike the *Spear Bearer*, Augustus's face is rendered with the kind of details that make this portrait an easily recognizable likeness.

To this combination of Greek and Roman traditions, the sculptor of the *Augustus of Primaporta* added mythological and historical imagery that exalts Augustus's family and celebrates his accomplishments. Cupid, son of the goddess Venus, rides a dolphin next to the emperor's right leg, a reference to the claim of the emperor's family, the Julians, to descent from the goddess Venus through her human son Aeneas. Augustus's anatomically conceived cuirass (torso armor) is also covered with figural imagery. Mid-torso is a scene representing Augustus's 20 BCE diplomatic victory over the Parthians; a Parthian (on the right) returns a Roman military standard to a figure variously identified as a Roman soldier or the goddess Roma. Looming above this scene at the top of the cuirass is a celestial deity who holds an arched canopy, implying that the peace signified by the scene below has cosmic implications. The personification of the earth at the bottom of the cuirass holds an overflowing cornucopia, representing the prosperity brought by Augustan peace.

THE ARA PACIS AUGUSTAE   One of the most extraordinary surviving Roman monuments from the time of Augustus is the **ARA PACIS AUGUSTAE**, or Altar of Augustan Peace (**FIG. 6-19**), begun in 13 BCE and dedicated in 9 BCE on the occasion of Augustus's triumphal return to the capital after three years spent establishing Roman rule in Gaul and Hispania. In its original location in the Campus Martius (Plain of Mars), the Ara Pacis was aligned with a giant sundial, marked out on the pavement with lines and bronze inscriptions and using as its pointer an Egyptian obelisk that Augustus had earlier brought from Heliopolis to signify Roman dominion over this ancient land.

The Ara Pacis itself consists of a walled rectangular enclosure surrounding an open-air altar, emulating Greek custom (**FIG. 6-20**). Made entirely of marble panels carved with elaborate sculpture, the monument presented powerful propaganda, uniting portraiture and allegory, religion and politics, the private and the public. On the inner walls, a series of foliate garlands hang in swags from ox skulls. The skulls symbolize sacrificial offerings at the altar during annual commemorations, and the garlands—including fruits and flowers from every season—signify the continuing peace and prosperity that Augustus brought to the Roman world.

On the exterior, this theme of natural prosperity continues in lower reliefs of lavish, scrolling acanthus leaves populated by animals. Above them, decorative allegory gives way to figural tableaux. On the front and back are framed allegorical scenes evoking the mythical history of Rome and the divine ancestry of Augustus. The longer sides portray two continuous processions, seemingly representing actual historical events rather than myth or allegory. Perhaps they document Augustus's triumphal return, or they could memorialize the dedication and first sacrifice performed by Augustus on the completed altar itself. In any event, the arrangement of the participants is emblematic of the fundamental dualism characterizing Roman rule under Augustus. On one side march members

6–19 ARA PACIS AUGUSTAE (ALTAR OF AUGUSTAN PEACE)
Rome. 13–9 BCE. View of west side. Marble, approx. 34′5″ × 38′ (10.5 × 11.6 m).

This monument was begun when Augustus was 50 (in 13 BCE) and was dedicated on Livia's 50th birthday (9 BCE).

Credit: © akg-images/Andrea Jemolo

of the Senate, a stately line of male elders. But on the other is Augustus's imperial family (**FIG. 6–21**)—men, women, and, notably, children, who stand in the foreground as Augustus's hopes for dynastic succession. Whereas most

6–20 RECONSTRUCTION DRAWING OF THE ARA PACIS AUGUSTAE

Credit: © Dorling Kindersley

of the adults maintain their focus on the ceremonial event, the imperial children are allowed to fidget, look at their cousins, or reach up to find comfort in holding the hands or tugging at the garments of the adults around them, one of whom puts her finger to her mouth in a shushing gesture, perhaps seeking to mitigate their distracting behavior. The lifelike aura brought by such anecdotal details underlines the earthborn reality of the ideology embodied here. Rome is now subject to the imperial rule of the family of Augustus, and this stable system will bring continuing peace and prosperity since his successors have already been born.

The processional friezes on the exterior sides of the enclosure wall clearly reflect Classical Greek works like the Ionic frieze of the Parthenon (SEE FIG. 5–40), with their three-dimensional figures wrapped in revealing draperies that also create rhythmic patterns of rippling folds. But unlike the Greek sculptors of the Parthenon, the Roman sculptors of the Ara Pacis depicted actual individuals participating in a specific event at a known time. The Classical style may evoke the general notion of a Golden Age, but the historical references and identifiable figures in the Ara Pacis procession associate that Golden Age specifically with Augustus and his dynasty.

6-21 IMPERIAL PROCESSION
Detail of a relief on the south side of the Ara Pacis. Height 5'2" (1.6 m).

The figures in this frieze represent members of Augustus's extended family, and scholars have proposed some specific, if tentative, identifications. The middle-aged man with the shrouded head at the far left is generally accepted to be a posthumous portrait of Marcus Agrippa, who would have been Augustus's successor had he not predeceased him in 12 BCE. The bored but well-behaved youngster pulling at Agrippa's robe—and being restrained gently by the hand of the man behind him—is probably Agrippa's son Gaius Caesar. The heavily swathed woman next to Agrippa on the right may be Augustus's wife, Livia, followed perhaps by Tiberius, who would become the next emperor. Behind Tiberius could be Antonia, the niece of Augustus, looking back at her husband, Drusus, Livia's younger son. She may grasp the hand of Germanicus, one of her younger children. The depiction of children and real women in an official relief was new to the Augustan period and reflects Augustus's desire to promote private family life as well as to emphasize his potential heirs and thus the continuity of his dynasty.

Credit: © akg-images/Andrea Jemolo

The Ara Pacis did not survive from antiquity in the form we see today. The monument eventually fell into disuse, ultimately into ruin. Remains were first discovered in 1568, but complete excavation took place only in 1937–1938 under the supervision of archaeologist Giuseppe Moretti, sponsored by the Italian dictator Benito Mussolini, who was fueled by his own ideological objectives. Once the monument had been unearthed, Mussolini had it reconstructed and commissioned a special building to house it, close to the **Mausoleum** (monumental tomb) of Augustus, all in preparation for celebrating the 2,000th anniversary of Augustus's birth, and associating the Roman imperial past with Mussolini's fascist state. The dictator even planned his own burial within Augustus's mausoleum.

More recently, the City of Rome commissioned American architect Richard Meier to design a new setting for the Ara Pacis, this time within a sleek, white box with huge walls of glass that allow natural light to flood the exhibition space (SEEN IN FIG. 6-19). Many Italian critics decried the Modernist design of Meier's building—completed in 2006—but this urban renewal project focused on the Ara Pacis has certainly revived interest in one of the most precious remains of Augustan Rome.

The Gemma Augustea

After Augustus's death in 14 CE, the Roman Senate deified him by decree, and his stepson Tiberius became emperor (ruled 14–37 CE). In acknowledgment of the lineage of both—Augustus from Julius Caesar and Tiberius from his father, Tiberius Claudius Nero, Livia's first husband—the dynasty is known as the Julio-Claudian (14–68 CE). It ended with the death of Nero in 68 CE.

An exquisite large onyx **cameo** (a gemstone carved in low relief) known as the **GEMMA AUGUSTEA** glorifies Augustus as triumphant over barbarians (a label for foreigners that the Romans adopted from the Greeks) and as the deified emperor (FIG. 6-22). The emperor, crowned with a victor's wreath, sits at the center right of the upper register. He has assumed the pose and identity of Jupiter, the king of the gods; an eagle, sacred to Jupiter, stands at his feet. Sitting next to him is a personification of Rome that seems to have Livia's features. The sea goat in the roundel between them may represent Capricorn, the emperor's zodiac sign.

Tiberius, as the adopted son of Augustus, steps out of a chariot at far left, returning victorious from the German

6-22 GEMMA AUGUSTEA

Early 1st century CE.
Onyx, 7½ × 9" (19 × 23 cm).
Kunsthistorisches Museum,
Vienna.

Credit: © KHM-
Museumsverband

front prepared to assume the throne as Augustus's chosen heir. Below this realm of godlike rulers, Roman soldiers are raising a post or standard on which armor captured from the defeated enemy is displayed as a trophy. The cowering, shackled barbarians on the bottom right wait to be tied to it. The artist of the Gemma Augustea brilliantly combines idealized, heroic figures based on Classical Greek art with recognizable Roman portraits, bringing together the dramatic action of Hellenistic art with Roman attention to descriptive detail and historical specificity.

Roman Cities

In good times and bad, individual Romans—like people everywhere at any time—tried to live a decent or even comfortable life with adequate shelter, food, and clothing. Romans loved to have contact with the natural world. The middle classes enjoyed their gardens, wealthy city dwellers maintained rural estates, and Roman emperors had country villas that were both functioning farms and places of recreation. Wealthy Romans even brought nature indoors by commissioning artists to paint landscapes on the interior walls of their homes. Through the efforts of the modern archaeologists who have excavated them, Roman cities and towns, houses, apartments, and country villas still evoke for us the ancient Roman way of life with amazing clarity.

Roman architects who designed new cities or expanded and rebuilt existing ones based their urban plans on the layout of Roman army camps. Like Etruscan towns, they were designed as a grid with two bisecting main streets crossing at right angles to divide the layout into quarters. The **forum** and other public buildings were generally located at this intersection, the site of the commander's headquarters in a military camp.

Much of the housing in a Roman city consisted of brick apartment blocks called *insulae*. These apartment buildings had internal courtyards, multiple floors joined by narrow staircases, and occasionally overhanging balconies. City dwellers—then as now—were social creatures who spent much of their lives in public markets, squares, theaters, baths, and neighborhood bars. The city dweller returned to the *insulae* to sleep, perhaps to eat. Even women enjoyed a public life outside the home—a marked contrast to the circumscribed lives of Greek women.

The affluent southern Italian city of Pompeii, a thriving center of between 10,000 and 20,000 inhabitants, gives a vivid picture of Roman city life. In 79 CE Mount Vesuvius erupted, burying the city under more than 20 feet of volcanic ash and preserving it until its rediscovery and excavation beginning in the eighteenth century (**FIGS. 6-23, 6-24**). Temples and government buildings surrounded a main square, or forum; shops and houses lined mostly straight, paved streets; and a protective wall enclosed the

6-23 AERIAL VIEW OF THE RUINS OF POMPEII

Destroyed 79 CE.

Credit: © David Hiser/National Geographic Creative/Corbis

6-24 DRAWING OF CENTRAL POMPEII IN ITS CURRENT STATE

Credit: © Dorling Kindersley

House of the Vettii

Stabian baths

theater

forum baths

market

forum

temple of Apollo

forum basilica

sea gate

heart of the city. The forum was the center of civic life in Roman cities, as the agora was in Greek cities. Business was conducted in its basilicas and porticos, religious duties performed in its temples, and speeches delivered in its open square. For recreation, people went to the nearby baths or to events in the theater or amphitheater.

Roman Houses

Wealthy city dwellers lived in private houses with enclosed gardens; these houses were often fronted by shops facing the street. The Romans emphasized the interior rather than the exterior in such gracious domestic architecture.

A Roman house usually consisted of small rooms laid out around one or two open courts, the atrium and the peristyle (**FIG. 6-25**). People entered the house from the street through a vestibule and stepped into the atrium, a large space with an **impluvium** (pool for catching rainwater). The peristyle was a planted courtyard, farther into the house and enclosed by columns. Off the peristyle was the formal reception room or office called the tablinum; here the head of the household conferred with clients. Portrait busts of the family's ancestors might be displayed in the tablinum or in the atrium. Private areas—such as the family dining room, sitting rooms, and bedrooms (*cubicula*)—and service areas—such as the kitchen and servants' quarters—could be arranged around the peristyle or the atrium.

6-25 PLAN AND RECONSTRUCTION DRAWING OF THE HOUSE OF THE SILVER WEDDING
Pompeii. 1st century CE.

Credit: Reprinted with the permission of Cambridge University Press

In Pompeii, where the mild southern climate permitted gardens to flourish year-round, the peristyle was often turned into an outdoor living room with painted walls, fountains, and sculpture, as in the mid-first-century CE remodeling of the second-century BCE **HOUSE OF THE VETTII** (**FIG. 6-26**). Since Roman houses were designed in

6-26 PERISTYLE GARDEN, HOUSE OF THE VETTII
Pompeii. Rebuilt 62–79 CE.

Credit: © Mimmo Jodice/Corbis

relation to a long axis that runs from the entrance straight through the atrium and into the peristyle, visitors were greeted at the door of the house with a deep vista, showcasing the lavish residence of their host and its beautifully designed and planted gardens extending into the distance.

Little was known about these gardens until archaeologist Wilhelmina Jashemski (1910–2007) excavated the peristyle in the House of G. Polybius in Pompeii, beginning in 1973. Earlier archaeologists had usually ignored, or unwittingly destroyed, evidence of gardens, but Jashemski developed a new way to find and analyze their layouts and the plants cultivated in them. Workers first removed layers of debris and volcanic material to expose the level of the soil as it was before the eruption in 79 CE. They then collected samples of pollen, seeds, and other organic material and carefully injected plaster into underground root cavities. When the surrounding earth was removed, the roots, now in plaster, enabled botanists to identify the types of plants and trees cultivated in the garden and to estimate their size.

The garden in the house of Polybius was surrounded on three sides by a portico, which protected a large cistern on one side that supplied the house and garden with water. Young lemon trees in pots lined the fourth side of the garden, and nail holes in the wall above the pots indicated that the trees had been espaliered—pruned and trained to grow flat against a support—a practice still in use today. Fig, cherry, and pear trees filled the garden space, and traces of a fruit-picking ladder, wide at the bottom and narrow at the top to fit among the branches, was found on the site.

An aqueduct built during the reign of Augustus eliminated Pompeii's dependence on wells and rainwater basins and allowed residents to add to their gardens pools, fountains, and flowering plants that needed heavy watering. In contrast to earlier, unordered plantings, formal gardens with low, clipped borders and plantings of ivy, boxwood, laurel, myrtle, acanthus, and rosemary—all mentioned by writers of the time—became fashionable. There is also evidence of topiary work (the clipping of shrubs and hedges into fanciful shapes), sculpture, and fountains. The peristyle garden of the House of the Vettii, for example, had more than a dozen fountain statues jetting water into marble basins (SEE FIG. 6–26). In the most elegant peristyles, mosaic decorations covered the floors, walls, and fountains.

Wall Painting

The interior walls of Roman houses were plain, smooth plaster surfaces with few architectural moldings or projections. On these invitingly blank fields artists created pictures at the House of the Vettii. Some used mosaic, but most painted with pigment suspended in a water-based solution of lime and soap, sometimes with a little wax. After such paintings were finished, they were polished with a special metal, glass, or stone burnisher and then buffed with a cloth. Many fine wall paintings in a series of developing styles have come to light through excavations, first in Pompeii and other communities surrounding Mount Vesuvius, near Naples, and more recently in and around Rome.

In the 1870s, German art historian August Mau (1840–1909) analyzed Pompeian wall painting and proposed a schematic organizing system that is still used by many today to categorize its stylistic development. In the earliest wall paintings from Pompeii, artists covered the walls with illusionistic paintings of thin slabs of colored marble and projecting architectural moldings. Mau referred to this as First-Style wall painting (c. 300–100 BCE). Later, painters began to extend the space of a room visually with scenes of figures on a shallow platform or with landscapes or cityscapes (SEE FIGS. 6–29, 6–30)—Mau's Second Style (c. 100–20 BCE). During the late first century BCE, Third-Style wall painting replaced vistas with solid planes of color decorated with fine, lively architectural and floral details and small, delicate vignettes (c. 20 BCE–c. 50 CE). The final phase of Pompeian wall painting, the Fourth Style (c. 50–79 CE), united all three earlier styles into compositions of enormous complexity (SEE FIG. 6–28), where some wall surfaces seem to recede or even disappear behind a maze of floating architectural forms, while other flat areas of color become the support for simulated paintings of narrative scenes or still lifes (compositions of inanimate objects).

HOUSE OF THE VETTII   Some of the finest surviving Roman wall paintings are found in the Pompeian House of the Vettii, whose peristyle garden we have already explored (SEE FIG. 6-26). The house was built to the axial house plan—with its entrance leading through an atrium to a peristyle garden (**FIG. 6-27**)—by two brothers, wealthy freed slaves A. Vettius Conviva and A. Vettius Restitutus. Between its damage during an earthquake in 62 CE and the eruption of Vesuvius in 79 CE, the walls of the house were repainted, and this spectacular Fourth-Style decoration was uncovered in a splendid state of preservation during excavations at the end of the nineteenth century.

A complex combination of painted fantasies fills the walls of a reception room off the peristyle garden (**FIG. 6-28**). At the base of the walls is a lavish frieze of simulated colored-marble revetment, imitating the actual stone veneers that are found in some Roman residences. Above this "marble" dado are broad areas of pure red or white, onto which are painted pictures resembling framed panel paintings, swags of floral garlands, or unframed figural vignettes. The framed picture here illustrates a Greek mythological scene from the story of Ixion, who was bound by Zeus to a spinning wheel in punishment for attempting

6-27 PLAN OF THE HOUSE OF THE VETTII
Pompeii. Rebuilt 62–79 CE.

6-27 PLAN OF THE HOUSE OF THE VETTII
Pompeii. Rebuilt 62–79 CE.

to seduce Hera. Between these pictorial fields, and along a long strip above them that runs around the entire room, are fantastic architectural vistas with multicolored columns and undulating entablatures that recede into fictive space through the use of fanciful linear perspective. The fact that this fictive architecture is occupied here and there by volumetric figures only enhances the sense of three-dimensional spatial definition.

VILLAS Villas were the country houses of wealthy Romans, and their plans, though resembling town houses, were often more expansive and irregular. The eruption of Vesuvius in 79 CE preserved not only the houses along the city streets within Pompeii, but also the so-called **VILLA OF THE MYSTERIES** just outside the city walls. Here a series of elaborate figural murals from the mid first century BCE (**FIG. 6–29**) seem to portray the initiation rites of a mystery religion, probably the cult of Bacchus, which were often performed in private homes as well as in special buildings or temples. Perhaps this room was a shrine or meeting place for such a cult to this god of vegetation, fertility, and

wine. Bacchus (or Dionysus) was one of the most important deities in Pompeii.

The entirely painted architectural setting consists of a simulated marble dado (similar to that in the House of the Vettii) and, around the top of the wall, an elegant frieze supported by painted pilaster strips. The figural scenes take place on a shallow "stage" along the top of the dado, with a background of a brilliant, deep red—now known as Pompeian red—that, as we have already seen, was very popular with Roman painters. The tableau unfolds around the entire room.

The walls of a room from another villa, this one at Boscoreale, farther removed from Pompeii and dating slightly later, open onto a fantastic urban panorama (**FIG. 6-30**). Surfaces seem to dissolve; a painted series of columns and lintels frames the view of a maze of complicated architectural forms, like the painted scenic backdrops of a stage. Indeed, the theater may have inspired this kind of decoration, as the theatrical masks hanging from the lintels seem to suggest. By using a kind of **intuitive perspective**, the artists have created the impression of real space

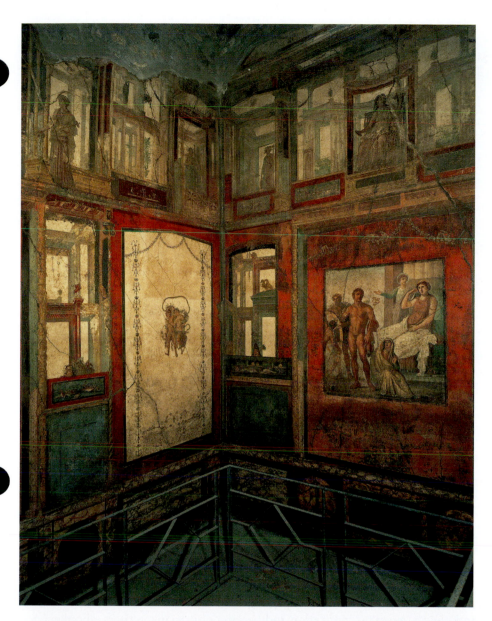

6-28 WALL PAINTING IN THE "IXION ROOM," HOUSE OF THE VETTII

Pompeii. Rebuilt 62–79 CE.

Credit: © Fotografica Foglia, Naples

6-29 INITIATION RITES OF THE CULT OF BACCHUS (?), VILLA OF THE MYSTERIES

Pompeii. Wall painting. c. 60–50 BCE. Photo taken after 2015 restoration.

Credit: © Fotografica Foglia, Naples - courtesy of the Ministero Beni e Att. Culturali e del Turismo - Suprintendenza Pompei

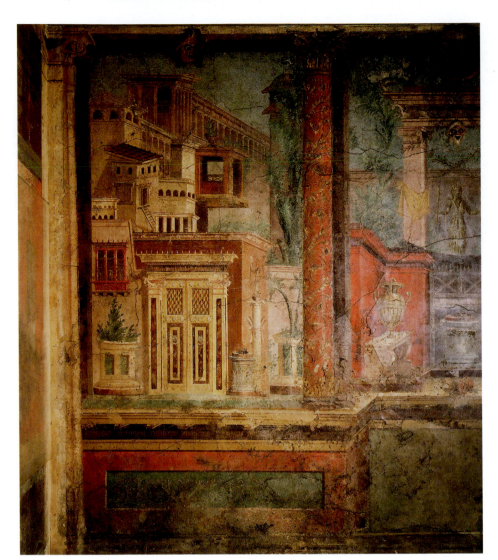

6–30 CITYSCAPE, HOUSE OF PUBLIUS FANNIUS SYNISTOR

Boscoreale. Detail of a wall painting from a bedroom. c. 50–30 BCE. Metropolitan Museum of Art, New York. Rogers Fund, 1903. (03.14.13).

Credit: © 2016. Image copyright The Metropolitan Museum of Art/Art Resource/Scala, Florence

beyond the wall. In intuitive perspective, architectural details follow diagonal lines that the eye interprets as parallel lines receding into the distance, and objects meant to be perceived as far away from the surface plane of the wall are shown gradually smaller and smaller than those intended to appear in the foreground.

Close to Rome, the late first-century BCE paintings on the dining-room walls of Livia's villa at Primaporta exemplify yet another approach to creating a sense of expanded space with murals (**FIG. 6–31**). Instead of rendering a stage set or opening onto an expansive architectural vista, the artists here created the illusion of being on a porch or pavilion looking out over a low wall into an orchard of flowering shrubs and heavily laden fruit trees populated by a variety of wonderfully observed birds—an idealized view of the natural world. Here the painters used **atmospheric perspective**, where the world becomes progressively less distinct as it recedes into the distance.

A PAINTER AT WORK This fresco—portraying a painter absorbed in her art—once decorated the walls of a house in Pompeii (**FIG. 6–32**). Like women in Egypt and

Crete, Roman women were far freer and more worldly than their Greek counterparts. Many received a formal education and became physicians, writers, shopkeepers, or even overseers in such male-dominated businesses as shipbuilding. But we have little information about the role women played in the visual arts, making the testimony of this picture precious.

The painter sits within a room that opens behind her to the outdoors, holding her **palette**, a sign of her profession. She wears a long robe covered by an ample mantle, and a gold headband holds back her hair; but lighting and composition highlight two other aspects of her body: her centralized face, which focuses intently on the subject of her painting—a sculptured rendering of the bearded fertility god Priapus appearing in the shadows of the right background—and her right arm, which extends downward so she can dip her brush into a paintbox that rests precariously on a column drum next to her folding stool. A small child steadies the panel on which she paints, and two elegantly posed and richly dressed women—perhaps her patrons—stand next to a pier behind her. The art she is practicing reflects well on her social position. Pliny

6–31 GARDEN VISTA, VILLA OF LIVIA AT PRIMAPORTA

Near Rome. Late 1st century BCE. Museo Nazionale Romano, Rome.

Like the garlands and curling vine scrolls on the Ara Pacis Augustae (SEE FIG. 6–19), the lush fertility of nature seems to celebrate the vitality and prosperity of Rome under Augustan peace.

Credit: © Vincenzo Pirozzi, Rome

the Elder claimed that "Among artists, glory is given only to those who paint panel paintings" (*Natural History*, 35.118). Wall paintings, he claimed, are of lesser value because they cannot be removed in case of fire. For this fresco, however, fixed positioning facilitated survival. When Mount Vesuvius erupted, it was wall paintings like this one that were preserved.

6–32 A PAINTER AT WORK

From the House of the Surgeon, Pompeii. 1st century BCE –1st century CE. Fresco, $17\frac{7}{8}'' \times 17\frac{3}{8}''$ (45.5 × 45.3 cm). Museo Archeologico Nazionale, Naples.

This painting of a female artist at work was conceived as a simulated panel painting, positioned on the yellow wall of a small room (compare the red wall in FIG. 6–29). It was revered so highly by the archaeologists who discovered it in 1771 that it was cut out of the wall to be exhibited as a framed picture in a museum, a practice that would be anathema today but was far from unusual in the eighteenth century.

Credit: © 2016. Photo Scala, Florence/Fotografica Foglia – courtesy of the Minstero Beni e Att. Culturali

STILL LIFES AND PORTRAITS In addition to cityscapes, landscapes, and figural tableaux, other subjects that appeared in Roman art included exquisitely rendered genre scenes (SEE FIG. 6–32), still lifes, and portraits. A still-life panel from Herculaneum, a community in the vicinity of Mount Vesuvius near Pompeii, depicts everyday domestic objects—still-green peaches and a glass jar half-filled with water (FIG. 6–33). The items have been carefully arranged on two stepped shelves to give the composition clarity and balance. Strong light floods the picture from left to right, casting shadows, picking up highlights, and enhancing the illusion of solid objects in real space.

Few Pompeian paintings are more arresting than a double portrait of a young husband and wife (FIG. 6–34) who look out from their simulated spatial world beyond the wall into the viewer's space within the room. The swarthy, wispy-bearded man addresses us with a direct stare and holds a scroll, a conventional sign of educational achievement seen frequently in Roman portraits. Though his wife overlaps him to stake her claim to the foreground, she gazes out at us less directly. She also holds fashionable attributes of literacy—a stylus she elevates in front of her chin and a folding writing tablet on which she would have

6–33 STILL LIFE, HOUSE OF THE STAGS (CERVI)
Herculaneum. Detail of a wall painting. Before 79 CE. Approx. 1′2″ × 1′1½″ (35.5 × 31.7 cm). Museo Archeologico Nazionale, Naples.

Credit: © akg-images/Erich Lessing

6–34 PORTRAIT OF A MARRIED COUPLE
Wall painting from Pompeii. Mid 1st century CE. Height 25½″ (64.8 cm). Museo Archeologico Nazionale, Naples.

Credit: © Fotografica Foglia, Naples - courtesy of the Ministero Beni e Att. Culturali used the stylus to inscribe words into a wax infill. This picture is comparable to modern studio portrait photography with its careful lighting and retouching, conventional poses and accoutrements. Its attention to physiognomic detail—note the differences in the spacing of the two figures' eyes and the shapes of their noses, ears, and lips—makes it clear that we are in the presence of actual human likenesses.

The Flavians

The Julio-Claudian dynasty ended with the suicide of Nero in 68 CE, which led to a brief period of civil war. Eventually an astute general, Vespasian, seized control of the government in 69 CE, founding a new dynasty known as the Flavian. Led by practical military men who inspired confidence and ruled for the rest of the first century, the Flavian dynasty restored the imperial finances and stabilized the frontiers. The Julio-Claudian fashion for classicizing imperial portraiture was replaced by a return to the ideal of time-worn faces with the effects of old age enhanced to project a sense of wisdom and accomplishment.

THE ARCH OF TITUS   When Domitian assumed the throne in 81 CE, he immediately commissioned a triumphal arch to honor the capture of Jerusalem in 70 CE by his brother and deified predecessor, Titus. Part architecture, part sculpture, and distinctly Roman, free-standing triumphal arches commemorate a triumph, or formal victory celebration, during which a victorious general or emperor paraded through Rome with his troops, captives, and booty. Constructed of concrete and faced with marble, **THE ARCH OF TITUS** (FIG. 6-35) is essentially a free-standing gateway whose passage is covered by a barrel vault. It served as a giant base, 50 feet tall, for a now-lost bronze statue of the emperor in a four-horse chariot, a typical triumphal symbol. Applied to the faces of the arch are columns in the Composite order supporting an entablature. The inscription on the uppermost story declares that the Senate and the Roman people erected the monument to honor Titus.

Titus's capture of Jerusalem ended a fierce campaign to crush a revolt of the Jews in Palestine.

6-35 THE ARCH OF TITUS
Rome. c. 81 CE (restored 1822–1824).
Concrete and white marble,
height 50′ (15 m).

The dedication inscribed across the tall attic story above the arch opening reads: "The Senate and the Roman people to the Deified Titus Vespasian Augustus, son of the Deified Vespasian." The perfectly sized and spaced Roman capital letters, meant to be read from a distance and cut with sharp terminals (serifs) to catch the light, established a standard that calligraphers and font designers still follow today.

Credit: © Rafael Ben-Ari/123RF

6-36 SPOILS FROM THE TEMPLE IN JERUSALEM
Relief in the passageway of the Arch of Titus. Marble, height 6′8″ (2.03 m).

Credit: © 2016. Photo Scala, Florence

The Romans sacked and destroyed the Temple in Jerusalem, carried off its sacred treasures, and displayed them in a triumphal procession in Rome (**FIG. 6-36**). A relief on the inside walls of the arch captures the drama of the occasion, depicting Titus's soldiers flaunting this booty as they carry it through the streets of Rome. The soldiers head toward the right through an arch, turned obliquely to project into the viewer's own space, thus allowing living spectators a sense of the press of a boisterous, disorderly crowd.

The mood of the procession depicted in this relief contrasts with the relaxed but formal solemnity of the procession portrayed on the Ara Pacis (SEE FIG. 6-21), but like the sculptors of the Ara Pacis, the sculptors of the Arch of Titus showed the spatial relationships among figures by rendering nearer elements in higher relief than those more distant. A **menorah** (seven-branched lampholder) from the Temple in Jerusalem dominates the scene with its relatively high relief.

THE COLOSSEUM Romans were huge sports fans, and the Flavian emperors catered to their tastes by building splendid facilities. Construction of Rome's greatest arena, the **FLAVIAN AMPHITHEATER** (**FIGS. 6-37, 6-38**), began under Vespasian in 70 CE and was completed under Titus, who dedicated it in 80 CE. The Flavian Amphitheater came to be known as the "Colosseum," because a gigantic statue of Nero called the *Colossus* stood next to it. "Colosseum" is a most appropriate description of this enormous entertainment center. Its outer wall stands 159 feet high. It is an oval,

measuring 615 by 510 feet, with a floor 280 by 175 feet. This floor was laid over a foundation of service rooms and tunnels that provided an area for the athletes, performers, animals, and equipment. The floor was covered by sand, *arena* in Latin, hence the English term "arena" for a building of this type.

Roman audiences watched a variety of athletic events, blood sports, and spectacles, including animal hunts, fights to the death between gladiators or between gladiators and wild animals, performances of trained animals and acrobats, and even mock sea battles, for which the arena would be flooded. The opening performances in 80 CE lasted 100 days, during which time it was claimed that 9,000 wild animals and 2,000 gladiators died for the amusement of the spectators.

The amphitheater is so remarkably efficient—with easy access, perfect sight lines, and effective crowd control—that stadiums today still use its plan. Some 50,000 spectators could move easily through the 76 entrance doors to the 3 levels of seats—laid over barrel-vaulted access corridors and entrance tunnels—and the standing area at the top. Each spectator had an uninterrupted view of the events below, and the walls on the top level supported a huge awning that could shade the seats. Sailors, who had experience in handling ropes, pulleys, and large expanses of canvas, worked the apparatus that extended the awning.

The curving, outer wall of the Colosseum consists of three levels of arcades (linear series of arches) surmounted by a wall-like attic (top) story. Each arch is framed by engaged columns. Entablature-like friezes mark the divisions between levels. Each level also uses a different architectural order, increasing in complexity from bottom to top: the plain Tuscan order on the ground level, Ionic on the second level, Corinthian on the third, and Corinthian pilasters on the fourth. The attic story is broken by small, square windows, which originally alternated with gilded-bronze shield-shaped ornaments called **cartouches**, supported on brackets that are still in place.

All these elements are purely decorative. As we saw in the Etruscan Porta Augusta (SEE FIG. 6–2), the addition of post-and-lintel decoration to arched structures was an Etruscan innovation. The systematic use of the orders in a logical succession from sturdy Tuscan to lighter Ionic to decorative Corinthian follows a tradition inherited from Hellenistic architecture. This orderly, dignified, and visually satisfying way of organizing the façades

6–37 RECONSTRUCTION DRAWING OF THE FLAVIAN AMPHITHEATER (COLOSSEUM)
Rome. 70–80 CE.

Credit: © Dorling Kindersley

6–38 OUTER WALL OF THE FLAVIAN AMPHITHEATER (COLOSSEUM)
Rome. 70–80 CE.

Credit: © 123RF.com

Elements of Architecture

ROMAN VAULTING

The Romans became experts in devising methods of covering large, open architectural spaces with concrete and masonry, using barrel vaults, groin vaults, or domes.

A **barrel vault** is constructed in the same manner as the round arch. In a sense, it is a series of connected arches extended in sequence along a line. The outward pressure exerted by the curving sides of the barrel vault requires buttressing within or outside the supporting walls.

When two barrel-vaulted spaces intersect each other at the same level, the result is a **groin vault**. Both the weight and

outward thrust of the groin vault are concentrated on four corner piers; only the piers require buttressing, so the walls on all four sides can be opened. The Romans used the groin vault to construct some of their grandest interior spaces.

A third type of vault brought to technical perfection by the Romans is the **dome**. The rim of the dome is supported on a circular wall, as in the Pantheon (SEE FIGS. 6–48, 6–49, 6–51). This wall is called a drum when it is raised on top of a main structure. Sometimes a circular opening, called an **oculus**, is left at the top.

barrel vault

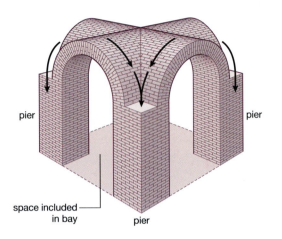

groin vault

of large buildings is still popular. Unfortunately, much of the Colosseum was dismantled in the Middle Ages as a source of marble, metal fittings, and materials for buildings such as churches.

PORTRAIT SCULPTURE Roman patrons continued to expect recognizable likenesses in their portraits, but this did not preclude idealization. A portrait sculpture of a **YOUNG FLAVIAN WOMAN** (**FIG. 6–39**) is idealized in a manner similar to the *Augustus of Primaporta* (SEE FIG. 6–18). Her features—a strong nose and jaw, heavy brows, deep-set eyes, and a long neck—are well observed and her hair is piled high in an extraordinary mass of ringlets following the latest court fashion. Executing the head required skillful chiseling and **drillwork**, a technique for rapidly cutting deep grooves with straight sides, used here to render the holes in the center of the curls. The overall effect is quite lifelike, as the play of light over the subtly sculpted marble surfaces simulates the textures of real skin and hair.

A contemporary bust of an older woman (**FIG. 6–40**) presents a strikingly different image of its subject. Although she also wears her hair in the latest fashion, it

is less elaborate than that of her younger counterpart. The work emphasizes not the fresh sheen of an unblemished face, but a visage clearly marked by the passage of time. We may regard this portrait as less idealized and more naturalistic, but for a Roman viewer, it conformed to an ideal of accomplishment by showcasing signs of aging, cherished since the Republican period as reflections of virtue and venerability.

The High Imperial Art of Trajan and Hadrian

What are the salient features of Roman art and architecture at the height of imperial power and expanse?

Domitian, the last Flavian emperor, was assassinated in 96 CE and succeeded by a senator, Nerva (ruled 96–98 CE), who designated as his successor Trajan, a general born in Spain who had commanded Roman troops in Germany. For nearly a century, the empire was under the control of brilliant administrators. Instead of depending on the vagaries

6–39 YOUNG FLAVIAN WOMAN

c. 90 CE. Marble, height 25″ (65.5 cm). Museo Capitolino, Rome.

Credit: © Araldo de Luca/Corbis

6–40 MIDDLE-AGED FLAVIAN WOMAN

Late 1st century CE. Marble, height 9½″ (24.1 cm). Musei Vaticani, Museo Gregoriano Profano, ex-Lateranese, Rome.

of fate (or genetics) to produce intelligent heirs, the emperors Nerva (ruled 96–98 CE), Trajan (ruled 98–117 CE), Hadrian (ruled 117–138 CE), and Antoninus Pius (ruled 138–161 CE) each selected an able administrator to follow himself, thus "adopting" his successor. Italy and the provinces flourished, and official and private patronage of the arts increased.

Under Trajan, the empire reached its greatest territorial expanse. By 106 CE, he had conquered Dacia, roughly present-day Romania (SEE MAP 6–1). His successor, Hadrian, consolidated the empire's borders and imposed far-reaching social, governmental, and military reforms. Hadrian was well educated and widely traveled, and his admiration for Greek culture spurred new building programs and classicizing works of art throughout the empire. Unfortunately, his successor, Marcus Aurelius (ruled 161–180 CE), broke the tradition of adoption and let his son, Commodus, inherit the throne. Within 12 years, Commodus (ruled 180–192 CE) had destroyed the stable government his predecessors had so carefully built.

Imperial Architecture

The Romans believed their rule extended to the ends of the Western world, but the city of Rome remained the nerve center of the empire. During his long and peaceful reign, Augustus had paved the city's old Republican Forum, restored its temples and basilicas, and followed Julius Caesar's example by building an Imperial Forum. These projects marked the beginning of a continuing effort to transform the capital into a magnificent monument to imperial rule. Such grand structures as the Imperial Forums, the Colosseum, the Circus Maximus (a track for chariot races), the Pantheon, and aqueducts stood amid the temples, baths, warehouses, and homes in the city center as expressions of successive emperors' beneficence and their desire to leave their mark on, and preserve their memory in, the capital. A model of Rome's city center makes apparent the dense building plan (FIG. 6–41).

THE FORUM OF TRAJAN   In about 110–113 CE, Trajan began the last and largest Imperial Forum on a large piece of property next to the earlier forums of Augustus and

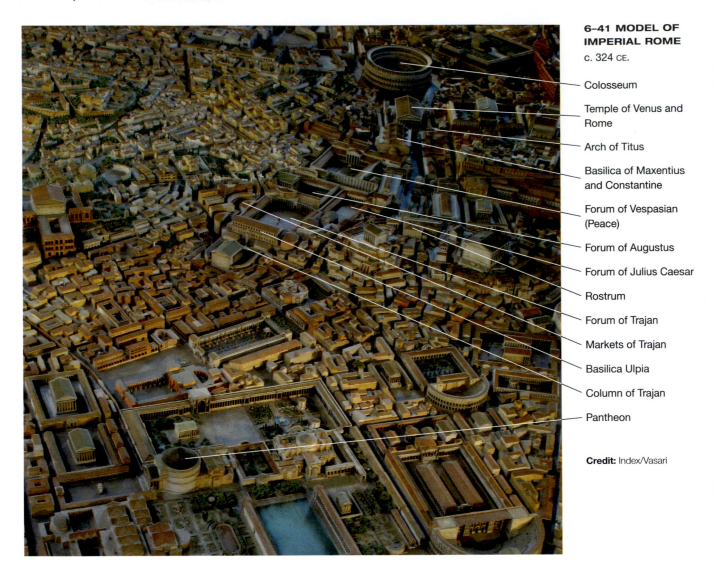

6–41 MODEL OF IMPERIAL ROME

c. 324 CE.

— Colosseum

— Temple of Venus and Rome

— Arch of Titus

— Basilica of Maxentius and Constantine

— Forum of Vespasian (Peace)

— Forum of Augustus

— Forum of Julius Caesar

— Rostrum

— Forum of Trajan

— Markets of Trajan

— Basilica Ulpia

— Column of Trajan

— Pantheon

Credit: Index/Vasari

Julius Caesar; Hadrian finished the project about 117 CE (**FIG. 6–42**). For this major undertaking, Trajan chose Apollodorus of Damascus, a Greek architect and experienced military engineer. A straight, central axis leads from the Forum of Augustus through a triple-arched gate surmounted by a bronze chariot group into a large, colonnaded square with a statue of Trajan on horseback at its center.

The **BASILICA ULPIA** (**FIG. 6–43**) closed off the courtyard at the north end. Dedicated in c. 112 CE, the building was named for the family to which Trajan belonged. A **basilica** was a large, rectangular building with an extensive interior space, adaptable for a variety of administrative governmental functions. The Basilica Ulpia was a court of law, but other basilicas served as imperial audience chambers, army drill halls, and schools. The Basilica Ulpia was a particularly grand interior space, 385 feet long (not including the apses) and 182 feet wide. A large central area (the **nave**) was flanked by double colonnaded aisles surmounted by open galleries or by a clerestory, an upper nave wall with windows. The timber truss roof had a span

of about 80 feet. The two **apses**, rounded extensions at each end of the building, provided imposing settings for judges when the court was in session.

During the site preparation for Trajan's forum, part of a commercial district had to be razed and excavated. To make up for the loss, Trajan ordered the construction of a handsome public market (**FIGS. 6–44, 6–45**). The market, comparable in size to a large modern shopping mall, had more than 150 individual shops on several levels and included a large, groin-vaulted main hall. In compliance with a building code that was put into effect after a disastrous fire in 64 CE, the market, like most Roman buildings of the time, was constructed of concrete (see "Concrete" on page 196) and faced with brick, with only occasional detailing in stone and wood.

Behind the Basilica Ulpia stood twin libraries built to house the emperor's collections of Latin and Greek manuscripts. These buildings flanked an open court, the location of the great spiral column commemorating Trajan's victory over the Dacians that was erected either c. 113 CE, at about

6-42 PLAN OF TRAJAN'S FORUM AND MARKET

c. 110–113 CE.

N

Temple to the Divine Trajan

Column of Trajan

Greek and Latin libraries

market hall

Markets of Trajan

Via Biberatica

Basilica Ulpia

Temple of Venus Genetrix in the Forum of Julius Caesar

equestrian statue of Trajan

0   50 m

0   100 ft

6-43 Gilbert Gorski RESTORED PERSPECTIVE VIEW OF THE CENTRAL HALL, BASILICA ULPIA

Rome. As it was c. 112 CE.

Trajan's architect was Apollodorus of Damascus. The building may have had clerestory windows instead of the gallery shown in this drawing. The Column of Trajan can be seen through the upper colonnade at right.

Credit: Dr. James E. Packer

6-44 RECONSTRUCTION DRAWING OF TRAJAN'S MARKET
Rome. As it was 100–112 CE.

Credit: Kevin Jones and Associates © Dorling Kindersley

the same time as the Basilica Ulpia, or by Hadrian after Trajan's death in 117 CE. The column became Trajan's tomb when Hadrian placed a golden urn containing his predecessor's ashes in its base.

THE COLUMN OF TRAJAN The relief decoration on the **COLUMN OF TRAJAN** spirals upward in a band that would stretch almost 625 feet if laid out straight. Like a giant, unfurled version of the scrolls housed in the libraries next to it, the column presents a continuous pictorial narrative of the Dacian campaigns of 102–103 and 105–106 CE (**FIG. 6-46**). The remarkable sculpture includes more than 2,500 individual figures linked by landscape and architecture and punctuated by the recurring figure of Trajan. The narrative band slowly expands from about 3 feet in height at the bottom of the column to 4 feet at the top, where it is farther from view. The natural and architectural elements in the scenes have been kept small so that the important figures can occupy as much space as possible.

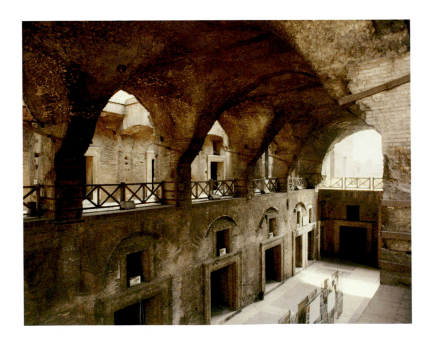

6-45 MAIN HALL, TRAJAN'S MARKET
Rome. 100–112 CE.

Credit: © 2016. Photo Scala, Florence - courtesy of the Ministero Beni e Att. Culturali

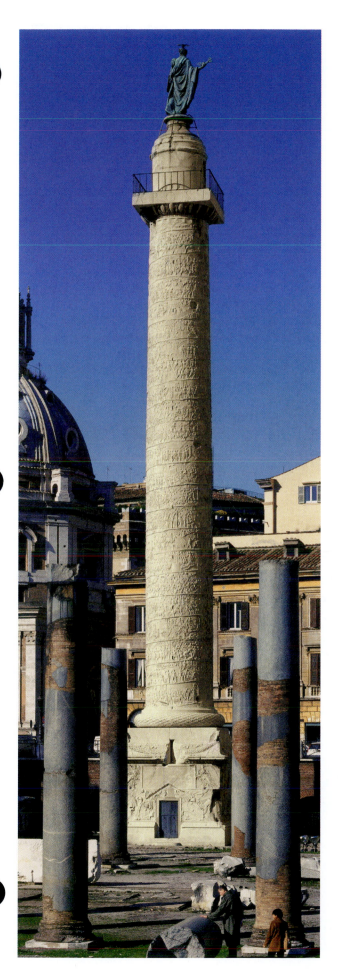

6-46 COLUMN OF TRAJAN

Rome. 113–116 CE, or after 117 CE. Marble, overall height with base 125′ (38 m); column alone 97′8″ (29.77 m); length of relief 625′ (190.5 m).

The height of the column may have recorded the depth of the excavation required to build the Forum of Trajan. The gilded bronze statue of Trajan that once stood on the top was replaced in 1588 CE with the statue of St. Peter seen today.

Credit: © Vincenzo Pirozzi, Rome

The scene at the beginning of the spiral, at the bottom of the column, shows Trajan's army crossing the Danube River on a pontoon bridge to launch the first Dacian campaign of 101 CE (**FIG. 6-47**). Soldiers construct battlefield headquarters in Dacia from which the men on the frontiers will receive orders, food, and weapons. In this spectacular piece of imperial ideology or propaganda, Trajan is portrayed as a strong, stable, and efficient commander of a well-run army, and his barbarian enemies are shown as worthy opponents of Rome.

6-47 ROMANS CROSSING THE DANUBE AND BUILDING A FORT

Detail of the lowest part of the Column of Trajan. 113–116 CE, or after 117 CE. Marble, height of the spiral band approx. 36″ (91 cm).

Credit: © 2016. Photo Scala, Florence - courtesy of the Ministero Beni e Att. Culturali

Elements of Architecture

CONCRETE

The Romans were pragmatic builders, and their practicality extended from recognizing and exploiting undeveloped potential in construction methods and physical materials to organizing large-scale building works. Their exploitation of the arch and the vault is typical of their adapt-and-improve approach. But their innovative use of concrete, beginning in the first century BCE, was a technological breakthrough of the greatest importance in the history of architecture.

In contrast to stone—which was expensive and difficult to quarry and move—the components of concrete were cheap, relatively light, and easily transported. Building stone structures required highly skilled masons, but a large, semiskilled workforce directed by a few experienced supervisors could construct brick-faced concrete buildings.

Roman concrete consisted of powdered lime, a volcanic sand called *pozzolana*, and various types of rubble, such as small rocks and broken pottery. Mixing these materials in water caused a chemical reaction that blended them, and they hardened into a strong, solid mass as they dried. At first, concrete was used mainly for poured foundations, but with technical advances it became indispensable for the construction of walls, arches, and vaults for ever-larger buildings such as

the Flavian Amphitheater (SEE FIG. 6–38) and the Market of Trajan (SEE FIG. 6–45). In the earliest concrete wall construction, workers filled a framework of rough stones with concrete. Soon they developed a technique known as *opus reticulatum*, in which the framework is a diagonal web of smallish bricks set in a cross pattern. Concrete-based construction freed the Romans from the limits of right-angle forms and comparatively short spans. With this new freedom, Roman builders pushed the established limits of architecture, creating some very large and highly original spaces by pouring concrete over wooden frameworks to mold it into complex curving shapes.

Concrete's one weakness was that it absorbed moisture and would eventually deteriorate if unprotected, so builders covered exposed concrete with a veneer, or facing, of finer materials—such as marble, stone, stucco, or painted plaster—to protect it. An essential difference between Greek and Roman architecture is that Greek builders reveal the building material itself and accept the design limitations of post-and-lintel construction, whereas Roman buildings expose only an externally applied surface covering. The sophisticated structural underpinnings are hidden from view.

6–48 PANTHEON
Rome. c. 110–128 CE.

Today a huge fountain dominates the square in front of the Pantheon. Built in 1578 by Giacomo della Porta, it now supports an Egyptian obelisk placed there in 1711 by Pope Clement XI.

Credit: © Vincenzo Pirozzi, Rome

6–49 RECONSTRUCTION DRAWING OF THE PANTHEON

Credit: © Dorling Kindersley

THE PANTHEON Perhaps the most remarkable ancient building surviving in Rome—and one of the marvels of world architecture in any age—is a temple to Mars, Venus, and the divine Julius Caesar known as the **PANTHEON** (**FIG. 6–48**). Although this monument was designed and constructed during the reigns of emperors Trajan and Hadrian, the long inscription on the architrave states that it was built by "Marcus Agrippa, son of Lucius, who was consul three times." Agrippa, the son-in-law and valued advisor of Augustus, sponsored a building on this site in 27–25 BCE. After a fire in 80 CE, Domitian either restored the Pantheon or built a new temple, which burned again after being struck by lightning in 110 CE. Although for some time scholars have believed that it was Hadrian who reconstructed the building in its current state in 118–128 CE, a recent study of the brick stamps has argued convincingly that the Pantheon was begun soon after 110 under Trajan, but completed during the reign of his successor, Hadrian. The Pantheon's spectacular and influential design may represent another work of Apollodorus of Damascus.

6–50 PLAN OF THE PANTHEON

Credit: After William L. MacDonald, The Architecture of the Roman Empire I: An Introductory Study. New Haven and London: Yale University Press, 1965, fig 9

The current setting of the temple gives little suggestion of its original appearance. Centuries of dirt and street construction hide its podium and stairs. Attachment holes in the pediment indicate the placement of bronze sculpture, perhaps an eagle within a wreath representing the imperial Jupiter. Today we can see the sides of the rotunda flanking the entrance porch, but when the Pantheon was constructed, the façade of this porch—resembling the façades of typical, rectangular temples—was literally all viewers could see of the building. Since their approach was controlled by an enclosed courtyard (SEE FIG. 6–41), the actual circular shape of the Pantheon was concealed.

Viewers were therefore surprised to pass through the rectilinear and restricted aisles of the portico and the huge main door to encounter the gaping space of the giant **rotunda** (circular room) topped with a vast, bowl-shaped dome, 143 feet in diameter and 143 feet from the floor at its summit (**FIGS. 6–49, 6–50**). Even without the controlled courtyard approach, encountering this space today is still an overwhelming experience—for many of

6–51 INTERIOR OF THE PANTHEON LOOKING UP INTO THE DOME

With light from the oculus on its coffered ceiling. c. 110–128 CE. Brick, concrete, marble veneer, diameter of dome 143′ (43.5 m).

Credit: © Insadco Photography/Alamy Stock Photo

us, one that is repeated on successive visits to the rotunda.

Standing at the center of this hemispherical temple (**FIG. 6–51**), the visitor feels isolated from the outside world and intensely aware of the shape and tangibility of the luminous space itself. Our eyes are drawn upward over the patterns made by the sunken panels, or **coffers**, in the dome's ceiling to the light entering the 29-foot-wide oculus, or round central opening. This disk of light illuminates a brilliant circle against the surface of the dome and moves around this microcosm throughout the day like a sun. Clouds travel across the opening as well; when rain falls in, it drains off through conduits on the floor planned by the original engineer. Occasionally a bird flies in.

The simple shape of the Pantheon's dome belies its sophisticated design and engineering. Marble veneer and richly colored architectural detail conceal the internal brick arches and concrete structure of the rotunda's 20-foot-thick walls. More than half of the original decoration— two tiers of columns, pilasters, and entablatures—survives. The simple repetition of square against circle, established on a large scale by juxtaposing the rectilinear portico against the circular rotunda, dominates the building's ornamentation. Seven **exedrae** (niches)—rectangular alternating with semicircular—punctuate the wall. Originally they held statues of gods. The boxlike coffers inside the dome, which help lighten the weight of the masonry, may once have contained gilded bronze rosettes or stars suggesting the heavens. In 609 CE, Pope Boniface IV rededicated the Pantheon as the Christian church of St. Mary of the Martyrs, thus ensuring its survival through the Middle Ages and down to our day.

HADRIAN'S VILLA AT TIVOLI   To imagine imperial Roman life at its most luxurious, one must go to Tivoli, a little more than 20 miles from Rome. **HADRIAN'S VILLA**, or country residence, was not a single building but an architectural complex of many buildings, lakes, and gardens spread over half a square mile (**FIG. 6–52**). Each section had its own inner logic and took advantage of natural

6-52 PLAN OF HADRIAN'S VILLA
Tivoli. c. 125–135 CE.

land formations and attractive views. Hadrian instructed his architects to re-create his favorite places throughout the empire so he could pretend to enjoy the Athenian Grove of Academe, the Painted Stoa from the Athenian Agora, and buildings of the Ptolemaic capital of Alexandria in Egypt.

Landscapes with pools, fountains, and gardens turned the villa into a place of delight. An area with a long reflecting pool, called **THE CANAL**, was framed by a colonnade with alternating semicircular and straight entablatures (**FIG. 6-53**). Copies of famous Greek

6-53 THE CANAL (REFLECTING POOL), HADRIAN'S VILLA
Tivoli. c. 125–135 CE.

Credit: © Vincenzo Pirozzi, Rome

statues—sometimes even originals—filled the spaces between columns. So great was Hadrian's love of Greek sculpture that he had the caryatids of the Erechtheion (SEE FIG. 5–46) replicated for his pleasure palace.

The individual buildings were not large, but they were extremely complex and imaginatively designed, exploiting fully the flexibility offered by concrete vaulted construction. Walls and floors had veneers of marble and travertine or of exquisite mosaics and paintings. A panel from one of the floor mosaics (FIG. 6–54) demonstrates the artistry of Hadrian's mosaicists. In a rocky landscape with only a few bits of greenery, a desperate male centaur raises a large boulder over his head to crush a tiger that has severely wounded a female centaur. Two other felines apparently took part in the attack—the white leopard on the rocks to the left and the dead lion at the feet of the male centaur. The artist rendered the figures with three-dimensional shading, foreshortening, and a great sensitivity to a range of figure types, including human torsos and animals in a variety of poses.

Roman Mosaics

Mosaics were used widely in Hellenistic times and became enormously popular for decorating homes in the Roman period. Mosaics were created with pebbles (SEE FIG. 5–58) or with small, regularly shaped pieces of colored stone and marble called tesserae. The stones were pressed into a kind of soft cement called grout. When the stones were firmly set, the spaces between them were also filled with grout. After the surface dried, it was cleaned and polished. Since the natural stones produced only a narrow range of colors, glass tesserae were also used to extend the palette as early as the third century BCE.

Some skilled mosaicists even copied well-known paintings, often by famous Greek artists. Employing a technique in which very small tesserae in a wide range of colors were laid down in irregular, curving lines, they effectively imitated painted brushstrokes. One example is **THE UNSWEPT FLOOR** (FIG. 6–55). Herakleitos, a second-century CE Greek mosaicist living in Rome, made this copy

6–54 BATTLE OF CENTAURS AND WILD BEASTS
From Hadrian's Villa, Tivoli. c. 125 CE. Mosaic, 23 × 36″ (58.4 × 91.4 cm). Staatliche Museen zu Berlin, Preussischer Kulturbesitz, Antikensammlung.

This floor mosaic may be a copy of a much-admired scene of a fight between centaurs and wild animals painted by the late fifth-century BCE Greek artist Zeuxis.

Credit: © 2016. Photo Scala, Florence/bpk, Bildagentur für Kunst, Kultur und Geschichte, Berlin

6–55 Herakleitos **THE UNSWEPT FLOOR**

Mosaic variant of a 2nd-century BCE painting by Sosos of Pergamon. 2nd century CE. Musei Vaticani, Museo Gregoriano Profano, Rome.

Credit: © akg-images/Pirozzi

of an original work by the renowned second-century BCE artist Sosos. Pliny the Elder, in his *Natural History*, mentions a mosaic of an unswept floor and another of doves that Sosos made in Pergamon.

A dining room would be a logical location for a floor mosaic of this theme with table scraps recreated in meticulous detail, even to the shadows they cast, and a mouse foraging among them. Guests reclining on their banquet couches would certainly have been amused by the pictures on the floor, and they could also have shown off their knowledge of the Greek precedent for the mosaic beneath their feet.

Imperial Portraits

Imperial portraits were objects of propaganda, proclaiming the accomplishments and pretensions of emperors. Marcus Aurelius, like Hadrian, was a successful military commander who was equally proud of his intellectual attainments. In a lucky error—or twist of fortune—a gilded-bronze equestrian statue of the emperor dressed as a military commander in a tunic and short, heavy cloak (**FIG. 6–56**) came mistakenly to be revered during the Middle Ages as a statue of Constantine, the first Christian emperor, and consequently escaped being melted down to recycle the bronze. The raised foreleg of the horse once trampled a crouching barbarian.

Marcus Aurelius's head, with its thick, curly hair and full beard (a fashion initiated by Hadrian), resembles traditional "philosopher" portraits from the Greek world. The emperor wears no armor and carries no weapons; like Egyptian kings, he conquers effortlessly by divine will. And like his illustrious predecessor Augustus, he reaches out to those around him in a rhetorical gesture of address. It is difficult to create an equestrian portrait in which the rider stands out as the dominant figure without making the horse look too small. The sculptor of this statue found a balance acceptable to viewers of the time and, in doing so, created a model for later artists.

6–56 EQUESTRIAN STATUE OF MARCUS AURELIUS

c. 176 CE. Bronze, originally gilded, height 11′6″ (3.5 m). Museo Capitolino, Rome.

Between 1187 and 1538, this statue stood in the piazza fronting the palace and church of St. John Lateran in Rome. In January 1538, Pope Paul III had it moved to the Capitoline Hill, and Michelangelo made it the centerpiece of his newly redesigned Capitoline Piazza. After being removed from its base for cleaning and restoration during the 1980s, it was taken inside the Capitoline Museum to protect it from air pollution, and a copy has replaced it in the piazza.

Credit: © akg-images/Pirozzi

6-57 COMMODUS AS HERCULES

From the Esquiline Hill, Rome. c. 191–192 CE. Marble, height 46½″ (118 cm). Palazzo dei Conservatori, Rome.

Credit: © Vincenzo Pirozzi, Rome fotopirozzi@inwind.it

Marcus Aurelius's son Commodus succeeded him as emperor. Commodus was a man without political skill, administrative competence, or intellectual distinction. During his unfortunate reign (180–192 CE), he devoted himself to luxury and frivolous pursuits, claiming at various times to be the reincarnation of Hercules and the incarnation of the god Jupiter. When he proposed to assume the consulship dressed and armed as a gladiator, his associates, including his mistress, arranged to have him strangled in his bath by a wrestling partner. In a spectacular marble bust, the emperor poses as **HERCULES** (**FIG. 6-57**), adorned with references to the hero's legendary labors: Hercules's club, the skin and head of the Nemean lion, and the golden apples from the Garden of the Hesperides. Commodus's likeness emphasizes his family resemblance to his more illustrious and powerful father (SEE FIG. 6-56), but the bust also captures his vanity through the grand pretensions of the costume and the Classical associations of the body type. The sculptor's sensitive modeling and expert drillwork exploit the play of light on the figure to bring out the textures of the hair, beard, facial features, and drapery and create an illusion of movement.

Funerary Sculpture

During the second and third centuries, a shift from cremation to inhumation created a growing demand for sarcophagi in which to bury the bodies of the deceased. Wealthy Romans commissioned thousands of massive and elaborate marble sarcophagi encrusted with sculptural relief, created in large production workshops throughout the Roman Empire.

In 1885, nine particularly impressive sarcophagi were discovered in private underground burial chambers built for use by a powerful, aristocratic Roman family—the Calpurnii Pisones. One of these sarcophagi, from c. 190 CE, portrays the **INDIAN TRIUMPH OF DIONYSUS** (see "Closer Look" on page 204). This is a popular theme in late second-century CE sarcophagi, but here the carved relief is of especially high quality—complex but highly legible at the same time. The mythological composition owes a debt to imperial ceremony: Dionysus, at far left in a chariot, receives from a personification of Victory standing behind him a laurel crown, identical to the headdress worn by Roman emperors during triumphal processions. Also derived from state ceremony is the display of booty and captives carried by the elephants at the center of the composition. But religion, rather than statecraft, is the real theme here. The set of sarcophagi to which this belongs proclaims the family's adherence to a mystery cult of Dionysus that focused on themes of decay and renewal, death and rebirth. The triumph of the deceased over death is the central message here, not one particular episode in the life of Dionysus himself.

A Closer Look

SARCOPHAGUS WITH THE INDIAN TRIUMPH OF DIONYSUS

Semele, mortal mother of the god Dionysus, gives birth prematurely and then dies. Once grown, Dionysus would travel to the underworld and bring his mother to paradise. Semele's death therefore suggests the promise of eternal life through her son.

These hooked sticks are identical to the *ankusha* still used by *mahouts* (elephant drivers) in India today.

As part of their worship, followers of Dionysiac mystery religions re-created the triumphant return of the god from India by parading in the streets after dark. A dancing maenad beats her tambourine here, suggesting the sounds and movements that would accompany such re-enactments.

The presence of exotic animals such as elephants, a lion, a giraffe, and panthers identifies this scene as Dionysus's triumphant return from India.

Snakes were not only used in the rites of Dionysiac mystery religions, they were also powerful symbols of rebirth and phallic fertility, making them especially appropriate in the context of a sarcophagus. Three snakes appear along the ground-line of the sculptural frieze.

The aged god Silenus leans on a *thyrsos* staff, a giant fennel stalk wound with ivy and topped with a pinecone, symbolizing fertility. Dionysus, with whom such staffs were associated, also carries one here as his triumphal scepter.

6-58 SARCOPHAGUS WITH THE INDIAN TRIUMPH OF DIONYSUS
c. 190 CE. Marble, 47½ × 92½ × 35¹³⁄₁₆″ (120.7 × 234.9 × 90.96 cm). The Walters Art Museum, Baltimore (23.31)

Credit: Photo © The Walters Art Museum, Baltimore

The Late Empire, Third and Fourth Centuries CE

What continues and what changes in the art and architecture of the Late Roman Empire?

The comfortable life suggested by the wall paintings in Roman houses and villas was to be challenged by hard times within a century. The reign of Commodus marked the beginning of a period of political and economic decline.

Barbarian groups had already begun moving into the empire in the time of Marcus Aurelius. Now they pressed on Rome's frontiers. Many crossed the borders and settled within them, disrupting provincial governments. As perceived threats spread throughout the empire, imperial rule became increasingly authoritarian. Eventually the army controlled the government, and the Imperial Guards set up and deposed rulers almost at will, often selecting candidates from among poorly educated, power-hungry provincial leaders in their own ranks.

The Severan Dynasty

Despite the pressures brought by political and economic change, the arts continued to flourish under the Severan emperors (193–235 CE) who succeeded Commodus. Septimius Severus (ruled 193–211 CE), who was born in Africa, and his Syrian wife, Julia Domna, restored public buildings, commissioned official portraits, and revitalized the old cattle market in Rome into a well-planned center of bustling commerce. Their sons, Geta and Caracalla, succeeded Septimius Severus as co-emperors in 211 CE, but Caracalla murdered Geta in 212 CE and then ruled alone until he in turn was murdered in 217 CE.

PORTRAITS OF CARACALLA   The Emperor Caracalla appears in his portraits as a fierce and courageous ruler, capable of confronting Rome's enemies and safeguarding the security of the Roman Empire. In the example shown here (**FIG. 6–59**), the sculptor has enhanced the intensity of the emperor's expression by producing strong contrasts of light and dark with chiseling and drillwork. Even the eyes have been drilled and engraved to catch the light in a way that makes them dominate Caracalla's expression. The contrast between this style and that of the portraits of Augustus is a telling reflection of the changing character of imperial rule. Augustus envisioned himself as the suave initiator of a Golden Age of peace and prosperity; Caracalla presents himself as a no-nonsense ruler of iron-fisted determination with a militaristic, close-cropped haircut and a glare of fierce intensity.

THE BATHS OF CARACALLA   The year before his death in 211 CE, Septimius Severus had begun a popular public-works project: the construction of magnificent new public baths on the southeast side of Rome as a new recreational and educational center. Caracalla completed and inaugurated the baths today known by his name in 216–217 CE. The impressive brick-and-concrete structure was hidden under a sheath of colorful marble and mosaic. The builders used soaring groin and barrel vaults, which allow the maximum space with the fewest possible supports. The groin vaults also made possible large windows in every bay (the space encompassed by each arch and its supports). Windows were important, since the baths depended on natural light and could only be open during daylight hours.

The **BATHS OF CARACALLA** (**FIG. 6–60**) were laid out on a strictly symmetrical plan. The bathing facilities were grouped in the center of the main building to make efficient use of the

6–59 CARACALLA

Early 3rd century CE. Marble, height 14½" (36.2 cm). Metropolitan Museum of Art, New York. Samuel D. Lee Fund, 1940. (40.11.1A).

Credit: © 2016. Image copyright The Metropolitan Museum of Art/Art Resource/ Scala, Florence. Photo: Schechter Lee

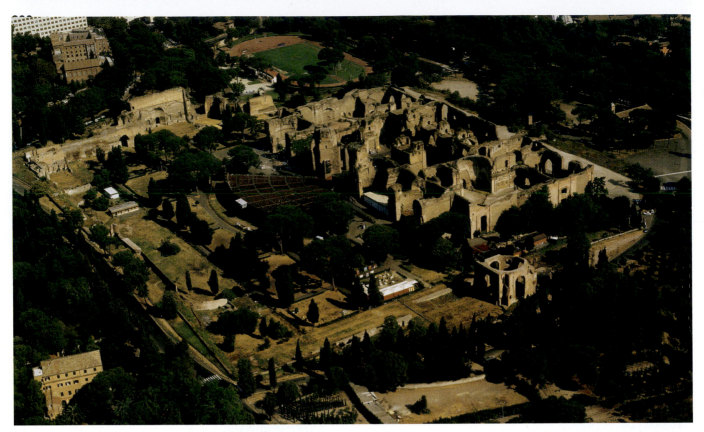

6–60A AERIAL VIEW OF THE BATHS OF CARACALLA
Rome. c. 211–217 CE.

Credit: © Alinari Archives/Corbis

6–60B PLAN OF THE BATHS OF CARACALLA
Rome. c. 211–217.

below-ground furnaces that heated them and to allow bathers to move comfortably from hot to cold pools and then finish with a swim. Many other facilities—exercise rooms, shops, latrines, and dressing rooms—were housed on each side of the bathing block. The bath buildings alone covered 5 acres. The entire complex, which included gardens, a stadium, libraries, a painting gallery, auditoriums, and huge water reservoirs, covered an area of 50 acres.

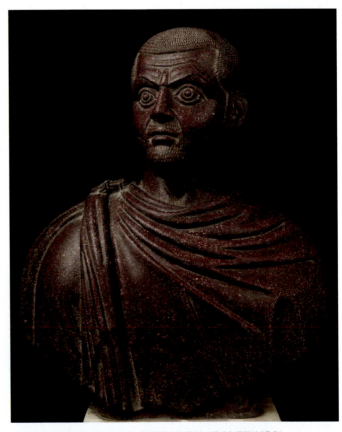

6–61 PORTRAIT OF A TETRARCH (GALERIUS?)
Early 4th century CE. Porphyry, 2′5½″ (65 cm). Egyptian Museum, Cairo.

Credit: Araldo de Luca

The Tetrarchy

Following the assassination of the last Severan emperor by one of his military commanders in 235 CE, Rome was plunged into a period of anarchy that lasted for 50 years. A series of soldier emperors attempted to rule the empire, but real order was only restored by Diocletian (ruled 284–305 CE), also a military commander. This brilliant politician and general reversed the empire's declining fortunes, but he also initiated an increasingly autocratic form of rule, and the social structure of the empire became increasingly rigid.

To divide up the task of defending and administering the Roman world and assure an orderly succession, in 286 CE Diocletian divided the empire in two. According to his plan, he would rule in the East with the title of "Augustus," while another Augustus, Maximian, would rule in the West. Then in 293 CE he devised a form of government called a tetrarchy, or "rule of four," in which each Augustus designated a subordinate and heir who held the title of "Caesar." Four individuals would rule the Roman Empire, which was now divided into four quadrants.

PORTRAITURE   The introduction of a radically new, hard style of geometricized abstraction, especially notable in portraits of the tetrarchs themselves, parallels Diocletian's political restructuring. A powerful bust of a tetrarch, startlingly alert with searing eyes (**FIG. 6–61**) embodies this strong stylistic shift away from the suave Classicism seen in the portrait of Commodus as Hercules (SEE FIG. 6–57). There is no clear sense of likeness. Who this individual is seems to be less significant than the powerful position he holds. Some art historians have interpreted this change in style as

a conscious embodiment of Diocletian's new concept of government, while others have pointed to parallels with the provincial art of Diocletian's Dalmatian homeland or with the Neoplatonic aesthetics of idealized abstraction promoted by Plotinus, a third-century CE philosopher who was widely read in the late Roman world. In any event, these riveting works represent not a degeneration of the Classical tradition but its conscious replacement by a different aesthetic viewpoint—militaristic, severe, and abstract rather than suave, slick, and classicizing.

This new mode is famously represented by a sculptural group of **THE TETRARCHS** (**FIG. 6–62**). The four

6–62 THE TETRARCHS

c. 300 CE. Porphyry, height of figures 51" (129 cm). Installed at the corner of the façade of the Cathedral of St. Mark, Venice.

This particular sculpture may have been made in Egypt and moved to Constantinople after 330 CE. Christian crusaders who looted Constantinople in 1204 CE took the statue to Venice and installed it at the Cathedral of St. Mark, where it remains today.

Credit: © Cameraphoto Arte, Venice

6–63 EXTERIOR OF THE AUDIENCE HALL OF CONSTANTIUS CHLORUS (NOW KNOWN AS THE BASILICA)

Trier, Germany. Early 4th century CE.

Credit: © Achim Bednorz, Cologne

figures are nearly identical, except that the senior Augusti have beards while their juniors, the Caesars, are clean-shaven. Dressed in military garb and clasping swords at their sides, they embrace each other in a show of imperial unity, proclaiming an alliance rooted in strength and vigilance. The sculpture is made of porphyry, an extremely hard, purple stone from Egypt that was reserved for imperial use (SEE FIG. 6–61).

ARCHITECTURE The tetrarchs ruled the empire from administrative headquarters in Milan (Italy), Trier (Germany), Thessaloniki (Greece), and Nicomedia (Turkey). Imposing architecture was created to house the government in these new capital cities. In Trier, for example, Constantius Chlorus (Caesar, 293–305; Augustus, 305–306 CE) and his son Constantine fortified the city with walls and a monumental gate that still stand. They built public amenities, such as baths, and a palace with a huge **AUDIENCE HALL**, later used as a Christian church (**FIG. 6–63**). This early fourth-century basilica's large size and simple plan and structure exemplify the architecture of the tetrarchs: no-nonsense, imposing buildings that would impress their subjects. The audience hall is a large rectangular building, 190 by 95 feet, with a strong directional focus given by a single apse opposite the door. Two rows of arched windows pierce the brick walls, originally stuccoed on the outside and covered with marble veneer inside.

A flat roof nearly 100 feet above the floor covers both the nave and the apse (**FIG. 6–64**). In a concession to the northern climate, the building was centrally heated with hot air flowing under the floor, a technique also used in

Roman baths. The windows of the apse create an interesting optical effect. Slightly smaller than the windows in straight side walls, they create the illusion of greater distance, so that the tetrarch enthroned in the apse would appear larger than life and the hall would seem longer than it actually is.

Constantine the Great

In 305 CE, Diocletian abdicated and forced his fellow Augustus, Maximian, to do so as well. The orderly succession he had planned, however, failed to occur, and a struggle for position and advantage followed almost immediately. Two main contenders appeared in the Western Empire: Maximian's son Maxentius and Constantine, son of Tetrarch Constantius Chlorus. Constantine emerged victorious in 312, defeating Maxentius at the Battle of the Milvian Bridge at the entrance to Rome.

According to Christian tradition, Constantine had a vision the night before the battle in which he saw a flaming cross in the sky and heard these words: "In this sign you shall conquer." The next morning he ordered that his army's shields and standards be inscribed with the monogram XP (the Greek letters *chi* and *rho*, standing for *Christos*). The victorious Constantine then showed his gratitude by ending the persecution of Christians and recognizing Christianity as a lawful religion. It is possible that his mother, Helena—a devout Christian, later canonized—influenced his decision. Whatever his motivation, Constantine and Licinius, who ruled the Eastern Empire, issued the Edict of Milan, an early model of religious toleration, in 313 CE.

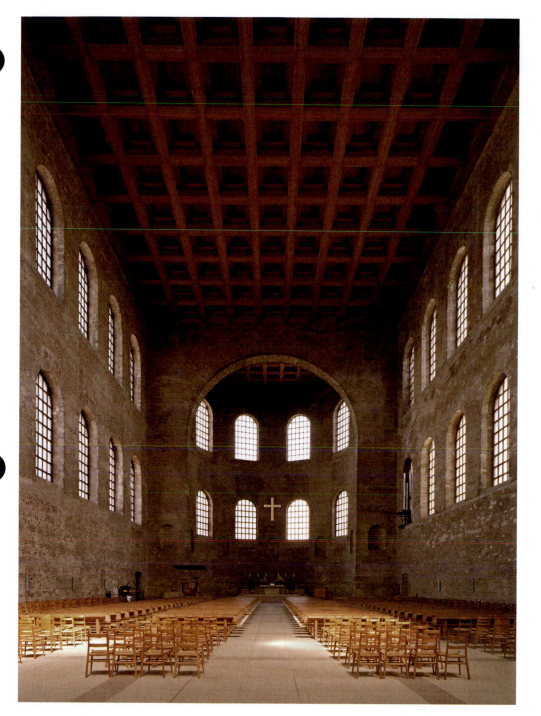

6–64 INTERIOR OF THE AUDIENCE HALL OF CONSTANTIUS CHLORUS (NOW KNOWN AS THE BASILICA)

Trier, Germany. Early 4th century CE. Height of room 100' (30.5 m).

Only the left wall and apse survive from the original Roman building. The hall became part of the bishop's palace during the medieval period.

Credit: © Achim Bednorz, Cologne

The Edict granted freedom to all religious groups, not just Christians. Constantine, however, remained the Pontifex Maximus of Rome's state religion. He also reaffirmed his devotion to the military's favorite god, Mithras, and to the Invincible Sun, Sol Invictus, a manifestation of Helios Apollo, the sun god. In 324 CE, Constantine defeated Licinius, his last rival, and ruled as sole emperor until his death in 337. After his last visit to Rome in 325, he made the port city of Byzantium the new capital of the Roman Empire and renamed it after himself: Constantinople (present-day Istanbul, in Turkey). Rome, which had already ceased to be the seat of government in the West, further declined in importance.

THE ARCH OF CONSTANTINE   In Rome, next to the Colosseum, the Senate erected a triumphal arch to commemorate Constantine's victory over Maxentius (**FIG. 6–65**), a huge, triple arch that dwarfs the nearby Arch of Titus (SEE FIG. 6–35). Its three barrel-vaulted passageways are flanked by columns on high pedestals and topped with a large attic story with elaborate sculptural decoration and a laudatory inscription: "To the Emperor Constantine from the Senate and the Roman People. Since through divine inspiration and great wisdom he has delivered the state from the tyrant and his party by his army and noble arms, [we] dedicate this arch, decorated with triumphal insignia." The "triumphal insignia" were in part appropriated from earlier monuments made for Constantine's illustrious predecessors—Trajan, Hadrian, and Marcus Aurelius. The reused items visually transferred the old Roman virtues of strength, courage, and piety associated with these earlier exemplary emperors to Constantine himself. New reliefs were made for the arch to recount the story of Constantine's victory and to symbolize his own power and generosity. They run in strips underneath the reused Hadrianic tondi (plural for tondo, a circular composition) (FIG. 6–66).

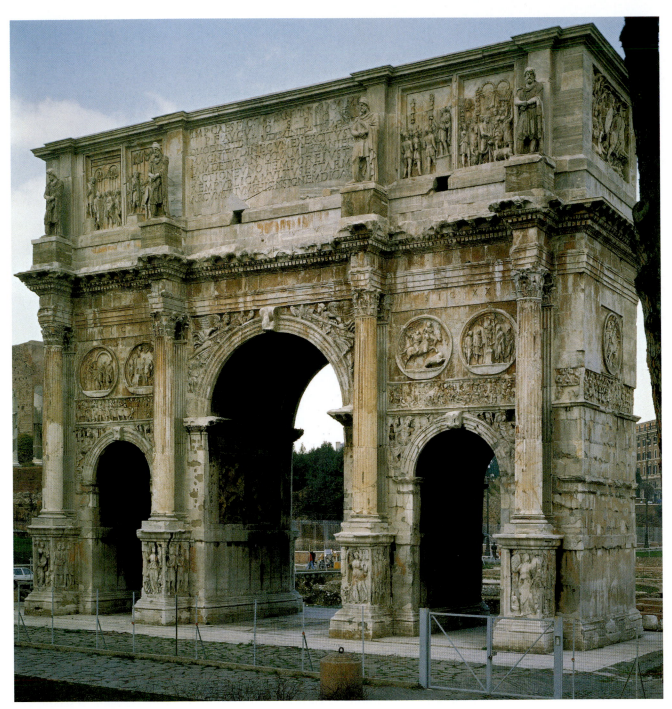

6–65 ARCH OF CONSTANTINE
Rome. 312–315 CE (dedicated July 25, 315). 69 × 85′ (21 × 26 m).

This massive, triple-arched monument to Emperor Constantine's victory over Maxentius in 312 CE is a wonder of recycled sculpture. On the attic story, flanking the inscription over the central arch, are relief panels taken from a monument celebrating the victory of Marcus Aurelius over the Germans in 174 CE. On the attached piers framing these panels are large statues of prisoners made to celebrate Trajan's victory over the Dacians in the second century CE. On the inner walls of the central arch and on the attic of the short sides (neither seen here) are reliefs also commemorating Trajan's conquest of Dacia. Over each of the side arches is a pair of large tondi (circular compositions) taken from a monument to Hadrian (SEE FIG. 6–66). The rest of the decoration is early fourth century CE, contemporary with the arch.

Credit: © akg-images/Pirozzi

6–66 HADRIAN/CONSTANTINE HUNTING BOAR AND SACRIFICING TO APOLLO; CONSTANTINE ADDRESSING THE ROMAN PEOPLE IN THE ROMAN FORUM

Tondi made for a monument to Hadrian and reused on the Arch of Constantine. c. 130–138 CE. Marble, diameter 6′6″ (2 m). Frieze by Constantinian sculptors 312–315 CE. Marble, height 3′4″ (1 m).

The two tondi were originally part of a lost monument erected by the emperor Hadrian (ruled 117–138 CE). The boar hunt demonstrates his courage and physical prowess, and his sacrificial offering to Apollo shows his piety and gratitude to the gods for their support. The classicizing heads, form-enhancing drapery, and graceful poses of the figures betray a debt to the style of Late Classical Greek art. In the fourth century CE, Constantine appropriated these tondi, had Hadrian's head recarved with his own or his father's features, and incorporated them into his own triumphal arch (SEE FIG. 6–65) so that the power and piety of this predecessor could reflect on him and his reign. In a strip of relief underneath the tondi, sculptors from his own time portrayed a ceremony performed by Constantine during his celebration of the victory over his rival, Maxentius, at the Battle of the Milvian Bridge (312 CE). Rather than the Hellenizing mode popular during Hadrian's reign, the Constantinian sculptors employ the blocky and abstract stylizations that became fashionable during the Tetrarchy.

Credit: © akg-images/Album/Prisma

Although the new Constantinian reliefs reflect the long-standing Roman predilection for depicting important events with recognizable detail, they nevertheless represent a significant change in style, approach, and subject matter (see lower figural frieze in FIG. 6–66). In this scene of Constantine addressing the Roman people in the Roman Forum, the Constantinian reliefs are easily distinguished from the reused Hadrianic tondi mounted just above them because of the faithfulness of the new reliefs to the avant-garde tetrarchic style we have already encountered in portraiture. The forceful, blocky, mostly frontal figures are compressed into the foreground plane. The participants to the sides, below the enthroned Constantine (his head is missing), almost congeal into a uniformly patterned mass that isolates the new emperor and connects him visually with the statues of his illustrious predecessors flanking him on the dais. This two-dimensional, hierarchical approach, with its emphasis on authority and power rather than on individualized outward form, is far removed from the classicizing illusionism of earlier imperial reliefs. It is one of the Roman styles that will be adopted by the emerging Christian Church.

THE BASILICA NOVA Constantine's rival Maxentius, who controlled Rome throughout his short reign (ruled 306–312), ordered the repair of older buildings there and had new ones built. His most impressive undertaking was a huge new basilica, just southeast of the Imperial Forums,

6-67 VIEW OF THE REMAINS OF THE BASILICA OF MAXENTIUS AND CONSTANTINE (BASILICA NOVA)
Rome. 306–313 CE.

Credit: © JIPEN/Shutterstock

6-68A RECONSTRUCTION DRAWING OF THE BASILICA OF MAXENTIUS AND CONSTANTINE (BASILICA NOVA)
Rome. 306–313 CE.

6-68B PLAN OF THE BASILICA OF MAXENTIUS AND CONSTANTINE (BASILICA NOVA)
Rome. 306–313 CE.

apse added later

barrel-vaulted bay

original apse

groin-vaulted nave

original entrance

groin-vaulted porch

barrel-vaulted bay

entrance added later

called the **BASILICA NOVA**, or New Basilica (**FIG. 6-67**). Now known as the Basilica of Maxentius and Constantine, this was the last important imperial government building erected in Rome. Like all basilicas, it functioned as an administrative center and provided a magnificent setting for the emperor when he appeared as supreme judge.

Earlier basilicas, such as Trajan's Basilica Ulpia (SEE FIG. 6–43), had been columnar halls, but Maxentius ordered his engineers to create the kind of large, unbroken, vaulted space found in public baths. Groin vaults covered the central hall, while the lower barrel vaults of the side aisles acted as buttresses, or projecting supports, for the central vault and allowed generous window openings in the clerestory areas over the side walls.

Three of these brick-and-concrete barrel vaults still loom over the streets of present-day Rome (SEE FIG. 6–67). The basilica originally measured 300 by 215 feet and the vaults of the central nave rose to a height of 114 feet. A groin-vaulted porch extended across the short side and sheltered a triple entrance to the central hall. At the opposite end of the long axis of the hall was an apse of the same width, which acted as a focal point for the building (**FIG. 6-68**). Christians would adopt this directional focus along a central axis from entrance to apse when designing basilican churches.

Constantine, seeking to impress the people of Rome with visible symbols of his authority, put his own stamp on projects Maxentius had started, including this one. He may have changed the orientation of the Basilica Nova by adding an imposing new entrance in the center of the long side facing the Via Sacra and a giant apse facing it across the three aisles. He also commissioned a colossal, 30-foot statue of himself for placement within an apse (**FIG. 6-69**). Sculptors used white marble for the head, chest, arms, and legs, and sheets of bronze for the drapery, all supported on a wooden frame. This statue became a permanent stand-in for the emperor, representing him whenever the conduct of business legally required his presence. The head combines features of traditional Roman portraiture with some of the abstract qualities evident in images of the tetrarchs (SEE FIG. 6–62). The defining characteristics of Constantine's face—his heavy jaw, hooked nose, and jutting chin—have been incorporated into a stylized, symmetrical pattern in which other features, such as his eyes, eyebrows, and hair, have been simplified into repeated geometric arcs. The result is a work that projects imperial power and dignity with no hint of human frailty or imperfection.

Roman Art after Constantine

Although Constantine was baptized only on his deathbed in 337, Christianity had become the official religion of the empire by the end of the fourth century, and non-Christians had become targets of persecution.

6-69 CONSTANTINE THE GREAT
From the Basilica of Maxentius and Constantine, Rome. 325–326 CE. Marble, height of head 8'6" (2.6 m). Palazzo dei Conservatori, Rome.

Credit: © Vincenzo Pirozzi, Rome

This religious shift, however, did not diminish Roman interest in the artistic traditions of their pagan Classical past. A large silver **PLATTER** dating from the mid fourth century CE (**FIG. 6-70**) proves that artists working for Christian patrons continued to use pagan themes, allowing them the opportunity to create elaborate figural compositions displaying the nude or lightly draped human body in complex, dynamic poses.

The Bacchic revelers on this platter whirl, leap, and sway in a dance to the piping of satyrs around a circular central medallion. In the centerpiece, nude females frolicking in the waves with fantastic sea creatures surround the head of the sea god Oceanus. In the figural composition that rings the outer circle, the figure of Bacchus is the one stable element. With a bunch of grapes in his right hand, a krater at his feet, and one foot on the haunches of his panther, he focuses his attention on a male follower begging for another drink. Only a few figures away, the drunken hero Hercules has lost his lion-skin mantle and collapsed in a stupor into the arms of two satyrs. The detail, clarity, and liveliness of this platter reflect the work of a virtuoso artist. Deeply engraved lines emphasize the contours of the subtly modeled bodies, echoing the technique of **undercutting** used to add depth to figures in stone and marble reliefs and suggesting a connection between silver-working and relief sculpture.

A farmer accidentally discovered this extraordinary platter—one of the greatest archaeological finds of the twentieth century—while plowing a field in 1942 outside the town of Mildenhall in Suffolk, England, located near the site of an ancient Roman villa. In total he unearthed 34 pieces of Roman silver tableware dating from the fourth century CE, including spoons engraved with Christian symbols. The find was not made public until four years later, since the farmer and his associates claimed they were unaware of how valuable it was, both materially and historically. When word of the discovery leaked out, however, the government confiscated the silver to determine if it was a "Treasure Trove"—gold or silver objects that have been intentionally hidden (rather than, for example, included in a burial) and that by law belong not to the finder, but to the Crown. The silver found at Mildenhall was deemed a "Treasure Trove" and is now one of the great glories of the British Museum in London.

The original owner of the hoard was thought to be a wealthy Roman Christian living in the provinces. Such opulent items were often hidden or buried to protect them from theft and looting, a sign of the breakdown of the Roman peace, especially in provincial areas. But there are those who do not believe the official story of the discovery. None of the silver in the hoard showed any sign of having been dented by a plow, and some believe that the quality and style of the objects are inconsistent with a provincial Roman context, especially so far in the hinterlands in England. Could the treasure have been looted from Italy during World War II, brought back to England (Mildenhall is not far from an American airfield), and buried to set up a staged discovery? The farmer who discovered the hoard and his associates, some argue, changed their story several times over the course of its history. Most scholars do believe the official story—that the silver was buried quickly for safekeeping by wealthy provincial Romans in Britain who felt threatened by a possible invasion or attack, and was forgotten (perhaps its owners were killed in the expected turmoil) until its accidental discovery in 1942. But when the history of art is founded on undocumented archaeological finds, there is usually some room for doubt.

Unlike the original owners of the Mildenhall platter, however, not all fourth-century Romans converted to Christianity. Among the champions of paganism were the Roman patricians Quintus Aurelius Symmachus and Virius Nicomachus Flavianus. A famous ivory diptych (**FIG. 6-71**) attests to the close relationship between their families, perhaps through marriage, as well as to their firmly held beliefs. A diptych was a pair of panels attached with hinges, not unlike the modest object held by the woman in FIGURE 6-34, but in this case made of a very precious material and

6-70 PLATTER

From Mildenhall, England. Mid 4th century CE. Silver, diameter approx. 24" (61 cm). British Museum, London.

Credit: © The Trustees of the British Museum. All rights reserved.

6–71 PRIESTESS OF BACCHUS (?)

Right panel of the diptych of Symmachus and Nicomachus. c. 390–401 CE.
Ivory, 11¾ × 4¾" (29.9 × 12 cm). Victoria & Albert Museum, London.

Credit: V&A Images/Victoria and Albert Museum

carved with reliefs on the exterior sides. On the interior of a diptych there were shallow, traylike recessions filled with wax, into which messages could be written with a stylus and sent with a servant as a letter to a friend or acquaintance, who could then smooth out the wax surface, incise a reply with his or her own stylus, and send the diptych back to its owner with the servant. Here, one family's name is inscribed at the top of each panel. On the panel inscribed "Symmachorum" (illustrated here), a stately, elegantly attired priestess burns incense at a beautifully decorated altar. On her head is a wreath of ivy, sacred to Bacchus. She is assisted by a small child, and the event takes place out of doors under an oak tree, sacred to Jupiter. Like the silversmiths, Roman ivory carvers of the fourth century CE were highly skillful, and their work was widely admired. They imitated the Augustan style effortlessly for conservative patrons like the Nicomachus and Symmachus families. The exquisite rendering of the drapery and foliage recalls the reliefs of the Ara Pacis (SEE FIG. 6–21).

Classical subject matter remained attractive to artists and patrons throughout the late Roman period. Even such great Christian thinkers as the fourth-century CE bishop Gregory of Nazianzus spoke out in support of the right of the people to appreciate and enjoy their Classical heritage, as long as it did not seduce them to return to pagan practices. As a result, stories of the ancient gods and heroes entered the secular realm as lively, visually delightful, even erotic decorative elements. As Roman authority gave way to local rule by powerful "barbarian" tribes in much of the West, many people continued to appreciate Classical learning and to treasure Greek and Roman art. In the East, patrons and artists cultivated Classical traditions, and they became an enduring element of Byzantine art.

Think About It

1   Characterize the salient stylistic features of the murals that survive from Roman houses in Pompeii, discussing specific examples from this chapter.

2   Explain how the Roman interest in portraits grew out of early funeral rituals and developed into a powerful aspect of imperial self-fashioning.

3   Describe and evaluate the subjects used in Etruscan tomb paintings and sarcophagi. How do Etruscan practices relate to what we have discovered about tombs in other ancient cultures?

4   Identify two key structural advances made by Roman builders and discuss their use in one large civic building. Why do you think the ancient Romans built on such a large scale?

Crosscurrents

Greek and Roman temples have features in common, but they are fundamentally different in important respects. Evaluate the significant similarities and dissimilarities by comparing these two buildings.

FIG. 5–37A

FIG. 6–17A

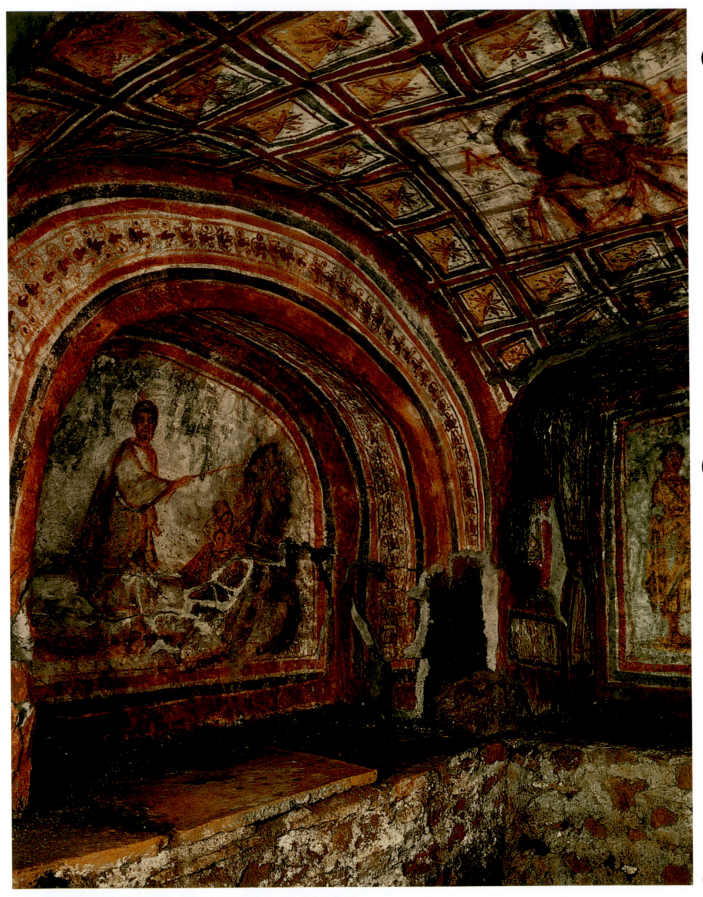

7-1 CUBICULUM OF LEONIS, CATACOMB OF COMMODILLA

Near Rome. Late 4th century.

Credit: Index Ricerca Iconografica

Chapter 7
Jewish and Early Christian Art

7.a Identify the visual hallmarks of Jewish and Early Christian art for formal, technical, and expressive qualities.

7.b Interpret the meaning of works of Jewish and Early Christian art based on their themes, subjects, and symbols.

7.c Relate Jewish and Early Christian artists and art to their cultural, economic, and political contexts.

7.d Apply the vocabulary and concepts relevant to Jewish and Early Christian art, artists, and art history.

7.e Interpret a work of Jewish and Early Christian art using the art historical methods of observation, comparison, and inductive reasoning.

7.f Select visual and textual evidence in various media to support an argument or an interpretation of a work of Jewish and Early Christian art.

In this painting in a Roman **catacomb** (underground cemetery) (**FIG. 7-1**), St. Peter, like Moses before him, strikes a rock and water flows from it (scene at left). Imprisoned in Rome at the end of his missionary journeys, Peter was said to have converted his fellow prisoners and jailers to Christianity, but he needed water with which to baptize them. Miraculously, a spring gushed forth at the touch of his staff. In spite of his all too human frailty, Peter became the rock (Greek *petros*) on which Jesus founded the Church. He was considered the first bishop of Rome, predecessor of today's pope. By including this episode from the life of Peter in the chamber's decoration, the early Christians who dug this catacomb as a place to bury their dead may have sought to emphasize the importance of their own city in Christian history.

In the star-studded heavens painted on the vault of this chamber floats the face of Christ, flanked by the first and last letters of the Greek alphabet, alpha and omega. Here Christ takes on the guise not of the youthful teacher or miracle worker seen so often in Early Christian art, but of a more mature Greek philosopher with long beard and hair. The **halo** (circle) of light around his head indicates his importance and his divinity, a symbol appropriated from the conventions of late Roman imperial art, where haloes often appeared around the heads of emperors.

These two catacomb paintings represent two major directions of Early Christian art—the narrative and the iconic—that will continue to be important as this visual tradition develops. The **narrative image** recounts an event drawn from St. Peter's life—striking the rock for water—which in turn evokes the establishment of the Church as well as the essential Christian rite of baptism. The **iconic image**—Christ's face flanked by alpha and omega—offers a tangible expression of an intangible concept. The letters signify the beginning and end of time, and, combined with the image of Christ, symbolically represent not a story, but an idea—the everlasting dominion of the heavenly Christ.

Throughout the long and continuing history of Christian art these two tendencies will be apparent—the narrative urge to tell a good story, in which moral or theological implications often have instructional value, and the desire to create iconic images that symbolize the core concepts and values of the developing religious tradition. In both cases, the works of art take on meaning only in relation to viewers' stored knowledge of Christian stories and beliefs. This art was made not to teach non-readers new stories or concepts, as is so often claimed, but rather to remind faithful viewers of stories they had already heard—perhaps to draw specific lessons in their retelling—or to highlight ideas that were central to religious belief and would guide the religious devotional practice it inspired.

Judaism and Christianity in the Late Roman World

What features of late antique Jewish and Christian art and architecture derive from Roman conventions?

Three religions that arose in the Near East still dominate the spiritual life of the Western world today: Judaism, Christianity, and Islam. All three are monotheistic—believing that the same God of Abraham created and rules the universe and hears the prayers of the faithful. Jews believe that God made a covenant, or pact, with their ancestors, the Hebrews, and that they are God's chosen people. They await the coming of a savior, the Messiah, "the anointed one." Christians believe that Jesus of Nazareth was that Messiah (the name Christ is derived from the Greek term meaning "Messiah"). They believe that in Jesus, God took human form, preached among men and women, suffered execution, rose from the dead, and ascended to heaven after establishing the Christian Church under the leadership of the apostles (his closest disciples). Muslims, while accepting the Hebrew prophets and Jesus as divinely inspired, believe Muhammad to be the last and greatest prophet of God (Allah), the Messenger of God through whom Islam was revealed some six centuries after Jesus's lifetime.

All three are "religions of the book," that is, they have written records of God's will and words: the Hebrew Bible; the Christian Bible, which includes the Hebrew Bible as its Old Testament as well as the Christian New Testament; and the Muslim Qur'an, believed to be the Word of God as revealed in Arabic directly to Muhammad through the archangel Gabriel.

Both Judaism and Christianity existed within the Roman Empire, along with various other religions devoted to the worship of many gods. The variety of religious buildings excavated in present-day Syria at the abandoned Roman outpost of Dura-Europos represents the cosmopolitan religious character of Roman society in the second and third centuries. The settlement—destroyed in 256 CE—included a Jewish house-synagogue, a Christian house-church, shrines to the Persian cults of Mithras and Zoroaster, and temples to Greek and Roman gods, including Zeus and Artemis.

Early Jewish Art

Although we concentrate here on the art and architecture of the late Roman world, Jewish art has a much longer history. The Jewish people trace their origin to a Semitic people called the Hebrews, who lived in the land of Canaan. Canaan, known since the second century CE by the Roman name Palestine, was located along the eastern edge of the Mediterranean Sea (MAP 7–1). According to the Torah—the first five books of the Hebrew Bible—God promised the

MAP 7–1 THE LATE ROMAN AND BYZANTINE WORLD

During the period that saw the early spread of Christianity and ultimately its legalization by Constantine, the Roman Empire still extended completely around the shores of the Mediterranean Sea.

7-2 ARK OF THE COVENANT AND MENORAHS
Wall painting in a Jewish catacomb, Villa Torlonia, Rome. 3rd century. 3'11" × 5'9" (1.19 × 1.8 m).

The menorah form probably derives from the ancient Near Eastern Tree of Life, symbolizing for the Jewish people both the end of exile and the paradise to come.

Credit: Soprintendenza Archeologica di Roma / IKONA

patriarch Abraham that Canaan would be a homeland for the Jewish people (Genesis 17:8), a belief that remains important for some Jews to this day.

Jewish settlement of Canaan probably began sometime in the second millennium BCE. According to Exodus, the second book of the Torah, the prophet Moses led the Hebrews out of slavery in Egypt to the promised land of Canaan. At one crucial point during the journey Moses climbed alone to the top of Mount Sinai, where God gave him the Ten Commandments, the cornerstone of Jewish law. The commandments, inscribed on tablets, were kept in a gold-covered wooden box known as the Ark of the Covenant.

Jewish law forbade the worship of idols, a prohibition that often made the representational arts—especially sculpture in the round—suspect. Nevertheless, artists working for Jewish patrons depicted both symbolic and narrative Jewish subjects, and they drew from the traditions of both Near Eastern and Classical Greek and Roman art.

THE FIRST TEMPLE IN JERUSALEM   In the tenth century BCE, the Jewish king Solomon built a temple in Jerusalem to house the Ark of the Covenant. According to the Hebrew Bible (2 Chronicles 2–7), he sent to nearby Phoenicia for cedar, cypress, and sandalwood and for a superb construction supervisor. The building later known as the First Temple was the spiritual center of Jewish life. Biblical texts describe courtyards, two bronze pillars (large, freestanding architectural forms), an entrance hall, a main hall, and the Holy of Holies, the innermost chamber that housed the Ark and its guardian cherubim, or attendant angels.

In 586 BCE, the Babylonians under King Nebuchadnezzar II conquered Jerusalem. They destroyed the Temple,

exiled the Jews, and carried off the Ark of the Covenant. When Cyrus the Great of Persia conquered Babylonia in 539 BCE, he permitted the Jews to return to their homeland (Ezra 1:1–4) and rebuild the Temple, which became known as the Second Temple. When Canaan became part of the Roman Empire, Herod the Great (king of Judaea, 37–34 BCE) restored the Second Temple. In 70 CE, Roman forces led by the general and future emperor Titus destroyed and looted the Second Temple and all of Jerusalem, a campaign the Romans commemorated on the Arch of Titus (SEE FIG. 6-36). The site of the Second Temple, the Temple Mount, is also an Islamic holy site, the Haram al-Sharif, and is now occupied by the shrine called the Dome of the Rock (SEE FIGS. 9-3, 9-4).

JEWISH CATACOMB ART IN ROME   Most of the earliest surviving examples of Jewish art date from the Hellenistic and Roman periods. Six Jewish catacombs, discovered on the outskirts of Rome and in use from the first to fourth centuries CE, display wall paintings with Jewish themes. In one example from the third century CE, two menorahs flank the long-lost **ARK OF THE COVENANT (FIG. 7-2)**. The continuing representation of the menorah, one of the precious objects looted from the Second Temple, kept the memory of the lost Jewish treasures alive.

SYNAGOGUES   Judaism has long emphasized religious learning. Jews gather in synagogues for study of the Torah—considered a form of worship. A synagogue can be any large room where the Torah scrolls are kept and read; it was also the site of communal social gatherings. Some synagogues were located in private homes or in buildings originally constructed like homes. The first synagogue in

7–3 WALL WITH TORAH NICHE

From a house-synagogue, Dura-Europos, Syria. 244–245 CE. Tempera on plaster, section approx. 40′ (12.19 m) long. Reconstructed in the National Museum, Damascus, Syria.

Credit: Princeton University Press/Art Resource, NY

Dura-Europos, Syria, consisted of an assembly hall, a separate alcove for women, and a courtyard. After a remodeling of the building completed in 244–245 CE, men and women shared the hall, and residential rooms were added. Two architectural features distinguished the assembly hall: a bench along its walls and a niche for the Torah scrolls (**FIG. 7–3**).

Scenes from Jewish history and the story of Moses, as recorded in Exodus, unfold in a continuous visual narrative around the room, employing the Roman tradition of epic historical presentation (SEE FIG. 6–47). In the scene of

THE CROSSING OF THE RED SEA (**FIG. 7–4**), Moses appears twice to signal sequential moments in the dramatic narrative. To the left he leans toward the army of Pharaoh, which is marching along the path that had been created for the Hebrews by God's miraculous parting of the waters, but at the right, wielding his authoritative staff, he returns the waters over the Egyptian soldiers to prevent their pursuit. Over each scene hovers a large hand, representing God's presence in both miracles—the parting and the unparting—using a symbol that will also be frequent in Christian art. Hierarchic scale makes it clear who is the

7–4 THE CROSSING OF THE RED SEA

Detail of a wall painting from a house-synagogue, Dura-Europos, Syria. 244–245 CE. National Museum, Damascus, Syria.

Credit: Image courtesy Yale University Art Gallery, Dura-Europos Collection

A Closer Look

THE MOSAIC FLOOR OF THE BETH ALPHA SYNAGOGUE

The shrine that holds the Torah is flanked by menorahs and growling lions, the latter perhaps as a security system to protect such sacred objects.

The figures in the four corners are winged personifications of the seasons; this figure holding a shepherd's crook and accompanied by a bird is Spring.

At the center of the zodiac wheel is a representation of the sun in a chariot set against a night sky studded with stars and a crescent moon.

The 12 signs of the zodiac appear in chronological order following a clockwise arrangement around the wheel of a year, implying perpetual continuity since the series has no set beginning and no end. This is Scorpio.

The peaceful coexistence of the lion and the ox (predator and prey) may represent a golden age or peaceable kingdom (Isaiah 11:6–9; 65:25).

Torah shrine and ritual objects.

- *The Metaphysical Realm*

The sun, seasons, and signs of the zodiac.

- *The Celestial Realm*

The Sacrifice of Isaac (Genesis 22:1–19).

- *The Terrestrial Realm*

This ram (identified by inscription) will ultimately take Isaac's place as sacrificial offering. Throughout the mosaic, animals are shown consistently in profile, human beings frontally.

These two texts—one in Aramaic and one in Greek—identify the artists of the mosaic as Marianos and his son Hanina, and date their work to the reign of either Emperor Justin I (518–527) or Justin II (565–578).

Abraham, preparing to sacrifice Isaac, is interrupted by the hand of God rather than by the angel specified in the Bible. Both Abraham and Isaac are identified by inscription, but Abraham's advanced age is signaled pictorially by the streaks of gray in his beard.

7–5 Marianos and Hanina **RITUAL OBJECTS, CELESTIAL DIAGRAM, AND SACRIFICE OF ISAAC**

Mosaic floor of the Beth Alpha Synagogue, Galilee, Israel. 6th century CE.

Credit: © akg-images/Bible Land Pictures/Jerusalem Photo: Zev Radovan hero in this two-part narrative, but the clue to his identity is provided only by the context of the story, which observers would have already known.

In addition to house-synagogues, Jews built meeting places designed on the model of the ancient Roman basilica. A typical basilica synagogue had a central nave; an aisle on both sides, separated from the nave by a line of columns; a semicircular apse with Torah shrine in the wall facing Jerusalem; and perhaps an atrium and porch, or **narthex** (vestibule). The small fifth-century CE synagogue at Beth Alpha—discovered between the Gilboa mountains and the River Jordan by farmers in 1928—fits well into this pattern with a three-nave interior, vestibule, and courtyard. Like some other very grand synagogues, it also has a mosaic floor, in this case a later addition from the sixth century. Most of the floor decoration is geometric in design, but in the central nave there are three complex panels full of figural compositions and symbols (see "Closer Look" on page 221) created using 21 separate colors of stone and glass tesserae. The images of ritual objects, a celestial diagram of the zodiac, and a scene of Abraham's near-sacrifice of Isaac, bordered by strips of foliate and geometric ornament, draw on both Classical and Near Eastern pictorial traditions.

Early Christian Art

At age 30, a Palestinian Jew named Jesus gathered a group of followers, male and female. Accounts of his life written by his followers credit him with performing miracles of healing and preaching on the value of loving God and neighbor, on the sanctity of social justice, on the forgiveness of sins, and on the promise of life after death. Christian belief holds that after his ministry on Earth Jesus was executed by crucifixion, and after three days rose from the dead.

The Christian scriptures include what Christians call the Old Testament (from the Hebrew Bible) and the New Testament (written well after Jesus's lifetime). The story of Jesus's life and collections of his teachings were recorded between about 70 and 100 CE in four Gospels at the beginning of the New Testament, attributed to four evangelists (from the Greek *evangelion*, meaning "good news"): Matthew, Mark, Luke, and John.

The New Testament also includes the Acts of the Apostles and the Epistles, 21 letters of advice and encouragement written to Christian communities in Greece, Asia Minor, and other parts of the Roman Empire. The final book is Revelation (or Apocalypse), a series of enigmatic visions and prophecies concerning the eventual triumph of God at the end of the world, written about 95 CE.

THE EARLY CHURCH   Jesus limited his ministry primarily to Jews; it was his apostles, as well as later followers such as Paul, who took his teachings to gentiles (non-Jews). Despite sporadic persecutions, Christianity persisted and spread throughout the Roman Empire. The imperial government formally recognized the religion in 313, and Christianity grew rapidly during the fourth century. As well-educated, upper-class Romans joined the Christian Church, they established increasingly elaborate organizational structures, rituals, doctrines, and works of art and architecture.

Christian communities became organized by geographic units, or dioceses, along the lines of Roman provincial governments. Senior church officials called bishops served as governors of dioceses made up of smaller units known as parishes and headed by priests. A bishop's church is a **cathedral**, a word derived from the Latin *cathedra*, which means "chair" but took on the meaning of "bishop's throne."

Communal Christian worship focused on the ritual consumption of bread and wine, identified as the Body and Blood of Christ, which Jesus had inaugurated at the Last Supper, a Passover Seder meal with his disciples just before his crucifixion. Around these acts developed a complicated religious ceremony, or liturgy, called the **Eucharist** (also known as Holy Communion or the Mass).

The earliest Christians gathered to worship in private apartments or houses or in buildings constructed after domestic models such as the third-century house-church excavated at Dura-Europos, Syria (see FIG. 7-6). As their worship became more ritualized and complex, however, they developed special buildings—churches and baptisteries—as well as specialized ritual equipment. They also began to use art to visualize their most important stories and ideas (SEE FIG. 7-1). The earliest surviving Christian art dates to the early third century and derives its styles and its imagery from Jewish and Roman visual traditions. In this process, known as **syncretism**, artists assimilate images from other traditions—either unconsciously or deliberately—and give them new meanings. For example, **orant** figures—worshipers with arms outstretched in prayer—can be pagan, Jewish, or Christian, depending on the context in which they occur. Perhaps the best-known syncretic image is the Good Shepherd. In pagan art, he was Apollo, or Hermes the shepherd, or Orpheus among the animals, or a personification of philanthropy. For Early Christians, he became the Good Shepherd of the Psalms (Psalm 23) and the Gospels (Matthew 18:12–14, John 10:11–16). Such images, therefore, do not have a stable meaning, but are associated with the meaning or meanings that a particular group of viewers brings to them. They remind rather than instruct.

DURA-EUROPOS   Our understanding of buildings used for worship by third-century Jews and Christians was greatly enhanced—even revolutionized—by the spectacular discoveries made in the 1930s while excavating the Roman military garrison and border town of Dura-Europos

7-6 RECONSTRUCTION OF BAPTISTERY, WITH FRAGMENTS OF ORIGINAL FRESCO

From Christian house-church, Dura-Europos, Syria. Before 256. Yale University Art Gallery, New Haven, Connecticut.

Credit: Image courtesy Yale University Art Gallery

(in present-day Syria). In 256, threatened by the Parthians attacking from the east, residents of Dura built a huge earthwork mound around their town in an attempt to protect themselves from the invading armies. In the process—since they were located on the city's margins right against its defensive stone wall— the houses used by Jews and Christians as places of worship were buried under the earthwork perimeter. In spite of this enhanced fortification, the Parthians conquered Dura-Europos. But since the victors never unearthed the submerged margins of the city, an intact Jewish house-synagogue and Christian house-church remained underground awaiting the explorations of modern archaeologists.

We have already seen the extensive strip narratives flanking the Torah shrine in the house-synagogue (SEE FIG. 7-3). The discovery of this expansive pictorial decoration contradicted a long-held scholarly belief that Jews of this period avoided figural decoration of any sort, in conformity with Mosaic law (Exodus 20:4). A few blocks down the street that ran along the city wall, a typical Roman house built around a central courtyard held another surprise. Only a discreet red cross above the door distinguished it from the other houses on its block, but the arrangement of the interior clearly documents its use as a Christian place of worship. A large assembly hall that could seat 60–70 people lies on one side of the courtyard, and across from it is a smaller but extensively decorated room with a water tank set aside for baptism, the central rite of Christian initiation (**FIG. 7-6**).

Along the walls of this room were scenes from Christ's miracles and a monumental portrayal of women visiting his tomb about to discover his resurrection. Even this early in Christian art, sacred spaces were decorated with pictures proclaiming the theological meaning of the rituals they housed. Above the baptismal basin is a **lunette** (semicircular wall section) with a painting (**FIG. 7-7**) in which Adam and Eve's fall from grace is juxtaposed with a larger image of the Good Shepherd (representing Jesus) who came to Earth to care for and guide his sheep (Christian believers) toward redemption and eternal life—a message that was especially appropriate juxtaposed with the rite of Christian baptism, which signaled the converts' passage from sin to salvation.

7-7 THE GOOD SHEPHERD WITH ADAM AND EVE AFTER THE FALL

Detail of lunette fresco in FIG. 7-6.

Credit: Image courtesy Yale University Art Gallery, Dura-Europos Collection

7-8 THE GOOD SHEPHERD, ORANTS, AND THE STORY OF JONAH

Painted ceiling of the Catacomb of SS. Peter and Marcellinus, Rome. Late 3rd–early 4th century.

Credit: Canali Photobank, Milan, Italy

CATACOMB PAINTING AND SCULPTURE   Christians, like Jews, used catacombs for burials and funeral ceremonies. They were not sites of communal worship. In the Christian Catacomb of Commodilla, dating from the fourth century, long rectangular niches in the walls called *loculi* each held two or three bodies. Affluent families created small rooms, or **cubicula** (singular, *cubiculum*), off the main passages to house sarcophagi (SEE FIG. 7–1). The *cubicula* were hewn out of tufo, a soft volcanic rock, then plastered and painted with imagery related to their owners' religious beliefs. The finest Early Christian catacomb paintings resemble murals in houses such as those preserved at Rome and Pompeii.

One fourth-century Roman catacomb contained remains, or relics, of SS. Peter and Marcellinus, two third-century Christians martyred for their faith. Here, the ceiling of a *cubiculum* is partitioned by a central **medallion**, or round compartment, and four semicircular lunettes, framed by arches (**FIG. 7–8**). At the center is a Good Shepherd, whose pose has roots in Classical sculpture. In its new context, the image was a reminder of Jesus's promise "I am the good shepherd. A good shepherd lays down his life for the sheep" (John 10:11).

The semicircular compartments surrounding the Good Shepherd tell the story of Jonah and the sea monster from the Hebrew Bible (Jonah 1–2), in which God caused Jonah to be thrown overboard, swallowed by the monster,

7-9 THE GOOD SHEPHERD

Eastern Mediterranean, probably Anatolia (present-day Turkey). Second half of the 3rd century. Marble, 19½ × 10 × 6″ (49.5 × 26 × 16.2 cm). Cleveland Museum of Art. John L. Severance Fund (1965.241).

Credit: Bridgeman Images

and released, repentant and unscathed, three days later. Christians reinterpreted this story as a parable of Christ's death and resurrection—and hence of the everlasting life awaiting true believers—and it was a popular subject in Christian catacombs. On the left, Jonah is thrown from the boat; on the right, the monster spits him up; and below, between these two scenes, Jonah reclines in the shade of a vine, a symbol of paradise. Orant figures stand between the lunettes, presumably images of the faithful Christians who were buried here.

SCULPTURE   Early Christian sculpture before the fourth century is rarer than painting. What survives are mainly sarcophagi and small statues and reliefs. A remarkable set of small marble figures, discovered in the 1960s and probably made in third-century Asia Minor, features a gracious **GOOD SHEPHERD** (**FIG. 7-9**). Because it was found with sculptures depicting Jonah—as we have already seen, a popular Early Christian theme—it is probably from a Christian context.

Imperial Christian Architecture and Art in Rome

How is Christian art and architecture transformed in Rome after its acceptance by Constantine?

When Constantine issued the Edict of Milan in 313 granting all people in the Roman Empire freedom to worship whatever god they wished, Christianity and Christian art and architecture entered a new phase. Sophisticated philosophical and ethical systems developed, incorporating many ideas from Greek and Roman pagan thought. Church scholars edited and commented on the Bible, and the papal secretary who would become St. Jerome (c. 347–420) undertook a new Bible translation from Hebrew and Greek versions into Latin, the language of the Western Church. The so-called Vulgate (from the same root as the word "vulgar," the Latin *vulgaris,* meaning "common" or "popular") became the official version of the Bible.

The developing Roman Christian community had special architectural needs. Greek temples had served as the house and treasury of the gods, forming a backdrop for ceremonies that took place at altars in the open air, but with Christianity, an entire community needed to gather inside a building to worship. Christians also needed locations for special activities such as the initiation of new members, private devotion, and burials. Beginning with the age of Constantine, **longitudinal-plan** pagan basilicas provided the model for congregational churches, and **central-plan** tombs provided a model for baptisteries and martyrs' shrines.

Old St. Peter's

Constantine ordered the construction of a large new basilican church to mark the place where Christians believed St. Peter was buried (**FIG. 7-10**). Our knowledge of what is now called Old St. Peter's (it was destroyed and replaced by a new building in the sixteenth century) is based on written descriptions, drawings made before and while it was being dismantled, the study of other churches inspired by it, and modern archaeological excavations at the site.

7-10 PLAN (A) AND RECONSTRUCTION DRAWING (B) OF OLD ST. PETER'S

c. 320–327; atrium added in later 4th century. Approx. 394' (120 m) long and 210' (64 m) wide.

Old St. Peter's included architectural elements in a longitudinal-plan arrangement that has characterized Christian basilican churches ever since. An atrium, or courtyard, in front of the basilica and a narthex across its width at the entrance end provided a place for people who had not yet been baptized. Five doorways—a large, central portal into the nave and two portals on each side—gave access to the church. Columns supporting an entablature lined the tall nave, forming what is called a nave colonnade, and above the entablature windows within the upper walls brought light directly into the nave space. Running parallel to the nave colonnade on each side was another row of columns that created shorter double side **aisles**; these columns supported round arches rather than an entablature (**FIG. 7–11**). The roofs of both nave and aisles were supported by wooden rafters. Sarcophagi and tombs lined the side aisles and graves were dug under the floor. At the apse end of the nave, Constantine's architects added an innovative **transept**—a perpendicular hall crossing in front of the apse, giving the plan of the building a T-shape. This area provided additional space for the large number of clergy serving the church, and it also accommodated pilgrims visiting the tomb of St. Peter. Old St. Peter's could hold at least 14,000 worshipers, and it remained the largest church in Christendom until the eleventh century.

Art and its Contexts

NAMING CHRISTIAN CHURCHES: DESIGNATION + DEDICATION + LOCATION

Christian churches are identified by a three-part descriptive title combining (1) designation (or type), (2) dedication (often to a saint), and (3) geographic location, in that order.

Designation: There are various types of churches fulfilling a variety of liturgical and administrative objectives, and the identification of a specific church often begins with an indication of its function within the system. For example, an **abbey church** or monastery church is the place of worship within a monastery or convent; a **pilgrimage church** is a site that attracts visitors wishing to venerate **relics** (material remains or objects associated with a saint) as well as attend services. A cathedral is a bishop's primary church (the word derives from the Latin *cathedra*, meaning "chair," since the chair or throne of a bishop is contained within his cathedral). A bishop's domain is called a diocese, and there can be only one church in the diocese designated as its bishop's cathedral, but a diocese has numerous parish churches where local residents attend regular services.

Dedication: Christian churches are always dedicated to Christ, the Virgin Mary, a saint, or a sacred concept or event, for example St. Peter's Basilica or the church of Hagia Sophia (Christ as the embodiment of Holy Wisdom). In short-hand identification, when we omit the church designation at the beginning, we always add an apostrophe and an *s* to a saint's name, as when using "St. Peter's" to refer to the Vatican Basilica of St. Peter in Rome.

Location: The final piece of information that clearly pinpoints the specific church indicated in a title is its geographic location, as in the church of San Vitale in Ravenna or the Cathedral of Notre-Dame (French for "Our Lady," referring to the Virgin Mary) in Paris. "Notre-Dame" alone usually refers to this Parisian cathedral, in spite of the fact that many contemporary cathedrals elsewhere (e.g. at Chartres and Reims) were also dedicated to "Notre-Dame." Similarly, "St. Peter's" usually means the Vatican church of the pope in Rome.

7-12 INTERIOR, CHURCH OF SANTA SABINA, ROME

View from the south aisle near the sanctuary toward the entrance. c. 422–432.

Credit: © akg-images/Andrea Jemolo

Santa Sabina

Old St. Peter's is gone, but the church of Santa Sabina in Rome, constructed by Bishop Peter of Illyria (a region in the Balkan peninsula) a century later between about 422 and 432, appears much as it did in the fifth century (**FIGS. 7-12, 7-13**). The basic elements of the Early Christian basilica are clearly visible here, inside and out: a nave lit by clerestory windows, flanked by single side aisles, and ending in a rounded apse.

Santa Sabina's exterior is simple brickwork. In contrast, the church's interior displays a wealth of marble veneer and 24 fluted marble columns with Corinthian capitals reused from a second-century pagan building. (Material reused from earlier buildings is known as **spolia**, Latin for "spoils.") The columns support round arches, creating a nave arcade, in contrast to the straight nave colonnade on an architrave in Old St. Peter's. The spandrels between the arches are faced with marble veneer that portrays chalices (wine cups) and paten (bread plates), essential equipment for the Eucharistic rite that took place at the altar. In such basilicas, the expanse of wall between the arcade and the clerestory typically had paintings or mosaics with biblical scenes, but here the decoration of the upper walls has been lost.

7-13 CHURCH OF SANTA SABINA, ROME

Exterior view from the southeast. c. 422–432.

Credit: © Vincenzo Pirozzi, Rome

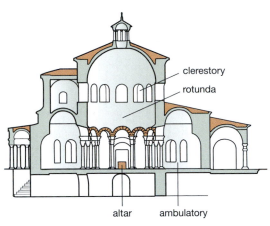

7-14 PLAN (A) AND SECTION (B) OF THE CHURCH OF SANTA COSTANZA, ROME
c. 350.

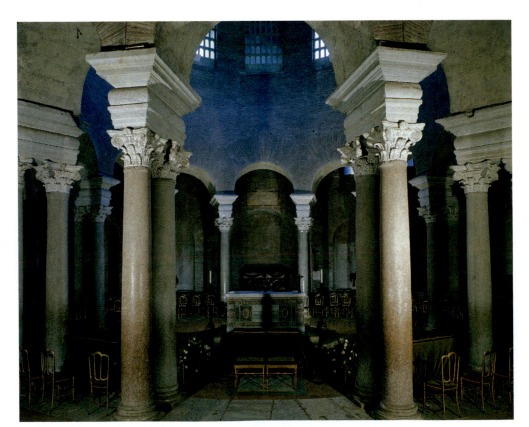

Santa Costanza

Central-plan Roman buildings with vertical (rather than longitudinal) axes served as models for Christian tombs, churches dedicated to or built over the tombs of martyrs, and baptisteries (where Christians "died"—giving up their old life—and were reborn as believers). One of the earliest surviving central-plan Christian buildings is the mausoleum of Constantina, daughter of Constantine. Her tomb was built outside the walls of Rome just before 350 (**FIG. 7-14**), and it was consecrated as a church in 1256, dedicated to Santa Costanza (the Italian form of Constantina, who was sanctified after her death).

The building is a tall rotunda with an encircling barrel-vaulted passageway called an **ambulatory**. Paired columns with Composite capitals and richly molded entablature blocks support the arcade and dome (**FIG. 7-15**). Unlike basilicas, where the longitudinal axis draws worshipers forward along a line from the entrance toward the apse, central-plan buildings such as this have a vertical axis from the center up through the dome, which may have functioned as a symbolic "vault of heaven."

Originally, the interior was entirely sheathed in mosaics and veneers of fine marble; mosaics still surviving in the ambulatory vault recall the syncretic images in the catacombs. In one section, for example, a bust portrait of Constantina at the crest of the vault is surrounded by a tangle of grapevines filled with **putti**—naked cherubs, derived from pagan art—who vie with the birds to harvest the grapes (**FIG. 7-16**). Along the bottom edges on each side, other *putti* drive wagonloads of grapes toward pavilions housing large vats in which more *putti* trample the grapes into juice for the making of wine. The technique and style are Roman; the subject is traditional, associated with Bacchus and his cult; but the meaning here is new. In a Christian context, the wine refers to the Eucharist and the trampling of grapes for the making of wine becomes an image of death and resurrection. Constantina's pagan

7-15 CHURCH OF SANTA COSTANZA, ROME
c. 350. View from ambulatory into rotunda.

Credit: © Vincenzo Pirozzi, Rome
fotopirozzi@inwind.it

7-16 HARVESTING OF GRAPES

Ambulatory vault, church of Santa Costanza, Rome. c. 350. Mosaic.

Credit: © 2016 Photo Scala, Florence

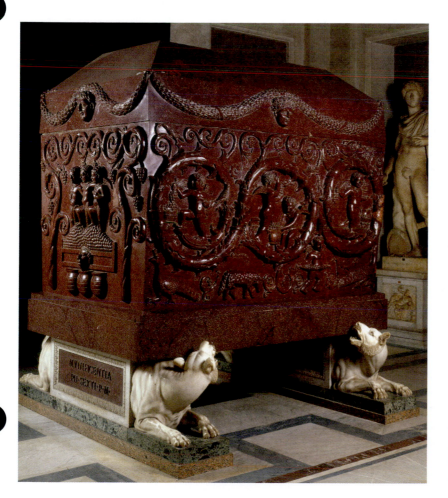

7-17 SARCOPHAGUS OF CONSTANTINA

c. 350. Porphyry, height 7′5″ (2.26 m).
Musei Vaticani, Rome.

Credit: © akg-images/Nimatallah

husband, however, may have appreciated the parallel, pagan reference.

Within her mausoleum, Constantina (d. 354) was buried within a spectacularly huge porphyry sarcophagus (**FIG. 7-17**) that was installed across from the entrance on the other side of the ambulatory in a rectangular niche (visible on the plan in FIG. 7-14; an in-place replica peeks over the altar in **FIG. 7-15**). The motifs are already familiar—the *putti* making wine that were in the mosaics of the ambulatory vaults. Here the scenes are framed by a huge, undulating grapevine whose subsidiary shoots curl above and below to fill the flat sides of the box. Striding along its base, peacocks symbolize eternal life in paradise, while a lone sheep could represent a member of Jesus's flock, presumably Constantina herself.

Sarcophagus of Junius Bassus

Carved about the same time as the Sarcophagus of Constantina but made of marble, the **SARCOPHAGUS OF JUNIUS BASSUS** (FIG. 7–18) is packed with figural scenes like the second-century CE Dionysiac sarcophagus (see "Closer Look" in Chapter 6 on page 204), only here they are separated into two registers, where columns, entablatures, and gables divide the space into fields for individual scenes. Junius Bassus was a Roman official who, as the inscription here tells us, was "newly baptized" and died on August 25, 359, at age 42.

In the center of both registers is a triumphant Christ. Above, he appears as a Roman emperor, distributing legal authority in the form of scrolls to flanking figures of SS. Peter and Paul and resting his feet on the head of Coelus, the pagan god of the heavens, here identifying Christ as ruler of the cosmos. In the bottom register, the earthly Jesus makes his triumphal entry into Jerusalem like a Roman emperor entering a conquered city. Jesus, however, rides on a humble ass rather than a powerful horse.

Even in the earliest Christian art, such as that in catacomb paintings and here on the sarcophagus of Junius Bassus, artists employed episodes from the Hebrew Bible allegorically since Christians saw them as prefigurations of important events in the New Testament. At the top left, Abraham passes the test of faith and need not sacrifice his son Isaac. Christians saw in this story an allegory that foreshadowed God's sacrifice of his own son, Jesus, which culminates not in Jesus's death, but in his resurrection. Under the triangular gable, second from the end at bottom right, the Hebrew Bible story of Daniel saved by God from the lions prefigures Christ's emergence alive from his tomb. At bottom far left, God tests the faith of Job, who provides a model for the sufferings of Christian martyrs. Next to Job, Adam and Eve have sinned to set in motion the entire Christian redemption story. Lured by the serpent, they have eaten the forbidden fruit and, conscious of their nakedness, are trying to hide their genitals with leaves.

Art and its Contexts

THE LIFE OF JESUS

Episodes from the life of Jesus as recounted in the Gospels form the principal subject matter of Christian visual art. What follows is a list of main events in his and his mother's life with parenthetical references when there are textual sources in the Gospel texts.

Maternity of Mary and Childhood of Jesus

Annunciation: The archangel Gabriel informs the Virgin Mary that God has chosen her to bear his Son. A dove often represents the Incarnation, her miraculous conception of Jesus through the Holy Spirit. (Lk 1:26–28)

Visitation: The pregnant Mary visits her older cousin Elizabeth, pregnant with the future St. John the Baptist. (Lk 1:29–45)

Nativity: Jesus is born in Bethlehem. The Holy Family—Jesus, Mary, and her husband, Joseph—is usually portrayed in a stable or, in Byzantine art, a cave. (Lk 2:4–7)

Annunciation to and Adoration of the Shepherds: Angels announce Jesus's birth to shepherds, who hurry to Bethlehem to honor him. (Lk 2:8–20)

Adoration of the Magi: Wise men from the east follow a bright star to Bethlehem to honor Jesus as king of the Jews, presenting him with precious gifts. Eventually these Magi became identified as three kings, often differentiated through facial type as young, middle-aged, and old. (Mat 2:1–12)

Presentation in the Temple: Mary and Joseph bring the infant Jesus to the Temple in Jerusalem, where he is presented to the high priest. (Lk 2:25–35)

Massacre of the Innocents and Flight into Egypt: An angel warns Joseph that King Herod plans to murder all male babies in Bethlehem to eliminate the threat of a newborn rival king. The Holy Family flees to Egypt. (Mat 2:13–16)

Jesus's Ministry

Baptism: At age 30, Jesus is baptized by John the Baptist in the River Jordan. The Holy Spirit appears in the form of a dove, and a heavenly voice proclaims Jesus as God's Son. (Mat 3:13–17, Mk 1:9–11, Lk 3:21–22)

Marriage at Cana: At his mother's request Jesus turns water into wine at a wedding feast, his first public miracle. (Jn 2:1–10)

Miracles of Healing: Throughout the Gospels, Jesus performs miracles of healing the blind, possessed (mentally ill), paralytic, and lepers; he also resurrects the dead.

Calling of Levi/Matthew: Jesus calls to Levi, a tax collector, "Follow me." Levi complies, becoming the disciple Matthew. (Mat 9:9, Mk 2:14)

Raising of Lazarus: Jesus brings his friend Lazarus back to life four days after his death. (Jn 11:1–44)

Transfiguration: Jesus reveals his divinity in a dazzling vision on Mount Tabor as his closest disciples—Peter, James, and John—look on. (Mat 17:1–5, Mk 9:2–6, Lk 9:28–35)

Tribute Money: Challenged to pay the temple tax, Jesus sends Peter to catch a fish, which turns out to have the required coin in its mouth. (Mat 17:24–27, Lk 20:20–25)

Jesus's Passion, Death, and Resurrection

Entry into Jerusalem: Jesus, riding an ass and accompanied by his disciples, enters Jerusalem, while crowds honor him,

7-18 SARCOPHAGUS OF JUNIUS BASSUS
Grottoes of St. Peter, Vatican, Rome. c. 359. Marble, 4 × 8′ (1.2 × 2.4 m).

Credit: © 2016. Photo Scala, Florence

spreading clothes and palm fronds in his path. (Mat 21:1–11, Mk 11:1–11, Lk 19:30–44, Jn 12:12–15)

Last Supper: During the Jewish Passover Seder, Jesus reveals his impending death to his disciples. Instructing them to drink wine (his blood) and eat bread (his body) in remembrance of him, he lays the foundation for the Christian Eucharist (Mass). (Mat 26:26–30, Mk 14:22–25, Lk 22:14–20)

Washing the Disciples' Feet: At the Last Supper, Jesus humbly washes the disciples' feet. (Jn 13: 4–12)

Agony in the Garden: In the Garden of Gethsemane on the Mount of Olives, Jesus struggles between his human fear of pain and death and his divine strength to overcome them. The apostles sleep nearby, oblivious. (Lk 22:40–45)

Betrayal/Arrest: Judas Iscariot (a disciple) has accepted a bribe to point out Jesus to an armed band of his enemies by kissing him. (Mat 26:46–49, Mk 14:43–46, Lk 22:47–48, Jn 18:3–5)

Jesus before Pilate: Jesus is taken to Pontius Pilate, Roman governor of Judaea, and charged with treason for calling himself king of the Jews. Pilate proposes freeing Jesus but is shouted down by the mob, which demands Jesus be crucified. (Mat 27:11–25, Mk 15:4–14, Lk 23:1–24, Jn 18:28–40)

Crucifixion: Jesus is executed on a cross, often shown between two crucified criminals and accompanied by the Virgin Mary, John the Evangelist, Mary Magdalen, and other followers standing at the foot of the cross. Roman soldiers sometimes torment Jesus, extending a sponge on a pole with vinegar instead of water for him to drink and stabbing him in the side with a spear. (Mat 27:35–50, Mk 15:23–37, Lk 23:38–49, Jn 19:18–30)

Descent from the Cross (Deposition): Jesus's followers take his body down from the cross. (Mat 27:55–59, Mk 15:40–46, Lk 23:50–56, Jn 19:38–40)

Lamentation/Pietà and Entombment: Jesus's sorrowful followers gather around his body to mourn and then place his body in a tomb. An image of the grieving Virgin alone with Jesus across her lap is known as a **pietà** (from Latin *pietas*, "pity"). (Mat 27:60–61, Jn 19:41–42)

Resurrection/Holy Women at the Tomb: Three days after his entombment, Christ rises from the dead, and his female followers—usually including Mary Magdalen—discover his empty tomb. An angel announces Christ's resurrection. (Mat 28, Mk 16, Lk 24:1–35, Jn 20)

Descent into Limbo/Harrowing of Hell (Anastasis): The resurrected Jesus descends into limbo, or hell, to free deserving predecessors, among them Adam, Eve, David, and Moses. (Apocryphal Gospel of Nicodemus, not in the New Testament)

Noli Me Tangere ("Do Not Touch Me"): Christ appears to Mary Magdalen as she weeps at his tomb. When she reaches out to him, he warns her not to touch him. (Lk 24:34–53, Jn 20:11–31)

Ascension: Christ ascends to heaven from the Mount of Olives, disappearing in a cloud, while his mother and apostles watch. (Acts 1)

Mary's Death

Dormition of the Virgin: Literally Mary's "falling asleep." She dies surrounded by the apostles, while her soul, in the form of a baby or child, appears above her in the arms of the risen Christ. (Not in the Gospels)

Assumption of the Virgin: Mary's body ascends to heaven. (Not in the Gospels)

On the upper right side, spread over two compartments, Jesus appears before Pontius Pilate, who is about to wash his hands, symbolizing his denial of responsibility for Jesus's death. Jesus's position here, held captive between two soldiers, recalls (and perhaps could also be read as) his arrest in Gethsemane, especially since the composition of this panel is reflected in the arrests of the apostles Peter (top, second frame from the left) and Paul (bottom, far right).

Ravenna and Thessaloniki

How do the art and architecture in the provincial capitals of Ravenna and Thessaloniki continue Imperial Roman conventions?

As the city of Rome's political importance dwindled, that of other imperial cities grew. In 395, Emperor Theodosius I split the Roman Empire into Eastern and Western divisions, each ruled by one of his sons. Heading the West, Honorius (ruled 395–423) first established his capital at Milan, but in 402, to escape the siege by Germanic settlers, he moved his government to Ravenna, on the east coast of Italy. Its naval base, Classis (present-day Classe), had been important since the early days of the empire. In addition to military security, Ravenna offered direct access by sea to Constantinople. When Italy fell in 476 to the Ostrogoths, Ravenna became one of their headquarters, but the beauty and richness of Early Christian buildings can still be experienced there in a remarkable group of especially well-preserved fifth- and sixth-century churches, baptisteries, and oratories, encrusted with mosaics.

The history of Thessaloniki (in present-day Greece) as an imperial capital dates back even earlier to the reorganization of Roman imperial government under Diocletian (see Chapter 6). Galerius—at first Diocletian's Caesar after the creation of the Tetrarchy in 293 and then emperor of the East from Diocletian's retirement in 305 to his own

7–19 ORATORY OF GALLA PLACIDIA, RAVENNA
c. 425–426.

Credit: © Gina Berto Vanni/Vanni Archive/Corbis

7-20 ORATORY OF GALLA PLACIDIA

View from entrance, barrel-vaulted arms housing sarchophagi, lunette mosaic of the martyrdom of St. Lawrence. c. 425–426.

Credit: Canali Photobank, Milan, Italy

death in 311—made Thessaloniki his capital, initiating an ambitious building program that included a hippodrome, a palace, and a triumphal arch. After Constantine eliminated his rivals and became sole emperor of the Roman world in 324, Thessaloniki decreased in importance, though it remained a provincial capital and the seat of a powerful bishop. The local Christian community dates to the first century CE. St. Paul's letters written to the church in Thessaloniki during the 50s became part of the New Testament.

The Oratory of Galla Placidia in Ravenna

One of the earliest surviving Christian structures in Ravenna is a magnificent **oratory** (small chapel) that was attached c. 425–426 to the narthex of the palace church of Santa Croce (**FIG. 7-19**). This building was dedicated to St. Lawrence, but today it bears the name of the remarkable Galla Placidia—daughter of Roman emperor Theodosius I, wife of a Gothic king, sister of emperors Honorius and Arcadius, and mother of Emperor Valentinian III. As regent for her son after 425, she ruled the Western Empire

until 437/438. The oratory came to be called the Mausoleum of Galla Placidia because she and her family were once believed to be buried there. This small building is **cruciform**, or cross-shape.

A barrel vault covers each arm of the oratory, and a pendentive dome—a dome continuous with its pendentives—covers the square space at the center (see "Pendentives and Squinches" in Chapter 8 on page 241). The interior of the chapel contrasts markedly with the unadorned exterior, a transition seemingly designed to simulate the passage from the real world into the supernatural realm (**FIG. 7-20**). The worshiper looking from the western entrance across to the eastern bay of the chapel sees brilliant mosaics in the vaults and panels of veined marble sheathing the walls below. Bands of luxuriant floral designs and geometric patterns cover the arches and barrel vaults, and figures of standing apostles, gesturing like orators, fill the upper walls of the central space. Doves flanking a small fountain between the apostles symbolize eternal life in heaven.

In the lunette at the end of the barrel vault opposite the entrance (seen here), a mosaic depicts the third-century St. Lawrence, to whom the building was dedicated. The triumphant martyr carries a cross over his shoulder like a

7-21 THE GOOD SHEPHERD
Lunette over the entrance, Oratory of Galla Placidia. c. 425–426. Mosaic.

Credit: © Cameraphoto Arte, Venice

trophy and gestures toward the fire-engulfed metal grill on which he was literally roasted at his martyrdom. At the left stands a tall cabinet containing the Gospels, signifying the faith for which he gave his life.

Opposite St. Lawrence, in a lunette over the entrance portal, is a mosaic of **THE GOOD SHEPHERD** (FIG. 7–21). A comparison with third- and fourth-century renderings of the same subject reveals significant changes in content and design.

The Rotunda Church of St. George in Thessaloniki

Galerius constructed within his palace complex in Thessaloniki a grand rotunda that may have been intended for his tomb. During the fifth century, this imperial building was converted into a church through the addition of an apse on the east side, an entrance on the west, and an ambulatory encircling the entire rotunda. The interior surface of

the huge dome—almost 100 feet in diameter—was covered with lavish golden mosaics, perhaps created by artists who were called here from Constantinople, which was developing into one of the great artistic centers of the Christian Roman world (FIG. 7–22).

Forming a circle around and above worshipers within the building, 16 standing figures of saints dressed in liturgical vestments make orant gestures of prayer, as if celebrating the liturgy in paradise concurrent with the services held here on earth. Behind them is a backdrop of elaborate architectural fantasies composed of Classical forms, decorated with gems, and inhabited by peacocks. The figures are equally Classical with their careful modeling, lavish drapery, and most notably their air of grace, eloquence, and composure. Classicizing features such as these will continue to develop as the Early Christian art of the Eastern Roman Empire blossoms into Byzantine art, which will flourish until the fifteenth century, centered in Constantinople.

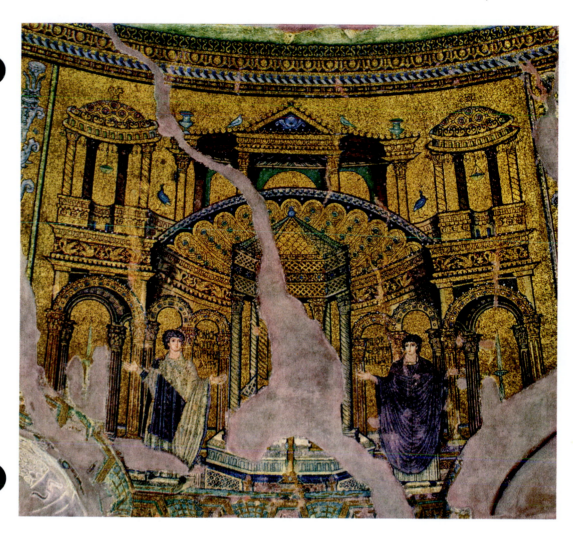

7-22 SS. ONESIPHOROS AND PORPHYRIOS STANDING BEFORE AN ARCHITECTURAL BACKDROP

Mosaics on the interior of the dome of the church of St. George (formerly the mausoleum of Galerius). Thessaloniki, northern Greece. Rotunda 4th century; mosaics 5th century.

Credit: Hirmer Fotoarchiv

Think About It

1   Discuss the Roman foundations of Early Christian sculpture, focusing your answer on the sarcophagus of Junius Bassus (**FIG. 7–18**). Look back to Chapter 6 to help form your ideas.

2   Distinguish the "iconic" from the "narrative" in two works of late antique Jewish or Christian art discussed in this chapter. How were these two traditions used by the communities that created these works?

3   How did the location of the Jewish and Christian buildings in Dura-Europos on the outskirts of the Roman Empire affect their design and decoration?

4   Identify the distinctive features of basilicas and central-plan churches, and discuss how the forms of these early churches were geared toward specific types of Christian worship and devotional practice.

Crosscurrents

Both Etruscans and Early Christians often painted the interior walls of their tombs. Discuss the themes chosen for the murals in these two examples. Are the images related to life, to death, or to life after death? How are the styles and subjects related to these two cultures?

FIG. 6–6

FIG. 7–1

8-1 DAVID BATTLING GOLIATH

One of the "David Plates," made in Constantinople. 629–630 CE. Silver, diameter 19⅞" (49.4 cm). Metropolitan Museum of Art, New York.

Credit: © 2016. Image copyright The Metropolitan Museum of Art/Art Resource/Scala, Florence

Chapter 8

Byzantine Art

⌄ Learning Objectives

8.a Identify the visual hallmarks of Byzantine art for formal, technical, and expressive qualities.

8.b Interpret the meaning of works of Byzantine art based on their themes, subjects, and symbols.

8.c Relate Byzantine artists and art to their cultural, economic, and political contexts.

8.d Apply the vocabulary and concepts relevant to Byzantine art, artists, and art history.

8.e Interpret a work of Byzantine art using the art historical methods of observation, comparison, and inductive reasoning.

8.f Select visual and textual evidence in various media to support an argument or an interpretation of a work of Byzantine art.

The robust figures on this huge silver plate (**FIG. 8-1**) enact three signature episodes in the youthful hero David's combat with the Philistine giant Goliath (1 Samuel 17:41–51). In the upper register, David—easily identified by his youth and as the "good guy" by his prominent halo—and Goliath challenge each other on either side of a seated Classical personification of the stream that will be the source of David's stones for the ensuing battle. The confrontation itself appears in the middle of the plate, in a broad figural frieze whose size signals its primary importance. Goliath is most notable here for his superior armaments—helmet, spear, sword, and an enormous shield. At the bottom, David, stones and slingshot flung behind him, seals his victory by severing the head of his foe, whose imposing weapons and armor are scattered uselessly behind him.

Some may be surprised to see a Judeo-Christian subject portrayed in a style that was developed for the exploits of Classical heroes, but this mixture of traditions is typical of the eclecticism that characterized the visual arts as the Christianized Roman world became the Byzantine Empire. Patrons saw no conflict between the artistic principles of the pagan past and the Christian teaching undergirding their imperial present. To them, this Jewish subject created for a Christian patron in a pagan style would have attracted notice only because of its sumptuousness and its artistic virtuosity.

This was one of nine "David Plates" unearthed in Cyprus in 1902. Control stamps—guaranteeing the purity of the material much like the stamps of "sterling" on silver today—date them to the reign of the Byzantine emperor Heraclius (ruled 613–641 CE). Displayed in the home of their owners, they were visual proclamations of wealth, education, and refined taste, just like collections of art and antiques in homes now. A constellation of iconographic and historical factors, however, allows us to uncover a subtler message. For the original owners, the single combat of David and Goliath might have recalled a situation involving their own emperor and enemies.

The reign of Heraclius was marked by war with the Sasanian Persians. A decisive moment in the final campaign of 628–629 CE occurred when Heraclius himself stepped forward for single combat with the Persian general Razatis, and the emperor prevailed, presaging Byzantine victory. Some contemporaries referred to Heraclius as a new David. Is it possible that the set of David Plates was produced for the emperor to offer as a diplomatic gift to one of his aristocratic allies, who subsequently took them to Cyprus? Perhaps the owners later buried them for safekeeping—like the early silver platter from Mildenhall (SEE FIG. 6–70).

Early Byzantine Art

How does early Byzantine art develop in the Eastern Roman Empire?

Art historians apply the term "Byzantine" broadly to the art and architecture of Constantinople—whose ancient name, before Constantine renamed the revitalized city after himself, was Byzantium—and of the regions under its influence. Constantine had chosen well in selecting the site of his new capital city—his "New Rome." Constantinople lay at the crossroads of the overland trade routes between Asia and Europe and the sea route connecting the Black Sea and the Mediterranean. Even as the territories controlled by Byzantine rulers diminished in size and significance up to the fall of Constantinople in 1453, Byzantine emperors continued to conceive themselves as successors to the rulers of ancient Rome, their domain as an extension of the Roman Empire, and their capital city as an enduring manifestation of the glory that was ancient Rome.

In this chapter, we will focus on what have been considered the three "golden ages" of Byzantine art. The Early Byzantine period, most closely associated with the reign of Emperor Justinian I (ruled 527–565), began in the fifth century and ended in 726 at the onset of the iconoclast controversy that led to the destruction of religious images. The Middle Byzantine period began in 843, when Empress Theodora (wife of Emperor Theophilus, 830–842, and regent of their son Emperor Michael III, 842–855) reinstated the veneration of icons, and continued until 1204, when Christian crusaders from western Europe occupied Constantinople. The Late Byzantine period began with the restoration of Byzantine rule in 1261 and ended with the empire's fall to the Ottoman Turks in 1453, at which point Russia succeeded Constantinople as the "Third Rome" and the center of the Eastern Orthodox Church. Late Byzantine art continued to flourish into the eighteenth century in Ukraine, Russia, and much of southeastern Europe.

MAP 8–1 THE LATE ROMAN AND BYZANTINE WORLD

The eastern shores of the Mediterranean, birthplace of Judaism and Christianity, were the focal point of the Byzantine Empire. The empire expanded farther west under Emperor Justinian, though by 1025 CE it had contracted again to the east.

The Golden Age of Justinian

The Eastern Roman Empire prospered during the fifth and sixth centuries, while invasions and religious controversy racked the Italian peninsula. In fact, during the sixth century under Emperor Justinian I and his wife, Empress Theodora (d. 548), Byzantine political power, wealth, and culture were at their peak. Imperial forces held northern Africa, Sicily, much of Italy, and part of Spain. Ravenna became the Eastern Empire's administrative capital in the west, and Rome remained under nominal Byzantine control until the eighth century.

HAGIA SOPHIA IN CONSTANTINOPLE In Constantinople, Justinian and Theodora embarked on a spectacular campaign of building and renovation, but little now remains of their architectural projects or of the old imperial capital itself. The church of Hagia Sophia, meaning "Holy Wisdom" (referring to the dedication of this church to Christ as the embodiment of divine wisdom) is a spectacular exception (**FIG. 8-2**). It replaced a fourth-century church destroyed when crowds, spurred on by Justinian's foes during the devastating urban Nika Revolt in 532, set the old church on fire and cornered the emperor within his palace. Theodora, a brilliant and politically shrewd woman, is said to have shamed Justinian, who was plotting to escape, into not fleeing the city, saying "Purple makes a fine shroud"—a reference to purple as the imperial color. Theodora meant that she would

rather remain and die an empress than flee and preserve her life. Taking up her words as a battle cry, Justinian led the imperial forces in crushing the rebels and restoring order, reputedly slaughtering 30,000 of his subjects in the process.

To design a new church that embodied imperial power and Christian glory, Justinian chose two scholar-theoreticians, Anthemius of Tralles and Isidorus of Miletus. Anthemius was a specialist in geometry and optics, and Isidorus a specialist in physics who had also studied vaulting. They developed an audacious and awe-inspiring design that was executed by builders who had refined their masonry techniques by building the towers and domed rooms that were part of the city's defenses.

The new Hagia Sophia was not constructed by the miraculous intervention of angels, as was rumored, but by mortal builders in only five years (532–537). Procopius of Caesarea, who chronicled Justinian's reign, claimed poetically that Hagia Sophia's gigantic dome seemed to hang suspended on a "golden chain from heaven." Legend has it that Justinian himself, aware that architecture can be a potent symbol of earthly power, compared his accomplishment with that of the legendary builder of the First Temple in Jerusalem, saying "Solomon, I have outdone you."

Hagia Sophia is an innovative hybrid of longitudinal and central architectural planning. The building is clearly dominated by the hovering form of its gigantic dome (**FIG. 8-3**). But flanking **conches**—halfdomes—extend the

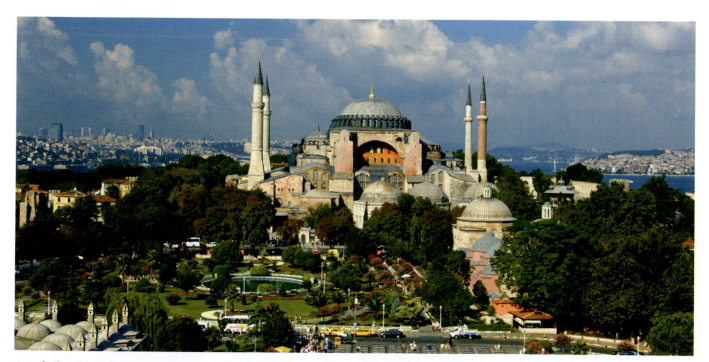

8-2 Anthemius of Tralles and Isidorus of Miletus **CHURCH OF HAGIA SOPHIA, CONSTANTINOPLE**
Present-day Istanbul. 532–537. View from the southwest.

The body of the original church is now surrounded by later additions, including the minarets built after 1453 by the Ottoman Turks. Today the building is a museum.

Credit: Photo © Ayhan Altun

8-3 INTERIOR OF THE CHURCH OF HAGIA SOPHIA

Credit: Photo © Ayhan Altun

8–4 PLAN (A) AND ISOMETRIC DRAWING (B) OF THE CHURCH OF HAGIA SOPHIA

central space into a longitudinal nave that expands outward from the central dome to connect with the narthex on one end and the halfdome of the sanctuary apse on the other. This processional core, called the **naos** in Byzantine architecture, is flanked by side aisles with **galleries** above them (**FIG. 8–4**).

Since its idiosyncratic mixture of basilica and rotunda precludes a ring of masonry underneath the dome to provide support around its circumference (as in the Pantheon,

SEE FIGS. 6–48, 6–49), the main dome of Hagia Sophia rests instead on four **pendentives** (triangular curving vault sections) that connect the base of the dome with the huge supporting piers at the four corners of the square area beneath it (see "Pendentives and Squinches" below). And since these piers are essentially submerged back into the darkness of the aisles, rather than expressed within the main space itself (SEE FIG. 8-4), the dome seems to float over a void.

Elements of Architecture
PENDENTIVES AND SQUINCHES

Pendentives and squinches are two methods of supporting a round dome or its drum over a square space. Pendentives are concave, triangular forms between the arches under a dome. They rise upward and inward to form a circular base of support on which the dome rests. **Squinches** are diagonal lintels placed across the upper corner of the wall and supported by an arch or a series of corbeled arches that give it a nichelike shape. Because squinches create an octagon, which is close in shape to a circle, they provide a solid base around the perimeter of a dome, usually elevated on a drum (a circular wall), whereas pendentives project the dome slightly inside the square space it covers, making it seem

to float. Byzantine builders preferred pendentives (as at Hagia Sophia, SEE FIG. 8–4), but elaborate, squinch-supported domes became a hallmark of Islamic architecture.

dome on squinches

dome on pendentives

The weightless effect was reinforced by the light-reflecting gold mosaic that covered the surfaces of dome and pendentives alike, as well as by the band of 40 windows that perforate the base of the dome right where it meets its support (SEE FIG. 8-3). This daring move challenges architectural logic by seeming to weaken the integrity of the masonry at the very place where it needs to be strong, but the windows created the circle of light that helps the dome appear to hover, and a reinforcement of buttressing on the exterior made the solution strong as well as shimmering. The origin of the dome on pendentives is obscure, but its large-scale use at Hagia Sophia was unprecedented and represents one of the boldest experiments in the history of architecture. It was to become the preferred method of supporting domes in Byzantine architecture.

The architects and builders of Hagia Sophia clearly stretched building materials to their physical limits, denying the physicality of the building in order to emphasize its spirituality. In fact, when the first dome fell in 558, it did so because a pier and pendentive shifted and because the dome was too shallow and exerted too much outward force at its base, not because the windows weakened the support. Confident of their revised technical methods, the architects designed a steeper dome that raised the summit 20 feet higher. They also added exterior buttressing. Although repairs had to be made in 869, 989, and 1346, the church has since withstood numerous earthquakes.

The liturgy used in Hagia Sophia in the sixth century has been lost, but it presumably resembled the rites described in detail for the church in the Middle Byzantine period. The celebration of the Eucharist took place behind a screen that separated the sanctuary from the nave. The emperor was the only layperson permitted to enter the sanctuary. Other men and women stood in the aisles or in the galleries, where they witnessed the processions of clergy moving in a circular path from the sanctuary into the nave and back five or six times during the ritual.

Hagia Sophia was thus a gigantic theater for public, imperial worship of God, created by a culture within which Church and state were inextricably intertwined. Justinian had the sanctuary embellished with 40,000 pounds of silver that he donated himself. This precious material was crafted into sumptuous decorations on the altar, ciborium (canopy sheltering the altar), ambo (pulpit), and screen. Since there was no figural decoration on the walls of the building in Justinian's time to focus the attention of viewers in any one place, worshipers standing on the church floor must have surveyed the whole expanse of the interior, shifting their attention from one shimmering vista to the next.

SAN VITALE IN RAVENNA In 540, Byzantine forces captured Ravenna from the Arian Christian Ostrogoths who had themselves taken it from the Romans in 476. Much of our knowledge of the art of this turbulent period comes from the well-preserved monuments in Ravenna. In 526, Ecclesius, bishop of Ravenna, commissioned two new churches, one for the city and one for its port, Classis. In the 520s, construction began on a central-plan church, a **martyrium** (church built over the grave of a martyr) dedicated to the fourth-century Roman martyr St. Vitalis (Vitale in Italian), but it was not finished until after Justinian had conquered Ravenna and established it as the administrative capital of Byzantine Italy (**FIG. 8-5**).

8-5 PLAN (A) AND CUTAWAY DRAWING (B) OF THE CHURCH OF SAN VITALE, RAVENNA
Under construction from c. 520; consecrated 547.

8–6 CHURCH OF SAN VITALE

View into the sanctuary toward the northeast. c. 547.

Credit: © 2016, Photo Scala, Florence

8–7 CHRIST ENTHRONED, FLANKED BY ANGELS, ST. VITALIS, AND BISHOP ECCLESIUS
Church of San Vitale, Ravenna. c. 547. Mosaic.

Credit: © akg-Images/Cameraphoto

wall shows an altar table set for the meal that Abraham offers to three disguised angels (Genesis 18:1–15), and next to it is a portrayal of his near-sacrifice of Isaac. In the spandrels and other framed wall spaces appear prophets and evangelists.

The framed wall spaces are bristling with symbolic references to Jesus, but the focus of the sanctuary program is the courtly tableau in the halfdome of the apse.

San Vitale was designed as a central-domed octagon surrounded by eight radiating exedrae (wall niches), surrounded in turn by an ambulatory and gallery, all covered by vaults. A rectangular sanctuary and semicircular apse project from one of the sides of the octagon, and circular rooms flank the apse. A separate oval narthex, set off-axis, joined church and palace and also led to cylindrical stair towers that gave access to the second-floor gallery.

The floor plan of San Vitale only hints at the effect of the complex, interpenetrating interior spaces of the church, an effect that was enhanced by the offset narthex with its double sets of doors leading into the church. People entering from the right saw only arched openings, whereas those entering from the left approached on an axis with the sanctuary visible straight ahead of them. The dome rests on eight large piers that frame the exedrae and the sanctuary. The undulating, two-story exedrae open through superimposed arcades into the outer aisles on the ground floor and into galleries on the second floor. They push out the circular central space and create an airy, floating sensation, reinforced by the liberal use of veined marble veneer and colored glass and gold mosaics in the surface decoration. As in Hagia Sophia, structure seems to dissolve into shimmering light and color.

Here, however, an elaborate program of figural mosaics focuses the worshiper's attention within the sanctuary (**FIG. 8–6**).

In the halfdome of the sanctuary apse St. Vitalis and Bishop Ecclesius flank an image of Christ enthroned. The other sanctuary images relate to its use for the celebration of the Eucharist. The lunette on the north

A youthful, classicizing Christ appears on axis (**FIG. 8–7**), dressed in imperial purple and enthroned on a cosmic orb in paradise, the setting indicated by the four rivers that flow from the ground underneath him. Two winged angels flank him like imperial bodyguards or attendants. In his left hand Christ holds a scroll with seven seals that he will open at his Second Coming at the end of time, proclaiming his authority not only over this age, but over the age to come. He extends his right hand to offer a crown of martyrdom to St. Vitalis, the saint to whom this church is dedicated. On the other side is the only figure in the tableau without a halo. Labeled as Bishop Ecclesius, he is the founder of San Vitale, who offers a model of the church itself to Christ. The artist has imagined a scene of courtly protocol in paradise, where Christ, as emperor, gives a gift to and receives a gift from members of the celestial entourage.

In separate, flanking rectangular compositions along the curving wall of the apse underneath the scene in the halfdome appear Justinian and Theodora and their retinues (Justinian can be seen in FIG. 8–6). The royal couple did not attend the dedication ceremonies for the church of San Vitale, conducted by Archbishop Maximianus in 547, and there is no evidence that they actually set foot in Ravenna, but these two large mosaic panels that face each other across its sanctuary picture their presence here in perpetuity. Justinian (**FIG. 8–8**), on the north wall, carries a large golden paten that will be used to hold the Eucharistic bread and stands next to Maximianus, who holds a golden, jewel-encrusted cross. The priestly celebrants at the right carry the Gospels encased in a golden, jeweled book cover, symbolizing the coming of Christ as the Word, and a censer containing burning incense to purify the altar prior to the Eucharist.

On the south wall, Theodora, standing beneath a fluted shell canopy and singled out by a golden halo and elaborate crown, carries a huge golden chalice studded with jewels (**FIG. 8-9**). The rulers present these gifts as precious offerings to Christ—emulating most immediately Bishop Ecclesius, who offers a model of the church to Christ in the halfdome of the apse, but also the three Magi who brought valuable gifts to the infant Jesus, depicted in "embroidery" at the bottom of Theodora's purple cloak. In fact, the paten and chalice offered by the royal couple will be used by this church to offer Eucharistic bread and wine to the local Christian community during the liturgy. In this way the entire program of mosaic decoration revolves around themes of offering, extended into the theme of the Eucharist itself.

Theodora's group stands beside a fountain, presumably in a courtyard leading to the entrance to the church. The open doorway and curtain are Classical space-creating devices, but here the mosaicists have deliberately avoided allowing their illusionistic power to overwhelm the mosaic's flat surface patterns. Notice, too, that the figures cast no shadows, and, though modeled, their outlines as

8-8 EMPEROR JUSTINIAN AND HIS ATTENDANTS, NORTH WALL OF THE APSE

Church of San Vitale, Ravenna. c. 547. Mosaic, 8'8" × 12' (2.64 × 3.65 m).

As head of state, the haloed Justinian wears a huge jeweled crown and a purple cloak; he carries a large golden paten that he is donating to San Vitale for the celebration of the Eucharist. Bishop Maximianus at his left holds a jeweled cross and another churchman holds a jewel-covered book. Government officials stand at Justinian's right, followed by barbarian mercenary soldiers, one of whom wears a neck torc, another a Classical cameo cloak clasp.

Credit: © Cameraphoto Arte, Venice

8-9 EMPRESS THEODORA AND HER ATTENDANTS, SOUTH WALL OF THE APSE

Church of San Vitale, Ravenna. c. 547. Mosaic, 8'8" × 12' (2.64 × 3.65 m).

Like Justinian, Theodora has a halo, wears imperial purple, and carries in her hands a liturgical vessel—the chalice that held the Eucharistic wine—that she will donate to the church. Her elaborate jewelry includes a wide collar of embroidered and jeweled cloth. A crown, hung with long strands of pearls (thought to protect the wearer from disease), frames her face. Her attendants also wear the rich textiles and jewelry of the Byzantine court.

Credit: © Cameraphoto Arte, Venice

silhouetted shapes are more prominent than their sense of three-dimensionality. Still, especially in Justinian's panel, a complex and carefully controlled system of overlapping allows us to see these figures clearly and logically situated within a shallow space, moving in a stately procession from left to right toward the entrance to the church and the beginning of the liturgy. So the scenes portrayed in these mosaic paintings are both flattened and three-dimensional, abstract and representational, patterned and individualized. Like Justinian and Theodora, their images are both there and not there at the same time.

THE MONASTERY OF ST. CATHERINE ON MOUNT SINAI

Justinian's imperial architectural projects extended across the breadth of the Byzantine Empire, emulating the example of the great emperors of ancient Rome. Soon after the dedication of San Vitale, he sponsored the reconstruction of the monastery of St. Catherine at Mount Sinai in Egypt (**FIG. 8–10**). This pilgrimage destination and spiritual retreat had been founded much earlier, during the fourth century, at the place where Moses had encountered God in the burning bush (Exodus 4 and 5) and in the shadow of the peak on which he had met God to receive the Ten Commandments (Exodus 19 and 20). Justinian's reconstruction focused on two aspects of the complex. In conjunction with the installation of a frontier garrison to protect both monks and pilgrims from Bedouin attacks on this remote border outpost, Justinian had the walls of the monastery fortified. He also commissioned a new church dedicated to the Virgin Mary and—according to inscriptions carved into the wooden beams that support its roof—built in memory of Theodora, who died in 548.

Procopius's description of this project focuses on the lives of the monks who lived there:

> On this Mount Sinai dwell monks whose life is a kind of careful rehearsal of death, and they enjoy without fear the solitude which is very precious to them. Since these monks have nothing to desire, for they are superior to all human wishes and they have no interest in owning anything or in caring for their bodies, nor do they seek pleasure in any other thing whatever, therefore the emperor Justinian built them a church which he dedicated to the Mother of God, so that they might be enabled to pass their lives within it, praying and holding services. (*Buildings*, V, viii, translated by H.B. Dewing, Loeb Library ed.)

The origins of monasticism in the eastern Christian world can be traced back to the third century, when some devout Christians began to retire into the desert to become hermits, living a secluded life of physical austerity and devoted to continual meditation and prayer. By the fourth century, groups of men and women began assembling around these hermits, ultimately forming independent secluded communities devoted to prayer and work. These monks and nuns practiced celibacy, poverty, and obedience to a spiritual leader, and they aspired to self-sufficiency so as to minimize contact with the outside world. The monastic movement grew rapidly; by 536 there were about 70 monasteries in Constantinople alone. Although they continued to function as retreats from the secular world—places where pious men and women could devote themselves almost exclusively to the contemplative life and safe havens for orphans, the poor, and the elderly—the monasteries, being tax-exempt, also amassed enormous wealth from the donations and bequests of the rich.

A local architect designed the new basilica church that

8–10 THE MONASTERY OF ST. CATHERINE, SINAI

Mount Sinai, Egypt. Fortifications and church constructed under the patronage of Emperor Justinian, c. 548–566.

Founded in the fourth century, this monastery was initially associated with the burning bush, since it was built on the site where Moses was believed to have encountered this startling theophany, but in the tenth or eleventh century it was rededicated to St. Catherine of Alexandria after acquiring her relics.

Credit: © age fotostock/Corbis RF/José Fuste Raga

8–11 THE TRANSFIGURATION OF CHRIST

Apse mosaic in the church of the Virgin, monastery of St. Catherine, Mount Sinai, Egypt. c. 565.

Framing the scene of the Transfiguration are medallion portraits of the 12 apostles, 2 monastic saints, and the 17 major and minor prophets. Sixth-century viewers would probably have associated David—in the medallion directly under Jesus and dressed in the robes and crown of a Byzantine emperor—with the patron, Emperor Justinian, and an inscription running above the lower row of medallions to the right identifies the monastic leaders at the time the mosaic was made and dates them to 565/6, near the time of Justinian's death.

Credit: © LatitudeStock/Alamy Stock Photo

Justinian commissioned for the monks and pilgrims of Mount Sinai. The building was constructed of local materials, but the sumptuous decoration of the sanctuary derives from more cosmopolitan artistic centers. The marble revetment that faces the lower walls of the apse was imported from an island quarry near Constantinople, and the artists who covered the halfdome of the apse and the end wall of the nave above it with powerful scenes in sumptuous mosaics were probably called in from Jerusalem, or even Constantinople. As at San Vitale, mosaic decoration is concentrated in the sanctuary, where the apse would have glistened with vivid color and divine light—a spotlighted destination at the end of the longitudinal axis of the processional nave (**FIG. 8–11**).

The mosaics integrate a series of stories and themes into a coherent program around the notion of theophany—the appearance of God to human beings. Two rectangular scenes on the end wall of the nave above the apse (only partially visible in FIG. 8-11) picture two local theophanies—Moses before the burning bush and Moses receiving the law. The halfdome of the apse highlights the Transfiguration, an episode from the life of Jesus during which he was transformed "on a high mountain" from human to divine and set between apparitions of Moses and Elijah before the eyes of Peter, James, and John, three of his disciples (Matthew 17:1–6, NRSV). The central figure of Jesus fits the description in the Gospel text—"his face shone like the sun, and his clothes became dazzling white." The artists have flattened Jesus's form and set him against a contrasting deep blue **mandorla** (body halo), through which pass rays of light emanating from him and touching the figures around him. Unlike Jesus, the three apostles below him—who "fell to the ground and were overcome by fear"—are active rather than static, aggressively three-dimensional rather than brilliantly flattened, in a visual contrast between celestial apparition and earthly form. The entire tableau takes place against a background of golden light, with no indication of a landscape setting other than the banded lines of color at the bottom of the scene.

Luxury Objects

The court workshops of Constantinople excelled in the production of luxurious small-scale works in gold, ivory, and textiles. The Byzantine elite also sponsored vital **scriptoria** (writing centers for scribes—professional document writers) for the production of **manuscripts** (handwritten books), often located within monasteries.

IVORY DIPTYCHS Commemorative ivory diptychs—two carved panels hinged together—originated with ancient Roman politicians elected to the post of consul. New consuls would send notices of their election to friends and colleagues by inscribing them in wax that filled a recessed rectangular area on the inner sides of a pair of ivory panels carved with elaborate decoration on the outside. Christians adapted the practice for religious use, inscribing a diptych with the names of people to be remembered with prayers during the liturgy.

This large panel portraying the **ARCHANGEL MICHAEL**—the largest surviving Byzantine ivory—was half of such a diptych (FIG. **8-12**). In his classicizing serenity, imposing physical presence, and elegant architectural setting, the archangel is comparable to the (supposed) priestess of Bacchus in the fourth-century pagan Symmachus diptych panel (SEE FIG. 6-71) and reminiscent of the standing saints in the dome mosaics of St. George in Thessaloniki (SEE FIG. 7-22). His relationship to the architectural

8-12 ARCHANGEL MICHAEL

Panel of a diptych, probably from the court workshop at Constantinople. Early 6th century. Ivory, 17 × 5½" (43.3 × 14 cm). British Museum, London.

Credit: © The Trustees of the British Museum. All rights reserved.

space and the frame around him, however, is more complex. His heels rest on the top step of a stair that clearly lies behind the columns and pedestals, but the rest of his body overlaps the architectural setting and thus seems to project in front of them—creating a striking tension between the celestial figure and his terrestrial backdrop.

The angel is outfitted as a divine messenger, holding a staff of authority in his left hand and a sphere symbolizing worldly power in his right. Within the arch is a similar cross-topped orb, set against the background of a scallop shell and framed by a wreath bound by a ribbon with long, rippling extensions. The lost half of this diptych would have completed the Greek inscription across the top, which reads: "Receive these gifts, and having learned the cause…." Perhaps the other panel contained a portrait of the emperor—many think he would be Justinian—or of another high official who presented the panels as a gift to an important colleague, acquaintance, or family member. Nonetheless, the emphasis here is on the powerfully classicized celestial messenger, who does not need to obey the laws of earthly scale or human perspective.

ILLUMINATED MANUSCRIPTS   Since people began to write, they have kept records on a variety of materials, including clay or wax tablets, pieces of broken pottery, papyrus, animal skins, and paper. Books have taken two forms: scroll and codex.

Scribes made scrolls from sheets of papyrus glued end to end or from thin sheets of cleaned, scraped, and trimmed sheepskin or calfskin, a material known as **parchment** or, when softer and lighter, **vellum** (an especially fine writing surface made from calfskin). Each end of the scroll was attached to a rod; readers slowly unfurled the scroll from one rod to the other as they read. Scrolls could be written to be read either horizontally or vertically.

At the end of the first century CE, the more practical and manageable **codex** (plural, codices)—sheets bound together like the modern book—replaced the scroll as the primary form of recording texts. The basic unit of the codex was the eight-leaf quire, made by folding a large sheet of parchment twice, cutting the edges free, then sewing the sheets together up the center. Heavy covers kept the sheets of a codex flat. The thickness and weight of parchment and vellum made it impractical to produce a very large manuscript, such as an entire Bible, in a single volume. As a result, individual sections were made into separate books.

Until the invention of printing in the fifteenth century, all books were manuscripts—that is, they were written by hand. Manuscripts often included illustrations, called **miniatures** (from *minium*, the Latin word for a reddish lead pigment). Manuscripts decorated with gold and colors were said to be **illuminated**.

Byzantine manuscripts were often made with very costly materials. For example, sheets of purple-dyed vellum and gold and silver inks were used to produce a codex now known as the Vienna Genesis. It was probably made in Syria or Palestine, and the purple vellum indicates that it may have been created for an imperial patron, since costly purple dye, made from the secretions of murex mollusks, was usually restricted to imperial use. The Vienna Genesis is written in Greek and illustrated with pictures that appear below the text at the bottom of the pages.

A painter who worked on the Vienna Genesis visualized the story of **REBECCA AT THE WELL** (FIG. 8-13) (Genesis 24) as a single composition. But—clinging to the **continuous narrative** tradition that had characterized the illustration of scrolls—this scene combines events that take place at different times in the story within a single narrative space. Rebecca, the heroine, appears at the left walking away from the walled city of Nahor with a large jug on her shoulder, going to fetch water. A colonnaded road leads toward a spring, personified by a reclining pagan water nymph who holds a flowing jar. In the foreground, Rebecca appears again, clearly identifiable by continuity of costume. Her jug now full, she encounters a thirsty camel driver and offers him water to drink. Since he is

8-13 REBECCA AT THE WELL
Page from a codex featuring the book of Genesis (known as the Vienna Genesis). Made in Syria or Palestine. Early 6th century. Tempera, gold, and silver paint on purple-dyed vellum, 13½ × 9⅞″ (33.7 × 25 cm). Österreichische Nationalbibliothek, Vienna.

Credit: B© Bildarchiv der Österreichischen Nationalbibliothek, Vienna. Cod. Theol. Gr. 31, pag. 13, fol. 7r (E19.237-D)

Abraham's servant, Eliezer, in search of a bride for Abraham's son Isaac, Rebecca's generosity results in her marriage to Isaac. The lifelike poses and rounded, full-bodied figures of this narrative scene conform to the conventions of traditional Roman painting. The sumptuous purple of the background and the glittering metallic letters of the text situate the book within the world of the privileged and powerful in Byzantine society.

SILVER The imperial court at Constantinople had a monopoly on the production of some luxury goods, especially those made of precious metals. A seventh-century court workshop seems to have been the origin of a spectacular set of nine silver plates portraying events in the early life of the biblical King David, including the plate that we examined at the beginning of the chapter (SEE FIG. 8–1).

The plates would have been made by hammering a large silver ingot (the plate in FIG. 8–1 weighs 12 pounds 10 ounces) into a round shape and raising on it the rough semblance of the human figures and their environment. With finer chisels, silversmiths then refined these shapes, and at the end of their work, they punched ornamental motifs and incised fine details. The careful modeling, lifelike postures, and intricate engraving document the highly refined artistry and technical virtuosity of these cosmopolitan artists at the imperial court, who still practiced a classicizing art that had characterized some works of Christian art for centuries (SEE FIGS. 7–9, 7–18, 7–21, 8–12).

Icons

Christians in the Byzantine world prayed to Christ, Mary, and the saints while gazing at images of them on independent panels known as **icons**. Church doctrine toward the veneration of icons was ambivalent.

Christianity inherited from Judaism an uneasiness with the power of religious images, rooted in the Mosaic prohibition of "graven images" (Exodus 20:4). The lingering effects of the early persecution of Christians because of their refusal to venerate images of Roman emperors only intensified this anxiety. But key figures of the Eastern Church, such as Basil the Great of Cappadocia (c. 329–379) and John of Damascus (c. 675–749), distinguished between idolatry—the worship of images—and the veneration of an idea or holy person depicted in a work of art. Icons were thus accepted as aids to meditation and prayer, intermediaries between worshipers and the holy personages they depicted. Honor showed to the image was believed to transfer directly to its spiritual prototype.

Surviving early icons are rare. A few precious examples exist at the monastery of St. Catherine on Mount

8–14 VIRGIN AND CHILD WITH SAINTS AND ANGELS

Icon. Second half of the 6th century. Encaustic on wood, 27 × 18⅞" (69 × 48 cm). Monastery of St. Catherine, Mount Sinai, Egypt.

Credit: © akg-images/Erich Lessing

Sinai, among them **VIRGIN AND CHILD WITH SAINTS AND ANGELS** (FIG. 8–14). As Theotokos (Greek for "bearer of God"), Jesus's earthly mother was viewed as a powerful, ever-forgiving intercessor, who could be counted on to appeal to her divine son for mercy on behalf of devout and repentant worshipers. The Virgin and Child are flanked here by Christian warrior-saints Theodore (left) and George (right)—both legendary figures said to have slain dragons, representing the triumph of the Church over the "evil serpent" of paganism. Angels behind them twist their heads to look heavenward. The artist has painted the Christ Child, the Virgin, and especially the angels, with an illusionism that renders them lifelike and three-dimensional in appearance. But the warrior-saints—who look out to meet directly the worshipful gaze of viewers—are more stylized. Here the artist barely hints at bodily form beneath the richly patterned textiles of their cloaks, and their faces are frozen in frontal stares of gripping intensity, addressing viewers directly.

Iconoclasm

During the eighth century, mounting discomfort with the place of icons in Christian devotion grew into a major controversy in the Byzantine world, and between 726 and 730, Emperor Leo III (ruled 717–741) imposed **iconoclasm** ("image breaking"), initiating the systematic destruction of images of saints and sacred stories on icons and in churches, as well as the persecution of those who made them and defended their use. Only a few early icons survived in isolated places like Mount Sinai, which was no longer a part of the Byzantine Empire at this time (FOR EXAMPLE, FIG. 8–14). Leo III's successor, Constantine V (ruled 741–775), enforced these policies and practices with even greater fervor, but at the end of the reign of Leo IV (ruled 775–780), his widow, Empress Irene, who ruled as regent for their son Constantine IV (ruled 780–797), put an end to iconoclasm in 787 through a church council held in Nicea. Leo V (ruled 813–820) instituted a second phase of iconoclasm in 813, and it remained imperial policy until March 11, 843, when the widowed Empress Theodora reversed her husband Theophilus's policy and reinstated the central place of images in Byzantine devotional practice.

A number of explanations have been proposed for these two interludes of Byzantine iconoclasm. Some Church leaders feared that the use of images in worship could lead to idolatry or at least distract worshipers from their spiritual exercises. Specifically, there were questions surrounding the relationship between images and the Eucharist, the latter considered by iconoclasts as sufficient representation of the presence of Christ in the church. But there was also anxiety in Byzantium about the weakening state of the empire, especially in relation to the advances of Arab armies into Byzantine territory. It was easy to pin

8-15 CRUCIFIXION AND ICONOCLASTS
From the Chludov Psalter. Mid 9th century. Tempera on vellum, 7¾ × 6″ (19.5 × 15 cm). State Historical Museum, Moscow.
MS. D. 29, fol. 67v.

This page and its illustration of Psalm 69:21—made soon after the end of the iconoclastic controversy in 843—record the iconophiles' harsh judgment of the iconoclasts. Painted in the margin at the right, a scene of the Crucifixion shows a soldier tormenting Christ with a vinegar-soaked sponge. In a striking visual parallel, two named iconoclasts—identified by inscription—in the adjacent picture along the bottom margin employ a whitewash-soaked sponge to obliterate an icon portrait of Christ, thus linking them by their actions with those who had crucified him.

these hard times on God's displeasure with the idolatrous use of images. Coincidentally, Leo III's success fighting the Arabs could be interpreted as divine sanction of his iconoclastic position, and its adoption might appease the iconoclastic Islamic enemy itself as well. Finally, since the production and promotion of icons was centered in monasteries—at that time rivaling the state in strength and wealth—attacking the use of images might check their growing power. Perhaps all these factors played a part, but with the triumph of the **iconophiles** (literally "lovers of images") in 843, the place of images in worship was again secure: Icons proclaimed Christ as God incarnate and facilitated Christian worship by acting as intermediaries between humans and saints. Those who had suppressed icons were considered heretics (FIG. 8–15).

Middle Byzantine Art

What traditions of Byzantine art and architecture are established during its middle period?

With the turmoil and destruction of iconoclasm behind them, Byzantine patrons and artists turned during the second half of the ninth century to ambitious projects of restoration and renewal, redecorating church interiors with figural images and producing new icons in a variety of media for the devotional practices of the faithful. This period also saw a renewal and expansion of the power and presence of monasteries in the Byzantine world. A new Macedonian dynasty of rulers—founded in 866 by Emperor Basil I (ruled 866–886) and continuing until 1056—increased Byzantine military might, leading to an expansion of imperial territory, only checked in the mid eleventh century by the growing power of the Turks, who dealt the Byzantine army a series of military setbacks that would continue to erode the empire until the fifteenth century. But after the empire stabilized under the Komnenian dynasty (1081–1185), it was not the Turks who instigated the end of the Middle Byzantine period. It ended abruptly when Christian crusaders from the west, who had set out on a holy war against Islam, diverted their efforts to conquering the wealthy Christian Byzantine Empire, taking Constantinople in 1204. The crusaders looted the capital and set up a Latin dynasty of rulers to replace the Byzantine emperors, who fled into exile.

The patronage of the Macedonian dynasty stimulated a new golden age of Byzantine art, often referred to as the "Macedonian Renaissance," since it was marked by an intensified interest in the styles and themes of Classical art, as well as by a general revitalization of intellectual life. As the Middle Byzantine period developed, the geography of Byzantine art changed significantly. As we have seen, early Byzantine civilization had been centered in lands along the rim of the Mediterranean Sea that had been within the Roman Empire. During the Middle Byzantine period, Constantinople's scope was reduced to present-day Turkey and other areas by the Black Sea, as well as the Balkan peninsula, including Greece, and southern Italy. The influence of Byzantine culture also extended into Russia and Ukraine, and to Venice, Constantinople's trading partner in northeastern Italy, at the head of the Adriatic Sea.

Architecture and Wall Painting in Mosaic and Fresco

Although the restitution of images led to the creation of new mosaics in the major churches of the capital, comparatively few Middle Byzantine churches in Constantinople have survived intact. Better-preserved examples of the central-plan domed churches that were popular in the

Byzantine world survive in Greece to the southwest and Ukraine to the northeast, and within the western medieval world are reflected in Venice. These structures document the Byzantine taste for a multiplicity of geometric forms, for verticality, and for rich decorative effects both inside and out.

APSE MOSAIC OF HAGIA SOPHIA   The upper parts of Justinian's church of Hagia Sophia were originally encrusted with broad expanses of gold mosaic framed by strips of vegetal and geometric ornament, but figural mosaics highlighting sacred individuals or sacred stories seem not to have been part of the original design. With the end of iconoclasm, however, there was an urgency to assert the significance of images within Byzantine churches, and the great imperial church of the capital was an important location to proclaim the orthodoxy of icons. By 867, mosaicists had inserted an iconic rendering of the Incarnation in the form of an image of the Virgin Mary holding the child Jesus in her lap (**FIG. 8-16**), flanked by angels and accompanied by an inscription claiming that "the images which the imposters [the iconoclast emperors] had cast down here, pious emperors have set up again."

8-16 VIRGIN AND CHILD IN THE APSE OF HAGIA SOPHIA

Constantinople (present-day Istanbul). Dedicated in 867. Mosaic.

Credit: Photo © Ayhan Altun

8–17 MONASTERY CHURCHES AT HOSIOS LOUKAS, STIRIS

Central Greece. Katholikon (left), early 11th century, and church of the Theotokos, late 10th century. View from the east.

Credit: © Ioannis Mantas/Alamy Stock Photo

The design of Hagia Sophia—especially the disposition of the sanctuary apse perforated from top to bottom with bands of windows—provided no obvious areas to highlight a figural mosaic, and working at the extreme height of the halfdome—where the mosaic is located—required the erection of immense wooden scaffolding to accommodate the artists at work (SEE FIG. 8-3, where the Virgin and Child appear at the top of the central lower apse, floating above the middle of the five windows at the bottom of the halfdome). Adding this mosaic was an expensive project.

Floating on an expansive sweep of gold mosaic with neither natural nor architectural setting—like a monumental icon presented for the perpetual veneration of the faithful—the Virgin and Child in Hagia Sophia recalls the pre-iconoclastic rendering on a surviving icon from Mount Sinai (SEE FIG. 8-14), but their gracefully modeled faces, their elegantly attenuated bodily proportions, and the jewel-studded bench that serves as their throne all proclaim the singular importance of their placement in Constantinople's principal imperial church. Co-emperors Michael III and Basil I were present in Hagia Sophia on March 29, 867, when the patriarch Photios preached the sermon at the dedication of the apse mosaics, laying claim to the historic moment this represented and challenging the rulers to maintain the orthodoxy it represented.

MONASTERY OF HOSIOS LOUKAS Although an outpost, Greece was part of the Byzantine Empire, and the eleventh-century Katholikon (main church) of the monastery of Hosios Loukas, built a few miles from the village of Stiris in central Greece, is an excellent example of Middle Byzantine architecture (FIG. 8-17). It stands next to the earlier church of the Theotokos (Virgin Mary) within the courtyard of the walled enclosure that contained the life of the monks (FIG. 8-18). They slept in individual rooms—called "cells"—incorporated into the walls around the periphery of the complex, and they ate their meals together in a long rectangular hall parallel to the main church.

The Katholikon has a compact central plan with a dome supported on squinches rising over an octagonal core (see "Pendentives and Squinches" on page 241). Outside, the rising forms of apses, walls, and roofs disguise the vaulting roofs of the interior. The Greek builders created a polychromed decorative effect on the exterior, alternating stones with bricks set both vertically and horizontally and using diagonally set bricks to form saw-toothed moldings. Inside the churches, the high central space carries the eyes of worshipers upward into the main dome, which soars above a ring of tall arched openings.

Unlike Hagia Sophia, with its clear, sweeping geometric forms, the Katholikon has a complex variety of architectural

warm rooms
for winter

monks' cells

8–18 PLAN OF THE
MONASTERY AT HOSIOS
LOUKAS
Including the two churches in
FIG. 8–17: Katholikon at lower
center, church of the Theotokos
above it and to the left.

old entrance

gardens

courtyard

gardens

older church
of the Virgin
(Theotokos)

underground
cistern

Katholikon
(main church
of Hosios Loukas)

refectory

current entrance

chapel and
clock tower

monks' cells

0   20m

shapes and spaces, including domes, groin vaults, barrel vaults, pendentives, and squinches, all built on a relatively small scale (**FIG. 8–19**). The barrel vaults and tall sanctuary apse with flanking rooms further complicate the spatial composition. Single, double, and triple windows create intricate and unusual patterns of light that illuminated a mosaic of Christ Pantokrator (now lost) looming at the center of the main dome. A mosaic of the Lamb of God surrounded by the Twelve Apostles at Pentecost fills the secondary,

sanctuary dome, and the apse halfdome presents a rendering of the Virgin and Child Enthroned reminiscent of the ninth-century mosaic in the apse halfdome of Hagia Sophia (SEE FIG. 8–16). Scenes of Christ's life on earth (the Nativity appears on the squinch visible in FIG. 8–19) and figures of saints fill the upper surfaces of the interior with brilliant color and dramatic images. As at Hagia Sophia, the lower walls are faced with a multicolored stone veneer. A screen with icons separates the congregation from the sanctuary.

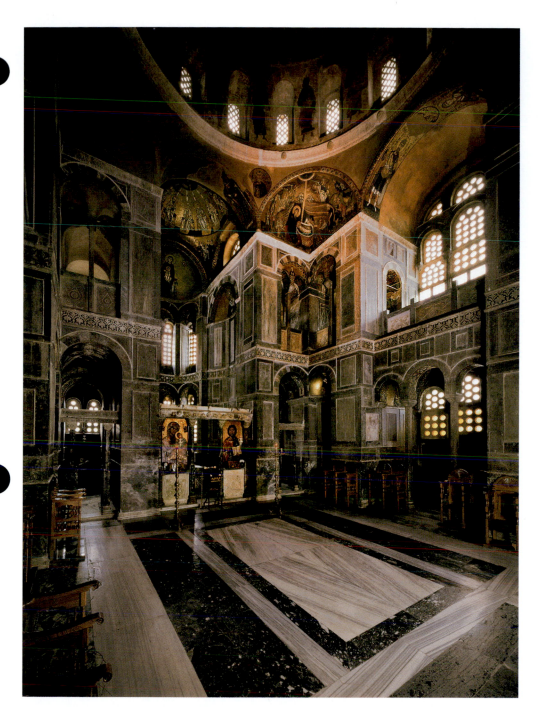

8-19 CENTRAL DOMED SPACE AND APSE (THE NAOS), KATHOLIKON
Monastery at Hosios Loukas. Early 11th century and later.

The subjects of the mosaics in Middle Byzantine churches such as the Katholikon at Hosios Loukas were organized into three levels according to meaning. Heavenly subjects like Christ Pantokrator, the Virgin Mary, Pentecost (Acts 2:1–3), or angels, appear on the tops of domes or in apse halfdomes. Below them, in a middle register are scenes from Christ's life on earth—here the Nativity in a squinch. Below, at the lowest level of mosaics are iconic representations of saints, closer to the viewer and thus more available for individual prayerful veneration.

Credit: © 2016. Image copyright The Metropolitan Museum of Art/ Art Resource/Scala, Florence. Photo: Bruce White Photography

CATHEDRAL OF SANTA SOPHIA IN KIEV   During the ninth century, the rulers of Kievan Rus—Ukraine, Belarus, and Russia—adopted Orthodox Christianity and Byzantine culture. These lands had been settled by eastern Slavs in the fifth and sixth centuries, but later were ruled by Scandinavian Vikings who had sailed down the rivers from the Baltic to the Black Sea. In Constantinople, the Byzantine emperor hired the Vikings as his personal bodyguards, and Viking traders established a headquarters in the upper Volga region and in the city of Kiev, which became the capital of the area under their control.

The first Christian member of the Kievan ruling family was Princess Olga (c. 890–969), who was baptized in Constantinople by the patriarch himself with the Byzantine emperor as her godfather. Her grandson Grand Prince Vladimir (ruled 980–1015) established Orthodox Christianity as the state religion in 988 and cemented his relations with the Byzantines by accepting baptism and marrying Anna, the sister of the powerful Emperor Basil II (ruled 976–1025).

Vladimir's son Grand Prince Yaroslav (ruled 1036–1054) founded the **CATHEDRAL OF SANTA SOPHIA** in Kiev (**FIG. 8-20**). The church—originally designed as a typical Byzantine multiple-domed cross—was expanded with double side aisles leading to five apses and incorporating a large central dome surrounded by 12 smaller domes, all of which creates a complicated and compartmentalized interior. The central domed space of the crossing, however,

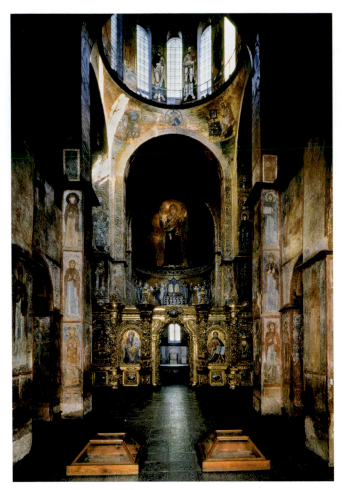

8-20 INTERIOR, CATHEDRAL OF SANTA SOPHIA, KIEV
1037–1046. Apse mosaics: Orant Virgin and Communion of the Apostles.

Credit: © 2016. Image copyright The Metropolitan Museum of Art/Art Resource/ Scala, Florence. Photo: Bruce White Photography

focuses attention on the nave and the main apse, where the walls glow with lavish decoration, including the mosaics of the central dome, the apse, and the arches of the crossing. The remaining surfaces are frescoed with scenes from the lives of Christ, the Virgin, the apostles Peter and Paul, and the archangels.

The Kievan mosaics established a standard iconographic system used in Russian Orthodox churches. A Christ Pantokrator fills the curving surface at the crest of the main dome (not visible above the window-pierced drum in FIG. 8-20). At a lower level, the apostles stand between the windows of the drum, with the four evangelists occupying the pendentives. An orant figure of the Virgin Mary seems to float in a golden heaven on the halfdome and upper wall of the apse, and on the wall below her is the Communion of the Apostles. Christ appears not once, but twice, in this scene, offering the Eucharistic bread and wine to the apostles, six on each side of the altar. With such extravagant use of costly mosaic, Prince Yaroslav made a powerful political declaration of his own power and wealth—and that of the Kievan Church as well.

MONASTERY CHURCH OF THE DORMITION AT DAPHNI The refined mosaicists who worked c. 1100 at the monastery church of the Dormition at Daphni, near Athens, seem to have conceived their compositions in relation to an intellectual ideal. They eliminated all "unnecessary" detail to focus on the essential elements of a narrative scene, conveying its mood and message in a moving but elegant style. The main dome of this church has retained its riveting image of the Pantokrator, centered at the crest of the dome like a seal of divine sanction and surveillance (FIG. 8-21). This imposing figure manages to be elegant and awesome at the same time. Christ blesses or addresses the assembled congregation with one hand, while the slender, attenuated fingers of the other spread to clutch a massive book securely. In the squinches of the corner piers are four signal episodes from his life: Annunciation, Nativity, Baptism, and Transfiguration.

A mosaic of the **CRUCIFIXION** from the lower part of the church (FIG. 8-22) exemplifies the focus on emotional appeal to individuals that appears in late eleventh-century Byzantine art. The figures inhabit an otherworldly space, a golden universe anchored to the material world by a few flowers, which suggest the promise of new life. A nearly nude Jesus is shown with bowed head and gently sagging body, his eyes closed in death. The witnesses have been reduced to two isolated mourning figures, Mary and the

8-21 CHRIST PANTOKRATOR WITH SCENES FROM THE LIFE OF CHRIST
Central dome and squinches, church of the Dormition, Daphni, Greece. c. 1100. Mosaic.

Credit: akg-images/Erich Lessing

8-22 CRUCIFIXION

Church of the Dormition, Daphni, Greece. c. 1100. Mosaic.

Credit: Studio Kontos Photostock

This depiction of the Crucifixion has symbolic as well as emotional power. The mound of rocks and the skull at the bottom of the cross represent Golgotha, the "place of the skull," the hill outside ancient Jerusalem where Adam was thought to be buried and where the Crucifixion was said to have taken place. Christians saw Jesus Christ as the new Adam, whose sacrifice on the cross saved humanity from the sins brought into the world by Adam and Eve. The arc of blood and water springing from Jesus's side refers to Eucharistic and baptismal rites. As Paul wrote in his First Letter to the Corinthians: "For just as in Adam all die, so too in Christ shall all be brought to life" (1 Corinthians 15:22). The timelessness and simplicity of this image were meant to aid the Christian worshiper seeking to achieve a mystical union with the divine through prayer and meditation, both intellectually and emotionally.

MONASTERY CHURCH OF ST. PANTELEIMON AT NEREZI

Dedicated in 1164, the church of St. Panteleimon—the Katholikon of the small monastery at Nerezi in Macedonia—was built under the patronage of Alexios Komnenos, nephew of Emperor John II (ruled 1118–1143). Here the wall paintings were created in fresco rather than mosaic, with a stylistic delicacy and **painterly** spontaneity characteristic of Byzantine art under the Komnenians. It represents well the growing emphasis on capturing the emotionalism of sacred narrative, already noted at Daphni. In the upper part of one wall, the scene of the **LAMENTATION** over the dead body of Christ (**FIG. 8-23**)—a nonbiblical episode that seems to have been developed during the twelfth century—forges a direct link with viewers'

young apostle John, to whom Jesus had just entrusted the care of his mother. The elegant cut of the contours and the eloquent restraint of the gestures only intensify the emotional power of the image. The nobility and suffering of these figures was meant to move monks and visiting worshipers toward a deeper involvement with their own meditations.

8-23 LAMENTATION

North wall of the church of the monastery of St. Panteleimon, Nerezi (near Skopje), Macedonia. 1164. Fresco.

Credit: © akg-images/Erich Lessing

emotions. The narrative emphasis is on the Virgin's anguish as she cradles the lifeless body of her son in the broad extension of her lap, pulling his head toward her, cheek to cheek, in a final embrace. Behind her, St. John bends to lift Jesus's hand to his cheek, conforming to a progressively descending diagonal arrangement of mourners that tumbles from the mountainous backdrop toward resolution in the limp torso of the savior. Such emotional expressions of human grief in human terms will be taken up again in Italy by Giotto over a century later (SEE FIG. 18–8).

THE CATHEDRAL OF ST. MARK IN VENICE The northeastern Italian city of Venice, set on the Adriatic at the crossroads of Europe and Asia Minor, was in certain ways an outpost of Byzantine art in Italy. Venice had been subject to Byzantine rule in the sixth and seventh centuries, and up to the tenth century, the city's ruler, the doge ("duke" in Venetian dialect), had to be ratified by the Byzantine

emperor. At the end of the tenth century, Constantinople granted Venice a special trade status that allowed its merchants to control much of the commerce between east and west, and the city grew enormously wealthy.

Venetian architects looked to Byzantine domed churches for inspiration in 1063, when the doge commissioned a church to replace the palace chapel that had housed the relics of St. Mark the apostle since they had been brought to Venice from Alexandria in 828/29 (**FIG. 8–24**). The **CATHEDRAL OF ST. MARK** is designed as a Greek cross, with arms of equal length. A dome covers each square unit—five great domes in all, separated by barrel vaults and supported by pendentives. Unlike Hagia Sophia in Constantinople, where the space seems to flow from the narthex up into the dome and through the nave to the apse, St. Mark's domed compartments produce a complex space in which each dome maintains its own separate vertical axis. As we have seen elsewhere, marble veneer covers the lower walls, and golden mosaics glimmer above on the vaults, pendentives, and domes.

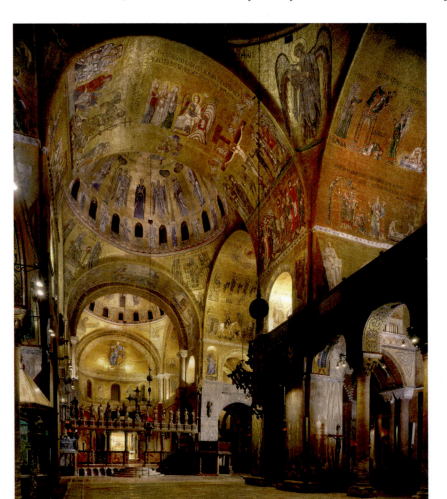

8–24A INTERIOR OF THE CATHEDRAL OF ST. MARK

Venice. Begun 1063. View looking toward apse.

This church is the third one built on the site. It was both the palace chapel of the doge and the burial place for the bones of the patron of Venice, St. Mark. The church was consecrated as a cathedral in 1807. The mosaics have been reworked continually to the present day.

Credit: © Cameraphoto Arte, Venice

8–24B PLAN OF THE CATHEDRAL OF ST. MARK

Venice. Begun 1063.

Precious Objects of Commemoration, Veneration, and Devotion

As in the Early Byzantine period, tenth-, eleventh-, and twelfth-century artists produced small, often portable, luxury items for wealthy members of the imperial court as well as for Church dignitaries. These patrons often commissioned such precious objects as official gifts for one another. They had to be portable, sturdy, and refined, representing the latest trends in style and subject. These works frequently combined exceptional beauty and technical virtuosity with religious meaning; many were icons or devotional objects. Ivory carving, gold and **enamel** work, fine books, and intricate panel paintings were especially prized.

IVORIES Standing slightly over 9 inches tall, the small ivory ensemble known as the **HARBAVILLE TRIPTYCH** (named after a nineteenth-century owner) was made as a portable devotional object with two hinged wings that could be folded shut for travel. Its privileged owner used this work as the focus for private prayer; its luxuriousness also signaled high status and wealth. When opened (**FIG. 8–25A**), the triptych features across the top of the central panel a tableau with an enthroned Christ flanked by Mary and St. John the Baptist. This is a composition known as the "Deësis" (meaning "entreaty" in Greek), which shows Mary and John interceding with Christ, presumably pleading for forgiveness and salvation for the owner of this work. St. Peter stands directly under Christ, gesturing upward toward him and flanked by four other apostles—SS. James, John, Paul, and Andrew, all identified by inscriptions. The figures in the outer panels (both back and front) are military saints, bishop saints, and martyrs.

These holy figures stand in spatial settings given definition only by the small bases under their feet, effectively removing their gently modeled forms from the physical world. As a whole, they represent a celestial court of saints attending the enthroned Christ in paradise, categorized into thematic groups in an organization that recalls the ordered distribution of subjects in a Middle Byzantine church (SEE FIGS. 8–19, 8–20). On the back of the central panel (**FIG. 8–25B**) is a symbolic

evocation of paradise itself in the form of a large, stable cross surrounded by luxurious vegetation inhabited by animals, presumably an evocation of the longed-for destination of the original owner, a reminder to focus attention

8–25A FRONT OF THE HARBAVILLE TRIPTYCH
From Constantinople. Mid 10th century. Ivory, closed 9½ × 5⅝" (24.2 × 14.3 cm); open 9½ × 11" (24.2 × 28 cm). Musée du Louvre, Paris.

Credit: Photo © RMN-Grand Palais (Musée du Louvre)/Daniel Arnaudet

8–25B BACK OF THE HARBAVILLE TRIPTYCH
From Constantinople. Mid 10th century. Ivory, closed 9½ × 5⅝" (24.2 × 14.3 cm); open 9½ × 11" (24.2 × 28 cm). Musée du Louvre, Paris.

Credit: Photo © RMN-Grand Palais (Musée du Louvre)/Daniel Arnaudet

8-26 CHRIST CROWNING EMPEROR ROMANOS II AND EMPRESS EUDOKIA

From Constantinople. 945–949. Ivory, 7⅜ × 3¾" (18.6 × 9.5 cm). Cabinet des Médailles, Bibliothèque Nationale, Paris.

Credit: Bibliothèque nationale de France

child—of the fusion of imperial authority with the religious faith that sanctioned and supported it. The carefully modeled figure of Christ, whose drapery is arranged to give three-dimensionality to his bodily form, offers a striking contrast to the stiff and flattened figures of the imperial couple, all but consumed by the elaborate decoration of their royal robes.

MANUSCRIPTS Painted books were some of the most impressive products of the Middle Byzantine period, and of the Macedonian Renaissance in particular. The luxurious Paris **Psalter** (named after its current library location) is a noteworthy example. This personal devotional book—meant to guide the prayer life of its aristocratic owner—includes the complete text of the Psalms and a series of odes or canticles drawn from the Bible that were a standard part of Byzantine psalters. The annotation of the biblical texts with passages from interpretive commentaries gives this book a scholarly dimension consistent with a revival of learning that took place under the Macedonian emperors. Indeed it seems to have been commissioned in Constantinople by the intellectual Emperor Constantine

on devotional practice and enlist the aid of the congregation of saints to assure the attainment of salvation. An abbreviated inscription above the cross—IC XC NIKA—backs up the pictorial reminder with words—"Jesus Christ is victorious."

Related to the Harbaville Triptych in both figure style and compositional format is an independent ivory panel portraying an emperor and empress standing on either side of and gesturing toward an elevated figure of Christ, who reaches out to touch their crowns (**FIG. 8-26**). The imperial figures are identified by inscription as Romanos and Eudokia—most likely Emperor Romanos II, son and co-emperor of Constantine VII Porphyrogenitos (ruled 945–959), and his first wife, Eudokia, the daughter of Hugo of Provence, King of Rome, whom Romanos married in 944 when she was only 4 years old and who died in 949. This is not a scene of coronation but an emblem—Eudokia, for instance, is represented as an adult rather than as a

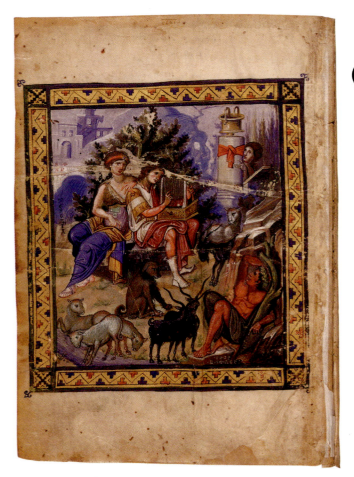

8-27 DAVID COMPOSING THE PSALMS

Page from the Paris Psalter. Constantinople. c. 950. Paint and gold on vellum, sheet size 14½ × 10½" (37 × 26.5 cm). Bibliothèque Nationale, Paris.

Credit: Bibliothèque nationale de France

VII Porphyrogenitos as a gift for his son Romanos II, whom we have already encountered (SEE FIG. 8–26).

This book is best known, however, neither for its learned texts nor for its imperial patron or owner, but for its set of 14 full-page miniatures. The fresh spontaneity of these paintings and the complicated abstraction underlying their compositional structure—salient stylistic features of the Macedonian Renaissance—make this book one of the true glories of Byzantine art. Eight of the framed miniatures portray episodes from the life of Israel's King David, who as a boy had saved the people of God by killing the giant Goliath (SEE FIG. 8–1) and who was traditionally considered the author of the Psalms. The first of these depicts David seated outdoors against a background of lush foliage while he composes the Psalms to the accompaniment of his harp (FIG. 8–27). Groups of animals surround him in the foreground, while his native city of Bethlehem looms through the atmospheric mist in the background.

The Macedonian Renaissance emphasis on a Classical revival is evident here in the personification of abstract ideas and landscape features: Melody, a languorous female figure, leans casually on David's shoulder to inspire his compositions, while another woman, perhaps Echo, peeks from behind a column in the right background. The swarthy reclining youth in the lower foreground is a personification of Mount Bethlehem, as we learn from his inscription. The motif of the dog watching over the sheep and goats while his master strums the harp invokes the Classical subject of Orpheus charming wild animals with music. The strongly modeled three-dimensionality of the forms, the integration of the figures into a three-dimensional space, and the use of atmospheric perspective all enhance the Classical flavor of the painting, in yet another example of the enduring vitality of pagan artistic traditions at the Christian court in Constantinople.

ICONS   In the centuries after the end of iconoclasm, one of the major preoccupations of Byzantine artists was the creation of independent devotional images in a variety of media. The revered twelfth-century icon of Mary and Jesus known as the **VIRGIN OF VLADIMIR** (FIG. 8–28) was probably painted in Constantinople but brought to Kiev. This distinctively humanized image is another example of the growing desire for a more immediate and personal religion that we have already seen in the Crucifixion mosaic at Daphni, dating slightly earlier. Here the artist used an established iconographic type known as the "Virgin of Compassion," showing Mary and the Christ Child pressing their cheeks together and gazing at each other with tender affection. This type of image is found as early as the tenth century and was believed to have been first painted by St. Luke, reproducing what he had seen in a vision. The *Virgin of Vladimir* was thought to protect the people of the city where it resided. It arrived in Kiev sometime in the

8-28 VIRGIN OF VLADIMIR
Probably from Constantinople. Faces, 12th century; the figures have been retouched. Tempera on panel, height approx. 31″ (78 cm). Tretyakov State Gallery, Moscow.

Credit: © 2016. Photo Scala, Florence

1130s, was subsequently taken to the city of Suzdal, and finally came to Vladimir in 1155. In 1480, it was moved to the Cathedral of the Dormition in the Moscow Kremlin.

Also from the twelfth century, but made from more precious materials and presenting a saintly image more hieratic than intimate, is a representation of the archangel Michael in silver-gilt and enamel (see "Closer Look" on page 262), whose technical virtuosity and sumptuous media suggest it may have been an imperial commission for use within the palace complex itself. St. Michael is dressed here as a confrontational military commander in the heavenly forces, a real contrast with the calmly classicizing angelic form he takes in the large ivory panel we examined from the Early Byzantine period (SEE FIG. 8–12).

This icon did not remain in Constantinople. It is now in the treasury of the Cathedral of St. Mark in Venice, one of many precious objects looted by Latin crusaders in 1204 at the fall of Constantinople during the ill-conceived Fourth Crusade. This devastating event brought an abrupt end to the Middle Byzantine period.

A Closer Look

ICON OF ST. MICHAEL THE ARCHANGEL

This bust portrait of Christ, created with **cloisonné** enamel, appears directly over the head of St. Michael, sanctioning his power with a gesture of blessing or recognition. The medallions on the upper corners portray SS. Peter and Menas, but the enamels once filling comparable medallions on the lower strip of the frame have been lost.

Heavily abbreviated inscriptions identify each saint by name.

In 1834, restorers replaced the wings of St. Michael, which are now probably disproportionately large in relation to the originals. In the same restoration, the precious gemstones once set into the frame were replaced with colored glass.

Four pairs of military saints in oval compartments flank St. Michael on the lateral strips of the frame. This entourage emphasizes the military character of St. Michael, who is dressed and equipped for battle as the leader of a heavenly army.

Luminous enamel (glass heated to the melting point at which it bonds to the underlying or surrounding metal) completely covers the face of St. Michael to give it the appearance of human flesh.

Lavish and intricate patterns created from enamel fill the background around St. Michael. Byzantine artists were virtuosos in the cloisonné technique, in which gold strips or wires are soldered to the underlying metal surface to separate the different colors of enamel from each other, forming a network of delicate gold lines that delineate the decorative forms and enliven the surface with reflected light.

A series of separately fabricated forms—haloed head, torso, legs, arms, wings, sword, and fully three-dimensional orb and sword—have been assembled to create the projecting figure of St. Michael.

8-29 ICON OF ST. MICHAEL THE ARCHANGEL
Made in Constantinople. 12th century. Silver-gilt on wood, cloisonné enamels, gemstones; 18⅛ × 13¾" (46 × 35 cm). Treasury of the Cathedral of St. Mark, Venice.

Credit: © Cameraphoto Arte, Venice

Late Byzantine Art

How is Byzantine art transformed during its late period?

A third great age of Byzantine art began in 1261 after the Byzantines expelled the Christian crusaders who had occupied Constantinople for nearly 60 years. Although the empire had been weakened and its domain decreased to small areas of the Balkans and Greece, the arts underwent a resurgence known as the Palaeologue Renaissance after the new dynasty of emperors who regained Constantinople.

The patronage of emperors, wealthy courtiers, and the Church stimulated renewed church building as well as the production of icons, books, and precious objects.

Constantinople: The Chora Church

In Constantinople, many existing churches were renovated, redecorated, and expanded during the Palaeologue Renaissance. Among these is the church of the monastery of Christ in Chora (meaning "in the country"), part of an influential monastery on the outskirts of Constantinople.

8-30 PLAN OF THE MONASTERY CHURCH OF CHRIST IN CHORA KARIYE MÜZESI, CONSTANTINOPLE

Present-day Istanbul. Original construction 1077–1081; expanded and refurbished c. 1315–1321.

Metochites became a powerful intellectual figure in Constantinople. As a poet, philosopher, and astronomer who wrote scores of complicated commentaries in an intentionally cultivated, arcane, and mannered literary style, he ridiculed a rival for his prose style of "excess clarity." In 1290, Emperor Andronicus II Palaeologus (ruled 1282–1328) called Metochites to court service, where the prolific young scholar became an influential senior statesman, ascending to the highest levels of the government and amassing power and wealth second only to that of the emperor himself. Metochites's political and financial status plummeted when the emperor was overthrown by his grandson in 1328. Stripped of his wealth and sent into exile, Metochites was allowed to return to the capital two years later, retiring to house arrest at the Chora monastery, where he died and was buried in 1332.

It is his association with this monastery that has become Theodore Metochites's greatest claim to enduring fame. He was at the peak of his power and wealth when he funded the expansion and restoration of the monastery's church, and the **FUNERARY CHAPEL** (or parekklesion) that was built adjacent to the main church (**FIG. 8-31**), was designed with the intention of creating a location for his own funeral and tomb.

The expansion of this church (known today as the Kariye Müzesi) was one of several projects that Theodore Metochites (1270–1332), a humanist poet and scientist and the administrator of the imperial treasury at Constantinople, sponsored between c. 1315 and 1321. He added a two-story annex on the north side, two narthexes on the west, and a parekklesion (side chapel) used as a funerary chapel on the south (**FIG. 8-30**). These structures contain the most impressive interior decorations remaining in Constantinople from the Late Byzantine period, rivaling in splendor and technical sophistication the works of the age of Justinian, but on a more intimate scale. The walls and vaults of the parekklesion are covered with frescos, and the narthex vaults are encrusted with mosaics.

Theodore Metochites was one of the most fascinating personalities of the Late Byzantine world. Son of an intellectual cleric who had been condemned and exiled for championing the union of the Roman and Byzantine Churches,

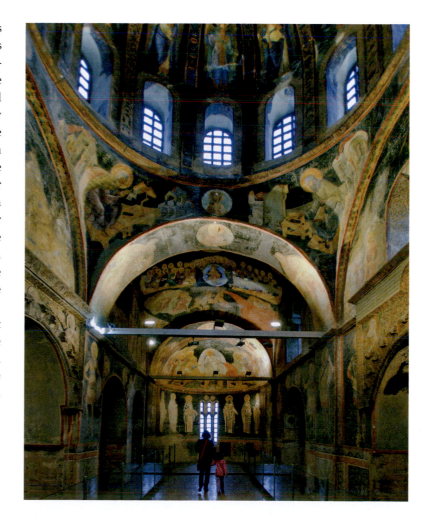

8-31 FUNERARY CHAPEL (PAREKKLESION)

Church of the monastery of Christ in Chora, present-day Istanbul. c. 1315–1321.

Credit: Photo © Ayhan Altun

8–32 ANASTASIS
Apse of the funerary chapel, church of the monastery of Christ in Chora, present-day Istanbul. c. 1321. Fresco.

Credit: Photo © Ayhan Altun

The extensive and highly integrated program of frescos covering every inch of the walls and vaults of this jewel-box space focuses on funerary themes and expectations of salvation and its rewards. Above a dado of imitation marble stands a frieze of 34 military saints ready to fulfill their roles as protectors of those buried in the chapel. Above them on the side walls of the main space are stories from the Hebrew Bible interpreted in Byzantine Christianity as prefigurations of the Virgin Mary's intercessory powers. A portrayal of Jacob's ladder (Genesis 28:11–19), for example, evokes her position between heaven and earth as a bridge from death to life. On the pendentives of the dome over the main space (two of which are seen in the foreground), famous Byzantine hymn writers sit at their desks surrounded by quotations from their work. These carefully chosen passages highlight texts associated with funerals, including one that refers to the story of Jacob's ladder.

The climax of the decorative program, however, is the powerful rendering of the **ANASTASIS** that occupies the halfdome of the apse (**FIG. 8–32**). In this popular Byzantine representation of the Resurrection—drawn not from the Bible but from the apocryphal Gospel of Nicodemus—Jesus demonstrates his powers of salvation by descending into limbo after his death on the cross to save his righteous Hebrew forebears from Satan's grasp. Here a boldly striding Christ—brilliantly outfitted in a pure white that makes him shine to prominence within the fresco program—lunges to rescue Adam and Eve from their tombs, pulling them upward with such force that they seem to float under the spell of his power. Satan lies tied into a helpless bundle at his feet, and patriarchs, kings, and prophets look on in admiration, perhaps waiting for their own turn to be rescued. During a funeral in this chapel, the head of the deceased would have been directed toward this engrossing

tableau, closed eyes facing upward toward a painting of the Last Judgment strategically positioned on the vault over the bier. In 1332, this was the location of Metochites's own dead body since this parekklesion was the site of his funeral. He may have been buried in one of the niche tombs cut into the walls of the chapel or within a tomb under the floor of the sanctuary itself, directly under the painted image of the archangel Michael, guardian of souls.

The mosaic decoration Metochites commissioned for the church's expansive narthexes, however, may be the most sumptuous product of his beneficence. Above an expanse of traditional marble revetment on the lower walls, mosaics cover every surface—the domical groin vaults, the wall lunettes, even the undersides of arches—with narrative scenes and their ornamental framework (**FIG. 8–33**). The small-scale figures of these mosaics seem to dance with enthusiasm through the narrative episodes they enact from the lives of Christ and his mother. Unlike the stripped-down narrative scenes of Daphni (SEE FIG. 8–22), here the artists have lavished special attention on the settings, composing their stories against backdrops of architectural fantasies and stylized plants. The architecture of the background is presented in an innovative system of perspective, charting its three-dimensionality not in relation to a point of convergence in the background—as will be the case in the linear, **one-point perspective** of fifteenth-century Florentine art—but projecting forward in relationship to a point in the foreground, thereby drawing attention to the figural scenes themselves.

The Chora mosaics build on the growing Byzantine interest in the expression of emotions within religious narrative, presenting a level of human tenderness that surpasses anything we have seen in Byzantine art thus far. The artists invite viewers to see the participants in these venerable, sacred stories as human beings just like themselves, only wealthier and holier. For example, the entire narrative field in one vault is devoted to a scene where the infant Mary is cuddled between her adoring parents, Joachim and Anna (**FIG. 8–34**; part of the scene is visible in FIG. 8–33). Servants on either side of the family look on with gestures and expressions of admiration and approval, perhaps modeling the response that is expected from viewers within the narthex itself. The human interaction extends to details such as the nuzzling of Mary's head into the beard of her father as she leans back to look into his eyes, and her tentative reach toward her mother's face at the same time. In another scene, the young Jesus rides on the shoulders of Joseph in a pose still familiar to fathers and children today. The informality and believability that these anecdotal details bring to sacred narrative recalls developments as far away as Italy, where at this same time Giotto and Duccio were using similar devices to bring their stories to life (see Chapter 18).

8-33 MOSAICS IN THE VAULTING OF THE INNER NARTHEX

Church of the monastery of Christ in Chora, present-day Istanbul. c. 1315–1321.

Credit: Photo © Ayhan Altun

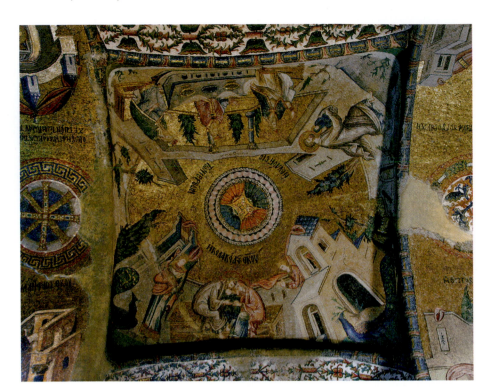

8–34 THE INFANT VIRGIN MARY CARESSED BY HER PARENTS JOACHIM AND ANNA

Lower half of this mosaic in the inner narthex, church of the monastery of Christ in Chora, present-day Istanbul. c. 1315–1321.

The Greek inscription placed over the family group identifies this scene as the fondling of the Theotokos (bearer of God).

Credit: Photo © Ayhan Altun

Icons

Late Byzantine artists of Constantinople created icons as well as painting murals and making mosaics on walls. Among the most dynamic and engaging is a representation of the Annunciation on one side of an early fourteenth-century double-sided icon (**FIG. 8-35**)—the other side has an image of the Virgin and Child—roughly contemporary with the redecoration of the Chora church. This icon was made in the capital, perhaps under imperial patronage, and sent from there to the archbishop of Ohrid. Over 3 feet tall, it was probably mounted on a pole and carried in processions, where both sides would be visible. Characteristic of Constantinopolitan art under the Palaeologues are the small heads, inflated bodies, and light shot-silk clothing of the figures; the forward-projecting perspective of the architecture of background and throne, similar in concept to that of the Chora mosaics (SEE FIG. 8-34); and the fanciful caryatids perched on the tops of the columns.

The practice of venerating icons intensified in Russia during the late Byzantine period; regional schools of icon painting flourished, fostering the work of remarkable artists. One of these was the renowned artist-monk Andrey Rublyov, who created a magnificent icon of **THE HOSPITALITY OF ABRAHAM** sometime between about 1410 and 1425 (**FIG. 8-36**). It was commissioned in honor of Abbot Sergius of the Trinity-Sergius Monastery, near Moscow. The theme is the Trinity, represented here by three identical angels. Rublyov's source for this idea was a story in the Hebrew Bible of the patriarch Abraham and his wife Sarah, who entertained three strangers who were in fact God represented by three divine beings in human form (Genesis 18). Tiny images of Abraham and Sarah's home and the oak of Mamre can be seen above the angels. The food the couple offered to the strangers becomes a chalice on an altarlike table.

Rublyov's icon clearly illustrates how Late Byzantine artists—like the artists of ancient Greece—relied on mathematical conventions to create ideal figures, giving their works remarkable consistency. But unlike the Greeks, who based their formulas on close observation of nature, Byzantine artists invented an ideal geometry to evoke a spiritual realm and conformed their representations of human forms and features to it. Here the circle forms the basic underlying structure for the composition. Despite this formulaic approach, talented artists like Rublyov worked within it to create a personal, expressive style. Rublyov relied on typical Late Byzantine conventions—salient contours, small heads and long bodies, and a focus on a limited number of figures—to capture the sense of the spiritual in his work, yet he distinguished his art by imbuing it with a sweet, poetic ambience.

The Byzantine tradition continued for centuries in the art of the Eastern Orthodox Church and is carried on to this day in Greek and Russian icon painting. But in Constantinople, Byzantine art—like the empire itself—came to an end in 1453. When the forces of the Ottoman sultan Mehmed II overran the capital, the Eastern Empire became part of the Islamic world. The Turkish conquerors were so impressed with the splendor of the Byzantine art and architecture in the capital, however, that they adopted its traditions and melded them with their own rich aesthetic heritage into a new, and now Islamic, artistic efflorescence.

8-35 ANNUNCIATION TO THE VIRGIN

Sent from Constantinople to the church of the Virgin Peribleptos, Ohrid, Macedonia. Early 14th century. Tempera on panel, 36⅝ × 26¾″ (93 × 68 cm). Icon Gallery, Ohrid, Macedonia.

Credit: © 2016. Photo Scala, Florence

8-36 Andrey Rublyov **THE HOSPITALITY OF ABRAHAM**

c. 1410–1425. Tempera on panel, 55½ × 44½″ (141 × 113 cm). Tretyakov State Gallery, Moscow.

Credit: © 2016. Photo Scala, Florence

Think About It

1   Characterize the role of the Classical tradition, already notable in the Early Christian period, in the developing history of Byzantine art. When was it used? In what sorts of contexts? Develop your discussion in relation to two specific examples from two different periods of Byzantine art.

2   Compare the portrayals of the Byzantine rulers in the mosaics of San Vitale in Ravenna (**SEE FIGS. 8–8, 8–9**) and those on a tenth-century ivory plaque (**SEE FIG. 8–26**). Discuss the subjects of the scenes themselves as well as the way the emperor and empress are incorporated within them.

3   How were images used in Byzantine worship? Why were images suppressed during iconoclasm?

4   How do the mosaics of the Chora Church in Constantinople emphasize the human dimensions of sacred stories? Consider in particular how the figures are represented, what kinds of stories are told, and in what way.

Crosscurrents

Both of these grand churches were built under the patronage of powerful rulers and were meant to glorify them as well as serve the Christian community. What features do they share? In what ways are they fundamentally different? What functions did they serve for both Church and state?

FIG. 7–10A

FIG. 8–4A

9–1 Yahya Ibn al-Wasiti THE MAQAMAT OF AL-HARIRI

From Baghdad, Iraq. 1237. Ink, pigments, and gold on paper, 13¾ × 10¼″ (35 × 25 cm). Bibliothèque Nationale, Paris. Arabic MS. 5847, fol. 18v.

Credit: Bibliothèque nationale de France

Chapter 9
Islamic Art

Learning Objectives

9.a Identify the visual hallmarks of Islamic art for formal, technical, and expressive qualities.

9.b Interpret the meaning of works of Islamic art based on their themes, subjects, and symbols.

9.c Relate Islamic artists and art to their cultural, economic, and political contexts.

9.d Apply the vocabulary and concepts relevant to Islamic art, artists, and art history.

9.e Interpret a work of Islamic art using the art historical methods of observation, comparison, and inductive reasoning.

9.f Select visual and textual evidence in various media to support an argument or an interpretation of a work of Islamic art.

THE MAQAMAT ("*Assemblies*") by al-Hariri (1054–1122) belongs to a popular Islamic literary genre of cautionary tales. Al-Hariri's stories revolve around a silver-tongued scoundrel named Abu Zayd, whose cunning inevitably triumphs over other people's naivety. His exploits take place in a world of colorful settings—including desert camps, ships, pilgrim caravans, apothecary shops, mosques, gardens, libraries, cemeteries, and courts of law. Comic stories of trickery in such settings would seem perfectly suited for illustration, and that is the case in this engaging manuscript, made in Baghdad during the thirteenth century. Human activity permeates the compositions. And the vivid visualizations provide us with rare windows into ordinary Muslim life: here, prayer in the congregational **mosque** (**FIG. 9–1**), a religious and social institution at the center of Islamic culture.

The congregation has gathered to hear a sermon preached by the deceitful Abu Zayd, who plans to make off with the alms collection. The men sit directly on the ground, as is customary not only in mosques, but in traditional dwellings. The listener in the front row tilts his chin upward to focus his gaze directly upon the speaker. He is framed and centered by the arch of the **mihrab** (the niche indicating the direction of Mecca) on the rear wall; his white turban contrasts noticeably with the darker gold background. Perhaps he stands in for the manuscript's readers who pause while perusing these illustrations to project themselves into the scene.

The columns of the mosque's arcades have ornamental capitals from which spring half-round arches. Glass mosque lamps hang from the center of each arch. Figures wear turbans and flowing, loose-sleeved robes with epigraphic borders (*tiraz*) embroidered in gold. Abu Zayd delivers his sermon from the steps of a **minbar** (pulpit) with an arched gateway opening at the lowest level. This *minbar* and the arcades that form the backdrop of the scene are reduced in scale so the painter can describe the entire setting and still make the figures the main focus of the composition. Likewise, although in an actual mosque the *minbar* would share the same wall as the *mihrab*, here they have been separated, perhaps to keep the *minbar* from hiding the *mihrab*, and to rivet our attention on what is most important—the rapt attention Abu Zayd commands from his captive audience, a group we ourselves join as we relish the anecdotal and pictorial delights of this splendid example of Islamic visual narrative.

Islam and Early Islamic Society

How do early Islamic society and culture foster the development of new forms of art and architecture?

Islam arose in seventh-century Arabia, a land of desert oases that was sparsely inhabited by tribal nomads and had no cities of great size. Yet under the leadership of its founder, the Prophet Muhammad (c. 570–632 CE), and his successors, Islam spread rapidly throughout northern

Africa, southern and eastern Europe, and into Asia, gaining territory and converts with astonishing speed. Because Islam encompassed geographical areas with a variety of long-established cultural traditions, and because it admitted diverse peoples among its converts, it absorbed and combined many different techniques and ideas about art and architecture. The result was a highly sophisticated artistic eclecticism.

Muslims ("those who have submitted to God") believe that in the desert outside of Mecca in 610 Muhammad received revelations that led him to found the religion called Islam ("submission to God's will"). Many powerful Meccans were hostile to the message preached by the young visionary, and in 622 he and his companions fled to Medina. There Muhammad built a house that became a gathering place for the converted and thus the first mosque. Muslims date their history as beginning with this *hijira* ("emigration").

In 630, Muhammad returned to Mecca with an army of 10,000, routed his enemies, and established the city as the spiritual capital of Islam. After his triumph, he went to the **KAABA** (**FIG. 9-2**), a cubelike, textile-draped shrine said to have been built for God by Ibrahim (Abraham) and Isma'il (Ishmael) and long the focus of pilgrimage and polytheistic worship. He emptied the shrine, repudiating its accumulated pagan idols, while preserving the enigmatic structure itself and dedicating it to God.

The Kaaba is the symbolic center of the Islamic world, the place to which all Muslim prayer is directed, and the ultimate destination of Islam's obligatory pilgrimage, the *hajj*. Each year, huge numbers of Muslims from all over the world travel to Mecca to circumambulate the Kaaba during the month of pilgrimage. The exchange of ideas that occurs during the intermingling of these diverse groups of pilgrims has contributed to Islam's cultural eclecticism.

Muhammad's act of emptying the Kaaba of its pagan idols instituted the fundamental practice of avoiding figural imagery in Islamic religious architecture. This did not, however, lead to a ban on art. Figural imagery is frequent in palaces and illustrated manuscripts, and Islamic artists also elaborated a rich vocabulary of nonfigural ornament, including complex geometric designs and scrolling foliate vines (that Europeans labeled **arabesques**), which were appropriate in all contexts. Islamic art revels in surface

9-2 THE KAABA, MECCA

The Kaaba represents the center of the Islamic world. Its cubelike form is draped with a black textile that is embroidered with a few Qur'anic verses in gold.

Credit: Ayazad/Fotolia

MAP 9–1 THE ISLAMIC WORLD

Within 200 years after 622 CE, the Islamic world expanded from Mecca to India in the east, and to Morocco and Spain in the west.

decoration and in manipulating line, color, and especially pattern, often highlighting the interplay of pure abstraction, organic form, and script.

According to tradition, the Qur'an assumed its final form during the time of the third caliph (successor to the Prophet), Uthman (ruled 644–656). As the language of the Qur'an, Arabic and its script have been a powerful unifying force within Islam. From the eighth through the eleventh centuries, Arabic was the universal language among scholars in the Islamic world and in some Christian lands as well. Inscriptions frequently ornament works of art, sometimes written clearly to provide a readable message, but in other cases written as complex patterns to also delight the eye.

The Prophet was succeeded by a series of caliphs. The accession of Ali as the fourth caliph (ruled 656–661) provoked a power struggle that led to his assassination and resulted in enduring divisions within Islam. Followers of Ali, known as Shi'ites (referring to the party or *shi'a* of Ali), regard him alone as the Prophet's rightful successor. Sunni Muslims, in contrast, recognize all of the first four caliphs as "rightly guided." Ali was succeeded by his rival Muawiya (ruled 661–680), a close relative of Uthman and the founder of the first Muslim dynasty, the Umayyad (661–750).

Islam expanded dramatically. Within two decades, seemingly unstoppable Muslim armies conquered the Sasanian Persian Empire, Egypt, and the Byzantine provinces of Syria and Palestine. By the early eighth century, the Umayyads had reached India, conquered northern Africa and Spain, and penetrated France before being turned back (**MAP 9–1**). In these newly conquered lands, the treatment of Christians and Jews who did not convert to Islam was not consistent, but in general, as "People of the Book"—followers of a monotheistic religion based on a revealed scripture—they enjoyed a protected status, though they were subject to a special tax and restrictions on dress and employment.

Muslims participate in congregational worship at a mosque (*masjid*, "place of prostration"). The Prophet Muhammad himself lived simply and instructed his followers in prayer at his house, now known as the Mosque of the Prophet, where he resided in Medina. This was a square enclosure that framed a large courtyard with rooms along the east wall where he and his family lived. Along the south wall, a thatched portico supported by palm-tree trunks sheltered both the faithful as they prayed and Muhammad as he spoke from a low platform. This simple arrangement inspired the design of later mosques. Without the architectural focus provided by chancels, altars, naves, or domes, the space of this prototypical hypostyle (multi-columned) mosque reflected the founding spirit of Islam in which the faithful pray as equals directly to God, led by an imam, but without the intermediary of a priesthood.

The Five Pillars of Islam

Islam emphasizes a direct personal relationship with God. The Pillars of Islam, sometimes symbolized by an open hand with the five fingers extended, enumerate the duties required of Muslims by their faith.

- The first pillar (*shahadah*) is to proclaim that there is only one God and that Muhammad is his messenger. While monotheism is common to Judaism, Christianity, and Islam, and Muslims worship the God of Abraham while also acknowledging Hebrew and Christian prophets such as Musa (Moses) and Isa (Jesus), Muslims deem the Christian Trinity polytheistic and assert that God was not born and did not give birth.

- The second pillar requires prayer (*salat*) to be performed by turning to face the Kaaba in Mecca five times daily: at dawn, noon, late afternoon, sunset, and nightfall. Prayer can occur almost anywhere, although the prayer on Fridays takes place in the congregational mosque. Because ritual ablutions are required for purity, mosque courtyards usually have fountains.

- The third pillar is the voluntary payment of annual tax or alms (*zakah*), equivalent to one-fortieth of one's assets. *Zakah* is used for charities such as feeding the poor, housing travelers, and paying the dowries of orphan girls. Among Shi'ites, an additional tithe is required to support the Shi'ite community specifically.

- The fourth pillar is the dawn-to-dusk fast (*sawm*) during Ramadan, the month when Muslims believe Muhammad received the revelations set down in the Qur'an. The fast of Ramadan is a communally shared sacrifice that imparts purification, self-control, and fellowship with others. The end of Ramadan is celebrated with the feast day 'Id al-Fitr (Festival of the Breaking of the Fast).

- For those physically and financially able to do so, the fifth pillar is the pilgrimage to Mecca (*hajj*), which ideally is undertaken at least once in the life of each Muslim. Among the extensive pilgrimage rites are donning simple garments to remove distinctions of class and culture; collective circumambulations of the Kaaba; kissing the Black Stone inside the Kaaba (probably a meteorite that fell in pre-Islamic times); and the sacrificing of an animal, usually a sheep, in memory of Abraham's readiness to sacrifice his son at God's command. The end of the *hajj* is celebrated by the festival 'Id al-Adha (Festival of Sacrifice).

The directness and simplicity of Islam have made the Muslim religion readily adaptable to numerous varied cultural contexts throughout history. The Five Pillars instill not only faith and a sense of belonging, but also a commitment to Islam in the form of actual practice.

Early Islamic Art and Architecture

What characterizes the early formation of Islamic art and architecture?

Under the caliphs of the Umayyad dynasty (661–750), while Mecca and Medina remained the holiest Muslim cities, the political center shifted to the Syrian city of Damascus, which became the Umayyad capital in 656. Throughout the Islamic empire the Umayyads built mosques and palaces that projected the authority of the new rulers and reflected the growing acceptance of Islam. In the eastern Mediterranean, they built shrines, mosques, and palaces under the influence of Roman and Byzantine architecture.

In 750 the Abbasid clan replaced the Umayyads in a coup d'état, ruling as caliphs until 1258 from Baghdad, in Iraq. Their long and cosmopolitan reign saw achievements in medicine, mathematics, the natural sciences, philosophy, literature, music, and art. They were generally tolerant of the ethnically diverse populations in the territories they subjugated, and they admired the past achievements of Roman civilization as well as the living traditions of Byzantium, Persia, India, and China, freely borrowing artistic techniques and styles from all of them.

In the tenth century, the Islamic world split into separate kingdoms ruled by independent caliphs. In addition to the Abbasids of Iraq, there was a Fatimid Shi'ite caliph ruling Tunisia and Egypt and a descendant of the Umayyads ruling Spain and Portugal (together then known as al-Andalus). The Islamic world did not reunite under the myriad dynasties who thereafter ruled from northern Africa to Asia, but loss in unity was gain to artistic diversity.

The Dome of the Rock

In the center of Jerusalem rises the Haram al-Sharif ("Noble Sanctuary"), a rocky outcrop from which Muslims believe Muhammad ascended to the presence of God on the "Night Journey" described in the Qur'an, as well as the site of the First and Second Jewish Temples. Jews and Christians variously associate this place with Solomon, the site of the creation of Adam, and the place where the patriarch Abraham prepared to sacrifice his son Isaac at the command of God. In 691–692, a domed shrine was built over the rock (**FIG. 9-3**), employing artists trained in the

9-3A EXTERIOR VIEW OF THE DOME OF THE ROCK, JERUSALEM
Israel. Begun 691.

Credit: © Zoonar GmbH/Alamy Stock Photo

Byzantine tradition to create the first great monument of Islamic art. By assertively appropriating a site holy to Jews and Christians, the Dome of the Rock manifested Islam's view of itself as completing and superseding the prophecies of those faiths.

Structurally, the Dome of the Rock imitates the centrally planned form of Early Christian and Byzantine

9-3B CUTAWAY DRAWING OF THE DOME OF THE ROCK, JERUSALEM
Israel. Begun 691.

Credit: © Dorling Kindersley

martyria (SEE FIGS. 7–14, 8–5). However, unlike the plain exteriors of its models, it is crowned by a golden dome that dominates the skyline. The ceramic tiles on the lower portion of the exterior were added later, but the opulent marble veneer and mosaics of the interior are original. The dome, surmounting a circular drum pierced with windows and supported by arcades of alternating **piers** and columns, covers the central space containing the rock (**FIG. 9–4**), and concentric aisles (ambulatories) permit devout visitors to circumambulate it.

Inscriptions from the Qur'an are interspersed with passages from other texts, including information about the building itself, to form a frieze around the inner and outer arcades. As pilgrims walk around the central space to read the inscriptions in brilliant gold mosaic on turquoise green ground, the building communicates both as a text and as a dazzling visual display. These inscriptions are especially notable because they are the oldest surviving written verses from the Qur'an and the first use of Qur'anic inscriptions in architecture. Below them, the walls are faced with marble—the veining of which creates abstract symmetrical patterns—and the rotunda is surrounded by columns of gray marble with gilded capitals. Above the calligraphic frieze is another mosaic frieze depicting symmetrical vine scrolls and trees in turquoise, blue, and green embellished with imitation jewels over a gold ground. The mosaics are variously thought to represent the gardens of Paradise and trophies of Muslim victories offered to God. Though the decorative program is extraordinarily rich, the focus of the building is neither art nor architecture but the plain rock it shelters.

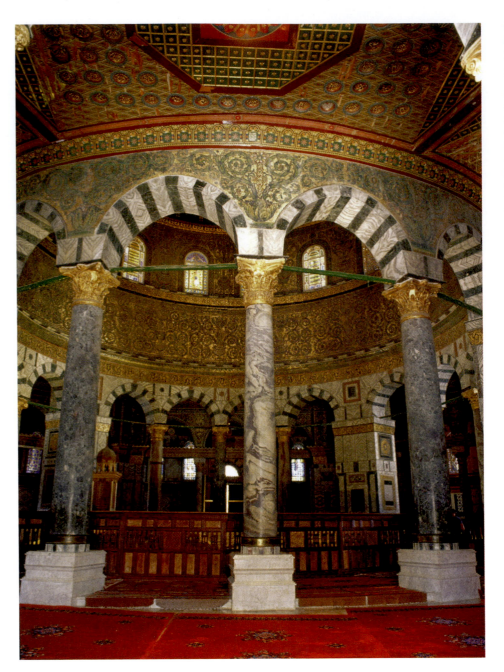

9-4 INTERIOR, DOME OF THE ROCK
Israel. Begun 691.

The arches of the inner and outer face of the central arcade are encrusted with golden mosaics, a Byzantine technique adapted for Islamic use to create ornament and inscriptions. The pilgrim must walk around the central space first clockwise and then counterclockwise to read the inscriptions. The carpets and ceilings are modern but probably reflect the original intent.

Credit: © akg-images/Jean-Louis Nou

The Great Mosque of Damascus

Muslim congregations gather on Fridays for regular worship in a mosque. The earliest mosque type followed the model of the Prophet's own house. The **GREAT MOSQUE** of Damascus (**FIG. 9–5**), built in 706 through the patronage of the Umayyad caliph al-Walid I (ruled 705–715), is a large rectangular space divided into a courtyard surrounded by arcaded porticos on three sides and a broad hypostyle prayer hall oriented toward Mecca. One of the hallmarks of the early hypostyle plan is its system of repeated bays and aisles that can easily be extended as the congregation grows in size. Another characteristic feature is the incorporation of large **minarets** (tall towers from which the faithful are called to prayer) that stand as powerful signs of Islam's presence in the city.

The **qibla** wall—the wall of the prayer hall that is closest to Mecca—included a *mihrab* niche, indicating the direction toward which prayer should be oriented. In the Great Mosque of Damascus, the *qibla* wall is given heightened importance by a perpendicular nave crowned by a dome and intersecting the three long aisles of the prayer hall to mark the axis that extends from the courtyard entrance to the *mihrab*. The *mihrab* (for a fourteenth-century example, SEE FIG. 9–22) belongs to the historical tradition of niches that signify a holy place—the Torah shrine in a synagogue, the frame for sculptures of gods or ancestors in Roman architecture, and the apse in a Christian church.

The design of the Damascus mosque and the architectural forms that compose it recall Roman and Byzantine architecture. An ancient Roman sanctuary platform was

9-5 VIEW FROM ABOVE OF THE GREAT MOSQUE, DAMASCUS
Syria. 706.

Credit: © akg-images/Gerard Degeorge

actually reused for its foundation, and Roman columns and carved stonework were incorporated into the building fabric during its construction. But the lavish glass mosaics encrusting the interior courtyard arcades (**FIG. 9-6**)—portraying lush landscapes and elaborate cityscapes—date from the period of Umayyad construction and were probably created by Byzantine artists from Constantinople.

9-6 MOSAICS ON THE COURTYARD ARCADE OF THE GREAT MOSQUE, DAMASCUS
Syria. 706–715.

Credit: © age fotostock/Mondadori Portfolio/Luca Mozzati

The Great Mosque of Cordoba

When the Umayyads were toppled in 750, a survivor of the dynasty, Abd al-Rahman I (ruled 756–788), fled across north Africa into southern Spain (al-Andalus) where with the support of Muslim settlers he established himself as the provincial ruler, or emir. This newly transplanted Umayyad dynasty ruled in Spain from its capital in Cordoba (756–1031). The Hispano-Umayyads were noted patrons of the arts, and one of the finest surviving examples of Umayyad architecture is the Great Mosque of Cordoba (**FIGS. 9–7, 9–8**).

In 785, the Umayyad conquerors began building the Cordoba mosque on the site of a Christian church built by the Visigoths, the pre-Islamic rulers of Spain. The choice of site was both practical—the Muslims had already been renting space within the church—and symbolic, an appropriation of place (similar to the Dome of the Rock) that affirmed their presence. Later rulers expanded the building three times, and today the walls enclose an area of about 620 by 460 feet, about a third of which is the courtyard. This patio was planted with fruit trees beginning in the early ninth century; today orange trees seasonally fill the space with color and sweet scent. Inside, the proliferation of pattern in the repeated columns and double flying arches is both colorful and dramatic. The marble columns and capitals in the hypostyle prayer hall were recycled from the Christian church that had formerly occupied the site, as well as from classical buildings in the region, which had been a wealthy Roman province. The mosque's interior incorporates *spolia* (reused) columns of slightly varying heights. There are two tiers of arches, one over the other, above these columns, the upper tier springing from rectangular piers that rise from the columns. This double-tiered design dramatically increases the height of the interior space, inspiring a sense of awe. The distinctively shaped **horseshoe arches**—a form known from Roman times and favored by the Visigoths—came to be

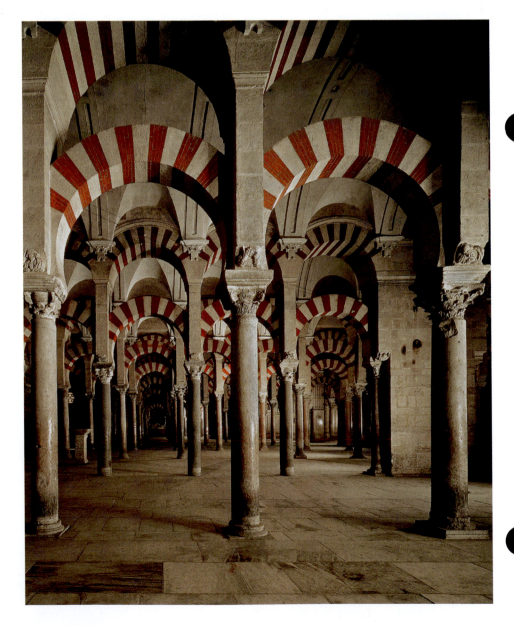

9–7 PRAYER HALL, GREAT MOSQUE, CORDOBA

Spain. Begun 785/786.

Credit: © Raffaello Bencini/Archivi Alinari, Firenze

Elements of Architecture
ARCHES

The simple **semicircular arch**, inherited from the Romans and Byzantines, has a single center point that is level with the points from which the arch springs.

Credit: Kathy Mrozek

The **horseshoe arch** pre-dates Islam but became the prevalent arch form in the West (SEE FIG. 9–7). The center point is above the level of the arch's springing point, so that it pinches inward above the capital.

The **pointed arch**, introduced after the beginning of Islam, has two (sometimes four) center points, the points generating different circles that overlap (SEE FIG. 9–16).

A **keel arch** has flat sides, and slopes where other arches are curved. It culminates at a pointed apex (SEE FIG. 9–22).

9-8 PLAN OF THE GREAT MOSQUE, CORDOBA
Begun 785/786.

closely associated with Islamic architecture in the West (see "Arches" above). Another distinctive feature of these arches, adopted from Roman and Byzantine precedents, is the alternation of white stone and red-brick voussoirs forming the curved arch. This mixture of materials may have helped the building withstand earthquakes.

In the final century of Umayyad rule, Cordoba emerged as a major commercial and intellectual hub and a flourishing center for the arts, surpassing Christian European cities in science, literature, and philosophy. As a sign of this new wealth, prestige, and power, Abd al-Rahman III (ruled 912–961) boldly reclaimed the title of caliph in 929. He and his son al-Hakam II (ruled 961–976) made the Great Mosque a focus of patronage, commissioning costly and luxurious renovations such as a new *mihrab* with three bays in front of it (**FIG. 9–9**). These capped the **maqsura**, an enclosure in front of the *mihrab* reserved for the ruler and other dignitaries, which became a feature of congregational mosques after an assassination attempt on one of the Umayyad rulers. A *minbar* formerly stood by the *mihrab* as the place for the prayer leader and as a symbol of

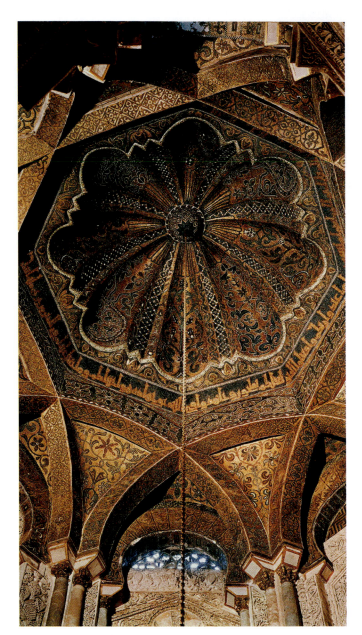

9–9 DOME IN FRONT OF THE MIHRAB, GREAT MOSQUE, CORDOBA

965.

Credit: © Raffaello Bencini/Archivi Alinari, Firenze

authority. The melon-shaped, ribbed dome over the central bay may be a metaphor for the celestial canopy. It seems to float upon a web of crisscrossing arches, the complexity of the design reflecting the Islamic interest in mathematics and geometry, not purely as abstract concepts but as sources for artistic inspiration. Lushly patterned mosaics with inscriptions, geometric motifs, and stylized vegetation clothe both this dome and the *mihrab* below in brilliant color and gold. These were installed by a Byzantine master sent by the emperor in Constantinople, who brought with him boxes of small glazed ceramic and glass pieces (tesserae). Such artistic exchange is emblematic of the interconnectedness of the medieval Mediterranean—through trade, diplomacy, and competition.

Minbar from the Kutubiya Mosque in Marrakesh

In the Kutubiya Mosque, the principal mosque of Marrakesh, Morocco, survives an exceptionally exquisite twelfth-century wooden **minbar** made originally for the Booksellers' Mosque in Marrakesh (**FIG. 9–10**). It consists of a staircase from which the weekly sermon was delivered to the congregation (SEE FIG. 9–1), and it is completely covered with intricate ornament. The sides are paneled in wooden marquetry with strapwork in a geometric pattern of eight-pointed stars and elongated hexagons inlaid with ivory (see "Ornament" on page 279). Wood carved in swirling vines fills the areas between the strapwork. Reflecting the arcades of its original architectural context, the risers of the stairs represent horseshoe arches (see "Arches" on page 277) resting on columns with ivory capitals and bases. This *minbar* is much like others across the Islamic world, but those at the Kutubiya Mosque and the Great Mosque of Cordoba were the finest, according to Ibn Marzuq (1311–1379), a distinguished preacher who had given sermons from 48 *minbars*.

9–10 MINBAR

From the Kutubiya Mosque, Marrakesh, Morocco. 1125–1130. Wood and ivory, 12′8″ × 11′4″ × 2′10″ (3.86 × 3.46 × 0.87 m). Badi Palace Museum, Marrakesh.

Credit: © akg-images/Erich Lessing

Art and its Contexts

ORNAMENT

Islamic art delights in complex ornament that sheathes surfaces, distracting the eye from the underlying structure or physical form.

Credit: © akg-images/François Guénet

ablaq masonry (Madrasa-Mausoleum-Mosque of Sultan Hasan, Cairo; SEE FIG. 9–16) juxtaposes stone of contrasting colors. The ornamental effect is enhanced here by the interlocking jigsaw shape of the blocks, called **joggled voussoirs**.

Credit: © Alen Laguta/123RF

cut tile (Shah-i Zinda, Samarkand; SEE FIG. 9–23), made up of dozens of individually cut ceramic tile pieces fitted precisely together, emphasizes the clarity of the colored shapes.

Credit: © VLADJ55/Shutterstock

muqarnas (Palace of the Lions, Alhambra, Granada; SEE FIG. 9–21) consist of small nichelike components, usually stacked in multiples as successive, non-load-bearing units in arches, cornices, and domes, hiding the transition from the vertical to the horizontal plane.

Credit: © akg Images/Erich Lessing

wooden strapwork (Kutubiya *minbar*, Marrakesh; SEE FIG. 9–10) assembles finely cut wooden pieces to create the appearance of geometrically interlacing ribbons, often framing smaller panels of carved wood and inlaid ivory or mother-of-pearl (shell).

Credit: © B.O'Kane/Alamy Stock Photo

mosaic (Dome of the Rock, Jerusalem; SEE FIG. 9–4) is comprised of thousands of small glass or glazed ceramic tesserae set on a plaster ground. Here the luminous white circular shapes are mother-of-pearl.

Credit: Loisclare/Fotolia

water (Court of the Myrtles, Alhambra, Granada) as a fluid architectural element reflects surrounding architecture, adds visual dynamism and sound, and, running in channels between areas, unites disparate spaces.

Credit: Credit: K.M. Westermann

chini khana (Ali Qapu Pavilion, Isfahan)—literally "china cabinet"—is a panel of niches, sometimes providing actual shelving, but used here for its contrast of material and void which reverses the typical figure–ground relationship.

Calligraphy

From the beginning, Arabic script was held in high esteem in Islamic society. Reverence for the Qur'an as the word of God extended—and continues to extend—by association to the act of writing itself, and **calligraphy** (the art of the finely written word) became one of the glories of Islamic art. Writing was not limited to books and documents but—as we have seen—was displayed on the walls of buildings and will appear on works in many media throughout the history of Islamic art. The written word played two roles: It could convey information about a building or object, describing its beauty or naming its patron, and it could delight the eye as a manifestation of beauty.

Arabic script is written from right to left, and a letter's form varies depending on its position in a word. With its rhythmic interplay between verticals and horizontals, Arabic lends itself to many variations. Calligraphers enjoyed the highest status of all artists in Islamic society. Apprentice scribes had to learn secret formulas for inks and paints and become skilled in the proper ways to sit, breathe, and manipulate their tools. They also had to absorb the complex literary traditions and number symbolism that had developed in Islamic culture. Their training was long and arduous, but unlike other artists, who were generally anonymous in the early centuries of Islam, outstanding calligraphers received public recognition.

Formal **Kufic** script (after Kufa, a city in Iraq) is blocky and angular, with strong upright strokes and long horizontals. It may have developed first for carved or woven inscriptions where clarity and practicality of execution were important. Most early Qur'ans were horizontal in orientation and had large Kufic letters creating only three to five lines per page. Visual clarity was essential because one book was often shared simultaneously by multiple readers. A page from a ninth-century Syrian Qur'an exemplifies the style common from the eighth to the tenth century (**FIG. 9-11**). Red diacritical marks (pronunciation guides) accent the dark brown ink; the surah ("chapter") title is embedded in the burnished ornament at the bottom of the sheet. Instead of page numbers, the brilliant gold of the framed words and the knoblike projection in the left-hand margin mark chapter breaks.

By the tenth century, more than 20 cursive scripts had come into use. They were standardized by Ibn Muqla (d. 940), an Abbasid official who fixed the proportions of the letters in each script and devised a method for teaching calligraphy that is still in use today. The Qur'an was usually written on parchment (treated sheep- or calfskin) and vellum (a fine parchment made of calfskin). Paper was first manufactured in Central Asia during the mid eighth century, having been introduced earlier by Buddhist monks. Muslims learned how to make high-quality, rag-based paper and eventually established their own paper mills. By about 1000, paper had largely replaced the more costly parchment for everything but Qur'an manuscripts, which adopted the new medium much later. It was a change as momentous as that brought about by movable type or the Internet, affecting not only the appearance of books but also their content. The inexpensive new medium sparked a surge in book production and a proliferation of increasingly elaborate and decorative cursive scripts, which had generally superseded Kufic by the thirteenth century.

Kufic script remained popular, however, in other media. It was the sole decoration on a type of white pottery made from the tenth century onward in and around the region of Nishapur (in Khurasan, in present-day Iran) and Samarkand (in present-day Uzbekistan) known as epigraphic ware. These elegant earthenware bowls and plates employ a clear lead glaze over a painted black inscription on a white slip ground (**FIG. 9-12**). Here the script's horizontals and verticals have been elongated to

9-11 PAGE FROM THE QUR'AN

Surah 2:286 and title of surah 3 in Kufic script. Syria. 9th century. Black ink, pigments, and gold on vellum; 8⅜ × 11⅛″ (21.8 × 29.2 cm). Metropolitan Museum of Art, New York. Rogers Fund, 1937. (37.99.2).

Credit: © 2016. Image copyright The Metropolitan Museum/ Art Resource/Scala, Florence

9-12 PLATE WITH KUFIC BORDER
From Khurasan. 10th–12th century. Earthenware with white and black slip, and lead glaze; diameter 14½" (33.8 cm). Musée du Louvre, Paris.

Credit: Photo © RMN/Thierry Ollivier

fill the plate's rim, stressing the letters' verticality in such a way that they seem to radiate from the bold spot at the center of the circle. The fine quality of the lettering indicates that a calligrapher furnished the model. The inscription translates as "Knowledge [or magnanimity]: the beginning of it is bitter to taste, but the end is sweeter than honey," an apt choice for tableware made to appeal to an educated patron. Inscriptions on Islamic ceramics provide a storehouse of such popular aphorisms.

Developments in Ceramics

In the ninth century, Islamic potters developed a means of producing a lustrous metallic surface on their ceramics. They may have learned the technique from Islamic glassmakers in Syria and Egypt, who had produced luster-painted vessels a century earlier. First the potters applied a paint laced with silver, copper, or gold oxides to the surface of already fired and glazed tiles or vessels. In a second firing with relatively low heat and less oxygen, these oxides burned away to produce a reflective, metallic sheen. The finished **lusterware** resembled precious metal. Lusterware tiles dated 862/863 decorated the *mihrab* of the Great Mosque at Kairouan. At first a carefully guarded secret of Abbasid potters in Iraq, lusterware soon spread throughout the Islamic world to North Africa, Egypt, Iran, Syria, and Spain.

Early potters covered the entire surface with luster, but soon they began to use luster to paint patterns using geometric designs, foliate motifs, animals, and human figures in brown, red, purple, and/or green. Most common was monochrome lusterware in shades of brown, as in this tenth-century jar from Iraq (**FIG. 9-13**). The form of the vessel is emphasized by the distribution of decorative motifs—the lip and neck are outlined with a framed horizontal band of scalloped motifs, the shoulder singled out with dots within circles (known as the "peacock's eye"

9-13 LUSTERWARE JAR
Iraq. 10th century. Glazed earthenware with luster, 11⅛ × 9⅛" (28.2 × 23.2 cm). Freer Gallery of Art, Smithsonian Institution, Washington, DC.

Credit: Bridgeman Images

9-14 MINA'I BOWL WITH BAHRAM GUR AND AZADA
Iran. 12th–13th century. *Mina'i* ware (stoneware with polychrome in-glaze and overglaze), diameter 8½" (21.6 cm). Metropolitan Museum of Art, New York.

Credit: © 2016 Image copyright The Metropolitan Museum of Art/Art Resource/Scala, Florence

foolishly belittled his skills as a hunter. To prove his peerless marksmanship, the king pins with his arrow the hoof and ear of a gazelle that had lifted its hind leg to scratch an itch. In this continuous narrative (representing multiple scenes from the same story within a single composition), the subsequent action is also portrayed: Azada trampled to death under the camel after Bahram Gur had pushed her from her mount as punishment for mocking him.

motif), and the height emphasized by boldly ornamented vertical strips with undulating outlines moving up toward pointed tops and dividing the surface of the jar into quadrants. Emphasis, however, is placed on representations of enigmatic human figures dressed in dark, hooded garments. They stand in bended postures and hold beaded strands while looking directly out toward viewers, engaged in an activity whose meaning and significance remains a mystery to us.

MINA'I WARE From the beginning, Islamic civilization in Iran was characterized by the production of exceptionally sophisticated and strikingly beautiful luxury ceramic ware. During the twelfth century, Persian potters developed a technique of multicolor ceramic overglaze painting known as *mina'i* ware, the Persian word for "enamel" (**FIG. 9-14**). *Mina'i* bowl, plate, and beaker decoration often references stories and subjects popular with potential owners. The circular scene at the bottom of this bowl is drawn from the royal life of Bahram Gur (Sasanian king Bahram V, ruled 420–438), legendary in the Islamic world for his prowess in love and hunting; this episode combines both. Bahram Gur rides proudly atop a large camel next to his favorite, the ill-fated lute player Azada, who has

Regional Dynasties

How do Islamic art and architecture develop in Egypt, Spain, Iran, Uzbekistan, and Afghanistan?

The Abbasid caliphate began a slow disintegration in the ninth century, and power in the Islamic world became distributed among more or less independent regional rulers. During the eleventh century, the Saljuqs, a Turkic people, swept from north of the Caspian Sea into Khurasan and took Baghdad in 1055, becoming the virtual rulers of the Abbasid lands. The Saljuqs united most of Iran and Iraq, establishing a dynasty that endured from 1037/38 to 1194. A branch of the dynasty, the Saljuqs of Rum, ruled much of Anatolia (Turkey) from the late eleventh to the beginning of the fourteenth century. The central and eastern Islamic world suffered a dramatic rift in the early thirteenth century when the nomadic Mongols—non-Muslims led by Genghiz Khan (ruled 1206–1227) and his successors—attacked northern China, Central Asia, and ultimately Iran. The Mongols captured Baghdad in 1258 and encountered weak resistance until they reached Egypt, where they were firmly defeated by the new ruler of the Mamluk dynasty (1250–1517). In Spain, the borders of Islamic territory were gradually pushed southward by Christian forces until the rule of the last Muslim dynasty there, the Nasrids (1230–1492), was ended. Morocco was ruled by the Berber Marinids from the mid thirteenth century until 1465.

Although the religion of Islam remained a dominant and unifying force throughout these developments, the history of later Islamic society and culture reflects largely regional phenomena. Only a few works have been selected here and in Chapter 24 to characterize Islamic art, and they by no means provide a comprehensive history.

The new dynasties built on a grand scale, expanding their patronage from mosques and palaces to include new functional buildings such as tombs, **madrasas** (colleges for religious and legal studies), public fountains, and urban hostels. To encourage long-distance trade, remote caravanserais (inns) were constructed for traveling merchants. A distinguishing characteristic of architecture in the later period is its complexity. Multiple building types were now combined in large and diverse complexes supported by perpetual endowments (called *waqf*) that funded not only the building, but its administration and maintenance. Increasingly, these complexes included the patron's own tomb, thus giving visual prominence to the act of individual patronage and expressing personal identity through commemoration. A new plan emerged, organized around a central courtyard framed by four large **iwans** (large vaulted halls with rectangular plans and monumental arched openings); this four-*iwan* plan was used for schools, palaces, and especially mosques.

The Mamluks in Egypt

Beginning in the eleventh century, Muslim rulers and wealthy individuals endowed hundreds of charitable complexes that displayed piety as well as personal wealth and status. The combined *madrasa*-mausoleum-mosque complex established in mid-fourteenth-century Cairo by the Mamluk Sultan Hasan (**FIG. 9–15**) is a splendid example. A deflected entrance—askew from the building's orientation—leads from the street, through a dark corridor, into a central, well-lit courtyard of majestic proportions. The complex has a classic four-*iwan* plan, each *iwan* serving as a classroom for students following a different branch of study who are housed in a surrounding, multi-storied cluster of tiny rooms.

The sumptuous *qibla iwan* served as the prayer hall for the complex (**FIG. 9–16**). Its walls are ornamented with typically Mamluk panels of sharply contrasting marbles (*ablaq* masonry, see "Ornament" on page 279) that culminate in a doubly recessed *mihrab* framed by slightly pointed arches on columns. The marble blocks of the arches are ingeniously joined in interlocking pieces called joggled voussoirs. The paneling is surmounted by a wide band of

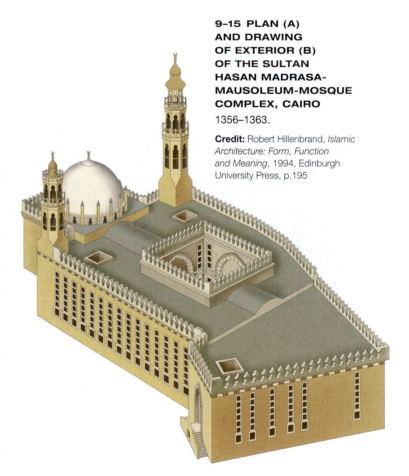

9–15 PLAN (A) AND DRAWING OF EXTERIOR (B) OF THE SULTAN HASAN MADRASA-MAUSOLEUM-MOSQUE COMPLEX, CAIRO
1356–1363.

Credit: Robert Hillenbrand, *Islamic Architecture: Form, Function and Meaning*, 1994, Edinburgh University Press, p.195

Kufic script in stucco set against a background of scrolling vines, both the text and the abundant foliage referring to the paradise that is promised to the faithful. Next to the *mihrab,* an elaborate *minbar* stands behind a platform for reading the Qur'an. Just beyond the *qibla iwan* is the patron's monumental domed tomb, ostentatiously asserting his identity with the architectural complex. The Sultan Hasan complex is vast in scale and opulent in decoration, but money was not a problem: The project was financed by the estates of victims of the bubonic plague that had raged in Cairo from 1348 to 1350.

GLASS, METALWORK, AND BOOK ARTS Partly because the mosque in the Sultan Hasan complex—and many smaller establishments—required hundreds of lamps, glassmaking was a booming industry in Egypt and Syria. Made of ordinary sand and ash, glass is the most ethereal of materials. The ancient Egyptians were producing glassware by the second millennium BCE (see Chapter 3), and the tools and techniques for making it have changed little since then. Islamic artists also used glass for beakers and bottles, but lamps, lit from within by oil and wick, glowed with special brilliance inside expansive architectural interiors (see "Closer Look" opposite).

Islamic metalsmiths enlivened the surface of vessels with scrolls, interlacing designs, human and animal figures, and calligraphic inscriptions. A shortage of silver in the mid twelfth century prompted the development of inlaid brasswork that used the more precious metal

sparingly, as in this basin (**FIG. 9-17**), among the finest works of metal produced by a Muslim artist. The dynamic surface is crowded with overlapping figures in vigorous poses that nevertheless remain distinct by means of hatching, modeling, and framing. The outside is divided into three bands. The upper and lower depict running animals, and the center shows scenes of horsemen flanked by attendants, soldiers, and falcons—scenes of the princely arts of horsemanship and hunting. In later metalwork, such pictorial cycles were replaced by elegant large-scale inscriptions.

The art of book production had flourished from the first century of Islam because an emphasis on the study of the Qur'an promoted a high level of literacy among both men and women. With the availability of paper, books on a wide range of religious as well as secular subjects became available, although since they were hand-copied, they always remained fairly costly. (Muslims did not adopt the printing press until the eighteenth and nineteenth centuries.) Libraries, often associated with *madrasas,* were endowed by members of the educated elite. Books made for royal patrons had luxurious bindings and highly embellished pages, the result of workshop collaboration between noted calligraphers and illustrators.

Mamluk manuscript illustrators executed intricate nonfigural designs filled with sumptuous botanical ornamentation for Qur'ans. As in architectural decoration, the exuberant ornament adheres to a strict geometric organization. On an impressive frontispiece, the design radiates on each page from a 16-pointed starburst, filling the central

9-16 QIBLA WALL WITH MIHRAB AND MINBAR
Sultan Hasan Madrasa-Mausoleum-Mosque Complex, Cairo. 1356–1363.

Credit: © B.O'Kane/Alamy Stock Photo

9–17 Muhammad Ibn al-Zain
BAPTISTERY OF ST. LOUIS
Syria or Egypt. c. 1300. Brass inlaid with silver and gold, 8¾ × 19¾″ (22.2 × 50.2 cm). Musée du Louvre, Paris.

Judging by its emblems and coats of arms, this beautifully crafted basin, with its princely themes of hunting and horsemanship, was made for an unidentified, aristocratic Mamluk patron. However, it became known as the Baptistery of St. Louis because it was acquired by the French sometime before the end of the fourteenth century (long after the era of St. Louis [king Louis IX, ruled 1226–1270]) and used for royal baptisms.

Credit: Photo © RMN-Grand Palais (Musée du Louvre)/Franck Raux

A Closer Look

A MAMLUK GLASS OIL LAMP

The inscription on the lamp's flared neck is a quotation from the Qur'an (surah 24:35): "God is the light of the heavens and the earth. His light might be compared to a niche that enshrines a lamp, the lamp within a crystal of star-like brilliance."

This emblem of a cup in a medallion is called a blazon. It identifies the commissioner of the lamp as a cup-bearer to the sultan. The use of blazons traveled to western Europe during the crusades, where it evolved into the system we know as heraldry.

During the thirteenth and fourteenth centuries, Mamluk glassmakers in Egypt and Syria imparted an elegant thinness to their vessels through refined glass-blowing and molding techniques. The blue, red, and gold enamel used to decorate the lamp was affixed to the glass surface by reheating the painted vessel.

This inscription around the body of the lamp identifies the patron, Sayf al-Din Qawsun (d. 1342), emir and cup-bearer of the Mamluk sultan al-Nasir Muhammad (ruled 1293–1341). It was probably intended for one of the patron's architectural commissions in Cairo.

The artist, 'Ali ibn Muhammad al-Barmaki, signed this work discreetly on the upper band of the foot, asking for God's protection.

9–18 'Ali ibn Muhammad al-Barmaki **GLASS OIL LAMP**
Cairo, Egypt. c. 1329–1335. Blown glass, polychrome enamel, and gold; diameter 9⅜″ (23.89 cm), height 14″ (35.56 cm). Metropolitan Museum of Art, New York.

Credit: © 2016. Image copyright The Metropolitan Museum of Art/Art Resource/Scala, Florence

9-19 QUR'AN FRONTISPIECE

Cairo. c. 1368. Ink, pigments, and gold on paper, 24 × 18″ (61 × 45.7 cm). National Library, Cairo. MS. 7.

The Qur'an to which this page belonged was donated in 1369 by Sultan Shaban to the *madrasa* established by his mother. A close collaboration between illuminator and scribe can be seen here and throughout the manuscript.

Credit: From: *Qur'ans of the Mamluks* by David James, fig. 132, p. 132. Courtesy of Alexandria Press

square (**FIG. 9-19**). The surrounding frames contain interlacing foliage and stylized flowers that embellish the holy scripture. The page's resemblance to court carpets was not coincidental. Designers often worked in more than one medium, leaving the execution of their efforts to specialized artisans. In addition to religious works, scribes copied and recopied famous secular texts—scientific treatises, manuals of all kinds, stories, and especially poetry. Painters supplied illustrations for these books and also created individual small-scale paintings—miniatures—that were collected by the wealthy and placed in albums.

The Nasrids in Spain

Muslim patrons also spent lavishly on luxurious palaces set in gardens. The Alhambra in Granada, in southeastern Spain, is an outstanding and sumptuous example. Built on the hilltop site of an early Islamic fortress, this palace complex was the seat of the Nasrids (1232–1492), the last Spanish Muslim dynasty, by which time Islamic territory

had shrunk from covering most of the Iberian peninsula to covering only the region around Granada. To the conquering Christians at the end of the fifteenth century, the Alhambra represented the epitome of luxury. Thereafter, they preserved the complex as much to commemorate the defeat of Islam as for its beauty. Essentially a small town extending for about half a mile along the crest of a high hill overlooking Granada, it included government buildings, royal residences, gates, mosques, baths, servants' quarters, barracks, stables, a mint, workshops, and gardens. Much of what one sees at the site today was built in the fourteenth century or by Christian patrons in later centuries.

The Alhambra offered dramatic views of the settled valley and snowcapped mountains around it, while enclosing gardens within its courtyards. One of these is the **COURT OF THE LIONS**, which stood at the heart of the so-called Palace of the Lions, the private retreat of Sultan Muhammad V (ruled 1354–1359 and 1362–1391). The Court of the Lions is divided into quadrants by cross-axial walkways—a garden form called a *chahar bagh*. The walkways carry channels that meet at a central marble fountain held aloft on the backs of 12 stone lions (**FIG. 9-20**). Water animates the fountain, filling the courtyard with the sound of its abundance. In an adjacent courtyard, the Court of the Myrtles, a basin's round shape responds to the naturally concentric ripples of the water that spouts from a central jet (see "Ornament" on page 279). Water has a practical role in the irrigation of gardens, but here it is raised to the level of an art form.

The Court of the Lions is encircled by an arcade of stucco arches embellished with **muqarnas** (nichelike components stacked in tiers, see "Ornament" on page 279) and supported on single columns or clusters of two and three. Second-floor **miradors**—windows that frame intentional views—look over the courtyard, which was originally either gardened or more likely paved, with aromatic citrus confined to corner plantings. Protected from view by the latticework screens in these windows, the women of the court, who did not appear in public, would watch the activities of the men below. At one end of the Palace of the Lions, a particularly magnificent *mirador* looks out onto a large, lower garden and the plain below. From here, the sultan literally oversaw the fertile valley that was his kingdom.

Pavilions used for dining and musical performances open off the Court of the Lions. One of these, the so-called Hall of the Abencerrajes, in addition to having excellent acoustics, is covered by a ceiling of dazzling geometrical complexity and exquisitely carved stucco (**FIG. 9-21**). The star-shaped vault is formed by a honeycomb of clustered *muqarnas* arches that alternate with corner squinches themselves filled with more *muqarnas*. The square room thus rises to an eight-pointed star, pierced by 16 windows, that culminates in a burst of *muqarnas* floating high overhead—a dematerialized architectural form, perceivable and yet ultimately unknowable, like the heavens themselves.

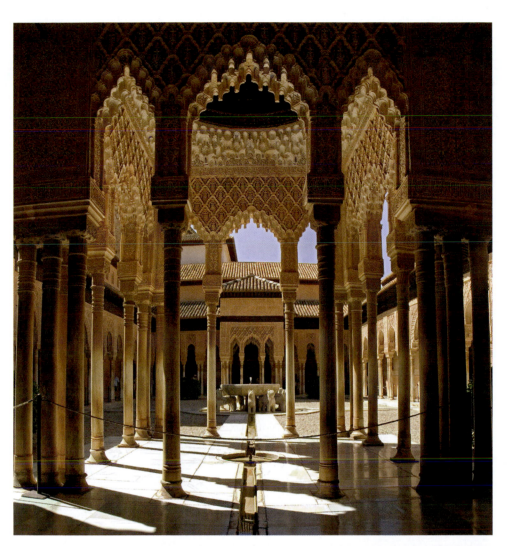

9-20 COURT OF THE LIONS, ALHAMBRA

Granada, Spain. 1354–1391.

Credit: Rafael Ramirez/Fotolia

9-21 MUQARNAS DOME, HALL OF THE ABENCERRAJES, PALACE OF THE LIONS, ALHAMBRA

Granada, Spain. 1354–1391.

The stucco *muqarnas* (stalactite) ornament does not support the dome but is actually suspended from it, composed of some 5,000 individual plaster pieces. Of mesmerizing complexity, the vault's effect can be perceived, but its structure cannot be fully comprehended.

Credit: © Roberto Tetsuo Okamura/ Shutterstock

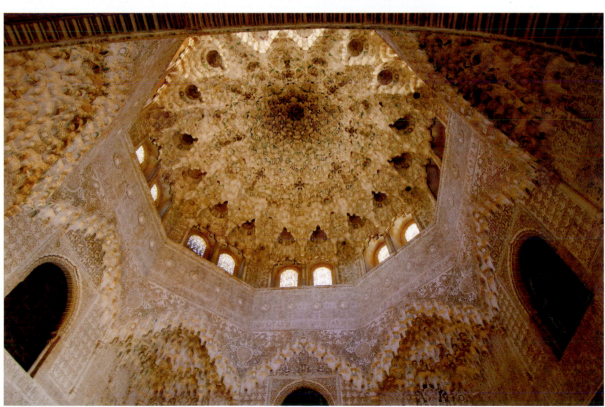

The Timurids in Iran, Uzbekistan, and Afghanistan

The Mongol invasions brought devastation and political instability, but also renewal and artistic exchange that provided the foundation for successor dynasties with a decidedly Eastern identity. One of the empires to emerge after the Mongols was the vast Timurid Empire (1370–1506), which conquered Iran, Central Asia, and the northern part of South Asia. Its founder, Timur (known in the West as Tamerlane), was a Mongol descendant, his lineage strengthened through marriage to a descendant of Genghiz Khan. Timur made his capital at Samarkand (in present-day Uzbekistan), which he embellished

9-22 TILE MOSAIC MIHRAB
From the Madrasa Imami, Isfahan, Iran. Founded 1354. Glazed and cut tiles, 11′3″ × 9′5¹¹⁄₁₆″ (3.43 × 2.89 m). Metropolitan Museum of Art, New York. Harris Brisbane Dick Fund. (39.20).

This *mihrab* has three inscriptions: the outer inscription, in cursive, contains Qur'anic verses (surah 9) that describe the duties of believers and the Five Pillars of Islam. Framing the niche's pointed arch, a Kufic inscription contains sayings of the Prophet. In the center, a panel with a line in Kufic and another in cursive states: "The mosque is the house of every pious person."

Credit: © 2016. Image copyright The Metropolitan Museum of Art/Art Resource/ Scala, Florence

by means of the forcible relocation of expert artists from the areas he conquered. Because the empire's compass was vast, Timurid art could integrate Chinese, Persian, Turkic, and Mediterranean artistic ideas into a Mongol base. Its architecture is characterized by axial symmetry, tall double-shelled domes (an inner dome capped by an outer shell of much larger proportions), modular planning with rhythmically repeated elements, and brilliant cobalt blue, turquoise, and white glazed ceramics. Although the empire itself lasted only 100 years after the death of Timur, its legacy endured in the art of the later Safavid dynasty in Iran and the Mughals of South Asia.

Made during a period of uncertainty as Iran shifted from Mongol to Timurid rule, this *mihrab* (1354), originally from a *madrasa* in Isfahan, is one of the finest examples of architectural ceramic decoration from this era (**FIG. 9-22**). More than 11 feet tall, it was made by painstakingly cutting each individual piece of tile, including the pieces making up the letters on the curving surface of the keel-profiled niche. The color scheme—white against turquoise and cobalt blue with accents of dark yellow and green—was typical of this type of decoration, as were the harmonious, dense, contrasting patterns of organic and geometric forms. The cursive inscription of the outer frame is rendered in elegant white lettering on a blue ground, while the Kufic inscription bordering the pointed arch reverses these colors for a striking contrast.

Near Samarkand, the preexisting Shah-i Zinda ("Living King") **FUNERARY COMPLEX** was adopted for the tombs of Timurid family members, especially princesses, in the late fourteenth and fifteenth centuries (**FIG. 9-23**). The mausolea are arrayed along a central avenue that descends from the tomb of Qutham b. Abbas (a cousin of the Prophet and a saint). The women sought burial in the vicinity of the holy man in order to gain *baraka* (blessing) from his presence. Like all Timurid architecture, the tombs reflect modular planning—noticeable in the repeated dome-on-square unit—and a preference for blue glazed tiles. The domes of the individual structures were double-shelled and, for exaggerated effect, stood on high drums inscribed with Qur'anic verses in interwoven Kufic calligraphy. The ornament on the exterior façades consists of an unusually exuberant array of patterns and techniques, from geometry to chinoiserie, and both painted and cut tiles (see "Ornament" on page 279). The tombs reflect a range of individual taste and artistic experimentation that was possible precisely because they were private commissions that served the patrons themselves, rather than the city or state (as in a congregational mosque).

BOOK ARTS One of the great royal centers of Islamic miniature painting was at Herat in western Afghanistan, where a Persian **school of painting** and calligraphy was

9-23 SHAH-I ZINDA FUNERARY COMPLEX
Samarkand, Uzbekistan. Late 14th–15th century.

Timurid princesses were buried here and built many of the tombs. The lively experimentation in varied artistic motifs indicates that women were well versed in the arts and empowered to exercise personal taste.

Credit: © Evgeniy Agarkov/Shutterstock

founded by the Timurids in the early fifteenth century. One of the most famous painters of the Herat School was Kamal al-Din Bihzad (c. 1450–1536/37), who worked under the patronage of Sultan Husayn Bayqara (ruled 1470–1506). When the Safavids supplanted the Timurids in 1506/07 and established their capital at Tabriz in northwestern Iran, Bihzad moved to Tabriz, where he headed the Safavid royal workshop.

Bihzad's key paintings, including his only signed works, appear in a manuscript of the thirteenth-century Persian poet Sa'di's *Bustan* ("Orchard") made for the royal library in 1488. Sa'di's narrative anthology in verse includes the story of Yusuf, the biblical Joseph, whose virtue was proven by resisting seduction by his master Potiphar's wife, named Zulayhka in the Islamic tradition (Genesis 39:6–12; Qur'an 12:23–25). Bihzad's vizualization of this event (**FIG. 9-24**) is one of the masterpieces of Persian narrative painting. The dazzling and elaborate

9-24 Kamal al-Din Bihzad **YUSUF FLEEING ZULAYHKA**
From a copy of the *Bustan* of Sa'di. Herat, Afghanistan. 1488.
Ink and pigments on paper, approx. 12 × 8½" (30.5 × 21.5 cm).
National Library, Cairo. (MS Adab Farsi 908, f. 52v).

Credit: © Roland and Sabrina Michaud/akg-images

architectural setting is inspired not by Sa'di's account, but by the Timurid poet Jami's more mystical version of the story (quoted in an architectural frame around the central *iwan* under the two figures), written only five years before Bihzad's painting. Jami sets his story in a seduction palace that Zulayhka had built specifically for this encounter, and into which she leads Yusuf ever inward from room to room, with entrance doors locked as they pass from one room to the next. As the scarlet-garbed Zulayhka lunges to possess him, the fire-haloed Yusuf flees her advances as the doors miraculously open in front of him.

The brilliant, jewel-like color of Bihzad's architectural forms and the exquisite detail with which each is rendered are salient characteristics of his style, as is the dramatic lunge of Zulayhka and Yusuf's balletic escape. The asymmetrical composition depends on a delicately balanced placement of flat screens of colorful ornament and two emphatically three-dimensional architectural features—a projecting balcony to the right and a zigzagging staircase to the left. Bihzad signed this work in a calligraphic panel over a window at upper left.

Art and Architecture of later Empires

What features characterize Islamic art and architecture under the Ottoman and Safavid dynasties?

In the pre-modern era, the introduction of gunpowder for use in cannons and guns caused a shift in military strategy. Isolated lords in lone castles could not withstand gunpowder sieges; power lay not in thick walls but in strong centralized governments that could invest in firepower and train armies in its use. Three great powers emerged in the Islamic world. To the west was the Ottoman Empire (1342–1918), which grew from a small principality in Asia Minor. In spite of setbacks inflicted by the Mongols, the Ottomans ultimately controlled Anatolia, western Iran, Iraq, Syria, Palestine, western Arabia (including Mecca and Medina), northern Africa (excepting Morocco), and part of eastern Europe. In 1453, their stunning capture of Constantinople (ultimately renamed Istanbul) brought the Byzantine Empire to an end. To the east of the Ottomans, Iran was ruled by the Safavid dynasty (1501–1732), distinguished for their Shi'ite branch of Islam. Their patronage of art and architecture brought a new refinement to artistic ideas and techniques drawn from the Timurid period. The other heirs to the Timurids were the Mughals of South Asia (1526–1858). The first Mughal emperor, Babur, invaded Hindustan (India and Pakistan) from Afghanistan, bringing with him a taste for Timurid gardens, architectural symmetry, and modular planning. Here we will focus on the Ottomans and the Safavids.

The Ottomans

Imperial Ottoman mosques were strongly influenced by Byzantine church plans. Prayer-hall interiors are dominated by ever-larger domed spaces uninterrupted by structural supports. Worship is directed, as in other mosques, toward a *qibla* wall and *mihrab* opposite the entrance.

Upon conquering Constantinople, Ottoman rulers converted the great Byzantine church of Hagia Sophia into a mosque, framing it with two graceful Turkish-style minarets in the fifteenth century and two more in the sixteenth century (SEE FIG. 8-2). In conformance with Islamic practice, the church's figural mosaics were destroyed or whitewashed. Huge calligraphic disks with the names of God (Allah), Muhammad, and the early caliphs were added to the interior in the mid nineteenth century (SEE FIG. 8-3). At present, Hagia Sophia is neither a church nor a mosque but a state museum.

SINAN Ottoman architects had already developed the domed, centrally planned mosque, but the vast open interior and structural clarity of Hagia Sophia inspired them to strive for a more ambitious scale. For the architect Sinan (c. 1489–1588), the development of a monumental, centrally planned mosque was a personal quest. Sinan began his career in the army, serving as engineer in the Ottoman campaigns at Belgrade, Vienna, and Baghdad. He rose through the ranks to become, in 1528, chief architect for Suleyman "the Magnificent," the tenth Ottoman sultan (ruled 1520–1566). Suleyman's reign marked the height of Ottoman power, and the sultan sponsored an ambitious building program on a scale not seen since the days of the Roman Empire. Serving Suleyman and his successor, Sinan is credited with more than 300 imperial commissions, including palaces, *madrasas* and Qur'an schools, tombs, public kitchens, hospitals, caravanserais, treasure houses, baths, bridges, viaducts, and 124 large and small mosques.

Sinan's crowning accomplishment, completed in about 1579 when he was over 80, was a mosque he designed in the provincial capital of Edirne for Suleyman's son, Selim II (ruled 1566–1574) (**FIG. 9-25**). The gigantic hemispheric dome that tops the Selimiye Mosque is more than 102 feet in diameter—larger than the dome of Hagia Sophia, as Sinan proudly pointed out. It crowns a building of extraordinary architectural coherence. The transition from square base to the central dome is accomplished by corner halfdomes that enhance the spatial plasticity and openness of the prayer hall's airy interior (**FIG. 9-26**). The eight massive piers that bear the dome's weight are visible both within and without; on the exterior they resolve in pointed towers that encircle the main dome, revealing the structural logic of the building and clarifying its form. In the arches that support the dome and span from one pier to the next—indeed at every level—light

9-25A PLAN OF THE MOSQUE OF SULTAN SELIM, EDIRNE

Western Turkey. 1568–1575.

Credit: Necipoglu Gülru, *The Age of Sinan: Architectural Culture in the Ottoman Empire*, 2005, London: Reaktion Books, p.239

9-25B EXTERIOR VIEW OF THE MOSQUE OF SULTAN SELIM, EDIRNE

Western Turkey. 1568–1575.

The minarets that pierce the sky around the prayer hall of this mosque, their sleek, fluted walls and needle-nosed spires soaring to more than 295 feet, are only 12½ feet in diameter at the base, an impressive feat of engineering. Only royal Ottoman mosques were permitted multiple minarets, and having more than two was unusual.

Credit: © Mehmet Cetin/Shutterstock

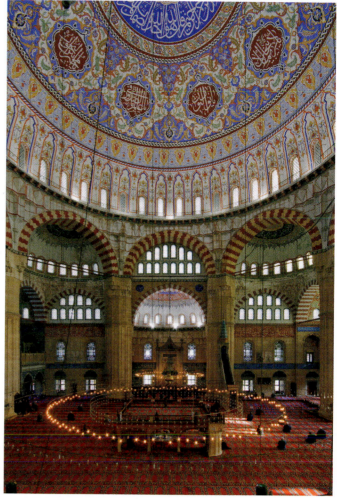

9-26 INTERIOR, MOSQUE OF SULTAN SELIM

Credit: Photo © Ayhan Altun

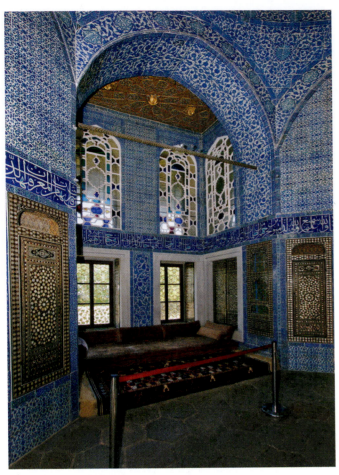

9-27 BAGHDAD KIOSK ALCOVE

Topkapi Palace, Istanbul. 1638.

Credit: Photo © Ayhan Altun

pours through windows into the interior, a space at once soaring and serene.

The interior was clearly influenced by Hagia Sophia—an open expanse under a vast dome floating on a ring of light—but it rejects Hagia Sophia's longitudinal pull from entrance to sanctuary. The Selimiye Mosque is truly a centrally planned structure. In addition to the mosque, the complex housed a *madrasa* and other educational buildings, a cemetery, a hospital, and charity kitchens, as well as the income-producing covered market and baths. Framed by the vertical lines of four minarets and raised on a platform at the city's edge, the Selimiye Mosque dominates the skyline.

TOPKAPI PALACE The Topkapi, the Ottomans' enormous palace in Istanbul, was a city unto itself. Built and inhabited from 1473 to 1853, it consisted of enclosures within walled enclosures, mirroring the immense political bureaucracy of the state. Inside, the sultan was removed from virtually all contact with the public. At the end of the inner palace, a free-standing pavilion, the Baghdad Kiosk (1638), provided him with a sumptuous retreat (**FIG. 9-27**). The kiosk consists of a low dome set above a cruciform hall with four alcoves. Each recess contains a low sofa (a Turkish word) laid with cushions and flanked by cabinets of wood inlaid with ivory and shell. Alternating with the cabinets are niches with ornate profiles; when stacked in profusion such niches—called *chini khana*—form decorative panels. On the walls, the blue-and-turquoise glazed tiles contain an inscription of the Throne

9-28 ILLUMINATED TUGRA OF SULTAN SULEYMAN

From Istanbul, Turkey. c. 1555–1560. Ink, paint, and gold on paper, removed from a *firman* and trimmed to 20½ × 25⅜" (52 × 64.5 cm). Metropolitan Museum of Art, New York. Rogers Fund, 1938. (38.149.1).

The *tugra* shown here is from a document endowing an institution in Jerusalem that had been established by Suleyman's powerful wife, Hurrem.

Credit: © 2016. Image copyright The Metropolitan Museum of Art/Art Resource/ Scala, Florence

9–29 PAINTED CERAMIC DISH WITH BIRDS AND FLOWERS
From Iznik, Turkey. c. 1575–1590. Stonepaste and polychrome painting under transparent glaze, diameter 11⅛" (28.4 cm). Metropolitan Museum of Art, New York. Gift of James J. Rorimer in appreciation of Maurice Dimand's curatorship, 1933–1959. (59.69.1).

Credit: © 2016. Image copyright The Metropolitan Museum of Art/Art Resource/Scala, Florence

in the body of the *tugra* may have been inspired by Chinese blue-and-white porcelain; similar designs appear on Ottoman ceramics and textiles.

The most important center for ceramic production under the Ottomans was Iznik (the Byzantine city of Nicea) in northwestern Turkey. Iznik potters specialized in polychrome underglaze painting, used on tiles made for architectural revetment as well as on plates and vessels intended for display. The three-color palette used on this dish (**FIG. 9-29**) is characteristic of their work. The sprawling floral spray that fills the interior—a rose, a tulip, and sprigs of honeysuckle and hyacinth—is a common motif in Iznik decoration, as is the energetic border of circles, spirals, and leaves, inspired by Chinese ceramics. The birds are more unusual. Perhaps they are the nightingales, which—with roses—are popular allegorical imagery in Ottoman love poetry.

Verse (Qur'an 2:255) which proclaims God's dominion "over the heavens and the earth," a reference to divine power that appears in many throne rooms and places associated with Muslim sovereigns. Sparkling light glows in the **stained glass** above.

CALLIGRAPHY AND CERAMICS   Following a practice begun by the Saljuqs and Mamluks, the Ottomans put calligraphy to political use, developing the design of imperial ciphers—**tugras**—into a specialized art form. Ottoman *tugras* combined the ruler's name and title with the motto "Eternally Victorious" into a monogram denoting the authority of the sultan and of those select officials who were also granted an emblem. *Tugras* appeared on seals, coins, and buildings, as well as on official documents called *firmans*, imperial edicts supplementing Muslim law. Suleyman issued hundreds of edicts, and a high court official supervised specialist calligraphers and illuminators who produced the documents with fancy *tugras* (**FIG. 9-28**).

Tugras were drawn in black or blue with three long, vertical strokes to the right of two concentric horizontal teardrops. Decorative foliage patterns fill the area within the script. By the 1550s, this fill decoration became more naturalistic, and in later centuries it spilled outside the emblems' boundary lines. This rare, oversized *tugra* has a sweeping, fluid but controlled line, drawn to set proportions. The color scheme of delicate floral interlace enclosed

The Safavid Dynasty

When Shah Isma'il (ruled 1501–1524) solidified Safavid rule over the land of the Timurids in the early years of the sixteenth century, he called Bihzad, the most distinguished member of the Herat School, to the capital city of Tabriz to supervise the Safavid royal workshop, which established a new golden age of book production by blending the Herat style with that of other regional Persian traditions. But it was Isma'il's son and successor, Shah Tahmasp (ruled 1524–1576), who emerged as the most important early patron.

SULTAN MUHAMMAD   As a child, Tahmasp was trained in the art of calligraphy and drawing in Herat, where Shah Isma'il had dispatched him to serve as titular governor. Shortly after succeeding his father, the youthful Tahmasp commissioned from the royal workshop in Tabriz a spectacular manuscript copy of the *Shahnama* ("Book of Kings"), Firdawsi's poetic history of Persian rulers written in the late tenth and early eleventh centuries.

9–30 Sultan Muhammad **THE "COURT OF GAYUMARS"**
From the *Shahnama* of Shah Tahmasp (fol. 20v). Tabriz, Iran.
c. 1525–1535. Ink, pigments, and gold on paper, page size
18½ × 12½″ (47 × 31.8 cm). Aga Khan Museum, Toronto. (AKM165).

Tahmasp's monumental volume—with pages 18½ inches tall, larger than any book produced during the Timurid period—consists of 742 folios whose margins are embellished with pure gold; 258 full-page pictures highlight the important kings and heroes of Persian royal history. The paintings were produced by a series of artists over an extended period during the 1520s and into the 1530s. This was the most important royal artistic project of the early Safavid period.

Among the most impressive paintings—indeed, a work that many consider the greatest of all Persian manuscript paintings—is a rendering of **THE "COURT OF GAYUMARS"** (**FIG. 9–30**) painted by Sultan Muhammad, the most renowned artist in the royal workshop. This assessment is not only modern. In 1544, Dust Muhammad—painter, chronicler, and **connoisseur**—cited this painting in particular when singling out Sultan Muhammad as the premier painter participating in the project, claiming that "although it has a thousand eyes, the celestial sphere

has not seen his like" (Blair and Bloom, page 168). Sultan Muhammad portrayed the idyllic reign of the legendary first Shah, Gayumars, who ruled from a mountaintop over a people who were the first to make clothing from leopard skins and develop the skill of cooking. The elevated and central figure of the king is surrounded by the members of his family and court, each rendered with individual facial features and varying body proportions to add a sense of naturalism to the unleashed fantasy characterizing the

9–31 ARDABIL CARPET
Produced in the Safavid royal workshops, probably for the shrine of Shaykh Safi al-Din in Ardabil, Iran. 1539–1540. Dyed wool pile, undyed silk warp and weft, 34′6″ × 17′6″ (10.51 × 5.34 m). Victoria and Albert Museum, London.

Credit: V&A Images/Victoria and Albert Museum

Technique

CARPET MAKING

Because textiles are made of organic materials that are destroyed through use, very few carpets from before the sixteenth century have survived. Carpets fall into two basic types: flat-weave carpets and pile, or knotted, carpets. Both can be made on either vertical or horizontal looms.

The best-known flat-weaves today are kilims, which are typically woven in wool with bold, geometric patterns and sometimes with brocaded details. Kilim weaving is done with a **tapestry** technique called slit tapestry (see A).

Knotted carpets are an ancient invention. The oldest known example, excavated in Siberia and dating to the fourth or fifth century LᴀD, has designs evocative of Achaemenid art, suggesting that the technique may have originated in Central Asia. In knotted carpets, the pile—the plush, thickly tufted surface—is made by tying colored strands of yarn, usually wool but occasionally silk for deluxe carpets, onto the vertical elements (the **warp**) of a yarn grid (see B and C). These knotted

loops are later trimmed and sheared to form the plush pile surface of the carpet. The **weft** strands (crosswise threads) are shot horizontally, usually twice, after each row of knots is tied, to hold the knots in place and to form the horizontal element common to all woven structures. The weft is usually an undyed yarn and is hidden by the colored knots of the warp. Two common knotting techniques are the asymmetrical knot (formerly called the Sehna knot), used in many carpets from Iran, Egypt, and Central Asia, and the symmetrical knot (formerly called the Gördes knot), more commonly used in Anatolian Turkish carpet weaving. The greater the number of knots, the shorter the pile. The finest carpets can have as many as 2,400 knots per square inch, each one tied separately by hand.

Although royal workshops produced luxurious carpets (SEE FIG. 9–31), most knotted rugs have traditionally been made in tents and homes by, depending on local custom, either women or men.

A Kilim weaving pattern used in flat-weaving

B Symmetrical knot, used extensively in Turkey

C Asymmetrical knot, used extensively in Iran

surrounding world. The landscape sparkles with brilliant color, encompassing the detailed delineation of lavish plant life as well as melting renderings of pastel rock formations, into which are tucked the faces of the spirits and demons animating this primitive paradise. Packed with surprises, this is a painting meant to be savored slowly by an elite audience within the Safavid court.

CARPETS   Shah Thamasp also sponsored royal workshops for the production of finely woven carpets that were often signed, an indication of the growing prestige associated with this medium. Maqsud of Kashan's name—presumably he was the designer—and the production date of 1539–40 (year 946 in the Islamic calendar) is woven into the design of one of the most spectacular surviving carpets of Thamasp's court, one of a pair that seem to have originally come from the funerary mosque of Shayke Safi al-Din in Ardabil (FIG. 9–31). This is a huge rug, measuring almost 35 by 18 feet, and densely woven with 340 knots in each

square inch (25 million knots in total). The central medallion—orbited by 16 radiating, pointed ovals in alternating colors—is flanked along the rug's long axis by two stylized representations of mosque lamps, one smaller than the other. Some have suggested that the difference in size may have been calculated to make the rug seem even longer when viewed from the end of the long rectangle when entering the room where it was displayed.

Rugs have long been used for Muslim prayer, which involves repeatedly kneeling and touching the forehead to the floor before God. While individuals often had their own small prayer rugs with representations of *mihrab* niches to orient them in prayer, many mosques were furnished with wool-pile rugs received as pious donations, such as this one from Ardabil. Rugs from Iran, Turkey, and elsewhere were historically highly valued by Westerners, who often displayed them on tables rather than floors. They remain one of the predominant forms of Islamic art known in the West.

ARCHITECTURE Whereas the Ottomans took their inspiration from works of the Byzantine Empire, the Safavids looked to Timurid architecture with its tall, double-shell domes sheathed in blue tiles. In the later Safavid capital of Isfahan, the typically Timurid taste for modular construction re-emerged on a grand scale that extended well beyond buildings to include avenues, bridges, public plazas, and gardens. To the preexisting city of Isfahan, Safavid Shah Abbas I (1588–1629) added an entirely new extension, planned around an immense central plaza (*maydan*) and a broad avenue called the Chahar Bagh that ran through a zone of imperial palace pavilions and gardens down to the river. The city's prosperity and beauty so amazed visitors who flocked from around the world to conduct trade and diplomacy that it led to the popular saying, "Isfahan is half the world."

With Isfahan's **MASJID-I SHAH**, or Royal Mosque (1611–1638), the four-*iwan* mosque plan reached its apogee (**FIG. 9–32**). Stately and huge, it anchors the south end of the city's *maydan*. Its 90-foot portal and the passageway through it aligns with the *maydan*, which is oriented astrologically, but the entrance corridor soon turns to conform to the prayer hall's orientation to Mecca. The portal's great *iwan* is framed by a *pishtaq* (a rectangular panel framing an *iwan*) that rises above the surrounding walls and is enhanced by the soaring verticality of its minarets.

9–32A PLAN OF THE MASJID-I SHAH, ISFAHAN
Iran. 1611–1638.

Credit: Drawing by Keith Turner after Henri Stierlin, courtesy of the Aga Khan Documentation Center at MIT.

The *iwan*'s profile is reflected in the repeated, double-tiered *iwans* that parade across the façade of the mosque courtyard and around the *maydan* as a whole. Achieving unity through the regular replication of a single element—here

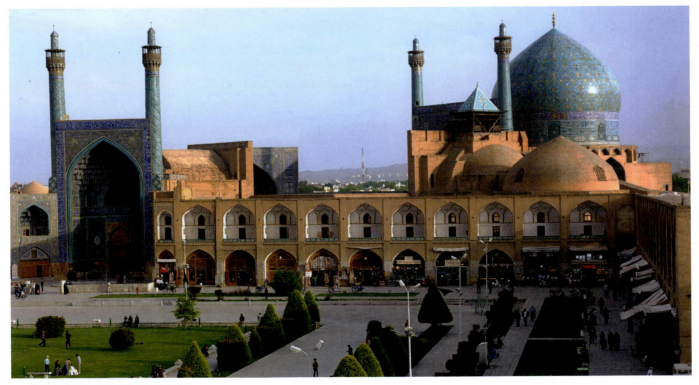

9–32B EXTERIOR VIEW OF THE MASJID-I SHAH, ISFAHAN
Iran. 1611–1638.

The tall, bulbous dome behind the *qibla iwan* and the large *pishtaqs* with minarets are pronounced vertical elements that made royal patronage visible not only from the far end of the *maydan* but throughout the city and beyond.

Credit: Klange76/Fotolia

the arch—is a hallmark of Safavid architecture inherited from Timurid aesthetics, but achieved on an unprecedented scale and integrated within a well-planned urban setting.

Into the Modern Era

Islamic art is not restricted to the distant past. But with the dissolution of the great Islamic empires and the formation of smaller nation-states during the twentieth century, questions of identity and its expression in art changed significantly. Muslim artists and architects began to participate in international movements that swept away many of the visible signs that formerly expressed their cultural character and difference. More recently, Islamic architects have sought to reconcile modernity with an Islamic cultural identity distinct from the West. In this spirit Iraqi architect Sami Mousawi and the Italian firm of Portoghesi-Gigliotti designed the **ISLAMIC CULTURAL CENTER** in Rome (completed 1992) with clean, modern lines, exposing the structure while at the same time taking full advantage of opportunities for ornament (**FIG. 9-33**). The structural logic appears in the prayer hall's concrete columns, which rise to meet abstract capitals in the form of plain rings, then spring upward to make a geometrically dazzling eight-pointed star supporting a dome of concentric circles. There are references here to the interlacing ribs of the *mihrab* dome in the Great Mosque of Cordoba (SEE FIG. 9–9), to the great domed spans of Sinan's prayer halls (SEE FIG. 9–26), and to the simple palm-tree trunks that supported the roof of the Mosque of the Prophet in Medina.

9-33 Paolo Portoghesi, Vittorio Gigliotti, and Sami Mousawi **ISLAMIC MOSQUE AND CULTURAL CENTER, ROME**
1984–1992.

The prayer hall, 197 × 131' (60 × 40 m), which has an ablution area on the floor below, can accommodate a congregation of 2,500 on its main floor and balconies. The large central dome, 65½' (20 m) in diameter, is surrounded by 16 smaller domes, all similarly articulated with concrete ribs.

Credit: © Gari Wyn Williams/Alamy Stock Photo

Think About It

1   Explain how the design of the mosque varies across the Islamic world with reference to three examples. Despite the differences, what features do mosques typically have in common?

2   Images of people are not allowed in Islamic religious contexts, but mosques and other religious buildings are lavishly decorated. What artistic motifs and techniques are used and why?

3   Compare the painted pages from sumptuous manuscripts in **FIGURES 9-24 and 9-30**. How does the comparison reveal the distinctive aspirations of religious and secular art in Islamic society? How are they different, and what features do they share?

4   Select an Islamic structure that is influenced by Roman or Byzantine architecture. Which forms are borrowed? Why and how, in their new Islamic context, are they transformed?

Crosscurrents

These buildings were constructed for worship during the formative years of Christianity and Islam. Explain why they appear similar and discuss the ways in which their designs are consistent with the religious and cultural contexts.

FIG. 7–10B

FIG. 9–5

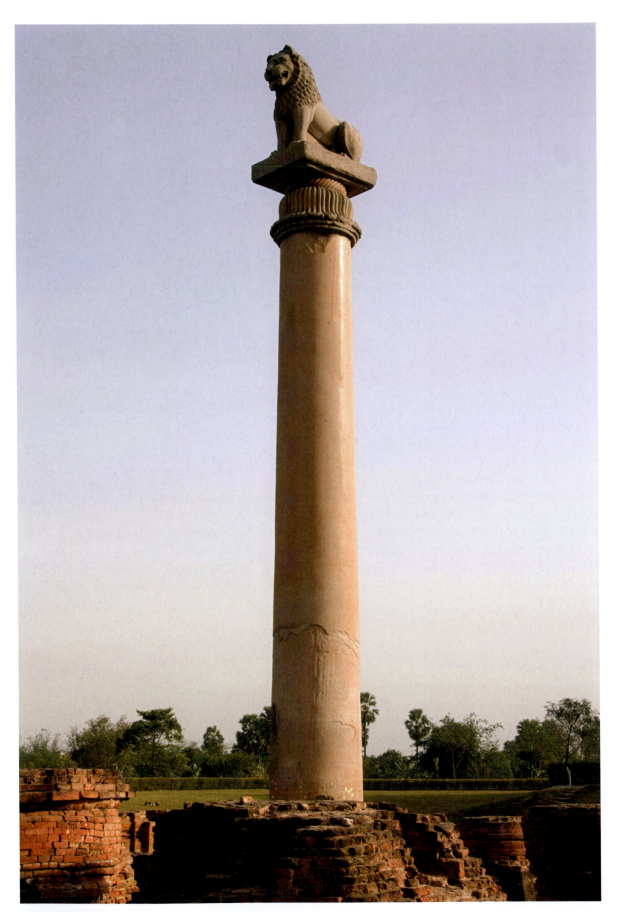

10-1 ASHOKAN PILLAR
Kutagarasala Vihara near Vaishali, Bihar, India. Maurya period, c. 279–232 BCE.

Credit: © Dinodia Photos/Alamy Stock Photo

Chapter 10
Art of South and Southeast Asia before 1200

∨ Learning Objectives

10.a Identify the visual hallmarks of South and Southeast Asian art for formal, technical, and expressive qualities.

10.b Interpret the meaning of works of South and Southeast Asian art based on their themes, subjects, and symbols.

10.c Relate South and Southeast Asian artists and art to their cultural, economic, and political contexts.

10.d Apply the vocabulary and concepts relevant to South and Southeast Asian art, artists, and art history.

10.e Interpret a work of South or Southeast Asian art using the art historical methods of observation, comparison, and inductive reasoning.

10.f Select visual and textual evidence in various media to support an argument or an interpretation of a work of South or Southeast Asian art.

The heroic qualities of the great ruler Ashoka Maurya are well recorded in the Indian cultural tradition. His accomplishments served as inspiration for later kings, like those of the Gupta dynasty, and Buddhist literary sources credit him with a wide range of miraculous deeds. But in spite of this fame, early historians had great difficulty distinguishing the historical man from the legend. In 1837, when examining inscriptions on a series of massive monolithic pillars (**FIG. 10–1**) in northern India, scholars realized that the designation "Beloved of the Gods" was one of King Ashoka's personal epithets. This realization made clear that the pillars dated to the time of King Ashoka (c. 273–232 BCE) and lifted some of the mystery surrounding this renowned figure. Once properly identified, his name appeared in numerous Maurya-dynasty inscriptions. What they reveal about the humanity of this man is in many ways more captivating than the larger-than-life figure encountered in the legends.

Notably, in his Thirteenth Rock Edict, Ashoka presents himself as a man weary of battle and intensely remorseful for the death and suffering generated by his political ambitions. In it, he recalls a horrific battle in the region of Kalinga that took place eight years into his reign. By his estimation 100,000 died and many thousands more were dispossessed or left in despair from the conflict. In surveying this carnage, Ashoka admits to being deeply pained and resolves henceforth to seek conquest through moral teachings (*dharma*) rather than by the sword. His profound

change of heart also proved to be a sound policy for establishing legal consistency over his vast empire. This stability stimulated a rich period of artistic production.

As part of this conversion, Ashoka supported religious institutions and gave special attention to the nascent Buddhist community. He also widely distributed royal inscriptions by having them carved directly onto boulders and mountainsides. These rock edicts were far more plentiful than the inscribed columns, commonly called Ashokan pillars, which are few in number and appear to have been concentrated in the heart of the Maurya empire. The remains of about 19 such pillars exist, but not all bear inscriptions that can be attributed with certainty to Ashoka. Most were placed at the sites of Buddhist monasteries along a route leading from Punjab in the northwest to Ashoka's capital, Pataliputra, in the northeast.

Pillars and pillared halls had been used as emblems of kingship in the Persian Achaemenid Empire (Chapter 2, pages 44–47), and it is possible that Ashoka was familiar with these precedents when he decided to display his words on columns detached from an architectural setting. Most of these edicts are inscribed in Prakrit, a language closely related to classical Sanskrit, but others were written in the languages spoken locally, like Greek and Aramaic. These observations are indicative of the size and reach of Ashoka's empire, which set the model for South Asian kingship over the centuries to come.

The Origins of Civilization in South Asia

What are the geographical and cultural contexts of the earliest art in South Asia?

It is difficult to make inclusive claims about South and Southeast Asia because the two areas were and are home to a broad range of ethnic communities, political units, language groups, and cultural traditions. One of the few things both regions share is the historical importance to trade networks and, consequently, an exposure to similar ideological and religious ideas, most notably Hinduism, Buddhism, and Islam. And the same proximity to the sea that played a role in trade also ensured exposure to the monsoon rains, which pull moisture from the oceans each summer and have traditionally enabled vigorous agricultural production. Due to their wealth and accessibility, both regions have historically been subject to periods of invasion, immigration, and colonization.

This sporadic influx of new peoples has, at times, been a source of great hardship, but each wave added to the rich diversity of these regions and contributed new layers to their remarkable artistic heritage.

The South Asian subcontinent, or Indian subcontinent, as it is commonly called, is a peninsular region that includes the present-day countries of India, Afghanistan, Pakistan, Nepal, Bhutan, Bangladesh, and Sri Lanka (**MAP 10–1**). This land mass is slowly pressing northward into the rest of Asia, and the collision has given rise to the Himalayas, the world's highest mountains, which capture the snows and feed the subcontinent's major rivers throughout the year. It is along these vast river systems that we can find the first evidence of organized settlements in the region.

The earliest civilization of South Asia was nurtured in the lower reaches of the Indus River, in present-day Pakistan and northwestern India. Known as the Indus or Harappan civilization (after Harappa, the first-discovered site), it flourished from approximately 2600 to 1900 BCE, or during roughly the same time as the Old Kingdom period

MAP 10–1 SOUTH AND SOUTHEAST ASIA

As the deserts in western China heat during the summer months, the hot air rises and pulls cool air north off the oceans. As this water-laden air hits the Himalayas and the Tibetan plateau, it drops the torrential monsoon rains over much of South and Southeast Asia.

10-2 SEAL IMPRESSIONS

A, D: horned animal; B: Bull; C: sacrificial rite to a goddess (?); E: yogi; F: three-headed animal. Indus Valley civilization, c. 2500–1500 BCE. Steatite, each seal approx. 1¼ × 1¼" (3.2 × 3.2 cm). National Museum of Karachi, Pakistan.

The more than 2,000 small seals and impressions that have been found offer an intriguing window on the Indus Valley civilization. Usually carved from steatite stone, the seals were coated with alkali and then fired to produce a lustrous, white surface. A perforated knob on the back of each may have been for suspending them. The most popular subjects are animals, most commonly a one-horned bovine standing before an altarlike object (A, D). The function of the seals may relate to trade but this remains uncertain since the script that is so prominent in the impressions has yet to be deciphered.

Credit: A-F, National Museum of Karachi, Karachi, Pakistan/Bridgeman Images

of Egypt, the Minoan civilization of the Aegean, and the dynasties of Ur and Babylon in Mesopotamia. In fact, there is evidence of trade contact between the Harappan civilization and Mesopotamia.

The presence of city mounds and the occasional discovery of small **SEALS** (such as those whose impressions are shown in **FIG. 10-2**) preserved the memory that an ancient civilization had existed in the Indus River Valley. Systematic excavations did not begin, however, until the 1920s, and they have continued to the present. These efforts have uncovered a number of major urban areas at points along the lower Indus River, including Harappa, Mohenjo-Daro, and Chanhu-Daro.

The Indus Civilization

MOHENJO-DARO   The ancient cities of the Indus Valley resemble each other in design and construction, suggesting a coherent culture. At Mohenjo-Daro, the best preserved of the sites, archaeologists discovered an elevated citadel area about 50 feet high, surrounded by a wall. Among the citadel's buildings is a remarkable **WATER TANK**, a large watertight pool that may have been a public bath but could also have had a ritual use (**FIG. 10-3**). Stretching out below the elevated area was the city, arranged in a gridlike plan with wide avenues and narrow side streets. Its houses, often two stories high, were generally built around a central courtyard. Like other Indus Valley cities, Mohenjo-Daro was constructed of fired brick, in contrast to the less durable sun-dried brick used in other cultures of the time. The city included a network of covered drainage systems that channeled away waste and rainwater. Clearly the technical and engineering skills of this civilization were highly advanced. At its peak, about 2500 to 2000 BCE,

10-3 LARGE WATER TANK, MOHENJO-DARO

Indus Valley (Harappan) civilization, c. 2600–1900 BCE.

This was possibly a public or ritual bathing area.

Credit: © akg-images/Gerard Degeorge

Mohenjo-Daro was approximately 6–7 square miles in size and had a population of about 20,000–50,000. The uniformity of its architecture and plans suggests some form of central political control, but in the absence of any clear political or religious structures we can say very little about how the cities were governed.

INDUS VALLEY SEALS   Although our knowledge of the Indus civilization is limited by the fact that we cannot read its writing, motifs on seals as well as the few discovered artworks strongly suggest continuities with later South Asian cultures. The seal in FIGURE 10-2E, for example, depicts a man in a meditative posture that resembles later forms of yoga, traditional physical and mental exercises usually undertaken for spiritual purposes. In FIGURE 10-2C, people with elaborate headgear stand in a row or procession observing a figure standing in a tree—possibly a goddess—and a kneeling worshiper. This scene may offer some insight into the religious or ritual customs of Indus people, whose deities may have been ancient prototypes of later Indian gods and goddesses.

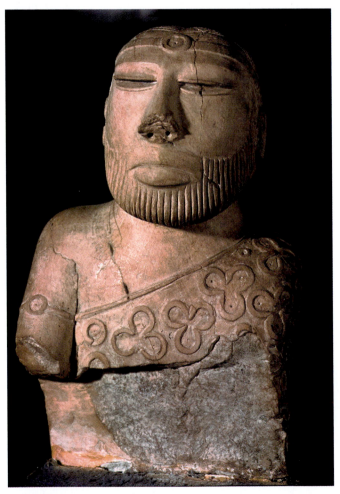

10-4 TORSO OF A "PRIEST-KING"
From Mohenjo-Daro. Indus Valley civilization, c. 2600–1900 BCE. Steatite, height 6⅞″ (17.5 cm). National Museum of Pakistan, Karachi.

Credit: © akg-images/Jean-Louis Nou

Numerous terra-cotta figurines and a few stone and bronze statuettes have been found at Indus sites. They reveal a confident maturity of artistic conception and technique. Both the terra-cotta and the stone figures foreshadow the later Indian artistic tradition in their sensuous naturalism.

"PRIEST-KING" FROM MOHENJO-DARO   The male torso sometimes called the "priest-king" (FIG. 10-4) suggests by this name a structure of society where priests functioned as kings—for which we have no evidence at all. Several features of this figure, including a low forehead, a broad nose, thick lips, and long slit eyes, are seen on other works from Mohenjo-Daro. The man's garment is patterned with a **trefoil** (three-lobed) motif. The depressions of the trefoil pattern were originally filled with red pigment, and the eyes were inlaid with colored shell or stone. Narrow bands with circular ornaments adorn the upper arm and the head. The headband falls in back into two long strands, which may be an indication of rank. Certainly, with its formal pose and simplified, geometric form, the statue conveys a commanding human presence.

NUDE TORSO FROM HARAPPA   Although its date is disputed, a nude **MALE TORSO** (FIG. 10-5) found at Harappa is an example of a contrasting naturalistic style of ancient Indus origin. Less than 4 inches tall, it is one of the most extraordinary portrayals of the human form to survive from any early civilization. Its lifelike rendering emphasizes the soft texture of the human body and the subtle nuances of muscular form. With these characteristics the Harappa torso forecasts the essential aesthetic attributes of later Indian sculpture.

The reasons for the demise of this flourishing civilization are not yet understood. Recent research has suggested that between 2000 and 1750 BCE there was a gradual breakdown of the architectural regularity characteristic of earlier periods. Many now think this was due to climate change and a dramatic shift in the course of local rivers. These changes made it impossible to practice the agriculture and river trade on which these cities depended. The cities of the Indus civilization declined, and predominantly rural and nomadic societies emerged.

The Vedic Period

About 2000 BCE nomadic herdsmen, the Aryans, entered India from Central Asia and the Russian steppes. Gradually they blended with the indigenous populations and introduced the horse and chariot, the Sanskrit language, a hierarchical social order, and religious practices that centered on the propitiation of gods through fire sacrifice. The earliest of their sacred writings, known as the Vedas, contain hymns to various gods including the divine king Indra. The importance of the fire sacrifice,

10–5 MALE TORSO

From Harappa. Indus Valley civilization, c. 2600–1900 BCE. Red sandstone, height 3¾" (9.5 cm). National Museum, New Delhi.

Credit: © akg-images/Jean-Louis Nou

the *Ramayana*, the most popular and enduring religious epic in India and Southeast Asia, were taking shape. These texts relate histories of gods and humans, bringing profound philosophical ideas to a more accessible and popular level. In this way, the religious tradition continued to evolve, emerging later as Hinduism, a loose term that encompasses the many religious forms that resulted from the mingling of Vedic culture with indigenous beliefs.

In this stimulating religious, philosophical, and literary climate, numerous religious communities arose, some of which did not accept the primacy of the Brahmins. Among these heterodox groups the Jains and the Buddhists were the most successful. The last of the 24 Jain spiritual pathfinders (*tirthankara*), Mahavira, is believed to have taught in the sixth century BCE. His were the earliest teachings ever to recognize nonviolence as a central moral principle. The Buddha Shakyamuni is thought to have lived shortly thereafter in the fifth century BCE. Both traditions espoused some basic Upanishadic tenets, such as the cyclical nature of existence and the need for liberation from the material world. However, they rejected the authority of the Vedas, and with it the legitimacy of the fire sacrifice and the hereditary class structure of Vedic society, including its powerful, exclusive priesthood. In further contrast with the Brahmins, who often held important positions in society, both Jainism and Buddhism were renunciant (*shramana*) traditions, centered on communities of monks and nuns who chose to separate themselves from worldly concerns. Over time, these communities did begin to play important social roles. But asceticism held, and continues to hold, an important place within most South Asian religious traditions.

overseen by a powerful priesthood—the Brahmins—and religiously sanctioned social classes, persisted through the Vedic period. At some point, the class structure became hereditary and immutable, with lasting consequences for Indian society.

During the latter part of this period, from about 800 BCE, the Upanishads were composed. These texts, written primarily by Brahmins, attempted to reform the Vedic ritual by emphasizing the unity between the individual and the divine. Some authors asserted that the material world is illusory and that only the universal divine (Brahman) is real and eternal. Others held that our existence is cyclical and that beings are caught in *samsara*, a relentless cycle of birth, life, death, and rebirth. Believers aspire to attain liberation from *samsara* and to unite the individual soul with the eternal, universal Brahman.

The latter portion of the Vedic period also saw the flowering of India's epic literature, written in the melodious and complex Sanskrit language. By around 400 BCE, the *Mahabharata*, the longest epic in world literature, and

The Flourishing of Buddhism and Hinduism

How does South Asian art develop with the flourishing of Buddhism and Hinduism across a series of regional dynasties through the twelfth century CE?

Buddhism

Many of the renunciant traditions developed from the efforts of gifted and insightful teachers. For the Buddhists, this man was Shakyamuni Buddha, who lived during the fifth century BCE in the present-day regions of southern Nepal and northern India. At his birth, it is believed, seers foretold that the infant prince, named Siddhartha Gautama, would become either a *chakravartin* (world-conquering ruler) or a *buddha* (literally an "awakened one" or a fully enlightened being). Hoping for a ruler like himself, Siddhartha's father tried to surround his son with pleasure and shield him from pain. Yet the prince was eventually exposed to the sufferings of old age, sickness, and death—the inevitable fate of all mortal beings. Deeply troubled by the human condition, Siddhartha at age 29 left the palace, his family, and his inheritance to live as an ascetic in the wilderness. After six years of meditation, he attained complete enlightenment at a site in India now called Bodh Gaya.

Following his enlightenment, the Buddha gave his first teaching in the Deer Park at Sarnath. Here he expounded the Four Noble Truths that are the foundation of Buddhism: (1) life is suffering; (2) this suffering has a cause, which is ignorance and desire; (3) this ignorance and desire can be overcome and extinguished; (4) the way to overcome them is by following the eightfold path of right view, right resolve, right speech, right action, right livelihood, right effort, right mindfulness, and right concentration. After the Buddha's death at age 80, his many disciples developed his teachings and established the world's oldest monastic institutions.

A buddha is not a god, but rather one who sees the ultimate nature of the world and is therefore no longer subject to *samsara*, the cycle of birth, death, and rebirth that otherwise holds all in its grip, whether they are gods, humans, animals, demons, tortured spirits, or hellish beings.

The early form of Buddhism, known as Theravada or Nikaya, stresses self-cultivation for the purpose of attaining *nirvana*, which is the extinction of *samsara* for oneself. Theravada Buddhism has continued mainly in Sri Lanka and Southeast Asia. Almost equally old is another form of Buddhism known as Mahayana, which became popular mainly in northern India; it eventually flourished in China, Korea, Japan, and in Tibet (as Vajrayana). Compassion for all beings is the foundation of Mahayana Buddhism, whose goal is not only *nirvana* for oneself but buddhahood (enlightenment) for every being throughout the universe. Many schools of Buddhism recognize buddhas other than Shakyamuni from the past, present, and future. One such is Maitreya, the next buddha destined to appear on earth. Several Buddhist schools also accept the existence of **bodhisattvas** ("those whose essence is wisdom"), saintly beings who are on the brink of achieving buddhahood but have vowed to help others achieve buddhahood before crossing over themselves. In art, bodhisattvas and buddhas are most clearly distinguished by their clothing and adornments: bodhisattvas wear the princely garb of India, while buddhas wear monks' robes.

The Maurya Period

In about 700 BCE, hundreds of years after their decline along the Indus, cities began to reappear on the subcontinent, particularly in the north, where numerous kingdoms arose. For most of its subsequent history, India was a shifting mosaic of regional kingdoms. From time to

10-6 LION CAPITAL

From Ashokan pillar at Sarnath, Uttar Pradesh, India. Maurya period, c. 250 BCE. Polished sandstone, height 7' (2.13 m). Archaeological Museum, Sarnath.

Credit: Borromeo/Art Resource, NY

time, however, a particularly powerful dynasty formed an empire. The first of these was the Maurya dynasty (c. 322–185 BCE), which claimed to rule over all but the southernmost portion of the subcontinent.

During the reign of the third Maurya king, Ashoka (ruled c. 273–232 BCE), Buddhism expanded from a religion largely localized in the Maurya heartland, a region known as Magadha, to one extending across the entire empire. Among the monuments Ashoka erected were monolithic pillars set up primarily at the sites of Buddhist monasteries. The fully developed Ashokan pillar—a slightly tapered sandstone shaft that usually rested on a stone foundation slab sunk more than 10 feet into the ground—rose to a height of around 50 feet (SEE FIG. 10-1). On it were often carved inscriptions relating to rules of *dharma,* the divinely ordained moral law believed to keep the universe from falling into chaos. Ideal kings were enjoined to uphold this law, and many later Buddhists interpreted the rules as also referring to Buddhist teachings. At the top were placed elaborate animal-shaped capitals carved from separate blocks of sandstone. Both shaft and capital were given the high polish characteristic of Maurya stonework. Scholars believe that the pillars, which served as royal standards, symbolized the **axis mundi** ("axis of the world"), joining earth with the cosmos and representing the vital link between the human and celestial realms.

LION CAPITAL FROM SARNATH   This capital (**FIG. 10–6**) originally crowned the pillar erected at Sarnath, the site of the Buddha's first sermon. It represents four addorsed, or back-to-back, Asiatic lions with open mouths standing atop a circular platform depicting a bull, horse, lion, and elephant separated by large chariot wheels. The base is an inverted lotus blossom whose bell shape formed a transition to the column. The deeply cut carving promotes an active play of light and shadow, resulting in details that must have been readily visible even when this image was placed high atop its pillar.

Some poetic references allude to the Buddha's sermon as the "Lion's Roar," whereas others refer to it as the turning of the "Wheel of the Law" (*dharmachakra*). This designation likens the Buddha's teachings to a chariot wheel and the sermon to the first push that set the wheel rolling across the world. The four lions and spoked wheels on the capital face the cardinal directions, thus referencing these descriptive titles.

However, the imagery works on two levels; it also holds important political associations. The lion may have served as a metaphor for the Buddha's preaching, but prior to that it was a symbol of kingship, and the elephant, horse, and bull were similarly potent as emblems of worldly and military power. When considered in conjunction with the wheel motifs, this imagery almost certainly also references the king as a *chakravartin*. This term refers to a universal king of such power that the wheels of his chariot pass everywhere unimpeded. The designation held great significance in South Asia, and Ashoka is here associating the worldly might of his empire with the moral authority of Buddhism. This relationship would have been further reinforced by the large wheel, now lost, that is believed to have rested atop the lions.

FEMALE FIGURE FROM DIDARGANJ   Alongside the formal religious institutions of the Brahmins, Buddhists, and Jains, there existed a host of popular religious practices centered on local gods of villages and fields who were believed to oversee worldly matters such as health, wealth, and fertility. A spectacular **FEMALE FIGURE HOLDING A FLY-WHISK**, or *chauri* (**FIG. 10–7**), found at Didarganj, near the Maurya capital of Pataliputra, may represent one such deity. Possibly representing a **yakshi**, a spirit associated with the productive and reproductive forces of nature,

10-7 FEMALE FIGURE HOLDING A FLY-WHISK
From Didarganj, Patna, Bihar, India. Probably Maurya period, c. 250 BCE. Polished sandstone, height 5'4¼" (1.63 m). Patna Museum, Patna.

Often identified as a *yakshi*, this sculpture has become one of the most famous works of Indian art. Holding a fly-whisk in her raised right hand, the figure wears only a long shawl and a skirtlike cloth. The nubbled tubes about her ankles probably represent anklets made of beaten gold. Her hair is bound behind in a large bun, and a small bun sits on her forehead. This hairstyle appears again in Indian sculpture of the later Kushan period (c. second century CE).

Credit: © akg-images/De Agostini Picture Lib./G. Nimatallah the figure embodies female associations with procreative abundance, bounty, and auspiciousness.

The statue's date is still debated by scholars, but many place it in the Maurya period. Sculpted from fine-grained sandstone, the statue conveys the *yakshi*'s authority through the frontal rigor of her pose, the massive volumes of her form, and the strong, linear patterning of her ornaments and dress. Alleviating and counterbalancing this hierarchical formality are her soft, youthful face, the precise definition of prominent features such as the stomach muscles, and the polished sheen of her exposed flesh. As noted above, this lustrous polish is a special feature of Maurya sculpture.

The Period of the Shunga and Early Satavahana

With the demise of the Maurya empire, India returned to rule by regional dynasties. Between the second century BCE and the early centuries CE, two of the most important of these dynasties were the Shunga dynasty (185–72 BCE) in central India and the Satavahana dynasty (third century BCE–third century CE), which initially ruled in central India and after the first century in the south. During this period, some of the most magnificent early Buddhist structures were created.

Elements of Architecture
STUPAS AND TEMPLES

Buddhist architecture in South Asia consists mainly of stupas and temples, often at monastic complexes containing *viharas* (monks' cells and common areas). These monuments may be either structural (built up from the ground) or rock-cut (hewn out of a mountainside). **Stupas** derive from burial mounds and contain relics beneath a solid, dome-shaped core. A major stupa is surrounded by a railing that creates a sacred path for ritual circumambulation at ground level. This railing is punctuated by gateways, called **toranas** in Sanskrit, aligned with the cardinal points of the compass. The stupa sits on a round or square terrace; stairs may lead to an upper circumambulatory path around the platform's edge. On top of the stupa a railing defines a square, from the center of which rises a mast supporting tiers of disk-shaped "umbrellas."

Hindu architecture in South Asia consists mainly of temples, either structural or rock-cut, executed in a number of styles and dedicated to diverse deities. The two general Hindu temple types

are the northern and southern styles, prevalent in northern India and southern India respectively. Within these broad categories is great stylistic diversity, though all are raised on plinths and dominated by their superstructures. In north India, the term **shikhara** is used to refer to the entire towerlike superstructure, which often curves inward, sloping more steeply near its peak. By contrast, the southern superstructure is comprised of angular, steplike terraces, and the term *shikhara* refers only to its **finial**, that is, the uppermost member of the superstructure. North Indian *shikharas* are crowned by **amalakas**. Inside, a series of **mandapas** (halls) leads to an inner sanctuary, the **garbhagriha**, which contains a sacred image. An axis mundi is imagined to run vertically up from the Cosmic Waters below the earth, through the *garbhagriha*'s image, and out through the top of the tower.

Jain architecture consists mainly of structural and rock-cut monasteries and temples that have much in common with their Buddhist and Hindu counterparts.

stupa

northern-style temple

southern-style temple

Religious monuments called stupas, solid mounds enclosing a relic, are fundamental to Buddhism (see "Stupas and Temples" opposite). The exact nature of the relic varies, but in ideal cases they are connected directly to the Buddha himself or to one of his important disciples. The form, size, and decoration of stupas differ from region to region, but their symbolic meaning remains virtually the same, and their plan is a carefully calculated **mandala**, or diagram of the cosmos as envisioned in Buddhism. Stupas are open to all for private worship.

The first stupas were constructed to house the Buddha's remains after his cremation. According to tradition, these relics were divided into eight portions and given to important kings, who then further divided and encased the remains in burial mounds. Since the early stupas held actual remains of the Buddha, they were venerated as his body and, by extension, his enlightenment and attainment of *nirvana* (liberation from rebirth). The method of veneration was, and still is, to circumambulate, or walk around, the stupa in a clockwise direction.

THE GREAT STUPA AT SANCHI   Probably no early Buddhist structure is more famous than the **GREAT STUPA** at Sanchi in central India (**FIG. 10-8**). Most likely dating to the time of Ashoka, the Great Stupa originally formed part of a large monastery complex crowning a hill. During the mid second century BCE, it was enlarged to its present size, and the surrounding stone railing was constructed. About 100 years later, elaborately carved stone gateways were added to the railing.

Representative of the early central Indian stupa type, the solid, hemispherical mound of the Great Stupa at Sanchi was built up from rubble and dirt, faced with dressed stone, and covered with a shining white plaster made from lime and powdered seashells. A 10-foot-tall stone railing demarcates a circumambulatory path at ground level. Another walkway, approached by a staircase on the south side, creates a second raised level for circumambulation. On top of the mound a square enclosure designated by another railing contains the top of a mast bearing three stone disks, or "umbrellas," of decreasing size. Interpreted in various ways, these disks are probably an architectural form derived from the parasols used to shade kings and indicate people of importance. They may also correspond to the "Three Jewels of Buddhism"—the Buddha, the Law, and the Monastic Order.

The railing provides a protective boundary and demarcates a ritual path around the central structure. Carved with octagonal uprights and lens-shaped crossbars, it probably simulates the wooden railings of the time. Four stone gateways, or *toranas*, aligned with the four cardinal directions punctuate the railing. An inscription on the south gateway indicates that it was provided by ivory carvers from the nearby town of Vidisha, while another inscription on the same *torana* specifies a gift during the reign of King Satakarni of the Satavahana dynasty, providing the first-century BCE date for the gateways. The vast majority of the inscriptions at Sanchi, however, record modest donations by individual devotees from all walks of life. This collaborative patronage points to Buddhism's expanding popularity.

10-8 STUPA 1 (THE GREAT STUPA) AT SANCHI
Madhya Pradesh, India. Founded 3rd century BCE; enlarged c. 150–50 BCE.
Credit: © veice/Shutterstock

Rising to a height of 35 feet, the gateways are the only elements of the Great Stupa at Sanchi to be ornamented with sculpture.

The four gates support a three-tiered array of architraves in which posts and crossbars are elaborately carved with symbols and scenes drawn mostly from the Buddha's life and the **Jataka tales**, stories of the Buddha's past lives. These relief sculptures employ two distinctive features of early South Asian visual narrative. The first is that the Buddha himself is not shown in human form prior to the late first century BCE. Instead, he is represented by symbols such as his footprints, an empty "enlightenment" seat, or a plank. The reasons for this absence are still widely debated but, since Vedic gods and Jinas are very rarely depicted in this period, it seems likely that this was the result of a wider cultural practice rather than a uniquely Buddhist prohibition. The second is that South Asian sculpture frequently employs continuous narrative. This means that several moments in time are represented in the same visual frame. This visual narrative technique is used in the portrayal of the Great Departure covering the outer surface of a curving architrave of the eastern *torana*.

The *toranas* are further decorated with free-standing sculptures depicting such subjects as *yakshis* and their male counterparts, *yakshas*, riders on real and mythical animals, and the Buddhist wheel. Forming a bracket between each capital and the lowest crossbar on the east gate is a sculpture of a **YAKSHI** (FIG. 10–10). These *yakshis* are some of the finest female figures in Indian art, and they make an instructive comparison with the Didarganj image of the Maurya period (SEE FIG. 10–7). The earlier figure was distinguished by a formal, somewhat rigid pose, an emphasis

A Closer Look
THE GREAT DEPARTURE

Before he became the Buddha, Prince Siddhartha resolved to give up his royal comforts in order to pursue the life of an ascetic. Confiding only in his charioteer Channa, the prince slipped out of his palace in the dead of night, and, mounting his horse, headed for the gates. The local gods, *yakshas*, were eager for the prince to succeed on his spiritual quest and cupped their hands under the horse's hooves so that no one would awaken from the noise. Indeed, in some versions, they carry the horse and its rider right over the palace walls. This story is depicted, using some distinctive forms of visual narrative, on the middle architrave of the east gate of the Great Stupa at Sanchi.

The presence of the prince is indicated by the riderless horses shaded by a royal parasol and fly-whisk. This is the same horse shown at various moments in the story.

All the action is organized geographically in the scene as it plays out between the palace and the forest. This tree indicates the transition into the forest setting.

The *yakshas* accompany the creature only when ridden by the prince. In the lower right, the horse and charioteer turn back on their own, unaccompanied by the local gods and leaving Shakyamuni to begin his life as an ascetic.

The footprints on the far right of the relief indicate the place Prince Siddhartha dismounted.

10–9 THE GREAT DEPARTURE
East *torana* (exterior middle architrave) of Stupa 1 (the Great Stupa) at Sanchi. 1st century BCE. Sandstone.

Credit: Dinodia/Bridgeman Images

carved from top to bottom like great pieces of sculpture, with all details completely finished in stone. The cool, dark interior and the echo that magnifies the smallest sound combine to promote a state of heightened awareness in these remarkable halls.

The monastic community used two types of rock-cut halls. The **vihara** functioned as the monks' living quarters, and the **chaitya** ("sanctuary") usually enshrined a stupa. A **CHAITYA HALL** at Karle (**FIG. 10–11**), dating from the first century BCE to the first century CE, is one of the largest and most fully developed examples of these early Buddhist works. At the entrance, columns once supported a wooden façade, in front of which stands a pillar, inspired by Ashokan precedents. The walls of the vestibule are carved in relief with rows of small balcony railings and arched windows, simulating the appearance of a great multi-storied palace. At the base of the side walls, enormous statues of elephants seem to support the entire structure on their backs. Dominating the upper portion of the main façade is a large, horseshoe-shaped opening that provides the hall's main source of light.

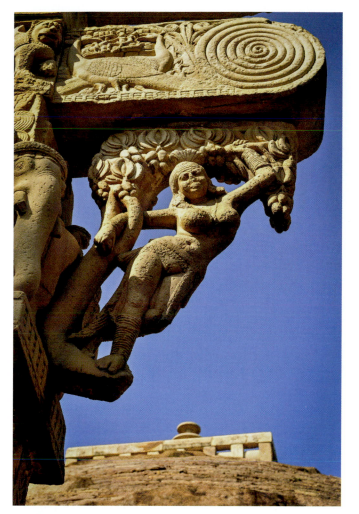

10–10 YAKSHI BRACKET FIGURE

East *torana* of the Great Stupa at Sanchi. 1st century BCE. Sandstone, height approx. 60″ (152.4 cm).

Credit: © veice/Shutterstock

on realistic details, and a clear distinction between clothed and nude parts of the body. In contrast, the Sanchi *yakshi* leans daringly into space with casual abandon, supported by one leg as the other charmingly crosses behind. Her diaphanous garment is noticeable only by its hems, and so she appears almost nude, which emphasizes her form. The mango tree on which she hangs is heavy with fruit, reasserting the fecundity and bounty associated with these mercurial deities. This semidivine figure's presence on a Buddhist gateway implies her role as a guardian or devotee, which, in turn, speaks to Buddhism's inclusiveness. Even deities were understood to benefit from the Buddha's teachings.

THE CHAITYA HALL AT KARLE From ancient times, caves have been considered hallowed places in India, because they were frequently the abodes of holy men and ascetics. Around the second century BCE, cavelike sanctuaries were hewn out of the stone plateaus in the region of south-central India known as the Deccan. Made for the use of Jain and Buddhist monks, these sanctuaries were

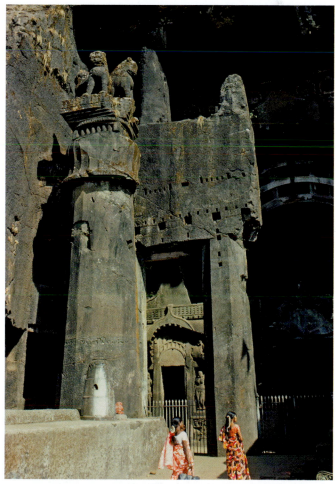

10–11 EXTERIOR OF CHAITYA HALL, KARLE

Maharashtra, India. 1st century BCE–1st century CE.

Credit: Image: Regents of the University of Michigan, History of Art Department, Visual Resources Collections

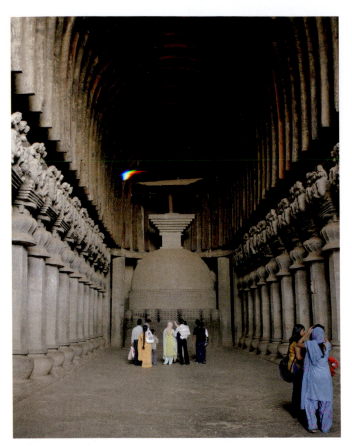

10-12 INTERIOR OF CHAITYA HALL, KARLE
Maharashtra, India. 1st century BCE–1st century CE.

Credit: © Ivan Vdovin/JAI/Corbis

The opening was originally fitted with a carved wooden screen, some of which remains, that filtered the light streaming inside.

Three entrances allow access to the interior. Flanking the doorways are sculpted panels of **mithuna** couples, amorous male and female figures that evoke the auspicious qualities of harmony and fertility in life. The **INTERIOR HALL** (FIG. 10-12), 123 feet long, has a 46-foot-high ceiling carved in the form of a barrel vault ornamented with arching wooden ribs. Both the interior and exterior of the hall were once brightly painted. Pillars demarcate a pathway for circumambulation around the stupa in the apse at the far end.

The side aisles are separated from the main aisle by closely spaced columns whose bases resemble a large pot set on a stepped pyramid of planks. The statues that comprise the upper capitals of these columns depict pairs of kneeling elephants, each bearing a *mithuna* couple. These figures, the only sculpture within this austere hall, may represent the nobility coming to pay homage. The pillars around the apse are plain, and the stupa is simple. A railing motif ornaments its base. The stupa was once topped with wooden umbrellas, only one of which remains. As with nearly everything in the cave, the stupa is carved from the rock of the cliff.

The Kushan Period

Around the first century CE, the regions of present-day Afghanistan, Pakistan, and north India came under the control of the Kushans, originally a nomadic people forced out of northwest China by the Han. Exact dates are uncertain, but they ruled from the first to the third century CE.

These heavily bearded warrior-kings made widespread use of royal portraiture on coins and in sculptural form. An image of **KING KANISHKA** (FIG. 10-13), whose reign is thought to have begun in 127 CE, represents one of the Kushans' most illustrious rulers. This boldly frontal work stands over 5 feet tall even with the head missing. The fact that his hands rest on his sword and massive club makes his martial authority clear even before reading the inscription, which identifies him as "The great king, king of kings." Attired in a coat and heavy felt riding boots, he is ill-suited for the warm South Asian climate; his garments reflect his Central Asian heritage. The hundreds of pearls that line the hem of his outfit are indicative of his great wealth and were particularly rare in the inland territories from which the Kushan migrated.

10-13 KING KANISHKA
Uttar Pradesh, India. c. 2nd–3rd century CE. Sandstone, height 5'3" (1.6 m). Government Museum, Mathura.

Credit: © T Paramjit/Ancient Art & Architecture Collection Ltd

These rulers were remarkably eclectic in their religious views and, judging from their coins, supported a wide range of religious institutions. In this tolerant climate, and perhaps spurred on by Kushan royal images, innovative figural art began to blossom in the Jain, Brahmanic, and Buddhist traditions.

Among these innovations are the first depictions of the Buddha himself in art. (Previously, as in the Great Stupa at Sanchi, the Buddha had been indicated solely by symbols.) Distinctive styles arose in the Gandhara region in the northwest (present-day Pakistan and Afghanistan) and in the important religious center of Mathura in central India. While the images from these Kushan-controlled regions are stylistically quite distinct, they shared a basic visual language, or iconography, in which the Buddha is readily recognized by specific characteristics. For instance, he wears a monk's robe, a long length of cloth draped over the left shoulder and around the body. The Buddha also is said to have had 32 major distinguishing marks, called **lakshanas**, some of which are reflected in the iconography (see "Buddhist Symbols" in Chapter 12 on page 370). These marks of a perfected being include a golden-colored body, long arms that reached to his knees, the impression of a wheel (*chakra*) on the palms of his hands and the soles of his feet, and the **urna**—a mark between his eyebrows. A prince in his youth, he had worn the customary heavy earrings, and so his earlobes are usually shown elongated. The top of his head is said to have had a protuberance called an **ushnisha**, which in images often resembles a bun or topknot and symbolizes his enlightenment.

THE GANDHARA STYLE Combining elements of Hellenistic, Persian, and Indian styles, Gandhara sculptors typically portrayed the Buddha as an athletic figure, more powerful and heroic than an ordinary human. Carved from gray schist, a fine-grained stone, this **STANDING BUDDHA** (**FIG. 10–14**) dates to the fully developed stage of the Gandhara style, during the second or early third century CE. The Buddha's body, whose contours are revealed through the folds of his garment, is broad and massive, with heavy shoulders and limbs and powerful legs. His left knee bends gently, suggesting a slightly relaxed posture.

The treatment of the robe is especially characteristic of the Gandhara manner. Naturalistic folds alternate with clinging cloth, setting up a clear, rhythmic pattern of heavy creases and shallow depressions. On the upper part of the figure, the folds break irregularly along the Buddha's left arm; below his waist they drape in a symmetric U shape. The strong tension of the complex fold pattern brings life and power to the figure. It resembles the treatment of togas on certain Roman statues (SEE FIG. 6–21) that exerted a strong influence on portrayals of the Buddha in Central and East Asia. The Gandhara region's relations with the Hellenistic world may have brought this strong

10–14 STANDING BUDDHA

From Gandhara, Pakistan. Kushan period, c. 2nd–3rd century CE. Gray schist, height 47¹⁄₂″ (1.2 m). Los Angeles County Museum of Art. Gift of Mr. and Mrs. Eric Lidow in honour of the museum's twenty-fifth anniversary (M.91.90)

Mediterranean feeling to its art. Pockets of Hellenistic culture had thrived in neighboring Bactria (present-day northern Afghanistan and southern Uzbekistan) since the fourth century BCE, when the Greeks under Alexander the Great had reached the borders of India. Also, Gandhara's position near the east–west trade routes stimulated contact with Roman culture in the Near East during the early centuries of the first millennium CE.

THE MATHURA STYLE   The second major style of Buddhist art in the Kushan period—that found at Mathura—was not allied with the Hellenistic-Roman tradition. Instead, the Mathura style evolved from representations of *yakshas*, the indigenous male nature deities. Early images of the Buddha produced at Mathura draw on this sculptural tradition, often portraying him in a frontal stance with broad shoulders and wide eyes.

The stele shown here (**FIG. 10-15**) is one of the finest of the early Mathura images. The sculptors worked in a distinctive red sandstone flecked with cream-colored spots. Carved in **high relief** (forms projecting strongly from the background), it depicts a seated Buddha with two attendants. His right hand is raised in a symbolic gesture meaning "have no fear." Images of the Buddha rely on a repertoire of such gestures, called **mudras**, to communicate certain ideas, such as teaching, meditation, or the attaining of enlightenment (see "Mudras" opposite). The Buddha's *urna*, his *ushnisha*, and the impressions of wheels on his palms and soles are all clearly visible in this figure. Behind his head is a large, circular halo; the scallop points of its border represent radiating light. Behind the halo are branches of the pipal tree, the tree under which the Buddha was seated when he achieved enlightenment. Two celestial beings hover above.

As in Gandhara sculptures, the Mathura work gives a powerful impression of the Buddha. The diaphanous quality of his robe is suited to the warm climate of Mathura, just as the thick robe of the Gandhara example is appropriate in the cooler weather of the northwest. The robe is pulled tightly over the body, allowing the fleshy form to be seen as almost nude. Where the pleats of the robe appear, such as over the left arm and fanning out between the legs, they are depicted abstractly through compact parallel formations of ridges with an incised line in the center of each ridge. This characteristic Mathura tendency to abstraction also appears in the face, whose features take on geometric shapes, as in the rounded forms of the widely opened eyes. Nevertheless, the torso with its subtle and soft modeling is strongly naturalistic. This Buddha's riveting outward gaze and alert posture impart an intense, concentrated energy that draws on imagery associated with nature deities and reveals a spiritual power contained in physical form.

Hinduism

Alongside the development of Buddhism, the older Vedic traditions underwent a long process of reform. These reforms were largely undertaken by members of the Brahmin community who had grown unsatisfied with the older systems of rituals. What emerged from these reforms was a series of practices and beliefs that we now collectively refer to as Hinduism. Hinduism is not one religion but many related beliefs and innumerable sects. It results from the mingling of Vedic beliefs with indigenous, local beliefs and practices. All three major Hindu sects draw upon the texts of the Vedas, which are believed to be sacred revelations set down about 1200–800 BCE. The gods lie outside the finite world, but they can appear in visible form to believers. Each Hindu sect takes its particular deity as supreme. By worshiping gods with rituals, meditation, and intense love, individuals may be reborn into increasingly higher positions until they escape the cycle of life, death, and rebirth, which is called *samsara*. The most popular deities are Vishnu, Shiva, and the Great Goddess, Devi. Deities are revealed and depicted in multiple aspects.

10-15 BUDDHA AND ATTENDANTS
From Katra Keshavdev, Mathura, Madhya Pradesh, India. Kushan period, c. late 1st–early 2nd century CE. Red sandstone, height 27¼" (69.2 cm). Government Museum, Mathura.

Credit: Photo: Frederick M. Asher

Art and its Contexts

MUDRAS

Mudras (Sanskrit for "signs") are ancient symbolic hand gestures that first appeared in a manual on dance, but came to be regarded as physical expressions of a particular action or state of being. In Buddhist art, they function iconographically. *Mudras* are also used during meditation to invoke specific states of mind. The following are the most common *mudras* in Asian art.

Dharmachakra mudra
Appears as if the subject is counting on his fingers. The gesture of teaching, setting the *chakra* (wheel) of the *dharma* (law or doctrine) in motion. Hands are at chest level.

Dhyana mudra
A gesture of meditation and balance, symbolizing the path toward enlightenment. Hands are in the lap, the lower representing *maya*, the physical world of illusion, the upper representing *nirvana*, enlightenment and release from the world.

Vitarka mudra
This variant of *dharmachakra mudra* stands for intellectual debate. The right and/or left hand is held at shoulder level with thumb and forefinger touching. The gesture resembles counting on the fingers with one hand.

Abhaya mudra
The gesture of reassurance, blessing, and protection, this *mudra* means "have no fear." The right hand is at shoulder level, with the palm outward.

Bhumisparsha mudra
This gesture calls upon the earth to witness Shakyamuni Buddha's enlightenment at Bodh Gaya. A seated figure's right hand reaches toward the ground, palm inward.

Varada mudra
The gesture of charity, symbolizing the fulfillment of all wishes. Alone, this *mudra* is made with the right hand; but when combined with *abhaya mudra* in standing Buddha figures (as is most common), the left hand is occasionally shown in *varada mudra*.

mudras

VISHNU: Vishnu is a regal god who works for the order and well-being of the world. He is often represented lying in a trance or asleep on the Cosmic Waters, where he dreams the world into existence. His attributes include the discus, conch shell, mace, and lotus. He usually has four arms and wears a crown and lavish jewelry. He rides a man-bird, Garuda. Vishnu appears in ten different incarnations (*avatara*), including Rama and Krishna, who have their own sects. Rama embodies virtue, and, assisted by the monkey king, he fights the demon Ravana. As Krishna, Vishnu is a supremely beautiful, blue-skinned youth who lives with the cowherds, loves the maiden Radha, and battles the demon Kansa.

SHIVA: Shiva is both creative and destructive, light and dark, male and female, ascetic and family man. His symbol is the *linga*, originally an upright phallus, which is typically represented as a low pillar set in a low base, or *yoni*, which represents the feminine. As an expression of his power and creative energy, he is often depicted as Lord of the Dance, dancing the Cosmic Dance, the endless cycle of death and rebirth, destruction and creation (SEE FIG. 10–33). He dances within a ring of fire, his four hands holding fire, carrying a drum, and gesturing to the worshipers. Shiva's animal vehicle is the bull. His consort is Parvati; their sons are the elephant-headed Ganesha, the remover of obstacles, and Karttikeya, often associated with war.

DEVI: Devi, the Great Goddess, controls material riches and fertility. She has forms indicative of beauty, wealth, and auspiciousness, but also forms of wrath, pestilence, and power. As the embodiment of cosmic energy, she provides the vital force to all the male gods. When armed and riding a lion (as the goddess Durga), she personifies righteous fury. As the goddess Lakshmi, she is the goddess of wealth and the auspicious.

There are countless other deities, but central to Hindu practice are *puja* (forms of worship) and *darshan* (beholding a deity), generally performed to obtain a deity's favor in the hope that this favor will lead to liberation from *samsara*. Because desire for the fruits of our actions traps us, the ideal is to consider all earthly endeavors as sacrificial offerings to a god. Pleased with our devotion, he or she may grant us an eternal state of pure being, pure consciousness, and pure bliss.

The Gupta Period and its Successors

The Guptas, who founded a dynasty in the eastern region of central India, expanded their territories during the fourth century CE to form an empire that encompassed northern and much of central India. Although Gupta rule was not long-lasting (ending in 550) or the most expansive, the influence of Gupta culture was tremendous and its impact was felt long after its decline. Renowned for their flourishing artistic, mathematical, and literary culture, the Guptas and their contemporaries brought forth some of India's most widely admired works of art. While Buddhism continued to be a major religion, the earliest surviving Hindu temples also date from this time.

By the fourth century the Vedic sacrifice, in which burnt offerings were ritually sent up to the gods, had given way to temple-based practices that invoked the divine presence into a sanctified architectural setting. These practices, collectively termed Hinduism by later observers, were still presided over by Brahmin priests but often brought new deities into prominence.

TEMPLE OF VISHNU AT DEOGARH   One of the earliest northern-style temples, dedicated to the Hindu god Vishnu, is at Deogarh in north-central India and dates to 530 CE (**FIG. 10–16**). The entire temple site is patterned on a *mandala*, or sacred diagram. Much of the central tower, or *shikhara*, has crumbled away, so we cannot determine its original shape with precision. Clearly a massive, solid structure built of large cut stones, it would have given the impression of a mountain, one of several metaphoric meanings of a Hindu temple. The temple has only one chamber, the *garbhagriha*, literally the womb chamber, which corresponds to the center of a *mandala*. As the deity's residence, the *garbhagriha* is likened to a sacred cavern within the "cosmic mountain" of the temple.

Large panels sculpted in relief with images of Vishnu appear as "windows" on the temple's exterior. These elaborately framed panels do not function literally to let light

10–16 VISHNU TEMPLE, DEOGARH
Uttar Pradesh, India. Gupta dynasty, c. 530 CE.

Credit: Borromeo/Art Resource, NY

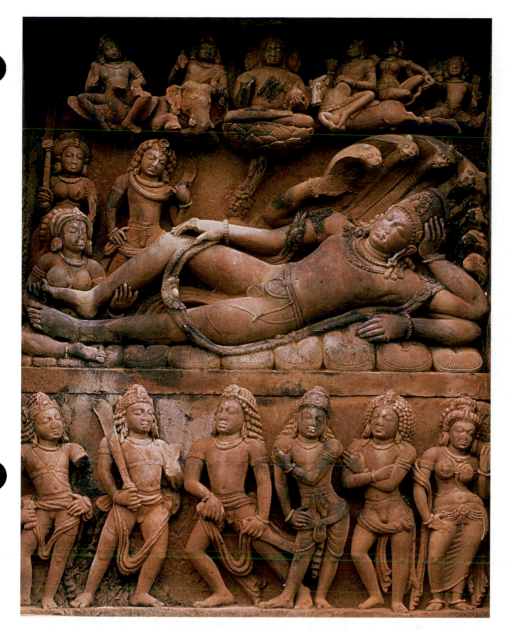

10–17 VISHNU LYING ON THE COSMIC WATERS
Relief panel in the Vishnu Temple, Deogarh. c. 530 CE. Sandstone, height approx. 5′ (1.5 m).

Credit: © akg-images/Jean-Louis Nou

richly ornamented. The ideal of the Gupta style is evident in the smooth, perfected shape of the body and in the lavishly detailed jewelry, including Vishnu's characteristic cylindrical crown. The four figures on the right in the frieze below Vishnu personify his four attributes. They stand ready to fight the appearance of evil, represented at the left of the frieze by two demons who threaten to kill Brahma and jeopardize all creation.

The birth of the universe and the appearance of evil are thus portrayed here in three clearly organized registers. Typical of Indian religious and artistic expression, these momentous events are set before our eyes not in terms of abstract symbols, but as a drama acted out by gods in superhuman form.

SEATED BUDDHA FROM SARNATH Buddhism continued to thrive during the Gupta period. Although the Gandhara style eventually declined in influence, the Mathura style gave rise to the Buddhist visual forms found over much of north India, including at sites like Sarnath.

A seated Buddha (**FIG. 10–18**) embodies the fully developed Sarnath Gupta style. Carved from fine-grained sandstone, the figure sits in a yogic posture making the teaching gesture indicative of the First Sermon. This event is further indicated by the devotees/listeners represented on the pedestal along with a wheel whose tread faces toward the viewer. The devotees, who may also represent the donors of this image, are joined in their devotion by two divine beings flying in from above. The Buddha's plain robe, portrayed with none of the creases and folds so prominent in the Kushan-period images, is typical of the Sarnath style. The body, clearly visible through the clinging robe, is graceful and slight, with broad shoulders and a well-proportioned torso. Only a few lines of the garment at the neck, waist, and hems interrupt the purity of its subtly

into the temple; they function symbolically to let the light of the deity *out* of the temple to be seen by those outside.

One panel depicts **VISHNU LYING ON THE COSMIC WATERS** at the beginning of creation (**FIG. 10–17**). He sleeps on the serpent of infinity, Ananta, whose body coils endlessly into space. Stirred by his female aspect (*shakti*, or female energy), personified here by the goddess Lakshmi, seen holding his foot, Vishnu dreams the universe into existence. From his navel springs a lotus (shown in this relief behind Vishnu), from which emerges the god Brahma (not to be confused with Brahman), who appears here as the central, four-headed figure in the row of gods portrayed above the reclining Vishnu. Brahma subsequently turns himself into the universe of space and time by thinking, "May I become many."

The sculptor has depicted Vishnu as a large, resplendent figure with four arms. His size and his multiple arms denote his omnipotence. He is lightly garbed but

10–18 BUDDHA PREACHING HIS FIRST SERMON
From Sarnath, Uttar Pradesh, India. Gupta period, c. 465–485 CE.
Sandstone, height 5′3″ (1.6 m). Archaeological Museum, Sarnath.

Credit: Luca Tettoni/Robert Harding

shaped surfaces; the face, smooth and ovoid, has the same refined elegance. The downcast eyes suggest otherworldly introspection, yet the gentle, open posture maintains a human quality. Behind the head is a large, circular halo. Carved in concentric circles of pearls and foliage, the ornate halo contrasts dramatically with the plain surfaces of the figure.

THE AJANTA CAVES   Prior to the late fifth century, the Vakataka dynasty had been subject to Gupta rule. Shortly after winning regional control, people affiliated with their court began to sponsor a new phase of construction at the rock-cut monastery of Ajanta. Each of these large caves, over 20 in all, appears to have had its own major patron. Whether inspired by devotion or competition, these caves are among the finest rock-cut architecture found anywhere. Adding to their importance is the fact that they preserve examples of wall painting, giving us a rare glimpse of a refined art form that has almost entirely been lost to time. Of these examples, Cave I, a large *vihara* hall with monks' chambers around the sides and a Buddha shrine chamber in the back, houses some of the finest. Murals painted in

mineral pigments on a prepared plaster surface cover the walls of the central court. Some depict episodes from the Buddha's past lives, while two large bodhisattvas, one of which is seen here (**FIG. 10–19**), flank the entrance to the shrine chamber.

Bodhisattvas are enlightened beings who postpone *nirvana* and buddhahood to help others achieve enlightenment. They are distinguished from buddhas in art by their princely garments. This bodhisattva is lavishly adorned with delicate ornaments: a bejeweled crown, large earrings, a pearl necklace, armbands, and bracelets. A striped cloth covers his lower body. The graceful bending posture and serene gaze impart a sympathetic attitude. The lotus flower in his right hand indicates his possible identity as the compassionate bodhisattva Avalokiteshvara.

The naturalistic style balances outline and softly graded color tones. Outline drawing, always a major ingredient of Indian painting, clearly defines shapes; tonal gradations impart the illusion of three-dimensional form, with lighter tones used for protruding parts such as the

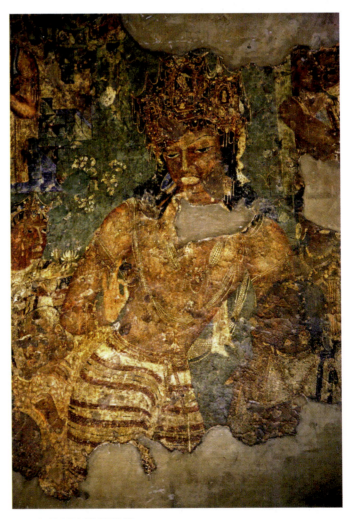

10–19 BODHISATTVA
Detail of a wall painting in Cave I, Ajanta, Maharashtra, India.
Vakataka dynasty, c. 475 CE.

Credit: © age fotostock/Dinodia

10–20 STANDING BUDDHA
Bamiyan, Afghanistan. c. 5th century CE. Sandstone coated in stucco, 165′ (50 m).

This photograph pre-dates the destruction of the Buddhas in 2001. Their recesses now stand empty.

Credit: Borromeo/Art Resource, NY

nose, brows, shoulders, and chest muscles. Together with the details of the jewels, these highlighted areas resonate against the subdued tonality of the figure. Sophisticated, realistic detail is balanced by the languorous human form. This particular synthesis is evident also in the Sarnath statue (SEE FIG. 10–18), which has much in common as well with the sculpture of Ajanta.

Other Developments, Fifth to the Seventh Centuries

After the fall of Gupta, north Indian empires struggled to match the splendor and stability of their predecessor, and by the late sixth century power shifted to the south where new and expansive empires emerged. These empires grew wealthy on trade and solidified their positions as transregional powers. As trade networks expanded, South Asian ideas and religions spread with them. This was good news for Buddhism, because as competition with Hinduism increased, the Buddhists found more receptive communities abroad.

THE BAMIYAN BUDDHAS   The Gupta and their feudatories were by no means the only kingdoms to flourish in fifth- to seventh-century South Asia. Bamiyan, about 155 miles northwest of Kabul, Afghanistan, was one example. Located just west of one of the most treacherous portions of the Silk Road, it was both a haven and crossroad on the lucrative trade routes that reached from China to the West. There, two enormous Buddhas were carved from

the rock of a cliff, one some 115 feet in height, the other about 165 feet tall (**FIG. 10–20**). Recorded by a Chinese pilgrim who came to Bamiyan in the seventh century, these Buddhas must date from before his visit. Buddhist travelers may have offered gifts of thanks or prayers for safety, depending on their destinations. On the right side of the smaller figure, pilgrims could walk within the cliff up a staircase that ended at the Buddha's shoulder. There they could look into the vault of the niche and see a painted image of the sun god, suggesting a metaphoric pilgrimage to the heavens. They could then circumambulate the figure at the level of the head and return to ground level by a staircase on the figure's left side. These huge figures likely served as the model for those at rock-cut sanctuaries in China, for example, at Yungang. Despite the historical and religious importance of these figures, and ignoring the pleas of world leaders, the Taliban demolished the Bamiyan Buddhas in 2001.

SIGIRIYA, SRI LANKA   Far away from Afghanistan, in the south, the palace site of **SIGIRIYA** was built on a dramatic plateau that rises abruptly above the forest canopy in north-central Sri Lanka (**FIG. 10–21**). According to the royal chronicles, this structure was built by King Kassapa in the late 400s CE after he usurped the throne from his father and drove off his brother. Visitors to the palace first passed through a broad moat and elaborate terraced gardens before beginning their ascent. At its base, the staircase passed through the chest of a massive sculptural lion, of which only the naturalistically rendered feet still exist.

10-21 SIGIRIYA
Matale District, Central Province, Sri Lanka. 5th century CE. Aerial view.

Credit: © Tuul and Bruno Morandi/Getty Images

As visitors climbed higher they were greeted by painted murals depicting elegant **HEAVENLY MAIDENS** moving among clouds (**FIG. 10-22**) before emerging at the top of the plateau. Only the foundations of the palace buildings, cisterns, and a few sculptures remain, but they are sufficient to convey a sense of the site's imposing splendor and spectacular elevation. Kassapa did not have long to enjoy his luxurious and well-fortified home, however, because within approximately 11 years the rightful heir, his brother Moggallana, returned with an army and took back the kingdom. After his victory, Moggallana gave Sigiriya to the Buddhists as a monastery.

TEMPLE OF SHIVA AT ELEPHANTA The Hindu god Shiva exhibits a wide range of aspects or forms, both gentle and wild: He is the Great Yogi who dwells for vast periods of time in meditation in the Himalayas; he is also the husband par excellence who makes love to the goddess Parvati for eons at a time; he is the Slayer of Demons; and he is the Cosmic Dancer who dances the destruction and re-creation of the world. Many of these forms of Shiva appear in the monumental relief panels adorning a cave-temple carved in the mid sixth century on the island of Elephanta off the coast of Mumbai in western India. The cave-temple is complex in layout and conception and is

10-22 HEAVENLY MAIDENS
Detail of wall painting, Sigiriya. 5th century CE.

Credit: Fuchsphotography/Fotolia

10–23 CAVE-TEMPLE OF SHIVA, ELEPHANTA

Maharashtra, India. Post-Gupta period, mid 6th century CE. View along the east–west axis to the *linga* shrine.

Credit: © age fotostock/Dinodia

a fine example of Hindu rock-cut architecture. While most temples have one entrance, this temple offers three—one facing north, one east, and one west. The interior, impressive in its size and grandeur, is designed along two main axes, one running north–south, the other east–west. The three entrances provide the only source of light, and the resulting cross- and back-lighting effects add to the sense of the cave as a place of mysterious, almost confusing complexity.

Along the east–west axis, large pillars cut from the rock appear to support the low ceiling and its beams, although, as with all architectural elements in a cave-temple, they are not structural (**FIG. 10–23**). The pillars form orderly rows, but the rows are hard to discern within the framework of the cave shape, which is neither square nor longitudinal, but formed of overlapping *mandalas* that create a symmetric yet irregular space. The pillars each have an unadorned, square base rising to nearly half the pillar's total height. Above is a circular column, which has a curved contour and a billowing "cushion" capital. Both column and capital are delicately fluted, adding a surprising refinement to these otherwise sturdy forms. The focus of the east–west axis is a square **linga shrine** (SEE FIG. 10–23, center left). A pair of colossal standing guardian figures flank each of its four entrances. In the center of the shrine is the *linga*, the abstracted symbol of Shiva that represents his presence as the unmanifest Formless One, or Brahman. Synonymous with Shiva, the *linga* is seen in nearly every Shiva temple and shrine.

The focus of the north–south axis, in contrast, is a relief on the south wall with a huge bust of Shiva representing his Sadashiva, or **ETERNAL SHIVA**, aspect (**FIG. 10–24**). Three heads rest upon the broad shoulders of the upper body, but five heads are implied: the fourth behind and the fifth, never depicted, on top. The head in the front depicts Shiva deep in introspection. The massiveness of the broad head, the large, barely delineated eyes, and the mouth with its heavy lower lip all suggest the

10–24 ETERNAL SHIVA

Rock-cut relief in the cave-temple of Shiva, Elephanta. Mid 6th century CE. Height approx. 11' (3.4 m).

Credit: © ephotocorp/Alamy Stock Photo

god's serious depths. Lordly and majestic, he easily supports his huge crown, intricately carved with designs and jewels, and the matted, piled-up hair of a yogi. On his left shoulder, his creative nature is depicted as female, with curled hair and a pearl-festooned crown. On his right shoulder, his wrathful, destroyer nature wears a fierce expression, and snakes adorn his ear and hand.

The Pallava Period

Rising to power in the late sixth century, the Pallava dynasty spread from its heartland in southeastern India, drawing wealth from overseas trade. The kingdom grew to its peak during the reigns of King Mahendravarman I (c. 600–630 CE) and his successor Narasimhavarman I (c. 630–668 CE), who was also referred to by his nickname "Mamalla" (which alludes to his skill at wrestling). Both men sponsored rock-cut shrines and sculpture at the coastal city of Mamallapuram, near Chennai. Often religious in subject matter, the carving is at times infused with a whimsical humor. This good-natured irreverence emerges most clearly in the Pallava literary tradition. One well-known farcical drama attributed to Mahendravarman himself pokes fun at Tantric ascetics, Buddhist monks, and Brahmin priests.

At Mamallapuram there are many large boulders and cliffs along the shore from which the Pallava-period stonecutters carved entire temples as well as reliefs. Among the most interesting of these rock-cut temples is a group known as the Five Rathas, which preserve diverse early architectural styles that probably reflect contemporary wood or brick structures.

DHARMARAJA RATHA AT MAMALLAPURAM   One of this group, today called the **DHARMARAJA RATHA** (**FIG. 10–25**), epitomizes the early southern-style temple. Each story of the superstructure is articulated by a cornice and carries a row of miniature shrines. Both shrines and cornices are decorated with a window motif from which faces peer. The shrines not only demarcate each story, but also provide loftiness for this palace intended to enshrine a god. The temple, square in plan, remains unfinished, and what would have been a pillared hall on the first floor was never hollowed out, suggesting that, like cave-temples, Dharmaraja Ratha was executed from the top downward. On the lower portion, only the columns and niches have been carved. The presence of a single deity in each niche forecasts the main trend in temple sculpture in the centuries ahead: The tradition of narrative reliefs declined, and the stories they told became concentrated in statues of individual deities, which conjure up entire mythological episodes through characteristic poses and a few symbolic objects. On the south side of this ratha, among the images of deities, is an unusual two-armed image identified as a representation of King Mamalla, who appears to be visually associating himself with Shiva. This practice of depicting royalty in the likeness of divinity became more common over time and was widely practiced in parts of Southeast Asia.

THE GREAT RELIEF AT MAMALLAPURAM   There are many possible ways to interpret an enormous relief at Mamallapuram (**FIG. 10–26**), and this ambiguity was almost certainly intended by its creators. In Sanskrit poetry, the use of overlapping meaning is called *slesha*, and it was appreciated for its sophistication. The most prominent interpretation of this scene is that it depicts the penance of a king, Bhagiratha, who sought to purify the bones of his deceased relatives by subjecting himself to terrible austerities. In response to his penance, the god Shiva sent the sacred Ganges River, represented by the natural cleft in the rock, to earth, thereby allowing the holy man to ensure his relatives some peace in their next lives. Bhagiratha is shown

10–25 DHARMARAJA RATHA, MAMALLAPURAM
Tamil Nadu, India. Pallava period, c. mid 7th century CE.

Credit: Arvind Balaraman/Fotolia

10-26 DESCENT OF THE GANGES

Rock-cut relief, Mamallapuram, Tamil Nadu, India. Mid 7th century CE. Granite, approx. 20′ (6 m).

Credit: Snowwhiteimages/Fotolia

staring directly at the sun through his parted fingers, standing for interminable periods on one foot, and in deep prayer before a temple. In the upper left part of the relief, Shiva, shown four-armed, appears before Bhagiratha to grant his wish. Elsewhere in the relief animal families are depicted, generally in mutually protective roles. But in a characteristically Pallava twist, this pious scene is mimicked by a cat who does his best to imitate Bhagiratha's pose (**FIG. 10-27**). The reference is to the story of an aging cat who pretends to be an ascetic who has renounced meat, so as to lure the local mice into complacency, much to their misfortune. This cautionary tale about false ascetics serves as an apt and humorous foil to the upper scene of consummate penance and faith. Both tales are set on the banks of the Ganges.

This richly carved relief was executed under the Pallava dynasty, which continued to flourish in southeastern India until the ninth century CE. The relief must have been visible to anyone heading inland from the sea and likely served as an allegory for benevolent kingship. It was possibly even an attempt to invoke the presence of the sacred Ganges River right at the heart of the Pallavas' southern empire.

10-27 CAT IN YOGIC POSTURE

Detail from rock-cut relief, Mamallapuram, Tamil Nadu, India. Mid 7th century CE.

Credit: Nstanev/Fotolia

The Eighth through Twelfth Centuries

During the eighth through twelfth centuries, regional styles developed in ruling kingdoms that were generally smaller than those that had preceded them. Hindu gods Vishnu, Shiva, and the Great Goddess (mainly Durga) grew increasingly popular. Monarchs rivaled each other in the building of temples to their favored deity, and complicated and subtle variations of the Hindu temple emerged with astounding rapidity in different regions. By around 1000 the Hindu temple reached unparalleled heights of grandeur and engineering.

KAILASHA TEMPLE, ELLORA   Occupied and expanded from the fifth to the tenth century, the rock-cut site of Ellora has 34 caves in all, variously dedicated to Buddhism, Jainism, and Hinduism. Among the most spectacular of these is "Cave" 16, the **KAILASHA TEMPLE** (**FIG. 10-28**), which

was most likely started in the reign of the Rashtrakuta king Krishna I (ruled 757–83 CE) and completed under his successors. In many ways, this structure marks the apex of the South Asian rock-cut tradition, as the skilled architects and artists successfully sculpted an entire two-story, highly ornamented Shiva temple out of a single mass of stone. The structure is set back in the mountainside, which required cutting straight down 107 feet so that the rock would be high enough to accommodate the stepped, southern-style tower.

Passing the outer gateway, devotees can circumambulate at ground level and admire the narrative sculptural scenes and large elephants that adorn the lower plinth. Alternately, visitors can climb an internal staircase to a second level where a relatively small shrine dedicated to Shiva's bull-mount, Nandi, faces the main temple across a bridge. The interior of the main temple hall (*mandapa*) was originally painted with additional narrative imagery. The *garbhagriha* can be circumambulated from the second story by coming out onto a balcony from which a

10-28 KAILASHA TEMPLE, CAVE 16, ELLORA
Aurangabad District, Maharashtra, India. Mid 8th century CE.

Credit: Michalknitl/Fotolia

10–29 KANDARIYA MAHADEVA TEMPLE, KHAJURAHO

Madhya Pradesh, India. Chandella dynasty, c. 1000 CE.

Credit: © Westend61 GmbH/Alamy Stock Photo

number of subsidiary shrines radiate. The narrative sculpture throughout the site depicts a wide range of deities and events from Hindu literature, many of which feature Shiva.

This site takes the metaphorical association between temples and mountains to an extreme as it is constructed, quite literally, from a mountain. Even the temple itself is named for Shiva's abode on Mount Kailasha in the Himalayas. Despite this association, remote mountainside locations better suited the needs of Buddhist and Jain monastic communities. Such locations proved to fit poorly with the public nature and ritual requirements of Hindu temples. The Kailasha Temple stands as the last of the great rock-cut Hindu temples. From this point on, architects and donors favored built structures placed in or near major urban centers.

KANDARIYA MAHADEVA TEMPLE, KHAJURAHO In 950 CE, the Chandella court moved against the weakened Pratihara dynasty, to whom they were vassals. This rebellion proved successful, and the Chandella marked their new status by undertaking an ambitious project of temple building. The earliest of these structures housed an image of Vishnu taken directly from their previous overlords, but this temple was only the first among many. Khajuraho remained the capital and main temple site for the Chandellas, who constructed more than 80 temples there, about 25 of which are well preserved.

The **KANDARIYA MAHADEVA** (**FIG. 10–29**), a temple dedicated to Shiva at Khajuraho, was probably built by a ruler of the Chandella dynasty in the late tenth or early eleventh century. In the northern style, a curvilinear *shikhara* rises over the *garbhagriha* of the temple. Extensively ornamented with additional halls on the front and porches to the sides and back, the temple rests on a stone terrace that sets off a sacred space from the mundane world. A steep flight of stairs at the front (to the right in the illustration) leads to a series of three *mandapas* (distinguished on the outside by pyramidal roofs), preceding the *garbhagriha*. The *mandapas* serve as spaces for ritual, such as dances performed for the deity, and for the presentation of offerings. The temple is built of stone blocks using only post-and-lintel construction. Despite this architectural challenge, the *shikhara* rises more than 100 feet over the *garbhagriha* and is crowned by a small *amalaka*, or bulbous ornament. The *shikhara* is bolstered by the many smaller subsidiary towers bundled around it. This decorative scheme adds a complex richness to the surface, but it also obscures the shape of the main *shikhara*, which is slender, with a swift and impetuous upward movement. The roofs of the *mandapas* contribute to the impression of rapid ascent by growing progressively taller as they near the *shikhara*.

Despite its apparent complexity, the temple has a clear structure and unified composition. Strong horizontal **moldings** (shaped or sculpted strips) and open spaces over the *mandapas* and porches separate the towers of the superstructure from the lower portion. Three rows of sculpture—some 600 figures—are integrated into the exterior walls. Approximately 3 feet tall and carved in high relief, the sculptures depict gods and goddesses, as well as figures in erotic postures.

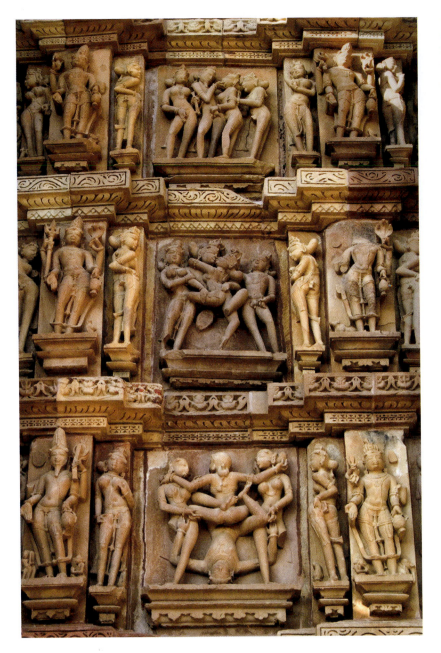

10-30 EROTIC SCULPTURES, KANDARIYA MAHADEVA TEMPLE
Detail of reliefs. Height of registers approx. 3'3" (1 m).
Sandstone, c. 1000 CE.

Credit: © Hitendra Sinkar/Alamy Stock Photo

ideal relationship between humans and deities. Rather than focusing on ritual and the performance of *dharma* according to the Vedas, *bhakti* stresses an intimate, personal, and loving relation with the god, and complete devotion and surrender to the deity. Tantrism, by contrast, is pursued under the guidance of a teacher and employs various techniques designed to help the devotee self-identify with the deity. Ultimately this leads to a profound understanding that there is no separation between oneself and the divine. Although not typical, both traditions have, at times, employed erotic or romantic imagery as a visual means of expressing ideas of devotion and unity.

GAL VIHARA, SRI LANKA During the twelfth century, when Buddhism had all but disappeared from India, it was still thriving in Sri Lanka. This island kingdom played a large role in exporting Buddhist ideas to parts of Southeast Asia, with which it had maintained close economic and cultural ties. Sri Lanka was central to strengthening and maintaining the conservative Theravada Buddhist traditions, especially by preserving scriptures and relics. Sri Lankan sculptors further refined Indian styles and iconography in colossal Buddhist sculptures but rarely initiated further elaboration on traditional Buddhist forms. Because the Buddha's image was believed to have been based on a portrait made during his lifetime, intentional variation was considered unnecessary and inaccurate.

The Khajuraho temples are especially well known for their **EROTIC SCULPTURES** (**FIG. 10-30**). These carvings are not placed haphazardly, but rather in a single vertical line at the juncture of the walls enclosing the *garbhagriha* and the last *mandapa*. Their significance is uncertain; perhaps they derive from the amorous couples (*mithuna*) found at the entrances of many temples and *chaityas*. It is also possible that they relate to two growing traditions within Hinduism: *tantra* and *bhakti*.

These terms are associated with two major religious movements that were developing throughout this period and affected Hindu practice and art: the tantric, or esoteric, and the *bhakti*, or devotional. Although both movements evolved throughout India, the influence of tantric sects appeared during this period primarily in the art of the north, while the *bhakti* movements found artistic expression across South Asia. *Bhakti* revolves around the

The construction of the Gal Vihara is linked to an ambitious series of construction projects undertaken by King Parakramabahu in the mid twelfth century. The rock-cut **PARINIRVANA OF THE BUDDHA** at this monastic complex (**FIG. 10-31**) is one of three colossal Buddhas at the site. This serene and dignified image restates one of the early themes of Buddhist art, that of the Buddha's final death and transcendence, with a sophistication of modeling and proportion that updates and localizes the classical Buddhist tradition. Postholes in the rock face reveal that this sculpture was originally housed in a wooden superstructure that has since decayed. Fortunately granite is

10-31 PARINIRVANA OF THE BUDDHA

Gal Vihara, near Polonnaruwa, Sri Lanka. 11th–12th century CE. Granite.

Credit: © ziggymars/123RF

more durable, and this fine example of Sri Lankan colossal sculpture has been preserved. This monastery, located north of the capital in Polonnaruwa, was occupied until the capital fell in the late 1200s.

The Chola Period

The Cholas, who succeeded the Pallavas in the mid ninth century, founded a dynasty that governed most of the far south of India well into the late thirteenth century. Their extensive trade networks and powerful navy also made them a potent cultural force in many parts of Southeast Asia over these centuries. The Chola dynasty reached its peak during the reign of Rajaraja I (ruled 985–1014). As an expression of gratitude for his many victories in battle, Rajaraja built the Rajarajeshvara Temple to Shiva in his capital, Thanjavur (formerly known as Tanjore). The name Rajarajeshvara means the temple of "Rajaraja's Lord," that is, Shiva, which also has the effect of linking the name of the king with that of Shiva. His patronage of the temple was in part a reflection of the fervent Shiva *bhakti* movement which had reached its peak by that time. Now commonly called the Brihadeshvara Temple (Temple of the Great Lord), this temple is a remarkable achievement of the southern style of Hindu architecture (**FIG. 10-32**). It stands within a huge walled compound near the banks of the Kaveri River. Although smaller shrines dot the compound, the Rajarajeshvara dominates the area.

10-32 RAJARAJESHVARA TEMPLE OF SHIVA, THANJAVUR

Tamil Nadu, India. Chola dynasty, 1003–1010 CE.

Credit: © 123RF.com

Rising to an astonishing height of 216 feet, this temple was probably the tallest structure in India in its time. Each story is decorated with miniature shrines, window motifs, and robust dwarf figures who seem to be holding up the next story. Like the contemporaneous Kandariya Mahadeva Temple at Khajuraho (SEE FIG. 10–29), the Rajarajeshvara has a longitudinal axis and greatly expanded dimensions, especially with regard to its superstructure, a four-sided, hollow pyramid. Typical of the southern style, the *mandapa* at the front of the Rajarajeshvara has a flat roof, as opposed to the pyramidal roofs of the northern style. The walls of the sanctum rise for two stories, with each story emphatically articulated by a large cornice. The interior was originally painted, and portions of this decoration have recently been uncovered as sections of the overpainting were removed. The exterior walls are ornamented with niches, each of which holds a single statue, usually depicting a form of Shiva. Because the Rajarajeshvara's superstructure is not obscured by its decorative motifs, it forcefully ascends skyward and is topped by an octagonal dome-shaped capstone. This huge capstone is exactly the same size as the *garbhagriha* housed 13 stories directly below. It thus evokes the shrine a final time before the eye ascends to the point separating the worldly from the cosmic sphere above.

Perhaps no sculpture is more representative of Hinduism than the statues of Shiva Nataraja, or Shiva as the Lord of Dance, a form perfected by sculptors under the royal patronage of the south Indian Chola dynasty during the late tenth to eleventh centuries (FIG. 10–33). The particularly striking Chola version of the Dancing Shiva was introduced and promoted primarily through the efforts of one woman, Queen Sembiyan Mahadevi. Donation records spanning over 60 years reveal that she was a major patron both of temple building and bronze casting, and many of her projects involved increasing the prominence of Shiva Nataraja. It was not unusual for Hindu royal families to associate themselves with a particular aspect of a deity, and her efforts were instrumental in forging such a bond between Shiva Nataraja and the Chola state.

By the thirteenth or fourteenth century, the dance of Shiva came to represent a dance of cosmic proportions, signifying the universe's cycle of death and rebirth; it is also a dance for each individual, signifying the liberation of the believer through Shiva's compassion. In the iconography of the Nataraja, this sculpture shows Shiva with four arms dancing on the prostrate body of Apasmara, a dwarf figure who symbolizes "becoming" and whom Shiva controls. Shiva's extended left hand holds a ball of fire; a circle of fire rings the god. The fire is emblematic of the destruction

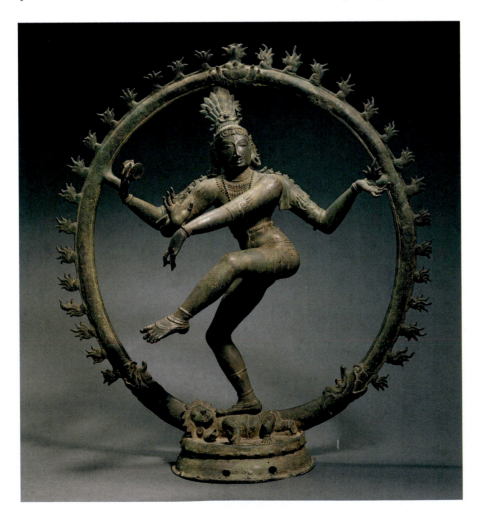

10–33 SHIVA NATARAJA (SHIVA AS LORD OF THE DANCE)

South India. Chola dynasty, 11th century CE. Bronze, 43⅞ × 40" (111.5 × 101.65 cm). Cleveland Museum of Art. Purchase from the J.H. Wade Fund (1930.331).

Credit: Bridgeman Images

of *samsara* and the physical universe as well as the destruction of *maya* (illusion) and our ego-centered perceptions. Shiva's back right hand holds a drum; its beat represents the irrevocable rhythms of creation and destruction, birth and death. His front right arm shows the *abhaya* "have no fear" *mudra* (see "Mudras" on page 313). The front left arm, gracefully stretched across his body with the hand pointing to his raised foot, signifies the promise of liberation.

The artist has rendered the complex pose with great clarity. The central axis, which aligns the nose, navel, and insole of the weight-bearing foot, maintains the figure's equilibrium while the remaining limbs extend asymmetrically far to each side. Shiva wears a short loincloth, a ribbon tied above his waist, and delicately tooled ornaments. The scant clothing reveals his perfected form with its broad shoulders tapering to a supple waist. The jewelry is restrained, and the detail does not detract from the beauty of the body. This work was made using the lost-wax method and is a testament to the extraordinary skill routinely exhibited by Chola artists.

Early Art and Architecture of Southeast Asia

How do Southeast Asian art and architecture develop through a series of early cultures and dynasties?

Geographically, Southeast Asia is part of the Asian continental plate and can be divided into two broad regions. The first part is its peninsular or mainland portion, which emerges from the southern edge of Asia and includes Myanmar, Cambodia, Laos, Malaysia, Singapore, Thailand, and Vietnam. The second region is comprised of a vast archipelago of islands that spreads out into the Pacific and Indian oceans. This maritime region includes the states of Brunei, East Timor, Indonesia, and the Philippines.

With its high mountainous interior and dense vegetation, Southeast Asia's earliest human settlements naturally formed along the rivers and coastlines, facilitating both food production and trade. Additionally, the presence of rich mineral deposits allowed for the development of metallurgy. Bronze casting developed early in the region, and the oldest bronze finds, located on the mainland, have been, with some disagreement, dated to 1500 BCE.

Early Southeast Asia

Archaeological work at sites such as Ban Chiang in northeastern Thailand has uncovered a wide range of bronze tools and jewelry as well as finely decorated ceramics. Because its distinctive bronzework has been found as far afield as Java, the archaeological site of Dongson in

northern Vietnam reveals evidence of short-range ocean trade having developed shortly after 600 BCE. By the first century CE, these trade networks had expanded, and evidence for a kingdom or collection of states called Funan in the southern reaches of the Southeast Asian peninsula is provided by third-century CE Chinese sources. As long-distance trade increased, the Southeast Asians found themselves in a strategic and lucrative location for controlling and mediating exchanges between East Asia and points west. Having no shortage of locally produced and highly prized commodities like hardwoods and spices, regional merchants were also active participants in this trade network. It was perhaps inevitable that over these centuries of trade, new ideas also arrived. By the sixth century CE there is ample evidence that Buddhism and Hinduism had taken firm root in the Mon kingdom of Dvaravati (present-day Thailand and southern Myanmar), as well as in the pre-Angkorian art of the Khmer (in today's Cambodia).

Sixth to the Ninth Century

As trade networks strengthened and expanded, Southeast Asian communities gained increased access to foreign goods and foreign ideas. The South Asian religions of Hinduism and Buddhism were of particular influence and gained popularity just as some of the earliest large-scale kingdoms were emerging. These religions supported and inspired emerging dynasties and became closely intertwined with early Southeast Asian concepts of kingship.

DVARAVATI-STYLE BUDDHA, THAILAND   The Mon ethnic group was among the first in Southeast Asia to adopt Buddhism. Starting in the sixth century CE they organized into a kingdom whose name, Dvaravati, is preserved thanks to a cache of ritual coins unearthed from a stupa in Nakhon Pathom, Thailand. The archaeological remains from this kingdom are quite varied in form, media, and subject, which is not surprising given that the Mon controlled this region until the Khmer gained influence in the tenth century.

Characteristic of the sculpture associated with early Mon sites are the standing Buddha images in bronze, as seen in an eighth-century example (**FIG. 10-34**). Stylistically, this image exhibits the arched brows, outlined facial features, and curled hair reminiscent of the Mathura style; however, the double robe is flattened in a distinctive manner against the body with a capelike angularity at its base. The iconography is consistent with that seen in South Asia, but Dvaravati Buddhas almost invariably display the same *mudra* in both hands, in this case the *vitarka*. The reasons for this insistence on symmetry are not known, but it suggests a local preference. The typically small size of these images may indicate that they were inspired by portable icons carried along the trade routes.

10-34 STANDING DVARAVATI BUDDHA
Mon Dvaravati style, from Thailand. 8th century CE. Bronze, 52"
(1.3 m). The Nelson-Atkins Museum of Art, Kansas City, Missouri.
Purchase: William Rockhill Nelson Trust (51-23).

HARIHARA, CAMBODIA Local preferences are exhibited clearly in a late seventh-century CE sculpture from Phnom Da, Cambodia. This pre-Angkorian Khmer work depicts a merged form of the Hindu gods Shiva and Vishnu known as **HARIHARA** (FIG. 10-35). Such images are only rarely encountered in South Asia, but in Southeast Asia, in the absence of a long history of sectarian differences between devotees of the two gods, this unified expression of Hindu divinity became extremely popular. Iconographically, the right side of the image depicts Shiva with his trident, matted hair, third eye, and animal skins. The left half, correspondingly, represents Vishnu, whose cylindrical crown, *chakra* (throwing disk), and fine garments indicate his identity. The artist has rendered this

complex subject with great skill, but in this early period the Khmer still did not fully trust the strength of the stone, so the sculptor cautiously linked the hands to the head with a supporting arch of stone.

BOROBUDUR, INDONESIA The mainland was not alone in transforming new ideas from abroad. The islands of Southeast Asia, Java in particular, produced some of the earliest and grandest responses to imported Buddhist ideas. The remarkable structure of **BOROBUDUR** (FIG. 10-36) was built in its central Java location by the Shailendra dynasty about the year 800. It appears to have been the endpoint of a processional road that linked this site with the Buddhist sacred structures at Mendut and Pawon. Borobudur has characteristics typical of a stupa as well as those suggestive of a three-dimensional *mandala*, or cosmic diagram, but many aspects of the structure's use are still poorly understood.

The monument itself rises more than 100 feet from ground level. This stepped pyramid of volcanic-stone blocks has five lower quadrilateral terraces that support three roughly circular terraces topped with a large, bell-shaped stupa, itself ringed by 72 smaller openwork stupas. Each of the squared terraces is enclosed by a high wall bearing extensive relief sculpture and adorned with Buddha images in niches and small, bell-shaped projections. The decoration on the lowest level was hidden for centuries because shortly after the monument was built, it was bolstered by a heavy architectural foot in order to stop the structure from spreading as the dirt in its core settled under the weight of the stone. During the restoration of the monument that began in 1975, these **bas-reliefs** were

10-35 HARIHARA
From Phnom Da, Angkor Barei, Cambodia. Pre-Angkorian Khmer, 7th century CE. Sandstone, 68" (76 cm). Musée Guimet, Paris.

Credit: Photo © RMN-Grand Palais (musée Guimet, Paris)/Thierry Ollivier

10-36 BOROBUDUR
Central Java, Magelang District, Indonesia. c. 800 CE. Aerial view.

Credit: © Luca Tettoni/ Corbis

exposed and carefully photographed. As with all sculpture at the site, the figures are elegant, with full, rounded bodies whose smooth forms are sporadically accentuated by delicately carved adornments.

The decorative program of these relief carvings displays a carefully calculated arrangement that moves from pragmatic moral lessons at the base up to more abstract religious ideas at the summit. The lowest gallery, which had been covered by the foot, depicts instructive scenes of karmic reward and punishment (**FIG. 10-37**). As one circumambulates to the next set of terraces, scenes of the Buddha's past lives and other moral tales share space with

10-37 SCENE OF DRUNKENNESS AND MODERATION
Borobudur, east side. Central Java, Indonesia. c. 800 CE.

This scene depicts a lesson from the Karmavibhanga on the rewards for moderation in food and drink. The figures on the upper right turn away from the scene of debauchery played out in front of them. In reward for this good judgment they are reborn as individuals with few diseases, indicated by the hearty couple surrounded by supplicants on the right side of the panel. The tree divides the cause from the effect.

Credit: © Ari Sanjaya/123RF

10–38 LORO JONGGRANG
Prambanan, Central Java, Indonesia. 9th century CE.

Credit: NJ/Fotolia

the life story of Shakyamuni Buddha. Moving upward, terraces four and five visually recount the story of Sudhana, an ordinary man who seeks personal enlightenment, eventually achieving it with the guidance of a bodhisattva. At this point visitors exit to the upper three circular terraces, whose rows of stupas and wide vista may be a metaphor for the enlightened state. Each of these perforated stupas holds a seated Buddha except for the large, central stupa, whose surface is solid. The placement of Buddha images on the monument and their differing *mudras* corresponds to the arrangement found in some Buddhist *mandalas* and points to another layer of meaning in this exceptionally complex architectural plan.

LORO JONGGRANG, INDONESIA Slightly later than Borobudur, but clearly influenced by its example, is the extensive site of **LORO JONGGRANG** in Prambanan, Java (**FIG. 10-38**). Although not a stepped pyramid, this Hindu monument employs a concentric plan and shares

Borobudur's repetition of bell-shaped forms. This temple complex was begun in the mid ninth century by the Sanjaya dynasty, regional rivals to the Shailendra, under the reign of Rakai Pikatan. It was then further expanded by later kings.

The buildings in the complex are arranged around the central temple dedicated to Shiva. The central sacred area, housing the biggest temples, is enclosed in an outer wall, beyond which the remains of 224 shrines are arrayed in four concentric squares. Most of these shrines are now badly damaged and their function is not clear, but some have speculated that their locations may reflect the social status of their donors. The towering central structure stands almost 155 feet high and is flanked by two somewhat smaller structures dedicated to Vishnu and Brahma, each just over 108 feet in height. The primary image of Shiva is an anthropomorphic representation rather than a *linga*. Its east-facing chamber is surrounded by subsidiary shrines aligned to the other

10-39 ABDUCTION OF SITA
Illustration of the *Ramayana*, relief 13, scene 2, Chandi Shiva, Prambanan, central Java, Indonesia. 9th century CE.

Credit: ©1983 Visual Resources Collections, Department of History of Art, Regents of the University of Michigan cardinal directions and housing images of deities associated with Shiva. The flanking temples have only one chamber each, which contain beautifully carved images of Vishnu and Brahma respectively. A row of three smaller chambers is located just across from the entrances to the main temples. It is believed that these buildings were dedicated to the mounts (*vahana*) of the three gods, but only the image of Shiva's mount, the bull Nandi, has survived. All the temples are raised on high plinths decorated with narrative scenes in relief.

A portion of these reliefs depicts scenes from the *Ramayana*. This Hindu epic was known in Indonesia from an early date, and aspects of the story were adjusted to better suit the needs and expectations of its Southeast Asian audience. Some of this local influence can be seen in a relief (**FIG. 10–39**) portraying the moment the wicked demon king Ravana (Rawana) abducts Sita, the wife of the hero Rama. Ravana, disguised as a Brahmin, seizes Sita in the midst of a Javanese village and in the process overturns a number of objects as the witnesses to the event react in horror and surprise. The wildlife in this panel exploit the distraction—a dog in the foreground grabs at food fallen from an overturned pot, a rat can be seen sneaking into the storehouse, and a monkey reaches for food held by a seated man. The addition of these details not mentioned in the text reinforces the shamefully animalistic nature of Ravana's actions, which ultimately lead to his own destruction. Typical for the art of Java in this period, the panel is full of activity; each event is accompanied by a host of attendants, onlookers, and references to the natural world.

Tenth to the Twelfth Century

By the tenth through twelfth centuries the powerful kingdoms in Angkor and Bagan were reaching their peaks. Their great wealth and success found expression in innovative forms of architectural construction whose ambitious design and grand scale took earlier forms of Southeast Asian construction to new heights.

ANANDA TEMPLE, MYANMAR   King Anawrahta came to power in 1044, uniting the disparate regional rulers in northern Myanmar under his rule and the local gods (*nats*) under Buddhism. Lavish temple-building projects were not just a means for the king to demonstrate his legitimacy and accrual of good *karma* (the concept that one's deeds, good or bad, eventually produce correspondingly positive or negative consequences); they were also seen as ensuring the welfare of state interests and public well-being. The focus of this fervent generosity was the Buddhist monastic order based near the capital in Bagan (also called Pagan). Over the course of generations of public and royal patronage this semiarid valley came to house several thousand spectacular Buddhist structures, large and small, in various states of repair.

Among these, one of the grandest is the **ANANDA TEMPLE** (**FIG. 10–40**), built in 1105 by King Kyanzittha, Anawrahta's adopted son and eventual successor. According to the legends, the head monk at Bagan, Shin Arahan, introduced the king to eight monks from India who were seeking support abroad. The ensuing discussions inspired the king to undertake a major act of patronage, which culminated in the construction of the Ananda Temple. The unique architectural plan of this temple is rather complex, but it can be envisioned as four temples placed up against the sides of a massive square-based stupa, which rises to almost 175 feet. The temples each face a cardinal direction and house large Buddha images covered in gold leaf, most of which have been renovated or replaced over the centuries. The walls of these temples have openings that make way for two covered circumambulation pathways. While most of the sculpture in niches along these pathways

10–40 ANANDA TEMPLE
Bagan, Mandalay Division, Myanmar. 12th century CE. Height approx. 35' (10.5 m).

Credit: Noelbynature/ Fotolia

10–41 PORTRAIT OF KING KYANZITTHA

West shrine, Ananda Temple, Bagan. 11th century CE.
Gilded lacquer, height 30" (76 cm).

Credit: Photo: John Listopad

remains, almost none of the painting does. The exterior is embellished with rising spires and flamelike decoration over the windows and doors. The central roof rises to the main tower in five tiers. These are decorated with horizontal bands of inset glazed ceramic plaques, many of which display scenes from the Buddha's past lives.

Of particular note are two gilded lacquer images of figures in postures of reverence flanking the Buddha image in the west-facing shrine. These images are believed to depict **KING KYANZITTHA** (FIG. 10–41), shown in elaborate attire, and his chief monk Shin Arahan, bald and in simple robes. The details of these figures have been somewhat obscured by accumulated layers of gold leaf, but this accretion may also have protected the lacquer from decay.

The Ananda is just one grand temple among many in Bagan. Unfortunately, misguided attempts by the government in Myanmar to restore these structures have resulted in conjectural and inaccurate renovations that have hidden or destroyed much of the early material.

ANGKOR WAT, CAMBODIA In 802, the Khmer king Jayavarman II, newly returned from Java, climbed Mount Kulen in what is now northwestern Cambodia. He was accompanied on this trip by a Brahmin who performed a ritual on the mountaintop that marked a special relationship between Jayavarman II and the Hindu god Shiva.

Thereafter, Jayavarman II and subsequent rulers in his lineage claimed the title of "god-king" (*devaraja*). The special religious status indicated by this designation was further solidified through architectural projects that invoked divine symbolism on behalf of the ruler. While Jayavarman II had ascended an actual mountain, his descendants opted to construct elaborate temple mountains near the major urban centers of Roluos and Angkor. These immense structures recalled the sacred mountains on which the gods dwell and marked the political and religious center of the Khmer empire.

Among the grandest and most unusual of these structures is Suryavarman II's temple mountain, known today as **ANGKOR WAT** (FIG. 10–42). Having come to power after a period of turmoil, Suryavarman II (ruled 1113–1150),

10–42 ANGKOR WAT

Angkor, Cambodia.
12th century CE.

Credit: © Olga Lipatova/Shutterstock

10-43 VISHNU CHURNING THE OCEAN OF MILK
Detail of relief sculpture, Angkor Wat. 12th century CE.

Credit: © Kevin R. Morris/Corbis

unlike most of his predecessors, chose to devote himself to the god Vishnu rather than to Shiva. He further broke with tradition by having his temple face west to the setting sun, a direction which had funerary associations.

The temple is a massive structure, comprised of three concentric galleries that frame a stepped pyramid crowned by five delicately tapered towers. This entire structure is surrounded by lakelike moats over 820 feet wide and crossed by walkways adorned with balustrades shaped like multi-headed serpents. The inner walls of the three outer galleries contain elaborate bas-relief sculptures,

many of which depict scenes from the great Hindu epics or glorified depictions of the king.

One relief on the east side of the outer gallery portrays a Hindu story known as the "Churning of the Ocean of Milk" (FIG. 10-43). In this tale, set in a time before the world was fully formed, Vishnu orchestrates the production of the elixir of immortality. He achieves this by wrapping the cosmic serpent around a great mountain emerging from the sea. Then by pulling on the serpent, the gods, working with their enemies, the *asura*, manage to churn up the elixir of immortality from the ocean's depths. This relief may hold a clue to understanding the monument as a whole. With its mountainlike towers, broad moat, and serpent balustrades, the entire complex at Angkor Wat parallels the setting of the legend and may speak to Suryavarman II's hopes for gaining a sort of immortality through his own special union with Vishnu.

Think About It

1   Consider the use of rock-cut architecture. What were the benefits and drawbacks to this architectural technique? How did it influence, and how was it influenced by, built architecture? Give examples.

2   Select one architectural work and one work of sculpture from this chapter. Explain how either Buddhist or Hindu ideas are expressed through their decoration, form, or iconography.

3   Describe the typical form of Indian temples, northern and southern. Directly contrast the stupa and the temple, paying attention to specific building features and how they are used.

4   How do sites like Mamallapuram, the Ananda Temple, and Angkor Wat help legitimize the authority of the ruler?

Crosscurrents

Water symbolism occurs frequently in the art of South and Southeast Asia. Consider how practical concerns over climate and commerce may have shaped the way this imagery was understood. Why would such symbolism be appropriate for royally sponsored sculpture, and what was its significance?

FIG. 10–26

FIG. 10–43

11–1 TERRA-COTTA SOLDIERS

From the mausoleum of Emperor Shihuangdi, Lintong, Shaanxi. Qin dynasty, c. 210 BCE. Earthenware, life-size.

Credit: National Geographic Image Collection

Chapter 11
Chinese and Korean Art before 1279

Learning Objectives

11.a Identify the visual hallmarks of early Chinese and Korean art for formal, technical, and expressive qualities.

11.b Interpret the meaning of works of early Chinese and Korean art based on their themes, subjects, and symbols.

11.c Relate early Chinese and Korean artists and art to their cultural, economic, and political contexts.

11.d Apply the vocabulary and concepts relevant to early Chinese and Korean art, artists, and art history.

11.e Interpret a work of early Chinese or Korean art using the art historical methods of observation, comparison, and inductive reasoning.

11.f Select visual and textual evidence in various media to support an argument or an interpretation of a work of early Chinese or Korean art.

As long as anyone could remember, the huge mound in Shaanxi Province in northern China had been just part of the landscape. But one day in 1974, peasants digging a well accidentally brought to light the first hint of riches. When archaeologists began to excavate, they were stunned by what they found: a vast underground army of some 8,000 life-size terra-cotta soldiers with 100 life-size ceramic horses standing in military formation and ready for battle (**FIG. 11–1**). For more than 2,000 years, while the tumultuous history of China unfolded overhead, they had guarded the tomb of Emperor Shihuangdi, the ruthless ruler who first united the states of China into an empire, the Qin. In ongoing excavations, additional bronze carriages and horses were found, further evidence of the technology and naturalism achieved during Qin Shihuangdi's reign.

China has had a long-standing fascination with antiquity, but archaeology is a relatively young discipline there. Only since the 1920s have scholars methodically dug into the layers of history, yet so much has been unearthed that ancient Chinese history has been rewritten many times. The archaeological record shows that Chinese civilization arose several millennia ago and was distinctive for its early advances in ceramics and metalwork, as well as for the elaborate working of jade. Early use of the potter's wheel, mastery of reduction firing, and invention of high-fired stoneware and porcelain distinguish the technological advancement of Chinese ceramics. Highly imaginative bronze casting and proficient techniques of mold making characterize early Chinese metalworking. Early attainments in jade reflect a technological competence with rotary tools and abrasion, as well as an aesthetic passion for the subtleties of shape, proportion, and surface texture.

Archaeology has supplemented our understanding of historically appreciated Chinese art forms, which explored human relationships and exemplified Confucian values, teaching the standards of conduct that underlie social order. Later, China also came to embrace the Buddhist tradition from India. In princely representations of Buddhist divinities and in sublime and powerful, but often meditative, figures of the Buddha, China's artists presented the divine potential of the human condition. Perhaps the most distinguished Chinese tradition is the presentation of philosophical ideals through the theme of landscape. Paintings of mountains and water in simple black ink became the ultimate artistic medium for expressing the vastness, abundance, and endurance of nature.

Chinese civilization radiated its influence throughout East Asia, repeatedly stimulating the growth of culture in Korea, which in turn transmitted influence to Japan.

The Middle Kingdom

How do the geography and early history of China lead to distinctive forms of art?

Among the cultures of the world, China is distinguished by its long, uninterrupted development, now traced back some 8,000 years. From Qin (pronounced "chin") comes our name for the country that the Chinese call the Middle Kingdom, the country in the center of the world. Present-day China occupies a large landmass in the center of East Asia, covering an area slightly larger than the continental United States. Within its borders lives one fifth of the human race.

The historical and cultural heart of China is the land watered by its three great rivers, the Yellow (Huang Ho), the Yangzi, and the Xi (**MAP 11-1**). The Qinling Mountains divide Inner China into north and south, regions with strikingly different climates, cultures, and historical fates. In the south, the Yangzi River flows through lush green hills to the fertile plains of the delta. Along the southern coastline, rich with natural harbors, arose China's port cities, the focus of a vast maritime trading network. The Yellow River, nicknamed "China's Sorrow" because of its disastrous floods, winds through the north—a dry land of steppe and desert, hot in the summer and lashed by cold winds in the winter. Over its vast and vulnerable frontier have come the nomadic invaders that are a recurring theme in Chinese history, but emissaries from Central Asia, India, Persia, and Europe also crossed this border.

Neolithic Cultures

Early archaeological evidence led scholars to believe that agriculture, the cornerstone technology of the Neolithic period, made its way to China from the ancient Near East. More recent findings, however, suggest that agriculture based on rice and millet arose independently in East Asia before 5000 BCE and that knowledge of Near Eastern grains followed some 2,000 years later. One of the clearest archaeological signs of Neolithic culture in China is evidence of the vigorous emergence of towns and cities. At Jiangzhai, near present-day Xi'an, for example, the foundations of more than 100 dwellings have been discovered surrounding the remains of a communal center, a cemetery, and a kiln. Dated to about 4000 BCE, the ruins point to the existence of a highly developed early society. Elsewhere, the foundations of the earliest-known Chinese palace have been uncovered and dated to about 2000 BCE.

PAINTED POTTERY CULTURES   In China, as in other places, distinctive forms of Neolithic pottery identify different cultures. One of the most interesting objects recovered is a shallow red **BOWL** with a turned-out rim (**FIG. 11-2**). Found in the village of Banpo near Xi'an and the Yellow

11-2 BOWL

From Banpo, near Xi'an, Shaanxi. Neolithic period, Yangshao culture, 5000–4000 BCE. Painted pottery, height 7" (17.8 cm). Banpo Museum.

Credit: Cultural Relics Publishing House

River, it was crafted sometime between 5000 and 4000 BCE. The bowl is an artifact of the Yangshao culture, one of the most important of the so-called Painted Pottery cultures of Neolithic China. Although not made on a potter's wheel, the bowl is perfectly round, and its surfaces are highly polished, bearing witness to a distinctly advanced technology. In addition, markings on shards from this location may be evidence of the beginnings of writing in China, which was fully developed by the second millennium BCE, in the later Bronze Age.

Inside the bowl, a pair of stylized fish suggests that fishing was an important activity for the villagers. The images between the two fish represent human faces flanked by fish, one on each side. Although there is no certain interpretation of the images, they may depict an ancestral figure who could assure an abundant catch, since the worship of ancestors and nature spirits was fundamental to later Chinese beliefs.

LIANGZHU CULTURE   Banpo lies near the great bend in the Yellow River, in the area traditionally regarded as the cradle of Chinese civilization, but archaeological finds have revealed that Neolithic cultures spread over a far broader geography. Recent excavations in sites more than 800 miles away, near Hangzhou Bay in the southeastern coastal region, have uncovered human and animal images—often masks or faces—more than 5,000 years old from the Liangzhu culture (**FIG. 11-3**). Large, round eyes, a flat nose, and a rectangular mouth protrude slightly from the background pattern of wirelike lines. Above the

MAP 11–1 CHINA AND KOREA

The map shows the borders of contemporary China and Korea. Bright-colored areas indicate the extent of China's Han dynasty (206 BCE–220 CE).

11-3 DRAWING OF THE MASK DECORATION ON A JADE CONG

Neolithic period, Liangzhu culture, 3200–2200 BCE.

Credit: Line drawing © Michael Sullivan, *The Arts of China, 5th Edtion, Revised and Expanded*. Published by the University of California Press, 2009, p. 12, fig. 1-14.

forehead a second, smaller face grimaces from under a huge headdress. The upper face may be human, perhaps riding the animal figure below. The drawing reproduces one of eight masks that were carved in low relief on the outside of a large jade *cong*, an object resembling a cylindrical tube encased in a rectangular block.

Another **CONG** (**FIG. 11–4**), also from Liangzhu, bears a lustrous, smooth finish and similar—if more stylized—mask motifs. Both *congs* were found near the remains of persons buried with what appear to be sets of numerous jade objects. The intricacy of these carvings documents the technical sophistication of the jade-working Liangzhu culture, which seems to have emerged around 3300 BCE. Jade, a stone cherished by the Chinese throughout their history, is extremely hard and is difficult to carve. Liangzhu artists must have used sand as an abrasive to slowly grind the stone down; modern artisans marvel at the refinement and virtuosity of the work they produced.

The meaning of the masklike image in FIGURE 11–3 is open to interpretation. Its combination of human and animal features seems to show how the ancient Chinese imagined supernatural beings, either deities or dead ancestors. Similar masks later formed the primary decorative motif of Bronze Age ritual objects. Still later, Chinese historians began referring to the ancient mask motif as the **taotie**, but the motif's original meaning had already been lost. The jade carving here seems to be a forerunner of this most central and mysterious image.

11–4 CONG

Neolithic period, Liangzhu culture, 3200–2200 BCE. Jade, 1⅞ × 2⅝″ (5 × 6.6 cm). Shanghai Museum.

The *cong* is one of the most prevalent and mysterious of early Chinese jade shapes. Originating in the Neolithic period, it continued to play a prominent role in burials through the Shang and Zhou dynasties. Many experts believe the *cong* was connected with the practice of contacting the spirit world.

Bronze Age China

How are the advanced metalworking traditions of Bronze Age China used within the cultures of the Shang and Zhou dynasties?

China entered its Bronze Age in the second millennium BCE. As with agriculture, scholars at first theorized that the technology had been imported from the Near East. Archaeological evidence now makes clear, however, that bronze casting using the **piece-mold casting** technique arose independently in China, where it eventually attained an extraordinary level of sophistication (see "Piece-Mold Casting" opposite).

Shang Dynasty

Traditional Chinese histories tell of three Bronze Age dynasties: the Xia, the Shang, and the Zhou. Experts at one time tended to dismiss the Xia and Shang as legendary, but twentieth-century archaeological discoveries fully established the historical existence of the Shang (c. 1700–1100 BCE) and point strongly to the historical existence of the Xia as well.

Shang kings ruled from a succession of capitals in the Yellow River Valley, where archaeologists have found walled cities, palaces, and vast royal tombs. The Shang were surrounded by many other states—some rivals, others clients—and their culture spread widely. Society seems to have been highly stratified, with a ruling group that had the bronze technology needed to make weapons and ritual vessels. They maintained their authority in part by claiming power as intermediaries between the supernatural and human realms. The chief Shang deity, Shangdi, may have been a sort of "Great Ancestor." It is thought that nature and fertility spirits were also honored, and that regular sacrifices were carried out to keep the spirits of dead ancestors vital so that they might help the living.

Shang priests communicated with the supernatural world through oracle bones. An animal bone or piece of tortoiseshell was inscribed with a question and heated until it cracked; the crack was then interpreted as an answer. Many oracle bones have been recovered and deciphered. They contain the earliest known form of Chinese writing, a script fully recognizable as the ancestor of the system still in use today (see "Chinese Characters" on page 340).

RITUAL BRONZES Shang tombs reveal a warrior culture of great splendor and violence. Many humans and animals were sacrificed to accompany the deceased into death. In one tomb, for example, chariots were found with the skeletons of their horses and drivers; in another, dozens of human skeletons lined the approaches to the central burial chamber. The tombs contain hundreds of jade,

Technique
PIECE-MOLD CASTING

The early piece-mold technique for bronze casting is different from the lost-wax process developed in the ancient Mediterranean and Near East. Although we do not know the exact steps ancient Chinese artists followed, we can deduce the general procedure for casting a vessel.

First, a model of the bronze-to-be was made of clay and dried. Then, to create a mold, damp clay was pressed onto the model; after the clay mold dried, it was cut away in pieces, which were keyed for later reassembly and then fired. The original model was shaved down to serve as the core for the mold. After this, the pieces of the mold were reassembled around the core and held in place by bronze spacers, which locked the core in position and ensured an even casting space around the core. The mold was then covered with another layer of clay, and a sprue, or pouring duct, was cut into the clay to receive the molten metal. A riser duct may also have been cut to allow the hot gases to escape. Molten bronze was then poured into the mold. When the metal cooled, the mold was broken apart to reveal a bronze copy of the original clay model. Finely cast relief decoration could be worked into the model or carved into the sectional molds, or both. Finally, the vessel could be burnished—a long process that involved scouring the surface with increasingly fine abrasives.

The vessel shown here is a **fang ding** recovered from the royal tombs near Yin, the last of the Shang capitals (present-day Anyang). A *ding* is a ceremonial rectangular cooking vessel standing on four legs that was used in Shang rituals and buried in Shang tombs. Weighing nearly 2,000 pounds, this *ding* is the largest Shang *ding* ever recovered.

Sectional clay molds for casting bronze vessels. This sketch is based on a vessel in the Zhengzhou Institute of Cultural Relics and Archaeology.

ivory, and lacquer objects, gold and silver ornaments, and bronze vessels. The enormous scale of Shang burials illustrates the great wealth of the civilization and the power of a ruling class able to consign such great quantities of treasure to the earth. It also documents this culture's reverence for the dead.

Bronze vessels are the most admired and studied of Shang artifacts. Like oracle bones and jade objects, they were connected with ritual practices, serving as containers for offerings of food and wine. A basic repertoire of about 30 shapes evolved. Some derive from earlier pottery forms, while others seem to reproduce wooden containers.

Still others are highly sculptural and take the form of fantastic composite animals. A ritual pouring vessel, known as a **GUANG** (FIG. **11-5**), shows a highly sculptural rendition of animal forms. The pouring spout and cover take the form of the head and body of a tiger, while the rear portion of the vessel and cover are conceived as an owl. Overall geometric decoration combines with suggestive zoomorphic forms. Such images seem to be related to the hunting life of the Shang, but their deeper significance is unknown. Shang creatures seem always to have a sense of mystery, evoking the Shang attitude toward the supernatural world.

11–5 COVERED RITUAL WINE-POURING VESSEL (GUANG) WITH TIGER AND OWL DÉCOR

Shang dynasty, 13th century BCE. Cast bronze, height with cover 9¾″ (25 cm), width including handle 12⅜″ (31.5 cm). Arthur M. Sackler Museum, Harvard University Art Museums, Cambridge, Massachusetts. Bequest of Grenville L. Winthrop (1943.52.103).

Credit: Bridgeman Images

Art and its Contexts
CHINESE CHARACTERS

Each word in Chinese is represented by its own unique symbol, called a character. Some characters originated as **pictographs**, images that mean what they depict. Writing reforms over the centuries have often disguised the resemblance, but if we place modern characters next to their ancestors, the pictures come back into focus:

	water	horse	moon	child	tree	mountain
Ancient						
Modern	水	馬	月	子	木	山

Other characters are ideographs, pictures that represent abstract concepts or ideas:

sun	+	moon	=	bright
日		月		明
woman	+	child	=	good
女		子		好

Most characters were formed by combining a radical, which gives the field of meaning, with a phonetic, which originally hinted at pronunciation. For example, words that have to do with water have the character for "water" 木 abbreviated to three strokes 氵 as their radical. Thus "to bathe," 沐 pronounced *mu*, consists of the water radical and the phonetic 木, which by itself means "tree" and is also pronounced *mu*. Here are other "water" characters. Notice that the connection to water is not always literal.

river	sea	weep	pure, clear	extinguish, destroy
河	海	泣	清	滅

These phonetic borrowings took place centuries ago. Many words have shifted in pronunciation, and for this and other reasons there is no way to tell how a character is pronounced or what it means just by looking at it. While at first this may seem like a disadvantage, in the case of Chinese it is advantageous. Spoken Chinese has many dialects. Some are so far apart in sound as to be virtually different languages. But while speakers of different dialects cannot understand each other, they can still communicate through writing, for no matter how they say a word, they write it with the same character. Writing has thus played an important role in maintaining the unity of Chinese civilization through the centuries.

Zhou Dynasty

Around 1100 BCE, the Shang were conquered by the Zhou from western China. During the Zhou dynasty (1100–221 BCE) a feudal society developed, with nobles related to the king ruling over numerous small states. (Zhou nobility are customarily ranked in English by such titles as duke and marquis.) The supreme deity became known as Tian, or Heaven, and the king ruled as the Son of Heaven. Later Chinese ruling dynasties continued to follow the belief that imperial rule emanated from a mandate from Heaven.

The first 300 years of this longest-lasting Chinese dynasty were generally stable and peaceful. In 771 BCE, however, the Zhou suffered defeat in the west at the hands of a nomadic tribe. Although they quickly established a new capital to the east, their authority had been crippled, and the later Eastern Zhou period was a troubled one. States grew increasingly independent, giving only nominal allegiance to the Zhou kings. Smaller states were swallowed up by their larger neighbors. During the time historians call the Spring and Autumn period (722–481 BCE), 10 or 12 states, later reduced to 7, emerged as powers. The ensuing Warring States period (481–221 BCE) saw intrigue, treachery, and increasingly ruthless warfare.

Against this background of social turmoil, China's great philosophers arose—such thinkers as Confucius (551–479 BCE), Laozi (flourished in sixth century BCE), Mozi (c. 470–391 BCE), and Zhuangzi (369–286 BCE). Traditional histories speak of China's "one hundred schools" of philosophy, indicating a shift of focus from the supernatural to the human world. Nevertheless, elaborate burials on an even larger scale than before reflected the continuation of traditional beliefs.

BRONZE BELLS Ritual bronze objects continued to play an important role during the Zhou dynasty, and new forms developed. One of the most spectacular recent discoveries is a carillon of 65 bronze components, mostly bells arranged in a formation 25 feet long (**FIG. 11-6**), found in the tomb of Marquis Yi of the state of Zeng. Each bell is precisely calibrated to sound two tones—one when struck at the center, another when struck at a corner. They are arranged in scale patterns in a variety of registers. Several musicians would have moved around the carillon, striking the bells in an appointed order.

Music may well have played a part in rituals for communicating with the supernatural, for the *taotie* typically appears on the front and back of each bell. The image is now much more intricate and stylized, a complexity made possible in part by the more refined lost-wax casting process (see "Lost-Wax Casting" in Chapter 14 on page 428), which had replaced the older piece-mold technique. The marquis, who died in 433 BCE, must have considered music important, for among the more than 15,000 objects recovered from his tomb were many musical instruments. Zeng was one of the smallest and shortest-lived states of the Eastern Zhou, but the contents of this tomb attest in quantity and quality to its high cultural level.

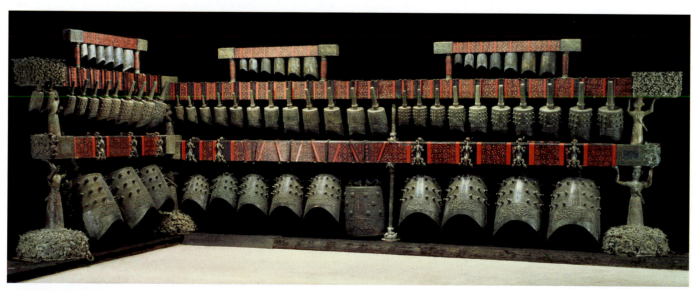

11-6 SET OF BELLS
From the tomb of Marquis Yi of Zeng, Suixian, Hubei. Zhou dynasty, 433 BCE. Bronze, with bronze and timber frame, frame height 9' (2.74 m), length 25' (7.62 m). Hubei Provincial Museum, Wuhan.

Credit: © Asian Art & Archaeology, Inc./Corbis

Early Chinese Empires

How do Chinese art and architecture develop during the Qin, Han, and Six dynasties periods?

Toward the middle of the third century BCE, the state of Qin launched military campaigns that led to its triumph over the other states by 221 BCE. For the first time in its history, China was united under a single ruler. This first emperor of Qin, Shihuangdi, a man of exceptional ability, power, and ruthlessness, was fearful of both assassination and rebellion. Throughout his life, he sought ways to attain immortality. Even before uniting China, he began his own mausoleum at Lintong, in Shaanxi Province. This project continued throughout his life and after his death, until rebellion abruptly ended the dynasty in 206 BCE. Since that time, the mound over the mausoleum has always been visible, but not until an accidental discovery in 1974 was its army of terra-cotta soldiers and horses revealed (SEE FIG. 11–1). Modeled from clay with individualized faces and meticulously rendered uniforms and armor and then fired, the figures claim a prominent place in the great tradition of Chinese ceramic art. The tomb itself has not yet been opened, but literary sources suggest that it reproduces the world as it was known to the Qin, with stars overhead and rivers and mountains below. Thus did the tomb's architects try literally to ensure that the underworld—the world of souls and spirits—would match the human world.

Qin rule was harsh and repressive. Laws were based on a totalitarian philosophy called legalism, and all other philosophies were banned, their scholars executed, and their books burned. Yet the Qin also established the mechanisms of centralized bureaucracy that molded China both politically and culturally into a single entity. Under the Qin, the country was divided into provinces and prefectures, the writing system and coinage were standardized, roads were built to link different parts of the country with the capital, and battlements on the northern frontier were connected to form the Great Wall. To the present day, China's rulers have followed the administrative framework first laid down by the Qin.

Han Dynasty

The commander who overthrew the Qin became the next emperor and founded the Han dynasty (206 BCE–220 CE). During this period China enjoyed peace, prosperity, and stability. Borders were extended and secured, and Chinese control over strategic stretches of Central Asia led to the opening of the Silk Road, a land route that linked China by trade all the way to Rome. In addition to spices, one of the precious goods traded was silk, which had been cultivated and woven in China since at least the third millennium BCE and treasured in Greece and Rome since the third century BCE (see "The Silk Road during the Tang Period" on page 353).

PAINTED BANNER FROM CHANGSHA The early Han dynasty marks the twilight of China's so-called mythocentric age, when people believed in a close relationship between the human and supernatural worlds. The most

11–7 PAINTED BANNER
From the tomb of the Marquess of Dai, Mawangdui, Changsha, Hunan. Han dynasty, c. 160 BCE. Colors on silk, height 6'8½" (2.05 m). Hunan Provincial Museum, Changsha.

Credit: © Asian Art & Archaeology, Inc./Corbis

Art and its Contexts

DAOISM

Daoism is an outlook on life that brings together many ancient ideas regarding humankind and the universe. Its primary text, a slim volume called the *Daodejing* (*The Way and Its Power*), is ascribed to the Chinese philosopher Laozi, who is said to have been a contemporary of Confucius (551–479 ʟᴍ). Later, a philosopher named Zhuangzi (369–286 ʟᴍ) explored many of the same ideas in a book that is known simply by his name: *Zhuangzi*. Together the two texts formed a body of ideas that crystallized into a school of thought during the Han period.

A *dao* is a way or path. The Dao is the Ultimate Way, the Way of the universe. The Way cannot be named or described, but it can be hinted at. It is like water. Nothing is more flexible and yielding, yet water can wear down the hardest stone. Water flows downward, seeking the lowest ground. Similarly, a Daoist sage seeks a quiet life, humble and hidden, unconcerned with worldly success. The Way is great precisely because it is small. The Way may be nothing, yet nothing turns out to be essential.

To recover the Way, we must unlearn. We must return to a state of nature. To follow the Way, we must practice *wu wei* (nondoing). "Strive for nonstriving," advises the *Daodejing*.

All our attempts at asserting ourselves, at making things happen, are like swimming against a current and are thus ultimately futile, even harmful. If we let the current carry us, however, we will travel far. Similarly, a life that follows the Way will be a life of pure effectiveness, accomplishing much with little effort.

It is often said that the Chinese are Confucians in public and Daoists in private, and the two approaches do seem to balance each other. Confucianism is a rational political philosophy that emphasizes propriety, deference, duty, and self-discipline. Daoism is an intuitive philosophy that emphasizes individualism, nonconformity, and a return to nature. If a Confucian education molded scholars outwardly into responsible, ethical officials, Daoism provided some breathing room for the artist and poet inside.

elaborate and best-preserved painting from this time is a T-shaped silk **BANNER** that summarizes this early world-view (**FIG. 11–7**). Found in the tomb of a noblewoman on the outskirts of present-day Changsha in Hunan Province, the banner dates from the second century BCE and is painted with scenes representing three levels of the universe—heaven, earth, and underworld—as well as a portrait of the deceased.

The heavenly realm appears at the top, in the crossbar of the T. In the upper-right corner is the sun, inhabited by a mythical crow; in the upper left, a mythical toad stands on a crescent moon. Between them is an image of the Torch Dragon, a primordial deity shown as a man with a long serpent's tail. Dragons and other celestial creatures swarm underneath him.

A gate guarded by two seated figures stands where the horizontal of heaven meets the banner's long, vertical stem. Two intertwined dragons loop through a circular jade piece known as a *bi*, itself usually a symbol of heaven, dividing this vertical segment into two areas. The portion above the *bi* represents the first stage of the heavenly realm. Here, the deceased woman and three attendants stand on a platform while two kneeling attendants welcome her. The portion beneath the *bi* represents the earthly world and the underworld. Silk draperies and a stone chime hanging from the *bi* form a canopy for the platform below. Like the bronze bells we saw earlier, stone chimes were ceremonial instruments dating from Zhou times. On the platform, ritual bronze vessels contain food and wine for the deceased, just as they did in Shang tombs. The squat, muscular man holding up the platform stands on a pair of fish whose

bodies form another *bi*. The fish and the other strange creatures in this section are inhabitants of the underworld.

Philosophy and Art

The Han dynasty marked the beginning of a new age, when the philosophical ideals of Daoism and Confucianism, formulated during the troubled times of the Eastern Zhou, became central to Chinese thought. Since this period, their influence has been continuous and fundamental.

DAOISM AND NATURE   Daoism emphasizes the close relationship between humans and nature. It is concerned with bringing the individual life into harmony with the Dao, or the Way, of the universe (see "Daoism" above). For some a secular, philosophical path, Daoism on a popular level developed into an organized religion, absorbing many traditional folk practices as well as the search for immortality.

Immortality was as intriguing to Han rulers as it had been to the first emperor of Qin. Daoist adepts experimented with diet, physical exercise, and other techniques in the belief that immortal life could be achieved on earth. A popular Daoist legend of the Land of Immortals in the Eastern Sea takes form in a bronze **INCENSE BURNER** from the tomb of Prince Liu Sheng, who died in 113 BCE (**FIG. 11–8**). Around the bowl, gold inlay outlines the stylized waves of the sea. Above them rises the mountainous island, crowded with birds, animals, and the immortals themselves, all cast in bronze with highlights of inlaid gold. This visionary world would have been shrouded in the shifting mist of incense when the burner was in use.

11–8 INCENSE BURNER
From the tomb of Prince Liu Sheng, Mancheng, Hebei. Han dynasty, 113 BCE. Bronze with gold inlay, height 10½" (26 cm). Hebei Provincial Museum, Shijiazhuang.

Technically, this exquisite work represents the ultimate development of the long and distinguished tradition of bronze casting in China.

Credit: © Asian Art & Archaeology, Inc./Corbis

CONFUCIANISM AND THE STATE   In contrast to the metaphysical focus of Daoism, Confucianism is concerned with the human world; its goal is the attainment of social harmony. To this end, it proposes a system of ethics based on reverence for ancestors and correct relationships among people. Beginning with self-discipline in the individual, Confucianism teaches how to rectify relationships within the family, and then, in ever-widening circles, with friends and others, all the way up to the level of the emperor and the state (see "Confucius and Confucianism" below).

Emphasis on social order and respect for authority made Confucianism especially attractive to Han rulers, who were eager to distance themselves from the disastrous legalism of the Qin. The Han emperor Wudi (ruled 141–87 BCE) made Confucianism the official imperial

Art and its Contexts
CONFUCIUS AND CONFUCIANISM

Confucius was born in 551 BCE into a declining aristocratic family in the state of Lu, roughly present-day Shandong Province. While still in his teens he set his heart on becoming a scholar; by his early twenties he had begun to teach.

By this time, wars for supremacy had begun among the various states of China, and the traditional social fabric seemed to be breaking down. Looking back to the early Zhou dynasty as a sort of golden age, Confucius thought about how a just and harmonious society could again emerge. For many years he sought a ruler who would put his ideas into effect, but to no avail. Frustrated, he spent his final years teaching. After his death in 479 BCE, his conversations with his students were collected by his disciples and their followers into a book known in English as the *Analects*, which is the only record of his teaching.

At the heart of Confucian thought is the concept of *ren* (human-heartedness). *Ren* emphasizes morality and empathy as the basic standards for all human interaction. The virtue of *ren* is most fully realized in the Confucian ideal of the *junzi* (gentleman). Originally indicating noble birth, the term was redefined to mean one who through education and self-cultivation had become a superior person, right-thinking and right-acting in all situations. A *junzi* is the opposite of a petty or small-minded person. His characteristics include moderation, integrity, self-control, loyalty, reciprocity, and altruism. His primary concern is justice.

Together with human-heartedness and justice, Confucius emphasized *li* (etiquette). *Li* includes everyday manners as well as ritual, ceremony, and protocol—the formalities of all social conduct and interaction. Such forms, Confucius felt, choreographed life so that an entire society moved in harmony. *Ren* and *li* operate in the realm of the Five Constant Relationships that define Confucian society: parent and child, husband and wife, elder sibling and younger sibling, elder friend and younger friend, ruler and subject. Deference to age is clearly built into this view, as is the deference to authority that made Confucianism attractive to emperors. Yet responsibilities flow the other way as well: The duty of a ruler is to earn the loyalty of subjects, of a husband to earn the respect of his wife, of age to guide youth wisely.

During the early years of the People's Republic of China, and especially during the Great Proletarian Cultural Revolution (1966–1976), Confucius and Confucian thought were denigrated. Recently, however, Confucian temples in Beijing and elsewhere have been restored. Notably, the Chinese government has used the philosopher's name officially in establishing hundreds of Confucius Institutes in more than 80 countries to promote the learning of the Chinese language abroad.

A Closer Look

A RECEPTION IN THE PALACE

Birds and small figures, possibly alluding to mythical creatures or immortals.

Women—and an empress?—receiving visitors on the upper floor.

The legendary archer Yi saves the world by shooting the extra sun-crows that were threatening it.

The procession of visitors in horse-drawn chariots on their way to the palace.

Men—and the emperor?—receiving visitors on the lower floor.

11–9 A RECEPTION IN THE PALACE

Detail from a rubbing of a stone relief in the Wu family shrine (Wuliangci). Jiaxiang, Shandong. Han dynasty, 151 CE. 27½ × 66½″ (70 × 169 cm). Princeton University Art Museum. Far Eastern Seminar Collection. (2002-307.24)

Credit: © 2016. Princeton University Art Museum/Art Resource NY/Scala, Florence. Photo: Bruce M. White

philosophy, and it remained the state ideology of China for more than 2,000 years, until the end of imperial rule in the twentieth century. Once institutionalized, Confucianism took on so many rituals that it eventually assumed the form and force of a religion. Han philosophers contributed to this process by infusing Confucianism with traditional Chinese cosmology. They emphasized the Zhou idea, taken up by Confucius, that the emperor ruled by the mandate of Heaven. Heaven itself was reconceived more abstractly as the moral force underlying the universe. Thus the moral system of Confucian society became a reflection of universal order.

Confucian subjects turn up frequently in Han art. Among the most famous examples are the reliefs from the Wu family shrines built in 151 CE in Jiaxiang. Carved and engraved in low relief on stone slabs, the scenes were meant to teach Confucian themes such as respect for the emperor, filial piety, and wifely devotion. Daoist motifs also appear, as do figures from traditional myths

and legends in a synchronism characteristic of Han art (see "Closer Look" above).

When compared with the Han-dynasty banner (SEE FIG. 11–7), this late Han relief clearly shows the change that took place in the Chinese worldview in the span of 300 years. The banner places equal emphasis on heaven, earth, and the underworld; human beings are dwarfed by a great swarm of supernatural creatures and divine beings. In the relief, the focus is clearly on the human realm and human behavior.

ARCHITECTURE Contemporary literary sources are eloquent on the wonders of the Han capital. Unfortunately, our only information about Han architecture is in the form of ceramic models of buildings found in tombs, where they were intended to house or support the dead in the afterlife. This model represents a typical Han dwelling (**FIG. 11–10**). Its four stories are crowned with a watchtower and face a small walled courtyard. Pigs and oxen probably occupied

11–10 TOMB MODEL OF A HOUSE AND TOWER
Eastern Han dynasty, 1st–mid 2nd century CE. Painted earthenware, 52 × 33½ × 27" (132.1 × 85.1 × 68.6 cm). The Nelson-Atkins Museum of Art, Kansas City, Missouri.

The main house in this ceramic model is assembled from a stack of 13 individual components. Hand-written inscriptions on several of them indicate their specific placement in the assembly process.

the ground floor, while the family lived in the upper stories, where larger windows provided light and air.

Aside from the multi-level construction, the most interesting feature of the house is the **bracketing** system (architectural elements projecting from the wall) that supports the rather broad eaves of its tiled roofs. Bracketing became a standard element of East Asian architecture, not only in private homes but more typically in palaces and temples (SEE FIG. 11–16). Another interesting aspect of the model is the elaborate painting on the exterior walls, much of it decorative but some of it illustrating structural features such as posts and lintels while other images evoke the world outdoors such as the trees flanking the gateway. Literary sources describe the walls of Han palaces as decorated with paint and lacquer, as well as inlaid with precious metals and stones.

Six Dynasties

With the fall of the Han in 220 CE, China splintered into three warring kingdoms. In 280 CE, the empire was briefly reunited, but invasions by nomadic peoples from central Asia, a source of disruption throughout Chinese history, soon forced the court to flee south. For the next three centuries, northern and southern China developed separately. In the north, 16 kingdoms carved out by invaders rose and fell before giving way to a succession of largely foreign dynasties. Warfare was commonplace. Tens of thousands of Chinese fled south, where six short-lived dynasties succeeded each other in an age of almost constant turmoil broadly known as the Six Dynasties period or the period of the Southern and Northern dynasties (265–589 CE).

In this chaotic context, the Confucian system lost influence. In the south, especially, many intellectuals—the creators and custodians of China's high culture—turned instead to Daoism, which contained a strong escapist element. Educated to serve the government, they increasingly withdrew from public life. They wandered the landscape, drank, wrote poems, practiced calligraphy, and expressed their disdain for the social world through willfully eccentric behavior.

The rarefied intellectual escape route of Daoism was available only to the educated elite. Most people sought answers in the magic and superstitions of Daoism in its religious form. Though weak and disorganized, the southern courts remained centers of traditional Chinese culture, and Confucianism survived as official doctrine. Yet ultimately it was a newly arrived religion—Buddhism—that flourished in the troubled China of the Six Dynasties.

PAINTING Although few paintings survive from the Six Dynasties, abundant literary sources describe the period as an important one for painting. Landscape, later a major theme of Chinese art, first appeared as an independent subject. Daoists wandered through China's countryside seeking spiritual refreshment, and both painters and scholars of the Six Dynasties found that wandering in the mind's eye through a painted landscape could serve the same purpose. This new emphasis on the spiritual value of painting contrasted with the Confucian view, which had emphasized its moral and didactic usefulness.

Reflections on painting traditions also inspired the first works on theory and aesthetics. Some of the earliest and most succinct formulations of the ideals of Chinese painting are the six principles set out by the scholar Xie He (active c. 500–535 CE). The first two principles in particular offer valuable insight into the context in which China's painters worked.

The first principle announces that "spirit consonance" imbues a painting with "life's movement." This "spirit" is the Daoist *qi*, the breath that animates all creation, the energy that flows through all things. When a painting has

11–11 Attributed to Gu Kaizhi **DETAIL OF ADMONITIONS OF THE IMPERIAL INSTRUCTRESS TO COURT LADIES**
Six Dynasties period or later, 5th–8th century CE. Handscroll, ink and colors on silk, 9¾" × 11′6″ (24.8 × 348.2 cm). British Museum, London.

Credit: © The Trustees of the British Museum. All rights reserved.

qi, it will be alive with inner essence, not merely outward resemblance. Artists must cultivate their own spirit so that this universal energy flows through them and infuses their work. The second principle recognizes that brushstrokes are the "bones" of a picture, its primary structural element. Traditionally, a Chinese painting is judged above all by the quality of its brushwork. Each brushstroke is a vehicle of expression; it is through the vitality of a painter's brushwork that "spirit consonance" makes itself felt.

We can sense this attitude already in the rapid, confident brushstrokes that outline the figures of the Han banner (SEE FIG. 11–7) and again in the more controlled, rhythmical lines of one of the most important works associated with the Six Dynasties period, a painted scroll known as **ADMONITIONS OF THE IMPERIAL INSTRUCTRESS TO COURT LADIES**. Attributed to the painter Gu Kaizhi (344–407 CE), it alternates illustrations and text to relate seven Confucian stories of wifely virtue from Chinese history, based on a text written as a reprimand of the empress. The first illustration depicts the courage of Lady Feng (FIG. 11–11). An escaped circus bear rushes toward her startled husband, a Han emperor. Behind his throne, two female servants have turned to run away. Before him, two male attendants try to fend off the bear with spears. Only Lady Feng is calm as she rushes forward to place herself between the beast and the emperor.

The figures are drawn with a brush in a thin, even-width line, and a few outlined areas are filled with color. Facial features, especially those of the men, are carefully delineated. Movement and emotion are shown through conventions—the scarves flowing from Lady Feng's dress, indicating that she is rushing forward, and the upturned strings on both sides of the emperor's head, suggesting his fear. There is no hint of a setting; the artist's careful placement of figures creates a sense of depth.

The painting is on silk, which was typically woven in bands about 12 inches wide and up to 20 or 30 feet long. Early Chinese painters thus developed the format used here, the **handscroll**—a long, narrow, horizontal composition compact enough to be held in the hand when rolled up. Handscrolls are intimate works, meant to be viewed by only two or three people at a time. They were not displayed completely unrolled as we commonly see them today in museums. Rather, viewers would open a scroll and savor it slowly from right to left, displaying only an arm's length at a time.

CALLIGRAPHY   The emphasis on the expressive quality and structural importance of brushstrokes finds its purest embodiment in calligraphy. The same brushes are used for both painting and calligraphy, and a relationship between them was recognized as early as Han times. In his teachings, Confucius had extolled the importance of the pursuit of knowledge and the arts. Among the visual arts, painting was felt to reflect moral concerns, while calligraphy was believed to reveal the character of the writer.

Calligraphy is regarded as one of the highest forms of artistic expression in China. For more than 2,000 years, China's literati—Confucian scholars and literary men who also served the government as officials—have been connoisseurs and practitioners of this art. During the fourth century CE, calligraphy came to full maturity. The most important practitioner of the day was Wang Xizhi (c. 307–365), whose works have served as models of excellence for subsequent generations. The example here comes from a letter, now somewhat damaged and mounted as part of an album, known as **FENG JU** (FIG. 11–12).

Feng Ju is an example of "running" or semicursive style, neither too formal nor too free but with a relaxed, easygoing manner. Brushstrokes vary in width and length,

11–12 Wang Xizhi **PORTION OF A LETTER FROM THE FENG JU ALBUM**

Six Dynasties period, mid 4th century CE. Ink on paper, 9¾ × 18½" (24.7 × 46.8 cm). National Palace Museum, Taibei, Taiwan, Republic of China.

The stamped characters that appear on Chinese artworks are seals—personal emblems. The use of seals dates from the Zhou dynasty, and to this day such seals traditionally employ the archaic characters, known appropriately as "seal script," of the Zhou or Qin. Cut in stone, a seal may state a formal, given name, or it may state any of the numerous personal names that China's painters and writers adopted throughout their lives. A treasured work of art often bears not only the seal of its maker, but also those of collectors and admirers through the centuries. In the Chinese view, these do not disfigure the work but add another layer of interest. This sample of Wang Xizhi's calligraphy, for example, bears the seals of two Song-dynasty emperors, a Song official, a famous collector of the sixteenth century, and two Qing-dynasty emperors of the eighteenth and nineteenth centuries.

Credit: © National Palace Museum, Taipei, Taiwan, Dist. RMN-Grand Palais/ image NPM

creating rhythmic vitality. Individual characters remain distinct, yet within each character the strokes are connected and simplified as the brush moves from one to the other without lifting off the page. The effect is fluid and graceful, yet strong and dynamic. Wang Xizhi's running style came to be officially accepted and learned along with other script styles by those who practiced this art.

BUDDHIST ART AND ARCHITECTURE   Buddhism originated in India during the fifth century BCE (see Chapter 10), then gradually spread north into central Asia. With the opening of the Silk Road during the Han dynasty, its influence reached China. To the Chinese of the Six Dynasties, beset by constant warfare and social devastation, Buddhism offered consolation in life and the promise

11–13 SEATED BUDDHA, CAVE 20, YUNGANG

Datong, Shanxi. Northern Wei dynasty, c. 460. Stone, height 45' (13.7 m).

Credit: Takashi Images/Fotolia

of salvation after death. The faith spread throughout the country across all social levels, first in the north, where many of the invaders promoted it as the official religion, then slightly later in the south, where it found its first great patron in the emperor Liang Wu Di (ruled 502–549 CE). Thousands of temples and monasteries were built, and many people became monks and nuns.

Almost nothing remains in China of the Buddhist architecture of the Six Dynasties, but we can see what it must have looked like in the Japanese Horyuji Temple (SEE FIG. 12–4), which was based on Chinese models of this period.

ROCK-CUT CAVES OF THE SILK ROAD The most impressive works of Buddhist art surviving from the Six Dynasties are the hundreds of northern rock-cut caves along the trade routes between Xinjiang in Central Asia and the Yellow River Valley. Both the caves and the sculptures that fill them were carved from the solid rock of the cliffs. Small caves high above the ground were retreats for monks and pilgrims, while larger caves at the base of the cliffs were wayside shrines and temples.

The caves at Yungang, near Datong in Shanxi Province in central China, contain many examples of the earliest phase of Buddhist sculpture in China, including the monumental **SEATED BUDDHA** in Cave 20 (**FIG. 11–13**). The figure was carved in the latter part of the fifth century by the imperial decree of a ruler of the Northern Wei dynasty (386–534 CE), the longest-lived and most stable of the northern kingdoms. Most Wei rulers were avid patrons of Buddhism, and under their rule the religion made its greatest advances in the north.

The front part of the cave has crumbled away, and the 45-foot statue, now exposed to the open air, is clearly visible from a distance. The elongated ears, protuberance on the head (*ushnisha*), and monk's robe are traditional attributes of the Buddha. The masklike face, full torso, massive shoulders, and shallow, stylized drapery indicate strong Central Asian influence. The overall effect of this colossus is remote and austere, less human than the more sensuous expression of the early Buddhist traditions in India.

Sui and Tang Dynasties

What significant contributions are made to the history of Chinese art under the Sui and Tang dynasties?

In 581 CE, a general from the last of the northern dynasties replaced a child emperor and established a dynasty of his own, the Sui. Defeating all opposition, he molded China into a centralized empire as it had been in Han times. The short-lived Sui dynasty fell in 618, but in reunifying the empire paved the way for one of the greatest dynasties in Chinese history: the Tang (618–907). Even today many Chinese living abroad still call themselves "Tang people." To them, Tang implies that part of the Chinese character that is strong and vigorous (especially in military power), noble and idealistic, but also realistic and pragmatic.

Buddhist Art and Architecture

The new Sui emperor was a devout Buddhist, and his reunification of China coincided with a fusion of the several styles of Buddhist sculpture that had developed. This new style is seen in a bronze **ALTAR TO AMITABHA BUDDHA** (**FIG. 11–14**), one of the many Buddhas of Mahayana Buddhism. Amitabha dwelled in the Western Pure Land, a paradise into which his faithful followers were promised rebirth. With its comparatively simple message of salvation, the Pure Land sect eventually became the most popular form of Buddhism in China and one of the most popular in Japan (see Chapter 12).

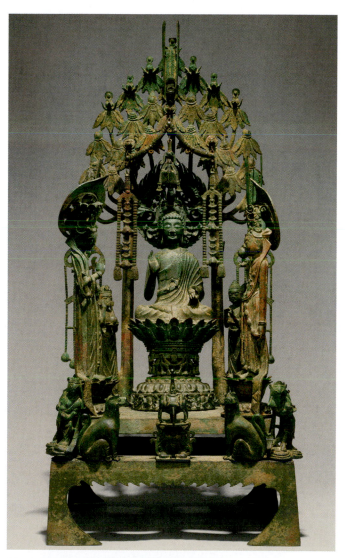

11–14 ALTAR TO AMITABHA BUDDHA
Sui dynasty, 593. Bronze, height 30⅛" (76.5 cm). Museum of Fine Arts, Boston. Gift of Mrs. W. Scott Fitz (22.407) and Gift of Edward Holmes Jackson in memory of his mother, Mrs. W. Scott Fitz (47.1407–1412).

Credit: Photograph © 2017 Museum of Fine Arts, Boston

The altar depicts Amitabha in his paradise, seated on a lotus throne beneath a canopy of trees. Each leaf cluster is set with jewels. Seven celestial figures sit on the topmost clusters, and ropes of "pearls" hang from the tree trunks. Behind Amitabha's head is a halo of flames. To his left, the bodhisattva Guanyin holds a pomegranate; to his right, another bodhisattva clasps his hands in prayer. Behind are four disciples who first preached the teachings of the Buddha. On the lower level, an incense burner is flanked by seated lions and two smaller bodhisattvas. Focusing on Amitabha's benign expression and filled with objects symbolizing his power, the altar combines the sensuality of Indian styles, the schematic abstraction of central Asian art, and the Chinese emphasis on linear grace and rhythm into a harmonious new style.

Buddhism reached its greatest development in China during the subsequent Tang dynasty, which for nearly three centuries ruled China and controlled much of Central Asia. Virtually the entire country adopted the Buddhist faith. A Tang vision of the popular Pure Land sect was expressed in a wall painting from a cave in Dunhuang (**FIG. 11–15**). A major stop along the Silk Road, Dunhuang has nearly 500 caves carved into its sandy cliffs, all filled with painted clay sculpture and decorated with wall paintings from floor to ceiling. The site was worked on continuously from the fourth to the fourteenth century, a period of almost 1,000 years. In the detail shown here, a seated Amitabha Buddha appears at center, flanked by four bodhisattvas, his messengers to the world. Two other groups of bodhisattvas are clustered at right and left. Great halls and towers rise in the background, representing the Western Paradise in terms of the grandeur of Tang palaces. Indeed, the aura of opulence could just as easily be that of the imperial court. This worldly vision of paradise provides our best indication of the splendor of Tang civilization at a time when Chang'an (present-day Xi'an) was probably the greatest city in the world.

The early Tang emperors proclaimed a policy of religious tolerance, but during the ninth century a conservative reaction developed. Confucianism was reasserted and Buddhism was briefly suppressed as a "foreign" religion. Thousands of temples, shrines, and monasteries were destroyed and innumerable bronze statues melted down. Fortunately, several Buddhist structures do survive from the Tang dynasty. One of them, the Nanchan Temple, is the earliest important surviving example of Chinese architecture.

11–15 THE WESTERN PARADISE OF AMITABHA BUDDHA
Detail of a wall painting in Cave 217, Dunhuang, Gansu. Tang dynasty, c. 750. 10'2" × 16' (3.1 × 4.86 m).

Credit: © dbimages/Alamy Stock Photo

11–16 NANCHAN TEMPLE, WUTAISHAN
Shanxi. Tang dynasty, 782.

Credit: © ChinaFotoPress/Getty Images

NANCHAN TEMPLE The Nanchan Temple shows characteristics of both temples and palaces of the Tang dynasty (**FIG. 11–16**). Located on Mount Wutai (Wutaishan) in the eastern part of Shanxi Province, this small hall was constructed in 782. The tiled roof, seen earlier in the Han tomb model (SEE FIG. 11–10), has taken on a curved silhouette. Quite subtle here, this curve became increasingly pronounced in later centuries. The very broad overhanging eaves are supported by a correspondingly elaborate bracketing system.

Also typical is the bay system of construction, in which a cubic unit of space, a bay, is formed by four posts and their lintels. The bay functioned in Chinese architecture as a **module**, a basic unit of construction. To create larger structures, an architect multiplied the number of bays. Thus, though modest in scope with only three bays, the Nanchan Temple still gives an idea of the vast, multistoried palaces of the Tang depicted in such paintings as FIGURE 11–15.

GREAT WILD GOOSE PAGODA The Great Wild Goose Pagoda of the Ci'en Temple in the Tang capital of Chang'an (present-day Xi'an) also survives (**FIG. 11–17**). The temple, constructed in 645 for the famous monk Xuanzang (600–664) on his return from a 16-year pilgrimage to India, was where he taught and translated the Sanskrit Buddhist scriptures he had brought back with him.

Built entirely in brick, the Great Wild Goose Pagoda nevertheless imitates the wooden architecture of the time. The walls are decorated in low relief to resemble bays, and bracket systems are reproduced under the projecting roofs of each story. Although modified and repaired in later times (its seven stories were originally five, and a new finial has been added), the pagoda still preserves the essence of Tang architecture in its simplicity, symmetry, proportions, and grace.

11–17 GREAT WILD GOOSE PAGODA AT CI'EN TEMPLE, CHANG'AN
Shanxi. Tang dynasty, first erected 645; rebuilt mid 8th century CE.

Credit: © Amy Harris/123RF.com

Elements of Architecture

PAGODAS

Pagodas developed from Indian stupas as Buddhism spread northeast along the Silk Road. Stupas merged with the watchtowers of Han-dynasty China in multi-storied stone or wood structures with projecting tiled roofs. This transformation culminated in wooden pagodas with upward-curving roofs supported by elaborate bracketing in China, Korea, and Japan. Buddhist pagodas retain the axis mundi masts of stupas. Like their South Asian prototypes, early East Asian pagodas were symbolic rather than enclosing structures. Later examples often provided access to the ground floor and sometimes to upper levels.

early stupa
India, 2nd century BCE

later stupa
Central Asia,
5th–6th century CE

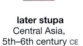

watchtower
China, Han dynasty,
c. 206 BCE–220 CE

stone pagoda
northwestern China,
c. 5th century CE

wooden pagoda
Japan, 7th century CE

Tang Figure Painting and Ceramics

Later artists looking back on their heritage recognized the Tang dynasty as China's great age of figure painting. Unfortunately, very few Tang **scroll paintings** still exist. However, the wall paintings of Dunhuang (SEE FIG. 11–15) give us some idea of the character of Tang figure painting, and we can look at copies of lost Tang paintings made by later Song-dynasty artists. **LADIES PREPARING NEWLY WOVEN SILK** is an outstanding example of such copies, this one attributed to Huizong (ruled 1101–1126 CE),

11–18 Attributed to Emperor Huizong **DETAIL OF LADIES PREPARING NEWLY WOVEN SILK**

Copy after a lost Tang-dynasty painting by Zhang Xuan. Northern Song dynasty, early 12th century CE. Handscroll with ink and colors on silk, 14⁹⁄₁₆ × 57³⁄₁₆″ (37 × 145.3 cm). Museum of Fine Arts, Boston. Special Chinese and Japanese Fund (12.886).

Confucius said of himself, "I merely transmit, I do not create; I love and revere the ancients." In this spirit, Chinese painters regularly copied paintings of earlier masters. Painters made copies both to absorb the lessons of their great predecessors and to perpetuate the achievements of the past. In later centuries, they took up the practice of regularly executing a work "in the manner of" some particularly revered ancient master. This was at once an act of homage, a declaration of artistic allegiance, and a way of reinforcing a personal connection with the past.

Credit: Photograph © 2017 Museum of Fine Arts, Boston

the last emperor of the Northern Song dynasty (**FIG. 11–18**). An inscription on the scroll identifies the Tang original as a famous work by Zhang Xuan, an eighth-century painter known for his depictions of women at the Tang court.

Since the original no longer exists, we cannot know how faithful the copy is, but its refined lines and bright colors seem to share the grace and dignity of Tang sculpture and architecture.

Art and its Contexts

THE SILK ROAD DURING THE TANG PERIOD

Under a series of ambitious and forceful Tang emperors, Chinese control once again extended over Central Asia. Goods, ideas, and influence flowed along the Silk Road. In the South China Sea, Arab and Persian ships carried on a lively trade with coastal cities. Chinese cultural influence in East Asia was so important that Japan and Korea sent thousands of students to study Chinese civilization.

Cosmopolitan and tolerant, Tang China was confident and curious about the world. Many foreigners came to the splendid new capital Chang'an (present-day Xi'an), and they are often depicted in the art of the period. A ceramic statue of a camel carrying a troupe of musicians (**FIG. 11–19**) reflects the Tang fascination with the "exotic" Turkic cultures of Central Asia. The three bearded musicians (one with his back to us) are Central Asian, while the two smooth-shaven ones are Han Chinese. Bactrian, or two-humped, camels, themselves exotic Central Asian "visitors," were beasts of burden in the caravans that traversed the Silk Road. The stringed lute (which the Chinese called the *pipa*) came from Central Asia to become a lasting part of Chinese music.

Stylistically, the statue reveals a new interest in naturalism, an important trend in both painting and sculpture. Compared with the rigid, staring ceramic soldiers of the first emperor of Qin (**SEE FIG. 11–1**), this Tang band is alive with gesture and expression. The camel throws its head back; the musicians are captured in mid-performance. Ceramic figurines such as this, produced by the thousands for tombs, offer glimpses into the gorgeous variety of Tang life. The statue's three-color glaze technique was a specialty of Tang ceramicists. The glazes—usually chosen from a restricted palette of amber-yellow, green, and blue—were splashed freely and allowed to run over the surface during firing to convey a feeling of spontaneity. The technique is emblematic of Tang culture itself in its colorful and cosmopolitan expressiveness.

The Silk Road had first flourished in the second century CE. A 5,000-mile network of caravan routes from the Han capital (near present-day Luoyang, Henan, on the Yellow River) to Rome, it brought Chinese luxury goods to Western markets.

The journey began at the Jade Gate (Yumen) at the westernmost end of the Great Wall, where Chinese merchants turned their goods over to Central Asian traders. Goods would change hands many more times before reaching the Mediterranean. Caravans headed first for the nearby desert oasis of Dunhuang. Here northern and southern routes diverged to skirt the vast Taklamakan Desert. At Khotan, in western China, farther west than the area shown in MAP 11–1, travelers on the southern route could turn off toward a mountain pass into Kashmir, in northern India. Or they could continue on, meeting up with the northern route at Kashgar, on the western border of the Taklamakan, before proceeding over the Pamir Mountains into present-day Afghanistan. From there, travelers could head toward present-day Pakistan and India, or travel west through present-day Uzbekistan, Iran, and Iraq, arriving finally at Antioch, in Syria, on the coast of the Mediterranean. After that, land and sea routes led to Rome.

11–19 CAMEL CARRYING A GROUP OF MUSICIANS
From a tomb near Xi'an, Shanxi. Tang dynasty, c. mid 8th century CE. Earthenware with three-color glazes, height 26⅛″ (66.5 cm). National Museum, Beijing.

Credit: Cultural Relics Publishing House

11-20 TWO EQUESTRIAN FIGURES
Tang dynasty, first half of 8th century CE.
Molded, reddish-buff earthenware with cold-painted pigments over white ground, height
(male figure) 14½" (37 cm). Arthur M. Sackler
Museum, Harvard Art Museums, Cambridge,
Massachusetts. Gift of Anthony M. Solomon
(2003.207.1-2).

This pair documents the participation of women
as well as men in sport and riding. Both have
pointed boots and are mounted on standing,
saddled, and bridled horses; their hands are
positioned to hold the reins. The male figure
wears a tall, elaborately embellished hat,
and the female figure has her hair arranged in
a topknot.

Credit: Bridgeman Images

Two earthenware **EQUESTRIAN FIGURES** (**FIG. 11–20**), a man and a woman made for use as tomb furnishings, reveal more directly the robust naturalism and exuberance of figural representation during the Tang period. Accurate in proportion and lively in demeanor, the statuettes are not glazed (as is the tomb figure in FIG. 11–19), but are "cold-painted" with pigments after firing to render details of costume and facial features.

Song Dynasty

What are the important developments in Chinese art during the Song dynasty?

A brief period of disintegration followed the fall of the Tang, but eventually China was again united, this time under the Song dynasty (960–1279). A new capital was founded at Bianjing (present-day Kaifeng), near the Yellow River. In contrast to the outgoing confidence of the Tang, the mood during the Song was more introspective, a reflection of China's weakened military situation. In 1126, the Jurchen tribes of Manchuria invaded China, sacked the capital, and took possession of much of the northern part of the country. Song forces withdrew south and established a new capital at Hangzhou. From this point on, the dynasty is known as the Southern Song (1127–1279), with the first portion called in retrospect the Northern Song (960–1126).

Although China's territory had diminished, its wealth had increased because of advances in agriculture, commerce, and technology begun under the Tang. Patronage was plentiful, and the arts flourished. Song culture is noted for its refined taste and intellectual grandeur. Where the Tang had reveled in exoticism, eagerly absorbing influences from Persia, India, and Central Asia, Song culture was more self-consciously Chinese. Philosophy experienced its most creative era since the "one hundred schools" of the Zhou. Song scholarship was brilliant, especially in history, and its poetry is noted for its depth. Perhaps the finest expressions of the Song, however, are in art, especially painting and ceramics.

No hint of political disruption or religious questioning intrudes on the sublime grace and beauty of this **SEATED GUANYIN BODHISATTVA** (**FIG. 11–21**), carved from wood in the eleventh or twelfth century in a territory on the northern border of Song China, a region ruled by the Liao dynasty (907–1125). Bodhisattvas are represented as young princes wearing royal garments and jewelry, their finery indicative of their worldly but virtuous lives. Guanyin is the Bodhisattva of Infinite Compassion, who appears in many guises, in this case as the Water and Moon Guanyin. He sits on rocks by the sea, in the position known as royal ease. His right arm rests on his raised and bent right knee and his left arm and foot hang down, the foot touching a lotus blossom.

Philosophy: Neo-Confucianism

Song philosophers continued the process, begun during the Tang, of restoring Confucianism to dominance. In strengthening Confucian thought, they drew on Daoist and especially Buddhist ideas, even as they openly rejected Buddhism itself as foreign. These innovations provided Confucianism with a new metaphysical aspect, allowing it to propose a richer, all-embracing explanation of the universe. This new synthesis of China's three main paths of thought is called Neo-Confucianism.

11–21 SEATED GUANYIN BODHISATTVA
Liao dynasty, 11th–12th century CE (the painting and gilding were restored in the 16th century). Wood with paint and gold, 95 × 65" (241.3 × 165.1 cm). The Nelson-Atkins Museum of Art, Kansas City, Missouri. Purchase: William Rockhill Nelson Trust (34–10).

Neo-Confucianism teaches that the universe consists of two interacting forces known as *li* (principle or idea) and *qi* (matter). All pine trees, for example, consist of an underlying *li* we might call "Pine Tree Idea" brought into the material world through *qi*. All the *li* of the universe, including humans, are but aspects of an eternal first principle known as the Great Ultimate (*taiji*), which is completely present in every object. Our task as human beings is to rid our *qi* of impurities through education and self-cultivation so that our *li* may realize its oneness with the Great Ultimate. This life-long process resembles the striving to attain buddhahood, and, if we persist in our attempts, one day we will be enlightened—the term itself coming directly from Buddhism.

Northern Song Painting

Neo-Confucian ideas found visual expression in art, especially in landscape, which became the most highly esteemed subject for painting. Northern Song artists studied nature closely to master its many appearances: the way each species of tree grows; the distinctive character of each rock formation; the changes of the seasons; the myriad birds, blossoms, and insects. This passion for descriptive detail was the artist's form of self-cultivation. Mastering outward forms showed an understanding of the principles behind them.

Yet despite the convincing accumulation of detail, Song landscape paintings do not record a specific site. The artist's goal was to paint the eternal essence of "mountain-ness," for example, not to reproduce the appearance of a particular mountain. Painting landscapes required artists to orchestrate their cumulative understanding of *li* in all its aspects—mountains and rocks, streams and waterfalls, trees and grasses, clouds and mist. A landscape painting thus expressed the desire for the spiritual communion with nature that was the key to enlightenment. As the tradition progressed, landscape also became a vehicle for conveying human emotions, even for speaking indirectly of one's own deepest feelings.

In the earliest times, art had reflected the mythocentric worldview of the ancient Chinese. Later, as religion came to dominate people's lives, the focus of art shifted, and religious images and human actions became important subjects. Subsequently, during the Song dynasty, artists developed landscape as the chief means of expression, preferring to avoid direct depiction of the human condition and to instead convey ideals in a symbolic manner. Chinese artistic expression thus moved from the mythical, through the religious and ethical, and finally to the philosophical and aesthetic.

FAN KUAN One of the first great masters of Song landscape was the eleventh-century painter Fan Kuan (active c. 990–1030 CE), whose surviving major work, **TRAVELERS AMONG MOUNTAINS AND STREAMS**, is regarded as one of the great monuments of Chinese art (**FIG. 11–22**). The work is physically large—almost 7 feet high—but the sense of monumentality also radiates from the composition itself.

The composition unfolds in three stages comparable to three acts of a drama. At the bottom a large, low-lying group of rocks establishes the extreme foreground. In anticipating the shape and substance of the mountains to come, the rocks introduce the main theme of the work, much as the first act of a drama introduces the principal characters. In the middle ground, travelers and their mules are coming from the right. Their size confirms our human scale—how small we are against the vastness of nature. This middle ground takes up twice as much picture surface as the foreground, and, like the second act of a play, shows variation and development. Instead of a solid mass, the rocks here are separated into two groups by a waterfall that is spanned by a bridge. In the hills to the right, the rooftops of a temple stand out above the trees.

11–22 Fan Kuan **TRAVELERS AMONG MOUNTAINS AND STREAMS**

Northern Song dynasty, early 11th century CE. Hanging scroll with ink and colors on silk, height 6'9½" (2.06 m). National Palace Museum, Taibei, Taiwan, Republic of China.

Credit: © Corbis

Mist veils the transition to the background, with the result that the mountain looms suddenly. This background area, almost twice as large as the foreground and middle ground combined, is the climactic third act of the drama. The mountain's ponderous weight increases as it extends upward, finally bursting into the sprays of energetic brushstrokes that describe the scrubby growth on top. To the right, a slender waterfall plummets, enhancing the mountain's upward thrust by contrast. The whole painting conveys the feeling of climbing a high mountain, leaving the human world behind to come face to face with the Great Ultimate in a spiritual communion.

All the elements are depicted with precise detail and in proper scale. Jagged brushstrokes describe the contours of rocks and trees and express their rugged character. Layers of short, staccato strokes (translated as "raindrop texture" from the Chinese) accurately mimic the texture of the rock surface. Spatial recession from foreground through middle ground to background is convincingly handled.

Although it contains realistic details, the landscape represents no specific place. In its forms, the artist expresses the ideal forms behind appearances; in the rational, ordered composition, he expresses the intelligence of the universe. The arrangement of the mountains, with the central peak flanked by lesser peaks on each side, seems to reflect both the ancient Confucian notion of social hierarchy, with the emperor flanked by his ministers, and the Buddhist motif of the Buddha with bodhisattvas at his side. The landscape, a view of nature uncorrupted by human habitation, expresses a kind of Daoist ideal. Thus we find the three strains of Chinese thought united, much as they are in Neo-Confucianism itself.

The ability of Chinese landscape painters to take us out of ourselves and to let us wander freely through their sites is closely linked to the avoidance of perspective as it is understood in the West. Fifteenth-century European painters, searching for fidelity to appearances, developed a scientific system for recording exactly the view that could be seen from a single, stable vantage point. In contrast, the goal of Chinese painting is to show a totality beyond what we are normally given to see. If the ideal for centuries of Western painters was to render what can be seen from a fixed viewpoint, that of Chinese artists was to reveal nature through a distant, all-seeing, and mobile viewpoint.

XU DAONING This sense of shifting perspective is clearest in the handscroll, where our vantage point changes constantly as we move through the painting. One of the finest handscrolls to survive from the Northern Song is **FISHING IN A MOUNTAIN STREAM** (FIG. 11–23), executed in the middle of the eleventh century by Xu Daoning (c. 970–c. 1052). Starting from a thatched hut in the right foreground, we follow a path that leads to a broad, open view of a deep vista dissolving into distant mists and mountain peaks. (Remember that viewers observed only a small section of the scroll at a time, moving from right to left. To mimic this effect, use two pieces of paper to frame a small viewing area, then move them slowly leftward.) Crossing over a small footbridge, we are brought back to the foreground with the beginning of a central group of high mountains that show extraordinary shapes. Again our path winds back along the bank, and we have a view of the highest peaks from another small footbridge. At the far side of the bridge, we find ourselves looking up into a deep valley, where a stream lures our eyes far into the distance. We can imagine ourselves resting in the small pavilion halfway up

11–23 Xu Daoning **SECTION OF FISHING IN A MOUNTAIN STREAM**
Northern Song dynasty, mid 11th century CE. Handscroll with ink on silk, 19″ × 6′10″ (48.9 cm × 2.09 m). The Nelson-Atkins Museum of Art, Kansas City, Missouri. Purchase, William Rockhill Nelson Trust (33–1559).

the valley on the right or perhaps fishing from the boats visible as the valley gives way to a second, smaller group of mountains, serving both as an echo of the central group and as a transition to the painting's finale, a broad, open vista. Gazing out into the distance and reflecting on our journey, we again feel that communion with nature that is the goal of Chinese artistic expression.

Such handscrolls have no counterpart in the Western visual arts and are often compared instead to the tradition of Western music, especially symphonic compositions. Both are generated from opening motifs that are developed and varied, both are revealed over time, and in both our sense of the overall structure relies on memory, for we do not see the scroll or hear the composition all at once.

ZHANG ZEDUAN   The Northern Song fascination with precision extended to details within landscape. The emperor Huizong, whose copy of *Ladies Preparing Newly Woven Silk* was seen in FIGURE 11–18, gathered around himself a group of court painters who shared his passion for quiet, exquisitely detailed, delicately colored paintings of birds and flowers. Other painters specialized in domestic

and wild animals, still others in palaces and buildings. One of the most spectacular products of this passion for observation is **PEACE REIGNS ALONG THE RIVER**, a long handscroll painted in the late eleventh or early twelfth century by Zhang Zeduan, an artist connected to the court (**FIG. 11–24**). Beyond its considerable visual delights, the painting is also a valuable record of daily life in the Song capital.

On the long expanse of the painted scroll an idealized view of city life unfolds. The scene reproduced here takes place at the Rainbow Bridge (its name derived from its shape), crowded with merchants and shoppers. The large boat approaching the bridge from the right is probably bringing goods from the southern part of China up the Grand Canal that ran through the city at that time. The sailors are preparing to pass beneath the bridge by lowering the sail and taking down the mast. Figures on ship and shore gesture wildly, shouting orders and advice, while a crowd gathers at the bridge railing to watch. Stalls on the bridge are selling food and other merchandise; wine shops and eating places line the banks of the canal. Some people are busy carrying goods, some are shopping, some are

11–24 Zhang Zeduan **SECTION OF PEACE REIGNS ALONG THE RIVER**
Northern Song dynasty, late 11th–early 12th century CE. Handscroll with ink and colors on silk, 9½″ × 7′4″ (24.8 cm × 2.28 m). The Palace Museum, Beijing.

Credit: Werner Forman Archive/ Palace Museum, Beijing

simply enjoying themselves. The bustling activity is meant to signify the economic prosperity that results from successful governance by the Northern Song emperor.

Little is known about the painter Zhang Zeduan other than that he was a member of the scholar-official class, the highly educated elite of imperial China. His painting demonstrates skill in the fine-line architectural drawing called *jiehua* ("ruled-line") painting. Interestingly, some of Zhang Zeduan's peers were already beginning to cultivate quite a different attitude toward painting as a form of artistic expression, one that placed overt display of technical skill at the lowest end of the scale of values. This emerging scholarly aesthetic, developed by China's literati, later came to dominate Chinese thinking about art.

Southern Song Painting and Ceramics

Landscape painting took a very different course after the fall of the north to the Jurchen in 1127 and the removal of the court to its new southern capital in Hangzhou.

XIA GUI   A new sensibility is reflected in the surviving portion of **TWELVE VIEWS OF LANDSCAPE** (**FIG. 11–25**) by Xia Gui (active c. 1195–1235), a member of the newly established Academy of Painters. In general, academy members continued to favor such subjects as birds and flowers in the highly refined, elegantly colored court style patronized earlier by Huizong (SEE FIG. 11–18). Xia Gui, however, was interested in landscape and cultivated his own style. Only the last four of the 12 views that originally made up this long handscroll have survived, but they are enough to illustrate the unique quality of his approach.

In contrast to the majestic, austere landscapes of the Northern Song painters, Xia Gui presents an intimate and lyrical view of nature. Subtly modulated, carefully controlled ink washes evoke a landscape veiled in mist, while a few deft brushstrokes indicate the details

showing through the mist—the grasses growing by the bank, the fishers at their work, the trees laden with moisture, the two bent-backed figures carrying their loads along the path that skirts the hill. Simplified forms, stark contrasts of light and dark, asymmetrical composition, and great expanses of blank space suggest a fleeting world that can be captured only in glimpses. The intangible has more presence than the tangible. By limiting himself to a few essential details, the painter evokes a deep feeling for what lies beyond.

This development in Song painting from the rational and intellectual to the emotional and intuitive had a parallel in philosophy. During the late twelfth century, a new school of Neo-Confucianism called School of the Mind insisted that self-cultivation could be achieved through contemplation, which might lead to sudden enlightenment. The idea of sudden enlightenment may have come from Chan Buddhism, better known in the West by its Japanese name, Zen. Chan Buddhists rejected formal paths to enlightenment such as scripture, knowledge, and ritual, in favor of meditation and techniques designed to "short-circuit" the rational mind. Xia Gui's painting seems to suggest this intuitive approach.

The subtle and sophisticated paintings of the Song were created for a highly cultivated audience who were equally discerning in other arts such as ceramics. Building on the considerable accomplishments of the Tang, Song potters achieved a technical and aesthetic perfection that has made their wares models of excellence throughout the world. Like their painter contemporaries, Song potters turned away from the exuberance of Tang styles to create more quietly beautiful pieces.

GUAN WARE   Among the most prized of the many types of Song ceramics is Guan ware, made mainly for imperial use (**FIG. 11–26**). The rounded body, high neck, and extended lip of this simple vessel show a strong sense of harmony. Enhanced by a lustrous grayish-blue glaze, the

11–25 Xia Gui **SECTION OF TWELVE VIEWS OF LANDSCAPE**
Southern Song dynasty, early 13th century CE. Handscroll with ink on silk, height 11″ (28 cm); length of extant portion 7′7½″ (2.31 m).
The Nelson-Atkins Museum of Art, Kansas City, Missouri. Purchase: William Rockhill Nelson Trust (32–159/2).

to be used deliberately in some of the most refined Song wares. In the play of irregular, spontaneous crackles over a perfectly regular, perfectly planned form we can sense the same spirit that hovers behind the self-effacing virtuosity and freely intuitive insights of Xia Gui's landscape.

In 1279 the Southern Song dynasty fell to the conquering forces of the Mongol leader Kublai Khan (1215–1294). China was subsumed into the vast Mongol empire. Mongol rulers founded the Yuan dynasty (1279–1368), setting up their capital in the northeast in what is now Beijing. Yet the cultural center of China remained in the south, in the cities that rose to prominence during the Song, especially Hangzhou. This separation of political and cultural centers, coupled with a lasting resentment toward "barbarian" rule, created the climate for later developments in Chinese art.

The Arts of Korea

What features characterize the early art of Korea from the Three Kingdoms period through the Goryeo dynasty?

Set between China and Japan, Korea occupies a peninsula in northeast Asia. Inhabited for millennia, the peninsula gave rise to a distinctively Korean culture during the Three Kingdoms period.

The Three Kingdoms Period

Traditionally dated 57 BCE–668 CE, the Three Kingdoms period saw the establishment of three independent nation-states: Silla in the southeast, Baekje in the southwest, and Goguryeo in the north. Large tomb mounds built during the fifth and sixth centuries CE are enduring monuments of this period.

A GOLD HEADDRESS   The most spectacular items recovered from these tombs are trappings of royal authority (**FIG. 11-27**). Made expressly for burial, this elaborate crown was assembled from cut pieces of thin gold sheet held together by gold wire. Spangles of gold embellish the crown, as do comma-shaped ornaments of green and white jadeite—a form of jade mineralogically distinct from the nephrite prized by the early Chinese. The tall, branching

11-26 GUAN WARE VESSEL
Southern Song dynasty, 13th century CE. Gray stoneware with crackled grayish-blue glaze, height 6⅝" (16.8 cm). Percival David Foundation of Chinese Art, British Museum, London.

Credit: © The Trustees of the British Museum. All rights reserved.

form flows without break from base to lip, evoking an introspective quality as eloquent as the blank spaces in Xia Gui's painting. The aesthetic of the Song is most evident in the crackle pattern on the glazed surface. The crackle technique was probably discovered accidentally, but it came

MAP 11–2 KOREA

The map shows Korea, with its division into North and South, and indicates major sites mentioned in this chapter.

11–27 CROWN

From the Gold Crown Tomb, Gyeongju, North Gyeongsang Province, Korea. Three Kingdoms period, Silla kingdom, probably 6th century CE. Gold with jadeite ornaments, height 17½″ (44.5 cm). National Museum of Korea, Seoul, Republic of Korea.

Credit: National Museum of Korea, Seoul, Republic of Korea

forms rising from the crown's periphery resemble trees and antlers. Within the crown is a conical cap woven of narrow strips of sheet gold and ornamented with appendages that suggest wings or feathers.

HIGH-FIRED CERAMICS   The tombs have also yielded ceramics in abundance. Most are containers for offerings of food placed in the tomb to nourish the spirit of the deceased. These items generally are of unglazed stoneware, a high-fired ceramic that is impervious to liquids, even without glaze.

The most imposing ceramic shapes are tall **STANDS** (**FIG. 11–28**), typically designed as a long, cylindrical shaft set on a bulbous base and used to support round-bottomed jars. Openwork apertures cut into the moist clay before firing lighten what otherwise would be rather ponderous forms. Few examples of Three Kingdoms ceramics exhibit surface ornamentation, other than an occasional combed wave pattern or an incised configuration of circles and **chevrons** (V shapes), but in this piece snakes inch their way up the shaft of the stand.

A BODHISATTVA SEATED IN MEDITATION   Buddhism was introduced into the Goguryeo kingdom from China in 372 CE and into Baekje by 384. Although it probably reached Silla in the second half of the fifth century, it gained recognition as the official religion of the Silla state only in 527.

At first, Buddhist art in Korea imitated Chinese examples. By the late sixth century, however, Korean sculptors had created a distinctive style, exemplified by a magnificent gilt-bronze image of a bodhisattva (probably the bodhisattva Maitreya) seated in meditation that likely dates to the early seventh century (**FIG. 11–29**). Although the pose derives from late sixth-century Chinese sculpture, the slender body, elliptical face, elegant drapery folds, and trilobed crown are distinctly Korean.

Buddhism was introduced to Japan from Korea—from the Baekje kingdom, according to literary accounts. Historical sources indicate that numerous Korean sculptors

11–28 CEREMONIAL STAND WITH SNAKE, ABSTRACT, AND OPENWORK DECORATION

Reportedly recovered in Andong, North Gyeongsang Province, Korea. Three Kingdoms period, Silla kingdom, 5th–6th century CE. Gray stoneware with combed, stamped, applied, and openwork decoration and with traces of natural ash glaze, height 23⅛″ (58.7 cm). Arthur M. Sackler Museum, Harvard Art Museums, Cambridge, Massachusetts. Partial gift of Maria C. Henderson and partial purchase through the Ernest B. and Helen Pratt Dane Fund for the Acquisition of Oriental Art (1991.501).

Credit: Bridgeman Images

11–29 BODHISATTVA SEATED IN MEDITATION

Korea. Three Kingdoms period, probably Silla kingdom, early 7th century CE. Gilt bronze, height 35⅞″ (91 cm). National Museum of Korea, Seoul, Republic of Korea (formerly in the collection of the Toksu Palace Museum of Fine Arts, Seoul).

Credit: Pictures from History/National Museum of Korea/Bridgeman Images

were active in Japan in the sixth and seventh centuries; several early masterpieces of Buddhist art in Japan show pronounced Korean influence (SEE FIG. 12–6).

The Unified Silla Period

In 660, the Silla kingdom conquered Baekje, and, in 668, through an alliance with Tang-dynasty China, it vanquished Goguryeo, uniting the peninsula under the rule of the Unified Silla dynasty, which lasted until 935. Buddhism prospered under Unified Silla, and many large, important temples were erected in and around Gyeongju, the Silla capital.

SEOKGURAM The greatest monument of the Unified Silla period is Seokguram, an artificial cave-temple constructed under royal patronage atop Mount Toham, near

Gyeongju. The temple is modeled after Chinese cave-temples of the fifth, sixth, and seventh centuries, which were in turn inspired by the Buddhist cave-temples of India.

Built in the mid eighth century of cut blocks of granite, Seokguram consists of a small rectangular antechamber joined by a narrow vestibule to a circular main hall with a domed ceiling. More than 11 feet in height, a huge seated Buddha dominates the main hall (FIG. 11–30). Seated on a lotus pedestal, the image represents the historical Buddha Shakyamuni at the moment of his enlightenment, as indicated by his earth-touching gesture, or *bhumisparsha mudra*.

11–30 SEATED SHAKYAMUNI BUDDHA

Seokguram Grotto, near Gyeongju, North Gyeongsang Province, Korea. Unified Silla period, c. 751 CE. Granite, height of Buddha 11′2½″ (3.42 m).

The Buddha's hands are in the *bhumisparsha mudra*, the earth-touching gesture symbolizing his enlightenment.

Credit: © Prisma Bildagentur AG/Alamy Stock Photo

The full, taut forms, diaphanous drapery, and anatomical details of his chest relate this image to eighth-century Chinese sculptures. Exquisitely carved low-relief images of bodhisattvas and lesser deities grace the walls of the ante-chamber, vestibule, and main hall.

The Goryeo Dynasty

Established in 918, the Goryeo dynasty eliminated the last vestiges of Unified Silla rule in 935; it would continue until 1392, ruling from its capital at Gaeseong—to the northwest of present-day Seoul and now in North Korea. A period of courtly refinement, the Goryeo dynasty is best known for its celadon-glazed ceramics.

CELADON-GLAZED CERAMICS The term **celadon** refers to a high-fired, transparent glaze of pale bluish-green

hue, typically applied over a pale gray stoneware body. Chinese potters invented celadon glazes and had initiated the continuous production of celadon-glazed wares as early as the first century CE. Korean potters began to experiment with such glazes in the eighth and ninth centuries, and soon the finest Goryeo celadons rivaled the best Chinese court ceramics. Although these wares were used by people of various socioeconomic classes during the Goryeo dynasty, the finest examples went to the palace, to nobles, or to powerful Buddhist clergy.

Prized for their classic simplicity, eleventh-century Korean celadons often have little decoration, but during the twelfth century potters added incised, carved, or molded embellishments, either imitating those of contemporary Chinese ceramics or exploring new styles and techniques of ornamentation. Most notable among their

11–31 MAEBYEONG BOTTLE WITH DECORATION OF BAMBOO AND BLOSSOMING PLUM TREE

Korea. Goryeo dynasty, late 12th–early 13th century CE. Inlaid celadon ware: light gray stoneware with decoration inlaid with black and white slips under celadon glaze, height 13¼″ (33.7 cm). Tokyo National Museum, Tokyo, Japan. (TG-2171).

Credit: TNM Image Archives

11–32 SEATED WILLOW-BRANCH GWANSE'EUM BOSAL (THE BODHISATTVA AVALOKITESHVARA)

Korea. Goryeo dynasty, late 14th century CE. Hanging scroll with ink, colors, and gold pigment on silk, height 62½" (159.6 cm). Arthur M. Sackler Museum, Harvard Art Museums, Cambridge, Massachusetts. Bequest of Grenville L. Winthrop (1943.57.12).

Credit: Bridgeman Images

inventions was inlaid decoration, in which black and white slips, or finely ground clays, were inlaid into the intaglio lines of decorative elements incised or stamped in the clay body, creating underglaze designs in contrasting colors, as seen in a bottle (**FIG. 11–31**) displaying three different pictorial scenes inlaid in black and white slips. The scene shown here depicts a clump of bamboo growing at the edge of a lake, the stalks intertwined with the branches of a blossoming plum tree (which flowers in late winter before sprouting leaves). Geese swim in the lake and butterflies flutter above, linking the several scenes around the bottle. Known as a *maebyeong* ("plum bottle"), such broad-shouldered vessels were used as storage jars for wine, vinegar, and other liquids. A small, bell-shaped cover originally capped the bottle, protecting its contents and complementing its curves.

BUDDHIST PAINTING Buddhism, the state religion of Goryeo, enjoyed royal patronage, allowing many temples to commission the very finest architects, sculptors, and painters. The most sumptuous Buddhist works produced during the Goryeo period were paintings. Created with ink and colors on silk, a fourteenth-century hanging scroll (**FIG. 11–32**) depicts Gwanse'eum Bosal (whom the Chinese called Guanyin), the bodhisattva of compassion. The rich colors and gold pigment reflect the luxurious taste of the period. Numerous paintings of this type were exported to Japan, where they influenced the course of Buddhist painting.

Think About It

1 To what extent is naturalism—the artistic goal of reproducing the visual appearance of the natural world—a motivating force in early Chinese and Korean art?

2 Compare and contrast the Chinese seated Guanyin bodhisattva (**FIG. 11–21**) and the Korean bodhisattva seated in meditation (**FIG. 11–29**). Define "bodhisattva," and examine how the artists gave visual expression to each deity's attributes.

3 Summarize the main principles of Confucianism. Then select a work from this chapter that gives visual form to Confucian philosophy and explain how it does so.

4 Select one of the Song-era Chinese landscape paintings included in this chapter. Describe it carefully and explain how it may embody philosophical or religious ideals.

Crosscurrents

These two imposing complexes from Egypt and China are royal tombs. Explain how they represent the political stature of the entombed and the beliefs of their cultures.

FIG. 3–4   FIG. 11–1

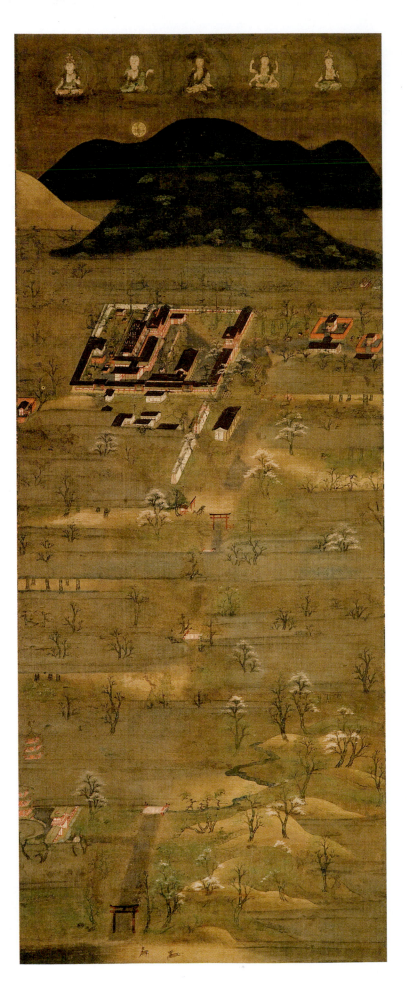

12–1 KASUGA SHRINE MANDALA

Kamakura period, early 14th century CE. Hanging scroll with ink, color, and gold on silk, $39\frac{1}{2} \times 15\frac{5}{8}''$ (100.3 × 39.8 cm). Mary Griggs Burke Collection. Gift of the Mary and Jackson Burke Foundation, 2015.

Credit: © 2016. Image copyright The Metropolitan Museum of Art/Art Resource, NY

Chapter 12
Japanese Art before 1333

Learning Objectives

12.a Identify the visual hallmarks of early Japanese art for formal, technical, and expressive qualities.

12.b Interpret the meaning of works of early Japanese art based on their themes, subjects, and symbols.

12.c Relate early Japanese artists and art to their cultural, economic, and political contexts.

12.d Apply the vocabulary and concepts relevant to early Japanese art, artists, and art history.

12.e Interpret a work of early Japanese art using the art historical methods of observation, comparison, and inductive reasoning.

12.f Select visual and textual evidence in various media to support an argument or an interpretation of a work of early Japanese art.

A group of Buddhist deities hovers at the top of this painting (**FIG. 12–1**), poised above a vast expanse of verdant hills and meadows filled with blossoming cherry and plum trees and a diagrammatic, bird's-eye view of a religious compound. The sacred site depicted in idealized but recognizable form is the Kasuga Shrine in Nara, dedicated to deities, known as *kami*, of Japan's native Shinto religion. It served as the family shrine for the most powerful aristocratic clan in ancient Japan, the Fujiwara, who chose the site for its proximity to their home, as well as for its natural beauty.

Life in Japan revolved around seasonal rhythms and the conceptions of *kami*, who give and protect life and embody the renewable, life-sustaining forces of nature. The *kami* were believed to have descended from the heavens at supremely beautiful places such as majestic mountains, towering waterfalls, old and gnarled trees, or unusual rock formations, thus rendering such locations holy—places where one might seek communion with *kami*. The deer prominently silhouetted at the very bottom of the painting are considered sacred messengers of *kami*. They roam freely in this area even today.

That foreign deities associated with Buddhism preside over a native Shinto shrine presented no anomaly. By the Heian period (794–1185 CE), the interaction of Buddhist and Shinto doctrines in Japan resulted from the belief that Buddhist deities were their original forms of *kami*. When Buddhism first entered Japan in the sixth century, the effort to integrate it with the indigenous Japanese religious belief system centered around *kami*, which only later came to be

called Shinto. Until the latter part of the nineteenth century, when the government forcibly separated the two religions and elevated Shinto to bolster worship of the emperor, Buddhism and Shinto were intimately intertwined, evolving together as complementary systems. Shinto explains the origins of the Japanese people and its deities protect them, while Buddhism offers salvation after death.

This painting encapsulates various aspects of ancient and early medieval Japanese art and culture. Like all religious art from early Japan, it was created to embody religious teachings and beliefs and was not considered a work of art. It represents how reverence for the natural world informed religious practice and visual vocabulary, and shows how the foreign religion of Buddhism was integrated with indigenous belief systems without sacrificing either. We will discover other creative syntheses of disparate traditions as we survey the art of early Japan.

The Origins of Art in Japan
What characterizes the earliest art produced by the prehistoric cultures of Japan?

Human habitation in Japan dates to around 30,000 years ago (**MAP 12–1**). Sometime after 15,000 years ago Paleolithic peoples gave way to Neolithic hunter-gatherers, who gradually developed the ability to make and use ceramics. Recent scientific dating methods have shown that some works of Japanese pottery date to earlier than 10,000 BCE.

MAP 12–1 JAPAN

Melting glaciers at the end of the Ice Age in Japan 15,000 years ago raised the sea level and formed the four main islands of Japan: Hokkaido, Honshu, Shikoku, and Kyushu.

Jomon Period

The early potters lived during the Jomon ("cord markings") period (c. 12,000–400 BCE), named for the patterns on much of the pottery they produced. They made functional earthenware vessels, probably originally imitating reed baskets, by building them up with coils of clay, then firing them in bonfires at relatively low temperatures (SEE FIG. 1-25). They also created small humanoid figures known as **dogu**, which were probably effigies that manifested a kind of sympathetic magic. Around 5000 BCE agriculture emerged with the planting and harvesting of beans and gourds.

Yayoi Period

During the succeeding Yayoi era (c. 400 BCE–300 CE), the introduction of rice cultivation by immigrants from Korea helped transform Japan into an agricultural nation. As it did elsewhere in the world, this shift to agriculture brought larger permanent settlements, class structure with the division of labor into agricultural and nonagricultural tasks, and more hierarchical forms of social organization. Korean settlers also brought metal technology. Bronze was used to create weapons as well as ceremonial objects such as bells. Iron metallurgy developed later in this period, eventually replacing stone tools in everyday life.

Kofun Period

Centralized government developed during the ensuing Kofun ("old tombs") period (c. 300–552 CE), named for its large royal tombs. With the emergence of a more complex social order, the veneration of leaders grew into the beginnings of an imperial system. Still in existence today in Japan, this system eventually explained that the emperor (or, very rarely, empress) descended directly from Shinto deities. When an emperor died, chamber tombs were constructed following Korean examples. Various grave goods were placed inside the tomb chambers, including large amounts of pottery, presumably to pacify the spirits of the dead and to serve the emperor in his next life. As part of a general cultural transfer from China through Korea, fifth-century potters in Japan gained knowledge of finishing techniques and improved kilns and began to produce high-fired ceramic ware.

The Japanese government has never allowed the major sacred tombs to be excavated, but much is known about the mortuary practices of Kofun-era Japan. Some huge tombs of the fifth and sixth centuries were constructed in a shape resembling a large keyhole and surrounded by moats dug to protect the sacred precincts. Tomb sites might extend over more than 400 acres, with artificial hills built over the tombs themselves. On the top of the hills were placed ceramic sculptures called **haniwa**.

HANIWA   The first *haniwa* were simple cylinders that may have held jars with ceremonial offerings. By the fifth century, these cylinders came to be made in the shapes of ceremonial objects, houses, and boats. Gradually, animals were added to the repertoire of *haniwa* subjects, including birds, deer, dogs, monkeys, cows, and horses. By the sixth century, **HANIWA** in human shapes were crafted, including males and females of various types, professions, and classes (FIG. **12-2**).

Haniwa embody aesthetic characteristics that we will encounter again in Japanese art. Their clay bodies were left

12-2 HANIWA

From Kyoto. Kofun period, 6th century CE. Earthenware, height 27"
(68.5 cm). Collection of the Tokyo National Museum. Important
Cultural Property.

There have been many theories on the function of *haniwa*. The
figures seem to have served as some kind of link between the world
of the dead, over which they were placed, and the world of the living,
from which they could be viewed. This figure has been identified
as a seated female shaman, wearing a robe, belt, and necklace
and carrying a mirror at her waist. In early Japan, shamans acted
as agents between the natural and the supernatural worlds, just as
haniwa figures were links between the living and the dead.

Credit: TNM Image Archives

unglazed and do not show a preoccupation with technical
virtuosity. Instead, their makers explored the expressive
potentials of simple and bold forms. *Haniwa* are never perfectly symmetrical; their slightly off-center eye-slits, irregular cylindrical bodies, and unequal arms seem to impart
the idiosyncrasy of life and individuality.

Shinto

As described at the beginning of this chapter, Shinto is
Japan's indigenous religious belief system. It encompasses
a variety of ritual practices that center around family, village, and devotion to *kami*. The term Shinto was not coined
until after the arrival of Buddhism in the sixth century CE;
as *kami* worship was influenced by and incorporated into
Buddhism it became more systematized, with shrines, a
hierarchy of deities, and more strictly regulated ceremonies.

THE ISE SHRINE One of the great Shinto monuments
is the Grand Shrine of Ise, on the coast southwest of Tokyo
(**FIG. 12-3**), where the main deity worshiped is the sun
goddess Amaterasu-o-mi-kami, the legendary progenitor
of Japan's imperial family. Japan's earliest written historical texts, recorded by the imperial court in the eighth century, claim that the Ise Shrine dates to the first century CE.
Although we do not know for certain if this is true, we do
know that it has been ritually rebuilt, alternately on two
adjoining sites, at 20-year intervals with few breaks since
the year 690, when the imperial family was solidifying its
hegemony. Its most recent rebuilding was in 2013 by carpenters who trained for the task from childhood. After the
kami is ceremonially escorted to the freshly copied shrine,
the old shrine is dismantled. Thus—like Japanese culture
itself—this exquisite shrine is both ancient and constantly
renewed. In this sense it embodies one of the most important characteristics of Shinto faith—ritual purification—
derived from respect for the cycle of the seasons in which
pure new life emerges in springtime and gives way to
death in winter, yet is reborn again in the following year.

Although Ise is visited by millions of pilgrims each
year, only members of the imperial family and a few Shinto
priests are allowed within the enclosure that surrounds its
inner shrine. Detailed documents on its appearance date
back to the tenth century, but shrine authorities denied
photographers access to its inner compound until 1953,
when the iconic photograph of it reproduced in FIGURE 12-3
was taken by a photographer officially engaged by a quasi-
governmental cultural relations agency. The reluctance of
shrine officials to permit photography even then may stem
from beliefs that such intimate pictures would violate the
privacy of the shrine's most sacred spaces.

Many aspects of the Ise Shrine are typical of Shinto
architecture, including the wooden piles that elevate the
building above the ground, a thatched roof held in place
by horizontal logs, the use of unpainted cypress wood,
and the overall feeling of natural simplicity rather than
overwhelming size or elaborate decoration. The building's
shape seems indebted to early raised granaries known
from drawings on bronze artifacts of the Yayoi period. The
sensitive use of unornamented natural materials suggests
an early origin for an aspect of Japanese taste that persists
to the present day.

Writing, Language, and Culture

Chinese culture enjoyed great prestige in East Asia. Written Chinese served as an international language of scholarship and cultivation, much as Latin did in medieval Europe. Educated Koreans, for example, wrote almost exclusively in Chinese until the fifteenth century. In Japan, Chinese continued to be used for certain kinds of writing, such as Buddhist *sutras*, philosophical and legal texts, and Chinese poetry (by Japanese writers), into the nineteenth century.

When it came to writing their own language, the Japanese initially borrowed Chinese characters, or *kanji*. Differences between the Chinese and Japanese languages made this system extremely unwieldy, so during the ninth century they developed two syllabaries, or *kana*, from simplified Chinese characters. (A syllabary is a system of lettering in which each symbol stands for a syllable.)

Katakana, consisting of angular symbols, was developed to aid pronunciation of Chinese Buddhist texts and now is generally used for foreign words. *Hiragana*, comprised of graceful, cursive symbols, was the written language the Japanese first used to write native poetry and prose. Eventually it came to be used to represent only the grammatical portions of the written Japanese language in conjunction with Chinese characters that convey meaning. Japanese written in *hiragana* was once called "women's hand" because its rounded forms looked feminine. During the Heian period *hiragana* was used to create a large body of literature, written either by women or sometimes for women by men.

A charming poem originated in Heian times to teach the new writing system. In two stanzas of four lines each, it uses almost all of the syllable sounds of spoken Japanese and thus almost every *kana* symbol.

12-3 MAIN HALL, INNER SHRINE, ISE
Mie Prefecture. Last rebuilt 2013. Photograph by Watanabe Yoshio (1907–2000), 1953. National Treasure.

Credit: Watanabe Yoshio/PPS

It was memorized as we would recite our ABC's. The first stanza translates as:

> Although flowers glow with color
> They are quickly fallen,
> And who in this world of ours
> Is free from change?
> (Translation by Earl Miner)

Like Chinese, Japanese is written in columns from top to bottom and across the page from right to left. (Following this logic, Chinese and Japanese handscrolls also read from right to left.) Below is the stanza written three ways. At the right, it appears in *katakana* glossed with the original phonetic value of each symbol. In the center, the stanza appears in flowing *hiragana*. To the left is the mixture of *kanji* and *hiragana* that eventually became standard.

kanji and *hiragana* mixed	*hiragana*	*katakana*
常ならむ 我世誰ぞ 散りぬるを 色は匂へど	つねならむ わかよたれそ ちりぬるを いろはにほへと	ツネナラム (Tsu-ne-na-ra-mu) ワカヨタレソ (Wa-ka-yo-ta-re-so) チリヌルヲ (Chi-ri-nu-ru-wo) イロハニホヘト (I-ro-ha-ni-ho-he-to)

Asuka and Nara Periods

How do the introduction and flourishing of Buddhism during the Asuka and Nara periods change Japanese art and architecture?

During the single century of the Asuka period (552–645 CE), new forms of philosophy, medicine, music, food, clothing, agriculture, city planning, religion, visual art, and architecture entered Japan from Korea and China at an astonishing pace. Most significant among these were Buddhism, a centralized governmental structure, and a system of writing. Each was adopted and gradually modified to suit local Japanese conditions, and each has had an enduring legacy.

Buddhism reached Japan in Mahayana form, with its many buddhas and bodhisattvas (see Chapter 10). After being accepted by the imperial family, it was soon adopted as a state religion. Buddhism represented not only different gods from Shinto but an entirely new concept of religion. Worship of Buddhist deities took place in temples situated close to imperial cities. The Chinese-influenced temples looked nothing like previous Japanese buildings. They housed anthropomorphic and elaborately symbolic Buddhist icons at a time when *kami* were not portrayed in human form (see "Buddhist Symbols" on page 370).

Yet Buddhism attracted followers because it offered a rich cosmology with profound teachings of meditation and enlightenment. The protective powers of its deities enabled the ruling elites to justify their own power, and they called upon Buddhist deities to nurture and protect the populace over whom they ruled. Many highly developed aspects of continental Asian art traveled to Japan with the new religion, including new methods of painting and sculpture.

Art and its Contexts

BUDDHIST SYMBOLS

A few of the most important Buddhist symbols, which have myriad variations, are described here in their most generalized forms.

Lotus flower: Usually shown as a white waterlily, the lotus (Sanskrit, *padma*) symbolizes spiritual purity, the wholeness of creation, and cosmic harmony. The flower's stem is an *axis mundi* ("axis of the world").

Lotus throne: Buddhas are frequently shown seated on an open lotus, either single or double, a representation of *nirvana* (SEE FIG. 12–10).

Chakra: An ancient sun symbol, the *chakra* (wheel) symbolizes both the various states of existence (the Wheel of Life) and the Buddhist doctrine (the Wheel of the Law). A *chakra*'s exact meaning depends on how many spokes it has.

Marks of a buddha: A buddha is distinguished by 32 physical attributes (*lakshanas*). Among them are a bulge on top of the head (*ushnisha*), a tuft of hair between the eyebrows (*urna*), and 1,000-spoked *chakras* on the soles of the feet.

Mandala: *Mandalas* are diagrams of cosmic realms, representing order and meaning within the spiritual universe. They may be simple or complex, three- or two-dimensional, and in a wide array of forms—such as an Indian stupa (SEE FIG. 10–8) or a Womb World *mandala* (SEE FIG. 12–8), an early Japanese type.

lotus flower

double lotus flower

chakra

ushnisha

urna

chakra

marks of a buddha

Credit:
Kathy Mrozek

Horyuji

The most significant surviving early Japanese temple is Horyuji, located on Japan's central plains not far from Nara. The temple was founded in 607 by Prince Shotoku (574–622), who ruled Japan as a regent and became the most influential early proponent of Buddhism. Rebuilt after a fire in 670, Horyuji is the oldest wooden temple in the world.

The main compound of Horyuji consists of a rectangular courtyard surrounded by covered corridors, one of which contains a gateway. Within the compound are two buildings: the **kondo** (main hall) and a five-story pagoda. In a simple asymmetrical layout, the large golden *kondo*

12–4 AERIAL VIEW OF THE HORYUJI COMPOUND
Pagoda to the west (left), golden hall (*kondo*) to the east (right). Nara Prefecture. Asuka period, 7th century CE. UNESCO World Heritage Site, National Treasure.

Credit: © Shashinkoubou

balances the tall, slender pagoda (**FIG. 12-4**). The *kondo*, filled with Buddhist images, is used for worship and ceremonies, while the pagoda serves as a **reliquary** and is not entered. Other monastery buildings lie outside the main compound, including an outer gate, a lecture hall, a repository for sacred texts, a belfry, and dormitories for monks.

Among the many treasures still preserved in Horyuji is a portable shrine decorated with paintings in lacquer. It is known as the Tamamushi Shrine after the *tamamushi* beetle, whose iridescent wings were originally affixed to the shrine to make it glitter, much like mother-of-pearl. Its architectural form replicates an ancient palace-form building type that pre-dates Horyuji itself.

HUNGRY TIGRESS JATAKA Paintings on the sides of the Tamamushi Shrine are among the few two-dimensional works of art to survive from the Asuka period. Most celebrated among them are two that illustrate Jataka tales, stories about former lives of the Buddha. One depicts the future Buddha nobly sacrificing his life in order to feed his body to a starving tigress and her cubs (**FIG. 12-5**).

12-5 HUNGRY TIGRESS JATAKA
Panel of the Tamamushi Shrine, Horyuji. Asuka period, c. 650 CE. Lacquer on wood, height of shrine 7′7½″ (2.33 m). Horyuji Treasure House, Nara. National Treasure.

Credit: © Iberfoto/Alinari Archives

12–6 Attributed to Tori Busshi **BUDDHA SHAKA AND ATTENDANT BODHISATTVAS IN THE HORYUJI KONDO**

Asuka period, c. 623 CE. Gilt bronze, height of seated figure 34½″ (87.5 cm). Horyuji, Nara Prefecture. National Treasure.

Credit: © Iberfoto/Alinari Archives

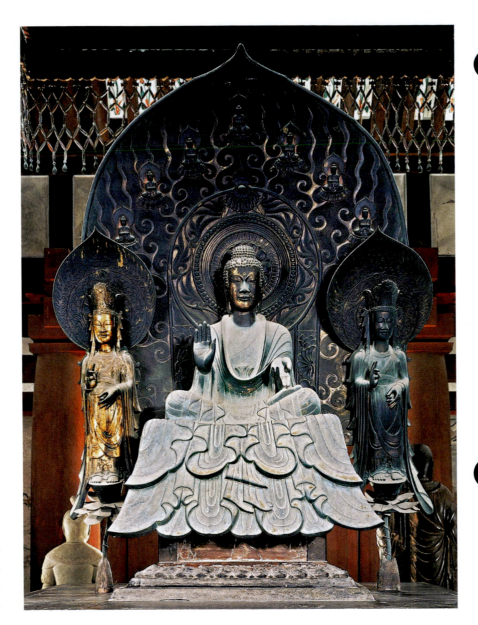

Since the tigers are at first too weak to eat him, he jumps off a cliff to break open his flesh. The painter has created a full narrative within a single frame. The graceful form of the Buddha appears three times in three sequential stages of the story, harmonized by the curves of the rocky cliff and tall wands of bamboo. First, he hangs his shirt on a tree, then he dives downward onto the rocks, and finally the starving animals devour his body. The elegantly slender renditions of the figure and the stylized treatment of the cliff, trees, and bamboo represent an international Buddhist style that was transmitted to Japan via China and Korea. Such illustrations of Jataka tales helped popularize Buddhism in Japan.

SHAKA TRIAD　　Another example of the international style of early Buddhist art at Horyuji is the sculpture called the Shaka Triad, traditionally attributed to sculptor Tori Busshi (**FIG. 12–6**). (Shaka is the Japanese name for Shakyamuni, the historical Buddha.) Tori Busshi (Busshi means Buddhist image-maker) may have been a descendant of Korean craftspeople who emigrated to Japan as part of an influx of Buddhists and artisans from Korea. The Shaka Triad reflects the strong influence of Chinese art of the Northern Wei dynasty (SEE FIG. 11–13). The frontal pose, the outsized face and hands, and the linear treatment of the drapery all suggest that the maker of this statue was well aware of earlier continental models, while the fine bronze casting of the figures shows his advanced technical skill.

Nara Period

The Nara period (645–794) is named for Japan's first permanent imperial capital, founded in 710. Previously, an emperor's death was thought to taint his entire capital city, so for reasons of purification (and perhaps also of politics), his successor usually selected a new site. As the government adopted ever more complex aspects of the Chinese political system, necessitating construction of huge administrative complexes, it abandoned this custom in the eighth century when Nara was founded. During this period, divisions of the imperial bureaucracy grew exponentially and hastened the swelling of the city's population to perhaps 200,000 people.

One result of the strong central authority was the construction in Nara of magnificent Buddhist temples and Shinto shrines that dwarfed those built previously. The expansive park in the center of Nara today is the site of the largest and most important of these, including the Shinto Kasuga Shrine depicted in FIGURE 12–1. The grandest of the Buddhist temples in Nara Park is Todaiji, which the deeply religious Emperor Shomu (ruled 724–749) conceived as the headquarters of a vast network of branch temples throughout the nation. Todaiji served as both a state-supported central monastic training center and as the setting for public religious ceremonies. The most spectacular of these took place in 752 and celebrated the consecration of the main Buddhist statue of the temple in a traditional "eye-opening" ceremony. The statue, a giant gilt-bronze image of the Buddha Birushana (Vairochana in Sanskrit), was inspired by the Chinese tradition of erecting monumental stone Buddhist statues in cave-temples (SEE FIG. 11–13).

The ceremony, which took place in the vast courtyard in front of the newly constructed Great Buddha Hall, was presided over by an illustrious Indian monk and included *sutra* chanting by over 10,000 Japanese Buddhist monks and sacred performances by 4,000 court musicians and dancers. Vast numbers of Japanese courtiers and emissaries from the Asian continent were the audience. Numerous ritual objects used in the ceremony came from exotic Asian and Near Eastern lands. The resulting cosmopolitan atmosphere reflected the position Nara then held as the eastern terminus of the Central Asian Silk Road.

Many of these treasures have been preserved in the Shosoin Imperial Repository at Todaiji, which today contains some 9,000 objects. The Shosoin came into being in the year 756 when Emperor Shomu died and his widow, the devout Buddhist empress Komyo, donated some 600 of his possessions to the temple, including a number of objects used during the Great Buddha's consecration ceremony. Many years later, objects used in Buddhist rituals and previously stored elsewhere at Todaiji were incorporated into the collection. The objects formerly owned by Emperor Shomu consisted mainly of his personal possessions, such as documents, furniture, musical instruments, games, clothing, medicine, weapons, some Buddhist ritual objects, and food and beverage vessels of metal, glass, and lacquer. Some of these had been made in Japan, while others came from as far away as China, India, Iran, Greece,

Rome, and Egypt. They reflect the vast international trade network that existed at this early date.

One of the items Empress Komyo donated in 756 is a magnificently crafted five-stringed lute (*biwa*) made of lacquered red sandalwood and chestnut and inlaid with mother-of-pearl, amber, and tortoiseshell. Its plectrum guard portrays a central Asian musician (his ethnicity apparent from his clothing and physical features) sitting on a camel and playing a lute (FIG. 12–7). This is the only existing example of an ancient five-stringed lute, an instrument invented in India and transmitted to China and Japan via the Silk Road. The Shosoin piece is generally identified as Chinese, but, as with many of the objects preserved in the Shosoin, the location of its manufacture is not certain. While it was most likely crafted in China and imported to Japan for use in the consecration ceremony (researchers have recently conclusively determined that it was indeed played), it is also plausible that Chinese (or Japanese) craftspeople made it in Japan using imported materials. Its meticulous workmanship is characteristic of the high level of craft production achieved by artists of this era.

Influenced by Emperor Shomu, the Buddhist faith permeated all aspects of Nara court society. Indeed, in 749 Shomu abdicated the throne to spend the remainder of his life as a monk. His daughter, also a devout Buddhist, succeeded him as empress but wanted to cede her throne to a Buddhist monk. This so dismayed her advisors that they moved the capital city away from Nara, where they felt Buddhist influence had become overpowering, and established a new one in Kyoto, within whose bounds only a few Buddhist temples would be allowed at first. The move of the capital to Kyoto marked the end of the Nara period.

12–7 FIVE-STRINGED LUTE (BIWA) WITH DESIGN OF A CENTRAL ASIAN MAN PLAYING A BIWA ATOP A CAMEL
Chinese. Tang dynasty, 8th century CE. Red sandalwood and chestnut inlaid with mother-of-pearl, amber, and tortoiseshell; length 42½" (108.1 cm), width 12" (30.9 cm), depth 3½" (9 cm). Shosoin Repository, Todaiji.

Credit: Shosoin, Todaiji, Nara

Heian Period

How are Japanese art and architecture transformed during the Heian period?

During the Heian period (794–1185) the Japanese fully absorbed and transformed their cultural borrowings from China and Korea. Generally peaceful conditions contributed to a new air of self-reliance, and the imperial government severed ties to China in the ninth century, a time when the power of related aristocratic families increased. An efficient method of writing the Japanese language was developed, and the rise of vernacular literature generated such prose masterpieces as Lady Murasaki's *The Tale of Genji*. During these four centuries of splendor and refinement, two major streams of Buddhism emerged—esoteric sects and, later, those espousing salvation in the Pure Land Western Paradise of the Buddha Amida.

Esoteric Buddhist Art

With the capital's move to Kyoto, the older Nara temples lost their influence. Soon two new esoteric sects of Buddhism, Tendai and Shingon, grew to dominate Japanese religious life. Strongly influenced by polytheistic religions such as Hinduism, Esoteric Buddhism (known as Tantric Buddhism in Nepal and Tibet) included a daunting number of deities, each with magical powers. The historical Buddha was no longer very important. Instead, most revered was the universal Buddha, called Dainichi ("Great Sun" in Japanese), who was believed to preside over the universe. He was accompanied by buddhas and bodhisattvas, as well as guardian deities who formed fierce counterparts to the more benign gods.

Esoteric Buddhism is hierarchical, and its deities have complex relationships to one another. Learning all the different gods and their interrelationships was assisted greatly by paintings, especially *mandalas*, cosmic diagrams

12–8 WOMB WORLD MANDALA

Heian period, late 9th century CE. Hanging scroll with colors on silk, 6′ × 5′1½″ (1.83 × 1.54 m). Toji, Kyoto. National Treasure.

Mandalas are used not only in teaching, but also as vehicles for practice. A monk, initiated into secret teachings, may meditate upon and assume the gestures of each deity depicted in the *mandala*, gradually working out from the center, so that he absorbs some of each deity's powers. The monk may also recite magical phrases, called mantras, as an aid to meditation. The goal is to achieve enlightenment through the powers of the different forms of the Buddha. *Mandalas* are created in sculptural and architectural forms as well as in paintings (SEE FIG. 10–36). Their integration of the two most basic shapes, the circle and the square, is an expression of the principles of ancient geomancy (divining by means of lines and figures) as well as Buddhist cosmology.

Credit: © Fine Art Images/ Superstock

of the universe that portray the deities in schematic order. The **WOMB WORLD MANDALA** from Toji, for example, is entirely filled with depictions of gods (**FIG. 12-8**). Dainichi is at the center, surrounded by buddhas of the four directions. Other deities, including some with multiple heads and limbs, branch out in diagrammatical order, each with a specific symbol of power and targeted to various levels of potential worshipers, some of whom needed to be frightened to awaken to Buddhist teaching. To believers, the *mandala* represents an ultimate reality beyond the visible world.

Perhaps the most striking attribute of many Esoteric Buddhist images is their sense of spiritual force and potency, especially in depictions of the wrathful deities, which are often surrounded by flames like those visible in the Womb World *mandala* just below the main circle of buddhas. With its intricate theology and complex doctrines, Esoteric Buddhism was a religion for the educated aristocracy, not for the masses. Its elaborate network of deities, hierarchy, and ritual found parallels in the elaborate social divisions of the Heian court.

Pure Land Buddhist Art

Rising militarism, political turbulence, and excesses of the imperial court marked the beginning of the eleventh century in Japan. To many, the unsettled times seemed to confirm the coming of *Mappo*, the Buddhist concept of a long-prophesied dark age of spiritual degeneration. Japanese of all classes reacted by increasingly turning to the promise of salvation after death through their faith in a Buddhist realm known as the Western Paradise of the Pure Land, a resplendent place filled with divine flowers and music. Amida (Amitabha in Sanskrit) and his attendant bodhisattvas preside there as divine protectors who compassionately accept all who submit wholeheartedly to their benevolent powers. Pure Land beliefs had spread to Japan from China by way of Korea, where they also enjoyed great popularity. They offered an easier and more immediate way to achieve salvation than the elaborate rituals of the esoteric sects. Pure Land Buddhism held that merely by chanting *Namu Amida Butsu* ("Hail to Amida Buddha"), the faithful would be reborn into the Western Paradise.

BYODOIN One of the most beautiful temples of Pure Land Buddhism is the Byodoin, located in the Uji Mountains not far from central Kyoto (**FIG. 12-9**). The temple itself was originally a secular villa whose form was intended to suggest the appearance of the palatial residence of Amida in his Western Paradise (SEE FIG. 11-15). It was built for a member of the powerful Fujiwara family who served as the leading counselor to the emperor. After the counselor's death in the year 1052, his descendants converted the palace into a memorial temple to honor his

12-9 BYODOIN (PHOENIX HALL), UJI
Kyoto Prefecture. Heian period, c. 1053 CE. UNESCO World Heritage Site, National Treasure.

Credit: © Kenneth Dedeu/Shutterstock

spirit. The Byodoin is often called the Phoenix Hall, not only for the pair of phoenix images on its roof, but also because the shape of the building itself suggests the mythical bird. Its thin columns give the Byodoin a sense of airiness, as though the temple could rise up through the sky to Amida's Western Paradise. The hall rests gently in front of an artificial pond created in the shape of the Sanskrit letter A, the sacred symbol for Amida.

The Byodoin's central image of Amida, carved by the master sculptor Jocho (died 1057), exemplifies the serenity and compassion of this Buddha (**FIG. 12-10**). When reflected in the water of the pond before it, the Amida image seems to shimmer in its private mountain retreat. Surrounding the Amida on the walls of the Byodoin are smaller wooden figures of bodhisattvas and angels, some playing musical instruments. Everything about the Byodoin was designed to simulate the appearance of the paradise that awaits the believer after death. Its remarkable state of preservation after more than 900 years allows visitors to experience the late Heian religious ideal at its most splendid.

Jocho's figure was not carved from a single block of wood like earlier sculpture, but from several blocks in his new **joined-block** method of construction (see "Joined-Block Wood Sculpture" opposite).

Secular Painting and Calligraphy

Parallel with the permeation of Buddhism during the Heian era (794–1185) was a refined secular culture that developed at court. Gradually over the course of these four centuries, the pervasive influence of Chinese culture in aristocratic society gave rise to new, uniquely Japanese developments. Above all, Heian court culture greatly valued refinement; pity any man or woman at court who was not accomplished in several forms of art. A woman would be admired for the way she arranged the 12 layers of her robes by color, or a man for knowing which kind of incense was being burned. Concurrently, court life became preoccupied by the poetical expression of human love. In this climate, women became a vital force in Heian society.

Although the status of women was to decline in later periods, they contributed greatly to art at the Heian court and became famous for their prose and poetry.

Although male courtiers continued to be required to read and write Chinese, both men and women of court society wrote prose and poetry in their native Japanese language using the newly devised *kana* script. They also used *kana* on text portions of new types of small-scale secular paintings: handscrolls or folding albums designed to be appreciated in private settings.

At the beginning of the eleventh century, the lady-in-waiting Lady Murasaki transposed the lifestyle of Heian aristocrats into fiction for the amusement of her fellow court ladies in *The Tale of Genji*, which some consider the world's first novel. Japanese today still admire this tale of 54 chapters as a pinnacle of Japanese literary achievement. (In 2009, the official 1,000-year anniversary of its completion, numerous exhibitions and celebrations took place throughout Japan.) Underlying the story of the love affairs of Prince Genji and his companions is the Heian conception of fleeting pleasures and ultimate sadness in life, an echo of the Buddhist view of the vanity of earthly pleasures.

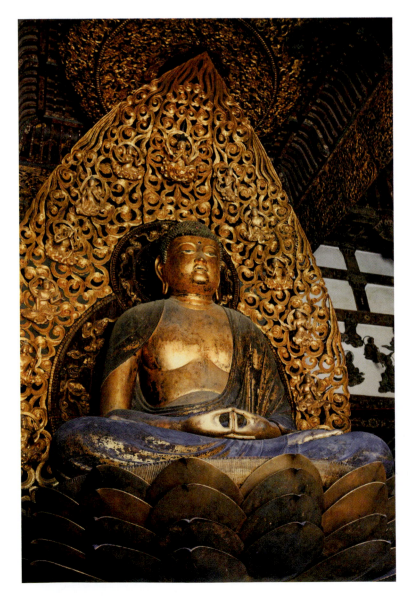

12–10 Jocho **AMIDA BUDDHA**
Byodoin (Phoenix Hall). Heian period, c. 1053 CE.
Gold leaf and lacquer on wood, height 9'8" (2.95 m).
National Treasure.

Credit: © Prisma Bildagentur AG/Alamy Stock Photo

Technique

JOINED-BLOCK WOOD SCULPTURE

Wood is a temperamental material because fluctuations in moisture content cause it to swell and shrink. Cut from a living, sap-filled tree, it takes many years to dry to a state of stability. While the outside of a piece of wood dries fairly rapidly, the inside yields its moisture only gradually, causing a difference in the rates of shrinkage between the inside and the outside, which induces the wood to crack. Consequently, a large statue carved from a single log must inevitably crack as it ages. Natural irregularities in wood, such as knots, further accentuate this problem. Thus, wood with a thinner cross section and fewer irregularities is less susceptible to cracking because it can dry more evenly. (This is the logic behind sawing logs into boards before drying.)

Japanese sculptors developed an ingenious and unique method, the joined-block technique, to reduce cracking in heavy wooden statues. This allowed them to create larger statues in wood than ever before, enabled standardization of body proportions, and encouraged division of labor among teams of carvers, some of whom became specialists in certain parts, such as hands or crossed legs or lotus thrones. To create large statues seated in the lotus pose, sculptors first put four blocks together vertically two by two in front and back, to form the main body, then added several blocks horizontally at what would become the front of the statue for the lap and knees. After carving each part, they assembled the figure and hollowed out the interior. This cooperative approach also had the added benefit of enabling workshops to produce large statues more quickly to meet a growing demand. Jocho is credited as the master sculptor who perfected this technique. The diagram shows how he assembled the Amida Buddha at the Byodoin (SEE FIG. 12–10).

Diagram of the joined-block wood sculpture technique used on the Amida statue by Jocho.

Credit: Kathy Mrozek

YAMATO-E HANDSCROLLS—THE TALE OF GENJI A new secular painting style arose called **yamato-e**, or native Japanese-style pictures; Yamato is the old Japanese word for Japan. One of the earliest surviving examples is an illustrated handscroll from the twelfth century depicting a series of scenes from *The Tale of Genji*. The handscroll alternates sections of text with illustrations of scenes from the story and features delicate lines, strong (but sometimes muted) mineral colors, and asymmetrical compositions. The paintings have a refined, subtle emotional impact. They generally show court figures in architectural settings, with the frequent addition of natural elements and gardens that help to convey the mood of the scene. Thus a blossoming cherry tree appears in a scene of happiness, while unkempt weeds appear in a depiction of loneliness. Such correspondences between nature and human emotion are an enduring theme of Japanese poetry and art. The figures in *The Tale of Genji* paintings do not show their emotions directly on their faces, which are rendered with a few simple lines. Instead, their feelings are conveyed by colors, poses, fluttering of curtains, and the overall composition of the scenes.

One scene portrays Prince Genji viewed from behind while visiting his favorite consort, Murasaki (not the same person as the author of the novel), who faces him across a narrow interior space (see "Closer Look" on page 378). Although Genji was especially fond of her, Murasaki could not become his principal wife because she was not from an aristocratic family. Here he comes to see her shortly before her death. One might expect the visualization of such a poignant moment to focus on the people involved. Instead the figures are relatively small and all but consumed by their clothing. The screens of the domestic interior dominate the scene, effectively squeezing Genji and Murasaki into a confined corridor. The composition, not the facial expressions or bodily postures, conveys the melancholy of the moment. The airy openness of the outdoor garden to the left—and the sketchy delicacy of the plants within it—heighten the sense of confinement and impending loss.

A Closer Look

THE TALE OF GENJI

Only 19 illustrated scenes survive from this earliest known example of an illustrated handscroll of *The Tale of Genji*, created about 100 years after the novel was written. Scholars assume that it originally contained illustrations from the entire novel of 54 chapters, approximately 100 pictures in all. Each scroll seems to have been produced by a team of artists. One was the calligrapher, most likely a member of the nobility.

Another was the master painter, who outlined two or three illustrations per chapter in fine brushstrokes and indicated the color scheme. Next, colorists went to work, applying layer after layer of color to build up patterns and textures. After they had finished, the master painter returned to reinforce outlines and apply the finishing touches, among them the details of the faces.

Thickly applied mineral colors are now cracking and flaking.

Following courtly convention, Murasaki's body is concealed beneath voluminous robes; she holds a fan to shield her face, and her loosened hair cascades around her face and over her clothes.

The roof has been removed so we can see what is happening.

Wooden verandas surrounded Japanese houses, merging interior and exterior to provide vantage points for admiring the gardens.

The non-individualized faces of the prince and his consort betray none of the emotional content of the scene.

Murasaki's daughter is discretely tucked between a "privacy" curtain and the wall.

12–11 SCENE FROM THE TALE OF GENJI
Heian period, 12th century CE. Handscroll with ink and colors on paper, 8⅝ × 18⅞" (21.9 × 47.9 cm). Gotoh Museum, Tokyo.

CALLIGRAPHY IN JAPANESE The text portions of the *The Tale of Genji* handscroll were written in *kana* script, which was also used to write poetry in Japanese. In the Heian period, the most significant form of native poetry was a 31-syllable format known as *waka*, which had first been composed earlier than the eighth century. During the Heian era, the finest *waka* by various writers were collected together and hand-copied in albums, the most popular of which featured writers collectively known as the Thirty-Six Immortal Poets, an anthology still appreciated by educated Japanese today. The earliest of many surviving examples of this iconic collection originally contained 39 volumes of poems. Two volumes were taken apart and sold in 1929, and now survive in single-page sections (**FIG. 12–12**). Collectively these separated volumes are known as the *Ishiyamagire* (Ishiyama fragments, named after Ishiyamadera, the temple that originally owned the volumes).

With its simple, flowing letters, characters, or syllables, interspersed occasionally with more complex Chinese characters, this style of writing gave a distinctive

12–12 BOOK PAGE FROM THE ISHIYAMAGIRE
Dispersed volumes, once owned by the Ishiyama Temple, of the anthology of the Thirty-Six Immortal Poets. Heian period, early 12th century CE. Ink with gold and silver on decorated and collaged paper, 8 × 6⅜″ (20.6 × 16.1 cm). Freer Gallery of Art, Smithsonian Institution, Washington, DC. (F1969.4).

Credit: Bridgeman Images

asymmetrical balance to the appearance of the written words. In these pages, the poems seem to float elegantly on fine dyed papers decorated with painting, block printing, scattered sheets, and particles of gold and silver, and sometimes paper collage. Often, as in FIGURE 12–12, the irregular pattern of torn paper edges adds a serendipitous element. The page shown here reproduces two verses by the eighth-century courtier Ki no Tsurayuki that express melancholy emotions. One reads:

> Until yesterday
> I could meet her,
> But today she is gone—
> Like clouds over the mountain
> She has been wafted away.

The spiky, flowing calligraphy, the patterning of the papers, the rich use of gold, and the suggestions of natural imagery all match the elegance of the poetry, epitomizing courtly Japanese taste.

YAMATO-E HANDSCROLLS—FROLICKING ANIMALS In its sedate and sophisticated portrayal of courtly life, *The Tale of Genji* scroll represents one side of *yamato-e*. But another style of native painting emerged contemporaneously. Characterized by bold, confident strokes of the brush and little if any use of color, it depicted subjects outside the court engaged in playful and irreverent activities. One of the early masterpieces of this style is a set of handscrolls known as *Frolicking Animals* (*Choju Giga*) that satirizes human behavior through animal antics. Freely executed entirely in black ink, the humorous parodies are attributed to Toba Sojo (1053–1140), abbot of a Buddhist monastery.

In one particularly amusing scene, a monkey—robed as a monk preoccupied with the passionate

12-13 Attributed to Toba Sojo **SCENE FROM FROLICKING ANIMALS**
Heian period, 12th century CE. Handscroll with ink on paper, height 12″ (30.5 cm). Kozanji, Kyoto. National Treasure.

Credit: TNM Image Archives

incantations that emerge from his gaping mouth like wisps of smoke—offers a peach branch on an altar, behind which a frog is posed as a buddha enthroned on a lotus leaf (**FIG. 12-13**). Around this monkey-monk is an assembly of animals—rabbits, monkey, foxes, and frog—representing monastic and secular worshipers, some bored and distracted, others focusing on their prayers, which are either read from texts or guided by the Buddhist prayer beads clutched in their hands. Although unlike the *Genji* scroll there is no accompanying text to *Frolicking Animals*, making it difficult to know exactly what was being satirized, the universality of the humorous antics remains.

Kamakura Period

How do the priorities of secular and religious patrons shape Japanese art of the Kamakura period?

The courtiers of the Heian era seem to have become so engrossed in their own refinement that they neglected their responsibilities for governing the country. Clans of warriors—samurai—from outside the capital grew increasingly strong. Two of these, the Taira and Minamoto, were especially powerful. They took opposing sides in the factional conflicts of the imperial court in order to control the weakened emperor and take charge of the government.

The Kamakura era (1185–1333) began when the head of the Minamoto clan, Yoritomo (1147–1199), defeated the Taira family and ordered the emperor to appoint him as

shogun (general-in-chief). To resist what he perceived as the softening effects of courtly life in Kyoto, he established his military capital in Kamakura, while the emperor continued to reside in Kyoto. Although Yoritomo's newly invented title of shogun nominally respected the authority of the emperor, it also assured him of supreme military and political power. The shogunate initiated by Yoritomo endured in various forms until 1868.

A Battle Handscroll

The battles for domination between the Minamoto and the Taira became famous not only in medieval Japanese history but also as subjects in literature and art. One of the great painted handscrolls depicting these battles is **NIGHT ATTACK ON THE SANJO PALACE** (**FIG. 12-14**). Though it was painted perhaps a century after the actual event, the artist conveyed the sense of eyewitness reporting even though imagining the scene from verbal—at best semifactual—descriptions. The style of the painting includes some of the brisk and lively linework of *Frolicking Animals* and also aspects of the more refined brushwork, use of color, and bird's-eye viewpoint of *The Tale of Genji* scroll. The relentless focus, however, is on the dynamic depiction of the savagery of warfare across expansive lateral compositions (see "Arms and Armor" opposite). Unlike the *Genji* scroll, *Night Attack* is full of action. The sense of energy and violence is pervasive, conveyed with sweeping power. There is no trace here of courtly poetic refinement and melancholy; the new world of the samurai is dominating the secular arts.

12–14 SECTION OF NIGHT ATTACK ON THE SANJO PALACE

Kamakura period, late 13th century CE. Handscroll with ink and colors on paper, 16¼″ × 22′ 9¹¹⁄₁₆″ (41.3 cm × 700.3 cm). Museum of Fine Arts, Boston. Fenollosa-Weld Collection (11.4000).

The battles between the Minamoto and Taira clans were fought primarily by mounted and armored warriors, who used swords as well as bows and arrows. In the year 1160, some 500 Minamoto rebels opposed to the retired emperor Go-Shirakawa carried out a daring raid on the Sanjo Palace. In a surprise attack in the middle of the night, they abducted the emperor. The scene was one of great carnage, much of it caused by the burning of the wooden palace. Despite the drama of the scene, this was not the decisive moment in the war. The Minamoto rebels would lose more-important battles to their Taira enemies, yet the Minamoto heirs to those who carried out this raid would eventually prove victorious, destroying the Taira clan in 1185.

Credit: Photograph © 2017 Museum of Fine Arts, Boston

Art and its Contexts

ARMS AND ARMOR

Battles such as the one depicted in *Night Attack on the Sanjo Palace* (SEE FIG. 12–14) were fought largely by archers on horseback. Samurai archers charged the enemy at full gallop and loosed their arrows just before they wheeled away. The scroll clearly shows their distinctive bow with its asymmetrically placed handgrip. The lower portion of the bow is shorter than the upper so it can clear the horse's neck. The samurai wear long, curved swords at their waists.

By the tenth century, Japanese swordsmiths had perfected techniques for crafting their legendarily sharp swords. Sword-makers face a fundamental difficulty: Steel hard enough to hold a razor-sharp edge is brittle and breaks easily, but steel resilient enough to withstand rough use is too soft to hold a keen edge. The Japanese ingeniously forged a blade which laminated a hard cutting edge within less brittle support layers.

The earliest form of samurai armor, illustrated here, known as *yoroi*, was intended for use by warriors on horseback, as seen in FIGURE 12–14. It was made of overlapping iron and lacquered leather scales, punched with holes and laced together with leather thongs and brightly colored silk braids. The principal piece wrapped around the chest, left side, and back. Padded shoulder straps hooked it together back to front. A separate piece of armor was tied to the body to protect the right side. The upper legs were protected by a four-sided skirt that attached to the body armor, while two large rectangular panels tied on with cords guarded the arms. The helmet was made of iron plates riveted together. From it hung a neck guard flared sharply outward to protect the face from arrows shot at close range.

helmet

detail of scales

body armor

Credit: Kathy Mrozek

Pure Land Buddhist Art

By the beginning of the Kamakura period, Pure Land Buddhist beliefs had swept throughout Japan, and several charismatic priests founded new sects to promote this ideology. They traveled throughout the country, spreading the new gospel in ways that appealed to people of all levels of education and sophistication. They were so successful that Pure Land Buddhist sects have remained the most popular form of Buddhism in Japan ever since.

RAIGO PAINTINGS Pure Land Buddhism taught that even one sincere invocation of the sacred chant could lead the most wicked sinner to the Western Paradise. Popular paintings called **raigo** ("welcoming approach") depicted the Amida Buddha, accompanied by bodhisattvas, coming down to earth to welcome the soul of the dying believer. Golden cords were often attached to these paintings, which were taken to the homes of the dying. A person near death held onto these cords, hoping that Amida would escort the soul directly to paradise.

Raigo paintings differ significantly in style from the complex *mandalas* and fierce guardian deities of Esoteric Buddhism. The earliest-known example of this subject is found on the walls and doors of the Byodoin, surrounding Jocho's sculpture of Amida (SEE FIG. 12–10). Like that statue, they radiate warmth and compassion. In the Kamakura

12–15 DESCENT OF AMIDA AND THE TWENTY-FIVE BODHISATTVAS
Kamakura period, 13th century CE. Hanging scroll with colors and gold on silk, 57¼ × 61½" (145 × 155.5 cm). Chion-in, Kyoto. National Treasure.

Credit: Photo Courtesy of Kyoto National Museum. Property of Chion-in period, *raigo* paintings were made in great numbers, reflecting the popularity of Pure Land Buddhism at that time. One magnificent example portrays Amida Buddha and 25 bodhisattvas descending over mountains (FIG. 12-15). The artist used gold paint and thin slivers of gold leaf cut in elaborate patterns to suggest the divine radiance of the deities. This painstaking cut–gold leaf technique, known as *kirikane*, is one of the great achievements of early Japanese Buddhist artists. It originated in China, but Japanese artists refined and perfected it. In this painting, the darkened silk behind the figures heightens the sparkle of their golden aura. In the flickering light of oil lamps and torches, *raigo* paintings would have appeared magical, whether in a temple or in a dying person's home.

One of the most remarkable aspects of this painting is its sensitive rendering of the landscape, full of rugged peaks and flowering trees. Perhaps this emphasis on the natural setting derives from a traditional Japanese appreciation for the beautiful land in which they dwelled, an appreciation that may stem from Shinto beliefs. In fact, Shinto pictures portraying the landscape of Japan as divine first appeared in the Kamakura period, just as Pure Land Buddhism was growing in popularity. One of these is the Kasuga Shrine *mandala* of FIGURE 12-1, demonstrating how Kamakura artists represented the merging of the two faiths of Buddhism and Shinto. The artist of this work made the shrine buildings resemble those of the palatial abode of Amida in his Western Paradise and rendered the landscape details with the radiant charm of Amida's heaven.

Zen Buddhist Art

Zen Buddhism was introduced to Japan from China, where it was already highly developed and known as Chan. Relations between the two countries had been interrupted during the Heian period. But during the Kamakura era, both emigrant Chinese and Japanese monks—who went to China to study Buddhism and returned home enthused about the new teachings they learned there—brought Zen to Japan. They secluded themselves in monasteries, leading an austere life of simplicity and self-responsibility.

Chan (Zen) monks modeled their behavior on that of the founder of their lineage, the mythical Indian Buddhist sage Daruma (Bodhidharma in Sanskrit), who emigrated to China in the sixth century CE and famously transmitted his teachings to a Chinese disciple who became the second Chan patriarch. This portrait of **DARUMA** (FIG. 12-16) is one of the earliest surviving examples of Japanese Zen painting. Using fine ink outlines and a touch of color for the robe and the figure's sandals, the artist portrays the Chan master seated meditating atop a rock with an unwavering gaze that is intended to convey his inner strength and serenity. At the top of the scroll is an inscription in Chinese by Yishan Yining (1247–1317), one of several influential

early Chinese Chan masters to emigrate to Japan. He had planned only to visit Japan as head of an official diplomatic delegation from China in 1299, but he stayed for the remainder of his life. Although the Japanese were wary of him at first, his sincere intentions to teach Chan and his erudite abilities quickly attracted influential supporters. Soon after arrival, Yishan was appointed as the tenth head abbot of the large Zen temple of Kenchoji in Kamakura, a post he held briefly before moving on to head several other Zen temples.

12-16 DARUMA

Inscription by Chinese Chan master Yishan Yining (1247–1317). Kamakura period, early 14th century CE. Hanging scroll with ink and colors on silk, 39⅝ × 20" (100.8 × 50.8 cm). Tokyo National Museum. Important Cultural Property.

Credit: TNM Image Archives

Kenchoji had been founded in 1253 by another emigrant Chan master, Lanxi Daolong (1213–1278). Lanxi was the first Chan master to travel to Japan. There, he was warmly received by the fifth Minamoto shogun, who

12–17 PORTRAIT OF THE CHINESE CHAN MASTER LANXI DAOLONG

Inscription by Lanxi Daolong. Kamakura period, 1271 CE. Hanging scroll with colors on silk, 41⅓ × 18″ (105 × 46.1 cm). Kenchoji, Kamakura. National Treasure.

Credit: Kenchoji, Kamakura

helped him plan construction of Kenchoji where, for the first time, authentic Chinese Chan Buddhism was to be taught in Japan. Kenchoji remains one of the most important Zen monasteries in Japan. The temple owns many formal portraits of its founder, including this one (**FIG. 12–17**), considered by many to be the best because it seems to capture Daolong's inner spirit as well as his outer form. This type of painting is peculiar to Chan and Zen sects and is known as *chinso*. These paintings were often gifts given by a master to disciples when they completed their formal training and departed to officiate at their own temples. The paintings served as personal reminders of the master's teachings and tangible evidence (like a diploma) of the disciples' right to transmit Zen teachings to their own pupils. Lanxi Daolong dedicated the inscription of this painting to an important regent (samurai official), a confidant of the shogun, and not an ordained Zen monk. This shows that Zen, from its early days in Japan, also strove to attract followers from among those in power who could not abandon their secular life for the rigorous, cloistered existence of Zen monks who lived in temples.

In some ways, Zen resembles the original teachings of the historical Buddha: it emphasizes individual enlightenment through meditation, without the help of deities or magical chants. It especially appealed to the self-disciplined spirit of samurai warriors, who were not satisfied with the older forms of Buddhism connected with the Japanese court. Zen was the last major form of Buddhism to reach Japan from the Asian mainland, and it had a profound and lasting impact on Japanese arts and culture.

Just as the *Night Attack* (SEE FIG. 12–14) reveals a propensity for recording the consequences of political turbulence by representing gruesome and detailed battle scenes in vivid colors, Kamakura-era Buddhist sculpture and painting also emphasized realism. Various factors account for this new taste. Society was dominated by samurai warriors, who possessed a more pragmatic outlook on the world than the Heian-period courtiers, who had lived a dreamlike, insular existence at court. In addition, renewed contacts with China introduced new styles for Buddhist art that emphasized lifelike portrayal. Finally, forging personal connections with heroic exploits and individuals—both past and present, political and religious—greatly concerned the people of the Kamakura period. Representing these figures in arresting pictorial and sculpted images helped reinforce legends and perpetuate their influence.

As the Kamakura era ended, the seeds of the future were planted both politically and culturally. The coming age witnessed the nation's continued dominance by the warrior class and the establishment of Zen as the religion of choice among those warriors who wielded power at the highest levels. As before, the later history of Japanese art continued to be marked by an intriguing interplay between native traditions and imported foreign tendencies.

Think About It

1   Discuss the influence of Chinese art on the early Japanese Buddhist complex at Horyuji, referring to Chapter 11 as necessary.

2   Compare the Heian-period Womb World *mandala* (**FIG. 12–8**) with the Kamakura-period *Descent of Amida and the Twenty-Five Bodhisattvas* (**FIG. 12–15**). How do these pictures embody the specific type of Buddhism from which each emerged? How would they have been used by believers?

3   Discuss a work of art in this chapter that combines aspects of the foreign traditions of Buddhism with native Shinto traditions. How do the artists blend the disparate traditions? How would the blending affect the way the work functioned within a religious context?

4   Characterize and compare one representative secular work of art from Heian courtly culture with one from the warrior culture that replaced it during the Kamakura period. How do these works relate to the political climates of these two distinct eras in early Japanese history?

Crosscurrents

These two works of art proclaim political power by documenting military conquest, but their artists chose vastly different media and contexts to achieve this goal. How do the differences between these battle narratives relate to the cultural context that gave rise to each? Be sure to consider the perspective of the viewer when forming your answer.

6–47

12–14

13-1 OFFERING 4, LA VENTA

Mexico. Olmec culture, c. 750–550 BCE. Jade, greenstone, granite, and sandstone; height of figures 6¼–7″ (16–18 cm). Museo Nacional de Antropología, Mexico City.

Credit: © akg-images/De Agostini Picture Lib./G. Dagli Orti

Chapter 13
Art of the Americas before 1300

Learning Objectives

13.a Identify the visual hallmarks of the art of early cultures in the Americas for formal, technical, and expressive qualities.

13.b Interpret the meaning of works of art of early cultures in the Americas based on their themes, subjects, and symbols.

13.c Relate artists and the art of early cultures in the Americas to their distinct cultural, economic, and political contexts.

13.d Apply the vocabulary and concepts relevant to the art, artists, and art history of early cultures in the Americas.

13.e Interpret a work of art of the early Americas using the art historical methods of observation, comparison, and inductive reasoning.

13.f Select visual and textual evidence in various media to support an argument or an interpretation of a work of art of the early Americas.

To modern viewers, this group of 16 stone figurines (**FIG. 13-1**) hints at a story or resembles a ritual in progress. Since they were "standing" in this manner when they were excavated in 1955 at the Olmec site of La Venta, in Mexico, we know these small statues were deposited as a group along with the six stela-like shafts of jade, called **celts**, lined up behind them. Their "standing" poses are identical and specific; they flex their knees so they can tuck in their tailbones, straighten their spines, and lift their heads while keeping their arms relaxed at their sides. Today this pose is used in practices such as tai chi to strengthen the body and maintain mental focus. Also, each figure appears to have cranial deformation, which would have been created intentionally shortly after birth, probably by bandaging the head for several months. With similar postures and heads, the figurines seem strikingly uniform.

If we look closely, however, we see that despite these obvious similarities, each figure is carved from a distinctive stone, with varying degrees of care. Each is slightly different in size and proportions. Recent scholarship proposes that these statuettes were made by different sculptors and used for other purposes before their burial in this cache. Their gender identity is also perplexing. While 14 wear male clothing and 2 have small breasts and a female pubic area, several of the "male" figures were originally ungendered or female. These figurines were seemingly brought to La Venta and may have been modified before their deposition around 750–550 BCE. At that time, La Venta was an important ritual center, the site of many buried offerings, or caches. These 16 figurines—known as Offering 4—were placed in a walled courtyard above a massive offering and adjacent to a long mound containing caches of royal regalia and numerous ceramic bowls. Perhaps the figurines were brought here to provide permanent representation of a village's spiritual practitioner in this important pilgrimage center.

About 100 years after the figurines were initially buried, someone checked to make sure they were still there. A hole was dug directly over the offering, but nothing was removed and the figurines were reburied. The precision of this later excavation shows that people remembered the exact location of the cache. This extraordinary find is an example of the importance of scientific archaeological excavations for understanding ancient art. Had these objects been torn out of the ground by looters and sold piecemeal on the black market, we might never have known that Olmec sculptures such as these were used to create meaningful installations, nor could we have imagined that once buried, art such as this could be remembered for so long.

The Rise of Civilizations in the Americas

What are the early geographic and cultural backgrounds for the development of art in the Western Hemisphere?

In recent years the question of the original settlement of the Americas has become an area of debate. The traditional view has been that human beings arrived in North and South America from Asia during the last Ice Age, when glaciers trapped enough of the world's water to lower the level of the oceans and expose a land bridge across the Bering Strait. Although most of present-day Alaska and Canada was covered by glaciers at that time, an ice-free corridor along the Pacific coast would have provided access from Asia to the south and east. Thus, this theory holds that sometime before 12,000 years ago, perhaps as early as 20,000 to 30,000 years ago, Paleolithic hunter-gatherers emerged from this corridor and began to spread out into two vast, uninhabited continents. This view is now challenged by the early dates of some new archaeological finds and by evidence suggesting the possibility of early connections with Europe as well, perhaps along the Arctic coast of the North Atlantic. Recently, some have theorized that Pacific Islanders could have sailed to the coast of Chile and spread out from there. In any event, by 10,000 to 12,000 years ago bands of hunters roamed throughout the Americas, and after the ice had retreated, the peoples of the Western Hemisphere were essentially cut off from the rest of the world until they were overrun by European invaders, beginning at the end of the fifteenth century CE.

In this isolation, the peoples of the Americas experienced cultural transformations similar to those seen elsewhere after the Paleolithic era. In most regions they developed an agricultural way of life. A trio of native

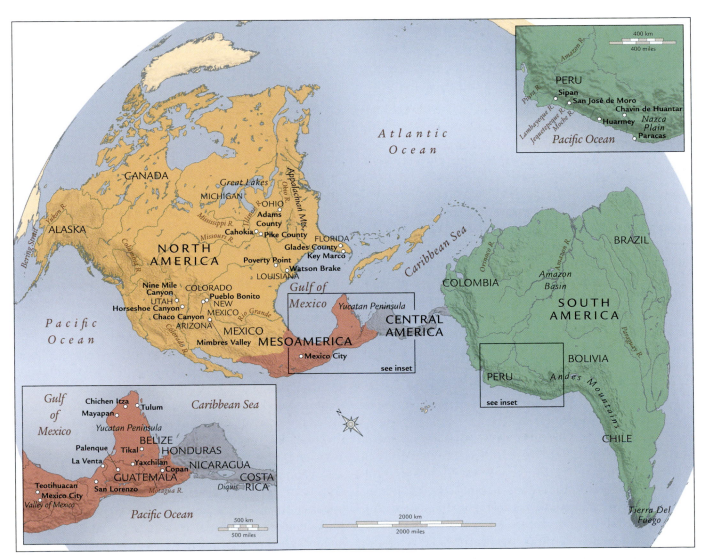

MAP 13–1 THE AMERICAS BEFORE 1300

Human beings moved across North America, then southward through Central America until they eventually reached the Tierra del Fuego region of South America.

plants—corn, beans, and squash—was especially important, but people cultivated potatoes, tobacco, cacao, tomatoes, and avocados as well. New World peoples also domesticated many animals: dogs, turkeys, guinea pigs, llamas, and their camelid cousins—alpacas, guanacos, and vicuñas.

As elsewhere, the shift to agriculture in the Americas was accompanied by population growth and, in some places, the rise of hierarchical societies, the appearance of ceremonial centers and towns with monumental architecture, and the development of sculpture, ceramics, and other arts. The people of Mesoamerica—the region that extends from central Mexico well into Central America—developed writing, astronomy, a complex and accurate calendar, and a sophisticated system of mathematics. Central and South American peoples had advanced metallurgy and produced exquisite gold, silver, and copper objects. The metalworkers of the Andes, the mountain range along the western coast of South America, began to produce metal jewelry, weapons, and agricultural implements in the first millennium CE, and people elsewhere in the Americas made tools, weapons, and art from other materials such as bone, ivory, stone, wood, and, where it was available, obsidian, a volcanic glass capable of a cutting edge 500 times finer than surgical steel. Basketry and weaving became major art forms. The inhabitants of the American Southwest built multi-storied, apartmentlike village and cliff dwellings, as well as elaborate irrigation systems with canals. Evidence of weaving in the American Southwest dates to about 7400 BCE.

The extraordinary early arts of the Americas served as an essential mode of communicating beliefs and displaying status. This chapter explores the accomplishments of selected cultures in five of those areas: Mesoamerica, Central America, the central Andes of South America, the Southeastern Woodlands and great river valleys of North America, and the North American Southwest.

Mesoamerica and Central America

What distinguishes the art and architecture of the Olmec, Teotihuacan, Maya, and Diquis cultures in Mesoamerica and Central America?

Ancient Mesoamerica encompasses the area from north of the Valley of Mexico (the location of Mexico City) to present-day Belize, Honduras, and western Nicaragua in Central America (**MAP 13-1**). The region is one of great contrasts, ranging from tropical rainforest to semiarid mountains. The civilizations that arose in Mesoamerica varied, but they were linked by cultural similarities and trade. Among their shared features were a ballgame with

religious and political significance (see "The Cosmic Ballgame" on page 390), monumental building construction, and a complex system of multiple calendars including a 260-day divinatory cycle and a 365-day ritual and agricultural cycle. Many Mesoamerican societies were sharply divided into elite and commoner classes.

The transition to farming began in Mesoamerica between 7000 and 6000 BCE, and by 3000 to 2000 BCE settled villages were widespread. The region's subsequent history is usually divided into three broad periods: Formative or Preclassic (1500 BCE–250 CE), Classic (250–900 CE), and Postclassic (900–1521 CE). This chronology derives primarily from the archaeology of the Maya—the people of Guatemala, southern Mexico, and the Yucatan Peninsula—with the Classic period bracketing the era during which the Maya erected dated stone monuments. As with the study of ancient Greek art, the term "Classic" reflects the view of early scholars that this period was a kind of golden age. Although this view is no longer current—and the periods are only roughly applicable to other cultures of Mesoamerica—the terminology has endured.

The Olmec

Mesoamericans used skillfully crafted objects to communicate with the powerful forces of nature. From the Gulf of Mexico to the Pacific, Formative Period peoples were developing technologies for marking time, maintaining health, and visualizing cherished ideas. Around 1700 BCE, the earliest major site along the Gulf Coast was not a village but a depository for precious objects. Within a spring at the base of Cerro Manatí, for over six centuries pilgrims deposited perfectly balanced and polished celts of imported jade and balls fashioned from local rubber, along with ceramics and seeds, before burying them under a thick layer of silt. Around 1300 BCE, the offerings were more frequently human busts carved of wood and wrapped in fiber bundles along with seeds, which were deposited in the spring along with more celts, wooden staffs, and a few infant bones.

At the same time, 11 miles away, a town—now called San Lorenzo—was developed on a leveled plateau surrounded by several watercourses and constructed low mounds. This first urban center in Mesoamerica flourished between 1300 and 900 BCE, and its inhabitants, in an astonishing explosion of creativity, created over 100 basalt sculptures of subjects for which there are no known precedents. After transporting basalt boulders from a volcano 30 miles away, they carved **COLOSSAL HEADS** (**FIG. 13-4**) weighing up to 25 tons, thrones depicting caves in rock walls with overhanging ledges, some remarkably naturalistic seated human figures, and a variety of animal forms.

Ten colossal heads have been excavated at San Lorenzo, and there is considerable speculation about what

Art and its Contexts

THE COSMIC BALLGAME

The ritual ballgame was one of the defining characteristics of Mesoamerican society. It was generally played on a long, rectangular court with a large, solid, heavy rubber ball. Using their elbows, knees, or hips—but not their hands—heavily padded players directed the ball toward a goal or marker. The rules, size, and shape of the court; the number of players on a team; and the nature of the goal varied. The largest surviving ballcourt, at Chichen Itza, is bigger than a modern football field. Large stone rings set in the walls of this court about 25 feet above the field served as goals. The **BALLCOURT** in **FIGURE 13-2** was constructed at the heart of the ceremonial center in the southernmost Maya city of Copan.

The game was a common subject in Mesoamerican art. This scene, painted on a **CYLINDRICAL VESSEL** (**FIG. 13-3**), shows four lords playing the ballgame, the architectural space of the ballcourt suggested by a few horizontal lines. The men wear elaborate headdresses and padded gear to protect them from the heavy rubber ball. The painter has chosen a moment of arrested movement: One player kneels to hit the ball—or has just hit it—while the others gesture and lean toward him.

The ballgame may have had religious and political significance: It is part of creation stories and was sometimes associated with warfare. Captive warriors might have been forced to play the game, and when the stakes were high the game may have culminated in human sacrifice.

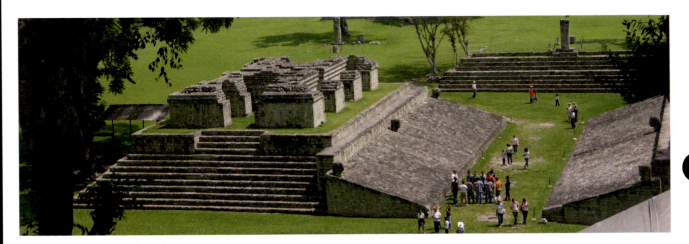

13-2 BALLCOURT
Copan, Honduras. Maya culture, c. 711–736 CE.

Credit: © Keren Su/Getty Images

13-3 CYLINDRICAL VESSEL WITH BALLGAME SCENE
Maya culture, 600–800 CE. Painted ceramic, diameter 6⅜″ (15.9 cm), height 8⅛″ (20.5 cm). Dallas Museum of Art. Gift of Mr. and Mrs. Raymond Nasher 1983.148.

This roll-out photograph shows the entire scene painted around the cylinder; a person holding the vessel would have to turn it to see what was happening. The text around the rim is a standard dedicatory inscription naming the vessel as one to be used for drinking chocolate, and tests of residues inside similar vessels have confirmed this use. Without sugar or milk, Maya chocolate was very different from ours; it was a frothy and bitter beverage consumed on courtly and ritual occasions.

Credit: Rollout photograph © Justin Kerr, K2803

they represent. All have broad features and flat noses, and all wear helmets. The overall shape is reminiscent of the rubber balls offered at El Manatí. As later civilizations would describe the ballgame, it had mythological cosmic and generative significance, and the decapitated heads of the heroic ballplayers were often used as a ball. These bodiless heads could represent balls or heroic ballplayers. However, some scholars think their monumentality and lack of uniformity suggests that they are more likely portraits of rulers. San Lorenzo was the most important town in the region. Despite evidence of social stratification and recognition that the elite must have amassed wealth, no deposits like those of El Manatí have been found in over 40 years of archaeology in the region.

However, the practice of buried offerings was revived at La Venta, which thrived from 1000 to 400 BCE. To initiate the second of four construction phases in an enclosed ritual courtyard, people carried 200 tons of serpentine (a dark green semiprecious mineral) from a source 180 miles away to create two massive offerings. These were 20-feet-deep pits, measuring 19 by 20 feet. Layers of pink, green, gold, and rose clay created settings for the serpentine blocks. The massive offerings served as effigies of lakes or springs, while on the uppermost layer, serpentine blocks formed a mosaic design that signified the sacred female earth surface, covered by an array of celts. Additional massive offerings initiated later phases of construction at La Venta. The number of small caches of stone figurines, celts, and jade ornaments in the form of earflares, hands, frogs, clamshells, canoes, and animal teeth increased, showing the growing importance of this center as a sacred site (SEE FIG. 13–1).

Meanwhile, like their counterparts at San Lorenzo, the La Venta Olmec built earthen mounds and set over 100 monumental sculptures in their plazas (FIG. 13–5). Unlike San Lorenzo, the mounds and enclosed

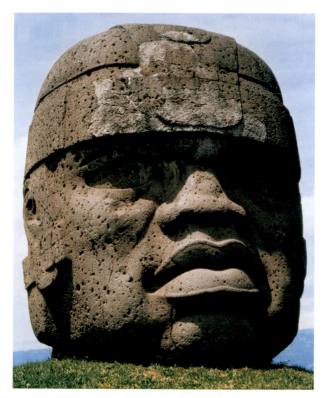

13–4 COLOSSAL HEAD, SAN LORENZO
Mexico. Olmec culture, c. 1200–900 BCE. Basalt, height 7′5″ (2.26 m). Anthropology Museum, Veracruz University, Jalapa.

Credit: Werner Forman Archive

13–5 GREAT PYRAMID AND PLAZA, LA VENTA
Mexico. Olmec culture, c. 900–400 BCE. Pyramid height approx. 100′ (30 m).

Credit: © 2016. Image copyright The Metropolitan Museum of Art/Art Resource/Scala, Florence

courtyard at La Venta were designed to symmetrically flank the site's central axis, which pointed south toward the nearest mountain on the horizon, presumably a sacred location. The sculptures included colossal heads, cave-niche thrones, basalt columns, and other enormous carvings. A 100-foot-high earthen mound in the center of the site was the largest in Mesoamerica at the time. These earthen forms and stone sculptures formed a processional narrative array along the central axis that portrayed the Olmec creation story. The climax of the story was portrayed in a series of gigantic stelai in the form of stylized human embryos from which maize sprouted; the fetuses, like the colossal heads, wore helmets.

The Olmec traded across Mesoamerica, obtaining jade from the Motagua River Valley in Honduras and malachite pigments from northwestern Mexico. As Formative Period people interacted, the ideas that Olmec art expressed so powerfully—about the parallels between maize plants and human life, reciprocal relations with natural forces, the preciousness of jade as a symbol of vital energy, and the cosmic ramifications of the ballgame—were adopted and transformed by groups throughout Mesoamerica. As Olmec civilization waned around 300 BCE, people in the Maya area and Teotihuacan in the Valley of Mexico forged new civilizations from these foundational ideas.

Teotihuacan

Located some 30 miles northeast of present-day Mexico City, the city of Teotihuacan experienced a period of rapid growth early in the first millennium CE. By 200 CE, it had emerged as Mesoamerica's first truly urban settlement,

13-7 PLAN OF THE CEREMONIAL CENTER OF TEOTIHUACAN

13-6 CEREMONIAL CENTER OF THE CITY OF TEOTIHUACAN
Mexico. Teotihuacan culture, c. 100–650 CE.

Credit: V Korostyshevskiy/Fotolia

13–8 PYRAMID OF THE FEATHERED SERPENT
The Ciudadela, Teotihuacan, Mexico. Teotihuacan culture, c. 200 CE.

Credit: NoraDoa/Fotolia

a significant center of commerce and manufacturing. At its height, between 300 and 650, Teotihuacan covered nearly 9 square miles and had a population of at least 125,000, making it the largest city in the Americas and one of the largest in the world at that time (**FIG. 13–6**). Its residents lived in walled "apartment compounds," and the entire city was organized on a grid (**FIG. 13–7**), its orientation chosen both for its calendrical significance and to respond to the surrounding landscape.

Although Teotihuacan declined after 650, it was never forgotten. Centuries later, it remained a legendary pilgrimage center. Aztec people (c. 1300–1525) revered the site, believing it to be the place where the gods created the sun and the moon, and they gave the city its name— "Teotihuacan," meaning place of divinity in the Nahuatl language of the Aztec. The names we use for its principal monuments are also Nahuatl. Despite a century of modern research, the ethnicity of the principal inhabitants of Teotihuacan remains unknown, because while they used a bit of pictographic writing, they did not name themselves or their city in their glyphs.

We do know about how the city developed. By 100 CE, planners established an orthogonal grid plan. The Avenue of the Dead (a series of plazas at different levels about 150 feet wide and over a mile long) runs 15 degrees east of north, or almost north–south, and creates a central axis like the one at earlier La Venta. All north–south streets and walls parallel this axis. The grid is further enforced by the Teotihuacan Measurement Unit (TMU) of 83 cm. All buildings and their components are even multiples of this measurement. Three pyramid complexes dominate the center of the city. At the north end of the central axis stands the Pyramid of the Moon, facing a large plaza flanked by

smaller, symmetrically placed platforms. It seems to echo the shape of the mountain behind it, and as one walks toward the pyramid, it looms above, eclipsing the mountain completely. The Pyramid of the Moon was enlarged several times, as were many Mesoamerican pyramids; each enlargement completely enclosed the previous structure and was accompanied by rich sacrificial offerings and caches including stone standing and seated figurines.

The largest of Teotihuacan's architectural monuments, the Pyramid of the Sun (SEE FIG. 13–6), located just to the east of the Avenue of the Dead, is slightly over 200 feet high and measures about 720 feet on each side at its base— similar in size to, but not as tall as, the largest Egyptian pyramid at Giza (see Chapter 3). The pyramid rises in a series of sloping steps to a flat platform where a small temple once stood. A monumental stone stairway led from level to level up the front of the pyramid to the temple platform. The exterior was faced with stone, which was then stuccoed and painted.

The Pyramid of the Sun was built over a tunnel that may have been an enlargement of a natural cave. Excavations from 2008 to 2011 within the tunnel revealed several burials and offering caches containing stone masks, anthropomorphic figurines, and shells. A similar tunnel has recently been discovered in the Ciudadela complex at the southern end of the ceremonial center. This complex consists of a series of temple platforms surrounding a plaza for religious and political gatherings of more than 60,000 people. The tunnel descends below the plaza floor, running eastward to terminate under the **PYRAMID OF THE FEATHERED SERPENT** (**FIG. 13–8**), and like the tunnel under the Pyramid of the Sun, this one also contained offerings. The pyramid uses the *talud-tablero* (slope-and-panel) system of construction that is a hallmark of the Teotihuacan architectural style. The *talud* (sloping base) of each platform supports a *tablero* (entablature) that rises vertically and is surrounded by a frame.

Archaeological excavations of the temple's early phase have revealed reliefs portraying undulating, feathered serpents floating in a watery space punctuated by aquatic shells. Their flat, angular, abstract style, typical of Teotihuacan art, is in marked contrast to the curvilinear, organic forms of Olmec art. While the bodies of the feathered serpents are rendered in low relief, in the vertical *tablero* sections three-dimensional sculptures of fanged serpent heads emerge from rings of stylized feathers. Each serpent carries on its body a squarish headdress with a protruding upper jaw; huge, round eyes originally inlaid with obsidian; and a pair of round goggles on its forehead between the eyes. These mosaic headdresses seem to represent an aspect of the Teotihuacan Storm God associated with warfare—other works of art at Teotihuacan and elsewhere in Mesoamerica show armed warriors wearing the same headdress. Inside the pyramid, this militaristic message was reinforced by the burials of dozens of sacrificial victims, some of them wearing necklaces made of human jawbones (or shell imitations thereof), their arms tied behind their backs.

The residential sections of Teotihuacan surrounded the city's center. The spacious palaces of the elite, with as many as 45 rooms and 7 patios, stood nearest the ceremonial center. Artisans, foreign traders, and peasants lived farther away, in more crowded compounds, all aligned with the Teotihuacan grid. Palaces and more humble homes alike were rectangular, one-story structures with high walls—plastered and covered with paintings—and suites of rooms arranged around open courtyards.

Teotihuacan's artists created wall paintings in a fresco technique, applying pigments directly on damp lime plaster. Once the paint was applied, the walls were polished to give them a smooth, shiny, and durable surface. The style, like that of the sculpture, was flat, angular, and abstract, often featuring processions of similarly dressed figures, rows of mythological animals, or other sequences of repeated images. Teotihuacan painters worked in several different color schemes, including a bright polychrome and a more restricted palette emphasizing tones of red. One detached fragment of a wall painting from the Techinantitla complex, which was 500 meters east of the Pyramid of the Moon, depicts a feathered serpent pouring liquids and flowers around trees (**FIG. 13-9**). In typical Central Mexican fashion, the trees (in the lower strip) appear in elevation view, with their roots showing below ground. Above each of the grey root systems sits a place glyph that forms a base for the trunk of the tree. This place name and tree configuration forms a toponym (place-name) in the Teotihuacan system of writing, and the visible roots of the trees implies attachment to each particular place. For example, the left-most place glyph is called "mask-step," followed by "yellow platform" and "hand-shell-yellow petals." Six more trees and glyphs (three more than are shown here) followed these first three around the room, then the nine place-trees series was repeated seven more times within the room. Such toponyms were integral to all Mesoamerican writing systems, both pictorial and phonetic.

Sometime in the early seventh century disaster struck Teotihuacan. The ceremonial center was sacked and

13-9 FEATHERED SERPENT AND FLOWERING TREES
Fragment of a fresco from Techinantitla building, Teotihuacan, Mexico. Teotihuacan culture, c. 500–650 CE. Earthen aggregate, lime plaster, and mineral pigments. 23¼ ×159½ × 2¼″ (59.1 × 405.1 × 5.7 cm). The Fine Arts Museums of San Francisco. Bequest of Harald Wagner (1985.104.1).

These fragments are among a group of numerous mural fragments that collector Harald Wagner unexpectedly bequeathed to the Fine Arts Museums of San Francisco in 1976. Because accessioning parts of ancient architectural complexes had been prohibited by the 1970 United Nations Educational, Scientific, and Cultural Organization Convention on cultural property, the museum was diligent in establishing the entry date of the pieces into the United States and initiated a cooperative effort among Mexican museums and conservation experts to jointly conserve the murals and return some of them to Mexico.

burned, and the city went into a permanent decline. Nevertheless, its influence continued as other centers throughout Mesoamerica, as far south as the Maya region, borrowed and transformed its imagery, as can be seen in the rectangular headdress and Storm God headdress ornament that Lady Xok wears on Yaxchilan Lintel 24 (SEE FIG. 13-14).

The Maya

More than any other ancient American civilization, the Maya developed their cities as works of art. Each of the hundreds of kingdoms that arose in the tropical rainforests of southeastern Mesoamerica created a unique visual identity by elaborating and individualizing the basic building forms—the plaza, pyramid, palace, and ballcourt—and by creating unusual modifications of the basic sculptural forms—the stela, lintel, altar, and throne. City founders chose to build near distinctive topographic features, and each city devised a strategy for the alignment of architecture to an astronomical phenomenon. Stucco reliefs transformed the flat walls of buildings into undulating forms that were brightly painted. Both images and hieroglyphs enlivened the surfaces, documenting the deeds of the rulers, their ancestors, and the city's patron deities. Decorated textiles, polychrome painted ceramics, and bark paper books added further visual complexity to the spectacle of the Maya court.

An increasingly detailed picture of the Maya has been emerging from recent archaeological research and from advances in deciphering their writing. That picture shows a society divided into competing city-states in a near-constant state of war with each other. A hereditary ruler and an elite class of nobles and priests governed each city-state, supported by a large group of farmer-commoners. Rulers established their legitimacy, maintained links with their divine ancestors, commemorated important calendrical dates, and sustained the gods through elaborate rituals, including ballgames, bloodletting ceremonies, and human sacrifice. Rulers commemorated such events and their military exploits on carved stelae.

Maya civilization emerged during the Late Preclassic period (400 BCE–250 CE), reached its peak in the southern lowlands of Mexico and Guatemala during the Classic period (250–900 CE), and shifted to the northern Yucatan Peninsula during the Postclassic period (900–1521 CE). Throughout this time, the Maya maintained strong ties with other regions of Mesoamerica: They inherited many ideas and technologies from the Olmec, had trade and military interactions with Teotihuacan, and, centuries later, were in contact with the Aztec Empire.

Art and its Contexts

MAYA WRITING

Maya writing is logosyllabic—it consists of ideographs or logographs that represent entire words as well as a set of symbols that stand for the sound of each syllable in the Maya language. Thus, a word like *balam* (jaguar) could be written in many different ways: with the logograph "BALAM," a picture of the head of a jaguar (top right); with three syllables, "ba-la-ma," for the sounds of the word *balam* (bottom right); or a combination of the two systems—the logograph "BALAM" complemented with one or more phonetic syllables, to make it clear which logograph was represented (and avoid the possibility of confusing this logograph with the symbol for *hix*, another kind of feline, for example) (middle right). The combination of these two systems allowed Maya scribes extraordinary flexibility, and some calligraphers seem to have delighted in finding as many different ways as possible to write the same word. Many Maya logographs remained very pictorial, like the glyph for jaguar illustrated here, which meant that Maya writing was never too distant from other kinds of image making. In fact, the same word, *ts'ib*, signified both writing and painting in the Classic Maya language.

With major advances in the decipherment of Maya hieroglyphic writing—beginning in the 1950s and continuing to this day—it has become clear that the inscriptions on Maya architecture and stelae are almost entirely devoted to a ceremonial recording of historical events. They document the dates of royal marriages, births of heirs, alliances between cities, and great military victories, and they tie these events to astronomical events and propitious dates in the Maya calendar. We know that the Maya also wrote books, but only four of these fragile manuscripts—called codices—have survived, all of them from the Postclassic period.

BALAM

ba-BALAM

BALAM-ma

ba-BALAM-ma

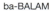

ba-la-ma

Credit: Kathy Mrozek

TIKAL The monumental buildings of Maya cities were masterly examples of the use of architecture for public display and as the backdrop for social and sacred ritual. Tikal (in present-day Guatemala) was one of the largest Maya cities, with a population of up to 70,000 at its height. Unlike Teotihuacan, with its grid plan, Maya cities, including Tikal, conformed to the uneven terrain of the rainforest. Plazas, pyramid-temples, ballcourts, and other structures stood on high ground connected by wide elevated roads, or causeways.

Tikal was settled in the Late Preclassic period, in the fourth century BCE, and continued to flourish through the Early Classic period. The kings of Tikal were buried in funerary pyramids like the one visible on the right in **FIGURE 13-10**, which was separated by a wide plaza from the royal palace to the south. Tikal suffered a major upheaval in 378 CE, recorded in texts from the city and surrounding centers, when some scholars believe the arrival of strangers from Teotihuacan precipitated the death of Tikal's king and the installation of a new ruler with ties to Central Mexico. Art from this period shows strong Teotihuacan influence in ceramic and architectural forms, though both were soon adapted to suit local Maya aesthetics. The city enjoyed a period of wealth and regional dominance until a military defeat led to a century of decline.

In the eighth century, Tikal finally succeeded in defeating the military alliance that dominated them when King Jasaw Chan K'awiil (ruled 682–734) captured Ich'aak K'ak, the king of mighty Calakmul. He initiated an extensive construction program, including ritual complexes for celebrating the K'atun, or 20-year period, which held the stela and altar that embodied both the K'atun and the ruler. His building program culminated in the construction of Temple I (SEE FIG. 13-10), a tall pyramid that faces a companion pyramid, Temple II, across a large central plaza. Containing Jasaw Chan K'awiil's tomb in the limestone bedrock below, Temple I rises above the forest canopy to a height of more than 140 feet. Its base has nine layers, probably reflecting the belief that the underworld had nine levels. Priests climbed the steep stone staircase on the exterior to the temple on top, which consists of two narrow, parallel rooms covered with a steep roof supported by corbel vaults. The crest that rises over the roof of the temple, known as a **roof comb**, was originally covered with brightly painted sculpture. Ritual performances on the narrow platform at the top of the pyramid would have been visible throughout the plaza. Inspired by Jasaw Chan K'awiil's building program, later kings of Tikal also built tall funerary pyramids that still tower above the rainforest canopy.

13-10 BASE OF NORTH ACROPOLIS (LEFT) AND TEMPLE I (RIGHT), TIKAL
Guatemala. Maya culture. North Acropolis, 4th century BCE–5th century CE; Temple I (Tomb of Jasaw Chan K'awiil), c. 734 CE.
Credit: © Daniel Loncarevic/Shutterstock

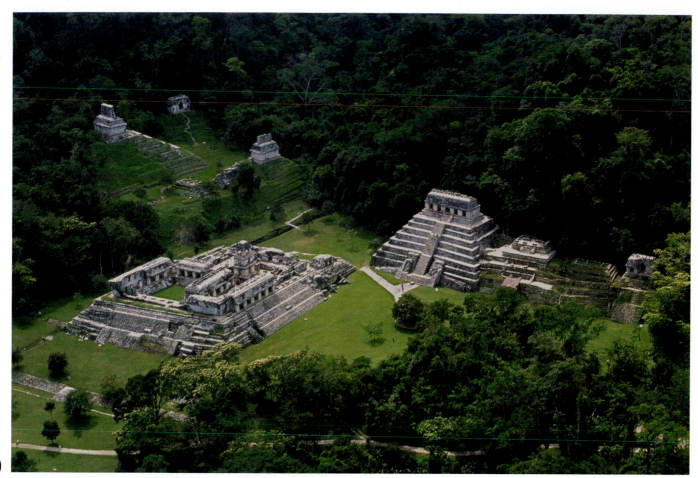

13–11 PALACE (FOREGROUND) AND TEMPLE OF THE INSCRIPTIONS, PALENQUE
Mexico. Maya culture. Palace, 5th–8th century CE; Temple of the Inscriptions (Tomb of Pakal the Great), c. 683 CE.

Credit: © Danny Lehman/Corbis

PALENQUE The small city-state of Palenque (in the present-day Mexican state of Chiapas) rose to prominence later than Tikal, during the Classic period. Hieroglyphic inscriptions record the beginning of its royal dynasty in 431 CE, but the city had only limited regional importance until the ascension of a powerful ruler, K'inich Janahb Pakal (*pakal* is Maya for "shield"), who ruled from 615 to 683. Known as Pakal the Great, he and his sons, who succeeded him, commissioned most of the structures visible at Palenque today. As at Tikal, urban planning responds to the landscape. Perched on a ridge over 300 feet above the swampy lowland plains, the buildings of Palenque are terraced into the mountains with a series of aqueducts channeling rivers through the urban core. The center of the city houses the palace, the Temple of the Inscriptions, and various temples (**FIG. 13–11**). Other temples, elite palaces, and a ballcourt surround this central group.

The palace was an administrative center as well as a royal residence. At its core was the throne room of Pakal the Great, a spacious structure whose stone roof imitated the thatched roofs of more humble dwellings. Over time, the palace grew into a complex series of buildings organized around four courtyards, where the private business of the court was transacted. From the outside, the palace presented an inviting façade of wide staircases and open colonnades decorated with stucco sculptures, but access to the interior spaces was tightly limited.

Next to the palace stands the Temple of the Inscriptions, Pakal the Great's funerary pyramid. Rising 75 feet above the plaza, it has nine levels like Temple I at Tikal (SEE FIG. 13–10). The shrine on the summit consists of a portico with five entrances and a vaulted inner chamber originally surmounted by a tall roof comb. Its façade still retains much of its stucco sculpture. The inscriptions that give the building its name consist of three large panels of text that line the back wall of the outer chamber at the top of the temple, linking Pakal's accomplishments to the mythical history of the city.

A corbel-vaulted stairway beneath the floor of the shrine at the top of Pakal's funerary pyramid zigzags down 80 feet to a small subterranean chamber that contained his tomb, discovered in 1952. A huge slab of carved limestone nearly filled the chamber. It covered a monolithic limestone sarcophagus with reliefs of ancestors merged with fruiting trees, both emerging from crevices in the earth to witness his death and rebirth, the subject of the elaborate relief sculpture on the lid (**FIG. 13–12**). Scholars have linked Pakal's unusual pose to birthing iconography. The Maya conventionalized symbol for a tree emerges from his midsection. In this case, logographs for "divinity" mark the tree, which is adorned with jade-beaded, square-nosed serpents on its branches, while a jade-bodied, double-headed serpent—a device held by rulers— wraps around it. The principal bird deity, which sits atop the tree, appears in Maya art during events of great creative and transformative power, and the jade beads and symbols of divinity that float around the tree provide the context for Pakal's rebirth. That this event occurs in the celestial realm is signaled by the solar, lunar, and planetary symbols in the "skybands" on the side borders.

Underneath the lid, archaeologists found the bones of Pakal in a uterus-shaped cavity within the sarcophagus.

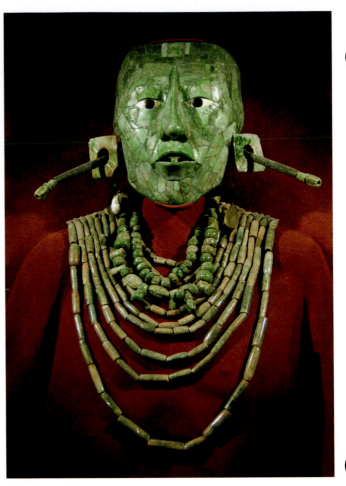

13–13 BURIAL MASK OF PAKAL THE GREAT
From Pakal's tomb, Temple of the Inscriptions, Palenque, Mexico. Maya culture, c. 683 CE. Jade, shell, and pearl; life-size mask. Museo Nacional de Antropología, Mexico City.

Credit: © akg-images/Album/J.Enrique Molina

13–12 REPRODUCTION OF LID OF THE SARCOPHAGUS OF PAKAL THE GREAT
From Pakal's tomb, Temple of the Inscriptions, Palenque, Mexico. Maya culture, c. 683 CE. Limestone, 12′1½″ × 7′1½″ (3.72 × 2.17 m).

Credit: © Fine Art Images/Alinari Archives, Firenze

Rich burial offerings covered him, including a jade mask, jewelry, and figurines. The mask (**FIG. 13–13**) shows the aesthetic modifications of Pakal's body during his lifetime. The shape of his head had been elongated during his infancy and an artificial bridge enhanced his long, curved nose. His compact chin and protruding lower lip conform to Maya ideals of beauty, and since the overall shape of his face is consistent with his portrayal in other portraits, this mask seems to have blended individual likeness with idealized conventions.

YAXCHILAN Yaxchilan differed from most Maya cities in its use of lintels as a major location for relief sculpture and in the prominence of women in its art. More than 60 lintels have been recovered. While some contain only hieroglyphic texts, most portray the rulers, royal women, and other nobles in elaborate costumes performing a variety of rituals. On Lintel 24, one of a series dedicated in 726 by Lady Xok (Shoke), she appears kneeling on the ground, drawing a thick, thorny cord through her tongue (see "Closer Look" opposite). Her husband, Shield Jaguar, stands next to her, holding a flaming torch, with which he may set fire to the strips of paper dotted with blood in the basket between them. The reason for the bloodletting may be linked to the fact that the date was an anniversary of Shield Jaguar's accession to the throne. This is one of the most explicit portrayals of bloodletting in Maya art as well as a rare depiction of a female perforating her tongue.

This lintel is unusual for another reason. Artist's signatures appear on some lintels, but the finished products appear to have been the result of the collaborative work of several hands. At least two sculptors seem to have created this scene, and one did something radical for Maya art. While the faces of both figures appear in strict profile view and Shield Jaguar's body takes the same orientation, Lady Xok's torso is frontal, and her right hand—highlighted against the ground at the center of the composition—twists

elegantly in a three-quarter view. This "3/4 artist" likely drew the composition, with its swirling flames and the foreshortening of Lady Xok's lower limbs and may also have written the text, with its irregular outlines and coarse detailing. A second artist, nicknamed "Elegant Knot," took charge of the delicate detailing of the complex textile patterns and knots, using carefully controlled parallel lines and regular edges.

POSTCLASSIC PERIOD   After warfare and environmental crisis led to the abandonment of the lowland Maya city-states around 800, the focus of Maya civilization shifted north to the Yucatan Peninsula. One of the principal cities of the Postclassic period was Chichen Itza, which means "at the mouth of the well of the Itza," and may refer to the deep *cenote* (sinkhole) at the site that was sacred to the

A Closer Look

SHIELD JAGUAR AND LADY XOK

Shield Jaguar's elaborate headgear includes the shrunken head of a sacrificial victim, proclaiming his past piety in another ritual pleasing to the gods.

The two inscriptions—almost acting as an internal frame for the standing figure—record the date and the nature of the ritual portrayed: bloodletting on October 28, 709. They also identify the standing king as Shield Jaguar and the kneeling woman as Lady Xok.

The sharply outlined subjects, as well as the way they project forward from a deeply recessed, blank background, focus viewers' attention on the bodies of Shield Jaguar and his kneeling wife, Lady Xok.

Shield Jaguar holds a huge torch, indicating that this ritual took place within a dark room or during the night.

Tasseled headdresses are associated with bloodletting rituals.

Lady Xok pulls a rope of thorns through her perforated tongue, while spiraling dotted lines show the blood she is sacrificing to the gods. The spiny rope falls to a basket with blood-spotted paper and a stingray spine (also sometimes used for bloodletting). This ritual of self-mutilation was required of royalty since it was believed to maintain royal rule and continuation of human life within the kingdom by gaining favor with the gods.

Lady Xok is lavishly dressed in a garment made of patterned fabric edged with a fringe. The mosaics on her cuffs and collar could be made of jade or shell.

13–14 SHIELD JAGUAR AND LADY XOK (LINTEL 24)
Yaxchilan, Mexico. Maya culture, 726 CE. Limestone, 43½ × 31¾″ (110.5 × 80.6 cm). British Museum, London.

Credit: Photograph © Justin Kerr, K2887

13–15 PYRAMID ("EL CASTILLO") WITH CHACMOOL IN FOREGROUND
Chichen Itza, Yucatan, Mexico. Maya culture, 9th–12th century CE.

From the top of the Temple of the Warriors, where a reclining *chacmool* sculpture graces the platform, there is a clear view of the radial pyramid nicknamed "El Castillo."

Credit: © akg-Images/ Hedda Eid

Maya. The city flourished from the ninth to the thirteenth century, and at its height covered about 6 square miles.

One of Chichen Itza's most conspicuous structures is a massive nine-level pyramid in the center of a large plaza, nicknamed **"EL CASTILLO"** ("the castle" in Spanish) **(FIG. 13–15)**. A stairway on each side of the radial pyramid leads to a square temple on the summit. At the spring and fall equinoxes, the setting sun casts undulating shadows on the stairway, forming bodies for the serpent heads carved at the base of the north balustrades, pointing toward the Sacred Cenote. Many prominent features of Chichen Itza are markedly different from earlier Maya sites and recall complexes in central Mexico, including long, colonnaded halls and inventive columns in the form of descending serpents. Brilliantly colored relief sculpture and painting covered the buildings of Chichen Itza. Many of the surviving works show narrative scenes that emphasize military conquests. Sculpture at Chichen Itza, including the serpent columns and balustrades and the half-reclining figures known as **chacmools**, has the sturdy forms, proportions, and angularity of architecture, rather than the curving complexity and subtle modeling of Classic Maya sculpture. The *chacmools* may represent fallen warriors and were used to receive sacrificial offerings.

After Chichen Itza's decline, Mayapan, in the middle of the Yucatan Peninsula, became the principal Maya center. But by the time the Spanish arrived in the early sixteenth century, Mayapan, too, had declined (destroyed in the mid fifteenth century), and smaller cities like Tulum, located on the Caribbean coast, were all that remained. The Maya people and much of their culture would survive the devastation of the conquest, adapting to the imposition of Hispanic customs and beliefs. However, many Maya continue to speak their own languages, venerate traditional sacred places, and follow traditional ways.

Central America

Unlike their neighbors in Mesoamerica, who lived in complex hierarchical societies, the people of Central America lived in extended family groups in towns led by chiefs. A notable example of these small chiefdoms was the Diquis culture (located in present-day Costa Rica), which lasted from about 700 to 1500 CE. The Diquis occupied fortified villages and seem to have engaged in constant warfare with one another. Although they did not produce monumental architecture or the large-scale sculpture found in other parts of Costa Rica, they created fine featherwork, ceramics, textiles, and objects of gold and jade.

Metallurgy and the use of gold and copper–gold alloys were widespread in Central America. The technique of lost-wax casting probably first appeared in present-day Colombia between 500 and 300 BCE. From there it spread north to the Diquis. A small, exquisite pendant **(FIG. 13–16)** illustrates the style and technique of Diquis goldwork. The pendant depicts a male figure wearing bracelets, anklets, and a belt with a snake-headed penis sheath. He plays a drum while holding the tail of a snake in his teeth and its head in his left hand. The wavy forms with serpent heads emerging from his scalp suggest an elaborate headdress, and the creatures emerging from his legs suggest some kind of reptile costume. The inverted triangles on the headdress probably represent birds' tails.

In Diquis mythology, serpents and crocodiles inhabited a lower world, humans and birds a higher one. Diquis art depicts animals and insects as fierce and dangerous. The man in the pendant is clearly a performer, and some have interpreted him as a shaman transforming himself into a composite serpent-bird or enacting a ritual snake dance surrounded by serpents or crocodiles. The scrolls on the sides of his head may represent a shaman's power

13-16 SUPERNATURAL FIGURE WITH DRUM AND SNAKE

Costa Rica. Diquis culture, c. 13th–16th century CE. Gold, 4¼ × 3¼″ (10.8 × 8.2 cm). Museos del Banco Central de Costa Rica, San José, Costa Rica.

Credit: Photo: John Bigelow Taylor

to hear and understand the speech of animals. Whatever its specific meaning, the pendant evokes a ritual of mediation between earthly and cosmic powers involving music, dance, and costume.

Whether gold figures of this kind were protective amulets or signs of high status, they were certainly more than personal adornment. Shamans and warriors wore gold to inspire fear, perhaps because gold was thought to capture the energy and power of the sun. This energy was also thought to allow shamans to leave their bodies and travel into cosmic realms.

South America: The Central Andes

What distinguishes the art and architecture of the early cultures in the central Andes?

Like Mesoamerica, the central Andes of South America— primarily present-day Peru and Bolivia—saw the development of complex hierarchical societies with rich and varied artistic traditions. The area is one of dramatic contrasts.

The narrow coastal plain, bordered by the Pacific Ocean on the west and the abruptly soaring Andes Mountains on the east, is one of the driest deserts in the world. Life here depends on the rich marine resources of the Pacific Ocean and the rivers that descend from the Andes, forming a series of valley oases. The Andes themselves are a region of lofty snowcapped peaks, high grasslands, steep slopes, and deep, fertile river valleys. The high grasslands are home to the Andean camelids that have served for thousands of years as beasts of burden and a source of wool and meat. The lush eastern slopes of the Andes descend to the tropical rainforest of the Amazon basin.

In contrast to developments in other parts of the world, Andean peoples developed monumental architecture and textiles long before ceramics and intensive agriculture, usually the two hallmarks of early civilization. Thus the earliest period of monumental architecture, beginning around 3000 BCE, is called the Preceramic period. On the coast, sites with ceremonial mounds and plazas were located near the sea, while in the highlands early centers consisted of multi-roomed, stone-walled structures with sunken central fire pits for burning ritual offerings. In the second millennium BCE (the Initial Period), as agriculture became more important both in the highlands and on the coast, the scale and pace of construction increased dramatically. Communities in the coastal valleys built massive, U-shaped ceremonial complexes, while highland religious centers focused on sunken, circular courtyards. By adding to these constructions bit by bit over generations and using older constructions as the nucleus of new buildings, relatively small communities could generate mountain-size pyramids.

Chavin de Huantar

Located on a trade route between the coast and the Amazon basin, the highland site of Chavin de Huantar was an important religious center between 900 and 200 BCE, home to a style of art that spread through much of the Andes. In Andean chronology, this era is known as the Early Horizon, the first of three so-called Horizon periods. The period was one of artistic and technical innovation in ceramics, metallurgy, and textiles.

The architecture of Chavin synthesizes coastal and highland traditions, combining the U-shaped pyramid typical of the coast with a sunken circular plaza lined with carved reliefs, a form common in the highlands. The often fantastical animals that adorn Chavin sculpture have features of jaguars, hawks, caimans, and other tropical Amazonian beasts.

Within the U-shaped Old Temple at Chavin is a maze-like system of narrow galleries, at the very center of which lies a sculpture called the **LANZÓN** (FIG. 13-17). Wrapped around a 15-foot-tall blade-shaped stone with a narrow projection at the top—a form that may echo the shape of traditional Andean planting sticks—this complex carving depicts a powerful creature with a humanoid body, clawed hands and feet, and enormous fangs. Its eyebrows and strands of hair terminate in snakes—a kind of composite and transformational imagery shared by many Chavin images. The creature is bilaterally symmetrical, except that it has one hand raised and the other lowered. Compact frontality, flat relief, curvilinear design, and the combination of human, animal, bird, and reptile parts characterize this early art.

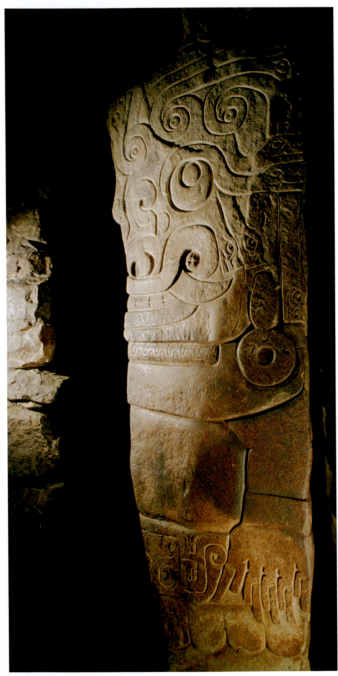

13-17 LANZÓN, CHAVIN DE HUANTAR
Peru. Chavin culture, c. 900 BCE. Granite, height 15' (4.5 m).

Credit: © akg-Images/Bildarchiv Steffens

It has been suggested that the Lanzón was an oracle (a chamber directly above the statue allowed priests' disembodied voices to filter into the room below), which would explain why people from all over the Andes made pilgrimages to Chavin, bringing exotic goods to the highland site and spreading the style of its art throughout the Andean region as they returned home.

The Paracas and Nazca Cultures

While Chavin de Huantar was flourishing as a highland center whose art was enormously influential, different valleys on the Pacific coast developed distinctive art styles and cultures.

PARACAS The Paracas culture of the Peruvian south coast flourished from about 600 BCE to 200 CE, overlapping the Chavin period. It is best known for its stunning textiles, which were found in cemeteries as wrappings, in many layers, around the bodies of the dead. Some bodies were wrapped in as many as 200 pieces of cloth.

Weaving is of great antiquity in the central Andes and continues to be among the most prized arts in the region (see "Andean Textiles" opposite). Fine textiles were a source of prestige and wealth.

The designs on Paracas textiles include repeated embroidered figures of warriors, dancers, composite creatures, and animals (**FIG. 13-18**). Tiny overlapping stitches on this example create a colorful, curvilinear pattern of paired fish—probably sharks, based on the placement of the gills—striking against the dark blue field and red border. Paracas embroiderers sometimes used as many as 22 different colors within a single figure, but only one simple stitch.

NAZCA The Nazca culture, which dominated portions of the south coast of Peru during the first seven centuries CE, overlapped the Paracas culture to the north. Nazca artisans wove fine fabrics and also produced multicolored pottery with painted and modeled images reminiscent of those on Paracas textiles.

The Nazca are best known for their colossal **earthworks**, or **geoglyphs**, which dwarf even the most ambitious twentieth-century environmental sculpture. On great stretches of desert they literally drew in the earth. By removing dark, oxidized stones, they exposed the light underlying stones. In this way they created gigantic images—including a **HUMMINGBIRD** with a beak 120 feet long (**FIG. 13-19**), a killer whale, a monkey, a spider, a duck, and other birds—similar to those with which they decorated their pottery. They also made abstract patterns and groups of straight, parallel lines that extend for up to 12 miles. The purpose and meaning of the glyphs remain a mystery, but the "lines" of stone are wide enough to have been ceremonial pathways.

Technique

ANDEAN TEXTILES

Textiles were one of the most important forms of art and technology in Andean society. Specialized fabrics were developed for everything from ritual burial shrouds and ceremonial costumes to rope bridges and knotted cords for record keeping. Clothing indicated ethnic group and social status and was customized for certain functions, the most rarefied being royal ceremonial garments made for specific occasions and worn only once. Andean textiles are among the most technically complex cloths ever made, and their creation consumed a major portion of societal resources.

Andean textile artists used two principal materials: cotton and camelid fiber. (Camelid fiber—llama, alpaca, guanaco, or vicuña hair—is the Andean equivalent of wool.) Cotton grows on the coast, while camelids—such as llamas and alpacas—thrive in the highlands. The presence of cotton fibers in the highlands and camelid fibers on the coast documents trade between the two regions from very early times and suggests that the production of textiles was an important factor in the domestication of both plants (cotton) and animals (camelids).

The earliest Peruvian textiles were made by twining, knotting, wrapping, braiding, and looping fibers. Those techniques continued to be used even after the invention of weaving looms in the early second millennium BCE. Most Andean textiles were woven on a simple, portable backstrap loom in which the undyed warp (the lengthwise threads) was looped and stretched between two bars. One bar was tied to a stationary object and the other strapped to the waist of the weaver. The weaver controlled the tension of the warp threads by leaning back and forth while threading a shuttle from side to side to insert the weft (crosswise threads). Changing the arrangement of the warp threads between each passage of the weft created a stable interlace of warp and weft: a textile.

Andean artists used a variety of different techniques to decorate their textiles, creating special effects that were prized for their labor-intensiveness and difficulty of manufacture as well as their beauty. In tapestry weaving, a technique especially suited to representational textiles, the weft does not run the full width of the fabric; each colored section is woven as an independent unit. **Embroidery** with needle and thread on an already woven textile allows even greater freedom from the rigid warp-and-weft structure of the loom, allowing the artist to create curvilinear forms with thousands of tiny stitches (SEE FIG. 13–18). As even more complex techniques developed, the production of a single textile might involve a dozen processes requiring highly skilled workers. Dyeing technology, too, was an advanced art form in the ancient Andes, with some textiles containing dozens of colors.

Because of their complexity, deciphering how these textiles were made can be a challenge, and investigators rely on contemporary Andean weavers—inheritors of this tradition—for guidance. Now, as then, fiber and textile arts are primarily in the hands of women.

13–18 MANTLE WITH DOUBLE FISH PATTERN
Paracas Necropolis, Peru. Paracas culture, 1st century CE. Cotton and camelid fiber, plain weave with stem-stitch embroidery, 118⅛ × 63¾" (3 × 1.62 m). Brooklyn Museum, New York. Alfred W. Jenkins Fund (34.1560).

13-19 EARTH DRAWING (GEOGLYPH) OF A HUMMINGBIRD, NAZCA PLAIN
Southwest Peru. Nazca culture, c. 1–700 CE. Length approx. 450′ (137 m); wingspan approx. 220′ (60.9 m).

Credit: © Stéphane Compoint

The Moche Culture

The Moche culture dominated the north coast of Peru from the Piura Valley to the Huarmey Valley—a distance of some 370 miles—between about 100 and 700 CE. Moche lords ruled each valley in this region from a ceremonial-administrative center. The largest of these, in the Moche Valley (from which the culture takes its name), contained the so-called Huaca del Sol (Pyramid of the Sun) and Huaca de la Luna (Pyramid of the Moon), both built of **adobe** brick (sun-baked blocks of clay mixed with straw). The Huaca del Sol, one of the largest ancient structures in South America, was originally 1,100 feet long by 500 feet wide, rising in a series of terraces to a height of 59 feet. Much of this pyramid was destroyed in the seventeenth century, when a Spanish mining company diverted a river through it to wash out the gold contained in its many burials. Recent excavations at the Huaca de la Luna have revealed brightly painted reliefs of deities, captives, and warriors, remade during successive renovations of the pyramid. This site had been thought to be the capital of the entire Moche realm, but the accumulating evidence indicates that the Moche maintained a decentralized social network.

The Moche were exceptional potters and metalsmiths. Vessels were made in the shapes of naturalistically modeled human beings, animals, and architectural structures, at times combined in complex figural scenes. They developed ceramic molds, which allowed them to mass-produce some forms. They also created **PORTRAIT VESSELS** that seem to preserve individual likenesses (**FIG. 13-20**) and recorded mythological narratives and ritual scenes in intricate fine-line painting. Similar scenes were painted on the walls of temples and administrative buildings. Moche metalsmiths, the most sophisticated in the central Andes, developed several innovative metal alloys.

THE TOMB OF THE WARRIOR PRIEST A central theme in Moche iconography is a ceremony in which prisoners captured in battle are sacrificed and several elaborately dressed figures then drink their blood. Archaeologists have labeled the principal figure in this sacrifice ceremony as the Warrior Priest and other important figures as the Bird Priest and the Priestess. The recent discovery of a number of spectacularly rich Moche tombs indicates that the sacrifice ceremony was an actual Moche ritual and that Moche lords and ladies assumed the roles of the principal figures. The occupant of a tomb at Sipán, in the Lambayeque Valley on the northwest coast, was buried with the regalia of the Warrior Priest. In tombs at the site of

San José de Moro, just south of Sipán, several women were buried with the regalia of the Priestess.

Among the riches accompanying the Warrior Priest at Sipán was a pair of exquisite gold-and-turquoise **EARSPOOLS**, each of which depicts three Moche warriors (**FIG. 13-21**). The central figure bursts into three dimensions, while his companions are shown in profile, in a flat inlay technique. All three are adorned with tiny gold-and-turquoise earspools, simpler versions of the object they themselves adorn. They wear gold-and-turquoise headdresses topped with delicate sheets of gold that resemble the crescent-shaped knives used in sacrifices. The central figure has a crescent-shaped nose ornament and carries a removable gold club and shield. A necklace of owl's-head beads strung with gold thread hangs around his shoulders; similar objects have been found in other tombs at Sipán. These earspools illustrate two of the most notable features of Moche art: its capacity for naturalism and its close attention to detail.

13-21 EARSPOOL
From Sipán, Peru. Moche culture, c. 300 CE. Gold, turquoise, quartz, and shell; diameter approx. 3″ (9.4 cm). Bruning Archaeological Museum, Lambayeque, Peru.

Credit: Photo: Susan Einstein

13-20 MOCHE PORTRAIT VESSEL
Peru. Moche culture, c. 100–700 CE. Clay, height 11″ (28 cm). Staatliche Museen zu Berlin, Ethnologisches Museum.

This is one of several portrait vessels made from the same mold that seems to portray a particular individual.

Credit: © 2016. Photo Scala, Florence/bpk, Bildagentur für Kunst, Kultur und Gechsichte, Berlin

North America

How do the art and architecture of early cultures differ across North America?

Compared to the densely inhabited agricultural regions of Mesoamerica and South America, most of North America remained sparsely populated. Early people lived primarily by hunting, fishing, and gathering edible plants. Agriculture was developed on a limited scale with the cultivation of squash, sunflowers, and other plants to supplement a diet comprised largely of game, fish, and berries.

The East

We are only beginning to understand the early culture of eastern North America. Archaeologists have discovered that people lived in communities that included both burial and ceremonial earthworks—mounds of earth-formed platforms that probably supported a chief's house and served as the shrines of ancestors and places for a sacred fire, tended by special guardians. Poverty Point, Louisiana, is one of the largest of the earthwork ceremonial centers (though not the earliest—this distinction goes to Watson

Brake, Louisiana, dating to 3400–3000 BCE). Dated between 1800 and 500 BCE—essentially contemporary with Stonehenge in England (SEE FIG. 1-22) and with Olmec constructions in Mexico (SEE FIG. 13-5)—Poverty Point consisted of huge, concentric earthen arcs three quarters of a mile wide.

The Woodland Period

The Woodland period (300 BCE–1000 CE) saw the creation of impressive earthworks along the great river valleys of the Ohio and Mississippi, where people built monumental mounds and buried individuals with valuable grave goods. Objects discovered in these burials indicate that the people of the Mississippi, Illinois, and Ohio river valleys traded widely with other regions of North and Central America. For example, the burial sites of the Adena (c. 1100 BCE–200 CE) and the Hopewell (c. 100 BCE–550 CE) cultures contained objects made with copper from present-day Michigan's Upper Peninsula, as well as cut sheets of mica from the Appalachian Mountains, turtle shells and sharks' teeth from Florida, and obsidian from Wyoming and Idaho. The pipes that the Hopewell people created from fine-grained pipestone for the ritual smoking of tobacco have been found from Lake Superior to the Gulf of Mexico.

The Hopewell carved their pipes with representations of forest animals and birds, sometimes with inlaid eyes and teeth of fresh-water pearls and bone. Combining realism and elegant simplification, a beaver crouching on a platform forms the bowl of a pipe found in present-day Illinois (FIG. 13-22). As in a modern pipe, the bowl—a hole in the beaver's back—could be filled with tobacco or other dried leaves, the leaves lighted, and smoke drawn through the hole in the stem. Using the pipe in this way, the smoker would be face to face with the beaver, whose shining pearl eyes may suggest an association with the spirit world.

The Mississippian Period

The Mississippian period (c. 700–1550 CE) is characterized by the widespread distribution of complex chiefdoms, both large and small, that proliferated throughout the region. The people of the Mississippian culture continued the mound-building tradition begun by the Adena, Hopewell, and others. From 1539 to 1543 Hernando de Soto encountered Mississippian societies while exploring the region, and this contact between native North American people and Europeans resulted in catastrophe. The Europeans introduced diseases, especially smallpox, to which native populations had had no previous exposure and hence no immunity. In short order, 80 percent of the native population perished, an extraordinary disruption of society, far worse than the Black Death in fourteenth-century Europe. By the time other Europeans reached the area, the great earthworks of the Mississippian culture had long been abandoned.

One of the most impressive Mississippian-period earthworks is the **GREAT SERPENT MOUND** in present-day Adams County, Ohio (FIG. 13-23). Researchers using carbon-14 dating have recently proposed dating the mound to about 1070 CE. There have been many interpretations of the twisting snake form, especially the "head" at the highest point, a Y shape and an oval enclosure that some see as the serpent opening its jaws to swallow a huge egg. Perhaps the people who built it were responding to the spectacular astronomical display of Halley's Comet in 1066.

Mississippian peoples built a major urban center known as Cahokia near the juncture of the Illinois, Missouri, and Mississippi rivers (now East St. Louis, Illinois). Although the site may have been inhabited as early as about 3000 BCE, most monumental construction at Cahokia took place between about 1000 and 1300 CE. At its height the city had a population of up to 15,000 people, with another 10,000 in the surrounding countryside (FIG. 13-24).

The most prominent feature of Cahokia—a feature also found at other Mississippian sites—is an enormous earth mound called Monk's Mound, covering 15 acres and originally 100 feet high. A small, rounded platform on its summit initially supported a wooden fence and a rectangular building. The mound is aligned with the sun at the equinox and may have had a special use during planting or harvest festivals. Smaller rectangular and rounded mounds in front of the principal

13-22 BEAVER EFFIGY PLATFORM PIPE
From Bedford Mound, Pike County, Illinois. Hopewell culture, c. 100–400 CE. Pipestone, river pearls, and bone, 4⁹⁄₁₆ × 1⁷⁄₈ × 2" (11.6 × 4.8 × 5.1 cm). Gilcrease Museum, Tulsa, Oklahoma.

Credit: Photo: John Bigelow Taylor

13–23 GREAT SERPENT MOUND

Adams County, Ohio. Mississippian culture, c. 1070 CE. Length approx. 1,254′ (328.2 m).

Credit: © Tony Linck/ SuperStock

mound surrounded a large, roughly rectangular plaza. The city's entire ceremonial center was protected by a stockade, or fence, of upright wooden posts. In all, the walled enclosure contained more than 100 mounds, platforms, wooden enclosures, and houses. The various earthworks functioned as tombs and bases for palaces and temples, and also served to make astronomical observations.

Postholes indicate that woodhenges (circles of wooden columns) were a significant feature of Cahokia. The largest (seen to the extreme left in FIG. 13–24) had 48 posts forming a circle with a diameter of about 420 feet. Sight lines between a 49th post set east of the center of the enclosure and points on the perimeter enabled early astronomers to determine solstices and equinoxes.

FLORIDA GLADES CULTURE   In 1895, excavators working in submerged mud and shell mounds off Key Marco on the west coast of Florida made a remarkable discovery: posts carved with birds and animals that had been preserved in the swamps. The large mound called Fort Center, in Glades County, Florida, gives the Florida Glades culture its name.

13–24 RECONSTRUCTION OF CENTRAL CAHOKIA

As it would have appeared about 1150 CE. Collinsville, Illinois. Mississippian culture, c. 1000–1300 CE. East–west length approx. 3 miles (4.82 km), north–south length approx. 2¼ miles (3.6 km); base of great mound 1,037 × 790′ (316 × 241 m), height approx. 100′ (30 m). Monk's Mound is the large platform in the center of the image.

Credit: Painting by William Iseminger, Reconstruction of Central Cahokia Mounds. c. 1150 CE. Courtesy of Cahokia Mounds State Historic Site

13–25 PELICAN FIGUREHEAD

Key Marco, Florida. Florida Glades culture, c. 1000 CE. Wood and paint, 4⅜ × 2⅜ × 3⅛″ (11.2 × 6 × 8 cm). University of Pennsylvania Museum of Archaeology and Anthropology, Philadelphia.

Credit: Courtesy of the Penn Museum, image #160303

At Key Marco, painted wooden animal and bird heads, a human mask, and the figure of a kneeling cat-human were found in circumstances that suggested a ruined shrine. Recently, carbon-14 dating of these items has confirmed a date of about 1000 CE. Although the heads are spare in details, the artists show a remarkable power of observation in reproducing the creatures they saw around them, such as the **PELICAN** in **FIGURE 13–25**. The surviving head, neck, and breast of the pelican are made of carved wood painted black, white, and gray (other images also had traces of pink and blue paint). The bird's outstretched wings were found nearby, but the wood shrank and disintegrated as it dried. Carved wooden wolf and deer heads were also found. Archaeologists think the heads might have been attached to ceremonial furniture or posts. Some see evidence here of a bird and animal cult or perhaps the use of birds and animals as clan symbols.

The Southwest

Farming cultures were slower to arise in the arid American Southwest, which became home to three major early cultures. The Hohokam culture, centered in the central and southern parts of present-day Arizona, emerged around 200 BCE and endured until sometime around 1300 CE. The Hohokam built large-scale irrigation systems, multi-story residences, and ballcourts that demonstrate ties with Mesoamerica. The Mimbres/Mogollon culture, located in the mountains of west-central New Mexico and east-central Arizona, flourished from about 200 to about 1150 CE. Potters made deep bowls painted with lively, imaginative, and sometimes complex scenes of humans and animals (**FIG. 13–26**). Much of our knowledge of this ceramic tradition is based on examples excavated in burials under the floors of Mimbres dwellings, where food bowls—most of them intentionally punctured before burial—were inverted and placed over the head of the deceased. Some experts believe these perforated bowls could have represented the dome of the sky and embodied ideas about the transport of the dead from the earth into the spirit world.

The third southwestern culture, the Ancestral Puebloans (formerly called Anasazi), emerged around 500 CE in the Four Corners region, where present-day Colorado, Utah, Arizona, and New Mexico meet. The Puebloans adopted the irrigation technology of the Hohokam and began building elaborate, multi-storied, apartmentlike "great houses" with many rooms for specialized purposes, including communal food storage and ritual.

As in Mimbres culture, Ancestral Puebloan people found aesthetic expression in their pottery. Women were the potters in ancient Pueblo society. They developed a functional, aesthetically pleasing, coil-built earthenware, or low-fired ceramic, initiating a tradition of ceramic production that continues to be important today among the Pueblo peoples of the Southwest. One type of vessel, a wide-mouthed **SEED JAR** with a globular body and holes

13–26 BOWL WITH SCORPIONS

Swarts Ruin, Southwest New Mexico. Mimbres culture, c. 1000–1150 CE. Earthenware with white slip and black paint, height 4¾″ (12 cm), diameter 11⅝″ (29.5 cm). Peabody Museum of Archaeology and Ethnology, Harvard University.

Credit: © President and Fellows of Harvard College, Peabody Museum of Archaeology and Ethnology, Harvard University, PM# 24-15-10/94585

13-27 SEED JAR
Ancestral Puebloan culture, c. 1150 CE. Earthenware with black-and-white pigment, diameter 14½" (36.9 cm). Saint Louis Art Museum.
Funds given by the Children's Art Festival (175:1981).

CHACO CANYON   Chaco Canyon, covering about 30 square miles in present-day New Mexico with nine great houses, or pueblos, was an important center of Ancestral Puebloan civilization. The largest-known "great house" is a ruin known as **"PUEBLO BONITO"** (**FIG. 13-28**), which was built in stages between the ninth and mid twelfth centuries. Eventually it included over 800 rooms in four or five stories, arranged in a D shape. Within the crescent part of the D, 32 **kivas** recall the round, semi-submerged pit houses of earlier Southwestern cultures. Here men performed religious rituals and instructed youths in their responsibilities. Interlocking pine logs formed a shallow, domelike roof with a hole in the center through which the men entered by climbing down a ladder. Based on what we know of later Pueblo beliefs, a small indentation in the floor of the kiva directly under the entrance and behind the fire pit may have symbolized the "navel of the earth"—the place where ancestors of the Ancestral Pueblo had emerged to settle on the earth in mythic "first times." The top of the kivas formed the floor of the communal plaza.

Pueblo Bonito stood at the hub of a network of wide, straight roads—almost invisible today, but discovered through aerial photography—that radiated out to some 70 other communities. They make no detour to avoid topographic obstacles; when they encounter cliffs, they become stairs. Their undeviating course suggests that they were more than practical thoroughfares: They may have served as processional ways. Given its place at the intersection

near the rim (**FIG. 13-27**), would have been suspended from roof poles by thongs attached to the jar's holes, out of reach of voracious rodents. The example shown here is decorated with black-and-white dotted squares and zig-zag patterns. The patterns conform to the body of the jar, enhancing its curved shape by focusing the energy of the design around its bulging expansion.

13-28 "PUEBLO BONITO"

Chaco Canyon, New Mexico. Ancestral Puebloan culture, 830–1150 CE.

Credit: © Richard A. Cooke/Corbis

13-29 "CLIFF PALACE"

Mesa Verde National Park, Colorado. Ancestral Puebloan culture, c. 1150–1300 CE.

Credit: © MarclSchauer/Shutterstock

of this road system and the prominence of kivas in the design of great houses such as Pueblo Bonito, some have suggested that Chaco Canyon may have been a gathering place or pilgrimage site for people from the entire region at specific times of year.

Though no one knows for certain why Chaco Canyon was abandoned, the Ancestral Puebloan population declined during a severe drought in the mid twelfth century, and building at Pueblo Bonito ceased around 1150. Ancestral Puebloans may have moved to the Rio Grande and Mogollon river valleys, where they built new apartmentlike dwellings on ledges under sheltering cliffs (**FIG. 13-29**). One of the most impressive surviving cliff

dwellings from this period is the "Cliff Palace" in Mesa Verde, Colorado, comprised of 150 rooms and 23 kivas, with an estimated population of about 100. Difficult as it must have been to live high on canyon walls and commute to farm the valley below, the cliff communities had the advantage of being relatively secure. The cliffs also acted as insulation, protecting the dwellings from the extremes of heat and cold that characterize this part of the world. The many rooms housed an entire community comfortably, and close proximity built communal solidarity.

ROCK ART The rock art of the American Southwest consists of pictographs, which are painted, and petroglyphs,

13-30 ANTHROPOMORPHS

The Great Gallery, Horseshoe (Barrier) Canyon, Utah. c. 1–1000 CE. Largest figure about 8′ (2.44 m) tall.

These may represent holy or priestly figures and are often associated with snakes, dogs, and other small, energetic creatures. Big-eyed anthropomorphs may be rain gods. Painters used their fingers and yucca-fiber brushes to apply the reddish pigment made from hematite (iron oxide).

Credit: © Whit Richardson/Aurora Open/ SuperStock

which are pecked or engraved. While occurring in numerous distinctive styles, rock art images include humans, animals, and geometric figures represented singly and in multi-figured compositions.

In the Great Gallery of Horseshoe Canyon, Utah, the painted human figures have long, decorated rectangular bodies and knoblike heads (**FIG. 13-30**). One large, wide-eyed figure popularly known as the "Holy Ghost" is nearly 8 feet tall. Archaeologists have dated these paintings to about 1,000 to 2,000 years ago; rock art is very difficult to date with any precision.

Petroglyphs are often found in places where the dark brown bacterial growths and staining known as **"desert varnish"** streak down canyon walls. To create an image, the artist scrapes through the layer of varnish, exposing the lighter sandstone beneath. In the petroglyphs of Nine Mile Canyon in central Utah—attributed to the Fremont people (800–1300 CE), who were agriculturists as well as hunters—a large human hunter draws his bow and arrow on a flock of bighorn sheep (**FIG. 13-31**). Other hunters and a large, rectangular, armless figure wearing a horned headdress mingle with the animals. The scene gives rise to the same questions and arguments we have noted with regard to the prehistoric art discussed in Chapter 1: Is this a record of a successful hunt, a ritual activity, or a mythic story?

Throughout the Americas for the next several hundred years artistic traditions would continue to emerge, develop, and be transformed as the indigenous peoples

of various regions interacted. But more than anything else, the sudden incursions of Europeans beginning in the late fifteenth century would have a dramatic and lasting impact on these civilizations and their art.

13-31 HUNTER'S MURAL
Nine Mile Canyon, Utah. Fremont people, 800–1300 CE.
Credit: © Ed Warner/Alamy Stock Photo

Think About It

1 Characterize and compare the differing figure styles of paintings from Teotihuacan and Maya culture as seen in **FIGURES 13-9** and **13-3**.

2 Discuss the significance of bloodletting as a recurring theme in early Mesoamerican art, focusing your answer on one specific work of art in this chapter.

3 Evaluate what we can learn about the broad cultural values of Olmec civilization from the figural group (**FIG. 13-1**) that was the subject of the opening discussion in this chapter.

4 Compare the architectural complexes of Teotihuacan and Chaco Canyon. Evaluate the arguments for understanding both of these early monuments of American art as ceremonial sites. What do we know of the rituals that would have been performed in each location?

Crosscurrents

Both of these works, representing activities and relationships critical to royal power, were created in pictorial relief sculpture. Compare the two very different techniques of carving and figural styles. How are style and technique related to the cultural traditions of the time when and place where they were made?

FIG. 3–28

FIG. 13–14

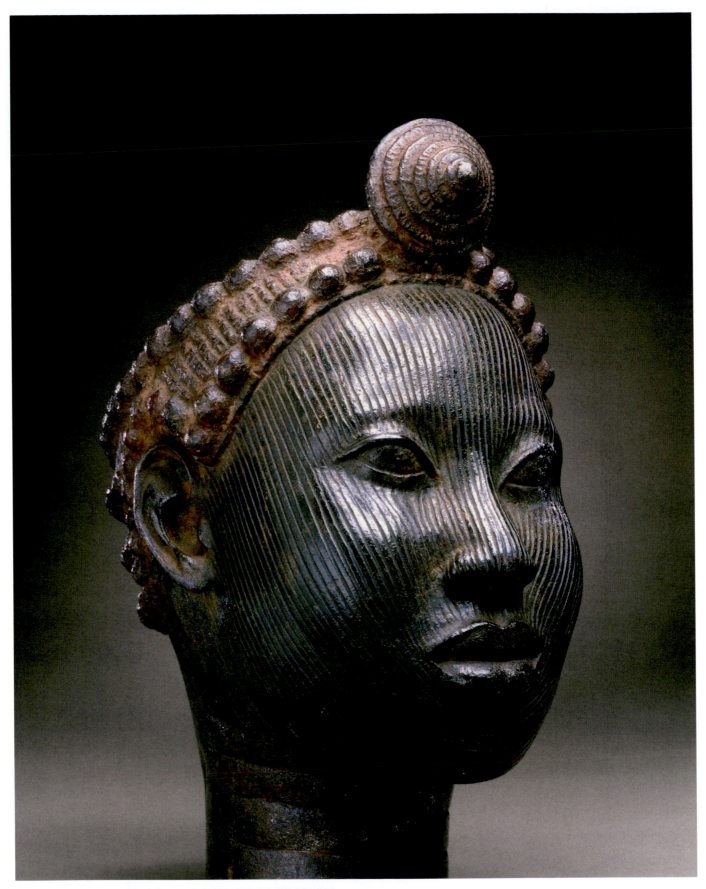

14-1 CROWNED HEAD OF A YORUBA RULER FROM IFE

Nigeria. Yoruba, 12th–15th century CE. Zinc brass, height 9⁷⁄₁₆″ (24 cm). National Commission for Museums and Monuments, Nigeria, Museum of Ife Antiquities.

Credit: *Photo © Dirk Bakker/Bridgeman Images*

Chapter 14
Arts of Africa to the Sixteenth Century

Learning Objectives

14.a Identify the visual hallmarks of the art of pre-1600 cultures in Africa for formal, technical, and expressive qualities.

14.b Interpret the meaning of works of pre-1600 cultures in Africa based on their themes, subjects, and symbols.

14.c Relate the art and artists in pre-1600 Africa to their distinct cultural, economic, and political contexts.

14.d Apply the vocabulary and concepts relevant to pre-1600 African art, artists, and art history.

14.e Interpret a work of pre-1600 African art using the art historical methods of observation, comparison, and inductive reasoning.

14.f Select visual and textual evidence in various media to support an argument or an interpretation of a work of pre-1600 African art.

The brass head seen here demonstrates the extraordinary talents of the artist who produced it using the lost-wax casting technique (**FIG. 14-1**). The modeling of the flesh—covered with thin, parallel **scarification** patterns (decorations made by scarring)—is remarkably sensitive, especially the subtle transitions around the nose and mouth.

This head portrays a Yoruba *oni* (king) and could represent either a male or female ruler. The full, delicate lips and expressive eyes bulge organically, stressing the artist's desire to connect human anatomy with the spiritual nature of the *oni*. The *oni* in fact was seen as an intermediary between Yoruba people and the spiritual realms of their gods, ancestors, and demons. The *oni* was understood to live in a human body, but be mostly spirit (or god-like) in nature.

Cast metal heads of kings and queens like the one seen here are part of a sculptural tradition that began in the city of Ife (also known as Ile-Ife) in about 1050 CE in what is today Nigeria. The Yoruba religion regards Ife as the "navel of the world," the site of creation where Ife's first ruler—Oni Oduduwa—came down from heaven to create Earth. By the eleventh century CE, Ife was a lively metropolis. It was, and remains, a sacred city for Yoruba people.

The Yoruba kings at Ife were but a small part of a tremendous series of ancient empires that stretched from West Africa to the central Saharan region (**MAP 14-1**). The Ghana and Akan empires south of the Sahara traded gold with those possessing salt in the north. Mobile populations such as the Fulani in the Sahara region and the Khoekhoe and San in the Kalahari region built wealth in herding domesticated animals across the savanna biomes of the continent. They displayed this wealth on their bodies in the form of elaborately made jewelry and clothing, as well as painstakingly elaborate hairstyles, body art, and patterned skin scarification. Nubian kings along the upper Nile influenced and were influenced by the Egyptian pharaohs farther downriver. Their temples and commemorative statues attest to their political power and artistic might.

By following the trade routes that linked African empires such as the Yoruba to each other and to the lands beyond their continent, we can gain insight into social, cultural, religious, and artistic desires of each region. Undoubtedly more research will lead to new interpretations and better understanding of the myriad of objects produced by Africans from prehistory to today. This is what makes the study of African art so exciting and dynamic, as well as vital to our understanding of art history around the world.

MAP 14–1 INDIGENOUS KINGDOMS IN 11TH–16TH CENTURY AFRICA

The Origins of Art in Africa

How do the prehistoric arts of Africa communicate spirituality, power, and identity?

Africa is a continent with over 54 countries and a twenty-first-century population estimated at 1.2 billion people, who speak more than 2,000 languages and live on a landmass large enough to encompass the entire United States three times over.

With such a sheer volume of cultures, arts, and languages, as well as a chronology going back 80,000 years, this field of study is constantly being updated and expanded, and it improves with each generation of scholarship. This chapter, therefore, can merely introduce some of the early artistic moments and monuments from across the continent of Africa, as we understand them at the beginning of the twenty-first century.

Concepts

Three concepts of great importance are present in the works of art covered in this chapter.

SPIRITUALITY   Whether prehistoric or from the 1500s, many works of art are created to honor, harness, or communicate with spiritual forces. Ancient African religions seem to have focused on the spiritual forces of animals and the shamanistic capacities of gifted human individuals to communicate with spirits beyond the visible world.

POWER   Massive architectural monuments for religious and political use clearly demonstrate the wealth, engineering expertise, and skill of the populations that built them. Trade networks that date back to prehistoric times created wealth and control for civilizations that were able to dominate the flow of goods from one area to the next.

Individual rulers commissioned works of art and architecture made from local and imported materials to display their control over their own people and their cosmopolitan connections to far-flung regions.

IDENTITY During these formative centuries, group identity and unity were more important than individual distinction. When rulers commissioned works of art representing people, even themselves, these images more accurately represented the role of their office than the likeness or personality of the individual. Thus "portraits," or personal likenesses of an individual, are not as important as the role of king, shaman, ancestor, historian, dancer, mother, or initiate. Societies were built on the organization of individuals into occupations that served the good of all. Works of art, like the *Crowned Head of a Yoruba Ruler* from Nigeria, represent the ideals of a good king or queen, without copying the particular king or queen's features.

Prehistoric Arts

Images painted on rocks are found throughout the African continent in places where the environment has been conducive to preservation. These rock paintings and engravings date back in some cases to 25,000 BCE. They range from highly abstract geometric designs to naturalistic representations of human and animal forms often arranged to tell stories. These include dramatic hunting scenes, views of domestic family life, and costumed dancing figures.

NAMIBIA AND SOUTH AFRICA Namibia is a sparsely populated country that is perhaps best known as a haven for safari vacationers and nature enthusiasts. Much of the country is on an elevated plateau that sits between the coastal Namib Desert in the west and the Kalahari Desert to the east. The dry climate has allowed for the preservation of countless works of rock art spread across the plateau, as well as in caves and rocky outcrops. The most famous rock art sites in Namibia are Twyfelfontein in the northwest, which is home to many scenes of herd animals, hunters, and groups of humans both painted and engraved on the rocky and hilly terrain, and the so-called "Apollo 11" cave in the southern part of the country.

The "Apollo 11" cave is the site of the earliest known figurative artworks on the African continent. They are animal figures dating to about 25,000 BCE, painted in red and black pigment on flat stones (**FIG. 14-2**). The stones were found in the late 1960s by archaeologist W.E. Wendt. He named the cave in honor of NASA's Apollo 11 mission, which had just successfully landed astronauts on the moon. While the name he gave to the cave has nothing to do with the ancient plaques he discovered there, it has stuck, and the site still goes by this appellation today.

The small slab seen here, despite being broken in half, contains the readily discernable image of an animal marked on the stone in a charcoal-based pigment. The animal is abstracted, with a large head and elongated thick neck, making it difficult to determine if the painter was attempting to render a specific species. More likely, the artist was attempting to capture the essence or spirit of the animal; in that case, naturalistic depiction would have been unnecessary, and perhaps even undesirable.

In parts of South Africa, the landscape is very similar to that in Namibia, making it home to an equally exciting number of carved and painted images on living rock. The majority of central and western South Africa is desert and semiarid desert, while a rocky escarpment, the

14-2 QUARTZITE SLABS DEPICTING ANIMALS

"Apollo 11" Cave. Namibia. c. 25,000 BCE. State Museum of Namibia, Windhoek.

Credit: Photo: W.E. Wendt. © State Museum of Namibia

14-3 "GAME PASS" SHELTER
Drakensberg, South Africa. San.

Credit: © Ariadne Van Zandbergen/Alamy Stock Photo

Drakensberg Mountain range, runs the length of its eastern region.

Numerous examples of rock painting are found in the Drakensberg Mountains. Almost 600 sites have been located in rock shelters and caves, with approximately 35,000 individual images catalogued. Around 2,400 years ago, ancestors of the San peoples began painting the walls of the Drakensberg cliffs. Ethnographic research among contemporary San people suggests possible interpretations for some of the paintings. For example, scholars have been studying contemporary San rituals performed to heal individuals or to cleanse communities. These ceremonies look very similar to images painted on the rock walls of the Drakensberg range. The San people have also continued their ancestral tradition of rock painting into today, making theirs one of the longest continually practiced art forms in the world.

In the **"GAME PASS" SHELTER** site seen here, the primary subject is a group of eland (a species of large-bodied antelope) with much smaller running and leaping humans positioned above them (**FIG. 14-3**). At its most literal, it is a scene of hunting, with men chasing the herd of eland. However, the artistic treatment of the eland certainly prioritizes them as the subject of this enormous wall painting.

The animals are painted in multiple hues of red, white, brown, and ocher. They overlap each other as well as appearing as solo depictions. The human figures, in contrast, are quite small and painted in only one color.

Game Pass is so named for the paintings along the wall but also for the vantage point it commands over the valley below. From here, hunters could watch undetected the movements of eland herds across the open plains. Most likely the paintings document this strategic viewing point and mark the site as a ritual location for hunters preparing physically and spiritually for the rigors of the hunt.

One small group of figures painted on the walls of Game Pass give proof to this theory. An eland is painted in profile with its rear legs stylized into a cross-legged pose that living animals do not make. A male figure stands behind the animal holding its tail and displaying the same awkward crossed-leg position. To the right of them, three human figures appear in contorted poses, and all the humans are painted with antelope hooves. Scholars interpret these gestures as those of a dying eland with a successful hunter who holds the animal directly while it dies in order to absorb its spiritual power. The three other human figures are interpreted as shamans in the middle of a trance who are also absorbing the spiritual energy of the eland before it dies. The transfer of energy between humans and animals via trance was and remains a vital component of San ritual hunting. Trance is still a respected and feared practice among the San today, who describe it as a ritual "death" that allows humans access to forces beyond their capacities.

ALGERIA   To the far north of the African continent, the mountains of the central Sahara Desert—principally the Tassili-n-Ajjer range in the south of present-day Algeria and the Acacus Mountains in present-day Libya—contain painted images that span the years between 8000 and 2000 BCE. They record not only the artistic and cultural development of the peoples who lived in the region, but also the transformation of the Sahara from fertile grassland to the vast desert we know today.

A variety of scenes found on rock walls in southern Algeria and Libya depict men and women dancing or performing various ceremonial activities (**FIG. 14–4**). The artists who created these works paid close attention to details of clothing, body decoration, and headdresses; in some examples the figures are depicted wearing masks that cover their faces. While scholars are still unsure of their exact meaning, some have suggested the figures are engaged in rituals intended to ensure adequate rainfall or success in hunting, or to honor their dead.

By 4000 BCE the savanna-like climate of the Sahara had become increasingly arid, and hippopotamuses, elephants, giraffes, and antelopes were disappearing from the region (and also as subjects in the rock art paintings of this time). Eventually, hunting gave way to herding as the primary life-sustaining activity of the Sahara's inhabitants. Paintings from Tassili-n-Ajjer dating to this period illustrate men and women gathered in front of round, thatched houses. As the men tend cattle, women prepare meals and care for children.

The continued drying of the Sahara into desert coincided with the rise of Egyptian civilization to the east. Similarities between Egyptian art and Saharan rock art include images of rams with disks between their horns. These were originally interpreted as evidence of Egyptian influence on the Saharan regions. Yet in light of the great age of Saharan rock art, it seems just as plausible that the influence flowed the other way, carried by people who migrated into the Nile Valley when the grasslands of the Sahara disappeared.

14–4 DANCERS IN CEREMONIAL ATTIRE
Section of rock wall painting, Tassili-n-Ajjer, Algeria. c. 5000–2000 BCE.

Credit: Dmitry Pichugin/Fotolia

North and East Africa

What features define the arts and architecture of the distinct cultures of North and East Africa, and what does this tell us about the political power of each culture?

The word "Africa" comes from the name given to a large territory encompassing what is today Tunisia, northern Algeria, and coastal Libya. Named by the Romans in the second century BCE when they annexed the city of Carthage in present-day Tunisia, "Africa Proconsularis" was one part of the much larger Roman Empire that at its height encompassed the entire Mediterranean Sea. Over time the name given to this colony eventually came to represent the entire continent.

Well before Rome folded northern Africa into its empire, the local populations had built sophisticated and long-standing empires and kingdoms. Dynastic and religious rulers in North and East Africa were natural trading partners, making use of trade route connections along the North African coast to Egypt and up the Nile to Nubia (now Sudan), as well as to the Axumite kingdom, which spread from present-day Ethiopia to Yemen and south to Sudan. Mercantile trade, exchange of objects of religious and royal value, and shared architectural technologies created the massive political and religious structures built across the region, many of which can still be seen today.

Ancient Nubia (Sudan)

Inhabited as of 5000 BCE, the lands of Nubia stretched from Khartoum, at the juncture of the Blue and White Nile rivers in what is now Sudan, north to the city of Aswan in present-day Egypt. At Aswan, the Nile is non-navigable due to a series of rapids known as the First Cataract, which served as the historical boundary between Egypt and Nubia. The Egyptians called the kingdom to their south "Kush." Powerful dynastic kings ruled over these lands from 2000 BCE up until the fourth century CE. When the Romans encountered the Kushites, they called them Nubians. Nubia has since been adopted to refer to the region and its inhabitants from 5000 BCE through the sixth century CE.

"I descended [the Nile] with three hundred [donkeys] laden with incense, ebony, grain, panthers, ivory, and every good product." Thus the Egyptian envoy Harkhuf described his return from Nubia in 2300 BCE. The riches of Nubia attracted merchants and envoys in ancient times, and trade brought the region into contact with not only Egyptians, but also Phoenicians, Greeks, and Romans.

THE KINGDOM OF KUSH   The Kushite kings and queens established themselves first at the city of Kerma (2000–1650 BCE) and subsequently at the cities of Napata and Meroë. During the Napatan period (800–270 BCE), Nubian kings also assumed control over Egypt, entering the dynastic line of pharaohs around 750 BCE and remaining kings of the combined Nubian and Egyptian kingdoms until around 661 BCE. As a result, the later sculpture and architecture of the Kushite kingdom reflect both Nubian and Egyptian influences.

A **COLOSSAL STATUE OF KING ASPELTA** dating to the Napatan period is one example (**FIG. 14–5**). Aspelta became the King of Kush after the sudden death of his older brother, Anlamani. In the statue, measuring over 10 feet in height, Aspelta assumes a posture seen in Egyptian sculptures of kings (SEE FIG. 3–10): arms held rigidly at the sides and the left leg forward in a striding position.

14-5 COLOSSAL STATUE OF KING ASPELTA
From Jebel Barkal, Sudan. Nubian, Napatan period, 593–568 BCE. Height 130¾″ (332.1 cm). Museum of Fine Arts, Boston (23.730), Harvard University/Boston Museum of Fine Arts Expedition 1916.

Credit: Photograph © 2017 Museum of Fine Arts, Boston

14–6 PYRAMIDS AT MEROË

Sudan. Nubian, 337 BCE–339 CE.

The damage seen to the pyramids in the background of this photograph was caused by looters and European explorers in the nineteenth century who dynamited the structures looking for the burial chambers and the troves of gold and valuable objects buried with each king and queen. Note that the two smaller pyramids at the front have been restored in modern times with lighter colored stone to distinguish the rebuilt sections from the original structures.

Credit: Robnaw/Fotolia

The sculptural treatment of the eyes also resembles Egyptian imagery with thick raised lines outlining the pupil. However, the designations that show him to be the king of Napata are Nubian. He wears a close-fitting cap on his head, and carved in low relief around his neck is a loop of cord that drapes over the front of each shoulder. These regalia are different than those used for Egyptian kings. Aspelta appears to have been the last Nubian king elected at the city of Napata. After his reign the Nubian kings moved farther south to establish their reign at the city of Meroë.

The Nubian **PYRAMIDS AT MEROË** were constructed between 337 BCE and 339 CE (**FIG. 14–6**) They are burial temples for Nubian rulers, both kings and queens. A clearly Nubian feature is the H-shaped entrance gateway known as a *bekhenet* in front of each burial pyramid. These sit in front of each major temple structure and symbolize the passage between the human realm and the world of the gods. The coffin containing the deceased king or queen would be moved through the doorway of the *bekhenet* into a small, rectangular tunnel that connected to the funerary chamber deep inside the pyramid behind it. While the use of a pyramid as a burial chamber is of ancient Egyptian influence, these are modified by Kushite architects to

distinguish them from those to the north. The pyramids at Meroë are not nearly as large as those in Giza, Egypt, for example, and they are narrower, shaped like isosceles triangles. In addition, each course of brickwork is slightly inset from the row beneath, creating horizontal ridges, unlike the smooth façades preferred by Egyptian pharaohs.

Ethiopia

Ethiopia's role in the history of humanity from prehistoric times to the present is unparalleled. This region is where our species, *homo sapiens*, first emerged; some of the oldest languages and alphabetic scripts in the world came from here; and it was home to some of the earliest incarnations of Christianity and Islam.

Ethiopia was a major contributor to the civilizations of the ancient world, including Greece, Egypt, Rome, Byzantium, and Arabia. In the second century BCE the kings in the Ethiopian highlands increased their importance through their control of trade routes from the African interior to the Red Sea port of Adulis. The city of Axum generated wealth for its kings by exporting ivory, gold, enslaved peoples, frankincense, myrrh, and salt. These ancient connections to vast swaths of human civilization have left a rich legacy in Ethiopia. Its people speak over 80 languages, and their written languages include the ancient Ge'ez (also Gə'əz) and Amharic scripts, both still in use today. Ethiopia was the sole territory on the African continent able to avoid territorial annexation by European nations during the colonial conquest. As a result, the colors of its flag—red, yellow, and green—were used by other African nations when they achieved independence from Europe in the mid twentieth century.

EARLY CHRISTIANITY   In the mid fourth century CE the Axumite king Ezana converted to Christianity. His conversion made Axum only the second politically Christian region in the world after Armenia, whose king Tiridates had converted his court in 301 CE.

The power and influence of the kings of Axum were only diminished by the displacement of the Red Sea trade routes after the Persian conquest of south Arabia, which among other things disrupted pilgrimage routes between Ethiopia and Jerusalem (the holy city revered by Christians, Jews, and Muslims). Subsequently, the Zagwe from Ethiopia's western highlands conquered Axum around 960 CE.

LIVING ROCK CHURCHES   In the mid twelfth century, Gebre (king) Mesqel Lalibela, a dynastic Zagwe ruler, wished to create a "new" Jerusalem in Ethiopia. He founded a holy site, which he named Lalibela after himself, in the highlands south of Axum. The numerous rock-hewn sanctuaries that were created in the hills above the city of Lalibela date from about 1181 to 1221. Rather than being built from the ground up, the churches and secondary structures were carved down from the ground level into living volcanic rock called tuff. In total, 11 churches were carved in close proximity to each other, creating a remarkable destination for Christian pilgrimages. UNESCO has declared all 11 churches at Lalibela a World Heritage Site.

BIETE GHIORGIS (CHURCH OF ST. GEORGE) possesses the most unique floor plan of the group, being in the shape of a square orthodox cross (**FIG. 14–7**). In order to construct it, a wide trench was first cut around what would become the 12 sides of the cross-shaped church. Stonemasons then carved out the windows on the uppermost level of the sanctuary and used these openings as a means by which to excavate the stone material from the inside ceiling of the church. Work progressed in this way

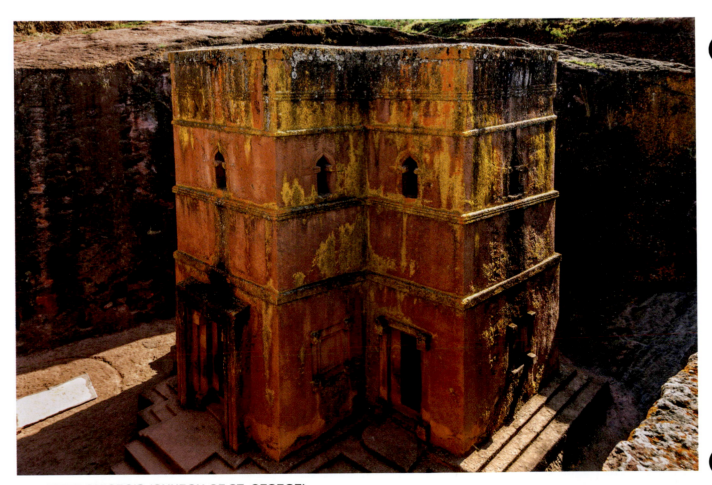

14-7 BIETE GHIORGIS (CHURCH OF ST. GEORGE)
Lalibela, Ethiopia. 13th century CE. Volcanic rock.

Credit: Milosk50/Fotolia

from roof to interior ceiling down through the levels of the structure until the desired "height" was reached. Finally the doors and windows of the ground-floor entry level could be carved. Then the exterior courtyard was widened and access tunnels dug to allow pilgrims and priests to enter the church. This top-down construction meant that each aspect of the structure had to be planned with precision before work could begin. The interior of the church is topped with a hemispherical domed ceiling in the style of the Byzantine churches that Ethiopian priests would have been familiar with from their pilgrimages to Jerusalem. This dome contains a large square cross carved in low relief, which mirrors a cross carved directly above it on the roof of the church. The exterior cross, while decorative, also serves in a drainage capacity: The channels formed by its sides carry water to the four downspouts at each side of the roof.

MANUSCRIPT ARTS Due to their long-standing connections with the ancient Christian world in the Middle East and then Byzantium and Rome, Ethiopian monks and monastic scribes most likely began using illuminated manuscripts from the moment the Axumite dynasty converted to Christianity in the fourth century. While their earliest texts do not survive, the scribes' practice of copying older manuscripts when they fell into disrepair means that many of the thirteenth- to twentieth-century manuscripts hearken back centuries in their texts and designs. We know that manuscripts from Byzantium and Rome were housed in Ethiopian repositories, while Ethiopian illuminated books also traveled to major Christian centers in Europe. Some Ethiopian Christian texts, such as **EUSEBIUS'S LETTER TO CARPIANUS**, illuminated by Mätre Krestos, were modeled on Byzantine predecessors (**FIG. 14–8**). However, these were always translated from the Greek or Latin into the local language of Ge'ez. Ge'ez remains the liturgical language of the Ethiopian Orthodox Church and is still the primary language used for religious documents.

Eusebius of Caesarea (c. 260–339 CE) was a Roman theologian and scholar who became Bishop of Caesarea (a coastal Roman city in the contemporary country of Israel). Among his most famous contributions to Christianity was his system of dividing the four Christian Gospels into canon tables, in order to identify where the four authors converged or diverged on their narrations of the life of Christ. In an important letter to a fellow Christian by the name of Carpianus, Eusebius explained how to use his table system.

From the time of its writing until about the fifteenth century, Eusebius's letter was often copied in Latin, Greek, or, in this case, Ge'ez at the beginning of illuminated manuscripts of Gospel books. After the letter, the canon tables would be presented, followed by pictures of the evangelists and scenes from the life of Christ.

14–8 Mätre Krestos **EUSEBIUS'S LETTER TO CARPIANUS** Gospel book. Tegray, northern Ethiopia. Early 14th century CE. Ink and pigment on parchment. The Walters Art Museum, Baltimore. Museum purchase with funds provided by the W. Alton Jones Foundation Acquisition Fund, 1996.

Mätre Krestos was a fourteenth-century monastic scribe in Tegray, in northern Ethiopia. His illuminations of Eusebius's letter and canon tables occupy 10 pages in his 248-page manuscript. Krestos had access to centuries-old Byzantine manuscripts, and some scholars believe his gospel is based on a sixth-century text that he may have used for reference. Like the earlier Byzantine models, Krestos uses a rounded arch to frame both the letter seen here and the canon tables that follow it. Surrounding the arch and its columns are birds of varying sizes. Birds were a favorite image in Ethiopian manuscripts, referring to the idea that the Holy Spirit took the form of a dove. Birds also appear in Early Christian versions of the Eusebian canon tables, a clear example of the convergence of local Ethiopian artistic preferences with those of early Christianity.

Tunisia

Present-day Tunisia is home to an extraordinarily long history of cultures. Berbers have been the area's inhabitants since prehistory. In the first millennium BCE, they were joined by Phoenicians, who established the ancient city of Carthage in 814 BCE. The Romans followed in the second century BCE, only to fall to the Byzantine Empire in 534 CE. Their leadership gave way to the Islamic conquest, which created the territory of Ifriqiya in the seventh century CE. Ifriqiya fell to the Ottoman Empire in the sixteenth century, the Ottomans fell to the French in 1881, and the French were forced out in 1956. Tunisia today bears both scars and glories from this history, and the Berbers are still a dynamic and powerful population in the area, as they were during and between all of the above political regimes. In 2010, the Tunisian revolution launched the Arab Spring, resulting in the Tunisian people taking the lead role in the movement toward democratic governance across North Africa.

ROMAN RUINS   Rome established its first colony in Tunisia in 146 BCE. Roman colonization of what is today Morocco, Algeria, Tunisia, Libya, and Egypt expanded until 117 CE and lasted intact until the end of the third century CE.

Around 238 CE, the aging Gordian I and his son, Gordian II, assumed dual control over the Roman colony of Africa Proconsularis and ordered the construction of a large **AMPHITHEATER AT EL JEM** (called Thysdrus by the Romans) to replace a smaller structure deemed insufficient (**FIG. 14–9**). The new amphitheater was to hold 35,000 spectators (although it arguably could have held almost double that) and was modeled on the Flavian Amphitheater (the Colosseum) in Rome (SEE FIGS. 6–37, 6–38). It is oval in form, four stories high, and measures 453 feet long by 374 feet wide. While smaller than the Colosseum, it was the largest amphitheater built by Rome on the African continent, and had it been completed, it would have rivaled the Colosseum in grandeur and capabilities.

The amphitheater at El Jem was never completed, however, because Gordian I suffered a military defeat at

14-9 ROMAN AMPHITHEATER AT EL JEM
Tunisia. c. 238 CE (never completed).

After the fall of the Roman Empire in North Africa, the El Jem amphitheater was used as a fortress and citadel by various clashing groups up through the seventeenth century. Damage to the amphitheater from cannon fire is still visible as a result. What remains of the amphitheater is well preserved, and UNESCO named it a World Heritage Site in 2010.

Credit: mrks_v/Fotolia

14–10 Ziadet-Allah I **GREAT MOSQUE OF KAIROUAN**
Tunisia. 836–875 CE.

Credit: Palmenpe/Fotolia

Carthage (the capital of the African colony) one month after assuming office and committed suicide. A rapid succession of Roman leaders came and went for the African colony. The North African chaos was surpassed only by greater chaos elsewhere in the Roman Empire, resulting in the eventual division of the empire into two parts.

ISLAMIC ARCHITECTURE The arrival of Islam in North Africa came as a result of long-standing trade routes along the Silk Road from China to southern Europe and sub-Saharan Africa. As the Middle East converted to follow the teachings of the prophet Muhammad in the seventh century, Arab traders in the region, who largely controlled the Silk Road trade through the Middle East, North Africa, and the western Mediterranean, brought their faith with them into North Africa. As the populations of northern Africa converted to the new religion, the need arose for both small neighborhood mosques (*masjid*) for prayers and large congregational or Friday mosques (*jama masjid*) for communal prayer and celebration.

There are no specific dictates in the Qur'an as to what a mosque must look like, only what it must achieve: a respectful, non-distracting space for prayer and purification. As a result, much religious architecture, whether in Tunisia or elsewhere, follows local architectural styles and material preferences.

The **GREAT MOSQUE OF KAIROUAN** (FIG. **14–10**) sits in the center of the religious city of Kairouan, which was founded in 670 CE by Uqba Ibn Nafi, an Arab general for the Umayyad Caliphate. The mosque was largely constructed between 836 and 875 CE, although it replaced a series of smaller mosques on the site going back to the original built by Uqba Ibn Nafi himself in 670. As it was conceived in 836 by Ziadet-Allah I, then emir of the ruling Aghlabid dynasty in Ifriqiya, the mosque has a hypostyle plan that follows an irregular rectangular format. It is built from local stone quarried and cut to look like bricks. Large arcades form bays and galleries surrounding a central open courtyard; this is derived from what the house of Prophet Muhammad is believed to have looked like in plan.

One of the most unusual features of this mosque is its reuse of marble and porphyry columns from antiquity. Columns in the prayer hall and courtyard are of Roman manufacture and were taken from Carthage and other sites. The columns are topped by capitals that do not always match the columns themselves; they came from various Roman and Byzantine temples that were dismantled during the seventh century. The columns are placed in pairs throughout, supporting the massive round arches of the arcades. Upon first glance, the arches also appear to be Roman in design, but they are actually modified in two substantial ways. Some are slightly pointed at the top, which allowed for the architect to span greater distances at a greater height, and all curve slightly inward at their bases where they meet the capitals of their columns. Each arch therefore looks like the letter C turned on its side: These are known as horseshoe arches. The mosque at Kairouan made the horseshoe arch synonymous with Islamic architecture as it was copied for centuries afterward and around the world. A dome sits on squinches at the *mihrab* wall of the mosque; this feature is both Byzantine and Islamic in origin.

The Great Mosque of Kairouan is the oldest surviving mosque on the African continent, and it bears remarkable witness to ninth-century changes in northern Tunisia. Kairouan was the founding capital city of Ifriqiya and the seat of the Aghlabid dynasty for the entirety of the ninth century. The mosque documents the Islamic victory over Roman and Byzantine empires, because it literally was built from their remains. Yet, at the same time, respect for the architectural traditions of earlier inhabitants of the area is obvious, as great care was taken to preserve the ancient columns and to use the local stone to tie the building to the indigenous history of this sacred site.

West and Central Africa

What are the features of West and Central African arts that reflect the societies and religions that produced them?

Historically, the Western and Central coastal cultures of the African continent have been the most well known to art historians. This is because of their long-standing contact with European nations, beginning during the fifteenth century, at the height of the European Renaissance. Art history and anthropology did not emerge as academic disciplines until the eighteenth century in Europe, as part of the Age of Enlightenment. By then, Europe's connections to West and Central Africa were 300 years old, and the arts of these areas formed the largest part of European art historical and anthropological research inquiries. Prior to the 1960s, in fact, a visit to any European or American art museum would reveal "African art" collections that were primarily the arts of Nigeria, the Ivory Coast, Sierra Leone, the Congo/Angola region, and Gabon. Greater surveys of the larger continent and the arts of northern, eastern, and southern Africa would not come until the end of the twentieth century and are still areas of growth for museum collection and display to this day.

That being said, the arts of West and Central Africa date back to well before the Common Era, and they are as diverse in nature as the cultures that produced them. Aesthetic objects in West and Central Africa served many societal needs: Some were for religious use; some were to honor ancestors and kings; some honored group identity, recorded history or promoted community; and some were for personal adornment and ornamentation. West and Central Africa hosted several of the major early kingdoms and empires on the African continent, including some of the wealthiest in the world during their time.

Mali

One of the first empires established in the territory now known as the Republic of Mali was the Ghana Empire that emerged in the fourth century CE; it ruled a large swath of what is now southern Mali, eastern Senegal, and southern Mauritania (SEE MAP 14-1). In the thirteenth century the Ghana Empire fell to the strengthening Mali Empire, from which the current country claims its name. Yet a third major empire arose here: The Songhai Empire dominated the area in the fifteenth through sixteenth centuries. Together these three empires were among the richest and most powerful the continent has ever known.

Islam had arrived very early in the ninth century due to the trade routes connecting the area to the northern Sahara empires. Rulers of the tenth-century Ghana Empire, as well as those of the subsequent Mali and Songhai empires, embraced the tradition. The cities of Timbuktu, Djenne, Gao, and Kano were early centers of Islamic learning and research in West Africa, roles they still occupy today.

GREAT MOSQUE OF DJENNÉ Archaeologists have determined that the city of Djenné was established by the third century CE, and that by the middle of the ninth century it had become a major urban center. Koi Konboro, the 26th king of Djenné, converted to Islam in the thirteenth century and transformed his palace into a huge mosque built from adobe brick (a sun-dried mixture of clay, mud, and dry fill). With its great surrounding wall and tall towers, locals claimed it was more beautiful and more lavishly decorated than the Kaaba, the central shrine of Islam, at Mecca.

Konboro's mosque eventually attracted the attention of austere Muslim rulers who objected to its sumptuous furnishings. Among these was the early nineteenth-century ruler Sekou Amadou, who destroyed the mosque by plugging the drains built to direct rain away from the fragile adobe surface. A few rainy seasons were all it took to melt the mosque into the ground. In the meantime, Amadou erected a new mosque nearby. But he and his followers were soon forced out of Mali by French colonial leaders, and the local community returned to Konboro's vision of a grand mosque at its original site. The current mosque, constructed between 1906 and 1907, sits on the ancient site and is of adobe construction in the style of the original (**FIG. 14-11**). Architect Ismaila Traoré, the head of

14–11 Ismaila Traoré (lead architect) and the Djenné Mason's Guild **GREAT MOSQUE AT DJENNÉ**
Eastern and northern façades. Mali. 1906–1907 CE.

The plan of the mosque is not quite rectangular. Inside, nine rows of heavy adobe columns, each 33′ (10 m) tall and linked by pointed arches, support a flat ceiling of palm logs, which is covered by adobe slip with raised conical air vents on the roof. A great double wall encloses an open courtyard on the west side (seen at the back right of the image). The main entrances to the men's prayer hall are in the north wall (to the right of the photograph).

Credit: Africanway/Fotolia

the Djenné **guild** (an artisans' organization) of masons, supervised the reconstruction.

The mosque's finials, or crowning ornaments, at the top of each tower are taken from Malian pre-Islamic shrine architecture and are symbols of fertility and purity. The façade and sides of the mosque are distinguished by tall, narrow engaged buttresses, which support the heavy arcades of the interior prayer hall. A significant feature of this mosque, and one incorporated into West African adobe architecture in general, is the **toron**: a wooden beam that projects from the exterior walls. Torons provide permanent supports for the wooden scaffolding erected each year so that the exterior of the mosque can be replastered. In addition they provide aesthetic interest, for they not only produce shadows that striate the surface of the mosque over the course of the day, but also break up the flat austerity of the windowless adobe walls.

CERAMICS   At a site near Djenné known as Djenné-Djenno or Old Jenné, excavations by both archaeologists and looters have uncovered hundreds of terra-cotta figures

dating from the thirteenth to the sixteenth century. The figures were polished, covered with a red clay slip, and fired at a low temperature.

A **HORSEMAN** sculpture armed with a quiver, arrows, and a dagger is a good example of the technique (**FIG. 14-12**). The rider and his horse were formed from coils of rolled clay, which were then smoothed together. The details of the face, clothing, and harness were subsequently carved, engraved, and painted on the figure prior to firing. The rider has a long, oval head and jutting chin; pointed oval eyes set in multiple framing lids; and a long, straight nose. He wears short pants and a helmet with a chinstrap, and his horse has an ornate bridle. Such elaborate trappings suggest that the horseman could be a guardian figure, hero, or even a deified ancestor.

To reduce the illegal looting and trading of these ceramics on the international art market, archaeologists have worked with the Malian government to put strict rules into place preventing them from being exported under any circumstances. Public museums and private collectors are now wrestling with the problem of

14-12 HORSEMAN
From Djenné-Djenno (Old Djenné), Mali. 13th–15th century CE.
Terra cotta, height 27¾″ (70.5 cm). National Museum of African Art,
Smithsonian Institution, Washington, DC. Museum Purchase (86.12.2).

Credit: Photo: Franko Khoury

determining if their Djenné-Djenno ceramics were looted,
bought, or sold illegally, in which case they would need to
be returned to Mali.

Nigeria

Nigeria today is the most populous nation on the continent, with over 181 million people. Perhaps startlingly,
considering its small size relative to other global nations, it
is also the eighth most populous nation in the world. More
than 250 ethnic groups are documented within its borders,
and Nigerians cumulatively speak over 500 indigenous
languages, with Hausa, Yoruba, Igbo (Ibo), and Fulani
being the most widespread.

Historically, the Yoruba (pronounced YOR-u-ba) claim
earliest settlement of the area; it is believed that the Yoruba language in fact goes back to the first millennium BCE.
Small, archaeologically well-known cities such as Nok and
Igbo-Ukwu were also present in the first millennium, but
the Yoruba were the first to organize into a kingdom with
far-reaching power and religious influence. Their capital,

Ife, was founded in the eighth century CE. It was a religious, linguistic, and artistic center from its inception, and
the arts it produced influenced every subsequent society
in the area—in particular, the Edo kingdom (thirteenth
through nineteenth centuries) based at Benin City to the
south of Ife.

ANCIENT NOK   Nok is a small town in the geographic
center of Nigeria. Masterful clay sculptures of humans
have been—and continue to be—found here, as well as in
neighboring regions. Many of the objects were not archaeologically excavated, however, and thus our knowledge of
their creation and function remains very limited. During
the 1950s, local miners digging for tin uncovered hundreds
of broken pieces from ceramic figures of humans and animals. Two types of dating, carbon-14 and thermolumines-
cence, subsequently fixed the ages of the Nok ceramics to
between 800 BCE and 600 CE, with most dating to a briefer
window from about 500 BCE to the very beginning of the
Common Era. These dates make the Nok ceramics some of
the oldest artworks from West Africa.

Nok ceramics range from miniatures to over-life-
size figures, and this head is the latter (**FIG. 14-13**). Most
remains are broken; scholars believe that heads like this

14-13 HEAD
From Nok, Nigeria. 500 BCE–200 CE. Terra cotta, height 14³⁄₁₆″ (36 cm).
National Museum Lagos, Nigeria.

Credit: Werner Forman Archive/National Museum, Lagos, Nigeria. Location: 02.

were originally attached to complete bodies either in wood or ceramic. The triangular or D-shaped eyes are characteristic of Nok style and also appear on sculptures of animals. Holes in the pupils, nostrils, and mouth allowed air to pass freely when the figure was fired.

IGBO-UKWU Located in southern Nigeria, the cultural heartland of the Igbo people, Igbo-Ukwu is one of the oldest archaeological sites in West Africa. To date, only three sites at Igbo-Ukwu have been archaeologically excavated: a burial for an important ruler, a storehouse of valued objects, and a midden (trash pit). These excavations revealed that bronze casting was a developed, specialized, and highly important method of art production in the region from as early as the ninth century. All objects recovered from these excavations are now in important museum collections around the world, foremost among them the National Museum in Lagos, Nigeria.

Like a number of other objects excavated at Igbo-Ukwu, the **ROPED POT ON A STAND** (**FIG. 14-14**) is a **skeuomorph**, an object created in a different material from an original but made to resemble it in form, shape, or texture. Scholars assume that the original item upon which this skeuomorph is based was a water vessel, made in ceramic, tied to a basketry or wooden base. Here, the object is made entirely of leaded bronze. The "rope" is nonfunctional, as the vessel is welded to its base, but its presence is required in order to refer to the original that this object replicates.

The vessel was made during the ninth or tenth century using the lost-wax method, although latex was most likely used instead of wax in this case. When it was found in the 1960s, scholars and artists debated for years whether it had been made from a single mold or cast in parts and soldered together. Microscopic analysis finally revealed that the flaring neck of the vessel (just below the rim) and the lower half of the pot stand were cast separately. Molten metal was then applied to the edges of the separate castings to join them. The knotted rope element was also cast separately and then slid over the vessel before the rim and lower half of the stand were attached to the pot.

Techniques for hammering and plating were known to the artists at Igbo-Ukwu, but they did not use them. Clearly, what was important to the culture at Igbo-Ukwu in the ninth and tenth centuries was to possess a unique, virtuoso style of cast-bronze metalwork that mimicked natural forms.

EDO KINGDOM AT BENIN CITY Benin City is a long-standing royal city in Nigeria. It is not to be confused with the present-day country of Benin (formerly Dahomey), which lies to the west of Nigeria. The population that has inhabited Benin City since at least the tenth century CE speaks Edo. They organized a sophisticated kingdom under the *oba* (king) Ogiso around 900, and a second

14-14 ROPED POT ON A STAND
From Igbo-Ukwu, Nigeria. 9th–10th century CE. Leaded bronze, height 12^{11}⁄$_{16}$" (32.3 cm). National Museum Lagos, Nigeria.

Credit: Photo © Dirk Bakker/Bridgeman Images

powerful dynasty arose under the warrior-king Eweka I in the thirteenth century. Eweka I is credited with bringing Benin City to the height of its power. From the twelfth through nineteenth centuries, in fact, Benin City was an internationally renowned sacred city, as well as the political capital of the Edo Empire. In the fifteenth and sixteenth centuries, three important *oba*, Ewuare, Ozolua, and Esigie, ignited an artistic revival in their capital. Thousands of art objects in cast brass, ivory, wood, and red ocean coral were created during their reigns. Many of the objects remaining to us from Benin City date to these centuries.

New research suggests that Oba Esigie (ruled 1517–1550s) and his son, Oba Orhogbua (ruled 1550s–1570s), commissioned the major group of decorative brass plaques that once adorned columns in the court chamber used by the *oba* and their retinues in the royal palace. The chamber was rectangular, with solid outer walls and a covered arcade supported by rectangular columns. The center of

Technique
LOST-WAX CASTING

In the lost-wax casting process a metal copy is produced from an original image made of wax. The usual metals for this casting process are bronze, an alloy of copper and tin, and brass, an alloy of copper and zinc. First, the sculptor models a wax original. Then the wax is dipped into clay slip and packed with hard clay to make a heat-resistant mold. Next, the wax is melted, leaving an empty cavity into which molten metal is poured. After the metal cools and solidifies, the mold is broken away and the metal copy is chased (trimmed of excess metal) and polished.

The progression of drawings here shows the steps used by the Benin sculptors of Africa. A heat-resistant "core" of clay (A) approximating the shape of the sculpture-to-be (and eventually becoming the hollow inside the sculpture) was covered by a layer of wax that had the thickness of the final sculpture. The sculptor carved or modeled (B) the details in the wax. Rods and a pouring cup made of wax (C) were attached to the model. A thin layer of fine, damp sand was pressed very firmly into the surface of the wax model, and then model, rods, and cup were encased in thick layers of clay (D). When the clay was completely dry, the mold was heated (E) to melt out the wax. The mold was then placed upside down in the ground to receive the molten metal (F). When the metal was completely cool, the outside clay cast and the inside core were broken up and removed (G), leaving the cast-brass sculpture. Details were polished to finish the piece, which could not be duplicated because the mold had been destroyed.

the room was open to the sky. More than 850 brass plaques in two sizes were produced for this chamber using the lost-wax casting method. Wide plaques were hung on the sides of the columns that faced the *oba* as he sat at the end of his audience hall on a dais, as well as on the opposite sides of the columns, where they faced visitors as they entered. A second set of narrow plaques hung on the sides of the columns that faced the side walls of the *oba*'s court, visible to those gathered along the walls to witness the audiences held by the *oba*. In this manner, each

14–15 PALACE PLAQUE OF A WAR CHIEF, WARRIORS, AND ATTENDANTS
Benin City Kingdom, Nigeria. Edo, 17th century CE. Brass, height 14¾ × 15½" (37.5 × 39.4 cm). The Nelson-Atkins Museum of Art, Kansas City, Missouri. Purchase: William Rockhill Nelson Trust (58.3).

of the columns was covered on all four sides, floor to ceiling, with plaques presenting a visual narrative of Esigie and Orhogbua, their courtiers, and the organization of Benin City royal society.

In the plaque seen here a warrior and his attendants are shown in service to the *oba*. The central figures on the plaque are in such high relief that they approach sculpture-in-the-round (**FIG. 14–15**). They are prominently raised from a textured background of foliate patterns representing four-petaled water flowers, the symbol of the water god Olokun, the patron deity of the *oba*.

The plaque uses hierarchical scale, which should not be confused with perspectival distance (in which objects

that are far away are represented as smaller than those that are close to the viewer). The warrior chief is larger in size and in the center of the composition, as he is more important than the figures that accompany him. He holds a spear in one hand and in the other an *eben* sword, a distinctive leaf-shaped sword only used by high-ranked court officials. Two lesser-ranked military officers carrying shields accompany him. Completing the group are a musician who plays a sideblown ivory oliphant (horn) that announces the warrior chief's presence, and an attendant who carries a ceremonial box for conveying gifts to the *oba*.

Another example of the virtuosity of artists in service to the *oba* at Benin City is the ivory **HIP PENDANT OF THE**

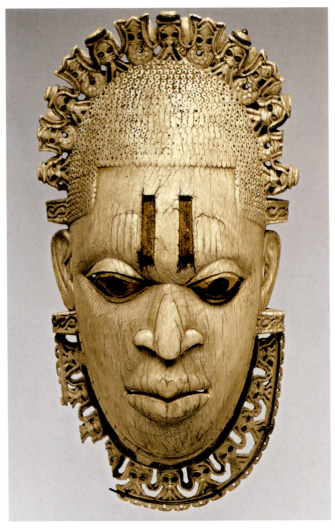

14–16 HIP PENDANT OF THE IYOBA (QUEEN MOTHER) IDIA

Benin City Kingdom, Nigeria. 16th century CE. Ivory, iron, and copper, height 9⅜" (23.8 cm). The Metropolitan Museum of Art, New York. The Michael C. Rockefeller Memorial Collection, Gift of Nelson A. Rockefeller (1978.412.323).

Credit: © 2016. Image copyright The Metropolitan Museum of Art/Art Resource/ Scala, Florence

IYOBA (QUEEN MOTHER) IDIA seen here (**FIG. 14–16**). It is one of two nearly matched ivory hip ornaments made at the same time for the famous Oba Esigie. One is in the Metropolitan Museum of Art in New York, and the other is held by the British Museum in London. Both represent the same woman, Idia, who held the title of *iyoba* (queen mother) while her son, Esigie, was *oba*.

Idia helped to negotiate the end of the war with the neighboring Igala in the early years of Esigie's reign, thus stabilizing the Edo Empire. For her efforts, Esigie created the title of *iyoba* for his mother. Most likely the two ivory pendants were made to commemorate her new status based on her political achievements.

The minutely detailed headdress and neck ruff of the pendant depict Portuguese men, identifiable through their round, European-style hats and long hair and beards. In Idia's headdress, each Portuguese face alternates with a mudfish, a local species of catfish recognizable by its broad flat body, whiskers, and eyes on the top of its head.

The Portuguese were an important symbol in Benin City art. They supplied coral, satin, hats, and other items of value to the *oba*, who in turn provided them with red pepper, metal, animal skins, and eventually ivory and captives to be sold as slaves. The Portuguese therefore became associated with the wealth and power of the *oba*; co-opting their image into the royal arts presented them as subjects to the king and queen mother, clearly under their economic and political control.

The mudfish seen in the ivory sculpture of Idia also signify the power of the *oba*. Mudfish have an extraordinary ability to dig into the mud of riverbanks and go into a state of hibernation during the dry season, waiting to re-emerge until the rains come. Some mudfish also carry an electrical charge. This ability to "defeat" death and electrocute enemies inspired their use as animal symbols for the *oba*.

Hip pendants were generally made of brass or bronze and worn where a man's rectangular cloth wrapper was knotted closed at his waist. In other sixteenth-century artworks from Benin City, we see warrior chiefs and kings wearing face pendants on their hips. Most of these depict kings, leopards, or the queen mother. Only a few ivory hip pendants have been found, making this piece and its partner at the British Museum almost unique in Edo art.

Cameroon

Cameroon is a relatively small country on the continent, roughly the size of Colorado and Utah combined. Yet over 240 languages are spoken there by a population of just under 22 million people. The earliest people in the area were the Bantu, who were skilled agriculturalists. About 2000 BCE, the Bantu migrated south for unknown reasons. They went on, however, to become the most dominant population in Central and Southern Africa.

MOUSGOUM ARCHITECTURE The Mousgoum people have lived in northern Cameroon on the river border between Cameroon and Chad, just south of Lake Chad, since at least the sixteenth or seventeenth century. They are primarily fishermen and farmers and are also very well respected for their architecture. The Mousgoum invented a style of adobe construction in which bricks are stacked in circular arrangements that decrease in diameter with each laid course. This produces a conical dome, or beehive, structure called a teleuk (**FIG. 14–17**).

As the Mousgoum add each subsequent ring of adobe brick to the dome, they cover the exterior of the teleuk in thick clay. The exterior clay is molded into a series of stacked, pointed ridges known as "feet." The tops of the

14–17 MOUSGOUM FAMILY ENCLOSURE WITH TELEUK HOUSES
Northern Cameroon. Adobe. Photo: Ernst M. Heims, 1911, from Adolf Friedrich, *From the Congo to the Niger and the Nile*, 1913.

This building type, as well as the circular arrangement of rooms in the family household, dates back to at least the sixteenth and seventeenth centuries. By the mid twentieth century, many Mousgoum had abandoned teleuk architecture and converted to construction in pre-fabricated cement block. However, in the late 1990s a revival of the style in the region began, with towns building teleukakay (teleuk plural) to serve as public community buildings and tourist centers, and individual families once again began incorporating the teleuk into their homesteads.

Credit: From: *Adolf Friedrich Duke of Mecklenburg, From the Congo to the Niger and the Nile: An account of the German Central African Expedition of 1910-1911*, Volume 1. London: Duckworth & Co, 1913, p.130.

ridges serve as places where the masons can stand as they stack the upper layers of the building. The feet also serve to guide rainwater off the structure during the rainy season, and they cast shadows on the walls' surfaces, reducing the amount of heat the structure absorbs from the sun. Lastly, the feet add aesthetic interest to the teleuk. When French colonial officials and missionaries began documenting Mousgoum buildings in the early twentieth century, they were so taken by the teleuk designs that they copied the style to build the French West African colonial pavilion that was exhibited at the 1931 International Colonial Exposition in Paris.

Teleuk architecture tells us much about Mousgoum society and culture. For example, family homes are constructed out of a circular ring of independent rooms. The two largest rooms house the father of the family and the grain produced by each family's farming activities. The mother of the family and any additional adult female relatives each have their own room, and small children and girls sleep with their mothers. Young men who have not yet established their own families share a room. Mousgoum society is organized around adults mentoring children of their own gender; this is reflected in the organization of family housing.

Republic of the Congo, Democratic Republic of the Congo, and Angola

Some of the biggest kingdoms on the continent were spread across what are now the Republic of the Congo, the Democratic Republic of the Congo, and Angola. The kingdoms of Loango, Kongo, Angola, and Benguela stretched across the coastal region, while inland, the kingdoms of the Luba, Kuba, Lunda, Matamba, and hundreds more existed for centuries. This region is home to some of the most valuable natural resources on earth. Huge copper and tin belts stretch through the region; diamonds, gold, copper, coltan (used in cell phones), lead, zinc, uranium, and more are also mined here.

The Republic of the Congo is the smallest of the three nations, separated from its much larger neighbor, the Democratic Republic of the Congo, by the enormous Congo River. All three of these entities are named for the Kingdom of Kongo, which controlled the region from the fourteenth through nineteenth centuries. The Democratic Republic of the Congo is large enough, in fact, to encompass all of Europe inside its borders, while Angola is about twice the size of Texas. The Bantu from Cameroon migrated to all three countries sometime during the first millennium BCE.

14–18 "THE BANSA, OR RESIDENCE OF THE KING OF KONGO, CALLED SÃO SALVADOR"
View of M'banza Kongo, capital city of the Kongo Kingdom, Angola. Engraving after Olfert Dapper, 17th century CE.

Credit: Thomas Astley, A new general collection of voyages and travels : consisting of the most esteemed relations, which have been hitherto published in any language; comprehending everything remarkable in its kind, in Europe, Asia, Africa, and America. London, 1745-47 [1968]. Volume 3/4, folding plate p.245. Picture Collection, The New York Public Library. Astor, Lenox and Tilden Foundations

Bantu languages are still widely spoken in the region and include Shona, Swahili, Luba, and Kongo. In Bantu languages, noun modifiers are attached to the beginnings of words, not at the end as in English. The prefix "ba-" means people and "ki-" means language. Therefore, it is most correct to state that the Bakongo speak Kikongo, the Bakuba speak Kikuba, and so on. In English usage, however, the prefixes are often dropped in order to avoid confusion.

THE KONGO KINGDOM The Kingdom of Kongo encompassed over 100,000 square miles of present-day northwestern Angola and the western part of the Democratic Republic of the Congo. In the fifteenth century, the capital city M'banza Kongo was the center of major trade networks, all of which were controlled by the Kongo king (**FIG. 14–18**).

Along with items made for trade, artists working for the kings of Kongo excelled at making luxury items for royal use. Textile squares, carved wooden cups, and

14–19 WOVEN AND CUT-PILE TEXTILE
Democratic Republic of the Congo. Kongo, before 1400 CE. Raffia, 18½ × 9½" (47 × 24 cm). Pitt Rivers Museum, University of Oxford, England. (1886.1.254.1).

This textile was dated by the Pitt Rivers Museum using carbon-14 analysis. When the textile first came into the museum's collection in 1886, its earliest documentation was a brief mention in a 1656 catalogue that may or may not have referred to this specific textile. Until carbon-14 dating was used in the twentieth century, this textile could only be dated as a "seventeenth-century" object. Carbon-14 dating proved that the textile was much older and had in fact been made before 1400.

Credit: Photo © Heini Schneebeli/Bridgeman Images

woven hats and garments formed the bulk of this industry. The textile seen here is a rare early example of one such royal item, and would have been highly prized by royal and elite individuals alike (**FIG. 14–19**).

A 1508 account of Kongo textiles by Portuguese sea captain Duarte Pacheco Pereira indicates how much these items were appreciated in Europe: "In the kingdom of the Congo they produce cloths from palm fibers with velvet-like pile of such beauty that better ones are not made in Italy."

Woven of raffia fiber with both raised and plushed bands and embroidered decorations, this small square was most likely made to serve two purposes: a valuable form of currency and a small section of a larger wearable garment.

In the textile's lightest bands, called "streets," the design was achieved by embroidering raffia fibers in a simple whipstitch pattern. The diamond or lozenge shapes, or "blocks," created between the lighter "streets" were embroidered in raffia dyed a darker color. The darkest color on the textile, used to form a border around the "streets," is done in a plush pile technique. Raffia fibers dyed a dark brown are pushed through from the back of the textile and then cut close to the surface to form a velvet-like pile. This gives the textile depth as well as visual contrast.

The primary symbol of the Kongo religion is a cosmogram, a cross shape within a diamond, usually with four circles drawn at each point of the diamond. This cosmogram is visible in the patterns of "streets" on this textile. The cosmogram represents the "Four Moments of the Sun"; the points on the diamond represent sunrise, midday, sunset, and night. These points also represent the four cardinal directions (north, south, east, and west) and four life stages (birth, adulthood, death, and ancestry/rebirth). Royal textiles such as this used cosmogram imagery to stress the kingdom's spirituality and the divine right of its kings to rule.

CHRISTIANITY IN THE KONGO KINGDOM The Kingdom of Kongo's religion surprised fifteenth- and sixteenth-century Portuguese and Dutch traders for its parallels with Christianity, including the cosmogram symbol, which to the Portuguese looked like their orthodox Christian cross. In fact, the Kongo readily assimilated European Christianity into their own religious practice.

In 1491, King Nzinga aNkuwa converted to Christianity, as did his son and successor Afonso I, who established Christianity as the official religion of the Kongo Kingdom. The conversions helped to solidify trade relations with the Portuguese, who had first arrived at M'banza Kongo in 1482. The ensuing trade in copper, salt, ivory, cloth, and, later, enslaved peoples brought increased prosperity to the kingdom.

Due to its shared geometry with the Kongo cosmogram, the crucifix became especially popular as a potent symbol of both Christian conversion and

adherence to traditional political and religious authorities. Cast in solid brass, this example somewhat mirrors a European prototype, but the imagery is restated in Kongolese terms (**FIG. 14–20**).

The features of the crucified Christ, as well as his hands and feet and those of the supporting figures, are stylized according to Kongo tradition. In the biblical telling, two thieves were crucified on either side of Jesus, while his mother Mary and many apostles watched his death. In the Kongo narration seen here, this well-known story is modified so that four of these individuals appear on the same cross as Jesus. The two thieves are depicted as small figures sitting on either side of Jesus's outstretched arms, while Mary kneels at his feet. The topmost figure may be John the Baptist, a saint or apostle, or even God the father. The Kongo artist has made the cross large enough to hold them all—in dramatic distinction from Portuguese depictions of the same subject, which would have been well known to this artist. The four supporting figures all kneel in prayer, which doubles in Kongo symbolism as clapping, a central African gesture of respect for another person.

14–20 CRUCIFIX

From the Democratic Republic of the Congo, Republic of the Congo, or Angola. Kongo, 16th–17th century CE. Solid cast brass, height 10¾" (27.3 cm). Metropolitan Museum of Art, New York. Gift of Ernst Anspach (1999.295.7).

Credit: © 2016. Image copyright The Metropolitan Museum of Art/Art Resource/ Scala, Florence

14–21 SITE OF GREAT ZIMBABWE

Credit: © akg-images/Interfoto

Southern Africa

How do the arts of early societies in Zimbabwe and South Africa transmit information about their societies and community structures?

Southern Africa is the traditional home of the San and Khoekhoe peoples and their ancestors. These groups were mobile and pastoral, herding their livestock across the vast savannas of the region. Encroached upon by the Bantu migrations from the north, the San and Khoekhoe were joined (and largely displaced) by the Zulu, Shona, Xhosa, and others. As we have seen, the region is famous for its rock art. It is also home to sites of architectural and artistic importance.

Zimbabwe

Known best for its national parks and safari excursions, Zimbabwe is the homeland of the Shona peoples. The country takes its name from the archaeological site of Great Zimbabwe, an early Shona kingdom that rose to prominence based on its trade networks with Arab merchants traversing the Indian Ocean.

GREAT ZIMBABWE At its height in the fourteenth century, **GREAT ZIMBABWE** is believed to have been a city of over 10,000 people, with the Great Enclosure serving as its religious and/or administrative hub (**FIG. 14-21**). The city was an important commercial center for the East African gold trade as well as commerce with Swahili traders along the coast. When Great Zimbabwe and its surrounding area were excavated in the early twentieth century, a large cache of goods including Portuguese medallions, Persian pottery from Iran, and even Chinese porcelain were found, testifying to the former extent of its trade.

The current ruins at Great Zimbabwe were originally three related sites. The oldest, known as Hill Ruin, was built on the top of a hill around 1250 CE. It sits atop a natural cave that has the unique feature of amplifying sound made from within it directly out and down to the valley below. About a century later, a second construction known as the Great Enclosure (c. 1350–1450 CE) was begun in the valley. The Great Enclosure consists of a 32-foot exterior wall with smaller concentric walls and solid stone tower structures inside. The third section of Great Zimbabwe, the Valley Ruins, is where the trade objects were found.

The exterior walls at the Great Enclosure were made from even, smoothly finished courses (rows) of locally quarried granite. The stones are carved to fit together so precisely that no mortar was needed to hold the walls together. The walls are still remarkably stable and have eroded very little over time. Near the top of the exterior wall, two rows of granite stones were carved in a double row of chevrons (diamond patterns), part of which is still visible at the ruins today.

Inside the Great Enclosure are two solid **CONICAL TOWERS**, the larger of which still stands over 30 feet tall (**FIG. 14–22**). Their exact original heights are unknown, but they were taller than the external walls. The larger conical tower is a massive stone construction made of very finely hewn granite. The stones fit together so tightly that

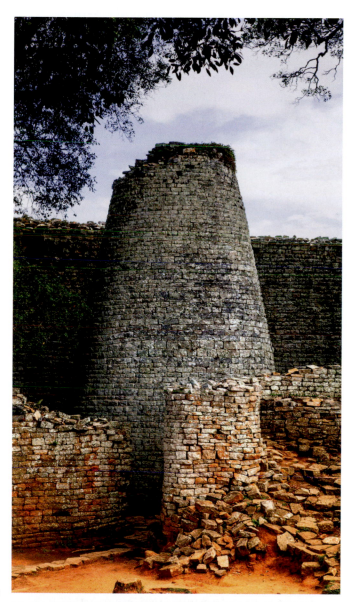

14–22 CONICAL TOWER IN THE GREAT ENCLOSURE
Great Zimbabwe, Zimbabwe. c. 1350–1450 CE. Stone, height 30'
(9.1 m).

Credit: © Lynn Y/Shutterstock

nothing can be slipped in between them; as a result, the tower looks as if it is made out of a solid stone block.

South Africa

When the government of South Africa officially ended the racially motivated segregationist practice of **apartheid** in 1994, the country took to euphemistically calling itself the "Rainbow Nation" based on its existing cultural diversity and its desire to recognize all the peoples that had been disenfranchised under the apartheid political system. While the contemporary dream for equality and freedom in South Africa is still a work in progress, culturally speaking, South Africa has always been a region of incredible artistic diversity.

MAPUNGUBWE HILL The Limpopo River forms South Africa's northeastern border with Zimbabwe and Botswana. The three countries converge where the Shashe River, which separates Zimbabwe and Botswana, joins the Limpopo. At this juncture lies the historical site of the Kingdom of Mapungubwe, which arose around 1220 CE as a regional kingdom. It remained viable only until about 1300, when its power was eclipsed by Great Zimbabwe to its north. It is believed that the inhabitants of the kingdom were Khoe or San peoples who located there due to the abundance of wildlife, including elephants, as well as for the agricultural fertility of the region. We know that trade for ivory was increasing during the period Mapungubwe was inhabited, and given its strategic location at the convergence of two rivers, we can safely understand that part, if not all, of the kingdom's wealth was procured through this trade.

Archaeological excavations determined that elite men and women lived separately from each other, while the general population lived apart from both elite genders. Those with elite status lived higher up on the hillside, while the lower classes were confined to the low-lying areas of the city. Several important burials were discovered in 1932; they have provided us with all the knowledge we have of Mapungubwe, as no other records survive.

In one tomb, archaeologists found a male skeleton assumed to be that of the king, or else an elite ruler. They found many gold objects buried with him, including a small rhinoceros made of gold known as the **MAPUNGUBWE GOLD RHINO** (**FIG. 14–23**). The rhinoceros was not solid gold, but rather gold sheeting that was pounded flat and then molded over a wooden sculpture. A bowl and a short scepter produced in the same technique of gold over wood were also in this grave. The man was buried in a seated position, knees drawn up to his chest, and holding the golden scepter in his hand. So far, more than 20 skeletons have been found at Mapungubwe Hill, three of them being elite burials.

The significance of this short-lived kingdom lies in the fact that it is one of the earliest examples of a kingdom

14–23 MAPUNGUBWE GOLD RHINO
From Mapungubwe Hill excavations, South Africa. 1220–1300 CE. 6 × 1⅝ × 2³⁄₁₆″ (152 × 42 × 55mm). The University of Pretoria, Department of UP Arts: Mapungubwe Collection.

In 2009, the South African post office issued a series of stamps featuring the Gold Rhino and a golden bowl and scepter from the Mapungubwe Hill World Heritage Site to commemorate this early civilization and its history.

and art objects and purchased the services of architects who returned home with him to build extravagant mosques and Islamic schools in Timbuktu. He was undoubtedly not the first king to make such an extensive voyage, however; the documentation of his trip indicates the strength of trade connections across northern Africa that were in place before his time.

East Africa, meanwhile, had been drawn since at least the beginning of the Common Era into the maritime trade that ringed the Indian Ocean and extended east to Indonesia and the South China Sea. Arab, Indian, and Persian ships plied the coastline. A new language, Swahili, evolved from centuries of contact between Arabic-speaking merchants and Bantu-speaking East Africans, and great port cities such as Kilwa, Mombasa, Dar es-Salaam, and Mogadishu arose.

with a stratified societal structure on the continent. It is also one of the first areas where goldsmithing developed in southern Africa. For these reasons, the site was designated as a UNESCO World Heritage Site in 2003.

International Art Trade

Who are the primary trade partners with early African regions and what are the important items of exchange?

Long-distance trade developed in African regions, as it did elsewhere in the world, to take advantage of products and raw materials that were produced in one place and desired in another. Along with agricultural and mercantile goods, items we now consider art moved along trade routes. Regular trade caravans are believed to have been crossing the Sahara Desert since the establishment of dynastic Egypt, and most likely much earlier than that.

North and East Africa

In the medieval period, Arab traders navigated the routes between Europe and sub-Saharan Africa bringing gold, salt, and spices from the kingdoms of Mali, Ghana, and the Songhai to trade partners as far north as the Netherlands. Islamic scholars chronicled these great West African empires, most famously that of Emperor Musa Keita I (known as Mansa Moussa) of Timbuktu, who in 1324 journeyed from Timbuktu in present-day Mali to Alexandria (Egypt) and then to Mecca (Saudi Arabia). He brought an entourage of tens of thousands of people with him and such a fortune in gold that he crashed the gold markets throughout the regions he visited, damage from which they took decades to recover. He traded gold for souvenirs

West and Central Africa

Trade in fine objects between regions in West and Central Africa and European partners began in earnest during the late fifteenth and early sixteenth centuries as a result of Portuguese advances in maritime navigation, which allowed them to navigate down the western coast of Africa, around the Cape of Good Hope, and over to East African port cities on their way to India. Encountering the continent firsthand, they were often astonished by what they found. "Dear King My Brother," wrote a fifteenth-century Portuguese king to his new trading partner, the *oba* (king) of Benin City in West Africa. The Portuguese king's respect was well founded—the Edo Empire at Benin City was vastly wealthier and more powerful than the small European country that had just stumbled upon it.

Benin City was not the only place where Europeans found artistic objects that fascinated them. The kingdoms of West and Central Africa supplied Europeans with the majority of their African art collections from the fifteenth through the nineteenth centuries. Over 800 African art objects brought to Europe between 1400 and 1800 still exist in collections today. Of these, over half originated in West Africa, and 113 came from Central Africa.

A Portuguese sea captain, Valentim Fernandez, commented that artists from Sierra Leone were "very talented in making ivory artifacts such as saltcellars and spoons; whatever sort of object is designed for them, they can carve it in ivory." Two objects of the sort described by Fernandez can be seen here. One is a Sapi-Portuguese **OLIPHANT (HUNTING HORN)**; virtually all its decorative motifs are European-inspired (**FIG. 14–24**). The mouthpiece is at the narrow end rather than on the side, as is typical for African horns. The carvings, including the coat of arms of Portugal and Spain, the motto of Spain's Ferdinand V, heraldic emblems, and hunting scenes, were derived from illustrations found in European prayer books and other publications given to the Sapi artist as source material.

However, not all of the designs found on some export ivories are derived from European sources. For example, the lidded **SALTCELLAR** seen here was also commissioned by a Portuguese individual, who described what he wanted to an artist working in coastal Sierra Leone (**FIG. 14–25**). Ivory saltcellars were popular items on aristocratic dining tables in the fifteenth and sixteenth

14–24 END-BLOWN OLIPHANT (HUNTING HORN)
From Sierra Leone. Bullom or Temne (Sapi) and Portuguese collaboration, late 15th century CE. Ivory and metal, length 25¼" (64.2 cm). National Museum of African Art, Smithsonian Institution, Washington, DC. Gift of Walt Disney World Co., a subsidiary of the Walt Disney Company (2005.6.9).

Credit: Photo: Frank Khoury

14–25 LIDDED SALTCELLAR
From Sierra Leone. Bullom or Temne (Sapi) and Portuguese collaboration, 15th–16th century CE. Ivory, height 11¾" (29.8 cm). Metropolitan Museum of Art, New York. Gift of Paul and Ruth W. Tishman (1991.435a,b).

Credit: © 2016. Image copyright The Metropolitan Museum of Art/Art Resource/Scala, Florence

centuries across Italy, Germany, and France. The round globe at the top is divided into two semispheres; the top one lifts off and table salt is kept in the bowl formed by the lower half. The floral and dot motifs on the top of the cellar display the artist's virtuosity with his chisel. The object is less than a foot tall, so this detail work is very delicate and difficult to achieve at such small scale. The lower half of the vessel is even more impressive. Alternating male and female figures with Sapi facial features and Sapi garments are separated from each other by crouching dogs, which are poised to leap up into the mouths of serpents that descend from a coil at the base of the globe. The serpents even have their tongues sticking out, a detail from nature that would have been sure to impress wealthy European patrons.

Europeans did not come empty-handed to West and Central Africa. They brought items of European

manufacture such as French fabrics, Dutch tableware, tools, and most significantly for the course of history, guns. They also transported items from the Far East to African trade partners. Indonesian batik fabrics and Chinese porcelain proved very popular with African buyers.

Foremost among all of the European goods exchanged in African markets, however, were the glass beads made in Venice, Bohemia, and the Netherlands. Glassmaking technology was widespread in Europe and rare in African nations, making the beads a highly desirable commodity. The bead trade was so extensive that by the mid nineteenth century, manufacturers in Europe were making cards with bead samples and prices on them so that wealthy prospective buyers (primarily kings and chiefs) in Africa could order their beads in advance, ensuring that they would have the newest and most fashionable styles from Europe (**FIG. 14–26**).

14–26 TRADE BEAD CARD
London, c. 1860s CE. Labeled "Beads employed in the African trade for ivory"; used in Ghana for trade with Asante. Group of 133 glass beads mounted on cardboard in 37 strings and 2 singles. British Museum, London. Gift of M. L. Levin (Af1863,0717.1).

Credit: © The Trustees of the British Museum. All rights reserved.

Southern Africa

Coastal South Africans primarily traded with Dutch partners early in the Atlantic trade system, as the Dutch had quickly supplanted the Portuguese in this area. Key goods were food and water needed to restock Dutch ships on their journey home from Indonesia. The Dutch offered metal, alcoholic beverages, and beads in exchange. Trade beads from Europe were also extremely popular elsewhere in southern Africa, and they were widely distributed north from the coast into regions now encompassed by Botswana, Zimbabwe, and Zambia.

As the European trade market grew in scope, Dutch and British populations began to settle in southern Africa, with the result that trade in this area moved away from foodstuffs for ships and toward raw materials (such as diamonds and minerals) that could be sent to Europe in exchange for goods of European manufacture supplied by the British.

By the seventeenth century, labor needs were increasing around the world to support large, European-run plantations producing sugar, cotton, tobacco, and agricultural items for international markets. Horrifically, from the seventeenth through nineteenth centuries, the most valuable and popular commodity traded in European and African exchanges was African people themselves. What had begun in the fifteenth century as a system for exchange of goods to the mutual benefit of Europe and Africa would become a brutal source of incalculable suffering, the repercussions of which are still felt today.

Think About It

1 Animals are often portrayed in a spiritual, rather than naturalistic, manner in prehistoric rock art. Discuss some of the techniques artists used to convey the spiritual qualities of the animals they painted.

2 Even when art objects and monuments were religious in nature, political power was often the means by which they could be produced. Select a religious object or monument from North or East Africa and discuss the role specific political forces played in its creation and history.

3 Give an example of an art object from West or Central Africa that conveys the cultural ideals of its society. What techniques did the artist employ to depict these social and cultural values in the object?

4 How did the architecture at Great Zimbabwe convey the city's political power to its neighbors and rivals?

5 How does studying the international trade of art objects across regions of Africa give us insight into the social, cultural, religious, and artistic desires of each region?

Crosscurrents

When the Kongolese people adopted Christianity in the late fifteenth century, they were interested in European depictions of Christ on the cross, but they did not adopt this imagery wholesale for their own Christian images. Discuss how this Kongolese image of the Crucifixion scene differs from that of the European example. What was important for the Kongolese artist to convey? Which elements does this Crucifixion share with European imagery, and which are new Kongolese innovations?

FIG. 8–22

FIG. 14–20

15–1 CHI RHO IOTA PAGE FROM THE BOOK OF KELLS

Probably made at Iona, Scotland. Late 8th or early 9th century. Oxgall inks and pigments on vellum, 12¾ × 9½″ (32.5 × 24 cm).
The Board of Trinity College, Dublin. MS. 58, fol. 34r.

Credit: © The Board of Trinity College, Dublin, Ireland/Bridgeman Images

Chapter 15
Early Medieval Art in Europe

⌄ Learning Objectives

15.a Identify the visual hallmarks of Early Medieval art for formal, technical, and expressive qualities.

15.b Interpret the meaning of works of Early Medieval art based on their themes, subjects, and symbols.

15.c Relate Early Medieval art and artists to their cultural, economic, and political contexts.

15.d Apply the vocabulary and concepts relevant to Early Medieval art, artists, and art history.

15.e Interpret a work of Early Medieval art using the art historical methods of observation, comparison, and inductive reasoning.

15.f Select visual and textual evidence in various media to support an argument or an interpretation of a work of Early Medieval art.

The explosion of ornament surrounding—almost suffocating—the words on this page from an early medieval manuscript clearly indicates the importance of what is being expressed (**FIG. 15–1**). The large Greek letters *chi rho iota* (*XPI*) abbreviate the word *Christi*, which starts the Latin phrase *Christi autem generatio*. The last word is written out fully and legibly at bottom right, clear of the decorative expanse. These words begin Matthew 1:18 (NRSV): "Now the birth of Jesus the Messiah took place in this way." So what is signaled here—not with a picture of the event, but with an ornamental celebration of its initial mention in the text—is Christ's first appearance within this Gospel book.

Known as the Book of Kells and produced in Ireland or Scotland sometime around the year 800, the lavish book not only contains the four biblical accounts of Christ's life; it would also have evoked Christ's presence on the altar of the monastery church where it was once housed. It is precisely the sort of ceremonial book carried in the hands of a deacon in Justinian's procession into San Vitale in Ravenna to begin the liturgy (SEE FIG. 8–8).

There is nothing explicitly Christian about the ornamental motifs on this page celebrating the first mention of the birth of Christ in the Gospels. The swirling spirals and interlaced tangles of stylized animal forms have their roots

in jewelry created by the migrating, so-called barbarian tribes that formed the "other" of the Greco-Roman world. But by this time, this ornamental repertory had been subsumed into the flourishing art of Irish monasteries. Irish monks became as famous for writing and copying books as for their intense spirituality and missionary fervor.

Wealthy, isolated, and undefended, Irish monasteries were easy victims to Viking attacks. In 806, monks fleeing Viking raids on the island of Iona (off the coast of present-day Scotland) established a refuge at Kells on the Irish mainland. They probably brought the Book of Kells with them. It was precious, and its production had entailed lavish expenditure: Four scribes and three major painters worked on it (modern scribes take about a month to complete such a page), 185 calves were slaughtered to make the vellum, and colors for some of its paintings came from as far away as Afghanistan.

Throughout the Middle Ages and across Europe, monasteries were principal centers of art and learning. While prayer and acts of mercy represented their primary vocation, some talented monks and nuns also worked as painters, jewelers, carvers, weavers, and embroiderers. Few, however, could claim a work of art as spectacular as this one.

The Early Middle Ages

***What are the geographical and historical backgrounds
for the early art and architecture of the European
Middle Ages?***

As Roman authority crumbled at the dissolution of the
Western Empire in the fifth century, it was replaced by rule
of people from outside the Romans' cultural orbit whom
the Romans—like the Greeks before them—called "barbarians," since they could only "barble" the Greek or Latin
languages (**MAP 15–1**). Thus far we have seen these "barbarians" as adversaries viewed through Greek and Roman
eyes—the defeated Gauls at Pergamon (SEE FIG. 5–62), the
captives on the Gemma Augustea (SEE FIG. 6–22), or the
enemy beyond the Danube River on Trajan's Column (SEE
FIG. 6–47). But by the fourth century many Germanic tribes
were allies of Rome. In fact, most of Constantine's troops
in the decisive battle with Maxentius at the Milvian Bridge
were Germanic "barbarians."

A century later the situation was entirely different. The
adventures of the Roman princess Galla Placidia, whom
we have already met as a patron of the arts (SEE FIG. 7–20),
bring the situation to life. She had the misfortune to be in
Rome when Alaric and the Visigoths sacked the city in 410
(the emperor and pope were living safely in Ravenna).
Carried off as a prize of war by the Goths, Galla Placidia
had to join their migrations through France and Spain and
eventually married the Gothic king, who was soon murdered. Back in Italy, married and widowed yet again, Galla
Placidia ruled the Western Empire as regent for her son
from 425 to 437/438. She died in 450, thus escaping yet
another sack of Rome, this time by the Vandals, in 455. The
fall of Rome shocked the Christian world, although the
wounds were more psychological than physical. Bishop
Augustine of Hippo (St. Augustine, d. 430) was inspired
to write *The City of God*, a cornerstone of Christian philosophy, as an answer to people who claimed that the Goths
represented the vengeance of the pagan gods on people
who had abandoned them for Christianity.

MAP 15–1 EUROPE OF THE EARLY MIDDLE AGES

This map shows the routes taken by the groups of people who migrated into and through the Western Roman world at the dawn of the Middle
Ages. Modern country names have been used here for convenience, but at this time, these countries as we know them did not yet exist.

Art and its Contexts

DEFINING THE MIDDLE AGES

The roughly 1,000 years of European history between the dissolution of the Western Roman Empire during the fifth century and the Florentine Renaissance in the fifteenth century are generally referred to as the Middle Ages, or the medieval period. These terms reflect the view of Renaissance humanists who regarded the period that preceded theirs as a "dark age" of ignorance, decline, and barbarism separating their own "golden age" from the golden ages of ancient Greece and Rome. Although scholars now acknowledge the ridiculousness of this self-serving formulation and recognize the millennium of the "Middle Ages" as a period

of great richness, complexity, creativity, and innovation, the term has endured.

Art historians commonly divide the Middle Ages into three periods: early medieval (ending c. 1000), Romanesque (eleventh and twelfth centuries), and Gothic (beginning in the mid twelfth and extending into the fifteenth century). In this chapter we can look at only a few of the many cultures that flourished during the early medieval period. For convenience, we will use modern geographic names as familiar points of reference (SEE MAP 15–1), but, in fact, European nations as we know them today did not yet exist.

Who were these people living outside of the Mediterranean orbit? Their wooden architecture has been lost to fire and decay, but their metalwork and its animal and geometric ornament have survived. They were hunters and fishermen, shepherds and farmers, living in villages with a social organization based on extended families and tribal loyalties. They engaged in pottery, weaving, and woodwork, and they fashioned metals into weapons, tools, and jewelry.

The Celts controlled most of western Europe (see "The Celts" in Chapter 5 on page 152), and the Germanic people—Goths and others—lived around the Baltic Sea. Increasing population evidently forced the Goths to begin to move south into better lands and climate around the Mediterranean and Black Sea, but the Romans had extended the borders of their empire across the Rhine and Danube rivers. Seeking the relative security and higher standard of living they saw in the Roman Empire, the Germanic people crossed the borders and settled within the Roman world.

The tempo of migration speeded up in the fifth century when the Huns from Central Asia swept down on western Europe; the Ostrogoths (Eastern Goths) moved into Italy and deposed the last Western Roman emperor in 476; the Visigoths (Western Goths) ended their wanderings in Spain; the Burgundians settled in Switzerland and eastern France; the Franks in Germany, France, and Belgium; and the Vandals crossed over into Africa, making Carthage their headquarters before circling back to Italy, sacking Rome in 455.

As these "barbarian" groups gradually converted to Christianity, the Church served to unify Europe's heterogeneous population. As early as 345, the Goths adopted Arian Christianity, beliefs considered heretical by the Church in Rome. (Arian Christians did not believe that Christ was divine or co-equal with God the Father.) Not until 589 did they accept Roman Christianity. But the

Franks under Clovis (ruled 481–511), influenced by his Burgundian wife Clotilda, converted to Roman Christianity in 496, beginning a fruitful alliance between French rulers and the popes. Kings and nobles defended the claims of the Roman Church, and the pope, in turn, validated their authority. As its wealth and influence increased throughout Europe, the Church emerged as the principal patron of the arts, commissioning buildings and liturgical equipment including altars, altar vessels, crosses, candlesticks, containers for the remains of saints (reliquaries), vestments (ritual garments), images of Christian symbols and stories, and copies of sacred texts.

"Barbarians" in Europe

What characterizes the metalworking traditions of migrating people from the east who settled in the former territory of the Western Roman Empire?

Weaving a rich fabric of themes and styles originating from inside and out of the empire, from pagan and Christian beliefs, and from urban and rural settlements, new artistic styles were born across Europe as people migrated from the east to settle within the former Western Roman Empire. Many of the "barbarian" groups were superb metalworkers and created magnificent, colorful jewelry with precious metals and inlays of gems. Most of the motifs were geometric or highly abstracted natural forms.

The Merovingians

Among the "barbarian" people who moved into the Western Roman world during the fifth century were the Franks, migrating westward from what is now Belgium and settling in the northern part of Roman Gaul (present-day France). There they were soon ruled by a succession of leaders from a dynasty named "Merovingian" after its legendary founder, Merovech. The Merovingians established a powerful kingdom during the reigns of Childeric I (ruled c. 457–481) and his son Clovis I, whose conversion to Christianity in 496 connected the Franks to the larger European world through an ecclesiastical network of communication and affiliation.

Some early illuminated books (books that include not only text but also pictures and decoration in color and gold) have been associated with the dynasty, but our knowledge of Merovingian art is based primarily on the jewelry that has been uncovered in the graves of kings, queens, and aristocrats, indicating that both men and women expressed their wealth in death as presumably in life by wearing earrings, necklaces, finger rings, bracelets, and weighty leather belts from which they suspended even more metalwork. One of the most spectacular royal tombs was that of Queen Arnegunde, unearthed during

excavations in 1959 at the Abbey of Saint-Denis, near Paris, which was a significant center of Merovingian patronage.

Arnegunde was discovered within a stone sarcophagus that had been undisturbed since her burial in c. 580–590. From her bodily remains, archaeologists determined that she was slight and blond, 5 feet tall, and about 70 years old at the time of her death. The inscription of her name on a gold ring on her left thumb provided the first clue to her identity, and her royal pedigree was confirmed by the sumptuousness of her clothing. She wore a short, purple silk tunic cinched at the waist by a substantial leather belt from which hung ornamental metalwork. Her stockings were supported by leather garters with silver strap tongues and dangling ornaments. Over this ensemble was a dark red gown embroidered in gold thread. This overgarment was open at the front, but clasped at neck and waist by round brooches and a massive buckle (**FIG. 15–2**).

15–2 JEWELRY OF QUEEN ARNEGUNDE
Discovered in her tomb, excavated at the Abbey of Saint-Denis, Paris. Burial c. 580–590. Gold, silver, garnets, and glass beads; length of pin 10⅜″ (26.4 cm). Musée des Antiquités Nationales, Saint-Germain-en-Laye, France.

Credit: Photo © RMN/Jean-Gilles Berizzi

These impressive objects were made by casting their general shape in two-piece molds, refining and **chasing** them with tools, and inlaying cut garnets to provide color and sparkle. Not long after Arnegunde's interment, Merovingian royalty ceased the practice of burying such precious items with the dead—encouraged by the Church to donate them instead to religious institutions in honor of the saints—but we are fortunate to have a few early examples that presumably document the way these royal figures presented themselves on state occasions.

The Norse

In Scandinavia (present-day Denmark, Norway, and Sweden), which was never part of the Roman Empire, people spoke variants of the Norse language and shared a mythology with other Germanic peoples. Scandinavian artists had exhibited a fondness for abstract patterning since early prehistoric times. During the first millennium BCE, trade, warfare, and migration had brought a variety of jewelry, coins, textiles, and other portable items into northern Europe, where artists incorporated the solar disks and stylized animals on these objects into their already rich artistic vocabulary.

By the fifth century CE, the so-called **animal style** dominated the arts, resulting in an impressive array of serpents, four-legged beasts, and squat human figures. The **GUMMERSMARK BROOCH** (**FIG. 15–3**), for example, is a large silver-gilt pin from Denmark, dating from the sixth century. Its elegant ornament consists of a large, rectangular panel connected by an arched bow to a medallion-like plate covering the pin's catch. The surface of the pin seethes with human, animal, and geometric forms. An eye-and-beak motif frames the rectangular panel, a man is compressed between dragons just below the bow, and a pair of monster heads and crouching dogs with spiraling tongues frame the covering of the catch.

Certain underlying principles govern animal-style design: The compositions are generally symmetrical, and artists depict animals in their entirety either in profile or from above. Ribs and spinal columns are exposed as if they had been x-rayed; hip and shoulder joints are pear-shape; tongues and jaws extend and curl; and legs end in large claws.

The northern jewelers carefully crafted their molds to produce a glittering surface on the cast metal, turning a process intended to speed production into an art form of great refinement.

Celts and Anglo-Saxons in Britain

After the Romans departed Britain at the beginning of the fifth century, Angles and Saxons from Germany and the Low Countries (present-day Belgium and Holland)

15–3 GUMMERSMARK BROOCH

Denmark. 6th century. Silver gilt, height 5¾" (14.6 cm). National Museum, Copenhagen.

Credit: Photo: Kit Weiss

and Jutes from Denmark crossed the sea to southeastern Britain. Gradually they extended their control northwest across the island. Over the next 200 years, the arts experienced a spectacular efflorescence. A fusion of Celtic, Roman, Germanic, and Norse cultures generated a new style of art, sometimes known as Hiberno-Saxon (from Hibernia, the Roman name for Ireland). Anglo-Saxon literature is filled with references to sumptuous jewelry and weapons made of or decorated with gold and silver. Some of these objects—Celtic and Scandinavian, as well as Anglo-Saxon—have survived.

The Anglo-Saxon epic *Beowulf*, composed as early as the seventh century, describes its hero's burial with a hoard of treasure in a grave mound near the sea. Such a burial site was discovered near the North Sea coast in Suffolk at a site called Sutton Hoo (*hoo* means "hill"). The grave's occupant

15-4 HINGED CLASP, FROM THE SUTTON HOO BURIAL SHIP

Suffolk, England. First half of 7th century. Gold plaques with granulation and inlays of garnet and checked millefiori glass, length 5″ (12.7 cm). British Museum, London.

Credit: © The Trustees of the British Museum. All rights reserved.

had been buried in a ship—90 feet long and designed for rowing, not sailing—whose traces in the earth were recovered by careful excavators. The wood and the hero's body had disintegrated, and no inscriptions record his name. He has sometimes been identified with the ruler Raedwald, who died about 625. Whoever he was, the treasures buried with him prove that he was a wealthy and powerful man. They include weapons, armor, other equipment to provide for the ruler's afterlife, and many luxury items. The objects from Sutton Hoo represent the broad multicultural heritage characterizing the British Isles at this time: Celtic, Scandinavian, and classical Roman, as well as Anglo-Saxon. There was even a Byzantine silver bowl.

One of the most exquisite finds was a gold clasp that once secured the leather body armor of its owner over his shoulder (**FIG. 15-4**). The two sides of the clasp—almost identical in design—would have been connected when a long gold pin, attached to one half by a delicate

RECOVERING THE PAST
SUTTON HOO

The story of the excavation of Sutton Hoo—unquestionably one of the most important archaeological discoveries in Britain—begins with Edith May Pretty, who decided late in her life to explore the burial mounds that were located on her estate in southeast Suffolk, securing the services of a local amateur archaeologist, Basil Brown. Excavations began in 1938 as a collaborative effort between the two of them, and in the following year they encountered the famous ship burial. As rumors spread of the importance of the find, its excavation was gradually taken over by renowned experts and archaeologists who moved from the remains of the ship to the treasures of the burial chamber for which Sutton Hoo is most famous. Police officers were posted to guard the site, and the treasures were sent for safekeeping to the British Museum in London, although, since Sutton Hoo was determined not to be "Treasure Trove" (buried objects meant to be retrieved by their original owners and now considered property of the Crown—see Chapter 6), it was Pretty's legal property. She, however, decided to donate the entire contents of the burial mound to the British Museum.

Excavation of Sutton Hoo was interrupted by World War II, but in 1945 Rupert Bruce-Mitford of the British Museum began a scholarly study of its treasures that would become his life's work. He not only subjected each piece to detailed scrutiny, but also proposed reconstructions of objects that were only partially preserved, such as the harp, helmet, and drinking horns. Using evidence that had been gathered in a famous murder case, he proposed that Sutton Hoo was actually a burial despite no human remains having ever been found, since they could have disappeared completely in the notably acidic soil of the mound. Other scholars used radiocarbon dating of timber fragments and close analysis of coins to focus the dating of the burial to c. 625, which happened to coincide with the death date of King Raedwald of East Anglia, the most popular candidate for the identity of the person buried at Sutton Hoo.

After heated discussions and considerable controversy, new excavations were carried out in the area around Sutton Hoo during the 1980s and 1990s. These revealed a series of other discoveries in what emerged as an important early medieval burial ground and proved that the area had been inhabited since the Neolithic period—but they uncovered nothing to rival the collection of treasures at Sutton Hoo.

but strong gold chain, was inserted through a series of aligned channels on the back side of the inner edge of each. The superb decoration of this work was created with thin pieces of garnet and blue-checkered glass (known as **millefiori**, from the Italian for "a thousand flowers") cut into precisely stepped geometric shapes and sinuous animal forms. The cut shapes were then inserted into channels and supplemented by granulation (the use of minute granules of gold fused to the surface; see also "Aegean Metalworking," page 93). Under the geometric pieces that form a rectangular patterned field on each side, jewelers placed gold foil stamped with incised motifs that reflect light back up through the transparent garnet to spectacular effect. Around these carpetlike rectangles are borders of interlacing snakes, and in the curving compartments to the outside stand pairs of semitransparent, overlapping boars stylized in ways that reflect the traditions of Scandinavian jewelry. Their curly tails overlap their rumps at the outer edges on each side of the clasp and connect through visible vertebrae along the arched backs to heads with floppy ears and extended tusks. Boars represented strength and bravery, important virtues in warlike Anglo-Saxon society.

The Early Christian Art of the British Isles

How do stylistic aspects of "barbarian" metalworking traditions continue in the Early Christian art of the British Isles?

Although the Anglo-Saxons who settled in Britain had their own gods and myths, Christianity survived. Monasteries flourished in the Celtic north and west, and

Christians from Ireland founded influential missions in Scotland and northern England. Cut off from Rome, these Celtic Christians developed their own liturgical practices, calendar, and distinctive artistic traditions. Then, in 597, Pope Gregory the Great (pontificate 590–604) dispatched missionaries from Rome to the Anglo-Saxon king Ethelbert of Kent, whose Christian wife, Bertha, was sympathetic to their cause. The head of this successful mission, the monk Augustine (St. Augustine of Canterbury, d. 604), became the first archbishop of Canterbury in 601. The Roman Christian authorities and the Irish monasteries, although allied in the effort to Christianize Britain, came into conflict over their divergent practices. The Roman Church eventually triumphed, but local traditions continued to influence British Christian art.

Illustrated Books

Among the richest surviving artworks of the period are lavishly decorated Gospel books, essential not only for spiritual and liturgical life within established monasteries, but also for the missionary activities of the Church, since a Gospel book was required in each new foundation. Often bound in gold and jeweled covers, they were placed on church altars, carried in processions, and even thought to protect parishioners from enemies, predators, diseases, and other misfortunes. The sumptuous books were produced by monks in local monastic workshops called scriptoria (see "The Medieval Scriptorium" below).

THE BOOK OF DURROW   One of the earliest surviving decorated Gospels of the period is the **BOOK OF DURROW**, dating to the second half of the seventh century (**FIG. 15–5**). The book's format reflects Roman Christian models, but its

Art and its Contexts

THE MEDIEVAL SCRIPTORIUM

Today books are made with computer software that can lay out pages, set type, and insert and prepare illustrations—and modern presses can produce hundreds of thousands of identical copies in full color. In medieval Europe, however, before the invention of printing from movable type in the mid-1400s, books were made by hand, one at a time. Each one was a time-consuming and expensive undertaking, and no two were exactly the same.

At first, medieval books were usually made by monks and nuns in a workshop called a scriptorium (plural, scriptoria) within the monastery. As the demand for books increased, rulers set up palace workshops employing both religious and lay scribes and artists, supervised by scholars. Books were written on carefully prepared animal skin—either vellum, which was fine

and soft, or parchment, which was heavier and shinier. Ink and water-based paints required time and experience to prepare, and many pigments—particularly blues and greens—were derived from costly semiprecious stones. In very rich books, artists also used gold leaf or gold paint.

Work on a book was often divided between scribes, who copied the text, and artists, who painted or drew illustrations, large initial letters, and other decorations. Occasionally, scribes and artists signed and dated their work on the last page, in what was called the **colophon**. One scribe even took the opportunity to warn: "O reader, turn the leaves gently, and keep your fingers away from the letters, for, as the hailstorm ruins the harvest of the land, so does the injurious reader destroy the book and the writing" (cited in Dodwell, p. 247).

15–5 SYMBOL OF THE EVANGELIST MATTHEW, GOSPEL BOOK OF DURROW

Page from the Gospel of Matthew. Probably made at Iona, Scotland, or in northern England. Second half of 7th century. Ink and tempera on parchment, $9\frac{5}{8} \times 6\frac{1}{8}''$ (24.4 × 15.5 cm). Trinity College, Dublin. MS. 57, fol. 21v.

Credit: © The Board of Trinity College, Dublin, Ireland/Bridgeman Images

paintings are an encyclopedia of Hiberno-Saxon design. Each of the four Gospels is introduced by a three-part decorative sequence: a page with the symbol of its evangelist author, followed by a page of pure ornament, and finally elaborate decoration highlighting the initial words of the text (the *incipit*).

The Gospel of Matthew is preceded by his symbol, the man, which demonstrates a great difference from the way humans were represented in the Greco-Roman tradition. The armless body is formed of a colorful checkered pattern recalling the rectangular panels of the Sutton Hoo clasp (SEE FIG. 15–4). Set on the body's rounded shoulders, a schematic, symmetrical, frontal face stares directly out at the viewer, and the tiny feet that emerge at its other end are seen from a contrasting profile view, as if to deny any hint of lifelike form or earth-based spatial placement. Equally prominent is the bold band of complicated but coherent interlacing ornament that borders the figure's field.

THE LINDISFARNE GOSPEL BOOK The **LINDISFARNE GOSPEL BOOK** (FIG. 15–6) is one of the most extraordinary manuscripts ever created, admired for the astonishing beauty of its words and pictures, but also notable for the wealth of information we have about its history. Two and a half centuries after it was made, a priest named Aldred added a colophon to the book, outlining with rare precision its history, as he knew it—that it had been written by Eadfrith, bishop of the island of Lindisfarne (698–721), and bound by Ethelwald, his successor. Producing this stupendous work of art was an expensive and laborious proposition—requiring 300 calfskins to make the vellum and pigments imported from as far away as the Himalayas for the decoration. Preliminary outlines were made for each of the pictures using compasses, dividers, straight edges, and sharp points of silver or lead—forerunner to our pencils.

The full pages of ornament set within cross-shape frameworks are breathtakingly complex visual puzzles that require patient and extended viewing. Hybrid animal

15–6 CARPET PAGE, LINDISFARNE GOSPEL BOOK

Lindisfarne, England. c. 715–720. Ink and tempera on vellum, $13\frac{3}{8} \times 9\frac{7}{16}''$ (34 × 24 cm). The British Library, London. Cotton MS.

Credit: © The British Library Board (Cotton Nero D. IV, f.26v)

15-7 PAGE WITH THE BEGINNING OF THE TEXT OF MATTHEW'S GOSPEL, LINDISFARNE GOSPEL BOOK

Lindisfarne. c. 715–720. Ink and tempera on vellum, 13⅜ × 9⁷⁄₁₆″ (34 × 24 cm). The British Library, London.

The words written in the right margin, just beside the frame, are an Old English gloss translating the Latin text, added here in the middle of the tenth century by the same Aldred who added the colophon. They represent the earliest surviving English text of the Gospels.

Credit: © The British Library Board (Cotton Nero D. IV, f.27)

forms tangle in acrobatic interlacing, disciplined by strict symmetry and sharp framing. Some have speculated that members of the religious community at Lindisfarne might have deciphered the patterns as a spiritual exercise.

This book was carried in processions and displayed on the altar, not shelved in a library to be consulted as a part of intellectual life. The text is heavily ornamented and abbreviated, making it difficult to read. The words that begin the Gospel of Matthew (**FIG. 15-7**)—*Liber generationis ihu xpi filii david filii abraham* ("The book of the generation of Jesus Christ, son of David, son of Abraham")—are jammed together, even stacked on top of each other. They are also surrounded by a proliferation of decorative forms deriving from barbarian visual traditions, which we have already seen moving from jewelry into books in the Book of Durrow (SEE FIG. 15–5) and the Book of Kells (SEE FIG. 15–1).

But the paintings in the Lindisfarne Gospels document more than the developing sophistication of an abstract artistic tradition. Instead of beginning each Gospel with a symbol of its author, the designer of this book introduced portraits of the evangelists writing their texts, drawing on a Roman tradition (**FIG. 15-8**). The monastic library at Wearmouth-Jarrow, near Lindisfarne, had a collection of Roman books, and an author portrait in one of them seems to have provided the model for an artist there to portray **EZRA RESTORING THE SACRED SCRIPTURES** within a huge Bible (**FIG. 15-9**). This painter worked to emulate Greco-Roman illusionistic traditions. Ezra is a modeled, three-dimensional form, sitting on a foreshortened bench and stool drawn in perspective to make them appear to recede into the distance. In the background, the obliquely placed books on the shelves of a cabinet seem to occupy the depth of its interior space.

Judging from the number of details these two portraits share, especially the figures' poses, the artist of the Matthew portrait in the Lindisfarne Gospels worked with the same Roman prototype. But instead of striving to capture the lifelike features of his Roman model, the Lindisfarne artist sought to undermine them. Matthew appears against a blank background. All indications of modeling have been stripped from his clothing to emphasize the decorative pattern and contrasting color created by the drapery folds. By carefully arranging the ornament on the legs of Matthew's bench, the three-dimensional shading and perspective seen in the portrait of Ezra have been suppressed. The footstool has been liberated from its support to float freely on the surface, while still resting under the evangelist's silhouetted feet. Playing freely with an acknowledged and well-understood alien tradition, the painter situates an enigmatic figure in the "background" at upper right behind a gathered drape—suspended from a curtain rod hanging from a screw eye sunk into the upper frame— that is not long enough to conceal the entire figure. Clearly there were important cultural reasons for such divergent reactions to a Mediterranean model—Wearmouth-Jarrow seeking to emphasize its Roman connections and Lindisfarne its indigenous roots. We are extremely fortunate to have two surviving works of art that embody the contrast so clearly.

THE BOOK OF KELLS   This chapter began with a close look at the most celebrated page in the Book of Kells—the page introducing Matthew's account of Jesus's birth (SEE FIG. 15-1). It is a dense thicket of patterns derived from metalworking traditions that embellish—in fact practically overwhelm—the Chi Rho monogram of Christ. The illuminators outlined each letter in the Chi Rho monogram, and then they subdivided the letters into panels filled with interlaced animals and snakes, as well as extraordinary spiral and knot motifs. The spaces

15–8 MATTHEW WRITING HIS GOSPEL, LINDISFARNE GOSPEL BOOK

Lindisfarne. c. 715–720. Ink and tempera on vellum, 13⅜ × 9⁷⁄₁₆″ (34 × 24 cm). The British Library, London.

The identity of the haloed figure peeking from behind the curtain is still a topic of debate. Some see him as Christ confronting us directly around the veil that separated the holy of holies from worshipers in the Jewish Temple; others think he is Moses, holding the closed book of the law that was meant to be seen in contrast to the open book into which Matthew writes his Gospel. Also curious here is the Greek form of "saint" in Matthew's title (*O Agios* or "the holy"), written, however, with letters from the Latin alphabet.

Credit: © The British Library Board (Cotton Nero D. IV, f.25v)

between the letters form a whirling ornamental field dominated by spirals.

In the midst of these abstractions, the painters inserted numerous pictorial and symbolic references to Christ—a fish (the Greek word for "fish," *ichthus*, comprises in its spelling the first letters of Jesus Christ, Son of God, Savior), moths (symbols of rebirth), the cross-inscribed wafer of the Eucharist, and numerous chalices and goblets. In a particularly intriguing image at bottom left, two cats pounce on a pair of mice nibbling the Eucharistic wafer, and two more mice torment the vigilant cats. This may be a metaphor for the struggle between good (cats) and evil (mice) or an acknowledgment of the perennial problem of keeping the sacred Host safe from rodents—or both.

15–9 EZRA RESTORING THE SACRED SCRIPTURES, IN THE BIBLE KNOWN AS THE CODEX AMIATINUS

Wearmouth-Jarrow, England. c. 700–715. Ink and tempera on vellum, 20 × 13½″ (50.5 × 34.3 cm). Biblioteca Medicea Laurenziana, Florence.

This huge manuscript (at over 2,000 pages, it weighs more than 75 pounds) is the earliest surviving complete text of the Bible in the Latin Vulgate translation of St. Jerome.

Credit: © 2016. Photo Scala, Florence - courtesy of the Ministero Beni e Att. Culturali

Irish High Crosses

Metalworking traditions influenced not only manuscript decoration, but also the monumental stone crosses erected in Ireland during the eighth century, called high crosses because of their size. The **SOUTH CROSS** of Ahenny, in County Tipperary, is an especially well-preserved example (**FIG. 15–10**). It seems to have been modeled on metal ceremonial or reliquary crosses, that is, cross-shape containers for holy relics. It is outlined with ropelike, convex moldings and covered with spirals and interlace. The large **bosses** (broochlike projections), which form a cross within this cross, resemble the jewels that were similarly placed on metal crosses. The circle enclosing the arms of high crosses has been interpreted as both a ring of heavenly light and a purely practical means of supporting the projecting arms.

15–10 SOUTH CROSS, AHENNY
County Tipperary, Ireland. 8th century. Sandstone.

Credit: Courtesy of Marilyn Stokstad

The Viking Era

What are the distinctive ornamental styles and enduring timber architectural traditions of the Vikings?

During the eighth century, seafaring bands of Norsemen known as Vikings (*viken*, "people from the coves") descended on the rest of Europe. Setting off in flotillas of as many as 350 ships, they explored, plundered, traded with, and colonized a vast area during the ninth and tenth centuries. The earliest recorded Viking incursions were two devastating attacks on wealthy isolated Christian monasteries: one in 793, on the religious community on Lindisfarne, off the northeast coast of England; and another in 795, at Iona, off Scotland's west coast.

Norwegian and Danish Vikings subsequently raided a vast territory stretching from Iceland and Greenland—where they settled in 870 and 985, respectively—to Ireland,

England, Scotland, and France. The Viking Leif Eriksson reached North America in 1000. In good weather a Viking ship could sail 200 miles in a day. In the early tenth century, the rulers of France bought off Scandinavian raiders (the Normans, or "northmen") with a large grant of land that became the duchy of Normandy. Swedish Vikings turned eastward and traveled down the Russian rivers to the Black Sea and Constantinople, where the Byzantine emperor recruited them to form an elite personal guard. Others, known as Rus, established settlements around Novgorod, one of the earliest cities in what would become Russia. They settled in Kiev in the tenth century and by 988 had become Orthodox Christians (see Chapter 8).

Carving in Wood and Stone

Since prehistoric times northerners had represented their ships as sleek sea serpents, and, as we saw at Sutton Hoo, they used them for burials as well as sea journeys. The ship of a dead warrior symbolized his passage to Valhalla (a legendary great hall that welcomed fallen warriors), and Viking chiefs were sometimes cremated in a ship in the belief that this hastened their journey. Women as well as men were honored by ship burials. A 75-foot-long ship, discovered in Oseberg, Norway, and dated c. 815–820, served as the vessel for two women on their journey to eternity in 834, a queen and her companion or servant. Although the burial chamber was long ago looted of jewelry and precious objects, the ship itself and its equipment attest to the wealth and prominence of its owner. A cart and four sleds, all made of wood with beautifully carved decorations, were stored on board. At least 12 horses, several dogs, and an ox had been sacrificed to accompany the women on their last journey.

The Oseberg ship itself was designed to be propelled by both sail and oars for travel in the relatively calm waters of fjords (narrow coastal inlets), not for voyages in the open sea. The rising prow spirals into a serpent's head, and bands of interlaced animals are carved in low relief along the edges (**FIG. 15-11**). Viking beasts are grotesque, broad-bodied creatures with bulging eyes, short muzzles, snarling mouths, and large teeth and claws. They adorned all sorts of Viking belongings—jewelry, houses, tent poles, beds, wagons, and sleds. Traces of color indicate that the carved wood of this ship was originally painted black, white, red, brown, and yellow.

All women, including the most elite, worked in the fiber arts. The Oseberg queen took her spindles (a frame for braiding), tablets for tablet-weaving, and two upright looms with her to the grave. Her cabin walls had been hung with tapestries, fragments of which survive. Women not only produced woven and embroidered garments and wall hangings, but also wove the huge sails of

15-11 GRIPPING BEASTS, DETAIL OF OSEBERG SHIP

c. 815–820. Wood. Vikingskiphuset, Universitets Oldsaksamling, Oslo, Norway.

Credit: © IAM/akg-images

waterproof unwashed wool that gave Viking ships their long-distance capability. The entire community—men and women—worked to create these ships, which represent the Vikings' most important surviving contribution to world architecture.

PICTURE STONES AT JELLING Both at home and abroad, the Vikings erected large memorial stones. Those covered mostly with inscriptions are called **rune stones** (runes are twiglike letters of an early Germanic alphabet). Those with figural decoration are called picture stones. Traces of pigments suggest that the memorial stones were originally painted in bright colors.

About 980, the Danish king Harald Bluetooth (c. 940–987) ordered a picture stone to be placed near an old, smaller rune stone and the family burial mounds at Jelling (**FIG. 15-12**). Carved in runes on a boulder 8 feet high is the inscription "King Harald had this memorial made for Gorm his father and Thyra his mother: that Harald who won for himself all Denmark and Norway and made the Danes Christians." Harald and the Danes had accepted Christianity in c. 960, but Norway did not become Christian until 1015.

During the tenth century, a new style emerged in Scandinavia and the British Isles, one that combined interlacing foliage and ribbons with animals that are more recognizable than the gripping beasts of the Oseberg ship. On one face of the larger Jelling stone the sculptor carved the image of Christ robed in the Byzantine manner, with arms outstretched as if crucified. He is entangled in a

15-12 ROYAL RUNE STONES, RIGHT-HAND STONE ORDERED BY KING HARALD BLUETOOTH

Jelling, Denmark. 983–985. Granite, 3-sided, height about 8' (2.44 m).

Credit: © Carmen Redondo/Corbis

double-ribbon interlace instead of nailed to a cross. A second side holds runic inscriptions, and a third, a striding creature resembling a lion fighting a snake. The loosely twisting double-ribbon interlace covering the surface of the stone could have been inspired by Hiberno-Saxon art.

Timber Architecture

The vast forests of Scandinavia provided the materials for timber buildings of many kinds. Two forms of timber construction evolved: one that stacked horizontal logs, notched at the ends, to form a rectangular building (the still-popular log cabin); and another that stood the wood on end to form a palisade or vertical plank wall, with timbers set directly in the ground or into a sill (a horizontal beam). More modest buildings consisted of wooden frames filled with wattle-and-daub. Typical buildings had a turf or thatched roof supported on interior posts. The same basic structure was used for almost all building types—feasting and assembly halls, family homes (which were usually shared with domestic animals), workshops, barns, and sheds. The great hall had a central open hearth (smoke escaped through a louver in the roof) and an off-center door designed to reduce drafts. People secured their residences and trading centers by building massive circular earthworks topped with wooden palisades.

THE BORGUND STAVE CHURCH Subject to decay and fire, early timber buildings have largely disappeared, leaving only postholes and other traces in the soil. In rural Norway, however, a few later **stave churches** survive—named for the four huge timbers (staves) that form their structural core. Borgund church (**FIG. 15–13**) has four corner staves supporting the central roof, with additional interior posts

15–13A EXTERIOR OF STAVE CHURCH, BORGUND, NORWAY
c. 1125–1150.

Credit: PHB.cz/Fotolia

15–13B CUTAWAY DRAWING OF STAVE CHURCH, BORGUND, NORWAY
c. 1125–1150.

Credit: Kathy Mrozek

that create the effect of a nave and side aisles, narthex, and **choir** (for the clergy). A rounded apse covered with a timber tower is attached to the choir. Steeply pitched roofs covered with wooden shingles protect the walls—planks slotted into the sills—from the rain and snow. Openwork timber stages set on the roof ridge create a tower and give the church a steep pyramidal shape. On all the gables either crosses or dragon heads protect the church and its congregation from trolls and demons.

The Vikings were not always victorious. Their colonies in Iceland and the Faeroe Islands survived, but in North America their trading posts eventually had to be abandoned. In Europe, south of the Baltic Sea, a new German dynasty challenged and then defeated the Vikings. By the end of the eleventh century the Viking era had come to an end.

Mozarabic Art in Spain

What style emerges from the synthesis of early Christian and Islamic traditions in the Mozarabic manuscripts of early medieval Spain?

In 711, Islamic invaders conquered Spain, ending Visigothic rule. Bypassing the small Christian kingdom of Asturias on the north coast, they crossed the Pyrenees Mountains into France, but in 732 Charles Martel and the Frankish army stopped them before they reached Paris. Islamic rulers remained in the Iberian peninsula (Spain and Portugal) for nearly 800 years, until the fall of Granada to the Christians in 1492.

With some exceptions, Christians and Jews who acknowledged the authority of the Islamic rulers and paid

15–14 Maius **WOMAN CLOTHED WITH THE SUN, THE MORGAN BEATUS**
Monastery of San Salvador at Tábara, León, Spain. 940–945. Tempera on vellum, 15⅛ × 22⅛" (38.5 × 56 cm). The Morgan Library and Museum, New York. MS. M644, fols. 152v–153r.

When the modern abstract French painter Fernand Léger (1881–1955; SEE FIG. 32–21) was visiting the great art historian Meyer Schapiro (1904–1996) in New York during World War II, the artist asked the scholar to suggest the single work of art that was most important for him to see while there. Schapiro took him to the Morgan Library to leaf through this manuscript. The strong impact it had on Léger can be clearly seen in the boldness of his later paintings.

Credit: © 2016. Photo Pierpont Morgan Library/Art Resource/Scala, Florence higher taxes because they were non-Muslims were left free to follow their own religious practices. The Iberian peninsula became a melting pot of cultures in which Muslims, Christians, and Jews lived and worked together, even as they were officially and firmly separated. Christians in the Muslim territories were called Mozarabs (from the Arabic *mustarib*, meaning "would-be Arab"). In an exchange of artistic influences, Christian artists incorporated some features of Islamic art into a colorful new style known as **Mozarabic**. When the Mozarabic communities migrated to northern Spain, which returned to Christian rule not long after the initial Islamic invasion, they took this Mozarabic style with them.

Beatus Manuscripts

One of the most influential books of the early Middle Ages was a Commentary on the Apocalypse compiled during the eighth century by Beatus, abbot of the monastery of San Martín at Liébana in the northern kingdom of Asturias. Beatus described the end of the world and the Last Judgment of the Apocalypse, rooted in the Revelation to John at the end of the New Testament, which vividly describes Christ's final, fiery triumph.

A lavishly illustrated copy of Beatus's Commentary, called the Morgan Beatus, was produced c. 940–945, probably at the monastery of San Salvador at Tábara, by an artist named Maius (d. 968), who both wrote the text and painted the illustrations. His gripping portrayal of the **WOMAN CLOTHED WITH THE SUN**, based on the biblical text of Apocalypse (Revelation) 12:1–18, extends over two pages to cover an entire opening of the book (**FIG. 15-14**). Maius has stayed close to the text in composing his tableau, which is dominated by the long, seven-headed, red dragon that slithers across practically the entire width of the picture to threaten at top left the "woman clothed with the sun, with the moon under her feet, and on her head a crown of twelve stars" (12:1). With his tail, at upper right, he sweeps a third of heaven's stars toward Earth while the woman's male child appears before the throne of God. Maius presents this complex allegory of the triumph of the Church over its enemies with a forceful, abstract, ornamental style that accentuates the nightmarish qualities of the events outlined in the text. The background has been distilled into horizontal strips of color; the figures become striped bundles of drapery capped with faces dominated by staring eyes and silhouetted, framing haloes. Apocalyptic events have been transformed by Maius into exotic abstractions that still maintain their power to captivate.

Another copy of Beatus's Commentary was produced about 30 years later for Abbot Dominicus of San Salvador at Tábara. A colophon identifies Senior as the scribe for this project. Emeterius and a woman named Ende

(or simply En), who signed herself "painter and servant of God," shared the task of illustration. For the first time in the West, a woman artist is identified by name with a specific surviving work of art. In an allegory of the triumph of Christ over Satan (**FIG. 15-15**), the painters show a peacock grasping a red-and-orange snake in its beak. The text explains that a bird with a powerful beak and beautiful plumage (Christ) covers itself with mud to trick the snake (Satan). Just when the snake decides the bird is harmless, the bird swiftly attacks and kills it. "So Christ in his Incarnation clothed himself in the impurity of our [human] flesh that through a pious trick he might fool the evil deceiver.... [W]ith the word of his mouth [he] slew the venomous killer, the devil" (cited in Williams, page 95).

15-15 Emeterius and Ende, with the scribe Senior
BATTLE OF THE BIRD AND THE SERPENT, COMMENTARY ON THE APOCALYPSE BY BEATUS AND COMMENTARY ON DANIEL BY JEROME
Made for Abbot Dominicus, probably at the monastery of San Salvador at Tábara, León, Spain. Completed July 6, 975. Tempera on parchment, 15¾ × 10¼" (40 × 26 cm). Cathedral Library, Gerona, Spain. MS. 7[11], fol. 18v.

Credit: Archivo Fotográfico Oronoz, Madrid

The Carolingian Empire

How do Roman traditions influence the development of art and architecture during the Carolingian Empire?

During the second half of the eighth century, a new force emerged on the Continent. Charlemagne (the French form of Carolus Magnus, Latin for "Charles the Great") established a dynasty and an empire known today as the Carolingian. He descended from a family that had followed the Merovingians in the late seventh century as rulers of the Franks in northern Gaul (parts of present-day France and Germany). Under Charlemagne (ruled 768–814), the Carolingian realm reached its greatest extent, encompassing western Germany, France, the Lombard kingdom in Italy,

15–16 EQUESTRIAN PORTRAIT OF CHARLES THE BALD (?)

9th century. Bronze, height 9½" (24.4 cm). Musée du Louvre, Paris.

Credit: © akg-images /Erich Lessing

and the Low Countries. Charlemagne imposed Christianity throughout this territory, and in 800, Pope Leo III (pontificate 795–816) crowned him emperor in a ceremony in St. Peter's Basilica in Rome, declaring him the rightful successor to Constantine, the first Christian emperor. This endorsement reinforced Charlemagne's authority and strengthened the bonds between the papacy and secular government in the West.

The Carolingian rulers' ascent to the Roman imperium, and the political pretensions it implied, are clearly signaled in a small bronze equestrian statue—once thought to be a portrait of Charlemagne himself but now usually identified with his grandson **CHARLES THE BALD** (FIG. 15–16). The idea of representing an emperor as a proud equestrian figure recalls the much larger image of Marcus Aurelius (SEE FIG. 6–56) that was believed during the Middle Ages to portray Constantine, the first Christian emperor. But unlike the bearded Roman, this Carolingian king sports a mustache, a Frankish sign of nobility that had also been common among the Celts (SEE FIG. 5–62). Works of art such as this are not a slavish mimicking of Roman prototypes, but a creative appropriation of Roman imperial typology to glorify rulers who are clearly Carolingian.

Charlemagne sought to restore the Western Empire as a Christian state and to revive the arts and learning: as inscribed on his official seal, "the Renewal of the Roman Empire." To lead this revival, he turned to Benedictine monks and nuns. By the early Middle Ages, monastic communities had spread across Europe. In the early sixth century, Benedict of Nursia (c. 480–547) wrote his *Rule for Monasteries*, and this set of guidelines for a secluded life of monastic work and prayer became the model for Benedictine monasticism, soon the dominant form throughout Europe. The Benedictines became Charlemagne's "cultural army," and the imperial court at Aachen, Germany, one of the leading intellectual centers of western Europe.

Architecture

To proclaim the glory of the new empire in monumental form, Charlemagne's architects turned for inspiration to two former Western imperial capitals, Rome and Ravenna. Charlemagne's biographer Einhard reported that the ruler "beyond all sacred and venerable places… loved the church of the holy apostle Peter in Rome." Not surprisingly, Constantine's basilica of St. Peter, with its long nave and side aisles ending in a transept and projecting apse (SEE FIG. 7–10A), served as a model for many important churches in Charlemagne's empire. The basilican plan, which had fallen out of favor since the Early Christian period, emerged again as the preferred arrangement of large congregational churches and would remain so throughout the Middle Ages and beyond.

CHARLEMAGNE'S PALACE AT AACHEN Charlemagne's palace complex provides an example of the Carolingian synthesis of Roman, Early Christian, and northern styles. Charlemagne, who enjoyed hunting and swimming, built a headquarters and palace complex amid the forests and natural hot springs of Aachen, in the northern part of his empire, and installed his court there in about 794. The palace complex included a large masonry audience hall and chapel facing each other across a large square (reminiscent of a Roman forum), and a monumental gateway supporting a hall of judgment. Other administrative buildings, a palace school, homes for his advisors and his large family, and workshops supplying all the needs of Church and state were mostly constructed using the wooden building traditions indigenous to this part of Europe.

The **PALACE CHAPEL** (FIG. **15–17**) functioned as Charlemagne's private place of worship, the church of his imperial court, a place for precious relics, and, after the emperor's death, the imperial mausoleum. The central, octagonal plan recalls the church of San Vitale in Ravenna (SEE FIG. 8–5), but the Carolingian architects added a monumental western entrance block. Known as a **westwork**, this structure combined a ground-floor narthex (vestibule) and an upper-story throne room which opened onto the chapel interior, allowing the emperor an unobstructed view of the liturgy at the high altar while assuring his privacy and safety. The room also opened outside into a large walled forecourt where the emperor could make public appearances and speak to assembled crowds.

The soaring core of the chapel is an octagon, surrounded at the ground level by an ambulatory (curving aisle passageway) and on the second floor by a gallery (upper-story passageway overlooking the main space) and rising to a clerestory above the gallery level and

15–17A INTERIOR VIEW, PALACE CHAPEL OF CHARLEMAGNE

Aachen (Aix-la-Chapelle), Germany. 792–805.

Extensive renovations took place here in the nineteenth century, when the chapel was reconsecrated as the cathedral of Aachen, and in the twentieth century, after it was damaged in World War II.

Credit: © Achim Bednorz, Cologne

15–17B SECTION DRAWING, PALACE CHAPEL OF CHARLEMAGNE

Aachen (Aix-la-Chapelle), Germany. 792–805.

Credit: Kathy Mrozek

under the octagonal dome. At the gallery level, two tiers of paired Corinthian columns and railings form a screen that re-emphasizes the flat, pierced walls of the octagon and enhances the clear, planar geometry of its design. The effect is quite different from the dynamic spatial play and undulating exedrae of San Vitale, but the veneer of richly patterned and multicolored stone—some imported from Italy—on the walls and the mosaics covering the dome at Aachen were clearly inspired by Byzantine architecture.

THE WESTWORK AT CORVEY Originally designed to answer practical requirements of protection and display in buildings such as Charlemagne's palace chapel, the soaring, multi-towered westwork came to function as the very visible sign of an important building; it is one of the hallmarks of Carolingian architecture. A particularly well-preserved example is the late ninth-century westwork at the

15–18 WESTWORK, ABBEY CHURCH OF CORVEY
Westphalia, Germany. Late 9th century (upper stories mid 12th century).

Credit: © Achim Bednorz, Cologne

ABBEY CHURCH OF CORVEY (FIG. 15–18). Even discounting the pierced upper story and towers that were added in the middle of the twelfth century, this is a broad and imposing block of masonry construction. The strong, austere exterior is a symmetrical arrangement of towers flanking a central core punched with a regular pattern of windows and doors, free of elaborate carving or decoration. In addition to providing private spaces for local or visiting dignitaries, the interiors of westworks may have been used for choirs—medieval musical graffiti were discovered inside this one—and they were the starting point for important liturgical processions.

THE SAINT GALL PLAN Monastic life centered on prayer and work, and since it also demanded seclusion, it required a special type of architectural planning. While contemplating how best to house a monastic community, Abbot Haito of Reichenau developed, at the request of his colleague Abbot Gozbert of Saint Gall, a conceptual plan for the layout of monasteries. This extraordinary ninth-century drawing survives in the library of the Abbey of Saint Gall in modern Switzerland and is known as the **SAINT GALL PLAN** (FIG. 15–19). This is not a blueprint in the modern sense, intended to guide the construction of an actual monastery, but a record of Carolingian thinking about the nature of monastic life. It does, however, reflect the basic layout of medieval monasteries, an efficient and functional arrangement that continues to be used by Benedictine monasteries today.

At the center of the Saint Gall plan is the **cloister**, an enclosed courtyard onto which open all the buildings that are central to the lives of monks. Most prominent is a large basilican church north of the cloister, with towers and multiple altars in nave and aisles as well as in the sanctuary at the east end, where monks would gather for communal prayer throughout the day and night. On the north side of the church were public buildings such as the abbot's house, the school, and the guesthouse. The monks' living quarters lie off the southern and eastern sides of the cloister, with a dormitory, a refectory (dining room), and work rooms. For night services the monks could enter the church directly from their dormitory. The kitchen, brewery, and bakery were attached to the refectory, and a huge cellar (indicated on the plan by giant barrels) was on the west side. Along the east edge of the plan are a cemetery, a hospital, and an educational center for novices (monks in training).

The Saint Gall plan indicates beds for 77 monks in the dormitory. Practical considerations for group living include latrines attached to every unit—dormitory, guesthouse, and abbot's house. Six beds and places in the refectory were reserved for visiting monks. In the surrounding buildings were special spaces for scribes and painters, who spent much of their day in the scriptorium studying and

15–19 SAINT GALL PLAN (ORIGINAL AND REDRAWN WITH CAPTIONS)

c. 817. Original in red ink on parchment, 28 × 44⅛" (71.1 × 112.1 cm). Stiftsbibliothek, Saint Gall, Switzerland. Cod. Sang. 1092.

Credit: (left) Stiftsbibliothek, St. Gallen; (right) Kathy Mrozek

copying books, and for teachers who staffed the monastery's schools and library. St. Benedict had directed that monks extend hospitality to all visitors, and the plan includes a hospice for the poor. South and west of the central core were workshops, farm buildings, and housing for the lay support staff.

Illustrated Books

Books played a central role in the efforts of Carolingian rulers to promote learning, propagate Christianity, and standardize church law and practice. Imperial workshops produced authoritative copies of key religious texts, weeding out the errors that had inevitably crept into books over centuries of copying them by hand. The scrupulously edited versions of ancient and biblical texts that emerged are among the lasting achievements of the Carolingian period. For example, the Anglo-Saxon scholar Alcuin of York, whom Charlemagne called to his court, spent the last eight years of his life producing a corrected copy of the Latin Vulgate Bible. His revision served as the standard text of the Bible for the remainder of the medieval period and is still in use.

Carolingian scribes also worked on standardizing script. Capitals (majuscules) based on ancient Roman inscriptions continued to be used for very formal writing, titles and headings, and luxury manuscripts. But they also developed a new, clear script called Carolingian minuscule, based on Roman forms but with a uniform lowercase alphabet that increased legibility and streamlined production. So, like those who transformed other revived Roman types—such as basilicas, central-plan churches, and equestrian Roman portraits—into creative new works, scribes and illuminators revitalized established traditions of book production. Notably, they returned the representation of lifelike human figures to a central position. For example, portraits of the evangelists (the authors of the Gospels) began to look like pictures of Roman authors.

As can be seen in a comparison of the author portraits in two Carolingian Gospel books, however, a common source in the Roman tradition did not preclude considerable variation in both style and expressive content.

15–20 PAGE WITH ST. MATTHEW THE EVANGELIST, CORONATION GOSPELS

Gospel of Matthew. Early 9th century. 12¾ × 9¹³⁄₁₆″ (32.4 × 24.9 cm). Kunsthistorisches Museum, Vienna. Inv.Nr. SK XIII 18, folio 15r

Tradition holds that this Gospel book was buried with Charlemagne in 814, and that in the year 1000 Emperor Otto III removed it from his tomb. Its title derives from its use in the coronation ceremonies of later German emperors.

Credit: © KHM-Museumsverband

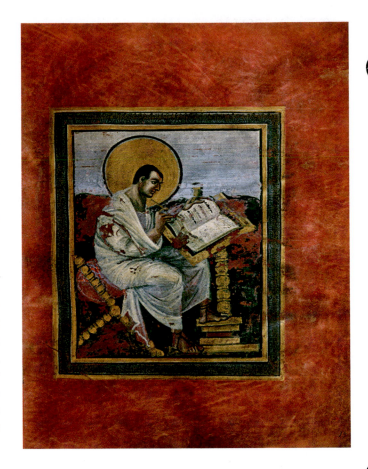

THE CORONATION GOSPELS   The portrait of Matthew (**FIG. 15–20**) in the early ninth-century **CORONATION GOSPELS** of Charlemagne conforms to the idealized, life-like representation of the Greco-Roman Classical tradition. The full-bodied, white-robed figure is modeled in brilliant white and subtle shading and seated on the cushion of a folding chair set within a freely painted landscape. The way his foot lifts up to rest on the solid base of his writing desk emphasizes his three-dimensional placement within an outdoor setting, and the frame enhances the Classical effect of a view seen through a window. Conventions for creating the illusion of solid figures in space may have been learned from Byzantine manuscripts in a monastic library or from artists fleeing Byzantium as a result of the iconoclastic controversy (see Chapter 8).

15–21 PAGE WITH ST. MATTHEW THE EVANGELIST, EBBO GOSPELS

Gospel of Matthew. Second quarter of 9th century. Ink, gold, and colors on vellum, each page 10¼ × 8¾″ (26 × 22.2 cm). Médiathèque d'Épernay, France. MS. 1, fol. 18v.

THE EBBO GOSPELS One of the most innovative and engaging Carolingian variations on Greco-Roman tradition is a Gospel book made for Archbishop Ebbo of Reims (archbishop 816–835, 840–841) at the nearby Abbey of Hautvillers (**FIG. 15-21**). The calm, carefully painted grandeur characterizing Matthew's portrait in the Coronation Gospels (SEE FIG. 15-20) has given way to spontaneous, calligraphic painting suffused with energetic abandon. The passion is apparent in the intensity of Matthew's gaze, but the whole composition is charged with energy, from the evangelist's wiry hairdo and rippling drapery to the rapidly sketched landscape and the windblown acanthus leaves of the frame. These forms are related to content, evoking the evangelist's spiritual excitement as he hastens to transcribe the Word of God delivered by the angel (also serving as Matthew's symbol), who is almost lost in the upper right corner. As if swept up in the saint's turbulent emotions, the footstool tilts precariously and the top of the desk seems about to detach itself from the pedestal.

THE UTRECHT PSALTER One of the most famous Carolingian manuscripts, the Utrecht Psalter (**FIG. 15-22**), is illustrated with ink drawings that match the linear vitality encountered in Ebbo's Gospel book. Psalms do not tell straightforward stories but use metaphor and allegory in poems of prayer; they are exceptionally difficult to illustrate. Some psalters bypass this situation by illustrating scenes from the life of the presumed author (SEE FIG. 8-27). The artists of the Utrecht Psalter, however, decided to interpret the words and images of individual psalms literally (see "Closer Look" on page 529). Sometimes the words are acted out, as in a game of charades.

A Closer Look

PSALM 23 IN THE UTRECHT PSALTER

The basilica curtains are drawn back to reveal an altar and hanging votive crown: "I will dwell in the house of the Lord forever" (verse 6).

The artist has situated the psalmist in a pasture filled with sheep, goats, and cattle "beside the still water" (verse 2) of a gently flowing stream.

The text of Psalm 23 (22 in the Latin Vulgate) begins here with the words *Dominus regit me* ("The Lord ruleth me"). This is the Latin translator's rewording of the Hebrew text of the opening, which is more familiar to Christians today as: "The Lord is my shepherd."

An angel supports the psalmist with a "rod and staff" while anointing his head with oil (verses 4 and 5).

"Thou preparest a table before me in the presence of mine enemies" (verse 5).

Enemies gather and shoot arrows, but the psalmist ignores them to focus on the table and the house of the Lord, holding a conspicuous cup in his hand, presumably overflowing (verses 5 and 6).

15-22 PSALM 23, THE UTRECHT PSALTER
c. 816–835. Ink on parchment, 13 × 9⅞" (33 × 25 cm). Utrecht University Library. MS. 32, fol. 13r.

15-23 CRUCIFIXION WITH ANGELS AND MOURNING FIGURES, LINDAU GOSPELS
Outer cover. c. 870–880. Gold, pearls, sapphires, garnets, and emeralds, 13¾ × 10⅞″ (36.9 × 27.5 cm). The Morgan Library and Museum, New York. MS. 1.

Credit: © 2016. Photo Pierpont Morgan Library/Art Resource/Scala, Florence

Metalwork

The sumptuously illustrated manuscripts of the medieval period represented an enormous investment of time, talent, and materials, so it is not surprising that they were often protected with equally sumptuous covers. But because these covers were made of valuable materials—ivory, enamelwork, precious metals, and jewels—they were frequently recycled or stolen. The elaborate book cover of gold and jewels now on the Carolingian manuscript known as the **LINDAU GOSPELS** (**FIG. 15-23**) was probably made between 870 and 880 at one of the monastic workshops of Charlemagne's grandson, Charles the Bald (ruled 840–877), but not for this book. Sometime before the sixteenth century it was reused on a late ninth-century manuscript from the monastery of Saint Gall.

The cross and the Crucifixion were common themes for medieval book covers. This one is crafted in pure gold with figures in repoussé (low relief produced by pushing or hammering up from the back of a panel of metal to produce raised forms on the front) surrounded by heavily jeweled frames. The jewels are raised on miniature arcades to allow reflected light to pass through them from beneath, imparting a lustrous glow, and also to allow light traveling in the other direction to reflect from the shiny surface of the gold.

Grieving angels hover above the arms of the cross, and earthbound mourners twist in agony below. Over Jesus's head personifications of the sun and the moon hide their faces in anguish. The gracefully animated poses of these figures, who seem to float around the jeweled bosses in the compartments framed by the arms of the cross, extend the expressive style of the Utrecht Psalter illustrations into another medium and a later moment. Jesus, on the other hand, has been modeled in a more rounded and calmer Classical style. He seems almost to be standing in front of the cross—straight, wide-eyed, with outstretched arms, as if to prefigure his ultimate triumph over death. The flourishes of blood that emerge from his wounds are almost decorative. There is little, if any, sense of his suffering.

Ottonian Europe

How do architecture, sculpture, and painting develop in Ottonian Europe?

In 843, the Carolingian Empire was divided into three parts ruled by three grandsons of Charlemagne. One of them was Charles the Bald, whom we have already encountered (SEE FIG. 15-16). Another, Louis the German, took the eastern portion, and when his family died out at the beginning of the tenth century, a new Saxon dynasty came to power in lands corresponding roughly to present-day Germany and Austria. We call this dynasty Ottonian

after its three principal rulers—Otto I (ruled 936–973), Otto II (ruled 973–983), and Otto III (ruled 983–1002; queens Adelaide and Theophanu ruled as regents for him, 983–994). After the Ottonian armies defeated the Vikings in the north and the Magyars (Hungarians) on the eastern frontiers, the resulting peace permitted increased trade and the growth of towns, making the tenth century a period of economic recovery. In 951, Otto I added northern Italy to his domain by marrying the widowed Lombard queen, Adelaide. He also re-established Charlemagne's Christian Roman Empire when he was crowned emperor by the pope in 962. The Ottonians and their successors so dominated the papacy and appointments to other high offices of the Church that in the twelfth century this union of Germany and Italy under a German ruler came to be known as the Holy Roman Empire. The empire survived in modified form as the Habsburg Empire into the early twentieth century.

The Ottonian ideology, rooted in unity of Church and state, takes visual form on an ivory plaque, one of several that may once have been part of the decoration of an altar or pulpit presented to Magdeburg Cathedral at the time of its dedication in 968 (**FIG. 15-24**). Otto I presents a model of the cathedral to Christ and St. Peter. Following hierarchic

15-24 OTTO I PRESENTING MAGDEBURG CATHEDRAL TO CHRIST

One of a series of 17 ivory plaques known as the Magdeburg Ivories, possibly carved in Milan. c. 962–968. Ivory, 5 × 4½" (12.7 × 11.4 cm). Metropolitan Museum of Art, New York. Gift of George Blumenthal, 1941 (41.100.157).

Credit: © 2016. Image copyright The Metropolitan Museum of Art/Art Resource/ Scala, Florence

scale, the mighty emperor is the smallest figure and the saints and angels, in turn, are taller than Otto but smaller than Christ. Otto is embraced by the patron saint of this church, St. Maurice, a third-century military commander who was martyred for refusing to worship pagan gods. The cathedral Otto holds is a basilica with prominent clerestory windows and a rounded apse. Like the Carolingian basilicas before it, it was intended to recall the Early Christian churches of Rome.

Architecture

As we have seen, Ottonian rulers sought to replicate the splendors of both the Christian architecture of Rome and the Christian empire of their Carolingian predecessors. German officials knew Roman basilicas well, since the German court in Rome was located near the Early Christian church of Santa Sabina (SEE FIGS. 7–12, 7–13). The buildings of Byzantium were another important influence, especially after Otto II married a Byzantine princess, cementing a tie with the East. But large timber-roofed basilicas were terribly vulnerable to fire. Magdeburg Cathedral burned down in 1008, only 40 years after its dedication; it was rebuilt in 1049, burned down again in 1207, and rebuilt yet again. In 1009, the Cathedral of Mainz burned down on the day of its consecration. The church of St. Michael at Hildesheim was destroyed in World War II. Luckily the convent church of St. Cyriakus at Gernrode, Germany, still survives.

THE CONVENT CHURCH OF ST. CYRIAKUS IN GERNRODE During the Ottonian Empire, aristocratic women often held positions of authority, especially as leaders of religious communities. When the provincial military governor Gero founded the convent

and **CHURCH OF ST. CYRIAKUS** in 961, he installed his widowed daughter-in-law as the convent's first abbess. The church was designed as a basilica with a westwork flanked by circular towers (**FIG. 15–25**). At the eastern end, a transept with chapels leads to a choir with an apse built over a crypt.

Like an Early Christian or Carolingian basilica, the interior of St. Cyriakus (SEE FIG. 15–25B) has a nave flanked by side aisles. But the design of the three-level wall elevation—nave arcade, gallery, and clerestory—creates a rhythmic effect distinct from the uniformity that characterized earlier basilicas. Rectangular piers alternate with round columns in the two levels of arcades, and at gallery level pairs of openings are framed by larger arches and then grouped in threes. The central rectangular piers, aligned on the two levels, bisect the walls vertically into two units, each composed of two broad arches of the nave arcade topped by three pairs of arches at the gallery level. This seemingly simple system with its rhythmic alternation of heavy and light supports, its balance of rectangular and rounded forms, and its combination of horizontal and vertical movements seems to prefigure the aesthetic exploration of wall design that will characterize the Romanesque architecture of the next two centuries.

Sculpture

Ottonian sculptors worked in ivory, bronze, wood, and other materials rather than stone. Like their Early Christian and Byzantine predecessors, they and their patrons focused on church furnishings and portable art rather than architectural sculpture. Drawing on Roman, Early Christian, Byzantine, and Carolingian models, they created large works in wood and bronze that would have a significant influence on later medieval art.

15–25A PLAN OF CHURCH OF ST. CYRIAKUS, GERNRODE
Harz, Saxony-Anhalt, Germany.
Begun 961; consecrated 973.

15–25B INTERIOR OF CHURCH OF ST. CYRIAKUS, GERNRODE

Harz, Saxony-Anhalt, Germany. Begun 961; consecrated 973.

Credit: © Achim Bednorz, Koln

15–26 GERO CRUCIFIX

Cologne Cathedral, Germany. c. 970. Painted and gilded wood, height of figure 6′2″ (1.88 m).

This life-size sculpture is both a crucifix to be suspended over an altar and a special kind of reliquary. A cavity in the back of the head was made to hold a piece of the Host, or Communion bread, already consecrated by the priest. Consequently, the figure not only represents the body of the dying Jesus but also contains a "relic" of the Eucharistic body of Christ. In fact, the Ottonian chronicle of Thietmar of Meresburg (written 1012–1018) claims that Gero himself placed a consecrated Host, as well as a fragment of the true cross, in a crack that formed within the head of this crucifix and prayed that it be closed, which it was.

Credit: Rheinisches Bildarchiv, Museen der Stadt Köln

THE GERO CRUCIFIX One of the few large works of carved wood to survive from the early Middle Ages is the **GERO CRUCIFIX** (FIG. 15–26). Archbishop Gero of Cologne (archbishop 969–976) commissioned the sculpture for his cathedral in about 970. The life-size figure of Christ is made of painted and gilded oak. The focus here is on Jesus's human suffering. He is shown as a tortured martyr, not as the triumphant hero of the Lindau Gospels cover (SEE FIG. 15–23). His broken body sags on the cross, and his head falls forward, eyes closed. The straight, linear fall of his golden drapery heightens the impact of his drawn face, emaciated arms and legs, sagging torso, and limp, bloodied hands. This is a poignant image of distilled anguish, meant to inspire pity and awe in its viewers.

THE HILDESHEIM DOORS Under the last of the Ottonian rulers, Henry II and Queen Kunigunde (ruled 1002–1024), Bishop Bernward of Hildesheim emerged as an important patron. His biographer, the monk Thangmar, described Bernward as a skillful goldsmith who closely supervised the artists working for him. Bronze doors made under his direction for the abbey church of St. Michael in Hildesheim—and installed by him in 1015, according to the inscription on them—represented the most ambitious bronze-casting project undertaken since antiquity (FIG. 15–27). Each door, including the impressive lion heads holding the ring handles, was cast as a single piece using the lost-wax process (see "Lost-Wax Casting" in Chapter 14 on page 428) and later detailed and reworked with chisels and fine tools. Rounded, animated figures populate spacious backgrounds. Architectural elements and features of the landscape are depicted in lower relief so that the figures stand out prominently, with their heads fully modeled in three dimensions. The result is lively, visually stimulating, and remarkably spontaneous in feeling for so monumental an undertaking.

The doors, standing more than 16 feet tall, portray events from the Hebrew Bible on the left (reading downward from the creation of Eve at the top to Cain's murder of Abel at the bottom) and from the New Testament on the right (reading upward from the Annunciation at the bottom to the *Noli me tangere* at the top). In each pair of scenes placed across from each other, the Hebrew Bible event is meant to prefigure or complement the New Testament event. For instance, the third panel down on the left shows Adam and Eve picking the forbidden fruit in the Garden of Eden, believed by Christians to be the source of human sin, suffering, and death. The paired scene on the right shows the Crucifixion of Jesus, whose sacrifice was believed to have atoned for Adam and Eve's original sin, bringing the promise of eternal life. At the center of the doors, six panels down—between the door pulls—Eve (left) and Mary (right) are paired, holding their sons. Cain (who murdered his brother) and Jesus (who was unjustly executed) signify the opposition of evil and good, damnation and salvation. Other telling combinations are the murder of Abel (the first sin) paired with the Annunciation (the advent of salvation) at the bottom, and the passing of blame from Adam and

Life in Paradise

Formation of Eve

Eve presented to Adam

The Fall

Temptation and Fall of Adam and Eve

Accusation and Judgment of Adam and Eve

Life in the World

Expulsion of Adam and Eve from Paradise

Adam and Eve Laboring

Eve's Children

Offerings by Cain (grain) and Abel (lamb)

Cain murders Abel

Promise of Return to Paradise

Noli me tangere

Three Marys at the Tomb

The Passion

Crucifixion

Judgment of Jesus by Pilate

Infancy of Jesus

Presentation of Jesus in the Temple

Adoration of the Magi

Mary's Child

Nativity

Annunciation

15–27 DOORS OF BISHOP BERNWARD

Cathedral of the Assumption of Mary, Hildesheim, Germany. 1015. Bronze, height 16′6″ (approx. 5 m).

Credit: Dommuseum Hildesheim. Photo: Florian Monheim

Eve to the serpent paired with Pilate washing his hands of any responsibility in the execution of Jesus, fourth from the top.

Illustrated Books

Like their Carolingian predecessors, Ottonian monks and nuns created richly illuminated manuscripts, which were often funded by secular rulers. Styles varied from place to place, depending on the traditions of the particular scriptorium, the models available in its library, and the creativity of its artists.

THE HITDA GOSPELS The presentation page of a Gospel book made in the early eleventh century for Abbess Hitda (d. 1041) of Meschede, near Cologne (**FIG. 15–28**) represents one of the most distinctive local styles. The abbess herself appears here offering the book to St. Walpurga, her convent's patron saint. The artist has angled the buildings of the sprawling convent in the background to frame the figures and draw attention to their interaction. The size of the architectural complex underscores the abbess's position of authority. The foreground—a rocky, undulating strip of landscape—is meant to be understood as holy ground, separated from the rest of the world by golden trees and the huge arch-shape aura that silhouettes St. Walpurga. The energetic spontaneity of the painting's style suffuses the scene with a sense of religious fervor appropriate to the visionary encounter.

THE GOSPELS OF OTTO III This Gospel book, made in a German monastery near Reichenau about 1000, shows another Ottonian painting style, in this case inspired by Byzantine art in its use of sharply outlined drawing and

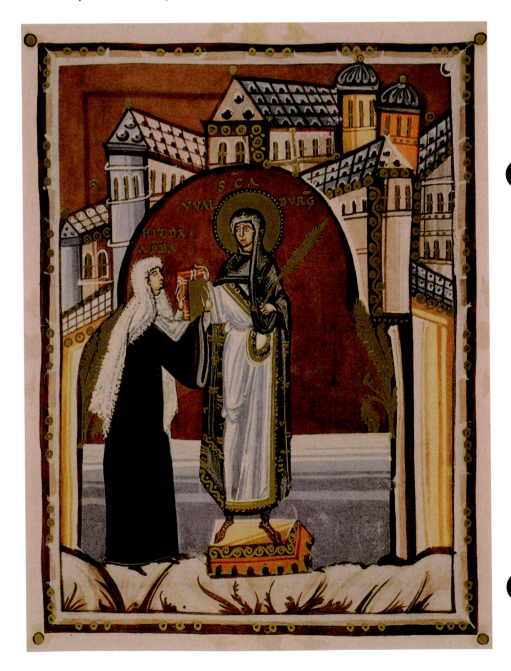

15–28 PRESENTATION PAGE WITH ABBESS HITDA AND ST. WALPURGA, HITDA GOSPELS

Early 11th century. Ink and colors on vellum, 11⅜ × 5⅝″ (29 × 14.2 cm). Universitäts- und Landesbibliothek, Darmstadt.

lavish fields of gold (**FIG. 15–29**). Backed by a more controlled and balanced architectural canopy than the one that sheltering Hitda and St. Walpurga, these tall, slender men gesture dramatically with long, thin fingers. The scene captures the moment when Jesus washes the feet of his disciples during their final meal together (John 13:1–17). At left is Peter, who had tried to stop his Savior from performing this ancient ritual of hospitality, with one leg reluctantly poised over the basin, while a centrally silhouetted and hierarchically scaled Jesus gestures emphatically to underscore the necessity and significance of the act. Another disciple at far right enthusiastically raises his leg to untie his sandals so he can be next in line. With selective stylization, the artist has transformed the Classical tradition into a style of stunning expressiveness and narrative power, features that will also characterize the figural styles associated with Romanesque art.

15–29 PAGE WITH CHRIST WASHING THE FEET OF HIS DISCIPLES, GOSPELS OF OTTO III
c. 1000. Ink, gold, and colors on vellum, approx. 13⅛ × 9½" (33.4 × 24.2 cm). Bayerische Staatsbibliothek, Munich. Clm 4453, fol. 237r.

Think About It

1   Characterize the styles of painting that developed in Spain for the illustration of commentaries on the Apocalypse and in the Ottonian world for visualizing sacred narratives. Focus your answer on specific examples discussed in this chapter.

2   Discuss the themes and subjects used for paintings in early medieval Gospel books by comparing two specific examples from different parts of Europe.

3   Explain the references to early Christian Roman traditions in Carolingian architecture. How did Carolingian builders transform their models?

4   Compare the renderings of the crucified Christ on the cover of the Lindau Gospels (**FIG. 15–23**) and on the Gero Crucifix (**FIG. 15–26**). Consider the differences in media and expressive effect, as well as in style and scale.

Crosscurrents

The equestrian portrait on the right consciously emulates the Roman tradition represented by the work on the left. For the early Middle Ages, this sort of creative appropriation was common artistic practice. Discuss what it tells us about the Carolingians, grounding your answer in a discussion of these two works.

FIG. 6–56

FIG. 15–16

16–1 CHRIST AND DISCIPLES ON THE ROAD TO EMMAUS

Cloister of the abbey of Santo Domingo, Silos, Castilla y Leon, Spain. c. 1100. Pier relief, figures nearly life-size.

Credit: Bridgeman Images

Chapter 16
Romanesque Art

⌄	**Learning Objectives**

16.a Identify the visual hallmarks of Romanesque art for formal, technical, and expressive qualities.

16.b Interpret the meaning of works of Romanesque art based on their themes, subjects, and symbols.

16.c Relate Romanesque art and artists to their cultural, economic, and political contexts.

16.d Apply the vocabulary and concepts relevant to Romanesque art, artists, and art history.

16.e Interpret a work of Romanesque art using the art historical methods of observation, comparison, and inductive reasoning.

16.f Select visual and textual evidence in various media to support an argument or an interpretation of a work of Romanesque art.

Three men seem to glide forward on tiptoe as their leader turns back (**FIG. 16–1**). Their bodies are smooth and elongated, their legs cross in gentle angles, and their shoulders, elbows, and fingers form soft curves. Draperies delicately delineate shallow contours, and the bearded faces stare out with large, wide eyes from under strong brows. The figures interrelate and interlock, pushing against the limits of their architectural frame.

Medieval viewers would have quickly identified the leader as Christ, not only by his commanding size, but specifically by his cruciform halo. The sanctity of his companions is signified by their own haloes. The scene reminds faithful Christians of the resurrected Christ and two of his disciples on the road from Jerusalem to Emmaus (Luke 24:13–35). Christ has the distinctive attributes of a medieval pilgrim—a hat, a satchel, and a walking stick. The scallop shell on his satchel is the badge worn by pilgrims to a specific site: the shrine of St. James at Santiago de Compostela. Early pilgrims who reached this destination in the far northwestern corner of the Iberian peninsula continued to the coast to pick up a shell as evidence of their journey. Soon shells were gathered (or fabricated from metal as brooches) and sold to the pilgrims—a lucrative business for both the sellers and the church. On the return journey home, the shell became the pilgrims' passport, a badge attesting to their piety and accomplishment.

Other distinctive badges were adopted at other pilgrimage sites, too.

This relief was carved on a corner pier in the cloister of the monastery of Santo Domingo in Silos, a major eleventh- and twelfth-century center of religious and artistic life south of the pilgrimage road across Spain (see "The Pilgrim's Journey to Santiago" on page 476). It engaged an audience of monks—who were well versed in the meaning of Christian images—through a sculptural style that we call Romanesque. Not since the art of ancient Rome half a millennium earlier had sculptors carved monumental figures in stone within an architectural fabric. During the early Middle Ages, sculpture was small-scale, independent, and created from precious materials—a highlighted object within a sacred space, rather than a part of the space's architectural envelope. But during the Romanesque period, narrative and iconic figural imagery in deeply carved ornamental frameworks was placed especially heavily around the entrances to churches, focusing attention on their compelling portal complexes. These public displays of Christian doctrine and moral teaching would have been part of the cultural landscape experienced by pilgrims journeying along the road to Santiago. Traveling as a pilgrim opened the mind to a world beyond the familiar towns and agricultural villages of home, signaling a new era in the social, economic, and artistic life of Europe.

MAP 16–1 EUROPE IN THE ROMANESQUE PERIOD

Although a few large political entities began to emerge in places like England and Normandy, Burgundy, and León/Castile, Europe remained a land of small economic entities. Pilgrimages, monasticism, and crusades acted as unifying international forces.

Romanesque Europe

What are the geographical and historical backgrounds for Romanesque art and architecture?

At the beginning of the eleventh century, Europe was still divided into many small political and economic units ruled by powerful families, such as the Ottonians in Germany (**MAP 16–1**). The nations we know today did not exist, although for convenience we shall use present-day names of countries. The king of France ruled only a small area around Paris known as the Île-de-France. The southern part of today's France had close linguistic and cultural ties to northern Spain; in the north the duke of Normandy (heir of the Vikings) and in the east the duke of Burgundy paid the French king only token homage.

When in 1066 Duke William II of Normandy (ruled 1035–1087) invaded England and, as William the Conqueror, became that country's new king, Norman nobles replaced the Anglo-Saxon nobility there, and England became politically and culturally allied with Normandy. As astute and skillful administrators, the Normans formed a close alliance with the Church, supporting it with grants of land and gaining in return the allegiance of abbots and bishops. Normandy became one of Europe's most powerful domains. During this period, the Holy Roman Empire, re-established by the Ottonians, encompassed much of Germany and northern Italy, while the Iberian peninsula remained divided between Muslim rulers in the south and Christian rulers in the north. By 1085, Alfonso VI of Castile and León (ruled 1065–1109) had conquered the Muslim stronghold of Toledo, a center of Islamic and Jewish culture in the kingdom of Castile. Catalunya (Catalonia) emerged as a power along the Mediterranean coast.

By the end of the twelfth century, however, a few exceptionally intelligent and aggressive rulers had begun to create national states. The Capetians in France and the Plantagenets in England were especially successful. In Germany and northern Italy, the power of local rulers and towns prevailed, and Germany and Italy remained politically fragmented until the nineteenth century.

Political, Economic, and Social Life

Although towns and cities with artisans and merchants grew in importance, Europe remained an agricultural society, and developing agricultural practices in this period led to expanded food supplies and population growth.

Land was the primary source of wealth and power for a hereditary aristocracy. Allegiances, obligations, and social relations among members of the upper echelons of society, as well as between them and the peasants who lived and worked on their land, were not static, but were subject to long- and short-term changes in power and wealth. Patterns of political and social dependencies, expectations, and obligations varied extensively from place to place and from community to community. Life was often difficult, and people from all levels of society were vulnerable to the violence of warfare—both local and general—as well as recurrent famine and disease.

The Church

In the early Middle Ages, Church and state had forged some fruitful alliances. Christian rulers helped ensure the spread of Christianity throughout Europe and supported monastic communities with grants of land. Bishops and abbots were often royal relatives, younger brothers and cousins, who supplied the rulers with crucial social and spiritual support and a cadre of educated administrators. As a result, secular and religious authority became tightly intertwined; this continued through the Romanesque period. Monasteries remained at the center of European culture, but there were two new cultural forces fostered by the Church: pilgrimages and crusades.

MONASTICISM   Although the first universities were established in the eleventh and twelfth centuries in the growing cities of Bologna, Paris, Oxford, and Cambridge, monastic communities continued to play a major role in intellectual life and—as in the early Middle Ages—provide valuable social services, including caring for the sick and destitute, housing travelers, and educating the elite. Because monasteries were major landholders, abbots and priors were part of the political power structure. The children of aristocratic families continued to join religious orders, strengthening links between monastic communities and the ruling elite.

As life in Benedictine communities grew increasingly comfortable and intertwined with the secular world, reform movements sought a return to earlier monastic austerity and spirituality. The first important group of reformers for the arts was the Burgundian congregation of Cluny, established in the tenth century. Later came the Cistercians, who sought reform of what they saw as Cluniac decadence and corruption of monastic values.

PILGRIMAGES   Pilgrimages to three of the holiest places of Christendom—Jerusalem, Rome, and Santiago de Compostela—increased (see "The Pilgrim's Journey to Santiago" on page 476), although the majority of pilgrimages were probably more local. Rewards awaited courageous travelers along the routes, whether long or short. Pilgrims on long journeys could venerate the relics of local saints along the route, and artists and architects were commissioned to create spectacular and enticing new buildings and works of art to capture their attention.

CRUSADES   In the eleventh and twelfth centuries, Christian Europe, previously on the defensive against the expanding forces of Islam, became the aggressor. In Spain, Christian armies of the north waged increasingly successful invasions against Islamic kingdoms in the south. At the same time, the Byzantine emperor asked the pope for help in his war with the Muslims surrounding his domain. The Western Church responded in 1095 by launching a series of holy wars, military offensives against Islamic powers known collectively as the crusades (from the Latin *crux*, referring to the cross crusaders wore).

This First Crusade was preached by Pope Urban II (pontificate 1088–1099) and fought by the lesser nobility of France, who had economic and political as well as spiritual objectives. The crusaders captured Jerusalem in 1099 and established a short-lived kingdom. The Second Crusade in 1147, preached by St. Bernard and led by France and Germany, accomplished nothing. In 1187, the Muslim leader Saladin united the Muslim forces and captured Jerusalem, inspiring the Third Crusade, led by German, French, and English kings. The Europeans recaptured some territory, but not Jerusalem, and in 1192 they concluded a truce with the Muslims, permitting the Christians access to the shrines in Jerusalem. Although the crusades were brutal military failures, the movement had far-reaching cultural and economic consequences, providing western Europeans with direct encounters with the more sophisticated material culture of the Islamic world and the Byzantine Empire. This in turn helped stimulate trade, and with trade came the development of an increasingly urban society during the eleventh and twelfth centuries.

Romanesque Architecture

How is architecture transformed across Europe during the Romanesque period?

The word "Romanesque," meaning "in the Roman manner," was coined in the early nineteenth century to describe early medieval European church architecture, which often displayed the solid masonry walls and rounded arches and vaults characteristic of imperial Roman buildings. Soon the term was applied to all the arts of the period from roughly the mid eleventh century to the second half of the twelfth century, even though that art derives from a variety of sources and reflects a multitude of influences, not just Roman.

This was a period of great construction activity in Europe. New castles, manor houses, churches, and monasteries arose everywhere. One eleventh-century monk claimed that the Christian faithful were so relieved to have passed through the apocalyptic anxiety that had gripped their world at the millennial change around the year 1000, that, in gratitude, "Each people of Christendom rivaled with the other, to see which should worship in the finest buildings. The world shook herself, clothed everywhere in a white garment of churches" (Radulphus Glaber, cited in Holt, vol. I, p. 18). The desire to glorify the house of the Lord and his saints (whose earthly remains in the form of relics kept their presence alive in the minds of the people) increased throughout Christendom.

Romanesque architecture and art was a trans-European phenomenon, but it was inflected regionally, and the style varied in character from place to place. Although timber remained common in construction, Romanesque builders used stone masonry extensively. Masonry vaults were stronger and more durable, and they enhanced the acoustical effect of Gregorian chant (plainsong, named after Pope Gregory the Great, pontificate 590–604). Stone towers sometimes marked the church as the most important building in the community. Portals were often encrusted with sculptures that broadcast the moral and theological messages of the Church to a wide public.

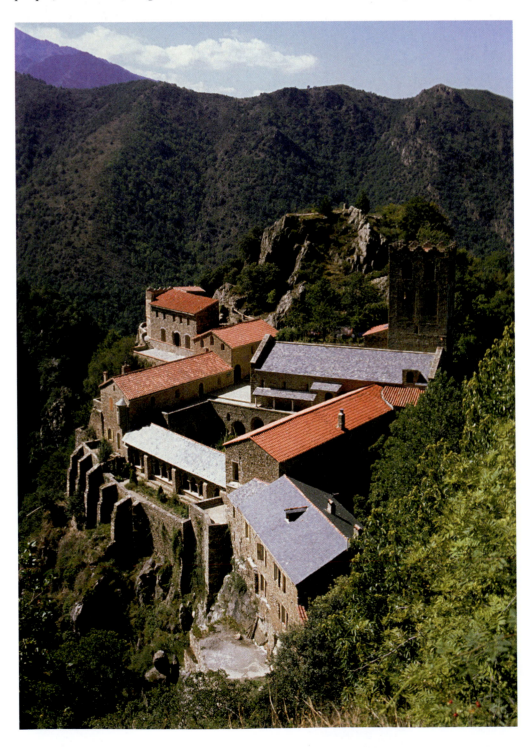

16–2 SAINT-MARTIN-DU-CANIGOU

French Pyrenees. 1001–1026.

Credit: © akg-images/Stefan Drechsel

"First Romanesque"

Soon after the year 1000, patrons and builders in Catalunya (northeast Spain), southern France, and northern Italy were already constructing all-masonry churches, employing the methods of late Roman builders. The picturesque Benedictine monastery of **SAINT-MARTIN-DU-CANIGOU**, nestled into the Pyrenees on a building platform stabilized by strongly buttressed retaining walls, is a typical example (**FIG. 16-2**). Patronized by the local Count Guifred, who took refuge in the monastery and died here in 1049, the complex is capped by a massive stone tower next to the sanctuary of the two-story church. Art historians call such early stone-vaulted buildings "First Romanesque," employing the term that Catalan architect and theorist Josep Puig I Cadafalch first associated with them in 1928.

THE CHURCH OF SANT VINCENÇ, CARDONA
Another fine example of "First Romanesque" is the **CHURCH OF SANT VINCENÇ** (St. Vincent) in the Catalan castle of Cardona (**FIG. 16-3**). Begun in the 1020s, it was consecrated in 1040. Castle residents entered the church through a two-story narthex into a nave with low narrow side aisles that permitted clerestory windows in the nave wall. The sanctuary was raised dramatically over an aisled crypt. The Catalan masons used local materials—small split stones, bricks, river pebbles, and very strong mortar—to raise plain walls and round barrel or groin vaults. Today we can admire their skillful stonework both inside and out, but the builders originally covered their masonry with stucco.

To strengthen the exterior walls and enrich their sculptural presence, the masons added vertical bands of projecting masonry (called strip buttresses) joined by arches and additional courses of masonry to counter the weight and outward thrust of the vault. On the interior these masonry strips project from the piers and continue up and over the vault, creating a series of **transverse arches**. Additional projecting bands line the underside of the arches of the nave arcade. The result is a compound, sculptural pier that works in concert with the transverse arches to divide the nave into a series of bays. This system of bay division became standard in Romanesque architecture. It is a marked contrast to the flat-wall continuity and undivided space within a pre-Romanesque church like the one in Gernrode (SEE FIG. 15–25).

Pilgrimage Churches

The growth of a cult of relics and the desire to visit holy shrines such as St. Peter's in Rome or St. James's in Spain, as well as the shrines of local saints, increasingly inspired Christians in western Europe to travel on pilgrimages (see "The Pilgrim's Journey to Santiago" on page 476). To accommodate the faithful and proclaim Church doctrine,

many monasteries—including those on the major pilgrimage routes—built large new churches, filled them with sumptuous altars and reliquaries, and encrusted them with elaborate stone sculpture on the exterior, especially around entrances.

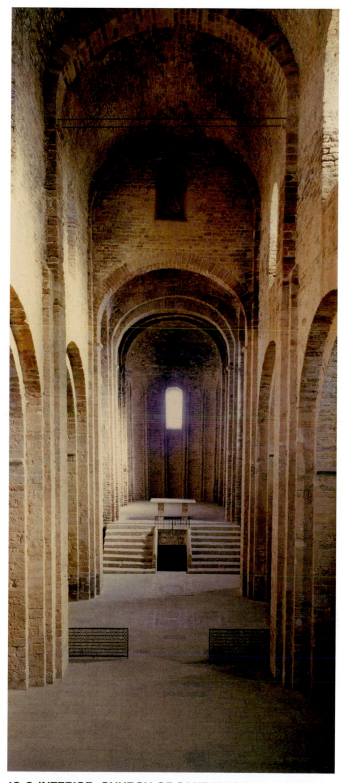

16-3 INTERIOR, CHURCH OF SANT VINCENÇ, CARDONA
Spain. 1020s–1030s.

Credit: Archivo Fotográphico Oronoz, Madrid

Art and its Contexts

THE PILGRIM'S JOURNEY TO SANTIAGO

Western Europe in the eleventh and twelfth centuries saw the growing popularity of religious pilgrimage—much of it local, but some of it international. The rough roads that led to the holiest destinations—the tomb of St. Peter and other martyrs in Rome, the church of the Holy Sepulcher in Jerusalem, and the cathedral of St. James in Santiago de Compostela in the northwest corner of Spain—were often crowded with pilgrims. Journeys could last a year or more; church officials going to Compostela were given 16 weeks' leave of absence. Along the way the pilgrims had to contend with bad food and poisoned water, as well as bandits and dishonest innkeepers and merchants.

In the twelfth century, the priest Aymery Picaud wrote a guidebook for pilgrims on their way to Santiago through what is now France. Like travel guides today, Picaud's book provided advice on local customs, comments on food and the safety of drinking water, and a list of useful words in the Basque language. In Picaud's time, four main pilgrimage routes to Santiago crossed France, merging into a single road in Spain at Puente la Reina and leading on from there through Burgos and León to Compostela (**MAP 16–2**). Conveniently spaced monasteries and churches offered food and lodging, as well as relics to venerate. Roads and bridges were maintained by a guild of bridge builders and guarded by the Knights of Santiago.

Picaud described the best-traveled routes and most important shrines to visit along the way. Chartres, for example, housed the tunic that the Virgin was said to have worn when she gave birth to Jesus. The monks of Vézelay had the bones of St. Mary Magdalen, and at Conques, the skull of Sainte Foy was to be found. Churches associated with miraculous cures—Autun, for example, which claimed to house the relics of Lazarus, raised by Jesus from the dead—were filled with the sick and injured praying to be healed.

MAP 16–2 THE PILGRIMAGE ROUTES TO SANTIAGO DE COMPOSTELA

THE CATHEDRAL OF ST. JAMES IN SANTIAGO DE COMPOSTELA   One major goal of pilgrimage was the **CATHEDRAL OF ST. JAMES** in Santiago de Compostela (**FIG. 16–4**), which held the body of St. James, the apostle to the Iberian peninsula. Builders of this and several other major churches along the roads leading through France to the shrine developed a distinctive plan designed to accommodate the crowds of pilgrims and allow them to move easily from chapel to chapel to venerate relics. This "pilgrimage plan" is a model of functional planning and traffic control. To the aisled nave the builders added aisled transepts with eastern chapels leading to an ambulatory (curving walkway) with additional radiating chapels around the apse. This expansion of the basilican plan allowed worshipers to circulate freely around the church's perimeter, visiting chapels and venerating relics without disrupting services within the main space.

At Santiago, pilgrims entered the church through large double doors at the ends of the transepts rather than through the western portal, which served ceremonial processions. Pilgrims from France entered the north transept portal; the approach from the town was through the south portal. All found themselves in a transept in which the design exactly mirrored the nave in height and structure (**FIG. 16–5**). Both nave and transept have two stories—an arcade and a gallery. Compound piers with attached half-columns on all four sides support the immense barrel vault and are projected over it vertically through a rhythmic series of transverse arches. They give sculptural form to the interior walls and also mark off individual vaulted bays in which the sequence is as clear and regular as the ambulatory chapels of the choir. Three different kinds of vaults are used here: barrel vaults with transverse arches cover the nave, groin vaults span the side aisles, and half-barrel or quadrant vaults cover the galleries and strengthen the building by countering the outward thrust of the high nave vaults and transferring it to the outer walls and buttresses. Without a clerestory, light enters the nave and transept only indirectly, through windows in the outer walls of the aisles and upper-level galleries. Light from the choir clerestory and the large windows of an octagonal **lantern** tower (a structure built above the height of the main

**16–4 PLAN (A) AND
RECONSTRUCTION DRAWING (B)
OF THE CATHEDRAL OF ST. JAMES,
SANTIAGO DE COMPOSTELA**

Galicia, Spain. 1078–1122; western portions
later. View from the east.

Credit: Kathy Mrozek

ceiling with windows that illuminate the space below) over the crossing would therefore spotlight the glittering gold and jeweled shrine of the principal relic at the high altar.

In its own time, Santiago was admired for the excellence of its construction—"not a single crack is to be found," said the twelfth-century pilgrims' guide, "admirable and beautiful in execution… large, spacious, well-lighted, of fitting size, harmonious in width, length, and height…." Pilgrims arrived at Santiago de Compostela weary after weeks or months of difficult travel through dense woods and mountains. Grateful to St. James for his protection along the way, they entered a church that welcomed them with open portals covered with the dynamic, moralizing sculpture that characterized Romanesque churches. The cathedral had no doors to close—it was open day and night.

**16–5 NAVE, CATHEDRAL
OF ST. JAMES, SANTIAGO DE COMPOSTELA**

1078–1122. View toward the choir.

Credit: © akg-images/Andrea Jemolo

Relics and Reliquaries

Christians turned to the heroes of the Church, especially martyrs who had died for their faith, to answer their prayers and to intercede with Christ on their behalf; prayers offered to saints while in close proximity to their relics were considered especially effective. Bodies, parts of bodies, and things associated with the Holy Family or the saints were kept in richly decorated containers called reliquaries. Reliquaries could be simple boxes, but they might also be created in more elaborate shapes, sometimes in the form of body parts such as arms, ribs, or heads. By the eleventh century, many different arrangements of crypts, chapels, and passageways gave people access to the relics kept in churches. When the Church decided that every altar required a relic, the saints' bodies and possessions were subdivided. In this way relics were multiplied; for example, hundreds of churches held relics of the true cross.

Owning and displaying these relics so enhanced the prestige and wealth of a community that people went to great lengths to acquire them, not only by purchase but also by theft. In the ninth century, for example, the monks of Conques stole the relics of the child martyr Sainte Foy (St. Faith) from her shrine at Agen. Such a theft was called "holy robbery," for the new owners insisted that it had been sanctioned by the saint, who had communicated to them her desire to move. In the late ninth or tenth century, the monks of Conques encased their new relic—the skull of Sainte Foy—in a gold and jeweled statue whose unusually large head was made from a reused late Roman work. During the eleventh century, they added the crown and more jeweled banding, and, over subsequent centuries, jewels, cameos, and other gifts added by pilgrims continued to enhance the statue's splendor (**FIG. 16–6**).

This type of reliquary—taking the form of a statue of the saint—was quite popular in the region around Conques, but not everyone was comfortable with the way these works functioned as cult images. Early in the eleventh century, Bernard of Angers prefaces his tendentious account of miracles associated with the cult of Sainte Foy by confessing his initial misgivings about such reliquaries, specifically the way simple folks adored them. Bernard thought it smacked of idolatry: "To learned people this may seem to be full of superstition, if not unlawful, for it seems as if the rites of the gods of ancient cultures, or that the rites of demons, are being observed" (*The Book of Sainte Foy*, p. 77). But when he witnessed firsthand the interaction of the reliquary statue with the faithful, he altered his position: "For the holy image is consulted not as an idol that requires sacrifices, but because it commemorates a martyr. Since reverence to her honors God on high, it was despicable of me to compare her statue to statues of Venus or Diana. Afterwards I was very sorry that I had acted so foolishly toward God's saint." (ibid., p. 78)

Cluny

In 909, the duke of Burgundy gave land for a monastery to Benedictine monks intent on strict adherence to the original rules of St. Benedict. They established the reformed congregation of Cluny. From its foundation, Cluny had an independent status; its abbot answered directly to the pope in Rome rather than to the local bishop or lord. This freedom, safeguarded by a series of long-lived and astute abbots, enabled Cluny to keep the profits from extensive gifts of both land and treasure. Independent, wealthy, and a center of culture and learning, Cluny and its affiliates became important patrons of architecture and art.

16–6 RELIQUARY STATUE OF SAINTE FOY (ST. FAITH)
Abbey church, Conques, France. Late 9th or 10th century with later additions. Silver gilt over a wood core, with gems and cameos of various dates. Height 33″ (85 cm). Church Treasury, Conques.

Credit: © akg-images/Erich Lessing

stables and guest house

abbot's residence

main gate

second church

monks' cloister

kitchen

monks' refectory

novices' dormitory

novices' cloister

monks' dormitory

third church

cemetery and chapel

infirmaries

latrines

16–7 RECONSTRUCTION DRAWING OF THE ABBEY OF CLUNY

Burgundy, France. 1088–1130. View from the east.

Credit: Stephen Conlin © Dorling Kindersley

The monastery of Cluny was a city unto itself. By the second half of the eleventh century, there were some 200 monks in residence, supplemented by many laymen on whom they depended for material support. Just as in the Saint Gall plan of the Carolingian period (SEE FIG. 15–19), the cloister lay at the center of this monastic community, joining the church with domestic buildings and workshops (FIG. 16–7). In wealthy monasteries such as Cluny, the arcaded galleries of the cloister had elaborate carved capitals as well as relief sculpture on piers (SEE FIG. 16–1). The capitals may have served as memory devices or visualized theology to direct and inspire the monks' thoughts and prayers.

Cluniac monks observed the traditional eight Benedictine Hours of the Divine Office (including prayers, scripture readings, psalms, and hymns) spread over the course of each day and night. Mass was celebrated after the third hour (terce), and the Cluniac liturgy was especially elaborate. During the height of this liturgy's use, plainsong, or Gregorian chant, filled the church with music 24 hours a day. And the design of the church at Cluny—like that of many of the churches of its numerous dependent

monasteries—was conceived largely as an elegant and extravagant setting for the performance of this liturgy. Cluniac churches were notable for their fine stone masonry with rich sculptured and painted decoration. In Burgundy the churches were distinguished by their use of classicizing elements drawn from Roman art, such as fluted pilasters and Corinthian capitals. Cluniac monasteries elsewhere, however, were free—perhaps even encouraged—to follow regional traditions and styles.

THE THIRD CHURCH AT CLUNY The original church at Cluny, a small, barnlike building, was soon replaced by a basilica with two towers and narthex on the west side and a choir with tower and chapels on the east. Hugh de Semur, abbot of Cluny for 60 years (1049–1109), began rebuilding the abbey church for the third time in 1088 (FIG. 16–8), financed by money paid in tribute by Muslims to victorious Christians in Spain. When King Alfonso VI of Castile and León captured Toledo in 1085, he sent 10,000 pieces of gold to Cluny; German rulers were also generous donors. Cluny III (as this third church is often referred to by art historians) was the largest church in Europe when it was completed in 1130: 550 feet long, with five aisles like Old St. Peter's in Rome. Built with superbly cut masonry and richly carved, painted, and furnished, it was a worthy home for the relics of St. Peter and St. Paul, which the monks had acquired from the church of St. Paul's Outside the Walls in Rome. It was also a fitting headquarters for a monastic order that eventually became so powerful within Europe that popes were chosen from its ranks.

In simple terms, the church was a basilica with five aisles, double transepts with chapels, and a high altar within the main choir space surrounded by an ambulatory and radiating chapels. The large number of chapels was necessary so that each monk-priest had an altar at which to perform daily Mass. Octagonal towers over the two crossings and additional towers over the transept arms created a dramatic pyramidal design at the east end. The nave had a three-part elevation. A nave arcade with tall compound piers, faced by pilasters to the inside and engaged columns at the sides, supported pointed arches lined by Classical ornament. At the next level a blind arcade and pilasters created a continuous sculptural strip that could have been modeled on an imperial Roman triumphal monument. Finally, triple clerestory windows in each bay let sunlight directly into the church around its perimeter. The pointed barrel vault with transverse arches rose to a daring height of 98 feet with a span of about 40 feet, made possible by giving the vaults a steep profile, rather than the weaker rounded profile used at Santiago de Compostela.

Cluny III was consecrated in 1130, but it no longer exists. The monastery was suppressed during the French Revolution, and this grandest of French Romanesque churches was sold stone by stone

for building materials. Today the site is an archaeological park, with only one transept arm from the original church still standing.

The Cistercians

New religious orders devoted to an austere spirituality arose in the late eleventh and early twelfth centuries. Among these were the Cistercians, who spurned Cluny's elaborate liturgical practices and aspects of their arts, especially figural sculpture in cloisters (see "St. Bernard and Theophilus: The Monastic Controversy over the Visual Arts" opposite). The Cistercian reform began in 1098 with the founding of the abbey of Cîteaux (Cistercium in Latin, hence the order's name). Led in the twelfth

16–8 RECONSTRUCTION DRAWING OF THE INTERIOR LOOKING TOWARD THE CHOIR, THIRD ABBEY CHURCH AT CLUNY

1088–1130. From Kenneth Conant, Carolingian and Romanesque Architecture, 800 to1200, Yale University Press, fig. 103.

Credit: Reproduced courtesy of Yale University Press, London.

Art and its Contexts

ST. BERNARD AND THEOPHILUS: THE MONASTIC CONTROVERSY OVER THE VISUAL ARTS

The twelfth century saw a heated controversy over the place and appropriateness of lavish art in monasteries. In a letter to William of Saint-Thierry, Bernard of Clairvaux wrote:

…in the cloisters, before the eyes of the brothers while they read—what is that ridiculous monstrosity doing, an amazing kind of deformed beauty and yet a beautiful deformity? What are the filthy apes doing there? The fierce lions? The monstrous centaurs? The creatures part man and part beast? The striped tigers? The fighting soldiers? The hunters blowing horns? You may see many bodies under one head, and conversely many heads on one body. On one side the tail of a serpent is seen on a quadruped, on the other side the head of a quadruped is on the body of a fish. Over there an animal has a horse for the front half and a goat for the back; here a creature which is horned in front is equine behind. In short, everywhere so plentiful and astonishing a variety of contradictory forms is seen that one would rather read in the marble than in books, and spend the whole day wondering at every single one of them than in meditating on the law of God. Good God! If one is not ashamed of the absurdity, why is one not at least troubled at the expense?

(Rudolph, *Things of Greater Importance*, pp. 11–12)

"Theophilus" is the pseudonym used by a monk who wrote a book during the first half of the twelfth century on the practice of artistic craft, voiced as a defense of the place of the visual arts within the monastic traditions of work and prayer. The book gives detailed instructions for panel painting, stained glass (colored glass assembled into ornamental or pictorial windows), and goldsmithing. In contrast to the stern warnings of Bernard, perhaps even in response to them, "Theophilus" assured artists that "God delights in embellishments" and that artists worked "under the direction and authority of the Holy Spirit."

He wrote:

Therefore, most beloved son, you should not doubt but should believe in full faith that the Spirit of God has filled your heart when you have embellished His house with such great beauty and variety of workmanship…

…do not hide away the talent given to you by God, but, working and teaching openly and with humility, you faithfully reveal it to those who desire to learn.

…if a faithful soul should see a representation of the Lord's crucifixion expressed in the strokes of an artist, it is itself pierced; if it sees how great are the tortures that the saints have endured in their bodies and how great the rewards of eternal life that they have received, it grasps at the observance of a better life; if it contemplates how great are the joys in heaven and how great are the torments in the flames of hell, it is inspired with hope because of its good deeds and shaken with fear on considering its sins.

(Theophilus, *On Divers Arts*, pp. 78–79)

As we will see in the next chapter, Abbot Suger of Saint-Denis shared the position of Theophilus, rather than that of Bernard, and from this standpoint would sponsor a reconstruction of his abbey church that gave birth to the Gothic style.

---

century by the commanding figure of Abbot (later St.) Bernard of Clairvaux, the Cistercians advocated strict mental and physical discipline and a life devoted to prayer and intellectual pursuits combined with shared manual labor. Like the Cluniacs, however, Cistercians depended on the work of laypeople. To seclude themselves as much as possible from the outside world, they settled in reclaimed swamps and wild forests, where they then farmed and raised sheep. In time, their monasteries extended from Russia to Ireland.

FONTENAY   Cistercian architecture embodies the ideals of the order—simplicity, austerity, and purity. Always practical, the Cistercians made a significant change to the already very efficient monastery plan. They placed key buildings such as the refectory at right angles to the cloister walk so they could easily be extended should the community grow. The cloister fountain was relocated from the center to the side, conveniently in front of the refectory, where the monks could wash when coming from their work in the fields for communal meals. For easy access to the sanctuary during their prayers at night, monks entered the church directly from the cloister into the south transept or from the dormitory by way of the "night stairs."

The **ABBEY OF NOTRE-DAME** in Fontenay, is among the best-preserved early Cistercian monasteries (**FIG. 16–9**). The abbey church, begun in 1139, has a regular geometric plan with a long bay-divided nave, rectangular chapels off the square-ended transept arms, and a shallow choir with a straight east wall. One of its characteristic features is the use of pointed barrel vaults over the nave and pointed arches in the nave arcade and side-aisle bays. Although pointed arches are usually associated with Gothic architecture, they are actually common in the Romanesque buildings of some regions, including Burgundy—we have already seen them at Cluny. Pointed arches are structurally more stable than round ones, directing more weight down into the floor instead of outward against the walls. Consequently, they can span greater distances at greater heights without collapsing.

16–9A PLAN OF THE ABBEY OF NOTRE-DAME, FONTENAY

Burgundy, France. 1139–1147.

Although Fontenay and other early Cistercian monasteries fully reflect the architectural developments of their time in masonry construction, vaulting, and planning, the Cistercians concentrated on harmonious proportions, superbly refined stonework, and elegantly carved foliate and ornamental decoration to achieve beauty in their architecture. The figural scenes and monstrous animals found on many Romanesque churches are avoided here. The large windows in the end wall, rather than a clerestory, provided light, concentrated here as at Santiago, on the sanctuary. The sets of triple windows may have reminded the monks of the Trinity. Some scholars have suggested that the numerical and proportional systems guiding the design of such seemingly simple buildings are saturated with the sacred numerical systems outlined by such eminent early theologians as St. Augustine of Hippo.

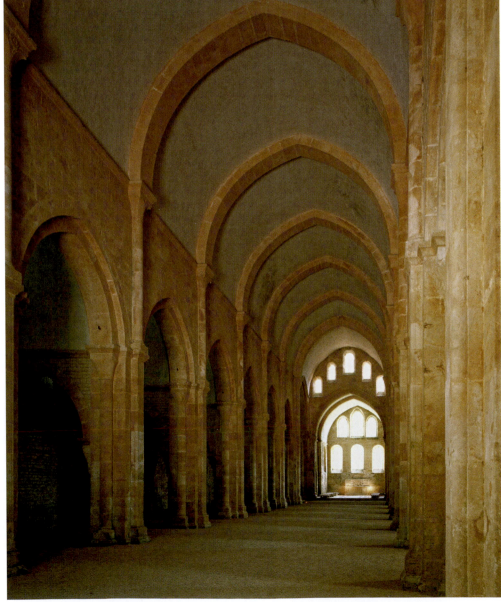

16–9B CHURCH INTERIOR OF THE ABBEY OF NOTRE-DAME, FONTENAY

Burgundy, France. 1139–1147. View toward the choir.

Credit: © akg-images/ Paul M.R. Maeyaert

16–10 CATHEDRAL COMPLEX, PISA

Tuscany, Italy. Cathedral, begun 1063; baptistery, begun 1153; campanile, begun 1174; Campo Santo, 13th century.

When finished in 1350, the Leaning Tower of Pisa stood 179 feet high. The campanile had begun to tilt while still under construction, and today it leans about 13 feet off the perpendicular. In the latest effort to keep it from toppling, engineers filled the base with tons of lead.

Credit: *Folco Quilici © Fratelli Alinari*

The streamlined but sophisticated architecture favored by the Cistercians spread from their homeland in Burgundy to become an international style. From Scotland and Poland to Spain and Italy, Cistercian designs and building techniques varied only slightly in relation to local building traditions. Cistercian experiments with masonry vaulting and harmonious proportions influenced the development of the French Gothic style in the middle of the twelfth century.

Regional Styles in Romanesque Architecture

The cathedral of Santiago de Compostela and the abbey church at Cluny reflect the cultural exchanges and international connections fostered by powerful monastic orders, and to a certain extent by travel along the pilgrimage roads, but Europe remained a land divided by competing kingdoms, regions, and factions. Romanesque architecture reflects this regionalism in the wide variety of its styles, traditions, and building techniques. Only a few examples can be examined here.

THE CATHEDRAL OF ST. MARY OF THE ASSUMPTION IN PISA   Throughout Italy artists looked to the still-standing remains of imperial Rome and early Christianity. The influence remained especially strong in Pisa, on the west coast of Tuscany. Pisa became a maritime power, competing with Barcelona and Genoa as well as the Muslims for control of trade in the western Mediterranean. In 1063, after a decisive victory over the Muslims, the jubilant Pisans began an imposing new cathedral dedicated to the Virgin Mary (**FIG. 16-10**). The cathedral was designed as a cruciform basilica by the master builder Busketos. A long nave with double side aisles (usually an homage to Old St. Peter's) is crossed by projecting transepts, designed like basilicas with their own aisles and apses. The builders added galleries above the side aisles, and a dome covers the crossing. Unlike Early Christian basilicas, the exteriors of Tuscan churches were richly decorated with marble—either panels of green and white marble or arcades. At Pisa, pilasters, applied arcades, and narrow galleries in white marble adorn the five-story façade.

In addition to the cathedral itself, the complex eventually included a baptistery, a campanile, and the later Gothic Campo Santo, a walled burial ground. The baptistery, begun in 1153, has arcading and galleries on the lower levels of its exterior that match those on the cathedral; the baptistery's present exterior dome and ornate upper levels were built later. The campanile (a free-standing bell tower now known for obvious reasons as "the Leaning Tower of Pisa") was begun in 1174 by master builder Bonanno Pisano. Built on inadequate foundations, it began to lean almost immediately. The cylindrical tower is encased in tier upon tier of marble columns. This creative reuse of the Classical theme of the colonnade, turning it into a decorative arcade, is characteristic of Tuscan Romanesque art.

THE BENEDICTINE CHURCH OF SAN CLEMENTE IN ROME The Benedictine **CHURCH OF SAN CLEMENTE** in Rome was rebuilt beginning in the eleventh century (it was consecrated in 1128) on top of the previous church, which had itself been built over a Roman sanctuary of Mithras. The architecture and decoration reflect a conscious effort to reclaim the artistic and spiritual legacy of the early church (**FIG. 16–11**). As with the columns of Santa Sabina (SEE FIG. 7–12), the columns in San Clemente are *spolia*: that is, they were reused from ancient Roman buildings. The church originally had a timber roof, now disguised by an ornate eighteenth-century ceiling. Even given the Romanesque emphasis on stone vaulting, the construction of timber-roofed buildings continued throughout the Middle Ages.

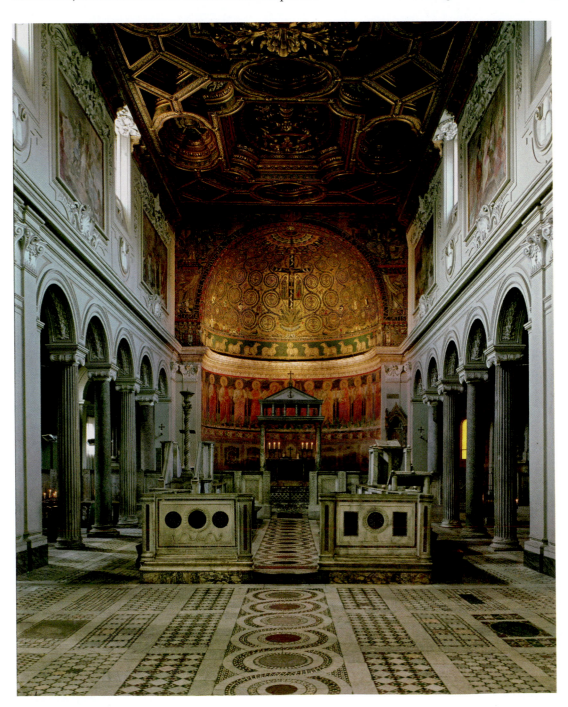

16–11 INTERIOR, CHURCH OF SAN CLEMENTE, ROME
Consecrated 1128.

San Clemente contains one of the finest surviving collections of early church furniture: choir stalls, pulpit, lectern, candlestick, and also the twelfth-century inlaid pavement. Ninth-century choir-screen panels were reused from the earlier church on the site. The upper nave wall and ceiling decoration date from the eighteenth century.

Credit: © akg-images/ Erich Lessing

16–12 STAGS DRINKING FROM STREAMS FLOWING UNDER THE CRUCIFIED CHRIST
Detail of mosaics in the apse of the church of San Clemente, Rome. Consecrated 1128.

Credit: © Dagli Orti G./De Agostini Picture Library, licenced via Alinari

At San Clemente, the nave ends in a semicircular apse opening directly off the rectangular hall without a sanctuary extension or transept crossing. To accommodate the increased number of participants in the twelfth-century liturgy, the liturgical choir for the monks was extended into the nave itself, defined by a low barrier made up of ninth-century relief panels reused from the earlier church. In Early Christian basilicas, the area in front of the altar had been similarly enclosed by a low stone parapet (SEE FIG. 7–12), and the Romanesque builders may have wanted to revive what they considered a glorious Early Christian tradition. A **baldacchino** (a canopy suspended over a sacred space, also called a ciborium) symbolizing the Holy Sepulcher covers the main altar in the apse.

The apse of San Clemente is richly decorated with marble revetment on the curving walls and mosaic in the semidome, in a system familiar from the Early Christian and Byzantine worlds (SEE FIGS. 7–20, 8–6). The mosaics recapture this past glory, portraying the trees and rivers of paradise in a lavish vine scroll inhabited by figures, in the midst of which emerges the crucified Christ flanked by Mary and St. John. Twelve doves on the cross and the 12 sheep that march in single file below represent the apostles. Stags drink from streams flowing from the base of the cross, an evocation of the tree of life in paradise (**FIG. 16–12**). An inscription running along the base of the apse explains, "We liken the Church of Christ to this vine that the law causes to wither and the Cross causes to bloom," a statement that recalls Jesus's reference to himself as the true vine and his followers as the branches (John 15:1–11). The learned monks of San Clemente would have been prepared to derive these and other meanings from the evocative symbols within this elaborate, glowing composition.

Although the subject of the mosaic recalls Early Christian art, the style and technique are clearly Romanesque. The artists have suppressed the sense of lifelike illusionism that characterized earlier mosaics in favor of ornamental patterns and schemas typical of the twelfth century. The doves silhouetted on the dark blue cross, the symmetrical repetition of circular vine scrolls, even the animals, birds, and humans among their leaves conform to an overriding formal design. With an irregular setting of mosaic tesserae in visibly rough plaster, the artists heighten color and increase the glitter of the pervasive gold field, allowing the mosaic to sparkle.

THE ABBEY CHURCH OF SAINT-SAVIN-SUR-GARTEMPE At the Benedictine **ABBEY CHURCH OF SAINT-SAVIN-SUR-GARTEMPE** in western France, a tunnel-like barrel vault runs the length of the nave and choir (**FIG. 16–13**). Without galleries or clerestory windows, the nave at Saint-Savin approaches the form of a "hall church," where the nave and aisles rise to an equal height. And unlike other churches we have seen (for example, FIG. 16–5), at Saint-Savin the barrel vault is unbroken by projecting transverse arches, making it ideally suited for paintings.

The paintings on the high vaults of Saint-Savin survive almost intact, presenting scenes from the Hebrew

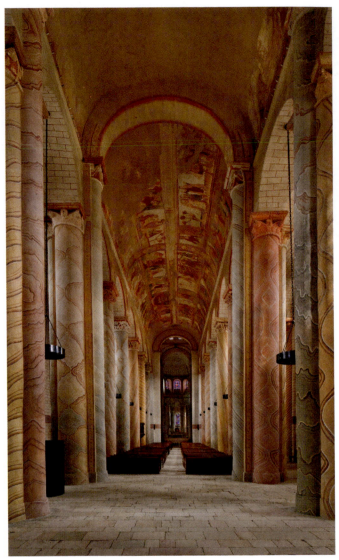

16-13 ABBEY CHURCH OF SAINT-SAVIN-SUR-GARTEMPE
Poitou, France. Choir c. 1060–1075; nave c. 1095–1115.

Credit: © Achim Bednorz, Cologne

Bible and New Testament. The nave was built c. 1095–1115, and the painters seem to have followed the masons immediately, probably using the same scaffolding. Perhaps their intimate involvement with the building process accounts for the vividness with which they portrayed the biblical story of the **TOWER OF BABEL** (FIG. 16–14).

According to the account in Genesis (11:1–9), God (represented here by a striding figure of Christ on the left) punished the prideful people who had tried to reach heaven by means of their own architectural ingenuity by scattering them and making their languages mutually unintelligible. The tower in the painting is Romanesque in style, reflecting the medieval practice of visualizing all stories in contemporary settings to stress their relevance for the contemporary audience. Workers haul heavy stone blocks toward the tower, presumably intending to lift them to masons on the top with the same hoist that has been used to haul up a bucket of mortar. The giant Nimrod, on the far right, simply hands over the blocks. These paintings embody the energy and narrative vigor that characterizes Romanesque art. A dynamic figure of God confronts the wayward people, stepping away from them even as he turns back, presumably to scold them. The dramatic movement, monumental figures, bold outlines, broad areas of color, and patterned drapery all promote the legibility of these pictures to viewers looking up in the dim light from far below. The team of painters working here did not use the *buon fresco* technique favored in Italy for its durability, but they did moisten the walls before painting, which allowed some absorption of pigments into the plaster and made them more permanent than paint applied to a dry surface.

SAN CLIMENT IN TAULL As we have seen at San Clemente in Rome and at Saint-Savin-sur-Gartempe (SEE FIGS.

16-14 TOWER OF BABEL
Detail of painting in nave vault, abbey church of Saint-Savin-sur-Gartempe, Poitou, France. c. 1115.

Credit: © akg-images/De Agostini Picture Lib.

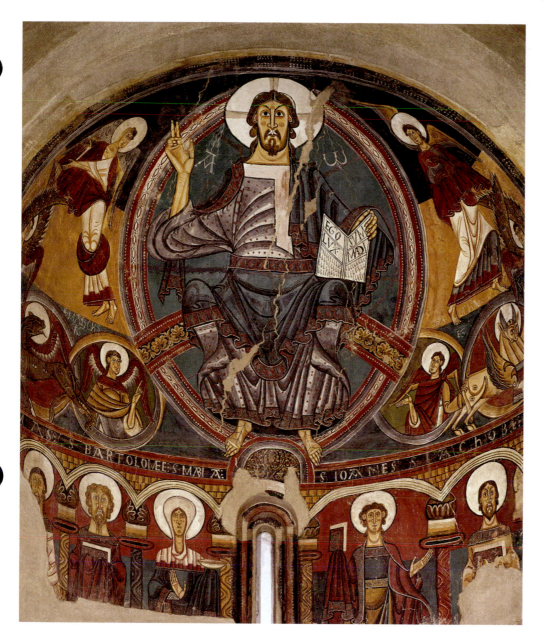

16–15 CHRIST IN MAJESTY

Detail of apse fresco, church of San Climent, Taull, Catalunya, Spain. Consecrated 1123. MNAC - Museu Nacional d'Art de Catalunya, Barcelona.

Credit: © akg-images/Album/Oronoz

16–11, 16–13), Romanesque church interiors were not bare expanses of stone, but were often covered with images that glowed in flickering candlelight amid clouds of incense. Outside Rome during the Romanesque period, murals largely replaced mosaics on the walls of churches. Wall painting was subject to the same influences as the other visual arts: that is, the mural painters could be inspired by illuminated manuscripts, or ivories, or enamels in their treasuries or libraries. Some artists must have seen examples of Byzantine art; others had Carolingian or even Early Christian models.

Artists in Catalunya brilliantly combined the Byzantine style with their own Mozarabic and Classical heritage in the apse paintings of the church of San Climent in the mountain village of Taull (Tahull), consecrated in 1123 just a few years before the church of San Clemente in Rome. The curve of the semidome of the apse contains a magnificently expressive **CHRIST IN MAJESTY** (FIG. 16–15) holding an open book inscribed *Ego sum lux mundi* ("I am the light of the world," John 8:12)—recalling in his commanding presence the imposing Byzantine depictions of Christ Pantokrator, ruler and judge of the world, in Middle Byzantine churches (SEE FIG. 8–21).

The San Climent artist was one of the finest painters of the Romanesque period, but where he came from and where he learned his art is unknown. His use of elongated oval faces, large staring eyes, and long noses, as well as the placement of figures against flat bands of color and his use of heavy outlines, reflect the Mozarabic past (SEE FIG. 15–14). At the same time, the influence of Byzantine art is revealed in his painting technique of modeling from light to dark through repeated colored lines of varying width in three shades—dark, medium, and light. Instead of blending the colors, he delights in the striped effect, as well as in the potential for pattern in details of faces, hair, hands, and muscles.

SPEYER AND DURHAM The imperial cathedral at Speyer in the Rhine River Valley was a colossal structure. An Ottonian, wooden-roofed church built between 1030 and 1060 was given a masonry vault c. 1080–1106 (**FIG. 16–16**). Massive compound piers mark each nave bay and support the transverse ribs of a groin vault that rises to a height of over 100 feet. The compound piers alternate with smaller piers supporting the vaults of the aisle bays. This rhythmic, alternating pattern of heavy and light elements, first suggested in Ottonian wooden-roofed architecture (SEE FIG. 15–25B), became an important design element in Speyer. Since groin vaults concentrate the weight and thrust of the vault on the four corners of the bay, they relieve the stress on the side walls of the building—so large windows can be safely inserted in each bay to flood the building with light.

The exterior of Speyer Cathedral emphasizes its Ottonian and Carolingian background. Soaring towers and wide transepts mark both ends of the building, although a narthex, not an apse, stands to the west. A large apse housing the high altar abuts the flat wall of the choir; transept

16–17 EXTERIOR, SPEYER CATHEDRAL
c. 1080–1106 and second half of the 12th century.

Credit: © akg-images/Erich Lessing

arms project at each side; a large octagonal tower rises over the crossing; and a pair of tall, slender towers flanks the choir (**FIG. 16–17**). A horizontal arcade forms an exterior gallery at the top of the apse and transept wall, recalling the Italian practice at Pisa (SEE FIG. 16–10).

In Durham, an English military outpost near the Scottish border, a prince-bishop held both secular and religious authority. For his headquarters he chose a defensive site where the bend in the River Wear formed a natural moat. Durham grew into a powerful fortified complex including a castle, a monastery, and a cathedral. The great tower of the castle defended against attack from the land, and an open space between buildings served as the courtyard of the castle and the cathedral green.

DURHAM CATHEDRAL, begun in 1087 and vaulted starting in 1093, is an impressive example of Norman Romanesque, but like most buildings that have been in continuous use, it has been altered several times (**FIG. 16–18**). The nave retains its Norman character, but the huge circular window lighting the choir is a later Gothic addition.

16–16 INTERIOR, SPEYER CATHEDRAL
Rhineland-Palatinate, Germany. As remodeled c. 1080–1106.

Credit: © akg-images/Bildarchiv Monheim

The cathedral's size and décor are ambitious. Enormous compound piers and robust columnar piers form the nave arcade and establish a rhythmic alternation. The columnar piers are carved with chevrons, spiral fluting, and diamond patterns, and some have scalloped, cushion-shape capitals. The richly carved arches that sit on them have multiple round moldings and chevron ornaments. All this carved ornamentation was originally painted.

Above the cathedral's massive piers and walls rises a new system of ribbed groin vaults. Romanesque masons in Santiago de Compostela, Cluny, Fontenay, Speyer, and Durham were all experimenting with stone vaulting—and adopted different solutions. The Durham builders divided each bay with two pairs of diagonal crisscrossing rounded ribs and so kept the crowns of the vaults close in height to the keystones of the pointed transverse arches. Although this allows the eye to run smoothly down the length of the vault, and from vault to vault down the expanse of the nave, the richly carved zigzagging moldings on the ribs themselves invite us to linger over each bay, acknowledging traditional Romanesque bay division. This new system of ribbed groin vaulting will become a hallmark of Gothic architecture, though there it will create a very different aesthetic effect.

16–18A PLAN OF DURHAM CATHEDRAL

Northern England. 1087–1133. Original east end replaced by a Gothic choir, 1242–c. 1280.

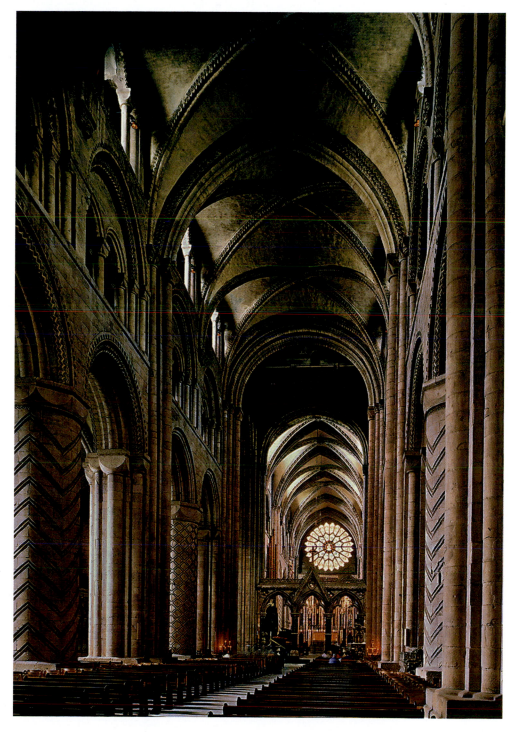

16–18B INTERIOR OF DURHAM CATHEDRAL

Northern England. 1087–1133. Original east end replaced by a Gothic choir, 1242–c. 1280. Vault height about 73′ (22.2 m).

Credit: © akg-images/A.F.Kersting

Secular Architecture

The need to provide for personal security in a time of periodic local warfare and political upheaval, as well as the desire to glorify the house of Christ and his saints, meant that communities used much of their resources to build castles and churches. Fully garrisoned, castles were sometimes as large as cities. In the twelfth century, **DOVER CASTLE** was a bold manifestation of military power that safeguarded the southeastern coast of England from invasion (**FIG. 16–19**). It illustrates the way in which a key defensive position developed over the centuries.

The Romans had built a lighthouse on the point where the English Channel separating England and France narrows. The Anglo-Saxons added a church (both lighthouse and church can be seen in FIG. 16–19 behind the tower, surrounded by the remains of earthen walls). In the early Middle Ages, earthworks topped by wooden walls provided a measure of security, and a wooden tower signified an important administrative building and residence. The advantage of fire-resistant walls was obvious, and in the twelfth and thirteenth centuries, military engineers replaced the timber tower and palisades with stone walls. They added the massive stone towers we see today.

The Great Tower, as it was called in the Middle Ages (later known as a **keep** in England and donjon in France), stood in a courtyard called the bailey, surrounded by additional walls. Ditches outside the walls added to their height. In some castles, ditches were filled with water to form moats. A gatehouse—perhaps with a drawbridge—controlled the entrance. In all castles, the bailey was filled with buildings, the most important of which was the lord's

16–19 DOVER CASTLE
Southern England.

Aerial view. Center: Norman Great Tower, surrounding earthworks and wall, twelfth century. Outer walls, thirteenth century. Modern buildings have red tiled roofs. The castle was used in World War II and is now a museum.

Credit: © Arcaid Images/Alamy Stock Photo

Elements of Architecture

THE ROMANESQUE CHURCH PORTAL

The most important imagery on a Romanesque portal appears on the semicircular **tympanum** directly over the door—often a hierarchically scaled image of abstract grandeur such as Christ in Majesty or Christ presiding over the Last Judgment—as well as on the lintel beneath it. **Archivolts**—curved moldings composed of the wedge-shaped stone voussoirs of the arch—frame the tympanum. On both sides of the doors, the **jambs** (vertical elements) and occasionally a central pier called the **trumeau** support the lintel and archivolts, providing further fields for figures, columns, or narrative friezes. The jambs can extend forward to form a porch.

hall; it was used to hold court and for feasts and ceremonial occasions. Timber buildings housed troops, servants, and animals. Barns, workshops, ovens, and wells were also needed—the castle had to be self-sufficient.

If enemies broke through the outer walls, the castle's defenders retreated to the Great Tower. In the thirteenth century, the builders at Dover doubled the walls and strengthened them with towers, even though the castle's position on cliffs overlooking the sea made scaling the walls nearly impossible. It could be forced to surrender only by starving its occupants.

During Dover Castle's heyday, improvements in farming and growing prosperity provided the resources for increased building activity across Europe. The secular and religious buildings that still stand—despite the ravages of weather, vandalism, neglect, and war—testify to the technical skills and creative ingenuity of the builders and the power, local pride, and faith of the patrons.

Romanesque Sculpture

Why is monumental architectural stone sculpture revived in the Romanesque period and how is the style extended into works in wood and bronze?

Architecture dominated the arts in the Romanesque period—not only because it required the material and human resources of entire communities, but because it provided the physical context for a revival of the art of monumental stone sculpture, which had been almost dormant in Europe for 500 years. The "mute" façades used in early medieval buildings (SEE FIG. 15–18) were transformed by Romanesque sculptors into "speaking" façades with richly carved portals that projected bold symbolic and

didactic programs to the outside world (SEE FIG. 16–21). Christ Enthroned in Majesty might be carved over the entrance, and increasing importance was accorded to the Virgin Mary. The prophets, kings, and queens of the Hebrew Bible were seen by medieval Christians as precursors of people and events in the New Testament, so they were depicted; we can also find representations of contemporary bishops, abbots, other noble patrons, and even ordinary folk. A profusion of monsters, animals, plants, geometric ornament, allegorical figures such as Lust and Greed, and depictions of real and imagined buildings surround the sculpture within its architectural setting. The elect rejoice in heaven with the angels; the damned suffer in hell, tormented by demons; biblical and historical tales come alive in a contemporary medieval setting, juxtaposed with scenes drawn from the viewer's everyday life.

These innovative portals are among the greatest artistic achievements of Romanesque art, taking the central messages of the Christian Church out of the sanctuary (SEE FIGS. 8–6, 8–11) and into the public spaces of medieval towns. And figural sculpture did not appear only at entrances—it was also on the capitals of interior and exterior piers and columns, as well as in friezes, on corbels, even peeking around cornices or from behind moldings. There was plenty of work for stone sculptors on Romanesque building sites.

Wiligelmo at the Cathedral of Modena

The spirit of ancient Rome pervades the sculpture of Romanesque Italy, and the sculptor Wiligelmo may have been inspired by Roman sarcophagi still visible in cemeteries when he carved horizontal reliefs across the west façade of Modena Cathedral, c. 1099. Wiligelmo took his

16–20 Wiligelmo **CREATION AND FALL OF ADAM AND EVE, WEST FAÇADE, MODENA CATHEDRAL**
Emilia, Italy. Building begun 1099; sculpture c. 1099. Height approx. 3′ (92 cm).

Credit: © 2016. Photo Scala, Florence

subjects here from Genesis, focusing on events from the **CREATION AND FALL OF ADAM AND EVE** (FIG. 16–20). On the far left, God, in a mandorla (body halo) supported by angels, appears as both Creator and Christ, identified by a cruciform halo. Following this iconic image, the narrative of creation unfolds in three scenes from left to right: God brings Adam to life, then brings forth Eve from Adam's side, and finally Adam and Eve cover their genitals in shame as they eat fruit from the forbidden tree, around which the wily serpent twists.

Wiligelmo's deft carving gives these figures a strong three-dimensionality. The framing arcade establishes a stagelike setting, with the rocks on which Adam lies and the tempting tree of paradise serving as stage props. Wiligelmo's figures exude life and personality; they convey an emotional connection with the narrative they enact. Bright paint, now almost all lost, must have increased their lifelike impact still further. An inscription at Modena proclaims, "Among sculptors, your work shines forth, Wiligelmo." This self-confidence turned out to be justified. Wiligelmo's influence can be traced throughout Italy and as far away as Lincoln Cathedral in England.

The Priory Church of Saint-Pierre at Moissac

The Cluniac priory of Saint-Pierre at Moissac was a major stop on the pilgrimage route to Santiago de Compostela. The shrine at the site dates back to the Carolingian period, and after affiliating with Cluny in 1047, the monastery prospered from the donations of pilgrims and local nobility, as well as from its control of shipping on the nearby Garonne River. During the twelfth century, Moissac's monks launched an ambitious building campaign, and much of the sculpture from the cloister (c. 1100, under Abbot Ansquetil) and the church portal and porch (1100–1130, under Abbot Roger) has survived. The quantity and quality of the carving here are outstanding.

A flattened figure of **CHRIST IN MAJESTY** dominates the huge tympanum (FIG. 16–21), visualizing a description of the Second Coming in Chapters 4 and 5 of Revelation. This gigantic Christ is an imposing, iconic image of enduring grandeur. He is enclosed by a mandorla; a cruciform halo rings his head. Although Christ is stable, even static, in this apocalyptic appearance, the four winged creatures symbolizing the evangelists—Matthew the man (upper left), Mark the lion (lower left), Luke the ox (lower right), and John the eagle (upper right)—who frame him on either side move with dynamic force, as if activated by his dramatic appearance. Rippling bands extend across the tympanum at Christ's sides and under him—perhaps representing waves in the "sea of glass like crystal" (Revelation 4:6). They delineate three registers in which 24 elders with "gold crowns on their heads" and either a harp or a gold bowl of incense (Revelation 4:4 and 5:8) twist to catch a glimpse of Christ's majestic arrival. Each of them takes an individually conceived pose and gesture, as if the sculptors were demonstrating their ability to represent three-dimensional human figures turning in space in a variety of postures, some quite challengingly contorted. Foliate and geometric ornament covers every surface surrounding this tableau. Monstrous heads in the lower corners of

16–21 SOUTH PORTAL, TYMPANUM SHOWING CHRIST IN MAJESTY, PRIORY CHURCH OF SAINT-PIERRE, MOISSAC
Tarn-et-Garonne, France. c. 1115.

Credit: © Achim Bednorz, Cologne

the tympanum spew ribbon scrolls, and other creatures appear at each end of the lintel, their tongues growing into ropes encircling acanthus rosettes.

Two side jambs and a trumeau (central portal pier) support the weight of the lintel and tympanum. These elements have scalloped profiles that playfully undermine the ability of the colonettes on the door jambs to perform their architectural function. They give a sense of instability to the lower part of the portal, as if to underline the ability of the stable figure of Christ in Majesty to provide his own means of support. St. Peter and the prophet Isaiah flank the doorway on the jambs. Peter, a tall, thin saint, steps away from the door but twists back to look through it.

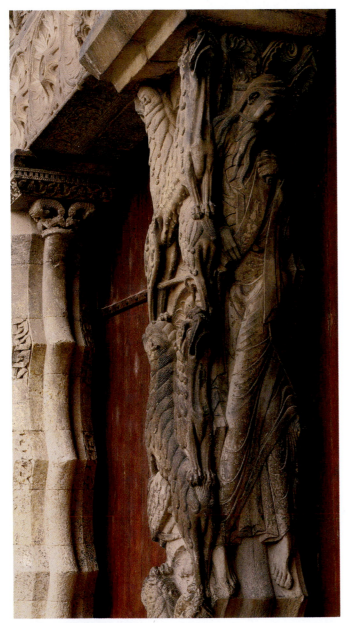

16-22 TRUMEAU, SOUTH PORTAL, PRIORY CHURCH OF SAINT-PIERRE, MOISSAC

c. 1115.

Credit: © Achim Bednorz, Cologne

The **TRUMEAU** (FIG. 16-22) is faced by a crisscrossing pair of lions. On the side visible here, a prophet, usually identified as Jeremiah, twists toward the viewer, with legs crossed in a pose that would challenge his ability to stand, much less move. The sculptors placed him in skillful conformity with the constraints of the scalloped trumeau; his head, pelvis, knees, and feet moving into the pointed cusps. This decorative scalloping, as well as the trumeau lions and lintel rosettes, may reveal the influence of Islamic art. Moissac was under construction shortly after the First Crusade, when many Europeans first encountered the Islamic art and architecture of the Holy Land. People from the region around Moissac participated in the crusade; perhaps they brought Islamic objects and ideas home with them.

A porch covering the area in front of the portal at Moissac provided a sheltered space for pilgrims to congregate and view the sculpture. The side walls of this porch are filled with yet more figural sculptures (FIG. 16-23), but the style of presentation changes here with the nature of the subject matter and the response that was sought from the audience. Instead of the stylized and agitated figures on the tympanum and its supports, here sculptors have substituted more lifelike and approachable human beings. Rather than embodying unchanging theological notions or awe-inspiring apocalyptic appearances, these figures convey human frailties and torments in order to persuade viewers to follow the Church's moral teachings.

Behind the double arcade framework of the lower part of the wall are hair-raising portrayals of the torments of those who fall prey to the two sins that particularly preoccupied twelfth-century moralists: avarice (greed and the hoarding of money) and lust (sexual misconduct). At bottom left, a greedy man is attacked by demons while the money bags around his neck weigh him down, strangling him. On the other side of the column, his counterpart, the female personification of lust (*luxuria*), is confronted by a pot-bellied devil while snakes bite at her breasts and another predator attacks her pubic area. In the scene that extends behind the column and across the wall above them, *luxuria* reappears, kneeling beside the deathbed of the miser, as devils make off with his money. These scenes are made as graphic as possible so that medieval viewers could identify with the situations, perhaps even feel the pain in their own bodies as a warning to avoid behaviors that lead to such gruesome consequences.

In the strip of relief running across the top of the wall, the mood is calmer, but the moral message remains clear, at least for those who know the story. The sculpture tells the tale of Lazarus and Dives (Luke 16:19–31), the most popular parable of Jesus in Romanesque art. The broad scene to the right shows the rich and greedy Dives, relishing the feast that is being laid before him by his servants and refusing to give even his table scraps to the leprous certainly evoked on the lower section of the wall in the torments of the miser, whom we can now identify with Dives himself. Clearly some knowledge is necessary to recognize the story of this sculpture, and a guide may have been present to aid those viewers who did not readily understand. Nonetheless, the moral of sin and its consequences can be read easily from the narrative presentation. This is not scripture for an illiterate population. It is a sermon sculpted in stone.

The Church of Saint-Lazare at Autun

A different sculptural style and another subject appear at Autun on the portal of the church of Saint-Lazare (see "Closer Look" on page 496), which was built in the first half of the twelfth century as part of a cathedral complex to house the relics of St. Lazarus, becoming the cathedral of Autun itself only in 1195. The tympanum portrays the Last Judgment, in which Christ—enclosed in a mandorla held by two svelte angels—has returned at the end of time to judge the cowering, naked humans whose bodies rise from their sarcophagi along the lintel at his feet. The damned writhe in torment at Christ's left (our right), while on the opposite side the saved savor serene bliss. The inscribed message on the side of the damned reads: "Here let fear strike those whom earthly error binds, for their fate is shown by the horror of these figures," and under the blessed: "Thus shall rise again everyone who does not lead an impious life, and endless light of day shall shine for him" (translations from Grivot and Zarnecki).

Another text, right under the feet of Christ, ascribes the Autun tympanum to a man named Gislebertus—*Gislebertus hoc fecit* ("Gislebertus made this"). Traditionally, art historians have interpreted this inscription as a rare instance of a twelfth-century artist's signature, assigning this façade and related sculpture to an individual named Gislebertus, who was at the head of a large workshop of sculptors. Recently, however, art historian Linda Seidel has challenged this reading, arguing that Gislebertus was actually a late Carolingian count who had made significant donations to local churches. Like the names inscribed on many academic buildings of American universities, this legendary donor's name would have been evoked here as a reminder of the long and rich history of secular financial support in Autun, and perhaps also as a challenge to those currently in power to respect and continue that venerable tradition of patronage themselves.

Thinner and taller than their counterparts at Moissac, stretched out and bent at sharp angles, the stylized figures at Autun are powerfully expressive and hauntingly beautiful. As at Moissac, a huge, **hieratic** (highly stylized) figure of Christ dominates the composition at the center of the tympanum, but the surrounding figures are not arranged here in regular compartmentalized tiers. Their posture

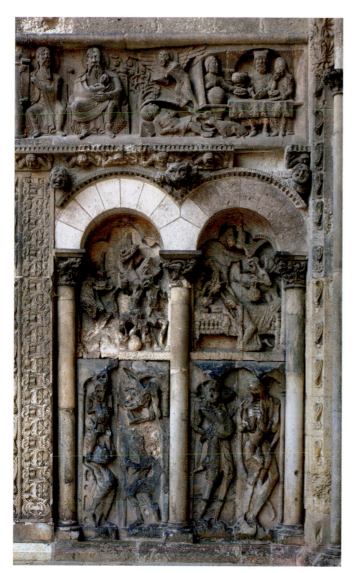

16–23 RELIEFS ON THE LEFT (WEST) WALL OF THE SOUTH PORCH, PRIORY CHURCH OF SAINT-PIERRE, MOISSAC

c. 1115.

The parable of Lazarus and Dives that runs across the top of this wall has retained its moral power to our own day. This was the text of Martin Luther King's last Sunday sermon, preached only a few days before his assassination in Memphis, where he was supporting a strike by sanitation workers. Perhaps he saw the parable's image of the table scraps of the rich and greedy as particularly appropriate to his context. Just as in this portal, in Dr. King's sermon the story was juxtaposed with other stories and ideas to craft its interpretive message in a way that was both clear and compelling for the audience addressed.

Credit: © Achim Bednorz, Cologne

beggar Lazarus, spread out at lower left. Under the table, dogs—unsatisfied by leftovers from Dives's feast—turn to lick the pus from Lazarus's sores as he draws his last breath. The angel above Lazarus, however, transfers his soul (once represented as a naked baby, now missing) to the lap of Abraham (a common image of paradise), where he is cuddled by the patriarch, the eternal reward for a pious life. The fate of Dives is not portrayed here, but it is

A Closer Look

THE LAST JUDGMENT TYMPANUM AT AUTUN

In one of the most endearing vignettes, an angel pushes one of the saved up through an open archway and into the glorious architectural vision of heaven. Another figure at the angel's side reaches up, impatient for his turn to be hoisted up into paradise.

Christ's mother, Mary, is enthroned as queen of heaven. Below, St. Peter—identified by the large keys slung over his shoulder—performs his duties as heavenly gatekeeper, clasping the hands of someone waiting to gain entrance.

This inscription proclaims "I alone dispose of all things and crown the just. Those who follow crime I judge and punish." Clearly, some of the viewers could read Latin.

The cross (a badge of Jerusalem) and scallop shell (a badge of Santiago de Compostela) identify these two figures as former pilgrims. The clear message is that participation in pilgrimage will be a factor in their favor at the Last Judgment.

The incised ornament on these sarcophagi is quite similar to that on ancient Roman sarcophagi, one of many indications that the Autun sculptors and masons knew the ancient art created when Autun was a Roman city.

Interestingly, hell is represented here as a basilica, with a devil emerging from the toothy maw that serves as a side entrance, capturing sinners for eternal torment. The devil uses a sharp hook to grab *luxuria*, the female personification of lust.

16–24 Gislebertus (?) THE LAST JUDGMENT
West portal tympanum, Cathedral of Saint-Lazare, Autun, Burgundy, France. c. 1120–1130 or 1130–1145.

Credit: © Achim Bednorz, Cologne

and placement conform to their involvement in the story they enact. Since that story is filled with human interest and anecdotal narrative detail, viewers can easily project themselves into what is going on. On the lintel, angels physically assist the resurrected bodies rising from their tombs, guiding them to line up and await their turn at being judged. Ominously, a pair of giant, pincerlike hands descends to snatch one of the damned on the right side of the lintel (as we look at it). Above these hands, the archangel Michael competes with devils over the fate of someone

whose judgment is being weighed on the scales of good and evil. The man himself perches on the top of the scale, hands cupped to his mouth to project his pleas for help toward the Savior. Another man hides nervously in the folds of Michael's robe, perhaps hoping to escape judgment or cowering from the prospect of eternal damnation.

By far the most riveting players in this drama are the grotesque, screaming demons who grab and torment the damned and even try to cheat by yanking the scales to favor damnation. The fear they inspire, as well as the poignant portrayal of the psychological state of those whom they torment, would have been reminders to medieval viewers to examine the way they were leading their own lives, or perhaps to seek the benefits of entering the doors in front of them to participate in the community of the Church.

16–25 THE MAGI ASLEEP (A) AND THE FLIGHT INTO EGYPT (B)

Capitals from the choir pier pilasters, Cathedral of Saint-Lazare, Autun, Burgundy, France. c. 1125.

Credit: Bridgeman Images

The creation of lively narrative scenes within the geometric confines of capitals (called **historiated capitals**) was an important Romanesque innovation in architectural sculpture. The same sculptors who worked on the Autun tympanum carved historiated capitals for pier pilasters inside the church. Two capitals (**FIG. 16–25**) depict scenes from the childhood of Jesus drawn from Matthew 2:1–18. In one capital, the Magi—who have previously adored and offered gifts to the child Jesus—are interrupted in their sleep by an angel who warns them not to inform King Herod of the location of the newborn king of the Jews. In an ingenious compositional device, the sculptor has shown the reclining Magi and the head of their bed as if viewed from above, whereas the angel and the foot of the bed are viewed from the side. This allows us to see clearly the angel—who is appearing to them in a dream—as he touches the hand of the upper Magus, whose eyes have popped open. As on the façade, the sculptor has conceived this scene in ways that emphasize the human qualities of its story, not its deep theological significance. With its charming, doll-like figures, the other capital shows an event that occurred just after the Magi's dream: Joseph, Mary, and Jesus are journeying toward Egypt to escape King Herod's order to murder all young boys so as to eliminate the newborn royal rival the Magi had journeyed to venerate.

Sculpture in Wood and Bronze

Painted wood was commonly used when abbey and parish churches of limited means commissioned statues. Wood was not only cheap, it was lightweight, a significant consideration since these devotional images were frequently carried in processions. But whereas wood seems to have been a sculptural medium that spread across Europe, three geographic areas—the Rhineland, the Meuse River Valley, and German Saxony—were the principal metalworking centers. Bronze sculpture was produced only for wealthy aristocratic and ecclesiastical patrons. It drew on a variety of stylistic sources, including the work of contemporary Byzantine and Italian artists, as well as Classical precedents as reinterpreted by the sculptors' Carolingian and Ottonian forebears.

CHRIST ON THE CROSS (MAJESTAT BATLLÓ) This mid-twelfth-century painted wooden crucifix from Catalunya, known as the **MAJESTAT BATLLÓ** (**FIG. 16–26**), presents a clothed, triumphant Christ, rather than the seminude figure we have seen at Byzantine Daphni (SEE FIG. 8–22) or on the Ottonian Gero Crucifix (SEE FIG. 15–26). This Christ's royal robes emphasize his kingship, although his bowed head, downturned mouth, and heavy-lidded eyes seem to convey sadness or introspection. The hem of his long, medallion-patterned tunic has pseudo-kufic

16-26 CRUCIFIX (MAJESTAT BATLLÓ)
Catalunya, Spain. Mid 12th century. Polychromed wood, height approx. 37¾" (96 cm). MNAC - Museu Nacional d'Art de Catalunya, Barcelona.

Credit: © 2016. Photo Scala, Florence

inscriptions—designs meant to resemble Arabic script—a reminder that silks from Islamic Spain were highly prized in Europe at this time.

MARY AS THE THRONE OF WISDOM Any Romanesque image of Mary seated on a throne and holding the Christ Child on her lap is known as "The Throne of Wisdom." In a well-preserved example in painted wood dating from the second half of the twelfth century (**FIG. 16-27**), Mother and Child are frontal and regal. Mary's thronelike bench symbolized the lion-throne of Solomon, the Hebrew Bible king who represented earthly wisdom in the Middle Ages. Mary, as Mother and "God-bearer" (the Byzantine *Theotokos*), gave Jesus his human nature. She forms a throne on which he sits in majesty, but she also represents the Church. Although the Child's hands are missing, we can assume that the young Jesus held a book—the Word of God—in his left hand and raised his right hand in blessing.

Such statues of the Virgin and Child served as cult objects on the altars of many churches during the twelfth century. They also sometimes took part in the liturgical dramas becoming popular in church services at this time. At the feast of the Epiphany, celebrating the arrival of the Magi to pay homage to the young Jesus, townspeople representing the Magi acted out their journey by searching through the church for the newborn king. The roles of Mary and Jesus were "acted" by such sculptures, which the "Magi" discovered on the altar. The Flight into Egypt capital from Autun in FIGURE 16–25 may record the theatrical use of a wooden statue, strapped to the back of a wooden donkey, that would have been rolled into the church on wheels, possibly referenced by the round forms at the base of the capital.

TOMB OF RUDOLF OF SWABIA The oldest-known bronze tomb effigy (recumbent portrait of the deceased) is that of **KING RUDOLF OF SWABIA** (**FIG. 16–28**), who died

16-27 VIRGIN AND CHILD
Auvergne region, France. Late 12th century. Oak with polychromy, height 31" (78.7 cm). Metropolitan Museum of Art, New York. Gift of J. Pierpont Morgan, 1916 (16.32.194).

Credit: © 2016. Image copyright The Metropolitan Museum of Art/Art Resource/ Scala, Florence

16–28 TOMB COVER WITH EFFIGY OF KING RUDOLF OF SWABIA

Saxony, Germany. c. 1080. Bronze with niello, approx. 6′5½″ × 2′2½″ (1.97 × 0.68 m). Cathedral of Merseburg, Germany.

Credit: © akg-images

16–29 Renier of Huy **BAPTISMAL FONT, NOTRE-DAME-AUX-FONTS**

Liège, Belgium. 1107–1118. Bronze, height 23⅝″ (60 cm), diameter 31¼″ (79 cm). Now in the church of Saint-Barthélemy, Liège.

Credit: © Achim Bednorz, Cologne

in battle in 1080. The spurs on his oversized feet identify him as a heroic warrior, and he holds a scepter and cross-surmounted orb, emblems of Christian kingship. Although the tomb is in the cathedral of Merseburg, in Saxony, the effigy has been attributed to an artist originally from the Rhine Valley. Nearly life-size, it was cast in one piece and gilded, though few traces of the gilding survive. The inscription around the frame was incised after casting, and glass paste or semiprecious stones may have originally been set into the eyes and crown. We know that during the battle that ultimately led to Rudolph's death he lost a hand—which was mummified separately and kept in a leather case—but the sculptor of his effigy presents him idealized and whole.

RENIER OF HUY Bronze sculptor Renier of Huy (Huy is near Liège in present-day Belgium) worked in the Mosan region under the profound influence of classicizing early medieval works of art, as well as the humanistic learning of Church scholars. Hellinus of Notre-Dame-aux-Fonts in Liège (abbot 1107–1118) commissioned a bronze **BAPTISMAL FONT** from Renier (**FIG. 16–29**) that was inspired by the basin carried by 12 oxen in Solomon's Temple in Jerusalem (I Kings 7:23–24).

Christian commentators identified the 12 oxen as the 12 apostles and the basin as the baptismal font, and this interpretation is given visual form in Renier's work. On the sides of the font are images of St. John the Baptist preaching and baptizing Christ, St. Peter baptizing the Roman soldier Cornelius, and St. John the Evangelist baptizing the philosopher Crato. Renier models sturdy but idealized bodies—nude or with clinging drapery—that move and gesture with lifelike conviction, infused with dignity, simplicity, and harmony. His understanding of human anatomy and movement must have derived from close observation of the people around him. He placed these figures within defined landscape settings, standing on an undulating ground-line, and separated into scenes by miniature trees. Water rises in a mound of rippling waves (in Byzantine fashion) to cover nude figures discreetly.

Textiles and Books

What are the characteristic features of the Romanesque style in textiles and manuscript painting?

Among the most admired arts during the Middle Ages were those that later critics patronized as the "minor" or "decorative" arts. Although small in scale, these works were often produced with technical virtuosity from very precious materials, and they were vital to the Christian mission and devotion of the institutions that housed them.

Artists in the eleventh and twelfth centuries were still often monks and nuns. They labored within monasteries as calligraphers and painters in scriptoria to produce books and as metalworkers to craft the enamel- and jewel-encrusted works used in liturgical services. They also embroidered the vestments, altar coverings, and wall hangings that clothed both celebrants and settings in the Mass. Increasingly, however, secular urban workshops supplied the aristocratic and royal courts with textiles, tableware, books, and weapons for their own use or as donations to religious institutions.

Chronicling History

Romanesque artists were commissioned not only to illustrate engaging stories and embody important theological ideas within the context of sacred buildings and sacred books. They also created visual accounts of secular history, where moralizing was one of the principal objectives of pictorial narrative.

THE WORCESTER CHRONICLE   The earliest-known illustrated history book, written in the twelfth century by a monk named John, is the **WORCESTER CHRONICLE** (**FIG. 16–30**). The pages shown here concern Henry I (ruled 1100–1135), the second of William the Conqueror's sons to sit on the English throne. The text relates a series of nightmares the king had in 1130, in which his subjects demanded tax relief. The artist depicts the dreams with energetic directness. On the first night, farmers confront the sleeping king; on the second, armed knights surround his bed; and on the third, monks, abbots, and bishops present their case. In the fourth illustration, the king travels in a storm-tossed ship and saves himself by promising God that he will rescind the tax increase for seven years. The author of the Worcester Chronicle assured his readers that this story came from a reliable source, the royal physician Grimbald, who appears in the margins next to three of the scenes. The farmers capture our attention today because we seldom see working men with their equipment and simple clothing depicted in painting from this time.

THE BAYEUX EMBROIDERY   Rarely has art spoken more vividly than in the eleventh-century **BAYEUX EMBROIDERY**, a strip of embroidered linen that recounts the history of the Norman Conquest of England. Its designer was a skillful storyteller who used a staggering number of images to tell the tale. In the 50 surviving scenes there are more than 600 human figures; 700 horses, dogs, and other creatures; and 2,000 inch-high letters. This work represents the kind of secular art that

16–30 John of Worcester **THOSE WHO WORK; THOSE WHO FIGHT; THOSE WHO PRAY—THE DREAM OF HENRY I, WORCESTER CHRONICLE**

Worcester, England. c. 1140. Ink and tempera on vellum, each page 12¾ × 9⅜" (32.5 × 23.7 cm). Corpus Christi College, Oxford.

Credit: By Permission of the President and Fellows of Corpus Christi College, Oxford (CCC Ms 157)

16–31 MESSENGERS SIGNAL THE APPEARANCE OF HALLEY'S COMET, THE BAYEUX EMBROIDERY

Norman–Anglo-Saxon, perhaps from Canterbury, Kent, England. c. 1066–1082. Linen with wool embroidery, height 20″ (50.8 cm). Centre Guillaume le Conquérant, Bayeux, France.

Credit: Musée de la Tapisserie, Bayeux, France/With special authorisation of the city of Bayeux/Bridgeman Images

Early in the story, the Anglo-Saxon nobleman Harold swears his allegiance to William, but later he betrays this vow, accepting the crown of England for himself. Harold begins as a heroic figure, but then events overtake him. After his coronation, cheering crowds celebrate—until Halley's Comet crosses the sky (**FIG. 16–31**). The Anglo-Saxons, seeing the comet as a portent of disaster, cringe and point at this brilliant ball of fire with a flaming tail, and a man rushes to inform the new king. Harold slumps on his throne in the Palace of Westminster. He foresees what is to come: Below his feet is his vision of a ghostly fleet of Norman ships already riding the waves. Duke William has assembled the last great Viking flotilla on the Normandy coast. Unworthy to be king, Harold dies in the ensuing battle at the hands of William and the Normans.

In another extended tableau, Duke William and his brother Odo, Bishop of Bayeux, are feasting before the battle (**FIG. 16–32**). Attendants bring in roasted birds on skewers, placing them on a makeshift table made of the knights' shields set on trestles. The diners, summoned by the blowing of a horn, gather at a curved table laden with food and drink. Bishop Odo—seated at the center, head and shoulders above William to his right—blesses the meal while others eat. The kneeling servant in the middle proffers a basin and towel so that the diners may wash their hands. The man on Odo's left points to the next event, a council

must once have been part of most royal courts. It could have been rolled up and transported from residence to residence as the noble Norman owner traveled throughout his domain, and some have speculated that it may have been the backdrop at banquets for stories sung by professional performers who could have received their cues from the identifying inscriptions that accompany most scenes. Eventually the embroidery was given to Bayeux Cathedral, perhaps by Bishop Odo, William's half brother; we know it was displayed around the walls of the cathedral on the feast of the relics.

Flanked by narrower bands of ornament, the broad, central narrative strip of the Bayeux Embroidery chronicles the events that led to Duke William of Normandy's conquest of England on October 14, 1066, when, after a long day of fighting, he became William the Conqueror, king of England. It may have been drawn by a Norman designer since there is a clear Norman bias in the telling of the story; it justifies William's conquest with the intensity of an eyewitness account. The style of the embroidery, however, suggests that Anglo-Saxons did the actual needlework.

16–32 BISHOP ODO BLESSING THE FEAST, THE BAYEUX EMBROIDERY

Norman–Anglo-Saxon, perhaps from Canterbury, Kent, England. c. 1066–1082. Linen with wool embroidery, height 20″ (50.8 cm). Centre Guillaume le Conquérant, Bayeux, France.

Credit: Musée de la Tapisserie, Bayeux, France/With special authorisation of the city of Bayeux/Bridgeman Images

16-33 DETAIL OF FIG. 16-32 HIGHLIGHTING THE EMBROIDERY STICHING

Credit: Musée de la Tapisserie, Bayeux, France/With special authorisation of the city of Bayeux/Bridgeman Images

of war between William (now the central and tallest figure), Odo, and a third man labeled "Rotbert," probably Robert of Mortain, another of William's half brothers. The text reads: "and here the servants (*ministra*) perform their duty. / Here they prepare the meal (*prandium*) / and here the bishop blesses the food and drink (*cibu et potu*). Bishop Odo. William. Robert."

The tragedy of this drama has spoken movingly to audiences over the centuries. It is the story of a good man—Harold—who, like Shakespeare's Macbeth, is overcome by his lust for power and so betrays his lord—Duke William. The images of this Norman invasion also spoke to people during the darkest days of World War II. When the Allies invaded Nazi-occupied Europe in June 1944, they took the same route in reverse from England to beaches on the coast of Normandy. The Bayeux Embroidery still speaks to us of the folly of human greed and ambition and of two battles that changed the course of history.

Although traditionally referred to as the "Bayeux Tapestry," this work is really an embroidery. In tapestry, the colored threads that create images or patterns are woven together during the process of production, completely covering the canvas ground that serves as their support; in embroidery, stitches are applied on top of a tightly woven fabric that serves as their support, as well as the ground behind the patterns they create (**FIG. 16-33**).

The embroiderers—probably Anglo-Saxon women based on the style—worked in tightly twisted wool that was dyed in eight colors and sewed onto fine linen cloth. They used only two stitches: the quick, overlapping stem stitch that produced a slightly jagged line or outline, and the time-consuming laid-and-couched work used to form blocks of color.

For the latter, the embroiderer first "laid" a series of long, parallel covering threads; then anchored them with a second layer of regularly spaced crosswise stitches; and finally tacked all the strands down with tiny "couching" stitches. Some of the laid-and-couched work was done in contrasting colors to achieve particular effects. The creative coloring is often fanciful: for example, some horses have legs in four different colors. Skin and other light-toned areas are represented by the bare linen cloth that formed the ground of the work.

Sacred Books

Monastic scriptoria continued to be the centers of illustrated book production, which increased dramatically during the twelfth century. But the scriptoria sometimes employed lay scribes and artists who traveled from place to place. In addition to the books needed for church services, scribes produced copies of sacred texts, scholarly commentaries, visionary devotional works, lives of saints, and collections of letters and sermons.

THE CODEX COLBERTINUS The portrait of **ST. MATTHEW** from the Codex Colbertinus (**FIG. 16-34**) is an entirely Romanesque conception, quite different from Hiberno-Saxon and Carolingian author portraits. Like the sculptured pier figures of Silos (**SEE FIG. 16-1**), the evangelist stands within an architectural frame that completely surrounds him. Instead of writing in his book, he blesses and holds it within the compact silhouette of his body. His dangling feet bear no weight, and his body has little sense of three-dimensionality, with solid blocks of color filling its strong outlines.

The text of Matthew's Gospel begins with a complementary block of ornament to the left of Matthew's portrait. The "L" of *Liber generationis* ("The book of the generation") is a framed picture formed of plants and animals—what art historians call a historiated initial. Dogs or catlike creatures and long-necked birds twist, claw, and bite each other and themselves while, in the center, two humans—one dressed and one nude—clamber up the letter. This manuscript was made in the region of Moissac at about the same time that sculptors were working on the abbey church, and the stacking of intertwined animals here recalls the outer face of the Moissac trumeau (SEE FIGS. 16–21, 16–22).

16–35 The Nun Guda **BOOK OF HOMILIES**
Westphalia, Germany. Early 12th century. Ink on parchment. Universitätsbibliothek Johann Christian Senckenberg, Frankfurt am Main, Germany. MS. Barth. 42, fol. 110v.

THE GERMAN NUN GUDA In another historiated initial, this one from Westphalia in Germany, the nun Guda has a more modest presentation. In a **BOOK OF HOMILIES** (sermons), she inserted her self-portrait into the letter *D* and signed it as scribe and painter, "Guda, the sinful woman, wrote and illuminated this book" (**FIG. 16–35**). This is a simple colored drawing with darker blocks of color in the background, but Guda and her monastic sisters played an important role in the production of books in the twelfth century, and not all of them remain anonymous. Guda's image is the earliest signed self-portrait by a woman in western Europe. Throughout the Middle Ages, women were involved in the production of books as authors, scribes, painters, and patrons.

A CISTERCIAN TREE OF JESSE The Cistercians were particularly devoted to the Virgin Mary and are also credited with popularizing themes such as the Tree of Jesse as a device for showing her position as the last link in the genealogy connecting Jesus to King David. (Jesse, the father of King David, was an ancestor of Mary and, through her, of Jesus.) A manuscript of St. Jerome's Commentary on Isaiah, made in the scriptorium of the Cistercian mother house of Cîteaux in Burgundy about 1125, contains an image of an abbreviated **TREE OF JESSE** (FIG. 16–36).

16–34 ST. MATTHEW FROM THE CODEX COLBERTINUS
c. 1100. Tempera on vellum, 7½ × 4" (19 × 10.16 cm). Bibliothèque Nationale, Paris. MS lat. 254, fol. 10r.

Credit: Bibliothèque nationale de France

A monumental Mary, with the Christ Child sitting on her veiled arm, stands over the forking branches of the tree, dwarfing the sleeping patriarch, Jesse, from whose body a small tree trunk grows. The long, vertical folds of Mary's voluminous drapery—especially the flourish at lower right, where a piece of her garment billows up, as if caught in an updraft—recall the treatment of drapery in the portal at Autun (SEE FIG. 16-24), also in Burgundy. The artist has drawn, rather than painted, with soft colors, using subtle tints that seem somehow in keeping with Cistercian restraint. Christ embraces his mother's neck, pressing his cheek against hers in a display of affection that recalls Byzantine icons of the period, like the *Virgin of Vladimir* (SEE FIG. 8-28). The foliate form Mary holds in her hands could be a flowering sprig from the Jesse Tree, or it could be a lily symbolizing her purity.

The building held by the angel on the left equates Mary with the Church, and the crown held by the angel on the right is hers as queen of heaven. The dove above her halo represents the Holy Spirit; Jesse Trees often have doves sitting in the uppermost branches. In the early decades of the twelfth century, Church doctrine came increasingly to stress the role of the Virgin Mary and the saints as intercessors who could plead for mercy on behalf of repentant sinners, and devotional images of Mary became increasingly popular during the later Romanesque period. As we will see, this popularity would continue into the Gothic period, not only in books but on the sculpted portals and within the stained-glass windows of cathedrals.

16-36 PAGE WITH THE TREE OF JESSE, EXPLANATIO IN ISAIAM (ST. JEROME'S COMMENTARY ON ISAIAH)
Abbey of Cîteaux, Burgundy, France. c. 1125. Ink and tempera on vellum, 15 × 4¾" (38 × 12 cm). Bibliothèque Municipale, Dijon, France. MS. 129, fol. 4v.

Credit: © 2016. Photo Scala, Florence

Hildegard also wrote important treatises on medicine and natural science, invented an alternate alphabet, and was one of the most gifted and innovative composers of her age, writing not only motets and liturgical settings, but also a musical drama that is considered by many to be the first opera. Clearly a major, multitalented figure in the intellectual and artistic life of her time—comparison with the later Leonardo da Vinci comes to mind—she also corresponded with emperors, popes, and the powerful abbots Bernard of Clairvaux and Suger of Saint-Denis.

Following a command she claimed to have received from God in 1141, and with the assistance of her nuns and the monk Volmar, Hildegard began to record the mystical visions she had been experiencing since she was just 5 years old. The resulting book, called the *Scivias* (from the Latin *scite vias lucis*, "know the ways of the light"), is filled not only with words but with striking images of the strange and wonderful visions themselves (FIG. 16-37).

The opening page (FIG. 16-38) shows Hildegard receiving a flash of divine insight, represented by the tongues of flame encircling her head—she said "a fiery light, flashing intensely, came from the open vault of heaven and poured through my whole brain"—while her scribe Volmar writes to her dictation. But was she also responsible for the arresting pictures that accompany the text in this book? Art historian Madeline Caviness thinks so, both because of their unconventional nature and because they conform in several ways to the "visionary" effects experienced by many people dur-

HILDEGARD OF BINGEN We might expect women to have had subordinate positions in the hierarchical and militaristic society of the twelfth century. On the contrary, aristocratic women took responsibility for managing estates during their male relatives' frequent absences in wars or while serving at court. And some women also achieved positions of authority and influence as the heads of religious communities. Notable among them was Hildegard of Bingen (1098–1179).

Born into an aristocratic German family, Hildegard transcended the barriers that limited most medieval women. She began serving as leader of her convent in 1136, and about 1147 she founded a new convent near Bingen.

ing migraines, which plagued Hildegard throughout her life but especially during her forties while she was composing the *Scivias*. She said of her visions, "My outward eyes are open. So I have never fallen prey to ecstasy in the visions, but I see them wide awake, day and night. And I am constantly fettered by sickness, and often in the grip of pain so intense that it threatens to kill me." (Translated in Newman, p. 16.)

Perhaps in this miniature Hildegard is using the large stylus to sketch on the wax tablets in her lap the pictures of her visions that were meant to accompany the verbal descriptions she dictates to Volmar, who sits at the right with a book in his hand, ready to write them down.

16-37 Hildegard of Bingen **THE UNIVERSE**
1927–1933 facsimile of Part I, Vision 3 of the *Liber Scivias* of Hildegard of Bingen. Original, 1150–1175.

Hildegard begins her description of this vision with these words: "After this I saw a vast instrument, round and shadowed, in the shape of an egg, small at the top, large in the middle, and narrowed at the bottom; outside it, surrounding its circumference, there was a bright fire with, as it were, a shadowy zone under it. And in that fire there was a globe of sparkling flame so great that the whole instrument was illuminated by it."

Credit: © akg-images/Erich Lessing

16-38 HILDEGARD AND VOLMAR
1927–1933 facsimile of the frontispiece of the *Liber Scivias* of Hildegard of Bingen. Original, 1150–1175.

This author portrait was once part of a manuscript of Hildegard's *Scivias* that many believe was made in her own lifetime, but it was lost in World War II. Today we can study its images only from prewar black-and-white photographs or from a full-color facsimile that was lovingly hand-painted by the nuns of the abbey of St. Hildegard in Eibingen under the direction of Joesepha Krips between 1927 and 1933, the source of both pictures reproduced here.

Credit: © akg-images/Erich Lessing

Think About It

1 Discuss what the term "Romanesque" means and distinguish some of the key stylistic features associated with architecture in this style.
2 Discuss the sculpture that was integrated into the exteriors of Romanesque churches. Why was it there? Whom did it address? What were the prominent messages? Refer to at least one church discussed in this chapter.
3 What is a pilgrimage site? How did pilgrimage sites function for medieval Christians? Ground your answer in a discussion of Santiago de Compostela, focusing on specific features that were geared toward pilgrims.
4 Analyze one example of a Romanesque work of art in this chapter that tells a story of human frailty. Who was the intended audience? How does its style relate to the intended moral message?

Crosscurrents

These pages served as the beginning of the Gospel of Matthew in two medieval manuscripts, one Hiberno-Saxon and the other Romanesque. Compare the designs of these two pages and the relationship that is established between words and images. How does the work of these two artists relate to work in other media during the period in which each was made?

FIG. 15-7

FIG. 16-34

17–1 SCENES FROM GENESIS

Detail of the Good Samaritan Window, south aisle of nave, Cathedral of Notre-Dame, Chartres, France. c. 1200–1210.
Stained and painted glass.

Credit: © 2016. A. Dagli Orti/Scala, Florence

Chapter 17
Gothic Art of the Twelfth and Thirteenth Centuries

Learning Objectives

17.a Identify the visual hallmarks of Gothic art and its regional variations for formal, technical, and expressive qualities.

17.b Interpret the meaning of works of Gothic art based on their themes, subjects, and symbols.

17.c Relate Gothic art and artists to their cultural, economic, and political contexts.

17.d Apply the vocabulary and concepts relevant to Gothic art, artists, and art history.

17.e Interpret a work of Gothic art using the art historical methods of observation, comparison, and inductive reasoning.

17.f Select visual and textual evidence in various media to support an argument or an interpretation of a work of Gothic art.

The Gothic style—originating in the powerful monasteries of the Paris region—dominated European art and architecture for 400 years. By the mid twelfth century, advances in building technology, increasing financial resources, and new intellectual and spiritual aspirations led to the development of a new art and architecture that expressed the religious and political values of monastic communities. Just as residents of twentieth-century American cities raced to erect higher and higher skyscrapers, the patrons of western Europe competed to build cathedrals and churches with ever-taller naves and towers, increasingly diaphanous walls of glowing glass, and breathtakingly airy interiors that seemed to open in all directions.

The light captured in stained-glass windows created luminous pictures and interior atmospheres that must have captivated worshipers whose everyday existence included little color. Gothic churches became the glorious jeweled houses of God: evocations of the heavenly Jerusalem and invitations to faithful living. And stained glass became the major medium of monumental painting.

This detail from the Good Samaritan Window at Chartres Cathedral (**FIG. 17-1**), created in the early years of the thirteenth century, well into the development of French Gothic architecture, includes scenes from Genesis, the first book of the Bible. The window portrays God's creation of Adam and Eve and continues with their subsequent temptation, fall into sin, and expulsion from the paradise of the Garden of Eden to lead a life of work and woe. Adam and Eve's story is used here to interpret the meaning of the parable of the Good Samaritan for medieval viewers, reminding them that Christ saves them from the original sin of Adam and Eve just as the Good Samaritan saves the injured and abused traveler (SEE FIG. 17-10). The stained-glass windows of Gothic cathedrals were radiant sermons, preached with pictures rather than with words. They were directed at a diverse audience of worshipers, drawn from a broad spectrum of medieval society, who derived multiple meanings from gloriously complicated works of art.

Gothic Europe

What are the cultural and historical backgrounds for Gothic art and architecture?

In the middle of the twelfth century, a distinctive new architecture known today as Gothic emerged in the Île-de-France, the French royal domain around Paris (**MAP 17-1**). The appearance there of a new style and technique of building coincided with the emergence of the monarchy as a powerful centralizing force. Within 100 years, an estimated 2,700 Gothic churches were built in the Île-de-France region alone.

Advances in building technology allowed progressively larger windows and ever loftier vaults, supported by exterior buttressing that was more and more streamlined and skeletal. The Gothic style spread throughout western Europe, gradually displacing Romanesque forms while taking on regional characteristics inspired by them.

MAP 17–1 EUROPE IN THE GOTHIC ERA

The color changes on this map chart the gradual expansion of territory ruled by the king of France during the period when Gothic was developing as a modern French style.

Gothic prevailed until about 1400, and even longer in some regions. It was adapted to all types of structures, including town halls and residences, as well as Christian churches and synagogues.

The term "Gothic" was popularized by the sixteenth-century Italian artist and historian Giorgio Vasari, who disparagingly attributed the by-then-old-fashioned style to the Goths, Germanic invaders who had "destroyed" the Classical civilization of the Roman Empire that Vasari preferred. In its own day the Gothic style was simply called "modern art" or the "French style."

The Rise of Urban and Intellectual Life

The Gothic period was an era of communal achievement and social change. Although Europe remained rural, towns became important centers of artistic patronage, fostering strong communal identity by public projects and ceremonies. Intellectual life was also stimulated by the interaction of so many people living side by side. Universities in Bologna, Padua, Paris, Cambridge, and Oxford supplanted monastic and cathedral schools as centers of learning. Brilliant teachers like Peter Abelard (1079–1142) drew crowds of students, and in the thirteenth century an Italian theologian, Thomas Aquinas (1225–1274), made Paris the intellectual center of Europe.

A system of reasoned analysis known as Scholasticism emerged from these universities, intent on reconciling Christian theology with Classical philosophy. Scholastic thinkers used a question-and-answer method of argument and arranged their ideas into logical outlines. Thomas Aquinas, the foremost Scholastic, applied Aristotelian logic to comprehend religion's supernatural aspects, setting up the foundation on which Catholic thought rests to this day. Some have seen a relationship between the development of these new ways of thinking and the geometrical order that permeates the design of Gothic cathedrals, as well as with the new interest in describing the appearance of the natural world in sculpture and painting.

The Age of Cathedrals

Urban cathedrals, the seats of the ruling bishops, superseded rural monasteries as centers of religious culture and patronage. So many cathedrals were rebuilt between 1150 and 1400—often to replace earlier churches destroyed in the fires that were a byproduct of population growth and housing density within cities—that some have dubbed the period the "Age of Cathedrals." Cathedral precincts functioned almost as towns within towns—containing a palace for the bishop, housing for the clergy, and workshops for the multitude of artists and laborers necessary to support building campaigns. These gigantic churches certainly dominated their urban surroundings. But even if their grandeur inspired admiration, their enormous expense and some bishops' intrusive displays of power inspired resentment, even rioting.

France and the Origins of the Gothic Style

How does the Gothic style originate at the monastery of Saint-Denis in the 1140s and develop in France over the next century?

The development and initial flowering of the Gothic style in France took place against the backdrop of the growing power of the Capetian monarchy. Louis VII (ruled 1137–1180) and Philip Augustus (ruled 1180–1223) consolidated royal authority in the Île-de-France and began to exert more control over powerful nobles in other regions. Louis VII's queen, Eleanor of Aquitaine, brought southwestern France into the royal domain, but when their marriage was annulled, Eleanor reclaimed her lands and married Henry Plantagenet—count of Anjou, duke of Normandy— who became King Henry II of England. The resulting tangle of conflicting claims kept France and England at odds for centuries.

As French kings continued to consolidate royal authority and increase their domains and privileges, the growing centralization of their government sparked a building boom in Paris, which developed from a small provincial town into a thriving urban center beginning in the middle of the twelfth century. Concentrated architectural activity in the capital provided the impetus—or perhaps simply the opportunity—for the developments in architectural technology and the new ways of planning and thinking about buildings that ultimately led to the birth of a new style.

The Birth of Gothic at the Abbey Church of Saint-Denis

Many consider the church of the Benedictine abbey of Saint-Denis, just north of Paris, to be the first Gothic building. This monastery had been founded in the fifth century over the tomb of St. Denis, the Early Christian martyr who had been sent from Rome to convert the local pagan population, becoming the first bishop of Paris. Early on, the abbey developed special royal significance. It housed tombs of the kings of France, the regalia of the French crown, and the relics of St. Denis, patron saint of France.

Construction began in the 1130s of a new church to replace the early medieval church at the abbey, under the supervision of Abbot Suger (abbot 1122–1151). Suger discusses the building of the church in a written account of his administration of the abbey, a rare firsthand chronicle and justification of a medieval building program. Suger prized magnificence, precious materials, and especially fine workmanship (see "Abbot Suger on the Value of Art in Monasteries" on page 512). He invited an international team of masons, sculptors, metalworkers, and glass painters, making this building site a major center of artistic exchange. Such a massive undertaking was extraordinarily expensive. The abbey received substantial annual revenues from the town's inhabitants, and Suger was not above forging documents to increase the abbey's landholdings, which constituted its principal source of income.

Suger began building c. 1135, with a conservative new west façade and narthex attached to the old church, but it was in the new choir—completed in three years and three months between July 14, 1140 and its consecration on June 11, 1144—where the fully formed Gothic architectural style may first have appeared. In his account of the reconstruction, Suger argues that the older building was inadequate to accommodate the crowds of pilgrims who arrived on feast days to venerate the body of St. Denis, and too modest to express the importance of the saint himself. In working with builders to conceive a radically new church design, he turned for inspiration to texts that were attributed erroneously to a follower of St. Paul named Dionysius (the Greek form of Denis), who considered radiant light a physical manifestation of God. Through the centuries, this Pseudo-Dionysius had become identified with the martyred Denis, so Suger was adapting what he believed was the patron saint's concept of divine luminosity in designing the new abbey church with walls composed essentially of stained-glass windows. In inscriptions he composed for the bronze doors (now lost), he was specific about the motivations for the church's innovative style: "being nobly bright, the work should lighten the minds, so that they may travel, through the true lights, to the True Light where Christ is the true door" (Panofsky, p. 49).

The **PLAN OF THE CHOIR** (**FIG. 17–2A**) retains key features of the Romanesque pilgrimage plan (SEE FIG. 16–4A), with a semicircular apse surrounded by an ambulatory, around which radiate seven chapels of uniform size. And the structural elements of the choir had already appeared in Romanesque buildings, including pointed arches, ribbed groin vaults, and external buttressing to relieve stress on the walls. The dramatic achievement of Suger's builders was the coordinated use of these features to create an architectural whole that emphasized open, flowing space enclosed by non-load-bearing walls of glowing stained glass (**FIG. 17–2B**). In Suger's words, the church becomes "a circular string of chapels by virtue of which the whole would shine with the wonderful and uninterrupted light of most luminous windows, pervading the interior beauty" (Panofsky, p. 101). And since Suger saw

the contemplation of light as a means of illuminating the soul and uniting it with God, he was providing his monks with an environment especially conducive to their primary vocation of prayer and meditation.

The revolutionary stained-glass windows of Suger's Saint-Denis were almost lost in the wake of the French Revolution, when this royal abbey represented everything the new leaders were intent on suppressing. Thanks to an enterprising antiquarian named Alexandre Lenoir, however, the twelfth-century windows, though removed from their architectural setting, were saved from destruction. During the nineteenth century, some stained glass returned to the abbey, but many panels are now in museums. One of the best-preserved—from a window that narrated Jesus's childhood—portrays **THE FLIGHT INTO EGYPT** (**FIG. 17–3**). The crisp elegance of the delineation of faces, foliage, and

17–2A PLAN OF THE CHOIR OF THE ABBEY CHURCH OF SAINT-DENIS
France. 1140–1144.

17–2B VIEW OF AMBULATORY AND APSE CHAPELS OF THE ABBEY CHURCH OF SAINT-DENIS
France. 1140–1144.

Envisioning the completion of the abbey church with a transept, and presumably also a nave, Abbot Suger had the following inscription placed in the church to commemorate the 1144 dedication of the choir: "Once the new rear part is joined to the part in front, the church shines with its middle part brightened. For bright is that which is brightly coupled with the bright, and bright is the noble edifice which is pervaded by the new light." (Panofsky, p. 51).

Credit: © akg-images/Bildarchiv Monheim

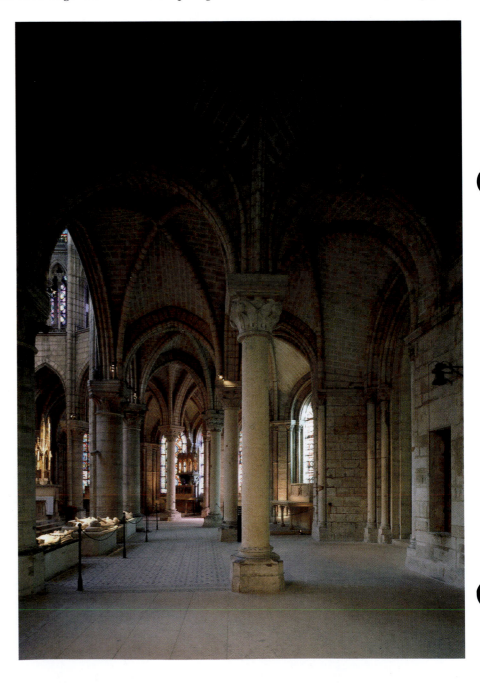

Elements of Architecture

RIB VAULTING

An important innovation of Romanesque and Gothic builders was **rib vaulting**. Rib vaults are a form of groin vault (see "Roman Vaulting" in Chapter 6 on page 190), in which the diagonal ridges (groins) rest on and are covered by curved moldings called ribs. After the walls and piers of the building reached the desired height, timber scaffolding to support these masonry ribs was constructed. When the mortar of the ribs was set, the web of the vault was then laid on forms built on the ribs themselves. After all the temporary forms were removed, the ribs may have provided strength at the intersections of the webbing to channel the vaults' thrust outward and downward to the foundations; they certainly add decorative interest. In short, ribs formed the "skeleton" of the vault; the webbing, a lighter masonry "skin." In Late Gothic buildings, additional decorative ribs give such vaults a lacelike appearance.

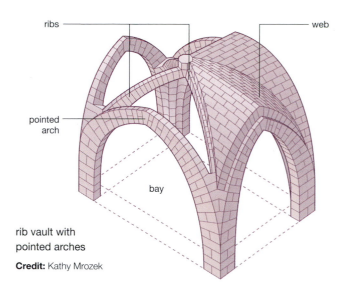

rib vault with
pointed arches

Credit: Kathy Mrozek

drapery—painted with vitreous enamel on the vibrantly colored pieces of glass that make up the panel (see "Stained Glass Windows" on page 512)—is almost as clear today as it was when the windows were new. One unusual detail—the Virgin reaching to pick a date from a palm tree that has bent down at the infant Jesus's command to accommodate her—is based on an apocryphal Gospel that was not included in the canonical Christian scriptures but remained a popular source for twelfth-century artists.

Louis VII and Eleanor of Aquitaine attended the consecration of the new choir in June 1144, along with a constellation of secular and sacred dignitaries. Since the bishops and archbishops of France were assembled at the consecration—celebrating Mass simultaneously at altars throughout the choir and crypt—they had the opportunity to experience firsthand this new Gothic style of building. The history of French architecture over the next few centuries indicates that they were quite impressed.

17-3 THE FLIGHT INTO EGYPT

Detail of the Incarnation (Infancy of Christ) Window, axial choir chapel, abbey church of Saint-Denis. c. 1140–1144. Glencairn Museum, Bryn Athyn, Pennsylvania.

Credit: © Glencairn Museum, Bryn Athyn, Pennsylvania.

Technique

STAINED-GLASS WINDOWS

The "wonderful and uninterrupted light" that Suger sought in the reconstruction of the choir of Saint-Denis in the 1140s was provided by stained-glass artists that—as he tells us—he called in from many nations to create glowing walls for the radiating chapels and perhaps the clerestory as well. As a result of their exquisite work, this influential building program not only constituted a new architectural style; it catapulted what had been a minor curiosity among pictorial techniques into the major medium of monumental European painting. For several centuries, stained glass would be integral to architectural design, not decoration added to an already completed building. Windows were produced at the same time that masons were building walls and carving capitals and moldings.

Our knowledge about the medieval art of stained glass is based on a precious twelfth-century text—*De Diversis Artibus* (*On Divers Arts*)—written by a German monk who called himself Theophilus Presbyter (see "St. Bernard and Theophilus" in Chapter 16 on page 481). In fact, the basic procedures of producing a stained-glass window have changed little since the Middle Ages. It is not a lost art, but it is a complex and costly process. The glass itself was made by bringing sand and ash to a molten state under intense heat and "staining" it with color through the addition of metallic oxides. This molten material was then blown and flattened into sheets. Guided by a **cartoon** (full-scale drawing) painted on a whitewashed board, the glass painter would cut from these sheets the individual shapes that would make up a figural scene or ornamental passage. A hot iron was used to crack the glass into a rough approximation that could later be refined by chipping away at the edges with an iron tool—a process called **grozing**—to achieve the precise shape needed in the composition.

The artists used a vitreous paint (made, Theophilus tells us, of iron filings and ground glass suspended in wine or urine) at full strength to block light and delineate features such as facial expressions or drapery folds. It could also be diluted to create modeling washes. Once painted, the pieces of glass would be fired in a kiln to fuse the painting with the glass surface. Only then did the artists assemble these shapes of color—like pieces of a complex compositional puzzle—with strips of lead (called **cames**), and subsequently mount a series of the resulting panels on an iron framework within the architectural opening to form an ensemble we call a stained-glass window. Lead was used in the assembly process because it was strong enough to hold the glass pieces together, but flexible enough to bend around their complex shapes and—perhaps more critically—absorb the impact from gusts of wind and prevent the glass itself from cracking.

Art and its Contexts

ABBOT SUGER ON THE VALUE OF ART IN MONASTERIES

Suger, who masterminded the reconstruction of the abbey church at Saint-Denis while he was its abbot (1122–1151), weighed in on the twelfth-century monastic debate concerning the appropriateness of elaborate art in monasteries (see "St. Bernard and Theophilus" in Chapter 16 on page 481), both through the magnificence of the new church he built and by the way he described and discussed the project in the account he wrote of his administration of the abbey.

These are his comments on the bronze doors, which were destroyed in 1794:

> Bronze casters having been summoned and sculptors chosen, we set up the main doors on which are represented the Passion of the Saviour and His Resurrection, or rather Ascension, with great cost and much expenditure for their gilding as was fitting for the noble porch…

The verses on the door are these:

> Whoever thou art, if thou seekest to extol the glory of these doors,
> Marvel not at the gold and the expense but at the craftsmanship of the work,
> Bright is the noble work; but being nobly bright, the work
> Should lighten the minds, so that they may travel, through the true lights,
> To the True Light where Christ is the true door,
> In what manner it be inherent in this world the golden door defines:
> The dull mind rises to truth through that which is material
> And, in seeing this light, is resurrected from its former subversion.

On the lintel, just under the large figure of Christ at the Last Judgment on the tympanum, Suger had inscribed:

> Receive, O stern Judge, the prayers of Thy Suger; grant that I be mercifully numbered among Thy own sheep.
>
> (Translations from Panofsky, pp. 47, 49)

The Cathedral of Notre-Dame at Chartres

The abbey church of Saint-Denis became the prototype for a new architecture of space and light based on a highly adaptable skeletal framework that supported rib vaulting on the points of slender piers—rather than along massive Romanesque walls—reinforced by external buttress systems. It initiated a period of competitive experimentation in France that resulted in ever-larger churches—principally cathedrals—enclosing increasingly taller interior spaces, walled with ever-greater expanses of stained glass.

The new Gothic conceptions of space and wall and the structural techniques that made them possible were developed further at the Cathedral of Notre-Dame at Chartres. The great cathedral dominates this town southwest of Paris and, for many people, is a near-perfect embodiment of the Gothic style. Constructed in several stages beginning in the mid twelfth century and extending into the mid thirteenth, with additions such as the north spire as late as the sixteenth century, Chartres Cathedral reflects the transition from an experimental twelfth-century architecture to a mature thirteenth-century style.

Chartres was the site of a pre-Christian virgin-goddess cult, and later, dedicated to the Virgin Mary, it became one of the oldest and most important Christian shrines in France. Its main treasure was a piece of linen believed to have been worn by the Virgin Mary when she gave birth to Jesus. This relic was a gift from the Byzantine empress Irene to Charlemagne, whose grandson Charles the Bald donated it to Chartres in 876. It was kept below the high altar in a huge basement crypt. The healing powers attributed to the cloth made Chartres a major pilgrimage destination, especially as the cult of the Virgin grew in popularity in the twelfth and thirteenth centuries. Its association with important market fairs—especially cloth markets—held at Chartres on the feast days of the Virgin put the textile relic at the intersection of local prestige and the local economy, increasing the income of the cathedral not only through pilgrimage but also through tax revenue it received from the markets.

The **WEST FAÇADE** of Chartres (**FIG. 17–4**) preserves an early sculptural program created within a decade of the reconstruction of Saint-Denis. Surrounding these three doors—the so-called Royal Portal, used only for important ceremonial entrances of the bishop and his retinue—sculpted figures calmly and comfortably fill their architectural settings.

On the central tympanum, Christ is enthroned in majesty, returning at the end of time surrounded by the four evangelists (**FIG. 17–5**). Although imposing, he seems more serene and human than in the hieratic and stylized portrayal of the same subject at the priory church at Moissac (SEE FIG. 16–21). The apostles, organized into four groups of

three, fill the lintel, and the 24 elders of the Apocalypse line the archivolts.

The right portal is dedicated to the Incarnation (God's first earthly appearance), highlighting the role of Mary in the early life of Christ, from the Annunciation to the Presentation in the Temple. On the left portal is the Ascension (the Incarnate God's return from earth to heaven). Jesus floats heavenward in a cloud supported by angels. Running across all three portals on the top of the jambs just underneath the level of the lintels, historiated capitals depict Jesus's life on earth in a series of small, lively narrative scenes.

17–4 WEST FAÇADE, CHARTRES CATHEDRAL (CATHEDRAL OF NOTRE-DAME)

France. West façade begun c. 1134; cathedral rebuilt after a fire in 1194; building continued to 1260; north spire 1507–1513.

Credit: © akg-images/Schütze/Rodemann

17–5 ROYAL PORTAL, WEST FAÇADE, CHARTRES CATHEDRAL
c. 1145–1155.

Credit: © Achim Bednorz, Cologne

Flanking all three openings on the jambs are column statues (**FIG. 17–6**) of kings, queens, and prophets from the Hebrew Bible, evocations of Christ's royal and spiritual ancestry as well as a reminder of the close ties between the Church and the French royal house. The prominence of kings and queens here is what has given the Royal Portal its name. The elegantly elongated proportions and linear, but lifelike, drapery of these column statues echo the cylindrical shafts behind them. Their meticulously carved, idealized heads radiate a sense of beatified calm. In fact, tranquility and order prevail in the overall design as well as in the individual components of this portal, a striking contrast to the dynamic configurations and energized figures on the portals of Romanesque churches.

17–6 ROYAL PORTAL, WEST FAÇADE, CHARTRES CATHEDRAL

Detail of prophets and ancestors of Christ (kings and queens of Judea), right side, central portal. c. 1145–1155.

Credit: © Achim Bednorz, Cologne

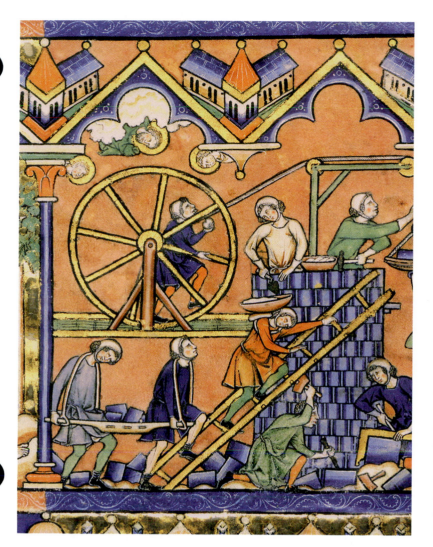

17–7 MASONS AT WORK
Detail of a miniature from a Picture Bible made in Paris. 1240s. The Morgan Library and Museum, New York. MS. M638, fol. 3r.

Credit: © 2016. Photo Pierpont Morgan Library/Art Resource/ Scala, Florence

ARCHITECTURE The bulk of Chartres Cathedral was constructed after a fire in 1194 destroyed an earlier Romanesque church but spared the Royal Portal, the windows above it, and the crypt with its precious relics. A papal representative convinced reluctant local church officials to rebuild. He argued that the Virgin had permitted the fire because she wanted a new and more beautiful church to be built in her honor. Between 1194 and about 1260 that new cathedral was built (see "The Gothic Church" on page 517).

Such a project required vast resources— money, raw materials, and skilled labor (see "Master Masons" below). A contemporary painting shows a building site with the **MASONS AT WORK** (**FIG. 17–7**). Carpenters have built scaffolds, platforms, and a lifting machine. Master stonecutters measure and cut the stones; workers carry and hoist the blocks by hand or with a lifting wheel. Thousands of stones had to be cut and placed accurately. Here a laborer carries mortar up a ladder to

Art and its Contexts
MASTER MASONS

Master masons oversaw all aspects of church construction in the Middle Ages, from design and structural engineering to construction and decoration. The master mason at Chartres coordinated the work of roughly 400 people, scattered with their equipment and supplies, across many locations, from distant stone quarries to high scaffolding. It has been estimated that this workforce set in place some 200 blocks of stone each day.

Funding shortages and technical delays, such as the need to let mortar harden for three to six months, made construction sporadic, so master masons and their crews moved constantly from job to job; often, several masters and many teams of masons contributed to the construction of a single building. Fewer than 100 master builders are estimated to have been responsible for all the major architectural projects around Paris during the century-long building boom there, some of them working on parts of as many as 40 churches. This was dangerous work. Masons were always at risk of injury, which could cut short a career in its prime. King Louis IX of

France actually provided sick pay to a mason injured in the construction of Royaumont Abbey in 1234, but not all workers were this lucky. Master mason William of Sens, who supervised construction at Canterbury Cathedral, fell from a scaffold. His injuries forced him to return to France in 1178 because of his inability to work. Some medieval contracts had pension arrangements or provisions that took potential injury or illness into account, but some did not.

Today, the names of more than 3,000 master masons are known to us, and the close study of differences in construction techniques often discloses the participation of specific masters. Master masons gained in prestige during the thirteenth century as they increasingly differentiated themselves from the laborers they supervised. In some cases their names were prominently inscribed in the labyrinths on cathedral floors. From the thirteenth century on, in what was then an exceptional honor, masters were buried along with patrons and bishops in the cathedrals they built.

men working on the top of the wall, where the lifting wheel delivers cut stones. To fund this work, bishops and cathedral officials usually pledged all or part of their incomes for up to ten years. Royal and aristocratic patrons joined in the effort. In a scheme that seems very modern, the churchmen at Chartres solicited contributions by sending the cathedral relics, including the Virgin's tunic, on tour as far away as England.

As the new structure rose higher during the 1220s, the work grew more costly and funds dwindled. But when the bishop and the cathedral clergy tried to make up the deficit by raising taxes, the townspeople drove them into exile for four years. This action in Chartres was not unique; people often opposed the building of cathedrals because of the burden of new taxes.

Building on the principles pioneered at Saint-Denis—a glass-filled masonry skeleton enclosing a large, open space—the masons at Chartres erected a church over 45 feet wide with vaults that soar approximately 120 feet above the floor. As at Saint-Denis, the plan is rooted in the Romanesque pilgrimage plan, but with a significantly enlarged sanctuary occupying a full third of the building (FIG. 17–8A). The Chartres builders codified what were to become the typical Gothic structural devices: pointed arches and ribbed groin vaults rising from compound piers over rectangular bays. The vaults were supported externally by the recently developed **flying buttress** system (SEE FIG. 17–9) in which arched exterior supports countered the lateral thrust of the nave vault and transferred its weight outward, over the side aisles, where it was resolved into and supported by a buttressing pier, rising from the ground. Flying buttresses permitted larger clerestory windows, nearly equal in height to the nave arcade (FIG. 17–8B). Paired **lancets** (tall openings with pointed tops) surmounted by small circular **rose windows** are created in a technique known as **plate tracery**—holes are cut into the stone wall and nearly half the wall surface is filled with stained glass. The band between the clerestory and nave arcade was now occupied by a **triforium** (arcaded wall passageway) rather than a tall gallery.

17–8B INTERIOR LOOKING EAST, CHARTRES CATHEDRAL
1194–c. 1220.

Credit: © Achim Bednorz, Cologne

17–8A PLAN, CHARTRES CATHEDRAL
1194–c. 1220.

Elements of Architecture

THE GOTHIC CHURCH

Most large Gothic churches in western Europe were built on the Latin cross plan, with a projecting transept marking the transition from nave to choir, an arrangement that derives ultimately from the fourth-century Constantinian basilica of Old St. Peter's (SEE FIG. 7–10A). The main entrance portal was generally on the west, with the choir and its apse on the east. A western narthex could precede the entrance to the nave and side aisles. An ambulatory with radiating chapels circled the apse and facilitated the movement of worshipers through the church. Many Gothic churches have a three-story elevation, with a triforium sandwiched between the nave arcade and a clerestory full of stained glass. Rib vaulting usually covered all spaces. Flying buttresses helped support the soaring nave vaults by transferring their outward thrust over the aisles to

massive, free-standing, upright external buttresses. Church walls were decorated inside and out with arcades of round or pointed arches, engaged columns and colonnettes, an applied filigree of **tracery**, and horizontal moldings called **stringcourses**. The pitched roofs above the vaults—necessary to shed rainwater from the building—were supported by wooden frameworks. A spire or crossing tower above the junction of the transept and nave was usually planned, though often never finished. Portal façades were also customarily marked by high, flanking towers or gabled porches ornamented with **pinnacles** and finials. Architectural sculpture proliferated on each portal's tympanum, archivolts, and jambs (SEE FIGS. 17–5, 17–6), and in France a magnificent rose window typically formed the centerpiece of the flat portal façades (**FIG. 17–9**).

17–9 SCHEMATIC DRAWING OF CHARTRES CATHEDRAL

STAINED GLASS   Chartres is distinctive among French Gothic buildings in that most of its stained-glass windows have survived. Stained glass is an enormously expensive and complicated medium of painting, but its effect on the senses and emotions made the effort worthwhile for medieval patrons and builders (see "Stained Glass Windows" on page 512). By 1260, glass painters had installed about 22,000 square feet of stained glass in 176 windows. Most of the glass dates from between about 1200 and 1250, but a few earlier windows from the 1150s—comparable in style to the windows of Suger's Saint-Denis—survived the fire of 1194 and remain in the west wall above the Royal Portal.

In the aisles and chapels, where the windows were low enough to be easily seen, there were elaborate multi-scene narratives, with small figures composed into individual episodes within the irregularly shaped compartments of windows, designed as stacked medallions set against dense, multicolored fields of ornament. Art historians refer to these as cluster medallion windows. The **GOOD SAMARITAN WINDOW** of c. 1200–1210 in the south aisle of the nave is a typical example of the design (**FIG. 17-10**). Its learned allegory on sin and salvation also typifies the complexity of Gothic narrative art.

The principal subject is a parable Jesus told his followers to teach a moral truth (Luke 10:25–37). The protagonist is a traveling Samaritan who cares for a stranger who has been beaten, robbed, and left for dead by thieves. Jesus's parable is an allegory for his imminent redemption of humanity's sins, and within this window a story from Genesis unfolds above the parable to make that association clear (SEE FIG. 17-1). Adam and Eve's fall introduced sin into the world, but Christ (the Good Samaritan) rescues humanity (the traveler) from sin (the thieves) and ministers to them within the Church, just as the Good Samaritan takes the wounded traveler for refuge and healing to an inn (bottom scene, FIG. 17-1). Stylistically, these willowy, expressive figures avoid the classicizing stockiness in Wiligelmo's folksy Romanesque rendering of the Genesis narrative at Modena (SEE FIG. 16-20). Instead they take the dancelike postures that will come to characterize Gothic figures as the style spreads.

In the clerestory windows, the Chartres glass painters mainly used not multi-scene narratives, but large-scale single figures that could be seen at a distance because of their size, bold drawing, and strong colors. Iconic ensembles were easier to "read" in lofty openings more removed from viewers, such as the huge north transept **ROSE WINDOW** (**FIG. 17-11**), which is over 42 feet in diameter. Surmounting five lancets, the ensemble proclaims the royal and

17-10 GOOD SAMARITAN WINDOW

South aisle of nave, Chartres Cathedral. c. 1200–1210.
Stained and painted glass.

Credit: Sonia Halliday Photographs

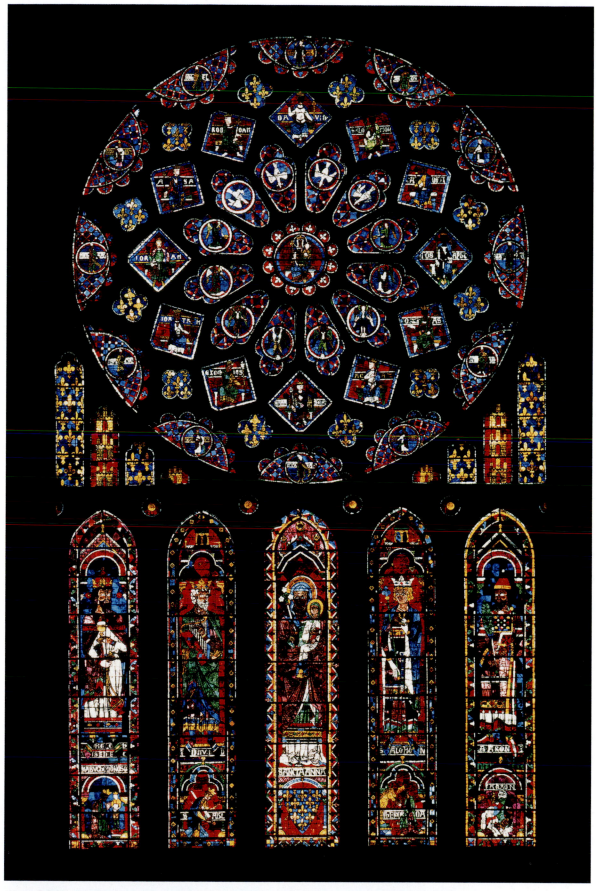

17–11 ROSE WINDOW AND LANCETS, NORTH TRANSEPT, CHARTRES CATHEDRAL
c. 1230–1235. Stained and painted glass.

Credit: © Angelo Hornak/Corbis

priestly heritage of Mary and Jesus and, through them, of the Church itself. In the central lancet, St. Anne holds her infant daughter Mary, flanked left to right by statuesque figures of Hebrew Bible leaders Melchizedek, David, Solomon, and Aaron. Above, in the very center of the rose window itself, Mary and Jesus are enthroned, surrounded by a radiating array of doves, angels, and Hebrew Bible kings and prophets.

This vast wall of glass was a gift from the young King Louis IX (ruled 1226–1270), perhaps arranged by his powerful mother, Queen Blanche of Castile (1188–1252), who ruled as regent (1226–1234) during Louis's minority. Royal heraldic emblems proclaim the window's association with the king. The arms of France—golden *fleurs-de-lis* on a blue ground—fill a prominent shield under St. Anne at the bottom of the central lancet. *Fleurs-de-lis* also appear in the graduated lancets bracketing the base of the rose window, and in a series of **quatrefoils** (four-lobed designs) within the rose itself. But also prominent is the Castilian device of golden castles on a red ground, a reference to the royal lineage of Louis's powerful mother. Light radiating from the deep blues and reds creates a hazy purple atmosphere in the soft light of the north side of the building. On a sunny day the masonry may seem to dissolve in color, but the bold theological and political messages of the rose window remain clear.

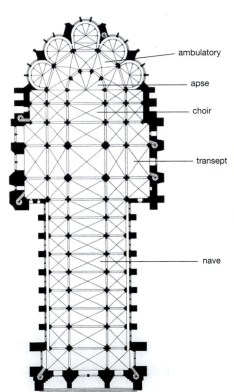

ambulatory

apse

choir

transept

nave

17–12 PLAN OF CATHEDRAL OF NOTRE-DAME, REIMS

France. Begun in 1211.

17–13 WEST FAÇADE, CATHEDRAL OF NOTRE-DAME, REIMS

Rebuilding begun 1211; façade begun c. 1225; to the height of rose window by 1260; finished for the coronation of Philip the Fair in 1286; towers left unfinished 1311; additional work 1406–1428.

Credit: © zechal/123RF

The Cathedral of Notre-Dame at Reims

Reims Cathedral, northeast of Paris in the region of Champagne, was the coronation church of the kings of France and, like Saint-Denis, had been a cultural and educational center since Carolingian times. When fire destroyed this historic building in 1210, the community at Reims began to erect a new Gothic structure, planned as a large basilica (**FIG. 17–12**). It is similar to the model set earlier at Chartres (SEE FIG. 17–8A), but at Reims priority is given to an extended nave rather than an expanded choir, perhaps a reference to the processional emphasis of the coronation ceremony. The cornerstone of the cathedral was laid in 1211, and work continued throughout the century. The expense of the project sparked such local opposition that twice in the 1230s revolts drove the archbishop and canons into exile. At Reims, five master masons directed the work on the cathedral over the course of a century—Jean d'Orbais, Jean le Loup, Gaucher de Reims, Bernard de Soissons, and Robert de Coucy.

The west front of the Cathedral of Reims is a magnificent ensemble in which almost every square inch of stone surface seems encrusted with sculptural decoration (**FIG.** 17–13). Its tall, gabled portals form a broad, horizontal base and project forward to display an expanse of sculpture, while the tympana they enclose are filled with stained-glass windows rather than stone carvings. Their soaring peaks—the middle one reaching to the center of the dominating rose window—unify the façade vertically. In a departure from tradition, Mary rather than Christ is featured in the central portal, a reflection of the growing popularity of her cult. Christ crowns her as queen of heaven in the central gable. The towers were later additions, as was the row of carved figures that runs from the base of one tower to the other above the rose window. This "gallery of kings" is the only strictly horizontal element of the façade.

The sheer quantity of sculpture envisioned for this elaborate cathedral front required the skills of many sculptors, working in an impressive variety of styles over several decades. Four figures from the right jamb of the **CENTRAL PORTAL** illustrate this rich stylistic diversity (**FIG. 17–14**). The pair on the right portrays the Visitation, in which Mary (left), pregnant with Jesus, visits her older cousin, Elizabeth (right), pregnant with St. John the Baptist. The sculptor of these figures, active in Reims about 1230–1235, drew heavily on ancient sources. Reims had been a major Roman city, and there were remaining Roman works at

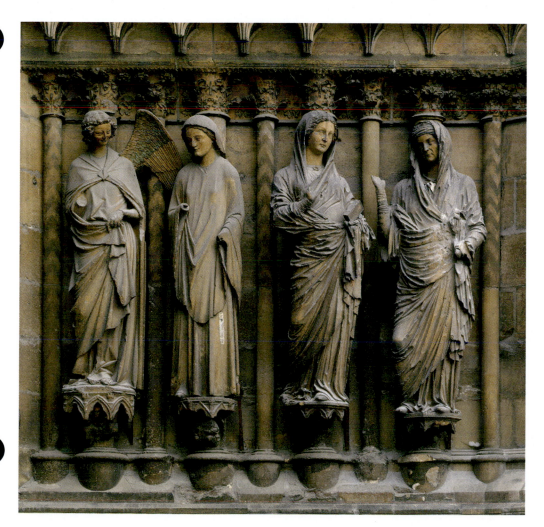

17–14 CENTRAL PORTAL, RIGHT SIDE, WEST FAÇADE, REIMS CATHEDRAL

Annunciation (left pair: Mary [right] c. 1240, angel [left] c. 1250) and Visitation (right pair: Mary [left] and Elizabeth [right] c. 1230).

Credit: © Angelo Hornak/Corbis

the disposal of medieval sculptors. The bulky bodies show the same solidity seen in Roman sculpture (SEE FIG. 6–15), and the women's full faces, wavy hair, and heavy mantles recall imperial portrait statuary, including the two imperial facial ideals of unblemished youth (Mary) and aged accomplishment (Elizabeth) (SEE FIGS. 6–39, 6–40). The figures shift their weight to one leg in contrapposto as they turn toward each other in conversation.

The pair to the left of the Visitation enacts the Annunciation, in which the archangel Gabriel announces to Mary that she will bear Jesus. This Mary's slight body, broad planes of simple drapery, restrained gesture, inward focus, and delicate features contrast markedly with the bold tangibility of the Mary in the Visitation next to her. She is clearly the work of a second sculptor. The archangel Gabriel (at the far left) represents a third artist, active at the middle of the century. This sculptor created tall, gracefully swaying figures with small, fine-featured heads, whose expressions, hairdos, and mannered poses of aristocratic refinement grew to characterize the figural arts in later Gothic sculpture and painting. These characteristics became the basis for what is called the International Gothic Style, fashionable across Europe well into the fifteenth century.

Inside the church (**FIG. 17–15**), the wall is designed, as at Chartres, as a three-story elevation with nave arcade and clerestory of equal height, divided by the continuous arcade of a narrow triforium passageway. The designer at Reims gives a subtle emphasis to the center of each bay in the wall elevation, coordinating the central division of the clerestory into two lancets with a slightly enlarged colonnette at the middle of the triforium. This design feature was

certainly noticed by one contemporary viewer, since it is (over)emphasized in the drawings Villard de Honnecourt made during a visit to Reims Cathedral c. 1230 (SEE FIG. 17–16). Villard also highlighted one of the principal innovations at Reims: the development of **bar tracery**, in which thin stone bars called **mullions** are inserted into an expansive opening in the wall to form a lacy framework for the stained glass (see the rose window in FIG. 17–15). Bar tracery replaced the older plate tracery—still used at Chartres (SEE FIG. 17–11)—and made possible even larger areas of stained glass in relation to wall surface.

A remarkable ensemble of sculpture and stained glass fills the interior west wall at Reims. A great rose window fills the clerestory level; a row of lancets illuminates the triforium; and a smaller rose window replaces the stone of the portal tympanum. The lower level is anchored visually

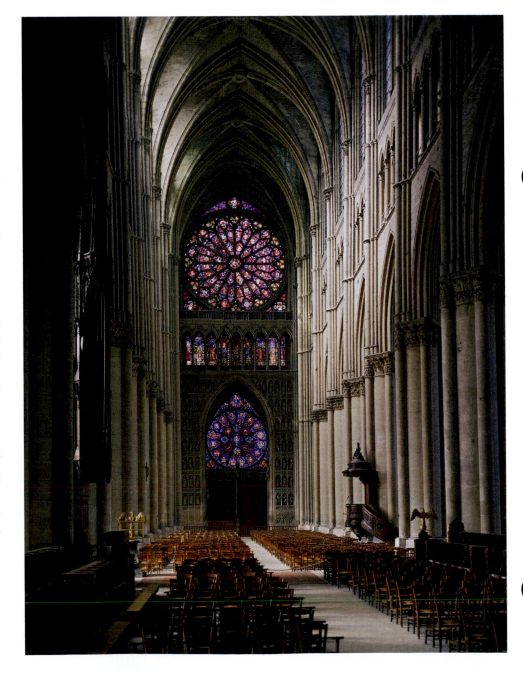

17–15 INTERIOR LOOKING WEST, REIMS CATHEDRAL
Begun 1211; nave c. 1220.

Credit: © akg-images/De Agostini Picture Lib./G. Dagli Orti

by an expanse of sculpture covering the inner wall of the façade. Here ranks of carved prophets and royal ancestors represented moral guides for the newly crowned monarchs who faced them while proceeding down the nave and out of the cathedral following the coronation ceremony as they began the job of ruling France.

Villard de Honnecourt

One of the most fascinating and enigmatic works surviving from Gothic France is a set of 33 sheets of parchment covered with about 250 drawings in leadpoint and ink, signed

17–17 Villard de Honnecourt **SHEET OF DRAWINGS WITH GEOMETRIC FIGURES**

c. 1230. Ink on vellum, 9¼ × 6″ (23.5 × 15.2 cm). Bibliothèque Nationale, Paris. MS. fr. 19093.

This page, labeled "help in drawing figures according to the lessons taught by the art of geometry," demonstrates how geometric configurations underlie the shapes of natural forms and the designs of architectural features. They seem to give insight into the design process of Gothic artists, but it is also possible that they represent the doodlings of a passionate amateur.

Credit: Bibliotheque nationale de France

17–16 Villard de Honnecourt **DRAWINGS OF THE INTERIOR AND EXTERIOR ELEVATION OF THE NAVE OF REIMS CATHEDRAL**

c. 1230. Ink on vellum, 9¼ × 6″ (23.5 × 15.2 cm). Bibliothèque Nationale, Paris. MS. fr. 19093.

Scholars still debate whether Villard's drawings of Reims Cathedral—the church he documented most extensively, with five leaves showing views and two containing details—were made from observing the building itself, during construction, or copied from construction drawings that had been prepared to guide the work of the masons. But in either case, what Villard documents here are those aspects of Reims that distinguish it from other works of Gothic architecture, such as the use of bar tracery, the enlarged central colonnettes of the triforium, the broad bands of foliate carving on the pier capitals, and the statues of angels that perch on exterior buttresses. He seems to have grasped what it was that separated this building from the other cathedrals rising across France at the same time.

Credit: Bibliotheque nationale de France

by a man named Villard from the Picardy town of Honnecourt and now bound into a book housed in the French National Library. Judging from the identifiable buildings that he recorded, Villard made these drawings in the 1220s and 1230s during extensive travels, mainly in France but also in Switzerland and Poland. Included are plans or individual details of the cathedrals of Cambrai, Chartres, Laon, and especially Reims (**FIG. 17–16**).

Villard seems simply to have drawn those things that interested him—animals, insects, human beings, church furnishings, buildings, and construction devices (**FIG. 17–17**). Although the majority of his drawings have nothing to do with architecture, his renderings of aspects of Gothic buildings have received the most attention since the book was rediscovered in the mid nineteenth century and have led to a widespread belief that he was an architect or master mason. There is no evidence for this. In fact, the evidence we have argues against it, since the architectural drawings appear to be the work of someone without a great deal of knowledge of the structural systems and design priorities of Gothic builders. This in no way diminishes the value of this amazing document, which allows us rare access into the mind of a curious, well-traveled thirteenth-century amateur who drew the things that caught his fancy in the extraordinary world around him.

Art in the Age of St. Louis

During the time of Louis IX (ruled 1226–1270; canonized as St. Louis in 1297), Paris became the artistic center of Europe. Artists from all over France were lured to the capital, responding to the growing local demand for new and remodeled buildings, as well as to the international demand for the extraordinary works of art that were the specialty of Parisian commercial workshops. Especially valued were richly illuminated manuscripts and small-scale objects in precious materials. The Parisian style of this period is often called the "Court Style," since its association with the court of St. Louis was one reason it spread beyond the capital to the courts of other European rulers. Parisian works became trans-European benchmarks of artistic quality and sophistication.

THE SAINTE-CHAPELLE IN PARIS The masterpiece of mid-thirteenth-century Parisian style is the Sainte-Chapelle (Holy Chapel) of the royal palace, commissioned by Louis IX to house his collection of relics of Christ's Passion, especially the Crown of Thorns. In many ways this huge chapel can be seen as the culmination of the Gothic style that emerged from Suger's pioneering choir at Saint-Denis. The interior walls have been reduced to a series of slender piers and mullions that act as skeletal support for a vast skin of stained glass (**FIG. 17-18**). The structure itself is stabilized by external buttressing that projects from the piers around the exterior of the building. Interlocking iron bars between the piers and concealed within the windows run around the entire building, adding further stabilization. The viewer inside is unaware of these systems of support, being focused instead on the kaleidoscopic nature of this jewelbox reliquary and the themes of sacred kingship that dominate the program of stained-glass windows.

The building project has a rich history. In 1237, Baldwin II, Latin ruler of Constantinople—a descendant of the crusaders who had snatched the Byzantine capital from Emperor Alexius III Angelus in 1204—was in Paris, offering to sell the relic of Christ's Crown of Thorns to his cousin, King Louis IX of France. The relic was at that time hocked in Venice, securing a loan to the

17-18 UPPER CHAPEL INTERIOR, THE SAINTE-CHAPELLE
Paris. 1239–1248.
Credit: © F1 ONLINE/SuperStock

cash-poor Baldwin, who had decided, rather than redeeming it, to sell it to the highest bidder. Louis purchased the relic in 1239, and on August 18, when the newly acquired treasure arrived at the edge of Paris, the humble king, barefoot, carried it through the streets of his capital to the royal palace. Soon after its arrival, plans were underway to construct a glorious new palace building to house it— the Sainte-Chapelle, completed for its ceremonial consecration on April 26, 1248. In the 1244 charter establishing services in the Sainte-Chapelle, Pope Innocent IV claimed that Christ had crowned Louis with his own crown, strong confirmation for Louis's own sense of the sacred underpinnings of his kingship.

The Sainte-Chapelle is an extraordinary manifestation of the Gothic style. The two-story building (**FIG. 17–19**)—there are both lower and upper liturgical spaces—is large for a chapel, and though it is now swallowed up by modern Paris, when it was built it was one of the tallest and most elaborately decorated buildings in the capital. The upper chapel is a completely open interior space surrounded by walls composed almost entirely of stained glass (SEE FIG. 17–18), presenting viewers with a glittering, multicolored expanse. Not only the king and his court experienced this chapel; members of the public came to venerate and celebrate the relic, as well as to receive the indulgences offered to pious visitors. The Sainte-Chapelle resembles a reliquary made of painted stone and glass instead of gold and gems, turned inside out so that we experience it from within. But this arresting visual impression is only part of the story.

The stained-glass windows present extensive narrative cycles related to the special function of this chapel. Since they are painted in a bold, energetic style, the stories are easily legible, in spite of their breadth and complexity. Around the sanctuary's **hemicycle** (apse or semicircular interior space) are standard themes relating to the celebration of the Mass. But along the straight side walls are broader, four-lancet windows whose narrative expanse is dominated by the exploits of the sacred kings and queens of the Hebrew Bible, heroes Louis claimed as his royal ancestors. Above the recessed niche where Louis sat at Mass was a window filled with biblical kings, whereas in the corresponding niche on the other side of the chapel, his mother, Queen Blanche of Castile, and his wife, Queen Marguerite of Provence, sat under windows devoted to the lives of Judith and Esther, alternatively appropriate role models for medieval queens. Everywhere we look we see kings being crowned, leading soldiers into holy warfare, or performing royal duties, all framed with heraldic references to Louis and the French royal house. There is even a window that includes scenes from the life of Louis IX himself.

17–19 SCHEMATIC DRAWING OF THE SAINTE-CHAPELLE

Paris. 1239–1248.

Credit: © Dorling Kindersley

17–20 HOLOFERNES'S ARMY CROSSING THE EUPHRATES RIVER
Detail of the Judith Window, from the Sainte-Chapelle, Paris. c. 1245. Stained, painted, and leaded glass, diameter 23⁵/₁₆″ (59.2 cm). Philadelphia Museum of Art.

Credit: © 2016. Photo The Philadelphia Museum of Art/Art Resource/Scala, Florence

the progressive climate of the mid-thirteenth-century Parisian art world.

ILLUMINATED MANUSCRIPTS   Paris gained renown in the thirteenth century not only for its new architecture and sculpture but also for the production of books. Manuscript painters flocked to Paris from other regions to join workshops supervised by university officials who controlled the production and distribution of books. These works ranged from small Bibles used as textbooks by university students to extravagant devotional and theological works filled with exquisite miniatures for wealthy patrons.

After the French Revolution, the Sainte-Chapelle was transformed into an archive, and some stained glass was removed to allow more light into the building. Deleted panels made their way onto the art market, and in 1803 the wealthy Philadelphia merchant William Powell bought three medallions from the Judith Window during a European tour; his collection was the first in America to concentrate on medieval art. One medallion portrays the armies of Holofernes crossing the Euphrates River (**FIG. 17–20**). A compact crowd of equestrian warriors to the right conforms to a traditional system of representing crowds as a measured, overlapping mass of essentially identical figures, but the warrior at the rear of the battalion breaks the pattern, turning to acknowledge a knight behind him. The foreshortened rump of this soldier's horse projects out into our space, as if he were marching from our real world into the fictive world of the window—an avant-garde touch from a major artist working in

17–21 QUEEN BLANCHE OF CASTILE AND KING LOUIS IX
From a Moralized Bible made in Paris. 1226–1234. Ink, tempera, and gold leaf on vellum, each page 15 × 10½″ (38 × 26.6 cm). The Morgan Library and Museum, New York. MS. M. 240, fol. 8r.

Credit: © 2016. Photo Pierpont Morgan Library/Art Resource, NY/Scala, Florence

A particularly sumptuous Parisian book from the time of Louis IX is a three-volume Moralized Bible from c. 1230, in which selected scriptural passages are paired with allegorical or moralized interpretations, using pictures as well as words to convey the message. The dedication page (**FIG. 17-21**) shows the teenage King Louis IX and his mother, Queen Blanche of Castile. The royal pair—emphasized by their elaborate thrones and slightly oversized heads—appear against a solid gold background under a multicolored architectural framework. Below them, a clerical scholar (left) dictates to a scribe, who seems to be working on a page from this very manuscript, with a column of roundels already outlined for paintings.

The design of stacked medallions—forming the layout for most of this monumental manuscript (**FIG. 17-22**)—clearly derives from stained-glass lancets with their columns of superimposed images (SEE FIG. 17-10). In the book, however, the schema combines pictures with words. Each page has two vertical strips of painted scenes set against a mosaiclike field and filled out by half-quatrefoils in the interstices—the standard format of mid-thirteenth-century windows. Adjacent to each medallion is an excerpt of text, either a summary of a scriptural passage or a terse contemporary interpretation or allegory. Both painted miniatures and texts alternate between scriptural summaries and their moralizing explications, outlined in words and visualized with pictures. This adds up to a very learned and complicated compilation, perhaps devised by clerical scholars at the University of Paris, but certainly painted by some of the most important professional artists in the cosmopolitan French capital.

England

How does the new French Gothic style combine with distinctive local materials and traditions in England?

Plantagenet kings ruled England from the time of Henry II and Eleanor of Aquitaine until 1485. Many were great patrons of the arts. During this period, London grew into a large city, but most people continued to live in rural villages and bustling market towns. Textile production dominated manufacture and trade, and fine embroidery continued to be an English specialty. The French Gothic style influenced English architecture and manuscript illumination, but these influences were tempered by local materials, methods, traditions, and tastes.

Manuscript Illumination

The universities of Oxford and Cambridge dominated intellectual life, but monasteries continued to house active scriptoria, in contrast to France, where book production became centralized in the professional workshops of Paris. By the end of the thirteenth century, secular workshops became increasingly active in England, meeting demand for books from students as well as from royal and noble patrons.

17-22 MORALIZATIONS FROM THE APOCALYPSE

From a Moralized Bible made in Paris. 1226–1234. Ink, tempera, and gold leaf on vellum, each page 15 × 10½″ (38 × 26.6 cm). The Morgan Library and Museum, New York. MS. M. 240, fol. 6r.

Credit: © 2016. Photo Pierpont Morgan Library/Art Resource, NY/Scala, Florence

MATTHEW PARIS The monastic tradition of history writing that we saw in the Romanesque Worcester Chronicle (SEE FIG. 16–30) flourished into the Gothic period at the Benedictine monastery of St. Albans, where monk Matthew Paris (d. 1259) compiled a series of historical works. Paris wrote the texts of his chronicles, and he also added hundreds of marginal pictures that were integral to his history writing. The tinted drawings have a freshness that reveals the artist as someone working outside the rigid strictures of compositional conventions—or at least pushing against them. In one of his books, Paris included an almost full-page, framed image of the Virgin and Child in a tender embrace (**FIG. 17-23**). Under this picture, outside the sacred space of Mary and Jesus, Paris drew a picture of himself—identified not by likeness but by a label with his name, strung out in alternating red and blue capital letters behind him. He looks not at the holy couple, but at the words in front of him. These offer his commentary on the image, pointing to the affection shown in the playful Christ Child's movement toward his earthly mother, but emphasizing the authority he has as the divine incarnation of his father. Matthew Paris seems almost to hold his words in his hands, pushing them upward toward the object of his devotion.

THE WINDMILL PSALTER The dazzling artistry and delight in ambiguity and contradiction that had marked early medieval manuscripts in the British Isles (SEE FIG. 15–1) also survived into the Gothic period in the Windmill Psalter of c. 1270–1280 (see "Closer Look" opposite).

The letter *B*—the first letter of Psalm 1, which begins with the words *Beatus vir qui non abit in consilio impiorum* ("Happy are those who do not follow the advice of the wicked", NRSV)—fills an entire left-hand page and outlines a densely interlaced thicket of tendrils and figures. This is a Tree of Jesse, a genealogical diagram of Jesus's royal and spiritual ancestors in the Hebrew Bible based on a prophesy in Isaiah 11:1–3. An oversized, semi-reclining figure of Jesse, father of King David, appears sheathed in a red mantle with the blue trunk of a vinelike tree emerging from his side. Above him is his majestically enthroned royal son, who, as an ancestor of Mary (shown just above him), is also an ancestor of Jesus, who appears at the top of the sequence. In the circling foliage flanking this sacred royal family tree is a series of prophets representing Jesus's spiritual heritage.

E, the second letter of the psalm's first word, appears at the top of the right-hand page and is formed from large tendrils emerging from delicate background vegetation to support characters in the story of the Judgment of Solomon portrayed within it (I Kings 3:16–27). Two women (one above the other at the right) claiming the same baby appear before King Solomon (enthroned on the crossbar) to settle their dispute. The king orders a guard to slice the baby in half

17-23 Matthew Paris **SELF-PORTRAIT KNEELING BEFORE THE VIRGIN AND CHILD**

From the *Historia Anglorum*, made in St. Albans, England. 1250–1259. Ink and color on parchment, 14 × 9¾" (35.8 × 25 cm). The British Library, London.

Credit: © The British Library Board (Royal 14 C VII, fol.6r)

A Closer Look

PSALM 1 IN THE WINDMILL PSALTER

Although this page initially seems to have been trimmed at left, the flattened outside edge of the roundels marks the original end of the page. What might have started as an independent Jesse Tree may later have been expanded into the initial B, widening the pictorial composition farther than originally planned.

The four evangelists appear in the corner roundels as personified symbols writing at desks.

The windmill that has given this psalter its name seems to be a religious symbol based on the fourth verse of this psalm: "Not so the wicked, not so: but like the dust, which the wind driveth from the face of the earth."

Tucked within the surrounds of the letter B are scenes from God's creation of the world, culminating in the forming of Adam and Eve. Medieval viewers would meditate on how the new Adam (Christ) and Eve (Mary)—featured in the Jesse Tree—had redeemed humankind from the sin of the first man and woman. Similarly, Solomon's choice of the true mother would recall Christ's choice of the true Church. Medieval manuscripts are full of cross-references and multiple meanings, intended to stimulate extended reflection and meditation, not embody a single truth or tell a single story.

Participants in this scene of the Judgment of Solomon have been creatively distributed within the unusual narrative setting of the letter *E*. Solomon sits on the crossbar; the two mothers are stacked one above the other; and the knight balancing the baby has to hook his toe under the curling extension of the crossbar to maintain his balance.

17–24 THE OPENING OF PSALM 1

From the Windmill Psalter, made in England, probably London. Late 13th century. Ink, color, and gold on vellum, each page 12¾ × 8¾″ (32.3 × 22.2 cm). The Morgan Library and Museum, New York. MS. M102, fols. 1v-2r.

Credit: © 2016. Photo Pierpont Morgan Library/Art Resource/Scala, Florence

with his sword and give each woman her share. This trick exposed the real mother, who hastened to give up her claim in order to save the baby's life. It has been suggested that the positioning of this story within the letter *E* may

have made a subtle association between Solomon and the reigning King Edward I. The rest of the psalm's five opening words appear on a banner carried by an angel who swoops down at the bottom of the *E*.

Architecture

The Gothic style in architecture appeared early in England, introduced by Cistercian and Norman builders and by traveling master masons. But in England there was less emphasis on height than in France. English churches have long, broad naves and screenlike façades.

SALISBURY CATHEDRAL   The thirteenth-century cathedral in Salisbury is an excellent example of English Gothic. It has unusual origins. The first cathedral in this diocese had been built within the castle complex of the local lord. In 1217, Bishop Richard Poore petitioned the pope to relocate the church, claiming the wind on the hilltop howled so loudly that the clergy could not hear themselves sing the Mass. A more pressing concern was probably his desire to escape the lord's control. As soon as he moved, the bishop established a new town called Salisbury. Material from the old church was carted down the hill and used in the new cathedral, along with dark, fossil-filled Purbeck stone from quarries in southern England and limestone imported from Caen. Building began in 1220, and most of the cathedral was finished by 1258, an unusually short period for such an undertaking (**FIG. 17–25**).

The west façade, however, was not completed until 1265. The small flanking towers project beyond the side walls and buttresses, giving the façade an increased width; the slightly later cloister and chapter house provided for the cathedral's clergy. The huge crossing tower (the French preferred a slender spire) and its 400-foot spire are a fourteenth-century addition, as are the flying buttresses, which were added to stabilize the tower. The crossing tower became the focal point of the building.

17–25 SALISBURY CATHEDRAL
England. Church building 1220–1258; west façade finished 1265; spire c. 1320–1330; cloister and chapter house 1263–1284.

Credit: © Skyscan/Corbis

17-26 PLAN OF SALISBURY CATHEDRAL

17-27 INTERIOR LOOKING EAST, SALISBURY CATHEDRAL

In the eighteenth century, the English architect James Wyatt subjected the building to radical renovations, during which the remaining stained glass and figure sculpture were removed or rearranged. Similar campaigns to refurbish medieval churches were common at the time. The motives of the restorers were complex and their results were far from our own notions of historical authenticity.

Credit: © Robert Preston Photography/Alamy Stock Photo

Salisbury has a distinctive plan (FIG. 17-26) with wide projecting double transepts, a square east end with a single chapel, and a spacious sanctuary—more like a monastic church. The nave interior reflects the Norman building tradition of heavy walls and a tall nave arcade topped with a gallery and a clerestory with simple lancet windows (FIG. 17-27). The walls alone are substantial enough to support the four-part ribbed vault. The emphasis on the horizontal movement of the arcades, unbroken by continuous vertical colonnettes extending from the compound piers, directs worshipers' attention forward toward the altar behind the choir screen. The use of color in the stonework is reminiscent of the decorative effects in Romanesque interiors. The shafts supporting the four-part rib vaults are made of dark Purbeck stone that contrasts with the lighter limestone of the rest of the interior. The original painting and gilding of the stonework would have enhanced the effect.

MILITARY AND DOMESTIC ARCHITECTURE Cathedrals were not the only Gothic buildings. Western European knights who traveled east during the crusades were impressed by the architectural forms they saw in Muslim castles and Byzantine fortifications. When they returned home, they had their own versions of these fortifications built. Castle gateways became more complex, nearly independent fortifications, often guarded by twin towers rather than just one. New rounded towers eliminated the corners that had made earlier square towers vulnerable to battering rams, and crenellations (notches) were added to tower tops to provide stone shields for more effective defense. The outer, enclosing walls were likewise strengthened. The open, interior space was enlarged and filled with more comfortable living quarters for the lord and wooden buildings to house the garrison and the support staff. Barns and stables for animals, including the extremely valuable war horses, were also erected within the enclosure.

17–28 EXTERIOR OF THE GREAT HALL, STOKESAY CASTLE
England. Late 13th century.

Credit: Fotomicar/Fotolia

STOKESAY CASTLE   Military structures were not the only secular buildings outfitted for defense. In uncertain times, the manor (a landed estate), which continued to be an important economic unit in the thirteenth century, also had to fortify its buildings. And country houses equipped with a tower and crenellated rooflines became a status symbol as well as a necessity. **STOKESAY CASTLE**, a remarkable fortified manor house, survives in England near the Welsh border. In 1291, a wool merchant, Lawrence of Ludlow, acquired the property of Stokesay and secured permission from King Edward I to fortify his dwelling— officially known as a "license to crenellate" (**FIG. 17–28**). Two towers—including a massive crenellated south tower—and a great hall still survive.

Life in the Middle Ages revolved around the hall. Windows on each side of Stokesay's hall open both toward the courtyard and out across a moat toward the countryside. By the thirteenth century, people began to expect some privacy as well as security; therefore at both ends of the hall are two-story additions that provided retiring rooms for the family and workrooms where women could spin and weave. Rooms at the north end could be reached from the hall, but the upper chamber at the south was accessible only by means of an exterior stairway. A tiny window— a peephole—let women and members of the household observe the often rowdy activities in the hall below. In layout, there was essentially no difference between this manor, far from the London court, and the mansions built by the nobility in the city. Palaces followed the same pattern of hall and retiring rooms; they were simply larger.

Germany and the Holy Roman Empire

How do the Gothic architecture and sculpture of Germany and the Holy Roman Empire compare with the foundational monuments in France?

The Holy Roman Empire, weakened by internal strife and a prolonged struggle with the papacy, ceased to be a significant power in the thirteenth century. England and France were becoming strong nation-states, and the empire's hold on southern Italy and Sicily ended at mid century with the death of Emperor Frederick II. Subsequent emperors—who were elected—had only nominal authority over a loose conglomeration of independent principalities, bishoprics, and free cities. As in England, the French Gothic style, avidly embraced in the western Germanic territories, shows regional adaptations and innovations.

Architecture

In the thirteenth century, the increasing importance of the sermon in church services led architects in Germany to develop the **hall church**, a type of open, light-filled interior space that had appeared in Europe in the early Middle Ages. Characterized by a nave and side aisles of equal height, these spacious and well-lit hall churches accommodated the large crowds drawn by charismatic preachers.

Chapter 17 Gothic Art of the Twelfth and Thirteenth Centuries **533**

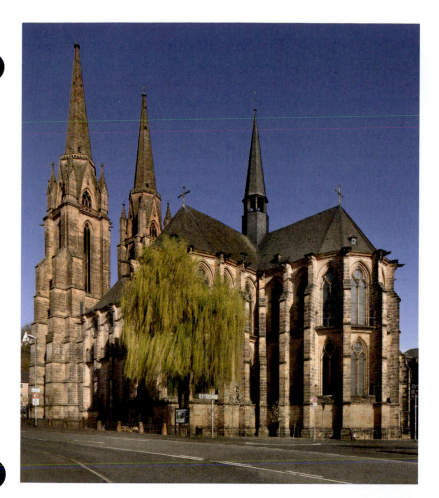

17-29 EXTERIOR, CHURCH OF ST. ELIZABETH OF HUNGARY

Marburg, Germany. 1235–1283.

Credit: © Achim Bednorz, Cologne

which is not the case. Inside, the closely spaced piers of the nave support the ribbed vault and, as with the buttresses, give the building a vertical, linear quality (**FIG. 17-30**). Light from the two stories of windows fills the interior, unimpeded by walls or galleries. The hall-church design was adopted widely for civic and residential buildings in Germanic lands and also for Jewish architecture.

THE OLD-NEW SYNAGOGUE Built in the third quarter of the thirteenth century using the hall-church design, Prague's **OLD-NEW SYNAGOGUE** (Altneuschul) is the oldest functioning synagogue in Europe and one of two principal synagogues serving the Jews of Prague (**FIG. 17-31**). Like a hall church, the vaults of the synagogue are all the same height. Unlike a basilican church, however, with its division into nave and side aisles, the Old-New Synagogue has only two aisles, each with three bays supported by the walls and

CHURCH OF ST. ELIZABETH OF HUNGARY IN MARBURG Perhaps the first true Gothic hall church, and one of the earliest Gothic buildings in Germany, was the **CHURCH OF ST. ELIZABETH OF HUNGARY** in Marburg (**FIG. 17-29**). The Hungarian princess Elizabeth (1207–1231) had been sent to Germany at age 4 to marry the ruler of Thuringia. He soon died of the plague, and she devoted herself to caring for people with incurable diseases. It was said that she died at age 24 from exhaustion, and she was canonized in 1235. Between 1235 and 1283, the knights of the Teutonic Order (who had moved to Germany from Jerusalem) built a church to serve as her mausoleum and pilgrimage center.

The plan of the church is an early German form with choir and transepts of equal size, each ending in apses. The elevation of the building, however, is new, with nave and aisles of equal height. On the exterior, tall buttresses emphasize its verticality, and the two rows of windows suggest a two-story building,

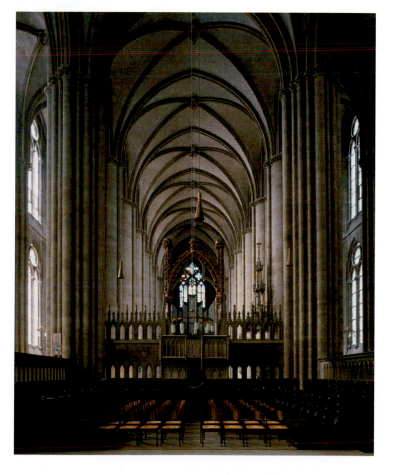

17-30 INTERIOR, CHURCH OF ST. ELIZABETH OF HUNGARY

Marburg, Germany. 1235–1283.

Credit: © Achim Bednorz, Cologne

17-31 INTERIOR, OLD-NEW SYNAGOGUE (ALTNEUSCHUL)
Prague, Bohemia (Czech Republic). c. late 13th century; *bimah* after 1483.

Credit: © akg-images/Erich Lessing

two octagonal piers. Each bay has Gothic four-part ribbed vaulting to which a nonfunctional fifth rib has been added. Some say that this fifth rib was added to undermine the cross form made by the intersecting diagonal ribs.

Medieval synagogues were both places of prayer and communal centers of learning and inspiration where men gathered to read and discuss the Torah. The synagogue had two focal points: a shrine for the Torah scrolls (the *aron*) and a raised platform for reading from them (the *bimah*). The congregation faced the Torah shrine, which was located on the east wall, in the direction of Jerusalem, while the reading platform stood in the center of the hall straddling the two center bays. In Prague it was surrounded by an ironwork open screen. The single entrance was placed off-center in a corner bay at the west end. Men worshiped and studied in the main space; women had to worship in annexes on the north and west sides.

Sculpture

Since the eleventh century, among the most creative centers of European sculpture were the Rhine River Valley and the region known as the Mosan (named after the Meuse River, in present-day Belgium), with centers in Liège and Verdun. Ancient Romans had built camps and cities in this area, and Classical influence lingered through the Middle Ages, when Nicholas of Verdun and his fellow goldsmiths initiated a new classicizing style in the arts.

SHRINE OF THE THREE KINGS For the archbishop of Cologne, Nicholas created the magnificent **SHRINE OF THE THREE KINGS** (c. 1190–c. 1205/1210), a reliquary for what were believed to be relics of the three Magi (**FIG. 17-32**). Shaped in the form of a basilican church, it is made of gilded bronze and silver set with gemstones and dark blue enamel plaques that accentuate its architectural details. Like his fellow Mosan artists, Nicholas was inspired by ancient Roman art still found in the region, as well as by classicizing Byzantine works. The figures are lifelike, fully modeled, and swathed in voluminous but revealing drapery. The three Magi and the Virgin fill the front gable end, and prophets and apostles sit in the niches in the two levels of arcading on the sides. The work combines robust, expressively mobile sculptural forms with a jeweler's exquisitely ornamental detailing to create an opulent, monumental setting for its precious contents.

17-32 Nicholas of Verdun and workshop **SHRINE OF THE THREE KINGS**

Cologne Cathedral, Germany. c. 1190–c. 1205/1210. Silver and gilded bronze with enamel and gemstones, 5′8″ × 6′ × 3′8″ (1.73 × 1.83 × 1.12 m).

Credit: © akg-images/Erich Lessing

17–33 ST. MAURICE
Magdeburg Cathedral, Germany. c. 1240–1250. Dark sandstone with traces of polychromy.

Credit: © akg-images/Hilbich

17–34 EKKEHARD AND UTA
West chapel, Naumburg Cathedral, Germany. c. 1245–1260. Stone with polychromy, height approx. 6'2″ (1.88 m).

Credit: © akg-images/Erich Lessing

ST. MAURICE A powerful current of realism runs through German Gothic sculpture. Some works seem to be carved after a living model. Among them is an arresting mid-thirteenth-century statue of **ST. MAURICE** in Magdeburg Cathedral (**FIG. 17–33**), the location of his relics since 968. The Egyptian Maurice, a commander in the Roman army, was martyred in 286 together with his Christian battalion while they were stationed in Germany. As patron saint of Magdeburg, he was revered by Ottonian emperors, who were anointed in St. Peter's in Rome at the altar of St. Maurice. He remained a favorite saint of military aristocrats. This is the first surviving representation of Maurice as a black African, an acknowledgment of his Egyptian origins and an aspect of the growing German interest in realism, which extends here to the detailed rendering of his costume of chain mail and riveted leather.

EKKEHARD AND UTA Equally portraitlike is the depiction of this couple, commissioned about 1245 by Dietrich II, bishop of Wettin, for the family funeral chapel, built at the west end of Naumburg Cathedral. Bishop Dietrich ordered life-size statues of 12 of his ancestors, who had been patrons of the church, to be placed on pedestals mounted at window level around the chapel.

In the representations of Margrave Ekkehard of Meissen (a margrave—count of the march or border—was a territorial governor who defended the frontier) and his Polish-born wife, Uta (**FIG. 17–34**), the sculptor created highly individualized figures and faces. Since these are eleventh-century people sculpted in the thirteenth century, we are not looking at their portrait likenesses, but it is still possible that live models were used to heighten the sense of a living presence in their portraits. But more than their faces contribute to this liveliness. The margrave nervously fingers the strap of the shield that is looped over his arm, and the coolly elegant Uta pulls her cloak around her neck as if to protect herself from the cold, while the extraordinary spread of her left hand is necessary to control the cloak's voluminous, thick cloth. The survival of original **polychromy** (multicolored painting on the surface of sculpture or architecture) indicates that color added to the impact of the figures. The impetus toward descriptive realism and psychological presence, initiated in the thirteenth century, will expand in the art of northern Europe into the fifteenth century and beyond.

Italy

What are the important developments in Italian sculpture and painting during the late Middle Ages?

The thirteenth century was a period of political division and economic expansion for the Italian peninsula. Part of southern Italy and Sicily was controlled by Frederick II von Hohenstaufen (1194–1250), Holy Roman Emperor from 1220. Frederick was a politically unsettling force. He fought with a league of north Italian cities and briefly controlled the Papal States. On his death, however, Germany and the Holy Roman Empire ceased to be an important factor in Italian politics and culture.

In northern Italy, in particular, organizations of successful merchants created communal governments in their prosperous and independent city-states and struggled against powerful families for political control. Artists began to emerge as independent agents, working directly with wealthy clients and with civic and religious institutions.

It was during this time that new religious orders known as the mendicants (begging monks) arose to meet the needs of the growing urban population. They espoused an ideal of poverty, charity, and love, and they dedicated themselves to teaching and preaching while living among the urban poor. Most notable in the beginning were the Franciscans, founded by St. Francis of Assisi (1182–1226; canonized in 1228). This son of a wealthy merchant gave away his possessions and devoted his life to God and the poor. As others began to join him, he wrote a simple rule for his followers, who were called brothers, or friars (from the Latin *frater*, meaning "brother"), and the pope approved the new order in 1209–1210.

Sculpture of the Pisano Family

During the first half of the thirteenth century, the culturally enlightened Frederick II fostered a Classical revival at his southern Italian court. In the Romanesque period, artists in southern Italy had already turned to ancient sculpture for inspiration, and Frederick, mindful of his imperial status as Holy Roman Emperor, encouraged this tendency to help communicate a message of power. He also encouraged artists to emulate the world around them. Nicola Pisano (active in Tuscany c. 1258–1278), who moved from the southern region of Apulia to Tuscany at mid century, became the leading exponent of this classicizing and naturalistic style.

NICOLA PISANO'S PULPIT AT PISA In an inscription on a free-standing marble **PULPIT** in the Pisa Baptistery (**FIG. 17-35**), Nicola identifies himself as a supremely self-confident sculptor: "In the year 1260 Nicola Pisano carved this noble work. May so gifted a hand be praised as it deserves." Columns topped with leafy Corinthian capitals

17-35 Nicola Pisano PULPIT
Baptistery, Pisa, Italy. 1260. Marble, height approx. 15′ (4.6 m).
Credit: © Studio Fotografico Quattrone, Florence

17–36 Nicola Pisano **ANNUNCIATION, NATIVITY, AND ADORATION OF THE SHEPHERDS**

Detail of pulpit, Baptistery, Pisa, Italy. 1260. Marble, 33½ × 44½″ (85 × 113 cm).

Credit: © Studio Fotografico Quattrone, Florence

support standing figures and Gothic trefoil arches, which in turn provide a platform for the six-sided pulpit. The columns rest on high bases carved with crouching figures, domestic animals, and shaggy-maned lions. Panels forming the pulpit enclosure illustrate New Testament subjects, each framed as an independent composition.

Each panel illustrates several scenes in a continuous narrative; **FIGURE 17-36** depicts the **ANNUNCIATION, NATIVITY, AND ADORATION OF THE SHEPHERDS**.

The Virgin reclines in the middle of the composition after having given birth to Jesus, who below receives his first bath from midwives. The upper left corner holds the Annunciation—the moment of Christ's conception, as announced by the archangel Gabriel. The scene in the upper right combines the Annunciation to the Shepherds with their Adoration of the Child. The viewer's attention moves from group to group within the shallow space, always returning to the regally detached Mother of God.

17–37 Giovanni Pisano **ANNUNCIATION, NATIVITY, AND ADORATION OF THE SHEPHERDS**

Detail of pulpit, Sant'Andrea, Pistoia, Italy. 1298–1301. Marble, 33 × 40⅛″ (83 × 102 cm).

Credit: © 2016. Photo Scala, Florence - courtesy Diocesi di Pistoia, Ufficio Beni Culturali

The format, style, and technique of Roman sarcophagus reliefs—readily accessible in the burial ground near the baptistery—may have provided Nicola's models for this carving. The sculptural treatment of the deeply cut, full-bodied forms is certainly Classical in inspiration, as are the heavy, placid faces.

GIOVANNI PISANO'S PULPIT AT PISTOIA   Nicola's son Giovanni (active c. 1265–1314) assisted his father while learning from him, and he may also have worked or studied in France. By the end of the thirteenth century, he had emerged as a versatile artist in his own right. Between 1298 and 1301, he and his workshop carved a pulpit for Sant'Andrea in Pistoia that is similar to his father's in conception but significantly different in style and execution. In his more dramatic rendering of the **ANNUNCIATION, NATIVITY, AND ADORATION OF THE SHEPHERDS**, Giovanni places graceful but energetic figures in an uptilted, deeply carved setting (**FIG. 17-37**). He replaces Nicola's imperious, stately Roman matron with a lithe, younger Mary, who recoils from Gabriel's advance at left, and at center, exhausted from giving birth, pulls at her bed-sheets for support while reaching toward her newborn baby. Sheep, shepherds, and angels spiral up through the trees at the right. Giovanni's sculpture is as dynamic as Nicola's is static.

Painting

The capture of Constantinople by crusaders in 1204 brought an influx of Byzantine art and artists to Italy. The imported style of painting, the *maniera greca* ("the Greek manner"), influenced thirteenth- and fourteenth-century Italian painting in style and technique and introduced a new emphasis on pathos and emotion.

PAINTED CRUCIFIXES   One example, a large wooden **CRUCIFIX** attributed to the thirteenth-century Florentine painter Coppo di Marcovaldo (**FIG. 17-38**), represents an image of a suffering Christ on the cross, a Byzantine type with closed eyes and bleeding, sagging body that encourages viewers to respond emotionally and empathetically to the image (SEE FIGS. 8-22, 15-26). This is a "historiated crucifix," meaning that narrative scenes flank Christ's body, in this case episodes from the story of his Passion. Such monumental crosses—this one is almost 10 feet high—were mounted on the choir screens that separated the clergy in the sanctuary from the laypeople in the nave, especially in the churches of the Italian mendicants. One such cross can be seen from behind with its wooden bracing in FIGURE 17-40, tilted out to lean toward the worshiper's line of vision and increase the emotional impact.

17–38 Coppo di Marcovaldo **CRUCIFIX**
From the Franciscan convent of Santa Chiara, San Gimignano, Italy. c. 1250–1270.
Tempera and gold on wood panel, 9'7⅜" × 8'1¼" (2.93 × 2.47 m). Pinacoteca, San Gimignano, Italy.

Credit: © 2016. Photo Fine Art Images/Heritage Images/Scala, Florence

THE CHURCH OF ST. FRANCIS AT ASSISI Two years after St. Francis's death in 1226, the church in his birthplace, Assisi, was begun. It was nearly finished in 1239 but was not dedicated until 1253. This building was unusually elaborate in its design, with upper and lower churches on two stories and a crypt at the choir end underneath both (**FIG. 17–39**). Both upper and lower churches have a single nave of four square vaulted bays, and both end in a transept and a single apse. The lower church has massive walls and a narrow nave flanked by side chapels. The upper church is a spacious, well-lit hall with excellent visibility and acoustics, designed to accommodate the crowds of pilgrims who came to see and hear the friars preach as well as to participate in church rituals and venerate the tomb of the saint. The church walls presented expanses of uninterrupted wall surface where sacred stories could unfold in murals. In the wall paintings of the upper church, the focus was on the story of Francis himself, presented as a model Christian life to which pilgrims, as well as resident friars, might aspire.

Scholars differ over whether the murals of the upper church were painted as early as 1290, but they agree on their striking narrative effectiveness. Like most Franciscan paintings, these scenes were designed to engage with viewers by appealing to their memories of their own life experiences, evoked by the inclusion of recognizable anecdotal details and emotionally expressive figures.

A good example is **THE MIRACLE OF THE CRIB AT GRECCIO** (**FIG. 17–40**), portraying St. Francis making the first Christmas manger scene in the church at Greccio.

The scene—like all Gothic visual narratives, set in the present, even though the event portrayed took place in the past—unfolds within a Gothic church that would have looked very familiar to late thirteenth-century viewers. A large wooden crucifix similar to the one by Coppo di Marcovaldo (SEE FIG. 17–38) has been suspended from a stand on top of a screen separating the sanctuary from the nave. The cross has been reinforced on the back and tilted forward to hover over people in the nave, whom we see crowding behind an open door in the choir screen. A pulpit, with stairs leading up to its entrance and candlesticks at its corners, rises above the screen at the left. An elaborate carved *baldacchino* (canopy) shelters the altar at the right, and an adjustable wooden lectern stands in front of the altar. Other small but telling touches include a seasonal liturgical calendar posted on the lectern, foliage swags decorating the *baldacchino*, and an embroidered altar cloth. Sound as well as sight is referenced in the figures of the friars who throw their heads back, mouths wide open, to provide the liturgical soundtrack to this cinematic tableau.

The focus on the sacred narrative is confined to a small area at lower right, where St. Francis reverently holds the Holy Infant above a plain, boxlike crib next to miniature representations of various animals that might have been

17–39 SCHEMATIC DRAWING OF THE CHURCH OF ST. FRANCIS, ASSISI
Umbria, Italy. 1228–1253.

Credit: Maltings Partnership © Dorling Kindersley

present at the Nativity, capturing the miraculous moment when the Christ Child appeared in the manger. But even if the story is about a miracle, it takes place in a setting full of worldly references that allowed contemporary viewers to imagine themselves as part of the scene, either as worshipers kneeling in front of the altar or as spectators pushing toward the doorway to get a better view. This narrative goal of engaging with viewers through references to their own lives, initiated during the Middle Ages, will continue into the Renaissance.

17–40 THE MIRACLE OF THE CRIB AT GRECCIO

From a cycle of the Life of St. Francis, church of St. Francis, Assisi. Late 13th or early 14th century. Fresco.

Credit: © 2016. Photo Scala, Florence

Think About It

1   Characterize the most important of the technological innovations and sociocultural formations that made the "Age of Cathedrals" possible.

2   Explain how manuscript illumination was used to convey complex theological ideas during the Gothic period. Analyze the iconography of one manuscript discussed in this chapter.

3   How was St. Francis's message of empathy conveyed in the frescos of the church of St. Francis in Assisi?

4   Analyze Salisbury Cathedral in England and the German church of St. Elizabeth of Hungary in Marburg. How does each reflect characteristics of French Gothic style, and how does each depart from that style and express architectural features characteristic of its own region?

Crosscurrents

These two works of art, one Romanesque and one Gothic, portray events from the same Bible story in a public context where they would have been seen by a diverse cross section of viewers. Compare the style of presentation. What features do these visual narratives have in common? How are they different? Is there a relationship between style, meaning, and medium?

FIG. 16–20

FIG. 17–1

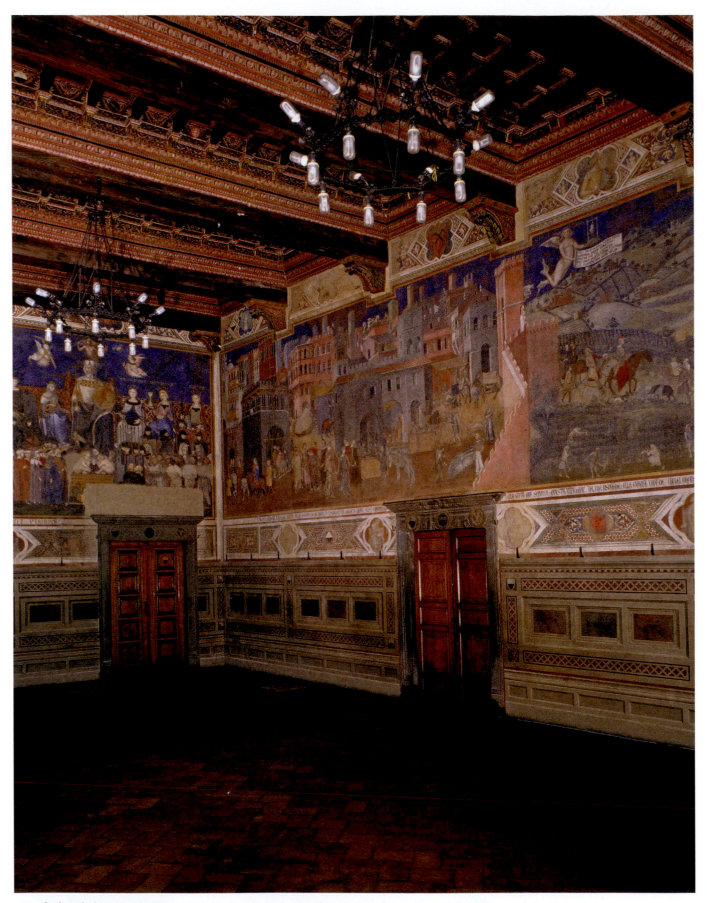

18–1 Ambrogio Lorenzetti **FRESCOS OF THE SALA DEI NOVE (OR SALA DELLA PACE)**

Palazzo Pubblico, Siena, Italy. 1338–1339. Length of long wall approx. 46′ (14 m).

Credit: © Studio Fotografico Quattrone, Florence

Chapter 18
Fourteenth-Century Art in Europe

Learning Objectives

18.a Identify the visual hallmarks of fourteenth-century European art for formal, technical, and expressive qualities.

18.b Interpret the meaning of works of fourteenth-century European art based on its themes, subjects, and symbols.

18.c Relate fourteenth-century European art and artists to their cultural, economic, and political contexts.

18.d Apply the vocabulary and concepts relevant to fourteenth-century European art, artists, and art history.

18.e Interpret a work of fourteenth-century European art using the art historical methods of observation, comparison, and inductive reasoning.

18.f Select visual and textual evidence in various media to support an argument or an interpretation of a work of fourteenth-century European art.

In 1338, the Nine—a council of merchants and bankers that governed Siena as an oligarchy—commissioned frescos from the renowned Sienese painter Ambrogio Lorenzetti (c. 1295–c. 1348) for three walls in the chamber of the Palazzo Pubblico where they met to conduct city business. This commission came at the moment of Siena's greatest prosperity and security since the establishment of their government in 1287.

Lorenzetti's frescos combine allegory with panoramic landscapes and cityscapes to visualize and justify the beneficial effects of the Sienese form of government. The moral foundation of the rule of the Nine is outlined in a complicated allegory in which seated personifications (far left in **FIG. 18–1**) of Concord, Justice, Peace, Strength, Prudence, Temperance, and Magnanimity, not only diagram good governance but actually reference the Last Judgment in a bold assertion of the relationship between secular rule and divine authority. This tableau contrasts with a similar presentation of bad government, where Tyranny is flanked by the personified forces that keep tyrants in power—Cruelty, Treason, Fraud, Fury, Division, and War. A group of scholars would have devised this complex program of symbols and meanings; it is unlikely that Lorenzetti would have known the philosophical works that underlie them. Lorenzetti's fame, however, and the wall paintings' secure position among the most remarkable surviving mural programs of the period, rests on the other part of this ensemble—the effects of good and bad government in city and country life (SEE FIG. 18–16).

Unlike the tableau showing the perils of life under tyrannical rule, the panoramic view of life under good government—which in this work of propaganda means life under the rule of the Nine—is well preserved. A vista of fourteenth-century Siena—identifiable by the cathedral dome and tower peeking over the rooftops in the background—showcases carefree life within shops, schools, taverns, and worksites, as the city streets bustle with human activity. Outside, an expansive landscape highlights agricultural productivity.

Unfortunately, within a decade of the frescos' completion, life in Siena was no longer so stable and carefree. The devastating bubonic plague came in 1348—Ambrogio Lorenzetti himself was probably one of the victims—and the rule of the Nine collapsed in 1355. But this glorious vision of joyful prosperity preserves the dreams and aspirations of a stable government using some of the most progressive and creative ideas in fourteenth-century Italian art, ideas we will see developed at the very beginning of the century, and whose history we will trace over the next two centuries through the Renaissance.

Fourteenth-Century Europe

What are the cultural and historical backgrounds for the transformation of European art during the fourteenth century?

Literary luminaries Dante, Petrarch, Boccaccio, Chaucer, and Christine de Pizan (see "A New Spirit in Fourteenth-Century Literature" below) and the visionary painters Giotto, Duccio, Jean Pucelle, and Master Theodoric participated in a cultural explosion that swept through fourteenth-century Europe, and especially Italy. The poet Petrarch (1304–1374) was a towering figure in this change, writing his love lyrics in Italian, the language of everyday life, rather than Latin, the language of ceremony and high art. Similarly, the deeply moving murals of Florentine painter Giotto di Bondone (c. 1277–1337) were rooted in his observation of the people around him, giving the characters in sacred narratives both great dignity and a striking new humanity. Even in Paris—still the artistic center of Europe as far as refined taste and technical sophistication were concerned—the painter Jean Pucelle began to show an interest in experimenting with established conventions.

Changes in the way that society was organized were also underway, and an expanding class of wealthy merchants supported the arts as patrons. Artisan guilds—organized by occupation—exerted quality control among members and supervised education through an apprenticeship system. Admission to a guild came after examination and the creation of a "masterpiece"—literally, a piece fine enough to achieve master status. The major guilds included cloth finishers, wool merchants, and silk manufacturers, as well as pharmacists and doctors. Painters belonged to the pharmacy guild, perhaps because they used mortars and pestles to grind their colors. Their patron saint, Luke, who was believed to have painted the first image of the Virgin Mary, was also a physician—or so they thought. Sculptors who worked in wood and stone had their own guild, while those who worked in metals belonged to another. Guilds provided social services for their members, including care of the sick and funerals for the deceased. Each guild had its patron saint, maintained a chapel, and participated in religious and civic festivals.

Despite the cultural flourishing and economic growth of the early decades, by the middle of the fourteenth century much of Europe was in crisis. Prosperity had fostered population growth, which began to exceed food production. A series of bad harvests compounded this problem with famine. To make matters worse, a prolonged conflict known as the Hundred Years' War (1337–1453) erupted between France and England. Then, in mid century, a lethal plague known as the Black Death swept across Europe (MAP 18–1), wiping out as much as 40 percent of the population. In spite of these catastrophic events, however, the strong current of cultural change still managed to persist through to the end of the century and beyond.

Art and its Contexts

A NEW SPIRIT IN FOURTEENTH-CENTURY LITERATURE

For Petrarch and his contemporaries, the essential qualifications for a writer were an appreciation of Greek and Roman authors and an ability to observe the people living around themselves. Although fluent in Latin, each chose to write in the language of their own time and place—whether Italian, English, or French. Leading the way was Dante Alighieri (1265–1321), who wrote *The Divine Comedy*, his great summation of human virtue and vice, in Italian, establishing his daily language as worthy to express great literary themes.

Francesco Petrarca, called simply Petrarch (1304–1374), raised the status of secular literature with his sonnets to his unattainable beloved, Laura, his histories and biographies, and his writings on the joys of country life in the Roman manner. Petrarch's imaginative updating of Classical themes in a work called *The Triumphs*—which examines the themes of Chastity triumphant over Love, Death over Chastity, Fame over Death, Time over Fame, and Eternity over Time—provided later Renaissance poets and painters with a wealth of allegorical subject matter.

The earthier Giovanni Boccaccio (1313–1375) perfected the art of the short story in *The Decameron*, a collection of amusing and moralizing tales told by a group of young Florentines who move to the countryside to escape the Black Death. With wit and sympathy, Boccaccio presents the full spectrum of daily life in Italy. Such secular literature, written in Italian as it was then spoken in Tuscany, provided a foundation for fifteenth-century Renaissance writers.

In England, Geoffrey Chaucer (c. 1342–1400) was inspired by Boccaccio to write his own series of stories, *The Canterbury Tales*, as if told by pilgrims traveling to the shrine of St. Thomas à Becket (1118?–1170) in Canterbury. Observant and witty, Chaucer depicted the pretensions and foibles, as well as the virtues, of humanity.

Christine de Pizan (1364–c. 1431), born in Venice but living and writing at the French court, became an author out of necessity when she was left a widow with three young children and an aged mother to support. Among her many works are a poem in praise of Joan of Arc and a history of famous women—including artists—from antiquity to her own time. In *The Book of the City of Ladies*, she defended women's abilities and argued for women's rights and status.

These writers, as surely as the visual artists Giotto, Duccio, Peter Parler, and Master Theodoric, led the way into a new era.

MAP 18–1 EUROPE IN THE FOURTEENTH CENTURY

Following its outbreak in the Mediterranean in 1347, the Black Death swept across the European mainland over the next four years.

Italy

How do political, religious, and cultural changes transform the artistic traditions of Florence and Siena during the first half of the fourteenth century?

As great wealth promoted patronage of art in fourteenth-century Italy, artists began to emerge as individuals in the modern sense, both in their own eyes and in the eyes of patrons. Although their methods and working conditions remained largely unchanged from the Middle Ages, artists in Italy contracted freely with wealthy townspeople and nobles as well as with civic and religious bodies. Perhaps it was their economic and social freedom that encouraged their self-confidence, individuality, and innovation.

Florentine Architecture and Metalwork

The typical medieval Italian city was a walled citadel on a hilltop. Houses clustered around a church and an open city square. Powerful families added towers to their houses, both for defense and as expressions of family pride. In Florence, by contrast, the ancient Roman city—with its axial rectangular plan and open city squares—formed the basis for the civic layout. The cathedral stood northeast of the ancient forum, and a street following the Roman plan connected it with the Piazza della Signoria, the seat of the government.

THE PALAZZO DELLA SIGNORIA The Signoria (ruling body, from *signore*, meaning "Lord") that governed Florence met in the **PALAZZO DELLA SIGNORIA**, a massive, fortified building with a bell tower 300 feet tall (**FIG. 18-2**). The building faces a large square, or piazza, which became the true center of Florence. The town houses around the piazza often had benches along their walls to provide convenient public seating. Between 1376 and 1382, master builders Benci di Cione and Simone Talenti constructed a huge **loggia**, or covered open-air corridor, at one side—now known as the Loggia dei Lanzi (Loggia of the Lancers)—to provide a sheltered place for ceremonies and speeches.

THE BAPTISTERY DOORS In 1330, Andrea Pisano (c. 1290–1348) was awarded the prestigious commission for a pair of gilded bronze doors for Florence's Baptistery of San Giovanni, situated directly in front of the cathedral. (Andrea's last name means "from Pisa," and he was not related to Nicola and Giovanni Pisano.) The doors were completed within six years and display 20 scenes from the **LIFE OF ST. JOHN THE BAPTIST** (the San Giovanni to whom the baptistery is dedicated), set above eight personifications of the Virtues (**FIG. 18-3**). The overall effect is two-dimensional and decorative: a grid of 28 rectangles with repeated quatrefoils filled with the graceful, patterned poses of delicate human figures. Within the quatrefoil frames, however, the figural compositions create the illusion of three-dimensional forms moving within natural and architectural spaces.

18-2 PIAZZA DELLA SIGNORIA WITH PALAZZO DELLA SIGNORIA (TOWN HALL) AND LOGGIA DEI LANZI (LOGGIA OF THE LANCERS)

Florence. Palazzo della Signoria, 1299–1310; Loggia dei Lanzi, 1376–1382.

Credit: © Achim Bednorz, Cologne

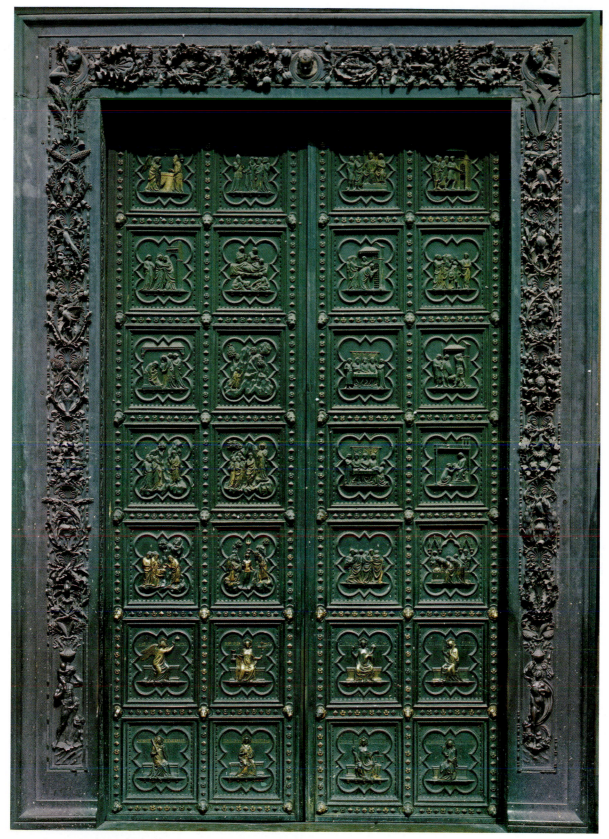

18–3 Andrea Pisano **LIFE OF ST. JOHN THE BAPTIST**

South doors, Baptistery of San Giovanni, Florence. 1330–1336. Gilded bronze, each panel 19¼ × 17″ (48 × 43 cm). Frame, Ghiberti workshop, mid 15th century.

The bronze vine scrolls filled with flowers, fruits, and birds on the lintel and jambs framing the door were added in the mid fifteenth century.

Credit: © Studio Fotografico Quattrone, Florence

18–4 Andrea Pisano **THE BAPTISM OF THE MULTITUDE**
Detail of the south doors, Baptistery of San Giovanni, Florence. 1330–1336. Gilded bronze, 19¼ × 17″ (48 × 43 cm).

Credit: Photo: David G. Wilkins

The scene of John baptizing a multitude (**FIG. 18–4**) takes place on a shelflike stage created by a forward extension of the rocky natural setting, which also expands back behind the figures into a corner of the quatrefoil frame. Composed as a rectangular group, the gilded figures present an independent mass of modeled forms. The illusion of three-dimensionality is enhanced by the way the curving folds of their clothing wrap around their bodies. At the same time, their graceful gestures and the elegant fall of their drapery reflect the soft curves and courtly postures of French Gothic art.

Florentine Painting

Florence and Siena, rivals in so many ways, each supported a flourishing school of painting in the fourteenth century. Both grew out of local thirteenth-century painting traditions and engendered individual artists who became famous in their own time. The Byzantine influence—the *maniera greca* ("Greek style")—continued to provide models of dramatic

pathos and narrative iconography, as well as stylized features including the use of gold for drapery folds and striking contrasts of highlights and shadows in the modeling of individual forms. By the end of the fourteenth century, the painter and commentator Cennino Cennini (see "Cennino Cennini on Panel Painting" on page 556) would be struck by the accessibility and modernity of Giotto's art, which, though it retained traces of the *maniera greca*, was moving toward the depiction of a lifelike, contemporary world anchored in solid, three-dimensional forms.

CIMABUE In Florence, this stylistic transformation began a little earlier than in Siena. About 1280, a painter named Cenni di Pepi (active c. 1272–1302), better known by his nickname "Cimabue," painted a panel portraying the **VIRGIN AND CHILD ENTHRONED** (**FIG. 18–5**), perhaps for the main altar of the church of Santa Trinità in Florence. At over 12 feet tall, this enormous egg-tempera panel painting set a new precedent for monumental altarpieces. Cimabue surrounds the Virgin and Child with angels and places a row of Hebrew Bible prophets beneath them. The hierarchically scaled figure of Mary holds the infant Jesus in her lap. Looking out at the viewer while gesturing toward her son as the path to salvation, she adopts a formula popular in Byzantine iconography since at least the sixth century (SEE FIG. 8–14).

Mary's huge throne, painted to resemble gilded bronze with inset enamels and gems, provides an architectural framework for the figures. Cimabue creates highlights on the drapery of Mary, Jesus, and the angels with thin lines of gold, as if to capture their divine radiance. The viewer seems suspended in space in front of the image, simultaneously looking down on the projecting elements of the throne and Mary's lap and looking straight ahead at the prophets at the base of the throne and the angels at each side. These spatial ambiguities, the subtle asymmetries within the centralized composition, the Virgin's engaging gaze, and the individually conceived faces of the old men give the picture a sense of life and the figures a sense of presence. Cimabue's ambitious attention to spatial volumes, his use of delicate light-to-dark modeling to simulate three-dimensional form, and his efforts to give naturalistic warmth to human figures had an impact on future Florentine painting.

18–5 Cimabue
VIRGIN AND CHILD ENTHRONED
Most likely painted for the high altar of the church of Santa Trinità, Florence. c. 1280. Tempera and gold on wood panel, 12′7″ × 7′4″ (3.53 × 2.2 m). Galleria degli Uffizi, Florence.

Credit: © Studio Fotografico Quattrone, Florence

GIOTTO DI BONDONE According to the sixteenth-century chronicler Giorgio Vasari, Cimabue discovered a talented shepherd boy, Giotto di Bondone (active c. 1300–1337) and taught him to paint; "not only did the young boy equal the style of his master, but he became such an excellent imitator of nature that he completely banished that crude Greek [Byzantine] style and revived the modern and excellent art of painting, introducing good drawing from live natural models, something which had not been done for more than two hundred years" (Vasari, translated by Bondanella and Bondanella, p. 16). After his training, Giotto may have collaborated on murals at the prestigious

church of St. Francis in Assisi. We know he worked for the Franciscans in Florence and absorbed facets of their teaching. St. Francis's message of humility, simple devotion, direct experience of God, and love for all creatures was gaining followers throughout western Europe, and it had a powerful impact on thirteenth- and fourteenth-century Italian literature and art.

Compared to Cimabue's *Virgin and Child Enthroned*, Giotto's altarpiece of the same subject (**FIG. 18–6**), painted about 30 years later for the church of the Ognissanti (All Saints) in Florence, exhibits greater spatial consistency and sculptural solidity while retaining some of Cimabue's

18–6 Giotto di Bondone **VIRGIN AND CHILD ENTHRONED**

Most likely painted for the high altar of the church of the Ognissanti (All Saints), Florence. 1305–1310. Tempera and gold on wood panel, 10′8″ × 6′8¼″ (3.53 × 2.05 m). Galleria degli Uffizi, Florence.

Credit: © Studio Fotografico Quattrone, Florence

Technique

BUON FRESCO

The two techniques used in mural painting are *buon* ("true") *fresco* ("fresh"), in which water-based paint is applied on wet plaster, and *fresco secco* ("dry"), in which paint is applied to a dry plastered wall. Both methods can be used on the same wall painting.

The advantage of *buon fresco* is its durability. A chemical reaction occurs as the painted plaster dries, which bonds the pigments into the wall surface. In *fresco secco*, by contrast, the color does not become part of the wall and tends to flake off over time. The chief disadvantage of *buon fresco* is that it must be done quickly without mistakes. The painter plasters and paints only as much as can be completed in a day, which explains the Italian term for each of these sections: **giornata**, or a day's work. The size of a *giornata* varies according to the complexity of the painting within it. A face, for instance, might take an entire day, whereas large areas of sky can be painted quite rapidly. In Giotto's Scrovegni Chapel, scholars have identified 852 separate *giornate*, some worked on concurrently within a single day by assistants in Giotto's workshop.

In medieval and Renaissance Italy, a wall to be frescoed was first prepared with a rough, thick undercoat of plaster known as the *arriccio*. When this was dry, assistants copied the master painter's composition onto it with reddish-brown pigment or charcoal. The artist made any necessary adjustments. These underdrawings, known as **sinopia**, have an immediacy and freshness that are lost in the finished painting. Work proceeded in irregularly shaped *giornate* conforming to the contours of major figures and objects. Assistants covered one section at a time with a fresh, thin coat of very fine plaster—the *intonaco*—over the *sinopia*, and when this was "set" but not dry, the artist worked with pigments mixed with water, painting from the top down so that drips fell on unfinished portions. Gilding and pigments such as ultramarine blue (which was unstable in *buon fresco*) would be added after the wall was dry using the *fresco secco* technique.

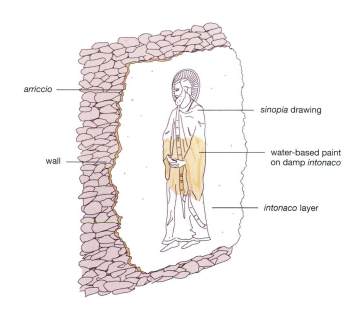

conventions. The position of the figures within a symmetrical composition reflects Cimabue's influence. Gone, however, are Mary's modestly inclined head and the delicate gold folds in her drapery. Instead, light and shadow play gently across her stocky form, and her action—holding her child's leg instead of pointing him out to us—seems less contrived. This colossal Mary overwhelms her slender Gothic tabernacle of a throne, where figures peer through openings and haloes overlap faces. In spite of the hierarchic scale, the formal, enthroned image, and the flat, gold background, Giotto has created the sense that these are fully three-dimensional beings, whose plainly draped, bulky bodies inhabit real space. The Virgin's torso is revealed by her thin tunic, and the angels are substantial solids whose foreshortened postures project from the foreground toward us, unlike those of Cimabue, who stay on the surface along lateral strips composed of overlapping screens of color.

Although Giotto was trained in the Florentine tradition, many of his principal works were produced elsewhere. After a sojourn in Rome during the last years of the thirteenth century, he was called to Padua in northern Italy soon after 1300 to paint frescos (see "*Buon Fresco*" above) for a new chapel being constructed at the site of an ancient Roman arena—explaining why it is often referred to as the Arena Chapel. The chapel was commissioned by Enrico Scrovegni, whose family fortune was made through the practice of usury, or charging interest when loaning money, a sin considered so grave at the time that it resulted in exclusion from the Christian sacraments. Enrico's father, Regibaldo, was an egregious case (he appears in Dante's *Inferno* as the prototypical usurer), but evidence suggests that Enrico followed in his father's footsteps, and the building of the Arena Chapel next to his new palatial residence seems to have been conceived at least in part as an attempt to atone not only for his father's sins, but also for his own. He was pardoned by Pope Benedict XI (pontificate 1303–1304).

That Scrovegni called two of the most famous artists of the time—Giotto and Giovanni Pisano (SEE FIG. 17–37)—to decorate his chapel indicates that his goals were to express his power, sophistication, and prestige, as well as to atone for his sins. The building itself has little architectural distinction. It is a simple, barrel-vaulted room with broad walls to showcase Giotto's paintings (**FIG. 18-7**). Giotto covered the entrance wall with the *Last Judgment* (not visible here) and the sanctuary wall with three highlighted scenes from the life of Christ. The Annunciation spreads over the two painted architectural frameworks on either side of the tall, arched opening into the sanctuary itself. Below this are, to the left, the scene of Judas receiving payment for betraying Jesus and, to the right, the scene of the Visitation, where the Virgin, pregnant with God incarnate, embraces her cousin Elizabeth, pregnant with St. John the Baptist. The compositions and color arrangement of these two scenes create a symmetrical pairing that encourages viewers to relate them, comparing the ill-gotten financial gains of Judas (a rather clear reference to Scrovegni usury) to the miraculous pregnancy that brought the promise of salvation.

Giotto subdivided the side walls of the chapel into framed pictures. A dado of faux-marble and allegorical **grisaille** paintings (monochrome paintings in shades of gray) of the Virtues and Vices support vertical bands painted to resemble marble inlay into which are inserted painted imitations of carved medallions. The central band of medallions spans the vault, crossing a brilliant, lapis-blue, star-spangled sky in which large portrait disks float like glowing moons. Set into this framework are three horizontal bands of rectangular narrative scenes from the life of the Virgin and her parents at the top and Jesus along the middle and lower registers, which make up the primary religious program of the chapel.

Both the individual scenes and the overall program display Giotto's genius for distilling complex stories into a series of compelling moments. He concentrates on the human dimensions of the unfolding drama—from touches of anecdotal humor to expressions of profound anguish—rather than on its symbolic or theological weight. His prodigious narrative skills are apparent in a set of scenes from Christ's life on the north wall (**FIG. 18-8**). At top left Jesus performs his first miracle, changing water into wine at the wedding feast at Cana. The wine steward—looking very much like the jars of new wine himself—sips the results.

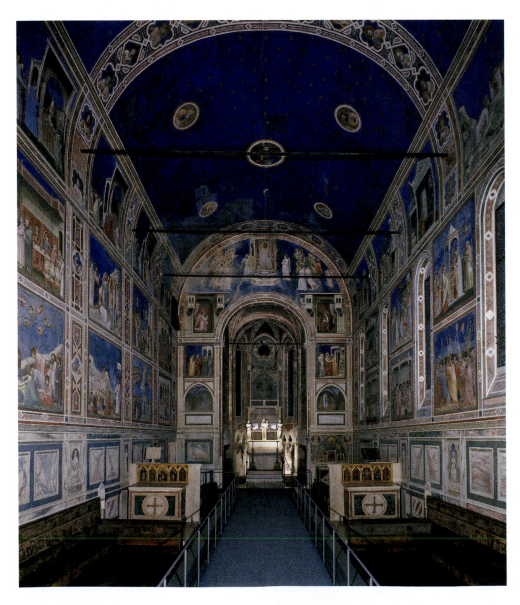

18-7 Giotto di Bondone **SCROVEGNI (ARENA) CHAPEL, VIEW TOWARD EAST WALL**

Padua. 1305–1306. Frescos.

Credit: © Studio Fotografico Quattrone, Florence

18–8 Giotto di Bondone **MARRIAGE AT CANA, RAISING OF LAZARUS, LAMENTATION, AND RESURRECTION/ NOLI ME TANGERE**

North wall of Scrovegni (Arena) Chapel, Padua. 1305–1306. Fresco, each scene approx. 6′5″ × 6′ (2 × 1.85 m).

Credit: © Studio Fotografico Quattrone, Florence

To the right is the Raising of Lazarus, where boldly modeled and individualized figures twist in space. Through their postures and gestures they react to the human drama by pleading for Jesus's help or by expressing either astonishment at the miracle or revulsion at the smell of death. Jesus is separated from the crowd. His transforming gesture is highlighted against the dark blue of the background, his profile face locked in communication with the similarly isolated Lazarus, whose eyes—still fixed in death—let us know that the miracle has not yet happened.

On the lower register, where Jesus's followers lament over his dead body, Giotto portrays palpable human suffering, drawing viewers into a circle of personal grief. The stricken Virgin pulls her dead son close, while John the Evangelist flings his arms back in convulsive despair and others hunch over the corpse. Much as Giotto linked the scene of Judas's pact and the Visitation across the

sanctuary arch, he links this scene to the mourning of Lazarus on the register above using the continuous diagonal implied by the sharply angled hillside behind both scenes, and the rhyming repetition of mourners in each scene—facing in opposite directions—who throw back their arms to express their emotional state. Viewers would know that the mourning in both scenes is resolved by resurrection, portrayed in the last picture in this set.

Following traditional medieval practice, the fresco program is full of scenes and symbols that are intended to be seen as coordinated or contrasting juxtapositions. What is new here is the way Giotto draws us into the experience of these events. This direct emotional appeal not only allows viewers to imagine the scenes in relation to their own life experiences, it also embodies the new Franciscan emphasis on personal devotion rooted in empathetic responses to sacred stories.

18–9 Giotto di Bondone
KISS OF JUDAS
South wall of Scrovegni
(Arena) Chapel, Padua.
1305–1306. Fresco,
6'6¾" × 6'7⁄8" (2 × 1.85 m).

Credit: © Studio Fotografico
Quattrone, Florence

One of the most gripping paintings in the chapel is Giotto's portrayal of the **KISS OF JUDAS**, the moment of betrayal that represents the first step on Jesus's road to the Crucifixion (**FIG. 18–9**). Savior and traitor are slightly off-center in the near foreground. The expansive sweep of Judas's strident yellow cloak—the same outfit he wore at the scene of his payment for the betrayal on the strip of wall to the left of the sanctuary arch—almost completely swallows Christ's body. Surrounding them, faces glare from all directions. A bristling array of weapons radiating from the confrontation draws attention to the encounter between Christ and Judas and documents the militarism of the arresting soldiers. Jesus stands solid, a model of calm resolve that recalls his visual characterization in the *Raising of Lazarus*, and forms a striking foil to the noisy and chaotic aggression that engulfs him. Judas, in simian profile, purses his lips for the kiss that will betray Jesus to his captors, setting up a mythic confrontation of good and evil. In a subplot to the left, Peter lunges forward to sever the ear of the high priest's assistant. They are behind another broad sweep of fabric, this one extended by a figure completely concealed except for the hand that pulls at Peter's cloak. Indeed, a broad expanse of cloth and lateral gestures creates a barrier along the picture plane—as if to protect viewers from the compressed chaos of the scene itself. Rarely has this poignant event been visualized with such riveting power.

Sienese Painting

Like their Florentine rivals, Sienese painters were rooted in thirteenth-century pictorial traditions, especially those of Byzantine art. Sienese painting emphasized the decorative potential of narrative painting with brilliant, jewel-like colors and elegantly posed figures. For this reason, some art historians consider Sienese art more conservative than Florentine art, but we will see that it has its own charm and its own narrative strategies.

DUCCIO DI BUONINSEGNA   Siena's foremost painter was Duccio di Buoninsegna (active 1278–1318), whose creative synthesis of Byzantine and French Gothic sources transformed the tradition in which he worked. Between 1308 and 1311, Duccio and his workshop painted a huge altarpiece commissioned for Siena Cathedral and known as the **MAESTÀ** ("Majesty") (**FIG. 18–10**). Creating this altarpiece—assembled from many wood panels bonded together before painting—was an arduous undertaking. The work was not only large—the central panel alone was 7 by 13 feet—but it had to be painted on both sides since it could be seen from all directions when installed on the main altar at the center of the sanctuary.

Because the *Maestà* was dismantled in 1771, its power and beauty can only be imagined from scattered parts, some still in Siena but others elsewhere. FIGURE 18–10A is a

18–10 Duccio di Buoninsegna **CONJECTURAL RECONSTRUCTION OF THE FRONT (A) AND BACK (B) OF THE MAESTÀ ALTARPIECE**
Made for Siena Cathedral. 1308–1311. Tempera and gold on wood, main front panel 7 × 13′ (2.13 × 4.12 m).

Credit: © Lew Minter

Technique

CENNINO CENNINI ON PANEL PAINTING

Il Libro dell' Arte (*The Book of Art*) of Cennino Cennini (c. 1370–1440) is a compendium of Florentine painting techniques from about 1400 that includes step-by-step instructions for making panel paintings, a process also used in Sienese paintings of the same period.

The wood for the panels, he explains, should be fine-grained, free of blemishes, and thoroughly seasoned by slow drying. The first step in preparing such a panel for painting was to cover its surface with clean white linen strips soaked in a **gesso** (primer) made from gypsum, a task, he tells us, best done on a dry, windy day. Gesso provided a ground, or surface, on which to paint, and Cennini specified that at least nine layers should be applied. The gessoed surface should then be burnished until it resembles ivory. Only then could the artist sketch the composition of the work with charcoal made from burned willow twigs. At this point, advised Cennini, "When you have finished drawing your figure, especially if it is in a very valuable [altarpiece], so that you are counting on profit and reputation from it, leave it alone for a few days, going back to it now and then to look it over and improve it wherever it still needs something. When it seems to you about right (and bear in mind that you may copy and examine things done by other good masters; that it is no shame to you), when the figure is satisfactory, take the feather and rub it over the drawing very lightly, until the drawing is practically effaced" (Cennini, trans. Thompson, p. 75). At this point, the final design would be inked in with a fine squirrel-hair brush. Gold leaf, he advises, should be affixed on a humid day, the tissue-thin sheets carefully glued down with a mixture of fine powdered clay and egg white on the reddish clay ground called bole. Then the gold is burnished with a gemstone or the tooth of a carnivorous animal. Punched and incised patterning should be added to the gold leaf later.

Fourteenth- and fifteenth-century Italian painters worked principally in tempera paint: powdered pigments mixed with egg yolk, a little water, and an occasional touch of glue. Apprentices were kept busy grinding pigments and mixing paints, setting them out for more senior painters in wooden bowls or shell dishes.

Cennini outlined a detailed and highly formulaic painting process. Faces, for example, were always to be done last, with flesh tones applied over two coats of a light greenish pigment and highlighted with touches of red and white. The finished painting was to be given a layer of varnish to protect it and intensify its colors.

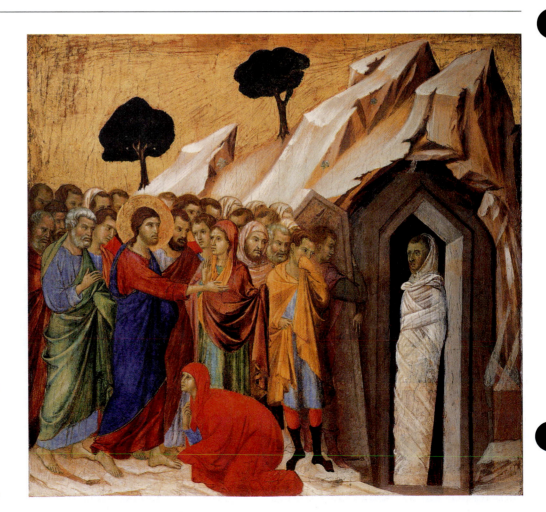

18–11 Duccio di Buoninsegna **RAISING OF LAZARUS**

From the predella of the back of the *Maestà* altarpiece (lower right corner of FIG. 18–10B), made for Siena Cathedral. 1308–1311. Tempera and gold on wood, 17⅛ × 18¼″ (43.5 × 46.4 cm). Kimbell Art Museum, Fort Worth, Texas.

Credit: © 2016. Photo Scala, Florence

18–12 Duccio di Buoninsegna **BETRAYAL OF JESUS**
From the back of the *Maestà* altarpiece (lower center of FIG. 18–10B), made for Siena Cathedral. 1308–1311.
Tempera and gold on wood, 22½ × 40″ (57.2 × 101.6 cm). Museo dell'Opera del Duomo, Siena.

Credit: © 2016. Photo Opera Metropolitana Siena/Scala, Florence

reconstruction of how the front of the original altarpiece might have looked. It is dominated by a large representation of the Virgin and Child in Majesty (thus its title of *Maestà*), flanked by 20 angels and 10 saints, including the 4 patron saints of Siena kneeling in the foreground. Above and below this lateral tableau were small narrative scenes from the last days of the life of the Virgin (above) and the infancy of Christ (spread across the **predella**, the lower zone of the altarpiece). An inscription running around the base of Mary's majestic throne places the artist's signature within an optimistic framework: "Holy Mother of God, be thou the cause of peace for Siena and life to Duccio because he painted thee thus." This was not Duccio's first work for the cathedral. In 1288, he had designed a stunning stained-glass window portraying the Death, Assumption, and Coronation of the Virgin for the huge circular opening in the east wall of the sanctuary. It would have hovered over the installed *Maestà* when it was placed on the altar in 1311.

The enthusiasm with which citizens greeted a great painting or altarpiece like the *Maestà* demonstrates the power of images as well as the association of such magnificent works with the glory of a city itself. According to a contemporary account, on December 20, 1311, the day that Duccio's altarpiece was carried from his workshop to the cathedral, all the shops were shut, and everyone in the city participated in the procession, with "bells ringing joyously, out of reverence for so noble a picture as is this" (Holt, p. 69).

On the back of the *Maestà* (SEE FIG. 18–10B) were episodes from the life of Christ focusing on his Passion. Sacred narrative unfolds in elegant episodes enacted by graceful figures who seem to dance their way through these stories while still conveying emotional content. Characteristic of Duccio's narrative style is the scene of the **RAISING OF LAZARUS (FIG. 18–11)**. Lyrical figures enact the event with graceful decorum, but their highly charged glances and expressive gestures—especially the bold reach of Christ—convey a strong sense of dramatic urgency that contrasts with the tense stillness that we saw in Giotto's rendering of this same moment of confrontation (SEE FIG. 18–8). Duccio's shading of drapery, like his modeling of faces, faithfully describes the figures' three-dimensionality, but the crisp outlines of the jewel-colored shapes created by their clothing, as well as the sinuous continuity of folds and gestures, generate rhythmic patterns crisscrossing the surface. Duccio's experimentation with the portrayal of space extends from the receding rocks of the mountainous landscape to the carefully studied interiors, including the tomb of Lazarus, the door of which was removed by a bystander to reveal Jesus's resurrected friend.

Duccio's rendering of the **BETRAYAL OF JESUS (FIG. 18–12)** is more expansive, both pictorially and temporally, occupying one of the broadest panels in the altarpiece (SEE FIG. 18–10B, lower center) and encompassing within one composition several moments in the sequential narrative of its subject matter. The tableau is centered and stabilized by the frontal figure of Jesus, whose dark mantle with its sinuous gold trim stands out from the densely packed, colorful crowd of figures surrounding him. Judas approaches from the left to identify Jesus. Although the heads of betrayer and betrayed touch in this moment, Duccio avoids the psychological power of Giotto's face-to-face confrontation in the Scrovegni Chapel (SEE FIG. 18–9). Flanking Duccio's stable, packed central scene of betrayal are two subsequent moments in the story, each pulling our attention to the sides. To the left, the apostle Peter lunges with a dynamic gesture to sever the ear of a member of the arresting party, while on the other side of the composition a group of apostles rushes to escape the central scene, abandoning Jesus to his fate. Through the postures and facial expressions of the many figures in this broad, continuous narrative, Duccio expresses the emotional charge of these pivotal moments in the narrative of Christ's Passion. At the same time, he creates a dazzling picture, as rich in color and linear elegance as it is faithful to the human dimensions of the situations it portrays.

SIMONE MARTINI   The generation of painters who followed Duccio continued to paint in the elegant style he established, combining the evocation of three-dimensional form with a graceful continuity of linear pattern. One of Duccio's most successful and innovative followers was Simone Martini (c. 1284–1344), whose paintings were in high demand throughout Italy, including in Assisi where he covered the walls of the St. Martin Chapel with frescos between 1312 and 1319. His most famous work, however, was commissioned in 1333 for the cathedral of his native Siena, an altarpiece of the **ANNUNCIATION** flanked by two saints (**FIG. 18–13**) that he painted in collaboration with his brother-in-law, Lippo Memmi.

18–13 Simone Martini and Lippo Memmi **ANNUNCIATION**
Made for Siena Cathedral. 1333. Tempera and gold on wood, 10′ × 8′9″ (3 × 2.67 m). Galleria degli Uffizi, Florence.

Credit: © Studio Fotografico Quattrone, Florence

Art and its Contexts

THE BLACK DEATH

A deadly outbreak of the bubonic plague, known as the Black Death after the dark sores that developed on the bodies of its victims, spread to Europe from Asia by both land and sea in the middle of the fourteenth century. At least half the urban population of Florence and Siena—some estimate 80 percent—died during the summer of 1348, probably including the artists Andrea Pisano and Ambrogio Lorenzetti. Death was so quick and widespread that basic social structures crumbled in the resulting chaos; people did not know where the disease came from, what caused it, or how long the pandemic would last.

Mid-twentieth-century art historian Millard Meiss proposed that the Black Death had a significant impact on the development of Italian art in the middle of the fourteenth century. Pointing to what he saw as a reactionary return to hieratic linearity in religious art, Meiss theorized that artists had retreated from the rounded forms that had characterized the work of Giotto to old-fashioned styles, and that this artistic change reflected a growing reliance on traditional religious values in the wake of a disaster that some interpreted as God's punishment of a world in moral decline.

An altarpiece painted in 1354–1357 by Andrea di Cione, nicknamed "Orcagna" ("Archangel"), under the patronage of Tommaso Strozzi—the so-called **STROZZI ALTARPIECE** (**FIG. 18–14**)—is the sort of painting that led Meiss to his interpretation. It is dominated by a central figure of Christ,

presumably enthroned, but without any hint of an actual seat, evoking the image of the judge at the Last Judgment, outside time and space. The silhouetted outlines of the standing and kneeling saints emphasize surface over depth; the gold floor beneath them does not offer any reassuring sense of spatial recession to contain them and their activity. Throughout, line and color are more prominent than form.

Recent art historians have stepped back from Meiss's contextual explanation of stylistic change. Some have pointed out logical relationships between style and subject in the works Meiss cites; others have seen in them a mannered outgrowth of current style rather than a reversion to an earlier style; still others have discounted the underlying notion that stylistic change is connected with social situations. But there is a clear relationship of works such as the Strozzi Altarpiece with death and judgment, sanctity, and the promise of salvation—themes also suggested in the narrative scenes on the predella: Thomas Aquinas's ecstasy during Mass, Christ's miraculous walk on water to rescue Peter, and the salvation of Emperor Henry II because of a pious donation. While these are not uncommon scenes in sacred art, it is easy to see a relationship between their choice as subject matter here and the specter cast by the Black Death over a world that had recently imagined its prosperity in art firmly rooted in references to everyday life (**SEE FIG. 18–16**).

18–14 Andrea di Cione (nicknamed "Orcagna") **ENTHRONED CHRIST WITH SAINTS, FROM THE STROZZI ALTARPIECE**
Strozzi Chapel, Santa Maria Novella, Florence. 1354–1357. Tempera and gold on wood, 9′ × 9′8″ (2.74 × 2.95 m).

Credit: © Studio Fotografico Quattrone, Florence

The smartly dressed figure of Gabriel—the extended flourish of his drapery behind him suggesting he has just arrived, and with some speed—raises his hand to address the Virgin. The words of his message are actually incised into the gold-leafed gesso of the background, running from his opened mouth toward the Virgin's ear: *Ave gratia plena dominus tecum* (Luke 1:28: "Hail, full of grace, the Lord is with thee"). Seemingly frightened—at the very least

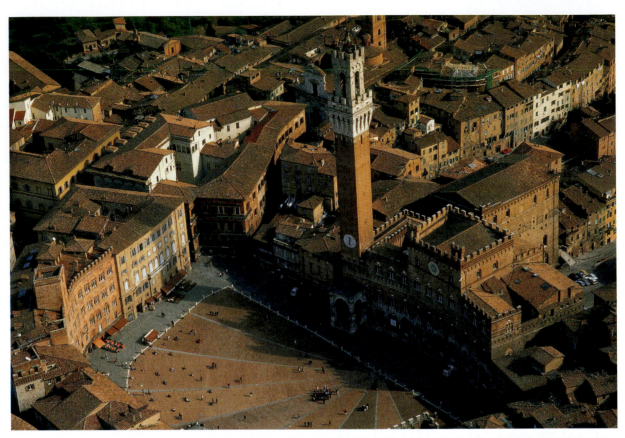

18–15 AERIAL VIEW OF THE CAMPO IN SIENA WITH THE PALAZZO PUBBLICO (CITY HALL INCLUDING ITS TOWER) FACING ITS STRAIGHT SIDE

Siena. Palazzo Pubblico 1297–c. 1315; tower 1320s–1340s.

Credit: © Archivi Alinari, Firenze

startled—by this unexpected celestial messenger, Mary recoils into her lavish throne, her thumb inserted into the book she had been reading to safeguard her place, while her other hand pulls at her clothing in an elegant gesture of nobility that relates back to the courtly art of thirteenth-century Paris (see Solomon, second lancet from the right in FIG. 17–11).

AMBROGIO LORENZETTI   The most important civic structure in Siena was the **PALAZZO PUBBLICO** (FIG. 18–15), the town hall which served as the seat of government, just as the Palazzo della Signoria did in rival Florence (SEE FIG. 18–2). There are similarities between these two buildings. Both are designed as strong, fortified structures sitting on the edge of a public piazza, and both have a tall tower, making them visible signs of the city from a considerable distance. The Palazzo Pubblico was constructed from 1297 to c. 1315, but the tower was not completed until 1348, when the bronze bell used to signal meetings of the ruling council was installed.

The interior of the Palazzo Pubblico was the site of important commissions by some of Siena's most famous artists. In c. 1315, Simone Martini painted a large mural of the Virgin in Majesty surrounded by saints—clearly based on Duccio's recently installed *Maestà*. Then, in 1338, the Siena city council commissioned Ambrogio Lorenzetti to paint frescos for the council room of the Palazzo known as the Sala dei Nove (Chamber of the Nine), or Sala della Pace (Chamber of Peace), on the theme of the contrast between good and bad government (SEE FIG. 18–1).

Lorenzetti painted the results of both good and bad government on the two long walls. For the expansive scene of **THE EFFECTS OF GOOD GOVERNMENT IN THE CITY AND IN THE COUNTRY**, and in tribute to his patrons, he created an idealized but recognizable portrait of the city of Siena and its immediate environs (FIG. 18–16). The cathedral dome and the distinctive striped campanile are visible in the upper left-hand corner; the streets are filled with the bustling activity of productive citizens who also have time for leisurely diversions. Lorenzetti shows the city from shifting viewpoints so we can see as much as possible, and renders its inhabitants larger in scale than the buildings around them to highlight their activity. Featured in the foreground is a circle of dancers—probably a professional troupe of male entertainers masquerading as women as part of a spring festival—and above them, at the top of the painting, a band of masons on exterior scaffolding is constructing the wall of a new building.

The Porta Romana, Siena's gateway leading to Rome, divides the thriving city from its surrounding countryside. In this panoramic landscape painting, Lorenzetti describes a natural world marked by agricultural productivity, showing activities of all seasons simultaneously—sowing, hoeing, and harvesting. Hovering above the gate that separates city life and country life is a woman clad in a wisp of transparent drapery, a scroll in one hand and a miniature gallows complete with a hanged man in the other. She represents Security, and her scroll bids those coming to the city to enter without fear because she has taken away the power of the guilty who would harm them.

18–16 Ambrogio Lorenzetti **THE EFFECTS OF GOOD GOVERNMENT IN THE CITY AND IN THE COUNTRY**
Sala dei Nove (also known as Sala della Pace), Palazzo Pubblico, Siena, Italy. 1338–1339. Fresco, total length approx. 46′ (14 m).
Credit: © Studio Fotografico Quattrone, Florence

The world of the Italian city-states—which had seemed so full of promise in Ambrogio Lorenzetti's *Good Government* fresco—was transformed into uncertainty and desolation by a series of natural and societal disasters as the middle of the century approached. In 1333, a flood devastated Florence, followed by banking failures in the 1340s, famine in 1346–1347, and epidemics of the bubonic plague, especially virulent in the summer of 1348. Some art historians have traced the influence of these calamities on the visual arts at the middle of the fourteenth century (see "The Black Death" on page 559). Yet as dark as those days must have seemed to the men and women living through them, the cultural and artistic changes initiated earlier in the century would persist. In a relatively short span of time, the European Middle Ages gave way in Florence to a new movement that would blossom in the Italian Renaissance.

France

What features characterize the small-scale works of art produced in Parisian workshops during the fourteenth century?

At the beginning of the fourteenth century, the royal court in Paris was still the arbiter of taste in western Europe, as it had been in the days of King Louis IX (St. Louis). During the Hundred Years' War, however, the French countryside was ravaged by armed struggles and civil strife. The power of the nobility, weakened significantly by warfare, was challenged by townsmen, who took advantage of new economic opportunities that opened up in the wake of the conflict. As centers of art and architecture, the duchy of Burgundy, England, and, for a brief moment, the court of Prague began to rival Paris.

French sculptors found lucrative new outlets for their work—not only in stone, but in wood, ivory, and precious metals, often decorated with enamel and gemstones—in the growing demand among wealthy patrons for religious art intended for homes as well as churches. Manuscript painters likewise created lavishly illustrated books for the personal devotions of the wealthy and powerful. And architectural commissions focused on exquisitely detailed chapels or small churches, often under private patronage, rather than on the building of grand cathedrals funded by Church institutions.

Manuscript Illumination

By the late thirteenth century, private prayer books became popular among wealthy patrons. Because they contained special prayers to be recited at the eight canonical devotional "hours" between morning and night, an individual copy of one of these books came to be called a **Book of Hours**.

Such a book included everything the layperson needed for pious practice—psalms, prayers and offices of the Virgin and other saints (such as the owner's patron or the patron of their home church), a calendar of feast days, and sometimes prayers for the dead. During the fourteenth century, a richly decorated Book of Hours was worn or carried like jewelry, counting among a noble person's most important portable possessions.

THE BOOK OF HOURS OF JEANNE D'ÉVREUX   King Charles IV gave his 14-year-old queen, Jeanne d'Évreux, a tiny Book of Hours illuminated by the Parisian painter Jean Pucelle, perhaps on the occasion of their marriage in 1324. When opened, it fits easily within one hand (see "Closer Look" opposite). This book was so precious to the queen that she mentioned it and its illuminator specifically in her will, leaving this royal treasure to King Charles V. Pucelle painted the book's pictures in *grisaille*. His style clearly derives from the courtly mode established in Paris at the time of Louis IX—softly modeled, voluminous draperies gathered loosely and falling in projecting diagonal folds around tall, elegantly posed figures with carefully coiffed, curly hair, broad foreheads, and delicate features. But his conception of space, with figures placed within coherent, discrete architectural settings, suggests a firsthand knowledge of contemporary Sienese art.

Jeanne appears in the initial *D* below the Annunciation, kneeling in prayer before a lectern, perhaps using this Book of Hours to guide her meditations, beginning with the words written on this page: *Domine labia mea aperies* (Psalm 51:15: "O Lord, open thou my lips"). The juxtaposition of the praying Jeanne with a scene from the life of the Virgin Mary suggests that the sacred scene is actually a vision inspired by Jeanne's meditations. The young queen might have identified with and sought to feel within herself Mary's joy at Gabriel's message. Given what we know of Jeanne's life and her royal husband's predicament, it might also have directed the queen's prayers toward the fulfillment of his wish for a male heir.

In the Annunciation, Mary is shown receiving the archangel Gabriel in a Gothic building that seems to project outward from the page toward the viewer, while rejoicing angels look on from windows under the eaves. The group of children at the bottom of the page at first glance seems to echo the angelic jubilation. Folklorists have suggested, however, that the children are playing "froggy in the middle" or "hot cockles," games in which one child was tagged by the others. To the medieval viewer, if the game symbolized the mocking of Christ or the betrayal of Judas, who "tags" his friend, it would have evoked a darker mood—referring to the picture on the other page of this opening and foreshadowing Jesus's imminent death even as his life is beginning.

A Closer Look

THE HOURS OF JEANNE D'ÉVREUX

In this opening Pucelle juxtaposes complementary scenes drawn from the Infancy and Passion of Christ, placed on opposing pages in a scheme known as the Joys and Sorrows of the Virgin. The "joy" of the Annunciation on the right is paired with the "sorrow" of the betrayal and arrest of Christ on the left.

Christ sways back as Judas betrays him with a kiss. The S-curve of his body mirrors the Virgin's pose on the opposite page, as both accept their fate with courtly decorum.

The prominent lamp held aloft by a member of the arresting battalion informs the viewer that this scene takes place at night, in the dark.

The angel who holds up the boxlike enclosure where the Annunciation takes place is an allusion to the legend of the miraculous transportation of this building from Nazareth to Loreto in 1294.

Christ reaches casually down to heal Malchus, the assistant of the high priest, whose ear Peter had just cut off in angry retaliation for his participation in the arrest of Jesus.

Visual puns, off-color jokes, and scenes of secular amusements from everyday life appear at the bottom of many pages of this book. Sometimes they relate to the themes of the sacred scenes above them. These comic knights riding goats may be a commentary on the lack of valor shown by the soldiers assaulting Jesus, especially if this wine barrel conjured up for Jeanne an association with the Eucharist.

The candle held by the cleric who guards the "door" to Jeanne's devotional retreat, as well as the rabbit emerging from its burrow in the marginal scene, are sexually charged symbols of fertility that seem directly related to the prayers of a child bride required to produce a male heir.

18–17 Jean Pucelle **THE KISS OF JUDAS AND THE ANNUNCIATION**

Two-page opening from the Hours of Jeanne d'Évreux. Paris. c. 1324–1328. *Grisaille* and color on vellum, each page 3⅝ × 2⁷/₁₆″ (9.2 × 6.2 cm). Metropolitan Museum of Art, New York. The Cloisters Collection (54.1.2), fols. 15v–16r.

Credit: © 2016. Image copyright The Metropolitan Museum of Art/Art Resource/ Scala, Florence

Metalwork and Ivory

Fourteenth-century French sculpture is intimate in character. Religious subjects became more emotionally expressive; objects became smaller and demanded closer scrutiny from the viewer. In the secular realm, tales of love and valor were carved on luxury items to delight the rich. Precious materials—gold, silver, and ivory—were preferred.

18–18 VIRGIN AND CHILD

c. 1324–1339. Silver gilt and enamel, height 27⅛" (69 cm). Musée du Louvre, Paris.

Credit: © Jacqueline Guillot/akg-images

A VIRGIN AND CHILD FROM SAINT-DENIS   A silver-gilt image of a standing **VIRGIN AND CHILD** (**FIG. 18–18**) is a rare survivor that verifies the acclaim that was accorded fourteenth-century Parisian goldsmiths. An inscription on the base documents the statue's donation to the abbey church of Saint-Denis in 1339 and the donor's name, the same Queen Jeanne d'Évreux whose Book of Hours we have just examined. In a style that recalls the work of artist Jean Pucelle in that Book of Hours, the Virgin holds Jesus in her left arm with her weight on her left leg, standing in a graceful, characteristically Gothic S-curve pose. Mary originally wore a crown, and she still holds a large enameled and jeweled *fleur-de-lis*—the heraldic symbol of royal France—which served as a reliquary container for strands of Mary's hair. The Christ Child, reaching out tenderly to caress his mother's face, is babylike in both form and posture. On the base, minuscule statues of prophets stand on projecting piers to separate 14 enameled scenes from Christ's Infancy and Passion, reminding us of the suffering to come. The apple in the baby's hand carries the theme further with its reference to Christ's role as the new Adam, whose sacrifice on the cross redeemed humanity from the first couple's fall into sin when Eve bit into the forbidden fruit.

AN IVORY CHEST WITH SCENES OF ROMANCE Fourteenth-century Paris was renowned for more than its goldsmiths (SEE FIG. 18–18). Among the most sumptuous and sought-after Parisian luxury products were small chests assembled from carved ivory plaques that were used by wealthy women to store jewelry or other personal treasures. The entirely secular subject matter of these chests explored romantic love. Indeed, they seem to have been courtship gifts from smitten men to desired women or wedding presents offered by grooms to their brides.

A chest from around 1330 to 1350, now in the Walters Museum (**FIG. 18–19**), is one of seven that have survived intact; there are fragments of a dozen more. It is a delightful and typical example. Figural relief covers five exterior sides of the box: around the perimeter and on the hinged top. The assembled panels were joined by hardware originally wrought in silver. Although some chests tell a single romantic story in sequential episodes, most, like this one, anthologize scenes drawn from a group of stories, combining courtly romance, secular allegory, and ancient fables.

On the lid of the Walters casket (**FIG. 18–20**), jousting is the theme. Spread over the central two panels, a single scene catches two charging knights in the heat of a tournament, while trumpeting heralds call the attention of spectators, lined up above in a gallery to observe this public display of virility. The panel at right mocks the very ritual showcased in the middle panels by pitting a woman against a knight, battling not with lances but with

18–19 SMALL IVORY CHEST WITH SCENES FROM COURTLY ROMANCES

Made in Paris. c. 1330–1350. Elephant ivory with modern iron mounts, height 4½ × 9¹¹⁄₁₆ × 4⅞" (11.5 × 24.6 × 12.4 cm). The Walters Art Museum, Baltimore. 71.264

Credit: Photo © The Walters Art Museum, Baltimore

18–20 ATTACK ON THE CASTLE OF LOVE

Top of the chest in FIG. 18–19.

Credit: Photo © The Walters Art Museum, Baltimore

18–21 TRISTAN AND ISEULT AT THE FOUNTAIN; CAPTURE OF THE UNICORN

Left short side of the chest in FIG. 18–19.

Credit: Photo © The Walters Art Museum, Baltimore

a long-stemmed rose (symbolizing sexual surrender) and an oak bough (symbolizing fertility). Instead of observing these goings-on, however, the spectators tucked into the upper architecture pursue their own flirtations. Finally, in the scene on the left, knights use crossbows and a catapult to hurl roses at the Castle of Love, while Cupid returns fire.

On the front of the chest (SEE FIG. 18–19), generalized romantic allegory gives way to vignettes from a specific story. At left, the long-bearded Aristotle teaches the young Alexander the Great, using exaggerated gestures and an authoritative text to emphasize his point. Today's lesson is a warning not to allow women to distract the young prince from his studies. The subsequent scene, however, pokes fun at the eminent teacher, who has become so smitten by a young beauty named Phyllis that he lets her ride

him around like a horse while his student observes from the castle in the background. The two scenes at right relate to an Eastern legend of the fountain of youth, popular in medieval Europe. A line of bearded elders approaches the fountain from the left, steadied by their canes; on the right, two newly rejuvenated couples, now nude, bathe and flirt within the fountain's basin. The man first in line for treatment looks suspiciously like the figure of Aristotle, forming a link between the two stories on the casket front.

Two other well-known medieval themes are juxtaposed on the left short side of the ivory chest (FIG. 18–21). At left, Tristan and Iseult have met secretly for an illicit romantic tryst, while Iseult's husband, King Mark, tipped off by an informant, observes them from a tree. But when they see his reflection in a fountain between them, they alter their behavior accordingly, and the king believes them innocent of the adultery he had (rightly) suspected. The medieval bestiary ("book of beasts") claimed that only a virgin could capture the mythical unicorn, which at right lays his head, with its aggressively phallic horn, into the lap of just such a pure maiden so that the hunter can take advantage of her alluring powers over the animal to kill it with his phallic counterpart of its horn, a large spear.

Unlike royal marriages of the time, which were essentially business contracts based on political or financial exigencies, the romantic love of the aristocratic wealthy involved passionate devotion. Images of gallant knights and their coy paramours captured the popular Gothic imagination and formed the principal subject matter on personal luxury objects—not only chests like this, but mirror backs, combs, writing tablets, even ceremonial saddles. These stories evoke themes that still captivate us: desire and betrayal, cruel rejection and blissful folly. In this way they allow us some access to the lives of the people who owned these precious objects, even if we ourselves are unable to afford them.

England

What is distinctive about English textiles and architecture during the fourteenth century?

Fourteenth-century England prospered in spite of the ravages of the Black Death and the Hundred Years' War with France. English life at this time is described in the brilliant social commentary of Geoffrey Chaucer in the *Canterbury Tales* (see "A New Spirit in Fourteenth-Century Literature" on page 544). The royal family—especially Edward I (ruled 1272–1307), the castle builder—and many nobles and bishops were generous patrons of the arts.

Embroidery: *Opus Anglicanum*

Since the thirteenth century, the English had been renowned for pictorial needlework, using colored silk and gold threads to create images as detailed as contemporary painters produced in manuscripts. Popular throughout Europe, the art came to be called *opus anglicanum* ("English work"). The popes had more than 100 pieces in the Vatican treasury. The names of several prominent embroiderers are known, but in the thirteenth century no one surpassed Mabel of Bury St. Edmunds, who created both religious and secular articles for King Henry III (ruled 1216–1272).

THE CHICHESTER-CONSTABLE CHASUBLE This *opus anglicanum* liturgical vestment, worn by a priest during Mass (**FIG. 18–22**), was embroidered c. 1330–1350 with

18–22 LIFE OF THE VIRGIN, BACK OF THE CHICHESTER-CONSTABLE CHASUBLE

From a set of vestments embroidered in *opus anglicanum* from southern England. c. 1330–1350. Red velvet with silk and metallic thread and seed pearls; length 4′3″ (129.5 cm), width 30″ (76 cm). Metropolitan Museum of Art, New York. Fletcher Fund, 1927 (27 162.1).

Credit: © 2016. Image copyright The Metropolitan Museum of Art/Art Resource/Scala, Florence.

images formed by subtle gradations of colored silk. Where gold threads were laid and couched (tacked down with colored silk), the effect resembles the burnished gold-leaf backgrounds of manuscript illuminations. The Annunciation, the Adoration of the Magi, and the Coronation of the Virgin are set in cusped, crocketed ogee (S-shape) arches, supported on animal-head corbels and twisting branches of oak leaves with seed-pearl acorns. Because the star and crescent moon in the Coronation of the Virgin scene are heraldic emblems of Edward III (ruled 1327–1377), perhaps he or a family member commissioned this luxurious vestment.

During the celebration of the Mass, especially as the priest moved, *opus anglicanum* would have glinted in the candlelight. Court dress was just as rich and colorful as the treasures on the altar, and at court such embroidered garments proclaimed the rank and status of the wearer. Such gold and bejeweled garments became so heavy that their wearers often needed help to move.

Architecture

In the later years of the thirteenth century and early years of the fourteenth, a distinctive and influential Gothic architectural style popularly known as the "Decorated style" developed in England. This change in taste has been credited to Henry III's ambition to surpass Louis IX, who was his brother-in-law, as a royal patron of the arts.

THE DECORATED STYLE AT EXETER One of the most complete Decorated-style buildings is **EXETER CATHEDRAL**. Thomas

of Witney began construction in 1313 and remained master mason from 1316 to 1342, supervising construction of the nave and redesigning upper parts of the choir. He left the towers of the original Norman cathedral, but turned the interior into a dazzling stone forest of colonnettes, moldings, and vault ribs (**FIG. 18-23**). From piers formed by a cluster of colonnettes rise multiple moldings that make the arcade seem to ripple. Bundled colonnettes spring from sculptured foliate corbels (brackets that project from a wall) between the arches and rise up the wall to support conical clusters of 13 ribs that meet at the summit of the vault, a modest 69 feet above the floor. The basic structure

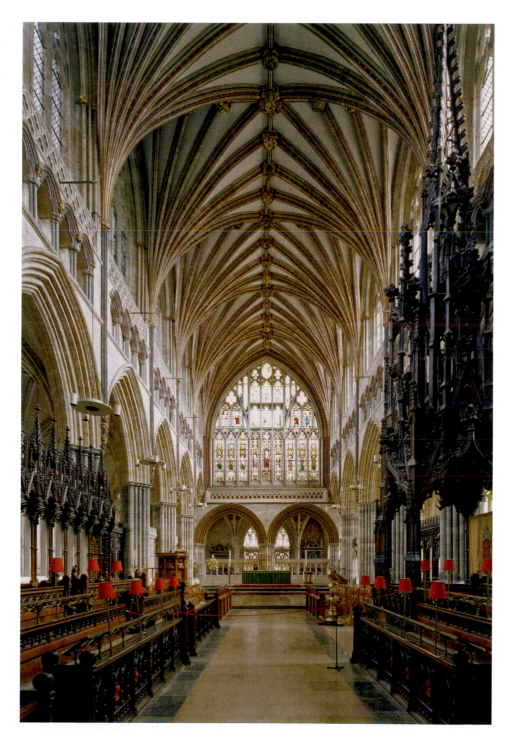

18-23 INTERIOR, EXETER CATHEDRAL

Devon, England. Thomas of Witney, choir, 14th century and bishop's throne, 1313–1317; Robert Lesyngham, east window, 1389–1390.

Credit: © akg/Bildarchiv Monheim

here is the four-part vault with intersecting cross-ribs, but the designer added additional ribs, called tiercerons, to create a richer linear pattern. Elaborately carved bosses (decorative knoblike elements) signal the point where ribs meet along the ridge of the vault. Large bar-tracery clerestory windows illuminate the 300-foot-long nave. Unpolished gray marble shafts, yellow sandstone arches, and a white French stone, shipped from Caen, add subtle gradations of color to the upper wall.

Detailed records survive for the building of Exeter Cathedral, documenting work over the period from 1279 to 1514, with only two short breaks. They record where masons and carpenters were housed (in a hostel near the cathedral) and how they were paid (some by the day with extra for drinks, some by the week, some for each finished piece); how materials were acquired and transported (including horseshoes and fodder for the horses); and, of course, payments for the building materials (not only stone and wood, but rope for measuring and parchment on which to draw forms for the masons). The bishops contributed generously to the building funds. This was not a labor only of love.

Thomas of Witney also designed the intricate, 57-foot-high bishop's throne (at right in FIG. 18-23), constructed by Richard de Galmeton and Walter of Memburg, who led a team of a dozen carpenters. The canopy resembles embroidery translated into wood, with its maze of pinnacles bursting with leafy crockets and tiny carved animals and heads. To finish the throne in splendor, Master Nicolas painted and gilded the wood. When the bishop was seated on his throne wearing embroidered vestments like the Chichester-Constable Chasuble (SEE FIG. 18–22), he must have resembled a golden image in a shrine—more a symbol of the power and authority of the Church than a specific human being.

THE PERPENDICULAR STYLE AT EXETER During the years following the Black Death, work at Exeter Cathedral came to a standstill. The nave had been roofed but not vaulted, and the windows had no glass. When work could be resumed, tastes had changed. The exuberance of the Decorated style gave way to an austere style in which rectilinear patterns and sharp, angular shapes replaced intricate curves, and luxuriant foliage gave way to simple, stripped-down patterns. This phase is known as the Perpendicular style.

In 1389–1390, well-paid master mason Robert Lesyngham rebuilt the great east window (SEE FIG. 18–23, far wall), designing its tracery in the new Perpendicular style. The window fills the east wall of the choir like a luminous altarpiece. A single figure in each light stands under a tall, painted canopy that flows into and blends with the stone tracery. The Virgin with the Christ Child stands in the center over the high altar with four female saints at the left

and four male saints on the right, including St. Peter, to whom the church is dedicated. At a distance, the colorful figures silhouetted against the silver *grisaille* glass become a band of color, reinforcing the rectangular pattern of the mullions and transoms. The combination of *grisaille*, silver-oxide stain (staining clear glass with shades of yellow or gold), and colored glass produces a glowing wall and casts a cool, silvery light over the nearby stonework.

Perpendicular architecture heralds the Renaissance style in its regularity, its balanced horizontal and vertical lines, and its plain wall or window surfaces. When Tudor monarchs introduced Renaissance art into the British Isles, builders were not forced to rethink the form and structure of their buildings; they simply changed the ornament from the pointed cusps and crocketed arches of the Gothic style to the round arches and columns and capitals of Roman Classicism. The Perpendicular style itself became an English architectural vernacular. It has even been popular in the United States, especially for churches and college buildings.

The Holy Roman Empire

How do the expressive qualities of the figural arts and the architectural supremacy of Prague lead to a distinctive form of Gothic in the Holy Roman Empire?

By the fourteenth century, the Holy Roman Empire existed more as idealized fiction than fact. The Italian territories had established their independence, and in contrast to England and France, Germany had become further divided into multiple states with powerful regional associations and princes. The Holy Roman emperors, now elected by Germans, concentrated on securing the fortunes of their families. They continued to be patrons of the arts, promoting local styles.

Mysticism and Suffering

The by-now-familiar ordeals of the fourteenth century—famines, wars, and plagues—helped inspire a mystical religiosity in Germany that emphasized both ecstatic joy and extreme suffering. Devotional images, known as *Andachtsbilder* in German, inspired worshipers to contemplate Jesus's first and last hours, especially during evening prayers, or vespers, giving rise to the term *Vesperbild* for the image of Mary mourning her son. Through such religious exercises, worshipers hoped to achieve understanding of the divine and union with God.

VESPERBILD In this well-known example (FIG. 18–24), blood gushes from the hideous rosettes that form the wounds of an emaciated and lifeless Jesus who teeters improbably on the lap of his hunched-over mother.

The Virgin's face conveys the intensity of her ordeal. Such images took on greater poignancy since they would have been compared, in the worshiper's mind, to the familiar, almost ubiquitous images of the young Virgin mother holding her innocent and loving baby Jesus.

THE HEDWIG CODEX The extreme physicality and emotionalism of the *Vesperbild* finds parallels in the actual lives of some medieval saints in northern Europe. St. Hedwig (1174–1243), married at age 12 to Duke Henry I of Silesia and mother of his seven children, entered the Cistercian convent of Trebniz (in present-day Poland) on her husband's death in 1238. She devoted the rest of her life to caring for the poor and seeking to emulate the suffering

of Christ by walking barefoot in the snow. As described in her *vita* (biography), she had a particular affection for a small ivory statue of the Virgin and Child, which she carried with her at all times; "she often took it up in her hands to envelop it in love, so that out of passion she could see it more often and through the seeing could prove herself more devout, inciting her to even greater love of the glorious Virgin. When she once blessed the sick with this image they were cured immediately" (translation from Schleif, p. 22). Hedwig was buried clutching the statue, and when her tomb was opened after her canonization in 1267, it was said that although most of her body had deteriorated, the fingers that still gripped the beloved object had miraculously not decayed.

18–24 VESPERBILD (PIETÀ)

From the Middle Rhine region, Germany. c. 1330. Wood and polychromy, height 34½" (88.4 cm). Landesmuseum, Bonn.

Credit: © akg-images/Erich Lessing

18–25 ST. HEDWIG OF SILESIA WITH DUKE LUDWIG I OF LIEGNITZ-BRIEG AND DUCHESS AGNES
Dedication page of the Hedwig Codex. 1353. Ink and paint on parchment, 13⁷⁄₁₆ × 9¾″ (34 × 25 cm). The J. Paul Getty Museum, Los Angeles. MS. Ludwig XI 7, fol. 12v.

A picture of Hedwig serves as the frontispiece (**FIG. 18-25**) of a manuscript of her *vita* known as the Hedwig Codex, commissioned in 1353 by one her descendants, Ludwig I of Liegnitz-Brieg. Duke Ludwig and his wife, Agnes, are shown here kneeling on either side of St. Hedwig, dwarfed by the saint's architectural throne and her own imposing scale. With her prominent, spidery hands, she clutches the famous ivory statue, as well as a rosary and a prayer book, inserting her fingers within it to maintain her place as if our arrival had interrupted her devotions. She has draped her leather boots over her right wrist in a reference to her practice of removing them to walk in the snow. Hedwig's highly volumetric figure stands in a swaying pose of courtly elegance derived from French Gothic, but the intensity of her gaze and posture are far removed from the mannered graciousness of the smiling angel of Reims (see statue at far left in FIG. 17-14), whose similar gesture and extended finger are employed simply to grasp his drapery and assure its elegant display.

The Supremacy of Prague

Charles IV of Bohemia (ruled 1346–1378) was raised in France, and his admiration for the French king Charles IV was such that he changed his own name from Wenceslas to Charles. He was officially crowned King of Bohemia in 1347 and Holy Roman Emperor in 1355. He established his capital in Prague, which, in the view of his contemporaries, replaced Constantinople as the "New Rome." Prague had a great university, a castle, and a cathedral overlooking a town that spread on both sides of a river joined by a stone bridge, a remarkable structure itself.

When Pope Clement VI made Prague an archbishopric in 1344, construction began on a new cathedral in the Gothic style to be named for St. Vitus. It would also serve as the coronation church and royal pantheon. But the choir was not finished for Charles's first coronation, so he brought Peter Parler from Swabia to complete it.

THE PARLER FAMILY   In 1317, Heinrich Parler, a former master of works on Cologne Cathedral, designed and began building the church of the Holy Cross in Schwäbisch Gmünd, in southwest Germany. In 1351, his son Peter

(c. 1330–1399), the most brilliant architect of this talented family, joined the workshop. Peter designed the choir (**FIG. 18–26**) in the manner of a hall church whose triple-aisled form was enlarged by a ring of deep chapels between the buttresses. The contrast between Heinrich's nave and Peter's choir (seen clearly in **FIG. 18–26B**) illustrates the increasing complexity of rib patterns covering the vaults, which emphasizes the unity of interior space rather than its division into bays.

Called by Charles IV to Prague in 1353, Peter turned the unfinished St. Vitus Cathedral into a "glass house," adding a vast clerestory and glazed triforium supported by double flying buttresses, all covered by net vaults that

18–26A Heinrich and Peter Parler **PLAN OF THE CHURCH OF THE HOLY CROSS, SCHWÄBISCH GMÜND**

Germany. Begun in 1317 by Heinrich Parler; choir by Peter Parler begun in 1351; vaulting completed 16th century.

Credit: © Achim Bednorz, Cologne

choir

nave

18–26B Heinrich and Peter Parler **INTERIOR OF THE CHURCH OF THE HOLY CROSS, SCHWÄBISCH GMÜND**

Germany. Begun in 1317 by Heinrich Parler; choir by Peter Parler begun in 1351; vaulting completed 16th century.

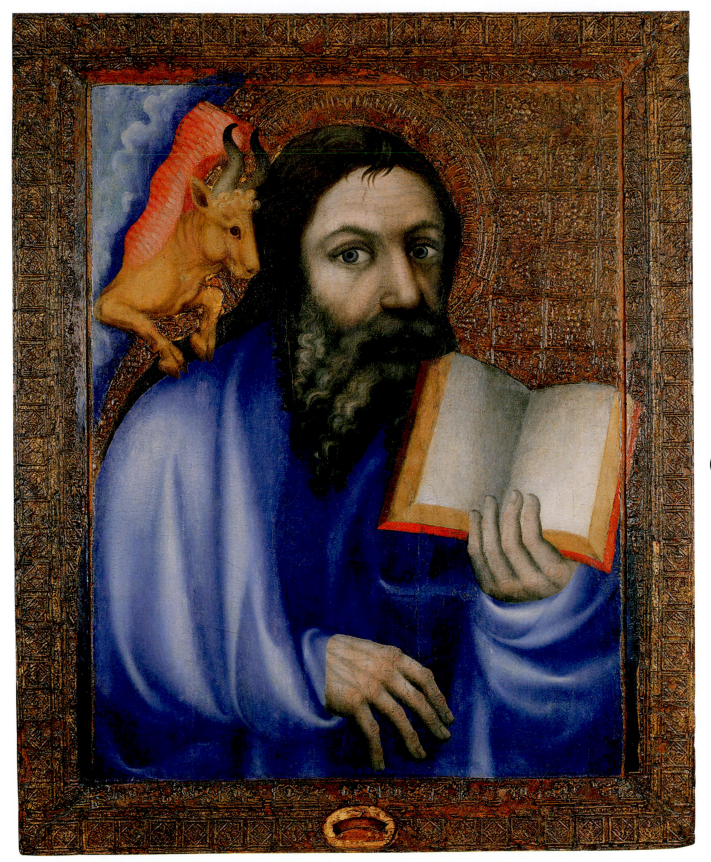

18–27 Master Theodoric **ST. LUKE**
Holy Cross Chapel, Karlstejn Castle, near Prague. 1360–1364. Paint and gold on panel, 45¼ × 37″ (115 × 94 cm).

Credit: Photo: Radovan Boček

created a continuous canopy over the space. Because of the success of projects such as this, Peter and his family became the most successful architects in the Holy Roman Empire. Their concept of space, luxurious decoration, and intricate vaulting dominated central European architecture for three generations.

MASTER THEODORIC At Karlstejn Castle, a day's ride from Prague, Charles IV built another chapel, covering the walls with gold and precious stones as well as with paintings. There were 130 paintings of the saints serving as reliquaries, with relics inserted into their frames. Master Theodoric, the court painter, provided drawings on the wood panels, and he painted about 30 images himself. Figures are crowded into—even extend over—their frames, emphasizing their size and power. Master Theodoric was head of the Brotherhood of St. Luke, and the way that his painting of **ST. LUKE** (**FIG. 18-27**), patron saint of painters, looks out at the viewer has suggested

to scholars that this may be a self-portrait. His personal style combined a preference for substantial bodies, oversized heads and hands, dour and haunted faces, and soft, deeply modeled drapery, with a touch of grace derived from the French Gothic style. The chapel, consecrated in 1365, so pleased the emperor that in 1367 he gave the artist a farm.

Prague and the Holy Roman Empire under Charles IV had become a multicultural empire where people of different religions (Christians and Jews) and ethnic heritages (German and Slav) lived side by side. But Charles died in 1378, and without his strong central government, political and religious dissent overtook the empire. Jan Hus, dean of the philosophy faculty at Prague University and a powerful reforming preacher, denounced the immorality he saw in the Church. He was burned at the stake, becoming a martyr and Czech national hero. The Hussite Revolution in the fifteenth century ended Prague's—and Bohemia's—leadership in the arts.

Think About It

1 Compare and contrast Giotto's and Duccio's renderings of the biblical story of Christ's Raising of Lazarus (**FIGS. 18-8, 18-11**).

2 Discuss Ambrogio Lorenzetti's engagement with secular subject matter in his frescos for Siena's Palazzo Pubblico (**FIG. 18-16**). How did these paintings relate to their sociopolitical context?

3 Discuss the circumstances surrounding the construction and decoration of the Scrovegni (Arena) Chapel, paying special attention to its relationship to the life and aspirations of its patron.

4 Choose one small work of art in this chapter that was crafted from precious materials with exceptional technical skill. Explain how it was made and how it was used. How does the work of art relate to its cultural and social contexts?

Crosscurrents

Depictions of the Virgin Mary holding the infant Jesus represent a theme that developed early in the history of European Christian art and continues to this day. Describe the relationship between the mother and child in these two examples. Characterize the difference in artistic style. How does the choice of medium contribute to the differences between them? How were they used?

 FIG. 16-27

 FIG. 18-18

Glossary

abacus (p. 110) The flat slab at the top of a **capital**, directly under the **entablature**.

abbey church (p. 226) An abbey is a monastic religious community headed by an abbot or abbess. An abbey church often has an especially large **choir** to provide space for the monks or nuns.

absolute dating (p. 12) A method, especially in archaeology, of assigning a precise historical date at which, or span of years during which, an object was made. Based on known and recorded events in the region, as well as technically extracted physical evidence (such as carbon-14 disintegration). See also **radiometric dating**, **relative dating**.

abstract (p. 8) Of art that does not attempt to describe the appearance of visible forms but rather to transform them into stylized patterns or to alter them in conformity to ideals.

academy (p. 942) An institution established for the training of artists. Academies date from the Renaissance and after; they were particularly powerful, state-run institutions in the seventeenth and eighteenth centuries. In general, academies replaced **guilds** as the venues where students learned the craft of art and were educated in art theory. Academies helped the recognition of artists as trained specialists, rather than craftspeople, and promoted their social status. An academician is an academy-trained artist.

acanthus (p. 111) A Mediterranean plant whose leaves are reproduced in Classical architectural ornament used on **moldings**, **friezes**, and **capitals**.

acroterion (*pl.* **acroteria**) (p. 111) An ornament at the corner or peak of a roof.

Action painting (p. 1091) Using broad gestures to drip or pour paint onto a pictorial surface. Associated with mid-twentieth-century American Abstract Expressionists, such as Jackson Pollock.

adobe (p. 404) Sun-baked blocks made of clay mixed with straw. Also: buildings made with this material.

aedicula (p. 622) A decorative architectural frame, usually found around a niche, door, or window. An aedicula is made up of a **pediment** and **entablature** supported by **columns** or **pilasters**.

aerial perspective (p. 633) See under **perspective**.

agora (p. 140) An open space in a Greek town used as a central gathering place or market. Compare **forum**.

aisle (p. 226) Passage or open corridor of a church, hall, or other building that parallels the main space, usually on both sides, and is delineated by a row, or **arcade**, of **columns** or **piers**. Called side aisles when they flank the **nave** of a church.

akropolis (p. 131) The citadel of an ancient Greek city, located at its highest point and housing temples, a treasury, and sometimes a royal palace. The most famous is the Akropolis in Athens.

album (p. 810) A book consisting of a series of paintings or prints (album leaves) mounted into book form.

allegory (p. 635) In a work of art, an image (or images) that symbolizes an idea, concept, or principle, often moral or religious.

alloy (p. 24) A mixture of metals; different metals melted together.

altarpiece (p. xxxvi) A painted or carved panel or ensemble of panels placed at the back of or behind and above an altar. Contains religious imagery (often specific to the place of worship for which it was made) that viewers can look at during liturgical ceremonies (especially the **Eucharist**) or personal devotions.

amalaka (p. 306) In Hindu architecture, the circular or square-shaped element on top of a spire (*shikhara*), often crowned with a **finial**, symbolizing the cosmos.

ambulatory (p. 228) The passage (walkway) around the **apse** in a church, especially a **basilica**, or around the central space in a **central-plan building**.

amphora (*pl.* **amphorae**) (p. 103) An ancient Greek or Roman jar for storing oil or wine, with an egg-shaped body and two curved handles.

animal style (p. 445) Decoration made of interwoven animals or serpents, often found in early medieval Northern European art.

ankh (p. 51) A looped cross signifying life, used by ancient Egyptians.

apartheid (p. 435) A political system in South Africa that used race as grounds for the segregation, discrimination, and political disenfranchisement of nonwhite South Africans. It officially ended in 1994.

appropriation (p. xxiv) The practice of some Postmodern artists of adopting images in their entirety from other works of art or from visual culture for use in their own art. The act of recontextualizing the appropriated image allows the artist to critique both it and the time and place in which it was created.

apse (p. 192) A large semicircular or polygonal (and usually **vaulted**) recess on an end wall of a building. In a Christian church, it often contains the altar. "Apsidal" is the adjective describing the condition of having such a space.

arabesque (p. 270) European term for a type of linear surface decoration based on foliage and calligraphic forms, thought by Europeans to be typical of Islamic art and usually characterized by flowing lines and swirling shapes.

arcade (p. 171) A series of **arches**, carried by **columns** or **piers** and supporting a common wall or **lintel**. In a blind arcade, the arches and supports are **engaged** and have a purely decorative function.

arch (p. 96) In architecture, a curved structural element that spans an open space. Built from wedge-shaped stone blocks called **voussoirs** placed together and held at the top by a trapezoidal **keystone**. It forms an effective space-spanning and weight-bearing unit, but requires **buttresses** at each side to contain the outward **thrust** caused by the weight of the structure. *Corbeled arch*: an arch or **vault** formed by **courses** of stones, each of which projects beyond the lower course until the space is enclosed; usually finished with a **capstone**. *Horseshoe arch*: an arch of more than a half-circle; typical of western Islamic architecture. *Round arch*: an arch that displaces most of its weight, or downward thrust, along its curving sides, transmitting that weight to adjacent supporting uprights (door or window **jambs**, **columns**, or **piers**). *Ogival arch*: a sharply pointed arch created by S curves. *Relieving arch*: an arch built into a heavy wall just above a **post-and-lintel** structure (such as a gate, door, or window) to help support the wall above by transferring the load to the side walls. *Transverse arch*: an arch that connects the wall **piers** on both sides of an interior space, up and over a stone **vault**.

Archaic smile (p. 117) The curved lips of ancient Greek statues in the period c. 600–480 BCE, usually interpreted as a way of animating facial features.

architrave (p. 110) The bottom element in an **entablature**, beneath the **frieze** and the **cornice**.

archivolt (p. 491) A band of **molding** framing an **arch**, or a series of stone blocks that form an arch resting directly on flanking **columns** or **piers**.

ashlar (p. 101) A highly finished, precisely cut block of stone. When laid in even **courses**, ashlar masonry creates a uniform face with fine joints. Often used as a facing on the visible exterior of a building, especially as a veneer for the **façade**. Also called **dressed stone**.

assemblage (p. 1040) Artwork created by gathering and manipulating two- and/or three-dimensional found objects.

astragal (p. 111) A thin convex decorative **molding**, often found on a Classical **entablature**, and usually decorated with a continuous row of beadlike circles.

atelier (p. 790) The studio or workshop of a master artist or craftsperson, often including junior associates and apprentices.

atmospheric perspective (p. 185) See under **perspective**.

atrial cross (p. 959) A cross placed in the **atrium** of a church. In Colonial America, used to mark a gathering and teaching place.

atrium (p. 160) An unroofed interior courtyard or room in a Roman house, sometimes having a pool or garden, sometimes surrounded by **columns**. Also: the open courtyard in front of a Christian church; or an entrance area in modern architecture.

automatism (p. 1072) A technique in which artists abandon the usual intellectual control over their brushes or pencils to allow the subconscious to create the artwork without rational interference.

avant-garde (p. 989) Term derived from the French military word meaning "before the group," or "vanguard." Avant-garde denotes those artists or concepts of a strikingly new, experimental, or radical nature for their time.

axis (p. xxviii) In pictures, an implied line around which elements are composed or arranged. In buildings, a dominant line around which parts of the structure are organized and along which human movement or attention is concentrated.

axis mundi (p. 305) A concept of an "axis of the world," which marks sacred sites and denotes a link between the human and celestial realms. For example, in South Asian art, the axis mundi can be marked by monumental free-standing decorative pillars.

baldacchino (p. 484) A canopy (whether suspended from the ceiling, projecting from

a wall, or supported by columns) placed over an honorific or sacred space such as a throne or church altar.

bar tracery (p. 522) See under **tracery**.

barbarian (p. 152) A term used by the ancient Greeks and Romans to label all foreigners outside their cultural orbit (for example, Celts, Goths, Vikings). The word derives from an imitation of what the "barblings" of their language sounded like to those who could not understand it.

barrel vault (p. 190) See under **vault**.

bas-relief (p. 328) Another term for low relief ("bas" is the French word for "low"). See under **relief sculpture**.

basilica (p. 192) A large rectangular building. Often built with a **clerestory**, side **aisles** separated from the center **nave** by **colonnades**, and an **apse** at one or both ends. Originally Roman centers for administration, later adapted to Christian church use.

bay (p. 171) A unit of space defined by architectural elements such as **columns**, **piers**, and walls.

beehive tomb (p. 100) A **corbel-vaulted** tomb, conical in shape like a beehive, and covered by an earthen mound.

Benday dots (p. 1108) In modern printing and typesetting, the individual dots that, together with many others, make up lettering and images. Often machine- or computer-generated, the dots are very small and closely spaced to give the effect of density and richness of tone.

bilum (p. 880) Netted bags made mainly by women throughout the central highlands of New Guinea. The bags can be used for everyday purposes or even to carry the bones of the recently deceased as a sign of mourning.

biomorphic (p. 1073) Denoting the biologically or organically inspired shapes and forms that were routinely included in abstracted Modern art in the early twentieth century.

black-figure (p. 108) A technique of ancient Greek **ceramic** decoration in which black figures are painted on a red clay ground. Compare **red-figure**.

blackware (p. 869) A **ceramic** technique that produces pottery with a primarily black surface with **matte** and glossy patterns on the surface.

blind arcade (p. 794) See under **arcade**.

bodhisattva (p. 304) In Buddhism, a being who has attained enlightenment but chooses to remain in this world in order to help others advance spiritually. Also defined as a potential buddha.

Book of Hours (p. 562) A prayer book for private use, containing a calendar, services for the canonical hours, and sometimes special prayers.

boss (p. 450) A decorative knoblike element that can be found in many places, e.g. at the intersection of a Gothic **rib vault** or as a buttonlike projection on metalwork.

bracket, bracketing (p. 346) An architectural element that projects from a wall to support a horizontal part of a building, 0such as beams or the eaves of a roof.

buon fresco (p. 89) See under **fresco**.

burin (p. 602) A metal instrument used in **engraving** to cut lines into the metal plate. The sharp end of the burin is trimmed to give a diamond-shaped cutting point, while the other end is finished with a wooden handle that fits into the engraver's palm.

buttress, buttressing (p. 171) A projecting support built against an external wall, usually to counteract the lateral **thrust** of a **vault** or **arch** within. In Gothic church architecture, a **flying buttress** is an arched bridge above the **aisle** roof that extends from the upper **nave** wall, where the lateral thrust of the main vault is greatest, down to a solid **pier**.

cairn (p. 18) A pile of stones or earth and stones that served both as a prehistoric burial site and as a marker for underground tombs.

calligraphy (p. 279) Handwriting as an art form.

calotype (p. 987) The first photographic process utilizing negatives and paper positives; invented by William Henry Fox Talbot in the late 1830s.

calyx krater (p. 121) See under **krater**.

came (*pl.* **cames**) (p. 512) A lead strip used in the making of leaded or **stained-glass** windows. Cames have an indented groove on the sides into which individual pieces of glass are fitted to make the overall design.

cameo (p. 177) Gemstone, clay, glass, or shell having layers of color, carved in low relief (see under **relief sculpture**) to create an image and ground of different colors.

camera obscura (p. 762) An early cameralike device used in the Renaissance and later for recording images from the real world. It consists of a dark box (or room) with a hole in one side (sometimes fitted with a lens). The camera obscura operates when bright light shines through the hole, casting an upside-down image of an object outside onto the inside wall of the box.

canon of proportions (p. 52) A set of ideal mathematical ratios in art based on measurements, as in the proportional relationships between the basic elements of the human body.

canopic jar (p. 54) In ancient Egyptian culture, a special jar used to store the major organs of a body before embalming.

capital (p. 68) The sculpted block that tops a **column**. According to the **conventions** of the orders, capitals include different decorative elements (see **order**). A *historiated capital* is one displaying a figural composition and/or narrative scenes.

capriccio (*pl.* *capricci*) (p. 931) A painting or print of a fantastic, imaginary landscape, usually with architecture.

capstone (p. 18) The final, topmost stone in a **corbeled arch** or **vault**, which joins the sides and completes the structure.

cartoon (p. 512) A full-scale drawing of a design that will be executed in another **medium**, such as wall painting, **tapestry**, or **stained glass**.

cartouche (p. 189) A frame for a **hieroglyphic** inscription formed by a rope design surrounding an oval space. Used to signify a sacred or honored name. Also: in architecture, a decorative device or plaque, usually with a plain center used for inscriptions or epitaphs.

caryatid (p. 110) A sculpture of a draped female figure acting as a **column** supporting an **entablature**.

cassone (*pl.* *cassoni*) (p. 630) An Italian dowry chest, often highly decorated with carvings, paintings, inlaid designs, and gilt embellishments.

catacomb (p. 217) An underground cemetery consisting of tunnels on different levels, having niches for urns and **sarcophagi** and often incorporating rooms (*cubicula*).

cathedral (p. 222) The principal Christian church in a diocese, the bishop's administrative center and housing his throne (*cathedra*).

celadon (p. 362) A high-fired, transparent **glaze** of pale bluish-green hue whose principal coloring agent is an oxide of iron. In China and Korea, such glazes were typically applied over a pale gray **stoneware** body, though Chinese potters sometimes applied them over **porcelain** bodies during the Ming (1368–1644) and Qing (1644–1911) dynasties. Chinese potters invented celadon glazes and initiated the continuous production of celadon-glazed wares as early as the third century CE.

cella (p. 110) The principal interior room at the center of a Greek or Roman temple within which the cult statue was usually housed. Also called the **naos**.

celt (p. 387) A smooth, oblong stone or metal object, shaped like an axe-head.

cenotaph (p. 783) A funerary monument commemorating an individual or group buried elsewhere.

centering (p. 171) A temporary structure that supports a masonry **arch**, **vault**, or **dome** during construction until the mortar is fully dried and the masonry is self-sustaining.

central-plan building (p. 225) Any structure designed with a primary central space surrounded by symmetrical areas on each side, e.g., a **rotunda**.

ceramics (p. 20) A general term covering all types of wares made from fired clay.

chacmool (p. 400) In Maya sculpture, a half-reclining figure probably representing an offering bearer.

chaitya (p. 309) A type of Buddhist temple found in India. Often built in the form of a hall or **basilica**, a *chaitya* hall is highly decorated with sculpture and usually is carved from a cave or natural rock location. It houses a sacred shrine or **stupa** for worship.

chamfer (p. 793) The slanted surface produced when an angle is trimmed or beveled, common in building and metalwork.

chasing (p. 445) Ornamentation made on metal by incising or hammering the surface.

château (*pl.* *châteaux*) (p. 704) A French country house or residential castle. A *château fort* is a military castle incorporating defensive works such as towers and battlements.

chattri (p. 793) In Indian architecture, a decorative pavilion with an umbrella-shaped **dome**.

chevron (p. 360) A decorative or heraldic motif of repeated *V*s; a zigzag pattern.

chiaroscuro (p. 650) An Italian word designating the contrast of dark and light in a painting, drawing, or print. *Chiaroscuro* creates spatial depth and volumetric forms through gradations in the intensity of light and shadow.

choir (p. 454) The part of a church reserved for the clergy, monks, or nuns, either between the **transept** crossing and the **apse** or extending farther into the **nave**; separated from the rest of the church by screens or walls and fitted with stalls (seats).

cista (*pl.* *cistae*) (p. 159) Cylindrical containers used in antiquity by wealthy women as a case for toiletry articles such as a mirror.

clerestory (p. 59) In a **basilica**, the topmost zone of a wall with windows, extending above the **aisle** roofs. Provides direct light into the **nave**.

cloisonné (p. 262) An **enameling** technique in which artists affix wires or strips to a metal surface to delineate designs and create compartments (*cloisons*) that they subsequently fill with enamel.

cloister (p. 458) An enclosed space, open to the sky, especially within a monastery, surrounded by an **arcaded** walkway, often having a fountain and garden. Since the most important monastic buildings (e.g., dormitory, refectory, church) open off the cloister, it represents the center of the monastic world.

codex (*pl.* **codices**) (p. 249) A book, or a group of **manuscript** pages (folios), held together by stitching or other binding along one edge.

coffer (p. 198) A recessed decorative panel used to decorate ceilings or **vaults**. The use of coffers is called coffering.

coiling (p. 863) A technique in basketry. In coiled baskets a spiraling coil, braid, or rope of material is held in place by stitching or interweaving to create a permanent shape.

collage (p. 917) A composition made of cut and pasted scraps of materials, sometimes with lines or forms added by the artist.

colonnade (p. 69) A row of **columns**, supporting a straight **lintel** (as in a **porch** or **portico**) or a series of **arches** (an **arcade**).

colophon (p. 447) The data placed at the end of a book listing the book's author, publisher, illuminator, and other information related to its production. In East Asian **handscrolls**, the inscriptions which follow the painting are also called colophons.

column (p. 111) An architectural element used for support and/or decoration. Consists of a rounded or polygonal vertical **shaft** placed on a base and topped by a decorative **capital**. In Classical architecture, columns are built in accordance with the rules of one of the architectural **orders**. They can be free-standing or attached to a background wall (**engaged**).

combine (p. 1100) Term used by Robert Rauschenberg to describe his works that combined painting and nontraditional sculptural elements.

commodification (p. 1100) Treating goods, services, ideas, or art merely as things to be bought or sold.

complementary color (p. 1011) The primary and secondary colors across from each other on the color wheel (red and green, blue and orange, yellow and purple). When juxtaposed, the intensity of both colors increases. When mixed together, they negate each other to make a neutral gray–brown.

Composite order (p. 162) See under **order**.

composite pose or **image** (p. 11) Combining different viewpoints within a single representation.

composition (p. xxv) The overall arrangement, organizing design, or structure of a work of art.

conch (p. 239) A halfdome.

connoisseur (p. 294) A French word meaning "an expert," and signifying one who studies and evaluates art based primarily on formal, visual, and stylistic analysis. A connoisseur studies the style and technique of an object to assess its relative quality and identify its maker through visual comparison with other works of secure authorship. See also **Formalism**.

continuous narrative (p. 249) See under **narrative image**.

contrapposto (p. 124) Italian term meaning "set against," used to describe the Classical convention of representing human figures with opposing alternations of tension and relaxation on either side of a central **axis** to give figures a sense of the potential for movement.

convention (p. 31) A traditional way of representing forms.

corbel, corbeling (p. 18) An early roofing and arching technique in which each **course** of stone projects slightly beyond the previous layer (a corbel) until the uppermost corbels meet; see also under **arch**. Also: **brackets** that project from a wall.

corbeled vault (p. 101) See under **vault**.

Corinthian order (p. 110) See under **order**.

cornice (p. 111) The uppermost section of a Classical **entablature**. More generally, a horizontally projecting element found at the top of a building wall or **pedestal**. A *raking cornice* is formed by the junction of two slanted cornices, most often found in **pediments**.

course (p. 101) A horizontal layer of stone used in building.

crenellation, crenellated (p. 44) Alternating high and low sections of a wall, giving a notched appearance and creating permanent defensive shields on top of fortified buildings.

crocket (p. 598) A stylized leaf used as decoration along the outer angle of spires, pinnacles, gables, and around **capitals** in Gothic architecture.

cruciform (p. 233) Of anything that is cross-shaped, as in the cruciform plan of a church.

cubiculum (*pl.* **cubicula**) (p. 224) A small private room for burials in a **catacomb**.

cuneiform (p. 29) An early form of writing with wedge-shaped marks impressed into wet clay with a **stylus**, primarily used by ancient Mesopotamians.

curtain wall (p. 1059) A wall in a building that does not support any of the weight of the structure.

cyclopean (p. 96) A method of construction using huge blocks of rough-hewn stone. Any large-scale, monumental building project that impresses by sheer size. Named after the Cyclopes (sing. Cyclops), one-eyed giants of legendary strength in Greek myths.

cylinder seal (p. 34) A small cylindrical stone decorated with **incised** patterns. When rolled across soft clay or wax, the resulting raised pattern or design served in Mesopotamian and Indus Valley cultures as an identifying signature.

dado (*pl.* **dadoes**) (p. 162) The lower part of a wall, differentiated in some way (by a **molding** or different coloring or paneling) from the upper section.

daguerreotype (p. 986) An early photographic process that makes a positive print on a light-sensitized copperplate; invented and marketed in 1839 by Louis-Jacques-Mandé Daguerre.

dendrochronology (p. xxxiii) The dating of wood based on the patterns of the tree's growth rings.

desert varnish (p. 411) A naturally occurring coating that turns rock faces into dark surfaces. Artists would draw images by scraping through the dark surface and revealing the color of the underlying rock. Extensively used in southwest North America.

diptych (p. xxxiii) Two panels of equal size (usually decorated with paintings or reliefs) hinged together.

dogu (p. 366) Small human figurines made in Japan during the Jomon period. Shaped from clay, the figures have exaggerated expressions and are in contorted poses. They were probably used in religious rituals.

dolmen (p. 17) A prehistoric structure made up of two or more large upright stones supporting a large, flat, horizontal slab or slabs.

dome (p. 190) A rounded **vault**, usually over a circular space. Consists of curved masonry and can vary in shape from hemispherical to bulbous to ovoidal. May use a supporting vertical wall (**drum**), from which the vault springs, and may be crowned by an open space (**oculus**) and/or an exterior **lantern**. When a dome is built over a square space, an intermediate element is required to make the transition to a circular drum. There are two systems. A dome on **pendentives** incorporates arched, sloping intermediate sections of wall that carry the weight and **thrust** of the dome to heavily **buttressed** supporting **piers**. A dome on **squinches** uses an arch built into the wall (squinch) in the upper corners of the space to carry the weight of the dome across the corners of the square space below. A halfdome or **conch** may cover a semicircular space.

domino construction (p. 1059) System of building construction introduced by the architect Le Corbusier in which reinforced concrete floor slabs are floated on six free-standing posts placed as if at the positions of the six dots on a domino playing piece.

Doric order (p. 110) See **order**.

dressed stone (p. 87) Another term for **ashlar**.

drillwork (p. 190) The technique of using a drill for the creation of certain effects in sculpture.

drum (p. 111) The circular wall that supports a **dome**. Also: a segment of the circular **shaft** of a **column**.

drypoint (p. 759) An **intaglio** printmaking process by which a metal (usually copper) plate is directly inscribed with a pointed instrument (**stylus**).The resulting design of scratched lines is inked, wiped, and printed. Also: the print made by this process.

earthenware (p. 21) A low-fired, opaque **ceramic** ware, employing humble clays that are naturally heat-resistant and remain porous after firing unless **glazed**. Earthenware occurs in a range of earth-toned colors, from white and tan to gray and black, with tan predominating.

earthwork (p. 402) Usually very large-scale, outdoor artwork that is produced by altering the natural environment.

echinus (p. 111) A cushionlike circular element found below the **abacus** of a Doric **capital**. Also: a similarly shaped **molding** (usually with egg-and-dart motifs) underneath the **volute**s of an Ionic capital.

electronic spin resonance (p. 13) Method that uses magnetic field and microwave irradiation to date material such as tooth enamel and its surrounding soil.

elevation (p. 110) The arrangement, proportions, and details of any vertical side or face of a building. Also: an architectural drawing showing an exterior or interior wall of a building.

embroidery (p. 403) Stitches applied in a decorative pattern on top of an already-woven fabric ground.

en plein air (p. 1003) French term (meaning "in the open air") describing the Impressionist practice of painting outdoors so artists could have direct access to the fleeting effects of light and atmosphere while working.

enamel (p. 259) Powdered, then molten, glass applied to a metal surface, and used by artists to create designs. After firing, the glass forms an opaque or transparent substance that fuses to the metal background. Also: an object created by the enameling technique. See also *cloisonné*.

encaustic (p. 1097) A painting **medium** using pigments mixed with hot wax.

engaged (p. 172) Of an architectural feature, usually a **column**, attached to a wall.

engraving (p. 602) An **intaglio** printmaking process of inscribing an image, design, or letters onto a metal or wood surface from which a print is made. An engraving is usually drawn with a sharp implement (**burin**) directly onto the surface of the plate. Also: the print made from this process.

entablature (p. 110) In the Classical **orders**, the horizontal elements above the **columns** and **capitals**. The entablature consists of, from bottom to top, an **architrave**, a **frieze**, and a **cornice**.

entasis (p. 110) A slight swelling of the **shaft** of a Greek **column**. The optical illusion of entasis makes the column appear from a distance to be straight.

esquisse (p. 962) French for "sketch." A quickly executed drawing or painting conveying the overall idea for a finished painting.

etching (p. 759) An **intaglio** printmaking process in which a metal plate is coated with acid-resistant resin and then inscribed with a **stylus** in a design, revealing the plate below. The plate is then immersed in acid, and the exposed metal of the design is eaten away by the acid. The resin is removed, leaving the design etched permanently into the metal and the plate ready to be inked, wiped, and printed.

Eucharist (p. 222) The central rite of the Christian Church, from the Greek word for "thanksgiving." Also known as the Mass or Holy Communion, it reenacts Christ's sacrifice on the cross and commemorates the Last Supper. According to traditional Catholic Christian belief, consecrated bread and wine become the body and blood of Christ; in Protestant belief, bread and wine symbolize the body and blood.

exedra (*pl.* **exedrae**) (p. 198) In architecture, a semicircular niche. On a small scale, often used as decoration, whereas larger exedrae can form interior spaces (such as an **apse**).

expressionism (p. 153) Artistic styles in which aspects of works of art are exaggerated to evoke subjective emotions rather than to portray objective reality or elicit a rational response.

façade (p. 53) The face or front wall of a building.

faience (p. 89) Type of **ceramic** covered with colorful, opaque glazes that form a smooth, impermeable surface. First developed in ancient Egypt.

fang ding (p. 339) A square or rectangular bronze vessel with four legs. The *fang ding* was used for ritual offerings in ancient China during the Shang dynasty.

fête galante (p. 926) A subject in painting depicting well-dressed people at leisure in a park or country setting. It is most often associated with eighteenth-century French Rococo painting.

filigree (p. 93) Delicate, lacelike ornamental work.

fillet (p. 111) The flat ridge between the carved-out **flutes** of a **column shaft**.

finial (p. 306) A knoblike architectural decoration usually found at the top point of a spire, pinnacle, canopy, or gable. Also found on furniture. Also the ornamental top of a staff.

flutes (p. 111) In architecture, evenly spaced, rounded parallel vertical grooves incised on **shafts** of **columns** or on columnar elements such as **pilasters**.

flying buttress (p. 516) See under **buttress**.

flying gallop (p. 89) A non-naturalistic pose in which animals are depicted hovering above the ground with legs fully extended backward and forward to signify that they are running.

foreshortening (p. xxvii) The illusion created on a flat surface by which figures and objects appear to recede or project sharply into space. Accomplished according to the rules of **perspective**.

formal analysis (p. xxv) An exploration of the visual character that artists bring to their works through the expressive use of elements such as line, form, color, and light, and through its overall structure or composition.

Formalism (p. 1089) An approach to the understanding, appreciation, and valuation of art based almost solely on considerations of form. The Formalist's approach tends to regard an artwork as independent of its time and place of making.

forum (p. 178) A Roman town center; site of temples and administrative buildings and used as a market or gathering area for the citizens.

fresco (p. 83) A painting technique in which water-based pigments are applied to a plaster surface. If the plaster is painted when wet, the color is absorbed by the plaster, becoming a permanent part of the wall (*buon fresco*). *Fresco secco* is created by painting on dried plaster, and the color may eventually flake off. Murals made by both these techniques are called frescos.

frieze (p. 110) The middle element of an **entablature**, between the **architrave** and the **cornice**. Usually decorated with sculpture, painting, or **moldings**. Also: any continuous flat band with **relief sculpture** or painted decoration.

frottage (p. 1072) A design produced by laying a piece of paper over a textured surface and rubbing with charcoal or other soft **medium**.

fusuma (p. 834) Sliding doors covered with paper, used in traditional Japanese construction. *Fusuma* are often highly decorated with paintings and colored backgrounds.

gallery (p. 241) A roofed passageway with one or both of its long sides open to the air. In church architecture, the story found above the side **aisles** of a church or across the width at the end of the **nave** or **transepts**, usually open to and overlooking the area below. Also: a building or hall in which art is displayed or sold.

garbhagriha (p. 306) From the Sanskrit word meaning "womb chamber," a small room or shrine in a Hindu temple containing its principal holy image.

genre painting (p. 727) A term used to loosely categorize paintings depicting scenes of everyday life, including (among others) domestic interiors, parties, inn scenes, and street scenes.

geoglyph (p. 402) Earthen design on a colossal scale, often created in a landscape as if to be seen from an aerial viewpoint.

gesso (p. 556) A primer made from glue, gypsum, and/or chalk, used as the ground of a wood panel or the priming layer of a canvas. Provides a smooth surface for painting.

gilding (p. 91) The application of paper-thin gold leaf or gold pigment to an object made from another **medium** (for example, a sculpture or painting). Usually used as a decorative finishing detail.

giornata (*pl.* **giornate**) (p. 551) Adopted from the Italian term meaning "a day's work," a *giornata* is the section of a **fresco** plastered and painted in a single day.

glazing (p. 613) In **ceramics**, an outermost layer of vitreous liquid (**glaze**) that, upon firing, renders the ware waterproof and forms a decorative surface. In painting, a technique used with oil **media** in which a transparent layer of paint (glaze) is laid over another, usually lighter, painted or glazed area. In architecture, the process of filling openings in a building with windows of clear or **stained glass**.

gold leaf (p. 47) Paper-thin sheets of hammered gold that are used in **gilding**. In some cases (such as Byzantine **icons**), also used as a ground for paintings.

gopura (p. 787) The towering gateway to an Indian Hindu temple complex.

Grand Manner (p. 940) An elevated style of painting popular in the eighteenth century in which the artist looked to the ancients and to the Renaissance for inspiration; for portraits as well as history painting, the artist would adopt the poses, compositions, and attitudes of Renaissance and antique models.

Grand Tour (p. 929) Popular during the eighteenth and nineteenth centuries, an extended tour of cultural sites in France and Italy intended to finish the education of a young upper-class person primarily from Britain or North America.

granulation (p. 93) A technique of decoration in which metal granules, or tiny metal balls, are fused onto a metal surface.

graphic arts (p. 711) A term referring to those arts that are drawn or printed and that utilize paper as the primary support.

grattage (p. 1073) A pattern created by scraping off layers of paint from a canvas laid over a textured surface. Compare **frottage**.

grid (p. 65) A system of regularly spaced horizontally and vertically crossed lines that gives regularity to an architectural plan or in the composition of a work of art. Also: in painting, a grid is used to allow designs to be enlarged or transferred easily.

grisaille (p. 552) A style of monochromatic painting in shades of gray. Also: a painting made in this style.

groin vault (p. 190) See under **vault**.

grozing (p. 512) Chipping away at the edges of a piece of glass to achieve the precise shape needed for inclusion in the composition of a **stained-glass** window.

guild (p. 425) An association of artists or craftspeople. Medieval and Renaissance guilds had great economic power, as they controlled the marketing of their members' products and provided economic protection, political solidarity, and training in the craft to its members. The painters' guild was usually dedicated to St. Luke, their patron saint.

hall church (p. 532) A church with **nave** and **aisles** of the same height, giving the impression of a large, open hall.

halo (p. 217) A circle of light that surrounds and frames the heads of emperors and holy figures to signify their power and/or sanctity. Also known as a nimbus.

handscroll (p. 347) A long, narrow, horizontal painting or text (or combination thereof) common in Chinese and Japanese art and of a size intended for individual use. A handscroll is stored wrapped tightly around a wooden pin and is unrolled for viewing or reading.

hanging scroll (p. 810) In Chinese and Japanese art, a vertical painting or text mounted within sections of silk. At the top is a semicircular rod; at the bottom is a round dowel. Hanging scrolls are kept rolled and tied except for special occasions, when they are hung for display, contemplation, or commemoration.

haniwa (p. 366) Pottery forms, including cylinders, buildings, and human figures, that were placed on top of Japanese tombs or burial mounds during the Kofun period (300–552 C.E.).

Happening (p. 1103) Term coined by Allan Kaprow in the 1960s to describe artworks incorporating elements of performance, theater, and visual images. Organized without a specific narrative or intent and with audience participation, the event proceeded according to chance and individual improvisation.

hemicycle (p. 525) A semicircular interior space or structure.

henge (p. 18) A circular area enclosed by stones or wood posts set up by Neolithic peoples. It is usually bounded by a ditch and raised embankment.

hierarchic scale (p. 27) The use of differences in size to indicate relative importance. For example, with human figures, the larger the figure, the greater her or his importance.

hieratic (p. 495) Highly stylized, severe, and detached, often in relation to a strict religious tradition.

hieroglyph (p. 53) Picture writing; words and ideas rendered in the form of pictorial symbols.

high relief (p. 312) See under **relief sculpture**.

historiated capital (p. 497) See under **capital**.

historicism (p. 981) The strong consciousness of and attention to the institutions, themes, styles, and forms of the past, made accessible by historical research, textual study, and archaeology.

history paintings (p. 942) Paintings based on historical, mythological, or biblical narratives. Once considered the noblest form of art, history paintings generally convey a high moral or intellectual idea and are often painted in a grand pictorial style.

horizon line (p. 581) A horizontal "line" formed by the implied meeting point of earth and sky. In linear perspective (under **perspective**), the **vanishing point** or points are located on this "line."

horseshoe arch (p. 277) See under **arch**.

hue (p. 79) Pure color. The saturation or intensity of the hue depends on the purity of the color. Its value depends on its lightness or darkness.

hydria (p. 142) A large ancient Greek or Roman jar with three handles (horizontal ones at both sides and one vertical at the back), used for storing water.

hypostyle hall (p. 66) A large interior room characterized by many closely spaced **columns** that support its roof.

icon (p. 250) An image representing a sacred figure or event in the Byzantine (later the Orthodox) Church. Icons are venerated by the faithful, who believe their prayers are transmitted through them to God.

iconic image (p. 217) A picture that expresses or embodies an intangible concept or idea.

iconoclasm (p. 251) The banning and/or destruction of images, especially **icons** and religious art. Iconoclasm in eighth- and ninth-century Byzantium and sixteenth- and seventeenth-century Protestant territories arose from differing beliefs about the power, meaning, function, and purpose of imagery in religion.

iconography (p. xxix) Identifying and studying the subject matter and **conventional** symbols in works of art.

iconology (p. xxx) Interpreting works of art as embodiments of cultural situation by placing them within broad social, political, religious, and intellectual contexts.

iconophile (p. 251) From the Greek for "lover of images." In periods of **iconoclasm**, iconophiles advocate the continued use of sacred images.

idealization (p. 136) A process in art through which artists strive to make their forms and figures attain perfection, based on pervading cultural values and/or their own personal ideals.

illumination (p. 249) A painting on paper or parchment used as an illustration and/or decoration in a **manuscript** or **album**. Usually richly colored, often supplemented by gold and other precious materials. The artists are referred to as illuminators. Also: the technique of decorating manuscripts with such paintings.

impasto (p. 761) Thick applications of paint that give a painting a palpable surface texture.

impluvium (p. 180) A pool under a roof opening that collected rainwater in the **atrium** of a Roman house.

impost block (p. 171) A block of masonry imposed between the top of a **pier** or above the **capital** of a **column** in order to provide extra support at the springing of an **arch**.

incising (p. 120) A technique in which a design or inscription is cut into a hard surface with a sharp instrument. Such a surface is said to be incised.

ink painting (p. 826) A monochromatic style of painting developed in China, using black ink with gray washes.

inlay (p. 29) To set pieces of a material or materials into a surface to form a design. Also: material used in or decoration formed by this technique.

installation, installation art (p. 1066) Contemporary art created for a specific site, especially a gallery or outdoor area, that creates a complete and controlled environment.

intaglio (p. 602) A technique in which the design is carved out of the surface of an object, such as an engraved seal stone. In the **graphic arts**, intaglio includes **engraving**, **etching**, and **drypoint**—all processes in which ink transfers to paper from incised, ink-filled lines cut into a metal plate.

intarsia (p. 636) Technique of **inlay** decoration using variously colored woods.

intuitive perspective (p. 182) See under **perspective**.

Ionic order (p. 110) See under **order**.

iwan (p. 283) In Islamic architecture, a large, vaulted chamber with a monumental arched opening on one side.

jamb (p. 491) In architecture, the vertical element found on both sides of an opening in a wall, and supporting an **arch** or **lintel**.

Japonisme (p. 1010) A style in French and American nineteenth-century art that was highly influenced by Japanese art, especially prints.

jasperware (p. 935) A fine-grained, unglazed, white **ceramic** developed in the eighteenth century by Josiah Wedgwood, often with raised designs remaining white above a background surface colored by metallic oxides.

Jataka tales (p. 308) In Buddhism, stories associated with the previous lives of Shakyamuni, the historical Buddha.

joggled voussoirs (p. 279) Interlocking **voussoirs** in an **arch** or **lintel**, often of contrasting materials for colorful effect.

joined-block sculpture (p. 376) Large-scale wooden sculpture constructed by a method developed in Japan. The entire work is made from smaller hollow blocks, each individually carved, and assembled when complete. The joined-block technique allowed production of larger sculpture, as the multiple joints alleviate the problems of drying and cracking found with sculpture carved from a single block.

kantharos (p. 121) A type of ancient Greek goblet with two large handles and a wide mouth.

keep (p. 490) The innermost and strongest structure or central tower of a medieval castle, sometimes used as living quarters, as well as for defense. Also called a donjon.

kente (p. 898) A cloth made by the Asante peoples of Ghana. It is woven in long, narrow strips featuring complex, irregular, geometric patterns. The strips are then sewn together to make a large rectangular fabric, which is worn by wrapping it around the body under the arms with one end draped up over one shoulder.

key block (p. 843) The master block in the production of a colored **woodblock print**, which requires different blocks for each color. The key block is a flat piece of wood upon which the outlines for the entire design of the print were first drawn on its surface and then all but these outlines were carved away with a knife. These outlines serve as a guide for the accurate **registration** or alignment of the other blocks needed to add colors to specific parts of a print.

keystone (p. 171) The topmost **voussoir** at the center of an **arch**, and the last block to be placed. The pressure of this block holds the arch together. Often of a larger size and/or decorated.

kiln (p. 21) An oven designed to produce enough heat for the baking, or firing, of clay, for the melting of the glass used in **enamel** work, and for the fixing of vitreous paint on **stained glass**.

kiva (p. 409) A subterranean, circular room used as a ceremonial center in some Native American cultures.

kondo (p. 370) The main hall inside a Japanese Buddhist temple where the images of Buddha are housed.

korambo (p. 879) A ceremonial or spirit house in Pacific cultures, reserved for the men of a village and used as a meeting place as well as to hide religious artifacts from the uninitiated.

kore (*pl.* **kourai**) (p. 116) An Archaic Greek statue of a young woman.

koru (p. 886) A design depicting a curling stalk with a bulb at the end that resembles a young tree fern; often found in Maori art.

kouros (*pl.* **kouroi**) (p. 116) An Archaic Greek statue of a young man or boy.

kowhaiwhai (p. 886) Painted curvilinear patterns often found in Maori art.

krater (p. 101) An ancient Greek vessel for mixing wine and water, with many subtypes that each have a distinctive shape. *Calyx krater:* a bell-shaped vessel with handles near the base that resembles a flower calyx. *Volute krater:* a krater with handles shaped like scrolls.

Kufic (p. 280) An ornamental, angular Arabic script.

kylix (p. 124) A shallow ancient Greek cup, used for drinking, with a wide mouth and small handles near the rim.

lacquer (p. 840) A type of hard, glossy surface varnish, originally developed for use on objects in East Asian cultures, made from the sap of the Asian sumac or from shellac, a resinous secretion from the lac insect. Lacquer can be layered and manipulated or combined with pigments and other materials for various decorative effects.

lakshana (p. 311) The 32 marks of the historical Buddha. The *lakshana* include, among others, the Buddha's golden body, his long arms, the wheel impressed on his palms and the soles of his feet, the *urna* between his eyes, and the *ushnisha* on his head.

lamassu (p. 41) Supernatural guardian-protector of ancient Near Eastern palaces and throne rooms, often represented sculpturally as a combination of the bearded head of a man, powerful body of a lion or bull, wings of an eagle, and the horned headdress of a god, usually possessing five legs.

lancet (p. 516) A tall, narrow window crowned by a sharply pointed arch, typically found in Gothic architecture.

lantern (p. 476) A turretlike structure situated on a roof, vault, or dome, with windows that allow light into the space below.

lekythos (*pl.* **lekythoi**) (p. 144) A slim ancient Greek oil vase with one handle and a narrow mouth.

linear perspective (p. 607) See under **perspective**.

linga shrine (p. 319) A place of worship centered on an object or representation in the form of a phallus or column (the *linga*), which symbolizes the power of the Hindu god Shiva.

lintel (p. 18) A horizontal element of any material carried by two or more vertical supports to form an opening.

literati painting (p. 807) A style of painting that reflects the taste of the educated class of East Asian intellectuals and scholars. Characteristics include an appreciation for the antique, small scale, and an intimate connection between maker and audience.

lithography (p. 969) Process of making a print (lithograph) from a design drawn on a flat stone block with greasy crayon. Ink is applied to the wet stone and adheres only to the greasy areas of the design.

loggia (p. 546) Italian term for a **gallery**. Often used as a corridor between buildings or around a courtyard, a loggia usually features an **arcade** or **colonnade**.

longitudinal-plan building (p. 225) Any structure designed with a rectangular shape and a longitudinal axis. In a cross-shaped building, the main arm of the building would be longer than any arms that cross it. For example, a **basilica**.

lost-wax casting (p. 36) A method of casting metal, such as bronze. A wax model is covered with clay and plaster, then fired, thus melting the model and leaving a hollow form. Molten metal is then poured into the hollow space and slowly cooled. When the hardened clay and plaster exterior shell is removed, a solid metal form remains to be smoothed and polished.

low relief (p. 40) See under **relief sculpture**.

lunette (p. 223) A semicircular wall area, framed by an **arch** over a door or window. Can be either plain or decorated.

lusterware (p. 281) Pottery decorated with metallic **glazes**.

madrasa (p. 283) An Islamic institution of higher learning, where teaching is focused on theology and law.

maenad (p. 105) In ancient Greece, a female devotee of the wine god Dionysos who participated in orgiastic rituals. Often depicted with swirling **drapery** to indicate wild movement or dance. Also called a Bacchante, after Bacchus, the Roman equivalent of Dionysos.

majolica (p. 585) Pottery painted with a tin **glaze** that, when fired, gives a lustrous and colorful surface.

mandala (p. 307) An image of the cosmos represented by an arrangement of circles or concentric geometric shapes containing diagrams or images. Used for meditation and contemplation by Buddhists.

mandapa (p. 306) In a Hindu temple, an open hall dedicated to ritual worship.

mandorla (p. 248) Light encircling, or emanating from, the entire figure of a sacred person.

manuscript (p. 248) A hand-written book or document.

maqsura (p. 277) An enclosure in a Muslim **mosque**, near the *mihrab*, designated for dignitaries.

martyrium (*pl.* **martyria**) (p. 242) A church, chapel, or shrine built over the grave of a Christian martyr.

mastaba (p. 54) A flat-topped, one-story structure with slanted walls built over an ancient Egyptian underground tomb.

matte (p. 585) Of a smooth surface that is without shine or luster.

mausoleum (p. 177) A monumental building used as a tomb. Named after the tomb of King Mausolos erected at Halikarnassos around 350 B.C.E.

medallion (p. 224) Any round ornament or decoration. Also: a large medal.

medium (*pl.* **media**) (p. xxv) The material from which a work of art is made.

megalith (*adj.* **megalithic**) (p. 17) A large stone used in some prehistoric architecture.

megaron (p. 95) The main hall of a Mycenaean palace or grand house.

memento mori (p. 925) From Latin for "remember that you must die." An object, such as a skull or extinguished candle, typically found in a *vanitas* image, symbolizing the transience of life.

menorah (p. 188) A Jewish lampstand with seven or nine branches; the nine-branched menorah is used during the celebration of Hanukkah. Representations of the seven-branched menorah, once used in the Temple of Jerusalem, became a symbol of Judaism.

metope (p. 111) The carved or painted rectangular panel between the **triglyphs** of a Doric **frieze**.

mihrab (p. 269) A recess or niche that distinguishes the wall oriented toward Mecca (*qibla*) in a **mosque**.

millefiori (p. 447) A glassmaking technique in which rods of differently colored glass are fused in a long bundle that is subsequently sliced to produce disks or beads with small-scale, multicolor patterns. The term derives from the Italian for "a thousand flowers."

minaret (p. 274) A tower on or near a **mosque** from which Muslims are called to prayer five times a day.

minbar (p. 269) A high platform or pulpit in a **mosque**.

miniature (p. 249) Anything small. In painting, miniatures may be illustrations within **albums** or **manuscripts** or intimate portraits.

mirador (p. 286) In Spanish and Islamic palace architecture, a very large window or room with windows, and sometimes balconies, providing views to interior courtyards or the exterior landscape.

mithuna (p. 310) The amorous male and female couples in Buddhist sculpture, usually found at the entrance to a sacred building. The *mithuna* symbolizes the harmony and fertility of life.

moai (p. 889) Statues found in Polynesia, carved from tufa, a yellowish brown volcanic stone, and depicting the human form. Nearly 1,000 of these statues have been found on the island of Rapa Nui but their significance has been a matter of speculation.

modeling (p. xxv) In painting, the process of creating the illusion of three-dimensionality on a two-dimensional surface by use of light and shade. In sculpture, the process of molding a three-dimensional form out of a malleable substance.

module (p. 351) A segment or portion of a repeated design. Also: a basic building block.

molding (p. 323) A shaped or sculpted strip with varying contours and patterns. Used as decoration on architecture, furniture, frames, and other objects.

mortise-and-tenon (p. 19) A method of joining two elements. A projecting pin (tenon) on one element fits snugly into a hole designed for it (mortise) on the other.

mosaic (p. 148) Image formed by arranging small colored stone or glass pieces (**tesserae**) and affixing them to a hard, stable surface.

mosque (p. 269) A building used for communal Islamic worship.

Mozarabic (p. 455) Of an eclectic style practiced in Christian medieval Spain when much of the Iberian peninsula was ruled by Islamic dynasties.

mudra (p. 312) A symbolic hand gesture in Buddhist art that denotes certain behaviors, actions, or feelings.

mullion (p. 522) A slender straight or curving bar that divides a window into subsidiary sections to create **tracery**.

muqarna (p. 286) In Islamic architecture, one of the nichelike components, often stacked in tiers to mark the transition between flat and rounded surfaces and often found on the **vault** of a **dome**.

naos (p. 241) The principal room in a temple or church. In ancient architecture, the **cella**. In a Byzantine church, the **nave** and **sanctuary**.

narrative image (p. 217) A picture that recounts an event drawn from a story, either factual (e.g. biographical) or fictional. In **continuous narrative**, multiple scenes from the same story appear within a single compositional frame.

narthex (p. 222) The vestibule or entrance porch of a church.

nave (p. 192) The central space of a church, two or three stories high and usually flanked by **aisles**.

ndop (p. 900) A Kikuba (Kuba) term meaning "statue." It is sculpted of wood to commemorate a Kuba king (*nyim*) and the role he serves in Kuba society.

necropolis (p. 54) A large cemetery or burial area; literally a "city of the dead."

nemes headdress (p. 51) The royal headdress of ancient Egypt.

niello (p. 93) A metal technique in which a black sulfur **alloy** is rubbed into fine lines engraved into metal (usually gold or silver). When heated, the alloy becomes fused with the surrounding metal and provides contrasting detail.

oculus (*pl.* **oculi**) (p. 190) In architecture, a circular opening. Usually found either as windows or at the apex of a **dome**. When at the top of a dome, an oculus is either open to the sky or covered by a decorative exterior **lantern**.

odalisque (p. 968) Turkish word for "harem slave girl" or "concubine."

oil paint (p. 585) Pigments suspended in a **medium** of oil and used for painting. Oil paint has particular properties that allow for greater ease of working: among others, a slow drying time (which allows for corrections), and a great range of relative opaqueness of paint layers (which permits a high degree of detail and luminescence).

oinochoe (p. 128) An ancient Greek jug used for wine.

olpe (p. 107) Any ancient Greek vessel without a spout.

one-point perspective (p. 264) See under **perspective**.

orant (p. 222) Of a standing figure represented praying with outstretched and upraised arms.

oratory (p. 233) A small chapel.

order (p. 111) A system of proportions in Classical architecture that includes every aspect of the building's plan, elevation, and decorative system. *Composite*: a combination of the Ionic and the Corinthian orders. The **capital** combines **acanthus** leaves with **volute** scrolls. *Corinthian*: the most ornate of the orders, the Corinthian includes a **base** and a **fluted column shaft** with a capital elaborately decorated with acanthus leaf carvings. Its **entablature** consists of an **architrave** decorated with **moldings**, a **frieze** often containing **relief sculpture**, and a **cornice** with **dentils**. *Doric*: the column shaft of the Doric order can be fluted or smooth-surfaced and has no base. The Doric capital consists of an undecorated **echinus** and **abacus**. The Doric entablature has a plain architrave, a frieze with **metopes** and **triglyphs**, and a simple cornice. *Ionic*: the column of the Ionic order has a base, a fluted shaft, and a capital decorated with volutes. The Ionic entablature consists of an architrave of three panels and moldings, a frieze usually containing sculpted relief ornament, and a cornice with dentils. *Tuscan*: a variation of Doric characterized by a smooth-surfaced column shaft with a base, a plain architrave, and an undecorated frieze. *Colossal* or giant: any of the above built on a large scale, rising through two or more stories

in height and often raised from the ground on a **pedestal**.

Orientalism (p. 982) A fascination with Middle Eastern cultures that inspired eclectic nineteenth-century European fantasies of exotic life that often formed the subject of paintings.

orthogonal (p. 141) Any line running back into the represented space of a picture perpendicular to the imagined **picture plane**. In **linear perspective**, all orthogonals converge at a single **vanishing point** in the picture and are the basis for a **grid** that maps out the internal space of the image. An orthogonal plan is any plan for a building or city that is based exclusively on right angles, such as the grid plan of many major cities.

pagoda (p. 352) An East Asian **reliquary** tower built with successively smaller, repeated stories. Each story is usually marked by an elaborate projecting roof.

painterly (p. 257) A style of painting which emphasizes the techniques and surface effects of brushwork (also color, light, and shade).

palace complex (p. 41) A group of buildings used for living and governing by a ruler and his or her supporters, usually fortified.

palazzo (p. 614) Italian term for palace, used for any large urban dwelling.

palette (p. 184) A hand-held support used by artists for arranging colors and mixing paint during the process of painting. Also: the choice of a range of colors used by an artist in a particular work, as typical of his or her style. In ancient Egypt, a flat stone used to grind and prepare makeup.

panel painting (p. xxxvii) Any painting executed on a wood support, usually planed to provide a smooth surface. A panel can consist of several boards joined together.

parchment (p. 249) A writing surface made from treated skins of animals. Very fine parchment is known as **vellum**.

parterre (p. 772) An ornamental, highly regimented flowerbed; especially as an element of the ornate gardens of a seventeenth-century palace or **château**.

passage grave (p. 18) A prehistoric tomb under a **cairn**, reached by a long, narrow, slab-lined access passageway or passageways.

pastel (p. 930) Dry pigment, chalk, and gum in stick or crayon form. Also: a work of art made with pastels.

pedestal (p. 110) A platform or base supporting a sculpture or other monument. Also: the block found below the base of a Classical **column** (or **colonnade**), serving to raise the entire element off the ground.

pediment (p. 110) A triangular gable found over major architectural elements such as Classical Greek **porticos**, windows, or doors. Formed by an **entablature** and the ends of a sloping roof or a raking **cornice**. A similar architectural element is often used decoratively above a door or window, sometimes with a curved upper **molding**. A *broken pediment* is a variation on the traditional pediment, with an open space at the center of the topmost angle and/or the horizontal cornice.

pendant (also **pendent**) (p. 652) One of a pair of artworks meant to be seen in relation to each other as a set.

pendentive (p. 241) The concave triangular section of a **vault** that forms the transition between a square or polygonal space and the circular base of a **dome**.

performance art (p. 1103) Works of art that are performed live by the artist and sometimes involve audience participation.

peristyle (p. 66) In Greek architecture, a surrounding **colonnade**. A peristyle building is surrounded on the exterior by a colonnade. Also: a peristyle court is an open colonnaded courtyard, often having a pool and garden.

perspective (p. xxiii) A system for representing three-dimensional space on a two-dimensional surface. *Atmospheric* or *aerial perspective*: a method of rendering the effect of spatial distance by subtle variations in color and clarity of representation. *Intuitive perspective*: a method of giving the impression of recession by visual instinct, not by the use of an overall system or program. *Oblique perspective*: an intuitive spatial system in which a building or room is placed with one corner in the **picture plane**, and the other parts of the structure recede to an imaginary **vanishing point** on its other side. Oblique perspective is not a comprehensive, mathematical system. *One-point* and multiple-point perspective (also called linear, scientific, or mathematical perspective): a method of creating the illusion of three-dimensional space on a two-dimensional surface by delineating a **horizon line** and multiple **orthogonal** lines. These recede to meet at one or more points on the horizon (vanishing point), giving the appearance of spatial depth. Called scientific or mathematical because its use requires some knowledge of geometry and mathematics, as well as optics. *Reverse perspective*: a Byzantine perspective theory in which the orthogonals or rays of sight do not converge on a vanishing point in the picture, but are thought to originate in the viewer's eye in front of the picture. Thus, in reverse perspective the image is constructed with orthogonals that diverge, giving a slightly tipped aspect to objects.

photomontage (p. 1053) A photographic work created from many smaller photographs arranged (and often overlapping) in a composition that is then rephotographed.

pictograph (p. 340) A highly stylized depiction serving as a symbol for a person or object. Also: a type of writing utilizing such symbols.

picture plane (p. 587) The theoretical plane corresponding with the actual surface of a painting, separating the spatial world evoked in the painting from the spatial world occupied by the viewer.

picturesque (p. 935) Of the taste for the familiar, the pleasant, and the agreeable, popular in the eighteenth and nineteenth centuries in Europe. Originally used to describe the "picturelike" qualities of some landscape scenes. When contrasted with the **sublime**, the picturesque stood for the interesting but ordinary domestic landscape.

piece-mold casting (p. 338) A casting technique in which the mold consists of several sections that are connected during the pouring of molten metal, usually bronze. After the cast form has hardened, the pieces of the mold are disassembled, leaving the completed object.

pier (p. 273) A masonry support made up of many stones, or rubble and concrete (in contrast to a column **shaft** which is formed from a single stone or a series of **drums**), often square or rectangular in plan, and capable of carrying very heavy architectural loads.

pietà (p. 231) A devotional subject in Christian religious art. After the Crucifixion the body of Jesus was laid across the lap of his grieving mother, Mary. When other mourners are present, the subject is called the Lamentation.

pietra serena (p. 613) A gray Tuscan sandstone used in Florentine architecture.

pilaster (p. 161) An **engaged** columnlike element that is rectangular in format and used for decoration in architecture.

pilgrimage church (p. 226) A church that attracts visitors wishing to venerate **relics** as well as attend religious services.

pinnacle (p. 517) In Gothic architecture, a steep pyramid decorating the top of another element such as a **buttress**. Also: the highest point.

plate tracery (p. 516) See under **tracery**.

plein air (p. 1003) See under **en plein air**.

plinth (p. 162) The slablike base or **pedestal** of a **column**, statue, wall, building, or piece of furniture.

podium (p. 141) A raised platform that acts as the foundation for a building, or as a platform for a speaker.

poesia (*pl.* **poesie**) (p. 668) Italian Renaissance paintings based on Classical themes, often with erotic overtones, notably in the mid-sixteenth-century works of the Venetian painter Titian.

polychromy (p. 537) Multicolored decoration applied to any part of a building, sculpture, or piece of furniture. This can be accomplished with paint or by the use of multicolored materials.

polyptych (p. xxxiii) An **altarpiece** constructed from multiple panels, sometimes with hinges to allow for movable wings.

porcelain (p. 20) A type of extremely hard and fine white **ceramic** first made by Chinese potters in the eighth century CE. Made from a mixture of kaolin and petuntse, porcelain is fired at a very high temperature, and the final product has a translucent surface.

porch (p. 110) The covered entrance on the exterior of a building. With a row of **columns** or **colonnade**, also called a **portico**.

portal (p. 40) A grand entrance, door, or gate, usually to an important public building, often decorated with sculpture.

portico (p. 63) In architecture, a projecting roof or porch supported by **columns**, often marking an entrance. See also **porch**.

post-and-lintel (p. 17) An architectural system of construction with two or more vertical elements (posts) supporting a horizontal element (**lintel**).

potassium-argon dating (p. 12) Archaeological method of **radiometric dating** that measures the decay of a radioactive potassium isotope into a stable isotope of argon, and inert gas.

potsherd (p. 21) A broken piece of **ceramic** ware.

poupou (p. 886) In Pacific cultures, a house panel, often carved with designs.

Prairie Style (p. 1061) Style developed by a group of Midwestern architects who worked together using the aesthetic of the prairie and indigenous prairie plants for landscape design to create mostly domestic homes and small public buildings.

predella (p. 557) The base of an **altarpiece**, often decorated with small scenes that are related in subject to that of the main panel or panels.

primitivism (p. 1037) The borrowing of subjects or forms, usually from non-European or prehistoric sources, by Western artists in an attempt to infuse work with expressive qualities attributed to other cultures, especially colonized cultures.

pronaos (p. 110) The enclosed vestibule of a Greek or Roman temple, found in front of the **cella** and marked by a row of **columns** at the entrance.

proscenium (p. 151) The stage of an ancient Greek or Roman theater. In a modern theater, the area of the stage in front of the curtain. Also: the framing **arch** that separates a stage from the audience.

psalter (p. 260) In Jewish and Christian scripture, a book of the Psalms (songs) attributed to King David.

psykter (p. 127) An ancient Greek vessel with an extended base to allow it to float in a larger **krater**; used to chill wine.

putto (*pl.* **putti**) (p. 228) A plump, naked little boy, often winged. In Classical art, called a cupid; in Christian art, a cherub.

pylon (p. 66) A massive gateway formed by a pair of tapering walls of oblong shape. Erected by ancient Egyptians to mark the entrance to a temple complex.

qibla (p. 274) The **mosque** wall oriented toward Mecca; indicated by the *mihrab*.

quatrefoil (p. 520) A four-lobed decorative pattern common in Gothic art and architecture.

quillwork (p. 861) A Native American technique in which the quills of porcupines and bird feathers are dyed and attached to materials in patterns.

radiometric dating (p. 12) Archaeological method of **absolute dating** by measuring the degree to which radioactive materials have degenerated over time. For dating organic (plant or animal) materials, one radiometric method measures a carbon isotope called radiocarbon, or carbon-14.

raigo (p. 382) A painted image that depicts the Amida Buddha and other Buddhist deities welcoming the soul of a dying believer to paradise.

raku (p. 838) A type of **ceramic** made by hand, coated with a thick, dark **glaze**, and fired at a low heat. The resulting vessels are irregularly shaped and glazed and are highly prized for use in the Japanese tea ceremony.

readymade (p. 913) An object from popular or material culture presented without further manipulation as an artwork by the artist.

récupération (p. 913) A French term for the West African method of using found objects to make fine-art sculptures and installations.

red-figure (p. 120) A technique of ancient Greek **ceramic** decoration characterized by red clay-colored figures on a black background. The figures are reserved against a painted ground and details are drawn, not engraved; compare **black-figure**.

register (p. 30) A device used in systems of spatial definition. In painting, a register indicates the use of differing ground-lines to differentiate layers of space within an image. In **relief sculpture**, the placement of self-contained bands of reliefs in a vertical arrangement.

registration marks (p. 843) In Japanese **woodblock prints**, two marks carved on the blocks to indicate proper alignment of the paper during the printing process. In multicolor printing, which used a separate block for each color, these marks were essential for achieving the proper position or registration of the colors.

relative dating (p. 12) Archaeological process of determining relative chronological relationships among excavated objects. Compare **absolute dating**.

relic (p. 226) Venerated object or body part associated with a holy figure, such as a saint, and usually housed in a **reliquary**.

relief sculpture (p. 5) A three-dimensional image or design whose flat background surface is carved away to a certain depth, setting off the figure. Called *high* or *low (bas-) relief* depending upon the extent of projection of the image from the background. Called *sunken relief* when the image is carved below the original surface of the background, which is not cut away.

reliquary (p. 371) A container, often elaborate and made of precious materials, used as a repository for sacred relics.

repoussé (p. 93) A technique of pushing or hammering metal from the back to create a protruding image. Elaborate reliefs are created by pressing or hammering metal sheets against carved wooden forms.

rhyton (p. 90) A vessel in the shape of a figure or an animal, used for drinking or pouring liquids on special occasions.

rib vault (p. 511) See under **vault**.

ridgepole (p. 17) A longitudinal timber at the apex of a roof that supports the upper ends of the rafters.

roof comb (p. 396) In a Maya building, a masonry wall along the apex of a roof that is built above the level of the roof proper. Roof combs support the highly decorated false **façades** that rise above the height of the building at the front.

rose window (p. 516) A round window, often filled with stained glass set into tracery patterns in the form of wheel spokes, found in the **façades** of the **naves** and **transepts** of large Gothic churches.

rosette (p. 108) A round or oval ornament resembling a rose.

rotunda (p. 197) Any building (or part thereof) constructed in a circular (or sometimes polygonal) shape, usually producing a large open space crowned by a **dome**.

round arch (p. 171) See under **arch**.

roundel (p. 161) Any ornamental element with a circular format, often placed as a decoration on the exterior of a building.

rune stone (p. 452) In early medieval northern Europe, a stone used as a commemorative monument and carved or inscribed with runes, a writing system used by early Germanic peoples.

rustication (p. 614) In architecture, the rough, irregular, and unfinished effect deliberately given to the exterior facing of a stone edifice. Rusticated stones are often large and used for decorative emphasis around doors or windows, or across the entire lower floors of a building.

sacra conversazione (p. 642) Italian for "holy conversation." Refers to a type of religious painting developed in fifteenth-century Florence in which a central image of the Virgin and Child is flanked by standing saints of comparable size who stand within the same spatial setting and often acknowledge each other's presence.

salon (p. 923) A large room for entertaining guests or a periodic social or intellectual gathering, often of prominent people, held in such a room. Also: a hall or **gallery** for exhibiting works of art.

sanctuary (p. 105) A sacred or holy enclosure used for worship. In ancient Greece and Rome, consisted of one or more temples and an altar. In Christian architecture, the space around the altar in a church called the chancel or presbytery.

sarcophagus (*pl.* **sarcophagi**) (p. 49) A stone coffin. Often rectangular and decorated with **relief sculpture**.

scarab (p. 51) In ancient Egypt, a stylized dung beetle associated with the sun and the god Amun.

scarification (p. 413) Ornamental decoration applied to the surface of the body by cutting the skin for cultural and/or aesthetic reasons.

school of artists or **painting** (p. 288) An art historical term describing a group of artists, usually working at the same time and sharing similar styles, influences, and ideals. The artists in a particular school may not necessarily be directly associated with one another, unlike those in a workshop or **atelier**.

scriptorium (*pl.* **scriptoria**) (p. 248) A room in a monastery for writing or copying **manuscripts**.

scroll painting (p. 352) A painting executed on a flexible support with rollers at each end. The rollers permit the horizontal scroll to be unrolled as it is studied or the vertical scroll to be hung for contemplation or decoration.

sculpture in the round (p. 5) Three-dimensional sculpture that is carved free of any background or block. Compare **relief sculpture**.

serdab (p. 54) In ancient Egyptian tombs, the small room in which the *ka* statue was placed.

sfumato (p. 650) Italian term meaning "smoky," soft, and mellow. In painting, the effect of haze in an image. Resembling the color of the atmosphere at dusk, *sfumato* gives a smoky effect.

sgraffito (p. 615) Decoration made by incising or cutting away a surface layer of material to reveal a different color beneath.

shaft (p. 111) The main vertical section of a **column** between the **capital** and the base, usually circular in cross section.

shaft grave (p. 98) A deep pit used for burial.

shikhara (p. 306) In the architecture of northern India, a conical (or pyramidal) spire found atop a Hindu temple and often crowned with an *amalaka*.

shoin (p. 835) A term used to describe the various features found in the most formal room of upper-class Japanese residential architecture.

shoji (p. 835) A standing Japanese screen covered in translucent rice paper and used in interiors.

siapo (p. 889) A type of *tapa* cloth found in Samoa and still used as an important gift for ceremonial occasions.

silkscreen printing (p. 1107) A technique of printing in which paint or ink is pressed through a stencil and specially prepared cloth to reproduce a design in multiple copies.

silverpoint (p. 591) A drawing technique using a stylus with a sharp silver tip to produce very fine, precise lines.

sinopia (*pl.* **sinopie**) (p. 551) Italian word taken from Sinope, the ancient city in Asia Minor that was famous for its red-brick pigment. In **fresco** paintings, a full-sized, preliminary sketch done in this color on the first rough coat of plaster or *arriccio*.

site-specific (p. 895) Commissioned and/or designed for a particular location.

skeuomorph (p. 427) A decorative object or design that mimics elements from a predecessor object that were integral to the function or structure of the predecessor.

slip (p. 120) A mixture of clay and water applied to a **ceramic** object as a final decorative coat. Also: a solution that binds different parts of a vessel together, such as the handle and the main body.

spandrel (p. 171) The area of wall adjoining the exterior curve of an **arch** between its **springing** and the **keystone**, or the area between two arches, as in an **arcade**.

spolia (p. 227) Fragments of older architecture or sculpture reused in a secondary context. Latin for "hide stripped from an animal."

springing (p. 171) The point at which the curve of an **arch** or **vault** meets with and rises from its support.

squinch (p. 241) An **arch** or **lintel** built across the upper corners of a square space, allowing a circular or polygonal **dome** to be securely set above the walls.

stained glass (p. 293) Glass stained with color while molten, using metallic oxides. Stained glass is most often used in windows, for which small pieces of different colors are precisely cut and assembled into a design, held together by lead **cames**. Additional details may be added with vitreous paint.

stave church (p. 453) A Scandinavian wooden structure with four huge timbers (staves) at its core.

stele (*pl.* **stelai**), also **stela** (*pl.* **stelae**) (p. 27) A stone slab placed vertically and decorated with inscriptions or reliefs. Used as a grave marker or commemorative monument.

stereobate (p. 111) In Classical architecture, the foundation upon which a temple stands.

still life (*pl.* **still lifes**) (p. xxx) A type of painting that has as its subject inanimate objects (such as food and dishes) or fruit and flowers taken out of their natural contexts.

stoa (p. 109) In Greek architecture, a long roofed walkway, usually having **columns** on one long side and a wall on the other.

stoneware (p. 21) A high-fired, vitrified, but opaque **ceramic** ware that is fired in the range of 1,200 to 1,400 degrees Centigrade. At that temperature, particles of silica in the clay bodies fuse together so that the finished vessels are impervious to liquids, even without glaze. Stoneware pieces are glazed to enhance their aesthetic appeal and to aid in keeping them clean. Stoneware occurs in a range of earth-toned colors, from white and tan to gray and black, with light gray predominating. Chinese potters were the first in the world to produce stoneware, which they were able to make as early as the Shang dynasty.

stringcourse (p. 517) A continuous horizontal band, such as a **molding**, decorating the face of a wall.

stucco (p. 74) A mixture of lime, sand, and other ingredients made into a material that can easily be molded or modeled. When dry, it produces a durable surface used for covering walls or for architectural sculpture and decoration.

stupa (p. 306) In Buddhist architecture, a bell-shaped or dome-like religious monument, made of piled earth, brick, or stone, and containing sacred **relics**.

style (p. xxxiii) A particular manner, form, or character of representation, construction, or expression that is typical of an individual artist or of a certain place or period.

stylobate (p. 111) In Classical architecture, the stone foundation on which a temple **colonnade** stands.

stylus (p. 29) An instrument with a pointed end (used for writing and printmaking), which makes a delicate line or scratch. Also: a special writing tool for **cuneiform** writing with one pointed end and one triangular.

sublime (p. 973) Of a concept, thing, or state of greatness or vastness with high spiritual, moral, intellectual, or emotional value; or something awe-inspiring. The sublime was a goal to which many nineteenth-century artists aspired in their artworks.

sunken relief (p. 73) See under **relief sculpture**.

symposium (p. 121) An elite gathering of wealthy and powerful men in ancient Greece that focused principally on wine, music, poetry, conversation, games, and love-making.

syncretism (p. 222) A process whereby artists assimilate and combine images and ideas from different cultural traditions, beliefs, and practices, giving them new meanings.

taotie (p. 338) A mask with a dragon- or animal-like face common as a decorative motif in Chinese art.

tapa (p. 889) A type of cloth used for various purposes in Pacific cultures, made from tree bark stripped and beaten, and often bearing subtle designs from the mallets used to work the bark.

tapestry (p. 295) Multicolored decorative weaving to be hung on a wall or placed on furniture. Pictorial or decorative motifs are woven directly into the supporting fabric, completely concealing it.

tatami (p. 835) Mats of woven straw used in Japanese houses as a floor covering.

temenos (p. 110) An enclosed sacred area reserved for worship in ancient Greece.

tempera (p. 144) A painting **medium** made by blending egg yolks with water, pigments, and occasionally other materials, such as glue.

tenebrism (p. 738) The use of strong *chiaroscuro* and artificially illuminated areas to create a dramatic contrast of light and dark in a painting.

terra cotta (p. 116) A **medium** made from clay fired over a low heat and sometimes left unglazed. Also: the orange–brown color typical of this medium.

tessera (*pl.* **tesserae**) (p. 148) A small piece of stone, glass, or other object that is pieced together with many others to create a **mosaic**.

thatch (p. 17) Plant material such as reeds or straw tied over a framework of poles to make a roof, shelter, or small building.

thermo-luminescence dating (p. 13) A method of **radiometric dating** that measures the irradiation of the crystal structure of material such as flint or pottery and the soil in which it is found, determined by how much a sample glows when it is heated.

tholos (p. 100) A small, round building. Sometimes built underground, as, for example, with a Mycenaean tomb.

thrust (p. 171) The outward pressure caused by the weight of a **vault** and supported by **buttressing**. See also under **arch**.

tondo (*pl.* **tondi**) (p. 128) A painting or **relief sculpture** of circular shape.

torana (p. 306) In Indian architecture, an ornamented gateway arch in a temple, usually leading to the **stupa**.

torc (p. 152) A circular neck ring worn by Celtic warriors.

toron (p. 425) In West African **mosque** architecture, one of the wooden beams that project from the walls. Torons are used as support for the scaffolding erected annually for the replastering of the building.

tracery (p. 517) Stonework or woodwork forming a pattern in the open space of windows or applied to wall surfaces. In *plate tracery*, a series of openings are cut through the wall. In *bar tracery*, **mullions** divide the space into segments to form decorative patterns.

transept (p. 226) The arm of a **cruciform** church perpendicular to the **nave**. The point where the nave and transept intersect is called the crossing. Beyond the crossing lies the **sanctuary**, whether **apse**, **choir**, or chevet.

transverse arch (p. 475) See under **arch**.

trefoil (p. 302) An ornamental design made up of three rounded lobes placed adjacent to one another.

triforium (p. 516) The element of the interior elevation of a church found directly below the **clerestory** and consisting of a series of arched openings in front of a passageway within the thickness of the wall.

triglyph (p. 111) Rectangular block between the **metope**s of a Doric **frieze**. Identified by the three carved vertical grooves, which approximate the appearance of the end of wooden beams.

triptych (p. 579) An artwork made up of three panels. The panels may be hinged together in such a way that the side segments (wings) fold over the central area.

trompe l'oeil (p. 587) A manner of representation in which artists faithfully describe the appearance of natural space and forms with the express intention of fooling the eye of the viewer, who may be convinced momentarily that the subject actually exists as three-dimensional reality.

trumeau (p. 491) A **column**, **pier**, or post found at the center of a large **portal** or doorway, supporting the **lintel**.

tugra (p. 293) A calligraphic imperial monogram used in Ottoman courts.

tukutuku (p. 886) Lattice panels created by women from the Maori culture and used in architecture.

Tuscan order (p. 161) See under **order**.

twining (p. 863) A basketry technique in which short rods are sewn together vertically. The panels are then joined together to form a container or other object.

tympanum (p. 491) In medieval and later architecture, the area over a door enclosed by an **arch** and a **lintel**, often decorated with sculpture or mosaic.

ukiyo-e (p. 842) A Japanese term for a type of popular art that was favored from the sixteenth century, particularly in the form of color **woodblock prints**. *Ukiyo-e* prints often depicted the world of the common people in Japan, such as courtesans and actors, as well as landscapes and myths.

undercutting (p. 214) A technique in sculpture by which the material is cut back under the edges so that the remaining form projects strongly forward, casting deep shadows.

underglaze (p. 813) Color or decoration applied to a **ceramic** piece before glazing.

upeti (p. 890) In Pacific cultures, a carved wooden design tablet, used to create patterns in cloth by dragging the fabric across it.

uranium-thorium dating (p. 12) Technique used to date prehistoric cave paintings by measuring the decay of uranium into thorium in the deposits of calcium carbonate that cover the surfaces of cave walls, to determine the minimum age of the paintings under the crust.

urna (p. 311) In Buddhist art, the curl of hair on the forehead that is a characteristic mark of a buddha. The *urna* is a symbol of divine wisdom.

ushnisha (p. 311) In Asian art, a round cranial bump or bun of hair symbolizing royalty and, when worn by a buddha, enlightenment.

vanishing point (p. 623) In a **perspective** system, the point on the **horizon line** at which **orthogonals** meet. A complex system can have multiple vanishing points.

vanitas (p. xxxii) An image, especially popular in Europe during the seventeenth century, in which all the objects symbolize the transience of life. *Vanitas* paintings are usually of **still lifes** or genre subjects.

vault (p. 18) An arched masonry structure that spans an interior space. *Barrel* or *tunnel vault*: an elongated or continuous semicircular vault, shaped like a half-cylinder. *Corbeled vault*: a vault made by projecting **courses** of stone; see also under **corbel**. *Groin* or *cross vault*: a vault created by the intersection of two barrel vaults of equal size which creates four side compartments of identical size and shape. *Quadrant vault*: a half-barrel vault. *Rib vault*: a groin vault with ribs (extra masonry) demarcating the junctions. Ribs may function to reinforce the groins or may be purely decorative.

veduta (*pl.* **vedute**) (p. 931) Italian for "vista" or "view." Paintings, drawings, or prints, often of expansive city scenes or of harbors.

vellum (p. 249) A fine animal skin prepared for writing and painting. See also **parchment**.

verism (p. 169) Style in which artists concern themselves with describing the exterior likeness of an object or person, usually by rendering its visible details in a finely executed, meticulous manner.

vihara (p. 309) From the Sanskrit term meaning "for wanderers." A *vihara* is, in general, a Buddhist monastery in India. It also signifies monks' cells and gathering places in such a monastery.

volute (p. 111) A spiral scroll, as seen on an Ionic **capital**.

votive figure (p. 31) An image created as a devotional offering to a deity.

voussoir (p. 171) Wedge-shaped stone block used to build an **arch**. The topmost voussoir is called a **keystone**. See also **joggled voussoirs**.

warp (p. 295) The vertical threads in a weaver's loom. Warp threads make up a fixed framework that provides the structure for the entire piece of cloth, and are thus often thicker than **weft** threads.

wattle and daub (p. 17) A wall construction method combining upright branches, woven with twigs (wattles) and plastered or filled with clay or mud (daub).

wax print fabric (p. 918) Cotton fabric printed to look like Indonesian batik cloth. Originally made in the Netherlands and exported to African coastal nations during the fifteenth through twenty-first centuries, it is now manufactured around the world, including in many African countries.

weft (p. 295) The horizontal threads in a woven piece of cloth. Weft threads are woven at right angles to and through the **warp** threads to make up the bulk of the decorative pattern. In carpets, the weft is often completely covered or formed by the rows of trimmed knots that form the carpet's soft surface.

westwork (p. 457) The monumental, west-facing entrance section of a Carolingian, Ottonian, or Romanesque church. The exterior consists of multiple stories between two towers; the interior includes an entrance vestibule, a chapel, and a series of **galleries** overlooking the **nave**.

white-ground (p. 143) A type of ancient Greek pottery in which the background color of the object was painted with a **slip** that turns white in the firing process. Figures and details were added by painting on or incising into this slip. White-ground wares were popular in the Classical period as funerary objects.

woodblock print (p. 602) A print made from one or more carved wooden blocks. In Japan, woodblock prints were made using multiple blocks carved in relief, usually with a block for each color in the finished print. See also **woodcut**.

woodcut (p. 602) A type of print made by carving a design into a wooden block. The ink is applied to the block with a roller. As the ink touches only on the surface areas and lines remaining between the carved-away parts of the block, it is these areas that make the print when paper is pressed against the inked block, leaving the carved-away parts of the design to appear blank. Also: the process by which the woodcut is made.

yaksha, yakshi (p. 305) The male (*yaksha*) and female (*yakshi*) nature spirits associated with fertility and abundance. Their sculpted images are often found on Buddhist and Hindu temples and other sacred places, particularly at the entrances.

yamato-e (p. 377) A native style of Japanese painting developed during the twelfth and thirteenth centuries, distinguished from Japanese painting styles that emulated Chinese traditions.

ziggurat (p. 29) In ancient Mesopotamia, a tall stepped tower of earthen materials, often supporting a shrine.

Bibliography

This bibliography is composed of books in English that are suggested "further reading" titles. Most are available in good libraries, whether college, university, or public. Recently published works have been emphasized so that the research information would be current. There are three classifications of listings: general surveys and art history reference tools, including journals and Internet directories; surveys of large periods that encompass multiple chapters (ancient art in the Western tradition, European medieval art, European Renaissance through eighteenth-century art, Modern art in the West, Asian art, African and Oceanic art, and art of the Americas); and books for individual Chapters 1 through 33.

General Art History Surveys and Reference Tools

Adams, Laurie Schneider. *Art Across Time.* 4th ed. New York: McGraw-Hill, 2011.

Barnet, Sylvan. *A Short Guide to Writing about Art.* 11th ed. Upper Saddle River, NJ: Pearson/Prentice Hall, 2010.

Bony, Anne. *Design: History, Main Trends, Main Figures.* Edinburgh: Chambers, 2005.

Boström, Antonia. *Encyclopedia of Sculpture.* 3 vols. New York: Fitzroy Dearborn, 2004.

Broude, Norma, and Mary D. Garrard, eds. *Feminism and Art History: Questioning the Litany.* Icon Editions. New York: Harper & Row, 1982.

Chadwick, Whitney. *Women, Art, and Society.* 4th ed. New York: Thames & Hudson, 2007.

Chilvers, Ian, ed. *The Oxford Dictionary of Art.* 4th ed. New York: Oxford Univ. Press, 2009.

Curl, James Stevens. *A Dictionary of Architecture and Landscape Architecture.* 2nd ed. Oxford: Oxford Univ. Press, 2006.

Davies, Penelope J.E., et al. *Janson's History of Art: The Western Tradition.* 8th ed. Upper Saddle River, NJ: Prentice Hall, 2010.

The Dictionary of Art. Ed. Jane Turner. 34 vols. New York: Grove's Dictionaries, 1996.

Frank, Patrick, Duane Preble, and Sarah Preble. *Prebles' Artforms.* 10th ed. Upper Saddle River, NJ: Pearson/ Prentice Hall, 2011.

Gaze, Delia, ed. *Dictionary of Women Artists.* 2 vols. London: Fitzroy Dearborn, 1997.

Griffiths, Antony. *Prints and Printmaking: An Introduction to the History and Techniques.* 2nd ed. London: British Museum Press, 1996.

Hadden, Peggy. *The Quotable Artist.* New York: Allworth Press, 2002.

Hall, James. *Dictionary of Subjects and Symbols in Art.* 2nd ed. Boulder, CO: Westview Press, 2008.

Holt, Elizabeth Gilmore, ed. *A Documentary History of Art.* 3 vols. New Haven: Yale Univ. Press, 1986.

Honour, Hugh, and John Fleming. *The Visual Arts: A History.* 7th ed. rev. Upper Saddle River, NJ: Pearson/ Prentice Hall, 2010.

Johnson, Paul. *Art: A New History.* New York: HarperCollins, 2003.

Kemp, Martin, ed. *The Oxford History of Western Art.* Oxford: Oxford Univ. Press, 2000.

Kleiner, Fred S. *Gardner's Art through the Ages.* Enhanced 15th ed. Belmont, CA: Thomson/ Wadsworth, 2011.

Kostof, Spiro. *A History of Architecture: Settings and Rituals.* 2nd ed. Revised Greg Castillo. New York: Oxford Univ. Press, 1995.

Levenson, Jay A., ed. *Circa 1492: Art in the Age of Exploration.* New Haven: Yale Univ. Press and the National Gallery of Art, Washington, DC, 1991.

MacGregor, Neil. *A History of the World in 100 Objects.* New York: Penguin Books, 2013.

Mackenzie, Lynn. *Non-Western Art: A Brief Guide.* 2nd ed. Upper Saddle River, NJ: Pearson/Prentice Hall, 2001.

Marmor, Max, and Alex Ross, eds. *Guide to the Literature of Art History 2.* Chicago: American Library Association, 2005.

Onians, John, ed. *Atlas of World Art.* New York: Oxford Univ. Press, 2004.

Sayre, Henry M. *Writing about Art.* 6th ed. Upper Saddle River, NJ: Pearson/Prentice Hall, 2009.

Sed-Rajna, Gabrielle. *Jewish Art.* Trans. Sara Friedman and Mira Reich. New York: Abrams, 1997.

Slatkin, Wendy. *Women Artists in History: From Antiquity to the Present.* 4th ed. Upper Saddle River, NJ: Pearson/ Prentice Hall, 2001.

Sutton, Ian. *Western Architecture: From Ancient Greece to the Present.* World of Art. New York: Thames & Hudson, 1999.

Trachtenberg, Marvin, and Isabelle Hyman. *Architecture, from Prehistory to Postmodernity.* 2nd ed. Upper Saddle River, NJ: Pearson/ Prentice Hall, 2002.

Tucker, Amy. *Visual Literacy: Writing about Art.* Boston: McGraw-Hill, 2002.

Watkin, David. *A History of Western Architecture.* 4th ed. New York: Watson-Guptill, 2005.

Art History Journals: A Selected List of Current Titles

African Arts. Quarterly. Los Angeles: Univ. of California at Los Angeles, James S. Coleman African Studies Center, 1967–.

American Art: The Journal of the Smithsonian American Art Museum. 3/year. Chicago: Univ. of Chicago Press, 1987–.

American Journal of Archaeology. Quarterly. Boston: Archaeological Institute of America, 1885–.

Antiquity: A Periodical of Archaeology. Quarterly. Cambridge: Antiquity Publications Ltd., 1927–.

Apollo: The International Magazine of the Arts. Monthly. London: Apollo Magazine Ltd., 1925–.

Archaeology Magazine. Bimonthly. New York: Archaeological Institute of America, 1948–.

Architectural History. Annually. Farnham, UK: Society of Architectural Historians of Great Britain, 1958–.

Archives of American Art Journal. Quarterly. Washington, DC: Archives of American Art, Smithsonian Institution, 1960–.

Archives of Asian Art. Annually. New York: Asia Society, 1945–.

Ars Orientalis: The Arts of Asia, Southeast Asia, and Islam. Annually. Ann Arbor: Univ. of Michigan Dept. of Art History, 1954–.

Art Bulletin. Quarterly. New York: College Art Association, 1913–.

Art History: Journal of the Association of Art Historians. 5/year. Oxford: Blackwell Publishing Ltd., 1978–.

Art in America. Monthly. New York: Brant Publications Inc., 1913–.

Art Journal. Quarterly. New York: College Art Association, 1960–.

The Art Newspaper. Monthly. London and New York: The Art Newspaper, 1990–.

Art Nexus. Quarterly. Bogota, Colombia: Arte en Colombia Ltda, 1976–.

Art Papers Magazine. Bimonthly. Atlanta: Atlanta Art Papers Inc., 1976–.

Artforum International. 10/year. New York: Artforum International Magazine Inc., 1962–.

Artibus Asiae. Biannually. Zürich: Museum Rietberg, 1925–.

Artnews. 11/year. New York: Artnews LLC, 1902–.

Bulletin of the Metropolitan Museum of Art. Quarterly. New York: Metropolitan Museum of Art, 1905–.

The Burlington Magazine. Monthly. London: Burlington Magazine Publications Ltd., 1903–.

Dumbarton Oaks Papers. Annually. Locust Valley, NY: J.J. Augustin Inc., 1940–.

Flash Art International. Bimonthly. Trevi, Italy: Giancarlo Politi Editore, 1980–.

Gesta. Semiannually. New York: International Center of Medieval Art, 1963–.

History of Photography. Quarterly. Abingdon, UK: Taylor & Francis Ltd., 1976–.

International Review of African American Art. Quarterly. Hampton, VA: International Review of African American Art, 1976–.

Journal of the American Research Center in Egypt. Annually. San Antonio: The American Research Center in Egypt, 1962–.

Journal of Design History. Quarterly. Oxford: Oxford Univ. Press, 1988–.

Journal of Egyptian Archaeology. Annually. London: Egypt Exploration Society, 1914–.

Journal of Hellenic Studies. Annually. London: Society for the Promotion of Hellenic Studies, 1880–.

Journal of Roman Archaeology. Annually. Portsmouth, RI: Journal of Roman Archaeology LLC, 1988–.

Journal of the Society of Architectural Historians. Quarterly. Chicago: Society of Architectural Historians, 1940–.

Journal of the Warburg and Courtauld Institutes. Annually. London: Warburg Institute, 1937–.

Leonardo: Art, Science, and Technology. 6/year. Cambridge, MA: MIT Press, 1968–.

Marg. Quarterly. Mumbai, India: Scientific Publishers, 1946–.

Master Drawings. Quarterly. New York: Master Drawings Association, 1963–.

Muqarnas. Annually. Cambridge, MA: E.J. Brill, 1983–.

October. Cambridge, MA: MIT Press, 1976–.

Oxford Art Journal. 3/year. Oxford: Oxford Univ. Press, 1978–.

Parkett. 3/year. Zürich, Switzerland: Parkett Verlag AG, 1984–.

Print Quarterly. Quarterly. London: Print Quarterly Publications, 1984–.

Simiolus: Netherlands Quarterly for the History of Art. Quarterly. Apeldoorn, Netherlands: Stichting voor Nederlandse Kunsthistorische Publicaties, 1966–.

Source: Notes in the History of Art. Quarterly. Chicago: Univ. of Chicago Press, 1981–.

Studies in Iconography. Annually. Kalamazoo: Medieval Institute Publications, Western Michigan Univ., 1993–.

Woman's Art Journal. Semiannually. Philadelphia: Old City Publishing Inc., 1980–.

Internet Directories for Art History Information: A Selected List

ALBERTI'S WINDOW: AN ART HISTORY BLOG,
http://albertis-window.com
Maintained by art historian Monica Bowen, this blog provides interesting and accessible posts for those curious about the history of art of various cultures and periods.

ARCHITECTURE AND BUILDING,
http://www.library.unlv.edu/arch/rsrce/webresources/
A directory of architecture websites collected by Jeanne Brown at the Univ. of Nevada at Las Vegas. Topical lists include architecture, building and construction, design, history, housing, planning, preservation, and landscape architecture. Most entries include a brief annotation and the last date the link was accessed by the compiler.

ART HISTORY RESOURCES ON THE WEB,
http://witcombe.sbc.edu/ARTHLinks.html
Authored by Professor Christopher L.C.E. Witcombe of Sweet Briar College in Virginia since 1995, the site includes an impressive number of links for various art historical eras as well as links to research resources, museums, and galleries. The content is frequently updated.

THE ART STORY,
http://www.theartstory.org
Dedicated to demonstrating the significance of modern and contemporary art, this site includes topic pages on the important artists, movements, and ideas from the mid nineteenth to the twenty-first century, as well as timelines and a blog with frequent posts examining a variety of related topics.

ART THROUGH TIME: A GLOBAL VIEW,
http://www.learner.org/courses/globalart/
Developed by Annenberg Learner, this 13-part series is a thematic and global overview of the history of art. The website makes use of videos, images, and text for each of the themes, which include the body, conflict, portraits, death, belief, cultures, dreams, history, ceremony, writing, domestic life, the natural world, and urban experience.

ART21,
http://www.art21.org/
Devoted to chronicling contemporary art and artists, this site provides access to films, articles, interviews, and other interpretive resources in order to introduce the public to contemporary art and the creative process.

ARTBABBLE,
http://www.artbabble.org/
An online community created by staff at the Indianapolis Museum of Art to showcase art-based video content, including interviews with artists and curators, original documentaries, and art installation videos. Partners and contributors to the project include ART21, Los Angeles County Museum of Art, the Museum of Modern Art, the New York Public Library, San Francisco Museum of Modern Art, and Smithsonian American Art Museum.

ARTCYCLOPEDIA: THE GUIDE TO GREAT ART ON THE INTERNET,
http://www.artcyclopedia.com
With more than 2,100 art sites and 75,000 links, this is one of the most comprehensive Web directories for artists and art topics. The primary search is by artist's name but access is also available by title of artwork, artistic movement, museum and gallery, nationality, period, and medium.

ARTSTOR,
http://www.artstor.org
Created by the Andrew W. Mellon Foundation, Artstor is a digital library of more than 1.9 million images for educational and research purposes gathered from institutions and databases around the world. The site also provides instructor resources, including curriculum and subject guides as well as tools for sharing and downloading images.

ARTSY,
https://www.artsy.net
With the goal of making the world's art accessible online, Artsy provides a rapidly expanding image database for works of art, design, and architecture from galleries, museums, estates, auctions, art fairs, and foundations. Especially strong in contemporary art and collecting, this site also continues to develop its pool of historical images and educational resources, including lesson plans.

EUROPEANA COLLECTIONS,
http://www.europeana.eu/portal/
Excellent for accessing more than 48 million European artworks, artifacts, videos, and books, this site offers compilations of collections by theme, period, location, or artist as well as online curated exhibitions, blog posts, and eBooks.

THE GETTY,
http://www.getty.edu/museum/index.html
The J. Paul Getty Museum's website is a great resource with access to the archived collection with thousands of downloadable images, art-historical research databases, and videos exploring works and themes related to the collection, conservation, and exhibitions.

GOOGLE ART PROJECT,
https://www.google.com/culturalinstitute/u/0/project/art-project
In 2011, Google launched this site in order to make the world's cultural heritage and objects more widely accessible for a global audience. Since then, they have compiled more than 700 digitized collections worldwide and have partnered with more than 850 institutions to provide access to high-resolution images and curated digital exhibitions.

HEILBRUNN TIMELINE OF ART HISTORY,
http://www.metmuseum.org/toah/
Illustrating the Metropolitan Museum of Art's collection, this resource compiles essays and images alongside chronologies to narrate the global history of art and culture. Includes the option to search for content by time period, region, or theme.

THE MODERN ART NOTES PODCAST,
https://manpodcast.com/
Hosted and produced by the historian and award-winning art critic Tyler Green, the MAN Podcast features hour-long interviews with artists, art historians, authors, curators, and conservators each week to discuss their work and topics current in the art world.

MoMA LEARNING,
http://www.moma.org/learn/moma_learning
The Museum of Modern Art's online resources for approaching modern and contemporary art. Organized by theme or artist, this site compiles lesson plans, PowerPoints, worksheets, and videos to engage students with the art in MoMA's collection.

MOTHER OF ALL ART AND ART HISTORY LINKS PAGES,
http://umich.edu/~motherha
Maintained by the Dept. of the History of Art at the Univ. of Michigan, this directory covers art history departments, art museums, and fine-arts schools and departments, as well as links to research resources. Each entry includes annotations.

VOICE OF THE SHUTTLE,
http://vos.ucsb.edu
Sponsored by Univ. of California, Santa Barbara, this directory includes more than 70 pages of links to humanities and humanities-related resources on the Internet. The structured guide includes specific subsections on architecture, on art (modern and contemporary), and on art history. Links usually include a one-sentence explanation, and the resource is frequently updated with new information.

Ancient Art in the Western Tradition, General

Amiet, Pierre. *Art in the Ancient World: A Handbook of Styles and Forms.* New York: Rizzoli, 1981.

Beard, Mary, and John Henderson. *Classical Art: From Greece to Rome.* Oxford History of Art. Oxford: Oxford Univ. Press, 2001.

Boardman, John. *Oxford History of Classical Art.* New York: Oxford Univ. Press, 2001.

Chitham, Robert. *The Classical Orders of Architecture.* 2nd ed. Boston: Elsevier/ Architectural Press, 2005.

Ehrich, Robert W., ed. *Chronologies in Old World Archaeology.* 3rd ed. 2 vols. Chicago: Univ. of Chicago Press, 1992.

Gerster, Georg. *The Past from Above: Aerial Photographs of Archaeological Sites.* Ed. Charlotte Trümpler. Trans. Stewart Spencer. Los Angeles: J. Paul Getty Museum, 2005.

Groenewegen-Frankfort, H.A., and Bernard Ashmole. *Art of the Ancient World: Painting, Pottery, Sculpture, Architecture from Egypt, Mesopotamia, Crete, Greece, and Rome.* Library of Art History. Upper Saddle River, NJ: Prentice Hall, 1972.

Haywood, John. *The Penguin Historical Atlas of Ancient Civilizations.* New York: Penguin, 2005.

Milleker, Elizabeth J., ed. *The Year One: Art of the Ancient World East and West.* New York: Metropolitan Museum of Art, 2000.

Nagle, D. Brendan. *The Ancient World: A Social and Cultural History.* 7th ed. Upper Saddle River, NJ: Pearson/ Prentice Hall, 2010.

Saggs, H.W.F. *Civilization before Greece and Rome.* New Haven: Yale Univ. Press, 1989.

Smith, William Stevenson. *Interconnections in the Ancient Near East: A Study of the Relationships between the Arts of Egypt, the Aegean, and Western Asia.* New Haven: Yale Univ. Press, 1965.

Tadgell, Christopher. *Imperial Form: From Achaemenid Iran to Augustan Rome.* New York: Whitney Library of Design, 1998.

———. *Origins: Egypt, West Asia, and the Aegean.* New York: Whitney Library of Design, 1998.

Trigger, Bruce G. *Understanding Early Civilizations: A Comparative Study.* New York: Cambridge Univ. Press, 2003.

Woodford, Susan. *The Art of Greece and Rome.* 2nd ed. New York: Cambridge Univ. Press, 2004.

European Medieval Art, General

Backman, Clifford R. *The Worlds of Medieval Europe.* 2nd ed. New York: Oxford Univ. Press, 2009.

Bennett, Adelaide Louise, et al. *Medieval Mastery: Book Illumination from Charlemagne to Charles the Bold: 800– 1475.* Trans. Lee Preedy and Greta Arblaster-Holmer. Turnhout: Brepols, 2002.

Benton, Janetta R. *Art of the Middle Ages.* World of Art. New York: Thames & Hudson, 2002.

Binski, Paul. *Painters.* Medieval Craftsmen. London: British Museum Press, 1991.

Brown, Sarah, and David O'Connor. *Glass-painters.* Medieval Craftsmen. London: British Museum Press, 1991.

Calkins, Robert G. *Medieval Architecture in Western Europe: From A.D. 300 to 1500.* New York: Oxford Univ. Press, 1998.

Cherry, John F. *Goldsmiths.* Medieval Craftsmen. London: British Museum Press, 1992.

Clark, William W. *The Medieval Cathedrals.* Westport, CT: Greenwood Press, 2006.

Coldstream, Nicola. *Masons and Sculptors.* Medieval Craftsmen. London: British Museum Press, 1991.

———. *Medieval Architecture.* Oxford History of Art. Oxford: Oxford Univ. Press, 2002.

De Hamel, Christopher. *Scribes and Illuminators.* Medieval Craftsmen. London: British Museum Press, 1992.

Duby, Georges. *Art and Society in the Middle Ages.* Trans. Jean Birrell. Malden, MA: Blackwell, 2000.

Fossier, Robert, ed. *The Cambridge Illustrated History of the Middle Ages.* Trans. Janet

Sondheimer and Sarah Hanbury Tenison. 3 vols. Cambridge: Cambridge Univ. Press, 1986–97.

Hoffman, Eva R., ed. *Late Antique and Medieval Art of the Mediterranean World.* Malden, MA: Blackwell Publishing Ltd., 2007.

Hürlimann, Martin, and Jean Bony. *French Cathedrals.* Rev. & enlarged ed. London: Thames & Hudson, 1967.

Jotischky, Andrew, and Caroline Susan Hull. *The Penguin Historical Atlas of the Medieval World.* New York: Penguin, 2005.

Kenyon, John. *Medieval Fortifications.* Leicester: Leicester Univ. Press, 1990.

Pfaffenbichler, Matthias. *Armourers.* Medieval Craftsmen. London: British Museum Press, 1992.

Rebold Benton, Janetta. *Art of the Middle Ages.* World of Art. New York: Thames & Hudson, 2002.

Rudolph, Conrad, ed. *A Companion to Medieval Art.* Blackwell Companions to Art History. Oxford: Blackwell, 2006.

Sekules, Veronica. *Medieval Art.* Oxford History of Art. New York: Oxford Univ. Press, 2001.

Snyder, James, Henry Luttikhuizen, and Dorothy Verkerk. *Art of the Middle Ages.* 2nd ed. Upper Saddle River, NJ: Pearson/ Prentice Hall, 2006.

Staniland, Kay. *Embroiderers.* Medieval Craftsmen. London: British Museum Press, 1991.

Stokstad, Marilyn. *Medieval Art.* 2nd ed. Boulder, CO: Westview Press, 2004.

———. *Medieval Castles.* Greenwood Guides to Historic Events of the Medieval World. Westport, CT: Greenwood Press, 2005.

European Renaissance through Eighteenth-Century Art, General

Black, C.F., et al. *Cultural Atlas of the Renaissance.* New York: Prentice Hall, 1993.

Blunt, Anthony. *Art and Architecture in France, 1500–1700.* 5th ed. Revised Richard Beresford. Pelican History of Art. New Haven: Yale Univ. Press, 1999.

Brown, Jonathan. *Painting in Spain: 1500–1700.* Pelican History of Art. New Haven: Yale Univ. Press, 1998.

Campbell, Stephen J., and Michael W. Cole. *Italian Renaissance Art.* New York: Thames & Hudson, 2014.

Cole, Bruce. *Studies in the History of Italian Art, 1250–1550.* London: Pindar Press, 1996.

Graham-Dixon, Andrew. *Renaissance.* Berkeley: Univ. of California Press, 1999.

Harbison, Craig. *The Mirror of the Artist: Northern Renaissance Art in Its Historical Context.* Perspectives. New York: Abrams, 1995.

Harris, Ann Sutherland. *Seventeenth-Century Art & Architecture.* 2nd ed. Upper Saddle River, NJ: Pearson/ Prentice Hall, 2008.

Harrison, Charles, Paul Wood, and Jason Gaiger. *Art in Theory 1648–1815: An Anthology of Changing Ideas.* Oxford: Blackwell, 2000.

Hartt, Frederick, and David G. Wilkins. *History of Italian Renaissance Art: Painting, Sculpture, Architecture*. 7th ed. Upper Saddle River, NJ: Pearson/Prentice Hall, 2011.

Jestaz, Bertrand. *The Art of the Renaissance*. Trans. I. Mark Paris. New York: Abrams, 1994.

Minor, Vernon Hyde. *Baroque & Rococo: Art & Culture*. New York: Abrams, 1999.

Paoletti, John T., and Gary M. Radke. *Art in Renaissance Italy*. 3rd ed. Upper Saddle River, NJ: Pearson/Prentice Hall, 2005.

Smith, Jeffrey Chipps. *The Northern Renaissance*. Art & Ideas. London and New York: Phaidon Press, 2004.

Stechow, Wolfgang. *Northern Renaissance, 1400–1600: Sources and Documents*. Upper Saddle River, NJ: Pearson/ Prentice Hall, 1966.

Summerson, John. *Architecture in Britain, 1530–1830*. 9th ed. Pelican History of Art. New Haven: Yale Univ. Press, 1993.

Waterhouse, Ellis K. *Painting in Britain, 1530–1790*. 5th ed. Pelican History of Art. New Haven: Yale Univ. Press, 1994.

Whinney, Margaret Dickens. *Sculpture in Britain: 1530–1830*. 2nd ed. Revised John Physick. Pelican History of Art. London: Penguin, 1988.

Modern Art in the West, General

Arnason, H.H., and Elizabeth C. Mansfield. *History of Modern Art: Painting, Sculpture, Architecture, Photography*. 6th ed. Upper Saddle River, NJ: Pearson/Prentice Hall, 2009.

Ballantyne, Andrew, ed. *Architectures: Modernism and After*. New Interventions in Art History, 3. Malden, MA: Blackwell, 2004.

Barnitz, Jacqueline. *Twentieth-Century Art of Latin America*. Austin: Univ. of Texas Press, 2001.

Bjelajac, David. *American Art: A Cultural History*. Rev. and expanded ed. Upper Saddle River, NJ: Pearson/Prentice Hall, 2005.

Bowness, Alan. *Modern European Art*. World of Art. New York: Thames & Hudson, 1995.

Brettell, Richard R. *Modern Art, 1851–1929: Capitalism and Representation*. Oxford History of Art. Oxford: Oxford Univ. Press, 1999.

Chipp, Herschel B. *Theories of Modern Art: A Source Book by Artists and Critics*. California Studies in the History of Art, 11. Berkeley: Univ. of California Press, 1984.

Clarke, Graham. *The Photograph*. Oxford History of Art. Oxford: Oxford Univ. Press, 1997.

Craven, David. *Art and Revolution in Latin America, 1910–1990*. New Haven: Yale Univ. Press, 2002.

Craven, Wayne. *American Art: History and Culture*. 2nd ed. Boston: McGraw-Hill, 2003.

Doordan, Dennis P. *Twentieth-Century Architecture*. New York: Abrams, 2002.

Doss, Erika. *Twentieth-Century American Art*. Oxford History of Art. Oxford: Oxford Univ. Press, 2002.

Edwards, Steve, and Paul Wood, eds. *Art of the Avant-Gardes*. Art of the 20th Century. New Haven: Yale Univ. Press, 2004.

Foster, Hal, et al. *Art Since 1900: Modernism, Antimodernism, Postmodernism*. New York: Thames & Hudson, 2004.

Gaiger, Jason, ed. *Frameworks for Modern Art*. Art of the 20th Century. New Haven: Yale Univ. Press, 2003.

———, and Paul Wood, eds. *Art of the Twentieth Century: A Reader*. New Haven: Yale Univ. Press, 2003.

Hamilton, George Heard. *Painting and Sculpture in Europe, 1880–1940*. 6th ed. Pelican History of Art. New Haven: Yale Univ. Press, 1993.

Hammacher, A.M. *Modern Sculpture: Tradition and Innovation*. Enl. ed. New York: Abrams, 1988.

Harris, Ann Sutherland, and Linda Nochlin. *Women Artists: 1550–1950*. Los Angeles: Los Angeles County Museum of Art, 1976.

Harrison, Charles, and Paul Wood, eds. *Art in Theory: 1900–2000*: An Anthology of Changing Ideas. 2nd ed. Malden, MA: Blackwell, 2003.

Hunter, Sam, John Jacobus, and Daniel Wheeler. *Modern Art: Painting, Sculpture, Architecture, Photography*. 3rd rev. & exp. ed. Upper Saddle River, NJ: Pearson/Prentice Hall, 2004.

Krauss, Rosalind E. *Passages in Modern Sculpture*. Cambridge, MA: MIT Press, 1977.

Mancini, JoAnne Marie. *Pre-Modernism: Art-World Change and American Culture from the Civil War to the Armory Show*. Princeton, NJ: Princeton Univ. Press, 2005.

Marien, Mary Warner. *Photography: A Cultural History*. 3rd ed. Upper Saddle River, NJ: Pearson/Prentice Hall, 2011.

Meecham, Pam, and Julie Sheldon. *Modern Art: A Critical Introduction*. 2nd ed. New York: Routledge, 2005.

Newlands, Anne. *Canadian Art: From Its Beginnings to 2000*. Willowdale, Ont.: Firefly Books, 2000.

Phaidon Atlas of Contemporary World Architecture. London: Phaidon Press, 2004.

Powell, Richard J. *Black Art: A Cultural History*. World of Art. 2nd ed. New York: Thames & Hudson, 2003.

Rosenblum, Naomi. *A World History of Photography*. 4th ed. New York: Abbeville Press, 2007.

Ruhrberg, Karl. *Art of the 20th Century*. Ed. Ingo F. Walther. 2 vols. New York: Taschen, 1998.

Scully, Vincent Joseph. *Modern Architecture and Other Essays*. Princeton, NJ: Princeton Univ. Press, 2003.

Stiles, Kristine, and Peter Selz. *Theories and Documents of Contemporary Art: A Sourcebook of Artists' Writings*. California Studies in the History of Art, 35. Berkeley: Univ. of California Press, 1996.

Tafuri, Manfredo. *Modern Architecture*. History of World Architecture. 2 vols. New York: Electa/Rizzoli, 1986.

Upton, Dell. *Architecture in the United States*. Oxford History of Art. Oxford: Oxford Univ. Press, 1998.

Wood, Paul, ed. *Varieties of Modernism*. Art of the 20th Century. New Haven: Yale Univ. Press, 2004.

Woodham, Jonathan M. *Twentieth-Century Design*. Oxford History of Art. Oxford: Oxford Univ. Press, 1997.

Asian Art, General

Addiss, Stephen, Gerald Groemer, and J. Thomas Rimer, eds. *Traditional Japanese Arts and Culture: An Illustrated Sourcebook*. Honolulu: Univ. of Hawai'i Press, 2006.

Barnhart, Richard M. *Three Thousand Years of Chinese Painting*. New Haven: Yale Univ. Press, 1997.

Blunden, Caroline, and Mark Elvin. *Cultural Atlas of China*. 2nd ed. New York: Checkmark Books, 1998.

Brown, Kerry, ed. *Sikh Art and Literature*. New York: Routledge in collaboration with the Sikh Foundation, 1999.

Chang, Léon Long-Yien, and Peter Miller. *Four Thousand Years of Chinese Calligraphy*. Chicago: Univ. of Chicago Press, 1990.

Chang, Yang-mo. *Arts of Korea*. Ed. Judith G. Smith. New York: Metropolitan Museum of Art, 1998.

Clark, John. *Modern Asian Art*. Honolulu: Univ. of Hawai'i Press, 1998.

Clunas, Craig. *Art in China*. 2nd ed. Oxford History of Art. Oxford: Oxford Univ. Press, 2009.

Coaldrake, William H. *Architecture and Authority in Japan*. London: Routledge, 1996.

Collcutt, Martin, Marius Jansen, and Isao Kumakura. *Cultural Atlas of Japan*. New York: Facts on File, 1988.

Craven, Roy C. *Indian Art: A Concise History*. Rev. ed. World of Art. New York: Thames & Hudson, 1997.

Dehejia, Vidya. *Indian Art*. Art & Ideas. London: Phaidon Press, 1997.

Fisher, Robert E. *Buddhist Art and Architecture*. World of Art. New York: Thames & Hudson, 1993.

Fu, Xinian. *Chinese Architecture*. Ed. & exp. ed., Nancy S. Steinhardt. New Haven: Yale Univ. Press, 2002.

Hearn, Maxwell K., and Judith G. Smith, eds. *Arts of the Sung and Yüan: Papers Prepared for an International Symposium*. New York: Dept. of Asian Art, Metropolitan Museum of Art, 1996.

Heibonsha Survey of Japanese Art. 31 vols. New York: Weatherhill, 1972–80.

Hertz, Betti-Sue. *Past in Reverse: Contemporary Art of East Asia*. San Diego: San Diego Museum of Art, 2004.

Japanese Arts Library. 15 vols. New York: Kodansha International, 1977–87.

Kerlogue, Fiona. *Arts of Southeast Asia*. World of Art. New York: Thames & Hudson, 2004.

Khanna, Balraj, and George Michell. *Human and Divine: 2000 Years of Indian Sculpture*. London: Hayward Gallery, 2000.

Lee, Sherman E. *A History of Far Eastern Art.* 5th ed. Ed. Naomi Noble Richards. New York: Abrams, 1994.

———. *China, 5000 Years: Innovation and Transformation in the Arts.* New York: Solomon R. Guggenheim Museum, 1998.

Leidy, Denise Patry. *The Art of Buddhism: An Introduction to Its History and Meaning.* Boston: Shambhala Publications, 2008.

Liu, Cary Y., and Dora C.Y. Ching, eds. *Arts of the Sung and Yüan: Ritual, Ethnicity, and Style in Painting.* Princeton, NJ: Art Museum, Princeton Univ., 1999.

McArthur, Meher. *The Arts of Asia: Materials, Techniques, Styles.* New York: Thames & Hudson, 2005.

———. *Reading Buddhist Art: An Illustrated Guide to Buddhist Signs and Symbols.* New York: Thames & Hudson, 2002.

Mason, Penelope. *History of Japanese Art.* 2nd ed. Upper Saddle River, NJ: Pearson/ Prentice Hall, 2005.

Michell, George. *Hindu Art and Architecture.* World of Art. London: Thames & Hudson, 2000.

———. *The Penguin Guide to the Monuments of India.* 2 vols. New York: Viking, 1989.

Mitter, Partha. *Indian Art.* Oxford History of Art. Oxford: Oxford Univ. Press, 2001.

Murase, Miyeko. *Bridge of Dreams: The Mary Griggs Burke Collection of Japanese Art.* New York: Metropolitan Museum of Art, 2000.

Nickel, Lukas, ed. *Return of the Buddha: The Qingzhou Discoveries.* London: Royal Academy of Arts, 2002.

Pak, Youngsook, and Roderick Whitfield. *Buddhist Sculpture: Handbook of Korean Art.* London: Laurence King Publishing, 2003.

Rawson, Philip. *The Art of Southeast Asia.* World of Art. London: Thames & Hudson, 1967.

Sullivan, Michael. *The Arts of China.* 5th ed., rev. & exp. Berkeley: Univ. of California Press, 2008.

Thorp, Robert L., and Richard Ellis Vinograd. *Chinese Art & Culture.* New York: Abrams, 2001.

Topsfield, Andrew, ed. *In the Realm of Gods and Kings: Arts of India.* London: Philip Wilson, 2004.

Tucker, Jonathan. *The Silk Road: Art and History.* Chicago: Art Media Resources, 2003.

Tregear, Mary. *Chinese Art.* Rev. ed. World of Art. New York: Thames & Hudson, 1997.

Vainker, S.J. *Chinese Pottery and Porcelain: From Prehistory to the Present.* New York: Braziller, 1991.

African and Oceanic Art and Art of the Americas, General

Anderson, Richard L., and Karen L. Field, eds. *Art in Small-Scale Societies: Contemporary Readings.* Upper Saddle River, NJ: Pearson/Prentice Hall, 1993.

Bassani, Ezio, ed. *Arts of Africa: 7000 Years of African Art.* Milan: Skira, 2005.

Benson, Elizabeth P. *Retratos: 2,000 Years of Latin American Portraits.* San Antonio, TX: San Antonio Museum of Art, 2004.

Berlo, Janet Catherine, and Lee Anne Wilson. *Arts of Africa, Oceania, and the Americas: Selected Readings.* Upper Saddle River, NJ: Prentice Hall, 1993.

Calloway, Colin G. *First Peoples: A Documentary Survey of American Indian History.* 3rd ed. Boston: Bedford/St. Martin's, 2008.

Coote, Jeremy, and Anthony Shelton, eds. *Anthropology, Art, and Aesthetics.* New York: Oxford Univ. Press, 1992.

Drewal, Henry, and John Pemberton III. *Yoruba: Nine Centuries of African Art and Thought.* New York: Center for African Art, 1989.

Evans, Susan Toby. *Ancient Mexico & Central America: Archaeology and Culture History.* 2nd ed. New York: Thames & Hudson, 2008.

———, and David L. Webster, eds. *Archaeology of Ancient Mexico and Central America: An Encyclopedia.* New York: Garland, 2001.

———, and Joanne Pillsbury, eds. *Palaces of the Ancient New World: A Symposium at Dumbarton Oaks,* 10th and 11th October, 1998. Washington, DC: Dumbarton Oaks Research Library and Collection, 2004.

Mack, John, ed. *Africa, Arts and Cultures.* London: British Museum Press, 2000.

Mexico: Splendors of Thirty Centuries. New York: Metropolitan Museum of Art, 1990.

Nunley, John W., and Cara McCarty. *Masks: Faces of Culture.* New York: Abrams in assoc. with the Saint Louis Art Museum, 1999.

Perani, Judith, and Fred T. Smith. *The Visual Arts of Africa: Gender, Power, and Life Cycle Rituals.* Upper Saddle River, NJ: Pearson/ Prentice Hall, 1998.

Phillips, Tom, ed. *Africa: The Art of a Continent.* New York: Prestel, 1995.

Rabineau, Phyllis. *Feather Arts: Beauty, Wealth, and Spirit from Five Continents.* Chicago: Field Museum of Natural History, 1979.

Scott, John F. *Latin American Art: Ancient to Modern.* Gainesville: Univ. Press of Florida, 1999.

Stepan, Peter. *Africa.* Trans. John Gabriel and Elizabeth Schwaiger. London: Prestel, 2001.

Visonà, Monica Blackmun, et al. *A History of Art in Africa.* 2nd ed. Upper Saddle River, NJ: Pearson/Prentice Hall, 2008.

Introduction

Acton, Mary. *Learning to Look at Paintings.* 2nd ed. New York: Routledge, 2009.

Arnold, Dana. *Art History: A Very Short Introduction.* Oxford and New York: Oxford Univ. Press, 2004.

Baxandall, Michael. *Patterns of Intention: On the Historical Explanation of Pictures.* New Haven: Yale Univ. Press, 1985.

Clearwater, Bonnie. *The Rothko Book.* London: Tate Publishing, 2006.

Decoteau, Pamela Hibbs. *Clara Peeters, 1594–ca.1640 and the Development of Still-Life Painting in Northern Europe.* Lingen: Luca Verlag, 1992.

Geertz, Clifford. "Art as a Cultural System." *Modern Language Notes* 91 (1976): 1473–1499.

Hochstrasser, Julie Berger. *Still Life and Trade in the Dutch Golden Age.* New Haven: Yale Univ. Press, 2007.

Holstein, Jonathan. *The Pieced Quilt: An American Design Tradition.* New York: Galahad Books, 1973.

Jolly, Penny Howell. "Rogier van der Weyden's Escorial and Philadelphia Crucifixions and Their Relation to Fra Angelico at San Marco." *Oud Holland* 95 (1981): 113–126.

Mainardi, Patricia. "Quilts: The Great American Art." *The Feminist Art Journal* 2/1 (1973): 1, 18–23.

Miller, Angela L., et al. *American Encounters: Art, History, and Cultural Identity.* Upper Saddle River, NJ: Pearson/ Prentice Hall, 2008.

Minor, Vernon Hyde. *Art History's History.* Upper Saddle River, NJ: Pearson/Prentice Hall, 2001.

Nelson, Robert S., and Richard Shiff, eds. *Critical Terms for Art History.* 2nd ed. Chicago: Univ. of Chicago Press, 2003.

Panofsky, Erwin. *Studies in Iconology: Humanistic Themes in the Art of the Renaissance.* New York: Oxford Univ. Press, 1939.

———. *Meaning in the Visual Arts.* Phoenix ed. Chicago: Univ. of Chicago Press, 1982.

Preziosi, Donald, ed. *The Art of Art History: A Critical Anthology.* 2nd ed. Oxford and New York: Oxford Univ. Press, 2009.

Rothko, Mark. *Writings on Art.* Ed. Miguel López-Remiro. New Haven: Yale Univ. Press, 2006.

———. *The Artist's Reality: Philosophies of Art.* Ed. Christopher Rothko. New Haven: Yale Univ. Press, 2004.

Schapiro, Meyer. "The Apples of Cézanne: An Essay on the Meaning of Still Life." *Art News Annual* 34 (1968): 34–53. Reprinted in *Modern Art 19th & 20th Centuries: Selected Papers* 2. London: Chatto & Windus, 1978.

Sowers, Robert. *Rethinking the Forms of Visual Expression.* Berkeley: Univ. of California Press, 1990.

Taylor, Joshua. *Learning to Look: A Handbook for the Visual Arts.* 2nd ed. Chicago: Chicago Univ. Press, 1981.

Tucker, Mark. "Rogier van der Weyden's 'Philadelphia Crucifixion.'" *Burlington Magazine* 139 (1997): 676–683.

Wang, Fangyu, et al., eds. *Master of the Lotus Garden: The Life and Art of Bada Shanren (1626–1705).* New Haven: Yale Univ. Press, 1990.

Chapter 1 Prehistoric Art

Aujoulat, Norbert. *Lascaux: Movement, Space, and Time.* New York: Abrams, 2005.

Bahn, Paul G. *The Cambridge Illustrated History of Prehistoric Art.* Cambridge Illustrated History. Cambridge: Cambridge Univ. Press, 1998.

Bataille, Georges. *The Cradle of Humanity: Prehistoric Art and Culture.* Ed. Stuart Kendall. Trans. Michelle Kendall and Stuart Kendall. New York: Zone Books, 2005.

Berghaus, Gunter. *New Perspectives on Prehistoric Art.* Westport, CT: Praeger, 2004.

Chippindale, Christopher. *Stonehenge Complete.* 3rd ed. New York: Thames & Hudson, 2004.

Clottes, Jean. *Chauvet Cave: The Art of Earliest Times.* Salt Lake City: Univ. of Utah Press, 2003.

———. *World Rock Art.* Trans. Guy Bennett. Los Angeles: Getty Conservation Institute, 2002.

———, and J. David Lewis-Williams. *The Shamans of Prehistory: Trance and Magic in the Painted Caves.* Trans. Sophie Hawkes. New York: Abrams, 1998.

Connah, Graham. *African Civilizations: An Archaeological Perspective.* 2nd ed. Cambridge: Cambridge Univ. Press, 2001.

Coulson, David, and Alec Campbell. *African Rock Art: Painting and Engravings on Stone.* New York: Abrams, 2001.

Cunliffe, Barry W., ed. *The Oxford Illustrated History of Prehistoric Europe.* New York: Oxford Univ. Press, 2001.

Forte, Maurizio, and Alberto Siliotti. *Virtual Archaeology: Re- Creating Ancient Worlds.* New York: Abrams, 1997.

Freeman, Leslie G. *Altamira Revisited and Other Essays on Early Art.* Chicago: Institute for Prehistoric Investigation, 1987.

Garlake, Peter S. *The Hunter's Vision: The Prehistoric Art of Zimbabwe.* Seattle: Univ. of Washington Press, 1995.

Gowlett, John A.J. *Ascent to Civilization: The Archaeology of Early Humans.* 2nd ed. New York: McGraw-Hill, 1993.

Guthrie, R. Dale. *The Nature of Paleolithic Art.* Chicago: Univ. of Chicago Press, 2005.

Jope, E.M. *Early Celtic Art in the British Isles.* 2 vols. New York: Oxford Univ. Press, 2000.

Kenrick, Douglas M. *Jomon of Japan: The World's Oldest Pottery.* New York: Kegan Paul, 1995.

Le Quellec, Jean-Loïc. *Rock Art in Africa: Mythology and Legend.* Trans. Paul Bahn. Paris: Flammarion, 2004.

Leakey, Richard E., and Roger Lewin. *Origins Reconsidered: In Search of What Makes Us Human.* New York: Doubleday, 1992.

Leroi-Gourhan, André. *The Dawn of European Art: An Introduction to Paleolithic Cave Painting.* Trans. Sara Champion. Cambridge: Cambridge Univ. Press, 1982.

Lewis-Williams, J. David. *The Mind in the Cave: Consciousness and the Origins of Art.* New York: Thames & Hudson, 2002.

O'Kelly, Michael J. *Newgrange: Archaeology, Art, and Legend.* New Aspects of Antiquity. London: Thames & Hudson, 1982.

Price, T. Douglas. *Images of the Past.* 5th ed. Boston: McGraw-Hill, 2008.

Renfrew, Colin, ed. *The Megalithic Monuments of Western Europe.* London: Thames & Hudson, 1983.

Sandars, N.K. *Prehistoric Art in Europe.* 2nd ed. Pelican History of Art. New Haven: Yale Univ. Press, 1992.

Sieveking, Ann. *The Cave Artists.* Ancient People and Places, vol. 93. London: Thames & Hudson, 1979.

Sura Ramos, Pedro A. *The Cave of Altamira.* Gen. Ed. Antonio Beltran. New York: Abrams, 1999.

White, Randall. *Prehistoric Art: The Symbolic Journey of Mankind.* New York: Abrams, 2003.

Chapter 2 Art of the Ancient Near East

Akurgal, Ekrem. *Ancient Civilizations and Ruins of Turkey: From Prehistoric Times until the End of the Roman Empire.* 5th ed. London: Kegan Paul, 2002.

Aruz, Joan, et al., eds. *Beyond Babylon: Art, Trade, and Diplomacy in the Second Millennium B.C.* New Haven: Yale Univ. Press, and Metropolitan Museum of Art, 2008.

———, ed. *Art of the First Cities: The Third Millennium B.C. from the Mediterranean to the Indus.* New York: Metropolitan Museum of Art, 2003.

Bahrani, Zainab. *The Graven Image: Representation in Babylonia and Assyria.* Archaeology, Culture, and Society Series. Philadelphia: Univ. of Pennsylvania Press, 2003.

Boardman, John. *Persia and the West: An Archaeological Investigation of the Genesis of Achaemenid Art.* New York: Thames & Hudson, 2000.

Bottero, Jean. *Everyday Life in Ancient Mesopotamia.* Trans. Antonia Nevill. Baltimore, MD: Johns Hopkins Univ. Press, 2001.

Charvat, Petr. *Mesopotamia before History.* Rev. & updated ed. New York: Routledge, 2002.

Crawford, Harriet. *Sumer and the Sumerians.* 2nd ed. New York: Cambridge Univ. Press, 2004.

Curtis, John, and Nigel Tallis, eds. *Forgotten Empire: The World of Ancient Persia.* Berkeley: Univ. of California Press, 2005.

Ferrier, R.W., ed. *The Arts of Persia.* New Haven: Yale Univ. Press, 1989.

Frankfort, Henri. *The Art and Architecture of the Ancient Orient.* 5th ed. Pelican History of Art. New Haven: Yale Univ. Press, 1996.

Haywood, John. *Ancient Civilizations of the Near East and Mediterranean.* London: Cassell, 1997.

Meyers, Eric M., ed. *The Oxford Encyclopedia of Archaeology in the Near East.* 5 vols. New York: Oxford Univ. Press, 1997.

Moorey, P.R.S. *Idols of the People: Miniature Images of Clay in the Ancient Near East.* The Schweich Lectures of the British Academy, 2001. New York: Oxford Univ. Press, 2003.

Polk, Milbry, and Angela M.H. Schuster. *The Looting of the Iraq Museum, Baghdad: The Lost Legacy of Ancient Mesopotamia.* New York: Abrams, 2005.

Reade, Julian. *Assyrian Sculpture.* Cambridge, MA: Harvard Univ. Press, 1999.

Roaf, Michael. *Cultural Atlas of Mesopotamia and the Ancient Near East.* New York: Facts on File, 1990.

Roux, Georges. *Ancient Iraq.* 3rd ed. London: Penguin, 1992.

Winter, Irene. "Sex, Rhetoric, and the Public Monument: The Alluring Body of the Male Ruler." In *Sexuality in Ancient Art*, eds. Natalie Kampen and Bettina A. Bergmann. Cambridge: Cambridge Univ. Press, 1996: 11–26.

Zettler, Richard L., and Lee Horne, eds. *Treasures from the Royal Tombs of Ur.* Philadelphia: Univ. of Pennsylvania, Museum of Archaeology and Anthropology, 1998.

Chapter 3 Art of Ancient Egypt

Ancient Egyptian Literature: An Anthology. Trans. John L. Foster. Austin: Univ. of Texas Press, 2001.

Arnold, Dieter. *Temples of the Last Pharaohs.* New York: Oxford Univ. Press, 1999.

Baines, John, and Jaromír Málek. *Cultural Atlas of Ancient Egypt.* Rev. ed. New York: Facts on File, 2000.

Egyptian Art in the Age of the Pyramids. New York: Metropolitan Museum of Art, 1999.

The Egyptian Book of the Dead: The Book of Going Forth by Day: Being the Papyrus of Ani (Royal Scribe of the Divine Offerings). 2nd rev. ed. Trans. Raymond O. Faulkner. San Francisco: Chronicle, 2008.

Freed, Rita E., Sue D'Auria, and Yvonne J. Markowitz. *Pharaohs of the Sun: Akhenaten, Nefertiti, Tutankhamen.* Boston: Museum of Fine Arts in assoc. with Bulfinch Press/ Little, Brown, 1999.

Hawass, Zahi A. *Tutankhamun and the Golden Age of the Pharaohs.* Washington, DC: National Geographic, 2005.

Ikram, Salima. *Death and Burial in Ancient Egypt.* Cairo: The American Univ. in Cairo Press, 2015.

Ikram, Salima, and Aidan Dodson. *The Mummy in Ancient Egypt: Equipping the Dead for Eternity.* London: Thames and Hudson, 1998.

Johnson, Paul. *The Civilization of Ancient Egypt.* Updated ed. New York: HarperCollins, 1999.

Kozloff, Arielle P. *Egypt's Dazzling Sun: Amenhotep III and His World.* Cleveland: Cleveland Museum of Art, 1992.

Lehner, Mark. *The Complete Pyramids.* New York: Thames & Hudson, 2008.

Málek, Jaromir. *Egypt: 4,000 Years of Art.* London: Phaidon Press, 2003.

Reeves, Nicholas, and Richard H. Wilkinson. *The Complete Valley of the Kings.* London: Thames and Hudson, 2008.

Robins, Gay. *The Art of Ancient Egypt.* Rev. ed. Cambridge, MA: Harvard Univ. Press, 2008.

Roehrig, Catharine H., Renee Dreyfus, and Cathleen A. Keller. *Hatshepsut, from Queen to Pharaoh.* New York: Metropolitan Museum of Art, 2005.

Russmann, Edna R. *Egyptian Sculpture: Cairo and Luxor*. Austin: Univ. of Texas Press, 1989.

Smith, Craig B. *How the Great Pyramid Was Built*. Washington, DC: Smithsonian Books, 2004.

Smith, William Stevenson. *The Art and Architecture of Ancient Egypt*. 3rd ed. Revised William Kelly Simpson. Pelican History of Art. New Haven: Yale Univ. Press, 1998.

Strouhal, Eugen. *Life of the Ancient Egyptians*. Trans. Deryck Viney. Norman: Univ. of Oklahoma Press, 1992.

Strudwick, Nigel, and Helen Strudwick. *Thebes in Egypt: A Guide to the Tombs and Temples of Ancient Luxor*. Ithaca, NY: Cornell Univ. Press, 1999.

Thomas, Thelma K. *Late Antique Egyptian Funerary Sculpture: Images for this World and for the Next*. Princeton, NJ: Princeton Univ. Press, 2000.

Tiradritti, Francesco. *Ancient Egypt: Art, Architecture and History*. Trans. Phil Goddard. London: British Museum Press, 2002.

The Treasures of Ancient Egypt: From the Egyptian Museum in Cairo. New York: Rizzoli, 2003.

Wilkinson, Richard H. *The Complete Temples of Ancient Egypt*. New York: Thames & Hudson, 2000.

———. *Reading Egyptian Art: A Hieroglyphic Guide to Ancient Egyptian Painting and Sculpture*. London: Thames & Hudson, 1992.

Winstone, H.V.F. *Howard Carter and the Discovery of the Tomb of Tutankhamen*. Rev. ed. Manchester: Barzan, 2006.

Ziegler, Cristiane, ed. *The Pharaohs*. New York: Rizzoli, 2002.

Zivie-Coche, Christiane. *Sphinx: History of a Monument*. Trans. David Lorton. Ithaca, NY: Cornell Univ. Press, 2002.

Chapter 4 Art of the Ancient Aegean

Castleden, Rodney. *The Knossos Labyrinth: A New View of the "Palace of Minos" at Knossos*. London: Routledge, 1990.

———. *Mycenaeans*. New York: Routledge, 2005.

Demargne, Pierre. *The Birth of Greek Art*. Trans. Stuart Gilbert and James Emmons. Arts of Mankind, vol. 6. New York: Golden, 1964.

Doumas, Christos. *The Wall-Paintings of Thera*. 2nd ed. Trans. Alex Doumas. Athens: Kapon Editions, 1999.

Fitton, J. Lesley. *Cycladic Art*. 2nd ed. London: British Museum Press, 1999.

Getz-Gentle, Pat. *Personal Styles in Early Cycladic Sculpture*. Madison: Univ. of Wisconsin Press, 2001.

Hamilakis, Yannis. ed. *Labyrinth Revisited: Rethinking "Minoan" Archaeology*. Oxford: Oxbow, 2002.

Hendrix, Elizabeth. "Painted Ladies of the Early Bronze Age." *The Metropolitan Museum of Art Bulletin New Series*, 55/3 (Winter 1997–1998): 4–15.

Higgins, Reynold A. *Minoan and Mycenean Art*. New. ed. World of Art. New York: Thames & Hudson, 1997.

Hitchcock, Louise. *Minoan Architecture: A Contextual Analysis*. Studies in Mediterranean Archaeology and Literature, Pocket-Book, 155. Jonsered: P. Åströms Förlag, 2000.

Hoffman, Gail L. "Painted Ladies: Early Cycladic II Mourning Figures?" *American Journal of Archaeology* 106/4 (October 2002): 525–550.

Immerwahr, Sara Anderson. *Aegean Painting in the Bronze Age*. University Park: Pennsylvania State Univ. Press, 1990.

Preziosi, Donald, and Louise Hitchcock. *Aegean Art and Architecture*. Oxford History of Art. Oxford: Oxford Univ. Press, 1999.

Shelmerdine, Cynthia W., ed. *The Cambridge Companion to the Aegean Bronze Age*. New York: Cambridge Univ. Press, 2008.

Strasser, Thomas F. "Location and Perspective in the Theran Flotilla Fresco." *Journal of Mediterranean Archaeology* 23/1 (2010): 3–26.

Chapter 5 Art of Ancient Greece

Barletta, Barbara A. *The Origins of the Greek Architectural Orders*. New York: Cambridge Univ. Press, 2001.

Beard, Mary. *The Parthenon*. Cambridge, MA: Harvard Univ. Press, 2003.

Belozerskaya, Marina, and Kenneth D.S. Lapatin. *Ancient Greece: Art, Architecture, and History*. Los Angeles: J. Paul Getty Museum, 2004.

Boardman, John. *Early Greek Vase Painting: 11th–6th Centuries B.C.: A Handbook*. World of Art. London: Thames & Hudson, 1998.

———. *Greek Sculpture: The Archaic Period: A Handbook*. World of Art. London: Thames & Hudson, 1991.

———. *Greek Sculpture: The Classical Period: A Handbook*. World of Art London: Thames & Hudson, 1985.

———. *Greek Sculpture: The Late Classical Period and Sculpture in Colonies and Overseas*. World of Art. New York: Thames & Hudson, 1995.

———. *The History of Greek Vases: Potters, Painters, and Pictures*. New York: Thames & Hudson, 2001.

Burn, Lucilla. *Hellenistic Art: From Alexander the Great to Augustus*. Los Angeles: J. Paul Getty Museum, 2004.

Clark, Andrew J., Maya Elston, and Mary Louise Hart. *Understanding Greek Vases: A Guide to Terms, Styles, and Techniques*. Los Angeles: J. Paul Getty Museum, 2002.

De Grummond, Nancy T. and Brunilde S. Ridgway. *From Pergamon to Sperlonga: Sculpture in Context*. Berkeley: Univ. of California Press, 2000.

Donohue, A.A. *Greek Sculpture and the Problem of Description*. New York: Cambridge Univ. Press, 2005.

Fullerton, Mark D. *Greek Art*. Cambridge: Cambridge Univ. Press, 2000.

Hard, Robin. *The Routledge Handbook of Greek Mythology*: Based on H.J. Rose's "Handbook of Greek Mythology." 7th ed. London: Routledge, 2008.

Hurwit, Jeffrey M. *The Acropolis in the Age of Pericles*. New York: Cambridge Univ. Press, 2004.

Karakasi, Katerina. *Archaic Korai*. Los Angeles: J. Paul Getty Museum, 2003.

Lawrence, A.W. *Greek Architecture*. 5th ed. Revised R.A. Tomlinson. Pelican History of Art. New Haven: Yale Univ. Press, 1996.

Martin, Roland. *Greek Architecture: Architecture of Crete, Greece, and the Greek World*. History of World Architecture. New York: Electa/ Rizzoli, 1988.

Neils, Jenifer. *The British Museum Concise Introduction to Ancient Greece*. Ann Arbor: Univ. of Michigan, 2008.

Osborne, Robin. *Archaic and Classical Greek Art*. Oxford History of Art. Oxford: Oxford Univ. Press, 1998.

Palagia, Olga, ed. *Greek Sculpture: Function, Materials, and Techniques in the Archaic and Classical Periods*. New York: Cambridge Univ. Press, 2006.

———, and J.J. Pollitt, eds. *Personal Styles in Greek Sculpture*. Yale Classical Studies, vol. 30. Cambridge: Cambridge Univ. Press, 1996.

Pedley, John Griffiths. *Greek Art and Archaeology*. 5th ed. Upper Saddle River, NJ: Pearson/Prentice Hall, 2012.

Pollitt, J.J. *Art and Experience in Classical Greece*. Cambridge: Cambridge Univ. Press, 1972; reprinted 1999.

———. *The Art of Ancient Greece: Sources and Documents*. 2nd ed. rev. Cambridge: Cambridge Univ. Press, 2001.

Ridgway, Brunilde Sismondo. *The Archaic Style in Greek Sculpture*. 2nd ed. Chicago: Ares, 1993.

———. *Fifth Century Styles in Greek Sculpture*. Princeton, NJ: Princeton Univ. Press, 1981.

———. *Fourth Century Styles in Greek Sculpture*. Wisconsin Studies in Classics. Madison: Univ. of Wisconsin Press, 1997.

———. *Hellenistic Sculpture 1: The Styles of ca. 331–200 B.C.* Wisconsin Studies in Classics. Madison: Univ. of Wisconsin Press, 1990.

Stafford, Emma J. *Life, Myth, and Art in Ancient Greece*. Los Angeles: J. Paul Getty Museum, 2004.

Stewart, Andrew F. *Greek Sculpture: An Exploration*. 2 vols. New Haven: Yale Univ. Press, 1990.

Whitley, James. *The Archaeology of Ancient Greece*. New York: Cambridge Univ. Press, 2001.

Chapter 6 Etruscan and Roman Art

Bianchi Bandinelli, Ranuccio. *Rome: The Centre of Power: Roman Art to A.D. 200*. Trans. Peter Green. Arts of Mankind, 15. London: Thames & Hudson, 1971.

———. *Rome: The Late Empire: Roman Art* A.D. *200–400.* Trans. Peter Green. Arts of Mankind, 17. New York: Braziller, 1971.

Borrelli, Federica. *The Etruscans: Art, Architecture, and History.* Ed. Stefano Peccatori and Stefano Zuffi. Trans. Thomas Michael Hartmann. Los Angeles: J. Paul Getty Museum, 2004.

Brendel, Otto J. *Prolegomena to the Study of Roman Art.* New Haven: Yale Univ. Press, 1979.

———. *Etruscan Art.* 2nd ed. Pelican History of Art. New Haven: Yale Univ. Press, 1995.

Conlin, Diane Atnally. *The Artists of the Ara Pacis: The Process of Hellenization in Roman Relief Sculpture.* Studies in the History of Greece & Rome. Chapel Hill: Univ. of North Carolina Press, 1997.

Cornell, Tim, and John Matthews. *Atlas of the Roman World.* New York: Facts on File, 1982.

D'Ambra, Eve. *Roman Art.* Cambridge: Cambridge Univ. Press, 1998.

Elsner, Jas. *Imperial Rome and Christian Triumph: The Art of the Roman Empire* A.D. *100–450.* Oxford History of Art. Oxford: Oxford Univ. Press, 1998.

Gabucci, Ada. *Ancient Rome: Art, Architecture, and History.* Eds. Stefano Peccatori and Stephano Zuffi. Trans. T.M. Hartman. Los Angeles: J. Paul Getty Museum, 2002.

Haynes, Sybille. *Etruscan Civilization: A Cultural History.* Los Angeles: J. Paul Getty Museum, 2000.

Holloway, R. Ross. *Constantine & Rome.* New Haven: Yale Univ. Press, 2004.

Kleiner, Fred. S. *A History of Roman Art.* Belmont, CA: Thomson/Wadsworth, 2007.

MacDonald, William L. *The Architecture of the Roman Empire: An Introductory Study.* Rev. ed. 2 vols. Yale Publications in the History of Art, 17, 35. New Haven: Yale Univ. Press, 1982.

———. *The Pantheon: Design, Meaning, and Progeny.* New foreword by John Pinto. Cambridge, MA: Harvard Univ. Press, 2002.

Mattusch, Carol C. *Pompeii and the Roman Villa: Art and Culture around the Bay of Naples.* Washington, DC: National Gallery of Art, 2008.

Mazzoleni, Donatella. *Domus: Wall Painting in the Roman House.* Los Angeles: J. Paul Getty Museum, 2004.

Packer, James E. *The Forum of Trajan in Rome: A Study of the Monuments in Brief.* Berkeley: Univ. of California Press, 2001.

Pollitt, J.J. *The Art of Rome, c. 753* B.C.*–337* A.D.*: Sources and Documents.* Upper Saddle River, NJ: Pearson/Prentice Hall, 1966.

Polybius. *The Histories.* Trans. W.R. Paton. 6 vols. Loeb Classical Library. Cambridge, MA: Harvard Univ. Press, 2000.

Ramage, Nancy H., and Andrew Ramage. *Roman Art: Romulus to Constantine.* 5th ed. Upper Saddle River, NJ: Pearson/Prentice Hall, 2009.

Spivey, Nigel. *Etruscan Art.* World of Art. New York: Thames & Hudson, 1997.

Stamper, John W. *The Architecture of Roman Temples: The Republic to the Middle Empire.* New York: Cambridge Univ. Press, 2005.

Stewart, Peter. *Statues in Roman Society: Representation and Response.* Oxford Studies in Ancient Culture and Representation. New York: Oxford Univ. Press, 2003.

Strong, Donald. *Roman Art.* 2nd ed. rev. & annotated. Ed. Roger Ling. Pelican History of Art. New Haven: Yale Univ. Press, 1995.

Ward-Perkins, J.B. *Roman Architecture.* History of World Architecture. New York: Electa/Rizzoli, 1988.

———. *Roman Imperial Architecture.* Pelican History of Art. New Haven: Yale Univ. Press, 1981.

Wilson Jones, Mark. *Principles of Roman Architecture.* New Haven: Yale Univ. Press, 2000.

Chapter 7 Jewish and Early Christian Art

Age of Spirituality: Late Antique and Early Christian Art, Third to Seventh Century. New York: Metropolitan Museum of Art, 1979.

Beckwith, John. *Early Christian and Byzantine Art.* 2nd ed. Pelican History of Art. New Haven: Yale Univ. Press, 1986.

Bleiberg, Edward, ed. *Tree of Paradise: Jewish Mosaics from the Roman Empire.* Brooklyn: Brooklyn Museum, 2005.

Cioffarelli, Ada. *Guide to the Catacombs of Rome and its Surroundings.* Rome: Bonsignori, 2000.

Fine, Steven. *Art and Judaism in the Greco–Roman World: Toward a New Jewish Archaeology.* New York: Cambridge Univ. Press, 2005.

Hachlili, Rachel. *Ancient Mosaic Pavements: Themes, Issues, and Trends.* Leiden: Brill, 2009.

Jensen, Robin Margaret. *Understanding Early Christian Art.* New York: Routledge, 2000.

Krautheimer, Richard, and Slobodan Curcic. *Early Christian and Byzantine Architecture.* 4th ed. Pelican History of Art. New Haven: Yale Univ. Press, 1992.

Levine, Lee I., and Zeev Weiss, eds. *From Dura to Sepphoris: Studies in Jewish Art and Society in Late Antiquity.* Journal of Roman Archaeology: Supplementary Series, no. 40. Portsmouth, RI: Journal of Roman Archaeology, 2000.

Lowden, John. *Early Christian and Byzantine Art.* Art & Ideas. London: Phaidon Press, 1997.

Mathews, Thomas F. *The Clash of Gods: A Reinterpretation of Early Christian Art.* Rev. ed. Princeton, NJ: Princeton Univ. Press, 1999.

Olin, Margaret. *The Nation without Art: Examining Modern Discourses on Jewish Art.* Lincoln: Univ. of Nebraska Press, 2001.

Olsson, Birger, and Magnus Zetterholm, eds. *The Ancient Synagogue from Its Origins until 200 C.E.: Papers Presented at an International Conference at Lund University, October 14–17, 2001.* Coniectanea Biblica: New Testament Series, 39. Stockholm: Almqvist & Wiksell International, 2003.

Rutgers, Leonard V. *Subterranean Rome: In Search of the Roots of Christianity in the Catacombs of the Eternal City.* Leuven: Peeters, 2000.

Sed-Rajna, Gabrielle. *Jewish Art.* Trans. Sara Friedman and Mira Reich. New York: Abrams, 1997.

Spier, Jeffrey, ed. *Picturing the Bible: The Earliest Christian Art.* New Haven: Yale Univ. Press, 2007.

Tadgell, Christopher. *Imperial Space: Rome, Constantinople and the Early Church.* New York: Whitney Library of Design, 1998.

Webb, Matilda. *The Churches and Catacombs of Early Christian Rome: A Comprehensive Guide.* Brighton, UK: Sussex Academic Press, 2001.

Weitzmann, Kurt. *Late Antique and Early Christian Book Illumination.* New York: Braziller, 1977.

Wharton, Annabel Jane. *Refiguring the Post-Classical City: Dura Europos, Jerash, Jerusalem and Ravenna.* Cambridge: Cambridge Univ. Press, 1995.

White, L. Michael. *The Social Origins of Christian Architecture.* 2 vols. Baltimore, MD: Johns Hopkins Univ. Press, 1990.

Chapter 8 Byzantine Art

Beckwith, John. *Early Christian and Byzantine Art.* 2nd ed. Pelican History of Art. New Haven: Yale Univ. Press, 1986.

Cormack, Robin. *Byzantine Art.* Oxford: Oxford Univ. Press, 2000.

———, and Maria Vassilaki, eds. *Byzantium, 330–1453.* London: Royal Academy of Arts, 2008.

Cutler, Anthony. *The Hand of the Master: Craftsmanship, Ivory, and Society in Byzantium (9th–11th Centuries).* Princeton, NJ: Princeton Univ. Press, 1994.

Eastmond, Antony, and Liz James, eds. *Icon and Word: The Power of Images in Byzantium: Studies Presented to Robin Cormack.* Burlington, VT: Ashgate, 2003.

Evans, Helen C., ed. *Byzantium: Faith and Power (1261–1557).* New York: Metropolitan Museum of Art, 2004.

———, and William D. Wixom, eds. *The Glory of Byzantium: Art and Culture of the Middle Byzantine Era,* A.D. *843–1261.* New York: Abrams, 1997.

Freely, John. *Byzantine Monuments of Istanbul.* Cambridge & New York: Cambridge Univ. Press, 2004.

Gerstel, Sharon. *Beholding the Sacred Mysteries: Programs of the Byzantine Sanctuary.* Seattle: College Art Association in association with Univ. of Washington Press, 1999.

———. *Rural Lives and Landscapes in Late Byzantium: Art, Archeology, and Ethnography.* Cambridge: Cambridge Univ. Press, 2015.

Gerstel, Sharon, and Robert Nelson. *Approaching the Holy Mountain: Art and Liturgy at St. Catherine's Monastery in the Sinai.* Turnhout: Brepols, 2010.

Grabar, André. *Byzantine Painting: Historical and Critical Study*. Trans. Stuart Gilbert. New York: Rizzoli, 1979.

Kitzinger, Ernst. *The Art of Byzantium and the Medieval West: Selected* Studies. Ed. W. Eugene Kleinbauer. Bloomington: Indiana Univ. Press, 1976.

———. *Byzantine Art in the Making: Main Lines of Stylistic Development in Mediterranean Art, 3rd–7th Century*. Cambridge, MA: Harvard Univ. Press, 1977.

Kleinbauer, W. Eugene. *Hagia Sophia*. London: Scala, 2004.

Krautheimer, Richard, and Slobodan Curcic. *Early Christian and Byzantine Architecture*. 4th ed. Pelican History of Art. New Haven: Yale Univ. Press, 1992.

Lowden, John. *Early Christian and Byzantine Art*. Art & Ideas. London: Phaidon Press, 1997.

Maguire, Henry. *The Icons of Their Bodies: Saints and Their Images in Byzantium*. Princeton, NJ: Princeton Univ. Press, 1996.

Mainstone, Rowland J. *Hagia Sophia: Architecture, Structure and Liturgy of Justinian's Great Church*. 2nd ed. New York: Thames & Hudson, 2001.

Mango, Cyril. *Art of the Byzantine Empire, 312–1453: Sources and Documents*. Upper Saddle River, NJ: Pearson/Prentice Hall, 1972.

Mathews, Thomas F. *Byzantium: From Antiquity to the Renaissance*. Perspectives. New York: Abrams, 1998.

Ousterhout, Robert. *Master Builders of Byzantium*. Princeton, NJ: Princeton Univ. Press, 1999.

Pentcheva, Bissera. *The Sensual Icon: Space, Ritual, and the Senses in Byzantium*. University Park: Pennsylvania State Univ. Press, 2010.

Procopius, with an English translation by H.B. Dewing. 7 vols. Loeb Classical Library. Cambridge, MA: Harvard Univ. Press, 1940.

Rodley, Lyn. *Byzantine Art and Architecture: An Introduction*. Cambridge: Cambridge Univ. Press, 1994.

Weitzmann, Kurt. *Place of Book Illumination in Byzantine Art*. Princeton, NJ: Art Museum, Princeton Univ., 1975.

Chapter 9 Islamic Art

Al-Faruqi, Isma'il R., and Lois Ibsen Al-Faruqi. *Cultural Atlas of Islam*. New York: Macmillan, 1986.

Atil, Esin. *The Age of Sultan Suleyman the Magnificent*. Washington, DC: National Gallery of Art, 1987.

Baker, Patricia L. *Islam and the Religious Arts*. London: Continuum, 2004.

Barry, Michael A. *Figurative Art in Medieval Islam and the Riddle of Bihzâd of Herât (1465–1535)*. Paris: Flammarion, 2004.

Blair, Sheila S., and Jonathan Bloom. *The Art and Architecture of Islam 1250–1800*. Pelican History of Art. New Haven: Yale Univ. Press, 1995.

Dodds, Jerrilynn D., ed. *Al-Andalus: The Art of Islamic Spain*. New York: Metropolitan Museum of Art, 1992.

Ecker, Heather. *Caliphs and Kings: The Art and Influence of Islamic Spain*. Washington, DC: Arthur M. Sackler Gallery, 2004.

Ettinghausen, Richard, Oleg Grabar, and Marilyn Jenkins-Madina. *Islamic Art and Architecture, 650–1250*. 2nd ed. Pelican History of Art. New Haven: Yale Univ. Press, 2001.

Frishman, Martin, and Hasan-Uddin Khan. *The Mosque: History, Architectural Development and Regional Diversity*. London: Thames & Hudson, 1994.

Grabar, Oleg. *The Formation of Islamic Art*. Rev. and enl. ed. New Haven: Yale Univ. Press, 1987.

———. *The Great Mosque of Isfahan*. New York: New York Univ. Press, 1990.

———. *Islamic Visual Culture, 1100–1800*. Burlington, VT: Ashgate, 2006.

———. *Mostly Miniatures: An Introduction to Persian Painting*. Princeton, NJ: Princeton Univ. Press, 2000.

———, Mohammad Al-Asad, Abeer Audeh, and Said Nuseibeh. *The Shape of the Holy: Early Islamic Jerusalem*. Princeton, NJ: Princeton Univ. Press, 1996.

Hillenbrand, Robert. *Islamic Art and Architecture*. World of Art. London: Thames & Hudson, 1999.

Irwin, Robert. *The Alhambra*. Cambridge, MA: Harvard Univ. Press, 2004.

Khalili, Nasser D. *Visions of Splendour in Islamic Art and Culture*. London: Worth Press, 2008.

Komaroff, Linda, and Stefano Carboni, eds. *The Legacy of Genghis Khan: Courtly Art and Culture in Western Asia, 1256–1353*. New York: Metropolitan Museum of Art, 2002.

Lentz, Thomas W., and Glenn D. Lowry. *Timur and the Princely Vision: Persian Art and Culture in the Fifteenth Century*. Los Angeles: Los Angeles County Museum of Art, 1989.

Necipolu, Gülru. *The Age of Sinan: Architectural Culture in the Ottoman Empire*. Princeton, NJ: Princeton Univ. Press, 2005.

Petruccioli, Attilio, and Khalil K. Pirani, eds. *Understanding Islamic Architecture*. New York: Routledge Curzon, 2002.

Roxburgh, David J., ed. *Turks: A Journey of a Thousand Years, 600–1600*. London: Royal Academy of Arts, 2005.

Sims, Eleanor, B.I. Marshak, and Ernst J. Grube. *Peerless Images: Persian Painting and Its Sources*. New Haven: Yale Univ. Press, 2002.

Stanley, Tim, Mariam Rosser-Owen, and Stephen Vernoit. *Palace and Mosque: Islamic Art from the Middle East*. London: V&A Publications, 2004.

Stierlin, Henri. *Islamic Art and Architecture*. New York: Thames & Hudson, 2002.

Tadgell, Christopher. *Four Caliphates: The Formation and Development of the Islamic Tradition*. London: Ellipsis, 1998.

Ward, R.M. *Islamic Metalwork*. New York: Thames & Hudson, 1993.

Watson, Oliver. *Ceramics from Islamic Lands*. New York: Thames & Hudson in assoc. with the al-Sabah Collection, Dar al-Athar al-Islamiyyah, Kuwait National Museum, 2004.

Chapter 10 Art of South and Southeast Asia before 1200

Atherton, Cynthia Packert. *The Sculpture of Early Medieval Rajasthan*. Studies in Asian Art and Archaeology, vol. 21. New York: Brill, 1997.

Behl, Benoy K. *The Ajanta Caves: Artistic Wonder of Ancient Buddhist India*. New York: Abrams, 1998.

Behrendt, Kurt A. *The Buddhist Architecture of Gandhara*. Handbook of Oriental Studies: Section Two: India, vol. 17. Boston: Brill, 2004.

Brown, Robert L., ed. *Art from Thailand*. Mumbai: Marg Publications, 1999.

Chakrabarti, Dilip K. *India, an Archaeological History: Palaeolithic Beginnings to Early Historic Foundations*. 2nd ed. New York: Oxford Univ. Press, 2009.

Craven, Roy C. *Indian Art: A Concise History*. Rev. ed. World of Art. New York: Thames & Hudson, 1997.

Czuma, Stanislaw J. *Kushan Sculpture: Images from Early India*. Cleveland: Cleveland Museum of Art, 1985.

Dehejia, Vidya. *Art of the Imperial Cholas*. New York: Columbia Univ. Press, 1990.

———. *The Sensuous and the Sacred: Chola Bronzes from South India*. New York: American Federation of Arts, 2002.

Dessai, Vishakha N., and Darielle Mason, eds. *Gods, Guardians, and Lovers: Temple Sculptures from North India, A.D. 700–1200*. New York: Asia Society Galleries, 1993.

Dhavalikar, Madhukar Keshav. *Ellora*. New York: Oxford Univ. Press, 2003.

Girard-Geslan, Maud. *Art of Southeast Asia*. Trans. J.A. Underwood. New York: Abrams, Inc., 1998.

Guy, John, ed. *Lost Kingdoms: Hindu-Buddhist Sculpture of Early Southeast Asia*. New Haven: Yale Univ. Press and Metropolitan Museum of Art, 2014.

Heller, Amy. *Early Himalayan Art*. Oxford: Ashmolean Museum, 2008.

Huntington, Susan L. *The Art of Ancient India: Buddhist, Hindu, Jain*. New York: Weatherhill, 1985.

———. *Leaves from the Bodhi Tree: The Art of Pala India (8th–12th Centuries) and Its International Legacy*. Dayton, OH: Dayton Art Institute, 1990.

Hutt, Michael. *Nepal: A Guide to the Art and Architecture of the Kathmandu Valley*. Boston: Shambhala, 1995.

Knox, Robert. *Amaravati: Buddhist Sculpture from the Great Stupa*. London: British Museum Press, 1992.

Khanna, Sucharita. *Dancing Divinities in Indian Art: 8th–12th Century A.D.* Delhi: Sharada Pub. House, 1999.

Kramrisch, Stella. *The Art of Nepal*. New York: Abrams, 1964.

———. *The Presence of Siva*. Princeton, NJ: Princeton Univ. Press, 1981.

Meister, Michael, ed. *Encyclopedia of Indian Temple Architecture*. 2 vols. in 7. Philadelphia: Univ. of Pennsylvania Press, 1983.

Michell, George. *Elephanta*. Bombay: India Book House, 2002.

———. *Hindu Art and Architecture*. World of Art. London: Thames & Hudson, 2000.

Mitter, Partha. *Indian Art*. Oxford History of Art. Oxford: Oxford Univ. Press, 2001.

Neumayer, Erwin. *Lines on Stone: The Prehistoric Rock Art of India*. New Delhi: Manohar, 1993.

Pal, Pratapaditya, ed. *The Ideal Image: The Gupta Sculptural Tradition and Its Influence*. New York: Asia Society, 1978.

Poster, Amy G. *From Indian Earth: 4,000 Years of Terracotta Art*. Brooklyn, NY: Brooklyn Museum, 1986.

Skelton, Robert, and Mark Francis. *Arts of Bengal: The Heritage of Bangladesh and Eastern India*. London: Whitechapel Art Gallery, 1979.

Stierlin, Henri. *Hindu India: From Khajuraho to the Temple City of Madurai*. Taschen's World Architecture. New York: Taschen, 1998.

Strachan, Paul. *Imperial Pagan: Art and Architecture of Old Burma*. Honolulu: Univ. of Hawai'i Press, 1990.

Tadgell, Christopher. *India and South-East Asia: The Buddhist and Hindu Tradition*. New York: Whitney Library of Design, 1998.

Williams, Joanna G. *Art of Gupta India, Empire and Province*. Princeton, NJ: Princeton Univ. Press, 1982.

Chapter 11 Chinese and Korean Art before 1279

Ciarla, Roberto, ed. *The Eternal Army: The Terracotta Soldiers of the First Chinese Emperor*. Vercelli: White Star, 2005.

Fong, Wen, ed. *Beyond Representation: Chinese Painting and Calligraphy, 8th–14th Century*. Princeton Monographs in Art and Archaeology, 48. New York: Metropolitan Museum of Art, 1992.

Fraser, Sarah Elizabeth. *Performing the Visual: The Practice of Buddhist Wall Painting in China and Central Asia, 618–960*. Stanford, CA: Stanford Univ. Press, 2004.

James, Jean M. *A Guide to the Tomb and Shrine Art of the Han Dynasty 206 B.C.–A.D. 220*. Chinese Studies, 2. Lewiston, NY: Mellen Press, 1996.

Karetzky, Patricia Eichenbaum. *Court Art of the Tang*. Lanham, MD: Univ. Press of America, 1996.

Kim, Kumja Paik. *Goryeo Dynasty: Korea's Age of Enlightenment, 918–1392*. San Francisco: Asian Art Museum—Chong-Moon Lee Center for Asian Art and Culture in cooperation with the National Museum of Korea and the Nara National Museum, 2003.

Ledderose, Lothat. *Ten Thousand Things: Module and Mass Production in Chinese Art*. Princeton: Princeton Univ. Press, 2000.

Li, Jian, ed. *The Glory of the Silk Road: Art from Ancient China*. Dayton, OH: Dayton Art Institute, 2003.

Little, Stephen, and Shawn Eichman. *Taoism and the Arts of China*. Chicago: Art Institute of Chicago, 2000.

Liu, Cary Y., Dora C.Y. Ching, and Judith G. Smith, eds. *Character & Context in Chinese Calligraphy*. Princeton, NJ: Art Museum, Princeton Univ., 1999.

Luo, Zhewen. *Ancient Pagodas in China*. Beijing, China: Foreign Languages Press, 1994.

Ma, Chengyuan. *Ancient Chinese Bronzes*. Ed. Hsio-Yen Shih. Hong Kong: Oxford Univ. Press, 1986.

Murck, Alfreda. *Poetry and Painting in Song China: The Subtle Art of Dissent*. Harvard-Yenching Institute Monograph Series. Cambridge, MA: Harvard Univ. Asia Center for the Harvard-Yenching Institute, 2000.

Ortiz, Valérie Malenfer. *Dreaming the Southern Song Landscape: The Power of Illusion in Chinese Painting*. Studies in Asian Art and Archaeology, vol. 22. Boston: Brill, 1999.

Paludan, Ann. *Chinese Tomb Figurines*. Hong Kong: Oxford Univ. Press, 1994.

Portal, Jane. *Korea: Art and Archaeology*. New York: Thames & Hudson, 2000.

Rawson, Jessica. *Mysteries of Ancient China: New Discoveries from the Early Dynasties*. London: British Museum Press, 1996.

Rhie, Marylin M. *Early Buddhist Art of China and Central Asia*. 2 vols in 3. Handbuch der Orientalistik. Vierte Abteilung; China, 12. Leiden: Brill, 1999.

Scarpari, Maurizio. *Splendours of Ancient China*. London: Thames & Hudson, 2000.

So, Jenny F., ed. *Noble Riders from Pines and Deserts: The Artistic Legacy of the Qidan*. Hong Kong: Art Museum, Chinese Univ. of Hong Kong, 2004.

Sturman, Peter Charles. *Mi Fu: Style and the Art of Calligraphy in Northern Song*. New Haven: Yale Univ. Press, 1997.

Wang, Eugene Y. *Shaping the Lotus Sutra: Buddhist Visual Culture in Medieval China*. Seattle: Univ. of Washington Press, 2005.

Watson, William. *The Arts of China to A.D. 900*. Pelican History of Art. New Haven: Yale Univ. Press, 1995.

———. *The Arts of China 900–1620*. Pelican History of Art. Reissue ed. 2003. New Haven: Yale Univ. Press, 2000.

Watt, James C.Y. *China: Dawn of a Golden Age, 200–750 A.D.* New York: Metropolitan Museum of Art, 2004.

Whitfield, Susan, and Ursula Sims-Williams, eds. *The Silk Road: Trade, Travel, War and Faith*. Chicago: Serindia Publications, 2004.

Wu Hung. *Monumentality in Early Chinese Art and Architecture*. Stanford, CA: Stanford Univ. Press, 1995.

Yang, Xiaoneng, ed. *The Golden Age of Chinese Archaeology: Celebrated Discoveries from the People's Republic of China*. Washington, DC: National Gallery of Art, 1999.

Chapter 12 Japanese Art before 1333

Cunningham, Michael R. *Buddhist Treasures from Nara*. Cleveland: Cleveland Museum of Art, 1998.

Gerhart, Karen. *The Material Culture of Death in Medieval Japan*. Honolulu: Univ. of Hawai'i Press, 2009.

Harris, Victor, ed. *Shinto: The Sacred Art of Ancient Japan*. London: British Museum Press, 2001.

Izutsu, Shinryu, and Shoryu Omori. *Sacred Treasures of Mount Koya: The Art of Japanese Shingon Buddhism*. Honolulu: Koyasan Reihokan Museum, 2002.

Kurata, Bunsaku. *Horyu-ji, Temple of the Exalted Law: Early Buddhist Art from Japan*. New York: Japan Society, 1981.

Levine, Gregory P.A., and Yukio Lippit. *Awakenings: Zen Figure Painting in Medieval Japan*. New York: Japan Society, 2007.

McCallum, Donald F. *The Four Great Temples: Buddhist Archaeology, Architecture, and Icons of Seventh-Century Japan*. Honolulu: Univ. of Hawai'i Press, 2009.

Mino, Yutaka. *The Great Eastern Temple: Treasures of Japanese Buddhist Art from Todai-ji*. Chicago: Art Institute of Chicago, 1986.

Mizoguchi, Koji. *An Archaeological History of Japan: 30,000 B.C. to A.D. 700*. Philadelphia: Univ. of Pennsylvania Press, 2002.

Murase, Miyeko. *The Tale of Genji: Legends and Paintings*. New York: Braziller, 2001.

Nishiwara, Kyotaro, and Emily J. Sano. *The Great Age of Japanese Buddhist Sculpture, A.D. 60–1300*. Fort Worth, TX: Kimbell Art Museum, 1982.

Pearson, Richard J. *Ancient Japan*. Washington, DC: Arthur M. Sackler Gallery, 1992.

Ten Grotenhuis, Elizabeth. *Japanese Mandalas: Representations of Sacred Geography*. Honolulu: Univ. of Hawai'i Press, 1999.

Washizuka, Hiromitsu, Park Youngbok, and Kang Woo-bang. *Transmitting the Forms of Divinity: Early Buddhist Art from Korea and Japan*. Ed. Naomi Noble Richard. New York: Japan Society, 2003.

Wong, Dorothy C., and Eric M. Field, eds. *Horyuji Reconsidered*. Newcastle: Cambridge Scholars, 2008.

Chapter 13 Art of the Americas before 1300

Benson, Elizabeth P., and Beatriz de la Fuente. *Olmec Art of Ancient Mexico*. Washington, DC: National Gallery of Art, 1996.

Berrin, Kathleen, ed. *Feathered Serpents and Flowering Trees: Reconstructing the Murals of Teotihuacan*. San Francisco: Fine Arts Museums of San Francisco, 1988.

Brody, J.J. *Anasazi and Pueblo Painting*. Albuquerque: Univ. of New Mexico Press, 1991.

Burger, Richard L. *Chavin and the Origins of Andean Civilization*. New York: Thames & Hudson, 1992.

Clark, John E., and Mary E. Pye, eds. *Olmec Art and Archaeology in Mesoamerica*. Studies in the History of Art, 58: Symposium Papers, 35. Washington, DC: National Gallery of Art, 2000.

Clayton, Lawrence A., Vernon J. Knight, and Edward Moore, eds. *The De Soto Chronicles: The Expedition of Hernando de Soto to North America, 1539–1543*. 2 vols. Tuscaloosa: Univ. of Alabama Press, 1993.

Coe, Michael D. and Rex Koontz. *Mexico: From the Olmecs to the Aztecs*. 5th ed. New York: Thames & Hudson, 2005.

———. *Breaking the Maya Code*. Rev. ed. New York: Thames & Hudson, 1999.

Donnan, Christopher. *Moche Portraits from Ancient Peru*. Austin: Univ. of Texas Press, 2003.

Fagan, Brian M. *Chaco Canyon: Archaeologists Explore the Lives of an Ancient Society*. New York: Oxford Univ. Press, 2005.

Hall, Robert L. *An Archaeology of the Soul: North American Indian Belief and Ritual*. Urbana: Univ. of Illinois Press, 1997.

Heyden, Doris, and Paul Gendrop. *Pre-Columbian Architecture of Mesoamerica*. Trans. Judith Stanton. History of World Architecture. New York: Electa/Rizzoli, 1988.

Korp, Maureen. *The Sacred Geography of the American Mound Builders*. Native American Studies. Lewiston, NY: Mellen Press, 1990.

Kubler, George. *The Art and Architecture of Ancient America: The Mexican, Maya, and Andean Peoples*. 3rd ed. with updated bib. Pelican History of Art. New Haven: Yale Univ. Press, 1993.

Labbé, Armand J. *Shamans, Gods, and Mythic Beasts: Colombian Gold and Ceramics in Antiquity*. New York: American Federation of Arts, 1998.

LeBlanc, Steven A. *Painted by a Distant Hand: Mimbres Pottery from the American Southwest*. Cambridge, MA: Peabody Museum Press, 2004.

Loendorf, Lawrence L., Christopher Chippindale, and David S. Whitley, eds. *Discovering North American Rock Art*. Tucson: Univ. of Arizona Press, 2005.

Martin, Simon, and Nikolai Grube. *Chronicle of the Maya Kings and Queens: Deciphering the Dynasties of the Ancient Maya*. 2nd ed. New York: Thames & Hudson, 2008.

Miller, Mary Ellen. *The Art of Mesoamerica: From Olmec to Aztec*. 4th ed. World of Art. London: Thames & Hudson, 2006.

———. *Maya Art and Architecture*. World of Art. London: Thames & Hudson, 1999.

———, and Simon Martin. *Courtly Art of the Ancient Maya*. San Francisco: Fine Arts Museums of San Francisco, 2004.

———, and Karl Taube. *The Gods and Symbols of Ancient Mexico and the Maya: An Illustrated Dictionary of Mesoamerican Religion*. London: Thames & Hudson, 1993.

Milner, George R. *The Moundbuilders: Ancient Peoples of Eastern North America*. Ancient Peoples and Places, 110. London: Thames & Hudson, 2004.

Noble, David Grant. *In Search of Chaco: New Approaches to an Archaeological Enigma*. Santa Fe, NM: School of American Research Press, 2004.

O'Connor, Mallory McCane. *Lost Cities of the Ancient Southeast*. Gainesville: Univ. Press of Florida, 1995.

Pasztory, Esther. *Teotihuacan: An Experiment in Living*. Norman: Univ. of Oklahoma Press, 1997.

Pillsbury, Joanne, ed. *Moche Art and Archaeology in Ancient Peru*. Studies in the History of Art: Center for Advanced Study in the Visual Arts, 63: Symposium Papers, 40. Washington, DC: National Gallery of Art, 2001.

Power, Susan C. *Early Art of the Southeastern Indians: Feathered Serpents & Winged Beings*. Athens: Univ. of Georgia Press, 2004.

Rohn, Arthur H., and William M. Ferguson. *Puebloan Ruins of the Southwest*. Albuquerque: Univ. of New Mexico Press, 2006.

Sharer, Robert J., and Loa P. Traxler. *The Ancient Maya*. 6th ed. Stanford, CA: Stanford Univ. Press, 2006.

Stierlin, Henri. *The Maya: Palaces and Pyramids of the Rainforest*. Cologne: Taschen, 2001.

Stone-Miller, Rebecca. *Art of the Andes: From Chavin to Inca*. 2nd ed. World of Art. New York: Thames & Hudson, 2002.

———. *To Weave for the Sun: Ancient Andean Textiles*. New York: Thames & Hudson 1994.

Townsend, Richard F., and Robert V. Sharp, eds. *Hero, Hawk, and Open Hand: American Indian Art of the Ancient Midwest and South*. Chicago: Art Institute of Chicago, 2004.

Von Hagen, Adriana, and Craig Morris. *The Cities of the Ancient Andes*. New York: Thames & Hudson, 1998.

Chapter 14 Arts of Africa to the Sixteenth Century

Bassani, Ezio, and M.D. McLeod. *African Art and Artefacts in European Collections: 1400–1800*. London: British Museum, 2000.

Blier, Suzanne Preston. *The Royal Arts of Africa: The Majesty of Form*. Perspectives. New York: Abrams, 1998.

Connah, Graham. *African Civilizations: An Archaeological Perspective*, 2nd ed. New York: Cambridge Univ. Press, 2001.

Gunsch, Kathryn Wysocki. *The Benin Plaques: A 16th Century Imperial Monument*. London: Ashgate, 2017 [in press].

LaGamma, Alisa. "*Ethiopia's Enduring Cultural Heritage*." Heilbrunn Timeline of Art History (September 2008). Accessed August 11, 2015. http://www.metmuseum.org/toah/hd/ethi/hd_ethi.htm.

Lamp, Frederick John. "Ancient Terracotta Figures from Northern Nigeria." *Yale University Art Gallery Bulletin* 53 (2011): 49–57.

Lewis-Williams, J. David. *San Rock Art. Ohio Short Histories of Africa*. Athens: Ohio Univ. Press, 2013.

Nelson, Steven. *From Cameroon to Paris: Mousgoum Architecture in and out of Africa*. Chicago and London: Univ. of Chicago Press, 2007.

Visonà, Monica Blackmun, Robin Poynor, and Herbert M. Cole. *A History of Art in Africa*. 2nd ed. Upper Saddle River, NJ: Pearson/Prentice Hall, 2008.

Walters Art Museum. "*Ethiopian Gospels*." The Walters Art Museum. Last modified 2015. Accessed August 12, 2015. http://art.thewalters.org/detail/31912/ethiopian-gospels-3/

Chapter 15 Early Medieval Art in Europe

Alexander, J.J.G. *Medieval Illuminators and Their Methods of Work*. New ed. New Haven: Yale Univ. Press, 1994.

The Art of Medieval Spain, A.D. 500–1200. New York: Metropolitan Museum of Art, 1993.

Backhouse, Janet, D.H. Turner, and Leslie Webster, eds. *The Golden Age of Anglo-Saxon Art, 966–1066*. Bloomington: Indiana Univ. Press, 1984.

Bandmann, Günter. *Early Medieval Architecture as Bearer of Meaning*. New York: Columbia Univ. Press, 2005.

Brown, Michelle P. *The Lindisfarne Gospels: Society, Spirituality and the Scribe*. Toronto: Univ. of Toronto Press, 2003.

Calkins, Robert G. *Illuminated Books of the Middle Ages*. Ithaca, NY: Cornell Univ. Press, 1983.

Carver, Martin. *Sutton Hoo: A Seventh-Century Princely Burial Ground and Its Context*. London: British Museum Press, 2005.

Davis-Weyer, Caecilia. *Early Medieval Art, 300–1150: Sources and Documents*. Upper Saddle River, NJ: Pearson/ Prentice Hall, 1971.

Diebold, William J. *Word and Image: An Introduction to Early Medieval Art*. Boulder, CO: Westview Press, 2000.

Dodwell, C.R. *Pictorial Arts of the West, 800–1200*. Pelican History of Art. New Haven: Yale Univ. Press, 1993.

Farley, Julia, and Fraser Hunter. *Celts: Art and Identity*. London: British Museum Press, 2015.

Farr, Carol. *The Book of Kells: Its Function and Audience*. London: British Library, 1997.

Fitzhugh, William W., and Elisabeth I. Ward, eds. *Vikings: The North Atlantic Saga*. Washington, DC: Smithsonian Institution Press, 2000.

Harbison, Peter. *The Golden Age of Irish Art: The Medieval Achievement, 600–1200*. London: Thames & Hudson, 1999.

Henderson, George. *From Durrow to Kells: The Insular Gospel-Books, 650–800*. London: Thames & Hudson, 1987.

Horn, Walter W., and Ernest Born. *Plan of Saint Gall: A Study of the Architecture and Economy of and Life in a Paradigmatic Carolingian Monastery.* California Studies in the History of Art, 19. 3 vols. Berkeley: Univ. of California Press, 1979.

Lasko, Peter. *Ars Sacra, 800–1200.* 2nd ed. Pelican History of Art. New Haven: Yale Univ. Press, 1994.

McClendon, Charles B. *The Origins of Medieval Architecture: Building in Europe, A.D. 600–900.* New Haven: Yale Univ. Press, 2005.

Mayr-Harting, Henry. *Ottonian Book Illumination: An Historical Study.* 2nd rev. ed. 2 vols. London: Harvey Miller, 1999.

Mentré, Mireille. *Illuminated Manuscripts of Medieval Spain.* New York: Thames & Hudson, 1996.

Nees, Lawrence. *Early Medieval Art.* Oxford History of Art. Oxford: Oxford Univ. Press, 2002.

Richardson, Hilary, and John Scarry. *An Introduction to Irish High Crosses.* Dublin: Mercier, 1990.

Schapiro, Meyer. *Language of Forms: Lectures on Insular Manuscript Art.* Ed. Jane Rosenthal. New York: Pierpont Morgan Library, 2006.

Stalley, R.A. *Early Medieval Architecture.* Oxford History of Art. Oxford: Oxford Univ. Press, 1999.

Wickham, Chris. *Framing the Early Middle Ages: Europe and the Mediterranean 400–800.* New York: Oxford Univ. Press, 2005.

Williams, John. *Early Spanish Manuscript Illumination.* New York: Braziller, 1977.

Wilson, David M. *Anglo-Saxon Art: From the Seventh Century to the Norman Conquest.* London: Thames & Hudson, 1984.

———, and Ole Klindt-Jensen. *Viking Art.* 2nd ed. Minneapolis: Univ. of Minnesota Press, 1980.

Chapter 16 Romanesque Art

Barral i Altet, Xavier. *The Romanesque: Towns, Cathedrals and Monasteries.* Taschen's World Architecture. New York: Taschen, 1998.

The Book of Sainte Foy. Ed. and trans. Pamela Sheingorn. Philadelphia: Univ. of Pennsylvania Press, 1995.

Cahn, Walter. *Romanesque Manuscripts: The Twelfth Century.* 2nd ed. 2 vols. A Survey of Manuscripts Illuminated in France. London: Harvey Miller, 1996.

Caviness, Madeline H. "Hildegard as Designer of the Illustrations to her Works." In *Hildegard of Bingen: The Context of her Thought and Art.* Ed. Charles Burnett and Peter Dronke. London: Warburg Institute, 1998: 29–63.

Davis-Weyer, Caecilia. *Early Medieval Art, 300–1150. Sources and Documents.* Upper Saddle River, NJ: Pearson/ Prentice Hall, 1971.

Dimier, Anselme. *Stones Laid before the Lord: A History of Monastic Architecture.* Trans. Gilchrist Lavigne. Cistercian Studies Series, no. 152. Kalamazoo, MI: Cistercian Publications, 1999.

Fergusson, Peter. *Architecture of Solitude: Cistercian Abbeys in Twelfth-Century England.* Princeton, NJ: Princeton Univ. Press, 1984.

Forsyth, Ilene H. *The Throne of Wisdom: Wood Sculptures of the Madonna in Romanesque France.* Princeton, NJ: Princeton Univ. Press, 1972.

Gaud, Henri, and Jean-François Leroux-Dhuys. *Cistercian Abbeys: History and Architecture.* Cologne: Könemann, 1998.

Gerson, Paula, ed. *The Pilgrim's Guide to Santiago de Compostela: A Critical Edition.* 2 vols. London: Harvey Miller, 1998.

Grivot, Denis, and George Zarnecki. *Gislebertus: Sculptor of Autun.* New York: Orion Press, 1961.

Hearn, M.F. *Romanesque Sculpture: The Revival of Monumental Stone Sculptures in the Eleventh and Twelfth Centuries.* Ithaca, NY: Cornell Univ. Press, 1981.

Hicks, Carola. *The Bayeux Tapestry: The Life Story of a Masterpiece.* London: Chatto & Windus, 2006.

Holt, Elizabeth Gilmore, ed. *A Documentary History of Art.* 2 vols. Princeton, NJ: Princeton Univ. Press, 1982–86.

Hourihane, Colum, ed. *Romanesque Art and Thought in the Twelfth Century: Essays in Honor of Walter Cahn.* The Index of Christian Art Occasional Papers 10. University Park, PA: Penn State Press, 2008.

Kubach, Hans E. *Romanesque Architecture.* History of World Architecture. New York: Electa/Rizzoli, 1988.

Minne-Sève, Viviane, and Hervé Kergall. *Romanesque and Gothic France: Architecture and Sculpture.* Trans. Jack Hawkes and Lory Frankel. New York: Abrams, 2000.

Newman, Barbara. *Sister of Wisdom: St. Hildegard's Theology of the Feminine.* 2nd ed. Berkeley: Univ. of California Press, 1997.

Rudolph, Conrad. *The "Things of Greater Importance": Bernard of Clairvaux's Apologia and the Medieval Attitude Toward Art.* Philadelphia: Univ. of Pennsylvania Press, 1990.

Schapiro, Meyer. *Romanesque Art: Selected Papers.* New York: George Braziller, 1977.

———. *The Romanesque Sculpture of Moissac.* New York: Braziller, 1985.

———. *Romanesque Architectural Sculpture: The Charles Eliot Norton Lectures.* Ed. Linda Seidel. Chicago: Univ. of Chicago Press, 2006.

Seidel, Linda. *Legends in Limestone: Lazarus, Gislebertus, and the Cathedral of Autun.* Chicago: Univ. of Chicago Press, 1999.

Sundell, Michael G. *Mosaics in the Eternal City.* Tempe: Arizona Center for Medieval and Renaissance Studies, 2007.

Swanson, R.N. *The Twelfth-Century Renaissance.* Manchester: Manchester Univ. Press, 1999.

Theophilus. *On Divers Arts: The Foremost Medieval Treatise on Painting, Glassmaking, and Metalwork.* Trans. John G. Hawthorne and Cyril Stanley Smith. New York: Dover, 1979.

Toman, Rolf, ed. *Romanesque: Architecture, Sculpture, Painting.* Trans. Fiona Hulse and Ian Macmillan. Cologne: Könemann, 1997.

Wilson, David M. *The Bayeux Tapestry: The Complete Tapestry in Color.* London: Thames & Hudson and New York: Knopf, 2004.

Zarnecki, George, Janet Holt, and Tristram Holland, eds. *English Romanesque Art, 1066–1200.* London: Weidenfeld and Nicolson, 1984.

Chapter 17 Gothic Art of the Twelfth and Thirteenth Centuries

Barnes, Carl F. *The Portfolio of Villard de Honnecourt: A New Critical Edition and Color Facsimile.* Burlington, VT: Ashgate, 2009.

Binding, Günther. *High Gothic: The Age of the Great Cathedrals.* Taschen's World Architecture. London: Taschen, 1999.

Binski, Paul. *Becket's Crown: Art and Imagination in Gothic England, 1170–1300.* New Haven: Yale Univ. Press, 2004.

Bony, Jean. *French Gothic Architecture of the 12th and 13th Centuries.* California Studies in the History of Art, 20. Berkeley: Univ. of California Press, 1983.

Camille, Michael. *Gothic Art: Glorious Visions.* Perspectives. New York: Abrams, 1996.

Coldstream, Nicola. *Masons and Sculptors.* Toronto & Buffalo, NY: Univ. of Toronto Press, 1991.

Crosby, Sumner M. *The Royal Abbey of Saint-Denis from Its Beginnings to the Death of Suger, 475–1151.* Yale Publications in the History of Art, 37. New Haven: Yale Univ. Press, 1987.

Erlande-Brandenburg, Alain. *Gothic Art.* Trans. I. Mark Paris. New York: Abrams, 1989.

Frankl, Paul. *Gothic Architecture.* Revised Paul Crossley. Pelican History of Art. New Haven: Yale Univ. Press, 2000.

Frisch, Teresa G. *Gothic Art, 1140–c.1450: Sources and Documents.* Upper Saddle River, NJ: Pearson/Prentice Hall, 1971.

Grodecki, Louis, and Catherine Brisac. *Gothic Stained Glass, 1200–1300.* Ithaca, NY: Cornell Univ. Press, 1985.

Jordan, Alyce A. *Visualizing Kingship in the Windows of the Sainte-Chapelle.* Turnhout: Brepols, 2002.

Moskowitz, Anita Fiderer. *Nicola & Giovanni Pisano: The Pulpits: Pious Devotion, Pious Diversion.* London: Harvey Miller, 2005.

Nussbaum, Norbert. *German Gothic Church Architecture.* Trans. Scott Kleager. New Haven: Yale Univ. Press, 2000.

Panofsky, Erwin. *Abbot Suger on the Abbey Church of St.- Denis and Its Art Treasures.* 2nd ed. Ed. Gerda Panofsky- Soergel. Princeton, NJ: Princeton Univ. Press, 1979.

Parry, Stan. *Great Gothic Cathedrals of France.* New York: Viking Studio, 2001.

Sauerländer, Willibald. *Gothic Sculpture in France, 1140–1270.* Trans. Janet Sandheimer. London: Thames & Hudson, 1972.

Scott, Robert A. *The Gothic Enterprise: A Guide to Understanding the Medieval Cathedral.* Berkeley: Univ. of California Press, 2003.

Simsom, Otto Georg von. *The Gothic Cathedral:*

Origins of Gothic Architecture and the Medieval Concept of Order. 3rd ed. exp. Bollingen Series. Princeton, NJ: Princeton Univ. Press, 1988.

Suckale, Robert, and Matthias Weniger. *Painting of the Gothic Era.* Ed. Ingo F. Walther. New York: Taschen, 1999.

Williamson, Paul. *Gothic Sculpture, 1140–1300.* Pelican History of Art. New Haven: Yale Univ. Press, 1995.

Chapter 18 Fourteenth-Century Art in Europe

Alexander, Jonathan, and Paul Binski, eds. *Age of Chivalry: Art in Plantagenet England, 1200–1400.* London: Royal Academy of Arts, 1987.

Backhouse, Janet. *Illumination from Books of Hours.* London: British Library, 2004.

Boehm, Barbara Drake, and Jirí Fajt, eds. *Prague: The Crown of Bohemia, 1347–1437.* New York: Metropolitan Museum of Art, 2005.

Bony, Jean. *The English Decorated Style: Gothic Architecture Transformed, 1250–1350.* The Wrightsman Lecture, 10. Oxford: Phaidon Press, 1979.

Cennini, Cennino. *The Craftsman's Handbook "Il libro dell'arte."* Trans. D.V. Thompson, Jr. New York: Dover, 1960.

Derbes, Anne, and Mark Sandona, eds. *The Cambridge Companion to Giotto.* Cambridge and New York: Cambridge Univ. Press, 2003.

Fajt, Jirí, ed. *Magister Theodoricus, Court Painter to Emperor Charles IV: The Pictorial Decoration of the Shrines at Karlstejn Castle.* Prague: National Gallery, 1998.

Holt, Elizabeth Gilmore, ed. *A Documentary History of Art.* 2 vols. Princeton, NJ, Princeton Univ. Press, 1982–86.

Ladis, Andrew. ed, *The Arena Chapel and the Genius of Giotto: Padua.* Giotto and the World of Early Italian Art, 2. New York: Garland, 1998.

Meiss, Millard. *Painting in Florence and Siena after the Black Death: The Arts, Religion, and Society in the Mid-Fourteenth Century.* 2nd ed. Princeton, NJ: Princeton Univ. Press, 1978.

Moskowitz, Anita Fiderer. *Italian Gothic Sculpture: c. 1250–c. 1400.* New York: Cambridge Univ. Press, 2001.

Norman, Diana, ed. *Siena, Florence, and Padua: Art, Society, and Religion 1280–1400.* 2 vols. New Haven: Yale Univ. Press, 1995.

Poeschke, Joachim. *Italian Frescoes, the Age of Giotto, 1280–1400.* New York: Abbeville Press, 2005.

Schleif, Corine. "St. Hedwig's Personal Ivory Madonna: Women's Agency and the Powers of Possessing Portable Figures." *The Four Modes of Seeing: Approaches to Medieval Imagery in Honor of Madeline Harrison Caviness.* Ed. Evelyn Staudinger Lane, Elizabeth Carson Paston, and Ellen M. Shortell. Farnham, Surrey: Ashgate, 2009: 282–403.

Vasari, Giorgio. *The Lives of the Artists.* Trans. Julia Conaway Bondanella and Peter Bondanella. Oxford World's Classics. New York: Oxford Univ. Press, 2008.

Welch, Evelyn S. *Art in Renaissance Italy, 1350–1500.* New ed. Oxford History of Art. Oxford: Oxford Univ. Press, 2000.

White, John. *Art and Architecture in Italy, 1250 to 1400.* 3rd ed. Pelican History of Art. Harmondsworth, UK: Penguin, 1993.

Wieck, Roger S. *Time Sanctified: The Book of Hours in Medieval Art and Life.* 2nd ed. New York: Braziller, 2001.

Text Credits

p.XXII, *The Random House Dictionary of the English Language, 2nd edition unabridged*, (Random House, 1966), Used by permission of Penguin Random House LLC. All rights reserved.

p.XXXIV, based on Mark Tucker "Rogier van der Weyden's 'Philadelphia Crucifixion'", *Burlington Magazine* Vol 139 (1997): 676–683. Reproduced by permission.

p.33, Lady Enheduanna, *The Exaltation of Inanna* translated by W. W. Hallo, (Yale University Press, 1968). Reproduced courtesy of Yale University Press and Yale Babylonian Collection.

p.49, "Tut-ankh-Amen's Inner Tomb is Opened Revealing Undreamed of Splendors, Still Untouched After 3,400 Years" *The New York Times*, February 17, 1923, copyright © NY Times, 1923. All rights reserved. Used by permission and protected by the Copyright Laws of the United States. The printing, copying, redistribution, or retransmission of this Content without express written permission is prohibited.

p.169, Horace, *The Epistles*, translated by Adam S. Kline, copyright © 2005. All rights reserved.

p.257, New Testament E-7 Long I Corinthians 15:20-28. *New American Bible (Revised Edition)* copyright © 2010, 1991, 1986, 1970. Confraternity of Christian Doctrine, Inc., Washington, DC. All Rights Reserved.

p.369, Earl Miner, *The Princeton Companion to Classical Japanese Literature*, (Princeton University Press, 1985) p.279, copyright © 1985. Reproduced by kind permission of the Estate of Earl Miner.

pp.455, 492, Scripture quotations from the ESV® Bible (The Holy Bible, English Standard Version®), copyright © 2001 by Crossway, a publishing ministry of Good News Publishers. Used by permission. All rights reserved.

pp.461, 713, Psalms 23:6 and 33:9, *Holy Bible, New International Version®* (Anglicised), NIV®, copyright © 1979, 1984, 2011 by Biblica, Inc.® Used by permission of Biblica, Zondervan, www.zondervan.com and Hodder and Stoughton. All rights reserved worldwide. The "NIV" and "New International Version" are trademarks registered in the United States Patent and Trademark Office by Biblica, Inc.™

p.481, "Things of Greater Importance", translated by Conrad Rudolph in *Bernard of Clairvaux's Apologia and the Medieval Attitude Toward Art*. (University of Pennsylvania Press, 1990) pp.11-12. Reprinted with permission of the University of Pennsylvania Press.

p.492, *Holy Bible. New Living Translation* copyright © 1996, 2004, 2007, 2013 by Tyndale House Foundation. Used by permission of Tyndale House Publishers Inc., Carol Stream, Illinois 60188. All rights reserved.

p.510, Erwin Panofsky, *Abbot Suger on the Abbey Church of St.-Denis and Its Art Treasures. 2nd edition*, edited by Gerda Panofsky-Soergel (Princeton University Press, 1979) p.51. Reproduced by permission.

Index

Figures in *italics* refer to illustrations; (c) refers to captions.